McGraw-Hill's

Essentials of Federal Taxation

McGraw-Hill's
Essentials of Federal Taxation

Brian C. Spilker
Brigham Young University
Editor

Benjamin C. Ayers
The University of Georgia

John A. Barrick
Brigham Young University

Edmund Outslay
Michigan State University

John R. Robinson
Texas A&M University

Connie D. Weaver
Texas A&M University

Ron G. Worsham
Brigham Young University

McGRAW-HILL'S ESSENTIALS OF FEDERAL TAXATION, 2019 EDITION, TENTH EDITION

Published by McGraw-Hill Education, 2 Penn Plaza, New York, NY 10121. Copyright © 2019 by McGraw-Hill Education. All rights reserved. Printed in the United States of America. Previous editions © 2018, 2017, and 2016. No part of this publication may be reproduced or distributed in any form or by any means, or stored in a database or retrieval system, without the prior written consent of McGraw-Hill Education, including, but not limited to, in any network or other electronic storage or transmission, or broadcast for distance learning.

Some ancillaries, including electronic and print components, may not be available to customers outside the United States.

This book is printed on acid-free paper.

1 2 3 4 5 6 7 8 9 LWI 21 20 19 18

ISBN   978-1-260-18967-4
MHID   1-260-18967-8
ISSN   2166-2711

Executive Portfolio Manager: *Kathleen Klehr*
Product Developers: *Danielle Andries, Erin Quinones*
Marketing Manager: *Zach Rudin*
Content Project Managers: *Lori Koetters, Jill Eccher, Brian Nacik*
Buyer: *Susan K. Culbertson*

Design: *Matt Backhaus*
Content Licensing Specialist: *Lorraine Buczek*
Cover Image: *© Robert Nicholas/AGE Fotostock*
Compositor: *Aptara®, Inc.*
Printer: *LSC Communications*

All credits appearing on page are considered to be an extension of the copyright page.

The Internet addresses listed in the text were accurate at the time of publication. The inclusion of a website does not indicate an endorsement by the authors or McGraw-Hill Education, and McGraw-Hill Education does not guarantee the accuracy of the information presented at these sites.

mheducation.com/highered

Dedications

We dedicate this book to:

My family, whose love and support helped make this book possible, and to Professor Dave Stewart for his great example and friendship over the last three decades.

Brian Spilker

My wife, Marilyn, daughters Margaret Lindley and Georgia, son Benjamin, and parents Bill and Linda.

Ben Ayers

My wife, Jill, and my children Annika, Corinne, Lina, Mitch, and Connor.

John Barrick

My family, Jane, Mark, Sarah, Chloe, Lily, Jeff, and Nicole, and to Professor James E. Wheeler, my mentor and friend.

Ed Outslay

JES, Tommy, and Laura.

John Robinson

My family: Dan, Travis, Alix, and Alan.

Connie Weaver

My wife, Anne, sons Matthew and Daniel, and daughters Whitney and Hayley.

Ron Worsham

About the Authors

Brian Spilker (PhD, University of Texas at Austin, 1993) is the Robert Call/Deloitte Professor in the School of Accountancy at Brigham Young University. He teaches taxation at Brigham Young University. He received both BS (Summa Cum Laude) and MAcc (tax emphasis) degrees from Brigham Young University before working as a tax consultant for Arthur Young & Co. (now Ernst & Young). After his professional work experience, Brian earned his PhD at the University of Texas at Austin. In 1996, he was selected as one of two nationwide recipients of the Price Waterhouse Fellowship in Tax Award. In 1998, he was a winner of the American Taxation Association and Arthur Andersen Teaching Innovation Award for his work in the classroom; he has also been awarded for his use of technology in the classroom at Brigham Young University. Brian researches issues relating to tax information search and professional tax judgment. His research has been published in journals such as *The Accounting Review, Organizational Behavior and Human Decision Processes, Journal of the American Taxation Association, Behavioral Research in Accounting, Journal of Accounting Education, Journal of Corporate Taxation,* and *Journal of Accountancy.*

Courtesy Brian Spilker

Ben Ayers (PhD, University of Texas at Austin, 1996) holds the Earl Davis Chair in Taxation and is the dean of the Terry College of Business at the University of Georgia. He received a PhD from the University of Texas at Austin and an MTA and BS from the University of Alabama. Prior to entering the PhD program at the University of Texas, Ben was a tax manager at KPMG in Tampa, Florida, and a contract manager with Complete Health, Inc., in Birmingham, Alabama. He is the recipient of 11 teaching awards at the school, college, and university levels, including the Richard B. Russell Undergraduate Teaching Award, the highest teaching honor for University of Georgia junior faculty members. His research interests include the effects of taxation on firm structure, mergers and acquisitions, and capital markets and the effects of accounting information on security returns. He has published articles in journals such as *The Accounting Review, Journal of Finance, Journal of Accounting and Economics, Contemporary Accounting Research, Review of Accounting Studies, Journal of Law and Economics, Journal of the American Taxation Association,* and *National Tax Journal.* Ben was the 1997 recipient of the American Accounting Association's Competitive Manuscript Award, the 2003 and 2008 recipient of the American Taxation Association's Outstanding Manuscript Award, and the 2016 recipient of the American Taxation Association's Ray M. Sommerfeld Outstanding Tax Educator Award.

Courtesy Ben Ayers

Courtesy John Barrick

John Barrick (PhD, University of Nebraska at Lincoln, 1998) is currently an associate professor in the Marriott School at Brigham Young University. He served as an accountant at the United States Congress Joint Committee on Taxation during the 110th and 111th Congresses. He teaches taxation in the graduate and undergraduate programs at Brigham Young University. He received both BS and MAcc (tax emphasis) degrees from Brigham Young University before working as a tax consultant for Price Waterhouse (now PricewaterhouseCoopers). After his professional work experience, John earned his PhD at the University of Nebraska at Lincoln. He was the 1998 recipient of the American Accounting Association, Accounting, Behavior, and Organization Section's Outstanding Dissertation Award. John researches issues relating to tax corporate political activity. His research has been published in journals such as *Organizational Behavior and Human Decision Processes, Contemporary Accounting Research,* and *Journal of the American Taxation Association.*

Courtesy Ed Outslay

Ed Outslay (PhD, University of Michigan, 1981) is a professor of accounting and the Deloitte/Michael Licata Endowed Professor of Taxation in the Department of Accounting and Information Systems at Michigan State University, where he has taught since 1981. He received a BA from Furman University in 1974 and an MBA and PhD from the University of Michigan in 1977 and 1981. Ed currently teaches graduate classes in corporate taxation, multiunit enterprises, accounting for income taxes, and international taxation. In February 2003, Ed testified before the Senate Finance Committee on the Joint Committee on Taxation's Report on Enron Corporation. MSU has honored Ed with the Presidential Award for Outstanding Community Service, Distinguished Faculty Award, John D. Withrow Teacher-Scholar Award, Roland H. Salmonson Outstanding Teaching Award, Senior Class Council Distinguished Faculty Award, MSU Teacher-Scholar Award, and MSU's 1st Annual Curricular Service-Learning and Civic Engagement Award in 2008. Ed received the Ray M. Sommerfeld Outstanding Tax Educator Award in 2004 and the Lifetime Service Award in 2013 from the American Taxation Association. He has also received the ATA Outstanding Manuscript Award twice, the ATA/Deloitte Teaching Innovations Award, and the 2004 Distinguished Achievement in Accounting Education Award from the Michigan Association of CPAs. In 2017, Ed received the American Accounting Association / J. Michael and Mary Ann Cook Prize given in "foremost recognition of an individual who consistently demonstrates the attributes of a superior teacher in the discipline of accounting." Ed has been recognized for his community service by the Greater Lansing Chapter of the Association of Government Accountants, the City of East Lansing (Crystal Award), and the East Lansing Education Foundation. He received a National Assistant Coach of the Year Award in 2003 from AFLAC and was named an Assistant High School Baseball Coach of the Year in 2002 by the Michigan High School Baseball Coaches Association.

John Robinson (PhD, University of Michigan, 1981) is the Patricia '77 and Grant E. Sims '77 Eminent Scholar Chair in Business. Prior to joining the faculty at Texas A&M, John was the C. Aubrey Smith Professor of Accounting at the University of Texas at Austin, Texas, and he taught at the University of Kansas where he was the Arthur Young Faculty Scholar. In 2009–2010 John served as the Academic Fellow in the Division of Corporation Finance at the Securities and Exchange Commission. He has been the recipient of the Henry A. Bubb Award for outstanding teaching, the Texas Blazer's Faculty Excellence Award, and the MPA Council Outstanding Professor Award. John also received the 2012 Outstanding Service Award from the American Taxation Association (ATA) and in 2017 was named the Ernst & Young and ATA Ray Sommerfeld Outstanding Educator. John served as the 2014–2015 president (elect) of the ATA and is the ATA's president for 2015–2016. John conducts research in a broad variety of topics involving financial accounting, mergers and acquisitions, and the influence of taxes on financial structures and performance. His scholarly articles have appeared in *The Accounting Review*, *The Journal of Accounting and Economics*, *Journal of Finance*, *National Tax Journal*, *Journal of Law and Economics*, *Journal of the American Taxation Association*, *The Journal of the American Bar Association*, and *The Journal of Taxation*. John's research was honored with the 2003 and 2008 ATA Outstanding Manuscript Awards. In addition, John was the editor of *The Journal of the American Taxation Association* from 2002–2005. Professor Robinson received his J.D. (*Cum Laude*) from the University of Michigan in 1979, and he earned a PhD in accounting from the University of Michigan in 1981. John teaches courses on individual and corporate taxation and advanced accounting.

Courtesy John Robinson

Connie Weaver (PhD, Arizona State University, 1997) is the KPMG Professor of Accounting at Texas A&M University. She received a PhD from Arizona State University, an MPA from the University of Texas at Arlington, and a BS (chemical engineering) from the University of Texas at Austin. Prior to entering the PhD Program, Connie was a tax manager at Ernst & Young in Dallas, Texas, where she became licensed to practice as a CPA. She teaches taxation in the Professional Program in Accounting and the Executive MBA program at Texas A&M University. She has also taught undergraduate and graduate students at the University of Wisconsin–Madison and the University of Texas at Austin. She is the recipient of several teaching awards, including the 2006 American Taxation Association/Deloitte Teaching Innovations award, the David and Denise Baggett Teaching award, and the college and university level Association of Former Students Distinguished Achievement award in teaching. Connie's current research interests include the effects of tax and financial incentives on corporate decisions and reporting. She has published articles in journals such as *The Accounting Review*, *Contemporary Accounting Research*, *Journal of the American Taxation Association*, *National Tax Journal*, *Accounting Horizons*, *Journal of Corporate Finance*, and *Tax Notes*. Connie is the senior editor of *The Journal of the American Taxation Association* and she serves on the editorial board of *Contemporary Accounting Research*.

Courtesy Connie Weaver

Ron Worsham (PhD, University of Florida, 1994) is an associate professor in the School of Accountancy at Brigham Young University. He teaches taxation in the graduate, undergraduate, MBA, and Executive MBA programs at Brigham Young University. He has also taught as a visiting professor at the University of Chicago. He received both BS and MAcc (tax emphasis) degrees from Brigham Young University before working as a tax consultant for Arthur Young & Co. (now Ernst & Young) in Dallas, Texas. While in Texas, he became licensed to practice as a CPA. After his professional work experience, Ron earned his PhD at the University of Florida. He has been honored for outstanding innovation in the classroom at Brigham Young University. Ron has published academic research in the areas of taxpayer compliance and professional tax judgment. He has also published legal research in a variety of areas. His work has been published in journals such as *Journal of the American Taxation Association*, *The Journal of International Taxation*, *The Tax Executive*, *Tax Notes*, *The Journal of Accountancy*, and *Practical Tax Strategies*.

Courtesy Ron Worsham

TEACHING THE CODE IN CONTEXT

   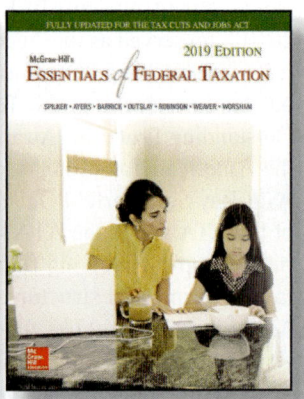

The bold innovative approach used by McGraw-Hill's Taxation series is quickly becoming the most popular choice of course materials among instructors and students. It's apparent why the clear, organized, and engaging delivery of content, paired with the most current and robust tax code updates, has been adopted by more than 600 schools across the country.

McGraw-Hill's Taxation is designed to provide a unique, innovative, and engaging learning experience for students studying taxation. The breadth of the topical coverage, **the storyline approach to presenting the material,** the emphasis on the tax and nontax consequences of multiple parties involved in transactions, and the integration of financial and tax accounting topics make this book ideal for the modern tax curriculum.

> "Do you want the best tax text? This is the one to use. It has a storyline in each chapter that can relate to real life issues."
>
> Leslie A. Mostow
> – University of Maryland, College Park

> "This text provides broad coverage of important topics and does so in a manner that is easy for students to understand. The material is very accessible for students."
>
> Kyle Post
> – Tarleton State University

Since the first manuscript was written in 2005, 449 professors have contributed 499 book reviews, in addition to 29 focus groups and symposia. Throughout this preface, their comments on the book's organization, pedagogy, and unique features are a testament to the **market-driven nature of *Taxation's* development.**

> "I think this is the best book available for introductory and intermediate courses in taxation."
>
> Shane Stinson
> – University of Alabama

A MODERN APPROACH FOR TODAY'S STUDENT

Spilker's taxation series was built around the following five core precepts:

1 **Storyline Approach:** Each chapter begins with a storyline that introduces a set of characters or a business entity facing specific tax-related situations. Each chapter's examples are related to the storyline, providing students with opportunities to **learn the code in context.**

2 **Integrated Examples:** In addition to providing examples in-context, we provide **"What if"** scenarios within many examples to **illustrate how variations in the facts might or might not change the answers.**

3 **Conversational Writing Style:** The authors took special care to write *McGraw-Hill's Taxation* in a way that fosters a friendly dialogue between the content and each individual student. The tone of the presentation is intentionally conversational—creating the impression of *speaking with* **the student,** as opposed to *lecturing to* the student.

4 **Superior Organization of Related Topics:** *McGraw-Hill's Taxation* provides two alternative topic sequences. In the *McGraw-Hill's Taxation of Individuals and Business Entities* volume, the individual topics generally follow the tax form sequence, with an individual overview chapter and then chapters on income, deductions, investment-related issues, and the tax liability computation. The topics then transition into business-related topics that apply to individuals. This volume then provides a group of specialty chapters dealing with topics of particular interest to individuals (including students), including separate chapters on home ownership, compensation, and retirement savings and deferred compensation. This volume concludes with a chapter covering the taxation of business entities. Alternatively, in the *Essentials of Federal Taxation* volume, the topics follow a more traditional sequence, with topics streamlined (no specialty chapters) and presented in more of a life-cycle approach.

5 **Real-World Focus:** Students learn best when they see how concepts are applied in the real world. For that reason, real-world examples and articles are included in **"Taxes in the Real World"** boxes throughout the book. These vignettes demonstrate current issues in taxation and show the relevance of tax issues in all areas of business.

> The in-text examples of how to complete tax returns(is a strength of this text). These help students improve their overall understanding of the material as it moves from something abstract to something tangible the student can produce."
>
> Christine Cheng–Louisiana State University

A STORYLINE APPROACH THAT RESONATES WITH STUDENTS

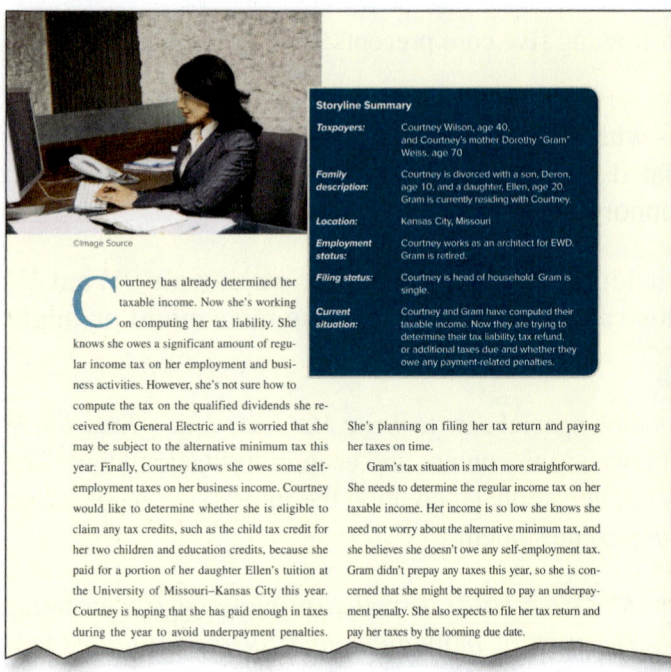

©Image Source

Storyline Summary

Taxpayers:	Courtney Wilson, age 40, and Courtney's mother Dorothy "Gram" Weiss, age 70
Family description:	Courtney is divorced with a son, Deron, age 10, and a daughter, Ellen, age 20. Gram is currently residing with Courtney.
Location:	Kansas City, Missouri
Employment status:	Courtney works as an architect for EWD. Gram is retired.
Filing status:	Courtney is head of household. Gram is single.
Current situation:	Courtney and Gram have computed their taxable income. Now they are trying to determine their tax liability, tax refund, or additional taxes due and whether they owe any payment-related penalties.

Courtney has already determined her taxable income. Now she's working on computing her tax liability. She knows she owes a significant amount of regular income tax on her employment and business activities. However, she's not sure how to compute the tax on the qualified dividends she received from General Electric and is worried that she may be subject to the alternative minimum tax this year. Finally, Courtney knows she owes some self-employment taxes on her business income. Courtney would like to determine whether she is eligible to claim any tax credits, such as the child tax credit for her two children and education credits, because she paid for a portion of her daughter Ellen's tuition at the University of Missouri–Kansas City this year. Courtney is hoping that she has paid enough in taxes during the year to avoid underpayment penalties.

She's planning on filing her tax return and paying her taxes on time.

Gram's tax situation is much more straightforward. She needs to determine the regular income tax on her taxable income. Her income is so low she knows she need not worry about the alternative minimum tax, and she believes she doesn't owe any self-employment tax. Gram didn't prepay any taxes this year, so she is concerned that she might be required to pay an underpayment penalty. She also expects to file her tax return and pay her taxes by the looming due date.

Each chapter begins with a storyline that introduces a set of characters facing specific tax-related situations. This revolutionary approach to teaching tax emphasizes real people facing real tax dilemmas. Students learn to apply practical tax information to specific business and personal situations. As their situations evolve, the characters are brought further to life.

> "Excellent text! Very readable, easy for students to read and understand. Storyline approach and integrated examples make it easy for students to relate to taxpayers and their tax situations."
>
> Sandra Owen
> – Indianan State University, Bloomington

Examples

Examples are the cornerstone of any textbook covering taxation. For this reason, *McGraw-Hill's Taxation* authors took special care to create clear and helpful examples that relate to the storyline of the chapter. Students learn to refer to the facts presented in the storyline and apply them to other scenarios—in this way, they build a greater base of knowledge through application. Many examples also include "What if?" scenarios that add more complexity to the example or explore related tax concepts.

> "The text is easy to read and provides many easy-to-follow examples throughout the chapter."
>
> Gloria Jean Stuart
> – Georgia Southern University

Example 2-1

Bill and Mercedes file their 2014 federal tax return on September 6, 2015, after receiving an automatic extension to file their return by October 15, 2015. In 2018, the IRS selects their 2014 tax return for audit. When does the statute of limitations end for Bill and Mercedes's 2014 tax return?

Answer: Assuming the six-year and "unlimited" statute of limitation rules do not apply, the statute of limitations ends on September 6, 2018 (three years after the later of the actual filing date and the *original* due date).

What if: When would the statute of limitations end for Bill and Mercedes for their 2014 tax return if the couple filed the return on March 22, 2015 (before the original due date of April 15, 2015)?

Answer: In this scenario the statute of limitations would end on April 15, 2018, because the later of the actual filing date and the original due date is April 15, 2015.

THE PEDAGOGY YOUR STUDENTS NEED TO PUT THE CODE IN CONTEXT

Taxes in the Real World

Taxes in the Real World are short boxes used throughout the book to demonstrate the real-world use of tax concepts. Current articles on tax issues, the real-world application of chapter-specific tax rules, and short vignettes on popular news about tax are some of the issues covered in Taxes in the Real World boxes.

> "The Spilker text makes tax easy for students to understand. **It integrates great real-world examples so students can see how topics will be applied in practice.** The integration of the tax form and exhibits of the tax forms in the text are outstanding."
>
> – Kristen Bigbee, Texas Tech University

TAXES IN THE REAL WORLD Tax Policy: Republicans versus Democrats

Oliver Wendell Holmes said "taxes are the price we pay to live in a civilized society." Both Democrats and Republicans desire the same things: a civilized society and a healthy economy. However, neither party can agree on what defines a civilized society or which path best leads to a healthy economy. The U.S. national debt is $20 trillion dollars and growing, yet the only thing we might agree on is that something has gone wrong. Regardless of which party or candidate you support, each party's agenda will affect your income and taxes in various ways.

To explore the divide, let's examine excerpts from each party's National Platform from our most recent presidential election (2016).

Republicans

"We are the party of a growing economy that gives everyone a chance in life, an opportunity to learn, work, and realize the prosperity freedom makes possible."

"Government cannot create prosperity, though government can limit or destroy it. Prosperity is the product of self-discipline, enterprise, saving and investment by individuals, but it is not an end in itself. Prosperity provides the means by which citizens and their families can maintain their independence from government, raise their children by their own values, practice their faith, and build communities of cooperation and mutual respect."

"Republicans consider the establishment of a pro-growth tax code a moral imperative. More than any other public policy, the way government raises revenue—how much, at what rates, under what circumstances, from whom, and for whom—

of taxes. Democrats will claw back tax breaks for companies that ship jobs overseas, eliminate tax breaks for big oil and gas companies, and crack down on inversions and other methods companies use to dodge their tax responsibilities . . . We will then use the revenue raised from fixing the corporate tax code to reinvest in rebuilding America and ensuring economic growth that will lead to millions of good-paying jobs."

"We will ensure those at the top contribute to our country's future by establishing a multi-millionaire surtax to ensure millionaires and billionaires pay their fair share. In addition, we will shut down the "private tax system" for those at the top, immediately close egregious loopholes like those enjoyed by hedge fund managers, restore fair taxation on multimillion dollar estates, and ensure millionaires can no longer pay a lower rate than their secretaries. At a time of near-record corporate profits, slow wage growth, and rising costs, we need to offer tax relief to middle-class families—not those at the top."

"We will offer tax relief to hard working, middle-class families for the cost squeeze they have faced for years from rising health care, childcare, education, and other expenses." https://www.democrats.org/party-platform#preamble

Conclusion

Each party fundamentally believes the government should create/maintain cities and states that form a civilized society, and that government should foster a healthy economy. However, they choose very different paths to reach this objec-

The Key Facts

The Key Facts provide quick synopses of the critical pieces of information presented throughout each chapter.

The **tax base** defines what is actually taxed and is usually expressed in monetary terms, whereas the **tax rate** determines the level of taxes imposed on the tax base and is usually expressed as a percentage. For example, a sales tax rate of 6 percent on a purchase of $30 yields a tax of $1.80 ($1.80 = $30 × .06).

Federal, state, and local jurisdictions use a large variety of tax bases to collect tax. Some common tax bases (and related taxes) include taxable income (federal and state income taxes), purchases (sales tax), real estate values (real estate tax), and personal property values (personal property tax).

Different portions of a tax base may be taxed at different rates. A single tax applied to an entire base constitutes a **flat tax**. In the case of **graduated taxes**, the base is divided

THE KEY FACTS

How to Calculate a Tax

- Tax = Tax base × Tax rate
- The tax base defines what is actually taxed and is usually expressed in monetary terms.
- The tax rate determines the level of taxes imposed

Exhibits

Today's students are visual learners, and *McGraw-Hill's Taxation* understands this student need by making use of clear and engaging charts, diagrams, and tabular demonstrations of key material.

> "It is easily accessible to students as it is written in easy-to-understand language, and contains sufficient examples to illustrate complicated tax concepts and calculations."
>
> Machiavelli Chao
> – University of California, Irvine: The Paul Merage School of Business

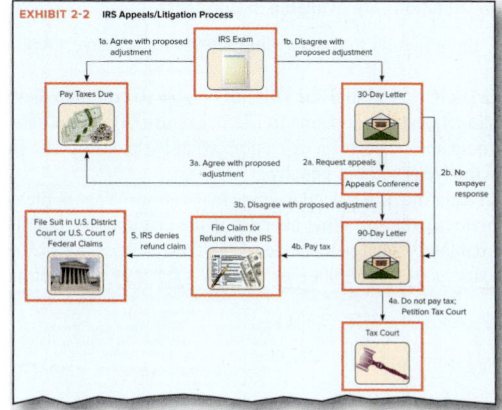

EXHIBIT 2-2   IRS Appeals/Litigation Process

PRACTICE MAKES PERFECT WITH A

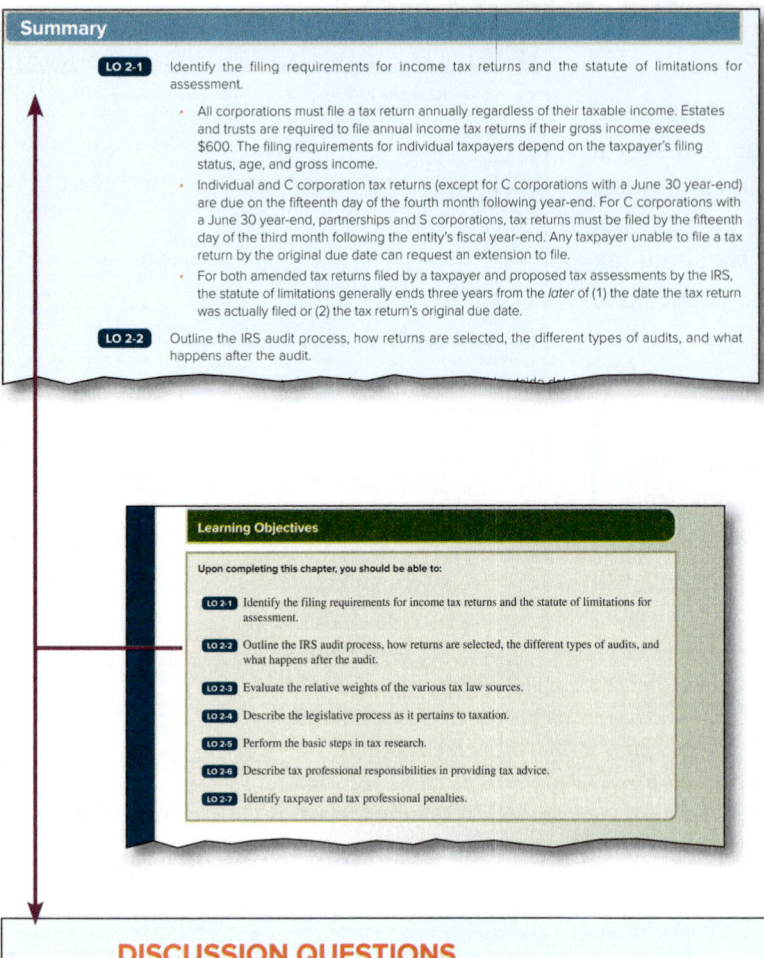

Summary

A unique feature of *McGraw-Hill's Taxation* is the end-of-chapter summary organized around learning objectives. Each objective has a brief, bullet-point summary that covers the major topics and concepts for that chapter, including references to critical exhibits and examples. All end-of-chapter material is tied to learning objectives.

Discussion Questions

Discussion questions, now available in *Connect*, are provided for each of the major concepts in each chapter, providing students with an opportunity to review key parts of the chapter and answer evocative questions about what they have learned.

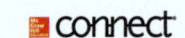

WIDE VARIETY OF ASSIGNMENT MATERIAL

Problems

Problems are designed to test the comprehension of more complex topics. Each problem at the end of the chapter is tied to one of that chapter's learning objectives, with multiple problems for critical topics.

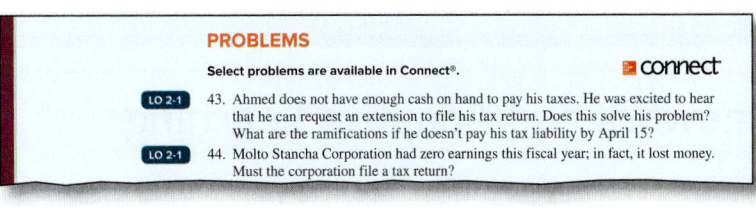

Tax Forms Problems

Tax forms problems are a set of requirements included in the end-of-chapter material of the 2019 edition. These problems require students to complete a tax form (or part of a tax form), provid-

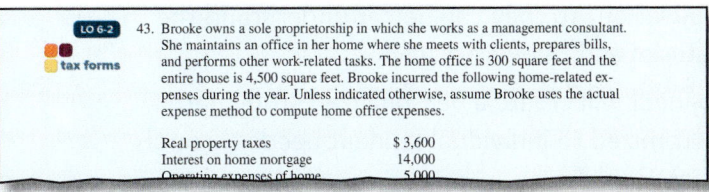

ing students with valuable experience and practice with filling out these forms. These requirements—and their relevant forms—are also included in *Connect*. Each tax form problem includes an icon to differentiate it from regular problems.

Research Problems

Research problems are special problems throughout the end-of-chapter assignment material. These require students to

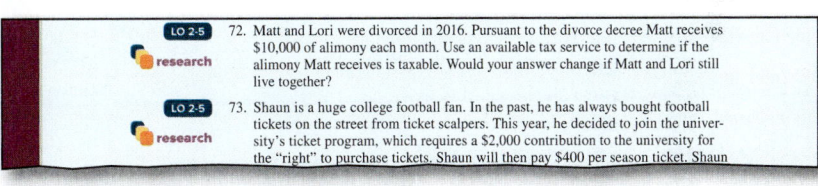

do both basic and more complex research on topics outside of the scope of the book. Each research problem includes an icon to differentiate it from regular problems.

Planning Problems

Planning problems are another unique set of problems included in the end-of-chapter assignment material. These re-quire students to test their tax planning

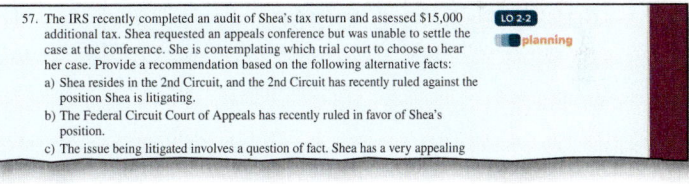

skills after covering the chapter topics. Each planning problem includes an icon to differentiate it from regular problems.

Comprehensive and Tax Return Problems

Comprehensive and tax return problems address multiple concepts in a single problem. Comprehensive problems are ideal for cumulative topics; for this rea-son, they are located at the end of all

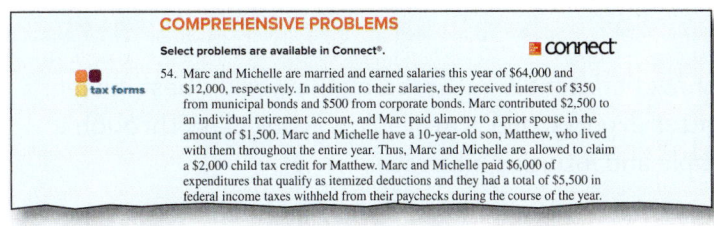

chapters. In the end-of-book Appendix C, we include tax return problems that cover multiple chap-ters. **Additional tax return problems are also available in *Connect* and *Instructor Resource Cen-ter*. These problems range from simple to complex and cover individual taxation, corporate taxation, partnership taxation, and S corporation taxation.**

McGraw-Hill Connect® is a highly reliable, easy-to-use homework and learning management solution that utilizes learning science and award-winning adaptive tools to improve student results.

Homework and Adaptive Learning

- Connect's assignments help students contextualize what they've learned through application, so they can better understand the material and think critically.

- Connect will create a personalized study path customized to individual student needs through SmartBook®.

- SmartBook helps students study more efficiently by delivering an interactive reading experience through adaptive highlighting and review.

Over **7 billion questions** have been answered, making McGraw-Hill Education products more intelligent, reliable, and precise.

Connect's Impact on Retention Rates, Pass Rates, and Average Exam Scores

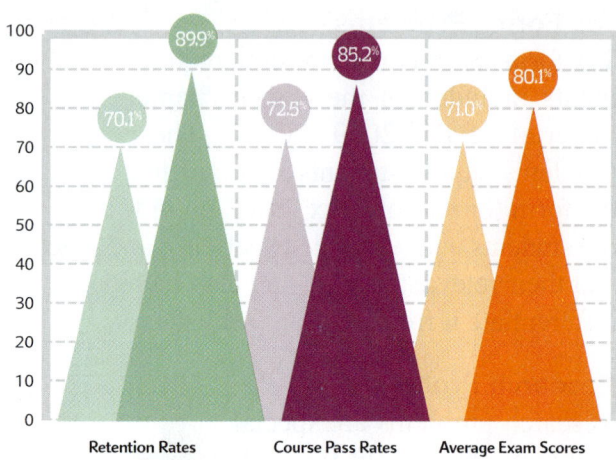

without Connect   with Connect

Using **Connect** improves retention rates by **19.8 percentage points**, passing rates by **12.7 percentage points**, and exam scores by **9.1 percentage points**.

73% of instructors who use **Connect** require it; instructor satisfaction **increases** by 28% when **Connect** is required.

Quality Content and Learning Resources

- Connect content is authored by the world's best subject matter experts, and is available to your class through a simple and intuitive interface.

- The Connect eBook makes it easy for students to access their reading material on smartphones and tablets. They can study on the go and don't need internet access to use the eBook as a reference, with full functionality.

- Multimedia content such as videos, simulations, and games drive student engagement and critical thinking skills.

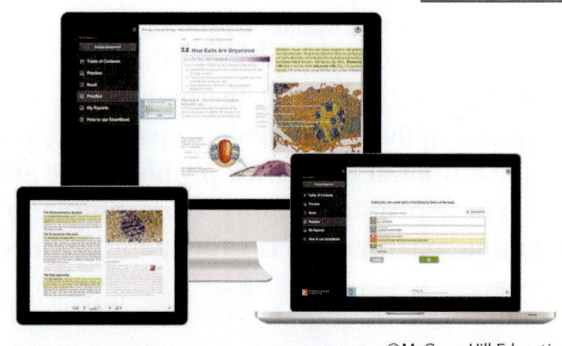

©McGraw-Hill Education

Robust Analytics and Reporting

©Hero Images/Getty Images

- Connect Insight® generates easy-to-read reports on individual students, the class as a whole, and on specific assignments.

- The Connect Insight dashboard delivers data on performance, study behavior, and effort. Instructors can quickly identify students who struggle and focus on material that the class has yet to master.

- Connect automatically grades assignments and quizzes, providing easy-to-read reports on individual and class performance.

Impact on Final Course Grade Distribution

without Connect		with Connect
22.9%	A	31.0%
27.4%	B	34.3%
22.9%	C	18.7%
11.5%	D	6.1%
15.4%	F	9.9%

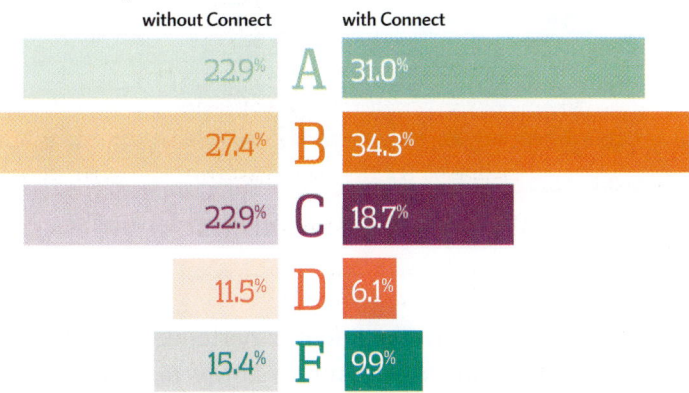

More students earn **As** and **Bs** when they use **Connect**.

Trusted Service and Support

- Connect integrates with your LMS to provide single sign-on and automatic syncing of grades. Integration with Blackboard®, D2L®, and Canvas also provides automatic syncing of the course calendar and assignment-level linking.

- Connect offers comprehensive service, support, and training throughout every phase of your implementation.

- If you're looking for some guidance on how to use Connect, or want to learn tips and tricks from super users, you can find tutorials as you work. Our Digital Faculty Consultants and Student Ambassadors offer insight into how to achieve the results you want with Connect.

DIGITAL LEARNING ASSETS TO IMPROVE STUDENT OUTCOMES

> "The quality of the online materials in Connect and Learnsmart are market-leading and unmatched in the tax arena."
>
> Jason W. Stanfield
> – Ball State University

Connect helps students learn more efficiently by providing feedback and practice material when they need it, where they need it. Connect grades homework automatically and gives immediate feedback on any questions students may have missed. The extensive assignable, gradable end-of-chapter content includes problems, comprehensive problems (available as auto-graded tax forms), and discussion questions. Also, select questions have been redesigned to test students' knowledge more fully. They now include tables for students to work through rather than requiring that all calculations be done offline.

Through November, Tex has received gross income of $120,000. For December, Tex is considering whether to accept one more work engagement for the year. Engagement 1 will generate $7,000 of revenue at a cost of $4,000, which is deductible for AGI. In contrast, engagement 2 will generate $7,000 of revenue at a cost of $3,000, which is deductible as an itemized deduction. Tex files as a single taxpayer. (use the tax rate schedules.)

a. Calculate Tex's taxable income assuming he chooses engagement 1 and assuming he chooses engagement 2. Assume he has no itemized deductions other than those generated by engagement 2.

	Description	Engagement 1	Engagement 2
(1)	Gross income before new work engagement	$ 120,000	$ 120,000
(2)	Income from engagement	7,000	7,000
(3)	Additional for AGI deduction	(4,000)	
(4)	Adjusted gross income	$ 123,000	$ 127,000
(5)	Greater		
(6)	Greater of itemized deductions or standard deduction		

Auto-Graded Tax Forms

The auto-graded **Tax Forms** in Connect provide a much-improved student experience when solving the tax-form based problems. The tax form simulation allows students to apply tax concepts by completing the actual tax forms online with automatic feedback and grading for both students and instructors.

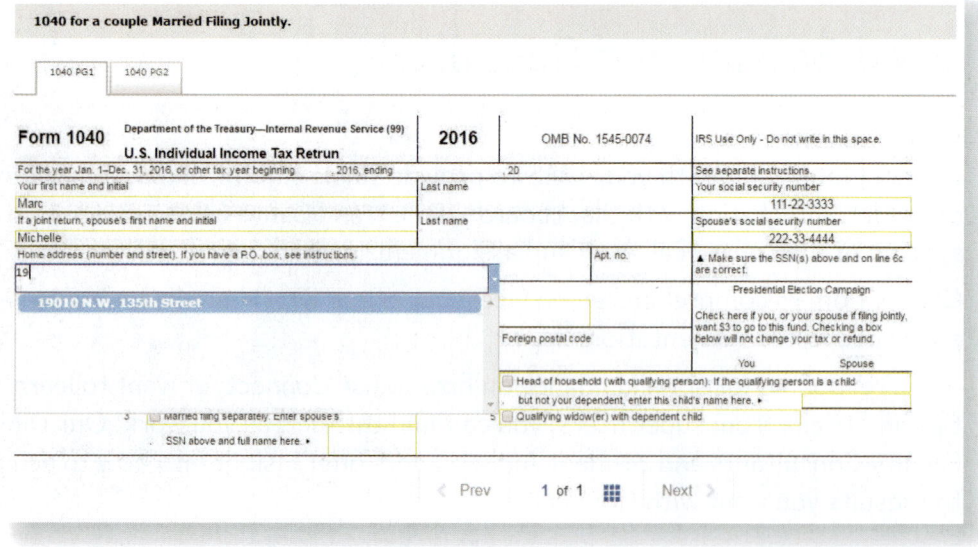

Guided Examples

The **Guided Examples,** or "hint" videos, in Connect provide a narrated, animated, step-by-step walk-through of select problems similar to those assigned. These short presentations can be turned on or off by instructors and provide reinforcement when students need it most.

TaxACT®

TaxAct Professional *McGraw-Hill's Taxation* can be packaged with tax software from TaxACT, one of the leading preparation software companies in the market today. The 2017 edition includes availability of both *Individuals* and *Business Entities* software, including the 1040 Forms and TaxACT Preparer's Business 3-Pack (with Forms 1065, 1120, and 1120S).

Please note, TaxACT is only compatible with PCs and not Macs. However, we offer easy-to-complete licensing agreement templates that are accessible within Connect and the Instructor Resources Center to enable school computer labs to download the software onto campus hardware for free.

Alfio, who is single and has no dependents, was planning on spending the weekend repairing his car. On Friday, Alfio's employer called and offered him $700 in overtime pay if he would agree to work over the weekend. Alfio could get his car repaired over the weekend at FixMyCar for $500. If Alfio works over the weekend, he will have to pay the $500 to have his car repaired but he will earn $700. Assume Alfio pays tax at a flat 20 percent rate.

b. If the cost of repairs is deductible:

Description	Amount
Overtime Pay	$700
Cost of Repairs	$500
Taxable Income	$200
Taxes on Pay	$ 40
Net Income	$160

So, he's $160 better off by working and having his car repaired by FixMyCar.

Roger's CPA

ROGER | *CPA Review* McGraw-Hill Education has partnered with Roger CPA Review, a global leader in CPA Exam preparation, to provide students a smooth transition from the accounting classroom to successful completion of the CPA Exam. While many aspiring accountants wait until they have completed their academic studies to begin preparing for the CPA Exam, research shows that those who become familiar with exam content earlier in the process have a stronger chance of successfully passing the CPA Exam.

Accordingly, students using these McGraw-Hill materials will have access to sample CPA Exam multiple-choice questions and Task-based Simulations from Roger CPA Review, with expert-written explanations and solutions. All questions are either directly from the AICPA or are modeled on AICPA questions that appear in the exam. Task-based Simulations are delivered via the Roger CPA Review platform, which mirrors the look, feel, and functionality of the actual exam.

McGraw-Hill Education and Roger CPA Review are dedicated to supporting every accounting student along their journey, ultimately helping them achieve career success in the accounting profession. For more information about the full Roger CPA Review program, exam requirements, and exam content, visit www.rogercpareview.com.

McGraw-Hill Customer Experience Group Contact Information

At McGraw-Hill, we understand that getting the most from new technology can be challenging. That's why our services don't stop after you purchase our products. You can contact our Product Specialists 24 hours a day to get product training online. Or you can search the knowledge bank of Frequently Asked Questions on our support website. For Customer Support, call **800-331-5094,** or visit www.mhhe.com/support. One of our Technical Support Analysts will be able to assist you in a timely fashion.

Four Volumes to Fit

McGraw-Hill's Taxation of Individuals is organized to emphasize topics that are most important to undergraduates taking their first tax course. The first three chapters provide an introduction to taxation and then carefully guide students through tax research and tax planning. Part II discusses the fundamental elements of individual income tax, starting with the tax formula in Chapter 4 and then proceeding to more discussion on income, deductions, investments, and computing tax liabilities in Chapters 5–8. Part III then discusses tax issues associated with business-related activities. Specifically, this part addresses business income and deductions, accounting methods, and tax consequences associated with purchasing assets and property dispositions (sales, trades, or other dispositions). Part IV is unique among tax textbooks; this section combines related tax issues for compensation, retirement savings, and home ownership.

McGraw-Hill's Taxation of Business Entities begins with the process for determining gross income and deductions for businesses, and the tax consequences associated with purchasing assets and property dispositions (sales, trades, or other dispositions). Part II provides a comprehensive overview of entities and the formation, reorganization, and liquidation of corporations. Unique to this series is a complete chapter on accounting for income taxes, which provides a primer on the basics of calculating the income tax provision. Included in the narrative is a discussion of temporary and permanent differences and their impact on a company's book "effective tax rate." Part III provides a detailed discussion of partnerships and S corporations. The last part of the book covers state and local taxation, multinational taxation, and transfer taxes and wealth planning.

Four Course Approaches

McGraw-Hill's Taxation of Individuals and Business Entities covers all chapters included in the two split volumes in one convenient volume. See Table of Contents.

McGraw-Hill's Essentials of Federal Taxation is designed for a one-semester course, covering the basics of taxation of individuals and business entities. To facilitate a one-semester course, *McGraw-Hill's Essentials of Federal Taxation* folds the key topics from the investments, compensation, retirement savings, and home ownership chapters in *Taxation of Individuals* into three individual taxation chapters that discuss gross income and exclusions, *for* AGI deductions, and *from* AGI deductions, respectively. The essentials volume also includes a two-chapter C corporation sequence that uses a life-cycle approach covering corporate formations and then corporate operations in the first chapter and nonliquidating and liquidating corporate distributions in the second chapter. This volume is perfect for those teaching a one-semester course and for those who struggle to get through the 25-chapter comprehensive volume.

SUPPLEMENTS FOR INSTRUCTORS

Assurance of Learning Ready

Many educational institutions today are focused on the notion of *assurance of learning,* an important element of many accreditation standards. *McGraw-Hill's Taxation* is designed specifically to support your assurance of learning initiatives with a simple, yet powerful, solution.

Each chapter in the book begins with a list of numbered learning objectives, which appear throughout the chapter as well as in the end-of-chapter assignments. Every test bank question for *McGraw-Hill's Taxation* maps to a specific chapter learning objective in the textbook. Each test bank question also identifies topic area, level of difficulty, Bloom's Taxonomy level, and AICPA and AACSB skill area.

AACSB Statement

McGraw-Hill Education is a proud corporate member of AACSB International. Understanding the importance and value of AACSB accreditation, *McGraw-Hill's Taxation* recognizes the curricula guidelines detailed in the AACSB standards for business accreditation by connecting selected questions in the text and the test bank to the general knowledge and skill guidelines in the revised AACSB standards.

The statements contained in *McGraw-Hill's Taxation* are provided only as a guide for the users of this textbook. The AACSB leaves content coverage and assessment within the purview of individual schools, the mission of the school, and the faculty. While *McGraw-Hill's Taxation* and the teaching package make no claim of any specific AACSB qualification or evaluation, we have, within the text and test bank, labeled selected questions according to the eight general knowledge and skill areas.

TestGen

TestGen is a complete, state-of-the-art test generator and editing application software that allows instructors to quickly and easily select test items from McGraw Hill's TestGen testbank content and to organize, edit, and customize the questions and answers to rapidly generate paper tests. Questions can include stylized text, symbols, graphics, and equations that are inserted directly into questions using built-in mathematical templates. With both quick-and-simple test creation and flexible and robust editing tools, TestGen is a test generator system for today's educators.

A HEARTFELT THANKS TO THE MANY COLLEAGUES WHO SHAPED THIS BOOK

The version of the book you are reading would not be the same book without the valuable suggestions, keen insights, and constructive criticisms of the list of reviewers below. Each professor listed here contributed in substantive ways to the organization of chapters, coverage of topics, and use of pedagogy. We are grateful to them for taking the time to read chapters or attend reviewer conferences, focus groups, and symposia in support of the development for the book:

Previous Edition Reviewers
Donna Abelli, *Mount Ida College*
Joseph Assalone, *Rowan College at Gloucester County*
Valeriya Avdeev, *William Paterson University*
Robyn Barrett, *St. Louis Community College*
Kevin Baugess, *ICDC College*
Christopher Becker, *Coastal Carolina University*
Jeanne Bedell, *Keiser University*
Marcia Behrens, *Nichols College*
Michael Belleman, *St. Clair County Community College*
David Berman, *Community College of Philadelphia*
Tim Biggart, *Berry College*

Cynthia Bird, *Tidewater Community College*
Lisa Blum, *University of Louisville*
Rick Blumenfeld, *Sierra College*
Cindy Bortman Boggess, *Babson College*
Cathalene Bowler, *University of Northern Iowa*
Justin Breidenbach, *Ohio Wesleyan University*
Suzon Bridges, *Houston Community College*
Stephen Bukowy, *UNC Pembroke*
Esther Bunn, *Stephen F. Austin State University*
Holly Caldwell, *Bridgewater College*
James Campbell, *Thomas College*
Alisa Carini, *UCSD Extension*

Ronald Carter, *Patrick Henry Community College*
Cynthia Caruso, *Endicott College*
Paul Caselton, *University of Illinois Springfield*
Amy Chataginer, *Mississippi Gulf Coast Community College*
Machiavelli Chao, *University of California, Irvine*
Max Chao, *University of California, Irvine*
Christine Cheng, *Louisiana State University*
Lisa Church, *Rhode Island College*
Marilyn Ciolino, *Delgado Community College*
Wayne Clark, *Southwest Baptist University*
Ann Cohen, *University at Buffalo, SUNY*
Sharon Cox, *University of Illinois–Urbana-Champaign*
Terry Crain, *University of Oklahoma–Norman*
Roger Crane, *Indiana University East*
Brad Cripe, *Northern Illinois University*
Curtis J. Crocker, *Southern Crescent Technical College*
Richard Cummings, *University of Wisconsin–Whitewater*
Joshua Cutler, *University of Houston*
William Dams, *Lenoir Community College*
Nichole Dauenhauer, *Lakeland Community College*
Susan Snow Davis, *Green River College*
Jim Desimpelare, *University of Michigan–Ann Arbor*
Julie Dilling, *Moraine Park Technical College*
Steve Dombrock, *Carroll University*
Dr. Vicky C. Dominguez, *College of Southern Nevada*
Michael P. Donohoe, *University of Illinois-Urbana-Champaign*
John Dorocak, *California State University–San Berdinado*
Amy Dunbar, *University of Connecticut–Storrs*
John Eagan, *Morehouse College*
Reed Easton, *Seton Hall University*
Elizabeth Ekmekjian, *William Paterson University*
Ann Esarco, *Columbia College Columbia*
Frank Faber, *St. Joseph's College*
Michael Fagan, *Raritan Valley Community College*
Frank Farina, *Catawba College*
Andrew Finley, *Claremont McKenna*
Tim Fogarty, *Case Western Reserve University*
Mimi Ford, *Middle Georgia State University*
Wilhelmina Ford, *Middle Georgia State University*
George Frankel, *San Francisco State University*
Lawrence Friedken, *Penn State University*
Stephen Gara, *Drake University*
Robert Gary, *University of New Mexico*
Greg Geisler, *University of Missouri–St. Louis*
Earl Godfrey, *Gardner Webb University*
Thomas Godwin, *Purdue University*
David Golub, *Northeastern University*
Marina Grau, *Houston Community College*
Brian Greenstein, *University of Delaware*
Patrick Griffin, *Lewis University*
Lillian Grose, *University of Holy Cross*
Rosie Hagen, *Virginia Western Community College*
Marcye Hampton, *University of Central Florida*
Cass Hausserman, *Portland State University*
Rebecca Helms, *Ivy Tech Community College*
Melanie Hicks, *Liberty University*
Mary Ann Hofmann, *Appalachian State University*
Robert Joseph Holdren, *Muskingum University*
Bambi Hora, *University of Central Oklahoma*
Carol Hughes, *Asheville Buncombe Technical Community College*

Helen Hurwitz, *Saint Louis University*
Rik Ichiho, *Dixie State University*
Kerry Inger, *Auburn University*
Paul Johnson, *Mississippi Gulf Coast CC–JD Campus*
Athena Jones, *University of Maryland University College*
Andrew Junikiewicz, *Temple University*
Susan Jurney, *University of Arkansas Fayetteville*
Sandra Kemper, *Regis University*
Jon Kerr, *Baruch College–CUNY*
Lara Kessler, *Grand Valley State University*
Janice Klimek, *University of Central Missouri*
Pamela Knight, *Columbus Technical College*
Satoshi Kojima, *East Los Angeles College*
Dawn Konicek, *Idaho State University*
Jack Lachman, *Brooklyn College*
Brandon Lanciloti, *Freed-Hardeman University*
Stacie Laplante, *University of Wisconsin–Madison*
Suzanne Laudadio, *Durham Tech*
Stephanie Lewis, *Ohio State University–Columbus*
Troy Lewis, *Brigham Young University*
Teresa Lightner, *University of North Texas*
Robert Lin, *California State University–East Bay*
Chris Loiselle, *Cornerstone University*
Bruce Lubich, *Penn State–Harrisburg*
Narelle Mackenzie, *San Diego State University, National University*
Michael Malmfeldt, *Shenandoah University*
Kate Mantzke, *Northern Illinois University*
Robert Martin, *Kennesaw State University*
Anthony Masino, *East Tennessee State University*
Paul Mason, *Baylor University*
Lisa McKinney, *University of Alabama at Birmingham*
Allison McLeod, *University of North Texas*
Lois McWhorter, *Somerset Community College*
Janet Meade, *University of Houston*
Michele Meckfessel, *University of Missouri–St. Louis*
Frank Messina, *University of Alabama at Birmingham*
R Miedaner, *Lee University*
Ken Milani, *University of Notre Dame*
Karen Morris, *Northeast Iowa Community College*
Stephanie Morris, *Mercer University*
Michelle Moshier, *University at Albany*
Leslie Mostow, *University of Maryland, College Park*
James Motter, *Indiana University-Purdue University Indianapolis*
Jackie Myers, *Sinclair Community College*
Michael Nee, *Cape Cod Community College*
Liz Ott, *Casper College*
Sandra Owen- *Indiana State University–Bloomington*
Edwin Pagan, *Passaic County Community College*
Jeff Paterson, *Florida State University*
Ronald Pearson, *Bay College*
Martina Peng, *Franklin University*
James Pierson, *Franklin University*
Sonja Pippin, *University of Nevada–Reno*
Anthony Pochesci, *Rutgers University*
Kyle Post, *Tarleton State University*
Christopher Proschko, *Texas State University*
Joshua Racca, *University of Alabama*
Francisco Rangel, *Riverside City College*
Pauline Ash Ray, *Thomas University*

Luke Richardson, *University of South Florida*
Rodney Ridenour, *Montana State University Northern*
John Robertson, *Arkansas State University*
Susan Robinson, *Georgia Southwestern State University*
Morgan Rockett, *Moberly Area Community College*
Miles Romney, *Michigan State University*
Ananth Seetharaman, *Saint Louis University*
Alisa Shapiro, *Raritan Valley Community College*
Deanna Sharpe, *University of Missouri*
Wayne Shaw, *Southern Methodist University*
Sonia Singh, *University of Florida*
Georgi Smatrakalev, *Florida Atlantic University*
Lucia Smeal, *Georgia State University*
Pamela Smith, *University of Texas at San Antonio*
Adam Spoolstra, *Johnson County Community College*
Joe Standridge, *Sonoma State*
Jason Stanfield, *Ball State University*
George Starbuck, *McMurry University*
James Stekelberg, *University of Arizona*
Shane Stinson, *University of Alabama*

Terrie Stolte, *Columbus State Community College*
Gloria Jean Stuart, *Georgia Southern University*
Kenton Swift, *University of Montana*
Erin Towery, *The University of Georgia*
Ronald Unger, *Temple University*
Karen Wallace, *Ramapo College*
Natasha Ware, *Southeastern University*
Luke Watson, *University of Florida*
Sarah Webber, *University of Dayton*
Cassandra Weitzenkamp, *Peru State College*
Marvin Williams, *University of Houston—Downtown*
Chris Woehrle, *American College*
Jennifer Wright, *Drexel University*
Massood Yahya-Zadeh, *George Mason University*
James Yang, *Montclair State University*
Scott Yetmar, *Cleveland State University*
Charlie Yuan, *Elizabeth City State University*
Xiaoli Yuan, *Elizabeth City State University*
Mingjun Zhou, *DePaul University*

Acknowledgments

We would like to thank the many talented people who made valuable contributions to the creation of this tenth edition. William A. Padley of Madison Area Technical College, Deanna Sharpe of the University of Missouri–Columbia, and Troy Lewis of Brigham Young University checked the page proofs and solutions manual for accuracy; we greatly appreciate the hours they spent checking tax forms and double-checking our calculations throughout the book. Teressa Farough, Troy Lewis of Brigham Young University, Lara Kessler of Grand Valley State University and Eric McLimore accuracy-checked the test bank. Thank you to Troy Lewis, Monika Turek, and Jason Stanfield for your contributions to the Smartbook revision for this edition. Special thanks to Troy Lewis of Brigham Young University for his sharp eye and valuable feedback throughout the revision process. Thanks as well to Marilyn Isaacks from Agate Publishing for managing the supplement process. Finally, William A. Padley of Madison Area Technical College, Deanna Sharpe of the University of Missouri–Columbia, and Vivian Paige of Old Dominion University greatly contributed to the accuracy of McGraw-Hill's *Connect* for the 2019 edition.

We also appreciate the expert attention given to this project by the staff at McGraw-Hill Education, especially Tim Vertovec, Managing Director; Kathleen Klehr, Executive Portfolio Manager; Danielle Andries, Senior Product Developer; Erin Quinones, Product Developer; Lori Koetters, Brian Nacik, and Jill Eccher, Content Project Managers; Matt Backhaus, Designer; Natalie King, Marketing Director; Zach Rudin, Marketing Manager; and Sue Culbertson, Senior Buyer.

Changes in *Essentials of Federal Taxation,* 2019 Edition

For the 2019 edition of McGraw-Hill's *Essentials of Federal Taxation,* many changes were made in response to feedback from reviewers and focus group participants:

- All **tax forms** have been **updated for the latest available tax form as of March 2018.** In addition, **chapter content** throughout the text has been **updated to reflect tax law changes through March 2018.**

Other notable changes in the 2019 edition include:

Chapter 1

- Updated tax rates for 2018 and Examples 1-3 through 1-7.
- Updated Social Security Wage base for 2018.
- Updated unified Tax Credit for 2018.
- Deleted Taxes in the Real World: Affordable Care Act amount for 2018 which was repealed.
- Updated Taxes in the Real World: National Debt for current debt limit.
- Updated Exhibit 1-4 for 2017 Federal revenues by source from Treasury.
- Updated Exhibit 1-5 for 2017 State revenues by source from U.S. Census.

Chapter 2

- Updated gross income thresholds by filing status for 2018 for new tax law changes.
- Updated discussion of filing requirements for married taxpayers for new tax law changes.
- Revised discussion of Preparer Tax Identification Numbers (PTIN).
- Revised end of chapter problems to reflect tax law changes.

Chapter 3

- Updated tax rates for 2018.
- Added Taxes in the Real World: Tax Reform and Tax Planning.
- Updated Exhibit 3-3 for new tax rates post TCJA.
- Modified Examples 3-7 and 3-8 to reflect changes in tax planning from TCJA.

Chapter 4

- Streamlined Learning Objective 4-1.
- Edited Learning Objective 4-2 to emphasize dependents instead of exemptions.
- Updated Exhibit 4-1 to reflect changes in the Individual Tax Formula

- Updated Exhibit 4-7 to reflect standard deduction amounts for 2018.
- Edited Exhibit 4-5 to remove moving expenses.
- Changed Example 4-2 to replace moving expenses with IRA contribution.
- Updated discussion of child tax credits to reflect new law.
- Updated examples to reflect changes in child tax credit under new tax law.
- Revised section on personal and dependency exemptions to emphasize who qualifies as a dependent of the taxpayer.
- Revised discussion of why determining filing status is important.
- Revised filing status discussion to emphasize claiming a dependent rather than claiming an exemption for a dependent.
- Edited flowcharts in appendices to emphasize claiming a dependent rather than claiming an exemption for a dependent.
- Added two new discussion questions to address questions relating to the new tax law.
- Deleted one problem dealing with dependency exemptions.
- Edited approximately 10 percent of the problems to reflect changes in the tax law allowing the deduction for qualified business income or dependency exemptions.
- Updated tax rates for 2018.
- Updated tax forms from 2016 to 2017 forms.

Chapter 5

- Revised discussion of claim of right doctrine for employees required to repay compensation for tax law changes.
- Updated discussion of alimony for tax law changes.
- Updated discussion of employee awards for length of service or safety awards for tax law changes.
- Clarified discussion of the deductibility of gambling expenses for tax law changes.
- Updated discussion of discharge of indebtedness for tax law changes.
- Revised discussion of fringe benefits and moving expenses for tax law changes.

- Added a discussion of accountable plan reimbursements.
- Updated for 2018 amounts for Flexible Spending Account contributions.
- Revised discussion of Section 529 plans for tax law changes.
- Added Taxes in the Real World on Bitcoin transactions.
- Added Taxes in the Real World on the taxation of prizes.
- Updated for 2018 foreign income exclusion amounts.
- Updated for annual gift tax exclusion and unified tax credit for 2018.
- Revised discussion of athletic scholarships.
- Updated U.S. Series EE Bond interest income exclusion for 2018.
- Updated inflation adjusted limits for defined benefit plans and defined contribution plans.
- Revised Appendix A and relate discussion about how taxpayers determine whether capital gains are taxed at 0, 15, 20, 25 or 28 percent or ordinary tax rates.
- Revised Exhibit 5-3 to reflect new maximum applicable tax rates that apply to capital gains.
- Updated tax forms from 2016 to 2017 forms.
- Updated end of chapter problems for tax law changes

Chapter 6

- Revised discussion of deductibility of business versus investment related expenses under for tax law changes.
- Revised Exhibit 6-1: Individual Business and Investment Related Deductions for AGI, from AGI, and Not Deductible.
- Added discussion for new excess business loss limitation.
- Revised discussion of the IRS method and the Tax Court method to reflect the circumstances in which each is more favorable given the new tax law.
- Clarified discussion about home office expense requirements.
- Revised discussion about home office expenses to indicate that employees can no longer claim the deduction.
- Revised discussion in IRA section to use modified AGI rather than AGI when describing deduction and contribution limitations.
- Updated modified AGI phase-out thresholds for deductible contributions to traditional IRAs and contributions to Roth IRAs.
- Revised discussion of moving expenses for tax law changes.

- Revised discussion of alimony deduction for tax law changes.
- Revised discussion of deduction for interest on qualified education loan for tax law changes.
- Eliminate discussion of expired deduction for qualified education expenses.
- Updated tax forms from 2016 to 2017 forms.
- Substantially revised end of chapter problems for tax law changes.

Chapter 7

- Updated AGI floor for medical expense itemized deduction for tax law change.
- Updated mileage rate for medical expense itemized deduction for 2018.
- Added discussion on new cap on itemized deductions for taxes.
- Revised discussion of mortgage interest deduction to reflect new cap on acquisition indebtedness and nondeductibility of interest on home-equity indebtedness.
- Revised discussion of investment interest expense deduction for tax law change that eliminates the deduction for investment expenses as itemized deductions.
- Revised discussion of charitable contributions for new 60 percent AGI limit for cash contributions to public charities and private operating foundations.
- Revised Exhibit 7-1: Summary of Charitable Contributions Limitation Rules.
- Revised discussion of casualty and theft losses on personal-use assets for tax law changes.
- Revised discussion of miscellaneous itemized deductions to reflect tax law changes that eliminated these deductions subject to 2 percent AGI floor (employee business expenses, tax preparation fees, hobby expenses, investment expenses)
- Eliminated discussion of itemized deduction and personal exemption phase-outs repealed by tax law changes.
- Updated standard deduction amounts for tax law changes.
- Eliminated discussion of personal and dependency exemptions repealed by tax law changes.
- Added discussion for new deduction for qualified business income.
- Updated tax forms from 2016 to 2017 forms.
- Substantially revised end of chapter problems for tax law changes.

Chapter 8

- Updated tax rate schedules to reflect tax law changes.
- Updated discussion of marriage penalty or benefit for tax law changes.

- Revised discussion of kiddie tax for tax law changes.
- Revised discussion of the tax calculation for preferentially taxed capital gains and dividends for tax law changes.
- Updated AMT discussion for new tax law changes related to adjustments, exemption amounts, and phase-out of exemptions.
- Updated AMT tax rate schedule for 2018.
- Updated Social Security Tax wage base and Self-Employment Tax base for 2018.
- Revised discussion of Medicare and additional Medicare tax.
- Updated discussion of child tax credit for tax law changes.
- Updated Lifetime Learning Credit phase-out for 2018.
- Updated discussion of education credits for expiration of the deduction for qualified education expenses.
- Updated Earned Income Credit amounts for 2018.
- Updated tax forms from 2016 to 2017 forms.
- Revised end of chapter problems for tax law changes.

Chapter 9

- Introduction was updated and the learning objectives were consolidated.
- Revised descriptions of deductions to reflect changes in the Tax Cuts and Jobs Act.
- Revised descriptions of general limitations on business deductions to reflect changes in the Tax Cuts and Jobs Act.
- Added text description and example of new business interest limitation.
- Revised text discussion of limitations on business deductions for meals and entertainment.
- Revised examples to reflect changes in the Tax Cuts and Jobs Act.
- Revised examples and text discussion for updated 2018 mileage rates.
- Added new TIRW to describe application of substantiation rules and the Cohan rule.
- Deleted discussion and illustration of domestic manufacturing deduction eliminated in the Tax Cuts and Jobs Act.
- Revised text description, examples, and Exhibit 9-2 to reflect changes in casualty loss deductions in the Tax Cuts and Jobs Act.
- Revised footnotes and added example of 52-53 week year.
- Revised text descriptions of cash method, UNICAP, and inventory accounting to reflect changes in the Tax Cuts and Jobs Act.
- Revised accounting for advanced payments of revenue to reflect accounting method changes in the Tax Cuts and Jobs Act.

- Revised accounting method changes to reflect new provisions in the Tax Cuts and Jobs Act updated dates in examples.
- Revised Exhibit 9-6 for changes in solutions due to accounting method changes in the Tax Cuts and Jobs Act.
- Eliminated discussion questions on domestic manufacturing deduction and added new discussion questions about business interest limitation.
- Revised discussion questions to reflect accounting method changes in the Tax Cuts and Jobs Act.
- Eliminated problems on domestic manufacturing deduction and added new problems with business interest limitation.
- Revised problems to reflect accounting method changes in the Tax Cuts and Jobs Act.

Chapter 10

- Modified story line to better apply to changes in tax law.
- Updated all examples for new purchase price on Teton's assets.
- Updated Exhibit 10-2 for Weyerhaueser's 2016 assets.
- Updated tax rates for 2018.
- Updated footnote 2 relating to depreciation allowed or allowable.
- Added new footnote to explain the opportunity to expense new roofs post TCJA.
- Added new preface to the depreciation section to explain impact of TCJA and under what conditions MACRS may be relevant.
- Moved the discussion about mid-quarter convention to new Appendix B.
- Added discussion to explain changes to qualified improvement property.
- Revised Example 10-7 (old 10-12) to include depreciation for two years on real property.
- Revised section on §179 amounts to reflect the larger 2018 amounts post-TCJA.
- Added footnote relating to definition of qualified real property for purposes of §179.
- Updated Examples 10-9 through 10-12 (old Examples 10-14 through 10-17) for 2018 §179 amounts.
- Substantially revised bonus depreciation section to include TCJA changes in percentages and qualified property.
- Added new Exhibit 10-8 to illustrate Bonus Depreciation Percentages.
- Added bonus depreciation Example 10-13.
- Revised listed property discussion to reflect removal of computer equipment as listed property.
- Updated discussion and Exhibit 10-9 (old 10-8) relating to automobile depreciation limits.

- Updated examples in listed property section to reflect TCJA changes.
- Added new discussion about the use of §179 for automobiles.
- Added new discussion and examples about the interaction of bonus depreciation and the automobile depreciation limitations. Includes new discussion of method for calculating depreciation on automobiles after year 1 when 100 percent bonus depreciation is taken.
- Added Taxes in the Real World: Cost Segregation.
- Updated Exhibit 10-10 (old 10-9) to reflect Teton's use of bonus depreciation in addition to §179 and MACRS for two years of asset acquisitions.
- Updated tax forms from 2016 to 2017 forms.
- Added new footnote 64 to describe treatment of R&D costs after 2021.
- Updated and revised end-of-chapter problems for §179 amounts and bonus depreciation rules post-TCJA.

Chapter 11

- Modified story line to better apply to changes in tax law
- Updated examples for new purchase price on Teton's assets.
- Updated Exhibit 11-4 for changes to capital gains threshold amounts.
- Added discussion about how changes to depreciation from TCJA might affect dispositions.
- Updated Exhibit 11-6 for changes to Teton's assets.
- Modified discussion on like-kind exchanges to reflect application to real property only.
- Modified Examples 11-15, 11-16, and 11-17 for like-kind exchanges.
- Updated discussion for involuntary conversion when contrasting qualified property to like-kind exchanges.
- Updated like-kind exchange EOC problems.
- Updated tax rates for 2018.
- Updated tax forms from 2016 to 2017 forms.

Chapter 12

- Clarified the discussion in "Rights, Responsibilities, and Legal Arrangements among Owners."
- Added mention of Certificate of Organization as a required filing to create a new LLC in certain states.
- Updated notes to Exhibit 12-1 to clarify that certain limited partnerships are eligible for IPOs.
- Replaced data in Taxes in the Real World on Comparing Entities Selected with more recent data from the IRS.
- Replaced the entire section on Double Taxation with new section on Taxation of Business Entity Income.

This section includes discussion of how flow-through entity income is taxed under new law and includes discussion on deduction for qualified business income and discussion of the self-employment tax for business owners.
- Revised discussion of how C corporations are taxed. This section includes discussion of the new tax rate for C corporations, the revised NOL rules, and the new DRD percentages.
- Added a section on owner compensation.
- Added section on deductibility of entity losses to include revised NOL rules for C corporations and the new excess loss limitation for noncorporate taxpayers.
- Updated Taxes in the Real Word: Best Entity Choice for Small Businesses? to reflect findings from a more recent study. Also, added information about the number of small businesses filing as partnerships and as S corporations.
- Revised discussion of Converting to Other Entity Types to reflect changes in the tax law and reasons why owners may wish to convert, given the new law.
- Revised the final discussion in the storyline. The taxpayer now chooses a C corporation rather than a partnership form for tax purposes.
- Revised Ethics discussion to include a situation where owner is potentially paying himself too little compensation.
- Changed or revised approximately 25 percent of the end of chapter problems.

Chapter 13

- Removed LO 5 dealing with alternative minimum tax including that section of the text and all related questions and problems in end of chapter materials.
- Revised tax liability section to include discussion of how corporations deal with minimum tax credit carryovers.
- Changed individual tax formula to reflect the deduction for qualified business income and the removal of deductions for personal and dependency exemptions.
- Updated Exhibit 13-3 to reflect changes in tax law for permanent book tax differences.
- Edited Exhibit 13-5 to show a bigger book-tax difference for depreciation.
- Updated dividends received discussion and related material to reflect new DRD percentages.
- Revised discussion about net operating losses to include discussion about the tax consequences of NOLs arising prior to 2018 and those arising after 2017.
- Revised discussion of contributions to capital for new tax law.
- Eliminated discussion of controlled groups (including old Exhibit 13-7 and related examples)

- Updated Taxes in the Real World about the government getting more corporate profits than shareholders to consider if this will change with the reduction in the corporate tax rate.
- Updated forms from 2016 to 2017.
- Updated Exhibits 13-8 and 13-9 to reflect taxable income given the new tax law.

Chapter 14

- Removed old LO3 dealing with constructive distributions and discussion of constructive dividends.
- Edited LO1 discussion to place less emphasis on tax strategies to mitigate or eliminate the double tax, given the significant reduction in corporate tax rates.
- Removed two discussion questions for LO1 and added one new discussion question.
- Edited discussion of adjustments to E&P, including Exhibit 14-1, to reflect new adjustments to E&P under the new tax law.
- Clarified that current E&P is calculated at end of the year without reduction for distributions made during the year.
- Revised chapter, including end of chapter problems to reflect 21 percent corporate tax rate.
- Removed problems dealing with constructive dividends.

Chapter 15

- Updated the discussion of self-employment income from partnerships to include the impact of recent case law.
- Revised the opening storyline of the chapter. The chapter assumes the taxpayer chooses to operate the business as a partnership for tax purposes.

- Added discussion on the new rule dealing with the availability of the cash method of accounting for partnerships.
- Added discussion on the new limitation on business interest deductions in the partnerships setting.
- Added discussion on new deduction for qualified business income.
- Added discussion on new excess business loss limitation and how it interacts with other loss limitation rules.
- Updated tax forms from 2016 to 2017 forms.
- Added material related to how the passive activity loss rules apply to publicly traded partnerships.
- Revised four problems to reflect changes in the Tax Cut and Jobs Act.

Chapter 16

- Clarified the approach for making a §754 election.
- Revised the definition of substantial built-in loss to reflect changes in the Tax Cut and Jobs Act.

Chapter 17

- Revised discussion of debt basis rules.
- Added discussion of 30 percent of taxable income limitation on the deduction for business interest expense under new tax law.
- Added discussion of deduction for qualified business income under new tax law.
- Added discussion of excess business loss limitation under new tax law.
- Added discussion of new PTTP distributions for eligible terminated S corporations under new tax law.
- Updated Social Security Tax wage base for 2018.
- Updated tax forms from 2016 to 2017 forms.
- Revised end of chapter problems for tax law changes.

NEW! Resources for 2017 Tax Cuts and Jobs Act—Available in 2018© and 2019©

- Brief Explainer Videos—Offers insights to students into new tax laws by comparing and contrasting with old tax code.
- Chapter Overviews—Identifies the tax law changes for each learning objective.
- Individual Chapter Guides—Provides summary description of new tax laws, expanding on the chapter overview.
- Problem Map—Marks the end-of-chapter content and test bank content affected by new tax laws in an easily navigable spreadsheet.

- Tagged Content in Connect—Added metadata tags to help instructors filter for end-of-chapter/test bank content impacted by 2017 tax reform.
- PowerPoints on Tax Changes—New slides detailing the updated laws on a chapter-by-chapter basis.
- Ongoing Author Webinars and Teaching Tips

As We Go to Press

The 2019 Edition is current through March, 2018. You can visit the *Connect Library* for updates that occur after this date.

Table of Contents

4   Individual Income Tax Overview, Dependents, and Filing Status

5   Gross Income and Exclusions

6   Individual *For* AGI Deductions

7   Individual *From* AGI Deductions

8   Individual Income Tax Computation and Tax Credits

11 Property Dispositions

12 Entities Overview

15 Forming and Operating Partnerships

16 Dispositions of Partnership Interests and Partnership Distributions

McGraw-Hill's

Essentials of Federal Taxation

1   An Introduction to Tax

Learning Objectives

Upon completing this chapter, you should be able to:

LO 1-1   Demonstrate how taxes influence basic business, investment, personal, and political decisions.

LO 1-2   Discuss what constitutes a tax and the general objectives of taxes.

LO 1-3   Describe the different tax rate structures and calculate a tax.

LO 1-4   Identify the various federal, state, and local taxes.

LO 1-5   Apply appropriate criteria to evaluate alternative tax systems.

©Andrew Rich/Getty Images

Storyline Summary

Taxpayer: Margaret

Employment status: Margaret is a full-time student at the University of Georgia.

Current situation: She is beginning her first tax class.

Margaret is a junior beginning her first tax course. She is excited about her career prospects as an accounting major but hasn't had much exposure to taxes. On her way to campus she runs into an old friend, Eddy, who is going to Washington, D.C., to protest recent proposed changes to the U.S. tax system. Eddy is convinced the IRS is evil and that the current tax system is blatantly unfair and corrupt. He advocates a simpler, fairer way of taxation. Margaret is intrigued by Eddy's passion but questions whether he has a complete understanding of the U.S. tax system. She decides to withhold all judgments about it (or about pursuing a career in taxation) until the end of her tax course. ■

WHO CARES ABOUT TAXES AND WHY?

A clear understanding of the role of taxes in everyday decisions will help you make an informed decision about the value of studying taxation or pursuing a career in taxation. One view of taxation is that it represents an inconvenience every April 15th (the annual due date for filing federal individual tax returns without extensions). However, the role of taxation is much more pervasive than this view suggests. Your study of this subject will provide you a unique opportunity to develop an informed opinion about taxation. As a business student, you can overcome the mystery that encompasses popular impressions of the tax system and perhaps, one day, share your expertise with friends or clients.

What are some common decisions you face that taxes may influence? In this course, we alert you to situations in which you can increase your return on investments by up to one-third! Even the best lessons in finance courses can't approach the increase in risk-adjusted return that smart tax planning provides. Would you like to own your home someday? Tax deductions for home mortgage interest and real estate taxes can reduce the after-tax costs of owning a home relative to renting. Thus, when you face the decision to buy or rent, you can make an informed choice if you understand the relative tax advantages of home ownership. Would you like to retire someday? Understanding the tax-advantaged methods of saving for retirement can increase the after-tax value of your retirement nest egg—and thus increase the likelihood that you can afford to retire, and do so in style. Other common personal financial decisions that taxes influence include: choosing investments, evaluating alternative job offers, saving for education expenses, and doing gift or estate planning. Indeed, taxes are a part of everyday life and have a significant effect on many of the personal financial decisions all of us face.

The role of taxes is not limited to personal finance. Taxes play an equally important role in fundamental business decisions such as the following:

- What organizational form should a business use?
- Where should the business locate?
- How should business acquisitions be structured?
- How should the business compensate employees?
- What is the appropriate mix of debt and equity for the business?
- Should the business rent or own its equipment and property?
- How should the business distribute profits to its owners?

Savvy business decisions require owners and managers to consider all costs and benefits in order to evaluate the merits of a transaction. Although taxes don't necessarily dominate these decisions, they do represent large transaction costs that businesses should factor into the financial decision-making process.

Taxes also play a major part in the political process. U.S. presidential candidates often distinguish themselves from their opponents based upon their tax rhetoric. Indeed, the major political parties generally have very diverse views of the appropriate way to tax the public.[1] Determining who is taxed, what is taxed, and how much is taxed are tough questions with nontrivial answers. Voters must have a basic understanding of taxes to evaluate the merits of alternative tax proposals. Later in this chapter, we'll introduce criteria you can use to evaluate alternative tax proposals.

---

[1]The U.S. Department of the Treasury provides a "history of taxation" on its website (www.treasury.gov/resource-center/faqs/Taxes/Pages/historyrooseveltmessage.aspx). You may find it interesting to read this history in light of the various political parties in office at the time.

TAXES IN THE REAL WORLD   Tax Policy: Republicans versus Democrats

Oliver Wendell Holmes said "taxes are the price we pay to live in a civilized society." Both Democrats and Republicans desire the same things: a civilized society and a healthy economy. However, neither party can agree on what defines a civilized society or which path best leads to a healthy economy. The U.S. national debt is $20 trillion dollars and growing, yet the only thing we might agree on is that something has gone wrong. Regardless of which party or candidate you support, each party's agenda will affect your income and taxes in various ways.

To explore the divide, let's examine excerpts from each party's National Platform from our most recent presidential election (2016).

Republicans

"We are the party of a growing economy that gives everyone a chance in life, an opportunity to learn, work, and realize the prosperity freedom makes possible."

"Government cannot create prosperity, though government can limit or destroy it. Prosperity is the product of self-discipline, enterprise, saving and investment by individuals, but it is not an end in itself. Prosperity provides the means by which citizens and their families can maintain their independence from government, raise their children by their own values, practice their faith, and build communities of cooperation and mutual respect."

"Republicans consider the establishment of a pro-growth tax code a moral imperative. More than any other public policy, the way government raises revenue—how much, at what rates, under what circumstances, from whom, and for whom—has the greatest impact on our economy's performance. It powerfully influences the level of economic growth and job creation, which translates into the level of opportunity for those who would otherwise be left behind."

"A strong economy is one key to debt reduction, but spending restraint is a necessary component that must be vigorously pursued." https://www.gop.com/platform/restoring-the-american-dream/

Democrats

"At a time of massive income and wealth inequality, we believe the wealthiest Americans and largest corporations must pay their fair share of taxes. Democrats will claw back tax breaks for companies that ship jobs overseas, eliminate tax breaks for big oil and gas companies, and crack down on inversions and other methods companies use to dodge their tax responsibilities . . . We will then use the revenue raised from fixing the corporate tax code to reinvest in rebuilding America and ensuring economic growth that will lead to millions of good-paying jobs."

"We will ensure those at the top contribute to our country's future by establishing a multimillionaire surtax to ensure millionaires and billionaires pay their fair share. In addition, we will shut down the "private tax system" for those at the top, immediately close egregious loopholes like those enjoyed by hedge fund managers, restore fair taxation on multimillion dollar estates, and ensure millionaires can no longer pay a lower rate than their secretaries. At a time of near-record corporate profits, slow wage growth, and rising costs, we need to offer tax relief to middle-class families—not those at the top."

"We will offer tax relief to hard working, middle-class families for the cost squeeze they have faced for years from rising health care, childcare, education, and other expenses." https://www.democrats.org/party-platform#preamble

Conclusion

Each party fundamentally believes the government should create/maintain cities and states that form a civilized society, and that government should foster a healthy economy. However, they choose very different paths to reach this objective. Democrats want to raise taxes on the wealthy and create government programs which cost more money, while Republicans wish to lower taxes and decrease government size and spending. Both motives are pure; however, current and cumulative deficits indicate that current revenue is insufficient to meet government spending. Solving these problems will require civil discourse, education and research/information in order to find realistic, effective solutions.

Republicans: https://www.gop.com/platform/restoring-the-american-dream/
Democrats: https://www.democrats.org/party-platform#preamble

In summary, taxes affect many aspects of personal, business, and political decisions. Developing a solid understanding of taxation should allow you to make informed decisions in these areas. Thus, Margaret can take comfort that her semester will likely prove useful to her personally. Who knows? Depending on her interest in business, investment, retirement planning, and the like, she may ultimately decide to pursue a career in taxation.

LO 1-2 # WHAT QUALIFIES AS A TAX?

"Taxes are the price we pay for a civilized society." —Oliver Wendell Holmes, Jr.

Taxes have been described in many terms: some positive, some negative, some printable, some not. Let's go directly to a formal definition of a tax, which should prove useful in identifying alternative taxes and discussing alternative tax systems.

A **tax** *is a payment required by a government that is unrelated to any specific benefit or service received from the government.* The general purpose of a tax is to fund the operations of the government (to raise revenue). Taxes differ from fines and penalties in that taxes are not intended to punish or prevent illegal behavior. Nonetheless, by allowing deductions from income, our federal tax system does encourage certain behaviors like charitable contributions, retirement savings, and research and development. Thus, we can view it as discouraging other legal behavior. For example, **sin taxes** impose relatively high surcharges on alcohol and tobacco products.[2] Cigarette taxes include a $1.01 per pack federal tax, a state tax in all 50 states, and also a few municipal taxes as well.[3]

Key components of the definition of a tax are that the payment is:

- Required (it is not voluntary);
- Imposed by a government agency (federal, state, or local); and
- Not tied directly to the benefit received by the taxpayer.

This last point is not to say that taxpayers receive no benefits from the taxes they pay. They benefit from national defense, a judicial system, law enforcement, government-sponsored social programs, an interstate highway system, public schools, and many other government-provided programs and services. The distinction is that taxes paid are not *directly* related to any specific benefit received by the taxpayer. For example, the price of admission to Yellowstone National Park is a fee rather than a tax because a specific benefit is received.

Can taxes be assessed for special purposes, such as a 1 percent sales tax for education? Yes. Why is an **earmarked tax,** a tax that *is* assessed for a specific purpose, still considered a tax? Because the payment made by the taxpayer does not directly relate to the specific benefit *received by the taxpayer.*

Example 1-1

Margaret travels to Birmingham, Alabama, where she rents a hotel room and dines at several restaurants. The price she pays for her hotel room and meals includes an additional 2 percent city surcharge to fund roadway construction in Birmingham. Is this a tax?

Answer: Yes. The payment is required by a local government and does not directly relate to a specific benefit that Margaret receives.

Example 1-2

Margaret's parents, Bill and Mercedes, recently built a house and were assessed $1,000 by their county government to connect to the county sewer system. Is this a tax?

Answer: No. The assessment was mandatory and it was paid to a local government. However, the third criterion was not met since the payment directly relates to a specific benefit (sewer service) received by the payees. For the same reason, tolls, parking meter fees, and annual licensing fees are also not considered taxes.

[2]Sin taxes represent an interesting confluence of incentives. On the one hand, demand for such products as alcohol, tobacco, and gambling is often relatively inelastic because of their addictive quality. Thus, taxing such a product can raise substantial revenues. On the other hand, one of the arguments for sin taxes is frequently the social goal of *reducing* demand for such products.

[3]Federal excise taxes on cigarettes are found in §5701(b). State taxes are as much as $4.35 per pack in New York, Anchorage, New York City, and Chicago impose municipal taxes as well.

HOW TO CALCULATE A TAX

In its simplest form, the amount of tax equals the tax base multiplied by the tax rate:

Eq. 1-1 $$\text{Tax} = \text{Tax Base} \times \text{Tax Rate}$$

The **tax base** defines what is actually taxed and is usually expressed in monetary terms, whereas the **tax rate** determines the level of taxes imposed on the tax base and is usually expressed as a percentage. For example, a sales tax rate of 6 percent on a purchase of $30 yields a tax of $1.80 ($1.80 = $30 × .06).

Federal, state, and local jurisdictions use a large variety of tax bases to collect tax. Some common tax bases (and related taxes) include taxable income (federal and state income taxes), purchases (sales tax), real estate values (real estate tax), and personal property values (personal property tax).

Different portions of a tax base may be taxed at different rates. A single tax applied to an entire base constitutes a **flat tax.** In the case of **graduated taxes,** the base is divided into a series of monetary amounts, or **brackets,** and each successive bracket is taxed at a different (gradually higher or gradually lower) percentage rate.

Calculating some taxes—income taxes for individuals or corporations, for example—can be quite complex. Advocates of flat taxes argue that the process should be simpler. But as we'll see throughout the text, most of the difficulty in calculating a tax rests in determining the tax *base*, not the tax rate. Indeed, there are only three basic tax rate structures (proportional, progressive, and regressive), and each can be mastered without much difficulty.

> **THE KEY FACTS**
>
> **How to Calculate a Tax**
>
> - Tax = Tax base × Tax rate
> - The tax base defines what is actually taxed and is usually expressed in monetary terms.
> - The tax rate determines the level of taxes imposed on the tax base and is usually expressed as a percentage.
> - Different portions of a tax base may be taxed at different rates.

DIFFERENT WAYS TO MEASURE TAX RATES

Before we discuss the alternative tax rate structures, let's first define three different tax rates that will be useful in contrasting the different tax rate structures: the marginal, average, and effective tax rates.

The **marginal tax rate** is the tax rate that applies to the *next additional increment* of a taxpayer's taxable income (or deductions). Specifically,

Eq. 1-2

$$\text{Marginal Tax Rate} = \frac{\Delta \text{Tax*}}{\Delta \text{Taxable Income}} = \frac{(\text{New Total Tax} - \text{Old Total Tax})}{(\text{New Taxable Income} - \text{Old Taxable Income})}$$

*Δ means *change in*.

where "old" refers to the current tax and "new" refers to the revised tax after incorporating the additional income (or deductions) in question. In graduated income tax systems, additional income (deductions) can push a taxpayer into a higher (lower) tax bracket, thus changing the marginal tax rate.

Example 1-3

Margaret's parents, Bill and Mercedes, file a joint tax return. They have $160,000 of taxable income this year (after all tax deductions). Assuming the following federal tax rate schedule applies, how much federal income tax will they owe this year?[4]

(continued on page 1-6)

---

[4]The tax rate schedules for single, married filing jointly, married filing separately, and head of household are included in Appendix D.

Married Filing Jointly (and Surviving Spouses)	
Not over $19,050	10% of taxable income
$19,050 to $77,400	$1,905 + 12% of taxable income in excess of $19,050
$77,400 to $165,000	$8,907 + 22% of taxable income in excess of $77,400
$165,000 to $315,000	$28,179 + 24% of taxable income in excess of $165,000
$315,000 to $400,000	$64,179 + 32% of taxable income in excess of $315,000
$400,000 to $600,000	$91,379 + 35% of taxable income in excess of $400,000
Over $600,000	$161,379 + 37% of taxable income in excess of $600,000

Answer: Bill and Mercedes will owe $27,079 computed as follows:

$$\$27,079 = \$8,907 + 22\%(\$160,000 - \$77,400)$$

Note that in this graduated tax rate structure, the first $19,050 of taxable income is taxed at 10 percent, the next $58,350 of taxable income (between $19,050 and $77,400) is taxed at 12 percent, and Bill and Mercedes's last $82,600 of taxable income (between $77,400 and $160,000) is taxed at 22 percent.

Many taxpayers incorrectly believe that all their income is taxed at their marginal rate. This mistake leads people to say, "I don't want to earn any additional money because it will put me in a higher tax bracket." Bill and Mercedes are currently in the 22 percent marginal tax rate bracket, but notice that not all their income is taxed at this rate. Their *marginal* tax rate is 22 percent. This means that small increases in income will be taxed at 22 percent, and small increases in tax deductions will generate tax *savings* of 22 percent. If Bill and Mercedes receive a large increase in income (or in deductions) such that they change tax rate brackets, we could not identify their marginal tax rate simply by knowing their current tax bracket.

Example 1-4

Bill, a well-known economics professor, signs a publishing contract with an $80,000 royalty advance. Using the rate schedule from Example 1-3, what would Bill and Mercedes's marginal tax rate be on this additional $80,000 of taxable income?

Answer: 23.88 percent, computed as follows:

Description	Amount	Explanation
(1) Taxable income with additional $80,000 of taxable income	$240,000.00	$80,000 plus $160,000 taxable income (Example 1-3)
(2) Tax on $240,000 taxable income	$ 46,179.00	Using the rate schedule in Example 1-3, $46,179 = $28,179 + 24% ($240,000 − $165,000)

Description	Amount	Explanation
(3) Taxable income before additional $80,000 of taxable income	$160,000.00	Example 1-3
(4) Tax on $160,000 taxable income	$ 27,079.00	Example 1-3
Marginal tax rate on additional $80,000 of taxable income	**23.88%**	$\dfrac{\Delta \text{Tax}}{\Delta \text{Taxable income}} = [(2) - (4)]/[(1) - (3)]$

Note that Bill and Mercedes's marginal tax rate on the $80,000 increase in taxable income rests *between* the 22 percent and 24 percent bracket rates because a portion of the additional income ($165,000 − $160,000 = $5,000) is taxed at 22 percent, with the remaining income ($240,000 − $165,000 = $75,000) taxed at 24 percent.

Example 1-5

Assume now that, instead of receiving a book advance, Bill and Mercedes start a new business that *loses* $90,000 this year (it results in $90,000 of additional tax deductions). What would be their marginal tax rate for these deductions?

Answer: 21.18 percent, computed as follows:

Description	Amount	Explanation
(1) Taxable income with additional $90,000 of tax deductions	$70,000	$160,000 taxable income (Example 1-3) less $90,000
(2) Tax on $90,000 taxable income	$ 8,019	Using the rate schedule in Example 1-3, $8,019 = $1,905 + 12% × ($70,000 − $19,050)
(3) Taxable income before additional $90,000 of tax deductions	$70,000	Example 1-3
(4) Tax on $70,000 taxable income	$27,079	Example 1-3
Marginal tax rate on additional $60,000 of tax deductions	**21.18%**	$\frac{\Delta \text{Tax}}{\Delta \text{Taxable income}} = [(2)-(4)]/[(1)-(3)]$

Bill and Mercedes's marginal tax rate on $90,000 of additional deductions (21.18 percent) differs from their marginal tax rate on $80,000 of additional taxable income (23.88 percent) in these scenarios because the relatively large increase in deductions in Example 1-5 causes some of their income to be taxed in a lower tax rate bracket, while the relatively large increase in income in Example 1-4 causes some of their income to be taxed in a higher tax rate bracket. Taxpayers often will face the same marginal tax rates for small changes in income and deductions.

The marginal tax rate is particularly useful in tax planning because it represents the rate of taxation or savings that would apply to additional taxable income (or tax deductions). In the Tax Planning Strategies and Related Limitations chapter, we discuss basic tax planning strategies that use the marginal tax rate.

The **average tax rate** represents a taxpayer's average level of taxation on each dollar of taxable income. Specifically,

Eq. 1-3
$$\text{Average Tax Rate} = \frac{\text{Total Tax}}{\text{Taxable Income}}$$

The average tax rate is often used in budgeting tax expense as a portion of income (i.e., determining what percent of taxable income earned is paid in tax).

The **effective tax rate** represents the taxpayer's average rate of taxation on each dollar of total income (sometimes referred to as economic income), including taxable *and* nontaxable income. Specifically,

Eq. 1-4
$$\text{Effective Tax Rate} = \frac{\text{Total Tax}}{\text{Total Income}}$$

Relative to the average tax rate, the effective tax rate provides a better depiction of a taxpayer's tax burden because it gives the taxpayer's total tax paid as a ratio of the sum of both taxable and nontaxable income earned.

Example 1-6

Assuming Bill and Mercedes have $160,000 of taxable income and $10,000 of nontaxable income, what is their average tax rate?

Answer: 16.92 percent, computed as follows:

Description	Amount	Explanation
(1) Taxable income	$160,000.00	
(2) Tax on $160,000 taxable income	$ 27,079.00	Example 1-3
Average tax rate	**16.92%**	$\dfrac{\text{Total tax}}{\text{Taxable income}} = (2)/(1)$

We should not be surprised that Bill and Mercedes's average tax rate is lower than their marginal tax rate because, although they are currently in the 22 percent tax rate bracket, not all of their taxable income is subject to tax at 22 percent. The first $19,050 of their taxable income is taxed at 10 percent, their next $58,350 is taxed at 12 percent, and only their last $82,000 of taxable income is taxed at 22 percent. Thus, their average tax rate is considerably lower than their marginal tax rate.

Example 1-7

Again, given the same income figures as in Example 1-6 ($160,000 of taxable income and $10,000 of nontaxable income), what is Bill and Mercedes's effective tax rate?

Answer: 15.93 percent, computed as follows:

Description	Amount	Explanation
(1) Total income	$170,000.00	$160,000 taxable income plus $10,000 in nontaxable income (Example 1-6)
(2) Tax on $160,000 taxable income	$ 27,079.00	Example 1-3
Effective tax rate	**15.93%**	$\dfrac{\text{Total tax}}{\text{Total income}} = (2)/(1)$

Should we be surprised that the effective tax rate is lower than the *average* tax rate? No, because except when the taxpayer has more nondeductible expenses (such as fines or penalties) than nontaxable income (such as tax-exempt interest), the effective tax rate will be equal to or less than the average tax rate.

TAX RATE STRUCTURES

There are three basic tax rate structures used to determine a tax: proportional, progressive, and regressive.

Proportional Tax Rate Structure

A **proportional tax rate structure,** also known as a flat tax, imposes a constant tax rate throughout the tax base. As the tax base increases, the taxes paid increase proportionally. Because this rate stays the same throughout all levels of the tax base, the marginal tax rate remains constant and, in fact, equals the average tax rate (see Exhibit 1-1). The new corporate tax rate, which is a constant rate of 21 percent, is an example of flat tax.

To calculate the tax owed for a proportional tax, simply use Equation 1-1 to multiply the tax base by the tax rate.

Eq. 1-5   Proportional tax = Tax base × Tax rate

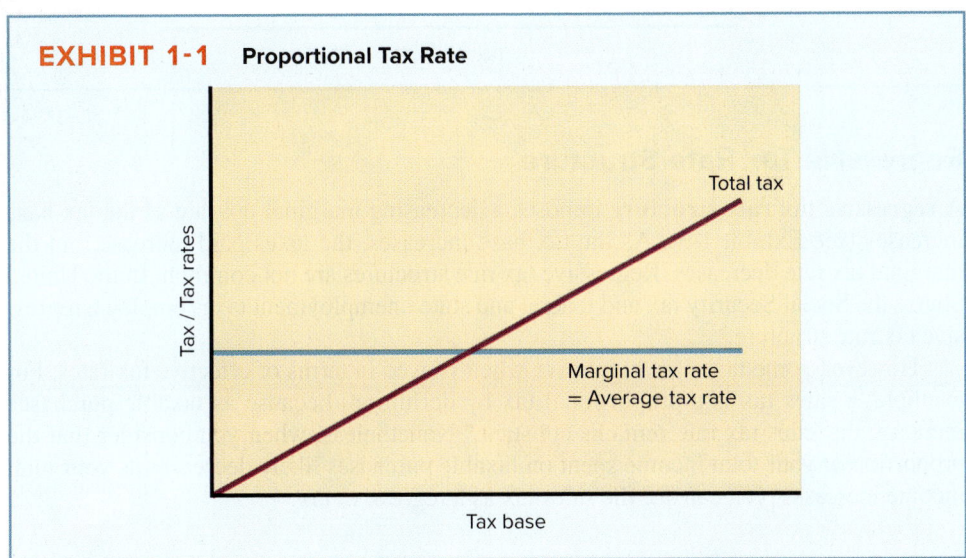

EXHIBIT 1-1   **Proportional Tax Rate**

Total tax

Marginal tax rate = Average tax rate

Tax / Tax rates

Tax base

Example 1-8

Knowing her dad is a serious Bulldog fan, Margaret buys a $100 sweatshirt in downtown Athens. The city of Athens imposes a sales tax rate of 7 percent. How much tax does Margaret pay on the purchase?

Answer: $100 purchase (tax base) × 7% (tax rate) = $7

Progressive Tax Rate Structure

A **progressive tax rate structure** imposes an increasing marginal tax rate as the tax base increases. Thus as the tax base increases, both the marginal tax rate and the taxes paid increase. Common examples of progressive tax rate structures include federal and most state income taxes. The tax rate schedule in Example 1-3 is a progressive tax rate structure. As illustrated in Exhibit 1-2, the average tax rate in a progressive tax rate structure will always be less than or equal to the marginal tax rate.

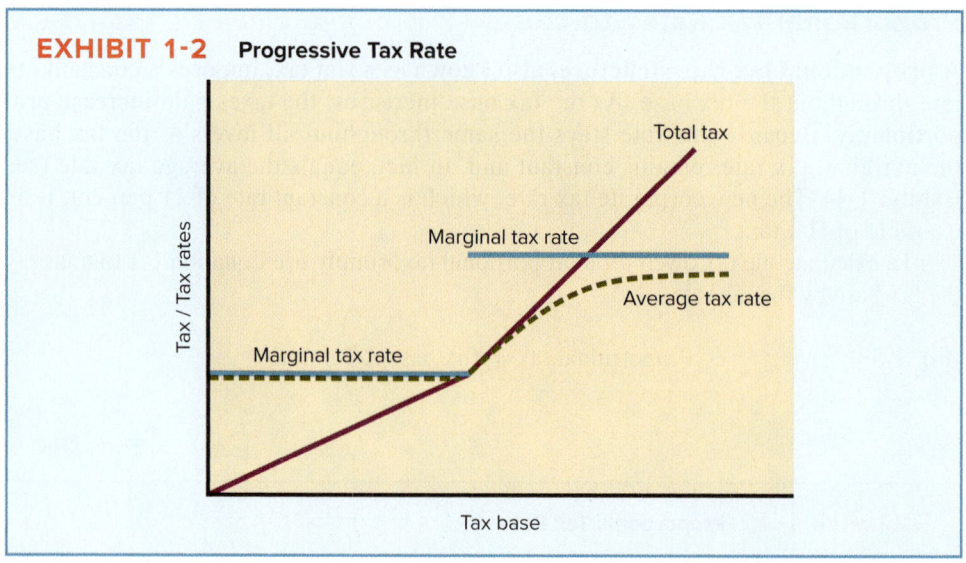

EXHIBIT 1-2   **Progressive Tax Rate**

Regressive Tax Rate Structure

A **regressive tax rate structure** imposes a decreasing marginal tax rate as the tax base increases (see Exhibit 1-3). As the tax base increases, the taxes paid increase, but the marginal tax rate decreases. Regressive tax rate structures are not common. In the United States, the Social Security tax and federal and state unemployment taxes employ a regressive tax rate structure.[5]

However, some taxes are regressive when viewed in terms of effective tax rates. For example, a sales tax is a proportional tax by definition, because as taxable purchases increase, the sales tax rate remains constant.[6] Nonetheless, when you consider that the proportion of your total income spent on taxable purchases likely decreases as your total income increases, you can see the sales tax as a regressive tax.

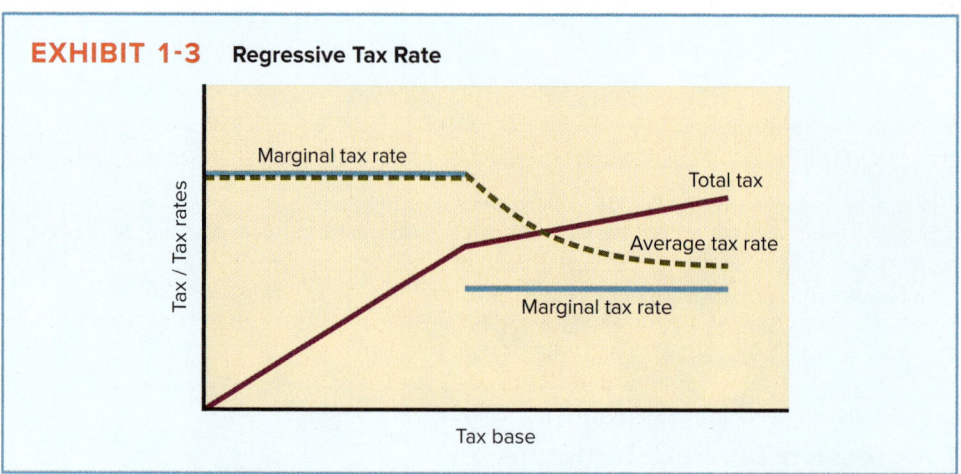

EXHIBIT 1-3   **Regressive Tax Rate**

---

[5]Wages subject to the Social Security tax (6.2 percent in 2018) are capped each year ($135,200 in 2018). Wages in excess of the cap are not subject to the tax. As might be expected, the maximum Social Security retirement benefit is capped as a function of the maximum wage base. Likewise, the federal and state unemployment tax bases and related unemployment benefits are capped.

[6]For example, a destitute taxpayer likely spends all he makes on food and other items subject to the sales tax; thus, all of his income is subject to a sales tax. In contrast, a wealthy taxpayer likely spends only a small fraction of his income on items subject to sales tax (while saving the rest). Thus, less of wealthy taxpayers' total income is subject to the sales tax, which ultimately results in a lower effective tax rate.

Example 1-9

Bill and Mercedes have two single friends, Elizabeth and Marc, over for dinner. Elizabeth earns $300,000 as CFO of a company and spends $70,000 on purchases subject to the 7 percent sales tax. Marc, who earns $75,000 as a real estate agent, spends $30,000 of his income on taxable purchases. Let's compare their marginal, average, and effective tax rates for the sales tax with those of Bill and Mercedes, who spend $50,000 of their income on taxable purchases:

	Elizabeth	Bill and Mercedes	Marc
(1) Total income	$300,000	$ 170,000	$ 75,000
(2) Total purchases subject to 7% sales tax	$ 70,000	$ 50,000	$ 30,000
(3) Sales tax paid	$ 4,900	$ 3,500	$ 2,100
Marginal tax rate	7.0%	7.0%	7.0%
Average tax rate (3)/(2)	7%	7%	7%
Effective tax rate (3)/(1)	1.6%	2.1%	2.8%

Is the sales tax regressive?

Answer: Yes. In terms of *effective* tax rates, the sales tax is regressive.

THE KEY FACTS

Tax Rate Structures

- A proportional tax rate structure
  - Imposes a constant tax rate throughout the tax base.
  - As a taxpayer's tax base increases, the taxpayer's taxes increase proportionally.
  - The marginal tax rate remains constant and always equals the average tax rate.
- A progressive tax rate structure
  - Imposes an increasing marginal tax rate as the tax base increases.
  - As a taxpayer's tax base increases, both the marginal tax rate and the taxes paid increase.
- A regressive tax rate structure
  - Imposes a decreasing marginal tax rate as the tax base increases.
  - As a taxpayer's tax base increases, the marginal tax rate decreases while the total taxes paid increases.

When we consider the marginal and average tax rates in Example 1-9, the sales tax has a proportional tax rate structure. But when we look at the *effective* tax rates, the sales tax is a regressive tax. Indeed, Marc, who has the smallest total income, bears the highest effective tax rate, despite all three taxpayers being subject to the same marginal and average tax rates. Why do we see such a different picture when considering the effective tax rate? Because unlike the marginal and average tax rates, the effective tax rate captures the *incidence* of taxation, which relates to the ultimate economic burden of a tax. Thus, a comparison of effective tax rates is more informative about taxpayers' relative tax burdens.

TYPES OF TAXES

LO 1-4

"You can't live with 'em. You can't live without 'em." This statement has often been used in reference to bosses, parents, spouses, and significant others. To some degree, it applies equally as well to taxes. Although we all benefit in multiple ways from tax revenues, and all civilized nations impose them, it would be hard to find someone who *enjoys* paying them. Most people don't object to the idea of paying taxes. Instead, it's the way taxes are levied that many people, like Margaret's friend Eddy, dislike. Hence, the search for the "perfect" tax can be elusive. The following paragraphs describe the major types of taxes currently used by federal, state, and local governments. After this discussion, we describe the criteria for evaluating alternative tax systems.

Federal Taxes

The federal government imposes a variety of taxes to fund federal programs such as national defense, Social Security, an interstate highway system, educational programs, and Medicare. Major federal taxes include the individual and corporate income taxes, employment taxes, estate and gift taxes, and excise taxes (each discussed in detail in the following paragraphs). Notably absent from this list are sales tax (a common tax levied by most state and local governments) and **value-added tax** (a type of sales tax also referred to as a VAT). Value-added taxes are imposed on the producers of goods and services

THE KEY FACTS

Federal Taxes

- Income tax
  - The most significant tax assessed by the U.S. government.
  - Represents approximately 60 percent (combined corporate and individual) of all tax revenues collected in the United States.
  - Levied on individuals, corporations, estates, and trusts.
- Employment and unemployment taxes
  - Second-largest group of taxes imposed by the U.S. government.

(continued)

- Employment taxes consist of the Old Age, Survivors, and Disability Insurance (OASDI) tax, commonly called the Social Security tax, and the Medical Health Insurance (MHI) tax, also known as the Medicare tax.
- Unemployment taxes fund temporary unemployment benefits for individuals terminated from their jobs without cause.
- Excise taxes
  - Third-largest group of taxes imposed by the U.S. government.
  - Levied on the *quantity* of products sold.
- Transfer taxes
  - Levied on the fair-market values of wealth transfers upon death or by gift.

based on the value added to the goods and services at each stage of production. They are quite common in Europe.

Income Tax   The most significant tax assessed by the U.S. government is the individual **income tax,** representing approximately 47.3 percent of all tax revenues collected in the United States in 2016. Despite the magnitude and importance of the federal income tax, its history is relatively short. Congress enacted the first U.S. personal income tax in 1861 to help fund the Civil War. This relatively minor tax (with a maximum tax rate of 5 percent) was allowed to expire in 1872. In 1892, Congress resurrected the income tax, but not without dissension among the states. In 1895, the income tax was challenged in *Pollock v. Farmers' Loan and Trust Company,* 157 U.S. 429 (1895). The U.S. Supreme Court ruled that the income tax was unconstitutional because direct taxes were prohibited by the Constitution unless the taxes were apportioned across states based upon their populations. This ruling, however, did not deter Congress. In July 1909, Congress sent a proposed constitutional amendment to the states to remove any doubt as to whether income taxes were allowed by the Constitution—and in February 1913, the 16th Amendment was ratified.

Congress then enacted the Revenue Act of 1913, which included a graduated income tax structure with a maximum rate of 6 percent. The income tax has been an important source of tax revenues for the U.S. government ever since. Today, income taxes are levied on individuals (maximum rate of 37 percent), corporations (flat rate of 21 percent), estates (maximum rate of 37 percent), and trusts (maximum rate of 37 percent). Higher income taxpayers must also pay a 3.8 percent tax on their net investment income. As Exhibit 1-4 illustrates, the individual income tax and employment taxes represent the largest sources of federal tax revenues. We discuss each of these taxes in greater detail later in the text.

Employment and Unemployment Taxes   Employment and unemployment taxes are the second-largest group of taxes imposed by the U.S. government. **Employment taxes** consist of the Old Age, Survivors, and Disability Insurance (OASDI) tax, commonly called the Social Security tax, and the Medical Health Insurance (MHI) tax, known as the Medicare tax. The **Social Security tax** pays the monthly retirement, survivor, and disability benefits for qualifying individuals, whereas the **Medicare tax** pays for medical insurance for individuals who are elderly or disabled. The tax base for the Social Security

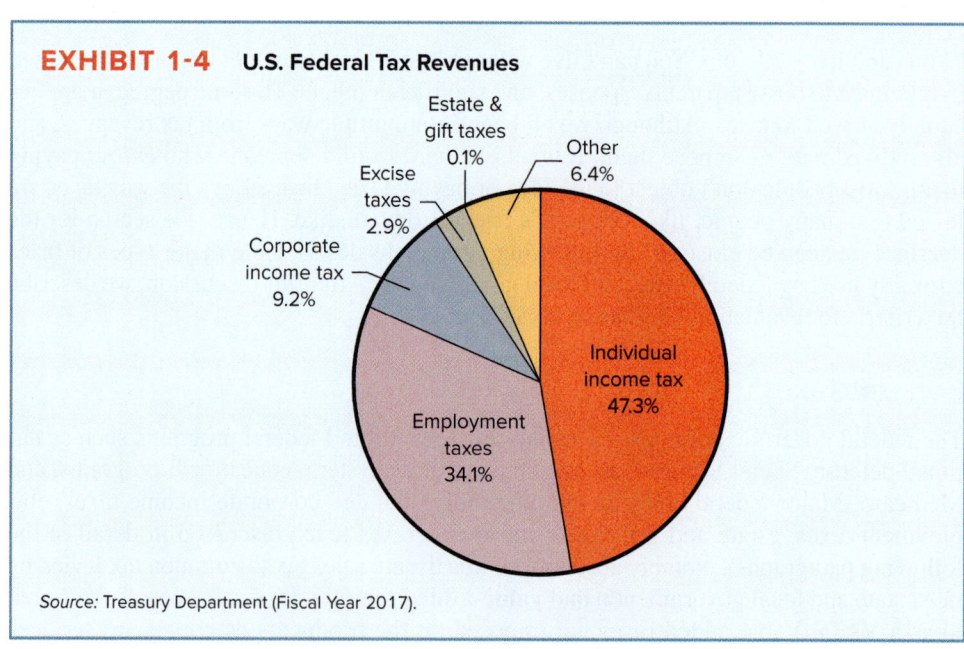

EXHIBIT 1-4   **U.S. Federal Tax Revenues**

Estate & gift taxes 0.1%
Other 6.4%
Excise taxes 2.9%
Corporate income tax 9.2%
Individual income tax 47.3%
Employment taxes 34.1%

Source: Treasury Department (Fiscal Year 2017).

and Medicare taxes is wages or salary, and the rates are 12.4 percent and 2.9 percent, respectively, in 2018. In 2018, the tax base for the Social Security tax is capped at $135,200 (wages over this cap are not subject to the tax). The tax base for the Medicare tax is not capped. Employers and employees split these taxes equally. Self-employed individuals, however, must pay these taxes in their entirety. In this case, the tax is often referred to as the **self-employment tax.** We discuss these taxes in more depth later in the text. There is a .9 percent Additional Medicare Tax levied on income earned by employees (employers are exempt) and self-employed taxpayers on income exceeding a threshold amount (see the Individual Income Tax Computation and Tax Credits chapter for details).

In addition to the Social Security and Medicare taxes, employers are also required to pay federal and state **unemployment taxes,** which fund temporary unemployment benefits for individuals terminated from their jobs without cause. As you might expect, the tax base for the unemployment taxes is also wages or salary. Currently, the federal unemployment tax rate is 6.0 percent. The wage base is the first $7,000 of wages received during the year. The U.S. government allows a credit for state unemployment taxes paid up to 5.4 percent. Thus, the effective federal unemployment tax rate may be as low as .6 percent (6.0% − 5.4% = .6%).[7]

Excise Taxes   **Excise taxes** are taxes levied on the retail sale of particular products. They differ from other taxes in that the tax base for an excise tax typically depends on the *quantity* purchased, rather than a monetary amount. The federal government imposes a number of excise taxes on goods such as alcohol, diesel fuel, gasoline, and tobacco products and on services such as telephone use, air transportation, and the use of tanning beds. In addition, states often impose excise taxes on these same items.

Example 1-10

On the drive home from Florida to Athens, Georgia, Margaret stops at Gasup-n-Go. On each gallon of gasoline she buys, Margaret pays 18.4 cents of federal excise tax and 7.5 cents of state excise tax (plus 4 percent sales tax). Could Margaret have avoided paying excise tax had she stopped in Florida instead?

Answer: No. Had she stopped in Florida instead, Margaret would have paid the same federal excise tax. Additionally, Florida imposes higher state taxes on gas.

Because the producer of the product pays the excise tax to the government, many people are not even aware that businesses build these taxes into the prices consumers pay. Nonetheless, consumers bear the burden of the taxes because of the higher price.

Transfer Taxes   Although they are a relatively minor tax compared to the income tax in terms of revenues collected, federal **transfer taxes**—estate and gift taxes—can be substantial for certain individual taxpayers and have been the subject of much debate in recent years. The **estate tax** (labeled the "death tax" by its opponents) and **gift taxes** are based on the fair market values of wealth transfers made upon death or by gift, respectively. In 2018, the maximum rate imposed on gifts is 37 percent. Most taxpayers, however, are not subject to estate and gift taxation because of the annual gift exclusion and gift and estate unified tax credits. The annual gift exclusion allows a taxpayer to transfer $15,000 of gifts per donee (gift recipient) each year without gift taxation. In 2018, the unified tax credit exempts from taxation $11,200,000 in bequests (transfers upon death) and gifts. Thus, only large transfers are subject to the gift and estate taxes.

[7]Although employers pay both federal and state unemployment taxes, all unemployment benefits actually are administered and paid by state governments.

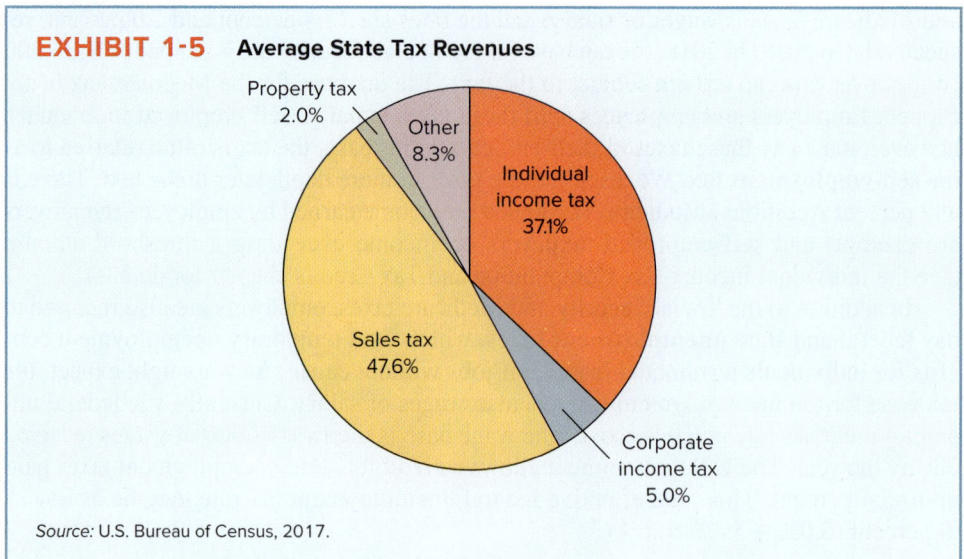

EXHIBIT 1-5 Average State Tax Revenues

- Property tax 2.0%
- Other 8.3%
- Individual income tax 37.1%
- Sales tax 47.6%
- Corporate income tax 5.0%

Source: U.S. Bureau of Census, 2017.

State and Local Taxes

Like the federal government, state and local governments (such as counties, cities, and school districts) use a variety of taxes to generate revenues for their programs (such as education, highways, and police and fire departments). Some of the more common **state** and **local taxes** include income taxes, sales and use taxes, excise taxes, and property taxes. Typically, as shown in Exhibit 1-5, the largest state tax revenues are generated by individual income taxes and state sales taxes—in contrast to federal revenues, which rely primarily on income and employment taxes. Local tax revenues are predominantly from sales and property taxes.

Income Taxes   Currently, most states and the District of Columbia impose income taxes on individuals and corporations who either reside in or earn income within the state.[8] This requires individuals living in these states to file a state tax return in addition to the federal return they already file. Calculations of individual and corporate taxable income vary with state law. Nonetheless, most state taxable income calculations largely conform to the federal taxable income calculations, with a limited number of modifications, although the tax rates are significantly less than the federal rate. The state of California is a notable exception because it has numerous modifications. Certain local governments such as New York City also impose an income tax and, again, the local calculations generally follow the respective state taxable income calculation.

Sales and Use Taxes   Most states, the District of Columbia, and local governments impose sales and use taxes. The tax base for a **sales tax** is the retail price of goods and some services, and retailers are responsible for collecting and remitting the tax; typically, sales tax is collected at the point of sale. The tax base for the **use tax** is the

[8]Currently, Alaska, Florida, Nevada, South Dakota, Texas, Washington, and Wyoming have no personal income tax, and New Hampshire and Tennessee only tax individual dividend and interest income. Nevada and Wyoming do not impose taxes on corporate income, and South Dakota only taxes banks. Washington imposes a gross receipts tax instead of a corporate income tax. Texas and Ohio have an activity-based tax that is based on net income or gross receipts.

retail price of goods owned, possessed, or consumed within a state that were *not* purchased within the state. The purpose of a use tax is to discourage taxpayers from buying goods out of state in order to avoid or minimize the sales tax in their home state. At the same time, by eliminating the incentive to purchase goods out of state, a use tax removes any competitive disadvantage a retailer may incur from operating in a state with a high sales tax. To avoid the potential of double taxing residents on sales taxes, states that impose a sales tax allow residents to take a credit for sales tax paid on goods purchased out of state.

Example 1-11

Margaret buys three new Lands' End shirts for her dad for $100. Because Lands' End does not have a business presence in Florida (Margaret's home state), it does not collect Florida sales tax on the $100 purchase. Does Margaret's purchase escape Florida taxation?

Answer: No. Because Florida has a 6 percent use tax, Margaret is liable for $6 in use tax on the purchase ($6 = $100 × .06).

Despite the potential importance of the use tax as a source of state tax revenue, states have only recently begun to enforce it. Poor compliance is therefore not surprising; indeed, many individuals have never heard of the use tax. While it is relatively easy to enforce it on goods obtained out of state if they are subject to a registration requirement, such as automobiles, it is quite difficult for states to tax most other out-of-state purchases. The state of Florida is not likely to search your closet to look for tax-evaded Lands' End shirts. Note, however, there are several bills before Congress to modernize Internet taxation and to try to subject all Internet sales to sales taxes.

Property Taxes   State and local governments commonly use two types of property taxes as sources of revenue: **real property taxes** and **personal property taxes.** Both are **ad valorem taxes,** meaning that the tax base for each is the fair market value of the property, and both are generally collected annually (if imposed at all).

Real property consists of land, structures, and improvements permanently attached to land, whereas *personal property* includes all other types of property, both tangible and intangible. Common examples of tangible personal property potentially subject to state and local taxation include automobiles, boats, private planes, business inventory, equipment, and furniture. Intangible personal property potentially subject to state and local taxation includes stocks, bonds, and intellectual property.

Of the two types, real property taxes are easier to administer because real property is not movable and purchases often have to be registered with the state, thereby making it easy to identify the tax base and taxpayer. Furthermore, the taxing body can estimate market values for real property without much difficulty. In contrast, personal property is generally mobile (thus easier to hide) and may be more difficult to value; therefore, personal property taxes are difficult to enforce. Accordingly, whereas all states and the District of Columbia provide for a real property tax, only a majority of states currently impose personal property taxes, most of which are assessed at the time of licensing or registration. However, most states do collect personal property taxes on business property.

Excise Taxes   We've said that the tax base for excise taxes is typically the quantity of an item or service purchased. States typically impose excise taxes on items subject to federal excise tax. Transactions subject to state excise tax often include the sale of alcohol, diesel fuel, gasoline, tobacco products, and telephone services.

Implicit Taxes

All the taxes discussed above are **explicit taxes;** that is, they are taxes directly imposed by a government and are easily quantified. **Implicit taxes,** on the other hand, are indirect taxes—not paid directly to the government—that result from a tax advantage the government grants to certain transactions to satisfy social, economic, or other objectives. Implicit taxes are defined as the reduced before-tax return that a tax-favored asset produces because of its tax-advantaged status. Let's examine this concept more closely.

First of all, what does it mean to be *tax-favored*? An asset is said to be tax-favored when the income the asset produces is either excluded from the tax base or subject to a lower (preferential) tax rate, or if the asset generates some other tax benefit such as large tax deductions. These tax benefits, *all other things equal*, result in higher after-tax profits (or lower after-tax costs) from investing in the tax-advantaged assets.

Why do tax-advantaged assets bear an implicit tax, or a reduced before-tax return as a result of the tax advantage? The answer is simple economics. The tax benefits associated with the tax-favored asset increase the demand for the asset. Increased demand drives up the price of the asset, which in turn reduces its before-tax return, which is an implicit tax by definition. Consider Example 1-12.

Example 1-12

Consider two bonds, one issued by the Coca-Cola Co. and the other issued by the State of Georgia. Both bonds have similar nontax characteristics (risk, for example), the same face value of $10,000, and the same market interest rate of 10 percent. The only difference between the two bonds is that the interest income from the Coca-Cola Co. bond is subject to a 20 percent income tax rate, whereas the interest income from the State of Georgia bond is tax-exempt with a 0 percent tax rate. Which of the two bonds is a better investment and should therefore have a higher demand?

	Price	Before-Tax* Return	Interest Income	Income† Tax	After-Tax Income	After-Tax* Return
Coca-Cola Bond	$10,000	10%	$1,000	$200	$ 800	8%
State of GA Bond	$10,000	10%	$1,000	$ 0	$1,000	10%

*Before-tax return is calculated as the before-tax income divided by the price of the bond. Likewise, after-tax return is calculated as the after-tax income divided by the price of the bond.
†Income tax equals the taxable interest income ($1,000) multiplied by the assumed income marginal tax rate (20 percent).

Answer: Compare the after-tax returns of the bonds. Given the difference between the return after taxes (10 percent vs. 8 percent), the better investment—again, all other investment features being equal—is the State of Georgia bond because it provides a higher *after*-tax return. Because all investors in this example should prefer to buy the State of Georgia bond, the demand for the bond will be high, and its price should increase. This increase in price leads to a lower before-tax return due to the bond's tax-favored status (this is an implicit tax).

Example 1-12 is a basic illustration of the need to consider the role of taxes in investment decisions. Without understanding the relative tax effects associated with each bond, we cannot correctly compare their after-tax returns.

At what point in Example 1-12 would you be indifferent between investing in the Coca-Cola Co. bond and the State of Georgia bond? Assuming both bonds have the same nontax characteristics, you would be indifferent between them when they both provide the same after-tax rate of return. This could occur if the State of Georgia raised the price of its bond from $10,000 to $12,500 ($1,000 interest/$12,500 price = 8% return). Or the State of Georgia could lower its bond interest payment from $1,000 to $800 ($800 interest/$10,000 price = 8% return). Either way, the State of Georgia benefits from selling the tax-exempt bonds—either at a higher price or at a lower interest rate relative to other bonds. Let's look more closely at this latter option, because it is, in fact, what many tax-exempt bond issuers choose to do.

	Price	Before-Tax Return	Interest Income	Income Tax	After-Tax Income	After-Tax Return
Coca-Cola Bond	$10,000	10%	$1,000	$200	$800	8%
State of GA Bond	$10,000	8%	$ 800	$ 0	$800	8%

At this point, assuming each bond has the same nontax characteristics, an investor should be indifferent between the Coca-Cola Co. bond and the State of Georgia bond. What is the tax burden on investors choosing the Coca-Cola Co. bond? Coca-Cola Co. bond investors are paying $200 of income taxes (explicit taxes). What is the tax burden on investors choosing the State of Georgia bond? While it is true they are subject to zero income taxes (explicit taxes), they are subject to implicit taxes in the form of the $200 less in interest income they accept. This $200 of reduced interest income (2 percent reduced before-tax rate of return) is an implicit tax. Although the investors in the State of Georgia bond are not paying this tax directly, they are paying it indirectly.

Does this happen in real life? Yes. Municipal bond interest income (interest income paid on bonds issued by state and local governments) generally is not subject to federal income taxation. Because of their tax-advantaged status, municipalities are able to pay a lower interest rate on their bond issuances and investors are willing to accept the lower rate. This type of indirect federal subsidy allows municipalities to raise money at a reduced cost without the need for direct federal subsidy or approval.

Although we were able to quantify the implicit taxes paid in the above example, in reality it is very difficult to estimate the amount of implicit taxes paid. For example, the federal government subsidizes housing by allowing taxpayers to deduct mortgage interest on their principal residence. Does this subsidy result in an implicit tax in the form of higher housing prices? Probably. Nonetheless, it would be difficult to quantify this implicit tax.

Despite the difficulty of quantifying implicit taxes, you should understand the concept of implicit taxes so you can make informed judgments about the attractiveness of alternative investments and the relative total tax burdens of tax-advantaged investments (considering both explicit and implicit taxes).

> **THE KEY FACTS**
>
> **Implicit Taxes**
>
> - Implicit taxes are indirect taxes that result from a tax advantage the government grants to certain transactions to satisfy social, economic, or other objectives.
> - Implicit taxes are defined as the reduced before-tax return that a tax-favored asset produces because of its tax-advantaged status.
> - Implicit taxes are difficult to quantify but important to understand in evaluating the relative tax burdens of tax-advantaged investments.

EVALUATING ALTERNATIVE TAX SYSTEMS

LO 1-5

Although it may appear that tax systems are designed without much forethought, in truth lawmakers engage in continuous debate over the basic questions of whom to tax, what to tax, and how much to tax. Margaret's friend Eddy is obviously upset with what he views as an unfair tax system. But fairness, as we will discuss shortly, is often like beauty—it is in the eye of the beholder. What is fair to one may seem blatantly unfair to others. In the following paragraphs, we offer various criteria (sufficiency, equity, certainty, convenience, and economy) you can use to evaluate alternative tax systems.[9] Satisfying everyone at the same time is difficult. Hence, the spirited debate on tax reform.

---

[9]Adam Smith identified and described the latter four criteria in *The Wealth of Nations*.

Sufficiency

Judging the **sufficiency** of a tax system means assessing the amount of the tax revenues it must generate and ensuring that it provides them. For a country's tax system to be successful, it must provide sufficient revenues to pay for governmental expenditures for a defense system, social services, and so on. This sounds easy enough: Estimate the amount of government expenditures that will be required, and then design the system to generate enough revenues to pay for these expenses. In reality, however, accurately estimating governmental expenditures and revenues is a rather daunting and imprecise process. Estimating governmental expenditures is difficult because it is impossible to predict the unknown. For example, in recent years governmental expenditures have increased due to the growth of Homeland Security, the Afghanistan and Iraq Wars, natural disasters, economic stimulus, and health care. Likewise, estimating governmental revenues is difficult because tax revenues are the result of transactions influenced by these same national events, the economy, and other factors. Thus, precisely estimating and matching governmental expenditures with tax revenues is nearly impossible.

The task of estimating tax revenues becomes even more daunting when the government attempts to make significant changes to the existing tax system or design a new one. Whenever Congress proposes changing who is taxed, what is taxed, or how much is taxed, its members must consider the taxpayer response to the change. That affects the amount of tax collected, and forecasters' prediction of what taxpayers will do affects the amount of revenue they estimate.

Static versus Dynamic Forecasting One option in forecasting revenue is to ignore how taxpayers may alter their activities in response to a tax law change and instead base projected tax revenues on the existing state of transactions, a process referred to as **static forecasting.** However, this type of forecasting may result in a large discrepancy in projected versus actual tax revenues if taxpayers do change their behavior.

The other choice is to attempt to account for possible taxpayer responses to the tax law change, a process referred to as **dynamic forecasting.** Dynamic forecasting is ultimately only as good as the assumptions underlying the forecasts and does not guarantee accurate results. Nonetheless, considering how taxpayers may alter their activities in response to a tax law change is a useful exercise to identify the potential ramifications of the change, even if the revenue projections ultimately miss the mark. For more information about the Congressional Revenue Estimating Process, including dynamic scoring, see the Joint Committee on Taxation explanation at https://www.jct.gov/publications. html?func=startdown&id=3720.

Example 1-13

The city of Heflin would like to increase tax revenues by $2,000,000 to pay for needed roadwork. A concerned taxpayer recently proposed increasing the cigarette excise tax from $1.00 per pack of cigarettes to $6.00 per pack to raise the additional needed revenue. Last year, 400,000 packs of cigarettes were sold in the city. Will the tax be successful in raising the $2,000,000 revenue?

Answer: Not likely. The proposed tax increase of $5, and the assumption that 400,000 packs will still be sold, is an example of static forecasting: It ignores that many taxpayers may respond to the tax change by quitting, cutting down, or buying cheaper cigarettes in the next town.

In some cases, static forecasting can lead to a tax consequence that is the opposite of the desired outcome. In Example 1-13, we might estimate that given Heflin's close proximity to other cities with a $1.00 cigarette tax, the number of packs of cigarettes sold within the city would drop significantly to, say, 50,000. In this case, the tax increase would actually *decrease* tax revenues by $100,000 ($400,000 existing tax − $300,000 new tax)—not a good outcome if the goal was to increase tax revenues.

Income versus Substitution Effects   Example 1-13 described proposed changes in an excise tax, which is a proportional tax. In terms of a progressive tax such as an *income* tax, a tax rate increase or an expansion of the tax base can result in one of two taxpayer responses, both of which are important for dynamic forecasting. The **income effect** predicts that when taxpayers are taxed more (when, say, a tax rate increases from 25 to 28 percent), they will work harder to generate the same after-tax dollars. The **substitution effect** predicts that when taxpayers are taxed more, rather than working more they will substitute nontaxable activities like leisure pursuits for taxable ones because the marginal value of taxable activities has decreased. Which view is accurate? The answer depends on the taxpayer. Consider the following examples.

Example 1-14

Margaret's friend George, who earns $40,000 taxable income as a mechanic, is taxed at an average rate of 10 percent (resulting in $4,000 of tax). If Congress increases the income tax rate such that George's average tax rate increases from 10 percent to 25 percent, how much more income tax will he pay?

Answer: It depends on whether the income effect or the substitution effect is operating. Assuming George is single and cannot afford a net decrease in his after-tax income, he will likely work more (the income effect rules). Prior to the tax rate increase, George had $36,000 of after-tax income ($40,000 taxable income less $4,000 tax). With the increased tax rate, George will have to earn $48,000 of taxable income to keep $36,000 after taxes [$48,000 − ($48,000 × .25) = $36,000]. Thus, if the income effect rules, the government will collect $12,000 of federal income tax from George, or $8,000 more than under the previous lower tax rate. In this scenario, the tax change increases government revenues because of the increased tax rate *and* the increased tax base.

   Whether the substitution effect or the income effect will describe any individual taxpayer's reaction to a tax increase is something we can only guess. But some factors—such as having higher disposable income—are likely to correlate with the substitution effect.

Example 1-15

What if: Now let's assume that George is married and has two young children. Both he and his wife work, and they file a tax return jointly with a 10 percent average tax rate. Either of their incomes is sufficient to meet necessities, even after the tax rate increase. But fixed child care costs make the marginal wage rate (the after-tax hourly wage less hourly child care cost) more sensitive to tax rate increases. In this case, the lower-earning spouse may choose to work less. Suppose George quits his full-time job and takes a part-time position that pays $10,000 to spend more time with his kids and to pursue his passion, reading sports novels. What are the taxes on George's income?

Answer: In this case, George will owe $2,500 tax ($10,000 × .25 = $2,500). Here, the substitution effect operates and the government collects much less than it would have if George had maintained his full-time position, because the tax rate increase had a negative effect on the tax base.

   As Examples 1-14 and 1-15 illustrate, the response to a tax law change can vary by taxpayer and can greatly affect the magnitude of tax revenues generated by the change. Herein lies one of the challenges in significantly changing an existing tax system or designing a new one: If a tax system fails to generate sufficient revenues, the government must seek other sources to pay for governmental expenditures. The most common source of these additional funds for the federal government is the issuance of debt instruments such as Treasury bonds. This, however, is only a short-term solution to a budget deficit. Debt issuances require both interest and principal payments, which require the federal government to identify even more sources of revenue to service the debt issued or to cut governmental spending (both of which may be unpopular choices with voters). A third option is for the government to default on its debt obligations. However, the costs of this option are potentially devastating. If the historical examples of Mexico, Brazil, Argentina, and Greece are any guide, a U.S. government default on its debt obligations would likely devalue the U.S. dollar severely and have extreme negative consequences for the U.S. capital markets.

The best option is for the government to match its revenues with its expenses—that is, not to spend more than it collects. State governments seem to be more successful in this endeavor than the U.S. federal government. Indeed, all states except Vermont require a balanced budget each year, whereas the federal government has had deficit spending for most of the last 40 years.

TAXES IN THE REAL WORLD National Debt

How much debt does the U.S. have today? About $20.2 trillion. Almost $14.7 trillion of the national debt is held by public investors, including individual bondholders, institutional investors, and foreign governments such as China, Japan, the United Kingdom, and Brazil. The $5.5 trillion remaining amount represents intragovernmental holdings—primarily Social Security.

Is $20.2 trillion too much to handle? The key issue is fiscal sustainability: the ability to pay off a debt in the future. Rising debt also has other negative consequences, such as higher interest payments, a need for higher taxes, restrictions on policy makers' fiscal policy choices, and the increased probability of a sudden fiscal crisis. If nothing is done to change the national debt trajectory, the debt will grow faster than the economy.

Is the national debt sustainable? The federal government has recently been recording budget deficits that are a larger share of the economy than any year since the end of World War II. With an aging population, Social Security and other benefits will require larger expenditures. By the end of the current decade, barring any significant policy shifts, the vast majority of federal tax revenue will be consumed by just four expenditures: interest on the debt, Medicare, Medicaid, and Social Security. To finance other government expenditures, including defense and all other discretionary programs, policy makers will have to borrow the money to pay for them.

Equity

We've looked at the challenges of designing a tax system that provides sufficient revenues to pay for governmental expenditures. An equally challenging issue is how the tax burden should be distributed across taxpayers. At the heart of this issue is the concept of **equity,** or fairness. Fairness is inherently subject to personal interpretation, and informed minds often disagree about what is fair. There is no "one-size-fits-all" definition of equity or fairness. Nonetheless, it is informative to consider in broad terms what makes a fair or equitable tax system.

In general terms, a tax system is considered fair or equitable if the tax is based on the taxpayer's ability to pay. Taxpayers with a greater ability to pay tax, pay more tax. In broad terms, each of the federal, state, and local taxes we've discussed satisfies this criterion. For example, those individuals with greater taxable income, purchases, property, and estates (upon death) generally pay higher dollar amounts in federal income tax, sales tax, property tax, and estate tax. If this is the case, why is there so much debate over the fairness of the U.S. income tax system? The answer is that equity is more complex than our first definition suggests. Let's take a closer look.

Horizontal versus Vertical Equity   Two basic types of equity are relevant to tax systems. **Horizontal equity** means that two taxpayers in similar situations pay the same tax. In broad terms, each of the federal, state, and local taxes discussed satisfy this definition. Two individual taxpayers with the same taxable income, same purchases, same value of property, and same estate value pay the same federal income tax, sales tax, property tax, and estate tax. However, on closer inspection we might argue that each of these tax systems is *not* horizontally equitable. Here are some examples:

THE KEY FACTS

Evaluating Alternative Tax Systems—Equity
- Questions of equity consider how the tax burden should be distributed across taxpayers.
- Horizontal equity means that two taxpayers in similar situations pay the same tax.
- Vertical equity is achieved when taxpayers with greater ability to pay tax, pay more tax than taxpayers with a lesser ability to pay tax.

- Two individual taxpayers with the same income will not pay the same federal income tax if one individual's income was earned as salary and the other individual's income was tax-exempt municipal bond interest income, dividend income, or capital gain(s) income, which can be subject to a lower tax rate.
- Two individuals with the same dollar amount of purchases will not pay the same sales tax if one buys a higher proportion of goods that are subject to a lower sales tax rate, such as groceries.
- Two individuals with real estate of the same value will not pay the same property tax if one individual owns farmland, which is generally subject to a lower property tax rate.
- Finally, two individuals with estates of the same value will not pay the same estate tax if one individual bequeaths more of her property to charity or a spouse, because these transfers are not subject to estate tax.

These failures of horizontal equity are due to what we call *tax preferences*. Governments provide tax preferences for a variety of reasons, such as to encourage investment or to further social objectives. Whether we view these tax preferences as appropriate greatly influences whether we consider a tax system to be fair in general and horizontally equitable in particular.

The second type of equity to consider in evaluating a tax system is **vertical equity.** Vertical equity is achieved when taxpayers with greater ability to pay tax, pay more tax than taxpayers with less ability to pay. We can think of vertical equity in terms of tax dollars paid or in terms of tax rates. Proponents of a flat income tax or of a sales tax—both of which are proportional tax rate structures—are more likely to argue that vertical equity is achieved when taxpayers with a greater ability to pay tax, simply pay more in tax *dollars*. Proponents of a progressive tax system are more likely to argue that taxpayers with a greater ability to pay should be subject to a higher tax *rate*. This view is based upon the argument that the *relative* burden of a flat tax rate decreases as a taxpayer's income increases. Which is the correct answer? There is no correct answer. Nonetheless, many feel very strongly regarding one view or the other.

Our discussion has focused on how we can view alternative tax rate structures in terms of vertical equity, ignoring the role that the tax base plays in determining vertical equity. Indeed, focusing on the tax rate structure in evaluating a tax system is appropriate only if the tax base chosen—whether it's taxable income, purchases, property owned, or something else—accurately portrays a taxpayer's ability to pay. This can be a rather strong assumption. Consider the sales tax in Example 1-9. Although taxable purchases in this example increase as the taxpayers' total incomes increase, total incomes increase at a much faster rate than taxable purchases. Thus, the gap between taxable purchases and total income widens as total income increases. The end result is that the effective tax rates for those with a greater ability to pay are *lower* than for those taxpayers with a lesser ability to pay, making this tax regressive. Regressive tax rate structures are generally considered not to satisfy vertical equity, unless you strongly believe that those with a greater ability to pay do so simply by paying more tax dollars, albeit at a lower tax rate. In sum, evaluating vertical equity in terms of effective tax rates may be much more informative than simply evaluating tax rate structures.

Certainty

Certainty means that taxpayers should be able to determine when to pay the tax, where to pay the tax, and how to determine the tax. Determining when and where to pay each of the taxes previously discussed is relatively easy. For example, individual federal income tax returns and the remaining balance of taxes owed must be filed with the Internal Revenue Service each year on or before April 15th. Likewise, sales taxes, property taxes, and excise taxes are each determined with relative ease: Sales taxes are based on the value of taxable purchases, property taxes are generally based on assessed property values, and excise taxes are based on the number of taxable units purchased. Indeed, these taxes are calculated for the taxpayer and often charged at regular intervals or at the point of purchase; they do not require a tax return.

In contrast, income taxes are often criticized as being too complex. What are taxable versus nontaxable forms of income? What are deductible/nondeductible expenses? When should income or expenses be reported? For wage earners with few investments, the answers to these questions are straightforward. For business owners and individuals with a lot of investments, the answers are nontrivial. Yearly tax law changes enacted by Congress can make it more difficult to determine a taxpayer's current tax liability, much less plan for the future.

Convenience

Convenience suggests that a tax system should be designed to facilitate the collection of tax revenues without undue hardship on the taxpayer or the government. Various tax systems meet this criterion by tying the collection of the tax as closely as possible to the transaction that generates it (when it is most convenient to pay the tax). For example, retailers collect sales taxes when buyers purchase goods. Thus, it is difficult for the buyer to avoid paying sales tax, assuming she is transacting with an ethical retailer. Likewise, employers withhold federal income and Social Security taxes directly from wage earners' paychecks, which speeds the government's collection of the taxes and makes it difficult for taxpayers to evade taxes. If tax withholdings are not sufficient relative to the taxpayer's anticipated income tax liability, or if the taxpayer is self-employed, he or she is required to make quarterly estimated tax installments. Individual quarterly estimated payments are due on April 15, June 15, September 15, and January 15, whereas corporate estimated tax payments are due on the 15th day of the third, sixth, ninth, and twelfth months of the corporation's fiscal year.

Economy

Economy requires that a good tax system should minimize the compliance and administration costs associated with the tax system. We can view economy from both the taxpayer's and the government's perspectives. Believe it or not, most tax systems fare well in terms of economy, at least from the government's perspective. For example, the current IRS budget represents approximately $\frac{1}{2}$ of a percent of every tax dollar collected. Compared to the typical costs of a collection agency, this is quite low.

How about from the taxpayer's perspective? Here the picture is a bit different. The sales tax imposes no administrative burden on the taxpayer and only small administrative costs on the local retailer. However, out-of-state sellers argue that collecting and remitting use taxes for thousands of state and city jurisdictions would be a substantial burden. Other taxes such as excise taxes and property taxes also impose minimal administrative costs on the taxpayer. In contrast, as we've seen, the income tax is often criticized for the compliance costs imposed on the taxpayer. Indeed, for certain taxpayers, record-keeping costs, accountant fees, attorney fees, and so on can be substantial. Advocates of alternative tax systems often challenge the income tax on this criterion.

Evaluating Tax Systems—The Trade-Off

At the heart of any debate about tax reform are fundamental decisions and concessions based on the five criteria we've just discussed. Interestingly enough, much of the debate regarding alternative tax systems can be reduced to a choice between simplicity and fairness. Those taxes that generally are simpler and easier to administer, such as the sales tax, are typically viewed as less fair. Those taxes that can be viewed as more fair, such as the federal income tax, often are more complex to administer. Thus, Margaret's friend Eddy faces a difficult choice about which type of tax system to advocate, as do all taxpayers. An understanding of the evaluative criteria should be helpful to anyone trying to reconcile the trade-offs among alternative tax proposals.

CONCLUSION

In almost any society, taxes are a part of life. They influence decisions about personal finance, investment, business, and politics. In this chapter, we introduced the basic concepts of why one should study tax, what a tax is, and how to calculate a tax. We also discussed various tax rates, tax rate structures, and different types of taxes imposed by federal, state, and local governments. Finally, we discussed the criteria that one might use to evaluate alternative tax rate systems. To make informed personal finance, investment, business, and political decisions, one must have a basic understanding of these items. In the following chapters we expand the discussion of how taxes influence these decisions while providing a basic understanding of our federal income tax system. Read on and learn more!

Summary

Demonstrate how taxes influence basic business, investment, personal, and political decisions.   **LO 1-1**

- Taxes are significant costs that influence many basic business, investment, and personal decisions.
  - *Business decisions* include what organizational form to take; where to locate; how to compensate employees; determining the appropriate debt mix; owning versus renting equipment and property; how to distribute profits; and so forth.
  - *Investment decisions* include alternative methods for saving for education or retirement, and so forth.
  - *Personal finance decisions* include evaluating job offers; gift or estate planning; owning a home versus renting; and so forth.
- Taxes also play a major part in the political process. Major parties typically have very diverse views on whom, what, and how much to tax.

Discuss what constitutes a tax and the general objectives of taxes.   **LO 1-2**

- The general purpose of taxes is to fund the government. Unlike fines or penalties, taxes are not meant to punish or prevent illegal behavior; but "sin taxes" (on alcohol, tobacco, tanning beds, etc.) are meant to discourage some behaviors.
- To qualify as a tax, three criteria are necessary: the payment must be (1) required (it is not voluntary), (2) imposed by a government (federal, state, or local), and (3) not tied directly to the benefit received by the taxpayer.

Describe the different tax rate structures and calculate a tax.   **LO 1-3**

- Tax = Tax rate × Tax base, where the tax base is what is taxed and the tax rate is the level of taxes imposed on the base. Different portions of a tax base may be taxed at different rates.

- There are three different tax rates that are useful in contrasting the different tax rate structures, tax planning, and/or assessing the tax burden of a taxpayer: the marginal, average, and effective tax rates.
- The *marginal* tax rate is the tax that applies to the next increment of income or deduction. The *average* tax rate represents a taxpayer's average level of taxation on each dollar of taxable income. The *effective* tax rate represents the taxpayer's average rate of taxation on each dollar of total income (taxable *and* nontaxable income).
- The three basic tax rate structures are proportional, progressive, and regressive.
    - A *proportional* tax rate structure imposes a constant tax rate throughout the tax base. As a taxpayer's tax base increases, the taxpayer's taxes increase proportionally. The marginal tax rate remains constant and always equals the average tax rate. A common example is a sales tax.
    - A *progressive* tax rate imposes an increasing marginal tax rate as the tax base increases. As a taxpayer's tax base increases, both the marginal tax rate and the taxes paid increase. A common example is the U.S. federal income tax.
    - A *regressive* tax rate imposes a decreasing marginal tax rate as the tax base increases. As a taxpayer's tax base increases, the marginal tax rate decreases while the total taxes paid increases.

LO 1-4   Identify the various federal, state, and local taxes.

- Federal taxes include the income tax, employment taxes (Social Security and Medicare taxes), unemployment taxes, excise taxes (levied on quantity purchased), and transfer taxes (estate and gift taxes).
- State and local taxes include the income tax (levied by most states), sales tax (levied on retail sales of goods and some services), use tax (levied on the retail price of goods owned or consumed within a state that were purchased out of state), property taxes (levied on fair market value of real and personal property), and excise taxes.
- Implicit taxes are indirect taxes that result from a tax advantage the government grants to certain transactions to satisfy social, economic, or other objectives. They are defined as the reduced before-tax return that a tax-favored asset produces because of its tax-advantaged status.

LO 1-5   Apply appropriate criteria to evaluate alternative tax systems.

- Sufficiency involves assessing the aggregate size of the tax revenues that must be generated and ensuring that the tax system provides these revenues. Static forecasting ignores how taxpayers may alter their activities in response to a proposed tax law change and bases projected tax revenues on the existing state of transactions. In contrast, dynamic forecasting attempts to account for possible taxpayer responses to a proposed tax law change.
- Equity considers how the tax burden should be distributed across taxpayers. Generally, a tax system is considered fair or equitable if the tax is based on the taxpayer's ability to pay—that is, taxpayers with a greater ability to pay tax, pay more tax. Horizontal equity means that two taxpayers in similar situations pay the same tax. Vertical equity is achieved when taxpayers with greater ability to pay tax, pay more tax relative to taxpayers with a lesser ability to pay tax.
- Certainty means taxpayers should be able to determine when, where, and how much tax to pay.
- Convenience means a tax system should be designed to facilitate the collection of tax revenues without undue hardship on the taxpayer or the government.
- Economy means a tax system should minimize its compliance and administration costs.

KEY TERMS

ad valorem taxes (1-15)	convenience (1-22)	effective tax rate (1-7)
average tax rate (1-7)	dynamic forecasting (1-18)	employment taxes (1-12)
bracket (1-5)	earmarked tax (1-4)	equity (1-20)
certainty (1-22)	economy (1-22)	estate tax (1-13)

excise taxes (1-13)

explicit taxes (1-16)

flat tax (1-5)

gift tax (1-13)

graduated taxes (1-5)

horizontal equity (1-21)

implicit taxes (1-16)

income effect (1-19)

income tax (1-12)

local tax (1-14)

marginal tax rate (1-5)

Medicare tax (1-12)

personal property tax (1-15)

progressive tax rate structure (1-9)

proportional tax rate structure (1-9)

real property tax (1-15)

regressive tax rate structure (1-10)

sales tax (1-14)

self-employment tax (1-13)

sin taxes (1-4)

Social Security tax (1-12)

state tax (1-14)

static forecasting (1-18)

substitution effect (1-19)

sufficiency (1-18)

tax (1-4)

tax base (1-5)

tax rate (1-5)

transfer taxes (1-13)

unemployment tax (1-13)

use tax (1-14)

value-added tax (1-11)

vertical equity (1-21)

DISCUSSION QUESTIONS

Discussion Questions are available in Connect®.

1. Jessica's friend Zachary once stated that he couldn't understand why someone would take a tax course. Why is this a rather naïve view?   **LO 1-1**

2. What are some aspects of business that require knowledge of taxation? What are some aspects of personal finance that require knowledge of taxation?   **LO 1-1**

3. Describe some ways in which taxes affect the political process in the United States.   **LO 1-1**

4. Courtney recently received a speeding ticket on her way to the university. Her fine was $200. Is this considered a tax? Why or why not?   **LO 1-2**

5. Marlon and Latoya recently started building a house. They had to pay $300 to the county government for a building permit. Is the $300 payment a tax? Why or why not?   **LO 1-2**

6. To help pay for the city's new stadium, the city of Birmingham recently enacted a 1 percent surcharge on hotel rooms. Is this a tax? Why or why not?   **LO 1-2**

7. As noted in Example 1-2, tolls, parking meter fees, and annual licensing fees are not considered taxes. Can you identify other fees that are similar?   **LO 1-2**

8. If the general objective of our tax system is to raise revenue, why does the income tax allow deductions for charitable contributions and retirement plan contributions?   **LO 1-2**

9. One common argument for imposing so-called sin taxes is the social goal of *reducing* demand for such products. Using cigarettes as an example, is there a segment of the population that might be sensitive to price and for whom high taxes might discourage purchases?   **LO 1-2**

10. Dontae stated that he didn't want to earn any more money because it would "put him in a higher tax bracket." What is wrong with Dontae's reasoning?   **LO 1-3**

11. Describe the three different tax rates discussed in the chapter and how taxpayers might use them.   **LO 1-3**

12. Which is a more appropriate tax rate to use to compare taxpayers' tax burdens— the average or the effective tax rate? Why?   **LO 1-3**

13. Describe the differences between proportional, progressive, and regressive tax rate structures.   **LO 1-3**

14. Arnold and Lilly have recently had a heated discussion about whether a sales tax is a proportional tax or a regressive tax. Arnold argues that a sales tax is regressive. Lilly counters that the sales tax is a flat tax. Who is correct?   **LO 1-3**

15. Which is the largest tax collected by the U.S. government? What types of taxpayers are subject to this tax?   **LO 1-4**

LO 1-4 16. What is the tax base for the Social Security and Medicare taxes for an employee or employer? What is the tax base for Social Security and Medicare taxes for a self-employed individual? Is the self-employment tax in addition to or in lieu of federal income tax?

LO 1-4 17. What are unemployment taxes?

LO 1-4 18. What is the distinguishing feature of an excise tax?

LO 1-4 19. What are some of the taxes that currently are unique to state and local governments? What are some of the taxes that the federal, state, and local governments each utilize?

LO 1-4 20. The state of Georgia recently increased its tax on a pack of cigarettes by $2. What type of tax is this? Why might Georgia choose this type of tax?

LO 1-4 21. What is the difference between a sales tax and a use tax?

LO 1-4 22. What is an ad valorem tax? Name an example of this type of tax.

LO 1-4 23. What are the differences between an explicit and an implicit tax?

LO 1-4 24. When we calculate average and effective tax rates, do we consider implicit taxes? What effect does this have on taxpayers' perception of equity?

LO 1-4 25. Benjamin recently bought a truck in Alabama for his business in Georgia. What different types of federal and state taxes may affect this transaction?

LO 1-5 26. Kobe strongly dislikes SUVs and is appalled that so many are on the road. He proposes to eliminate the federal income tax and replace it with a $50,000 annual tax per SUV. Based on the number of SUVs currently owned in the United States, he estimates the tax will generate exactly the amount of tax revenue currently collected from the income tax. What is wrong with Kobe's proposal? What type of forecasting is Kobe likely using?

LO 1-5 27. What is the difference between the income and substitution effects? For which types of taxpayers is the income effect more likely descriptive? For which types of taxpayers is the substitution effect more likely descriptive?

LO 1-5 28. What is the difference between horizontal and vertical equity? How do tax preferences affect people's view of horizontal equity?

LO 1-3 **LO 1-5** 29. Montel argues that a flat income tax rate system is vertically equitable. Oprah argues that a progressive tax rate structure is vertically equitable. How do their arguments differ? Who is correct?

LO 1-3 **LO 1-5** 30. Discuss why evaluating vertical equity simply based on tax rate structure may be less than optimal.

LO 1-4 **LO 1-5** 31. Compare the federal income tax to sales taxes using the "certainty" criterion.

LO 1-5 32. Many years ago a famous member of Congress proposed eliminating federal income tax withholding. What criterion for evaluating tax systems did this proposal violate? What would likely have been the result of eliminating withholding?

LO 1-5 33. "The federal income tax scores very high on the economy criterion because the current IRS budget is relatively low compared to the costs of a typical collection agency." Explain why this statement may be considered wrong.

PROBLEMS

Select problems are available in Connect®.

LO 1-3 34. Chuck, a single taxpayer, earns $75,000 in taxable income and $10,000 in interest from an investment in City of Heflin bonds. Using the U.S. tax rate schedule, how much federal tax will he owe? What is his average tax rate? What is his effective tax rate? What is his current marginal tax rate?

35. Using the facts in problem 34, if Chuck earns an additional $40,000 of taxable in-come, what is his marginal tax rate on this income? What is his marginal rate if, instead, he had $40,000 of additional deductions?

36. Campbell, a single taxpayer, earns $400,000 in taxable income and $2,000 in inter-est from an investment in State of New York bonds. Using the U.S. tax rate sched-ule, how much federal tax will she owe? What is her average tax rate? What is her effective tax rate? What is her current marginal tax rate?

37. Using the facts in problem 36, if Campbell earns an additional $15,000 of taxable income, what is her marginal tax rate on this income? What is her marginal rate if, instead, she had $15,000 of additional deductions?

38. Jorge and Anita, married taxpayers, earn $150,000 in taxable income and $40,000 in interest from an investment in City of Heflin bonds. Using the U.S. tax rate schedule for married filing jointly (see Example 1-3), how much federal tax will they owe? What is their average tax rate? What is their effective tax rate? What is their current marginal tax rate?

39. Using the facts in problem 38, if Jorge and Anita earn an additional $100,000 of taxable income, what is their marginal tax rate on this income? What is their marginal rate if, instead, they report an additional $100,000 in deductions?

40. Scot and Vidia, married taxpayers, earn $240,000 in taxable income and $5,000 in interest from an investment in City of Tampa bonds. Using the U.S. tax rate sched-ule for married filing jointly (see Example 1-3), how much federal tax will they owe? What is their average tax rate? What is their effective tax rate? What is their current marginal tax rate?

41. Using the facts in problem 40, if Scot and Vidia earn an additional $80,000 of taxable income, what is their marginal tax rate on this income? How would your answer differ if they, instead, had $80,000 of additional deductions?

42. Melinda invests $200,000 in a City of Heflin bond that pays 6 percent interest. Alternatively, Melinda could have invested the $200,000 in a bond recently issued by Surething Inc. that pays 8 percent interest and has risk and other nontax charac-teristics similar to the City of Heflin bond. Assume Melinda's marginal tax rate is 25 percent.

a) What is her after-tax rate of return for the City of Heflin bond?

b) How much explicit tax does Melinda pay on the City of Heflin bond?

c) How much implicit tax does she pay on the City of Heflin bond?

d) How much explicit tax would she have paid on the Surething Inc. bond?

e) What would have been her after-tax rate of return on the Surething Inc. bond?

43. Hugh has the choice between investing in a City of Heflin bond at 6 percent or in-vesting in a Surething bond at 9 percent. Assuming that both bonds have the same nontax characteristics and that Hugh has a 40 percent marginal tax rate, in which bond should he invest?

44. Using the facts in problem 43, what interest rate does Surething Inc. need to offer to make Hugh indifferent between investing in the two bonds?

45. Fergie has the choice between investing in a State of New York bond at 5 percent and a Surething bond at 8 percent. Assuming that both bonds have the same nontax characteristics and that Fergie has a 30 percent marginal tax rate, in which bond should she invest?

46. Using the facts in problem 45, what interest rate does the State of New York bond need to offer to make Fergie indifferent between investing in the two bonds?

LO 1-3 47. Given the following tax structure, what minimum tax would need to be assessed on Shameika to make the tax progressive with respect to average tax rates?

Taxpayer	Salary	Muni-Bond Interest	Total Tax
Mihwah	$10,000	$10,000	$600
Shameika	$50,000	$30,000	$???

LO 1-3 48. Using the facts in problem 47, what minimum tax would need to be assessed on Shameika to make the tax progressive with respect to effective tax rates?

LO 1-3 LO 1-5 49. Song earns $100,000 taxable income as an interior designer and is taxed at an average rate of 20 percent (i.e., $20,000 of tax). If Congress increases the income tax rate such that Song's average tax rate increases from 20 percent to 25 percent, how much more income tax will she pay assuming that the income effect is descriptive? What effect will this tax rate change have on the tax base and tax collected?

LO 1-3 LO 1-5 50. Using the facts from problem 49, what will happen to the government's tax revenues if Song chooses to spend more time pursuing her other passions besides work in response to the tax rate change and earns only $75,000 in taxable income? What is the term that describes this type of reaction to a tax rate increase? What types of taxpayers are likely to respond in this manner?

LO 1-5 51. Given the following tax structure, what tax would need to be assessed on Venita to make the tax horizontally equitable?

Taxpayer	Salary	Total Tax
Mae	$10,000	$ 600
Pedro	$20,000	$ 1,500
Venita	$10,000	$???

LO 1-5 52. Using the facts in problem 51, what is the minimum tax that Pedro should pay to make the tax structure vertically equitable based on the tax rate paid? This would result in what type of tax rate structure?

LO 1-5 53. Using the facts in problem 51, what is the minimum tax that Pedro should pay to make the tax structure vertically equitable with respect to the amount of tax paid? This would result in what type of tax rate structure?

LO 1-5 54. Consider the following tax rate structure. Is it horizontally equitable? Why or why not? Is it vertically equitable? Why or why not?

Taxpayer	Salary	Total Tax
Rajiv	$10,000	$600
LaMarcus	$20,000	$600
Dory	$10,000	$600

LO 1-5 55. Consider the following tax rate structure. Is it horizontally equitable? Why or why not? Is it vertically equitable? Why or why not?

Taxpayer	Salary	Total Tax
Marilyn	$10,000	$ 600
Kobe	$20,000	$3,000
Alfonso	$30,000	$6,000

LO 1-5 56. Consider the following tax rate structure. Is it horizontally equitable? Why or why not? Is it vertically equitable? Why or why not?

Taxpayer	Salary	Total Tax
Rodney	$10,000	$600
Keisha	$10,000	$600

57. Lorenzo is considering starting a trucking company either in Texas or Oklahoma. He will relocate his family, which includes his wife, children, and parents, to reside in the same state as his business. What types of taxes may influence his decision of where to locate his business?

58. Congress would like to increase tax revenues by 10 percent. Assume that the average taxpayer in the United States earns $65,000 and pays an average tax rate of 15 percent. If the income effect is in effect for all taxpayers, what average tax rate will result in a 10 percent increase in tax revenues? This is an example of what type of forecasting?

59. Locate the IRS website at www.irs.gov/. For every $100 the IRS collected, how much was spent on the IRS's collection efforts? What tax system criterion does this information help you to evaluate with respect to the current U.S. tax system?

LO 1-5

research

60. Using the Internet, find a comparison of income tax rates across states. What state currently has the highest income tax rate? In considering individual tax burdens across states, what other taxes should you consider?

LO 1-4

research

ROGER | *CPA Review*

Sample CPA Exam questions from Roger CPA Review are available in Connect as support for the topics in this text. These Multiple Choice Questions and Task-Based Simulations include expert-written explanations and solutions and provide a starting point for students to become familiar with the content and functionality of the actual CPA Exam.

Tax Compliance, the IRS, and Tax Authorities

Learning Objectives

Upon completing this chapter, you should be able to:

LO 2-1 Identify the filing requirements for income tax returns and the statute of limitations for assessment.

LO 2-2 Outline the IRS audit process, how returns are selected, the different types of audits, and what happens after the audit.

LO 2-3 Evaluate the relative weights of the various tax law sources.

LO 2-4 Describe the legislative process as it pertains to taxation.

LO 2-5 Perform the basic steps in tax research.

LO 2-6 Describe tax professional responsibilities in providing tax advice.

LO 2-7 Identify taxpayer and tax professional penalties.

©Robert Nicholas/AGE Fotostock

Storyline Summary

Taxpayers: Bill and Mercedes

Family description: Bill and Mercedes are married with one daughter, Margaret, and live in Tampa, Florida.

Employment status: Bill is an economics professor; Mercedes is a small business owner.

Filing status: Married, filing jointly

Current situation: Bill and Mercedes face an IRS audit involving a previous year's interest deductions.

Bill and Mercedes received a notice from the Internal Revenue Service (IRS) that their return is under audit for certain interest deductions. As you might expect, they are quite concerned, especially because it has been several years since they claimed the deductions and they worry that all their supporting documentation may not be in place. Several questions run through their minds. How could the IRS audit a return that was filed so long ago? Why was their tax return selected, and what should they expect during the audit? The interest deductions they reported were based on advice from their CPA. What would cause the IRS and a CPA to interpret the law differently? What is their financial exposure if the deductions are ultimately disallowed? Will they have to pay interest and penalties in addition to the tax they might owe? ■

Even the most conservative taxpayer is likely to feel anxiety after receiving an IRS notice. This chapter will help answer Bill and Mercedes's questions and provide an overview of the audit process and tax research. While all taxpayers should understand these basics of our tax system, aspiring accountants should be especially familiar with them.

LO 2-1   TAXPAYER FILING REQUIREMENTS

To file or not to file? Unlike Hamlet's "to be or not to be," this question has a pretty straightforward answer. Filing requirements are specified by law for each type of taxpayer. All corporations must file a tax return annually regardless of their taxable income. Estates and trusts are required to file annual income tax returns if their gross income exceeds $600.[1]

The filing requirements for individual taxpayers are a little more complex. Specifically, they depend on the taxpayer's filing status (single, married filing jointly, and so on, discussed in more detail in the Individual Income Tax Overview, Dependents, and Filing Status chapter), age, and gross income (income before deductions). Exhibit 2-1 lists the 2018 gross income thresholds for taxpayers based on their filing status, gross income, and age. As detailed in Exhibit 2-1, the gross income thresholds are calculated as the sum of the standard deduction and additional deductions for taxpayers age 65 or older.[2] These amounts are indexed for inflation and thus change each year. For certain taxpayers, such as the self-employed and those claimed as dependents by another taxpayer, lower gross income thresholds apply.

EXHIBIT 2-1   **2018 Gross Income Thresholds by Filing Status**

Filing Status and Age (in 2018)	2018 Gross Income	Explanation
Single	$12,000	$12,000 standard deduction
Single, 65 or older	$13,600	$12,000 standard deduction + $1,600 additional deduction
Married, filing a joint return	$24,000	$24,000 standard deduction
Married, filing a joint return, one spouse 65 or older	$25,300	$24,000 standard deduction + $1,300 additional deduction
Married, filing a joint return, both spouses 65 or older	$26,600	$24,000 standard deduction + $2,600 additional deductions (2)
Married, filing a separate return	$ 0	
Head of household	$18,000	$18,000 standard deduction
Head of household, 65 or older	$19,600	$18,000 standard deduction + $1,600 additional deduction
Surviving spouse with a dependent child	$24,000	$24,000 standard deduction
Surviving spouse, 65 or older, with a dependent child	$25,300	$24,000 standard deduction + $1,300 additional deduction

Source: www.irs.gov

Whether a taxpayer is due a refund (which occurs when taxes paid exceed tax liability) does *not* determine whether a taxpayer must file a tax return. Gross income determines whether a tax return is required. Further, note that even a taxpayer whose gross income falls below the respective threshold is not precluded from filing a tax return.

[1]Estates file income tax returns during the administration period (i.e., before all of the estate assets are distributed).

[2]IRC §6012. We describe the standard deduction in detail later in the text. A married taxpayer is required to file a tax return (regardless of gross income) if: (i) such individual and his spouse, at the close of the taxable year, did not have the same household as their home; (ii) the individual's spouse files a separate return; or (iii) the individual or his spouse is a dependent of another taxpayer who has income (other than earned income) in excess of $500.

Indeed, taxpayers due a refund *should* file a tax return to receive the refund (or claim a refundable tax credit), even if they are not required to file a tax return.

Tax Return Due Date and Extensions

Like the filing requirements, due dates for tax returns vary based on the type of taxpayer. Individual tax returns are due on the fifteenth day of the fourth month following year-end— that is, April 15 for calendar-year individuals. (Due dates that fall on a Saturday, Sunday, or holidays are automatically extended to the next day that is not a Saturday, Sunday, or holiday.) Similarly, tax returns for taxable corporations ("C" corporations) are generally due on the fifteenth day of the fourth month following the corporation's year-end. The exception is for tax returns for C corporations with a June 30 year-end, which are due on the fifteenth day of the third month (September 15th). For both partnerships and S corporations (generally nontaxable corporations), tax returns must be filed by the fifteenth day of the third month following the entity's year-end (March 15 for calendar-year partnerships or S corporations). Any individual, partnership, or S corporation unable to file a tax return by the original due date can, by that same deadline, request a six-month extension to file, which is granted automatically by the IRS. Similarly, C corporations may request an automatic five-, six-, or seven-month extension to file depending on the corporation's year-end.[3]

An extension allows the taxpayer to delay filing a tax return but does *not* extend the due date for tax payments. Thus, when a taxpayer files an extension, she must estimate how much tax will be owed. If a taxpayer fails to pay the entire balance of tax owed by the original due date of the tax return, the IRS charges the taxpayer interest on the underpayment from the due date of the return until the taxpayer pays the tax.[4] The interest rate charged depends on taxpayer type (individual or corporation) and varies quarterly with the federal short-term interest rate.[5] For example, the interest rate for tax underpayments for individuals equals the federal short-term rate plus three percentage points.[6]

What happens if the taxpayer does not file a tax return by the time required, whether April 15 or an extended deadline? As you might guess, the IRS imposes penalties on taxpayers failing to comply with the tax law. In many cases, the penalties can be quite substantial (see later discussion in this chapter). In the case of failure to file a tax return, the penalty equals 5 percent of the tax due for each month (or partial month) that the return is late. However, the maximum penalty is generally 25 percent of the tax owed, and the failure-to-file penalty does not apply if the taxpayer owes no tax.

Statute of Limitations

Despite the diligent efforts of taxpayers and tax professionals, it is quite common for tax returns to contain mistakes. Some may be to the taxpayer's advantage and others may be to the government's advantage. Regardless of the nature of the mistake, the taxpayer is obligated to file an amended return to correct the error (and request a refund or pay a deficiency) if the statute of limitations has not expired for the tax return. Likewise, the IRS can propose adjustments to the taxpayer's return if the statute of limitations for the return has not expired.

By law, the **statute of limitations** defines the period in which the taxpayer can file an amended tax return or the IRS can assess a tax deficiency for a specific tax year. For both amended tax returns filed by a taxpayer and proposed tax assessments by the IRS, the statute of limitations generally ends three years from the *later* of (1) the date the tax return was actually filed or (2) the tax return's original due date.

[3]June 30 year-end C corporations may request a seven-month extension. All other C corporations may request a six-month extension.

[4]The tax law also imposes a penalty for late payment in addition to the interest charged on the underpayment. We briefly discuss this penalty later in the chapter and in the Individual Income Tax Computation and Tax Credits chapter.

[5]The federal short-term rate is determined from a one-month average of the market yields from marketable obligations of the United States with maturities of three years or less.

[6]This same interest rate applies to individuals who overpay their taxes (i.e., receive a tax refund and interest payment as a result of an IRS audit or from filing an amended tax return).

The statute of limitations for IRS assessment can be extended in certain circumstances. For example, a six-year statute of limitations applies to IRS assessments if the taxpayer omits items of gross income that exceed 25 percent of the gross income reported on the tax return. For fraudulent returns, or if the taxpayer fails to file a tax return, the news is understandably worse. The statute of limitations remains open indefinitely in these cases.

Example 2-1

Bill and Mercedes file their 2014 federal tax return on September 6, 2015, after receiving an automatic extension to file their return by October 15, 2015. In 2018, the IRS selects their 2014 tax return for audit. When does the statute of limitations end for Bill and Mercedes's 2014 tax return?

Answer: Assuming the six-year and "unlimited" statute of limitation rules do not apply, the statute of limitations ends on September 6, 2018 (three years after the later of the actual filing date and the *original* due date).

What if: When would the statute of limitations end for Bill and Mercedes for their 2014 tax return if the couple filed the return on March 22, 2015 (before the original due date of April 15, 2015)?

Answer: In this scenario the statute of limitations would end on April 15, 2018, because the later of the actual filing date and the original due date is April 15, 2015.

Taxpayers should prepare for the possibility of an audit by retaining all supporting documents (receipts, canceled checks, etc.) for a tax return until the statute of limitations expires. After the statute of limitations expires, taxpayers can discard the majority of supporting documents but should still keep a copy of the tax return itself, as well as any documents that may have ongoing significance, such as those establishing the taxpayer's *basis* or original investment in existing assets like personal residences and long-term investments.

LO 2-2 IRS AUDIT SELECTION

Why me? This is a recurring question in life and definitely a common taxpayer question after receiving an IRS audit notice. The answer, in general, is that a taxpayer's return is selected for audit because the IRS has data suggesting the taxpayer's tax return has a high probability of a significant understated tax liability. Budget constraints limit the IRS's ability to audit a majority or even a large minority of tax returns. Currently, fewer than 1 percent of all tax returns are audited. Thus, the IRS must be strategic in selecting returns for audit in an effort to promote the highest level of voluntary taxpayer compliance and increase tax revenues.

Specifically, how does the IRS select tax returns for audit? The IRS uses a number of computer programs and outside data sources (newspapers, financial statement disclosures, informants, and other public and private sources) to identify tax returns that may have an understated tax liability. Common computer initiatives include the **DIF (Discriminant Function) system,** the **document perfection program,** and the **information matching program.** The most important of these initiatives is the DIF system. The DIF system assigns a score to each tax return that represents the probability the tax liability on the return has been underreported (a higher score = a higher likelihood of underreporting). The IRS derives the weights assigned to specific tax return attributes from historical IRS audit adjustment data from the National Research Program.[7] The DIF system then uses these (undisclosed) weights to score each tax return based on the tax return's characteristics. Returns with higher DIF scores are reviewed to determine whether an audit is the best course of action.

---

[7]Similar to its predecessor, the Taxpayer Compliance Measurement Program, the National Research Program (NRP) analyzes a large sample of tax returns that are randomly selected for audit. From these randomly selected returns, the IRS identifies tax return characteristics (e.g., deductions for a home office, unusually high tax deductions relative to a taxpayer's income) associated with underreported liabilities, weights these characteristics, and then incorporates them into the DIF system. The NRP analyzes randomly selected returns to ensure that the DIF scorings are representative of the population of tax returns.

All returns are checked for mathematical and tax calculation errors, a process referred to as the document perfection program. Individual returns are also subject to the information matching program. This program compares the taxpayer's tax return to information submitted to the IRS from other taxpayers like banks, employers, mutual funds, brokerage companies, and mortgage companies. Information matched includes items such as wages (Form W-2 submitted by employers), interest income (Form 1099-INT submitted by banks), and dividend income (Form 1099-DIV submitted by brokerage companies). For tax returns identified as incorrect via the document perfection and information matching programs, the IRS recalculates the taxpayer's tax liability and sends a notice explaining the adjustment. If the taxpayer owes tax, the IRS will request payment of the tax due. If the taxpayer overpaid tax, the IRS will send the taxpayer a refund of the overpayment.

In addition to computer-based methods for identifying tax returns for audit, the IRS may use a number of other audit initiatives that target taxpayers working in certain industries, engaging in certain transactions like the acquisition of other companies, or having specific attributes like home office deductions. Taxpayers of a given size and complexity, such as large publicly traded companies, may be audited every year.

TAXES IN THE REAL WORLD   Turning in Your Neighbor Can Pay Big Bucks

The Wall Street Journal reported that in April 2011 the IRS made its first payment under a new taxpayer whistleblower program that promises large rewards for turning in tax cheats. Under the large-award whistleblower program (where unpaid taxes, interest, and penalties exceed $2 million and the tax cheat, if an individual, has gross income exceeding $200,000 in at least one year), whistleblowers can be paid between 15 and 30 percent of the taxes, interest, and penalties collected by the IRS. Under the small-award whistleblower program (tax, interest, and penalty underpayments of $2 million or less), the IRS may pay whistleblowers up to 15 percent of the unpaid taxes and interest collected. Whistleblowers use IRS Form 211 (www.IRS.gov) to apply for the program, and as you might expect, all whistleblower payments received are fully taxable. In its first payment, the IRS awarded $4.5 million to a former in-house accountant for a large financial services firm. Given the potential windfall to whistleblowers, you might expect a long line of "concerned" citizens applying for the program. You would be correct. As of January 2017, the IRS Commissioner announced that the IRS has paid out more than $465 million in awards since 2007, on collection of $3.4 billion based on whistleblower information.

Source: Based on: "Taxes: How to Turn in Your Neighbor to the IRS," *The Wall Street Journal,* WSJ.com, September 3, 2011.

How was Bill and Mercedes's tax return selected for audit? Given the audit focus on certain deductions, the IRS likely selected their return for audit because the amount or type of the deductions resulted in a high DIF score. IRS personnel then determined that the deductions warranted further review and, thus, selected the tax return for audit.

ETHICS

After Bill and Mercedes's tax return was selected for audit, Bill read on the Internet speculation that filing a paper tax return (instead of filing electronically) and extending a tax return deadline decrease the chance of IRS audit. Bill has convinced Mercedes that they need to use these strategies in the future and look for other ways to avoid audit. Has Bill crossed an ethical boundary?

Types of Audits

The three types of IRS audits are correspondence, office, and field examinations. **Correspondence examinations** are the most common. These audits, as the name suggests, are conducted by mail and generally are limited to one or two items on the taxpayer's return. Of the three types of audits, correspondence audits are generally the narrowest in scope and the least complex. The IRS typically requests supporting documentation for one or more items on the taxpayer's return, like charitable contributions deducted, for example. When appropriate documentation is promptly supplied, these audits typically can be concluded relatively quickly. Of course, they can also be expanded to address other issues that arise as a result of the IRS's inspection of taxpayer documents.

Office examinations are the second most common audit. As the name suggests, the IRS conducts them at its local office. These audits are typically broader in scope and more complex than correspondence examinations. Small businesses, taxpayers operating sole proprietorships, and middle- to high-income individual taxpayers are more likely, if audited, to have office examinations. In these examinations, the taxpayer receives a notice that identifies the items subject to audit, requests substantiation for these items as necessary, and notifies the taxpayer of the date, time, and location of the exam. Taxpayers may attend the examination alone or with representation, such as their tax adviser or attorney, or simply let their tax adviser or attorney attend on their behalf.

Field examinations are the least common audit. The IRS conducts these at the taxpayer's place of business or the location where the taxpayer's books, records, and source documents are maintained. Field examinations are generally the broadest in scope and the most complex of the three audit types. They can last months to years and generally are limited to business returns and the most complex individual returns.

What type of exam do you think Bill and Mercedes will have? Because their return is an individual tax return and the audit is restricted to a relatively narrow set of deductions, their return will likely be subject to a correspondence audit. If the audit were broader in scope, an office examination would be more likely.

After the Audit After the examination, the IRS agent provides a list of proposed adjustments (if any) to the taxpayer for review. If he or she agrees to the proposed changes, the taxpayer signs an agreement form (Form 870) and pays the additional tax owed or receives the proposed refund. If the taxpayer disputes the proposed changes, the taxpayer will receive a **30-day letter** giving him or her 30 days to either (1) request a conference with an appeals officer, who is independent and resides in a separate IRS division from the examining agent, or (2) agree to the proposed adjustment. An appeals officer would consider the merits of the unresolved issues as well as the "hazards of litigation"—that is, the probability that the IRS will lose if the case is brought to court and the resulting costs of a taxpayer-favorable ruling. If the taxpayer chooses the appeals conference and reaches an agreement with the IRS there, the taxpayer can then sign Form 870. If the taxpayer and IRS still do not agree on the proposed adjustment at the appeals conference, or the taxpayer chooses not to request an appeals conference, the IRS will send the taxpayer a **90-day letter.** See Exhibit 2-2.

Why would a taxpayer prefer one trial court over others? To understand this, we must appreciate the basic distinguishing factors of each. First and foremost, it is relatively common for the U.S. Tax Court, local U.S. District Court, or the U.S. Court of Federal Claims to interpret and rule differently on the same basic tax issue. Given a choice of courts, the taxpayer should prefer the court most likely to rule favorably on his or her particular issues. The courts also differ in other ways. For example, the U.S. District Court is the only court that provides for a jury trial; the U.S. Tax Court is the only court that allows tax cases to be heard *before* the taxpayer pays the disputed liability and the only court with a small claims division (hearing claims involving disputed liabilities of $50,000 or less); and the U.S. Tax Court judges are tax experts, whereas the U.S. District Court and U.S. Court of Federal Claims judges are generalists. The taxpayer should consider each of these factors in choosing a trial court. For example, if the taxpayer feels very confident in her tax return position but does not have sufficient funds to pay the disputed liability, she will prefer the U.S. Tax Court. If, instead, the taxpayer is litigating a tax return position

---

THE KEY FACTS

IRS Audits

- The three types of IRS audits are correspondence, office, and field examinations.
- After the audit, the IRS will send the taxpayer a 30-day letter, which provides the taxpayer the opportunity to pay the proposed assessment or request an appeals conference.
- If an agreement is not reached at appeals or the taxpayer does not pay the proposed assessment, the IRS will send the taxpayer a 90-day letter.
- After receiving the 90-day letter, the taxpayer may pay the tax or petition the U.S. Tax Court to hear the case.
- If the taxpayer chooses to pay the tax, the taxpayer may then request a refund of the tax and eventually sue the IRS for refund in the U.S. District Court or the U.S. Court of Federal Claims.

EXHIBIT 2-2   IRS Appeals/Litigation Process

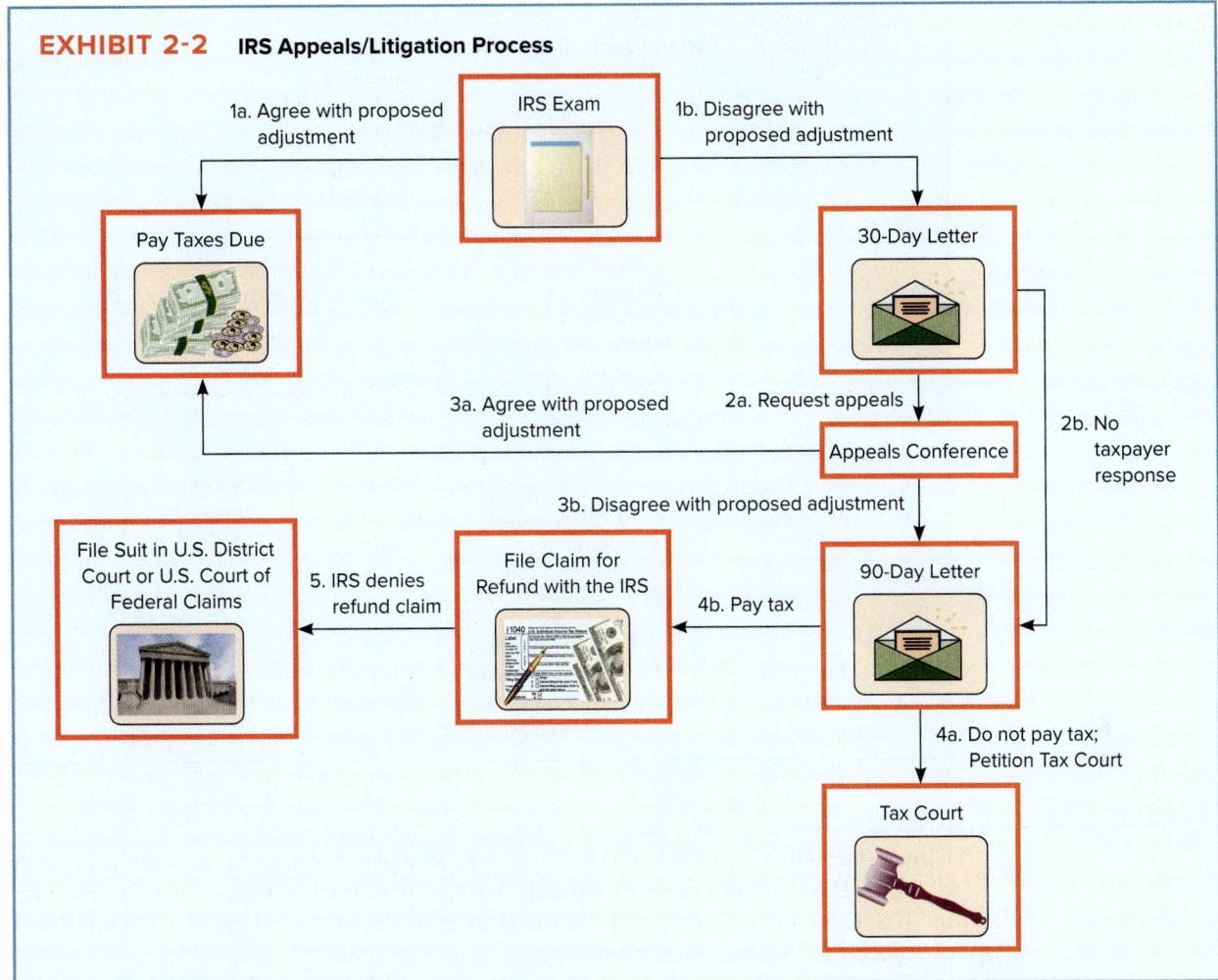

IRS Exam: ©Imageroller/Alamy Stock Photo; Supreme Court: ©McGraw-Hill Education/Jill Braaten, photographer (also known as a *statutory notice of deficiency*) explains that the taxpayer has 90 days to either (1) pay the proposed deficiency or (2) file a petition in the U.S. Tax Court to hear the case.[8] The **U.S. Tax Court** is a national court whose judges are tax experts who hear only tax cases. If the taxpayer would like to litigate the case but prefers it to be heard in the local **U.S. District Court** or the **U.S. Court of Federal Claims,** the taxpayer must pay the tax deficiency first, then request a refund from the IRS, and then sue the IRS for refund in the court after the IRS denies the refund claim.

that is low on technical merit but high on emotional appeal, a jury trial in the local U.S. District Court may be the best option.

What happens after the taxpayer's case has been decided in a trial court? The process may not be quite finished. After the trial court's verdict, the losing party has the right to request one of the 13 **U.S. Circuit Courts of Appeals** to hear the case. Exhibit 2-3 depicts the specific appellant courts for each lower-level court. Both the U.S. Tax Court and local U.S. District Court cases are appealed to the specific U.S. Circuit Court of Appeals based on the taxpayer's residence.[9] Cases litigated in Alabama, Florida, and Georgia, for example, appeal to the U.S. Circuit Court of Appeals for the 11th Circuit, whereas those tried in Louisiana, Mississippi, and Texas appeal to the 5th Circuit. In contrast, all U.S. Court of Federal Claims cases appeal to the U.S. Circuit Court of Appeals for the Federal

---

[8]If the taxpayer lacks the funds to pay the assessed tax, there is legitimate doubt as to whether the taxpayer owes part or all of the assessed tax, or collection of the tax would cause the taxpayer economic hardship or be unfair or inequitable, the taxpayer can request an offer in compromise with the IRS to settle the tax liability for less than the full amount assessed by completing Form 656.

[9]Decisions rendered by the U.S. Tax Court Small Claims Division cannot be appealed by the taxpayer or the IRS.

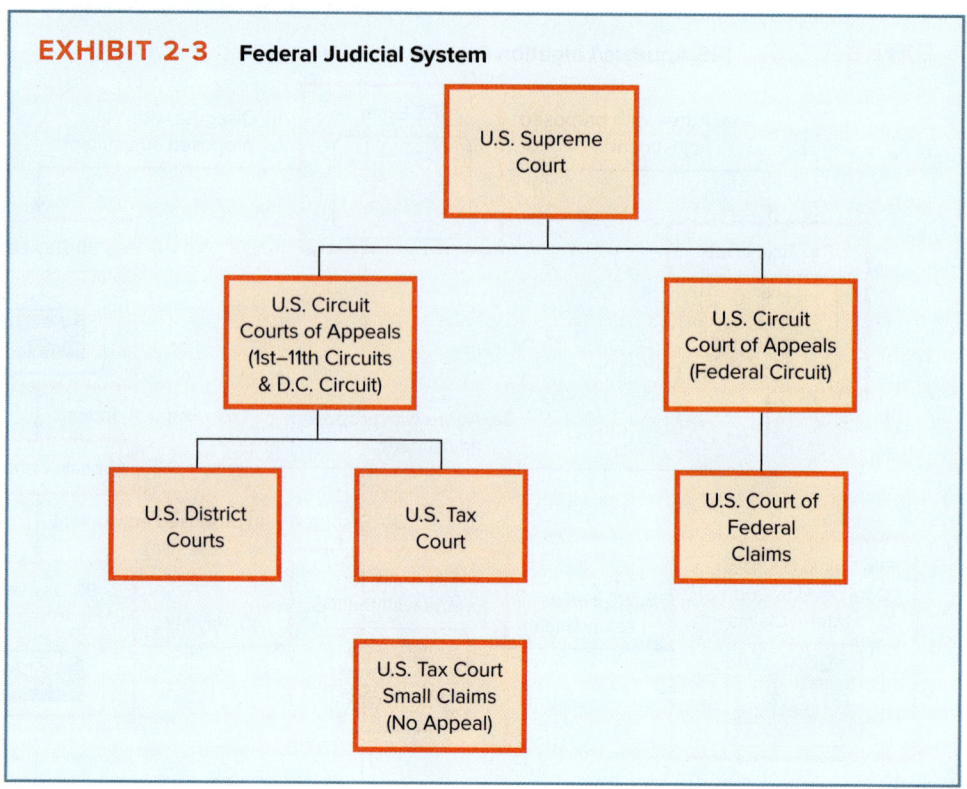

EXHIBIT 2-3 Federal Judicial System

Circuit (located in Washington, D.C.). Exhibit 2-4 depicts the geographic regions for each of the 11 U.S. Circuit Courts of Appeals defined by numerical region. Not depicted are the U.S. Circuit Court of Appeals for the District of Columbia and the U.S. Circuit Court of Appeals for the Federal Circuit.

Through the initial selection of a trial court—U.S. District Court, U.S. Tax Court, or U.S. Court of Federal Claims—the taxpayer has the ability to determine which circuit court would hear an appeal of the case (the U.S. Circuit Court of Appeals based on residence or the U.S. Circuit Court of Appeals for the Federal Circuit). Alternative circuit courts may interpret the law differently, and therefore, in choosing a trial-level court, the taxpayer should consider the relevant circuit courts' judicial histories to determine which circuit court (and thus, which trial court) would be more likely to rule in his or her favor.

After an appeals court hears a case, the losing party has one last option to receive a favorable ruling: a petition to the **U.S. Supreme Court** to hear the case. However, given the quantity of other cases appealed to the U.S. Supreme Court that are of national importance, the Supreme Court agrees to hear only a few tax cases a year—cases with great significance to a broad cross-section of taxpayers or cases litigating issues in which there has been disagreement among the circuit courts. For most tax cases, the Supreme Court refuses to hear the case (denies the ***writ of certiorari***) and litigation ends with the circuit court decision.

Although litigation of tax disputes is quite common, taxpayers should carefully consider the pros and cons. Litigation can be very costly financially and emotionally, and thus it is more appropriately used as an option of last resort, after all other appeal efforts have been exhausted.

What is the likely course of action for Bill and Mercedes's audit? It is too soon to tell. Before you can assess the likely outcome of their audit, you need a better understanding of both the audit issue and the relevant tax laws that apply to the issue. The next section explains alternative tax law sources. After we discuss the various sources of our tax laws,

EXHIBIT 2-4   Geographic Boundaries for the U.S. Circuit Courts of Appeals

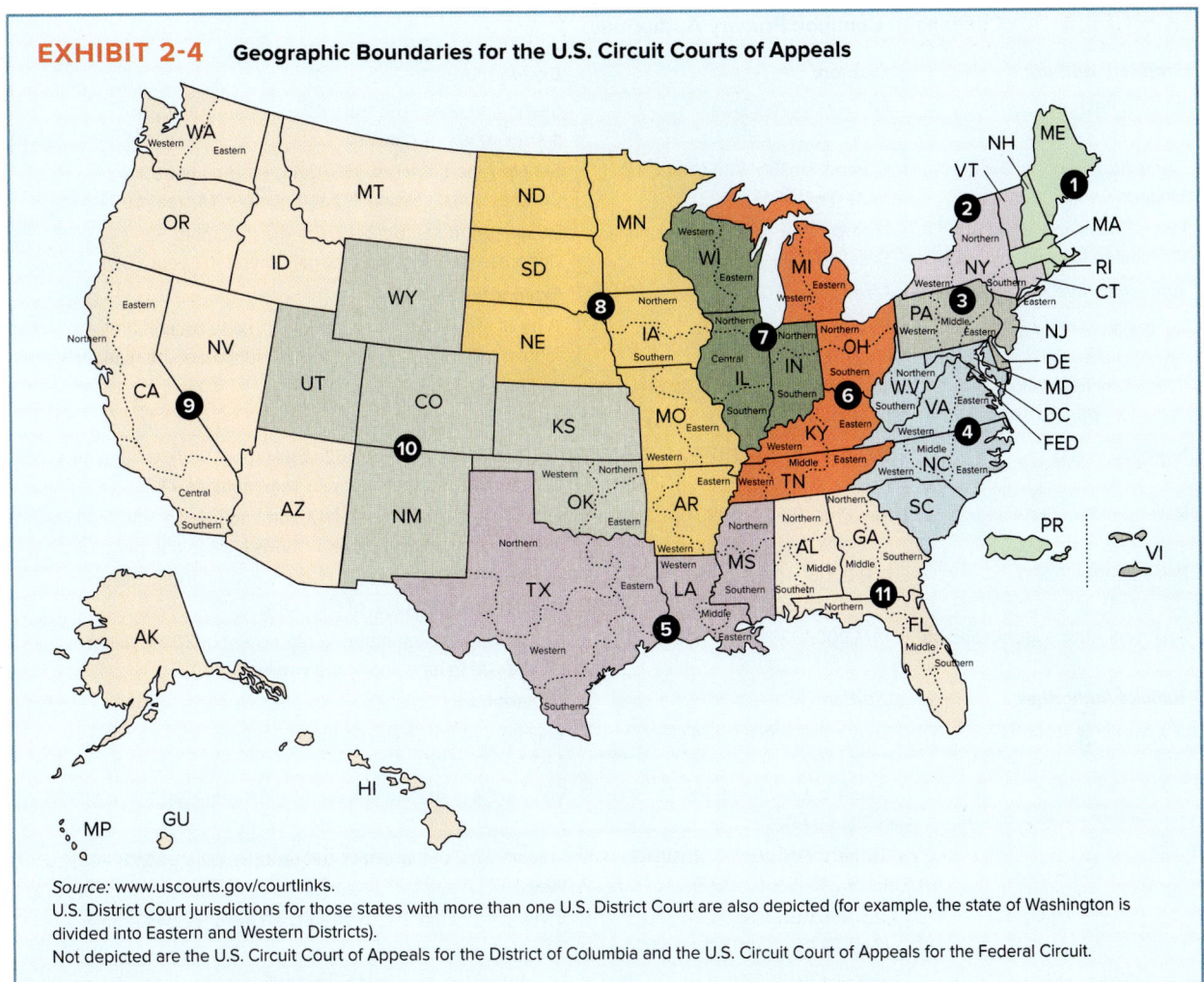

Source: www.uscourts.gov/courtlinks.
U.S. District Court jurisdictions for those states with more than one U.S. District Court are also depicted (for example, the state of Washington is divided into Eastern and Western Districts).
Not depicted are the U.S. Circuit Court of Appeals for the District of Columbia and the U.S. Circuit Court of Appeals for the Federal Circuit.

we'll describe how Bill and Mercedes (or their CPA) can research the sources to identify the best possible course of action.[10]

TAX LAW SOURCES

LO 2-3 LO 2-4

There are two broad categories of tax authorities: primary authorities and secondary authorities. **Primary authorities** are official sources of the tax law generated by the legislative branch (statutory authority issued by Congress), judicial branch (rulings by the U.S. District Courts, U.S. Tax Court, U.S. Court of Federal Claims, U.S. Circuit Courts of Appeals, or U.S. Supreme Court), and executive/administrative branch (Treasury and IRS pronouncements). Exhibit 2-5 displays the most common primary sources, their respective citations, and related explanations. We'll discuss each of these authorities below.

Secondary authorities are unofficial tax authorities that interpret and explain the primary authorities, such as tax research services (discussed below), tax articles from professional journals and law reviews, newsletters, and textbooks. For quick questions, practitioners often use the *CCH Master Tax Guide* or *RIA Federal Tax Handbook*.

---

[10]Accountants should be mindful to not engage in the unauthorized practice of law. In years past, several court cases have addressed this issue without providing a clear understanding between practicing tax accounting and the unauthorized practice of law. At present, tax accountants are not likely to overstep their responsibilities if they limit their advice to tax issues and leave the general legal advice and drafting of legal documents to attorneys.

EXHIBIT 2-5 **Citations to Common Primary Authorities**

Statutory Authorities:	Citation:	Explanation:
Internal Revenue Code	IRC Sec. 162(e)(2)(B)(i)	Section number 162, subsection e, paragraph 2, subparagraph B, clause i
Committee Reports: Senate Finance Committee Report	S. Rep. No. 353, 82d Cong., 1st Sess. 14 (1951)	Senate report number 353, Congress number 82, Congressional session 1, page number 14, year 1951
House Ways and Means Committee Report	H. Rep. No. 242, 82d Cong., 1st Sess. 40 (1951)	House report number 242, Congress number 82, Congressional session 1, page number 40, year 1951
Administrative Authorities:	**Citation:**	**Explanation:**
Final Regulation	Reg. Sec. 1.217-2(c)(1)	Type of regulation (1 = income tax), code section 217, regulation number 2, paragraph c, subparagraph number 1
Temporary Regulation	Temp. Reg. Sec. 1.217-2(c)(1)	Same as final regulation
Proposed Regulation	Prop. Reg. Sec. 1.217-2(c)(1)	Same as final regulation
Revenue Ruling	Rev. Rul. 77-262, 1977-2 C.B. 41	Ruling number 77-262 (262nd ruling of 1977), volume number of cumulative bulletin 1977-2, page number 41
Revenue Procedure	Rev. Proc. 99-10, 1999-1 C.B. 272	Procedure number 99-10 (10th procedure of 1999), volume number of cumulative bulletin 1999-1, page number 272
Private Letter Ruling	PLR 200601001	Year 2006, week number 01 (1st week of 2006), ruling number 001 (1st ruling of the week)
Technical Advice Memorandum	TAM 200402001	Year 2004, week number 02 (2nd week of 2004), ruling number 001 (1st ruling of the week)
Judicial Authorities:	**Citation:**	**Explanation:**
U.S. Supreme Court	*Comm. v. Kowalski,* 434 U.S. 77 (S. Ct., 1977)	Volume 434 of the United States Reporter, page 77, year 1977
	Comm. v. Kowalski, 98 S. Ct. 315 (S. Ct., 1977)	Volume 98 of the West court reporter, page 315, year 1977
	Comm. v. Kowalski, 77-2 USTC par. 9,748 (S. Ct., 1977)	Volume 77-2 of the CCH court reporter, paragraph 9,748, year 1977
	Comm. v. Kowalski, 40 AFTR2d 77-6128 (S. Ct., 1977)	Volume 40 of the RIA AFTR2d court reporter, paragraph 77-6128, year 1977
U.S. Circuit Court of Appeals	*Azar Nut Co. v. Comm.,* 931 F.2d 314 (5th Cir., 1991)	Volume 931 of the West F.2d court reporter, page 314, circuit 5th, year 1991
	Azar Nut Co. v. Comm., 91-1 USTC par. 50,257 (5th Cir., 1991)	Volume 91-1 of the CCH USTC court reporter, paragraph 50,257, circuit 5th, year 1991
	Azar Nut Co. v. Comm., 67 AFTR2d 91-987 (5th Cir., 1991)	Volume 67 of the RIA AFTR2d court reporter, paragraph 91-987, year 1991
U.S. Tax Court—Regular decision	*L.A. Beeghly,* 36 TC 154 (1962)	Volume 36 of the Tax Court reporter, page 154, year 1962
U.S. Tax Court—Memorandum decision	*Robert Rodriguez,* RIA TC Memo 2005-012	Paragraph number 2005-012 of the RIA Tax Court Memorandum reporter
	Robert Rodriguez, 85 TCM 1162 (2005)	Volume 85 of the CCH Tax Court Memorandum reporter, page 1162, year 2005
U.S. Court of Federal Claims	*J.R. Cohen v. U.S.,* 510 F. Supp. 297 (Fed. Cl., 1993)	Volume 510 of the West F. Supp. court reporter, page 297, year 1993
	J.R. Cohen v. U.S., 72 AFTR2d 93-5124 (Fed. Cl., 1993)	Volume 72 of the RIA AFTR2d court reporter, paragraph 93-5124, year 1993
	J.R. Cohen v. U.S., 93-1 USTC par. 50,354 (Fed. Cl., 1993)	Volume 93-1 of the CCH USTC court reporter, paragraph 50,354, year 1993
U.S. District Court	*Waxler Towing Co., Inc. v. U.S.,* 510 F. Supp. 297 (W.D, TN, 1981)	Volume 510 of the West F. Supp. court reporter, page 297, Western District (W.D.), state Tennessee, year 1981
	Waxler Towing Co., Inc. v. U.S., 81-2 USTC par. 9,541 (W.D., TN, 1981)	Volume 81-2 of the CCH USTC court reporter, paragraph 9,541, Western District (W.D.), state Tennessee, year 1981
	Waxler Towing Co., Inc. v. U.S., 48 AFTR2d 81-5274 (W.D., TN, 1981)	Volume 48 of the RIA AFTR2d court reporter, paragraph 81-5274, Western District (W.D.), state Tennessee, year 1981

EXHIBIT 2-6   Common Secondary Tax Authorities

Tax Research Services:	*Professional Journals:*
BNA Tax Management Portfolios	*Journal of Accountancy*
CCH Standard Federal Tax Reporter	*Journal of Taxation*
CCH Tax Research Consultant	*Practical Tax Strategies*
RIA Federal Tax Coordinator	*Taxes*
RIA United States Tax Reporter	*Tax Adviser*
Newsletters:	*Quick Reference Sources:*
Daily Tax Report	*IRS Publications*
Federal Tax Weekly Alert	*CCH Master Tax Guide*
Tax Notes	*RIA Federal Tax Handbook*
Law Reviews:	*Textbooks:*
Tax Law Review (New York University School of Law)	*McGraw-Hill's Taxation of Individuals and Business Entities*
Virginia Tax Review (University of Virginia School of Law)	*McGraw-Hill's Essentials of Federal Taxation*

Secondary authorities may be very helpful in understanding a tax issue, but they hold little weight in a tax dispute (hence their "unofficial" status). Thus, tax advisers should always be careful to verify their understanding of tax law by examining primary authorities directly and to *never* cite secondary authority in a research memo. Exhibit 2-6 lists some of the common sources of secondary authority.

TAXES IN THE REAL WORLD   Google: Not Authoritative on Tax Matters

While Internet super giant Google may be the king of all cyberspace knowledge, the Tax Court ruled in *Woodard v. Comm.*, TC Summary Opinion 2009-150, that a Google search does not constitute reasonable cause to excuse a Harvard MBA/CPA from taking an incorrect tax return position. The Tax Court noted that although the taxpayer had not worked as an accountant for years before filing his tax return, "his accounting degree, MBA, and CPA training, no matter how stale, undoubtedly taught him what sources could be relied upon as definitive; such as, for example, the Internal Revenue Code and the income tax regulations, both of which are readily available on the Internet."

Legislative Sources: Congress and the Constitution

The three legislative or statutory tax authorities are the U.S. Constitution, the Internal Revenue Code, and tax treaties. The **U.S. Constitution** is the highest authority in the United States, but it provides very little in the way of tax law since it contains no discussion of tax rates, taxable income, or other details. Instead, the 16th Amendment provides Congress the ability to tax income directly, from whatever source derived, without apportionment across the states.

Various attempts to amend the U.S. Constitution with regard to taxation—for example, one effort to repeal the 16th Amendment entirely and one to require a two-thirds majority in both houses to raise taxes—have so far met with failure.

Internal Revenue Code

The second (and main) statutory authority is the **Internal Revenue Code of 1986,** as amended, known as the Code. The Internal Revenue Code has the same authoritative weight as tax treaties and Supreme Court rulings. Thus, a taxpayer should feel very confident in a tax return position, such as taking a deduction, that is specifically allowed by the Code. The Internal Revenue Code is unique in that all federal tax authorities—all administrative and judicial authorities except tax treaties

EXHIBIT 2-7 Tax Legislation Process

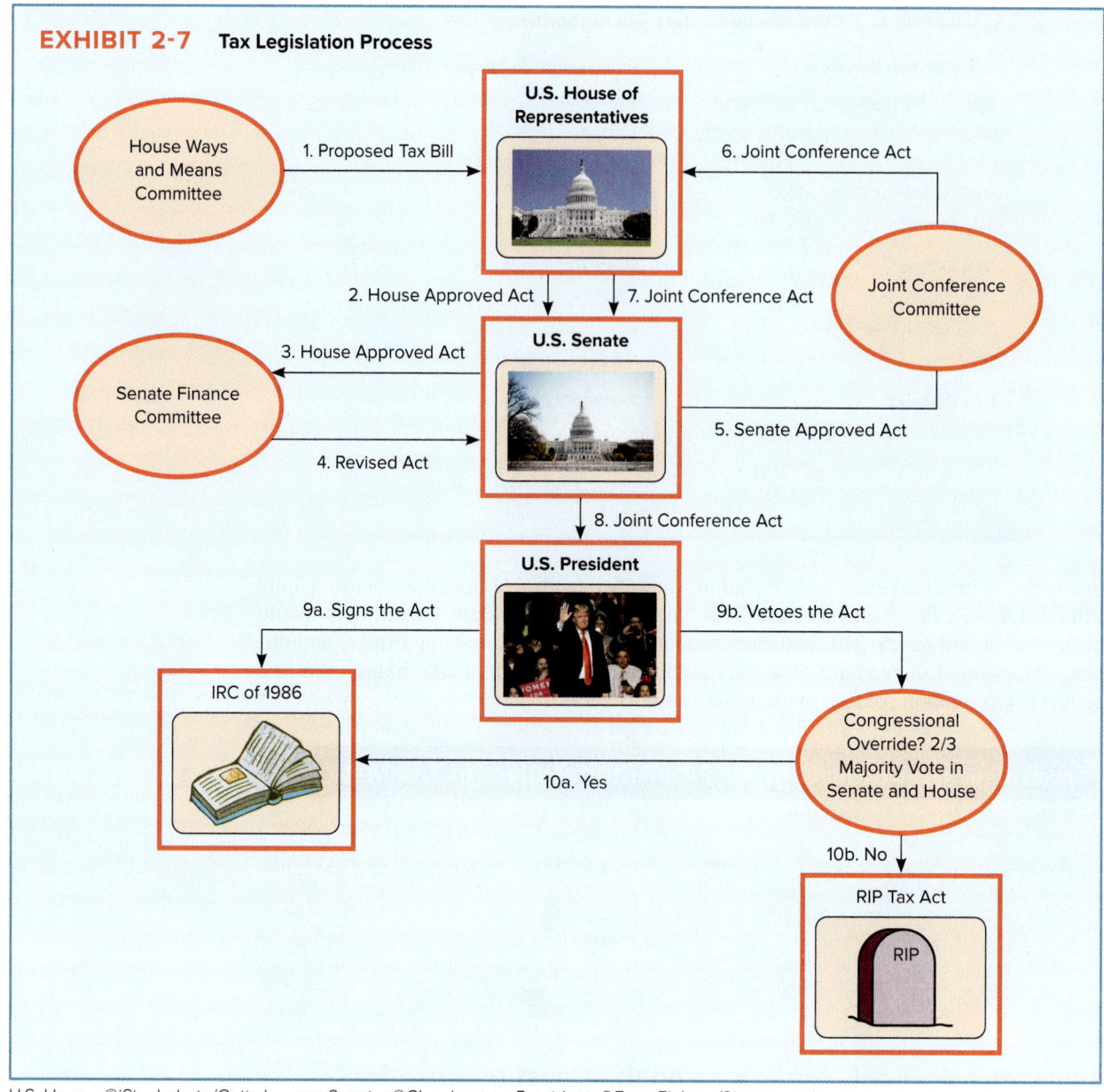

U.S. House: ©iStockphoto/Getty Images; Senate: ©Glow Images; President: ©Evan El-Amin/Shutterstock

and the Constitution—can be seen as an interpretation of it. Hence, understanding the relevant code section(s) is critical to being an efficient and effective tax professional.

Congress enacts tax legislation virtually every year that changes the Code; 1986 was simply the last major overhaul. Prior to 1986, tax law changes were incorporated into the Internal Revenue Code of 1954, the year a new numbering system and other significant changes were introduced. Before that, tax law changes were incorporated into the Internal Revenue Code of 1939, which was the year the tax law was first codified.

The Legislative Process for Tax Laws Exhibit 2-7 illustrates the legislative process for enacting tax laws. As required by the U.S. Constitution (Article 1, Section 7), "All bills for raising revenue shall originate in the House of Representatives." The Senate may propose tax legislation, but the first to formally consider a bill will be the House, typically within its Ways and Means Committee. After the committee debates the proposed legislation and drafts a bill, the bill goes to the House of Representatives floor for debate and ultimately a vote (either yea or nay without modification). If the bill is approved, it becomes an *act* and is sent to the Senate, which typically refers the act to the Senate Finance Committee. Not to be outdone by the House, the Senate Finance Committee usually amends the act during its deliberations. After the revised act passes the Senate Finance Committee, it goes to the Senate for debate and vote. Unlike representatives, senators may modify the proposed legislation during their debate.

If the Senate passes the act, both the House and Senate versions of the legislation are sent to the Joint Conference Committee, which consists of members of the House Ways and Means Committee and the Senate Finance Committee. During the Joint Conference Committee deliberations, committee members debate the two versions of the proposed legislation. Possible outcomes for any specific provision in the proposed legislation include adoption of the Senate version, the House version, or some compromise version of the two acts. Likewise, the Joint Conference Committee may simply choose to eliminate specific provisions from the proposed legislation or fail to reach a compromise, thereby terminating the legislation.

After the Joint Conference Committee approves the act, the revised legislation is sent to the House and Senate for vote. If both the House and Senate approve it, the act is sent to the president for his or her signature. If the president signs the act, it becomes law and is incorporated into the Internal Revenue Code of 1986 (Title 26 of the U.S. Code, which contains *all* codified laws of the United States). If the president vetoes the legislation, Congress may override the veto with a two-thirds positive vote in both the House and the Senate.

The House Ways and Means Committee, Senate Finance Committee, and Joint Conference Committee each produce a committee report that explains the current tax law, proposed change in the law, and reasons for the change. These committee reports are considered statutory sources of the tax law and may be very useful in interpreting tax law changes and understanding congressional intent. These committee reports are especially important after new legislation has been enacted because, with the exception of the Code, there will be very little authority interpreting the new law (i.e., no judicial or administrative authorities because of the time it takes for the new law to be litigated or for the IRS to issue interpretative guidance).

Basic Organization of the Code

The Internal Revenue Code is divided into subtitles, chapters, subchapters, parts, subparts, and sections. All existing and any new tax laws are placed in the Code within a specific subtitle, chapter, subchapter, part, subpart, and section. When referencing a tax law, the researcher generally refers to the law simply by its code section. Code sections are numbered from 1 to 9834, with gaps in the section numbers to allow new code sections to be added to the appropriate parts of the Code as needed. Each code section is further divided into subsections, paragraphs, subparagraphs, and clauses to allow more specific reference or citation. See Exhibit 2-5 for an example code citation and explanation.

Memorizing the various subtitles and chapters of the Code has limited value (except to impress your friends at parties). However, understanding the *organization* of the Code is important, especially for the aspiring tax accountant. (See Exhibit 2-8.) First, you must understand the organization of a code section, its subsections, paragraphs, subparagraphs, and clauses to be able to cite the respective law correctly as, for example, IRC Sec. 162(b)(2). Second, note that many provisions in the Code apply only to specific parts of the Code. For example, it is quite common for a code section to include the phrase "for purposes of this chapter, ..." If you do not understand what laws are encompassed in the chapter, it will be very difficult for you to interpret the code section and determine its applicability to a research question.

Finally, remember that code sections addressing similar transactions, such as deductions, or topics, such as C corporations, are grouped together. Consider a researcher faced with the question of whether an item of income is taxable. If the researcher understands the organization of the Code, she can quickly focus her research on code sections 61–140, which provide a broad definition of gross income, list items specifically included in gross income, and identify items specifically excluded from gross income.

EXHIBIT 2-8 **Example of Code Organization**

Subtitle A—Income Taxes

Chapter 1—Income Taxes

Subchapter A—Determination of Tax Liability

Part I—Definition of Gross Income, Adjusted Gross Income, Taxable Income, etc. (Sec. 61–68)

Sec. 61—Gross Income Defined

Sec. 62—Adjusted Gross Income Defined

Sec. 63—Taxable Income Defined

Subsection 63(c)—Standard Deduction

Paragraph 63(c)(2)—Basic Standard Deduction

Subparagraph 63(c)(2)(A)

Clause 63(c)(2)(A)(i)

Part II—Items Specifically Included in Gross Income (Sec. 71–90)

Sec. 71—Alimony

Sec. 72—Annuities

Sec. 73—Services of Child

Sec. 74—Prizes & Awards

Part III—Items Specifically Excluded from Gross Income (Sec. 101–140)

Sec. 101—Certain Death Benefits

Sec. 102—Gifts and Inheritances

Sec. 103—Interest on State & Local Bonds

Tax Treaties   **Tax treaties** are negotiated agreements between countries that describe the tax treatment of entities subject to tax in both countries, such as U.S. citizens earning investment income in Spain. The U.S. president has the authority to enter into a tax treaty with another country after receiving the Senate's advice. If you are a U.S. citizen earning income abroad or an accountant with international clients, you need knowledge of U.S. tax laws, the foreign country's tax laws, and the respective tax treaty between the U.S. and the foreign country for efficient tax planning. Because the focus in this text is on U.S. tax laws, we only briefly mention the importance of tax treaties as a statutory authority.

Example 2-2

Bill recently spent a summer in Milan, Italy, teaching a graduate level economics course. While in Italy he earned a $20,000 stipend from Bocconi University and some interest in a temporary banking account that he established for the trip. What tax laws must Bill consider to understand any tax liability from his $20,000 stipend?

Answer: U.S. tax laws, Italian tax laws, and the U.S.–Italy tax treaty will determine the tax consequences of the amounts Bill earned in Italy.

THE KEY FACTS

Judicial Authorities

- Our judicial system has the ultimate authority to interpret the Internal Revenue Code and settle disputes between taxpayers and the IRS.
- The Supreme Court is the highest judicial authority.
- Beneath the Supreme Court, the decisions of the 13 Circuit Courts of Appeals represent the next highest judicial authority.

(continued)

Judicial Sources: The Courts

Our judicial system has the ultimate authority to interpret the Internal Revenue Code and settle disputes between the IRS and taxpayers. As Exhibit 2-3 illustrates, there are five basic sources of judicial authority (three trial-level courts, 13 U.S. Circuit Courts of Appeals, and the Supreme Court). We've noted that the Supreme Court, along with the Code, represents the highest tax-specific authority. An important distinction between the two, however, is that the Supreme Court does not establish law but instead simply interprets and applies the Code (along with other authorities). Thus, the Code and the Supreme Court should never be in conflict.[11]

[11]The Supreme Court does have the authority to declare a Code provision unconstitutional.

Below the Supreme Court, the decisions of the 13 U.S. Circuit Courts of Appeals represent the next highest judicial authority. The lowest level of judicial authority consists of three different types of trial-level courts (94 U.S. District Courts that hear cases involving taxpayers that reside within their respective district, the U.S. Court of Federal Claims, and the U.S. Tax Court). Given that the U.S. Tax Court hears only tax cases and that its judges are "tax experts," its decisions typically have more weight than those rendered by a district court or the U.S. Court of Federal Claims.[12] Likewise, because the U.S. Court of Federal Claims hears a much narrower set of issues than U.S. District Courts (only monetary claims against the U.S. government), its decisions have more weight than district court decisions.

In rendering court decisions, all courts apply the judicial doctrine of ***stare decisis.*** This doctrine means that a court will rule consistently with (a) its previous rulings (unless, due to evolving interpretations of the tax law over time, the court decides to overturn an earlier decision) and (b) the rulings of higher courts with appellate jurisdiction (the courts its cases are appealed to). The implication of *stare decisis* is that a circuit court will abide by Supreme Court rulings and its own rulings, whereas a trial-level court will abide by Supreme Court rulings, its respective circuit court's rulings, and its own rulings. For example, a district court in California would follow U.S. 9th Circuit and Supreme Court rulings as well as the court's own rulings.

The doctrine of *stare decisis* presents a special problem for the U.S. Tax Court because it appeals to different circuit courts based on the taxpayer's residence. To implement the doctrine of *stare decisis*, the tax court applies the **Golsen rule.**[13] The Golsen rule simply states that the tax court will abide by rulings of the circuit court that has appellate jurisdiction for a case.

> **THE KEY FACTS**
> - The lowest level of judicial authority consists of three different types of trial-level courts (U.S. District Courts, U.S. Court of Federal Claims, and the U.S. Tax Court).
> - U.S. Tax Court decisions typically are considered to have more authoritative weight than decisions rendered by a district court or the U.S. Court of Federal Claims.
> - All courts apply the judicial doctrine of *stare decisis*, which means that a court will rule consistently with its previous rulings and the rulings of higher courts with appellate jurisdiction.

Example 2-3

What if: If Bill and Mercedes opt to litigate their case in the U.S. Tax Court, by which circuit court's rulings will the court abide?

Answer: Because Bill and Mercedes live in Florida, the U.S. Tax Court will abide the circuit court with appellate jurisdiction in Florida, which happens to be the U.S. 11th Circuit Court.

Administrative Sources: The U.S. Treasury

Regulations, Revenue Rulings, and Revenue Procedures The Treasury Department, of which the IRS is a bureau, is charged with administering and interpreting the tax laws of the United States, among other duties such as printing money and advising the president on economic issues. **Regulations** are the Treasury Department's official interpretation of the Internal Revenue Code, have the highest authoritative weight, and often contain examples of the application of the Code that may be particularly helpful to the tax researcher. Regulations are issued in three different forms: final, temporary, and proposed. The names are very descriptive. **Final regulations** are regulations that have been issued in final form, and thus, unless or until revoked, they represent the Treasury's interpretation of the Code. **Temporary regulations** have a limited life (three years for regulations issued after November 20, 1988). Nonetheless, during their life, they carry the same authoritative weight as final regulations. Finally, all regulations are issued in the form of **proposed regulations** first, to allow public comment on them. Proposed regulations do not carry the same authoritative weight as temporary or final regulations.

In addition to being issued in three different forms, regulations also serve three basic purposes: interpretative, procedural, and legislative. Most regulations are issued as

> **THE KEY FACTS**
> **Administrative Authorities**
> - The Treasury Department is charged with administering and interpreting the tax laws.
> - Regulations
>   - Regulations are the Treasury Department's official interpretation of the Internal Revenue Code and have the highest authoritative weight.
>   - Regulations are issued in three different forms (proposed, temporary, and final) and serve three basic purposes (interpretative, procedural, and legislative).

---

[12]The Tax Court renders both "regular" and "memorandum" decisions. Regular decisions involve new or unusual points of law, whereas memorandum decisions involve questions of fact or the application of existing law. Both decisions have similar authoritative weight. Decisions issued by the Tax Court's Small Claims division may not be cited as precedent.

[13]54 TC 742 (1970).

(continued)

- Revenue rulings and revenue procedures
    - Revenue rulings and revenue procedures are second in administrative authoritative weight after regulations.
    - Revenue rulings address the application of the Code and regulations to a specific factual situation.
    - Revenue procedures explain in greater detail IRS practice and procedures in administering the tax law.
- Letter rulings
    - Letter rulings are less authoritative but more specific than revenue rulings and regulations.
    - Private letter rulings represent the IRS's application of the Code and other tax authorities to a specific transaction and taxpayer.

interpretative or procedural regulations. As the names suggest, **interpretative regulations** represent the Treasury's interpretation of the Code. In Bill and Mercedes's case, these might be the regulations issued under IRC Sec. 163, which discuss interest deductions. **Procedural regulations** explain Treasury Department procedures as they relate to administering the Code. Again, for Bill and Mercedes's case, these might be the regulations issued under IRC Sec. 6501 regarding the statute of limitations for IRS assessment and collection. **Legislative regulations,** the rarest type, are issued when Congress specifically directs the Treasury Department to create regulations to address an issue in an area of law. In these instances, the Treasury is actually writing the law instead of interpreting the Code. Because legislative regulations represent tax law instead of an interpretation of tax law, legislative regulations generally have been viewed to have more authoritative weight than interpretative and procedural regulations. However, in *Mayo Foundation for Medical Education & Research v. U.S.,* 131 S.Ct. 704 (2011), the Supreme Court held (subject to specific conditions) that all Treasury regulations warrant deference. It is thus a very difficult process to challenge any regulation, and taxpayers are cautioned not to take tax return positions inconsistent with regulations.

Revenue rulings and revenue procedures are second in administrative authoritative weight after regulations. But unlike regulations, revenue rulings address the application of the Code and regulations to a specific factual situation. Thus, while **revenue rulings** have less authoritative weight, they provide a much more detailed interpretation of the Code as it applies to a specific transaction and fact pattern. For example, Rev. Rul. 87-22 discusses the deductions of prepaid interest (points) a taxpayer may claim when refinancing the mortgage for a principal residence, whereas the Code and regulations do not specifically address this issue. Although revenue rulings are binding on the IRS (until revoked, superseded, or modified), courts may agree or disagree with a revenue ruling. Thus, while revenue rulings should be carefully evaluated because they represent the IRS's interpretation, courts may provide a different interpretation of the tax law that a taxpayer might choose to follow. **Revenue procedures** are also much more detailed than regulations. They explain in greater detail IRS practice and procedures in administering the tax law. For example, Rev. Proc. 87-56 provides the specific depreciation lives for depreciable assets (discussed in the Property Acquisition and Cost Recovery chapter). As with revenue rulings, revenue procedures are binding on the IRS until revoked, modified, or superseded.

Letter Rulings Below revenue rulings and revenue procedures in authoritative weight rest letter rulings. As you might guess, letter rulings are less authoritative but more specific than revenue rulings and regulations. Letter rulings generally may not be used as precedent by taxpayers. However, they may be cited as authority to avoid the substantial understatement of tax penalty under IRC Sec. 6662 imposed on taxpayers and the related tax practitioner penalty under IRC Sec. 6694 (discussed later in this chapter). **Private letter rulings** represent the IRS's application of the Code and other tax authorities to a specific transaction and taxpayer. Private letter rulings are issued in response to a taxpayer request and are common for proposed transactions with potentially large tax implications. For example, companies commonly request a private letter ruling to ensure that a proposed corporate acquisition meets the definition of a tax-free exchange. However, the IRS also maintains a list of certain issues on which it refuses to rule, such as the tax consequences of proposed federal tax legislation. Each year, the IRS publishes an updated list of these transactions in a revenue procedure.

Other types of letter rulings include determination letters and technical advice memorandums. **Determination letters,** issued by local IRS directors, are generally not controversial. An example of a determination letter is the request by an employer for the IRS to rule that the taxpayer's retirement plan is a "qualified plan." **Technical advice memorandums** differ from private letter rulings in that they are generated for completed transactions and usually are requested by an IRS agent during an IRS audit.

Is this a comprehensive list of IRS pronouncements? No. In addition to the pronouncements listed above, the IRS issues several less common types, which are beyond the scope of this text. A couple of other pronouncements, however, warrant some discussion. As we mentioned above, the IRS and taxpayers litigate tax cases in a number of courts and jurisdictions. Obviously, the IRS wins some of these cases and loses others. Except for Supreme Court cases, whenever the IRS loses, it may issue an **acquiescence** or **nonacquiescence** as guidance for how the IRS intends to respond to the loss. Although an acquiescence indicates that the IRS has decided to *follow* the court's adverse ruling in the future, it does not mean that the IRS *agrees* with it. Instead, it simply means that the IRS will no longer litigate this issue.

A nonacquiescence has the exact opposite implications and alerts taxpayers that the IRS does plan to continue to litigate this issue. Finally, the IRS also issues **actions on decisions,** which explain the background reasoning behind an IRS acquiescence or non-acquiescence.[14] What are noticeably absent from the list of administrative authorities? IRS publications and tax return form instructions. *Neither are considered primary authorities and should not be cited as precedent. Likewise, it is not advisable to rely on either to avoid taxpayer or tax practitioner penalties.*

TAX RESEARCH

LO 2-5

Now that you have a basic understanding of the different types of tax authority, why do you think that the IRS and taxpayers disagree with respect to the tax treatment of a transaction? In other words, why would the IRS and Bill and Mercedes's CPA reach different conclusions regarding the deductibility of certain expenses? The answer is that, because the Code does not specifically address the tax consequences of each transaction type or every possible variation of a particular transaction, the application of the tax law is subject to debate and differing interpretations by the IRS, courts, tax professionals, taxpayers, and so on. Tax research, therefore, plays a vital role in allowing us to identify and understand the varying authorities that provide guidance on an issue; assess the relative weights of differing authorities; understand the risks associated with different tax return positions; and ultimately, draw an appropriate conclusion regarding the application of the tax law to the issue. The following paragraphs describe the basic process of tax research that tax professionals use to identify and analyze tax authorities to answer tax questions. We will then revisit Bill and Mercedes's issue and view the research memo prepared by their CPA.

Step 1: Understand Facts

To answer a tax question, you must understand it. To understand the question, you must know the facts. There are two basic types of facts: open facts and closed facts. *Open facts* have not yet occurred, such as the facts associated with a proposed transaction. *Closed facts* have already occurred. The distinction between open and closed facts is important because, unlike closed facts, open facts can be altered, and different facts may result in very different tax consequences. Open facts allow the taxpayer to arrange a transaction to achieve the most advantageous outcome. Thus, they are especially important in tax planning.

How do you establish the facts for a research question? Interview clients, speak with third parties such as attorneys and brokers, and review client documents such as contracts, prior tax returns, wills, trust documents, deeds, and corporate minutes. When interviewing clients, remember that not many are tax experts. Thus, it is up to the tax professional to ask the correct initial and follow-up questions to obtain all the relevant facts. Also consider nontax factors, such as a client's personal values or objectives, because these often put constraints on tax-planning strategies.

Step 2: Identify Issues

A tax professional's ability to identify issues is largely a function of his or her type of tax expertise. A tax expert in a particular area will typically be able to identify quickly the

> ### THE KEY FACTS
> **Tax Research**
> - The five steps in tax research are (1) understand the facts, (2) identify issues, (3) locate relevant authorities, (4) analyze the tax authorities, and (5) document and communicate research results.
> - The two types of tax services that tax professionals use in tax research are annotated tax services, arranged by code section, and topical services, arranged by topic.
> - Research questions often consist of questions of fact or questions of law.
>   - The answer to a question of fact hinges upon the facts and circumstances of the taxpayer's transaction.
>   - The answer to a question of law hinges upon the interpretation of the law, such as interpreting a particular phrase in a code section.
> - When the researcher identifies that different authorities have conflicting views, she should evaluate the "hierarchy," jurisdiction, and age of the authorities.
> - Once the tax researcher has identified relevant authorities, she must make sure that the authorities are still valid and up to date.
>
> *(continued)*

---

[14]Actions on decisions have no precedential value but may be cited as authority to avoid the substantial understatement of tax penalty under IRC Sec. 6662 imposed on taxpayers and the related tax practitioner penalty under IRC Sec. 6694 (discussed later in this chapter).

> • The most common end product of a research question is a research memo, which has five basic parts: (1) facts, (2) issues, (3) authority list, (4) conclusion, and (5) analysis.

specific tax issues that relate to transactions in that area. For example, an expert in corporate acquisitions would quickly identify the tax consequences and specific issues of alternative acquisition types. A novice, on the other hand, would likely identify broader issues first and then more specific issues as he or she researched the relevant tax law.

What's the best method to identify tax issues? First of all, get a good understanding of the client's facts. Then, combine your understanding of the facts with your knowledge of the tax law. Let's consider the example of Bill and Mercedes's interest deduction. For an expert in this particular area, the issues will be immediately evident. For a novice, the initial response may take the form of a series of general questions: (1) Is this item of expense deductible? (2) Is that item of income taxable? (3) In what year should the expense be deducted? (4) In what year should the item of income be taxed? After you identify these types of general issues, your research will enable you to identify the more specific issues that ultimately determine the tax ramifications of the transaction.

Example 2-4

Elizabeth, Bill and Mercedes's friend who is a shareholder and the CFO of a company, loaned money to her company to help it avoid declaring bankruptcy. Despite Elizabeth's loan, the company did file for bankruptcy, and Elizabeth was not repaid the loan. What issues would a researcher consider?

Answer: The first questions to ask are whether Elizabeth can deduct the bad debt expense and, if so, as what type of deduction? As the researcher delves more into the general issue, he would learn that the type of deduction depends on whether Elizabeth's debt is considered a business or nonbusiness bad debt. This more specific issue depends on whether Elizabeth loaned the money to the company to protect her job (business bad debt) or to protect her stock investment in the company (nonbusiness bad debt). Bad-debt expenses incurred for nonbusiness debts (investment-related debts) are deducted as capital losses and thus subject to limitations (discussed in the Gross Income and Exclusions chapter), whereas bad-debt expenses for business debts (business-related debts) are ordinary deductions and not limited.

Why might this case be a good one to litigate in U.S. District Court?

Answer: Because a jury might be more likely to be convinced to assess Elizabeth's motives favorably.

Step 3: Locate Relevant Authorities

Step three in the research process is to locate the relevant authorities (code sections, regulations, court cases, revenue rulings) that address the tax issue. Luckily, tax services can aid the researcher in identifying relevant authorities. Most, if not all, of these services are available on the Internet (with a subscription) and thus offer the flexibility to conduct research almost anywhere.[15]

There are two basic types of tax services: annotated and topical. **Annotated tax services** are arranged by Internal Revenue Code section. That is, for each code section, an annotated service includes the code section; a listing of the code section history; copies of congressional committee reports that explain changes to the code section; a copy of all the regulations issued for the specific code section; the service's unofficial explanation of the code section; and brief summaries (called annotations) of relevant court cases, revenue rulings, revenue procedures, and letter rulings that address issues specific to the code section. Two examples of annotated tax services are Commerce Clearing House's (CCH) Standard Federal Tax Reporter and Research Institute of America's (RIA) United States Tax Reporter.

---

[15]www.IRS.gov contains a lot of information (tax forms, IRS publications, etc.) that may be especially useful for answering basic tax questions. In addition, tax publishers, such as CCH and RIA, produce quick reference tax guides (e.g., the *CCH Master Tax Guide* or the *RIA Federal Tax Handbook*) that may be used to answer basic tax questions.

Topical tax services are arranged by topic, such as taxable forms of income, tax-exempt income, and trade or business expenses. For each topic, the services identify tax issues that relate to each topic and then explain and cite authorities relevant to the issue (code sections, regulations, court cases, revenue rulings, etc.). Beginning tax researchers often prefer topical services, because they generally are easier to read. Some examples of topical federal tax services include BNA's Tax Management Portfolios, CCH's Tax Research Consultant, and RIA's Federal Tax Coordinator.

How does a researcher use these services? An expert would probably go directly to the relevant portions of an annotated or topical service. A novice may conduct a keyword search in the service, use the tax service's topical index, or browse the tax service to identify the relevant portions. Some suggestions for identifying keywords: Try to describe the transaction in three to five words. An ideal keyword search typically includes (1) the relevant area of law and (2) a fact or two that describes the transaction. Try to avoid keywords that are too broad (income, deduction, taxable) or too narrow.

Example 2-5

Bill and Mercedes refinanced the mortgage on their principal residence a couple of years ago when their original mortgage's four-year balloon payment came due. Their mortgage institution charged Bill and Mercedes $3,000 of points (prepaid interest) upon the refinancing in order to give them a reduced interest rate. On their CPA's advice, Bill and Mercedes deducted the $3,000 in the year they paid it, but upon audit, the IRS disallowed the deduction. What is the research issue?

Answer: The issue is, should Bill and Mercedes have deducted the $3,000 of points in the year they paid it?

What are some keywords that could identify the relevant tax authority?

Answer: Points (area of law), interest (area of law), refinancing (fact that describes the transaction).

Keyword searching is more an art than an exact science. As you gain a better understanding of different areas of the tax law, you'll become much more efficient at using keywords. If keyword searching is not proving beneficial, check your spelling, make sure you're searching within the correct database, rethink your keywords, use another research method, use another tax service, or as a last resort, take a break.

While utilizing keyword searches or other research methods to identify potentially relevant areas of law and tax authorities, constantly ask yourself whether you are indeed in the correct area of law. Once the answer to this question is an authoritative yes, you can delve deeper into the area of law and related authorities to answer the question.

Step 4: Analyze Tax Authorities

Once a researcher identifies relevant authorities, she must read carefully to ensure she fully understands them, as well as their application to the research problem. Two basic types of issues researchers will encounter are questions of fact and questions of law.

The answer to a **question of fact** hinges upon the facts and circumstances of the taxpayer's transaction. For example, whether a trade or business expense is "ordinary," "necessary," "reasonable," and thus deductible, is a question of fact. If you're researching a question of fact, understand *which* facts determine the answer—in this case, which facts make an expense "ordinary," "necessary," and "reasonable" and which do not. In this type of question, the researcher will focus on understanding how various facts affect the research answer and identifying authorities with fact patterns similar to her client's.

The answer to a **question of law** hinges upon the interpretation of the law, such as a particular phrase in a code section (see the sample research memo in Exhibit 2-9 for an example of a question of law). If a researcher is faced with this type of question, she will

EXHIBIT 2-9 **Sample Internal Research Memo**

Below is the memo Bill and Mercedes's CPA drafted after researching their issue.

Date:	July 8, 2018
Preparer:	Joe Staff
Reviewer:	Sandra Miller
Subject:	Deductibility of Points Paid in Refinancing
Facts:	Four years ago Bill and Mercedes's credit union provided them a $250,000 mortgage loan for their new home. The mortgage loan was a four-year interest-only note with a balloon payment at the end of four years. Bill and Mercedes (Floridians residing in the 11th Circuit) chose this type of loan to allow them to minimize their mortgage payment until their other house was sold. After 18 months, Bill and Mercedes sold their other house and refinanced their original short-term loan with a 15-year conventional mortgage. The credit union charged Bill and Mercedes $3,000 in points (prepaid interest) upon the refinancing.
Issue:	Can Bill and Mercedes deduct the points in the year they paid them?
Authorities:	IRC Sec. 461(g).
	Rev. Rul. 87-22, 1987-1 CB 146.
	J.R. Huntsman v. Comm. (8 Cir., 1990), 90-2 USTC par. 50,340, rev'g 91 TC 917 (1988).
	AOD 1991-002.
	P.G. Cao v. Comm. (9 Cir., 1996), 96-1 USTC par. 50,167, aff'g 67 TCM 2171 (1994).
Conclusion:	Because Bill and Mercedes's refinancing represents an integrated step in securing permanent financing for their home, substantial authority supports their deduction of the $3,000 in points this year.
Analysis:	IRC Sec. 461(g)(1) provides that cash-method taxpayers (Bill and Mercedes) must amortize prepaid interest (points) over the life of the loan instead of receiving a current deduction. IRC Sec. 461(g)(2) provides an exception to the general rule of Sec. 461(g)(1). Specifically, IRC Sec. 461(g)(2) allows cash-method taxpayers to deduct points in the year paid if the related debt was incurred "in connection with the purchase or improvement of," and secured by, the taxpayer's principal residence. The question whether Bill and Mercedes should amortize or currently deduct the points paid to refinance the mortgage on their principal residence depends upon the interpretation of "in connection with the purchase or improvement of" found in IRC Sec. 461(g)(2).
	There are two basic interpretations of "in connection with the purchase or improvement of." In Revenue Ruling 87-22, the IRS rules that points incurred in refinancing a mortgage on a taxpayer's residence are deductible in the year paid to the extent that the taxpayer uses the loan proceeds to improve the taxpayer's residence. Thus, points paid to simply refinance an existing mortgage without improving the residence must be amortized over the life of the loan.
	In contrast, in *J.R. Huntsman v. Comm.*, the 8th Circuit Court interpreted the phrase "in connection with the purchase or improvement of" much more broadly and held that points incurred to refinance a mortgage on the taxpayer's principal residence are currently deductible if the refinancing represents an *integrated step to secure permanent financing* for the taxpayer's residence. The facts in *J.R. Huntsman v. Comm.* are very similar to Bill and Mercedes's facts. Like Bill and Mercedes, the taxpayers in *J.R. Huntsman v. Comm.* also purchased their principal residence using a short-term loan with a "balloon" payment. When the balloon payment came due, the taxpayers obtained a permanent mortgage on their home (a 30-year conventional mortgage). The 8th Circuit Court held that in this case the permanent mortgage was acquired to extinguish the short-term financing and finalize the purchase of the home. "Thus, where taxpayers purchase a principal residence with a short-term three-year loan secured by a mortgage on the residence, and replace the loan with permanent financing . . . , the permanent mortgage obtained is sufficiently in connection with the purchase of the home to fall within the exception provided for by section 461(g)(2)."
	In Action on Decision 1991-002, the IRS has indicated that it will not follow the *J.R. Huntsman v. Comm.* decision outside the 8th Circuit (in the 11th Circuit where Bill and Mercedes live). Nonetheless, other courts (the 9th Circuit in *P.G. Cao v. Comm.*) have indicated a willingness to apply the 8th Circuit's interpretation of IRC Sec. 461(g)(2). That is, they have allowed deductibility of points incurred in refinancing if the refinancing occurred to secure permanent financing, instead of for some other reason such as to secure a lower interest rate.
	Given the similarity in facts between Bill and Mercedes's refinancing and those in *J.R. Huntsman v. Comm.* (refinancing of a short-term note to secure permanent financing), substantial authority supports a current deduction of the points paid.

spend much of her time researching the various interpretations of the code section and take note of which authorities interpret the code differently and why.

For many tax questions, the answer is clear with no opposing interpretations or contrary authorities. For other questions, the researcher may identify that different authorities have conflicting views. In this situation, the tax researcher should evaluate the hierarchical level, jurisdiction, and age of the authorities, placing more weight on higher and newer authorities that have jurisdiction over the taxpayer. A tax researcher will become more adept at this process as she gains experience.

Once the tax researcher has identified relevant authorities, she must make sure the authorities are still valid and up to date. For court cases, a **citator**—a research tool that allows you to check the status of several types of tax authorities—can be used to review the history of a case to find out, for example, whether it was subsequently appealed and overturned and to identify subsequent cases that cite it. Favorable citations (for example, a citation of the case by another authority in support of its ruling) strengthen a case. In contrast, unfavorable ones weaken it (for example, a citation of the case by another authority that questions or limits the case's decision). Citators can also check the status of revenue rulings, revenue procedures, and other IRS pronouncements. Checking the status of the Code is fairly simple: just locate the current version. Checking the status of regulations is a little more complicated. Most tax services alert researchers if a regulation has not been updated for certain changes in the Code. If this is the case, the researcher should evaluate whether the changes in the Code make the regulation obsolete.

As you will see in the analysis section of the sample research memo drafted by Bill and Mercedes's CPA (see Exhibit 2-9), whether they should amortize (deduct over the life of the loan) or currently deduct the points paid to refinance the mortgage on their principal residence is a question of law that ultimately depends upon the interpretation of a particular phrase: "in connection with the purchase or improvement of" found in IRC Sec. 461(g)(2). Is there a correct answer to this question? No. There is no clear-cut answer. Rather, this is a situation where the tax professional must use professional judgment. Because there is substantial authority supporting the current deduction of the points (discussed in detail in the sample memo), Bill and Mercedes should be able to deduct the points currently without risk of penalty. However, they should be aware that the IRS has clearly stated in an action on decision that it will fight this issue outside the 8th Circuit— for example, in the 11th Circuit, where Bill and Mercedes live.

Step 5: Document and Communicate the Results

After a researcher finishes her research, the final step of the process is to document and communicate the results. The most common end product of a research question is the internal research memo the researcher drafts for her supervisor's attention. The memo has five basic parts: (1) facts, (2) issues, (3) authority list, (4) conclusion, and (5) analysis. The purpose of the memo is to inform the reader of the answer to a research question, and thus, it should be written in an objective manner by discussing all relevant authorities to the research question, including those authorities that support, as well as those that conflict with, the answer. Below are some suggestions for each part of the memo. Compare these to the execution within the sample internal research memo presented in Exhibit 2-9.

Facts   Discuss facts relevant to the question presented—that is, facts that provide necessary background of the transaction (generally, who, what, when, where, and how much) and those facts that may influence the research answer. Keeping the fact discussion relatively brief will focus the reader's attention on the relevant characteristics of the transaction.

Issues   State the specific issues that the memo addresses. This section confirms that you understand the research question, reminds the reader of the question being analyzed, and allows future researchers to determine whether the analysis in the memo is relevant. Issues should be written as specifically as possible and limited to one or two sentences per issue.

Authorities In this section, cite the relevant tax authorities that apply to the issue, such as the IRC, court cases, and revenue rulings. How many authorities should you cite? Enough to provide a clear understanding of the issue and interpretation of the law. Remember, in order to reach an accurate assessment of the strength of your conclusion, you should consider authorities that may support your desired conclusion, as well as those that may go against it.

Conclusion There should be one conclusion per issue. Each conclusion should answer the question as briefly as possible and, preferably, indicate why the answer is what it is.

Analysis The goal of the analysis is to provide the reader a clear understanding of the area of law and specific authorities that apply. Typically, you will organize an analysis to discuss first the general area(s) of law (the code section), and then the specific authorities (court cases, revenue rulings) that apply to the research question. How many authorities should you discuss? As many as necessary to provide the reader an understanding of the issue and relevant authorities. After you discuss the relevant authorities, apply the authorities to your client's transaction and explain how the authorities result in your conclusion.

Client Letters In addition to internal research memos, tax professionals often send their clients letters that summarize their research and recommendations. Basic components of the client letter include: (1) research question and limitations, (2) facts, (3) analysis, and (4) closing. Below are some suggestions for each part of the client letter. Compare these to the execution within the sample client letter presented in Exhibit 2-10.

Research Question and Limitations After the salutation (Dear Bill and Mercedes) and social graces (I enjoyed seeing you last week . . .), clearly state the research question addressed and any disclaimers related to the work performed. This portion of the letter ensures that the tax professional and client have a mutual understanding of the question researched and any limitations on the research performed. As in a memo, issues should be written as specifically as possible and be limited to one or two sentences. Most accounting firms have standard boilerplate language regarding the limitations on work performed that is included in every client letter.

Facts Briefly summarize the facts relevant to the question presented—that is, facts that provide necessary background of the transaction and those facts that may influence the research answer. Keeping the fact discussion relatively brief will focus the client's attention on the relevant characteristics of the transaction.

Analysis Summarize the relevant authorities (including citations in most situations) and their implications for the client's research question using precise language appropriate for the client's level of tax expertise. The length of this portion of the letter will vary with the complexity of the research question and the client's interest in understanding the specific research details.

Closing In this section, summarize the key outcome(s) of the research conducted and any recommended client action, thank the client for requesting your service, and remind the client to contact you with additional questions or for further assistance.

In the case of Bill and Mercedes's interest deduction, their CPA recommended a tax return position that the IRS disallowed upon audit. Did their CPA violate her professional responsibilities by recommending a position the IRS disallowed? Good question. Let's take a look at the rules governing tax professional responsibilities.

EXHIBIT 2-10   **Sample Client Letter**

Below is the client letter that Bill and Mercedes's CPA sent to them.

Dear Bill and Mercedes,

I enjoyed seeing you last week at the Tampa Bay Boys and Girls Clubs charity auction. What a great event for such a worthy cause!

Thank you for requesting my advice concerning the tax treatment of the points paid when refinancing your mortgage.

My research is based upon the federal income tax laws that apply as of the date of this letter and the facts that you have provided as follows: Four years ago your credit union provided you a $250,000 interest-only note on your home that required a balloon payment at the end of four years. You chose this type of loan to minimize your mortgage payment until your previous house sold. After 18 months, you sold your previous house and refinanced the original short-term loan with a 15-year conventional mortgage. The credit union charged you $3,000 in points upon the refinancing.

After a thorough review of the applicable tax authority, I found there is substantial authority supporting a current deduction of the $3,000 points paid. IRC Sec. 461(g)(2) allows cash-method taxpayers to deduct points in the year paid if the related debt was incurred "in connection with the purchase or improvement of," and secured by, the taxpayer's principal residence. There are two basic interpretations of "in connection with the purchase or improvement of." The IRS has ruled (Revenue Ruling 87-22) that points paid to simply refinance an existing mortgage without improving the residence must be amortized over the life of the loan. In contrast, in *J.R. Huntsman v. Comm.*, the 8th Circuit Court held that points incurred to refinance a mortgage on the taxpayer's principal residence are currently deductible if the refinancing represents an *integrated step to secure permanent financing* for the taxpayer's residence.

The facts in *J.R. Huntsman v. Comm.* are very similar to your facts. Like you, the taxpayers in *J.R. Huntsman v. Comm.* purchased their principal residence using a short-term loan with a balloon payment. When the balloon payment came due, the taxpayers obtained a permanent mortgage on their home. The 8th Circuit Court held that in this case the permanent mortgage was acquired to finalize the purchase of the home and allowed the current deduction of the points.

J.R. Huntsman v. Comm. provides substantial authority to support a current deduction of the $3,000 points paid to refinance your initial short-term mortgage. In addition, other courts have applied the 8th Circuit's interpretation of IRC Sec. 461(g)(2), which adds "strength" to the 8th Circuit decision. However, the IRS has indicated that it will not follow the *J.R. Huntsman v. Comm.* decision outside the 8th Circuit (in the 11th Circuit where you live). Accordingly, the IRS would likely disallow the $3,000 deduction upon audit, and thus, while you have substantial authority to deduct the points currently, there is risk in doing so.

I would be happy to discuss this issue with you in more depth since these types of issues are always difficult. Likewise, if you have any other questions or issues with which I may assist you, please do not hesitate to contact me. Thank you again for requesting my advice.

Sincerely,

Sandra Miller, CPA

TAX PROFESSIONAL RESPONSIBILITIES

LO 2-6

Tax practitioners are subject to a variety of statutes, rules, and codes of professional conduct. Some examples include the American Institute of CPAs (AICPA) Code of Professional Conduct, the AICPA **Statements on Standards for Tax Services (SSTS),** the IRS's Circular 230, and statutes enacted by a CPA's specific state board of accountancy. Tax practitioners should absolutely have a working knowledge of these statutes, rules, and guidelines because (1) they establish the professional standards for the practitioner and (2) failure to comply with the standards could result in adverse consequences for the tax professional, such as being admonished, suspended, or barred from practicing before the IRS; being admonished, suspended, or expelled from the AICPA; or suffering suspension or revocation of the CPA license. Given the voluminous nature of applicable statutes, rules, and codes, we will simply provide a brief overview of the major common sources of tax professional standards.

CPAs who are members of the AICPA are bound by the AICPA Code of Professional Conduct and Statements on Standards for Tax Services. Other tax professionals use these provisions as guidance of professional standards. The AICPA Code of Professional Conduct is not specific to tax practice and provides broader professional standards that are especially relevant for auditors—that is, for those independent CPAs charged with examining an entity's financial statements. Provisions included in the Code of Professional Conduct address the importance of a CPA maintaining independence from the client and using due professional care in carrying out responsibilities. Additional provisions limit the acceptance of contingent fees, preclude discreditable acts such as signing a false return, and prohibit false advertising and charging commissions. Most of these provisions rightly fall under the heading of common sense. Nonetheless, a regular review should prove useful to the practicing CPA.

The AICPA's Statements on Standards for Tax Services (SSTS) recommend appropriate standards of practice for tax professionals and are intended to complement other provisions that govern tax practice (e.g., Circular 230 discussed below). One objective of these standards is to encourage increased understanding by the Treasury, IRS, and the public of a CPA's professional standards. Many state boards of accountancy have adopted similar standards, thus making the SSTS especially important. Currently, seven SSTS describe the tax professional standards when recommending a tax return position, answering questions on a tax return, preparing a tax return using data supplied by a client, using estimates on a tax return, taking a tax return position inconsistent with a previous year's tax return, discovering a tax return error, and giving tax advice to taxpayers. Exhibit 2-11 provides a brief summary of each SSTS. Most important from a research perspective, SSTS No. 1 provides that a tax professional must comply with the standards imposed by the applicable tax authority when recommending a tax return position or preparing or signing a tax return. IRC Sec. 6694 provides these standards for federal tax purposes.

IRC Sec. 6694 imposes a penalty on a *tax practitioner* for any position that is not supported by **substantial authority.**[16] A good tax professional evaluates whether supporting authority is substantial based upon the supporting and opposing authorities' weight and relevance. Substantial authority suggests the probability that the taxpayer's position will be sustained upon audit or litigation is in the 35 to 40 percent range or above. The tax practitioner can also avoid penalty under IRC Sec. 6694 if the tax return position has at least a reasonable basis (is supported by one or more tax authorities) and the position is disclosed on the taxpayer's return.

Example 2-6

Did Bill and Mercedes's CPA meet her professional standards as provided by SSTS No. 1?

Answer: Yes. Based on *J.R. Huntsman v. Comm.*, it is safe to conclude that there is a 35 to 40 percent or greater probability that the current points deduction will be sustained upon judicial review. Specifically, Bill and Mercedes's facts are very similar to those in *J.R. Huntsman v. Comm.*, and subsequent courts have interpreted the phrase "in connection with" consistently with *J.R. Huntsman v. Comm.*

Circular 230, issued by the IRS, provides regulations governing tax practice and applies to all persons practicing before the IRS. There are five parts of Circular 230. Subpart A describes who may practice before the IRS (CPAs, attorneys, enrolled agents) and

---

[16]The "more likely than not" standard, defined as a greater than 50 percent chance of a position being sustained on its merits, applies to tax shelters and other reportable transactions specified by the IRS.

EXHIBIT 2-11   Summary of the AICPA Statements on Standards for Tax Services

SSTS No 1: Tax Return Positions

A tax professional should comply with the standards, if any, imposed by the applicable tax authority for recommending a tax return position, or preparing or signing a tax return. If the tax authority has no written standards (or if they are lower than the following standard), the tax professional may recommend a tax return position or prepare or sign a return when she has a good-faith belief that the position has a realistic possibility of being sustained if challenged, or if there is a reasonable basis for the position and it is *adequately disclosed* on the tax return.

SSTS No. 2: Answers to Questions on Returns

A tax professional should make a reasonable effort to obtain from the taxpayer the information necessary to answer all questions on a tax return.

SSTS No. 3: Certain Procedural Aspects of Preparing Returns

In preparing or signing a tax return, a tax professional may rely without verification on information that a taxpayer or a third party has provided, unless the information appears to be incorrect, incomplete, or inconsistent.

SSTS No. 4: Use of Estimates

Unless prohibited by statute or rule, a tax professional may use taxpayer estimates in preparing a tax return if it is impractical to obtain exact data and if the estimated amounts appear reasonable based on the facts and circumstances known by the professional.

SSTS No. 5: Departure from a Position Previously Concluded in an Administrative Proceeding or Court Decision

A tax professional may sign a tax return that contains a departure from a position previously concluded in an administrative or court proceeding if the tax professional adheres to the standards of SSTS No. 1. This rule does not apply if the taxpayer is bound to a specific tax treatment in the later year, such as by a formal closing agreement with the IRS.

SSTS No. 6: Knowledge of Error: Return Preparation and Administrative Proceedings

A tax professional must advise the taxpayer promptly of an error and its potential consequences when she learns of an error in a previously filed tax return, an administrative hearing (such as an audit), or the taxpayer's failure to file a required return. The tax professional should include a recommendation for appropriate measures the taxpayer should take. The professional is not obligated to inform the IRS of the error, nor may she do so without the taxpayer's permission, except when required by law. However, in an administrative proceeding only, the tax professional should request the taxpayer's agreement to disclose the error to the IRS. If the taxpayer refuses to disclose the error to the IRS, the professional may consider terminating the professional relationship with the taxpayer.

SSTS No. 7: Form and Content of Advice to Taxpayers

In providing advice to taxpayers, tax professionals must use judgment that reflects professional competence and serves the taxpayer's needs. The professional should ensure that the standards under SSTS No. 1 are satisfied for all advice rendered. The professional is not obligated to communicate with a taxpayer when subsequent events affect advice previously provided except when implementing plans associated with the advice provided or when the professional is obligated to do so by specific agreement.

AICPA Statements

THE KEY FACTS

Tax Professional Responsibilities

- Tax practitioners are subject to a variety of statutes, rules, and codes of professional conduct.
- The AICPA's seven Statements on Standards for Tax Services (SSTS) recommend appropriate standards of practice for tax professionals.
  - Many state boards of accountancy have adopted standards similar to the SSTS standards.
- Circular 230 provides regulations governing tax practice and applies to all persons practicing before the IRS.
  - There is a good bit of overlap between Circular 230 and the AICPA SSTS.

what practicing before the IRS means (tax return preparation, representing clients before the IRS, and so on).[17] Subpart B describes the duties and restrictions that apply to individuals governed by Circular 230. Included in Subpart B are provisions discussing the submission of records to the IRS, guidelines when a practitioner discovers a tax return error, restrictions on charging contingency fees, prohibition of sharing employment with someone suspended from practicing before the IRS, stringent rules relating to providing advice for tax shelters, and standards for when a practitioner can recommend a tax return

[17]Similar to attorneys and CPAs, enrolled agents and registered tax return preparers can represent taxpayers before the IRS. To become an enrolled agent, you must have either worked for the IRS for five years or pass a comprehensive examination.

position.[18] Subparts C and D explain sanctions and disciplinary proceedings for practitioners violating the Circular 230 provisions. Subpart E concludes with a few miscellaneous provisions (such as the Circular 230 effective date). There is a good bit of overlap between Circular 230 and the AICPA SSTS.

Although Circular 230 provides many rules governing tax practice, the Internal Revenue Code and other Treasury regulations often contain requirements specific to tax professionals. Thus, it is important for tax professionals to keep abreast of all applicable guidance, regardless of the specific authoritative source. A good example of this is the tax-preparer registration requirement in Reg. §1.6109-2, which requires that all paid tax-return preparers apply for and receive a preparer tax identification number (PTIN). Although not a particularly daunting registration requirement, it is important nonetheless as failure to include the tax-return preparer's PTIN on tax returns is subject to a $50 penalty per violation.

LO 2-7   TAXPAYER AND TAX PRACTITIONER PENALTIES

THE KEY FACTS

Taxpayer and Tax Practitioner Penalties

- The IRS can impose both criminal and civil penalties to encourage tax compliance by both tax professionals and taxpayers.
- The standard of conviction is higher in a criminal trial, but the penalties are also much higher.
- A taxpayer will not be subject to an underpayment penalty if there is substantial authority that supports the tax return position.
- A tax practitioner will also not be subject to penalty for recommending a tax return position if there is substantial authority that supports the position.

In addition to motivating good behavior via tax professional standards, the IRS can impose both criminal and civil penalties to encourage tax compliance by both tax professionals and taxpayers. **Civil penalties** are much more common, generally come in the form of monetary penalties, and may be imposed when tax practitioners or taxpayers violate tax statutes without reasonable cause—say, as the result of negligence, intentional disregard of pertinent rules, willful disobedience, or outright fraud. Some common examples of civil penalties are listed in Exhibit 2-12.

Criminal penalties are much less common than civil penalties, although they have been used to incarcerate some notorious criminals who escaped conviction for other crimes. (Prohibition-era mobster Al Capone was convicted and put in prison for tax evasion.) Criminal penalties are commonly charged in tax evasion cases, which include willful intent to defraud the government, but are imposed only after normal due process, including a trial. Compared to civil cases, the standard of conviction is higher in a criminal trial; guilt must be proven beyond a reasonable doubt (versus the "clear and convincing evidence" standard for civil tax fraud). However, the penalties are also much higher, such as fines up to $100,000 for individuals plus a prison sentence.

Assuming the IRS assesses additional tax upon audit, will the taxpayer always be subject to penalty? No. While the taxpayer will have to pay interest on the underpayment, he or she will *not* be subject to an underpayment penalty *if there is substantial authority that supports the tax return position*.[19] As discussed above, substantial authority suggests that the probability the taxpayer's position will be sustained upon audit or litigation is in the 35 to 40 percent range or higher.

Example 2-7

What is Bill and Mercedes's exposure to penalties in their IRS audit?

Answer: None. Why? Because "substantial tax authority" supports their tax return position and the disputed tax liability is relatively small (the tax savings on a $3,000 tax deduction), Bill and Mercedes have no penalty exposure. Nonetheless, Bill and Mercedes will owe interest on the disputed tax liability unless the IRS recants its position in the audit or appeals process (or if the case is litigated and Bill and Mercedes win).

---

[18]Circular 230 imposes the same tax practitioner standards as in IRC Sec. 6694 for when a tax practitioner generally may recommend a tax return position (substantial authority and no disclosure or reasonable basis with disclosure).

[19]The taxpayer can also avoid penalty if the tax return position has at least a reasonable basis (i.e., supported by one or more tax authorities) and the position is disclosed on the taxpayer's return (IRC Sec. 6662).

EXHIBIT 2-12   **Civil Penalties Imposed for Tax Violations**

Taxpayers		Tax Practitioners	
Failure to file a tax return	5% of tax due per month (or partial month). Maximum penalty is 25% of net tax due. If the tax return is not filed within 60 days of the due date (including extensions), the minimum penalty is the smaller of $210 or 100% of the unpaid tax.	Failure to provide a copy of the tax return to a taxpayer	$50 per violation
Failure to pay tax owed	0.5% of tax due per month (or partial month). Reduces the failure to file a tax return penalty, if applicable. Maximum combined failure to file and failure to pay tax penalty is 5% of net tax due per month not to exceed 25% of net tax due. Minimum combined penalty if the tax return is not filed within 60 days of the due date (including extensions) is the smaller of $210 or 100% of the unpaid tax.	Failure to sign a tax return	$50 per violation
Failure to make estimated payments	Penalty varies with federal short-term interest rate and underpayment.	Failure to include the tax practitioner's ID number on the tax return	$50 per violation
Substantial understatement of tax	20% of understatement	Failure to keep a listing of taxpayers or tax returns	$50 per violation
Underpayment of tax due to transactions lacking economic substance	20% or 40% of understatement		
Providing false withholding information	$500	Failure to keep a listing of employees	$50 per violation
Fraud	75% of liability attributable to fraud	Understatement due to unreasonable position	Greater of $1,000 or 50% of income derived from preparing the taxpayer's tax return.
		Willful understatement of tax	Greater of $5,000 or 75% of income derived from preparing the taxpayer's tax return.
		Organizing, promoting, etc. an abusive tax shelter	Lesser of $1,000 or 100% of gross income derived from tax shelter. If activity is based on fraudulent statements, the penalty equals 50% of gross income derived from tax shelter.
		Aiding and abetting the understatement of a tax liability	$1,000 ($10,000 if related to corporate taxes).

As we explained in Example 2-6, Bill and Mercedes's CPA met her professional standards (as defined currently in SSTS No. 1) by recommending a tax return position that meets the "Substantial Authority" standard. Likewise, because substantial tax authority supports the tax return position, Bill and Mercedes's CPA should also not have penalty exposure under IRC Sec. 6694.

CONCLUSION

Now that we have a full understanding of the issue under audit for Bill and Mercedes, what is their likely outcome? Another good question. The IRS has stated that it will continue to disallow a current deduction for points incurred for refinanced mortgages. Nonetheless, the courts appear to follow *J.R. Huntsman v. Comm.*, and therefore, the IRS stands a strong possibility of losing this case if litigated. In an IRS appeals conference, the appeals officer may consider the hazards of litigation. Accordingly, Bill and Mercedes have a good likelihood of a favorable resolution at the appeals conference.

In this chapter we discussed several of the fundamentals of tax practice and procedure: taxpayer filing requirements, the statute of limitations, the IRS audit process, the primary tax authorities, tax research, tax professional standards, and taxpayer and tax practitioner penalties. For the tax accountant, these fundamentals form the basis for much of her work. Likewise, tax research forms the basis of much of a tax professional's compliance and planning services. Even for the accountant who doesn't specialize in tax accounting, gaining a basic understanding of tax practice and procedure is important. Assisting clients with the IRS audit process is a valued service that accountants provide, and clients expect all accountants to understand basic tax procedure issues and how to research basic tax issues.

Summary

LO 2-1 Identify the filing requirements for income tax returns and the statute of limitations for assessment.

- All corporations must file a tax return annually regardless of their taxable income. Estates and trusts are required to file annual income tax returns if their gross income exceeds $600. The filing requirements for individual taxpayers depend on the taxpayer's filing status, age, and gross income.
- Individual and C corporation tax returns (except for C corporations with a June 30 year-end) are due on the fifteenth day of the fourth month following year-end. For C corporations with a June 30 year-end, partnerships and S corporations, tax returns must be filed by the fifteenth day of the third month following the entity's fiscal year-end. Any taxpayer unable to file a tax return by the original due date can request an extension to file.
- For both amended tax returns filed by a taxpayer and proposed tax assessments by the IRS, the statute of limitations generally ends three years from the *later* of (1) the date the tax return was actually filed or (2) the tax return's original due date.

LO 2-2 Outline the IRS audit process, how returns are selected, the different types of audits, and what happens after the audit.

- The IRS uses a number of computer programs and outside data sources to identify tax returns that may have an understated tax liability. Common computer initiatives include the DIF (Discriminant Function) system, the document perfection program, and the information matching program.
- The three types of IRS audits consist of correspondence, office, and field examinations.
- After the audit, the IRS will send the taxpayer a 30-day letter, which provides the taxpayer the opportunity to pay the proposed assessment or request an appeals conference. If an agreement is not reached at appeals or the taxpayer does not pay the proposed assessment,

the IRS will send the taxpayer a 90-day letter. At this time, the taxpayer may pay the tax or petition the U.S. Tax Court to hear the case. If the taxpayer chooses to pay the tax, the taxpayer may then request a refund of the tax and eventually sue the IRS for a refund in the U.S. District Court or the U.S. Court of Federal Claims.

Evaluate the relative weights of the various tax law sources.   `LO 2-3`

- Primary authorities are official sources of the tax law generated by the legislative branch (statutory authority issued by Congress), judicial branch (rulings by the U.S. District Court, U.S. Tax Court, U.S. Court of Federal Claims, U.S. Circuit Courts of Appeals, or U.S. Supreme Court), or executive/administrative branch (Treasury and IRS pronouncements). Secondary authorities are unofficial tax authorities that interpret and explain the primary authorities.

Describe the legislative process as it pertains to taxation.   `LO 2-4`

- Exhibit 2-7 illustrates the legislative process for enacting tax law changes. Bills proceed from the House Ways and Means Committee to the House of Representatives. If approved, the act is sent to the Senate Finance Committee with a revised version then sent to the U.S. Senate. If approved, the Joint Conference Committee considers the acts passed by the House of Representatives and Senate. If a compromise is reached, the revised act is sent to the House of Representatives; if approved, it is then sent to the Senate; and if approved by the Senate, it is then sent to the president. If signed by the president, the act is incorporated into the IRC of 1986. If the president vetoes the legislation, Congress may override the veto with a two-thirds positive vote in both the House of Representatives and Senate.

Perform the basic steps in tax research.   `LO 2-5`

- The five basic steps in tax research are (1) understand the facts, (2) identify issues, (3) locate relevant authorities, (4) analyze the tax authorities, and (5) document and communicate research results.
- When the researcher identifies that different authorities have conflicting views, she should evaluate the "hierarchy," jurisdiction, and age of the authorities, placing more weight on higher and newer authorities that have jurisdiction over the taxpayer.

Describe tax professional responsibilities in providing tax advice.   `LO 2-6`

- Tax practitioners are subject to a variety of statutes, rules, and codes of professional conduct. Some examples include the American Institute of CPAs (AICPA) Code of Professional Conduct, the AICPA Statements on Standards for Tax Services (SSTS), the IRS's Circular 230, and statutes enacted by a CPA's specific state board of accountancy.
- The AICPA's Statements on Standards for Tax Services (SSTS) recommend appropriate standards of practice for tax professionals. Many state boards of accountancy have adopted similar standards, thus making the SSTS especially important. Currently, there are seven SSTS (summarized in Exhibit 2-11) that describe the tax professional standards.
- Circular 230 provides regulations governing tax practice and applies to all persons practicing before the IRS. There is a good bit of overlap between Circular 230 and the AICPA SSTS.

Identify taxpayer and tax professional penalties.   `LO 2-7`

- The IRS can impose both criminal and civil penalties to encourage tax compliance by both tax professionals and taxpayers. Civil penalties are much more common, generally come in the form of monetary penalties, and may be imposed when tax practitioners or taxpayers violate tax statutes without reasonable cause. Some common examples of civil penalties are listed in Exhibit 2-12.
- Criminal penalties are much less common than civil penalties and are commonly charged in tax evasion cases. Compared to civil cases, the standard of conviction is higher in a criminal trial, but the penalties are also much higher.
- A taxpayer will not be subject to an underpayment penalty if there is substantial authority that supports the tax return position.
- A tax practitioner will also not be subject to penalty for recommending a tax return position if there is substantial authority that supports the position.

KEY TERMS

30-day letter (2-6)
90-day letter (2-6)
acquiescence (2-17)
action on decision (2-17)
annotated tax service (2-18)
Circular 230 (2-24)
citator (2-21)
civil penalties (2-26)
correspondence examination (2-5)
criminal penalties (2-26)
determination letters (2-16)
DIF (Discriminant Function) system (2-4)
document perfection program (2-4)
field examination (2-6)
final regulations (2-15)
Golsen rule (2-15)

information matching program (2-4)
Internal Revenue Code of 1986 (2-11)
interpretative regulations (2-16)
legislative regulations (2-16)
nonacquiescence (2-17)
office examination (2-6)
primary authorities (2-9)
private letter rulings (2-16)
procedural regulations (2-16)
proposed regulations (2-15)
question of fact (2-19)
question of law (2-19)
regulations (2-15)
revenue procedures (2-16)
revenue rulings (2-16)
secondary authorities (2-9)
stare decisis (2-15)

Statements on Standards for Tax Services (SSTS) (2-23)
statute of limitations (2-3)
substantial authority (2-24)
tax treaties (2-14)
technical advice memorandum (2-16)
temporary regulations (2-15)
topical tax service (2-19)
U.S. Circuit Courts of Appeals (2-7)
U.S. Constitution (2-11)
U.S. Court of Federal Claims (2-7)
U.S. District Court (2-7)
U.S. Supreme Court (2-8)
U.S. Tax Court (2-7)
writ of certiorari (2-8)

DISCUSSION QUESTIONS

Discussion Questions are available in Connect®.

LO 2-1 1. Name three factors that determine whether a taxpayer is required to file a tax return.

LO 2-1 2. Benita is concerned that she will not be able to complete her tax return by April 15. Can she request an extension to file her return? By what date must she do so? Assuming she requests an extension, what is the latest date that she could file her return this year without penalty?

LO 2-1 3. Agua Linda Inc. is a calendar-year corporation. What is the original due date for the corporate tax return? What happens if the original due date falls on a Saturday?

LO 2-2 4. Approximately what percentage of tax returns does the IRS audit? What are the implications of this number for the IRS's strategy in selecting returns for audit?

LO 2-2 5. Explain the difference between the DIF system and the National Research Program. How do they relate to each other?

LO 2-2 6. Describe the differences between the three types of audits in terms of their scope and taxpayer type.

LO 2-2 7. Simon just received a 30-day letter from the IRS indicating a proposed assessment. Does he have to pay the additional tax? What are his options?

LO 2-2 8. Compare and contrast the three trial-level courts.

LO 2-3 9. Compare and contrast the three types of tax law sources and give examples of each.

LO 2-3 10. The U.S. Constitution is the highest tax authority but provides very little in the way of tax laws. What are the next highest tax authorities beneath the U.S. Constitution?

LO 2-3 11. Jackie has just opened her copy of the Code for the first time. She looks at the table of contents and wonders why it is organized the way it is. She questions whether it makes sense to try and understand the Code's organization. What are some reasons why understanding the organization of the Internal Revenue Code may prove useful?

LO 2-3 12. Laura Li, a U.S. resident, worked for three months this summer in Hong Kong. What type of tax authority may be especially useful in determining the tax consequences of her foreign income?

13. What are the basic differences between regulations, revenue rulings, and private letter rulings? `LO 2-3`

14. Under what circumstance would the IRS issue an acquiescence? A nonacquiescence? An action on decision? `LO 2-3`

15. Carlos has located a regulation that appears to answer his tax research question. He is concerned because the regulation is a temporary regulation. Evaluate the authoritative weight of this type of regulation. Should he feel more or less confident in his answer if the regulation is a proposed regulation? `LO 2-3`

16. Tyrone recently read a regulation that Congress specifically requested the IRS to issue. What type of regulation is this? How does this regulation's authoritative weight compare to other regulations? `LO 2-3`

17. In researching a tax question, you find only one authority (a trial-level court opinion) that is directly on point. Which court would you least prefer to have hear this case and why? `LO 2-3`

18. What is *stare decisis* and how does it relate to the Golsen rule? `LO 2-3`

19. Mason was shocked to learn that the current Code is the Internal Revenue Code of 1986. He thought that U.S. tax laws change more frequently. What is wrong with Mason's perception? `LO 2-4`

20. Describe in general the process by which new tax legislation is enacted. `LO 2-4`

21. What are the three committees that debate proposed tax legislation? What documents do these committees generate, and how might they be used? `LO 2-4`

22. The president recently vetoed a tax act passed by the House and Senate. Is the tax act dead? If not, what will it take for the act to be passed? `LO 2-4`

23. What are the five basic parts of an internal research memo? `LO 2-5`

24. What is the difference between primary and secondary authorities? Explain the role of each authority type in conducting tax research. `LO 2-5`

25. Jorge is puzzled that the IRS and his CPA could legitimately reach different conclusions on a tax issue. Why does this happen? `LO 2-5`

26. What is the difference between open and closed facts? How is this distinction important in conducting tax research? `LO 2-5`

27. In writing a research memo, what types of facts should be included in the memo? `LO 2-5`

28. Amber is a tax expert, whereas Rob is a tax novice. Explain how their process in identifying tax issues may differ. `LO 2-5`

29. Discuss the basic differences between annotated and topical tax services. How are these services used in tax research? `LO 2-5`

30. In constructing a keyword search, what should the keyword search include? `LO 2-5`

31. Lindsey has become very frustrated in researching a tax issue using keyword searches. What suggestions can you give her? `LO 2-5`

32. Nola, a tax novice, has a fairly simple tax question. Besides tax services, what are some sources that she can use to answer her question? `LO 2-5`

33. Armando identifies a tax research question as being a question of fact. What types of authorities should he attempt to locate in his research? `LO 2-5`

34. How are citators used in tax research? `LO 2-5`

35. What is the general rule for how many authorities a research memo should discuss? `LO 2-5`

36. Identify some of the sources for tax professional standards. What are the potential ramifications of failing to comply with these standards? `LO 2-6`

37. Levi is recommending a tax return position to his client. What standard must he meet to satisfy his professional standards? What is the source of this professional standard? `LO 2-6`

38. What is Circular 230? `LO 2-6`

LO 2-7   39. What are the basic differences between civil and criminal tax penalties?

LO 2-7   40. What are some of the most common civil penalties imposed on taxpayers?

LO 2-7   41. What are the taxpayer's standards to avoid the substantial understatement of tax penalty?

LO 2-7   42. What are the tax practitioner's standards to avoid a penalty for recommending a tax return position?

PROBLEMS

Select problems are available in Connect®.

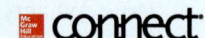

LO 2-1   43. Ahmed does not have enough cash on hand to pay his taxes. He was excited to hear that he can request an extension to file his tax return. Does this solve his problem? What are the ramifications if he doesn't pay his tax liability by April 15?

LO 2-1   44. Molto Stancha Corporation had zero earnings this fiscal year; in fact, it lost money. Must the corporation file a tax return?

LO 2-1   45. The estate of Monique Chablis earned $450 of income this year. Is the estate required to file an income tax return?

LO 2-1   46. Jamarcus, a full-time student, earned $2,500 this year from a summer job. He had no other income this year and will have zero federal income tax liability this year. His employer withheld $300 of federal income tax from his summer pay. Is Jamarcus required to file a tax return? Should Jamarcus file a tax return?

LO 2-1   47. Shane has never filed a tax return despite earning excessive sums of money as a gambler. When does the statute of limitations expire for the years in which Shane has not filed a tax return?

LO 2-1   48. Latoya filed her tax return on February 10 this year. When will the statute of limitations expire for this tax return?

LO 2-1   49. Using the facts from the previous problem, how would your answer change if Latoya understated her income by 40 percent? How would your answer change if Latoya intentionally failed to report as taxable income any cash payments she received from her clients?

LO 2-2   50. Paula could not reach an agreement with the IRS at her appeals conference and has just received a 90-day letter. If she wants to litigate the issue but does not have sufficient cash to pay the proposed deficiency, what is her best court choice?

LO 2-2   51. In choosing a trial-level court, how should a court's previous rulings influence the choice? How should circuit court rulings influence the taxpayer's choice of a trial-level court?

LO 2-2   52. Sophia recently won a tax case litigated in the 7th Circuit. She has just heard that the Supreme Court denied the *writ of certiorari*. Should she be happy or not, and why?

LO 2-2   53. Campbell's tax return was audited because she failed to report interest she earned on her tax return. What IRS audit selection method identified her tax return?

LO 2-2   54. Yong's tax return was audited because he calculated his tax liability incorrectly. What IRS audit procedure identified his tax return for audit?

LO 2-2   55. Randy deducted a high level of itemized deductions two years ago relative to his income level. He recently received an IRS notice requesting documentation for his itemized deductions. What audit procedure likely identified his tax return for audit?

LO 2-2   56. Jackie has a corporate client that has recently received a 30-day notice from the IRS with a $100,000 tax assessment. Her client is considering requesting an appeals conference to contest the assessment. What factors should Jackie advise her client to consider before requesting an appeals conference?

57. The IRS recently completed an audit of Shea's tax return and assessed $15,000 additional tax. Shea requested an appeals conference but was unable to settle the case at the conference. She is contemplating which trial court to choose to hear her case. Provide a recommendation based on the following alternative facts:

    a) Shea resides in the 2nd Circuit, and the 2nd Circuit has recently ruled against the position Shea is litigating.

    b) The Federal Circuit Court of Appeals has recently ruled in favor of Shea's position.

    c) The issue being litigated involves a question of fact. Shea has a very appealing story to tell but little favorable case law to support her position.

    d) The issue being litigated is highly technical, and Shea believes strongly in her interpretation of the law.

    e) Shea is a local elected official and would prefer to minimize any local publicity regarding the case.

`LO 2-2`
`planning`

58. Juanita, a Texas resident (5th Circuit), is researching a tax question and finds a 5th Circuit case ruling that is favorable and a 9th Circuit case that is unfavorable. Which circuit case has more "authoritative weight" and why? How would your answer change if Juanita were a Kentucky resident (6th Circuit)?

`LO 2-3`

59. Faith, a resident of Florida (11th Circuit), recently found a circuit court case that is favorable to her research question. Which two circuits would she prefer to have issued the opinion?

`LO 2-3`

60. Robert has found a "favorable" authority directly on point for his tax question. If the authority is a court case, which court would he prefer to have issued the opinion? Which court would he least prefer to have issued the opinion?

`LO 2-3`

61. Jamareo has found a "favorable" authority directly on point for his tax question. If the authority is an administrative authority, which specific type of authority would he prefer to answer his question? Which administrative authority would he least prefer to answer his question?

`LO 2-3`

62. For each of the following citations, identify the type of authority (statutory, administrative, or judicial) and explain the citation.

    a) Reg. Sec. 1.111-1(b)

    b) IRC Sec. 469(c)(7)(B)(i)

    c) Rev. Rul. 82-204, 1982-2 C.B. 192

    d) *Amdahl Corp.,* 108 TC 507 (1997)

    e) PLR 9727004

    f) *Hills v. Comm.,* 50 AFTR2d 82-6070 (11th Cir., 1982)

`LO 2-3`

63. For each of the following citations, identify the type of authority (statutory, administrative, or judicial) and explain the citation.

    a) IRC Sec. 280A(c)(5)

    b) Rev. Proc. 2004-34, 2004-1 C.B. 911

    c) *Lakewood Associates*, RIA TC Memo 95-3566

    d) TAM 200427004

    e) *U.S. v. Muncy*, 2008-2 USTC par. 50,449 (E.D., AR, 2008)

`LO 2-3`

64. Justine would like to clarify her understanding of a code section recently enacted by Congress. What tax law sources are available to assist Justine?

`LO 2-4`

65. Aldina has identified conflicting authorities that address her research question. How should she evaluate these authorities to make a conclusion?

`LO 2-5`

66. Georgette has identified a 1983 court case that appears to answer her research question. What must she do to determine if the case still represents "current" law?

`LO 2-5`

67. Sandy has determined that her research question depends upon the interpretation of the phrase "not compensated by insurance." What type of research question is this?

`LO 2-5`

LO 2-5

research

68. J. C. has been a professional gambler for many years. He loves this line of work and believes the income is tax-free.

   a) Use an available tax research service to determine whether J. C.'s thinking is correct. Is the answer to this question found in the Internal Revenue Code? If not, what type of authority answers this question?

   b) Write a memo communicating the results of your research.

LO 2-5

research

69. Katie recently won a ceramic dalmatian valued at $800 on a television game show. She questions whether this prize is taxable since it was a "gift" she won on the show.

   a) Use an available tax research service to answer Katie's question.

   b) Write a letter to Katie communicating the results of your research.

LO 2-5

research

70. Pierre recently received a tax penalty for failing to file a tax return. He was upset to receive the penalty, but he was comforted by the thought that he will get a tax deduction for paying the penalty.

   a) Use an available tax research service to determine if Pierre is correct.

   b) Write a memo communicating the results of your research.

LO 2-5

research

71. Paris was happy to provide a contribution to her friend Nicole's campaign for mayor, especially after she learned that charitable contributions are tax deductible.

   a) Use an available tax service to determine whether Paris can deduct this contribution.

   b) Write a memo communicating the results of your research.

LO 2-5

research

72. Matt and Lori were divorced in 2016. Pursuant to the divorce decree Matt receives $10,000 of alimony each month. Use an available tax service to determine if the alimony Matt receives is taxable. Would your answer change if Matt and Lori still live together?

LO 2-5

research

73. Shaun is a huge college football fan. In the past, he has always bought football tickets on the street from ticket scalpers. This year, he decided to join the university's ticket program, which requires a $2,000 contribution to the university for the "right" to purchase tickets. Shaun will then pay $400 per season ticket. Shaun understands that the price paid for the season tickets is not tax deductible as a charitable contribution. However, contributions to a university are typically tax deductible.

   a) Use an available tax service to determine how much, if any, of Shaun's $2,000 contribution for the right to purchase tickets is tax deductible.

   b) Write a letter to Shaun communicating the results of your research.

LO 2-5

research

74. Latrell recently used his Delta Skymiles to purchase a free round-trip ticket to Milan, Italy (value $1,200). The frequent flyer miles used to purchase the ticket were generated from Latrell's business travel as a CPA. Latrell's employer paid for his business trips, and he was not taxed on the travel reimbursement.

   a) Use an available tax research service to determine how much income, if any, Latrell will have to recognize as a result of purchasing an airline ticket with Skymiles earned from business travel.

   b) Write a memo communicating the results of your research.

LO 2-5

research

75. Benjamin, a self-employed bookkeeper, takes a CPA review course ($1,500 cost) to help prepare for the CPA exam.

   a) Use an available tax research service to determine if Benjamin may deduct the cost of the CPA exam course.

   b) Write a memo communicating the results of your research.

76. Randy has found conflicting authorities that address a research question for one of his clients. The majority of the authorities provide an unfavorable answer for his client. According to Randy's estimates, if the client takes the more favorable position on its tax return then there is approximately a 48 percent chance that the position will be sustained upon audit or judicial proceeding. If the client takes this position on its tax return, will Randy be subject to penalty? Will the client potentially be subject to penalty?

    LO 2-6

77. Using the same facts from the previous problem, how would your answer change if Randy estimates that there is only a 20 percent chance that the position will be sustained upon audit or judicial proceeding?

    LO 2-6

78. Sasha owes additional tax imposed in a recent audit. In addition to the tax, will she be assessed other amounts? If so, how will these amounts be determined?

    LO 2-7

79. Maurice has a client that recently asked him about the odds of the IRS detecting cash transactions not reported on a tax return. What are some of the issues that Maurice should discuss with his client?

    LO 2-7

ROGER | *CPA Review*

Sample CPA Exam questions from Roger CPA Review are available in Connect as support for the topics in this text. These Multiple Choice Questions and Task-Based Simulations include expert-written explanations and solutions and provide a starting point for students to become familiar with the content and functionality of the actual CPA Exam.

Tax Planning Strategies and Related Limitations

©Chris Ryan/AGE Fotostock

Storyline Summary

Taxpayers: Bill and Mercedes

Family description: Bill and Mercedes are married with one daughter, Margaret.

Employment status: Bill is an economics professor; Mercedes is a small business owner.

Filing status: Married, filing jointly

Current situation: Bill and Mercedes want to engage in low risk tax planning strategies.

While working with their CPA during their audit, Bill and Mercedes decide to inquire about low risk tax planning opportunities. Specifically, they would like to gain a better understanding of how to maximize their after-tax income without increasing their potential for another audit. (Although it was fun and educational, one audit is enough!) Mercedes is convinced that, as a small business owner (Lavish Interior Designs Inc.), she pays more than her fair share of taxes. Likewise, Bill, an avid investor, wonders whether he is missing the mark by not considering taxes in his investment decisions. ■

Bill and Mercedes have come to the right place. This chapter describes the basic tax planning concepts that form the basis of the simplest to most complex tax planning transactions. In the process we also discuss the judicial doctrines that serve as basic limits on tax planning.

BASIC TAX PLANNING OVERVIEW

LO 3-1

Effective tax planning requires a basic understanding of the roles that tax and nontax factors play in structuring business, investment, and personal decisions. Although tax factors may not be the sole or even the primary determinant of a transaction or its structure, taxes can significantly affect the costs or benefits associated with business, investment, and personal transactions. Thus, the tax implications of competing transactions warrant careful consideration. Likewise, nontax factors, such as the taxpayer's financial goals or legal constraints, are an integral part of every transaction.

In general terms, effective tax planning maximizes the taxpayer's after-tax wealth while achieving the taxpayer's nontax goals. Maximizing after-tax wealth is not necessarily the same as minimizing taxes. Specifically, maximizing after-tax wealth requires us to consider both the tax and nontax costs and benefits of alternative transactions, whereas tax minimization focuses solely on a single cost—taxes. Indeed, if the goal of tax planning were simply to minimize taxes, the simplest way to achieve it would be to earn no income at all. Obviously, this strategy has potential limitations—most notably, the unattractive nontax consequence of poverty. Thus, it is necessary to consider the nontax ramifications of any planning strategy.

Virtually every transaction includes three parties: the taxpayer, the other transacting party, and the uninvited silent party that specifies the tax consequences of the transaction—the government. Astute tax planning requires an understanding of the tax and nontax costs from the perspectives of both the taxpayer *and* the other parties. For example, it would be impossible for an employer to develop an effective compensation plan without considering the tax and nontax costs associated with different compensation arrangements from both the employer's and the employees' perspectives. With sound tax planning, the employer can design a compensation package that generates value for employees while reducing costs for the employer. (One way to achieve this goal is through the use of nontaxable fringe benefits, such as health insurance, which are deductible expenses to the employer but not taxable income to employees.) Throughout the text, we highlight situations where this multilateral approach to tax planning is especially important.

In this chapter we discuss three basic tax planning strategies that represent the building blocks of tax planning:

1. *Timing* (deferring or accelerating taxable income and tax deductions).
2. *Income shifting* (shifting income from high- to low-tax-rate taxpayers).
3. *Conversion* (converting income from high- to low-tax-rate activities).

TIMING STRATEGIES

LO 3-2 LO 3-3
LO 3-6

One of the cornerstones of basic tax planning is the idea of *timing*. *When* income is taxed or an expense is deducted affects the associated "real" tax costs or savings. This is true for two reasons. First, the time when income is taxed or an expense is deducted affects the *present value* of the taxes paid on income or the tax savings on deductions. Second, the tax costs of income and tax savings of deductions vary as *tax rates* change. The tax costs on income are higher when tax rates are higher and lower when tax rates are lower. Likewise, the tax savings on deductions are higher when tax rates are higher and lower when tax rates are lower. Let's look at the effects of present value and tax rates on the timing strategy.

Present Value of Money

The concept of **present value**—also known as the time value of money—basically states that $1 received today is worth *more* than $1 received in the future. Is this true, or is this some type of new math?

It's true. Assuming an investor can earn a positive **after-tax rate of return** such as 5 percent, $1 invested today should be worth $1.05 in one year.[1] Specifically,

Eq. 3-1

$$\text{Future Value} = \text{Present Value} \times (1 + r)^n$$
$$= \$1 \times (1 + .05)^1 = \$1.05$$

where $1 is the present value, r is the after-tax rate of return (5 percent), and n is the investment period (1 year). Hence, $1 today is equivalent to $1.05 in one year. The implication of the time value of money for tax planning is that the timing of a cash inflow or a cash outflow affects the present value of the income or expense.

Example 3-1

Bill is given the choice of receiving a $1,000 nontaxable gift today or a $1,000 nontaxable gift in one year. Which would Bill prefer? Assume Bill could invest $1,000 today and earn an 8 percent return after taxes in one year. If he receives the gift today, how much would the $1,000 be worth in one year?

Answer: The $1,000 gift today would be worth $1,080 in one year, and thus Bill should prefer to receive the gift today. Specifically,

$$\text{Future Value} = \text{Present Value} \times (1 + r)^n$$
$$= \$1,000 \times (1 + .08)^1 = \$1,080$$

In terms of *future value*, the choice in the above example between receiving $1,000 today and $1,000 in one year simplifies to a choice between $1,080 and $1,000. For even the least materialistic individual, choosing $1,080—that is, $1,000 *today*—should be straightforward.

Often tax planners find it useful to consider sums not in terms of future value, but rather in terms of present value. How would we restate the choice in Example 3-1 in terms of present value? Obviously, the present value of receiving $1,000 today is $1,000, but what is the *present value* of $1,000 received in one year? The answer depends on the **discount factor,** which we derive from the taxpayer's expected after-tax rate of return. The discount factor is very useful for calculating the present value of future inflows or outflows of cash. We can derive the discount factor for a given rate of return simply by rearranging the future value equation (Eq. 3-1) from above:

Eq. 3-2

$$\text{Present Value} = \text{Future Value}/(1 + r)^n$$
$$= \$1/(1 + .08)^1 = \$0.926$$
$$\text{Therefore, the discount factor} = 0.926$$

THE KEY FACTS

Present Value of Money

- The concept of present value—also known as the time value of money—states that $1 received today is worth *more* than $1 received in the future.
- The implication of the time value of money for tax planning is that the timing of a cash inflow or a cash outflow affects the present value of the income or expense.
- Present Value = Future Value/$(1 + r)^n$.
- When we are considering cash inflows, higher present values are preferred; when we are considering cash outflows, lower present values are preferred.

---

[1]Assuming a constant marginal tax rate (t), after-tax rate of return (r) may be calculated as follows: $r = R \times (1 - t)$, where R is the taxpayer's before-tax rate of return.

EXHIBIT 3-1 **Present Value of a Single Payment at Various Annual Rates of Return**

Year	4%	5%	6%	7%	8%	9%	10%	11%	12%
1	.962	.952	.943	.935	.926	.917	.909	.901	.893
2	.925	.907	.890	.873	.857	.842	.826	.812	.797
3	.889	.864	.840	.816	.794	.772	.751	.731	.712
4	.855	.823	.792	.763	.735	.708	.683	.659	.636
5	.822	.784	.747	.713	.681	.650	.621	.593	.567
6	.790	.746	.705	.666	.630	.596	.564	.535	.507
7	.760	.711	.665	.623	.583	.547	.513	.482	.452
8	.731	.677	.627	.582	.540	.502	.467	.434	.404
9	.703	.645	.592	.544	.500	.460	.424	.391	.361
10	.676	.614	.558	.508	.463	.422	.386	.352	.322
11	.650	.585	.527	.475	.429	.388	.350	.317	.287
12	.625	.557	.497	.444	.397	.356	.319	.286	.257
13	.601	.530	.469	.415	.368	.326	.290	.258	.229
14	.577	.505	.442	.388	.340	.299	.263	.232	.205
15	.555	.481	.417	.362	.315	.275	.239	.209	.183

Applying the discount factor, we can see that $1,000 received in one year is worth $926 in today's dollars. Thus, in terms of present value, Bill's choice in Example 3-1 simplifies to a choice between a cash inflow of $1,000 today and a cash inflow worth $926 today. Again, choosing $1,000 today is pretty straightforward.

Exhibit 3-1 provides the discount factors for a lump sum (single payment) received in *n* periods using various rates of return. Tax planners frequently utilize such tables for quick reference in calculating present value for sums under consideration.

Example 3-2

At a recent holiday sale, Bill and Mercedes purchased $1,000 worth of furniture with "no money down and no payments for one year!" How much money is this deal really worth? (Assume their after-tax rate of return on investments is 10 percent.)

Answer: The discount factor of .909 (Exhibit 3-1, 10% Rate of Return column, Year 1 row) means the present value of $1,000 is $909 ($1,000 × .909 = $909)—so Bill and Mercedes save $91 ($1,000 − $909 = $91).

While Example 3-1 considers a $1,000 cash inflow, Example 3-2 addresses a $1,000 cash *outflow*. In terms of present value, choosing between paying $1,000 today and paying $1,000 in a year simplifies to choosing a cash outflow of either $1,000 (by paying today) or $909 (by paying in one year). Most people would prefer to pay $909. Indeed, financial planners always keep the following general rule of thumb in mind: When considering *cash inflows, prefer higher present values;* when considering *cash outflows, prefer lower present values.*

The Timing Strategy When Tax Rates Are Constant

In terms of tax planning, remember that *taxes paid* represent cash *outflows*, while *tax savings* generated from tax deductions are cash *inflows*. This perspective leads us to two basic tax-related timing strategies when tax rates are constant (not changing):

1. Accelerate tax deductions (deduct in an earlier period).
2. Defer recognizing taxable income (recognize in a later period).

Accelerating tax deductions to an earlier period increases the present value of the tax savings from the deduction. That is, tax savings received now have a higher present value than the same amount received a year from now.

Deferring income to a later period decreases the present value of the tax cost of the income. That is, taxes paid a year from now have a lower present value than taxes paid today. These two strategies are summarized in Exhibit 3-2.

EXHIBIT 3-2   **The Timing Tax Strategy When Tax Rates Are Constant**

Item	Recommendation	Why?
Tax deductions	Accelerate tax deductions into earlier years.	Maximizes the present value of tax savings from deductions.
Taxable income	Defer taxable income into later tax years.	Minimizes the present value of taxes paid.

Example 3-3

Mercedes, a calendar-year taxpayer, uses the cash method of accounting for her small business.[2] On December 28, she receives a $10,000 bill from her accountant for consulting services related to her small business. She can avoid late payment charges by paying the $10,000 bill before January 10 of next year. Let's assume that Mercedes's marginal tax rate is 32 percent *this year and next* and that she can earn an after-tax rate of return of 10 percent on her investments. When should she pay the $10,000 bill—this year or next?

Answer: If Mercedes pays the bill this year, she will receive a tax deduction on this year's tax return.[3] If she pays the bill in January, she will receive a tax deduction on next year's tax return (one year later). She needs to compare the after-tax costs of the accounting service, using the present value of the tax savings for each scenario:

Description	Option 1: Pay $10,000 bill *this year*	Option 2: Pay $10,000 bill *next year*
Present Value Comparison		
Tax deduction	$10,000	$10,000
Marginal tax rate	× 32%	× 32%
Tax savings	$ 3,200	$ 3,200
Discount factor	× 1	× .909
Present value tax savings	$ 3,200	$ 2,909
After-tax cost of accounting services:		
Before-tax cost	$10,000	$10,000
Less: Present value tax savings	− 3,200	− 2,909
After-tax cost of accounting services	$6,800	$ 7,091

Since Mercedes would surely rather spend $6,800 than $7,091 for accounting services, paying the bill in December is the clear winner.

---

[2]In the Business Income, Deductions, and Accounting Methods chapter, we discuss the basic accounting methods (e.g., cash vs. the accrual method), which influence the timing of when income and deductions are recognized for tax purposes.

[3]Accelerating her payment from January 10 to December 31 will increase the present value of the $10,000 cash outflow by 10 days. Thus, there is a minor present value cost associated with accelerating her payment.

In terms of accelerating deductions, the intent of the timing strategy is to accelerate the tax deduction significantly *without* accelerating the actual cash outflow that generates the expense. Indeed, if we assume a marginal rate of 32 percent and an after-tax return of 8 percent, accelerating a $1,000 cash outflow by one year to realize $320 in tax savings actually *increases* the after-tax *cost* of the expense from $629.68 to $680.

	Present Value Comparison	
Description	**Present value of net cash outflow *today***	**Present value of net cash outflow in *one year***
Cash outflow	$1,000	$1,000.00
Less: Tax savings (outflow × 32% tax rate)	− 320	− 320.00
Net cash outflow	$ 680	$ 680.00
Present value factor	× 1	× .926
Present value of net cash outflow today	$ 680	$ 629.68

Generally speaking, whenever a taxpayer can accelerate a deduction without also substantially accelerating the cash outflow, the timing strategy will be more beneficial.

Is the accelerating deductions strategy utilized in the real world? Yes. While it is particularly effective for cash-method taxpayers, who can often control the year in which they pay their expenses, all taxpayers have *some* latitude in timing deductions. Common examples of the timing strategy include accelerating depreciation deductions for depreciable assets, using LIFO instead of FIFO for inventory, and accelerating the deduction of certain prepaid expenses.[4] For large corporations, the benefits associated with this timing strategy can be quite substantial. Thus, tax planners spend considerable time identifying the proper period in which to recognize expenses and evaluating opportunities to accelerate deductions.

Are there certain taxpayer or transaction attributes that enhance the advantages of accelerating deductions? Absolutely. Higher tax rates, higher rates of return, larger transaction amounts, and the ability to accelerate deductions by two or more years all increase the benefits of accelerating deductions. To demonstrate this for yourself, simply rework Example 3-3 and substitute any of the following: 50 percent tax rate, 12 percent after-tax rate of return, $100,000 expense, or a five-year period difference in the timing of the expense deduction. The benefits of accelerating deductions become much more prominent with these changes.

Deferring income recognition is an equally beneficial timing strategy, especially when the taxpayer can defer the recognition of income significantly without deferring the actual receipt of income very much. Consider the following example.

Example 3-4

In early December, Bill decides he would like to sell $100,000 of his Dell Inc. stock, which cost $20,000 10 years ago. Assume Bill's tax rate on the $80,000 gain will be 15 percent and his typical after-tax rate of return on investments is 7 percent. What effect would deferring the sale to January have on Bill's after-tax income on the sale?

---

[4]See the discussion of accounting methods in the Business Income, Deductions, and Accounting Methods chapter.

Answer:

	Present Value Comparison	
Description	**Option 1: Sell the $100,000 stock in December[5]**	**Option 2: Sell the $100,000 stock in January[5]**
Sales price	$100,000	$100,000
Less: Cost of stock	− 20,000	− 20,000
Gain on sale	$ 80,000	$ 80,000
Marginal tax rate	× 15%	× 15%
Tax on gain	$ 12,000	$ 12,000
Discount factor	× 1	×.935
Present value tax cost	$ 12,000	$ 11,220
After-tax income from sale:		
Before-tax income	$100,000	$100,000
Less: Present value tax cost	− 12,000	− 11,220
After-tax income from sale	**$ 88,000**	**$ 88,780**

Bill would doubtlessly prefer to earn $88,780 to $88,000, so from a tax perspective, selling the Dell Inc. stock in January is preferable. An important nontax issue for Bill to consider is the possibility that the stock price may fluctuate between December and January.

Income deferral represents an important aspect of investment planning, retirement planning, and certain property transactions. Income-related timing considerations also affect tax planning for everyday business operations, such as determining the appropriate period in which to recognize income (e.g., cash or accrual accounting method for income and deduction recognition, and depreciation methods).

Do certain taxpayer or transaction attributes enhance the advantages of deferring income? Yes. The list is very similar to that for accelerating deductions: Higher tax rates, higher rates of return, larger transaction amounts, and the ability to defer revenue recognition for longer periods of time increase the benefits of deferral. To demonstrate this for yourself, simply rework Example 3-4 using any of the following: 50 percent tax rate, 12 percent after-tax rate of return on investments, or $200,000 gain.[6]

The Timing Strategy When Tax Rates Change

When tax rates change, the timing strategy requires a little more consideration because the tax costs of income and the tax savings from deductions will now vary. The higher the tax rate, the higher the tax savings for a tax deduction. The lower the tax rate, the lower

THE KEY FACTS

The Timing Strategy

- The time at which income is taxed or an expense is deducted affects the *present value* of the taxes paid on income or tax savings on deductions.
- The tax costs of income and tax savings of deductions vary as *tax rates* change.
- When tax rates are constant, tax planners prefer to defer income and accelerate deductions.
- When tax rates are increasing, the taxpayer must calculate the optimal tax strategies for deductions and income.
- When tax rates are decreasing, taxpayers should accelerate tax deductions into earlier years and defer taxable income to later years.

---

[5]This will require Bill to pay the tax on the gain no later than April 15 of the following year (i.e., three months after the sale for option 1 and 15 months after the sale for option 2). If Bill and Mercedes's current-year withholding and estimated payments do not equal or exceed 110 percent of their previous year's tax liability, they will have to make an estimated payment by January 15 to avoid the failure to make estimated tax payment penalty (discussed later in the Individual Income Tax Computation and Tax Credits chapter). This example assumes that Bill and Mercedes can avoid the underpayment of estimated tax penalty discussed in the Individual Income Tax Computation and Tax Credits chapter by paying 110 percent of their previous year's tax liability in both options 1 and 2. Thus, they can defer paying the tax on the gain until April 15 of the year following the sale.

[6]In Example 3-4, increasing the deferral period (e.g., from one to five years) also increases the benefits of tax deferral but requires additional assumptions regarding the expected five-year return of the Dell Inc. stock (assuming he does not sell the stock for five years) and his new investment (assuming he sells the Dell Inc. stock and immediately reinvests the after-tax proceeds).

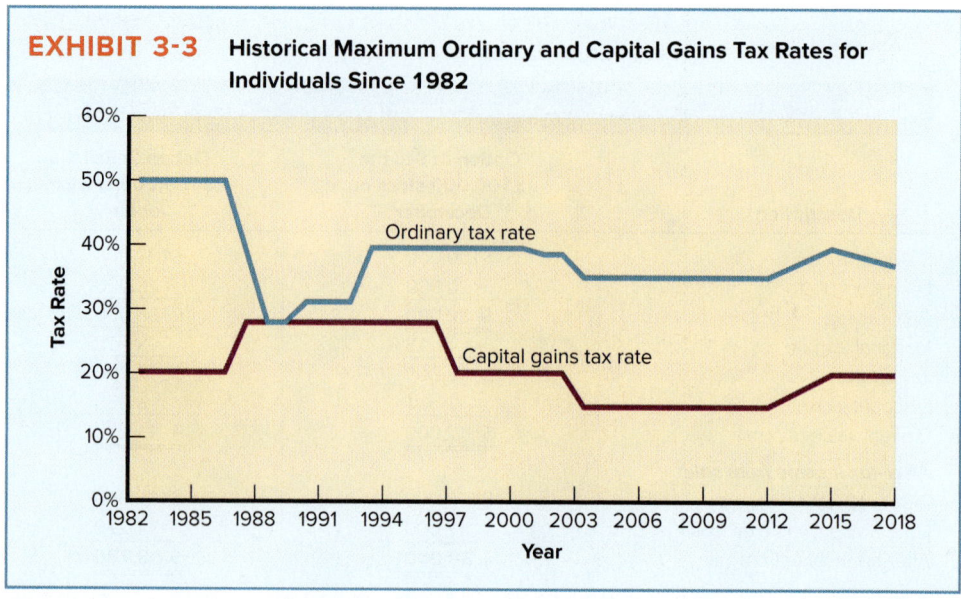

EXHIBIT 3-3   Historical Maximum Ordinary and Capital Gains Tax Rates for Individuals Since 1982

the tax costs for taxable income. *All other things being equal, taxpayers should prefer to recognize deductions during high-tax-rate years and income during low-tax-rate years.* The implication is that before a taxpayer implements the timing strategies suggested above (accelerate deductions, defer income), she should consider whether her tax rates are likely to change. In fact, as we discuss below, increasing tax rates may even suggest the taxpayer should *accelerate* income and *defer* deductions.

What would cause a taxpayer's marginal tax rate to change? The taxpayer's taxable income can change for a variety of reasons, such as changing jobs, retiring, or starting a new business. Indeed, in the Introduction to Tax chapter, we demonstrated how a taxpayer's marginal tax rate changes as income or deductions change. Marginal tax rates can also change because of tax legislation. We discussed the tax legislative process in the Tax Compliance, the IRS, and Tax Authorities chapter and noted that Congress frequently enacts tax legislation because lawmakers use taxes to raise revenue, stimulate the economy, and so on. For example, the Tax Cuts and Jobs Act enacted on December 22, 2017 lowered the top ordinary tax rate from 39.6 percent to 37 percent. In the last 35 years, Congress has changed the maximum statutory tax rates that apply to ordinary income, such as wages and business income, or capital gains, such as gains from the sale of stock, for individual taxpayers no fewer than eleven times (see Exhibit 3-3).

Let's take a look at how changing tax rates affect the timing strategy recommendations. Exhibit 3-4 presents recommendations for when tax rates are increasing. The taxpayer must actually calculate the optimal tax strategies for deductions and income when tax rates are increasing. Specifically, because accelerating deductions causes them to be

EXHIBIT 3-4   The Timing Tax Strategy When Tax Rates Are Increasing

Item	Recommendation	Why?
Tax deductions	Requires calculation to determine optimal strategy.	The taxpayer must calculate whether the benefit of accelerating deductions outweighs the disadvantage of recognizing deductions in a *lower*-tax-rate year.
Taxable income	Requires calculation to determine optimal strategy.	The taxpayer must calculate whether the benefit of deferring income outweighs the disadvantage of recognizing income in a *higher*-tax-rate year.

recognized in a *lower*-tax-rate year, the taxpayer must calculate whether the benefit of accelerating the deduction outweighs the disadvantage. Likewise, because deferring income causes income to be recognized in a *higher*-tax-rate year, the taxpayer must calculate whether the benefit of deferring income outweighs the disadvantage.

Example 3-5

Having decided she needs new equipment for her business, Mercedes is now considering whether to make the purchase and claim a corresponding $10,000 deduction at year-end or next year. Mercedes anticipates that, with the new machinery, her business income will rise such that her marginal rate will increase from 24 percent this year to 32 percent next year. Assuming her after-tax rate of return is 8 percent, what should Mercedes do?

Answer: Given rising tax rates, Mercedes must calculate the after-tax cost of the equipment for *both* options and compare present values.

	Present Value Comparison	
Description	**Option 1: Pay $10,000 bill *this year***	**Option 2: Pay $10,000 bill *next year***
Tax deduction	$10,000	$10,000
Marginal tax rate	× 24%	× 32%
Tax savings	$ 2,400	$ 3,200
Discount factor	× 1	× .926
Present value tax savings	$ 2,400	$ 2,963
After-tax cost of equipment:		
Before-tax cost	$10,000	$10,000
Less: Present value tax savings	− 2,400	− 2,963
After-tax cost of equipment	$ 7,600	$ 7,037

Paying the $10,000 next year is the clear winner.

In the above example, if the choice were either to recognize $10,000 of *income* this year or next, the *amounts* would be exactly the same but the conclusion would be different, and Mercedes would prefer to receive $7,600 of after-tax income this year instead of $7,037. (Remember, when considering cash *inflows*, we prefer the *higher* present value.) Are these always the answers when tax rates are increasing? No, the answer will depend on both the taxpayer's after-tax rate of return and the magnitude of the tax rate increase.

Now let's consider the recommendations when tax rates are *decreasing*—a common scenario when an individual reaches retirement. Exhibit 3-5 presents the timing strategy

EXHIBIT 3-5   **The Timing Tax Strategy When Tax Rates Are Decreasing**

Item	Recommendation	Why?
Tax deductions	Accelerate tax deductions into earlier years.	Maximizes the present value of tax savings from deductions due to the acceleration of the deductions into *earlier* years with a *higher* tax rate.
Taxable income	Defer taxable income into later tax years.	Minimizes the present value of taxes paid due to the deferral of the income to later years with a *lower* tax rate.

TAXES IN THE REAL WORLD Tax Reform and Tax Planning

How does tax reform affect taxpayers' tax planning? It depends! There is little debate that tax reform affects taxpayers' decisions, but *how* it affects their decisions is a function of the enacted tax laws, and taxpayers' circumstances. Provisions to reduce the tax rate, eliminate the interest deduction on corporate debt, and change the tax treatment of capital expenditures affect the after-tax cost of investments, making them more difficult to appropriately value. As a result, it is more difficult for taxpayers to determine the appropriate tax planning strategy.

For companies in the business of investing, such as private equity firms and real estate investment companies, the various tax provisions can have a big and potentially negative impact. For example, it is fairly common for private equity firms to use leveraged buyouts to acquire portfolio companies. Eliminating interest deductions reduces the value of the portfolio companies and, consequently, reduces the profitability of private

equity firms. Therefore, this provision might encourage taxpayers to reduce debt usage on investment purchases (an example of the conversion strategy). Capital intensive businesses will see tax benefits from a tax provision that allows full expensing of capital investments, leading to their use of the timing strategy to purchase assets in the time period when these assets can be immediately expensed rather than depreciated. Similarly, a reduction in tax rates can generate additional tax benefits by encouraging taxpayers to accelerate deductions in a year with higher tax rates or to defer income so it is realized in a year with lower tax rates, a basic tax timing strategy.

With tax reform, it is certain that taxpayers are assessing how their tax strategies might change.

Source: Based on: "Tax reform uncertainty testing alternative investors," http://www.pionline.com/article/20170417/PRINT/304179983/tax-reform-uncertainty-testing-alternative-investors, April 17, 2017.

THE KEY FACTS

Limitations to the Timing Strategy

- Timing strategies contain several inherent limitations.
- Whenever a taxpayer is unable to accelerate a deduction without also accelerating the cash outflow, the timing strategy will be less beneficial.
- Tax law generally requires taxpayers to continue their investment in an asset in order to defer income recognition for tax purposes.
- A deferral strategy may not be optimal if the taxpayer has severe cash flow needs, if continuing the investment would generate a low rate of return compared to other investments, if the current investment would subject the taxpayer to unnecessary risk, and so on.
- The constructive receipt doctrine, which provides that a taxpayer must recognize income when it is actually *or* constructively received, also restricts income deferral for cash-method taxpayers.

recommendations in this case. The recommendations are clear. Taxpayers should accelerate tax deductions into earlier years to reap the tax savings from *accelerating* deductions to *higher*-tax-rate years. Likewise, taxpayers should defer taxable income to later years to enjoy the tax benefits of *deferring* taxable income to *lower*-tax-rate years.

Limitations to Timing Strategies   Timing strategies contain certain inherent limitations. First, tax laws generally require taxpayers to continue their investment in an asset in order to defer income recognition for tax purposes. In other words, deferral is generally not an option if a taxpayer has "cashed out" of an investment.[7] For example, Bill could not sell his Dell stock in December and then choose not to recognize the income until January. A deferral strategy may not be optimal if (1) the taxpayer has severe cash flow needs, (2) continuing the investment would generate a low rate of return compared to other investments, or (3) the current investment would subject the taxpayer to unnecessary risk. For example, the risk that the value of Bill's investment in Dell Inc. will decline from December to January in Example 3-4 may lead Bill to forgo deferring his stock sale until January. Again, the astute taxpayer considers both the tax *and* nontax ramifications of deferring income.

A second limitation results from the **constructive receipt doctrine,** which also restricts income deferral for cash-method taxpayers.[8] Unlike accrual-method taxpayers, cash-method taxpayers report income for tax purposes when the income is *received*, whether it is in the form of cash, property, or services.[9] The cash method affords taxpayers

---

[7]See the discussion of like-kind exchanges in the Property Dispositions chapter.

[8]Later in this chapter we discuss other judicial doctrines that apply to all planning strategies.

[9]As we discuss in depth in the Business Income, Deductions, and Accounting Methods chapter, accrual-method taxpayers report income when it is earned. In general, income is deemed earned when all events have occurred that fix the taxpayer's right to the income and the income can be estimated with reasonable accuracy. Thus, income recognition for accrual-method taxpayers generally is not tied to payment. Receipt of prepaid income by accrual-method taxpayers may trigger income recognition in certain circumstances. The constructive receipt doctrine may apply in these situations.

some leeway in determining when to recognize income, because such taxpayers can control when they bill their clients. However, the constructive receipt doctrine provides that a taxpayer must recognize income when it is actually *or* constructively received. Constructive receipt is deemed to have occurred if the income has been credited to the taxpayer's account or if the income is unconditionally available to the taxpayer, the taxpayer is aware of the income's availability, and there are no restrictions on the taxpayer's control over the income.

Example 3-6

Mercedes's brother-in-law, Carlos, works for King Acura, which recently instituted a bonus plan that pays year-end bonuses each December to employees rated above average for their customer service. Carlos is expecting a $10,000 bonus this year that will be paid on December 31. Thinking he'd prefer to defer this income until next year, Carlos plans to take a vacation on December 30 so that he will not receive his bonus check until January. Will Carlos's strategy work?

Answer: No, the constructive receipt doctrine applies here. Because Carlos's check was unconditionally available to him on December 31, he was aware of its availability, and there were no restrictions on his control over the income on that date, Carlos must report the income in the current year.

What could taxpayers do to avoid Carlos's problem in the future? They could request that their employer institute a company policy of paying bonuses on January 1, which would allow all employees to report the bonus income in that year. However, if the employer is a cash-method taxpayer, this creates a potential conflict with its employees.[10] Such an employer would most likely prefer to deduct the bonus in the current year, which requires the bonuses to be paid in December. This conflict would not exist if the employer were an accrual-method taxpayer, because paying the bonuses in January would not affect its ability to deduct the bonuses in the previous year.[11]

INCOME-SHIFTING STRATEGIES

LO 3-4 **LO 3-6**

We've seen that the value of a tax deduction, or the tax cost of income, varies with the marginal tax rate. We've also seen that tax rates can vary across time, which leads to basic tax planning strategies regarding when to recognize deductions and income. Tax rates can also vary across *taxpayers* or *jurisdictions* (states, countries), which leads to still other tax planning strategies—for example, shifting income from high-tax-rate taxpayers to low-tax-rate taxpayers or shifting deductions from low-tax-rate taxpayers to high-tax-rate taxpayers.

The type of taxpayers who benefit most from this strategy are (1) related parties, such as family members or businesses and their owners, who have varying marginal tax rates and are willing to shift income for the benefit of the group; and (2) taxpayers operating in multiple jurisdictions with different marginal tax rates. In any case, tax planners should seek only legitimate methods of shifting income that will withstand IRS scrutiny. In the following section we discuss transactions between family members, followed by a discussion of transactions between owners and their businesses, and finally a discussion of income shifting across jurisdictions.

---

[10]Because King Acura carries inventory, the cash method is not allowed for transactions related to its inventory (e.g., cost of goods sold, sales, etc.). However, King Acura is permitted to use the cash method for other transactions. This mixed method is referred to as the "hybrid" method of accounting.

[11]§267(a)(2). When an employee/shareholder and an employer/corporation are related (i.e., the employee/shareholder owns more than 50 percent of the value of the employer corporation), the corporation is not allowed to deduct the compensation expense until the employee/shareholder includes the payment in income.

Transactions between Family Members and Limitations

One of the most common examples of income shifting is high-tax-rate parents shifting income to low-tax-rate children. For example, Bill and Mercedes have a 32 percent marginal tax rate, whereas their daughter, Margaret, has a 10 percent marginal tax rate. Assuming their marginal tax rates remain constant with relatively modest changes in income, every $1 of income that Bill and Mercedes shift to Margaret reduces the family's tax liability by 22 cents [$1 × (32% − 10%)]. Thus, if Bill and Mercedes shift $10,000 of taxable income to Margaret, the family's after-tax income will increase by $2,200. Can taxpayers legally do this? Yes and no. As you might expect, there are limitations on this type of income shifting.

The **assignment of income doctrine** requires income to be taxed to the taxpayer who actually earns it.[12] Merely attributing your paycheck or dividend to another taxpayer does not transfer the tax liability associated with the income. The assignment of income doctrine implies that, in order to shift income to a taxpayer, that taxpayer must actually earn the income. For example, if Mercedes would like to shift some of her business income to Margaret, Margaret must actually earn it. One way to accomplish this would be for Mercedes to employ Margaret in her business and pay her a $10,000 salary. The effects of this transaction are to decrease Mercedes's taxable income by $10,000 because of tax-deductible salary expense, and to increase Margaret's income by the $10,000 taxable salary. What if Margaret is paid $10,000 to answer Mercedes's business phone one Saturday afternoon every month? Does this seem reasonable? Not likely. The IRS frowns upon this type of aggressive strategy.

Indeed, the IRS closely scrutinizes such **related-party transactions**—that is, financial activities among family members (also among owners and their businesses, or among businesses owned by the same owners). Unlike **arm's length transactions,** in which each transacting party negotiates for his or her own benefit, related-party transactions are useful for taxpayers who are much more willing to negotiate for their own common good to the detriment of the IRS. For example, would Mercedes pay an unrelated party $10,000 to answer the phone once a month? Doubtful.[13]

Are there other ways to shift income to children? For example, could Bill shift some of his investment income to Margaret? Yes, but there's a catch. The assignment of income applies what is referred to as the "fruit and the tree" analogy [*Lucas v. Earl* (S. Ct., 1930), 8 AFTR 10287]. For the owner to avoid being taxed on the fruit from the tree (the income), the owner must transfer the tree. Thus, to shift investment income, Bill would also have to transfer ownership in the underlying investment assets to Margaret.[14] Is there a problem with this requirement? Not for Margaret. However, Bill would likely prefer to maintain his wealth. The nontax disadvantages of transferring wealth to implement the income-shifting strategy often outweigh the tax benefits of the transfer. For example, most parents either could not afford to or would have serious reservations about transferring significant wealth to their children—a prime example of how nontax costs may override tax considerations.

Transactions between Owners and Their Businesses and Limitations

Income shifting is not limited to transactions within a family unit. One of the most common examples occurs between owners and their businesses. Let's consider Mercedes's interior design business. Currently, Mercedes operates her business as a sole proprietorship. A sole proprietorship (unlike a C corporation) is not a separate reporting entity, and thus, Mercedes reports her business income and deductions on her individual tax return. Shifting

---

[12]Later in this chapter we discuss other judicial doctrines that apply to all planning strategies.

[13]The Internal Revenue Code also contains specific provisions to curtail benefits from related-party transactions. For example, as we discuss in the Property Dispositions chapter, §267 disallows a tax deduction for losses on sales to related parties (even if the sale was consummated at the asset's fair market value).

[14]Further, as we discuss in the Individual Income Tax Computation and Tax Credits chapter, the "kiddie tax" may apply when parents shift too much investment income to children. The kiddie tax restricts the amount of a child's investment income that can be taxed at the child's (lower) tax rate subjects the rest to trust (higher) tax rates.

income to or from her sole proprietorship offers no benefit because all of her sole proprietorship income is reported on her tax return, regardless of whether it is attributed to her personally or to her business. On the other hand, if Mercedes operated her interior design business as a C corporation, shifting income to or from the C corporation may make good financial sense because the corporation would be a separate entity with tax rates distinct from Mercedes's individual tax rate. Shifting income to herself from the C corporation may allow Mercedes to decrease the tax on her business profits, thereby increasing her after-tax income. This strategy may become more common with the recent significant drop in the corporate tax rates compared to the small decrease in individual tax rates. Example 3-7 illustrates the savings obtainable from this strategy.

Example 3-7

Mercedes is considering incorporating her interior design business. She projects $200,000 of business profit next year. Excluding this profit, Bill and Mercedes expect $70,000 of taxable income next year. If Mercedes would like to minimize her current-year tax liability, should she incorporate her business? (Use the married filing jointly and corporate tax rates in Appendix D to answer this question.)

Answer: If Mercedes does not incorporate her business, the first $7,400 of her business profits will be taxed at 12 percent (from $70,000 to $77,400 of taxable income, the marginal tax rate is 12 percent. The next $87,600 (from $77,400 to $165,000 of taxable income) would be taxed at 22 percent. The remaining $105,000 (from $165,000 to $270,000 of taxable income) would be taxed at 24 percent. Upon reviewing the corporate tax rate schedule, you should note that the corporate tax rate is a flat 21 percent, and is lower than Bill and Mercedes's current marginal tax rate of 24 percent. Thus, there appears to be some opportunity for Mercedes to reduce her current-year tax liability by incorporating her business.[15]

In order to shift income from the corporation to the owner, the corporation must create a tax deduction for itself in the process. Compensation paid to employee–owners is the most common method of shifting income from corporations to their owners. Compensation expense is deductible by the corporation and is generally taxable to the employee. Having the business owner rent property to the corporation or loan money to the corporation are also effective income-shifting methods, because both transactions generate tax deductions for the corporation and income for the shareholder. Because corporations don't get a tax deduction for dividends paid, paying dividends is *not* an effective way to shift income. Having a corporation pay dividends actually results in "double taxation"—the profits generating the dividends are taxed first at the corporate level, and then at the shareholder level. Depending on the taxpayer's tax rate and their dividend tax rate, this strategy may be a good one though under the new tax law it can be quite complicated, and recommending this tax planning strategy without analyzing the taxpayer's situation may not be a good way to keep your job as a tax consultant.

After a taxpayer identifies the opportunity and appropriate method to shift income (compensation paid to a related party), he or she can easily determine the optimal amount to shift depending on the taxpayers' marginal tax rates.

Example 3-8

Assuming Mercedes's goal is to minimize her current-year federal income tax liability, how much of the $200,000 business income should her corporation report?

Answer: It should report $192,600. Comparing the two tax rate schedules reveals how to calculate this number.

(continued on page 3-14)

---

[15]Note that this is a simplified discussion of one of many tax issues associated with incorporating a business and assumes Mercedes's business does not qualify for the deduction for qualified business income discussed in the Individual From AGI Deductions chapter. In addition, as discussed later in this chapter, Mercedes must consider the judicial doctrines (economic substance, business purpose, etc.) in making this decision. She also needs to consider further tax planning opportunities described in the following example.

Step 1: Would Mercedes rather have income taxed at 21 percent (the corporation's tax rate) or 12 percent (Bill and Mercedes's marginal tax rate before recognizing any profit from Mercedes's business)? Twelve percent is the obvious answer. To take advantage of Bill and Mercedes's 12 percent tax bracket, Mercedes should shift $7,400 of the expected $200,000 in profits to herself and Bill—via a salary paid to Mercedes.

Step 2: Assuming Bill and Mercedes report $77,400 of income, their marginal tax rate will now be 22 percent, and thus Mercedes's choice is to have additional income taxed at 22 percent (Bill and Mercedes's marginal tax rate) or at 21 percent (the corporation's tax rate). Twenty-one percent is the clear answer. To take advantage of the 21 percent corporate tax rate, the corporation should retain the remaining $192,600 of the expected $200,000 in profits.

How much current federal income tax does this strategy save Bill and Mercedes? The corporation's and Bill and Mercedes's combined federal income tax liability will be $49,353 ($40,446 for the corporation plus $8,907 for Bill and Mercedes) compared to $53,379 for Bill and Mercedes if the business is operated as a sole proprietorship. Thus, they will save $4,026.[16]

Are there nontax disadvantages of the income-shifting-via-incorporating strategy? Yes. For example, one nontax disadvantage for Mercedes is that her new corporation now has $152,154 of her after-tax profits ($192,600 profits less $40,446 of corporate tax). If Mercedes has personal cash-flow needs that require use of the $152,154, this is not a viable strategy. Indeed, it's advantageous only if the business owner intends to reinvest the business profits into the business. Furthermore, any subsequent transactions between Mercedes and the corporation would clearly be related-party transactions. Thus, Mercedes should be prepared for IRS scrutiny.[17]

As the above example illustrates, tax-avoiding strategies can be quite beneficial and as Bill and Mercedes's personal (nonbusiness) income increases (i.e., their tax bracket increases on personal income), the strategies will produce even greater tax savings. With the decrease in the corporate tax rate from 35 percent to 21 percent, we are likely to see an increasing preference for businesses to operate as corporations. However, tax planning strategies also entail some financial risks if they fail to pass muster with the IRS.

ETHICS

Agnes Meher is the owner of LuPat, a profitable construction company that she operates as a sole proprietorship. As a sole proprietor, Agnes reports the business income from LuPat on her individual tax return. Agnes expects the business to generate $400,000 of taxable income this year. Combined with her other income, this will put her in the top tax bracket (37 percent). Agnes has two children named Ellie Mae and Spencer, ages 9 and 11, respectively, who do not currently have any taxable income. Agnes would like to shift some of her income from LuPat to Ellie Mae and Spencer to reduce the overall tax burden from the business income. To shift the income, Agnes hired Ellie Mae and Spencer to perform some janitorial and clerical services for LuPat, paying each child $20,000. What do you think of Agnes's strategy?

---

[16]This strategy will result in the eventual double taxation of the income retained in Mercedes's corporation. Specifically, Mercedes will eventually have to pay tax on the income retained by the corporation, either in the form of taxable dividends from the corporation or a taxable gain when she sells or liquidates the corporation. The present value of this additional layer of tax reduces the tax savings from this strategy. The longer that the second layer of tax is deferred, the more advantageous this strategy will be. In addition, the example ignores employment-related taxes. These calculations are beyond the scope of this chapter.

[17]The taxpayer should maintain documentation for related-party transactions (e.g., notes for related-party loans and contemporaneous documentation of reasonable compensation paid to related parties).

Income Shifting across Jurisdictions and Limitations

Taxpayers that operate in multiple jurisdictions (states, countries) also apply the income-shifting strategy. Specifically, income earned in different jurisdictions—whether in the United States or abroad, and for state income tax purposes, income earned in different states—is often taxed very differently. With a proper understanding of the differences in tax laws across jurisdictions, taxpayers can use these differences to maximize their after-tax wealth.

Example 3-9

Carlos's employer, King Acura, has two locations. Its main location is in South Dakota (a state with no corporate tax), with a secondary location in North Dakota (maximum corporate state tax rate of 4.31 percent). What tax planning strategy may save money for King Acura?

Answer: The most obvious strategy is to shift income from the North Dakota location to the South Dakota location, thereby reducing King Acura's state income tax liability by about 4.31 cents for every dollar of income shifted.[18]

A number of possibilities exist to execute a strategy such as King Acura's in Example 3-9. Assuming that the North Dakota and South Dakota locations exchange cars, the firm could shift income via *transfer pricing* (using the price the South Dakota location charges the North Dakota location for cars transferred to North Dakota). Likewise, if the South Dakota location (the corporate headquarters) provides a legitimate support function for the North Dakota location, the firm should allocate a portion of the overhead and administrative expenses from the South Dakota location to the North Dakota location.

What are some of the limitations of income shifting across jurisdictions? First, taxing authorities are fully aware of the tax benefits of strategically structuring transactions across tax borders (across countries or states). Thus, the IRS closely examines transfer pricing on international transactions. Similarly, state tax authorities scrutinize interstate transactions between related taxpayers. Second, when taxpayers locate in low-tax-rate jurisdictions to, in effect, shift income to a tax-advantaged jurisdiction, they may bear **implicit taxes** (i.e., additional costs attributable to the jurisdiction's tax advantage). For example, the demand for workers, services, or property in low-tax-rate jurisdictions, whether a foreign country or a low-tax state, may increase the nontax costs associated with operating a business there enough to offset the tax advantages. Finally, negative publicity from moving operations (and jobs) from the United States to a lower-tax jurisdiction may more than offset any tax benefits associated with these strategies.

THE KEY FACTS

The Income-Shifting Strategy

- Income shifting exploits the differences in tax rates across taxpayers or jurisdictions.
- Common examples of income shifting include high-tax-rate parents shifting income to low-tax-rate children, businesses shifting income to their owners, and taxpayers shifting income from high-tax jurisdictions to low-tax jurisdictions. The assignment of income doctrine requires income to be taxed to the taxpayer who actually earns the income.
- The IRS closely monitors income-shifting strategies that involve related-party transactions.

CONVERSION STRATEGIES

LO 3-5

We've now seen how tax rates can vary across time and taxpayers. They can also vary across different *activities*. For example, ordinary income such as salary, interest income, and business income received by individual taxpayers is taxed at their ordinary marginal

---

[18]Because state taxes are deductible for federal tax purposes, every dollar of state taxes reduced with this strategy will increase King Acura's federal income tax liability by its federal marginal tax rate (e.g., 21 percent). Thus, the net tax savings for every dollar of income shifted from North Dakota to South Dakota will be 3.4 percent, which equals the state tax savings (4.31 percent) less the federal tax increase resulting from the lost state tax deduction (4.31% × 21%).

tax rates. Long-term capital gains, which are gains from the sale of investment assets held longer than one year, and dividends are taxed at lower tax rates (currently a maximum of 20 percent), and still other forms of income like nontaxable compensation benefits and municipal bond interest are tax-exempt. Expenses from different types of activities may also be treated very differently for tax purposes. Business expenses are generally fully tax deductible, whereas tax deductions for investments may be limited, and tax deductions for personal expenses may be completely disallowed. In sum, the tax law does not treat all types of income or deductions the same. This understanding forms the basis for the conversion strategy—recasting income and expenses to receive the most favorable tax treatment.

To implement the conversion strategy, the taxpayer must be aware of the underlying differences in tax treatment across various types of income, expenses, and activities and have some ability to alter the nature of the income or expense to receive the more advantageous tax treatment. To analyze the benefits of the conversion strategy, you often compare the after-tax rates of return of alternative investments rather than the **before-tax rates of return.** Given a stationary marginal tax rate, you can calculate an investment's after-tax rate of return as follows:

Eq. 3-3

$$\text{After-Tax Rate of Return} = \text{Before-Tax Rate of Return} - (\text{Before-Tax Rate of Return} \times \text{Marginal Tax Rate})$$

which simplifies to

Eq. 3-4

$$\text{After-Tax Rate of Return} = \text{Before-Tax Rate of Return} \times (1 - \text{Marginal Tax Rate})$$

Example 3-10

Bill is contemplating three different investments, each with the same amount of risk:

1. A high-dividend stock that pays 8.5 percent dividends annually but has no appreciation potential.
2. Taxable corporate bonds that pay 9 percent interest annually.
3. Tax-exempt municipal bonds that pay 6 percent interest annually.

Assuming that dividends are taxed at 20 percent and that Bill's marginal tax rate on ordinary income is 32 percent, which investment should Bill choose?

Answer: To answer this question, we must compute Bill's after-tax rate of return for each investment. The after-tax rates of return for the three investments are

Investment Choice	Computation	After-Tax Rate of Return
High-dividend stock	$8.5\% \times (1 - 20\%) =$	6.8%
Corporate bond	$9\% \times (1 - 32\%) =$	6.1
Municipal bond	$6\% \times (1 - 0\%) =$	6.0

Accordingly, Bill should choose the dividend-yielding stock.

What marginal tax rate on ordinary income would make Bill indifferent between the dividend-yielding stock and the corporate bond?

Answer: The dividend-yielding stock has an after-tax rate return of 6.8 percent. For Bill to be indifferent between this stock and the corporate bond, the corporate bond would need a 6.8 percent after-tax rate of return. We can use Equation 3-4 to solve for the marginal tax rate.

After-Tax Rate of Return = Before-Tax Rate of Return × (1 − Marginal Tax Rate)

6.8% = 9% × (1 − Marginal Tax Rate)

Marginal Tax Rate = 24.44%

Let's check this answer: After-Tax Rate of Return = 9% × (1 − 24.44%) = 6.8%

Example 3-10 shows how taxpayers may compare investments when the investment period is one year. However, when taxpayers hold investments for more than a year they potentially receive benefits from combining the timing strategy and the conversion strategy. First, they may be able to defer recognizing gains on the assets until they sell them—the longer the deferral period, the lower the present value of the tax when taxpayers ultimately sell the assets. Second, they may pay taxes on the gains at preferential rates. For example, taxpayers who invest in a corporate stock (capital asset) that does not pay dividends will defer gain on any stock appreciation until they sell the stock, and because it is a capital asset held longer than one year, their gains will be taxed at the lower preferential tax rate for long-term capital gains. These tax advantages provide taxpayers with a greater after-tax rate of return on these investments than they would obtain from less tax-favored assets that earn equivalent before-tax rates of return. Investors who quickly sell investments pay taxes on gains at higher, ordinary rates and incur significantly greater transaction costs. Nevertheless, taxpayers should balance the tax benefits available for holding assets with the risk that the asset values will have declined by the time they want to sell the assets.

To compare investments with differing time horizons, taxpayers use the annualized after-tax rate of return. In general, the after-tax rate of return on any investment is $(FV/I)^{1/n} - 1$ where FV is the future value after taxes, I is the investment (in after-tax dollars), and n is the number of investment periods.[19]

Example 3-11

What if: Assume Bill decides to purchase Intel stock for $50,000 and hold the shares for five years. If the Intel stock grows at a constant 8 percent before-tax rate and does not pay any dividends, how much cash will Bill accumulate after taxes after five years, assuming a long-term capital gains tax rate of 20 percent?

Answer: $68,773, computed as follows:

Description	Amount	Explanation
(1) Proceeds from sale	$ 73,466	$[\$50,000 \times (1 + 0.08)^5]$
(2) Basis in shares	50,000	This is the investment in the shares.
(3) Gain realized on sale	$ 23,466	(1) − (2)
(4) Tax rate on gain	× 20%	Low rate for long-term capital gain*
(5) Tax on gain	$ 4,693	(3) × (4)
After-tax cash after 5 years	**$68,773**	(1) − (5)

*Assumes Bill doesn't have any capital losses.

What annual after-tax rate of return will Bill earn on the money invested?

Answer: 6.58 percent $[(\$68,773/\$50,000)^{1/5} - 1]$.

What if: What would be the after-tax rate of return if Bill held the stock for 18 years?

(*continued on page 3-18*)

[19]Financial calculators designate this calculation as the IRR or internal rate of return.

Answer: 7.03 percent, computed as follows:

Description	Amount	Explanation
(1) Proceeds from sale	$199,801	[$50,000 × (1 + 0.08)^{18}]
(2) Basis in shares	50,000	This is the investment in the shares.
(3) Gain realized on sale	$149,801	(1) − (2)
(4) Tax rate on gain	× 20%	Low rate for long-term capital gain*
(5) Tax on gain	$ 29,960	(3) × (4)
After-tax cash after 18 years	$169,841	(1) − (5)
After-tax rate of return after 18 years	**7.03%**	[($169,841/$50,000)$^{1/18}$ − 1]

*Assumes Bill doesn't have any capital losses.

What if: How does Bill's rate of return on the Intel stock held for five years compare to a taxable corporate bond that pays 9 percent interest annually and is held for five years?

Answer: The annualized rate of return on the stock held for five years is 6.58 percent, as shown above. Because the interest on the taxable corporate bond is taxed annually, the annual after-tax rate of return does not change with the investment horizon and will equal 6.1 percent, as shown in Example 3-10 [9% × (1 − 32%)]. In this situation, the combined tax benefits from the timing and conversion strategies cause the stock investment to generate a higher annualized after-tax return than the taxable corporate bond even though its pretax return is lower.

Limitations of Conversion Strategies

Like other tax planning strategies, conversion strategies face potential limitations. The Internal Revenue Code itself also contains several specific provisions that prevent the taxpayer from changing the nature of expenses, income, or activities to a more tax-advantaged status, including (among many others) the depreciation recapture rules discussed in the Property Dispositions chapter and the luxury auto depreciation rules discussed in the Property Acquisition and Cost Recovery chapter. In addition, as discussed in the Introduction to Tax chapter, implicit taxes may reduce or eliminate the advantages of tax-preferred investments (such as municipal bonds or any investment taxed at preferential tax rates) by decreasing their before-tax rate of returns. Thus, implicit taxes may reduce the advantages of the conversion strategy.

LO 3-6

ADDITIONAL LIMITATIONS TO TAX PLANNING STRATEGIES: JUDICIALLY-BASED DOCTRINES

The IRS has several other doctrines at its disposal for situations in which it expects taxpayer abuse. These doctrines have developed from court decisions and apply across a wide variety of transactions and planning strategies (timing, income shifting, and conversion). The **business purpose doctrine,** for instance, allows the IRS to challenge and disallow business expenses for transactions with no underlying business motivation, such as the travel cost of a spouse accompanying a taxpayer on a business trip. The **step-transaction doctrine** allows the IRS to collapse a series of related transactions into one transaction to determine the tax consequences of the transaction. The **substance-over-form doctrine** allows the IRS to consider the transaction's substance regardless of its form and, where appropriate, to reclassify the transaction according to its substance. Finally, the **economic substance doctrine** requires transactions to meet two criteria to obtain tax benefits. First, a transaction must meaningfully change a taxpayer's economic position (excluding any federal income tax effects). Second, the taxpayer must have a substantial purpose (other than tax avoidance) for the transaction. Economic substance is clearly related to several other doctrines such as the business purpose, step-transaction, and substance-over-form doctrines; however, the economic substance doctrine was incorporated into the Internal Revenue Code in 2010 as §7701(o). This codification standardizes the requirement for transactions to meet both tests. None of the other doctrines have yet been codified.

The courts have been inconsistent with the application of the tests, with some requiring the transaction to meet either the business purpose or economic substance and others requiring that it meet both tests. A key part of the codification of the economic substance doctrine is a stiff penalty of 40 percent of the underpayment for failing to meet the requirements—reduced to 20 percent if the taxpayer makes adequate disclosure. In the Tax Compliance, the IRS, and Tax Authorities chapter, we noted that the Internal Revenue Code is the ultimate tax authority. The business purpose, step-transaction, substance-over-form, and economic substance doctrines allow the IRS to state the tax consequences of transactions that follow only the form of the Internal Revenue Code and not the spirit.

You can often assess whether the business purpose, step-transaction, or substance-over-form doctrines apply by using the "smell test." If the transaction "smells bad," one of these doctrines likely applies. (Transactions usually "smell bad" when the primary purpose is to avoid taxes and not to accomplish an independent business objective.) For example, using the substance-over-form doctrine, the IRS would likely reclassify most of the $10,000 paid to Margaret for answering the phone one Saturday afternoon a month as a gift from Mercedes to Margaret (see the earlier discussion of income shifting and transactions between family members), even though the transaction was structured as compensation and Margaret did do some work for her mother. This recharacterization would unwind the income-shifting benefits for the amount considered to be a gift, because gifts to family members are not tax deductible. In sum, the *substance* of the transaction must be justifiable, not just the form.

TAX AVOIDANCE VERSUS TAX EVASION

Each of the general tax planning strategies discussed in this book falls within the confines of legal **tax avoidance.** Tax avoidance has long been endorsed by the courts and even Congress. Recall, for example, that Congress specifically encourages tax avoidance by excluding municipal bond income from taxation, preferentially taxing dividend and capital gain income, and enacting other provisions. Likewise, the courts have often made it quite clear that taxpayers are under no moral obligation to pay more taxes than required by law. As an example, in *Commissioner v. Newman,* 159 F.2d 848 (2 Cir., 1947), which considered a taxpayer's ability to shift income to his children using trusts, Judge Learned Hand included the following statement in his dissenting opinion:

> Over and over again courts have said that there is nothing sinister in so arranging one's affairs as to keep taxes as low as possible. Everybody does so, rich or poor; and all do right, for nobody owes any public duty to pay more than the law demands: taxes are enforced exactions, not voluntary contributions. To demand more in the name of morals is mere cant.

In contrast to tax avoidance, **tax evasion**—that is, the willful attempt to defraud the government—falls outside the confines of legal tax avoidance and thus may land the perpetrator within the confines of a federal prison. (Recall from the Tax Compliance, the IRS, and Tax Authorities chapter that the rewards of tax evasion include stiff monetary penalties and imprisonment.) When does tax avoidance become tax evasion? Very good question. In many cases a clear distinction exists between avoidance (such as not paying tax on municipal bond interest) and evasion (not paying tax on a $1,000,000 game show prize). In other cases, the line is less clear. In these situations, professional judgment, the use of a smell test, and consideration of the business purpose, step-transaction, substance-over-form, and economic substance doctrines may prove useful.

TAXES IN THE REAL WORLD Cheating the IRS

Few people like to pay taxes, but most of us do so. Some, however, try to cheat the IRS, including the rich and famous (among them, Mike "The Situation" Sorrentino, Chris Tucker, and rapper DMX). Folks who are trying to escape the reach of the IRS may fail to file tax returns, claim deductions to which they're not entitled, make up fake business expenses, or otherwise try to disguise how much money they really made. These tax evaders cost the government a lot of money. The average annual "tax gap" for 2008–2010, the most recent period for which the IRS has estimated the amount of owed taxes that weren't paid on time, is $458 billion (see https://www.irs.gov/newsroom/the-tax-gap).

The main cause of the tax gap is underreporting income, accounting for $376 billion of the IRS's missing money. Not filing returns and underpaying taxes owed were two other causes. Some of that money fails to make it into the hands of the government through innocent accounting mistakes or the inability of taxpayers to pay even though they want to. But some of it goes missing due to deliberate fraud.

In fiscal year (FY) 2016, the IRS initiated 3,395 criminal investigations related to tax code violations (these aren't the same as audits, which are much more common—1.03 million individuals were audited in FY 2016). The number of criminal investigations is relatively small, especially considering the millions of taxpayers in the United States. But once the IRS starts an investigation, there's a good chance it will lead to a conviction and prison time for the offender. The IRS boasts of a 79.5 percent conviction rate (2,699 sentenced/3,395 investigations) on these criminal tax cases.

Source: "Avoid an Audit: 6 Tax Lessons from Celebrities." http://www.cheatsheet.com/personal-finance/5-lessons-from-celebrity-tax-cheats.html/?a=viewall April 4, 2016 and the IRS Criminal Divisions 2016 Annual Report. https://www.irs.gov/pub/foia/ig/ci/2016_annual_report_02092017.pdf.

As you might expect, tax evasion is a major problem for the IRS that vigorous prosecution alone has not been able to solve. Is tax evasion a victimless crime? No. Because the federal government must replace lost tax revenues by imposing higher taxes on others, honest taxpayers are the true victims of tax evasion. Currently, the most recent federal government estimates indicate that tax evasion costs the federal government more than $450 billion annually in lost tax revenues. As citizens and residents of the United States, each of us must recognize our obligation to support our country. As future accountants and business professionals, we also must recognize the inherent value of high ethical standards, which call for us to do the right thing in *all* situations. Business professionals have learned over and over that the costs of doing otherwise far exceed any short-term gains.

CONCLUSION

In this chapter we discussed three basic tax planning strategies—timing, income shifting, and conversion—and their related limitations. Each of these strategies exploits the variation in taxation across different dimensions. The timing strategy exploits the variation in taxation across time: The real tax costs of income decrease as taxation is deferred; the real tax savings associated with tax deductions increase as tax deductions are accelerated. However, because tax rates may change over time and the tax costs of income and tax savings of deductions vary with tax rates, tax planning should consider the effects of such changes on the timing strategy. The income-shifting strategy exploits the variation in taxation across taxpayers or jurisdictions. The assignment of income doctrine limits aggressive attempts to shift income across taxpayers. In addition, related-party transactions receive close IRS attention given the increased likelihood of taxpayer abuses in these transactions. Finally, the conversion strategy exploits the variation in taxation rates across activities, although implicit taxes may reduce the advantages of this strategy. In addition to limitations specific to each planning strategy, the judicial doctrines of business purpose, step-transaction, and substance-over-form broadly apply to a wide range of transactions and planning strategies.

The timing, income-shifting, and conversion strategies represent the building blocks for the more sophisticated tax strategies that tax professionals employ on a daily basis. Combining an understanding of these basic tax planning strategies with knowledge of our tax law will provide you with the tools necessary to identify, evaluate, and implement tax planning strategies. Throughout the remainder of the text, we will discuss how these strategies can be applied to different transactions.

Summary

Identify the objectives of basic tax planning strategies.   **LO 3-1**

- Effective tax planning maximizes the taxpayer's after-tax wealth while achieving the taxpayer's nontax goals. Maximizing after-tax wealth is not necessarily the same as tax minimization. Maximizing after-tax wealth requires one to consider both the tax and nontax costs and benefits of alternative transactions, whereas tax minimization focuses solely on a single cost (i.e., taxes).
- Virtually every transaction involves three parties: the taxpayer, the other transacting party, and the uninvited silent party that specifies the tax consequences of the transaction (i.e., the government). Astute tax planning requires an understanding of the tax and nontax costs from the taxpayer's *and* the other parties' perspectives.

Apply the timing strategy.   **LO 3-2**

- One of the cornerstones of basic tax planning involves the idea of *timing*—that is, *when* income is taxed or an expense is deducted affects the associated "real" tax costs or savings. This is true for two reasons. First, the timing of when income is taxed or an expense is deducted affects the *present value* of the taxes paid on income or the tax savings on deductions. Second, the tax costs of income and the tax savings from deductions vary as *tax rates* change.
- When tax rates are constant, tax planners prefer to defer income (i.e., to reduce the present value of taxes paid) and accelerate deductions (i.e., to increase the present value of tax savings). Higher tax rates, higher rates of return, larger transaction amounts, and the ability to accelerate deductions or defer income by two or more years increase the benefits of the timing strategy.
- When tax rates change, the timing strategy requires a little more consideration because the tax costs of income and the tax savings from deductions vary as *tax rates* change. When tax rates are increasing, the taxpayer must calculate the optimal tax strategies for deductions and income. When tax rates are decreasing, the recommendations are clear. Taxpayers should accelerate tax deductions into earlier years and defer taxable income to later years.
- Timing strategies contain several inherent limitations. Generally speaking, whenever a taxpayer must accelerate a cash outflow to accelerate a deduction, the timing strategy will be less beneficial. Tax law generally requires taxpayers to continue their investment in an asset in order to defer income recognition for tax purposes. A deferral strategy may not be optimal if the taxpayer has severe cash flow needs, if continuing the investment would generate a low rate of return compared to other investments, if the current investment would subject the taxpayer to unnecessary risk, and so on. The constructive receipt doctrine, which provides that a taxpayer must recognize income when it is actually or constructively received, also restricts income deferral for cash-method taxpayers.

LO 3-3 Apply the concept of present value to tax planning.

- The concept of present value—also known as the time value of money—basically states that $1 today is worth *more* than $1 in the future. For example, assuming an investor can earn a positive return (e.g., 5 percent after taxes), $1 invested today should be worth $1.05 in one year. Hence, $1 today is equivalent to $1.05 in one year.
- The implication of the time value of money for tax planning is that the timing of a cash inflow or a cash outflow affects the present value of the income or expense.

LO 3-4 Apply the income shifting strategy.

- The income-shifting strategy exploits the differences in tax rates across taxpayers or jurisdictions. Three of the most common examples of income shifting are high-tax-rate parents shifting income to low-tax-rate children, businesses shifting income to their owners, and taxpayers shifting income from high-tax jurisdictions to low-tax jurisdictions.
- The assignment of income doctrine requires income to be taxed to the taxpayer who actually earns the income. In addition, the IRS closely monitors such related-party transactions—that is, financial activities among family members, among owners and their businesses, or among businesses owned by the same owners. Implicit taxes may also limit the benefits of income shifting via locating in tax-advantaged jurisdictions.

LO 3-5 Apply the conversion strategy.

- Tax law does not treat all types of income or deductions the same. This understanding forms the basis for the conversion strategy—recasting income and expenses to receive the most favorable tax treatment. To implement the conversion strategy, one must be aware of the underlying differences in tax treatment across various types of income, expenses, and activities and have some ability to alter the nature of the income or expense to receive the more advantageous tax treatment.
- Common examples of the conversion strategy include investment planning to invest in assets that generate preferentially taxed income; compensation planning to restructure employee compensation from currently taxable compensation to nontaxable or tax-deferred forms of compensation; and corporate distribution planning to structure corporate distributions to receive the most advantageous tax treatment.
- The Internal Revenue Code contains specific provisions that prevent the taxpayer from changing the nature of expenses, income, or activities to a more tax-advantaged status. Implicit taxes may also reduce or eliminate the advantages of conversion strategies.

LO 3-6 Describe basic judicial doctrines that limit tax planning strategies.

- The constructive receipt doctrine, which may limit the timing strategy, provides that a taxpayer must recognize income when it is actually *or* constructively received. Constructive receipt is deemed to have occurred if the income has been credited to the taxpayer's account or if the income is unconditionally available to the taxpayer, the taxpayer is aware of the income's availability, and there are no restrictions on the taxpayer's control over the income.
- The assignment of income doctrine requires income to be taxed to the taxpayer who actually earns the income. The assignment of income doctrine implies that, in order to shift income to a taxpayer, that taxpayer must actually earn the income.
- The business purpose, step-transaction, and substance-over-form doctrines apply across a wide variety of transactions and planning strategies (timing, income shifting, and conversion).
- The business purpose doctrine allows the IRS to challenge and disallow business expenses for transactions with no underlying business motivation, such as the travel cost of a spouse accompanying a taxpayer on a business trip.
- The step-transaction doctrine allows the IRS to collapse a series of related transactions into one transaction to determine the tax consequences of the transaction.
- The substance-over-form doctrine allows the IRS to consider the transaction's substance regardless of its form and, where appropriate, reclassify the transaction according to its substance.

- The codified economic substance doctrine requires transactions to have a substantial purpose and to meaningfully change a taxpayer's economic position in order for a taxpayer to obtain tax benefits.

Contrast tax avoidance and tax evasion. **LO 3-7**

- Tax avoidance is the legal act of arranging one's transactions, and so on, to minimize taxes paid. Tax evasion is the willful attempt to defraud the government (i.e., by not paying taxes legally owed). Tax evasion falls outside the confines of legal tax avoidance.
- In many cases a clear distinction exists between avoidance (e.g., not paying tax on municipal bond interest) and evasion (e.g., not paying tax on a $1,000,000 game show prize). In other cases, the line between tax avoidance and evasion is less clear. In these situations, professional judgment, the use of a "smell test," and consideration of the business purpose, step-transaction, and substance-over-form doctrines may prove useful.

KEY TERMS

after-tax rate of return (3-3)	constructive receipt doctrine (3-10)	related-party transaction (3-12)
arm's length transactions (3-12)	discount factor (3-3)	step-transaction doctrine (3-18)
assignment of income doctrine (3-12)	economic substance doctrine (3-19)	substance-over-form doctrine (3-18)
before-tax rate of return (3-16)	implicit tax (3-15)	tax avoidance (3-19)
business purpose doctrine (3-18)	present value (3-3)	tax evasion (3-19)

DISCUSSION QUESTIONS

Discussion Questions are available in Connect®.

1. "The goal of tax planning is to minimize taxes." Explain why this statement is not true. **LO 3-1**
2. Describe the three parties engaged in every business transaction and how understanding taxes may aid in structuring transactions. **LO 3-1**
3. In this chapter we discuss three basic tax planning strategies. What different features of taxation does each of these strategies exploit? **LO 3-1**
4. What are the two basic timing strategies? What is the intent of each? **LO 3-2**
5. Why is the timing strategy particularly effective for cash-method taxpayers? **LO 3-2**
6. What are some common examples of the timing strategy? **LO 3-2**
7. What factors increase the benefits of accelerating deductions or deferring income? **LO 3-2**
8. How do changing tax rates affect the timing strategy? What information do you need to determine the appropriate timing strategy when tax rates change? **LO 3-2** **LO 3-3**
9. Describe the ways in which the timing strategy has limitations. **LO 3-2** **LO 3-6**
10. The concept of the time value of money suggests that $1 today is not equal to $1 in the future. Explain why this is true. **LO 3-3**
11. Why is understanding the time value of money important for tax planning? **LO 3-3**
12. What two factors increase the difference between present and future values? **LO 3-3**
13. What factors have to be present for income shifting to be a viable strategy? **LO 3-4**
14. Name three common types of income shifting. **LO 3-4**
15. What are some ways that a parent could effectively shift income to a child? What are some of the disadvantages of these methods? **LO 3-4**
16. What is the key factor in shifting income from a business to its owners? What are some methods of shifting income in this context? **LO 3-4**

LO 3-4 17. Explain why paying dividends is not an effective way to shift income from a corporation to its owners.

LO 3-5 18. What are some of the common examples of the conversion strategy?

LO 3-5 19. What is needed to implement the conversion strategy?

LO 3-5 20. Explain how implicit taxes may limit the benefits of the conversion strategy.

LO 3-5 **LO 3-6**
planning 21. Clark owns stock in BCS Corporation that he purchased in January of the current year. The stock has appreciated significantly during the year. It is now December of the current year, and Clark is deciding whether or not he should sell the stock. What tax and nontax factors should Clark consider before making the decision on whether to sell the stock now?

LO 3-5 22. Do after-tax rates of return for investments in either interest- or dividend-paying securities increase with the length of the investment? Why or why not?

LO 3-5 23. Cameron purchases stock in both Corporation X and Corporation Y. Neither corporation pays dividends. The stocks both earn an identical before-tax rate of return. Cameron sells stock in Corporation X after three years and he sells the stock in Corporation Y after five years. Which investment likely earned a greater after-tax return? Why?

LO 3-5 24. Under what circumstances would you expect the after-tax return from an investment in a capital asset to approach that of tax-exempt assets (assuming equal before-tax rates of return)?

LO 3-5
planning 25. Laurie is thinking about investing in one or several of the following investment options:

Corporate bonds (ordinary interest paid annually)
Dividend-paying stock (qualified dividends)
Life insurance (tax-exempt)
Savings account
Growth stock

a) Assuming all of the options earn similar returns before taxes, rank Laurie's investment options from highest to lowest according to their after-tax returns.
b) Which of the investments employ the deferral and/or conversion tax planning strategies?
c) How does the time period of the investment affect the returns from these alternatives?
d) How do these alternative investments differ in terms of their nontax characteristics?

LO 3-5 26. What is an "implicit tax" and how does it affect a taxpayer's decision to purchase municipal bonds?

LO 3-6 27. Several judicial doctrines limit basic tax planning strategies. What are they? Which planning strategies do they limit?

LO 3-6 28. What is the constructive receipt doctrine? What types of taxpayers does this doctrine generally affect? For what tax planning strategy is the constructive receipt doctrine a potential limitation?

LO 3-6 29. Explain the assignment of income doctrine. In what situations would this doctrine potentially apply?

LO 3-6 30. Relative to arm's-length transactions, why do related-party transactions receive more IRS scrutiny?

LO 3-6 31. Describe the business purpose, step-transaction, and substance-over-form doctrines. What types of tax planning strategies may these doctrines inhibit?

LO 3-7 32. What is the difference between tax avoidance and tax evasion?

LO 3-7 33. What are the rewards of tax avoidance? What are the rewards of tax evasion?

LO 3-7 34. "Tax avoidance is discouraged by the courts and Congress." Is this statement true or false? Please explain.

PROBLEMS

Select problems are available in Connect®.

35. Yong recently paid his accountant $10,000 for elaborate tax planning strategies that exploit the timing strategy. Assuming this is an election year and there could be a power shift in the White House and Congress, what is a potential risk associated with Yong's strategies?

    LO 3-2
    planning

36. Billups, a physician and cash-method taxpayer, is new to the concept of tax planning and recently learned of the timing strategy. To implement the timing strategy, Billups plans to establish a new policy that allows all his clients to wait two years to pay their co-pays. Assume that Billups does not expect his marginal tax rates to change. What is wrong with his strategy?

    LO 3-2   LO 3-3
    planning

37. Tesha works for a company that pays a year-end bonus in January of each year (instead of December of the preceding year) to allow employees to defer the bonus income. Assume Congress recently passed tax legislation that decreases individual tax rates as of next year. Does this increase or decrease the benefits of the bonus deferral this year? What if Congress passed legislation that increased tax rates next year? Should Tesha ask the company to change its policy this year? What additional information do you need to answer this question?

    LO 3-2   LO 3-3
    planning

38. Isabel, a calendar-year taxpayer, uses the cash method of accounting for her sole proprietorship. In late December she received a $20,000 bill from her accountant for consulting services related to her small business. Isabel can pay the $20,000 bill anytime before January 30 of next year without penalty. Assume her marginal tax rate is 40 percent this year and next year, and that she can earn an after-tax rate of return of 12 percent on her investments. When should she pay the $20,000 bill—this year or next?

    LO 3-2   LO 3-3
    planning

39. Using the facts from the previous problem, how would your answer change if Isabel's after-tax rate of return were 8 percent?

    LO 3-2   LO 3-3
    planning

40. Manny, a calendar-year taxpayer, uses the cash method of accounting for his sole proprietorship. In late December he performed $20,000 of legal services for a client. Manny typically requires his clients to pay his bills immediately upon receipt. Assume Manny's marginal tax rate is 37 percent this year and next year, and that he can earn an after-tax rate of return of 12 percent on his investments. Should Manny send his client the bill in December or January?

    LO 3-2   LO 3-3
    planning

41. Using the facts from the previous problem, how would your answer change if Manny's after-tax rate of return were 8 percent?

    LO 3-2   LO 3-3
    planning

42. Reese, a calendar-year taxpayer, uses the cash method of accounting for her sole proprietorship. In late December, she received a $20,000 bill from her accountant for consulting services related to her small business. Reese can pay the $20,000 bill anytime before January 30 of next year without penalty. Assume Reese's marginal tax rate is 32 percent this year and will be 37 percent next year, and that she can earn an after-tax rate of return of 12 percent on her investments. When should she pay the $20,000 bill—this year or next?

    LO 3-2   LO 3-3
    planning

43. Using the facts from the previous problem, when should Reese pay the bill if she expects her marginal tax rate to be 35 percent next year? 24 percent next year?

    LO 3-2   LO 3-3
    planning

44. Hank, a calendar-year taxpayer, uses the cash method of accounting for his sole proprietorship. In late December, he performed $20,000 of legal services for a client. Hank typically requires his clients to pay his bills immediately upon receipt. Assume his marginal tax rate is 32 percent this year and will be 37 percent next year, and that he can earn an after-tax rate of return of 12 percent on his investments. Should Hank send his client the bill in December or January?

    LO 3-2   LO 3-3
    planning

LO 3-2 **LO 3-3**
planning
45. Using the facts from the previous problem, when should Hank send the bill if he expects his marginal tax rate to be 35 percent next year? 24 percent next year?

LO 3-3
46. Geraldo recently won a lottery and chose to receive $100,000 today instead of an equivalent amount in 10 years, computed using an 8 percent rate of return. Today, he learned that interest rates are expected to increase in the future. Is this good news for Geraldo given his decision?

LO 3-3
planning
47. Assume Rafael can earn an 8 percent after-tax rate of return. Would he prefer $1,000 today or $1,500 in five years?

LO 3-3
planning
48. Assume Ellina earns a 10 percent after-tax rate of return and that she owes a friend $1,200. Would she prefer to pay the friend $1,200 today or $1,750 in four years?

LO 3-3
planning
49. Jonah has the choice of paying Rita $10,000 today or $40,000 in 10 years. Assume Jonah can earn a 12 percent after-tax rate of return. Which should he choose?

LO 3-3
planning
50. Bob's Lottery Inc. has decided to offer winners a choice of $100,000 in 10 years or some amount currently. Assume that Bob's Lottery Inc. earns a 10 percent after-tax rate of return. What amount should Bob offer lottery winners currently, in order for him to be indifferent between the two choices?

LO 3-4
planning
51. Tawana owns and operates a sole proprietorship and has a 37 percent marginal tax rate. She provides her son, Jonathon, $8,000 a year for college expenses. Jonathon works as a pizza delivery person every fall and has a marginal tax rate of 15 percent.

a) What could Tawana do to reduce her family tax burden?

b) How much pretax income does it currently take Tawana to generate the $8,000 (after taxes) given to Jonathon?

c) If Jonathon worked for his mother's sole proprietorship, what salary would she have to pay him to generate $8,000 after taxes (ignoring any Social Security, Medicare, or self-employment tax issues)?

d) How much money would the strategy in part (c) save?

LO 3-4
planning
52. Moana is a single taxpayer who operates a sole proprietorship. She expects her taxable income next year to be $250,000, of which $200,000 is attributed to her sole proprietorship. Moana is contemplating incorporating her sole proprietorship. Using the single individual tax brackets and the corporate tax rate, find out how much current tax this strategy could save Moana (ignore any Social Security, Medicare, or self-employment tax issues). How much income should be left in the corporation?

LO 3-4
planning
53. Orie and Jane, husband and wife, operate a sole proprietorship. They expect their taxable income next year to be $450,000, of which $250,000 is attributed to the sole proprietorship. Orie and Jane are contemplating incorporating their sole proprietorship. Using the married-joint tax brackets and the corporate tax rate, find out how much current tax this strategy could save Orie and Jane. How much income should be left in the corporation?

LO 3-4
planning
54. Hyundai is considering opening a plant in two neighboring states. One state has a corporate tax rate of 10 percent. If operated in this state, the plant is expected to generate $1,000,000 pretax profit. The other state has a corporate tax rate of 2 percent. If operated in this state, the plant is expected to generate $930,000 of pretax profit. Which state should Hyundai choose? Why do you think the plant in the state with a lower tax rate would produce a lower before-tax income?

LO 3-4 **LO 3-6**
planning
55. Bendetta, a high-tax-rate taxpayer, owns several rental properties and would like to shift some income to her daughter, Jenine. Bendetta instructs her tenants to send their rent checks to Jenine so Jenine can report the rental income. Will this shift the income from Bendetta to Jenine? Why, or why not?

56. Using the facts in the previous problem, what are some ways that Bendetta could shift some of the rental income to Jenine? What are the disadvantages associated with these income-shifting strategies?

57. Daniel is considering selling two stocks that have not fared well over recent years. A friend recently informed Daniel that one of his stocks has a special designation, which allows him to treat a loss up to $50,000 on this stock as an ordinary loss rather than the typical capital loss. Daniel figures that he has a loss of $60,000 on each stock. If Daniel's marginal tax rate is 35 percent and he has $120,000 of other capital gains (taxed at 15 percent), what is the tax savings from the special tax treatment?

58. Dennis is currently considering investing in municipal bonds that earn 6 percent interest, or in taxable bonds issued by the Coca-Cola Company that pay 8 percent. If Dennis's tax rate is 22 percent, which bond should he choose? Which bond should he choose if his tax rate is 32 percent? At what tax rate would he be indifferent between the bonds? What strategy is this decision based upon?

59. Helen holds 1,000 shares of Fizbo Inc. stock that she purchased 11 months ago. The stock has done very well and has appreciated $20/share since Helen bought the stock. When sold, the stock will be taxed at capital gains rates (the long-term rate is 15 percent and the short-term rate is the taxpayer's marginal tax rate). If Helen's marginal tax rate is 35 percent, how much would she save by holding the stock an additional month before selling? What might prevent Helen from waiting to sell?

60. Anne's marginal income tax rate is 32 percent. She purchases a corporate bond for $10,000 and the maturity, or face value, of the bond is $10,000. If the bond pays 5 percent per year before taxes, what is Anne's annual after-tax rate of return from the bond if the bond matures in one year? What is her annual after-tax rate of return if the bond matures in 10 years?

61. Irene is saving for a new car she hopes to purchase either four or six years from now. Irene invests $10,000 in a growth stock that does not pay dividends and expects a 6 percent annual before-tax return (the investment is tax deferred). When she cashes in the investment after either four or six years, she expects the applicable marginal tax rate on long-term capital gains to be 25 percent.

   a) What will be the value of this investment four years from now? Six years from now?

   b) When Irene sells the investment, how much cash will she have after taxes to purchase the new car (four and six years from now)?

62. Komiko Tanaka invests $12,000 in LymaBean, Inc. LymaBean does not pay any dividends. Komiko projects that her investment will generate a 10 percent before-tax rate of return. She plans to invest for the long term.

   a) How much cash will Komiko retain, after taxes, if she holds the investment for five years and then sells it when the long-term capital gains rate is 15 percent?

   b) What is Komiko's after-tax rate of return on her investment in part (a)?

   c) How much cash will Komiko retain, after taxes, if she holds the investment for five years and then sells when the long-term capital gains rate is 25 percent?

   d) What is Komiko's after-tax rate of return on her investment in part (c)?

   e) How much cash will Komiko retain, after taxes, if she holds the investment for 15 years and then sells when the long-term capital gains rate is 15 percent?

   f) What is Komiko's after-tax rate of return on her investment in part (e)?

63. Alan inherited $100,000 with the stipulation that he "invest it to financially benefit his family." Alan and his wife Alice decided they would invest the inheritance to help them accomplish two financial goals: purchasing a Park City vacation home and saving for their son Cooper's education.

	Vacation Home	Cooper's Education
Initial investment	$50,000	$50,000
Investment horizon	5 years	18 years

Alan and Alice have a marginal income tax rate of 32 percent (capital gains rate of 15 percent) and have decided to investigate the following investment opportunities.

	5 Years	Annual After-Tax Rate of Return	18 Years	Annual After-Tax Rate of Return
Corporate bonds (ordinary interest taxed annually)	5.75%		4.75%	
Dividend-paying stock (no appreciation and dividends are taxed at 15%)	3.50%		3.50%	
Growth stock	FV = $65,000		FV = $140,000	
Municipal bond (tax-exempt)	3.20%		3.10%	

Complete the two annual after-tax rates of return columns for each investment and provide investment recommendations for Alan and Alice.

64. Duff is really interested in decreasing his tax liability, and by his very nature he is somewhat aggressive. A friend of a friend told him that cash transactions are more difficult for the IRS to identify and, thus, tax. Duff is contemplating using this "strategy" of not reporting cash collected in his business to minimize his tax liability. Is this tax planning? What are the risks with this strategy?

65. Using the facts from the previous problem, how would your answer change if, instead, Duff adopted the cash method of accounting to allow him to better control the timing of his cash receipts and disbursements?

66. Using an available tax service or the Internet, identify three basic tax planning ideas or tax tips suggested for year-end tax planning. Which basic tax strategy from this chapter does each planning idea employ?

67. Jayanna, an advertising consultant, is contemplating instructing some of her clients to pay her in cash so that she does not have to report the income on her tax return. Use an available tax service to identify the three basic elements of tax evasion and penalties associated with tax evasion. Write a memo to Jayanna explaining tax evasion and the risks associated with her actions.

68. Using the IRS website (https://www.irs.gov/uac/The-Tax-Gap), how large is the current estimated "tax gap" (i.e., the amount of tax underpaid by taxpayers annually)? What group of taxpayers represents the largest "contributors" to the tax gap?

ROGER | *CPA Review*

Sample CPA Exam questions from Roger CPA Review are available in Connect as support for the topics in this text. These Multiple Choice Questions and Task-Based Simulations include expert-written explanations and solutions and provide a starting point for students to become familiar with the content and functionality of the actual CPA Exam.

Individual Income Tax Overview, Dependents, and Filing Status

Learning Objectives

Upon completing this chapter, you should be able to:

LO 4-1 Describe the formula for calculating an individual taxpayer's taxes payable or refund.

LO 4-2 Explain the requirements for determining who qualifies as a taxpayer's dependent.

LO 4-3 Determine a taxpayer's filing status.

©Creatas Images/Getty Images

Tara Hall just completed a unit on individual taxation in her undergraduate tax class at South Dakota State University. She was excited to share her knowledge with her parents, Rodney and Anita Hall, as they prepared their tax return. Rodney and Anita have been married for over 25 years, and they have filed a joint tax return each year. The Halls' 12-year-old son Braxton lives at home but Tara, who is 21, lives nearby in the university dorms. Further, in January of this year, Rodney's younger brother Shawn moved in with the Halls. The Halls expect Shawn to live with them for at least one year and maybe two. Every year Rodney and Anita use tax-preparation software to complete their tax return, but they are not always sure they understand the final result. This year, with Tara's help, they hope that will change. ∎

Storyline Summary

Taxpayers:	Rodney and Anita Hall
Other household members:	Tara, their 21-year-old daughter, and Braxton, their 12-year-old son. Shawn, Rodney's brother, also lives with the Halls.
Location:	Brookings, South Dakota
Employment status:	Rodney is a manager for a regional grocery chain. His annual salary is $74,000. Anita works as a purchasing-card auditor at South Dakota State University. Her annual salary is $56,000.
Current situation:	Determining their tax liability

This chapter and the next four discuss the fundamental elements of the individual income tax formula. This is the overview chapter; the other chapters provide more depth on individual income tax topics. Here we introduce the individual income tax formula, summarize its components, describe requirements for determining who qualifies as a taxpayer's dependent, and explain how to determine a taxpayer's filing status. The Gross Income and Exclusions chapter explains gross income, the chapters on individual deductions describe deductible expenses to determine adjusted gross income and taxable income. Finally, the Individual Income Tax Computation and Tax Credits chapter addresses issues associated with calculating a taxpayer's tax liability and discusses tax return filing concerns.

LO 4-1   THE INDIVIDUAL INCOME TAX FORMULA

Each year, individuals file tax returns to report their **taxable income,** the tax base for the individual income tax, to the Internal Revenue Service.[1] Exhibit 4-1 presents a simplified formula for calculating taxable income. As we discuss in more detail below, this formula reflects recent tax law changes.

EXHIBIT 4-1   Individual Tax Formula

	Gross income
Minus:	*For AGI (above the line) deductions*
Equals:	Adjusted gross income (AGI)
Minus:	*From AGI (below the line) deductions:*
	(1) *Greater* of
	(a) Standard deduction or
	(b) Itemized deductions and
	(2) Deduction for qualified business income
Equals:	Taxable income
Times:	Tax rates
Equals:	Income tax liability
Plus:	Other taxes
Equals:	Total tax
Minus:	Credits
Minus:	Prepayments
Equals:	Taxes due or (refund)

Beginning with gross income, this formula is embedded in the first two pages of the individual income tax Form 1040, the form individuals generally use to report their taxable income.[2] Exhibit 4-2 presents the first two pages of the 2017 Form 1040 edited to replace the line on page 2 for personal and dependency exemption deductions with the deduction for qualified business income. The 2018 tax forms, which will reflect recent tax law changes, were unavailable at the time we went to press. The last line on page 1 of Form 1040 is **adjusted gross income (AGI),** an important reference point in the income tax formula. Let's look at the components of the individual tax formula and provide a brief description of each of the key elements.

Gross Income

The U.S. tax laws are based on the **all-inclusive income concept.** Under this concept, **gross income** generally includes all **realized income** from *whatever source derived.*[3] Realized income is income generated in a transaction with a second party in which there

[1]See Exhibit 1 in the Tax Compliance, the IRS, and Tax Authorities chapter for a description of who must file a tax return.

[2]To see the 1913 version of the individual tax form, go to http://www.irs.gov/pub/irs-utl/1913.pdf.

[3]§61(a).

Form **1040** Department of the Treasury—Internal Revenue Service (99)
U.S. Individual Income Tax Return **2017** OMB No. 1545-0074 | IRS Use Only—Do not write or staple in this space.

For the year Jan. 1–Dec. 31, 2017, or other tax year beginning _____ , 2017, ending _____ , 20 ___

See separate instructions.

Your first name and initial | Last name | **Your social security number**

If a joint return, spouse's first name and initial | Last name | **Spouse's social security number**

Home address (number and street). If you have a P.O. box, see instructions. | Apt. no.

▲ Make sure the SSN(s) above and on line 6c are correct.

City, town or post office, state, and ZIP code. If you have a foreign address, also complete spaces below (see instructions).

Presidential Election Campaign
Check here if you, or your spouse if filing jointly, want $3 to go to this fund. Checking a box below will not change your tax or refund. ☐ You ☐ Spouse

Foreign country name | Foreign province/state/county | Foreign postal code

Filing Status

Check only one box.

1 ☐ Single
2 ☐ Married filing jointly (even if only one had income)
3 ☐ Married filing separately. Enter spouse's SSN above and full name here. ▶
4 ☐ Head of household (with qualifying person). (See instructions.)
If the qualifying person is a child but not your dependent, enter this child's name here. ▶
5 ☐ Qualifying widow(er) (see instructions)

Exemptions

6a ☐ **Yourself.** If someone can claim you as a dependent, **do not** check box 6a . . . . .
b ☐ **Spouse** . . . .

Boxes checked on 6a and 6b

c **Dependents:**

(1) First name Last name	(2) Dependent's social security number	(3) Dependent's relationship to you	(4) ✓ if child under age 17 qualifying for child tax credit (see instructions)
			☐
			☐
			☐
			☐

If more than four dependents, see instructions and check here ▶ ☐

No. of children on 6c who:
• lived with you
• did not live with you due to divorce or separation (see instructions)

Dependents on 6c not entered above

d Total number of exemptions claimed . . . .

Add numbers on lines above ▶

Income

Attach Form(s) W-2 here. Also attach Forms W-2G and 1099-R if tax was withheld.

If you did not get a W-2, see instructions.

7 Wages, salaries, tips, etc. Attach Form(s) W-2 . . . . | 7
8a **Taxable** interest. Attach Schedule B if required . . . . | 8a
b **Tax-exempt** interest. **Do not** include on line 8a . . . | 8b
9a Ordinary dividends. Attach Schedule B if required . . . . | 9a
b Qualified dividends . . . . | 9b
10 Taxable refunds, credits, or offsets of state and local income taxes . . . . . | 10
11 Alimony received . . . . | 11
12 Business income or (loss). Attach Schedule C or C-EZ . . . . | 12
13 Capital gain or (loss). Attach Schedule D if required. If not required, check here ▶ ☐ | 13
14 Other gains or (losses). Attach Form 4797 . . . . | 14
15a IRA distributions . | 15a | b Taxable amount . . . | 15b
16a Pensions and annuities | 16a | b Taxable amount . . . | 16b
17 Rental real estate, royalties, partnerships, S corporations, trusts, etc. Attach Schedule E | 17
18 Farm income or (loss). Attach Schedule F . . . . | 18
19 Unemployment compensation . . . . | 19
20a Social security benefits | 20a | b Taxable amount . . . | 20b
21 Other income. List type and amount _____ | 21
22 Combine the amounts in the far right column for lines 7 through 21. This is your **total income** ▶ | 22

Adjusted Gross Income

23 Educator expenses | 23
24 Certain business expenses of reservists, performing artists, and fee-basis government officials. Attach Form 2106 or 2106-EZ | 24
25 Health savings account deduction. Attach Form 8889 . | 25
26 Moving expenses. Attach Form 3903 . . . . . . | 26
27 Deductible part of self-employment tax. Attach Schedule SE . | 27
28 Self-employed SEP, SIMPLE, and qualified plans . . | 28
29 Self-employed health insurance deduction . . . | 29
30 Penalty on early withdrawal of savings . . . . . | 30
31a Alimony paid **b** Recipient's SSN ▶ | 31a
32 IRA deduction . . . . | 32
33 Student loan interest deduction . . . . | 33
34 Reserved for future use . . . . | 34
35 Domestic production activities deduction. Attach Form 8903 | 35
36 Add lines 23 through 35 . . . . | 36
37 Subtract line 36 from line 22. This is your **adjusted gross income** . . . . . ▶ | 37

For Disclosure, Privacy Act, and Paperwork Reduction Act Notice, see separate instructions. | Cat. No. 11320B | Form **1040** (2017)

(continued)

EXHIBIT 4-2   Form 1040, pages 1 and 2 (*continued*)

Form 1040 (2017)   Page **2**

Tax and Credits	38	Amount from line 37 (adjusted gross income)	38	
	39a	Check if: ☐ **You** were born before January 2, 1953, ☐ Blind. ☐ **Spouse** was born before January 2, 1953, ☐ Blind. } **Total boxes checked ▶ 39a**		
	b	If your spouse itemizes on a separate return or you were a dual-status alien, check here ▶ 39b ☐		
Standard Deduction for— • People who check any box on line 39a or 39b **or** who can be claimed as a dependent, see instructions. • All others: Single or Married filing separately, $6,350 Married filing jointly or Qualifying widow(er), $12,700 Head of household, $9,350	40	**Itemized deductions** (from Schedule A) **or** your **standard deduction** (see left margin)	40	
	41	Subtract line 40 from line 38	41	
	42	**Exemptions.** If line 38 is $156,900 or less, multiply $4,050 by the number on line 6d. Otherwise, see instructions	42	
	43	**Taxable income.** Subtract line 42 from line 41. If line 42 is more than line 41, enter -0-	43	
	44	**Tax** (see instructions). Check if any from: **a** ☐ Form(s) 8814 **b** ☐ Form 4972 **c** ☐	44	
	45	**Alternative minimum tax** (see instructions). Attach Form 6251	45	
	46	Excess advance premium tax credit repayment. Attach Form 8962	46	
	47	Add lines 44, 45, and 46 ▶	47	
	48	Foreign tax credit. Attach Form 1116 if required	48	
	49	Credit for child and dependent care expenses. Attach Form 2441	49	
	50	Education credits from Form 8863, line 19	50	
	51	Retirement savings contributions credit. Attach Form 8880	51	
	52	Child tax credit. Attach Schedule 8812, if required	52	
	53	Residential energy credit. Attach Form 5695	53	
	54	Other credits from Form: **a** ☐ 3800 **b** ☐ 8801 **c** ☐	54	
	55	Add lines 48 through 54. These are your **total credits**	55	
	56	Subtract line 55 from line 47. If line 55 is more than line 47, enter -0- ▶	56	
Other Taxes	57	Self-employment tax. Attach Schedule SE	57	
	58	Unreported social security and Medicare tax from Form: **a** ☐ 4137 **b** ☐ 8919	58	
	59	Additional tax on IRAs, other qualified retirement plans, etc. Attach Form 5329 if required	59	
	60a	Household employment taxes from Schedule H	60a	
	b	First-time homebuyer credit repayment. Attach Form 5405 if required	60b	
	61	Health care: individual responsibility (see instructions) Full-year coverage ☐	61	
	62	Taxes from: **a** ☐ Form 8959 **b** ☐ Form 8960 **c** ☐ Instructions; enter code(s)	62	
	63	Add lines 56 through 62. This is your **total tax** ▶	63	
Payments If you have a qualifying child, attach Schedule EIC.	64	Federal income tax withheld from Forms W-2 and 1099	64	
	65	2017 estimated tax payments and amount applied from 2016 return	65	
	66a	**Earned income credit (EIC)**	66a	
	b	Nontaxable combat pay election 66b		
	67	Additional child tax credit. Attach Schedule 8812	67	
	68	American opportunity credit from Form 8863, line 8	68	
	69	Net premium tax credit. Attach Form 8962	69	
	70	Amount paid with request for extension to file	70	
	71	Excess social security and tier 1 RRTA tax withheld	71	
	72	Credit for federal tax on fuels. Attach Form 4136	72	
	73	Credits from Form: **a** ☐ 2439 **b** ☐ Reserved **c** ☐ 8885 **d** ☐	73	
	74	Add lines 64, 65, 66a, and 67 through 73. These are your **total payments** ▶	74	
Refund Direct deposit? See instructions.	75	If line 74 is more than line 63, subtract line 63 from line 74. This is the amount you **overpaid**	75	
	76a	Amount of line 75 you want **refunded to you.** If Form 8888 is attached, check here ▶ ☐	76a	
	▶ b	Routing number ___ ▶ c Type: ☐ Checking ☐ Savings		
	▶ d	Account number ___		
	77	Amount of line 75 you want **applied to your 2018 estimated tax ▶** 77		
Amount You Owe	78	**Amount you owe.** Subtract line 74 from line 63. For details on how to pay, see instructions ▶	78	
	79	Estimated tax penalty (see instructions) 79		

Third Party Designee
Do you want to allow another person to discuss this return with the IRS (see instructions)?   ☐ **Yes.** Complete below.   ☐ **No**
Designee's name ▶   Phone no. ▶   Personal identification number (PIN) ▶ _____

Sign Here
Joint return? See instructions. Keep a copy for your records.

Under penalties of perjury, I declare that I have examined this return and accompanying schedules and statements, and to the best of my knowledge and belief, they are true, correct, and accurately list all amounts and sources of income I received during the tax year. Declaration of preparer (other than taxpayer) is based on all information of which preparer has any knowledge.

Your signature	Date	Your occupation	Daytime phone number
Spouse's signature. If a joint return, **both** must sign.	Date	Spouse's occupation	If the IRS sent you an Identity Protection PIN, enter it here (see inst.)

Paid Preparer Use Only

Print/Type preparer's name	Preparer's signature		Date	Check ☐ if self-employed	PTIN
Firm's name ▶				Firm's EIN ▶	
Firm's address ▶				Phone no.	

Go to *www.irs.gov/Form1040* for instructions and the latest information.   Form **1040** (2017)

is a measurable change in property rights between parties (for example, appreciation in a stock investment would not represent realized income unless the taxpayer sold the stock).

Certain tax provisions allow taxpayers to permanently exclude specific types of realized income from gross income (excluded income items are never taxable) and other provisions allow taxpayers to defer including certain types of realized income items in gross income until a subsequent year (deferred income items are included in gross income in a later year). Realized income items that taxpayers permanently exclude from taxation are referred to as **exclusions.** Realized income items that taxpayers include in gross income in a subsequent year are called **deferrals.** Exhibit 4-3 provides a partial listing of common income items included in gross income, their character (discussed below), and where in the text we provide more detail on each income item. Exhibit 4-4 provides a partial listing of common exclusions and deferrals and indicates where in the text we discuss each in more detail.

EXHIBIT 4-3   Partial Listing of Common Income Items

Income Item	Character	Discussed in More Detail in These Chapters
Compensation for services including fringe benefits	Ordinary	Gross Income and Exclusions
Business income	Ordinary	Business Income, Deductions, and Accounting Methods
Gains from selling property	Ordinary or capital[4]	Gross Income and Exclusions and Property Dispositions
Interest and dividends	Ordinary or qualified dividend	Gross Income and Exclusions
Rents and royalties	Ordinary	Gross Income and Exclusions, and Individual For AGI Deductions
Alimony (pre-2019 decree) and annuities	Ordinary	Gross Income and Exclusions
Income from the discharge of indebtedness	Ordinary	Gross Income and Exclusions

EXHIBIT 4-4   Partial Listing of Common Exclusions and Deferrals

Exclusion or Deferral Item	Exclusion or Deferral	Discussed in These Chapters
Interest income from municipal bonds	Exclusion	Gross Income and Exclusions
Gift and inheritance	Exclusion	Gross Income and Exclusions
Gain on sale of personal residence	Exclusion	Gross Income and Exclusions
Life insurance proceeds	Exclusion	Gross Income and Exclusions
Installment sale	Deferral	Property Dispositions
Like-kind exchange	Deferral	Property Dispositions

Character of Income   While gross income increases taxable income dollar for dollar, certain types of gross income are treated differently than other types of gross income for purposes of computing a taxpayer's taxable income and income tax liability. For example, one type of income may be taxed at a different rate than another type of

---

[4]Dispositions of assets used in a trade or business for more than a year generate an intermediate character of income called §1231 gain or loss. Ultimately, §1231 gains and losses are treated as either ordinary or capital on the tax return.

income. The *type* of income is commonly referred to as the **character of income.** The most common characters of income are as follows:

- Ordinary: This is income or loss that is taxed at the ordinary rates provided in the tax rate schedules in Appendix D, or that offsets income taxed at these rates, and is not capital in character.

- Capital: These are gains or losses on the disposition or sale of capital assets. In general, capital assets are all assets *other than*

    1. Accounts receivable from the sale of goods or services.
    2. Inventory and other assets held for sale in the ordinary course of business.
    3. Assets used in a trade or business, including supplies.[5]

Nonbusiness assets such as personal-use automobiles or personal residences and assets held for investment such as stocks and bonds are capital assets.

Capital gains and losses are further characterized as long-term (when the taxpayer owns the capital asset for more than one year before selling it) or short-term (when the taxpayer owns the capital asset for one year or less before selling it). A gain on a sale of a capital asset is generally included in gross income. If the gain is a long-term capital gain, it is generally taxed at a 15 percent tax rate (taxed at 20 percent for high-income taxpayers and 0 percent for low-income taxpayers). If the gain is a short-term capital gain, the gain is taxed at ordinary income rates. Note that even though a short-term capital gain is taxed at ordinary rates, it is still considered to be a capital gain and not ordinary income.

A loss on the sale of a capital asset—no matter how long the taxpayer holds the asset before selling—generates a deduction for the taxpayer in the year of sale (a *for* AGI deduction, as discussed below). However, the deduction for the loss is limited to $3,000 for the year (losses in excess of the limit are carried forward indefinitely). If the taxpayer sells a personal-use asset like a personal automobile or personal residence at a loss, the loss is not deductible.

When a taxpayer sells more than one capital asset during the year, the gains and losses are netted together. A net loss is subject to the $3,000 annual deduction limit. A net gain may be taxed at 15, 20, or 0 percent or at the ordinary rates depending on the outcome of the netting process and the taxpayer's taxable income. We discuss the netting process in detail in the Investments chapter.[6]

- Qualified dividend: Shareholders receiving dividends from corporations include the dividend income in gross income. If the dividend meets the qualified dividend requirements, it is generally taxed at a rate of 15 percent (taxed at 20 percent for high-income taxpayers and 0 percent for low-income taxpayers).[7] If a dividend does not meet the qualified dividend requirement, it is taxed at ordinary rates. Because qualified dividends (and long-term capital gains) are taxed at a **preferential tax rate** (a rate lower than the ordinary income rate), qualified dividends (and long-term capital gains) can be referred to as **preferentially taxed income.** While qualified dividends are taxed at the same rate as long-term capital gains, qualified dividends are not included in the capital gain and loss netting process. Therefore, qualified dividend is a separate and distinct character from capital.

Example 4-1

Rodney earned a salary of $74,000, and Anita earned a salary of $56,000. The Halls also received $600 of interest income from investments in corporate bonds and $300 of interest income from investments in municipal bonds. This was their only realized income during the year. What is the Halls' gross income?

---

[5]See §1221(a) for the definition of a capital asset.

[6]As we discover in the Investments chapter, certain capital gains may be taxed at a maximum rate of 25 percent and others may be taxed at a maximum rate of 28 percent.

[7]A qualified dividend generally includes dividends distributed by a U.S. corporation if the shareholder meets certain holding period requirements for the stock. These requirements are discussed in more detail in the Investments chapter.

Answer: $130,600, computed as follows:

Description	Amount	Explanation
(1) Rodney's salary	$ 74,000	
(2) Anita's salary	56,000	
(3) Interest from corporate bonds	600	
Gross income	**$130,600***	(1) + (2) + (3)

*The $300 of interest income from municipal bonds is excluded from gross income.

What is the character of the salary, the interest income from the corporate bonds, and the interest income from the investments in municipal bonds?

Answer: The salary and interest income from corporate bonds are ordinary income. The interest income from the municipal bonds is excluded from gross income.

What if: Suppose this year the Halls sold shares of stock in XYZ Corporation at a $4,000 gain (their only transaction involving a capital asset). They purchased the stock three years ago. What would be the character of the gain? At what rate would the gain be taxed?

Answer: This is a long-term capital gain because stock is a capital asset and the Halls owned the stock for more than a year before selling. Given their income level, the gain would be taxed at a maximum rate of 15 percent.

What if: Suppose this year the Halls sold stock at a $4,000 loss (their only transaction involving a capital asset). They purchased the stock three years ago. What is the character of the loss? How much of the loss may the Halls deduct this year?

Answer: This is a long-term capital loss, because the stock is a capital asset and the Halls owned the stock for more than a year before selling. The Halls can deduct $3,000 of the loss as a *for* AGI deduction this year. The remaining $1,000 loss is carried over to next year.

What if: Suppose this year the Halls sold a personal automobile at a $4,000 loss. They purchased the automobile three years ago. What is the character of the loss? How much of the loss may the Halls deduct in the current year?

Answer: This is a long-term capital loss, because the automobile is a capital asset and the Halls owned the auto for more than a year before selling. However, the Halls are not allowed to deduct any of the $4,000 loss this year or any year because the automobile is a personal-use asset.

Deductions

Deductions reduce a taxpayer's taxable income. However, they are not necessarily easy to come by because, in contrast to the all-inclusive treatment of income, deductions are *not allowed unless a specific tax law allows them*. Thus, deductions are a matter of **legislative grace.** The tax laws provide for two distinct types of deductions in the individual tax formula: for adjusted gross income (AGI) deductions and from AGI deductions. As indicated in the individual tax formula, gross income minus **for AGI deductions** equals AGI, and AGI minus **from AGI deductions** equals taxable income. Congress identifies whether the deductions are *for* or *from* AGI when it enacts new legislation that grants deductions. The distinction between the deduction types is particularly important because AGI is a reference point often used in determining the extent to which taxpayers are allowed to claim certain tax benefits. For example, taxpayers with AGI in excess of certain thresholds lose tax benefits from items such as the child tax credit and education credits (we discuss credits below).

For AGI Deductions

For AGI deductions tend to be deductions associated with business activities and certain investing activities. Because *for* AGI deductions reduce AGI (deducted on page 1 of Form 1040), they are referred to as **"deductions above the line."** The "line" in this case is AGI, which is the last line on page 1 of Form 1040 (see Exhibit 4-2). Prior to 2018, moving expenses were a common for AGI deduction. However, the recent tax law eliminated moving expenses as a deduction for all taxpayers but members of the armed forces. Exhibit 4-5 provides a partial listing of common *for* AGI deductions under new tax law and indicates where in the text we discuss them.

THE KEY FACTS

For and From AGI Deductions

- *For* AGI deductions
  - Reduce AGI.
  - Are referred to as deductions "above the line."
  - Are generally more valuable than *from* AGI deductions.
- *From* AGI deductions
  - Deduct *from* AGI to determine taxable income.
  - Are referred to as deductions "below the line."

EXHIBIT 4-5 **Partial Listing of Common *for* AGI Deductions**

For AGI Deduction	Discussed in More Detail in These Chapters
Alimony paid (pre-2019 decree)	Individual For AGI Deductions
Health insurance deduction for self-employed taxpayers	Individual For AGI Deductions
Rental and royalty expenses	Individual For AGI Deductions
Capital losses (*net* losses limited to $3,000 for the year)	Gross Income and Exclusions
One-half of self-employment taxes paid	Individual Income Tax Computation and Tax Credits
Business expenses	Business Income, Deductions, and Accounting Methods
Losses on dispositions of assets used in a trade or business	Property Dispositions
Contributions to qualified retirement accounts [e.g., 401Ks and individual retirement accounts (IRAs)]	Individual For AGI Deductions

Example 4-2

Rodney made a $5,000 deductible (for AGI) contribution to his individual retirement account (IRA). What is the Halls' adjusted gross income?

Answer: $125,600, computed as follows:

Description	Amount	Explanation
(1) Gross income	$ 130,600	Example 4-1
(2) IRA contribution	(5,000)	*For* AGI deduction (see Exhibit 4-5)
Adjusted gross income	**$125,600**	(1) + (2)

From AGI Deductions From AGI deductions are commonly referred to as **"deductions below the line"** because they are deducted after AGI has been determined (deducted on page 2 of Form 1040). For years prior to 2018, from AGI deductions included **itemized deductions,** the **standard deduction,** and personal and dependency exemptions. However, beginning in 2018 the new tax law added a from AGI deduction that is generally equal to 20 percent of a taxpayer's qualified business income (QBI) and it eliminates the deduction for personal and dependency exemptions. While the deduction for QBI is a from AGI deduction, it is not an itemized deduction. Thus, beginning in 2018, individuals can deduct the QBI deduction and *either* their itemized deductions *or* a fixed amount called the standard deduction as from AGI deductions. Taxpayers generally deduct the higher of the standard deduction or itemized deductions. Exhibit 4-6 identifies the primary categories of itemized deductions.

EXHIBIT 4-6 **Primary Categories of Itemized Deductions**

- *Medical and dental expenses:* Deductible to the extent these expenses exceed 7.5 percent of AGI.
- *Taxes:* State and local income taxes, sales taxes, real estate taxes, personal property taxes, and other taxes (an aggregate $10,000 deduction limitation applies to taxes).
- *Interest expense:* Mortgage and investment interest expense.
- *Gifts to charity (charitable contributions).*
- *Other miscellaneous deductions:* Gambling losses (to the extent of gambling winnings) and certain other deductions.

Note: Itemized deductions are detailed on Schedule A of Form 1040. We discuss itemized deductions in more depth in the Individual From AGI Deductions chapter.

The amount of the standard deduction varies by taxpayer filing status (we discuss filing status in more detail later in the chapter); the government indexes this deduction for inflation. Exhibit 4-7 presents the basic standard deduction amounts by filing status for 2017 and 2018. The new tax law significantly increased the standard deduction amounts for 2018. Special rules may alter the allowable standard deduction for certain taxpayers. We discuss these departures from the basic standard deduction amounts in the Individual From AGI Deductions chapter.

EXHIBIT 4-7 Standard Deduction Amounts by Filing Status*

	2017	2018
Married filing jointly	$12,700	$24,000
Qualifying widow or widower	12,700	24,000
Married filing separately	6,350	12,000
Head of household	9,350	18,000
Single	6,350	12,000

*Married taxpayers 65 years of age or over and/or blind are entitled to an additional standard deduction of $1,300 ($1,300 for age and another $1,300 for blindness); single and head of household taxpayers 65 years of age or over and/or blind are entitled to an additional standard deduction of $1,600 (one for age and another for blindness). (See the Individual From AGI Deductions chapter for more detail.) For individuals claimed as a dependent on another tax return, the 2018 standard deduction is the greater of (1) $1,050 or (2) $350 plus earned income not to exceed the standard deduction amount for those who are not dependents (see the Individual Income Tax Computation and Tax Credits chapter for more detail).

Example 4-3

Rodney and Anita Hall annually file a joint tax return. They paid a total of $11,000 for expenditures that qualified as itemized deductions and they had no qualified business income (QBI). What is the total amount of *from* AGI deductions Rodney and Anita are allowed to deduct on their tax return?

Answer: $24,000, computed as follows:

Description	Amount	Explanation
(1) Standard deduction	$24,000	Married filing joint filing status (see Exhibit 4-7)
(2) Itemized deductions	11,000	
(3) Greater of (1) or (2)	24,000	The standard deduction exceeds itemized deductions.
(4) QBI deduction	0	No qualified business income
Total deductions *from* AGI	**$24,000**	(3) + (4). (Also referred to as deductions "below the line.")

What if: What would be the amount of the Halls' *from* AGI deductions if, instead of the original facts, Rodney and Anita had paid a total of $11,000 in expenditures that qualified as itemized deductions and they were allowed to claim a $1,000 QBI deduction based on $5,000 of qualified business income they reported?

Answer: $25,000, computed as follows:

Description	Amount	Explanation
(1) Standard deduction	$24,000	Married filing joint filing status (see Exhibit 4-7)
(2) Itemized deductions	11,000	
(3) Greater of (1) or (2)	24,000	The standard deduction exceeds itemized deductions.
(4) QBI deduction	1,000	QBI of $5,000 × 20%
Total deductions *from* AGI	**$25,000**	(3) + (4). (Also referred to as deductions "below the line.")

What if: What would be the amount of the Halls' *from* AGI deductions if, instead of the original facts, Rodney and Anita had paid a total of $28,000 in expenditures that qualified as itemized deductions?

(continued on page 4-10)

Answer: $28,000, computed as follows:

Description	Amount	Explanation
(1) Standard deduction	$24,000	Married filing joint filing status (see Exhibit 4-7)
(2) Itemized deductions	28,000	
(3) Greater of (1) or (2)	28,000	The standard deduction exceeds itemized deductions.
(4) QBI deduction	0	No qualified business income
Total deductions *from* AGI	**$28,000**	(3) + (4). (Also referred to as deductions "below the line.")

Income Tax Calculation

After determining taxable income, taxpayers can generally calculate their regular income tax liability using either a **tax table** or a **tax rate schedule,** depending on their filing status and income level (taxpayers with taxable income under $100,000 generally must use the tax tables).[8] See Appendix D for the regular tax rate schedules. However, as we discussed above, certain types of income included in taxable income are taxed at rates different from those in the tables or tax rate schedules. The 2017 tax rate schedules had seven different income tax brackets (10, 15, 25, 28, 33, 35, and 39.6 percent). The 2018 tax rate schedules also have seven different income tax brackets but the rates change for all but the first bracket (10, 12, 22, 24, 32, 35, and 37 percent). Overall, for a given level of taxable income, a taxpayer's tax liability will generally be lower under the 2018 tax rate schedules.

Example 4-4

With Tara's help, the Halls have determined their taxable income to be $101,600, as follows:

Description	Amount	Explanation
(1) Adjusted gross income	$125,600	Example 4-2
(2) *From* AGI deductions	$ (24,000)	Example 4-3
Taxable income	**$101,600**	(1) + (2)

They have also determined that all of their income is ordinary income. What is their tax liability?

Answer: $14,231. See the married filing jointly tax rate schedule in Appendix D. {$8,907 + $5,324 [22% × ($101,600 − $77,400)]}.

What if: Using the tax rate schedules, what would the Halls' tax liability be if their taxable income were $12,000 (all ordinary income)?

Answer: $1,200 ($12,000 × 10%).

What if: Assume that in addition to the $101,600 of ordinary income, the Halls also reported $5,000 of long-term capital gain subject to a 15 percent tax rate. How much tax would they pay on the additional $5,000 gain?

Answer: $750 ($5,000 × 15%). Long-term capital gains (gains on the sale of a capital asset owned for more than a year) are generally taxed at a 15 percent rate. Note that the Halls' taxable income is $106,600. $101,600 of the income is taxed at ordinary rates and $5,000 is taxed at the preferential percent rate.

[8]For administrative convenience and to prevent low- and middle-income taxpayers from making mathematical errors using a rate schedule, the IRS provides tax tables that present the gross tax for various amounts of taxable income. For simplicity, we use the tax rate schedule to determine tax liabilities in the examples presented in this text.

Other Taxes

In addition to the individual income tax, individuals may also be required to pay other taxes such as the **alternative minimum tax (AMT)** or **self-employment taxes.** These taxes are imposed on tax bases other than the individual's regular taxable income. Furthermore, taxpayers with relatively high AGI are subject to a 3.8 percent net investment income tax on unearned (investment) income and a .9 percent additional Medicare tax on earned income. We discuss these taxes in more detail in the Individual Income Tax Computation and Tax Credits chapter.

Tax Credits

Individual taxpayers may reduce their tax liabilities by **tax credits** to determine their total taxes payable. Like deductions, tax credits are specifically granted by Congress and are narrowly defined. Unlike deductions, which reduce *taxable income*, tax credits *directly reduce taxes payable*. Thus, a $1 deduction reduces taxes payable by $1 times the marginal tax rate while a $1 credit reduces taxes payable by $1. Common tax credits include the child tax credit [$2,000 per qualifying child (under the age of 17 at year end), up from $1,000 per child under 2017 tax law and a $500 credit for other qualifying dependents], the child and dependent care credit, the earned income credit, the American opportunity credit, and the lifetime learning credit. We discuss credits in more detail in the Individual Income Tax Computation and Tax Credits chapter.

Tax Prepayments

After calculating the total tax and subtracting their available credits, taxpayers determine their taxes due (or tax refund) by subtracting tax prepayments from the total tax remaining after credits. Tax prepayments include: (1) **withholdings,** or income taxes withheld from the taxpayer's salary or wages by her employer, (2) **estimated tax payments** the taxpayer makes for the year (paid directly to the IRS), and (3) tax that the taxpayer overpaid on the prior-year tax return that the taxpayer elects to apply as an estimated payment for the current tax year instead of receiving as a refund.

   If tax prepayments exceed the total tax after subtracting credits, the taxpayer receives a tax refund (or elects to apply the refund as an estimated tax payment) for the difference. If tax prepayments are less than the total tax after credits, the taxpayer owes additional tax and potentially a penalty for the underpayment.

Example 4-5

Based on their calculation in Example 4-4, Rodney and Anita Hall's tax liability is $14,231. The Halls had $12,100 of federal income taxes withheld by their employers from their paychecks and are able to claim a $2,000 child tax credit for their 12-year-old son Braxton and a $500 child tax credit for Tara. What is the Halls' tax due or tax refund?

Answer: $369 tax refund, computed as follows:

Description	Amount	Explanation
(1) Tax liability	$ 14,231	Example 4-4
(2) Tax credits	(2,500)	Child tax credit: $2,000 for Braxton and $500 for Tara.
(3) Tax prepayments	(12,100)	
Tax refund	**$ (369)**	(1) + (2) + (3)

Although it is not explicitly stated in the individual tax formula, a taxpayer's filing status affects many parts of the tax formula, including the standard deduction amount and the applicable income tax rate schedule, among others. In the next section, we describe the rules for determining a taxpayer's filing status. However, because a taxpayer's filing status may depend on whether the taxpayer has dependents for tax purposes, we first discuss how to identify who qualifies as a taxpayer's dependent.

LO 4-2   DEPENDENTS OF THE TAXPAYER

For 2017, taxpayers could claim and deduct a personal exemption for themselves. Married taxpayers filing jointly could claim and deduct two personal exemptions (one for each spouse). Individual taxpayers could generally claim and deduct a personal exemption for themselves (unless they qualified as a dependent of another taxpayer). Further, to provide some tax relief for those supporting others, a taxpayer was allowed to claim and deduct an exemption for each person who qualified as the taxpayer's dependent. For 2017, taxpayers could deduct (from AGI) $4,050 for each exemption they could claim.

However, under new tax law effective in 2018, the deduction for personal and dependency exemptions is reduced to zero. Nevertheless, as mentioned previously, it remains necessary to determine who qualifies as a dependent of the taxpayer for purposes of determining filing status, eligibility for certain tax credits, and other tax-related computations.

Dependency Requirements

To qualify as a dependent of another, an individual:

1. Must be a citizen of the United States or a resident of the United States, Canada, or Mexico.
2. Must *not* file a joint return with his or her spouse unless there is no tax liability on the couple's joint return and there would not have been any tax liability on either spouse's tax return if they had filed separately.[9]
3. Must be considered either a **qualifying child** *or* a **qualifying relative** of the taxpayer.[10]

While the requirements for determining a qualifying child and a qualifying relative have some similarities, the qualifying relative requirements are broader in scope.

Qualifying Child   To be considered a qualifying child of a taxpayer, an individual must satisfy the following four tests: (1) relationship, (2) age, (3) residence, and (4) support.[11]

Relationship test.   A qualifying child must be an eligible relative of the taxpayer. Eligible relatives include the taxpayer's:

- Child or descendant of a child. For this purpose, a child includes a taxpayer's adopted child, stepchild, and eligible foster child.

---

[9]Rev. Rul. 54-567, 1954-2 C.B. 108.

[10]§152.

[11]Technically, an individual is not eligible to be a qualifying child of another if she filed a joint return with her spouse (other than to claim a refund) [see §152(c)(1)(E)]. However, because this is also a requirement to be claimed as a dependent, we do not discuss the requirement separately here.

- Sibling or descendant of sibling. For this purpose, a sibling includes a taxpayer's half-brother, half-sister, stepbrother, or stepsister.

Under this definition, the taxpayer's grandchild would qualify as an eligible relative, as would the taxpayer's sister's grandchild.

Age test.   A qualifying child must be younger than the taxpayer and *either* (1) under age 19 at the end of the year or (2) under age 24 at the end of the year *and* a full-time student.[12] A person is a full-time student if she was in school full-time during any part of each of five calendar months during the calendar year.[13] An individual of any age who is permanently and totally disabled is deemed to have met the age test.[14]

Residence test.   A qualifying child must have the same principal residence as the taxpayer for *more* than half the year. Time that a child or the taxpayer is *temporarily* away from the taxpayer's home because the child or taxpayer is ill, is pursuing an education, or has other special circumstances is counted as though the child or taxpayer were living in the taxpayer's home.[15]

Support test.   A qualifying child must *not* have provided more than half of his or her *own* support (living expenses) for the year. Such support generally includes:

- Food, school lunches, toilet articles, and haircuts.
- Clothing.
- Recreation—including toys, summer camp, horseback riding, entertainment, and vacation expenses.
- Medical and dental care.
- Child care expenses.
- Allowances and gifts.
- Wedding costs.
- Lodging.
- Education—including board, uniforms at military schools, and tuition. When determining who provided the support for a taxpayer's *child* who is a full-time student, scholarships are excluded from the computation.[16]

Example 4-6

Rodney and Anita have two children: Braxton, age 12, who lives at home, and Tara, age 21, who is a full-time student and does not live at home. Tara earned $9,000 from a summer job, but she did *not* provide more than half of her own support during the year. Are Braxton and Tara qualifying dependent children of Rodney and Anita?

(continued on page 4-14)

---

[12]§152(c)(3)(A).
[13]§152(f)(2).
[14]§152(c)(3)(B).
[15] Reg. §1.152-1(b).
[16]§152(f)(5) and §152(f)(1). This provision requires that the student be a son, daughter, stepson, stepdaughter, or an eligible foster child of the taxpayer.

Answer: Yes, see analysis of factors below:

Test	Braxton	Tara
Relationship	Yes, son.	Yes, daughter.
Age	Yes, under age 19 at end of year (and younger than his parents).	Yes, under age 24 at year-end *and* full-time student (and younger than her parents).
Residence	Yes, lived at home entire year.	Yes, time away at college is considered as time at home if Tara plans to live in her parents' home again at some point (it is a temporary absence).
Support	Yes, does not provide more than half of own support.	Yes, does not provide more than half of own support.

Because they both meet all the requirements, Braxton and Tara are qualifying children to the Halls. So, both Braxton and Tara are the Halls' dependents.

What if: Suppose Tara provided more than half of her own support. Would she be considered a qualifying child of her parents?

Answer: No. She would fail the support test.

What if: Assume the original facts apply but now Tara is age 25. Would she be considered a qualifying dependent child of her parents?

Answer: No. She would fail the age test. Note, however, that Tara could still qualify as her parents' dependent as a qualifying relative (see Example 4-8 below).

What if: Assume the original facts, except now suppose that Braxton is Anita's stepbrother's son. Would Braxton be considered a qualifying dependent child of Rodney and Anita?

Answer: Yes. Braxton meets the relationship test because he is the descendant of Anita's stepbrother (sibling).

Tiebreaking rules. The requirements for determining who is a qualifying child leave open the possibility that one person could be a qualifying child to more than one taxpayer. In these circumstances, the taxpayer who has priority for claiming the person as a dependent is based on the following tiebreaking rules:

1. If the person is a qualifying child of a parent, the parent is entitled to claim the person as a dependent. This situation could arise, for example, when a child lives with her mother *and* her grandparents. In this case, the mother has priority for claiming the the child as a dependent over the grandparents.

2. If the individual is a qualifying child to both parents, the parent with whom the child has resided for the longest period of time during the year has priority for claiming the person as a dependent. This situation may arise in a year when the child lives with both parents for more than half of the year, but the parents separate or divorce in the latter part of the year. Note, however, that for a child of divorced parents, the noncustodial parent (the parent the child does not live with) can claim the child as a dependent qualifying child if the custodial parent signs a form indicating that he or she will not claim the child as a dependent and the noncustodial parent attaches the form to his or her tax return.[17]

3. Finally, if the child resides with each parent for equal amounts of time during the year or the qualifying child resides with a taxpayer who is not the child's parent, the taxpayer with the *highest AGI* has priority for claiming the child as a dependent.[18]

[17]See §152(e). The custodial signs Form 8332, and the noncustodial parent attaches it to his or her tax return.

[18]However, if the parents may claim the child as a qualifying child but no parent does so, another taxpayer may claim the individual as a qualifying child but only if the other individual's AGI is higher than the AGI of any parent of the child [§152(c)(4)(C)].

Example 4-7

In the previous example, we established that Rodney and Anita's son Braxton is their qualifying dependent child. Braxton's Uncle Shawn—Rodney's brother—lived in the Halls' home (the same home Braxton lived in) for more than 11 months during the year. Does Braxton meet the requirements to be considered Shawn's qualifying child?

Answer: Yes, see analysis of factors below.

Test	Braxton
Relationship	Yes, son of Shawn's brother.
Age	Yes, under age 19 at end of year (and younger than Shawn).
Residence	Yes, lived in same residence as Shawn for more than half the year.
Support	Yes, does not provide more than half of his own support.

Thus, Braxton is considered to be Rodney and Anita's qualifying child *and* he is considered to be Shawn's qualifying child. Under the tiebreaker rules, who is allowed to claim Braxton as a dependent for the year?

Answer: Rodney and Anita. Under the first tiebreaking rule, Rodney and Anita are allowed to claim Braxton as a dependent because they are Braxton's parents.

What if: Suppose Shawn is Rodney's cousin. Would Braxton be considered Shawn's qualifying child?

Answer: No, Braxton does not meet the relationship test for Shawn if he is Rodney's cousin. Braxton is not the descendant of Shawn's sibling.

Qualifying Relative   A qualifying relative is a person who is *not* a qualifying child *and* satisfies (1) a relationship test, (2) a support test, and (3) a gross income test.

Relationship test.   As you might expect, the relationship test for a qualifying relative is more inclusive than the relationship test for a qualifying child. A person meets the qualifying relative relationship test who either (1) has a qualifying family relationship with the taxpayer or (2) meets the qualifying relative "member of the household" test. A qualifying family relationship with the taxpayer includes the following:

- A descendant or ancestor of the taxpayer. For this purpose, a child includes a taxpayer's adopted child, stepchild, and eligible foster child, and a parent includes a stepmother and stepfather.
- A sibling of the taxpayer, including a stepbrother or a stepsister.
- A son or daughter of the brother or sister of the taxpayer (cousins do not qualify).
- A sibling of the taxpayer's mother or father.
- An in-law (mother-in-law, father-in-law, sister-in-law, brother-in-law, son-in-law, or daughter-in-law) of the taxpayer.

A person meets the qualifying relative "member of the household" test if that person has the same principal place of abode as the taxpayer for the entire year (*even if the person does not have a qualifying family relationship with the taxpayer*).[19]

Support test.   The support test generally requires that the taxpayer pay more than half the qualifying relative's support/living expenses (note that this is a different support test than the support test for a qualifying child). As we discussed above, support/

---

[19]A person is considered to live with the taxpayer for the entire year if he or she was either born during the year or died during the year and resided with the taxpayer for the remaining part of the year.

living expenses include rent, food, medicine, and clothes, among other things. Just as with the qualifying child support test, scholarships of children of a taxpayer who are full-time students are excluded from the support test.[20] Under a multiple support agreement, taxpayers who don't pay over half of an individual's support may still be allowed to claim the individual as a dependent under the qualifying relative rules if the following apply:[21]

1. No one taxpayer paid over one-half of the individual's support.
2. The taxpayer and at least one other person provided more than half the support of the individual, and the taxpayer and the other person(s) would have been allowed to claim the individual as a dependent except for the fact that they did not provide over half of the support of the individual.
3. The taxpayer contributed *over* 10 percent of the individual's support for the year.
4. Each other person who provided *over* 10 percent of the individual's support [see requirement (2) above] provides a signed statement to the taxpayer agreeing not to claim the individual as a dependent. The taxpayer includes the names, addresses, and Social Security numbers of each other person on Form 2120, which the taxpayer attaches to her Form 1040.

Multiple support agreements are commonly used in situations when siblings support elderly parents.

Gross income test.   The gross income test requires that a qualifying relative's gross income for the year be *less* than $4,150 in 2018.[22]

Example 4-8

What if: Suppose Tara is age 25, is a full-time student, and does not live with her parents. Tara earned $3,000 from a summer job, and her parents provided more than half her support. Does Tara qualify as her parents' dependent?

Answer: Yes, as their qualifying relative. She is too old to be their qualifying child.

Test	Explanation
Relationship	Yes, Rodney and Anita's daughter.
Support	Yes, the Halls provide more than half of Tara's support.
Gross income	Yes, Tara's gross income for the year is less than $4,150.

Tara's parents may claim her as a dependent. Note that if Tara's gross income were at least $4,150, she would *not* qualify as her parents' dependent.

Example 4-9

In determining who qualified as their dependents, Rodney and Anita evaluated whether Shawn is their *qualifying relative*. Assuming Shawn's gross income for the year is $42,000, the Halls provided food and lodging for Shawn valued at $8,000, and Shawn paid for his other living expenses valued at $14,000, is Shawn a qualifying relative of the Halls?

---

[20]§152(f)(5) and §152(f)(1). Just as with a qualifying child, this provision requires that the student be a son, daughter, stepson, stepdaughter, or an eligible foster child of the taxpayer.

[21]§152(d)(3).

[22]This is the amount that taxpayers could have deducted for each personal or dependency exemption in 2018 before the new tax law eliminated the deduction for exemptions.

Answer: No, as analyzed below.

Test	Explanation
Relationship	Yes, Rodney's brother.
Support	No, the Halls provided $8,000 of support to Shawn, but Shawn provided $14,000 of his own support. Because the Halls provided less than half of Shawn's support, Shawn does not pass the support test.
Gross income	No, Shawn's gross income for the year is $42,000, which exceeds $4,150, so Shawn fails the gross income test.

Because Shawn fails the support test and the gross income test, he is not a qualifying relative of the Halls. Consequently, they cannot claim Shawn as a dependent.

What if: Assume that Shawn received $5,000 of tax-exempt interest during the year and that this is his only source of income. Does he fail the gross income test? (Note, however, that Shawn would still fail the support test so he would not be a qualifying relative of the Halls no matter the outcome of the gross income test.)

Answer: No. Because tax-exempt interest is excluded from gross income, Shawn's gross income is $0, so he passes the gross income test.

What if: Assume the original facts in the example except now suppose that Shawn paid for his $14,000 of living expenses with interest he had received from tax-exempt bonds. Would Shawn pass the support test?

Answer: No. The Halls would not have provided more than half of Shawn's support. The fact that Shawn received the money he spent on his support from tax-exempt income does not matter. All that matters is that he provided more than half of his own support.

What if: Assume that Anita's 92-year-old grandfather Juan lives in an apartment by himself near the Halls' residence. His gross income for the year is $3,000. Assuming the Halls provide more than half of Juan's living expenses for the year, would Juan be a qualifying relative of the Halls?

Answer: Yes, as analyzed below.

Test	Explanation
Relationship	Yes, Anita's grandfather.
Support	Yes, as assumed in the facts, the Halls provide more than half of Juan's support.
Gross income	Yes, Juan's gross income for the year is $3,000, which is less than $4,150, so Juan passes the gross income test.

What if: Assume that Anita's 92-year-old grandfather Juan lives in an apartment by himself and reports gross income for the year of $3,000. Anita provided 40 percent of Juan's support, Juan provided 25 percent of his own support, Anita's brother Carlos provided 30 percent of the support, and Anita's sister Kamella provided 5 percent of Juan's support. Who is eligible to claim Juan as a dependent under a multiple support agreement?

Answer: Anita and Carlos. Anita and Carlos are eligible because (1) no one taxpayer provided more than half of Juan's support, (2) Anita and Carlos together provided more than half of Juan's support and Juan would have been both Anita's and Carlos's qualifying relative except for the fact that neither provided over half of Juan's support, and (3) Anita and Carlos each provided over 10 percent of Juan's support (Kamella provided only 5 percent of Juan's support so she is not eligible). Anita and Carlos will need to agree on who will claim Juan as a dependent. Assuming they agree that Anita will claim Juan as a dependent, she will need to receive a signed statement from Carlos agreeing not to claim Juan as a dependent and she will need to attach Form 2120 to her (and Rodney's) tax return providing Carlos's name, address, and Social Security number.

What if: Assume the facts in the prior what-if scenario in which Anita is allowed to claim Juan as a dependent under a multiple support agreement. If Anita is not allowed to deduct a dependency exemption for Juan, why should Anita care whether Juan is her dependent or not?

Answer: While, under the new tax law, Anita is not entitled to a dependency exemption deduction for Juan, she is eligible to claim a $500 child tax credit for Juan because he is Anita's dependent and he is not a qualifying child.

What if: Assume Juan lives in an apartment by himself and is a friend of the family but is unrelated to either Rodney or Anita. His gross income is $3,000 and the Halls provide over half of his support. Is Juan a qualifying relative of the Halls?

(continued on page 4-18)

Answer: No, as analyzed below.

Test	Explanation
Relationship	No, not related to the Halls and his principal place of abode is not in the Halls' household for the *entire* year. If the Halls' home was his principal place of abode for the entire year, he would have met the relationship test even though he's not actually related to anyone in the Hall family.
Support	Yes, as assumed in the facts, the Halls provide more than half of Juan's support.
Gross income	Yes, Juan's gross income for the year is $3,000, which is less than $4,150, so Juan passes the gross income test.

The Halls would not be able to claim Juan as a dependent because he fails the qualifying relative relationship test under this set of facts.

The rules for determining who is a qualifying child and who is a qualifying relative for tax purposes overlap to some extent. The primary differences between the two sets of rules are:

1. The relationship requirement is more broadly defined for qualifying relatives than for qualifying children.
2. Qualifying children are subject to age restrictions while qualifying relatives are not.
3. Qualifying relatives are subject to a gross income restriction while qualifying children are not.
4. Taxpayers need not provide more than half a qualifying child's support (though the child cannot provide more than half of her own support), but they must provide more than half of the support of a qualifying relative.
5. Qualifying children are subject to a residence test (they must have the same primary residence as the taxpayer for more than half the year), while qualifying relatives are not. Exhibit 4-8 summarizes the dependency requirements.

EXHIBIT 4-8   **Summary of Dependency Requirements**

Test	Qualifying Child	Qualifying Relative
Relationship	Taxpayer's child, stepchild, foster child, sibling, half-brother or half-sister, stepbrother or stepsister, or a descendant of any of these relatives.	Taxpayer's descendant or ancestor, sibling, stepmother, stepfather, stepbrother or stepsister, son or daughter of taxpayer's sibling, sibling of the taxpayer's mother or father, in-laws, and anyone else who has the same principal place of abode as the taxpayer for the entire year (even if not otherwise related).
Age	Younger than the taxpayer claiming the individual as a qualifying child and under age 19 or a full-time student under age 24. Also anyone totally and permanently disabled.	Not applicable.
Residence	Lives with taxpayer for more than half of the year (includes temporary absences for things such as illness and education).	Not applicable.
Support	The qualifying child must not provide more than half of his or her own support.	Taxpayer must have provided more than half of the support for the qualifying relative.
Gross income	Not applicable.	Gross income less than $4,150 in 2018.
Other	Not applicable.	Not a qualifying child.

Finally, an individual who is a dependent of another is not allowed to claim any dependents.[23] Appendix A at the end of this chapter provides a flowchart for determining whether an individual qualifies as the taxpayer's dependent.

ETHICS

Blake was 21 years of age at the end of the year. During the year, he was a full-time college student. He also worked part-time and earned $8,000, which he used to pay all $6,000 of his living expenses. Blake's parents, Troy and Camille, claimed him as a dependent on their joint tax return. After filing the return, Troy told Blake they owed him $3,001 for his annual living expenses. What do you think of Troy and Camille's strategy to claim Blake as a dependent?

FILING STATUS

LO 4-3

Each year taxpayers determine their **filing status** according to their marital status at year-end and whether they have any dependents. A taxpayer's filing status is important because, as we discussed above, it determines:

- The applicable tax rate schedule for determining the taxpayer's tax liability.
- The taxpayer's standard deduction amount.
- The AGI threshold for reductions in certain tax benefits such as the itemized deduction for medical expenses and certain tax credits, among other benefits.

Each year, all taxpayers filing tax returns file under one of the following five filing statuses:

1. Married filing jointly
2. Married filing separately
3. Qualifying widow or widower (surviving spouse)
4. Single
5. Head of household

Married Filing Jointly and Married Filing Separately

Married couples may file tax returns jointly (**married filing jointly**) or separately (**married filing separately**). To be married for filing status purposes, taxpayers must be married on the last day of the year. When one spouse dies during the year, at the end of the year the surviving spouse is considered to be *married* to the spouse who died unless the surviving spouse has remarried during the year. Married couples filing joint returns combine their income and deductions and agree to share joint and several liability for the tax liability on the return. That is, they are both ultimately responsible for seeing that the tax is paid.

When married couples file separately, each spouse reports the income he or she received during the year and the deductions he or she is claiming on a tax return separate from that of the other spouse.[24] So that married taxpayers can't file separately to gain more combined tax benefits than they would be entitled to if they were to file jointly, tax-related items for married filing separate (MFS) taxpayers—such as tax rate schedules and standard deduction amounts, among others—are generally one-half what they are for married filing joint (MFJ) taxpayers. Also, if one spouse deducts itemized deductions, the other spouse is required to deduct itemized deductions even if his or her standard deduction amount is more than the total itemized deductions. Thus, only in unusual circumstances does it make economic sense for *tax* purposes for married couples to file separately.

---

[23] See §152(b)(1).

[24] As we discuss in the Gross Income and Exclusions chapter, under community property laws of certain states, one spouse may be treated as receiving income earned by the other spouse.

THE KEY FACTS

Filing Status for Married Taxpayers

- Married filing jointly
  - Taxpayers are legally married as of the last day of the year.
  - When one spouse dies during the year the surviving spouse is still considered to be married for tax purposes during the year of the spouse's death.
  - Both spouses are ultimately responsible for paying the joint tax.
- Married filing separately
  - Taxpayers are legally married as of the last day of the year.
  - Generally no tax advantage to filing separately (usually a disadvantage).
  - Each spouse is ultimately responsible for paying his or her own tax.
  - Couples may choose to file separately (generally for nontax reasons).
- Qualifying widow or widower
  - When a taxpayer's spouse dies, the surviving spouse can file as a qualifying widow or widower for two years after the year of the spouse's death if the surviving spouse remains unmarried and maintains a household for a dependent child.

However, it may be wise for married couples to file separately for *nontax* reasons. For example, a spouse who does not want to be liable for the other spouse's income tax liability, or a spouse who is not in contact with the other spouse, may want to file separately (see abandoned spouse discussion below).

Example 4-10

Rodney and Anita Hall are married at the end of the year. What is their filing status?

Answer: Married filing jointly, unless they choose to file separately.

What if: Assume that in 2018 the Halls file a joint return. In 2019, Rodney and Anita divorce and the IRS audits their 2018 tax return and determines that, due to overstating their deductions, the Halls underpaid their taxes by $2,000. Who must pay the tax?

Answer: Both Rodney and Anita are responsible for paying. If the IRS can't locate Rodney, it can require Anita to pay the full $2,000 even though she earned $56,000 and Rodney earned $74,000.

What if: Assume that in 2018 the Halls file separate tax returns. In 2019, Rodney and Anita divorce and the IRS audits the Halls' separate tax returns. It determines that by overstating deductions, Rodney understated his tax liability by $1,500 and Anita understated her tax liability by $500. Further, the IRS cannot locate Rodney. What is the maximum amount of taxes Anita is liable for?

Answer: $500. Because she filed a separate return, she is responsible for the tax liability associated with her separate tax return, and she is not responsible for the taxes associated with Rodney's tax return.

TAXES IN THE REAL WORLD   Tax Status for Same-Sex Married Couples

In June 2013, the Supreme Court struck down the federal "Defense of Marriage Act" (DOMA) which meant that same-sex couples who were married in a state that authorized and recognized same-sex marriages would now be treated as married for federal income tax purposes. However, couples who were in a registered domestic partnership, civil union, or other similar formal relationship recognized under state law were *not* recognized as married for federal income tax purposes.

In June 2015, the Supreme Court ruled that the 14th Amendment of the Constitution guarantees a right to same-sex marriage. This ruling unifies marital status at the federal and state levels. A taxpayer's marital status is important for determining income tax filing status and has implications for other areas of the tax law (estate and gift tax, for example).

Source: Obergefell vs. Hodges, 576 U.S. _____ (2015).

Qualifying Widow or Widower (Surviving Spouse)

When a taxpayer's spouse dies, the taxpayer is no longer legally married. However, to provide tax relief for widows and widowers *with dependents*, taxpayers who meet certain requirements qualify for **qualifying widow or widower** filing status, also called surviving spouse status, for up to two years *after* the end of the year in which the other spouse died. Recall that for tax purposes, they are still considered to be married at the end of the year of the spouse's death. Taxpayers are eligible for qualifying widow or widower filing status if they (1) remain unmarried and (2) pay over half the cost of maintaining a household where a child who qualifies as the taxpayer's dependent lived for the entire year (except for temporary absences).[25]

---

[25]§2(a).

The dependent child must be a child or stepchild (including an adopted child but not a foster child) of the taxpayer.

Example 4-11

What if: Assume that last year Rodney passed away, and during the current year Anita did not remarry but maintained a household for Braxton and Tara, her dependent children. Under these circumstances, what is Anita's filing status for the current year?

Answer: Qualifying widow. Last year, the year of Rodney's death, Anita qualified to file a joint return with Rodney. This year, she is a qualifying widow because she has not remarried and she has maintained a household for the entire year for her dependent children. She will qualify as a surviving spouse next year (two years after Rodney's death) if she does not remarry and she continues to maintain a household for Braxton and/or Tara for the entire year.

Single

Unmarried taxpayers who do not qualify for head of household status (discussed below) file as **single** taxpayers. As we discuss below, an unmarried taxpayer generally must have a dependent who is a qualifying person to qualify for head of household filing status.

Example 4-12

Shawn Hall, Rodney's brother, was divorced in January and is unmarried at the end of the year. Shawn does not claim any dependents. What is his filing status?

Answer: Single. Because Shawn is unmarried at the end of the year, and he does not have any dependents, his filing status is single.

Head of Household

In terms of tax rate schedules and standard deduction amounts, the **head of household** filing status is less favorable than the married filing jointly and qualifying widow or widower filing statuses. However, it is more favorable than married filing separately and single filing statuses (see tax rates and standard deduction amounts provided in Appendix D). To qualify for head of household filing status, a taxpayer must:

- Be unmarried (or be considered unmarried under the provisions discussed below) at the end of the year.
- Not be a qualifying widow or widower.
- Pay more than half the costs of keeping up a home for the year.
- Have a "qualifying person" live in the taxpayer's home for more than half the year (except for temporary absences such as military service, illness, or schooling). However, if the qualifying person is the taxpayer's *dependent* parent, the parent is not required to live with the taxpayer. A qualifying person may not qualify more than one person for head of household filing status. Exhibit 4-9 describes who is considered a qualifying person for purposes of head of household filing status.[26]

[26]§2(b). The new tax law imposes due diligence requirements for paid preparers in determining eligibility for a taxpayer to file as head of household and a $500 penalty each time a paid preparer fails to meet these requirements. See §6695(g).

THE KEY FACTS

Filing Status for Unmarried Taxpayers
- Single
  - Unmarried taxpayers at year-end who do not qualify for head of household.
- Head of household
  - Unmarried taxpayers or taxpayers considered to be unmarried at year-end.
  - Must pay more than half of the costs of maintaining a household in which a qualifying person lives for more than half of the tax year or must pay more than half of the costs for maintaining a separate household for a parent who qualifies as taxpayer's dependent.

EXHIBIT 4-9 **Who Is a Qualifying Person for Determining Head of Household Filing Status?**
(Adapted from Table 4 in IRS Publication 501)

IF the person is the taxpayer's . . .	And . . .	THEN, the person is . . .
Qualifying child	the person is single,	a qualifying person, whether or not the taxpayer can claim the person as a dependent.**
	the person is married and the taxpayer may claim the person as a dependent,	a qualifying person.**
	the person is married and the taxpayer may not claim the person as a dependent,	not a qualifying person.
Qualifying relative who is the taxpayer's mother or father	the taxpayer may not claim the taxpayer's mother or father as a dependent,	not a qualifying person.
	the taxpayer may claim the taxpayer's mother or father as a dependent,	a qualifying person even if the taxpayer's mother or father did not live with the taxpayer. However, the taxpayer must have paid more than half the costs to maintain the household of the mother or father.
Qualifying relative other than the taxpayer's mother or father	the person did not live with the taxpayer for more than half the year,	not a qualifying person.
	the taxpayer can claim the person as a dependent, the person lived with the taxpayer for more than half the year, and the person is related to the taxpayer through a qualifying family relationship,	a qualifying person.
	the person is the taxpayer's qualifying relative only because the person lived with the taxpayer as a member of the taxpayer's household for the entire year (the person does not have a qualifying family relationship with the taxpayer),	not a qualifying person.
	the taxpayer cannot claim the person as a dependent or the taxpayer can claim the person as a dependent only because of a multiple support agreement,	not a qualifying person.

*Appendix B at the end of this chapter includes a flowchart for determining whether a person is a qualifying person for head of household filing status.
**If a custodial parent allows the noncustodial parent to claim the child as a dependent under a divorce decree, the agreement is ignored for purposes of this test.
Source: Adapted from Table 4 in IRS Publication 501.

Example 4-13

What if: Assume Rodney and Anita divorced last year. During the current year, Braxton lives with Anita for the entire year and Anita pays all the costs of maintaining the household for herself and Braxton. Under these circumstances, what is Anita's filing status for the year?

Answer: Head of household. Anita is unmarried at the end of the year, she provides more than half the costs of maintaining her household, Braxton lives with her for more than half of the year, and Braxton is her qualifying child.

What if: Assume Rodney and Anita divorced last year. During the current year, Braxton lives with Anita for the entire year, and Anita pays all the costs of maintaining the household for herself and Braxton. Assume that Anita allowed Rodney to claim Braxton as a dependent under the divorce decree. Under these circumstances, what is Anita's filing status for the year?

Answer: Head of household. Braxton is a qualifying person for Anita (the custodial parent) even though Anita is not claiming Braxton as a dependent. Braxton is not a qualifying person for Rodney (the noncustodial parent).

What if: Assume that Rodney and Anita divorced last year. If Braxton is Anita's cousin (rather than her son) and he lives with Anita in her home from June 15 through December 31, what is Anita's filing status for the year?

Answer: Single. Anita does not qualify for head of household filing status because Braxton is not her qualifying child (he fails the relationship test) or her qualifying relative (he fails the relationship test because he did not live in Anita's home for the entire year and he does not have a qualifying family relationship with Anita because he is her cousin).

What if: Assume that Rodney and Anita divorced last year, Braxton is Anita's cousin, and Braxton lives with Anita in her home for the entire year. What is Anita's filing status for the year?

Answer: Single. Even though Braxton is Anita's qualifying relative, Braxton meets the qualifying relative relationship test only because he lived with Anita for the entire year (not because he had a qualifying family relationship with her). Therefore, while Anita may claim Braxton as a dependent, she does not qualify for the head of household filing status.

What if: Assume Rodney's brother Shawn lived with the Halls, but Shawn paid more than half the costs of maintaining a separate apartment that is the principal residence of his mother, Sharon. Sharon's gross income is $1,500. Because Shawn provided more than half of Sharon's support during the year, and because Sharon's gross income was only $1,500, she qualifies as Shawn's dependent relative. In these circumstances, what is Shawn's filing status?

Answer: Head of household. Shawn paid more than half the costs of maintaining a separate household where his mother resides, and his mother qualifies as his dependent.

If Sharon's gross income were at least $4,150, she would fail the dependency gross income test and would not qualify as Shawn's dependent. If she did not qualify as his dependent, she would not be a qualifying person, and Shawn would not qualify for the head of household filing status. Also, if Sharon were Shawn's grandmother rather than his mother, she would not be a qualifying person (no matter the amount of her gross income) and Shawn would not qualify for head of household status. Sharon must be Shawn's parent in order for her to qualify Shawn as a head of household.

Married Individuals Treated as Unmarried (Abandoned Spouse)   In certain situations a couple may be legally married at the end of the year but living apart. Although the couple could technically file a joint tax return, this is often not desirable from a nontax perspective, because each spouse would be assuming responsibility for paying tax on income earned by either spouse whether it was reported or not. However, because both spouses are married at the end of the year, their only other option is to file under the tax-unfavorable married filing separately filing status.

To provide tax relief in these situations, the tax laws treat a married taxpayer *as though he or she were unmarried* at the end of the year if the taxpayer meets the following requirements:

- The taxpayer is married at the end of the year (or is not *legally* separated from the other spouse).
- The taxpayer does not file a joint tax return with the other spouse.
- The taxpayer pays *more than half* the costs of maintaining his or her home for the entire year, and this home is the principal residence for a child (who qualifies as the taxpayer's dependent[27]) for *more than half* the year (the child must be a child of the taxpayer, including adopted child, stepchild, or eligible foster child[28]).
- The taxpayer lived apart from the other spouse for the last six months of the year (the other spouse did not live at all in the taxpayer's home during the last six months—temporary absences due to illness, education, business, vacation, or military service count as though the spouse still lived in the taxpayer's home).

If the taxpayer meets these requirements, he or she also meets the head of household filing status requirements and may file as head of household for the year. The primary objective of this tax rule is to provide tax relief to one spouse who has been abandoned by or separated from the other spouse and left to care for a dependent child. Thus, a married taxpayer who qualifies as unmarried under this provision is

---

[27]A taxpayer meets this test if the taxpayer (custodial parent) cannot claim the child as a dependent only because he or she agreed under a divorce decree to allow the noncustodial to claim the child as a dependent.
[28]§152(f).

frequently referred to as an **abandoned spouse.** Nevertheless, the provision may still apply even when no spouse has been abandoned. For example, a couple may separate by mutual consent. Further, if both spouses meet the requirements, both spouses may qualify as being unmarried in the same year and thus both may qualify for head of household filing status.

Example 4-14

What if: Assume that last year, Rodney and Anita informally separated (they did not *legally* separate). Rodney moved out of the home and into his own apartment. Anita stayed in the Halls' home with Braxton. During the current year, Anita paid more than half the costs of maintaining the home for herself and Braxton. Even though Rodney and Anita were legally married at the end of the year, they filed separate tax returns. Under these circumstances, is Anita considered to be married or unmarried for tax purposes?

Answer: Unmarried. Anita meets the requirements for being treated as unmarried determined as follows (see requirements above):

- Anita is married to Rodney at the end of the year.
- Anita filed a tax return separate from Rodney's.
- Anita paid more than half the costs of maintaining her home, and her home was the principal residence for Braxton, who is her dependent child.
- Rodney did not live in Anita's home for the last six months of the year (in fact, he didn't live there at any time during the entire year).

What if: Given that Anita meets the requirements for being treated as unmarried, what is her filing status?

Answer: Head of household. Since Anita meets the abandoned spouse requirements she also meets the head of household filing status requirements. Without the abandoned spouse rule, Anita would have been required to file as married filing separately. Rodney's filing status, however, is married filing separately. Note, however, that if Rodney's new residence became Tara's principal residence, Rodney would also be treated as unmarried and would be eligible for head of household filing status.

Appendix C at the end of this chapter includes a flowchart for determining a taxpayer's filing status.

SUMMARY OF INCOME TAX FORMULA

Tara crunched some numbers and put together a summary of her parents' taxable income calculation. She determined that her parents will receive a $369 tax refund when they file their tax return. Tara's summary is provided in Exhibit 4-10, and Exhibit 4-11 presents pages 1 and 2 of the Halls' Form 1040.

EXHIBIT 4-10   **Taxable Income and Tax Calculation Summary for Rodney and Anita Hall**

Description	Amount	Explanation
(1) Gross income	130,600.00	Example 4-1
(2) For AGI deductions	(5,000.00)	Example 4-2, line (2)
(3) Adjusted gross income	$ 125,600.00	(1) + (2)
(4) From AGI deductions	$ (24,000.00)	Example 4-3
(5) Taxable income	$101,600.00	(3) + (4)
(6) Income tax liability	$ 14,231.00	Example 4-4
(7) Credits	(2,500.00)	Example 4-5, line (2)
(8) Tax prepayments	(12,100.00)	Example 4-5, line (3)
Tax (refund)	$ (369.00)	(9) + (10) + (11)

EXHIBIT 4-11   Form 1040

Form **1040**	Department of the Treasury—Internal Revenue Service (99) **U.S. Individual Income Tax Return**	**2017**	OMB No. 1545-0074	IRS Use Only—Do not write or staple in this space.

For the year Jan. 1–Dec. 31, 2017, or other tax year beginning	, 2017, ending	, 20	See separate instructions.

Your first name and initial	Last name	Your social security number
Rodney	Hall	2 2 4 5 6 1 2 4 5

If a joint return, spouse's first name and initial	Last name	Spouse's social security number
Anita	Hall	3 2 4 4 3 3 4 7 8

Home address (number and street). If you have a P.O. box, see instructions. — Apt. no.

665 Henry Avenue

▲ Make sure the SSN(s) above and on line 6c are correct.

City, town or post office, state, and ZIP code. If you have a foreign address, also complete spaces below (see instructions).

Brookings, SD, 57007

Foreign country name	Foreign province/state/county	Foreign postal code

Presidential Election Campaign
Check here if you, or your spouse if filing jointly, want $3 to go to this fund. Checking a box below will not change your tax or refund. ☐ You   ☐ Spouse

Filing Status

Check only one box.

1. ☐ Single
2. ☑ Married filing jointly (even if only one had income)
3. ☐ Married filing separately. Enter spouse's SSN above and full name here. ▶
4. ☐ Head of household (with qualifying person). (See instructions.) If the qualifying person is a child but not your dependent, enter this child's name here. ▶
5. ☐ Qualifying widow(er) (see instructions)

Exemptions

6a	☑ **Yourself.** If someone can claim you as a dependent, **do not** check box 6a	Boxes checked on 6a and 6b	**2**
b	☑ **Spouse**		

If more than four dependents, see instructions and check here ▶ ☐

c Dependents: (1) First name Last name	(2) Dependent's social security number	(3) Dependent's relationship to you	(4) ✓ if child under age 17 qualifying for child tax credit (see instructions)
Tara Hall	2 4 2 6 8 9 9 4 5	Daughter	☐
Braxton Hall	2 4 2 2 3 7 8 4 5	Son	☑
			☐
			☐

No. of children on 6c who:
• lived with you **2**
• did not live with you due to divorce or separation (see instructions)

Dependents on 6c not entered above

Add numbers on lines above ▶ **4**

d	Total number of exemptions claimed		

Income

Attach Form(s) W-2 here. Also attach Forms W-2G and 1099-R if tax was withheld.

If you did not get a W-2, see instructions.

7	Wages, salaries, tips, etc. Attach Form(s) W-2	7	130,000
8a	**Taxable** interest. Attach Schedule B if required	8a	600
b	**Tax-exempt** interest. **Do not** include on line 8a	8b 300	
9a	Ordinary dividends. Attach Schedule B if required	9a	
b	Qualified dividends	9b	
10	Taxable refunds, credits, or offsets of state and local income taxes	10	
11	Alimony received	11	
12	Business income or (loss). Attach Schedule C or C-EZ	12	
13	Capital gain or (loss). Attach Schedule D if required. If not required, check here ▶ ☐	13	
14	Other gains or (losses). Attach Form 4797	14	
15a	IRA distributions 15a	b Taxable amount	15b	
16a	Pensions and annuities 16a	b Taxable amount	16b	
17	Rental real estate, royalties, partnerships, S corporations, trusts, etc. Attach Schedule E	17	
18	Farm income or (loss). Attach Schedule F	18	
19	Unemployment compensation	19	
20a	Social security benefits 20a	b Taxable amount	20b	
21	Other income. List type and amount	21	
22	Combine the amounts in the far right column for lines 7 through 21. This is your **total income** ▶	22	130,600

Adjusted Gross Income

23	Educator expenses	23			
24	Certain business expenses of reservists, performing artists, and fee-basis government officials. Attach Form 2106 or 2106-EZ	24			
25	Health savings account deduction. Attach Form 8889	25			
26	Moving expenses. Attach Form 3903	26			
27	Deductible part of self-employment tax. Attach Schedule SE	27			
28	Self-employed SEP, SIMPLE, and qualified plans	28			
29	Self-employed health insurance deduction	29			
30	Penalty on early withdrawal of savings	30			
31a	Alimony paid b Recipient's SSN ▶	31a			
32	IRA deduction	32	5,000		
33	Student loan interest deduction	33			
34	Reserved for future use	34			
35	Domestic production activities deduction. Attach Form 8903	35			
36	Add lines 23 through 35	36		5,000	
37	Subtract line 36 from line 22. This is your **adjusted gross income** ▶	37		125,600	

For Disclosure, Privacy Act, and Paperwork Reduction Act Notice, see separate instructions.   Cat. No. 11320B   Form **1040** (2017)

(continued)

EXHIBIT 4-11   *(continued)*

Form 1040 (2017)   Page **2**

Tax and Credits	38	Amount from line 37 (adjusted gross income)		38	125,600
	39a	Check if: ☐ **You** were born before January 2, 1953, ☐ Blind. ☐ **Spouse** was born before January 2, 1953, ☐ Blind. } Total boxes checked ▶ 39a			
	b	If your spouse itemizes on a separate return or you were a dual-status alien, check here▶ 39b☐			
Standard Deduction for—	40	**Itemized deductions** (from Schedule A) **or** your **standard deduction** (see left margin) . .		40	24,000
• People who check any box on line 39a or 39b or who can be claimed as a dependent, see instructions.	41	Subtract line 40 from line 38		41	101,600
	42	**Exemptions.** If line 38 is $156,900 or less, multiply $4,050 by the number on line 6d. Otherwise, see instructions		42	
	43	**Taxable income.** Subtract line 42 from line 41. If line 42 is more than line 41, enter -0- . .		43	101,600
	44	**Tax** (see instructions). Check if any from: **a** ☐ Form(s) 8814 **b** ☐ Form 4972 **c** ☐ _____		44	14,231
• All others:	45	**Alternative minimum tax** (see instructions). Attach Form 6251		45	
Single or Married filing separately, $6,350	46	Excess advance premium tax credit repayment. Attach Form 8962		46	
	47	Add lines 44, 45, and 46 . . . . ▶		47	14,231
Married filing jointly or Qualifying widow(er), $12,700	48	Foreign tax credit. Attach Form 1116 if required	48		
	49	Credit for child and dependent care expenses. Attach Form 2441	49		
	50	Education credits from Form 8863, line 19 . . .	50		
Head of household, $9,350	51	Retirement savings contributions credit. Attach Form 8880	51		
	52	Child tax credit. Attach Schedule 8812, if required . . .	52	2,500	
	53	Residential energy credit. Attach Form 5695	53		
	54	Other credits from Form: **a** ☐ 3800 **b** ☐ 8801 **c** ☐ _____	54		
	55	Add lines 48 through 54. These are your **total credits**		55	2,500
	56	Subtract line 55 from line 47. If line 55 is more than line 47, enter -0- . . . . ▶		56	11,731
Other Taxes	57	Self-employment tax. Attach Schedule SE		57	
	58	Unreported social security and Medicare tax from Form: **a** ☐ 4137 **b** ☐ 8919 . .		58	
	59	Additional tax on IRAs, other qualified retirement plans, etc. Attach Form 5329 if required . .		59	
	60a	Household employment taxes from Schedule H		60a	
	b	First-time homebuyer credit repayment. Attach Form 5405 if required		60b	
	61	Health care: individual responsibility (see instructions) Full-year coverage ☐		61	
	62	Taxes from: **a** ☐ Form 8959 **b** ☐ Form 8960 **c** ☐ Instructions; enter code(s) _____		62	
	63	Add lines 56 through 62. This is your **total tax** . . . . ▶		63	11,731
Payments	64	Federal income tax withheld from Forms W-2 and 1099 . .	64	12,100	
	65	2017 estimated tax payments and amount applied from 2016 return	65		
If you have a qualifying child, attach Schedule EIC.	66a	**Earned income credit (EIC)**	66a		
	b	Nontaxable combat pay election 66b			
	67	Additional child tax credit. Attach Schedule 8812	67		
	68	American opportunity credit from Form 8863, line 8 . . .	68		
	69	Net premium tax credit. Attach Form 8962	69		
	70	Amount paid with request for extension to file	70		
	71	Excess social security and tier 1 RRTA tax withheld	71		
	72	Credit for federal tax on fuels. Attach Form 4136	72		
	73	Credits from Form: **a** ☐ 2439 **b** ☐ Reserved **c** ☐ 8885 **d** ☐ _____	73		
	74	Add lines 64, 65, 66a, and 67 through 73. These are your **total payments** . . . . . ▶		74	12,100
Refund	75	If line 74 is more than line 63, subtract line 63 from line 74. This is the amount you **overpaid**		75	369
	76a	Amount of line 75 you want **refunded to you.** If Form 8888 is attached, check here . ▶ ☐		76a	369
Direct deposit? See instructions.	▶ b	Routing number _____ ▶ c Type: ☐ Checking ☐ Savings			
	▶ d	Account number _____			
	77	Amount of line 75 you want **applied to your 2018 estimated tax** ▶ 77			
Amount You Owe	78	**Amount you owe.** Subtract line 74 from line 63. For details on how to pay, see instructions ▶		78	
	79	Estimated tax penalty (see instructions) 79			

Third Party Designee	Do you want to allow another person to discuss this return with the IRS (see instructions)? ☐ **Yes.** Complete below. ☐ **No**
	Designee's name ▶ _____ Phone no. ▶ _____ Personal identification number (PIN) ▶ ☐☐☐☐☐

Sign Here	Under penalties of perjury, I declare that I have examined this return and accompanying schedules and statements, and to the best of my knowledge and belief, they are true, correct, and accurately list all amounts and sources of income I received during the tax year. Declaration of preparer (other than taxpayer) is based on all information of which preparer has any knowledge.
Joint return? See instructions. Keep a copy for your records.	Your signature	Date	Your occupation	Daytime phone number
	Spouse's signature. If a joint return, **both** must sign.	Date	Spouse's occupation	If the IRS sent you an Identity Protection PIN, enter it here (see inst.) ☐☐☐☐☐☐

Paid Preparer Use Only	Print/Type preparer's name	Preparer's signature	Date	Check ☐ if self-employed	PTIN
	Firm's name ▶			Firm's EIN ▶	
	Firm's address ▶			Phone no.	

Go to *www.irs.gov/Form1040* for instructions and the latest information.   Form **1040** (2017)

CONCLUSION

Recently enacted tax law introduced changes to the individual income tax formula. This chapter presents an overview of the individual income tax formula under the new tax law and provides rules for determining who qualifies as a taxpayer's dependents and for determining a taxpayer's filing status. In the Gross Income and Exclusions chapter, we turn our attention to determining gross income. In the individual deductions chapters, we describe deductions available to taxpayers when computing their taxable income. In the Individual Income Tax Computation and Tax Credits chapter, we conclude our review of the individual income tax formula by determining how to compute a taxpayer's tax liability and her taxes due or tax refund.

Appendix A   Dependency Exemption Flowchart (Part I)

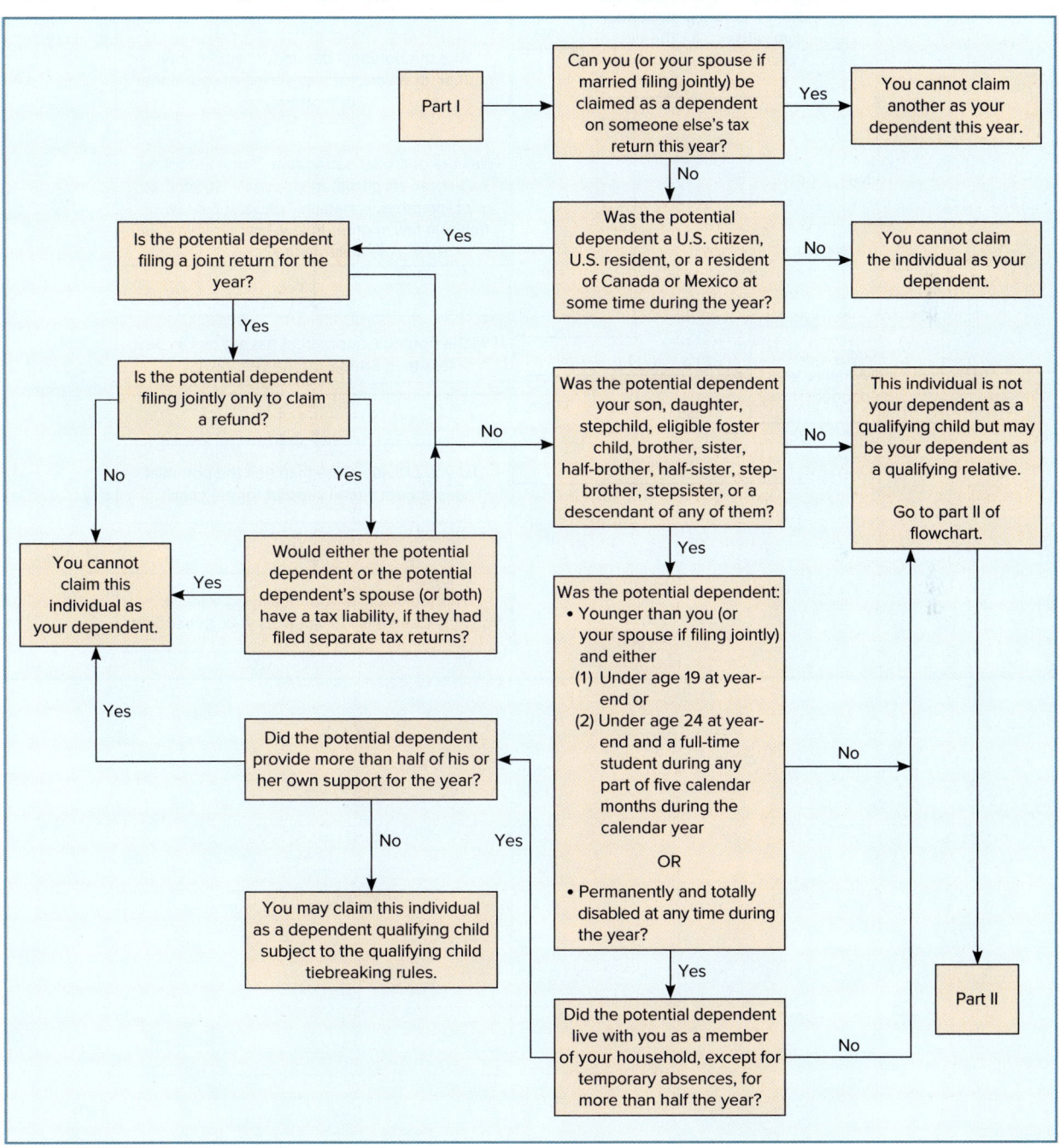

Appendix A   (Part II)

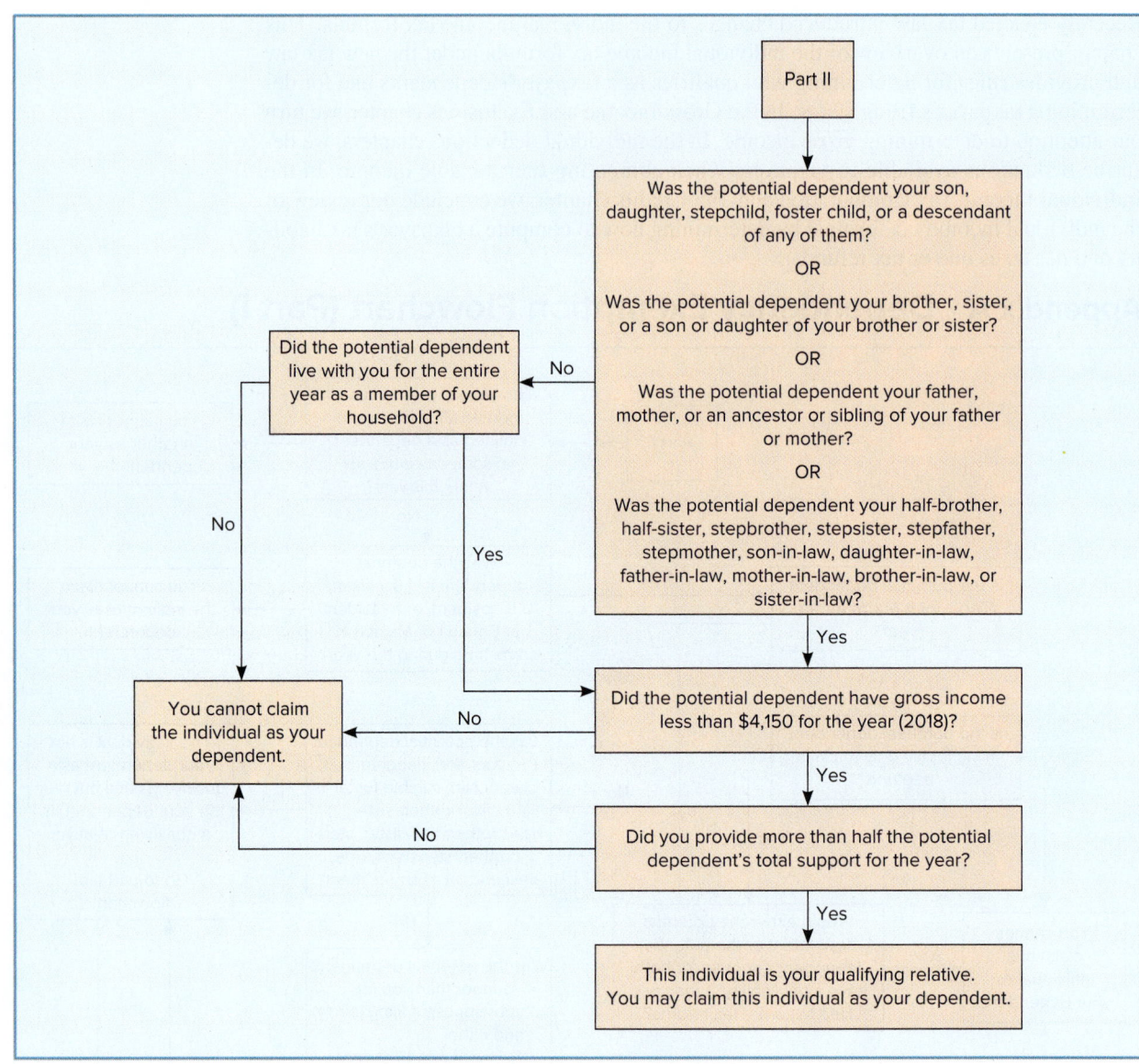

Appendix B   Qualifying Person for Head of Household Filing Status Flowchart

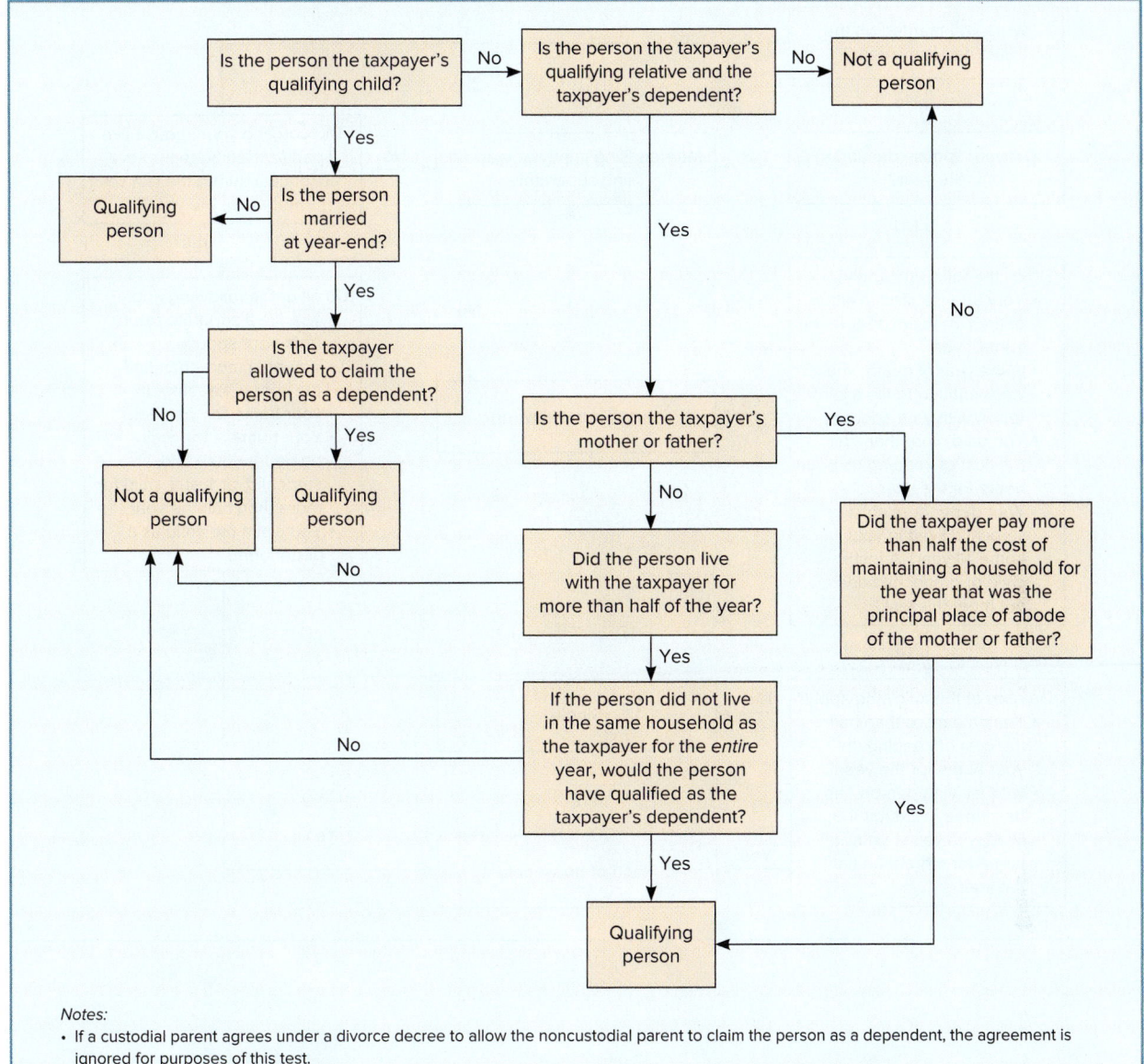

Notes:

- If a custodial parent agrees under a divorce decree to allow the noncustodial parent to claim the person as a dependent, the agreement is ignored for purposes of this test.
- If the taxpayer can claim the person as a dependent only because of a multiple support agreement, that person is not a qualifying person.
- One qualifying person may not qualify more than one person for head of household filing status.

Appendix C   Determination of Filing Status Flowchart

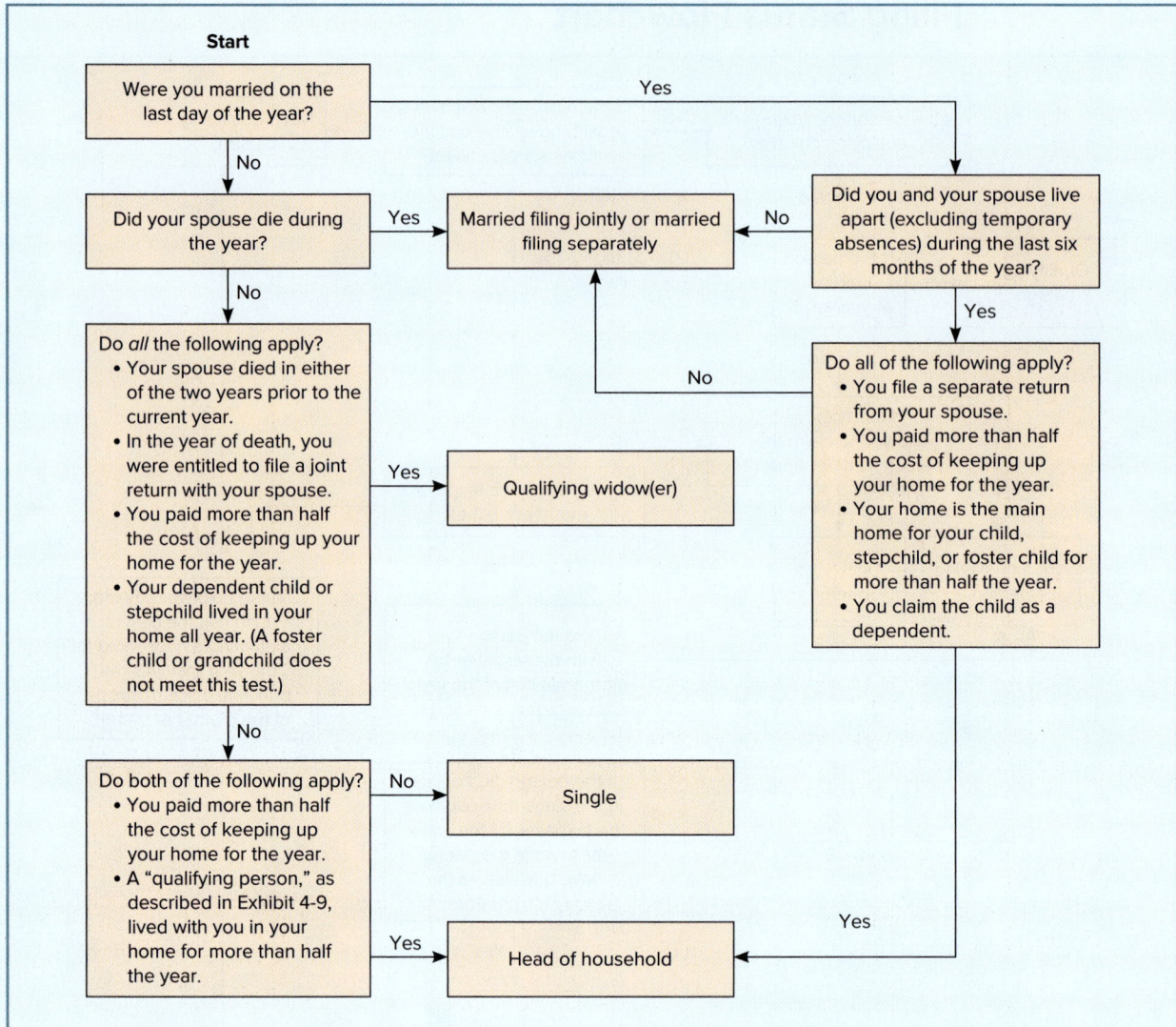

Summary

LO 4-1   Describe the formula for calculating an individual taxpayer's taxes payable or refund.

- Generally, taxpayers are taxed on all income they realize during the year, no matter the source. However, the tax laws allow taxpayers to permanently exclude or to defer to a later year certain types of income they realize during the year.

- Income items that taxpayers are allowed to permanently exclude from income are called *exclusions*. Realized income items that taxpayers are not taxed on until a future period are called *deferrals*.

- Taxpayers include gross income on their tax returns.

- The character of the income determines how the income is treated for tax purposes, including, potentially, the rate at which the income is taxed.

- Ordinary income is taxed at the rates provided in the tax rate schedules; long-term capital gains (after a netting process) and qualified dividends are taxed at a maximum rate of 0, 15, or 20 percent, depending on the taxpayer's taxable income.

- Capital gains and losses arise from the sale or disposition of capital assets. In general a capital asset is any asset other than accounts receivable from the sale of goods or services, inventory, and assets used in a trade or business. If a capital asset is owned for more than a year before it is sold, the capital gain or loss is long-term. Otherwise, it is short-term.

- Taxpayers may deduct up to $3,000 of net capital loss for the year (excess of capital losses over capital gains for the year) against ordinary income. The remainder is suspended and carried over to the next year.

- Even though a personal-use asset meets the capital asset definition, a taxpayer is not allowed to deduct a loss on the sale or disposition of a personal-use asset.

- Deductions reduce a taxpayer's taxable income. The two types of deductions are *for* AGI deductions and *from* AGI deductions.

- Gross income minus *for* AGI deductions equals adjusted gross income (AGI). *For* AGI deductions are deductions "above the line," the last line on the front page of the individual tax form, Form 1040.

- *For* AGI deductions tend to relate to business activities and certain investment activities.

- AGI minus *from* AGI deductions equals taxable income.

- *From* AGI deductions include the deduction for qualified business income and either the standard deduction or itemized deductions. *From* AGI deductions are referred to as "deductions below the line."

- AGI is an important reference point in the individual tax formula because it is often used in other tax-related calculations.

- Taxpayers generally deduct itemized deductions when the amount of the itemized deductions exceeds the standard deduction. The standard deduction varies by filing status and is indexed for inflation. Special rules may alter the standard deduction amount for certain taxpayers.

- Taxpayers are no longer allowed to deduct amounts for personal and dependency exemptions.

- Taxpayers generally calculate the tax on their taxable income by referring to tax tables or tax rate schedules.

- Taxpayers may be required to pay the alternative minimum tax (AMT), self-employment tax, the 3.8 percent net investment income tax on unearned (investment) income, and/or the .9 percent additional Medicare tax on earned income in addition to their regular income tax.

- Tax credits reduce taxpayers' tax liability dollar for dollar, while deductions decrease taxable income dollar for dollar.

- Taxpayers prepay taxes during the year through withholdings by employers, estimated tax payments, or prior-year overpayments applied toward the current-year tax liability.

- If tax prepayments exceed the taxpayer's total tax after credits, the taxpayer receives a refund. If tax prepayments are less than the total tax after credits, the taxpayer owes additional tax with his or her tax return.

Explain the requirements for determining who qualifies as a taxpayer's dependent.   **LO 4-2**

- Individuals who qualify as the dependent of another are not allowed to claim any dependents.

- Taxpayers may claim as dependents those who (1) are citizens of the United States or residents of the United States, Canada, or Mexico and (2) meet the joint tax return test, and are considered either a qualifying child or a qualifying relative of the taxpayer.

- A child must meet a relationship test, an age test, a residence test, and a support test to qualify as a qualifying child.

- A person who is not a qualifying child may be considered a qualifying relative by meeting a relationship test, a support test, and a gross income test.

LO 4-3   Determine a taxpayer's filing status.

- Taxpayers may file their tax returns as married filing jointly, married filing separately, qualifying widow or widower (also referred to as surviving spouse), single, or head of household.

- Married taxpayers may file a joint return or they may file separately. It is generally more advantageous for tax purposes to file jointly, if married. However, for nontax reasons, it may be advantageous to file separately.

- Each spouse is ultimately responsible for paying the tax on a joint return no matter who received the income.

- For two years after the year in which one spouse dies, the surviving spouse may file as a qualifying widow or widower as long as he or she (1) remains unmarried and (2) maintains a household for a dependent child (child, stepchild, or adopted child).

- Unmarried taxpayers who do not qualify for head of household status file as single taxpayers.

- An unmarried taxpayer who is not a qualifying widow or widower may file as head of household if the person pays more than half the costs of maintaining a household that is, for *more* than half the taxable year, the principal place of abode for a qualifying person (if the qualifying person is a parent, the parent need not reside with the taxpayer). In general, for an individual to be a qualifying person, the taxpayer must be able to claim the person as a dependent and the person must be considered to be related to the taxpayer even if the person does not live with the taxpayer for the entire year. That is, the taxpayer and the person must be related through a qualifying family relationship. See Exhibit 4-9 for a flow-chart for determining whether an individual is a qualifying person for purposes of determining head of household filing status.

KEY TERMS

abandoned spouse (4-24)

adjusted gross income (AGI) (4-2)

all-inclusive income concept (4-2)

alternative minimum tax (AMT) (4-11)

character of income (4-6)

deductions (4-7)

deductions above the line (4-7)

deductions below the line (4-8)

deferrals (4-5)

estimated tax payments (4-11)

exclusions (4-5)

filing status (4-19)

for AGI deductions (4-7)

from AGI deductions (4-7)

gross income (4-2)

head of household (4-21)

itemized deductions (4-8)

legislative grace (4-7)

married filing jointly (4-19)

married filing separately (4-19)

preferential tax rate (4-6)

preferentially taxed income (4-6)

qualifying child (4-12)

qualifying relative (4-12)

qualifying widow or widower (4-20)

realized income (4-2)

self-employment taxes (4-11)

single (4-21)

standard deduction (4-8)

tax credits (4-11)

taxable income (4-2)

tax rate schedule (4-10)

tax tables (4-10)

withholdings (4-11)

DISCUSSION QUESTIONS

Discussion Questions are available in Connect®.

LO 4-1   1. How are realized income, gross income, and taxable income similar, and how are they different?

LO 4-1   2. Are taxpayers required to include all realized income in gross income? Explain.

LO 4-1   3. All else being equal, should taxpayers prefer to exclude income or to defer it? Why?

LO 4-1   4. Why should a taxpayer be interested in the character of income received?

LO 4-1   5. Is it easier to describe what a capital asset is or what it is not? Explain.

6. Are all capital gains (gains on the sale or disposition of capital assets) taxed at the same rate? Explain. **LO 4-1**

7. Are taxpayers allowed to deduct net capital losses (capital losses in excess of capital gains)? Explain. **LO 4-1**

8. Compare and contrast *for* and *from* AGI deductions. Why are *for* AGI deductions likely more valuable to taxpayers than *from* AGI deductions? **LO 4-1**

9. What is the difference between gross income and adjusted gross income, and what is the difference between adjusted gross income and taxable income? **LO 4-1**

10. How do taxpayers determine whether they should deduct their itemized deductions or utilize the standard deduction? **LO 4-1**

11. How was the income tax formula for individuals changed for 2018 by the new tax law? **LO 4-1**

12. Why are some deductions called "above the line" deductions and others called "below the line" deductions? What is the "line"? **LO 4-1**

13. If taxpayers are not allowed to claim deductions for dependency exemptions, is it necessary to determine who qualifies as a taxpayer's dependents? Briefly explain. **LO 4-1**

14. What is the difference between a tax deduction and a tax credit? Is one more beneficial than the other? Explain. **LO 4-1**

15. What types of federal income-based taxes, other than the regular income tax, might taxpayers be required to pay? In general terms, what is the tax base for each of these other taxes on income? **LO 4-1**

16. Identify three ways taxpayers can pay their income taxes to the government. **LO 4-1**

17. If a person meets the qualifying relative tests for a taxpayer, is that person automatically considered to be a dependent of the taxpayer? **LO 4-1**

18. Emily and Tony are recently married college students. Can Emily qualify as her parents' dependent? Explain. **LO 4-2**

19. Compare and contrast the relationship test requirements for a qualifying child with the relationship requirements for a qualifying relative. **LO 4-2**

20. In general terms, what are the differences in the rules for determining who is a qualifying child and who qualifies as a dependent as a qualifying relative? Is it possible for someone to be a qualifying child and a qualifying relative of the same taxpayer? Why or why not? **LO 4-2**

21. How do two taxpayers determine who has priority to claim a person as a dependent if the person is a qualifying child of two taxpayers when neither taxpayer is a parent of the child (assume the child does not qualify as a qualifying child for either parent)? How do parents determine who claims the child as a dependent if the child is a qualifying child of both parents when the parents are divorced or file separate tax returns? **LO 4-2**

22. Isabella provides 30 percent of the support for her father Hastings, who lives in an apartment by himself and has no gross income. Is it possible for Isabella to claim her father as a dependent? Explain. **LO 4-2**

23. What requirements do an abandoned spouse and a qualifying widow or widower have in common? **LO 4-3**

24. True or False. For purposes of determining head of household filing status, the taxpayer's mother or father is considered to be a qualifying person of the taxpayer (even if the mother or father does not qualify as the taxpayer's dependent) as long as the taxpayer pays more than half the costs of maintaining the household of the mother or father. Explain. **LO 4-3**

LO 4-3   25. Is a qualifying relative always a qualifying person for purposes of determining head of household filing status?

LO 4-3   26. For tax purposes, why is the married filing jointly tax status generally preferable to the married filing separately filing status? Why might a married taxpayer prefer *not* to file a joint return with the taxpayer's spouse?

LO 4-3   27. What does it mean to say that a married couple filing a joint tax return has joint and several liability for the taxes associated with the return?

PROBLEMS

Select problems are available in Connect®.

LO 4-1   28. Jeremy earned $100,000 in salary and $6,000 in interest income during the year. Jeremy's employer withheld $11,200 of federal income taxes from Jeremy's paychecks during the year. Jeremy has one qualifying dependent child who lives with him. Jeremy qualifies to file as head of household and has $23,000 in itemized deductions.

a) Determine Jeremy's tax refund or taxes due.

b) Assume that in addition to the original facts, Jeremy has a long-term capital gain of $4,000. What is Jeremy's tax refund or tax due including the tax on the capital gain?

c) Assume the original facts except that Jeremy had only $7,000 in itemized deductions. What is Jeremy's tax refund or tax due?

LO 4-1   29. David and Lilly Fernandez have determined their tax liability on their joint tax return to be $1,700. They have made prepayments of $1,500 and also have a child tax credit of $2,000. What is the amount of their tax refund or taxes due?

LO 4-1
planning   30. Rick, who is single, has been offered a position as a city landscape consultant. The position pays $125,000 in cash wages. Assume Rick has no dependents. Rick deducts the standard deduction instead of itemized deductions.

a) What is the amount of Rick's after-tax compensation (ignore payroll taxes)?

b) Suppose Rick receives a competing job offer of $120,000 in cash compensation and nontaxable (excluded) benefits worth $5,000. What is the amount of Rick's after-tax compensation for the competing offer? Which job should he take if taxes are the only concern?

LO 4-1
planning   31. Through November, Cameron has received gross income of $120,000. For December, Cameron is considering whether to accept one more work engagements for the year. Engagement 1 will generate $7,000 of revenue at a cost to Cameron of $3,000, which is deductible for AGI. In contrast, engagement 2 will generate $5,000 of qualified business income (QBI) which is eligible for the 20% QBI deduction. Cameron files as a single taxpayer.

a) Calculate Cameron's taxable income assuming he chooses engagement 1 and assuming he chooses engagement 2. Assume he has no itemized deductions.

b) Which engagement maximizes Cameron's after-tax cash flow? Explain.

LO 4-1
planning   32. Nitai, who is single and has no dependents, was planning on spending the weekend repairing his car. On Friday, Nitai's employer called and offered him $500 in overtime pay if he would agree to work over the weekend. Nitai could get his car repaired over the weekend at Autofix for $400. If Nitai works over the weekend, he will have to pay the $400 to have his car repaired but he will earn $500. Assume Nitai pays tax at a flat 12 percent rate.

a) Strictly considering tax factors, should Nitai work or repair his car if the $400 he must pay to have his car fixed is not deductible?

b) Strictly considering tax factors, should Nitai work or repair his car if the $400 he must pay to have his car fixed is deductible *for* AGI?

33. Rank the following three single taxpayers in order of the magnitude of taxable income (from lowest to highest) and explain your results. **LO 4-1 LO 4-2**

	Ahmed	Baker	Chin
Gross income	$90,000	$90,000	$90,000
Deductions *for* AGI	14,000	7,000	0
Itemized deductions	$0	$7,000	$14,000
Deduction for qualified business income	0	2,000	10,000

34. Aishwarya's husband passed away in 2017. She needs to determine whether Jasmine, her 17-year-old stepdaughter, who is single, qualifies as her dependent in 2018. Jasmine is a resident but not a citizen of the United States. She lived in Aishwarya's home from June 15 through December 31, 2018. Aishwarya provided more than half of Jasmine's support for 2018. **LO 4-2**

   a) Is Aishwarya allowed to claim Jasmine as a dependent for 2018?

   b) Would Aishwarya be allowed to claim Jasmine as a dependent for 2018 if Aishwarya provided more than half of Jasmine's support in 2018, Jasmine lived in Aishwarya's home from July 15 through December 31 of 2018, and Jasmine reported gross income of $5,000 for the year?

   c) Would Aishwarya be allowed to claim Jasmine as a dependent for 2018 if Aishwarya provided more than half of Jasmine's support in 2018, Jasmine lived in Aishwarya's home from July 15 through December 31 of 2018, and Jasmine reported gross income of $2,500 for the year?

35. The Samsons are trying to determine whether they can claim their 22-year-old adopted son, Jason, as a dependent. Jason is currently a full-time student at an out-of-state university. Jason lived in his parents' home for three months of the year and he was away at school for the rest of the year. He received $9,500 in scholarships this year for his outstanding academic performance and earned $4,800 of income working a part-time job during the year. The Samsons paid a total of $5,000 to support Jason while he was away at college. Jason used the scholarship, the earnings from the part-time job, and the money from the Samsons as his only sources of support. **LO 4-2**

   a) Can the Samsons claim Jason as their dependent?

   b) Assume the original facts except that Jason's grandparents, not the Samsons, provided him with the $5,000 worth of support. Can the Samsons (Jason's parents) claim Jason as their dependent? Why or why not?

   c) Assume the original facts except substitute Jason's grandparents for his parents. Determine whether Jason's grandparents can claim Jason as a dependent.

   d) Assume the original facts except that Jason earned $5,500 while working part-time and used this amount for his support. Can the Samsons claim Jason as their dependent? Why or why not?

36. John and Tara Smith are married and have lived in the same home for over 20 years. John's uncle Tim, who is 64 years old, has lived with the Smiths since March of this year. Tim is searching for employment but has been unable to find any—his gross income for the year is $2,000. Tim used all $2,000 toward his own support. The Smiths provided the rest of Tim's support by providing him with lodging valued at $5,000 and food valued at $2,200. **LO 4-2**

   a) Are the Smiths able to claim Tim as a dependent?

   b) Assume the original facts except that Tim earned $10,000 and used all the funds for his own support. Are the Smiths able to claim Tim as a dependent?

c) Assume the original facts except that Tim is a friend of the family and not John's uncle.

d) Assume the original facts except that Tim is a friend of the family and not John's uncle and Tim lived with the Smiths for the entire year.

LO 4-2 37. Francine's mother Donna and her father Darren separated and divorced in September of this year. Francine lived with both parents until the separation. Francine does *not* provide more than half of her own support. Francine is 15 years old at the end of the year.

a) Is Francine a qualifying child to Donna?

b) Is Francine a qualifying child to Darren?

c) Assume Francine spends more time living with Darren than Donna after the separation. Who may claim Francine as a dependent?

d) Assume Francine spends an equal number of days with her mother and her father and that Donna has AGI of $52,000 and Darren has AGI of $50,000. Who may claim Francine as a dependent?

LO 4-2 38. Jamel and Jennifer have been married 30 years and have filed a joint return every year of their marriage. Their three daughters, Jade, Lindsay, and Abbi, are ages 12, 17, and 22, respectively, and all live at home. None of the daughters provides more than half of her own support. Abbi is a full-time student at a local university and does not have any gross income.

a) Which, if any, of the daughters qualify as dependents of Jamel and Jennifer?

b) Assume the original facts except that Abbi is married. She and her husband live with Jamel and Jennifer while attending school and they file a joint return. Abbi and her husband reported a $1,000 tax liability on their tax return. If all parties are willing, can Jamel and Jennifer claim Abbi as a dependent on their tax return? Why or why not?

c) Assume the same facts as part (b), except that Abbi and her husband report a $0 tax liability on their joint tax return. Also, if the couple had filed separately, Abbi would not have had a tax liability on her return but her husband would have had a $250 tax liability on his separate return. Can Jamel and Jennifer claim Abbi as a dependent on their tax return? Why or why not?

d) Assume the original facts except that Abbi is married. Abbi files a separate tax return. Abbi's husband files a separate tax return and reports a $250 tax liability on the return. Can Jamel and Jennifer claim Abbi as a dependent?

LO 4-2 **LO 4-3** 39. Dean Kastner is 78 years old and lives by himself in an apartment in Chicago. Dean's gross income for the year is $2,500. Dean's support is provided as follows: Himself (5 percent), his daughters Camille (25 percent) and Rachel (30 percent), his son Zander (5 percent), his friend Frankie (15 percent), and his niece Sharon (20 percent).

a) Absent a multiple support agreement, of the parties mentioned in the problem, who may claim Dean as a dependent?

b) Under a multiple support agreement, who is eligible to claim Dean as a dependent? Explain.

c) Assume that Camille is allowed to claim Dean as a dependent under a multiple support agreement. Camille is single, and Dean is her only dependent. What is Camille's filing status?

LO 4-2 40. Mel and Cindy Gibson's 12-year-old daughter Rachel was abducted on her way home from school on March 15, 2018. Police reports indicated that a stranger had physically dragged Rachel into a waiting car and sped away. Everyone hoped that the kidnapper and Rachel would be located quickly. However, as of the end of the year, Rachel was still missing. The police were still pursuing several promising

leads and had every reason to believe that Rachel was still alive. In 2019, Rachel was returned safely to her parents.

a) Are the Gibsons allowed to claim Rachel as a dependent for 2018 even though she only lived in the Gibsons' home for two-and-one-half months? Explain and cite your authority.

b) Assume the original facts except that Rachel is unrelated to the Gibsons but she has been living with them since January 2013. The Gibsons have claimed Rachel as a dependent for the years 2013 through 2017. Are the Gibsons allowed to claim Rachel as a dependent for 2018? Explain and cite your authority.

41. Kimberly is divorced and the custodial parent of a three-year-old girl named Bailey. Kimberly and Bailey live with Kimberly's parents, who pay all the costs of maintaining the household (such as mortgage, property taxes, and food). Kimberly pays for Bailey's clothing, entertainment, and health insurance costs. These costs comprised only a small part of the total costs of maintaining the household. Kimberly does not qualify as her parents' dependent. `LO 4-2` `LO 4-3`

a) Determine the appropriate filing status for Kimberly.

b) What if Kimberly lived in her own home and provided all the costs of maintaining the household?

42. Lee is 30 years old and single. Lee paid all the costs of maintaining his household for the entire year. Determine Lee's filing status in each of the following alternative situations: `LO 4-2` `LO 4-3`

a) Lee is Ashton's uncle. Ashton is 15 years old and has gross income of $5,000. Ashton lived in Lee's home from April 1 through the end of the year.

b) Lee is Ashton's uncle. Ashton is 20 years old, not a full-time student, and has gross income of $7,000. Ashton lived in Lee's home from April 1 through the end of the year.

c) Lee is Ashton's uncle. Ashton is 22 years old and was a full-time student from January through April. Ashton's gross income was $5,000. Ashton lived in Lee's home from April 1 through the end of the year.

d) Lee is Ashton's cousin. Ashton is 18 years old, has gross income of $3,000, and is not a full-time student. Ashton lived in Lee's home from April 1 through the end of the year.

e) Lee and Ashton are cousins. Ashton is 18 years old, has gross income of $3,000, and is not a full-time student. Ashton lived in Lee's home for the entire year.

43. Ray Albertson is 72 years old and lives by himself in an apartment in Salt Lake City. Ray's gross income for the year is $3,000. Ray's support is provided as follows: himself (9 percent), his daughters Diane (20 percent) and Karen (15 percent), his sons Mike (20 percent) and Kenneth (10 percent), his friend Milt (14 percent), and his cousin Henry (12 percent). `LO 4-2` `LO 4-3`

a) Absent a multiple support agreement, of the parties mentioned in the problem, who may claim Ray as a dependent?

b) Under a multiple support agreement, who is eligible to claim Ray as a dependent? Explain.

c) Assume that under a multiple support agreement, Diane claims Ray as a dependent. Diane is single with no other dependents. What is her filing status?

44. Juan and Bonita are married and have two dependent children living at home. This year, Juan is killed in an avalanche while skiing. `LO 4-3`

a) What is Bonita's filing status this year?

b) Assuming Bonita doesn't remarry and still has two dependent children living at home, what will her filing status be next year?

c) Assuming Bonita doesn't remarry and doesn't have any dependents next year, what will her filing status be next year?

LO 4-3 45. Gary and Lakesha were married on December 31 last year. They are now preparing their taxes for the April 15 deadline and are unsure of their filing status.

a) What filing status options do Gary and Lakesha have for last year?

b) Assume instead that Gary and Lakesha were married on January 1 of this year. What is their filing status for last year (neither has been married before and neither had any dependents last year)?

LO 4-3 46. Elroy, who is single, has taken over the care of his mother Irene in her old age. Elroy pays the bills relating to Irene's home. He also buys all her groceries and provides the rest of her support. Irene has no gross income.

a) What is Elroy's filing status?

b) Assume the original facts except that Elroy has taken over the care of his grandmother, Renae, instead of his mother. What is Elroy's filing status?

c) Assume the original facts except that Elroy's mother, Irene, lives with him and receives an annual $5,700 taxable distribution from her retirement account. Elroy still pays all the costs to maintain the household. What is his filing status?

LO 4-3 47. Kano and his wife, Hoshi, have been married for 10 years and have two children under the age of 12. The couple has been living apart for the last two years and both children live with Kano. Kano has provided all the means necessary to support himself and his children. Kano and Hoshi do not file a joint return.

a) What is Kano's filing status?

b) Assume the original facts except that Kano and Hoshi separated in May of the current year. What is Kano's filing status?

c) Assume the original facts except that Kano and Hoshi separated in November of this year. What is Kano's filing status?

d) Assume the original facts except that Kano's parents, not Kano, paid more than half of the cost of maintaining the home in which Kano and his children live. What is Kano's filing status?

LO 4-3 48. Horatio and Kelly were divorced at the end of last year. Neither Horatio nor Kelly remarried during the current year and Horatio moved out of state. Determine the filing status of Horatio and Kelly for the current year in the following independent situations:

a) Horatio and Kelly did not have any children and neither reported any dependents in the current year.

b) Horatio and Kelly had one child, Amy, who turned 10 years of age in the current year. Amy lived with Kelly for all of the current year and Kelly provided all of her support.

c) Assume the same facts as in part (b) but Kelly allowed Horatio to claim Amy as a dependent under the divorce decree even though Amy did not reside with Horatio at all during the current year.

d) Assume the original facts except that during the current year Madison, a 17-year-old friend of the family, lived with Kelly (for the entire year) and was fully supported by Kelly.

e) Assume the original facts except that during the current year Kelly's mother, Janet, lived with Kelly. For the current year, Kelly was able to claim Janet as a dependent under a multiple support agreement.

LO 4-2 **LO 4-3** 49. In each of the following *independent* situations, determine the taxpayer's filing status and the number of dependents the taxpayer is allowed to claim.

a) Frank is single and supports his 17-year-old brother, Bill. Bill earned $3,000 and did not live with Frank.

b) Geneva and her spouse reside with their son, Steve, who is a 20-year-old undergraduate student at State University. Steve earned $13,100 at a part-time summer job, but he deposited this money in a savings account for graduate school. Geneva paid all of the $12,000 cost of supporting Steve.

c) Hamish's spouse died last year and Hamish has not remarried. Hamish supports his father, Reggie, age 78, who lives in a nursing home and had interest income this year of $2,500.

d) Irene is married but has not seen her spouse since February. She supports her spouse's 18-year-old child, Dolores, who lives with Irene. Dolores earned $4,500 this year.

e) Assume the same facts as in part (d). Also, assume that Craig is Irene's husband. Craig supports his 12-year-old son Ethan, who lives with Craig. Ethan did not earn any income.

50. In each of the following *independent* cases, determine the taxpayer's filing status and the number of dependents the taxpayer is allowed to claim.   **LO 4-2**   **LO 4-3**

a) Alexandra is a blind widow (her spouse died five years ago) who provides a home for her 18-year-old nephew, Newt. Newt's parents are dead and so Newt supports himself. Newt's gross income is $5,000.

b) Bharati supports and maintains a home for her daughter, Daru, and son-in-law, Sam. Sam earned $15,000 and filed a joint return with Daru, who had no income.

c) Charlie intended to file a joint return with his spouse, Sally. However, Sally died in December. Charlie has not remarried.

d) Deshi cannot convince his spouse to consent to signing a joint return. The couple has not separated.

e) Edith and her spouse support their 35-year-old son, Slim. Slim is a full-time college student who earned $5,500 over the summer in part-time work.

51. Jasper and Crewella Dahvill were married in year 0. They filed joint tax returns in years 1 and 2. In year 3, their relationship was strained and Jasper insisted on filing a separate tax return. In year 4, the couple divorced. Both Jasper and Crewella filed single tax returns in year 4. In year 5, the IRS audited the couple's joint year 2 tax return and each spouse's separate year 3 tax returns. The IRS determined that the year 2 joint return and Crewella's separate year 3 tax return understated Crewella's self-employment income, causing the joint return year 2 tax liability to be understated by $4,000 and Crewella's year 3 separate return tax liability to be understated by $6,000. The IRS also assessed penalties and interest on both of these tax returns. Try as it might, the IRS has not been able to locate Crewella, but they have been able to find Jasper.   **LO 4-3**

a) What amount of tax can the IRS require Jasper to pay for the Dahvill's year 2 joint return? Explain.

b) What amount of tax can the IRS require Jasper to pay for Crewella's year 3 separate tax return? Explain.

52. Janice Traylor is single. She has an 18-year-old son named Marty. Marty is Janice's only child. Marty has lived with Janice his entire life. However, Marty recently joined the Marines and was sent on a special assignment to Australia. During the current year, Marty spent nine months in Australia. Marty was extremely homesick while in Australia, since he had never lived away from home. However, Marty knew this assignment was only temporary, and he couldn't wait to come home and find his room just the way he left it. Janice has always filed as head of household, and Marty has always been considered a qualifying child (and he continues to meet all the tests with the possible exception of the residence test due to his stay in Australia). However, this year Janice is unsure whether she qualifies as head of household due to Marty's nine-month absence during the year. Janice has come to you for advice on whether she qualifies for head of household filing status. What do you tell her?   **LO 4-3**   **research**

53. Doug Jones submitted his 2018 tax return on time and elected to file a joint tax return with his wife, Darlene. Doug and Darlene did not request an extension for their 2018 tax return. Doug and Darlene owed and paid the IRS $124,000 for their 2018 tax year. Two years later, Doug amended his return and claimed married filing   **LO 4-3**   **research**

separate status. By changing his filing status, Doug sought a refund for an overpayment for the tax year 2018 (he paid more tax in the original joint return than he owed on a separate return). Is Doug allowed to change his filing status for the 2018 tax year and receive a tax refund with his amended return?

COMPREHENSIVE PROBLEMS

Select problems are available in Connect®.

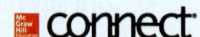

tax forms

54. Marc and Michelle are married and earned salaries this year of $64,000 and $12,000, respectively. In addition to their salaries, they received interest of $350 from municipal bonds and $500 from corporate bonds. Marc contributed $2,500 to an individual retirement account, and Marc paid alimony to a prior spouse in the amount of $1,500. Marc and Michelle have a 10-year-old son, Matthew, who lived with them throughout the entire year. Thus, Marc and Michelle are allowed to claim a $2,000 child tax credit for Matthew. Marc and Michelle paid $6,000 of expenditures that qualify as itemized deductions and they had a total of $5,500 in federal income taxes withheld from their paychecks during the course of the year.

a) What is Marc and Michelle's gross income?

b) What is Marc and Michelle's adjusted gross income?

c) What is the total amount of Marc and Michelle's deductions *from* AGI?

d) What is Marc and Michelle's taxable income?

e) What is Marc and Michelle's taxes payable or refund due for the year? (Use the tax rate schedules.)

f) Complete the first two pages of Marc and Michelle's Form 1040 (use the most recent form available).

tax forms

55. Demarco and Janine Jackson have been married for 20 years and have four children who qualify as their dependents (Damarcus, Janine, Michael, and Candice). The couple received salary income of $100,000, qualified business income of $10,000 from an investment in a partnership, and they sold their home this year. They initially purchased the home three years ago for $200,000 and they sold it for $250,000. The gain on the sale qualified for the exclusion from the sale of a principal residence. The Jacksons incurred $16,500 of itemized deductions, and they had $3,550 withheld from their paychecks for federal taxes. They are also allowed to claim a child tax credit for each of their children. However, because Candice is 18 years of age, the Jacksons may claim a child tax credit for other qualifying dependents for Candice.

a) What is the Jacksons' taxable income, and what is their tax liability or (refund)?

b) Complete the first two pages of the Jacksons' Form 1040 (use the most recent form available).

c) What would their taxable income be if their itemized deductions totaled $28,000 instead of $16,500?

d) What would their taxable income be if they had $0 itemized deductions and $6,000 of *for* AGI deductions?

e) Assume the original facts but now suppose the Jacksons also incurred a loss of $5,000 on the sale of some of their investment assets. What effect does the $5,000 loss have on their *taxable income*?

f) Assume the original facts but now suppose the Jacksons own investments that appreciated by $10,000 during the year. The Jacksons believe the investments will continue to appreciate, so they did not sell the investments during this year. What is the Jacksons' taxable income?

56. Camille Sikorski was divorced last year. She currently provides a home for her 15-year-old daughter Kaly. Kaly lived in Camille's home for the entire year, and Camille paid for all the costs of maintaining the home. She received a salary of $105,000 and contributed $6,000 of it to a qualified retirement account (a *for* AGI deduction). She also received $10,000 of alimony from her former husband. Finally, Camille paid $15,000 of expenditures that qualified as itemized deductions.

    a) What is Camille's taxable income?

    b) What would Camille's taxable income be if she incurred $24,000 of itemized deductions instead of $15,000?

    c) Assume the original facts but now suppose Camille's daughter, Kaly, is 25 years old and a full-time student. Kaly's gross income for the year was $5,000. Kaly provided $3,000 of her own support, and Camille provided $5,000 of support. What is Camille's taxable income?

57. Tiffany is unmarried and has a 15-year-old qualifying child. Tiffany has determined her tax liability to be $3,525, and her employer has withheld $1,500 of federal taxes from her paycheck. Tiffany is allowed to claim a $2,000 child tax credit for her qualifying child. What amount of taxes will Tiffany owe (or what amount will she receive as a refund) when she files her tax return?

 **ROGER** | *CPA Review*

Sample CPA Exam questions from Roger CPA Review are available in Connect as support for the topics in this text. These Multiple Choice Questions and Task-Based Simulations include expert-written explanations and solutions and provide a starting point for students to become familiar with the content and functionality of the actual CPA Exam.

Gross Income and Exclusions

©Image Source

The past year was a year of change for Courtney Wilson. After her divorce from Al Wilson, Courtney assumed sole custody of their 10-year-old son, Deron, and their 20-year-old daughter, Ellen. Looking for a fresh start in January, Courtney quit her job as an architect in Cincinnati, Ohio, and moved to Kansas City, Missouri. Courtney wanted to pursue several promising job opportunities in Kansas City and be close to Ellen while she attends the University of Missouri–Kansas City. Courtney's 70-year-old mother "Gram" also lives in Kansas City and is in relatively good health. However, Courtney's father, "Gramps," passed away last December from cancer. At Courtney's insistence, Gram moved in with Courtney and Deron in April.

In late April, Courtney broke her wrist in a mountain biking accident and was unable to work for two weeks. Thankfully, Courtney's disability insurance paid her for lost wages during her time away from work.

While her personal life has been in disarray, Courtney's financial prospects have been improving. Shortly after arriving in Kansas City, Courtney was fortunate to land a job as an architect with Earth Wise Design (EWD). EWD provided Courtney the following compensation and benefits this year:

- Salary $118,000.
- Medical and life insurance premiums.
- Contribution of 10 percent of her base salary to her qualified retirement account.
- No-interest loan with a promise to forgive the loan principal over time if she continues her employment with EWD.
- Performance bonus for her first year on the job.

Courtney also received other payments unrelated to her employment with EWD as follows:

- Alimony from her ex-husband Al.
- Child support from her ex-husband Al.
- Consulting income.
- Dividend, interest, and rental income.
- Refund of state taxes she paid last year.

Before Gram moved in with Courtney, she lived alone in an apartment in Kansas City. After Gramps died, Gram was dependent on her Social Security

Storyline Summary

Taxpayers:	Courtney Wilson, age 40 Courtney's mother, Dorothy "Gram" Weiss, age 70
Family description:	Courtney is divorced with a son, Deron, age 10, and a daughter, Ellen, age 20. Gram is currently residing with Courtney.
Location:	Kansas City, Missouri
Employment status:	Courtney works as an architect for EWD. Her salary is $118,000. Gram is unemployed.
Current situation:	Determining what income is taxable.

benefits. In early April, Gram received the proceeds from Gramps's life insurance policy. She invested part of the proceeds in an annuity contract that will pay Gram a fixed amount per year. Gram also invested some of the proceeds in the stock of a local corporation. She used the rest of the life insurance proceeds to purchase a certificate of deposit and start a savings account. Gram also spent some of her spare time completing sweepstakes entries. Her hard work paid off when she won a WaveRunner in a sweepstakes contest.

Until their divorce, Courtney's husband always prepared their income tax return. Since EWD hired her, Courtney has become anxious about her income tax and whether her withholding will be sufficient to cover her tax bill. Courtney is also worried about Gram's tax situation, because Gram did not make any tax payments this year. ■

In the previous chapter, we presented an overview of individual taxation. In this chapter, we begin to dig deeper into the tax formula to determine a taxpayer's gross income. We focus on whether income is included or excluded from a taxpayer's gross income rather than the rate at which the income is taxed. In the next three chapters, we continue to work through the individual tax formula to determine the tax liabilities for Courtney and Gram. The Individual *For* AGI Deductions chapter describes deductible expenses to determine adjusted gross income, the Individual *From* AGI Deductions chapter describes deductible expenses *from* AGI, and the Individual Income Tax Computation and Tax Credits chapter addresses issues associated with calculating the tax liability, tax credits, and tax return filing concerns.

LO 5-1 ## REALIZATION AND RECOGNITION OF INCOME

As we learned in the previous chapter, **gross income** is income that taxpayers realize, recognize, and report on their tax returns for the year. In the previous chapter, we discussed gross income in general terms. In this chapter we explain the requirements for taxpayers to recognize gross income, and we discuss the most common sources of gross income.

What Is Included in Gross Income?

The definition of gross income for tax purposes is provided in §61(a) as follows:

> GENERAL DEFINITION.—Except as otherwise provided in this subtitle, gross income means all income *from whatever source derived* (emphasis added).

In addition to providing this all-inclusive definition of income, §61 includes a list of examples of gross income such as compensation for services, business income, rents, royalties, interest, and dividends. However, it is clear that unless a tax provision says otherwise, gross income includes *all* income. Thus, gross income is *broadly* defined. Reg. §1.61-(a) provides further insight into the definition of gross income as follows:

> Gross income means all income from whatever source derived, unless excluded by law. Gross income includes income realized in any form, whether in money, property, or services.

Based on §61(a), Reg. §1.61-(a), and various judicial rulings, taxpayers *recognize* gross income when (1) they receive an economic benefit, (2) they realize the income, *and* (3) no tax provision allows them to exclude or defer the income from gross income for that year.[1] Let's address each of these three requirements for recognizing gross income.

Economic Benefit   Taxpayers must receive an economic benefit (i.e., receive an item of value) to have gross income. Common examples where a taxpayer receives economic benefit include receiving compensation for services (the compensation could be in the form of cash, other property, or even services received), proceeds from property sales (typically cash, property, or debt relief), and income from investments or business activities (such as business income, rents, interest, and dividends). How about when a taxpayer borrows money? Is the economic benefit criterion met? No, because when a taxpayer borrows money, the economic benefit received (the cash received) is completely offset by the liability the taxpayer is required to pay from borrowing the funds (the debt amount).

Realization Principle   As indicated in Reg. §1.61-(a), the tax definition of income adopts the **realization principle.** Under this principle, income is realized when (1) a taxpayer engages in a transaction with another party, and (2) the transaction results in a measurable change in property rights. In other words, assets or services are exchanged for cash, claims to cash, or other assets with determinable value.

The concept of realization for tax purposes closely parallels the concept of realization for financial accounting purposes. Requiring a transaction to trigger realization reduces the uncertainty associated with determining the *amount* of income because a change in rights can typically be traced to a specific moment in time and is generally accompanied by legal documentation.

Example 5-1

In April, Gram used part of the life insurance proceeds she received from Gramps's death to purchase 50 shares in Acme Corporation for $30 per share. From April to the end of December, the value of the shares fluctuated between $40 and $25, but on December 31, the shares were worth $35. If Gram does *not* sell the shares, how much income from her stockholdings in Acme Corporation does she *realize* for the year?

Answer: $0. Unless Gram sells the stock, she does not enter into a transaction resulting in a measurable change of property rights with a second party. Thus, she does not realize income even though she experienced an economic benefit from the appreciation of the stock from $30 per share to $35 per share.

Adopting the realization principle for defining gross income provides two major advantages. First, because parties to the transaction must agree to the value of the exchanged property rights, the transaction allows the income to be measured objectively. Second, the transaction often provides the taxpayer with the **wherewithal to pay** taxes (at least when the taxpayer receives cash in the transaction). That is, the transaction itself provides the taxpayer with the funds to pay taxes on income generated by the transaction. Thus, it reduces the possibility that the taxpayer will be required to sell other assets to pay the taxes on the income from the transaction. Note, however, when taxpayers receive property or services in a transaction (instead of cash), realization has also occurred (despite the absence of wherewithal to pay).

---

[1]For tax purposes it matters not whether income is obtained through legal or illegal activities (e.g., embezzlement). See *Eugene James v. U.S.* (1961, S. Ct.), 7 AFTR 2d 1361.

Recognition   Taxpayers who realize an economic benefit must include the benefit in gross income unless a specific provision of the tax code says otherwise. That is, taxpayers are generally required to *recognize* all realized income by reporting it as gross income on their tax returns. However, as we describe later in this chapter, through exclusions Congress allows taxpayers to permanently exclude certain types of income from gross income and through deferrals it allows taxpayers to defer certain types of income from gross income until a subsequent year. Thus, it is important to distinguish between realized and recognized income.

Other Income Concepts

The tax laws, administrative authority, and judicial rulings have established several other concepts important for determining an individual's gross income.

Form of Receipt   A common misperception is that taxpayers must receive cash to realize and recognize gross income. However, Reg. §1.61-(a) indicates that taxpayers realize income whether they receive money, property, *or* services in a transaction. For example, **barter clubs** facilitate the exchange of rights to goods and services between members, many of whom have the mistaken belief that they need not recognize income on the exchanges. However, when members exchange property, they realize and recognize income at the market price, the amount that outsiders are willing to pay for the goods or services. Also, other taxpayers who exchange or trade goods or services with each other must recognize the value of the goods or services as income, even when they do not receive any cash. Indeed, taxpayers have the legal and ethical responsibility to report realized income (assuming no exclusion provision applies) no matter the form of its receipt or whether the IRS knows the taxpayer received the income.

Example 5-2

What if: Suppose during March, Gram paid no rent to her neighbor (also her landlord). Although the neighbor typically charges $350 per month for rent, he allowed Gram to live rent-free in exchange for babysitting his infant son. What income would Gram and Gram's neighbor realize and recognize on this exchange?

Answer: $350. Gram and the neighbor each would recognize $350 of income for March. The neighbor recognizes $350 of rental receipts because this is the value of the babysitting services the neighbor received in lieu of a cash payment for rent from Gram (an economic benefit the neighbor realized through the exchange). Gram recognizes $350 of babysitting income, because this is the value of the services provided to her neighbor (an economic benefit was realized because Gram was not required to pay rent).

TAXES IN THE REAL WORLD   Bitcoin—Taxable?

With the proliferation of virtual currency (like bitcoin), you would expect the IRS to provide guidance as to how virtual currency transactions are taxed. You expect correctly. In IRS Notice 2014-21, the IRS ruled that virtual currency is treated as property. Taxpayers who receive it as payment for goods or services must include in gross income the fair market value of the virtual currency measured in U.S. dollars on the date of payment or receipt. For this purpose, receiving bitcoin is just like receiving cash.

What happens when a taxpayer disposes of virtual currency (e.g., buying something with bitcoin)? Unlike cash, because virtual currency is treated as property, a taxpayer will generally have a gain or loss on the exchange of virtual currency. The gain or loss is determined by comparing the fair market value of the property, cash, or services received to the taxpayer's cost basis (investment) in the virtual currency. The character of the gain or deductibility of the loss on the exchange depends on how the taxpayer "holds" the virtual currency (either as a capital asset or ordinary income property).

Return of Capital Principle   When taxpayers sell assets, they must determine the extent to which they include the sale proceeds in gross income. Initially, the IRS was convinced that Congress's all-inclusive definition of income required taxpayers to include *all* sale proceeds in gross income. Taxpayers, on the other hand, argued that a portion of proceeds from a sale represented a return of the cost or capital investment in the underlying property (called **tax basis**). The courts determined that when receiving a payment for property, taxpayers are allowed to recover the cost of the property tax-free. Consequently, when taxpayers sell property, they are allowed to reduce the sale proceeds by their unrecovered investment in the property to determine the realized gain from the sale.[2] When the tax basis exceeds the sale proceeds, the **return of capital** principle generally applies to the extent of the sale proceeds. The excess of basis over sale proceeds is generally not considered to be a return of capital, but rather a loss that is deductible only if specifically authorized by the tax code. Below, we revisit the return of capital principle when we discuss asset dispositions.

The return of capital principle gets complicated when taxpayers sell assets and collect the sale proceeds over several periods. In these cases, the principle is usually modified by law to provide that the return of capital occurs pro rata as the proceeds are collected over time. We discuss this issue in more detail later in this chapter when we discuss the taxation of annuities.

Recovery of Amounts Previously Deducted   A refund is not typically included in gross income because it usually represents a return of capital. For example, a refund of $1,000 on an auto purchased for $12,000 simply reduces the net cost of the vehicle to $11,000. Likewise, a $200 refund of a $700 business expense is not included in gross income but instead reduces the net expense to $500. However, if the refund is made for an expenditure deducted in a *previous* year, then under the **tax benefit rule** the refund is included in gross income to the extent that the prior deduction produced a tax benefit.[3] For example, suppose an individual paid a $1,000 business expense claimed as a *for* AGI deduction in 2017, but $250 of the expense was subsequently reimbursed in 2018. Because the $250 business deduction produced a tax benefit in 2017 (reduced taxable income), the $250 refund in 2018 would be included in income.

The application of the tax benefit rule is more complex for individuals who itemize deductions. An itemized deduction only produces a tax benefit to the extent that total itemized deductions exceed the standard deduction. For example, suppose that an individual's total itemized deductions exceeded the standard deduction by $100. A refund of $150 of itemized deductions would cause the individual's itemized deductions to fall $50 beneath the standard deduction. If the refund occurred in the same year as the expense, the individual would have elected the standard deduction, and the refund would have caused taxable income to increase by only $100 (the difference between claiming the standard deduction and the total itemized deductions that would have been claimed in the absence of any refund). If the refund occurs the year after the deduction is claimed, then only $100 of the $150 refund would be included in gross income under the tax benefit rule. The $100 is added to taxable income in the year of the refund because this is the increment in taxable income that would have resulted if the refund was issued in the year the itemized deduction was claimed.

Example 5-3

In 2017 Courtney paid $3,500 in Ohio state income taxes, and she included this payment with her other itemized deductions when she filed her federal income tax return in March of 2018. Courtney filed her 2017 federal return as a head of household and claimed $15,600 of itemized deductions. She also filed an Ohio state income tax return in March of 2018 and discovered she only owed $3,080 in Ohio income tax for 2017. Hence, Courtney received a $420 refund of her Ohio income tax in June of 2018. How much of the $420 refund, if any, is Courtney required to include in her gross income in 2018? The answer depends upon the standard deduction for 2017. Help Courtney apply the tax benefit rule (the standard deduction for head of household filling status in 2017 was $9,350).

(*continued on page 5-6*)

[2]§1001(a).
[3]§111.

Answer: All $420. Courtney is required to include the entire refund in her 2018 gross income because her itemized deduction for the $420 of state income taxes that she overpaid last year reduced her taxable income by $420. Accordingly, because she received a tax benefit (deduction) for the entire $420 overpayment, she must include it all in gross income in 2018. See the following for the calculation of the amount of tax benefit Courtney received from the $420 overpayment of taxes in 2017.

Deduction	Amount	Explanation
(1) Itemized deductions	$15,600	
(2) 2017 standard deduction	9,350	Head of household filing status
(3) Reduction in taxable income	15,600	Greater of (1) and (2)
(4) Itemized deductions adjusted for the $420 refund	15,180	(1) − $420
(5) Reduction in taxable income after adjustment for the $420 refund	15,180	Greater of (2) and (4)
Tax benefit due to prior deduction of $420 refund	**$ 420**	(3) − (5)

What if: Let's consider alternative fact patterns provided in Scenarios A and B to further illustrate the application of the tax benefit rule.

Scenario A: In 2017 Courtney's itemized deductions, including $3,500 in state taxes, were $5,500.

Scenario B: In 2017 Courtney's itemized deductions, including $3,500 in state taxes, were $9,550.

How much of the $420 refund would Courtney include in her 2018 gross income in Scenarios A and B?

Answer Scenario A: $0. As computed below, Courtney received $0 tax benefit from the $420 tax overpayment in 2017, so she need not include any of the refund in her gross income.

Answer Scenario B: $200. As computed below, Courtney received a $200 tax benefit (reduction in taxable income) from the $420 state tax overpayment in 2017, so she must include $200 of the refund in her 2018 gross income.

Deduction	Scenario A Amount	Scenario B Amount	Explanation
(1) Itemized deductions	$5,500	$9,550	
(2) 2017 standard deduction	9,350	9,350	Head of household filing status
(3) Reduction in taxable income	9,350	9,550	Greater of (1) and (2)
(4) Itemized deductions adjusted for the $420 refund	5,080	9,130	(1) − $420
(5) Reduction in taxable income adjusted for the $420 refund	9,350	9,350	Greater of (2) and (4)
Tax benefit due to prior deduction of $420 refund	**$ 0**	**$ 200**	(3) − (5)

When Do Taxpayers Recognize Income?

Individual taxpayers generally file tax returns reporting their taxable income for a calendar-year period, whereas corporations often use a fiscal year-end. In either case, the taxpayer's method of accounting generally determines the year in which realized income is recognized and included in gross income.

Accounting Methods   Most large corporations use the accrual method of accounting. Under the **accrual method,** income is generally recognized when earned, and expenses are generally deducted in the period when liabilities are incurred. In contrast, most individuals use the **cash method** as their overall method of accounting.[4] Under the cash method, taxpayers recognize income in the period they receive it (in the form of cash,

---

[4]Taxpayers involved in a business may use the accrual or hybrid overall method of accounting. We discuss these methods in the Business Income, Deductions, and Accounting Methods chapter.

property, or services), rather than when they actually earn it. Likewise, cash-method taxpayers claim deductions when they make expenditures, rather than when they incur liabilities. The cash method greatly simplifies the computation of income for the overwhelming majority of individuals, many of whom have neither the time nor the training to apply the accrual method. Another advantage of the cash method is that taxpayers may have some control over when income is received and expenses are paid. Because of this control, taxpayers can more easily use the timing tax planning strategy (described in the Tax Planning Strategies and Related Limitations chapter) to lower the present value of their tax bill.

Constructive Receipt   Taxpayers using the cash method of accounting may try to shift income from the current year to the next year when they receive payments near year-end. For instance, taxpayers may merely delay cashing a check or avoid picking up a compensation payment until after year-end. The courts responded to this ploy by devising the **constructive receipt doctrine.**[5] The constructive receipt doctrine states that a taxpayer realizes and recognizes income when it is actually or *constructively* received. Constructive receipt is deemed to occur when the income has been credited to the taxpayer's account or when the income is unconditionally available to the taxpayer, the taxpayer is aware of the income's availability, and there are no restrictions on the taxpayer's control over the income.

> **THE KEY FACTS**
>
> **Income Recognition**
>
> - Cash-method taxpayers recognize income when it is received.
> - Income is realized regardless of whether payments are received in money, property, *or* services.
> - Income is taxed in the period in which a cash-method taxpayer has a right to receive payment without substantial restrictions.

Example 5-4

Courtney is a cash-method taxpayer. Based on her outstanding performance, Courtney earned a $4,800 year-end bonus. On December 28, Courtney's supervisor told her that her bonus was issued as a separate check and that Courtney could pick up the check in the accounting office anytime. Courtney did not pick up the check until January 2 of the next year, and she did not cash it until late January. When does Courtney realize and recognize the $4,800 income?

Answer: On December 28 of the tax year in question. Courtney *constructively* received the check that year because it was unconditionally available to her on December 28, she was aware of the check's availability, and there were no restrictions on her control over the check. Courtney must include the $4,800 bonus in gross income for that year, even though she did not actually receive the funds until late January of the next year.[6]

Claim of Right   The **claim of right doctrine** is another judicial doctrine created to address the timing of income recognition. This doctrine applies to situations in which a taxpayer receives income in one period but is required to return the payment in a subsequent period. The claim of right doctrine states that income has been realized if a taxpayer receives income and there are no restrictions on the taxpayer's use of the income (e.g., the taxpayer does not have an obligation to repay the amount). A common example of the claim of right doctrine is a cash bonus paid to employees based on company earnings. Despite *potentially* having to repay the bonuses (e.g., in the case of a "clawback" provision that requires repayment if the company has an earnings restatement), the employees would include the bonuses in gross income in the year received because there are no restrictions on their use of the income.[7]

---

[5]Justice Holmes summarized this doctrine as follows: "The income that is subject to a man's unfettered command and that he is free to enjoy at his own option may be taxed to him as his income, whether he sees fit to enjoy it or not." *Corliss v. Bowers* (S. Ct., 1930), 281 US 376.

[6]Note also that Courtney's employer would include her bonus on Courtney's W-2 for the year in which it issued the check.

[7]§1341 provides relief for a taxpayer who recognizes taxable income because of the claim of right doctrine and in a later year determines that she does not have a claim of right. Specifically, §1341 provides that if a taxpayer recognizes taxable income in an earlier year because she has a "claim of right" (unrestricted right) to the income received, a deduction is then allowable in a later year because she did not have an unrestricted right to the income, and if the related tax deduction exceeds $3,000, then the tax imposed in the later year is the lesser of (1) the tax for the taxable year computed with the deduction or (2) the tax for the taxable year computed without the deduction, less a tax credit for the previous tax paid on the item of income. Beginning in 2018, individuals who are required to repay compensation previously recognized in a prior year under the claim of right doctrine are not allowed a deduction for the repayment if the amount does not exceed $3,000.

Who Recognizes the Income?

In addition to determining *when* taxpayers realize and recognize income, it is important to consider *who* (which taxpayer) recognizes the income. This question often arises when taxpayers attempt to shift income to other related taxpayers through the income-shifting strategy. For example, a father (with a high marginal income tax rate) might wish to assign his paycheck to his minor child (with a low marginal income tax rate) to minimize their collective tax burden.

Assignment of Income

The courts developed the **assignment of income doctrine** to prevent taxpayers from arbitrarily transferring the taxation on their income to others. In essence, the assignment of income doctrine holds that the taxpayer who earns income from services must recognize the income. Likewise, income from property, such as dividends and interest, is taxable to the person who actually owns the income-producing property.[8] For example, interest income from a bond is taxable to the person who owns the bond during the time the interest income accrues. Thus, to shift income from property to another person, a taxpayer must also transfer the *ownership* in the property to the other person.

Example 5-5

What if: Courtney would like to begin saving for Deron's college tuition. If Courtney were to direct EWD to deposit part of her salary in Deron's bank account, who would pay tax on the salary income?

Answer: Courtney would be taxed on her entire salary as income because she earned the income.[9] The payment to Deron would be treated as a gift and would not be taxable to him (gifts are excluded from the recipient's income, as discussed later in the chapter).

What if: Suppose that Courtney wanted to shift her rental income to Deron. What would Courtney need to do to ensure that her rental income is taxed to Deron?

Answer: Courtney would have to transfer her ownership in the rental property to Deron in order for Deron to be taxed on the rental income.[10]

Community Property Systems

While most states use a common law system, nine states (Arizona, California, Idaho, Louisiana, Nevada, New Mexico, Texas, Washington, and Wisconsin) implement **community property systems.** Under community property systems, the income earned from services by one spouse is treated as though it were earned equally by both spouses. Also, property acquired by either spouse during the marriage is usually community property and is treated as though it is owned equally by each spouse.[11] Property that a spouse brings into a marriage is treated as that spouse's separate property. For federal income tax purposes, the community property system has the following consequences:

- Half of the income earned from the *services* of one spouse is included in the gross income of the other spouse.
- Half of the income from property held as *community* property by the married couple is included in the gross income of each spouse.

---

[8]This rule of thumb is also referred to as the "fruit and the tree" doctrine because of the analogy to fruit belonging to the tree upon which it was grown. See *Lucas v. Earl* (1930) 281 US 111 and *Helvering v. Horst* (1940) 311 US 112.

[9]Note also, that EWD has the responsibility of issuing a W-2 to the taxpayer who provided the services—Courtney in this case.

[10]As explained in the Individual Income Tax Computation and Tax Credits chapter, the tax savings from such a transfer would be mitigated in the calculation of Deron's tax by the so-called "kiddie" tax. Likewise, Courtney should consider the gift tax implications of this transfer before transferring the property to Deron.

[11]Property acquired during the marriage via gift or inheritance or purchased with a spouse's separate property is considered separate property.

- In five community property states (Arizona, California, Nevada, New Mexico, and Washington), all of the income from property owned *separately* by one spouse is included in that spouse's gross income.
- In Texas, Louisiana, Wisconsin, and Idaho, half of the income from property owned *separately* by one spouse is included in the gross income of each spouse.

In contrast, for federal income tax purposes, the common law system has the following consequences:

- All of the income earned from the *services* of one spouse is included in the gross income of the spouse who earned it.
- For property owned *separately*, all of the income from the separately owned property is included in that spouse's gross income.
- For property owned *jointly* (i.e., not separately), each co-owner is taxed on the income attributable to his or her share of the property. For example, suppose that a parcel of property is jointly owned by husband and wife. One-half of the income from the property would be included in the gross income of each spouse. Similarly, income from property owned by three or more persons would be included in the gross income of each co-owner based on his or her respective ownership share.

Example 5-6

In the year prior to their divorce, Courtney and Al Wilson lived in Ohio, a common law state and file married filing separately. That year, Al earned $90,000 of annual salary and Courtney earned $60,000. How much of the income earned by Al and by Courtney in the year prior to the divorce did Al report on his individual tax return? How much income did Courtney report on her individual tax return?

Answer: Because they resided in a common law state, Al reports the $90,000 that he earned on his own tax return, and Courtney reports the $60,000 she earned on her own tax return.

What if: How much of this income would Al have been required to include on his individual tax return, and how much of this income would Courtney have been required to report on her individual tax return, if they lived in California, a community property state?

Answer: If they resided in a community property state, both Al and Courtney would have included $75,000 of the $150,000 the couple had jointly earned [(Al's $90,000 + Courtney's $60,000)/2] on their respective individual tax returns.

If a couple files a joint tax return, the community property rules do not affect the aggregate taxes payable by the couple, because the income of both spouses is aggregated on the return. However, when couples file separate tax returns, their combined tax liability may depend on whether they live in a common law state, a community property state that shares income from separate property equally between spouses, or a community property state that does not split income from separate property between spouses.[12]

TYPES OF INCOME

LO 5-2

Now that we have a basic understanding of the general definition of gross income and related concepts, let's turn our attention to specific *types* of income subject to taxation. Our discussion is organized around income from services, income from property, and other sources of income.

---

[12]§66 provides rules that allow spouses living apart in community property states to be taxed on his or her own income from services if (1) the taxpayers live apart for the entire year, (2) they do not file a joint tax return with each other, and (3) they do not transfer any of the income from services between each other.

Income from Services

Income from labor is one of the most common sources of gross income, and it is rarely exempt from taxation. This income includes salary, wages, unemployment compensation, and fees that a taxpayer earns through services in a nonemployee capacity. Income from services is often referred to as **earned income** because it is generated by the efforts of the taxpayer (this also includes business income earned by a taxpayer even if the taxpayer's business is selling inventory).

To facilitate the employees' reporting of their salaries and wages, employees receive a Form W-2 from their employers at the end of each year, which summarizes their salary and wage compensation and tax withholding. Gross income includes all forms of compensation unless the tax law provides a specific exclusion. Later in this chapter, we discuss specific exclusions for employer-provided benefits.

Example 5-7

EWD pays Courtney a salary of $118,000. In addition, Courtney earned and received $19,500 in fees from consulting work she did on weekends independent of her employment with EWD. She incurred $1,500 in miscellaneous expenses for supplies and transportation while doing the consulting work. What is Courtney's total *income* from services (earned income) from her employment and from her self-employment activities?

Answer: $136,000, consisting of her $118,000 of salary and her $19,500 business income from her consulting activities, less the $1,500 of expenses related to her consulting activities. Note that business deductions are *for* AGI deductions that taxpayers subtract from their gross business income to derive net business income or loss, reported on page 1 of Form 1040. We discuss these deductions in greater detail in the Individual *For* AGI Deductions chapter.

Employee Stock Options   In addition to receiving cash compensation, employees may receive equity-based compensation in the form of stock options or stock awards. Stock options are classified for tax purposes as either nonqualified options (NQOs) or incentive stock options (ISOs). ISOs satisfy certain tax code requirements and provide favorable tax treatment for employees, whereas NQOs do not. For either type of option, employees experience no tax consequences on the **grant date** of the option (the date the options are allocated to the employees) and the **vesting date** (the date when the options can be exercised). However, when they exercise NQOs, employees report ordinary income equal to the total **bargain element** of the stock acquired (the difference in the fair market value of the stock acquired and the purchase price).[13] For NQOs, the employee's basis in the stock acquired is its fair market value, which is the sum of the amount paid for the stock (the **exercise price**) and the bargain element.[14] In contrast, when they exercise ISOs, employees don't report any income for regular tax purposes (as long as they don't immediately sell their shares), and their basis in the shares acquired with ISOs is the exercise price. (However, the bargain element is included in income for alternative minimum tax purposes. We discuss the alternative minimum tax in the Individual Income Tax Computation and Tax Credits chapter.) The holding period for stock shares acquired with NQOs and ISOs begins on the **exercise date** (the date the options are exercised).

[13]When employees exercise NQOs and the related stock is subject to sale restrictions, the employees report ordinary income at the time the restrictions lapse equal to the difference in the fair market value of the stock at the date the restrictions lapse and the purchase price.

[14]Restricted stock (stock employees receive as compensation that may be sold only after the passage of time or after certain performance targets are achieved) is taxed like NQOs with two important distinctions: while employees receiving NQOs are taxed as compensation on the bargain element of the shares when they exercise their options, employees receiving restricted stock are taxed on the *full fair market value* of the shares *on the date the restricted stock vests* (the selling restrictions lapse). Any subsequent appreciation in the value of the stock is taxed as either long-term or short-term capital gain(s) or loss(es) when the taxpayer sells the stock, depending on the holding period and future movement of the stock price. The employee's holding period for the stock begins on the vesting date.

Employees who acquire shares through the exercise of ISOs have an additional benefit: *If they hold such shares for at least two years after the grant date and one year after the exercise date*, they will treat the difference between the sale proceeds and the tax basis (the exercise price) as a long-term capital gain in the year of disposition.[15] Thus, unlike NQOs, the bargain element is treated as a long-term capital gain and is not subject to tax until the stock is sold. If, however, the employee does not meet the two-year and one-year holding requirements, the premature sale of the stock is classified as a disqualifying disposition, and the bargain element is taxed at the time of sale as if the option had been an NQO (i.e., as compensation income). Any remaining gain on the sale is treated as a capital gain.[16]

Example 5-8

What if: Suppose that in addition to her salary, Courtney acquires 20,000 shares of EWD with NQOs (20,000 NQOs × 1 share per NQO) and 5,000 shares with ISOs (5,000 ISOs × 1 share per ISO). Given that the fair market value of EWD stock is $20 per share on the exercise date and the exercise price is $5 per share for the NQOs and ISOs, how much income will Courtney report on the day she exercises the options?

Answer: $300,000 ordinary income from the NQOs, calculated below, and $0 for the ISOs (she must include the bargain element of $75,000 on the 5,000 ISOs in her AMT calculation).

Description	Amount	Explanation
(1) Shares acquired with NQOs	20,000	
(2) Market price per share	$ 20	
(3) Exercise price	5	
(4) Bargain element per share	$ 15	(2) − (3)
Bargain element (ordinary income)	**$300,000**	(1) × (4)

What is Courtney's basis in the 20,000 shares she acquired with NQOs?

Answer: $400,000. [$100,000 (20,000 shares × $5 per share exercise price) + $300,000 (bargain element taxed as ordinary income).]

What is Courtney's basis in the 5,000 shares she acquired through ISOs?

Answer: $25,000. (5,000 shares acquired × $5 per share exercise price.)

Example 5-9

What if: Suppose that five years after Courtney exercised her NQOs and acquired 20,000 EWD shares with a basis of $20 per share, she sold all of the shares for $25 per share. What is the amount and character of the gain she will recognize on the sale?

Answer: $100,000 long-term capital gain, calculated as follows:

Description	Amount	Explanation
(1) Amount realized (sale proceeds)	$ 500,000	(20,000 × $25)
(2) Tax basis	400,000	Example 5-8
Long-term capital gain recognized	**$100,000**	(1) − (2)

What if: If Courtney sold the shares for $25 per share six months after she exercised them, what would be the character of the $100,000 gain she would recognize on the sale?

Answer: Short-term capital gain, because she held the shares for one year or less before selling them.

---

[15]§422(a)(1).

[16]If the stock is sold at a loss, the employee would treat the loss as a capital loss and would not recognize the prior bargain element as compensation income. If the stock is sold at a gain (but at less than the original bargain element of the stock), the employee simply recognizes the difference between the sales price and exercise price as compensation income.

Example 5-10

What if: Suppose that five years after Courtney exercised her ISOs and acquired 5,000 EWD shares with a basis of $5 per share, she sold all of the shares for $25 per share. What are the amount and the character of the gain she will recognize on the sale?

Answer: Courtney will recognize a $100,000 long-term capital gain, calculated as follows:

Description	Amount	Explanation
(1) Amount realized	$ 125,000	(5,000 × $25)
(2) Tax basis	25,000	Example 5-8
Long-term capital gain recognized	**$100,000**	(1) – (2)

Example 5-11

What if: Assume that Courtney exercised her ISOs and executed a same-day sale of the 5,000 shares on the vesting date (January 1, year 3) when the share price was $15. What is the amount and character of income she will recognize on these transactions?

Answer: $50,000 ordinary income. Because Courtney's sale is a disqualifying disposition (she did not hold the shares for at least one year), the transactions are recast as though she exercised nonqualified options. See computations below.

Description	Amount	Explanation
(1) Shares acquired with ISOs that were disqualified (became NQOs)	5,000	
(2) Market price per share	$ 15	
(3) Exercise price	5	Example 5-8
(4) Bargain element per share	$ 10	(2) – (3)
Bargain element (ordinary income)	**$50,000**	(1) × (4)

Income from Property

Income from property, often referred to as **unearned income,** may take different forms, such as gains or losses from the sale of property, dividends, interest, rents, royalties, and annuities.[17] The tax treatment of unearned income depends upon the type of income and, in some circumstances, the type of transaction generating the income. For example, as discussed in the Individual Income Tax Overview, Dependents, and Filing Status chapter, qualified dividends and long-term capital gains are taxed at preferential tax rates, whereas other unearned income is generally taxed at ordinary tax rates. Likewise, while gains or losses are typically recognized in the current period, certain types of gains and losses are postponed indefinitely. We discuss annuity income, property dispositions, and capital gains and losses briefly in the following paragraphs. We discuss income from the sale of business assets in more detail in the Property Dispositions chapter.

Example 5-12

Courtney owns 1,000 shares of GE stock that she registered in a dividend reinvestment plan. Under this plan, all dividends are automatically used to purchase more shares of the stock. This year, GE declared and paid $700 in dividends on Courtney's stock. Must Courtney include the dividend in her gross income for the year?

Answer: Yes. Courtney includes the $700 of dividends (unearned income) in her gross income. The fact that Courtney chose to reinvest the dividends does not affect their taxability, because she received an economic benefit and change in property rights associated with the dividend.

[17]The tax definition of unearned income is different from the financial accounting definition. Unearned income for financial accounting purposes is a liability that represents advance payments for goods or services.

Example 5-13

Gram purchased a $100,000, three-year certificate of deposit (CD) with a portion of the life insurance proceeds she received on Gramps's death. At year-end, her CD account is credited with $4,100 of interest, and her savings account is credited with $650 of interest. Courtney had a total of $271 of interest credited to her savings account and $50 credited to her checking account during the year. How much interest must Gram and Courtney include in their gross income for the year?

Answer: Gram must include the $4,100 of interest credited to her CD account and the $650 of interest credited to her savings account this year, regardless of whether she withdraws the interest or not. Courtney must include the $271 of interest credited to her savings account and the $50 credited to her checking account, regardless of whether she withdraws the interest or not.[18]

Example 5-14

Courtney owns a condo in town that she rents to tenants. This year, the condo generated $14,000 of rental revenue. Courtney incurred $4,000 in real estate taxes, $2,500 in utility expenses, $500 in advertising expenses, and $2,000 of depreciation and other expenses associated with the rental. What effect does the rental have on Courtney's *gross income*? What effect does the rental have on Courtney's *taxable income*?

Answer: The rent increases Courtney's *gross income* by $14,000. However, after considering her allowable deductions for the rental, Courtney will only report $5,000 of *taxable income* from rental activities, computed as follows:

Description	Amount
Rental revenue	$14,000
Less allowable deductions:	
Real estate taxes	$(4,000)
Utilities	(2,500)
Advertising	(500)
Depreciation and other expenses	(2,000)
Total rental expenses	(9,000)
Net rental (taxable) income	$ 5,000

Annuities   An **annuity** is an investment that pays a stream of equal payments over time. Individuals often purchase annuities as a means of generating a fixed income stream during retirement. There are two basic types of annuities: (1) annuities paid over a fixed period and (2) annuities paid over a person's life (for as long as the person lives). The challenge from a tax perspective is to determine how much of each annuity payment represents gross income (income taxed at ordinary tax rates) and how much represents a nontaxable *return of capital* (return of the original investment). For both types of annuities, the tax law deems a *portion* of each annuity payment as a nontaxable return of capital and the remainder as gross income. Taxpayers use the *annuity exclusion ratio* to determine the portion of each payment that is a nontaxable return of capital.

$$\text{Annuity exclusion ratio} = \frac{\textit{Original investment}}{\textit{Expected value of annuity}} = \text{Return of capital } \textit{percentage}$$

[18]While taxpayers generally recognize interest income when they receive the interest payments, special rules apply to the timing and amount of interest from bonds when there is a bond discount (bonds are issued at an amount below maturity value) or a bond premium (bonds are issued at an amount above the maturity value). Specifically, taxpayers must amortize the bond discount and include in income the current-year amortization plus any interest received. In contrast, taxpayers may elect to amortize a bond premium. In this scenario, the current-year amortization offsets a portion of the interest payments received. Different rules apply for bond discounts if the taxpayer purchases the bond in the secondary bond market at a discount. In this case, the taxpayer can elect but is not required to amortize the bond discount.

For fixed annuities, the expected value is the number of payments times the amount of the payment. In other words, for an annuity payable over a fixed term the return of capital is simply the original investment divided by the number of payments. The number of payments, however, is uncertain for annuities paid over a person's life. For these annuities, taxpayers must use IRS tables to determine the expected value based upon the taxpayer's life expectancy at the start of the annuity.[19] To calculate the expected value of the annuity, the number of annual payments from the table (referred to as the expected return multiple) is multiplied by the annual payment amount. Taxpayers with an annuity paid over the life of one person (a single-life annuity) use the expected return multiple from the table, a portion of which is presented in Exhibit 5-1.

EXHIBIT 5-1   **Table for Expected Return Multiple for Ordinary Single-Life Annuity**

Age at Annuity Starting Date	Expected Return Multiple
68	17.6
69	16.8
70	16.0
71	15.3
72	14.6

Some annuities provide payments over the lives of two people. For example, a taxpayer may purchase an annuity that provides an annual payment each year until both the taxpayer *and* the taxpayer's spouse pass away. This type of annuity is called a joint-life annuity. The IRS provides a separate table for determining the expected number of payments from joint-life annuities.

A taxpayer receiving a life annuity who lives longer than his or her estimated life expectancy will ultimately receive more than the expected number of payments. The entire amount of these "extra" payments is included in the taxpayer's gross income because the taxpayer has completely recovered her investment in the annuity by the time she receives them. If the taxpayer dies *before* receiving the expected number of payments, the amount of the unrecovered investment (the initial investment less the amounts received, which is treated as a nontaxable return of capital) is deducted on the taxpayer's final income tax return.[20]

Example 5-15

In January of this year, Gram purchased an annuity from UBET Insurance Co. that will pay her $10,000 per year for the next 15 years. Gram received the first $10,000 payment in December. Gram paid $99,000 for the annuity and will receive $150,000 over the life of the annuity (15 years × $10,000 per year). How much of the $10,000 payment Gram receives in December should she include in her gross income?

Answer: $3,400. Because Gram purchased a fixed-payment annuity, the portion of the annuity payment included in gross income is calculated as follows:

Description	Amount	Explanation
(1) Investment in annuity contract	$99,000	
(2) Number of payments	15	
(3) Return of capital per payment	$ 6,600	(1)/(2)
(4) Amount of each payment	$10,000	
Gross income per payment	**$ 3,400**	(4) − (3)

[19]See Reg. §1.72-9. Special rules under §72(d) apply to annuities from qualified retirement plans. These rules only apply when a taxpayer makes an after-tax contribution to a qualified employer retirement plan (which is uncommon). In most cases, taxpayers only make pretax contributions to qualified retirement plans, which results in fully taxable annuity distributions.

[20]The unrecovered cost of the annuity is deducted as a miscellaneous itemized deduction. See §72(b)(3) and §67(b)(10).

What if: Assume the annuity Gram purchased pays her $1,000 per month over the remainder of her life. Gram (70 years old) paid $99,000 for the annuity, and she received her first $1,000 payment in December of this year. How much income would she recognize on the $1,000 payment?

Answer: $484.40, computed as follows:

Description	Amount	Explanation
(1) Investment in annuity contract	$ 99,000	
(2) Expected return multiple	16	Exhibit 5-1, 70 years old
(3) Amount of each payment	$ 1,000	
(4) Expected return	$192,000	(2) × (3) × 12 months
(5) Return of capital percentage	51.56%	(1)/(4)
(6) Return of capital per payment	$ 515.60	(3) × (5)
Taxable income per payment	**$ 484.40**	(3) − (6)

After Gram receives her entire $99,000 as a return of capital, each subsequent $1,000 annuity payment will be fully taxable.

Property Dispositions   Taxpayers can realize a gain or loss when disposing of an asset. Consistent with the return of capital principle we discussed above, taxpayers are allowed to recover their investment in property (tax basis) before they realize any gain. A loss is realized when the proceeds are less than the tax basis in the property. Because the return of capital principle generally applies only to the extent of the sale proceeds, a loss does not necessarily reduce the taxpayer's taxable income. A loss will reduce the taxpayer's taxable income only if the loss is deductible. Exhibit 5-2 presents a general formula for computing the gain or loss from the sale of an asset.

EXHIBIT 5-2   Formula for Calculating Gain (Loss) from Sale of an Asset

Sales proceeds
Less: Selling expenses
= Amount realized
Less: Tax basis (investment) in property sold
= Gain (Loss) on sale

Example 5-16

On December 31, Gram sold her 50 shares of Acme Corporation stock for $40 per share. Gram also paid $150 in broker's commissions on the sale. Gram originally purchased the shares in April of this year for $30 per share. How much gross income does Gram recognize from the stock sale?

Answer: Gram recognizes $350 gross income on the sale, computed as follows:

Sale proceeds ($40 × 50 shares)	$2,000
Less: Selling expenses	−150
= Amount realized	$1,850
Less: Tax basis (investment) in property sold ($30 × 50 shares)	−1,500
Gain (Loss) on sale	**$ 350**

Because a taxpayer cannot accurately compute the gain or loss on the sale of a capital asset without knowing its basis, it is important for taxpayers to maintain accurate records to track their basis in capital assets. This process is relatively straightforward for unique assets such as a taxpayer's personal residence or individual jewels in a taxpayer's jewelry collection. However, capital assets such as shares of stock are much more homogeneous and difficult to track. For example, a taxpayer may purchase blocks of stock in a given corporation at different times over a period of several years, paying a different price per share for each block of stock acquired. When the taxpayer sells shares of this stock in subsequent years, what basis does she use to compute gain or loss? Taxpayers who haven't adequately tracked the basis in their stock are required to use the **first-in, first-out (FIFO) method** of determining the basis of the shares they sell.[21] However, if they maintain good records, they can use the **specific identification method** to determine the basis of the shares they sell. (Brokers are now required to track and report basis for stock acquired on or after January 1, 2011.) Taxpayers using the specific identification method can choose to sell their high-basis stock first, minimizing their gains or increasing their losses on stock dispositions.

The rate at which taxpayers are taxed on gains from property dispositions and the extent to which they can deduct losses from property dispositions depends on whether they used the asset for business purposes, investment purposes, or personal purposes. For example, as we discussed in the Individual Income Tax Overview, Dependents, and Filing Status chapter, long-term capital gains realized by individuals are taxed at preferential tax rates, and deductions for net capital losses realized by individuals are limited to $3,000 per year. In contrast, losses realized on assets used for personal purposes are generally not deductible. In the following paragraphs, we discuss the taxation of capital gains and losses in more detail. In the Property Dispositions chapter, we discuss the gains on the sale of business assets.

Capital Gains and Losses Capital assets are typically investment-type assets and personal-use assets.[22] Thus, artwork, corporate stock, bonds, your personal residence, and even your iPad are capital assets. When a taxpayer sells a capital asset for more than its tax basis, the taxpayer recognizes a capital gain; if a taxpayer sells a capital asset for less than its tax basis, the taxpayer recognizes a capital loss (to the extent the loss is deductible). Taxpayers selling capital assets that they hold for a year or less recognize **short-term capital gains or losses.**[23] Alternatively, taxpayers selling capital assets they hold for more than a year recognize **long-term capital gains or losses.** The holding period begins on the day after acquisition and includes the day of sale. Short-term capital gains are taxed at ordinary rather than preferential rates. In contrast, long-term capital gains are taxed at preferential rates.

Not all long-term capital gains are created equal. Although long-term capital gains are generally taxed at 0 percent, 15 percent, or 20 percent depending on the taxpayer's income, there are several exceptions to the general rule. For example, certain long-term capital gains are taxed at a maximum rate of 25 percent (unrecaptured §1250 gain is discussed in the Property Dispositions chapter), gains from the sale of collectibles are taxed at a maximum 28 percent rate, and §1202 gains are taxed at a 0 percent tax rate. Collectibles consist of works of art, any rug or antique, any metal or gem, any stamp or coin, any alcoholic beverage, or any other similar item held for more than one year.[24] Section 1202 gains are gains from the sale of qualified small business stock held for *more*

---

[21]Reg. §1.1012-1(c)(1).

[22]§1221 defines capital assets in the negative. This code section excludes inventory, depreciable property, or real property used in a trade or business; certain self-created intangibles, accounts, or notes receivable; U.S. government publications; certain commodities derivative financial instruments; certain hedging transactions; and supplies from the definition of a capital asset.

[23]Nonbusiness bad debt is treated as a short-term capital loss no matter how long the debt was outstanding before it became worthless. Whether a bad debt is considered to be a business bad debt for individuals depends on the facts and circumstances. In general, if the taxpayer experiencing the loss is in the business of loaning money, the bad debt should be considered to be business bad debt; otherwise, the bad debt will likely be considered nonbusiness bad debt.

[24]§408(m).

than five years.[25] When taxpayers sell qualified small business stock that was (a) acquired after September 27, 2010, and (b) held for more than five years, they may exclude (subject to limitations) 100 percent of the gain on the sale from regular taxable income.[26]

Exhibit 5-3 presents the maximum tax rates applicable to capital gains.

EXHIBIT 5-3   Classification of Capital Gains by Maximum Applicable Tax Rates

Short-Term or Long-Term Gain	Type	Maximum Rate
Short term	All	37%*
Long term	Collectibles	28%*
Held > 5 years	Qualified small business stock purchased after September 27, 2010	0%
Long term	Unrecaptured §1250 gain from depreciable realty	25%*
Long term	All remaining capital gain (and §1231 gains) not included elsewhere	20%†

*Lower rates will apply when the taxpayer's ordinary rate is less than the rates reflected in this exhibit.
†The preferential tax rate varies with the taxpayer's taxable income. See Appendix D at the end of the text for the tax brackets by filing status that apply to preferentially taxed capital gains and dividends.

Netting Process for Gains and Losses   To determine the appropriate tax treatment for the capital gains and losses recognized during the year, the taxpayer must engage in a netting process. This netting process can be complex when taxpayers recognize capital losses and long-term capital gains subject to different maximum tax rates. Because 25 percent and 28 percent capital gains are less common, we limit our discussion of the netting for taxpayers who do not recognize any 25 percent or 28 percent rate long-term capital gains. For details regarding the netting process including 25 percent and 28 percent gains, see Appendix A at the end of the chapter.

Step 1: Net all short-term gains and short-term losses, including any short-term capital loss carried forward from a prior year. If the net amount is positive, it is termed a **net short-term capital gain (NSTCG).** If the net amount is negative, it is called a **net short-term capital loss (NSTCL).**

Step 2: Net long-term gains and losses, including any long-term capital loss carried forward from a prior year. If the net amount is positive, the amount is called a **net long-term capital gain (NLTCG).** If negative, the amount is termed a **net long-term capital loss (NLTCL).**

Step 3: If Step 1 and Step 2 both yield gains—*or* if they both yield losses—the netting process ends. Otherwise, net the short- and long-term outcomes against each other to yield a final net gain or net loss, which may be either classified as short term (if the NSTCG exceeds the NLTCL or if the NSTCL exceeds the NLTCG) or long term (if the NLTCG exceeds the NSTCL or if the NLTCL exceeds the NSTCG). When net long-term capital gains exceed net short-term capital losses, if any, the taxpayer is said to have a net capital gain.

[25]§1(h)(7). In general, §1202 defines qualified small business stock as stock received at *original issue* from a C corporation with a gross tax basis in its assets both before and after the issuance of no more than $50,000,000 and with at least 80 percent of the value of its assets used in the active conduct of certain qualified trades or businesses.

[26]The exclusion decreases to 75 percent for qualified small business stock acquired after February 17, 2009, and before September 28, 2010. For qualified small business stock acquired after August 10, 1993, and before February 18, 2009, the exclusion is 50 percent. The gain excluded from sale of qualified small business stock is not an AMT preference item for stock acquired after September 27, 2010, but the gain excluded is an AMT preference item for stock acquired before September 28, 2010.

Example 5-17

What if: Gram decided to pursue her life-long dream of owning a fully loaded Winnebago. To come up with the necessary cash, she sells the following investments:

Stock	Market Value	Basis	Capital Gain/Loss	Scenario 1 Type	Scenario 2 Type
A	$40,000	$ 5,000	$ 35,000	Long	Short
B	20,000	30,000	(10,000)	Long	Short
C	20,000	12,000	8,000	Short	Long
D	17,000	28,000	(11,000)	Short	Long

What is the amount and nature of Gram's capital gains and losses (Scenario 1)?

Answer: $22,000 net capital gain (treated as long-term capital gain), computed as follows:

Step 1: Net short-term gains and short-term losses. The $8,000 short-term gain on stock C is netted against the $11,000 short-term loss on stock D, yielding an NSTCL of $3,000.

Step 2: Net long-term gains and long-term losses. The $35,000 long-term gain on stock A is netted against the $10,000 long-term loss on stock B, producing an NLTCG of $25,000.

Step 3: Net the results of Step 1 and Step 2. The NSTCL from Step 1 is netted with the NLTCG from Step 2 yielding a $22,000 net capital gain [($3,000) + $25,000] taxable at long-term capital gains rates.

What if: Consider the original facts, except that Scenario 2 dictates the long- and short-term capital gains. What is the amount and character of Gram's net gain (or loss) on the sale of the shares in this situation?

Answer: $22,000 net short-term capital gain computed as follows:

Step 1: The gain from stock A would first be netted with the loss from stock B to produce a $25,000 NSTCG [$35,000 + ($10,000)].

Step 2: The loss from stock D and the gain from stock C are combined to provide a $3,000 NLTCL [($11,000) + $8,000].

Step 3: The results from Step 1 and Step 2 are netted to reach a $22,000 net short-term capital gain [$25,000 NSTCG + ($3,000) NLTCL].

THE KEY FACTS

Capital Gains and Losses

- Capital assets are typically investment-type assets and personal-use assets.
- Taxpayers selling capital assets that they hold for a year or less recognize short-term capital gains or losses. Alternatively, taxpayers selling capital assets they hold for more than a year recognize long-term capital gains or losses. Short-term capital gains are taxed at ordinary rather than preferential rates. In contrast, long-term capital gains are taxed at preferential rates.
- To determine the appropriate tax treatment for the capital gains and losses recognized during the year, the taxpayer must engage in a netting process. This netting process can be complex when taxpayers recognize capital losses and long-term capital gains subject to different maximum tax rates.

After completing the netting process, taxpayers must calculate the tax consequences of the resulting outcomes. Net short-term capital gains are included in gross income and taxed as ordinary income. As we discussed and illustrated in the Individual Income Tax Overview, Dependents, and Filing Status chapter, net long-term capital gains are included in gross income and generally are taxed at 0 percent, 15 percent, or 20 percent depending on the taxpayer's taxable income and tax brackets for preferentially taxed capital gains and dividends. Taxpayers can deduct up to $3,000 ($1,500 if married filing separately) of net capital losses against ordinary income. Net capital losses in excess of $3,000 ($1,500 if married filing separately) retain their short- or long-term character and are carried forward and treated as though they were incurred in the subsequent year. Short-term losses are applied first to reduce ordinary income when the taxpayer recognizes both short- and long-term net capital losses. Capital loss carryovers for individuals never expire.

Losses on Sales to Related Persons　　When taxpayers sell assets at a loss to related parties, they are not able to deduct the loss.[27] Instead, the related person acquiring the asset adds the disallowed loss to her basis in the asset and may eventually be allowed to deduct all, a portion, or none of the disallowed loss on a subsequent sale.

Wash Sales　　Consider the case of a taxpayer attempting to do some tax planning near the end of the year: She has invested in the stock of several corporations; some of these investments have appreciated while others have declined in value. The taxpayer wants to

---

[27]§267(a).

capture the tax benefit of the stock losses in the current year to offset ordinary income (up to $3,000) or to offset other capital gains she has already recognized during the year. However, she can't deduct the losses until she sells the stock. Why might this be a problem? If the taxpayer believes that the stocks with unrealized losses are likely to appreciate in the near future, she may prefer *not* to sell those stocks but rather to keep them in her investment portfolio. What might this taxpayer do to deduct the losses while continuing to hold the investment in the stocks? For one, she might be tempted to sell the stocks and then immediately buy them back. Or, she might buy more of the same stock and then sell the stock she originally held to recognize the losses. With this strategy, she hopes to realize (and then recognize or deduct) the losses and, at the end of the day, still hold the stocks in her investment portfolio.

Although this might sound like a great plan, certain wash sale tax rules prevent this strategy from accomplishing the taxpayer's objective. A **wash sale** occurs when an investor sells or trades stock or securities at a loss *and* within 30 days *either before or after* the day of sale buys substantially identical stocks or securities.[28] Because the day of sale is included, the 30-days-before-and-after period creates a 61-day window during which the wash sale provisions may apply.[29] When the wash sale provisions apply to a sale of stock, realized losses are not recognized; instead, the amount of *the unrecognized loss is added to the basis of the newly acquired stock.* Congress created this rule to prevent taxpayers from accelerating losses on securities that have declined in value without actually altering their investment in the securities. The 61-day period ensures that taxpayers cannot deduct losses from stock sales without exposing themselves to the risk that the stock they sold will subsequently increase in value.

Example 5-18

What if: Courtney owns 100 shares of Cisco stock that she purchased in June 2017 for $50 a share. On December 21, 2018, Courtney sells the shares for $40 a share to generate cash for the holidays. This sale generates a capital loss of $1,000 [$4,000 sale proceeds (100 × $40) − $5,000 tax basis ($50 × 100)]. Later, however, Courtney decides that Cisco might be a good long-term investment. On January 3, 2019 (13 days later), Courtney purchases 100 shares of Cisco stock for $41 a share ($4,100). Does Courtney *realize* a short- or long-term capital loss on the December 21 sale?

Answer: Long-term capital loss. She held the stock for more than one year (June 2017 to December 2018) before selling.

How much of the realized $1,000 long-term capital loss can Courtney recognize or deduct on her 2018 tax return?

Answer: Zero. Because Courtney sold the stock at a loss and purchased the same stock within the 61-day period centered on the date of sale (30 days before December 21 and 30 days after December 21), the wash sale rules disallow the loss in 2018. Had Courtney waited just another 18 days to repurchase the Cisco shares, she could have avoided the wash sale rules. In that case, under the general rules for capital loss deductibility, Courtney *would* be able to deduct the $1,000 capital loss from the sale against her ordinary income on her 2018 income tax return.

What tax basis will Courtney have in the Cisco stock she purchased (or repurchased) on January 3, 2019?

Answer: $5,100. Under the wash sale rules, Courtney adds the $1,000 disallowed loss to the basis of the stock she purchased on January 3. Thus, she now owns 100 shares of Cisco stock with a $5,100 basis in the shares, which is $1,000 more than she paid for it.

How much of the $1,000 realized loss would Courtney have recognized if she had only purchased 40 shares of Cisco stock instead of 100 shares on January 3, 2019?

Answer: $600. The wash sale rules disallow the loss to the extent taxpayers acquire other shares in the 61-day window. In this situation, Courtney only acquired 40 percent (40 of 100) of the shares she sold at a loss within the window. Consequently, she must disallow 40 percent, or $400, of the loss, and she is allowed to deduct the remaining $600 loss.

---

[28]Substantially identical stocks or securities include contracts or options to buy substantially identical securities. However, corporate bonds and preferred stock are not generally considered substantially identical to common stock of the same corporation.

[29]§1091.

Other Sources of Gross Income

Taxpayers may receive income from sources other than their efforts (earned income from wages or business) and their property (unearned income such as dividends and interest). In this section we briefly summarize other common types of gross income. If by chance you encounter other types of income that are not specifically discussed here, remember that the tax law is based upon the all-inclusive income concept. That is, unless a specific provision grants exclusion or deferral, economic benefits that are realized generate gross income. This basic understanding of the structure of our tax law (and research skills to investigate the taxability of specific income types) will serve you well as you evaluate whether realized income should be included in gross income.

Income from Flow-Through Entities

Individuals may invest in various business entities. The type of entity for tax purposes for a business affects how the income generated by the business is taxed. For example, income earned by a corporation (other than an S corporation) is taxed at the entity level as opposed to the owner level. In contrast, the income and deductions from a **flow-through entity,** such as a partnership or S corporation (a corporation electing S corporation status), "flow through" to the owners of the entity (partners or shareholders). That is, the owners report income or deductions as though they operated a portion of the business personally. Specifically, each partner or S corporation shareholder reports his or her share of the entity's income and deductions, generally in proportion to his or her ownership percentage, on his or her individual tax return.[30]

Because different types of income and deductions may be treated differently for tax purposes (e.g., qualified dividends are eligible for a special low tax rate), each item the partners or shareholders report on their tax returns retains its underlying tax characteristics. That is, the partners are treated as if they personally received their share of each item of the flow-through entity's income. For example, corporate dividend income paid to a partnership is reported and taxed as dividend income on the partners' individual tax returns. Also, it is important to note that owners of flow-through entities are taxed on their share of the entity's income whether or not cash is distributed to them. When owners receive cash distributions from the entity, the distributions are generally treated as a return of capital to the extent of their investment (tax basis) in the entity and, therefore, not included in the owner's gross income. Distributions reduce the owner's tax basis in the entity, and distributions in excess of basis are taxable. Partnerships and S corporations report to each partner or shareholder that partner or shareholder's share of partnership and S corporation income (or loss) on Schedule K-1 filed with the partnership and S corporation's annual information returns (Form 1065 and 1120S, respectively).[31]

Example 5-19

What if: Suppose that Courtney is a 40 percent partner in KJZ partnership. KJZ reported $20,000 of business income and $3,000 of interest income for the year. KJZ also distributed $1,000 of cash to Courtney. What amount of gross income from her ownership in KJZ partnership would Courtney report for the current year?

Answer: $9,200, consisting of $8,000 of business income ($20,000 × 40%) and $1,200 of interest income ($3,000 × 40%). Courtney would not include the $1,000 distribution in her gross income to the extent that the distribution does not exceed her basis in the partnership. We discuss the basis rules for partners and S corporation shareholders in the Forming and Operating Partnerships, Dispositions of Partnership Interests and Partnership Distributions, and S Corporations chapters.

---

[30]The deduction of losses from partnerships and S corporations are subject to several limitations that we discuss in the Individual Deductions chapter.

[31]See Forms 1065 and 1120S on the IRS website, www.irs.gov.

Alimony When couples legally separate or divorce, one spouse may be required to provide financial support to the other in the form of **alimony.** The tax law defines and specifies the following terms for alimony: (1) a transfer of *cash* is made under a written separation agreement or divorce decree; (2) the separation or divorce decree does not designate the payment as something other than alimony; (3) in the case of legally separated (or divorced) taxpayers under a separation or divorce decree, the spouses do not live together when the payment is made; and (4) the payments cannot continue after the death of the recipient.[32]

For tax purposes, a transfer between former spouses represents alimony only if it meets this definition. For any divorce or separation agreement executed before January 1, 2019, if a payment meets the definition of alimony, then the amount of the payment is included in the gross income of the person receiving it and it is deductible *for* AGI by the person paying it. Thus, alimony shifts income from one spouse to the other.[33] In contrast, for any divorce or separation agreement executed after December 31, 2018, alimony payments are not included in the gross income of the person receiving the payments and are not deductible by the person paying alimony.

Example 5-20

In addition to paying child support, under the divorce decree executed in 2017 Al is required to pay Courtney $20,000 cash each year until she dies. The decree does not designate this amount as a payment for something other than alimony, and Al and Courtney do not live together. Does this payment qualify as alimony?

Answer: Yes. These payments qualify as alimony for tax purposes because (1) they are cash payments made under a divorce decree, (2) they are not designated as something other than alimony, (3) Al and Courtney do not live together, and (4) the payments cease on Courtney's death. In the current year, Al made a $20,000 alimony payment to Courtney. Courtney includes all $20,000 in her gross income. To ensure that the income is taxed only once, Al is allowed to treat the entire payment as a deduction *for* AGI.

What if: Suppose that Courtney and Al's divorce agreement was executed in 2019. What amount of the $20,000 payment would Courtney include in her gross income and would Al deduct?

Answer: Because the divorce agreement was executed after December 31, 2018, Courtney would not include the $20,000 payment in gross income, and Al would not treat the payment as a deduction for AGI.

There may be other types of payments that *do not qualify as alimony*. These include (1) property divisions (who gets the car, house, or china?) and (2) child support payments fixed by the divorce or separation agreement.[34] In any event, if a transfer of property between spouses does *not* meet the definition of alimony, the *recipient* of the transfer *excludes* the value of the transfer from income, and the person transferring the property is not allowed to deduct the value of the property transferred.

---

[32]Source: §71(b). In addition, certain payments to third parties on behalf of the spouse, such as mortgage payments, can also qualify as payments in cash.

[33]To minimize tax-avoidance income shifting between a higher tax rate payor of alimony and a lower tax rate recipient of alimony pursuant to divorce agreement or separation agreement executed before 2019, Congress enacted a complex set of restrictions called the anti-front loading rules that make it difficult for taxpayers to disguise property payments as alimony payments.

[34]Source: §71(c). A payment that is not specifically designated as child support may nonetheless be treated as child support if the payment is reduced on the happening of a specific contingency related to the child. For example, a payment that ceases once a child reaches the age of 18 would be treated as child support.

Example 5-21

As required by the divorce decree, Al made $10,000 in child support payments during the year to Courtney to help her support Deron. Al is required to make child support payments until Deron is 18 years old. Is the current-year payment considered alimony?

Answer: No. The $10,000 of child support payments are not income to Courtney. They are not alimony because the divorce decree specifies that they are for child support. Consequently, Courtney does not include these payments in gross income, and Al does not deduct them.

Example 5-22

As part of the divorce agreement executed in 2017, Al transferred his interest in their joint residence to Courtney. The couple did not have any outstanding debt on the home. At the time of the divorce, the home was valued at $500,000 and Al's share was valued at $250,000. What were the tax consequences of the home ownership transfer to Courtney?

Answer: Because the transfer was not a cash transfer, it did not qualify as alimony. Consequently, Courtney would not have recognized the $250,000 as income, and Al would not have deducted the $250,000 transfer.

Prizes, Awards, and Gambling Winnings   Prizes, awards, and gambling winnings, such as raffle or sweepstakes prizes or lottery winnings, are included in gross income.

Example 5-23

After devoting much of her free time during the year to filling out sweepstakes entries, Gram hit the jackpot. She won a WaveRunner worth $7,500 in a sweepstakes sponsored by *Reader's Digest*. How much of the prize, if any, must Gram include in her gross income?

Answer: Gram must include the full $7,500 value of the WaveRunner in her gross income. Note that because she must pay taxes on the winnings, she is not really getting the WaveRunner for "free."

There are three specific, narrowly defined exceptions to this rule. First, awards for scientific, literary, or charitable achievement such as the Nobel prize are excluded from gross income, *but only if* (1) the recipient was selected without any action on his part to enter the contest or proceeding, (2) the recipient is not required to render substantial future services as a condition to receive the prize or award, and (3) the payer of the prize or award transfers the prize or award to a federal, state, or local governmental unit or qualified charity such as a church, school, or charitable organization designated by the taxpayer.[35] The obvious downside of this exception is that the award recipient does not actually get to receive or keep the cash from the award. However, for tax purposes it is more beneficial for the recipient to exclude the award from income entirely by immediately transferring it to a charitable organization than it is to receive the award, recognize the income, and then contribute funds to a charity for a charitable deduction. Designating the award for payment to a federal, state, or local governmental unit or qualified charity has the same effect as claiming the transfer as a deduction *for* AGI. However, by receiving the award, recognizing the income, and then contributing funds to a charity, the taxpayer is deducting the donation as a deduction *from* AGI. As we discussed in the Individual Tax Overview, Dependents, and Filing Status chapter, deductions *for* AGI are likely more advantageous than deductions *from* AGI.

The second exception is for employee *awards for length of service or safety achievement*.[36] These nontaxable awards are limited per employee per year to $400 of tangible property

---

[35]Source: §74(b).

[36]Prizes or awards from an employer-sponsored contest are fully taxable.

other than cash, cash equivalents, gift cards, gift coupons or gift certificates, or vacations, meals, lodging, tickets to theater or sporting events, stocks, bonds, other securities, and other similar items.[37] The award is not excluded from the employee's income if circumstances suggest it is disguised compensation.[38]

The third narrowly defined exception is for the value of any awards (medals) and prize money received by Team USA athletes from the U.S. Olympic Committee on account of competition in the Olympic and Paralympic games. While there is no limit on the exclusion amount, the exclusion does *not* apply to a taxpayer for any year in which the taxpayer's AGI (after excluding the award) exceeds $1 million ($500,000 for a married individual filing a separate return).[39]

TAXES IN THE REAL WORLD   You've Won a Brand New Car!

Who hasn't dreamed of hearing that famous phrase on the "Price Is Right"? Well, while many have dreamed of winning the Showcase Showdown, those who have had the pleasure of doing so have learned that those fabulous prizes come with substantial extras in the form of federal and state income taxes and even sales taxes. Indeed, winners of those fabulous new model cars get the pleasure of paying sales tax on the cars before they are handed the keys and federal and California income taxes in the year of their big win and 15 minutes of fame. To add a bit of insult to injury, taxes are paid on the value of the MSRP (manufacturer suggested retail price) of the car—not on the value that might be negotiated at the dealer. Nonetheless, a win is a win, even if it is not quite as lucrative as imagined.

Taxpayers must include the *gross* amount of their gambling winnings for the year in gross income.[40] Taxpayers are allowed to deduct their gambling losses and related gambling expenses to the extent of their gambling winnings, but the losses and related expenses are usually deductible as miscellaneous itemized deductions.[41] For professional gamblers, however, the losses and related expenses are deductible (to the extent of gambling winnings) *for* AGI.

ETHICS

While vacationing you find a $100 bill on the beach. Nobody saw you find it. Assuming the find meets the definition of gross income, would you report it as taxable income? Why or why not? Would your answer differ if you found $100,000 instead of $100?

Social Security Benefits   Over the last 40 years, the taxation of Social Security benefits has changed considerably. Forty years ago, Social Security benefits were completely excluded from income. Today, taxpayers may be required to include *up to* 85 percent of the benefits in gross income *depending* on the amount of the taxpayer's filing status, Social Security benefits, and *modified* AGI.[42] Modified AGI is regular AGI (excluding Social Security benefits) plus tax-exempt interest income, excluded foreign income

---

[37]§74(c).

[38]The $400 limit is increased to $1,600 for qualified award plans (written plans that do not discriminate in favor of highly compensated employees). However, the *average* cost of all qualified plan awards from an employer is limited to $400. Managers, administrators, clerical employees, or professional employees are not eligible for an exclusion for a safety award.

[39]§74(d).

[40]Subject to *de minimis* rules, payers of gambling winnings report winnings to recipients and the IRS on Form W-2G.

[41]See Rev. Rul. 83-130, 1983-2 CB 148.

[42]§86(d) applies to monthly benefits under title II of the Social Security Act and tier 1 railroad retirement benefits. The Social Security Administration reports Social Security benefits on Form SSA-1099.

(discussed later in the chapter), and certain other deductions *for* AGI.[43] The calculation of the amount of Social Security benefits to be included in income is depicted on the IRS worksheet in Appendix B at the end of this chapter.[44] The calculation is complex, to say the least. However, the taxability of Social Security benefits can be summarized as follows:

Single taxpayers:

1. If modified AGI + 50 percent of Social Security benefits ≤ $25,000, Social Security benefits are not taxable.
2. If $25,000 < modified AGI + 50 percent of Social Security benefits ≤ $34,000, taxable Social Security benefits are the lesser of (a) 50 percent of the Social Security benefits or (b) 50 percent of (modified AGI + 50 percent of Social Security benefits – $25,000).
3. If modified AGI + 50 percent of Social Security benefits > $34,000, taxable Social Security benefits are the lesser of (a) 85 percent of Social Security benefits or (b) 85 percent of (modified AGI + 50 percent of Social Security benefits – $34,000), plus the lesser of (1) $4,500 or (2) 50 percent of Social Security benefits.

Taxpayers filing married separate:

Taxable Social Security benefits are the lesser of (a) 85 percent of the Social Security benefits or (b) 85 percent of the taxpayer's modified AGI + 50 percent of Social Security benefits.

Taxpayers filing married joint:

1. If modified AGI + 50 percent of Social Security benefits ≤ $32,000, Social Security benefits are not taxable.
2. If $32,000 < modified AGI + 50 percent of Social Security benefits ≤ $44,000, taxable Social Security benefits are the lesser of (a) 50 percent of the Social Security benefits or (b) 50 percent of (modified AGI + 50 percent of Social Security benefits – $32,000).
3. If modified AGI + 50 percent of Social Security benefits > $44,000, taxable Social Security benefits are the lesser of (a) 85 percent of Social Security benefits or (b) 85 percent of (modified AGI + 50 percent of Social Security benefits – $44,000), plus the lesser of (1) $6,000 or (2) 50 percent of Social Security benefits.

The implications of the above calculations are that the Social Security benefits of taxpayers with relatively low taxable income are not taxable, and that 85 percent of the Social Security benefits of taxpayers with moderate to high taxable income is taxable.

Example 5-24

Gram received $7,200 of Social Security benefits this year. Suppose that Gram's modified AGI is $16,000. What amount of the Social Security benefits must Gram include in her gross income?

Answer: $0. Gram's modified AGI plus one-half of her Social Security benefits is $19,600 [$16,000 modified AGI + ($7,200 Social Security benefits × 50%)], which is below $25,000. Hence, Gram may *exclude* the entire $7,200 of Social Security income from gross income.

What if: Assume that Gram received $7,200 of Social Security benefits this year and that her modified AGI is $50,000. What amount of benefits must Gram include in her gross income?

Answer: $6,120 ($7,200 × 85%).

What if: Assume that Gram received $7,200 of Social Security benefits this year and that her modified AGI is $26,400. What amount of benefits must Gram include in her gross income?

Answer: $2,500. Gram is single and her modified AGI + 50 percent of Social Security benefits falls between $25,000 and $34,000. Her taxable Social Security benefits are the lesser of (a) 50 percent of the Social Security benefits ($7,200 × 50% = $3,600) or (b) 50 percent of [$26,400 modified AGI + $3,600 (50 percent of Social Security benefits) – $25,000] = $2,500. Thus, her taxable Social Security benefits are $2,500.

---

[43]See §86(b)(2).

[44]Because the 2018 worksheet was not available at the time the book went to press, we include the 2017 worksheet in Appendix B at the end of the chapter. The 2017 worksheet can be used to determine the taxable portion of Social Security benefits received in 2018.

What if: Assume that Gram received $7,200 of Social Security benefits this year and that her modified AGI is $31,400. What amount of benefits must Gram include in her gross income?

Answer: $4,450. Gram is single and her modified AGI + 50 percent of Social Security benefits exceeds $34,000. Her taxable Social Security benefits are the lesser of (a) 85 percent of Social Security benefits ($7,200 × 85% = $6,120) or (b) 85 percent of [$31,400 modified AGI + $3,600 (50 percent of Social Security benefits) − $34,000] = $850, plus the lesser of (1) $4,500 or (2) 50 percent of Social Security benefits (50% × $7,200 = $3,600). This calculation simplifies to the lesser of (a) $6,120 or (b) $4,450 ($850 + lesser of (1) $4,500 or (2) $3,600). Thus, Gram's taxable Social Security benefits are $4,450.

Imputed Income   Besides realizing *direct* economic benefits like wages and interest, taxpayers sometimes realize *indirect* economic benefits that they must include in gross income as **imputed income.** Bargain purchases (such as goods sold by an employer to an employee at a discount) and below-market loans (such as a loan from an employer to an employee at a zero or unusually low interest rate) are two common examples of taxable indirect economic benefits. Both bargain purchases and below-market loans generally result in tax consequences (such as gross income or taxable gifts) if the purchase or loan transaction is not an "arms-length" transaction (such as transactions between an employer and employee, owner and entity, or among family members).

For bargain purchases, the tax consequences vary based on the relationship of the parties. For example, a bargain purchase by an employee from an employer results in taxable compensation income to the employee, a bargain purchase by a shareholder from a corporation results in a taxable dividend to the shareholder, and a bargain purchase between family members is deemed to be a gift from one family member to the other (as discussed later in the chapter, gifts are nontaxable for income tax purposes but are potentially subject to gift tax, to be paid by the person making the gift).

Although the general rule is that bargain purchases by an employee from an employer creates taxable compensation income to the employee, the tax law does provide a limited exclusion for employee bargain purchases. Specifically, employees may exclude (a) a discount on employer-provided goods as long as the discount does not exceed the employer's gross profit percentage on all property offered for sale to nonemployee customers and (b) up to 20 percent employer-provided discount on services. Discounts in excess of these amounts are taxable as compensation.[45]

Example 5-25

To create more space for Gram, Courtney received EWD architectural design services as part of her compensation package and at a substantial discount. EWD's services were valued at $35,000, but Courtney was charged only $22,000. How much of the discount must Courtney include in gross income?

Answer: $6,000, computed as follows:

Description	Amount	Explanation
(1) Value of services EWD provided to Courtney	$35,000	
(2) Courtney's cost of the services	22,000	
(3) Discount on services	$13,000	(1) − (2)
(4) Excludable discount	7,000	(1) × 20%
Discount in excess of 20% is included in gross income	**$ 6,000**	(3) − (4)

For below-market loans, the indirect economic benefit conveyed to the borrower (such as an employee, shareholder, or family member) is a function of the amount of the loan and the difference in the market interest rate and the rate actually charged by the lender (such as an employer, corporation, or family member). To eliminate any tax

[45]Source: §132(a)(2).

advantages of below-market loans, the tax law generally requires the lender and borrower to treat the transaction as if:

1. The borrower paid the lender the difference between the applicable federal interest rate (compounded semiannually) and the actual interest paid. This difference is called *imputed interest*.
2. The lender then returned the imputed interest to the borrower.

The deemed "payment" of the imputed interest in these transactions is treated as interest income to the lender and interest expense to the borrower. The deductibility of the interest expense for the borrower depends on how she used the loan proceeds (for business, investment, or personal purposes). As we learn in the next chapter, business interest expense is a deduction *for* AGI, investment interest expense is an itemized deduction subject to limitations, and personal interest is generally not deductible. The tax consequences of the "return" of the imputed interest from the lender to the borrower vary based on the relationship of the parties (similar to the case of a bargain purchase). For example, the return of the imputed interest from an employer lender to an employee borrower is treated by both parties as taxable compensation paid to the employee, the return of the imputed interest from a corporation to a shareholder is considered a dividend, and a return of imputed interest by a family member to another family member is considered a gift. The imputed interest rules generally do not apply to aggregate loans of $10,000 or less between the lender and borrower [§7872(c)].[46]

Example 5-26

At the beginning of January, EWD provides Courtney with a $100,000 zero-interest loan. Assume the applicable federal interest rate (compounded semiannually) is 4 percent. Courtney used the loan proceeds to acquire several personal-use assets (an automobile and other items). What amount is Courtney required to include in gross income in the current year?

Answer: $4,000, computed as follows:

Description	Amount	Explanation
(1) Loan principal	$100,000	
(2) Applicable federal interest rate compounded semiannually	4%	
(3) Interest on loan principal at federal rate	$ 4,000	(1) × (2)
(4) Interest paid by Courtney	0	
Imputed interest included in Courtney's gross income	**$ 4,000**	(3) − (4)

Courtney will include the $4,000 imputed interest in gross income as compensation and will also incur an imputed interest expense of $4,000 for the year. EWD will (a) deduct $4,000 of compensation expense and (b) report $4,000 of interest income. In this example, we assume Courtney used the proceeds for personal purposes so she is not allowed to deduct the interest expense.

What if: Assume the same facts except that EWD had loaned Courtney $10,000 at a zero-interest rate. How much imputed interest income would Courtney be required to include in her gross income for the year?

Answer: $0. The imputed interest rules don't apply because the loan did not exceed $10,000.

Discharge of Indebtedness

In general, when a taxpayer's debt is forgiven by a lender (the debt is discharged), the taxpayer must include the amount of debt relief in gross income.[47]

---

[46]For "gift" loans (for example, loans between individuals), the $10,000 *de minimis* exception is not available for loan proceeds used to purchase or carry income-producing assets. Likewise, the $10,000 *de minimis* exception is not available for compensation-related loans or corporate-shareholder loans where the principal purpose of the loans is to avoid federal tax. For gift loans of $100,000 or less, the imputed interest is limited to the borrower's net investment income (investment income, such as interest income or other investment income not taxed at preferential rates, less related investment expenses). If the borrower's net investment income is $1,000 or less, the imputed interest rules do not apply. §7872(d). The exception for gift loans of $100,000 or less is *not available* for loans where the principal purpose of the loans is to avoid federal tax.

[47]§61(a)(12). Income from discharge of indebtedness is also realized when debt is forgiven by lenders other than employers such as banks and credit card companies.

Example 5-27

In the previous example, Courtney borrowed $100,000 from EWD. Because EWD wants to keep Courtney as an employee, it agrees to forgive $10,000 of loan principal at the end of each year that Courtney stays on board. On December 31 of this year, EWD formally cancels $10,000 of Courtney's indebtedness. How much of this debt relief is Courtney required to include in gross income?

Answer: All $10,000 is included in Courtney's gross income.

To provide tax relief for insolvent taxpayers—taxpayers with liabilities, including tax liabilities, exceeding their assets—a **discharge of indebtedness** is *not* taxable if the taxpayer is insolvent before *and* after the debt forgiveness.[48] If the discharge of indebtedness makes the taxpayer solvent, the taxpayer recognizes gross income to the extent of his solvency.[49] For example, if a taxpayer is discharged of $30,000 of debt and this causes him to be solvent by $10,000 (after the debt relief, the taxpayer's assets exceed his liabilities by $10,000), the taxpayer must include $10,000 in gross income.[50]

EXCLUSION AND DEFERRAL PROVISIONS

LO 5-3

So far in this chapter, we've discussed various types of income taxpayers must realize and recognize by reporting it on their tax returns in the current year. However, there are specific types of income that taxpayers realize but are allowed to permanently *exclude* from gross income or temporarily *defer* from gross income until a subsequent period. *Exclusions* and *deferrals* are the result of *specific congressional action* and are *narrowly* defined. Because taxpayers are not required to recognize income that is excluded or deferred, we refer to tax laws allowing exclusions or deferrals as **nonrecognition provisions.** Nonrecognition provisions result from various policy objectives. In very general terms, Congress allows most exclusions and deferrals for two primary reasons: (1) to subsidize or encourage particular activities or (2) to be fair to taxpayers (such as mitigating the inequity of double taxation).

Common Exclusions

Because exclusion provisions allow taxpayers to permanently remove certain income items from their tax base, they are particularly taxpayer-friendly. We begin by introducing three common exclusion provisions: the exclusions of municipal bond interest, gain on the sale of a personal residence, and fringe benefits. We continue with a survey of other exclusion provisions based on their underlying purpose: education, double taxation, and sickness and injury.[51]

Municipal Bond Interest
The most common example of an exclusion provision is the exclusion of interest on **municipal bonds.** Municipal bonds include bonds issued by state and local governments located in the United States, and this exclusion is generally recognized as a subsidy to state and local governments (the exclusion allows state and

---

[48]§108(a)(1)(B).

[49]§108(a)(3).

[50]Other circumstances in which taxpayers may exclude a discharge of indebtedness are beyond the scope of this chapter. See §108(f) for discussion of the limited exclusions of student loan forgiveness for loans requiring students to work for a specified time in certain professions or student loans forgiven on account of death or total and permanent disability of the student. See §108(a)(1)(E) for discussion of the exclusion of up to $2,000,000 of home mortgage forgiveness from 2007 through 2017. See §108(i) for a discussion for the deferral of debt forgiveness income for businesses reacquiring debt at a discounted price in 2009 and 2010. This provision allows a taxpayer to recognize the debt forgiveness income ratably over the five-year period 2014 through 2018.

[51]Another common exclusion we discuss in the Individual *For* AGI Deductions chapter is the exclusion of earnings on "Roth" retirement savings accounts.

local governments to offer bonds at a lower before-tax interest rate). In contrast, interest on U.S. government obligations (such as Treasury bills) is taxable for federal tax purposes but is tax-exempt for state and local tax purposes.

Example 5-28

Courtney holds a $10,000 City of Cincinnati municipal bond. The bond pays 5 percent interest annually. Courtney acquired the bond a few years ago. The city used the proceeds from the bond issuance to help pay for renovations on a major league baseball stadium. In late December, Courtney received $500 of interest income from the bond for the year. How much of the $500 interest from the municipal bond may Courtney *exclude* from her gross income?

Answer: All $500 because the interest is from a municipal bond.

Gains on the Sale of Personal Residence   The tax law provides several provisions that encourage or subsidize home ownership, and the exclusion of the gain on the sale of a personal residence is a common example of one such provision. Specifically, taxpayers meeting certain home ownership *and* use requirements can permanently exclude up to $250,000 ($500,000 if married filing jointly) of realized gain on the sale of their principal residence.[52] Gain in excess of the excludable amount generally qualifies as long-term capital gain subject to tax at preferential rates. To satisfy the ownership test, the taxpayer must have owned the residence (house, condominium, trailer, or houseboat) for a total of two or more years during the five-year period ending on the date of the sale. To satisfy the use test, the taxpayer must have *used* the property as her principal residence for a total of two or more years (noncontiguous use is permissible) during the five-year period ending on the date of the sale. The tax law limits each taxpayer to one exclusion every two years. Married couples filing joint returns are eligible for the full $500,000 exclusion if *either* spouse meets the ownership test and *both* spouses meet the principal-use test. However, if *either* spouse is ineligible for the exclusion because he or she personally used the $250,000 exclusion on another home sale during the two years before the date of the current sale, the couple's available exclusion is reduced to $250,000.

Example 5-29

What if: Assume that in October of this year, Courtney sold her home in Cincinnati. Courtney and her ex-husband purchased the home four years ago for $400,000, and Courtney received the house in the divorce settlement and lived there until she moved to Kansas City in January. She sold the home for $550,000. How much taxable gain does she recognize on the sale of the home?

Answer: $0. Because Courtney satisfies the two-year ownership and two-year use test, she may exclude up to $250,000 of gain from the sale of her home. Thus, Courtney may exclude the entire $150,000 gain that she realized on the sale ($550,000 sales price less $400,000 basis).

What if: Assume the same facts except Courtney sold the home for $700,000. How much taxable gain does she recognize on the sale of the home?

Answer: $50,000. Because Courtney satisfies the two-year ownership and two-year use test, she may exclude $250,000 of the $300,000 gain from the sale of her home ($700,000 sales price less $400,000 basis). Thus, Courtney recognizes a $50,000 taxable gain on the sale.

Fringe Benefits   In addition to paying salary and wages, many employers provide employees with **fringe benefits.** For example, an employer may provide an employee with an automobile to use for personal purposes, pay for an employee to join a health

---

[52]§121.

club, pay for an employee's moving expenses, or pay for an employee's home security. In general, the value of these benefits is *included* in the employee's gross income as compensation for services. However, certain fringe benefits, called "qualified" fringe benefits, are excluded from gross income.[53] Exhibit 5-4 lists some of the most common fringe benefits excluded from an employee's gross income.

In addition to excluded fringe benefits, many employers make contributions to retirement plans on behalf of their employees. Subject to specific rules that we discuss in the Individual *For* AGI Deductions chapter, these contributions (as well as employee contributions from salary) are not currently included in the employee's gross income but are deferred until the employee withdraws the contributions and related earnings from the plan.

Example 5-30

EWD paid $6,000 this year for Courtney's health insurance premiums and $150 in premiums for her $40,000 group-term life insurance policy. How much of the $6,150 in benefits can Courtney exclude from her gross income?

Answer: Courtney can exclude all $6,150 in benefits from her gross income. All health insurance premiums paid by an employer on an employee's behalf are excluded from the employee's income. In addition, premiums employers pay on an employee's behalf for group-term life insurance (up to $50,000 of coverage) are also excluded from the employee's gross income.

Example 5-31

In December, Courtney mailed a newsletter to several dozen friends and relatives with a recent picture of her son, daughter, and mother. Courtney printed both the newsletter and the photos on printers at work (with permission of EWD). Courtney would have paid $55 for the duplicate newsletters and photos at a nearby copy center. How much of this $55 benefit that Courtney received from EWD may she *exclude* from her gross income?

Answer: All $55 is excluded. The $55 benefit is considered a nontaxable *de minimis* (so minor to merit disregard) fringe benefit because it is small in amount and infrequent.

Employee expense reimbursement.   As a common fringe benefit, many employees are reimbursed for their employee business expenses by their employers. If an employee is required to submit documentation supporting expenses to receive reimbursement and the employer reimburses only legitimate business expenses, then the employer's reimbursement plan qualifies as an **accountable plan.** Under an accountable plan (which is the most common method for reimbursement), employees *exclude* expense reimbursements from gross income and do *not* deduct the reimbursed expenses. In contrast, if employees receive employer reimbursements for legitimate business expenses but do not have to submit documentation supporting the expenses, the reimbursement is considered taxable compensation, and the employee is *not* allowed to deduct the expenses as employment-related expenses (reimbursed or not). You can imagine that employees really favor accountable plans.

---

[53]Most nontaxable fringe benefits are listed with "items specifically excluded from gross income" in §§101–140 of the Internal Revenue Code. Employers are generally prohibited from discriminating among employees with respect to nontaxable fringe benefits (i.e., they cannot offer them only to executives). Note that §132 provides an exclusion of qualified moving expense reimbursements for members of the Armed Forces of the United States on active duty who move pursuant to a military order. This exclusion is not available to other individuals.

EXHIBIT 5-4   Common Qualified Fringe Benefits (excluded from employee's gross income)

Item	Description
Medical and dental health insurance coverage (§106)	An employee may exclude from income the cost of medical and insurance coverage and dental health insurance premiums the employer pays on an employee's behalf.[54]
Life insurance coverage (§79)	Employees may exclude from income the value of life insurance premiums the employer pays on an employee's behalf for up to $50,000 of group-term life insurance.
De minimis (small) benefits [§132(a)(4)]	As a matter of administrative convenience, Congress allows employees to exclude from income relatively small and infrequent benefits employees receive at work (such as limited use of a business copy machine).
Meals and lodging provided for the employer's convenience (§119)	Employees may exclude employer-provided meals and lodging if they (1) are provided on the employer's business premises to the employee (and spouse and dependents); (2) are provided for the employer's convenience (such as allowing the employee to be on-call 24 hours a day or continue working on-site over lunch); and (3) the employee accepts the lodging as a condition of employment (for lodging only).
Employee educational assistance programs (§127)	Employees may exclude up to $5,250 of employer-provided educational assistance benefits covering tuition, books, and fees for any instruction that improves the taxpayer's capabilities, whether or not job-related or part of a degree program.
No additional cost services [§132(a)(1)]	Employees may exclude the value of services provided by an employer that generate no substantial costs to the employer (such as free flight benefits for airline employees on a space-available basis or free hotel service for hotel employees).
Qualified employee discounts [§132(a)(2)]	Employees may exclude (a) a discount on employer-provided goods as long as the discount does not exceed the employer's gross profit percentage on all property offered for sale to customers and (b) up to 20 percent employer-provided discount on services. Discounts in excess of these amounts are taxable as compensation. See Example 5-25.
Dependent care benefits (§129)	Employees may exclude up to $5,000 for benefits paid or reimbursed by employers for caring for children under age 13 or dependents or spouses who are physically or mentally unable to care for themselves.
Working condition fringe benefits [§132(a)(3)]	Employees may exclude from income any benefit or reimbursement of a benefit provided by an employer that would be deductible as an ordinary and necessary expense by the employee if the employee had paid the expense.
Qualified transportation benefits [§132(a)(5)]	Employees may exclude up to $260 per month of employer-provided parking and up to $260 per month of the combined value of employer-provided mass transit passes and the value of a carpool vehicle for employee use.
Cafeteria plans (§125)	Cafeteria plans allow employees to choose between various nontaxable fringe benefits (such as health insurance and dental insurance) and cash. These benefits are tax-free to the extent the taxpayer chooses nontaxable fringe benefits and taxable to the extent the employee receives cash.
Flexible spending accounts (§125)	Flexible spending accounts (or FSAs) allow employees to set aside a portion of their *before*-tax salary for payment of health and/or dependent-care benefits. These amounts must be used by the end of the year or within the first two and a half months of the next plan year, or employees forfeit the unused balance. In lieu of allowing the two-and-a-half-month grace period at the beginning of each new year, employers can allow employees to carry over up to $500 of unused amounts to be used anytime during the next year (it is the employer's choice). This option does not apply to dependent-care flexible spending accounts. For 2018, the amount of before-tax salary an employee may set aside for medical expenses is limited to $2,650 and the before-tax amount that may be set aside for dependent-care expenses is limited to $5,000.

[54]The cost of medical coverage paid by an employer and offered through a health insurance exchange is not an excludable benefit unless the employer is a small employer that elects to make all of its full-time employees eligible for plans offered through the small business health options program (SHOP). For this purpose, a small employer is an employer that employed an average of at least one but 100 or fewer employees during business days in the prior year, and employs at least one employee on the first day of the plan year. In 2015, SHOP is open to employers with 50 or fewer full-time equivalent employees. Beginning in 2016, some states opened SHOPs to employers with up to 100 full-time equivalent employees.

TAXES IN THE REAL WORLD   Have Phone, Will Call Tax-Free

In years past, the IRS classified employee cell phones issued by employers as a taxable benefit (i.e., taxable compensation) and required employees to keep detailed records to substantiate business versus personal use of the phone. As you might expect, the classification and record-keeping requirements were not met with great enthusiasm. In 2011, the IRS reversed its course and now considers an employer-issued cell phone as an excludable fringe benefit (both for business and personal use) when the phone is provided primarily for noncompensatory business reasons. Even better, the IRS no longer requires record keeping for employees to receive the tax-free treatment. See Notice 2011-72.

Education-Related Exclusions

As an incentive for taxpayers to participate in higher education (education beyond high school), Congress excludes certain types of income if the funds are used for higher education. In the following paragraphs, we discuss exclusions for scholarships and exclusions for certain types of investment plans used to save for college.[55]

Scholarships   College students seeking a degree can exclude from gross income scholarships (including Pell grants) that pay for tuition, fees, books, supplies, and other equipment *required* for the student's courses.[56] Any excess scholarship amounts (such as for room or board) are fully taxable. The scholarship exclusion applies only if the recipient is *not* required to perform services in exchange for receiving the scholarship. "Scholarships" that represent compensation for past, current, or future services are fully taxable. However, tuition waivers or reductions provided by an educational institution for undergraduate courses for student employees or for graduate courses for teaching or research assistants are not taxable.

What about athletic scholarships? Good question. The IRS has ruled that the value of athletic scholarships is excludable from gross income if the scholarship: (1) is awarded to students by a university that *expects* but *does not require* the students to participate in a particular sport; (2) requires no particular activity in lieu of participation; and (3) is not canceled if the student cannot participate.[57] Like other scholarships, athletic scholarships are only excludable from gross income to the extent they pay for tuition, fees, books, supplies, and other equipment required for the student's courses. Any excess amount (for example, for room and board) is taxable.

THE KEY FACTS

Education Exclusions

- Students seeking a college degree can exclude scholarships that pay for required tuition, fees, books, and supplies.
- Taxpayers are allowed to exclude earnings on investments in 529 plans and Coverdell education savings accounts if they use the earnings to pay for qualified educational expenditures.
- Taxpayers can elect to exclude interest earned on Series EE savings bonds when the redemption proceeds are used to pay qualified higher education expenses.
- The exclusion of interest on Series EE savings bonds is restricted to taxpayers with modified AGI below specific limits.

Example 5-32

Ellen, Courtney's daughter, received a $700 scholarship from the University of Missouri–Kansas City that pays $400 of her tuition and provides $300 cash for books. Ellen spent $350 on books. How much of the scholarship may she exclude from gross income?

Answer: All $700 is excluded. Ellen may exclude all of the scholarship for tuition and she may exclude the $300 cash she received for books because she spent all $300 purchasing her books for school.

What if: How much is Ellen allowed to exclude if she spent only $250 on books?

Answer: $650 is excluded. Ellen excludes all of the scholarship for her tuition and $250 of the $300 in cash payments because she spent $250 on books. She must include the excess cash payment of $50 ($300 − $250) in her gross income.

---

[55]A detailed explanation is available in IRS Publication 970 *Tax Benefits for Education* available on the IRS website at www.irs.gov.

[56]§117(b)(2).

[57]Source: Rev. Rul. 77-263, 1977-2 CB 47.

Other Educational Subsidies   Taxpayers are allowed to exclude from gross income earnings on investments in qualified education plans such as 529 plans and Coverdell education savings accounts as long as they use the earnings to pay for qualifying educational expenditures.

529 plans allow parents, grandparents, and other individuals to contribute up to the maximum allowed by state-sponsored 529 plans to fund the qualified educational costs of future *college* students and, subject to limitations, educational costs of students at public, private or religious elementary or secondary schools.[58] Earnings in 529 plans are distributed tax-free provided they are used for qualified education expenses (no annual limit) or tuition expense attributable to public, private, or religious elementary or secondary schools (subject to a $10,000 limit per beneficiary per year). Qualified higher education expenses include tuition, books, supplies, required equipment and supplies, computer equipment and software, and reasonable room and board costs of attending a higher education institution. If, on the other hand, distributions are made to the beneficiary for other purposes or exceed the $10,000 limit for tuition expenses attributable to public, private, or religious elementary or secondary schools, the earnings distributed are taxed to the beneficiary at the beneficiary's tax rate and are subject to an additional 10 percent penalty, while distributions of the original investment (contributions) to the beneficiary are treated as gifts.[59] Similarly, distributions to contributors (e.g., parents, grandparents) that represent earnings on their contributions are included in contributors' gross income and also subject to the 10 percent penalty.

With a Coverdell account, yearly contributions to the account are limited to $2,000 for each beneficiary, and distributions may be used to pay for qualified educational costs of kindergarten through 12th grade and qualified higher-education expenses such as tuition, books, fees, supplies, and reasonable room and board.[60] The $2,000 contribution limit for Coverdell accounts phases out as AGI (modified to include certain types of excluded foreign income) increases from $190,000 to $220,000 for married filing jointly taxpayers, and from $95,000 to $110,000 for all other taxpayers.

U.S. Series EE bonds.   The federal government issues bonds that allow taxpayers to acquire the bonds at a discount and redeem the bonds for a fixed amount over stated time intervals. These bonds don't generate any cash in the form of interest until the taxpayer redeems the bond. At redemption, the amount of the redemption price in excess of the acquisition price is interest included in gross income.[61] U.S. Series EE bonds fall into this category. However, an exclusion is available for interest from Series EE bonds. This exclusion requires that the redemption proceeds be used to pay for higher-education expenses of the taxpayer, the taxpayer's spouse, or a dependent of the taxpayer. Qualified higher-education expenses include the tuition and fees required for enrollment or attendance at an eligible educational institution. Taxpayers may also exclude the interest income if they contribute the proceeds to a qualified tuition program.

The exclusion is partially reduced or eliminated for taxpayers exceeding a fixed level of modified adjusted gross income (adjusted gross income before the educational savings bond exclusion, the foreign earned income exclusion, and certain other deductions).[62] If the taxpayer's modified AGI exceeds the thresholds in the redemption year, the exclusion is phased out (gradually reduced) until all of the interest from the bonds is taxed.[63]

---

[58]Contribution limits vary according to the state administering the 529 plan. In addition, more than half the states offer a state tax deduction or credit to residents contributing to the 529 plan sponsored by the state in which the contributors reside.

[59]Under §529(c)(3), multiple distributions received under these circumstances are treated as annuities. As a result, a portion of each distribution would be treated as a gift with the remainder treated as income.

[60]§530(b). This definition of qualified higher education expenses is consistent with the definition used in §221(d)(2) to determine if interest paid on education-related loans is deductible (see the Individual *For* AGI Deductions chapter).

[61]Alternatively, taxpayers can elect to include the annual increase in the redemption value in gross income rather than waiting to recognize all the income on redemption. See §454(a).

[62]§135(c)(4).

[63]In 2018, the phase-out range begins at $119,300 of modified adjusted gross income for married taxpayers filing joint returns. For all other taxpayers, the phase-out range begins at $79,550.

Exclusions That Mitigate Double Taxation

Congress provides certain exclusions that eliminate the potential double tax that may arise for gifts, inheritances, and life insurance proceeds.

Gifts and Inheritances

Individuals may transfer property to other taxpayers without receiving or expecting to receive value in return. If the *transferor* is alive at the time of the transfer, the property transfer is called a **gift.** If the property is transferred from the decedent's estate (the *transferor* is deceased), it is called an **inheritance.** These transfers are generally subject to a federal transfer tax, *not* the income tax. Gifts are typically subject to the federal gift tax and inheritances are typically subject to a federal estate tax.[64] Thus, gift and estate taxes are imposed on *transfer* of the property and *not included in income by the recipient.* Congress excludes property transferred as gifts and inheritances from income taxation to avoid the potential double taxation (transfer and income taxation) on these transfers.

Example 5-33

Ellen graduated from high school last year. As a graduation present, Gram purchased a $1,500 travel package for Ellen, so that Ellen could go on a Caribbean cruise. Last year, Ellen also received an inheritance of $2,000 from Gramps's estate. How much gross income does Ellen recognize on the $1,500 gift she received from Gram and the $2,000 inheritance she received from Gramps's estate?

Answer: $0. Ellen is allowed to exclude the entire gift and the entire amount of the inheritance from her gross income. Consequently, she does not recognize any gross income from these transactions.

Life Insurance Proceeds

In some ways, life insurance proceeds are similar to inheritances. When the owner of the life insurance policy dies, the beneficiary receives the death benefit proceeds. The decedent (or the decedent's estate) is generally subject to estate taxation on the amount of the insurance proceeds. In order to avoid potential double taxation on the life insurance proceeds, the tax laws allow taxpayers receiving life insurance proceeds to exclude the proceeds from gross income.[65] However, when the insurance proceeds are paid over a period of time rather than in a lump sum, a portion of the payments represents interest and must be included in gross income. In addition, the life insurance proceeds exclusion generally does not apply when a life insurance policy is transferred to another party for valuable consideration. In this case, the eventual life insurance proceeds collected by the purchaser are excluded up to the sum of the purchase price of the policy and any subsequent premiums, with remaining proceeds taxable as ordinary income.[66]

What happens if a taxpayer cashes out a policy before death? The tax treatment varies based on the specific facts. Generally, if a taxpayer simply cancels a life insurance contract and is paid the policy's cash surrender value, she would recognize ordinary income to the extent the proceeds received exceed previous premiums paid. If premiums paid exceed the proceeds received, the loss is not deductible. If, however, the taxpayer is terminally ill (medically certified with an illness expected to cause death within 24 months), early receipt of life insurance proceeds in the form of **accelerated death benefits** is not taxable. If a taxpayer is chronically ill (medically certified to require substantial assistance for daily living activities or due to cognitive impairment), life insurance proceeds are not taxable to the extent they are used to pay for the taxpayer's long-term care.

---

[64]As a general rule, for 2018, the federal gift tax does not apply to relatively small gifts ($15,000 or less per person per year), and the federal estate tax only applies to transfers from larger estates (over $11,200,000).

[65]§101. The exclusion does not apply if the insurance policy is sold by the owner.

[66]This exception to the exclusion does not apply if the recipient of the policy is the insured, a partner of the insured, a partnership in which the insured is a partner, or a corporation in which the insured is an officer or shareholder. This exception also does not apply to policies transferred by gift or tax-free exchange. §101(a)(2).

Example 5-34

What if: Gramps received $200,000 of accelerated death benefits from a life insurance policy last year when he was diagnosed with terminal cancer with an expected life of less than one year. How much gross income would the $200,000 payment generate?

Answer: None, because Gramps was medically certified as terminally ill with an illness expected to cause death within 24 months.

What if: Due to financial issues, Gramps several years ago transferred a $100,000 life insurance policy on his life to a business associate for $5,000. Since that time, the business associate continued to pay the annual premiums on the policy (totaling $20,000 before Gramps's death). Upon Gramps's death, the life insurance company paid the business associate the policy's $100,000 face value. How much of the $100,000 payment is taxable?

Answer: $75,000. Because the business associate purchased the life insurance policy from Gramps for valuable consideration, she may exclude the $100,000 proceeds up to the sum of the purchase price of the policy ($5,000) and any subsequent premiums ($20,000), with the remaining proceeds ($100,000 − $5,000 − $20,000 = $75,000) taxable as ordinary income.

Foreign-Earned Income   U.S. citizens are subject to tax on all income whether it is generated in the United States or in foreign countries. Because most foreign countries also impose tax on income earned within their borders, U.S. citizens could be subject to both U.S. and foreign taxation on income earned abroad. To provide relief from this potential double taxation, Congress allows taxpayers to exclude foreign-earned income (income from foreign sources for personal services performed) up to an annual maximum amount. Income from pensions, annuities, salary paid by the U.S. government, or deferred compensation does not qualify for the exclusion. The maximum exclusion is indexed for inflation, and in 2018 the maximum is $103,900. Rather than claim this exclusion, taxpayers may deduct foreign taxes paid as itemized deductions or they may claim the foreign tax credit for foreign taxes paid on their foreign-earned income.[67]

To determine whether claiming the annual exclusion, the deduction, or the foreign tax credit is most advantageous, taxpayers should compare the tax effects of each option. To claim the annual exclusion instead of the foreign tax deduction or credit, the taxpayer must elect to do so using Form 2555. Taxpayers who elect to use the exclusion may revoke the election for later years and use the foreign tax credit or deduct foreign taxes paid. However, once a taxpayer revokes the exclusion election, she may not reelect to use the exclusion before the sixth tax year after the tax year the revocation was made.

As you might expect, individuals must meet certain requirements to qualify for the foreign-earned income exclusion. To be eligible for the annual exclusion, a taxpayer must have her tax home in a foreign country and (1) be considered a resident of the foreign country by living in the country for the entire year (calendar year) or (2) live in the foreign country for 330 days in a consecutive 12-month period, which might occur over two tax years. The *maximum* exclusion is reduced pro rata for each day during the calendar year that is not part of the qualifying 12-month period.

Taxpayers meeting the requirement for the foreign-earned income exclusion may also exclude from income reasonable housing costs (paid by an employer) that exceed 16 percent of the statutory foreign-earned income exclusion amount for the year (exceed 16 percent × $103,900 = $16,624 in 2018). The exclusion, however, is limited to a maximum of 14 percent of the statutory exclusion amount (14 percent × $103,900 = $14,546 in 2018). Thus, in 2018, if a taxpayer incurs housing costs (provided by an employer) exceeding $16,624, she may exclude such excess costs up to $14,546 (thus, the first $16,624 of employer-provided housing costs are included in gross income).[68] The housing exclusion

---

[67]See §911(b)(2) and the Individual *From* AGI Deductions chapter and the Business Income, Deductions, and Accounting Methods chapter.

[68]§911(c).

limit is also subject to daily proration if the taxpayer's qualifying 12-month period occurs over two tax years.

Example 5-35

What if: Assume Courtney is considering a transfer to EWD's overseas affiliate. If she transfers, she anticipates she will earn approximately $120,000 in salary. How much of her expected $120,000 annual salary will Courtney be allowed to exclude from her gross income assuming she meets the residency requirements?

Answer: She is eligible to exclude $103,900 of her $120,000 of compensation from U.S. taxation in 2018. However, her entire $120,000 salary may be subject to the foreign country's income tax.

What if: Assume Courtney decides to transfer, but she expects her 12-month qualifying period to include only 200 days in the first year and 140 days in the second year. How much of her expected $65,000 salary in the first year will she be allowed to exclude from gross income?

Answer: $56,932 [$103,900 full exclusion × 200/365 (days in foreign country/days in year)].

What if: Assume that Courtney expects her 12-month qualifying period to include 200 days in the first year and that she expects her salary to be $45,000 during this period. How much of her expected $45,000 salary will she be allowed to exclude from gross income?

Answer: All $45,000. She can exclude up to $56,932 of salary from income (see above computation).

What if: Assume that if Courtney transfers, EWD's overseas affiliate will also pay for her housing while overseas ($25,000 per year). How much of the $25,000 housing payments may Courtney exclude assuming she lives in the country for the entire year?

Answer: $8,376. Since Courtney meets the requirements for the foreign-earned income exclusion, she may exclude the employer-provided housing costs that exceed $16,624 (16% × $103,900), up to a maximum exclusion of $14,546 (14% × $103,900). Thus, Courtney may exclude $8,376 [the lesser of (a) $8,376 ($25,000 housing cost less $16,624) or (b) $14,546].

Sickness and Injury-Related Exclusions

The tax laws provide several exclusion provisions for taxpayers who are sick or injured. One explanation for these exclusions is that payments for sickness or injury are considered returns of (human) capital.

Workers' Compensation   The provision for workers' compensation is relatively straightforward. Taxpayers receive workers' compensation benefits when they are unable to work because of a work-related injury. Any payments a taxpayer receives from a state-sponsored workers' compensation plan are excluded from the taxpayer's income.[69] Note that this treatment is *opposite* that of *unemployment* compensation, which is fully taxable.

Payments Associated with Personal Injury   Historically, the question of which payments associated with a personal injury were excludable was controversial. In 1996 Congress settled the matter by deciding that all payments associated with compensating a taxpayer for a *physical* injury (including payments for past, current, and future lost wages) are excluded from gross income. That is, the tax laws specify that any *compensatory damages* on account of a *physical injury* or *physical sickness* are nontaxable. Thus, damages taxpayers receive for emotional distress associated with a physical injury are excluded.

In contrast, *punitive damages* are *fully taxable*, because they are intended to punish the harm-doer rather than to compensate the taxpayer for injuries. Likewise, taxpayers receiving damages for emotional distress that are not associated with a physical injury must include those payments in income. In general, all other awards (those that do not relate to physical injury or sickness or are payments for the medical costs of treating emotional distress) are included in gross income.

[69]§104.

Example 5-36

In February, Courtney's cousin, Kelsey, was struck and injured by a bus while walking in a crosswalk. Because the bus driver was negligent, the bus company settled Kelsey's claim by paying her $1,500 for medical expenses and $500 for emotional distress associated with the accident. How much of the $2,000 Kelsey received from the bus company may she *exclude* from her gross income?

Answer: All $2,000. Kelsey may exclude the $1,500 she received for medical expenses and the $500 payment she received for emotional distress because these damages were associated with Kelsey's physical injury.

What if: Assume Kelsey sued the bus company and was awarded $5,000 in punitive damages. How much of the $5,000 would Kelsey be able to exclude from her gross income?

Answer: $0. Payments for punitive damages are not excludable. Kelsey would be required to include the entire $5,000 in her gross income.

THE KEY FACTS

Exclusions Related to Sickness and Injury

- Payments from workers' compensation plans are excluded from gross income.
- Payments received as compensation for a *physical* injury are excluded from gross income, but punitive damages are included in gross income.
- Reimbursements by health and accident insurance policies for medical expenses paid by the taxpayer are excluded from gross income.
- Disability payments received from an *employee-purchased* policy are excluded from gross income.

Health Care Reimbursement   Any reimbursement a taxpayer receives from a health and accident insurance policy for medical expenses paid by the taxpayer during the current year is excluded from gross income. The exclusion applies regardless of whether the taxpayer, her employer, or someone else purchased the health and accident policy for the taxpayer. Of course, the tax benefit rule may require inclusion of reimbursements of medical expenses that were deducted by the taxpayer in a prior year.

Disability Insurance   The exclusion provisions for **disability insurance** are more restrictive than those for workers' compensation payments or reimbursements from a health and accident insurance plan. Disability insurance, sometimes called *wage replacement insurance*, pays the insured individual for wages lost when the individual misses work due to injury or disability. If an individual purchases disability insurance directly, the cost of the policy is not deductible, but any disability benefits are excluded from gross income.

Disability insurance may also be purchased on an individual's behalf by an employer. The employer may allow employees to choose whether the premiums paid on their behalf are to be considered taxable compensation or a nontaxable fringe benefit. If the premiums are taxable compensation to the employee, the policy is considered to have been purchased by the employee. If the premium paid for by the employer is a nontaxable fringe benefit to the employee, the policy is considered to have been purchased by the employer. This distinction is important because only payments taxpayers receive from an *employee-purchased* policy are excluded from their gross income. If the employer pays the premiums for an employee as a nontaxable fringe benefit, the employee must include all disability benefits in gross income.

Example 5-37

Courtney purchased disability insurance last year. In late April of this year, she broke her wrist in a mountain biking accident and could not work for two weeks. Courtney's doctor bills totaled $2,000, of which $1,600 was reimbursed by her health insurance purchased by EWD. How much of the $1,600 health insurance reimbursement for medical expenses is Courtney allowed to *exclude* from her gross income?

Answer: All $1,600 is excluded. All medical expense reimbursements from health insurance are excluded from a taxpayer's gross income.

Courtney also received $600 for lost wages due to the accident from her disability insurance policy. How much of the $600 is Courtney allowed to exclude from her gross income?

Answer: All $600 is excluded. Courtney can exclude the entire amount because she paid the premiums on the policy.

What if: How much of the $600 payment for lost wages from the disability insurance policy would Courtney exclude if EWD paid the disability insurance premium on her behalf as a nontaxable fringe benefit?

Answer: $0 would be excluded. In this circumstance the policy would be considered to be purchased by the employer, so Courtney would not be allowed to exclude any of the $600 payment from gross income. She would include the payment in gross income and be taxed on the entire $600.

What if: How much of the $600 payment for lost wages from the disability insurance policy would Courtney be allowed to exclude if she paid half the cost of the policy with after-tax dollars and EWD paid the other half as a taxable fringe benefit?

Answer: All $600 would be excluded. Because Courtney paid for the entire cost of the policy with after-tax dollars, she is allowed to exclude all of the disability insurance benefit. Note that if EWD had paid for half the cost of the policy as a nontaxable fringe benefit, Courtney would have been able to exclude $300, not $600.

Deferral Provisions

We've described exclusion provisions that allow taxpayers to permanently eliminate certain types of income from their tax base. Other code sections, called *deferral provisions*, allow taxpayers to defer (but not permanently exclude) the recognition of certain types of realized income. Transactions generating deferred income include installment sales, like-kind exchanges, involuntary conversions, and contributions to qualified retirement accounts. In the following paragraphs, we briefly describe the basic tax rules for contributions to employer-provided qualified retirement plans. In the Individual *For* AGI Deductions chapter, we discuss contributions to individual retirement accounts. We "defer" our discussion of the remaining transactions to subsequent chapters.

Employer-Provided Qualified Retirement Plans   Many employers help employees save for retirement by sponsoring retirement plans on behalf of their employees. These plans may be "qualified" retirement plans or "nonqualified" deferred compensation plans. Qualified plans are subject to certain restrictions not applicable to nonqualified plans. Both qualified and nonqualified plans are useful tools through which employers can achieve various compensation-related goals.[70]

Employer-provided qualified plans can be generally classified as **defined benefit plans** or **defined contribution plans.** As the name suggests, defined benefit plans spell out the specific benefit the employee will receive on retirement based on a fixed formula. The fixed formula is usually a function of years of service and employees' compensation levels as they near retirement. For employees who retire in 2018, the maximum annual benefit an employee can receive is the *lesser* of (1) 100 percent of the average of the employee's three highest years of compensation or (2) $220,000.[71] Defined benefit plans are typically funded through a combination of employer contributions and employee contributions of a portion of their salary. Neither contribution is taxable (except employee contributions are still subject to FICA taxes), as employees are subject to tax on the distributions from defined benefit plans, not the contribution.

In contrast to defined benefit plans, defined contribution plans specify the maximum annual contributions that employers and employees may contribute to the plan. Employers may provide different types of defined contribution plans, such as 401(k) plans (used by for-profit companies), 403(b) plans (used by nonprofit organizations,

---

[70]The tax treatment for employees for nonqualified deferred compensation plans is similar to that of qualified retirement plans. Specifically, employees are generally not subject to tax until they actually receive distributions from the nonqualified deferred compensation plans. Because qualified retirement plans are more common, we limit our discussion to these plans.

[71]§415(b)(1). The maximum benefit is adjusted annually for inflation.

including educational institutions), 457 plans (used by government agencies), profit-sharing plans, and money purchase pension plans.[72] They may even offer multiple defined contribution plans. For 2018, the sum of employer *and* employee contributions to an employee's defined contribution account(s) is limited to the *lesser* of (1) $55,000 ($61,000 for employees who are at least 50 years of age by the end of the year) or (2) 100 percent of the employee's compensation for the year.[73] *Employee* contributions to an employee's 401(k) account are limited to $18,500 (or $24,500 for employees that reach age 50 by the end of the year).[74] While this limit applies only to employee contributions, the $55,000 (or $61,000) limit still applies to the sum of employer and employee contributions. For example, if an employee under age 50 contributes the maximum $18,500 to her employer-sponsored 401(k) plan in 2018, the employer's contribution would be limited to $36,500 ($55,000 − $18,500).[75] Because of this limit on employer contributions, highly compensated employees may not be able to receive the full employer match available to other employees. As with defined benefits, neither employer nor employee contributions to defined contribution plans are taxable [neither are included in taxable salary, except for Roth 401(k) plans] as employees are subject to tax on the distributions from defined contribution plans, not the contribution.[76] Employee contributions, however, are still subject to FICA taxes.

Example 5-38

EWD provides a 401(k) plan in which it contributes an amount equal to 10 percent of Courtney's salary of $118,000 without any employee contributions. What are the tax consequences to Courtney?

Answer: Courtney will not be subject to current tax on EWD's $11,800 contribution.

What if: EWD provides a 401(k) plan that allows employees to contribute 10 percent of their salary with a 100 percent matching contribution by EWD. What are the tax consequences to Courtney if she chooses to contribute 10 percent of her salary to the plan?

Answer: Courtney's taxable salary for income tax purposes will be reduced to $106,200 [$118,000 − 10% × $118,000], but she will still be subject to FICA taxes on her entire salary ($118,000) before the 401(k) contributions. Courtney will also not be subject to tax on EWD's matching contribution of $11,800.

When employees receive distributions (that is, take withdrawals) from defined benefit or defined contribution plans [other than Roth 401(k) plans], the distributions are taxed as ordinary income. However, when employees receive distributions from these plans either

---

[72]401(k), 403(b), and 457 plans reflect the Code sections describing the plans.

[73]Source: §415(c)(1). The amount is indexed for inflation under §415(d)(1)(C).

[74]§402(g)(1). The amount is indexed for inflation under §402(g)(4).

[75]If an employee participates in more than one defined contribution plan, these limits apply to the total employee and employer contributions to all defined contribution plans. Thus, in a situation where the employee participates in more than one defined contribution plan, the contribution limits for any one defined contribution plan may be less than the overall contribution limits described here.

[76]When employers provide a Roth 401(k) plan, *employees* may elect to contribute to the Roth 401(k) *instead of or in addition to* contributing to a traditional 401(k) plan. However, *employer* contributions to an employee's 401(k) account must go to the employee's *traditional* 401(k) account rather than the employee's Roth 401(k) account. In contrast to contributions to traditional 401(k) plans, employee contributions of their salary to Roth 401(k) accounts are taxable, whereas *qualified* distributions from a Roth 401(k) account are excluded from gross income. Qualified distributions from Roth 401(k) accounts are those made after the employee's account has been open for five taxable years *and* the employee is at least 59½ years of age. All other distributions are nonqualified distributions. Nonqualified distributions of the taxpayer's account *contributions* are not subject to tax because the taxpayer did not deduct these amounts. In contrast, nonqualified distributions of the account *earnings* are fully taxable and are subject to the 10 percent early distribution penalty. If less than the entire balance in the plan is distributed, the nontaxable portion of the distribution is determined by multiplying the amount of the distribution by the ratio of account contributions to the total account balance.

too early or too late, they must pay a penalty in addition to the income taxes they owe on the distributions. Generally, employees who receive distributions before they reach:

- 59½ years of age or
- 55 years of age *and* have separated from service (retired or let go by employer)

are subject to a 10 percent nondeductible penalty on the amount of the early distributions.

Taxpayers who fail to receive a minimum distribution for (pertaining to) a particular year are also penalized. The year for which taxpayers must receive their *first* minimum distribution is the *later* of:

- the year in which the employee reaches 70½ years of age or
- the year in which the employee retires.

Taxpayers must receive this distribution no later than April 1 of the year after the year to which the first minimum distribution pertains.[77] Taxpayers generally must receive minimum distributions for subsequent years by the end of the years to which they pertain. Thus, a retired taxpayer who turns 70½ years of age in 2018 must receive a minimum distribution for 2018 by April 1, 2019. The same taxpayer must receive a minimum distribution for 2019 by December 31, 2019.

The amount of the minimum required distribution for a particular year is the taxpayer's account balance at the end of the year *prior to* the year to which the distribution pertains multiplied by a percentage from an IRS Uniform Lifetime Table. The percentage is based on the taxpayer's age at the end of the year to which the distribution pertains. The consequences for failing to receive timely minimum distributions are even more severe than receiving distributions too early. Taxpayers incur a 50 percent nondeductible penalty on the amount of a minimum distribution the employee should have received but did not. For this reason, it is vital that payouts from plans be monitored to avoid not only the 10 percent premature distribution penalty, but also the 50 percent penalty for late withdrawals. Because defined benefit plans typically don't permit payout arrangements that would trigger the early distribution or minimum distribution penalties, these penalties are of greater concern to participants in defined contribution plans.

> ### THE KEY FACTS
> #### Employer-Provided Qualified Retirement Plans
>
> - Employer-provided qualified plans can be generally classified as defined benefit plans or defined contribution plans.
> - Defined benefit plans spell out the specific benefit the employee will receive on retirement based on a fixed formula, whereas defined contribution plans specify the maximum annual contributions that employers and employees may contribute to the plan.
> - Employer and employee contributions to defined benefit or defined contribution plans are generally not taxable.
> - When employees receive distributions from defined benefit or defined contribution plans [other than Roth 401(k) plans], the distributions are taxed as ordinary income. However, when employees receive distributions either too early or too late, they must pay a penalty in addition to the income taxes they owe on the distributions.

Example 5-39

What if: Assume when she reaches 60 years of age, Courtney retires from EWD and receives a $60,000 distribution from her 401(k) account in the year she retires. Assuming her marginal ordinary tax rate is 32 percent, what amount of tax will Courtney pay on the distribution?

Answer: $19,200 ($60,000 × 32%).

What if: Assume when Courtney is 57 years of age and still employed by EWD, she requests and receives a $60,000 distribution from her 401(k) account. What amount of tax and penalty is Courtney required to pay on the distribution?

Answer: $19,200 taxes ($60,000 × 32%) + $6,000 penalty ($60,000 × 10%).

What if: Assume Courtney is let go from EWD when she is 57 years old. In that same year, she requests and receives a $60,000 distribution from her 401(k) account. What amount of tax and penalty is Courtney required to pay on the distribution?

Answer: $19,200 taxes ($60,000 × 32%) + $0 penalty (she is over 55 years of age and has separated from service with EWD).

---

[77]The amount of the required minimum distribution *for the year* in which a retired employee turns 70½ is the same whether the employee receives the distribution in the year she turns 70½ or whether she defers receiving the distribution until the next year (no later than April 1).

INCOME SUMMARY

At the end of the year, Courtney calculated her income and Gram's income. Exhibit 5-5 presents Courtney's income calculation, Exhibit 5-6 displays how this income would be reported on the front page of Courtney's tax return, and Exhibit 5-7 presents Gram's income calculation. Note that Courtney's actual *gross* income equals her total income on page 1 of her Form 1040 plus her $1,500 consulting expenses (see Example 5-7) and her $9,000 deductions for rental expenses (see Example 5-14), which are both *for* AGI deductions. Because Gram doesn't have any business, rental, or royalty deductions, her gross income is equal to her total income on line 22 of page 1 of her tax return.

EXHIBIT 5-5   Courtney's Income

Description	Amount	Reference
(1) Salary (line 7, 1040 page 1)	$ 118,000	Example 5-7
(2) Employment bonus award (line 7, 1040 page 1)	4,800	Example 5-4
(3) Discount architectural design services (line 7, 1040 page 1)	6,000	Example 5-25
(4) Compensation on below-market loan from EWD (line 7, 1040 page 1)	4,000	Example 5-26
(5) Discharge of indebtedness (line 7, 1040 page 1)	10,000	Example 5-27
(6) Interest income (line 8a, 1040 page 1)	321	Example 5-13
(7) Dividends (lines 9a and 9b, 1040 page 1)	700	Example 5-12
(8) State tax refund (line 10, 1040 page 1)	420	Example 5-3
(9) Alimony (line 11, 1040 page 1)	20,000	Example 5-20
(10) Net business income (line 12, 1040 page 1)	18,000	Example 5-7
(11) Net rental income (line 17, 1040 page 1)	5,000	Example 5-14
Total income as presented on line 22 of front page of 1040 (see Exhibit 5-6)	**$187,241**	Sum of (1) through (11)

EXHIBIT 5-6   Courtney's Tax Return

(total income as reported on 1040 page 1, lines 7–22)

Income					
	7	Wages, salaries, tips, etc. Attach Form(s) W-2	7		142,800
	8a	**Taxable** interest. Attach Schedule B if required	8a		321
	b	**Tax-exempt** interest. **Do not** include on line 8a	8b	500	
Attach Form(s) W-2 here. Also attach Forms W-2G and 1099-R if tax was withheld.	9a	Ordinary dividends. Attach Schedule B if required	9a		700
	b	Qualified dividends	9b	700	
	10	Taxable refunds, credits, or offsets of state and local income taxes	10		420
	11	Alimony received	11		20,000
	12	Business income or (loss). Attach Schedule C or C-EZ	12		18,000
	13	Capital gain or (loss). Attach Schedule D if required. If not required, check here ▶ ☐	13		
If you did not get a W-2, see instructions.	14	Other gains or (losses). Attach Form 4797	14		
	15a	IRA distributions .	15a		b Taxable amount . . .	15b		
	16a	Pensions and annuities	16a		b Taxable amount . . .	16b		
	17	Rental real estate, royalties, partnerships, S corporations, trusts, etc. Attach Schedule E	17		5,000
	18	Farm income or (loss). Attach Schedule F	18		
	19	Unemployment compensation	19		
	20a	Social security benefits	20a		b Taxable amount . . .	20b		
	21	Other income. List type and amount _____	21		
	22	Combine the amounts in the far right column for lines 7 through 21. This is your **total income** ▶	22		187,241

EXHIBIT 5-7   **Gram's Income**

Deduction	Amount	Reference
Interest income	$ 4,750	Example 5-13
Annuity income	3,400	Example 5-15
Gain on stock sale	350	Example 5-16
Sweepstakes winnings (WaveRunner)	7,500	Example 5-23
Income for current year	**$16,000**	

CONCLUSION

In this chapter we explained the basic concepts of income realization and recognition, identified and discussed the major types of income, and described common income exclusions and deferrals. We discovered that many exclusions are related to specific congressional objectives, but that absent a specific exclusion or deferral provision, realized income should be included in gross income. In the next three chapters, we turn our attention to the deductions available to taxpayers when computing their taxable income, and we conclude our review of the individual income tax formula by determining how to compute taxpayers' tax liability and their taxes due or tax refund. We will continue to follow Courtney and Gram in their quest to determine their taxable income and corresponding tax liability.

Appendix A   Netting Gains and Losses from 0/15/20 Percent, 25 Percent, and 28 Percent Capital Assets

When taxpayers sell long-term capital assets and recognize gains subject to the 25 percent and/or 28 percent capital gains rates, we must expand the basic netting process described in the chapter. In these situations, apply the following steps to determine the amount of gain taxable at the different tax rates:

Step 1: Net all short-term capital gains and short-term capital losses, including any short-term capital loss carried forward from the prior year. A net positive amount is a net short-term capital gain. A net negative amount is a net short-term capital loss. If there are no long-term capital gains or losses, the netting process is complete. Otherwise, continue to Step 2.

Step 2: Separate long-term capital gains and losses into three separate rate groups (28 percent, 25 percent, and 0/15/20 percent). Place any net long-term capital loss carried over from the prior year into the 28 percent rate group. Sum the gains and losses within each group. The outcome will be a net 28 percent gain or loss, a 25 percent gain (there are no 25 percent losses), and/or a net 0/15/20 percent gain or loss. Proceed to Step 3.

Step 3: (A) If none of the long-term rate groups from Step 2 nets to a gain, transfer the net loss (if any) in the 0/15/20 percent rate group to the 28 percent rate group, combine it with the loss in that group (if any), and proceed to Step 4.

(B) If none of the long-term rate groups from Step 2 nets to a loss, proceed to Step 6.

(C) Combining net gains and losses in long-term rate groups:

1. If Step 2 results in net losses in both the 28 percent and 0/15/20 percent rate groups, combine the net losses and then apply them to offset gains in the 25 percent rate group. If the losses exceed the gain, the result is a net long-term capital loss. Proceed to Step 4. If the gain exceeds the losses, the result is a net long-term capital gain. Proceed to Step 6.

2. If the Step 2 outcomes include a net loss in the 28 percent rate group and net gains in the other rate groups, apply the net loss from the 28 percent rate group to the gain in the 25 percent rate group until the 25 percent rate group gain is reduced to zero. Then offset any remaining 28 percent rate group loss against the net gain in the 0/15/20 percent rate group. If the net loss from the 28 percent rate group exceeds the net gains from the other rate groups, the net loss is a net long-term capital loss. Proceed to Step 4. If gain remains in the 25 percent and/or 0/15/20 percent rate groups after applying the loss, the result is a net long-term capital gain. Proceed to Step 6.

3. If the amounts from Step 2 include a net loss in the 0/15/20 percent rate group and net gains in the 28 percent and/or the 25 percent rate groups, apply the net loss from the 0/15/20 percent rate group to the net gain in the 28 percent rate group until the net gain is reduced to zero. Then offset any remaining loss against the gain in the 25 percent rate group. If the net loss from the 0/15/20 percent rate group exceeds the net gains from the other rate groups, the net loss is a net long-term capital loss. Proceed to Step 4. If gain remains in the 28 percent and/or 25 percent rate groups after applying the loss, the result is a net long-term capital gain. Proceed to Step 6.

Step 4: If there is no net short-term capital gain or loss from Step 1, the netting process is complete; apply the net capital loss deduction limitations as described previously and ignore the remaining steps. If the result from Step 1 is a net short-term capital loss and the result from Step 3 is a net long-term capital loss, the netting process is complete: apply the net capital loss deduction limitations described previously and ignore the remaining steps. Otherwise, continue on to Step 5.

Step 5: If Step 1 produces a net short-term capital gain and Step 3 produces a net long-term capital loss, sum the net short-term capital gain and the net long-term capital loss.

(a) If the outcome is a net loss, the netting process is complete. Apply the net capital loss deduction limitations described previously.

(b) If the outcome is a net gain, the net gain is treated the same as a net short-term capital gain and is taxed at ordinary rates. The netting process is complete.

Step 6: If there is no net short-term capital gain or loss from Step 1, the netting process is complete. The tax on the net long-term capital gain remaining in each long-term group is determined as described in the next section. If the Step 1 outcome is a net short-term capital gain, skip to Step 7. If the Step 1 outcome is a net short-term capital loss *and* Step 3 results in a net gain in any (or all) of the long-term rate groups, first use the short-term capital loss to offset the gain in the 28 percent rate group (if any), then the gain in the 25 percent rate group (if any), and finally the gain in 0/15/20 percent rate group (if any).

(a) If the net short-term capital loss exceeds all gains in the long-term rate groups, the netting process is complete. Apply the net capital loss deduction limitations described previously.

(b) If the net short-term capital loss does not offset all of the gain in any (or all) of the long-term rate groups, the netting process is complete. The result is a net capital gain. The tax on the gain remaining in each long-term group is determined as described in the next section.

Step 7: If Step 1 produces a net short-term capital gain *and* Step 3 produces a net long-term capital gain(s), the netting process is complete. The tax on the remaining gains is determined as described in the next section.

Example 5A-1

What if: Assume that Gram sold stocks, gold coins, and a rental home (with $50,000 of accumulated depreciation) as follows:

Capital Asset	Market Value	Tax Basis	Capital Gain/Loss	Scenario 1 Type
A stock	$ 40,000	$ 5,000	$ 35,000	Long 0/15/20%
B stock	20,000	30,000	(10,000)	Long 0/15/20%
C stock	20,000	12,000	8,000	Short
D stock	17,000	28,000	(11,000)	Short
Gold coins	4,000	3,000	1,000	Long 28%
Rental home	200,000	80,000	120,000	Long 25% and 0/15/20%*
Overall gain			**$143,000**	

*$50,000 of the gain is 25 percent gain (§1250 unrecaptured gain from the accumulated depreciation on the property—see the Property Dispositions chapter), and the remaining $70,000 is 0/15/20 percent gain.

Assuming Gram did not sell any other capital assets during the year, she recognizes an overall capital gain of $143,000. What is (are) the maximum tax rate(s) applicable to this gain?

Answer: $95,000 of gain is subject to a 0/15/20 percent maximum rate and $48,000 of gain is subject to a 25 percent rate, computed as follows:

Step 1: $3,000 net short-term capital loss [$8,000 + ($11,000)].

Step 2: Stock A and Stock B are placed in the 0/15/20 percent group, the gold coins are placed in the 28 percent group, $50,000 of the gain from the sale of the rental home is placed in the 25 percent group, and the remaining $70,000 gain from the rental home is placed in the 0/15/20 percent group. The sum of the gains and losses in each group results in a net 28 percent gain of $1,000, a 25 percent gain of $50,000, and a net $95,000 gain in the 0/15/20 percent group.

Step 3: 3(A) does not apply. 3(B) applies because all of the long-term rate groups have a net gain from Step 2. We proceed to Step 6.

Step 4: Not required.

Step 5: Not required.

Step 6: Move the $3,000 loss from Step 1 into the 28 percent group to offset the $1,000 gain. Next, move the remaining $2,000 loss [$1,000 gain on gold + ($3,000) short-term loss from Step 1] into the 25 percent group to offset the $50,000 gain. The netting process is complete at this point because the net short-term capital loss does not offset all of the gains in the long-term rate groups (Step 6[b]) and only gains remain in the long-term rate groups.

Step 7: Not required.

(continued on page 5-44)

Gram's netting process is reflected in the following table:

Description	Short-Term	Long-Term Overall	Long-Term 28%	Long-Term 25%	Long-Term 0/15/20%
Stock C	$8,000				
Stock D	(11,000)				
Step 1:	(3,000)				
Coins		$ 1,000	1,000		
Unrecaptured §1250 gain		50,000		50,000	
Remaining gain from rental property		70,000			70,000
Stock A		35,000			35,000
Stock B		(10,000)			(10,000)
Step 2:		$146,000)			
Steps 4 and 5:			$1,000	$50,000	$95,000
Step 6:	(3,000) →		(3,000)		
Step 7			(2,000) →	(2,000)	
Step 8				48,000	
Summary				$48,000	$95,000
Applicable Rate				25%	0/15/20%

EFFECT OF 25 PERCENT AND 28 PERCENT CAPITAL GAINS ON TAX LIABILITY

Determining the effects of capital gains on a taxpayer's tax liability is also a bit more complex if the taxpayer recognizes 25 percent or 28 percent capital gains. To do so, follow these basic guidelines:

- If the taxpayer's ordinary taxable income (total taxable income excluding long-term capital gains and qualified dividends) falls within the 20 percent tax bracket for long-term capital gains (see Appendix D for the tax brackets by filing status for 0 percent, 15 percent, and 20 percent long-term capital gains and dividends), the capital gains for each of the 0/15/20 percent, 25 percent, and 28 percent groups are taxed at their maximum rates.

- If the taxpayer's total taxable income (including capital gains and qualified dividends) falls within the 0 percent tax bracket for long-term capital gains (see Appendix D), the capital gains for the 0/15/20 percent group are taxed at 0 percent, and the 25 percent and 28 percent gains are taxed at the taxpayer's ordinary rates. Thus, the taxpayer's tax is calculated using the ordinary tax rates on the taxpayer's taxable income including the 25 percent and 28 percent gains (and excluding the 0/15/20 percent gains, which are taxed at 0 percent).

- For other situations, use the following steps to determine the tax on the gains:

  Step 1: Fill up the 10, 12, 22, 24, 32, 35, and 37 percent tax rate brackets with taxable income, exclusive of long-term capital gains (and qualified dividends) subject to preferential rates.

  Step 2: Next, if there is any remaining space below the beginning of the 32 percent bracket after step 1, add any 25 percent rate capital gains to the amount from step 1 until reaching the end of the 24 percent bracket. This 25 percent rate capital gain is taxed at the ordinary rates provided in the tax rate schedule.

  Step 3: Next, if, after including all of the 25 percent gain (step 2), there is still space remaining below the beginning of the 32 percent bracket, add any 28 percent rate capital gain until reaching the end of the 24 percent bracket. This 28 percent rate capital gain is taxed at the ordinary rates provided in the tax rate schedule.

  Step 4: Next, use the taxpayer's taxable income after Step 3 as a starting point and refer to the tax brackets that apply to preferentially taxed capital gains and dividends (see Appendix D). Take the taxpayer's taxable income after Step 3 and add any 0/15/20 percent capital gains (and qualified dividends). Any 0/15/20 percent capital gains and qualified dividends that fall within the 0 percent tax bracket are taxed at 0 percent, and any 0/15/20 percent capital gains and qualified dividends that fall within the 15 percent tax bracket are taxed at 15 percent. Any remaining 0/15/20 capital gains and qualified dividends are taxed at 20 percent.

Step 5: Finally, any remaining 25 percent rate capital gain (not taxed in step 2) is taxed at 25 percent. Any remaining 28 percent rate capital gain (not taxed in step 3) is taxed at 28 percent. If, however, a taxpayer's tax liability would be lower using the ordinary tax rates for all ordinary income and capital gains (which is possible but not typical), the taxpayer would simply owe tax based on the ordinary tax rates.

Example 5A-2

What if: Let's return to the facts of the previous example where Gram recognized a $48,000 25 percent net capital gain and a $95,000 0/15/20 percent net capital gain. Also, assume that Gram's taxable income for 2018 before considering the net capital gains is $10,000. Gram's filing status is single. What is Gram's gross tax liability for the year?

Answer: $22,949.50, computed as follows:

Amount and Type of Income	Applicable Rate	Tax	Explanation
$9,525; ordinary	10%	$ 952.50	$9,525 × 10%. The first $9,525 of Gram's $10,000 of ordinary income is taxed at 10 percent (see single tax rate schedule for this and other computations).
$475; ordinary	12%	57.00	$475 × 12%. Gram's remaining $475 of ordinary income ($10,000 − $9,525) is taxed at 12 percent.
$28,700; 25 percent capital gains	12%	3,444.00	$28,700 × 12%. The end of Gram's 12 percent tax bracket is $38,700 minus $10,000 ($9,525 + $475) already taxed. Gram's ordinary tax rate of 12 percent is lower than the maximum 25 percent rate for these gains, so they are taxed at the lower ordinary rate.
$19,300; 25 percent capital gains	22%	4,246.00	$19,300 × 22%. $48,000 total 25% gain minus $28,700 25 percent gain already taxed at 12 percent. Gram's ordinary tax rate of 22 percent is lower than the maximum 25 percent rate for these gains, so they are taxed at the lower ordinary rate.
$95,000; 0/15/20 percent capital gains	15%	14,250.00	$95,000 × 15%. When added to Gram's taxable income through Step 3 ($58,000), all of the 0/15/20 percent gains fall within the 15 percent tax bracket for preferentially taxed capital gains (between $38,600 and $425,800), so they are taxed at 15 percent.
Gross tax liability		**$22,949.50**	

Appendix B   2017 Social Security Worksheet from Form 1040

2017 Form 1040—Lines 20a and 20b

Social Security Benefits Worksheet—Lines 20a and 20b   *Keep for Your Records*

Before you begin:
- ✓ Complete Form 1040, lines 21 and 23 through 32, if they apply to you.
- ✓ Figure any write-in adjustments to be entered on the dotted line next to line 36 (see the instructions for line 36).
- ✓ If you are married filing separately and you lived apart from your spouse for all of 2017, enter "D" to the right of the word "benefits" on line 20a. If you don't, you may get a math error notice from the IRS.
- ✓ Be sure you have read the *Exception* in the line 20a and 20b instructions to see if you can use this worksheet instead of a publication to find out if any of your benefits are taxable.

1. Enter the total amount from **box 5** of **all** your **Forms SSA-1099** and **Forms RRB-1099.** Also, enter this amount on Form 1040, line 20a .... **1.** _____

2. Multiply line 1 by 50% (0.50) .... **2.** _____

3. Combine the amounts from Form 1040, lines 7, 8a, 9a, 10 through 14, 15b, 16b, 17 through 19, and 21 .... **3.** _____

4. Enter the amount, if any, from Form 1040, line 8b .... **4.** _____

5. Combine lines 2, 3, and 4 .... **5.** _____

6. Enter the total of the amounts from Form 1040, lines 23 through 32, plus any write-in adjustments you entered on the dotted line next to line 36 .... **6.** _____

7. Is the amount on line 6 less than the amount on line 5?

    ☐ **No.** (STOP)   None of your social security benefits are taxable. Enter -0- on Form 1040, line 20b.

    ☐ **Yes.** Subtract line 6 from line 5 .... **7.** _____

8. If you are:
    - Married filing jointly, enter $32,000
    - Single, head of household, qualifying widow(er), or married filing separately and you **lived apart** from your spouse for all of 2017, enter $25,000
    - Married filing separately and you lived with your spouse at any time in 2017, skip lines 8 through 15; multiply line 7 by 85% (0.85) and enter the result on line 16. Then, go to line 17

    .... **8.** _____

9. Is the amount on line 8 less than the amount on line 7?

    ☐ **No.** (STOP)   None of your social security benefits are taxable. Enter -0- on Form 1040, line 20b. If you are married filing separately and you **lived apart** from your spouse for all of 2017, be sure you entered "D" to the right of the word "benefits" on line 20a.

    ☐ **Yes.** Subtract line 8 from line 7 .... **9.** _____

10. Enter: $12,000 if married filing jointly; $9,000 if single, head of household, qualifying widow(er), or married filing separately and you **lived apart** from your spouse for all of 2017 .... **10.** _____

11. Subtract line 10 from line 9. If zero or less, enter -0- .... **11.** _____

12. Enter the **smaller** of line 9 or line 10 .... **12.** _____

13. Enter one-half of line 12 .... **13.** _____

14. Enter the **smaller** of line 2 or line 13 .... **14.** _____

15. Multiply line 11 by 85% (0.85). If line 11 is zero, enter -0- .... **15.** _____

16. Add lines 14 and 15 .... **16.** _____

17. Multiply line 1 by 85% (0.85) .... **17.** _____

18. **Taxable social security benefits.** Enter the **smaller** of line 16 or line 17. Also enter this amount on Form 1040, line 20b .... **18.** _____

TIP *If any of your benefits are taxable for 2017 **and** they include a lump-sum benefit payment that was for an earlier year, you may be able to reduce the taxable amount. See* Lump-Sum Election *in Pub. 915 for details.*

Summary

Apply the concept of realization and explain when taxpayers recognize gross income.   **LO 5-1**

- Income is typically realized with a transaction that allows economic benefit to be identified and measured.
- Unless realized income is deferred or excluded, it is included in gross income in the period dictated by the taxpayer's accounting method.
- The accrual method of accounting recognizes income in the period it is earned, and this method is typically used by large corporations.
- The cash method of accounting recognizes income in the period received, and this method offers a simple and flexible method of accounting typically used by individuals.
- The return of capital principle, constructive receipt doctrine, and assignment of income doctrine affect how much income is recognized, when income is recognized, and who recognizes income, respectively.

Understand the distinctions between the various sources of income, including income from services and property.   **LO 5-2**

- Income from services is called earned income, whereas income from property is called unearned income.
- A portion of annuity payments and proceeds from sales of property is a nontaxable return of capital.
- Taxpayers selling capital assets that they hold for a year or less recognize short-term capital gains or losses. Alternatively, taxpayers selling capital assets they hold for more than a year recognize long-term capital gains or losses. Short-term capital gains are taxed at ordinary rather than preferential rates. Long-term capital gains are taxed at preferential rates.
- Earned and unearned income generated by flow-through business entities is reported by partners and Subchapter S shareholders.
- Other sources of income include alimony payments, unemployment compensation, Social Security benefits, prizes and awards, bargain purchases, imputed interest on below-market loans, and discharge of indebtedness.

Apply basic income exclusion and deferral provisions to compute gross income.   **LO 5-3**

- Interest received from holding state and local indebtedness (municipal interest) is excluded from gross income.
- A taxpayer satisfying certain home ownership and use requirements can permanently exclude up to $250,000 ($500,000 if married filing jointly) of realized gain on the sale of her principal residence.
- Employment-related nonrecognition provisions include a variety of excludable fringe benefits.
- Gifts, inheritances, life insurance proceeds, and foreign-earned income up to $103,900 (in 2018) are excluded from gross income in order to mitigate the effects of double taxation.
- Common injury-related nonrecognition provisions include the exclusions for workers' compensation, personal injury payments and reimbursements from health insurance policies, and certain payments from disability policies.
- Employer and employee contributions to defined benefit or defined contribution plans are generally not taxable. When employees receive distributions from defined benefit or defined contribution plans [other than Roth 401(k) plans], the distributions are taxed as ordinary income.

KEY TERMS

accelerated death benefits (5-33)	assignment of income doctrine (5-8)	community property systems (5-8)
accountable plan (5-29)	bargain element (5-10)	constructive receipt doctrine (5-7)
accrual method (5-6)	barter clubs (5-4)	defined benefit plans (5-37)
alimony (5-21)	cash method (5-6)	defined contribution plans (5-37)
annuity (5-13)	claim of right doctrine (5-7)	disability insurance (5-36)

discharge of indebtedness (5-27)
earned income (5-10)
exercise date (5-10)
exercise price (5-10)
first-in, first-out (FIFO)
    method (5-16)
flow-through entity (5-20)
fringe benefits (5-28)
gift (5-33)
grant date (5-10)
gross income (5-2)
imputed income (5-25)

inheritance (5-33)
long-term capital gains or losses (5-16)
municipal bond (5-27)
net long-term capital gain
    (NLTCG) (5-17)
net long-term capital loss
    (NLTCL) (5-17)
net short-term capital
    gain (NSTCG) (5-17)
net short-term capital
    loss (NSTCL) (5-17)
nonrecognition provisions (5-27)

realization principle (5-3)
return of capital (5-5)
short-term capital gains or
    losses (5-16)
specific identification method (5-16)
tax basis (5-5)
tax benefit rule (5-5)
unearned income (5-12)
vesting date (5-10)
wash sale (5-19)
wherewithal to pay (5-3)

DISCUSSION QUESTIONS

Discussion Questions are available in Connect®.

LO 5-1   1. Based on the definition of gross income in §61 and related regulations, what is the general presumption regarding the taxability of income realized?

LO 5-1   2. Based on the definition of gross income in §61, related regulations, and judicial rulings, what are the three criteria for recognizing taxable income?

LO 5-1   3. Describe the concept of realization for tax purposes.

LO 5-1   4. Compare and contrast realization of income with recognition of income.

LO 5-1   5. Tim is a plumber who joined a barter club. This year Tim exchanges plumbing services for a new roof. The roof is properly valued at $2,500, but Tim would have only billed $2,200 for the plumbing services. What amount of income should Tim recognize on the exchange of his services for a roof? Would your answer change if Tim would have normally billed $3,000 for his services?

LO 5-1   6. Andre constructs and installs cabinets in homes. Blair sells and installs carpet in apartments. Andre and Blair worked out an arrangement whereby Andre installed cabinets in Blair's home and Blair installed carpet in Andre's home. Neither Andre nor Blair believes they are required to recognize any gross income on this exchange because neither received cash. Do you agree with them? Explain.

LO 5-1   7. What issue precipitated the return of capital principle? Explain.

LO 5-1   8. Compare how the return of capital principle applies when (1) a taxpayer sells an asset and collects the sale proceeds immediately and (2) a taxpayer sells an asset and collects the sale proceeds over several periods (an installment sale). If Congress wanted to maximize revenue from installment sales, how would it have applied the return of capital principle for installment sales?

LO 5-1   9. This year Jorge received a refund of property taxes that he deducted on his tax return last year. Jorge is not sure whether he should include the refund in his gross income. What would you tell him?

LO 5-1   10. Describe in general how the cash method of accounting differs from the accrual method of accounting.

LO 5-1   11. Janet is a cash-method, calendar-year taxpayer. She received a check for services provided in the mail during the last week of December. However, rather than cash the check, Janet decided to wait until the following January because she believes that her delay will cause the income to be realized and recognized next year. What would you tell her? Would it matter if she didn't open the envelope? Would it matter if she refused to check her mail during the last week of December? Explain.

12. The cash method of accounting means that taxpayers don't recognize income unless they receive cash or cash equivalents. True or false? Explain. **LO 5-1**

13. Contrast the constructive receipt doctrine with the claim of right doctrine. **LO 5-1**

14. Dewey is a lawyer who uses the cash method of accounting. Last year Dewey provided a client with legal services worth $55,000, but the client could not pay the fee. This year Dewey requested that in lieu of paying Dewey $55,000 for the services, the client could make a $45,000 gift to Dewey's daughter. Dewey's daughter received the check for $45,000 and deposited it in her bank account. How much of this income is taxed, if any, to Dewey? Explain. **LO 5-1**

15. Clyde and Bonnie were married this year. Clyde has a steady job that will pay him about $37,000, while Bonnie does odd jobs that will produce about $28,000 of income. They also have a joint savings account that will pay about $400 of interest. If Clyde and Bonnie reside in a community property state and file married-separate tax returns, how much gross income will Clyde and Bonnie each report? Is there any difference if they reside in a common law state? Explain. **LO 5-1**

16. Distinguish earned income from unearned income, and provide an example of each. **LO 5-2**

17. From an employee perspective, how are incentive stock options treated differently than nonqualified stock options for tax purposes? In general, for a given number of options, which type of stock option should employees prefer? **LO 5-2**

18. Jim purchased 100 shares of stock this year and elected to participate in a dividend reinvestment program. This program automatically uses dividends to purchase additional shares of stock. This year Jim's shares paid $350 of dividends and he used these funds to purchase additional shares of stock. These additional shares are worth $375 at year-end. What amount of dividends, if any, should Jim declare as income this year? Explain. **LO 5-2**

19. Jerry has a certificate of deposit at the local bank. The interest on this certificate was credited to his account on December 31 of last year, but he didn't withdraw the interest until January of this year. When is the interest income taxed? **LO 5-2**

20. Conceptually, when taxpayers receive annuity payments, how do they determine the amount of the payment they must include in gross income? **LO 5-2**

21. George purchased a life annuity to provide him monthly payments for as long as he lives. Based on IRS tables, George's life expectancy is 100 months. Is George able to recover his cost of the annuity if he dies before he receives 100 monthly payments? Explain. What happens for tax purposes if George receives more than 100 payments? **LO 5-2**

22. Brad purchased land for $45,000 this year. At year-end Brad sold the land for $51,700 and paid a sales commission of $450. What effect does this transaction have on Brad's gross income? Explain. **LO 5-2**

23. What is the deciding factor in determining whether a capital gain is a short-term or long-term capital gain? What tax rates apply to short-term gains versus long-term capital gains? **LO 5-2**

24. What is a "wash sale"? What is the purpose of the wash sale tax rules? **LO 5-2**

25. Tomiko is a 50 percent owner (partner) in the Tanaka partnership. During the year, the partnership reported $1,000 of interest income and $2,000 of dividends. How much of this income must Tomiko include in her gross income? **LO 5-2**

26. Clem and Ida have been married for several years, but in 2018 they finalized their divorce. In the divorce decree, Clem agreed to deed his car to Ida and pay Ida $10,000 per year for four years (but not beyond her death). Will either of these transfers qualify as alimony for tax purposes? Explain. **LO 5-2**

27. Larry Bounds has won the Gold Bat Award for hitting the longest home run in Major League Baseball this year. The bat is worth almost $35,000. Under what conditions can Larry exclude the award from his gross income? Explain. **LO 5-2**

LO 5-2   28. Rory and Nicholi, single taxpayers, each annually receive Social Security benefits of $15,000. Rory's taxable income from sources other than Social Security exceeds $200,000. In contrast, the Social Security benefits are Nicholi's only source of income. What percentage of the Social Security benefits must Rory include in his gross income? What percentage of Social Security benefits is Nicholi required to include in his gross income?

LO 5-2   29. Rolando purchases a golf cart from his employer, E-Z-Go Golf Carts, for a sizable discount. Explain the rules for determining if Rolando's purchase results in taxable income for him.

LO 5-2   30. When an employer makes a below-market loan to an employee, what are the tax consequences to the employer and employee?

LO 5-2   31. Explain why an insolvent taxpayer is allowed to exclude income from the discharge of indebtedness if the taxpayer remains insolvent after receiving the debt relief.

LO 5-3   32. What are the basic requirements to exclude the gain on the sale of a personal residence?

LO 5-3   33. Explain why an employee should be concerned about whether his employer reimburses business expenses using an "accountable" plan?

LO 5-3   34. Cassie works in an office and has access to several professional color printers. Her employer allows Cassie and her fellow employees to use the printers to print color postcards for the holidays. This year Cassie printed out two dozen postcards worth almost $76. Must Cassie include this amount in her gross income this year? Explain your answer.

LO 5-3   35. What are some common examples of taxable and tax-free fringe benefits?

LO 5-3   36. Explain how state and local governments benefit from the provisions that allow taxpayers to exclude interest on state and local bonds from their gross income.

LO 5-3   37. Explain why taxpayers are allowed to exclude gifts and inheritances from gross income even though these payments are realized and clearly provide taxpayers with wherewithal to pay.

LO 5-3   38. Describe the kinds of insurance premiums an employer can pay on behalf of an employee without triggering includible compensation to the employee.

LO 5-3   39. How are state-sponsored 529 educational savings plans taxed if investment returns are used for educational purposes? Are the returns taxed differently if they are not ultimately used to pay for education costs?

LO 5-3   40. Jim was injured in an accident and his surgeon botched the medical procedure. Jim recovered $5,000 from the doctors for pain and suffering and $2,000 for emotional distress. Determine the taxability of these payments and briefly explain to Jim the apparent rationale for including or excluding these payments from gross income.

LO 5-3   41. Tom was just hired by Acme Corporation and has decided to purchase disability insurance. This insurance promises to pay him weekly benefits to replace his salary should he be unable to work because of disability. Disability insurance is also available through Acme as part of its compensation plan. Acme pays these premiums as a nontaxable fringe benefit, but the plan promises to pay about 10 percent less in benefits. If Tom elects to have Acme pay the premiums, then his compensation will be reduced by an equivalent amount. Should tax considerations play a role in Tom's choice to buy disability insurance through Acme or on his own? Explain.

LO 5-3   42. How are defined benefit plans different from defined contribution plans? How are they similar?

LO 5-3   43. What are the consequences if a taxpayer takes a distribution from a retirement plan either too early or too late? Describe the rules for determining if a distribution is too early or too late.

PROBLEMS

Select problems are available in Connect®.

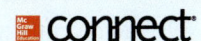

44. For the following independent cases, determine whether economic income is present and, if so, whether it must be included in gross income (i.e., is it realized and recognized for tax purposes?).

    a) Asia owns stock that is listed on the New York Stock Exchange, and this year the stock increased in value by $20,000.

    b) Ben sold stock for $10,000 and paid a sales commission of $250. Ben purchased the stock several years ago for $4,000.

    c) Bessie is a partner in SULU Enterprises LLC. This year SULU reported that Bessie's share of rental income was $2,700 and her share of municipal interest was $750.

45. Devon owns 1,000 shares of stock worth $10,000. This year he received 200 additional shares of this stock from a stock dividend. His 1,200 shares are now worth $12,500. Must Devon include the dividend paid in stock in income?

46. XYZ declared a $1 per share dividend on August 15. The date of record for the dividend was September 1 (the stock began selling *ex-dividend* on September 2). The dividend was paid on September 10. Ellis is a cash-method taxpayer. Determine if he must include the dividends in gross income under the following independent circumstances.

    a) Ellis bought 100 shares of XYZ stock on August 1 for $21 per share. Ellis received $100 on September 10. Ellis still owns the shares at year-end.

    b) Ellis bought 100 shares of XYZ stock on August 1 for $21 per share. Ellis sold his XYZ shares on September 5 for $23 per share. Ellis received the $100 dividend on September 10 (note that even though Ellis didn't own the stock on September 10, he still received the dividend because he was the shareholder on the record date).

    c) Ellis bought 100 shares of XYZ stock for $22 per share on August 20. Ellis received the $100 dividend on September 10. Ellis still owns the shares at year-end.

47. For the following independent cases, determine whether economic income is present and, if so, whether it must be included in gross income. Identify a tax authority that supports your analysis.

    a) Hermione discovered a gold nugget (valued at $10,000) on her land.

    b) Jay embezzled $20,000 from his employer and has not yet been apprehended.

    c) Keisha found $1,000 inside an old dresser. She purchased the dresser at a discount furniture store at the end of last year and found the money after the beginning of the new year. No one has claimed the money.

48. Although Hank is retired, he is an excellent handyman and often works part-time on small projects for neighbors and friends. Last week his neighbor, Mike, offered to pay Hank $500 for minor repairs to his house. Hank completed the repairs in December of this year. Hank uses the cash method of accounting and is a calendar-year taxpayer. Compute Hank's gross income for this year from each of the following alternative transactions:

    a) Mike paid Hank $200 in cash in December of this year and promised to pay the remaining $300 with interest in three months.

    b) Mike paid Hank $100 in cash in December of this year and gave him a negotiable promissory note for $400 due in three months with interest. Hank sold the note in January for $350.

    c) Mike gave Hank tickets to the big game in January. The tickets have a face value of $50 but Hank could sell them for $400. Hank went to the game with his son.

LO 5-1

LO 5-1

research

LO 5-1

research

LO 5-1

research

LO 5-1

d) Mike bought Hank a new set of snow tires. The tires typically sell for $500, but Mike bought them on sale for $450.

LO 5-1 49. Jim recently joined the Austin Barter Club, an organization that facilitates the exchange of services between its members. This year Jim provided lawn-mowing services to other club members. Jim received the following from the barter club. Determine the amount, if any, Jim should include in his gross income in each of the following situations:

a) Jim received $275 of car repair services from another member of the club.

b) Jim received a $150 credit that gave him the option of receiving a season pass at a local ski resort from another member of the club. However, he forgot to request the pass by the end of the ski season and his credit expired.

c) Jim received a $450 credit that can only be applied for goods or services from club members next year.

LO 5-1

research

50. Last year Acme paid Ralph $15,000 to install a new air-conditioning unit at its headquarters building. The air conditioner did not function properly, and this year Acme requested that Ralph return the payment. Because Ralph could not repair one critical part in the unit, he refunded the cost of the repair, $5,000, to Acme.

a) Is Ralph required to include the $15,000 payment he received last year in his gross income from last year?

b) What are the tax implications of the repayment if Ralph was in the 35 percent tax bracket when he received the $15,000 payment from Acme, but was in the 24 percent tax bracket when he refunded $5,000 to Acme?

LO 5-1 51. Louis files as a single taxpayer. In April of this year he received a $900 refund of state income taxes that he paid last year. How much of the refund, if any, must Louis include in gross income under the following independent scenarios? Assume the standard deduction last year was $6,350.

a) Last year Louis claimed itemized deductions of $6,600. Louis's itemized deductions included state income taxes paid of $1,750.

b) Last year Louis had itemized deductions of $4,800 and he chose to claim the standard deduction. Louis's itemized deductions included state income taxes paid of $1,750.

c) Last year Louis claimed itemized deductions of $7,790. Louis's itemized deductions included state income taxes paid of $2,750.

LO 5-1 52. L. A. and Paula file as married taxpayers. In August of this year, they received a $5,200 refund of state income taxes that they paid last year. How much of the refund, if any, must L. A. and Paula include in gross income under the following independent scenarios? Assume the standard deduction last year was $12,700.

a) Last year L. A. and Paula had itemized deductions of $10,200, and they chose to claim the standard deduction.

b) Last year L. A. and Paula claimed itemized deductions of $23,300. Their itemized deductions included state income taxes paid of $7,500.

c) Last year L. A. and Paula claimed itemized deductions of $15,500. Their itemized deductions included state income taxes paid of $10,500.

LO 5-1 53. Clyde is a cash-method taxpayer who reports on a calendar-year basis. This year Paylate Corporation has decided to pay Clyde a year-end bonus of $1,000. Determine the amount Clyde should include in his gross income this year under the following circumstances:

a) Paylate Corporation wrote the check and put it in his office mail slot on December 30 of this year, but Clyde did not bother to stop by the office to pick it up until after year-end.

b) Paylate Corporation mistakenly wrote the check for $100. Clyde received the remaining $900 after year-end.

c) Paylate Corporation mailed the check to Clyde before the end of the year (and it was delivered before year-end). Although Clyde expected the bonus payment, he decided not to collect his mail until after year-end.

d) Clyde picked up the check in December, but the check could not be cashed immediately because it was postdated January 10.

54. Identify the amount, if any, that these individuals must include in gross income in the following independent cases. Assume that the individuals use the cash method of accounting and report income on a calendar-year basis.   `LO 5-1`

     a) Elmer was an extremely diligent employee this year and his employer gave him three additional days off with pay (Elmer's gross pay for the three days totaled $1,200, but his net pay was only $948).

     b) Amax purchased new office furniture and allowed each employee to take home old office furniture valued at $250.

55. Cammie received 100 NQOs (each option provides a right to purchase 10 shares of MNL stock for $10 per share) at the time she started working for MNL Corporation four years ago, when MNL's stock price was $8 per share. Now that MNL's stock price is $40 per share, she intends to exercise all of her options. After acquiring the 1,000 MNL shares with her options, she held the shares for more than one year and sold them at $60 per share. What are Cammie's tax consequences on the grant date, the exercise date, and the date she sold the shares, assuming her ordinary marginal rate is 32 percent and her capital gains rate is 15 percent?   `LO 5-2`

56. Mark received 10 ISOs at the time he started working for Hendricks Corporation five years ago, when Hendricks's price was $5 per share (each option gives him the right to purchase 10 shares of Hendricks Corporation stock for $5 per share). Now that Hendricks's share price is $35 per share, he intends to exercise all options and hold all of his shares for more than one year. Assume that more than a year after exercise, Mark sells the stock for $35 a share. What are Mark's tax consequences on the grant date, the exercise date, and the date he sells the shares, assuming his ordinary marginal rate is 32 percent and his long-term capital gains rate is 15 percent?   `LO 5-2`

57. Ralph owns a building that he is trying to lease. Ralph is a calendar-year, cash-method taxpayer and is trying to evaluate the tax consequences of three different lease arrangements. Under lease 1, the building rents for $500 per month, payable on the first of the next month, and the tenant must make a $500 security deposit that is refunded at the end of the lease. Under lease 2, the building rents for $5,500 per year, payable at the time the lease is signed, but no security deposit is required. Under lease 3, the building rents for $500 per month, payable at the beginning of each month, and the tenant must pay a security deposit of $1,000 that is to be applied toward the rent for the last two months of the lease.   `LO 5-2`   **research**

     a) What amounts are included in Ralph's gross income this year if a tenant signs lease 1 on December 1 and makes timely payments under that lease?

     b) What amounts are included in Ralph's gross income this year if the tenant signs lease 2 on December 31 and makes timely payments under that lease?

     c) What amounts are included in Ralph's gross income this year if the tenant signs lease 3 on November 30 and makes timely payments under that lease?

58. Anne purchased an annuity from an insurance company that promised to pay her $20,000 per year for the next 10 years. Anne paid $145,000 for the annuity, and in exchange she will receive $200,000 over the term of the annuity.   `LO 5-2`

     a) How much of the first $20,000 payment should Anne include in gross income?

     b) How much income will Anne recognize over the term of the annuity?

59. Larry purchased an annuity from an insurance company that promises to pay him $1,500 per month for the rest of his life. Larry paid $170,820 for the annuity. Larry is in good health and he is 72 years old. Larry received the first annuity payment of   `LO 5-2`

$2,400 this year if the interest rate on the loan had been set at the prevailing federal interest rate.

a) Wally used the funds as a down payment on a speedboat and repaid the $20,000 loan (including $200 of interest) at year-end. Does this loan result in any income to either party, and if so, how much?

b) Assume instead that Pay More forgave the loan and interest on December 31. What amount of gross income does Wally recognize this year? Explain.

LO 5-3   70. Jimmy has fallen on hard times recently. Last year he borrowed $250,000 and added an additional $50,000 of his own funds to purchase $300,000 of undeveloped real estate. This year the value of the real estate dropped dramatically, and Jimmy's lender agreed to reduce the loan amount to $230,000. For each of the following independent situations, indicate the amount Jimmy must include in gross income and explain your answer:

a) The real estate is worth $175,000 and Jimmy has no other assets or liabilities.

b) The real estate is worth $235,000 and Jimmy has no other assets or liabilities.

c) The real estate is worth $200,000 and Jimmy has $45,000 in other assets but no other liabilities.

LO 5-3

research   71. Grady is a 45-year-old employee with AMUCK Garbage Corporation. AMUCK pays group-term life insurance premiums for employees, and Grady chose the maximum face amount of $120,000. What amount, if any, of the premium AMUCK paid on his behalf must Grady include in his gross income for the year? Provide a tax authority to support your answer.

LO 5-3   72. Fred currently earns $9,000 per month. Fred has been offered the chance to transfer for three to five years to an overseas affiliate. His employer is willing to pay Fred $10,000 per month if he accepts the assignment. Assume that the maximum foreign-earned income exclusion for next year is $103,900.

a) How much U.S. gross income will Fred report if he accepts the assignment abroad on January 1 of next year and works overseas for the entire year? If Fred's employer also provides him free housing (cost of $20,000), how much of the $20,000 is excludable from Fred's income?

b) Suppose that Fred's employer has offered Fred a six-month overseas assignment beginning on January 1 of next year. How much U.S. gross income will Fred report next year if he accepts the six-month assignment abroad and returns home on July 1 of next year?

c) Suppose that Fred's employer offers Fred a permanent overseas assignment beginning on March 1 of next year. How much U.S. gross income will Fred report next year if he accepts the permanent assignment abroad? Assume that Fred will be abroad for 305 days out of 365 next year. If Fred's employer also provides him free housing (cost of $16,000 next year), how much of the $16,000 is excludable from Fred's income?

LO 5-3   73. For each of the following situations, indicate how much the taxpayer is required to include in gross income and explain your answer:

a) Steve was awarded a $5,000 scholarship to attend State Law School. The scholarship pays Steve's tuition and fees.

b) Hal was awarded a $15,000 scholarship to attend State Hotel School. All scholarship students must work 20 hours per week at the school residency during the term.

LO 5-3   74. Cecil cashed in a Series EE savings bond with a redemption value of $14,000 and an original cost of $9,800. For each of the following independent scenarios, calculate the amount of interest Cecil will include in his gross income assuming he files as a single taxpayer:

a) Cecil plans to spend all of the proceeds to pay his son's tuition at State University. Cecil's son is a full-time student, and Cecil claims his son as a dependent. Cecil estimates his modified adjusted gross income at $63,100.

b) Assume the same facts in part (a), except Cecil plans to spend $4,200 of the proceeds to pay his son's tuition at State University, and Cecil estimates his modified adjusted gross income at $60,600.

75. Grady is a member of a large family and received the following payments this year. For each payment, determine whether the payment constitutes realized income and determine the amount of each payment Grady must include in his gross income.   **LO 5-3**

a) A gift of $20,000 from Grady's grandfather.

b) 1,000 shares of GM stock worth $120 per share inherited from Grady's uncle. The uncle purchased the shares for $25 each, and the shares are worth $125 at year-end.

c) A gift of $50,000 of Ford Motor Bonds. Grady received the bonds on October 31, and he received $1,500 of semiannual interest from the bonds on December 31.

d) A loan of $5,000 for school expenses from Grady's aunt.

76. Bart is the favorite nephew of his aunt Thelma. Thelma transferred several items of value to Bart. For each of the following transactions, determine the effect on Bart's gross income.   **LO 5-3**

a) Thelma gave Bart an auto worth $22,000. Thelma purchased the auto three years ago for $17,000.

b) Thelma elects to cancel her life insurance policy, and she gives the cash surrender value of $15,000 to Bart.

c) Bart is the beneficiary of a $100,000 whole life insurance policy on the life of Thelma. Thelma died this year, and Bart received $100,000 in cash.

d) Bart inherited 500 shares of stock from Thelma's estate. Thelma purchased the shares many years ago for $1,200, and the shares are worth $45,000 at her death.

77. Terry was ill for three months and missed work during this period. During his illness, Terry received $4,500 in sick pay from a disability insurance policy. What amounts are included in Terry's gross income under the following independent circumstances?   **LO 5-3**

a) Terry has disability insurance provided by his employer as a nontaxable fringe benefit. Terry's employer paid $2,800 in disability premiums for Terry this year.

b) Terry paid $2,800 in premiums for his disability insurance this year.

c) Terry's employer paid the $2,800 in premiums for Terry, but Terry elected to have his employer include the $2,800 as compensation on Terry's W-2.

d) Terry has disability insurance whose cost is shared with his employer. Terry's employer paid $1,800 in disability premiums for Terry this year as a nontaxable fringe benefit, and Terry paid the remaining $1,000 of premiums from his after-tax salary.

78. Tim's parents plan to provide him with $50,000 to support him while he establishes a new landscaping business. In exchange for the support, Tim will maintain the landscape at his father's business. Under what conditions will the transfer of $50,000 be included in Tim's gross income? Explain. Do you have a recommendation for Tim and his parents?   **LO 5-3**   **planning**

79. What amounts are included in gross income for the following taxpayers? Explain your answers.   **LO 5-3**

a) Janus sued Tiny Toys for personal injuries from swallowing a toy. Janus was paid $30,000 for medical costs and $250,000 for punitive damages.

b) Carl was injured in a car accident. Carl's insurance paid him $500 to reimburse his medical expenses and an additional $250 for the emotional distress Carl suffered as a result of the accident.

c) Ajax published a story about Pete and as a result Pete sued Ajax for damage to his reputation. Ajax lost in court and paid Pete an award of $20,000.

d) Bevis was laid off from his job last month. This month he drew $800 in unemployment benefits.

LO 5-3 80. This year, Janelle received $200,000 in life insurance proceeds. Under the following scenarios, how much of the $200,000 is taxable?

a) Janelle received the proceeds upon the death of her father, Julio.

b) Janelle received the $200,000 proceeds because she was diagnosed with colon cancer (life expectancy of six months), and she needed the proceeds for her care.

c) The proceeds related to a life insurance policy she purchased for $35,000 from a friend in need. After purchase, Janelle paid annual premiums that total $22,000.

LO 5-3 81. This year, Leron and Sheena sold their home for $750,000 after all selling costs. Under the following scenarios, how much taxable gain does the home sale generate for Leron and Sheena?

a) Leron and Sheena bought the home three years ago for $150,000 and lived in the home until it sold.

b) Leron and Sheena bought the home one year ago for $600,000 and lived in the home until it sold.

c) Leron and Sheena bought the home five years ago for $500,000. They lived in the home for three years until they decided to buy a smaller home. Their home has been vacant for the past two years.

LO 5-3 82. Dontae's employer has offered him the following employment package. What is Dontae's gross income from his employment?

Salary	$400,000
Health insurance	10,000
Dental insurance	1,500
Membership to Heflin Country Club	20,000
Season tickets to Atlanta Braves games	5,000
Tuition reimbursement for graduate courses	4,000
Housing allowance (for a McMansion in his neighborhood of choice)	40,000

LO 5-3 83. Allie received a $50,000 distribution from her 401(k) account this year that she established while working for Big Stories Inc. Assuming her marginal ordinary tax rate is 24 percent, how much tax and penalty will Allie pay on the distribution under the following circumstances?

a) Allie is 45 and still employed with Big Stories Inc.

b) Allie is 56 and was terminated from Big Stories Inc. this year.

c) Allie is 67 and retired.

COMPREHENSIVE PROBLEMS

Select problems are available in Connect®.

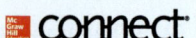

84. Charlie was hired by Ajax this year as a corporate executive and a member of the board of directors. During the current year, Charlie received the following payments or benefits paid on his behalf.

Salary payments	$92,000
Contributions to qualified pension plan	10,200
Qualified health insurance premiums	8,400
Year-end bonus	15,000
Annual director's fee	10,000
Group-term life insurance premiums (face = $40,000)	750
Whole life insurance premiums (face = $100,000)	1,420
Disability insurance premiums (no special election to treat as taxable benefit)	4,350

a) Charlie uses the cash method and calendar year for tax purposes. Calculate Charlie's gross income for the current year.

b) Suppose that Ajax agrees to pay Charlie an additional $100,000 once Charlie completes five years of employment. Will this agreement alter Charlie's gross income this year relative to your part (a) answer? Explain.

c) Suppose that in exchange for his promise to remain with the firm for the next four years, Ajax pays Charlie four years of director's fees in advance. Will this arrangement alter Charlie's gross income this year relative to your part (a) answer? Explain.

d) Assume that in lieu of a year-end bonus Ajax transfers 500 shares of Bell stock to Charlie as compensation. Further assume that the stock is listed at $35 per share and Charlie will sell the shares by year-end, at which time he expects the price to be $37 per share. Will this arrangement alter Charlie's gross income this year relative to your part (a) answer? Explain.

e) Suppose that in lieu of a year-end bonus Ajax makes Charlie's house payments (a total of $23,000). Will this arrangement alter Charlie's gross income this year relative to your part (a) answer? Explain.

85. Irene is disabled and receives payments from a number of sources. The interest payments are from bonds that Irene purchased over past years and a disability insurance policy that Irene purchased herself. Calculate Irene's gross income.

Interest, bonds issued by City of Austin, Texas	$ 2,000
Social Security benefits	8,200
Interest, U.S. Treasury bills	1,300
Interest, bonds issued by Ford Motor Company	1,500
Interest, bonds issued by City of Quebec, Canada	750
Disability insurance benefits	19,500
Distributions from qualified pension plan	5,400

86. Ken is 63 years old and unmarried. He retired at age 55 when he sold his business, Understock.com. Though Ken is retired, he is still very active. Ken reported the following financial information this year. *Assume* Ken files as a single taxpayer. Determine Ken's gross income and complete page 1 of Form 1040 for Ken.

tax forms

a) Ken won $1,200 in an illegal game of poker (the game was played in Utah, where gambling is illegal).

b) Ken sold 1,000 shares of stock for $32 a share. He inherited the stock two years ago. His tax basis (or investment) in the stock was $31 per share.

c) Ken received $25,000 from an annuity he purchased eight years ago. He purchased the annuity, to be paid annually for 20 years, for $210,000.

d) Ken received $13,000 in disability benefits for the year. He purchased the disability insurance policy last year.

e) Ken decided to go back to school to learn about European history. He received a $500 cash scholarship to attend. He used $300 to pay for his books and tuition, and he applied the rest toward his new car payment.

f) Ken's son, Mike, instructed his employer to make half of his final paycheck of the year payable to Ken as a gift from Mike to Ken. Ken received the check on December 30 in the amount of $1,100.

g) Ken received a $610 refund of the $3,600 in state income taxes his employer withheld from his pay last year. Ken claimed $6,400 in itemized deductions last year (the standard deduction for a single filer was $6,350).

h) Ken received $30,000 of interest from corporate bonds and money market accounts.

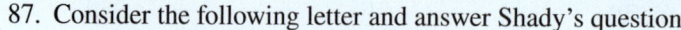

tax forms

87. Consider the following letter and answer Shady's question.

To my friendly student tax preparer:

Hello, my name is Shady Slim. I understand you are going to help me figure out my gross income for the year . . . whatever that means. It's been a busy year and I'm a busy man, so let me give you the lowdown on my life and you can do your thing.

I was unemployed at the beginning of the year and got $2,000 in unemployment compensation. I later got a job as a manager for Roca Cola. I earned $55,000 in base salary this year. My boss gave me a $5,000 Christmas bonus check on December 22. I decided to hold on to that check and not cash it until next year, so I won't have to pay taxes on it this year. Pretty smart, huh? My job's pretty cool. I get a lot of fringe benefits like a membership to the gym that costs $400 a year and all the Roca Cola I can drink, although I can't really drink a whole lot—I figure $40 worth this year.

As part of my manager duties, I get to decide on certain things like contracts for the company. My good buddy, Eddie, runs a bottling company. I made sure that he won the bottling contract for Roca Cola for this year (even though his contract wasn't quite the best). Eddie bought me a Corvette this year for being such a good friend. The Corvette cost $50,000 and I'm sure he bought it for me out of the goodness of his heart. What a great guy!

Here's a bit of good luck for the year. Upon leaving my office one day, I found $8,000 lying in the street! Well, one person's bad luck is my good luck, right?

I like to gamble a lot. I won a $32,000 poker tournament in Las Vegas this year. Can you believe that I didn't lose anything this year?

Speaking of the guys, one of them hit me with his car as we were leaving the game one night. He must have been pretty ticked that he lost! I broke my right leg and my left arm. I sued the guy and got $11,000 for my medical expenses, $3,000 to pay my psychotherapist for the emotional problems I had relating to the injuries (I got really depressed!), and I won $12,000 in punitive damages. That'll teach him that he's not so tough without his car!

Another bit of bad luck. My uncle Monty died this year. I really liked the guy, but the $200,000 inheritance I received from him made me feel a little better about the loss. I did the smart thing with the money and invested it in stocks and bonds and socked a little into my savings account. As a result, I received $600 in dividends from the stock, $200 in interest from the municipal bonds, and $300 in interest from my savings account.

My ex-wife, Alice, is still paying me alimony. She's a lawyer who divorced me in 2015 because I was "unethical" or something like that. Since she was making so much money and I was unemployed at the time, the judge ruled that she had to pay ME alimony. Isn't that something? She sent me $3,000 in alimony payments this year. She still kind of likes me, though. She sent me a check for $500 as a Christmas gift this year. I didn't get her anything, though.

So there you go. That's this year in a nutshell. Can you figure out my gross income and complete page 1 of Form 1040 for me? And since you're a student, this is free, right? Thanks, I owe you one! Let me know if I can get you a six-pack of Roca Cola or something.

88. Diana and Ryan Workman were married on January 1 of last year. Diana has an eight-year-old son, Jorge, from her previous marriage. Ryan works as a computer programmer at Datafile Inc. (DI) earning a salary of $96,000. Diana is self-employed and runs a day care center. The Workmans reported the following financial information pertaining to their activities during the current year.

tax forms

a) Ryan earned a $96,000 salary for the year.

b) Ryan borrowed $12,000 from DI to purchase a car. DI charged him 2 percent interest ($240) on the loan, which Ryan paid on December 31. DI would have charged Ryan $720 if interest had been calculated at the applicable federal interest rate. Assume that tax avoidance was not a motive for the loan.

c) Diana received $2,000 in alimony and $4,500 in child support payments from her former husband. They divorced in 2016.

d) Diana won a $900 cash prize at her church-sponsored Bingo game.

e) The Workmans received $500 of interest from corporate bonds and $250 of interest from a municipal bond. Diana owned these bonds before she married Ryan.

f) The couple bought 50 shares of ABC Inc. stock for $40 per share on July 2. The stock was worth $47 a share on December 31. The stock paid a dividend of $1.00 per share on December 1.

g) Diana's father passed away on April 14. She inherited cash of $50,000 from her father and his baseball card collection, valued at $2,000. As the beneficiary of her father's life insurance policy, Diana also received $150,000.

h) The couple spent a weekend in Atlantic City in November and came home with gross gambling winnings of $1,200.

i) Ryan received $400 cash for reaching 10 years of continuous service at DI.

j) Ryan was hit and injured by a drunk driver while crossing a street at a crosswalk. He was unable to work for a month. He received $6,000 from his disability insurance. DI paid the premiums for Ryan, but they reported the amount of the premiums as compensation to Ryan on his year-end W-2.

k) The drunk driver who hit Ryan in part (j) was required to pay his $2,000 medical costs, $1,500 for the emotional trauma he suffered from the accident, and $5,000 for punitive damages.

l) For meeting his performance goals this year, Ryan was informed on December 27 that he would receive a $5,000 year-end bonus. DI (located in Houston, Texas) mailed Ryan's bonus check from its payroll processing center (Tampa, Florida) on December 28. Ryan didn't receive the check at his home until January 2.

m) Diana is a 10 percent owner of MNO Inc., a Subchapter S corporation. The company reported ordinary business income for the year of $92,000. Diana acquired the MNO stock two years ago.

n) Diana's day care business collected $35,000 in revenues. In addition, customers owed her $3,000 at year-end. During the year, Diana spent $5,500 for supplies, $1,500 for utilities, $15,000 for rent, and $500 for miscellaneous expenses. One customer gave her use of his vacation home for a week (worth $2,500) in exchange for Diana allowing his child to attend the day care center free of charge. Diana accounts for her business activities using the cash method of accounting.

o) Ryan's employer pays the couple's annual health insurance premiums of $5,500 for a qualified plan.

Required:

A) Assuming the Workmans file a joint tax return, determine their gross income.

B) Using your answer in part A, complete page 1 of Form 1040 through line 22 for the Workmans.

C) Assuming the Workmans live in California, a community property state, and that Diana and Ryan file separately, what is Ryan's gross income?

D) Using your answer in part C, complete page 1 of Form 1040 through line 22 for Ryan Workman.

ROGER | *CPA Review*

Sample CPA Exam questions from Roger CPA Review are available in Connect as support for the topics in this text. These Multiple Choice Questions and Task-Based Simulations include expert-written explanations and solutions and provide a starting point for students to become familiar with the content and functionality of the actual CPA Exam.

Individual *For* AGI Deductions

Upon completing this chapter, you should be able to:

LO 6-1 Identify *for* AGI deductions directly related to business activities.

LO 6-2 Describe the loss limitation rules for passive activities, the rental use of a home, and home office deductions.

LO 6-3 Explain *for* AGI deductions indirectly related to business activities and *for* AGI deductions that subsidize specific activities.

©Image Source

Storyline Summary

Taxpayers:	Courtney Wilson, age 40, and Courtney's mother, Dorothy "Gram" Weiss, age 70
Family description:	Courtney is divorced with a son, Deron, age 10, and a daughter, Ellen, age 20. Gram is currently residing with Courtney. Ellen is currently a full-time student.
Location:	Kansas City, Missouri
Employment status:	Courtney works as an architect for EWD. Gram is retired.
Filing status:	Courtney files as head-of-household. Gram files as a single taxpayer.
Current situation:	Courtney and Gram are trying to determine their allowable deductions and compute their adjusted gross income.

Now that Courtney has determined her gross income, she still must determine her deductions to compute her adjusted gross income (AGI). Fortunately, Courtney keeps detailed records of all the expenditures she believes to be deductible. Besides expenses associated with her week-end consulting work and rental property, Courtney incurred some significant costs moving from Cincinnati to Kansas City. She also paid self-employment taxes on her consulting income. Courtney is confident some of these items are deductible, but she isn't quite sure which items are deductible and how much.

Gram's deductions *for* AGI are likely to be more limited. The only item that she identified that might affect her AGI is a penalty that she paid for cashing in her certificate of deposit early. ■

In the previous chapter, we determined *gross income* for both Courtney and Gram. To compute their taxable income, however, we need to identify their deductions. As emphasized previously, taxpayers are not allowed to deduct expenditures unless there is a specific tax law authorizing the deductions. And as we learn in this chapter, Congress grants many deductions for taxpayers for a variety of reasons.

As we discussed in the Individual Income Tax Overview, Dependents, and Filing Status chapter, deductions appear in one of two places in the individual income tax formula. Deductions "*for* AGI" (also called deductions "above the line") are subtracted directly from gross income.[1] Next, deductions "*from* AGI" (also called deductions "below the line") are subtracted directly from AGI, resulting in taxable income. Deductions *for* AGI are generally preferred over deductions *from* AGI because deductions above the line reduce taxable income dollar for dollar. In contrast, deductions *from* AGI sometimes have no effect on taxable income. Further, because many of the limitations on tax benefits for higher income taxpayers are based upon AGI, deductions *for* AGI often reduce these limitations, thereby increasing potential tax benefits. Thus, it's important to determine both the amount of the deduction and whether it's a deduction *for* AGI or *from* AGI. In this chapter, we describe the deductions *for* AGI and related loss limitation rules for passive activities, the rental use of a home, and home office deductions. In the Individual *From* AGI Deductions chapter we tackle itemized deductions, the standard deduction, and the deduction for qualified business income.

DEDUCTIONS *FOR* AGI—OVERVIEW

Congress allows taxpayers to claim a variety of deductions *for* AGI.[2] To provide an overview, we select a cross-section of deductions *for* AGI and classify them into three categories:

1. Deductions *directly* related to **business activities.**
2. Deductions *indirectly* related to business activities.
3. Deductions subsidizing specific activities.

We've organized our discussion around these categories to illustrate the variety of deductions *for* AGI and explain why Congress provides preferential treatment for certain deductions.

 ## DEDUCTIONS DIRECTLY RELATED TO BUSINESS ACTIVITIES

As a matter of equity, Congress allows taxpayers involved in business activities to deduct expenses incurred to generate business income. That is, because taxpayers include the revenue they receive from doing business in gross income, they should be allowed to deduct against gross income the expenses they incur to generate those revenues.

To begin, we must define "business activities" and, for reasons we discuss below, we must distinguish business activities from **investment activities.** In general, for tax purposes, activities are either *profit-motivated* or motivated by personal objectives. Profit-motivated activities are, in turn, classified as either (1) business activities or (2) investment activities. Business activities are sometimes referred to as a **trade or business,** and these activities require a relatively high level of involvement or effort. For example,

---

[1]Most, but not all, deductions *for* AGI appear on lines 23 through 35 on page 1 of Form 1040. The term "above the line" refers to the placement of deductions *for* AGI before the last line of the first page of Form 1040. This last line is the taxpayer's AGI.

[2]§62 identifies deductions *for* AGI.

if an individual is a full-time employee, the individual is in the business of being an employee. Self-employed individuals are also engaged in business activities. Unlike business activities, investment activities are profit-motivated activities that *don't* require a high degree of involvement or effort.[3] Instead, investment activities involve investing in property for appreciation or for income payments. An individual who occasionally buys land or stock in anticipation of appreciation or dividend payments is engaged in an investment activity.

Example 6-1

Suppose that Courtney purchased a parcel of land for its appreciation potential. Would her ownership in the land be considered a business or investment activity?

Answer: Courtney's activity would most likely be considered an investment activity, because she acquired the land for its appreciation potential and she does not plan to exercise any special effort to develop the property or to become actively involved in other real estate speculation.

What if: Suppose that Courtney frequently buys and sells land or develops land to sell in small parcels to those wanting to build homes. Would Courtney's activity be considered a business or investment activity?

Answer: Courtney's activity would most likely be considered a business activity because she is actively involved in generating profits from the land by developing it rather than simply holding the land for appreciation.

The distinction between business and investment activities is critical for determining whether a deduction associated with the activity is above or below the line or even deductible. With one exception, business expenses are deducted *for* AGI. The lone exception is unreimbursed employee business expenses, which, unfortunately, are not deductible for years beginning after 2017.[4] In contrast, investment-related expenses, if deductible at all, are deductible as itemized deductions with one exception. Expenses associated with rental and royalty activities are deductible *for* AGI regardless of whether the activity qualifies as an investment or a business. Exhibit 6-1 summarizes the rules for classifying business and investment-related expenses as *for* AGI deductions, *from* AGI deductions, or not deductible.

EXHIBIT 6-1   Individual Business and Investment-Related Expense Deductions *for* AGI, *from* AGI, and Not Deductible

	Deduction Type		
Activity Type	**Deduction *for* AGI**	**Deduction *from* AGI** (itemized deduction)	**Not Deductible**
Business activities	Self-employed business expenses	N/A	Unreimbursed employee business expenses
Investment activities	Rental and royalty expenses	Investment interest expense	Other investment expenses

[3]§162 generally authorizes trade or business expense deductions, while §212 generally authorizes deductions for investment activities. The distinction between these activities is discussed in the Business Income, Deductions, and Accounting Methods chapter.

[4]Prior to 2018, both unreimbursed employee business expenses and other investment expenses were deductible from AGI as miscellaneous itemized deductions subject to a 2 percent of AGI floor.

Trade or Business Expenses

Congress limits business deductions to expenses directly related to the business activity and expenses that are **ordinary and necessary** for the activity.[5] This means that deductible expenses must be appropriate and helpful for generating a profit. Although business deductions are one of the most common deductions *for* AGI, they are not readily visible on the front page of Form 1040. Instead, these deductions are reported with business revenues on Schedule C of Form 1040. Schedule C, presented in Exhibit 6-2, is essentially an income statement for the business that identifies typical ordinary and necessary business expenses. Taxpayers transfer the *net* income or loss from Schedule C to Form 1040 (page 1), line 12.

EXHIBIT 6-2   **Parts I and II from Schedule C Profit or Loss from Business**

Part I   Income

1	Gross receipts or sales. See instructions for line 1 and check the box if this income was reported to you on Form W-2 and the "Statutory employee" box on that form was checked . . . . ▶ ☐	1	
2	Returns and allowances	2	
3	Subtract line 2 from line 1	3	
4	Cost of goods sold (from line 42)	4	
5	**Gross profit.** Subtract line 4 from line 3	5	
6	Other income, including federal and state gasoline or fuel tax credit or refund (see instructions)	6	
7	**Gross income.** Add lines 5 and 6 . . . . ▶	7	

Part II   Expenses. Enter expenses for business use of your home **only** on line 30.

8	Advertising	8		18	Office expense (see instructions)	18	
9	Car and truck expenses (see instructions)	9		19	Pension and profit-sharing plans .	19	
				20	Rent or lease (see instructions):		
10	Commissions and fees .	10		a	Vehicles, machinery, and equipment	20a	
11	Contract labor (see instructions)	11		b	Other business property . . .	20b	
12	Depletion	12		21	Repairs and maintenance . . .	21	
13	Depreciation and section 179 expense deduction (not included in Part III) (see instructions)	13		22	Supplies (not included in Part III) .	22	
				23	Taxes and licenses	23	
				24	Travel, meals, and entertainment:		
14	Employee benefit programs (other than on line 19) . .	14		a	Travel	24a	
				b	Deductible meals and entertainment (see instructions) .	24b	
15	Insurance (other than health)	15					
16	Interest:			25	Utilities	25	
a	Mortgage (paid to banks, etc.)	16a		26	Wages (less employment credits) .	26	
b	Other	16b		27a	Other expenses (from line 48) . .	27a	
17	Legal and professional services	17		b	**Reserved for future use** . . .	27b	

28	**Total expenses** before expenses for business use of home. Add lines 8 through 27a . . . . ▶	28	
29	Tentative profit or (loss). Subtract line 28 from line 7	29	
30	Expenses for business use of your home. Do not report these expenses elsewhere. Attach Form 8829 unless using the simplified method (see instructions). **Simplified method filers only:** enter the total square footage of: (a) your home: _____ and (b) the part of your home used for business: _____ . Use the Simplified Method Worksheet in the instructions to figure the amount to enter on line 30	30	
31	**Net profit or (loss).** Subtract line 30 from line 29. • If a profit, enter on both **Form 1040, line 12** (or **Form 1040NR, line 13**) and on **Schedule SE, line 2.** (If you checked the box on line 1, see instructions). Estates and trusts, enter on **Form 1041, line 3.** • If a loss, you **must** go to line 32.	31	
32	If you have a loss, check the box that describes your investment in this activity (see instructions). • If you checked 32a, enter the loss on both **Form 1040, line 12,** (or **Form 1040NR, line 13**) and on **Schedule SE, line 2.** (If you checked the box on line 1, see the line 31 instructions). Estates and trusts, enter on **Form 1041, line 3.** • If you checked 32b, you **must** attach **Form 6198.** Your loss may be limited.	32a ☐ All investment is at risk. 32b ☐ Some investment is not at risk.

For Paperwork Reduction Act Notice, see the separate instructions.   Cat. No. 11334P   Schedule C (Form 1040) 2017

Example 6-2

Besides being employed by EWD, Courtney is also a self-employed architectural consultant (a business activity). This year her consulting activity generated $19,500 of revenue and incurred $1,500 in expenses (primarily travel and transportation expenses). How does she report the revenue and deductions from the activity?

Answer: Courtney reports the $19,500 of revenue and deducts the $1,500 of business expenses *for* AGI on her Schedule C. Her net income of $18,000 from her consulting activities is included on the front page (line 12) of her individual tax return.

---

[5]§162. In the Business Income, Deductions, and Accounting Methods chapter, we address the requirements for deductible business expenses in detail.

Rental and Royalty Expenses

Taxpayers are allowed to deduct their expenses associated with generating rental or royalty income *for* AGI.[6] Like business expenses, rental and royalty expenses do not appear directly on the front page of Form 1040. Instead, rental and royalty deductions are reported with rental and royalty revenues on Schedule E of Form 1040.[7] Schedule E, presented in Exhibit 6-3, is essentially an income statement for the taxpayer's rental or royalty activities. Taxpayers transfer the *net* income or loss from Schedule E to Form 1040 (page 1), line 17.

EXHIBIT 6-3　Page 1 of Schedule E Rental or Royalty Income

Income:		Properties:	A	B	C
3	Rents received	3			
4	Royalties received	4			
Expenses:					
5	Advertising	5			
6	Auto and travel (see instructions)	6			
7	Cleaning and maintenance	7			
8	Commissions.	8			
9	Insurance	9			
10	Legal and other professional fees	10			
11	Management fees	11			
12	Mortgage interest paid to banks, etc. (see instructions)	12			
13	Other interest.	13			
14	Repairs.	14			
15	Supplies	15			
16	Taxes	16			
17	Utilities.	17			
18	Depreciation expense or depletion	18			
19	Other (list) ▶ _____	19			
20	Total expenses. Add lines 5 through 19	20			
21	Subtract line 20 from line 3 (rents) and/or 4 (royalties). If result is a (loss), see instructions to find out if you must file **Form 6198**	21			
22	Deductible rental real estate loss after limitation, if any, on **Form 8582** (see instructions)	22	( )	( )	( )
23a	Total of all amounts reported on line 3 for all rental properties	23a			
b	Total of all amounts reported on line 4 for all royalty properties	23b			
c	Total of all amounts reported on line 12 for all properties	23c			
d	Total of all amounts reported on line 18 for all properties	23d			
e	Total of all amounts reported on line 20 for all properties	23e			
24	**Income.** Add positive amounts shown on line 21. **Do not** include any losses		24		
25	**Losses.** Add royalty losses from line 21 and rental real estate losses from line 22. Enter total losses here .		25	( )	
26	**Total rental real estate and royalty income or (loss).** Combine lines 24 and 25. Enter the result here. If Parts II, III, IV, and line 40 on page 2 do not apply to you, also enter this amount on Form 1040, line 17, or Form 1040NR, line 18. Otherwise, include this amount in the total on line 41 on page 2 . . .		26		

For Paperwork Reduction Act Notice, see the separate instructions.　　Cat. No. 11344L　　Schedule E (Form 1040) 2017

Rental and royalty endeavors are most commonly considered to be investment activities, but like trade or business expenses, rental and royalty deductions are claimed above the line.[8] Perhaps rental and royalty expenses are deductible *for* AGI because Congress believes that these activities usually require more taxpayer involvement than other types of investment activities. Despite this preferential treatment, the deductibility of rental losses (where expenses exceed income) are subject to limitations (basis, at-risk, passive loss, and excess business loss rules). We discuss these limitations in the next section.

---

[6]§212(a)(4).

[7]Rental income and expenses for renting personal property (e.g., equipment, furniture, etc.) instead of real property is generally reported on Schedule C (not Schedule E). If the rental of personal property is not considered a trade or business, the rental income and expenses are reported on lines 21 and 36, respectively, of Form 1040.

[8]Royalties are received for allowing others to use property or rights to property. For example, royalties are paid for allowing others to use or sell copyrighted material, such as books or plays, or extract natural resources from property. The amount of the royalty is often a percentage of total revenues derived from the property or rights to property.

Courtney owns a condominium that she rents to tenants. This year she received $14,000 in rental revenue and incurred $9,000 of expenses associated with the rental, including management fees, maintenance, and depreciation. How does she report the revenue and expenses for tax purposes?

Answer: Courtney reports the $14,000 of rental receipts and deducts the $9,000 of rental expenses *for* AGI on Schedule E. The net rental income of $5,000 is reported on the front page (line 17) of her individual tax return.

Losses on Dispositions

As we discuss in more detail in the Property Dispositions chapter, taxpayers disposing of business assets at a loss are allowed to deduct the losses *for* AGI. Also, individual taxpayers selling investment (capital) assets at a loss are allowed to deduct the "capital" losses against other capital gains. If the capital losses exceed the capital gains, they can deduct up to $3,000 as a net capital loss in a particular year. Losses in excess of the $3,000 limit are carried forward indefinitely to subsequent years, when they are deductible subject to the same limitations.

Flow-Through Entities

Income from flow-through entities such as partnerships, LLCs, and S corporations passes through to the owners of those entities, with the related business income reported on Schedule E of the tax returns of the owners. Similarly, any expenses and losses incurred by the entity pass through to the entity owners, who typically treat them as deductions *for* AGI, subject to certain restrictions (basis, at-risk, passive loss rules and excess business loss limitation) that we discuss next.

LO 6-2   LOSS LIMITATION RULES

As we have discussed, deductions associated with trade or business-related activities are deducted as *for* AGI deductions. Trade or business deductions simply reduce the net income from the business activity and are fully deductible. If, however, the activities generate losses, the losses are subject to a variety of loss limitation provisions. In the following paragraphs, we describe the limitations that apply across trade or business activities, rental and royalty activities, and flow-through entities as well as provisions that specifically apply to the rental use of a home and home office deductions.

Tax Basis, At-Risk, and Passive Loss Rules

A taxpayer may invest directly in an income-producing enterprise by purchasing rental property or by forming a business as a sole proprietor. Similarly, a taxpayer could invest in a partial interest in a trade or business or rental activity by acquiring an ownership interest in a **flow-through entity** that does not pay taxes, such as a partnership, limited liability company (taxed as a partnership), or an S corporation (taxed similar to a partnership by shareholders' election). No matter whether an investor makes a direct investment in rental property or in a sole proprietorship or makes an indirect investment in a business or rental activity through a partnership, limited liability company, or S corporation, the *actual operating income or loss* from these investments flows through to the taxpayer as it is earned and is treated as ordinary income or ordinary loss. If trade or business or rental activities (held either directly or indirectly through flow-through entities) generate ordinary operating income, taxpayers report it on their tax returns, and it is taxed at ordinary rates. However, if these activities generate operating losses, the operating losses must clear three hurdles to be deductible currently. The three loss limits are the tax-basis, at-risk, and the passive loss limits.[9] In addition, for losses that clear each of the three hurdles, taxpayers are not allowed to deduct excess business losses as described below.

Tax-Basis and At-Risk Rules   The tax-basis hurdle limits a taxpayer's deductible operating losses to the taxpayer's tax basis in the business or rental activity. Any losses not deductible because of the tax-basis hurdle are carried forward and are deductible if and when the taxpayer generates more tax basis to absorb the loss. This limitation is very similar to loss limitations that apply when a taxpayer sells an investment asset such as corporate stock or another similar capital asset. Recall that the formula for determining gain or loss on an exchange is the amount realized less the taxpayer's adjusted basis in the property. If a taxpayer were to sell an asset for nothing, the loss would be the amount of her tax basis in the property, but no more.

Obviously, in order to apply the tax-basis loss limitation, we must first determine the taxpayer's tax basis in the activity. Very generally speaking, the tax basis is the taxpayer's investment in the activity adjusted for certain items (namely, income, debt, and investments). The adjustments are beyond the scope of this chapter; however, tax basis is discussed in later chapters relating to flow-through entities.

When a loss from a business or business-related activity clears the tax-basis hurdle, it next must clear an at-risk hurdle on its journey toward deductibility.[10] The **at-risk rules** are meant to limit the ability of investors to deduct "artificial" ordinary losses produced with certain types of debt. These rules serve to limit ordinary losses to a taxpayer's economic risk in an activity. Generally, a taxpayer is considered to be at risk in an activity to the extent of any cash or the basis of any property personally contributed to the activity and certain other adjustments similar (but not identical) to those for tax basis. Because the computation of tax basis and at-risk amount are so similar, a taxpayer's tax basis and her at-risk amount in the activity are frequently the same so that when she clears the tax-basis hurdle for deducting a loss, she also clears the at-risk hurdle. If the at-risk amount does differ from the tax basis, the at-risk amount will be less than the tax basis.[11] Losses that clear the tax-basis hurdle but do not clear the at-risk hurdle are suspended until the taxpayer generates more at-risk amounts to absorb the loss or until the activity is sold, when they may offset the seller's gain from the disposition of the activity.

Example 6-4

What if: Assume that Courtney used $10,000 of her savings to acquire a 5 percent interest in a limited partnership (a flow-through entity) called Color Comfort Sheets (CCS). Courtney's share of CCS's loss for the year is $15,000. What amount of this loss is Courtney allowed to deduct after applying the tax basis and at-risk limitations?

Answer: $10,000. Because Courtney's tax basis and at-risk amount in her CCS interest are both $10,000 (the amount of cash invested), $10,000 of the loss clears the tax-basis hurdle and then the at-risk hurdle. Thus, Courtney may deduct $10,000 of the $15,000 loss before considering the passive activity loss limits discussed below. The suspended $5,000 loss carries over to next year and may be deducted when Courtney has additional tax-basis and at-risk amounts.

---

[9]Trade or business losses from sole proprietorships (reported on Schedule C) in which the taxpayer is actively involved and not just an investor generally are not restricted by these three limits. Instead, these losses typically are fully deductible as *for* AGI deductions.

[10]§465.

[11]A detailed discussion of these adjustments is beyond the scope of this chapter. However, a basic difference between the at-risk amount and tax basis is that the types of debt that increase a taxpayer's at-risk amount are more restrictive than the types of debt that increase tax basis. Hence, the at-risk amount will always be less than or equal to tax basis.

Passive Activity Income and Losses   Even when a taxpayer has a sufficient tax basis and sufficient amounts at risk to absorb a loss from a business-related activity, the loss may still be limited by the **passive activity loss rules.** Prior to 1986, investors were able to use ordinary losses from certain passive activities to offset portfolio income (interest, dividends, and capital gains), salary income, and self-employment income, including income from other trades or businesses they were actively involved in managing. During this time, a tax shelter industry thrived by marketing investments to wealthy investors designed primarily to generate ordinary losses that could be used to shield other income from tax. To combat this practice, Congress introduced the passive activity loss rules.[12] Specifically, these rules limit the ability of investors in certain passive activities involving interests in trades or businesses and in rental property, including real estate, to use their ordinary losses from these activities currently to reduce taxable income from other sources.[13] The passive activity loss rules are applied to any losses that clear the tax-basis and at-risk loss limits.

Passive Activity Definition   The passive activity loss rules define a passive activity as "any activity which involves the conduct of a trade or business, and in which the taxpayer does not materially participate." According to the tax code, participants in rental activities, including rental real estate, and limited partners in partnerships are generally deemed to be passive participants, and participants in all other trade or business activities are passive unless their involvement in an activity is "regular, continuous, and substantial." Clearly, these terms are quite subjective and difficult to apply. Fortunately, regulations provide more certainty in this area by listing seven separate tests for material participation.[14] An individual, other than a limited partner without management rights, can be classified as a material participant in an activity by meeting any one of the seven tests in Exhibit 6-4. Investors who purchase rental property or an interest in a trade or business without intending to be involved in the management of the trade or business are classified as passive participants, and these activities are classified as passive activities with respect to them.

EXHIBIT 6-4   Tests for Material Participation

Individuals are generally considered material participants for the activity if they meet any *one* of these tests:

1. The individual participates in the activity more than 500 hours during the year.
2. The individual's activity constitutes substantially all of the participation in such activity by all individuals, including nonowners.
3. The individual participates more than 100 hours during the year, and the individual's participation is not less than any other individual's participation in the activity.
4. The activity qualifies as a "significant participation activity" (more than 100 hours spent during the year), and the aggregate of all "significant participation activities" is greater than 500 hours for the year.
5. The individual materially participated in the activity for any 5 of the preceding 10 taxable years.
6. The individual materially participated for any three preceding years in any personal service activity (personal services in health, law, accounting, architecture, etc.).
7. Taking into account all the facts and circumstances, the individual participates on a regular, continuous, and substantial basis during the year.

---

[12]§469.

[13]Before passage of the passive activity loss rules, the "at-risk rules" in §465 were adopted in an attempt to limit the ability of investors to deduct "artificial" ordinary losses. Given the similarity of the at-risk and tax-basis computations, especially for real estate investments, the at-risk rules were not entirely successful at accomplishing this objective. The passive activity loss rules were adopted as a backstop to the at-risk rules, and both sets of rules may potentially apply to a given activity.

[14]§1.469-5T.

Income and Loss Categories   Under the passive activity loss rules, each item of a taxpayer's income or loss for the year is placed in one of three categories. Losses from the passive category cannot offset income from other categories. The three different categories are as follows:

1. *Passive activity income or loss*—income or loss from an activity in which the taxpayer is not a material participant.
2. *Portfolio income*—income from investments including capital gains and losses, dividends, interest, annuities, and royalties.
3. *Active business income*—income from sources in which the taxpayer is a material participant. For individuals, this includes salary and self-employment income.

The impact of segregating taxpayers' income in these categories is to limit their ability to apply passive activity losses against income in the other two categories. In effect, passive activity losses are suspended and remain in the passive income or loss category until the taxpayer generates passive income, either from the passive activity producing the loss or from some other passive activity, or until the taxpayer sells the entire activity that generated the passive loss in a taxable transaction. On the sale, current and suspended passive losses from the activity are first applied to reduce gain from the sale of the activity, then to reduce net passive income from other passive activities, and then to reduce nonpassive income.[15]

Example 6-5

What if: Let's return to the facts in the previous example, where Courtney's share of CCS's loss is $15,000, her tax basis in her CCS interest is $10,000, and her at-risk amount in the activity is also $10,000. Further assume that Courtney received $142,800 in salary and other benefits, $321 of taxable interest income, $20,000 in alimony, and $700 of dividends. Finally, assume that Courtney earned $18,000 from her consulting activities and had $5,000 of net rental income from her condo. How would each of these income or loss items be allocated among the passive, portfolio, and active income and loss categories?

Answer: Courtney's $10,000 loss from CCS remaining after applying the tax-basis and at-risk loss limits is placed in the passive category because, as a limited partner, Courtney did not materially participate in the activity. Further, her $5,000 of net income from her rental condo is included in the passive category because rental activities are generally considered to be passive. The $321 of taxable interest income and $700 of dividends are included in the portfolio income category. Finally, the $142,800 of salary and other benefits, $20,000 of alimony, and $18,000 of consulting income (she is a material participant as her activity constitutes substantially all of the participation in the activity by all individuals) are included in the active income category.

What if: What is Courtney's AGI for the year assuming, other than the items described above, no other items affect her AGI?

Answer: $181,821, computed as follows:

Description	Amount	Explanation
(1) Active income	$180,800	Salary and other benefits of $142,800; alimony of $20,000; consulting income of $18,000.
(2) Portfolio income	1,021	Interest of $321; dividends of $700.
(3) Passive income	0	$5,000 of passive income from the rental condo and $10,000 of passive losses that clear the tax-basis and at-risk hurdles. The $10,000 passive loss is deductible only to the extent of the $5,000 passive income (resulting in $0 net passive income in AGI). The remaining $5,000 passive loss is a suspended passive loss.
AGI	**$181,821**	(1) + (2) + (3)

(continued on page 6-10)

---

[15]§469(g).

What if: In addition to the facts above, assume that at the beginning of next year Courtney sells her limited partnership interest in CCS for $12,000. If Courtney's tax basis on the date of sale is $0, what effect does the sale have on her AGI?

Answer: $7,000 increase in AGI, computed as follows:

Description	Amount	Explanation
(1) Capital gain	$12,000	Gain recognized = $12,000 − $0 tax basis.
(2) Ordinary loss	(5,000)	The $5,000 loss previously suspended at the basis level is not deductible upon the sale because Courtney's tax basis remains at $0. However, Courtney can deduct the $5,000 loss that was suspended last year at the passive loss level.
Increase in AGI	**$ 7,000**	(1) + (2)

Rental Real Estate Exception to the Passive Activity Loss Rules Tax laws are renowned for exceptions to rules and, not surprisingly, the general rule that passive activity losses cannot be used to offset nonpassive types of income is subject to a few important exceptions. The one we choose to discuss here applies to lower-to-middle income individuals with rental real estate.[16] A taxpayer who is an **active participant in a rental activity** may be allowed to deduct up to $25,000 of the rental loss against other types of income. To be considered an active participant, the taxpayer must (1) own at least 10 percent of the rental property and (2) participate in the process of making management decisions such as approving new tenants, deciding on rental terms, and approving repairs and capital expenditures.

Consistent with a number of tax benefits, the exception amount for active owners is phased out as adjusted gross income increases: The $25,000 maximum exception amount is phased out by 50 cents for every dollar the taxpayer's adjusted gross income (before considering the rental loss) exceeds $100,000. Consequently, the entire $25,000 deduction is phased out when the taxpayer's adjusted gross income reaches $150,000.

Example 6-6

What if: Assume that Jeb Landers, Courtney's uncle, owns and rents a condominium. Jeb is involved in approving new tenants for the rental home and in managing its maintenance. During the year, he reported a net loss of $5,000 from the rental activity, and he had sufficient tax-basis and at-risk amounts to absorb the loss. Further, his only sources of income during the year were $126,000 of salary and $22,000 of long-term capital gains. Given Jeb's $5,000 loss from his rental home, how much of the loss could he deduct currently?

Answer: $1,000. Because Jeb meets the definition of an "active participant" and has adjusted gross income of less than $150,000, before considering his rental loss, he may deduct a portion of the loss against his other income. His $1,000 deduction is computed as follows:

Description	Amount	Explanation
(1) Maximum deduction available before phase-out	$25,000	
(2) Phase-out of maximum deduction	24,000	[($148,000 − 100,000) × .5]
(3) Maximum deduction in current year	1,000	(1) − (2)
(4) Rental loss in current year	5,000	
(5) Rental loss deductible in current year	**1,000**	Lesser of (3) or (4)
Passive loss carryforward	4,000	(4) − (5)

[16]§469(b)(7) provides another important exception to the general rule that all real estate activities are passive. To overcome this presumption, taxpayers must spend more than half their time working in real estate trades or businesses and for more than 750 hours during the year. This exception benefits individuals that spend a substantial amount of time in activities like real estate development and construction.

> **What if:** Assume that Jeb's salary for the year had been $50,000 and he reported $22,000 from the sale of his stock. How much of his rental loss could he deduct currently?
>
> **Answer:** Because Jeb's adjusted gross income is only $72,000 under this scenario, he could deduct his entire $5,000 rental loss during the year.

Excess Business Loss Limitation

For years beginning after 2017, taxpayers are not allowed to deduct an **"excess business loss"** for the year. Rather, excess business losses are carried forward to subsequent years as a net operating loss carryforward. The excess business loss limitation applies to losses that are otherwise deductible under the basis, at-risk, and passive loss rules. An excess business loss for the year is the excess of aggregate business deductions for the year over the sum of aggregate business gross income or gain of the taxpayer plus a threshold amount. The threshold amount for 2018 is $500,000 for married taxpayers filing jointly and $250,000 for other taxpayers. The threshold amounts are indexed for inflation. In the case of partnership or S corporation business losses, the provision applies at the partner or shareholder level.

Example 6-7

> **What if:** Suppose that Courtney invested in a partnership, and that this year her share of business losses from the partnership are $270,000. Assume that the $270,000 loss is deductible under the basis, at-risk, and passive loss rules. How much of the loss would be deductible?
>
> **Answer:** $250,000. Deductible net business losses are limited to $250,000 ($500,000 for taxpayers married filing jointly). The $20,000 excess business loss would be carried forward next year as a net operating loss.

Loss Limitation Rules—Rental Use of the Home

A taxpayer with the financial wherewithal to do so may purchase a second home as a vacation home, a rental property, or a combination of the two. A taxpayer may own a second home outright or may share ownership with others through a timeshare or fractional ownership arrangement. The nontax benefits of owning a second home include a fixed vacation destination, the ability to trade the use of the home with an owner of a home in a different destination, the opportunity for generating income through rentals, and the potential appreciation of the second home as an investment. The nontax costs of owning a second home include the initial cost of the home, the extra cost of maintaining the home, the hassle of dealing with renters or property managers, and the downside risk associated with holding the second home as an investment.

The tax consequences of owning a second home depend on whether the home qualifies as a residence and on the number of days the taxpayer rents out the home. The home is categorized in one of three ways:

1. Residence with minimal rental use (rents home for 14 or fewer days).
2. Residence with significant rental use (rents home for 15 or more days).
3. Nonresidence.

A property is considered a "residence" for tax purposes if the taxpayer uses the home for personal purposes for *more than* the greater of 14 days or 10 percent of the number of rental days during the year. For example, if a taxpayer rents her home for 200 days and uses it for personal purposes for 21 days or more, the home is considered to be a residence

THE KEY FACTS

Rental Use of the Home

- Tax treatment depends on amount of personal and rental use. The three categories are:
  1. Residence with minimal rental use (personal residence).
  2. Residence with significant rental use (vacation home).
  3. Nonresidence (rental property).

for tax purposes. If the same taxpayer used the home for personal purposes for 20 days, the home would be considered a nonresidence for tax purposes. Personal use includes days the taxpayer or the taxpayer's relative stays in the home (even if rented at fair market value to the relative), as well as any days rented to anyone else at less than fair market value.

Residence with Minimal Rental Use

The law is simple for homeowners who rent a home that qualifies as a residence for a minimal amount of time during the year. That is, they live in it for at least 15 days and they rent it for 14 or fewer days. Taxpayers are not required to include the gross receipts in rental income and are not allowed to deduct any expenses related to the rental.[17] The owner is, however, allowed to deduct qualified residence interest (see discussion in the Individual *From* AGI Deductions chapter) and real property taxes on the second home as itemized deductions.

Example 6-8

What if: Courtney purchased a vacation home in a golf community in Scottsdale, Arizona, in January 2018. She spent 10 days vacationing in the home in early March and another 15 days vacationing in the home in mid-December. In early February, she rented the home for 14 days to a group of golfers who were in town to attend a PGA Tour golf tournament and play golf. Courtney received $6,000 in rent from the group, and Courtney incurred $1,000 of expenses relating to the rental home. Courtney did not rent the property again for the rest of the year. How much will the $5,000 net income from the rental increase her taxable income?

Answer: Zero! Because Courtney lived in the home for at least 15 days (25 days) and rented the home for 14 or fewer days (14) during 2018, she does not report the rental income to the IRS, and she does not deduct expenses associated with the rental. Note that Courtney can also deduct the mortgage interest and real property taxes on the property for the *full year* as itemized deductions.

A taxpayer with a strategically located second (or even first) home can take advantage of this favorable tax rule by renting the property and excluding potentially large rental payments from those in town to attend high-profile events such as certain college football games (e.g., games for the University of Notre Dame or The University of Texas at Austin), the Olympics, the Masters golf tournament, the Super Bowl, and Mardi Gras.

ETHICS

Tabitha lives in a college town and spends each May traveling abroad. Because the local university offers a three-week Maymester, she has started to rent her home each May for the Maymester (23 days in total) to college students, who often find it difficult to arrange such a short-term rental. Tabitha structures the rental for students to pay for 14 days with 9 days on either side of the lease for students to move in or move out. Tabitha does not report the rental income from the leases because of the 14-day rule. Would you feel comfortable signing Tabitha's tax return?

Residence with Significant Rental Use (Vacation Home)

When a home qualifies as a residence and the taxpayer rents out the home for 15 days or more, the rental revenue is included in gross income, expenses to obtain tenants (advertising and realtor commissions) are deductible as direct rental expenses, and expenses relating to the home are allocated between personal and rental use. The expenses allocated to personal use are not deductible unless they are deductible under nonrental tax provisions as itemized deductions. (The most common of these deductions are mortgage interest and real property taxes, but this would also include casualty losses on a home in a federally declared disaster area.)

[17]§280A(g).

When the gross rental revenue exceeds the sum of the direct rental expenses and the expenses allocated to the rental use of the home, the taxpayer is allowed to deduct the expenses in full. However, when these expenses exceed the rental revenue, the deductibility of the expenses is limited. In these situations, taxpayers divide the rental expenses into one of three categories or "tiers." The tier 1, 2, and 3 expenses for rental property are described in Exhibit 6-5.

EXHIBIT 6-5   Rental Expenses by Tier and Deduction Sequence

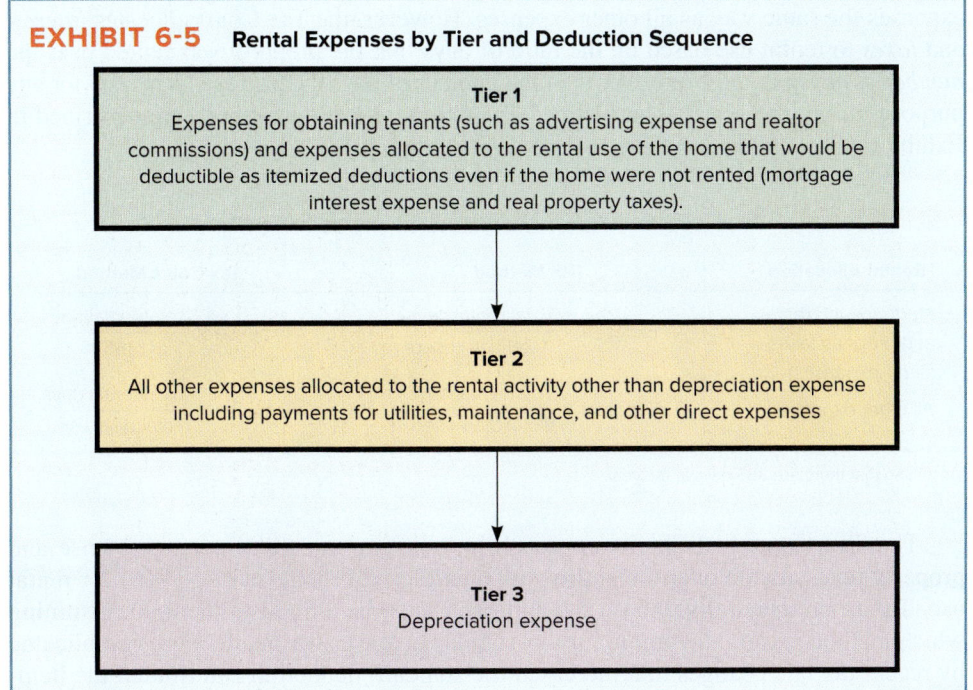

Tier 1
Expenses for obtaining tenants (such as advertising expense and realtor commissions) and expenses allocated to the rental use of the home that would be deductible as itemized deductions even if the home were not rented (mortgage interest expense and real property taxes).

Tier 2
All other expenses allocated to the rental activity other than depreciation expense including payments for utilities, maintenance, and other direct expenses

Tier 3
Depreciation expense

The taxpayer first deducts tier 1 expenses (expenses to obtain tenants and mortgage interest and real property taxes allocated to rental use[18]) in full. This is true even when tier 1 expenses exceed the gross rental revenue.[19] Second, the taxpayer deducts tier 2 expenses.[20] However, the tier 2 expense deductions are limited to the gross rental revenue in excess of tier 1 expenses. Any tier 2 expenses not deducted in the current year due to the income limitation are suspended and carried forward to the next year. Finally, the taxpayer deducts tier 3 expenses (depreciation). The tier 3 expense deduction is limited to the gross rental revenue in excess of tier 1 and tier 2 expenses. Any tier 3 expenses not deductible because of the income limitation are suspended and carried forward to the next year. The nondeductible tier 3 expense does not reduce the basis in the home. The three tier deduction sequence is designed to maximize taxpayer deductions for expenses that would be deductible even without any rental use of the home (most commonly, mortgage interest and real property taxes) and to minimize the allowable depreciation deductions for the home. This sequence is more favorable for taxpayers who do not itemize deductions or whose potential mortgage interest and/or real property tax deductions are limited and it is less favorable to other taxpayers.

[18]Technically, expenses to obtain tenants (advertising and realtor commissions) are a reduction in gross rental income for tax purposes. However, we classify them as tier 1 expenses to simplify the discussion.

[19]The rental activity associated with a home falling into the residence with significant rental use category is not considered to be a passive activity, so income or loss generated from the activity is not considered to be passive income or passive loss [§469(j)].

[20]§280A(c)(5). Also see IRS Publication 537, "Residential Rental Property (Including Rental of Vacation Homes)."

As we mentioned above, expenses associated with the rental use of the home must be allocated between rental use and personal use of the home. These expenses are *generally* allocated to rental use based on the ratio of the number of days of rental use to the total number of days the property was used for rental and personal purposes (see Exhibit 6-6). All expenses not allocated to rental use are allocated to personal use.

The only potential exception to the general allocation rule involves the allocation of mortgage interest expense and real property taxes (both tier 1 expenses). The IRS and the Tax Court disagree on how to allocate these particular expenses. The IRS allocates these expenses the same way as all other expenses. However, the Tax Court allocates *interest* and *taxes* to rental use based on the ratio of days that the property was rented over the *number of days in the year*, rather than the number of days the property was used for any purpose during the year.[21] The IRS and Tax Court allocation methods are described in Exhibit 6-6 (assuming that there are 365 days in the year).

EXHIBIT 6-6   Tax Court versus IRS Method of Allocating Expenses

Rental Allocation	IRS Method	Tax Court Method
Mortgage interest and property taxes (tier 1 expenses)	Expense $\times \dfrac{\text{Total rental days}}{\text{Total days used}}$	Expense $\times \dfrac{\text{Total rental days}}{365^*}$
All other expenses	Expense $\times \dfrac{\text{Total rental days}}{\text{Total days used}}$	Expense $\times \dfrac{\text{Total rental days}}{\text{Total days used}}$

*Assuming that there are 365 days in the year.

The Tax Court justifies its approach by pointing out that interest expense and property taxes accrue over the entire year regardless of the level of personal or rental use. Taxpayers generally choose the approach most beneficial to them. Determining which method is more favorable for a particular taxpayer was made more complicated by recent tax law changes that increased the standard deduction and limited the itemized deduction for taxes. When the gross income limitation does not apply, the IRS method is generally more favorable because it allocates more mortgage interest and real property taxes to rental use where they are deductible as for AGI deductions. Under the Tax Court method more mortgage interest and real property taxes would be allocated to personal use where they may or may not provide tax benefit depending on whether the taxpayer itemizes deductions and whether the taxpayer has reached the $10,000 limit for deducting taxes. When the gross income limitation applies, the Tax Court method is likely more favorable for taxpayers who receive tax benefit from additional mortgage interest and real property tax itemized deductions because it maximizes their total current year deductions (for AGI plus itemized deductions) from the property relative to the IRS method. On the other hand, when the gross income limitation applies, the IRS method likely favors taxpayers who do not itemize deductions or who do not receive full tax benefit from the additional itemized deductions that would be provided by the Tax Court method (they are already capped on the itemized deduction for taxes or the full amount of mortgage interest and real property taxes is not above the standard deduction amount when combined with other itemized deductions). For these taxpayers, the trade-off is they have more excess tier 2 and tier 3 deductions that they carryover and deduct in a subsequent year instead of having more itemized deductions that provide little to no tax benefit. In any event, use of the Tax Court method likely involves more risk of IRS scrutiny than the IRS method.

---

[21]The Tax Court method of allocating these expenses is also referred to as the Bolton method after the taxpayer in the court case in which the Tax Court approved this method of allocating deductions. While the court case initially was tried in the Tax Court, the decision in favor of the taxpayer was appealed to the Ninth Circuit Court that also ruled in favor of the taxpayer and sanctioned the use of the Tax Court or Bolton method of allocating interest expense. *Bolton v. Commissioner,* 82-2 USTC par. 9699 (9 Cir., 1982), aff'g 77 TC 104 (1981).

Example 6-9

What if: At the beginning of 2018, Courtney purchased a vacation home in Scottsdale, Arizona, for $400,000. She paid $100,000 down and financed the remaining $300,000 with a 6 percent mortgage secured by the home. During the year, Courtney used the home for personal purposes for 30 days and rented the home for 200 days. Thus, the home falls into the residence with significant rental use category. She received $37,500 of rental revenue and incurred $500 of rental advertising expenses. How are her expenses allocated to the rental use under the IRS and Tax Court methods?

Answer: See the following summary of allocation of expenses associated with the home:

Allocation Method to Rental Use				
Expense	**Amount**	**Tier**	**IRS Method (200/230)**	**Tax Court Method (200/365 Tier 1 200/230 Other)**
Advertising*	$ 500	1	$ 500	$ 500
Interest	18,000	1	15,652	9,863
Real estate taxes	5,000	1	4,348	2,740
Total tier 1 expenses	$23,500	1	$20,500	$13,103
Utilities	4,500	2	$ 3,913	$ 3,913
Repairs	1,800	2	1,565	1,565
Insurance	3,500	2	3,043	3,043
Maintenance	3,200	2	2,783	2,783
Total tier 2 expenses	$13,000	2	$11,304	$11,304
Tier 3: Depreciation	13,939	3	$12,121	$12,121
Total expenses	$50,439			

*Advertising is a direct expense of the rental, so it is fully deductible against rental revenue.

Net Income from Rental	IRS Method	Tax Court Method
Rental receipts	$37,500	$37,500
Less tier 1 expenses	(20,500)	(13,103)
Income after tier 1 expenses	17,000	24,397
Less tier 2 expenses	(11,304)	(11,304)
Income after tier 2 expenses	5,696	13,093
Less tier 3 expenses	(5,696)	(12,121)
Taxable rental income	$ 0	$ 972
Interest itemized deduction	$ 2,348	$ 8,137
Real property tax itemized deduction	652	2,260
Deductible rental expenses (sum of tier 1, 2, and 3 expenses)	37,500	36,528
Total personal and rental expenses	$40,500	$46,925

At first glance, it appears that the Tax Court method is more favorable for Courtney. After all, Courtney is able to claim $6,425 more total deductions under the Tax Court method compared to the IRS method ($46,925 minus $40,500). While the IRS method allows Courtney to deduct $972 more for AGI (rental) deductions than the Tax Court method ($37,500 minus $36,528), the Tax Court method allows Courtney to potentially deduct $5,789 more in mortgage interest expense ($8,137 minus $2,348) and $1,608 more in real property taxes ($2,260 minus $652) as itemized deductions. However, on closer inspection, it is not clear whether the Tax Court or the IRS method is more favorable for two reasons. First, the Courtney is allowed to carry forward to next year the $6,425 of depreciation expense that she did not deduct this year under the IRS method. That is, she was not able to deduct the $6,425 this year but she will be able to deduct it in a subsequent year if she generates enough income. Second, Courtney reports $1,608 more in real property taxes under the Tax Court method than under the IRS method. However, as we will learn in chapter 7 (see Example 7-5), Courtney exceeds the $10,000 limit on the itemized deduction for taxes so the additional $1,608 of real property taxes does not increase her itemized deductions and it provides no tax benefit. The Tax Court gives Courtney more deductions in the current year but the IRS method gives her more deductions in the current plus future years (assuming she generates enough income).

THE KEY FACTS

Rental Use of the Home

• Nonresidence (rental property):
  • Rental use is at least one day and personal use is no more than the greater of (1) 14 days or (2) 10 percent of rental days.
  • Allocate expenses to rental and personal use.
  (continued)

- Rental deductions in excess of rental income are deductible subject to passive loss limitation rules.
- Interest expense allocated to personal use is not deductible.

Taxpayers report their rental activities on Schedule E of Form 1040. The deductible tier 1, tier 2, and tier 3 expenses are *for* AGI deductions. Exhibit 6-7 displays the completed Schedule E for Courtney's "what if" Scottsdale vacation home using the Tax Court method.

Nonresidence (Rental Property)   For property in this category, the taxpayer includes the rental revenue in gross income and deducts all rental expenses allocated to the rental use of the property as *for* AGI deductions (all on Schedule E). When the property is used for even a day for personal purposes, the expenses must be allocated between the rental usage and the personal usage.[22] In this situation, however, the law does not allow the taxpayer to deduct mortgage interest not allocated to rental use because the taxpayer does not meet the minimum amount of personal use required for the deduction (the home is not a qualified residence). However, the taxpayer is still allowed to deduct, as an itemized deduction, real property taxes not allocated to the rental. In contrast to the residence with significant rental use category, if the rental expenses exceed the gross income from the home in this category, the deductibility of the loss is not subject to a gross income limitation but it is subject to the passive activity restrictions discussed previously.[23]

Example 6-10

What if: Suppose that at the beginning of 2018, Courtney purchased a vacation home in Scottsdale, Arizona, for $400,000. She paid $100,000 down and financed the remaining $300,000 with a 6 percent mortgage secured by the home. During the year, Courtney *did not use the home for personal purposes*, and she rented the home for 200 days. She received $37,500 in gross rental revenue for the year and incurred $50,439 of expenses relating to the rental property. How much can Courtney deduct in this situation?

Answer: The good news is that the deductions are not limited to gross income from the rental so she can deduct all $50,439, generating a $12,939 loss on the property ($37,500 − $50,439). The bad news is that, as we discussed above, the loss is subject to the passive loss rules. If Courtney is considered to actively participate in the rental, she may be able to deduct some or all of the $12,939 loss depending on whether her AGI is ultimately $100,000, between $100,000 and $150,000, or greater than or equal to $150,000. If her AGI is greater than $150,000, she will only be able to deduct the passive loss against other passive income (or carry the loss forward).

Exhibit 6-8 summarizes the tax rules relating to a home used for rental purposes depending on the extent of rental (and personal) use.

Business Use of Home Deduction Limitations

Because a personal residence is a personal-use asset, utility payments and depreciation due to wear and tear are not deductible expenses. However, taxpayers who use their home—or at least part of their home—for business purposes may be able to deduct expenses associated with their home use if they meet certain stringent requirements.[24]

To qualify for **home office deductions,** a taxpayer must use her home—or part of her home—exclusively and regularly as either:

1. The principal place of business for any of the taxpayer's trade or businesses, or
2. As a place to meet with patients, clients, or customers in the normal course of business.

Taxpayers fail the exclusive use test if they use the area of the home in question for both business and personal purposes.

[22]§280A(e).

[23]If the home rental is deemed to be a not-for-profit activity, the loss is subject to the hobby loss rules in §183 (discussed in the Individual *From* AGI Deductions chapter).

[24]§280A. If taxpayers rent the home they occupy and they meet the requirements for business use of the home, they can deduct part of the rent they pay. To determine the amount of the deduction, multiply the rental payment by the percentage of the home used for business purposes.

EXHIBIT 6-7   Courtney's Schedule E for Vacation Home Rental

SCHEDULE E (Form 1040)	**Supplemental Income and Loss**	OMB No. 1545-0074
	(From rental real estate, royalties, partnerships, S corporations, estates, trusts, REMICs, etc.)	**2017**
Department of the Treasury Internal Revenue Service (99)	▶ Attach to Form 1040, 1040NR, or Form 1041. ▶ Go to *www.irs.gov/ScheduleE* for instructions and the latest information.	Attachment Sequence No. **13**

Name(s) shown on return	Your social security number
Courtney Wilson	**123-45-6789**

Part I   **Income or Loss From Rental Real Estate and Royalties**   **Note:** If you are in the business of renting personal property, use **Schedule C** or **C-EZ** (see instructions). If you are an individual, report farm rental income or loss from **Form 4835** on page 2, line 40.

A Did you make any payments in 2017 that would require you to file Form(s) 1099? (see instructions) . . . . .   ☐ Yes ☑ No
B If "Yes," did you or will you file required Forms 1099? . . . .   ☐ Yes ☐ No

1a	Physical address of each property (street, city, state, ZIP code)
A	**100 Dream Home Way, Scottsdale, Arizona 85250**
B	
C	

1b	Type of Property (from list below)	2	For each rental real estate property listed above, report the number of fair rental and personal use days. Check the **QJV** box only if you meet the requirements to file as a qualified joint venture. See instructions.		Fair Rental Days	Personal Use Days	QJV
A	3			**A**	200	30	☐
B				**B**			☐
C				**C**			☐

Type of Property:
1 Single Family Residence   3 Vacation/Short-Term Rental   5 Land   7 Self-Rental
2 Multi-Family Residence   4 Commercial   6 Royalties   8 Other (describe)

Income:	Properties:		A	B		C
3	Rents received	3	37,500			
4	Royalties received	4				
Expenses:						
5	Advertising	5	500			
6	Auto and travel (see instructions)	6				
7	Cleaning and maintenance	7	2,783			
8	Commissions.	8				
9	Insurance	9	3,043			
10	Legal and other professional fees	10				
11	Management fees	11				
12	Mortgage interest paid to banks, etc. (see instructions)	12	9,863			
13	Other interest.	13				
14	Repairs.	14	1,565			
15	Supplies	15				
16	Taxes	16	2,740			
17	Utilities	17	3,913			
18	Depreciation expense or depletion	18	12,121			
19	Other (list) ▶ _____	19				
20	Total expenses. Add lines 5 through 19	20	36,528			
21	Subtract line 20 from line 3 (rents) and/or 4 (royalties). If result is a (loss), see instructions to find out if you must file **Form 6198**	21	972			
22	Deductible rental real estate loss after limitation, if any, on **Form 8582** (see instructions)	22	(	)(	)(	)
23a	Total of all amounts reported on line 3 for all rental properties	23a	37,500		
b	Total of all amounts reported on line 4 for all royalty properties	23b			
c	Total of all amounts reported on line 12 for all properties	23c	9,863		
d	Total of all amounts reported on line 18 for all properties	23d	12,121		
e	Total of all amounts reported on line 20 for all properties	23e	36,528		
24	**Income.** Add positive amounts shown on line 21. **Do not** include any losses	24		972
25	**Losses.** Add royalty losses from line 21 and rental real estate losses from line 22. Enter total losses here .	25	(	)
26	**Total rental real estate and royalty income or (loss).** Combine lines 24 and 25. Enter the result here. If Parts II, III, IV, and line 40 on page 2 do not apply to you, also enter this amount on Form 1040, line 17, or Form 1040NR, line 18. Otherwise, include this amount in the total on line 41 on page 2 . . .	26		972

For Paperwork Reduction Act Notice, see the separate instructions.   Cat. No. 11344L   Schedule E (Form 1040) 2017

EXHIBIT 6-8   Summary of Tax Rules Relating to Home Used for Rental Purposes

	Residence with Minimal Rental Use	Residence with Significant Rental Use	Nonresidence
Classification test	Reside in home for at least 15 days and rent home for fewer than 15 days during the year.	Rent home for 15 days or more and use home for personal purposes for more than the greater of (1) 14 days or (2) 10 percent of the total rental days.	Rent home for at least one day, with personal use of home not to exceed the greater of (1) 14 days or (2) 10 percent of the rental days.
Rental revenue	Exclude from gross income.	Include in gross income.	Include in gross income.
Direct rental expenses unrelated to home use	Not deductible.	Fully deductible *for* AGI (loss not subject to passive activity loss rules).	Deductible *for* AGI but subject to passive activity loss rules.
Treatment of mortgage interest and real property taxes	Deductible as itemized deductions.	Allocate between personal-use days and rental days; interest and taxes allocated to rental days are deductible as rental expenses; interest and taxes allocated to personal-use days are deductible as itemized deductions.	Allocated between personal-use days and rental days; interest and taxes allocated to rental days are deductible as rental expenses; taxes allocated to personal-use days are deductible as itemized deductions; interest allocated to personal-use days is not deductible.
Treatment of all other expenses	Not deductible.	Allocate between personal-use days and rental days; expenses allocated to personal-use days are not deductible; expenses allocated to rental days are deductible as rental expenses to the extent of rental revenue minus the sum of direct rental expenses, rental mortgage interest, and real property taxes when expenses allocated to rental days exceed the rental income.	Allocated between personal-use days and rental days; expenses allocated to personal-use days are not deductible; expenses allocated to rental days are deductible and can generate loss but loss is subject to passive activity loss rules.
Excess expenses	Not applicable.	Rental expenses in excess of rental income minus the sum of direct rental expenses, rental mortgage interest, and real property taxes are carried forward to the next year.	Not applicable; rental expenses are deductible, even if they create a rental loss (subject to passive activity loss rules).

Example 6-11

What if: Courtney uses a large room in her basement as her office for her consulting business. The room has been wired for all of her office needs. Once or twice a week, Courtney sits at the desk in the room and surfs the web to read up on her favorite sports teams. Is the office space eligible for a home office deduction?

Answer: No. The office is not used exclusively for Courtney's business.

The exclusive use rule does not apply if the taxpayer either:

- Uses part of the home for the storage of inventory or product samples, or
- Uses part of the home as a day care facility.

When a taxpayer has more than one business location, including the home, which one is her principal place of business? This is a facts-and-circumstances determination based upon:

- The relative importance of the activities performed at each place where the taxpayer conducts business (more income from an activity generally means it's a more important activity), and
- The total time spent doing work at each location.

However, by definition, a taxpayer's principal place of business also includes the place of business used by the taxpayer for the administrative or management activities of the taxpayer's trade or business *if there is no other fixed location of the trade or business where the taxpayer conducts substantial administrative or management activities of the trade or business.*[25]

If a taxpayer meets with clients or patients in her home during the normal course of business, she qualifies for the home office deduction even if the home is not her principal place of business. However, the clients or patients must visit the taxpayer's home *in person*. Communication through telephone calls or other types of communication technology does not qualify.

Example 6-12

What if: Courtney uses a large room in her basement as her office for her consulting business. The room has been wired for all of her office needs, and Courtney uses the room exclusively for her business use. Does this space qualify for the home office deduction?

Answer: Yes. While Courtney will spend a good deal of time meeting with clients on location, she has no other fixed location for her trade or business. Further, the office is used exclusively for business purposes. Consequently, Courtney qualifies for the home office deduction subject to certain limitations described below.

Self-employed taxpayers deduct home office expenses on Schedule C. In contrast, for years after 2017, employees cannot deduct home office expenses (as employee expenses are generally nondeductible after 2017).[26]

TAXES IN THE REAL WORLD   If You Want the Bathroom to Qualify as a Home Office, You Better Lock It and Keep the Key

The IRS and a taxpayer with seven years of IRS work experience recently did battle over home office expenses in the Tax Court. The taxpayer operates an accounting business, and he uses a bedroom in his residence exclusively for his accounting business. The taxpayer included the bathroom adjacent to the bedroom in his home office square footage. However, because the taxpayer testified that his children and personal guests occasionally used the bathroom, the Tax Court determined that the bathroom was not used exclusively for business purposes (the children and personal guests may beg to differ), and it disallowed the expenses associated with the bathroom square footage. See Luis Balas, T.C. Memo. 2011-201 (2011).

---

[25]§280A(c)(1).

[26]IRS Publication 587, Business Use of Your Home, page 4, provides a flowchart for determining whether taxpayers are allowed to deduct home office expenses. Prior to 2018, an *employee* (not a self-employed taxpayer) who otherwise met the requirements for a home office deduction was allowed a deduction only if: (a) the employee's use of the home was considered to be for the convenience of the employer and not just something helpful or useful for the employee, and (b) the employee does not rent part of the home to the employer. The deductible home office expenses for employees prior to 2018 were generally miscellaneous itemized deduction subject to a 2 percent AGI floor (except real estate taxes, mortgage interest, and casualty losses).

Direct versus Indirect Expenses   When a taxpayer qualifies for home office deductions, she is allowed to deduct only actual expenses that are related—either directly or indirectly—to the business. Direct expenses are expenses incurred in maintaining the room or part of the home that is set aside for business use. Direct expenses include painting or costs of other repairs to the area of the home used for business.[27] These expenses are deductible in full as home office expenses. Indirect expenses are expenses incurred in maintaining and using the home. Indirect expenses include insurance, utilities, interest, real property taxes, general repairs, and depreciation on the home as if it were used entirely for business purposes. In contrast to direct expenses, only indirect expenses allocated to the home office space are deductible.

How do taxpayers allocate indirect expenses to the home office space? If the rooms in the home are roughly of equal size, the taxpayer may allocate the indirect expenses to the business portion of the home based on the number of rooms. In a 10-room home, a taxpayer using one room for qualifying business use is allowed to deduct 10 percent of the indirect expenses. Alternatively, the taxpayer may allocate indirect expenses based on the amount of the space or square footage of the business-use room relative to the total square footage in the home. If the home is 5,000 square feet and the home office is 250 square feet, the taxpayer may deduct 5 percent of the indirect expenses. Unrelated expenses, such as painting a room not used for business purposes, are not deductible.

In lieu of allocating actual expenses to home office use, the IRS allows taxpayers to use an optional simplified method for computing home office expenses.[28] Under the simplified method, taxpayers are not allowed to deduct any *actual* expenses relating to qualified business use of the home (including depreciation). Instead, taxpayers electing the simplified method deduct, subject to limitations described below, the allowable business use square footage of the office (not to exceed 300 feet) multiplied by $5 per square foot. Thus, this method generates a maximum deduction of $1,500 (300 square feet × $5 per square foot). In addition, taxpayers using this method are allowed to deduct all of their home mortgage interest and real property taxes as itemized deductions on Schedule A. Taxpayers may choose from year to year whether to use the simplified method or the actual expense method.

Example 6-13

What if: Courtney moved into her new $400,000, 5,000-square-foot home on January 15, 2018, and set up a 500-square-foot home office in the basement on that same date for her consulting business. Through the end of the calendar year, Courtney incurred several expenses relating to the home (see table below). Assuming she qualifies for the home office deduction, she would sum the direct expenses and the indirect expenses allocated to the office. She would allocate the indirect expenses based on the square footage of the office compared to the rest of the home. Using the actual expense method, what amount of home-related expenses would qualify as home office expenses?

---

[27]The basic local telephone service charge, including taxes, for the first telephone line into a home is a nondeductible personal expense. However, charges for business long-distance phone calls on that line, as well as the cost of a second line into the home used exclusively for business, are deductible business expenses. However, these expenses are not deducted as home office expenses. Rather, these expenses are deducted separately on the appropriate form or schedule. Taxpayers filing Schedule C (Form 1040) would deduct these expenses as utilities.

[28]Rev. Proc. 2013-13.

Answer: $3,643, as calculated below. All direct expenses and 10 percent of the indirect expenses would be allocated to the home office (500 office square footage/5,000 home square footage). Courtney would allocate the expenses as follows:

Total Expense	Type	(A) Amount	(B) Office %	(A) × (B) Home Office Expense
Painting office	Direct	$ 200	100%	$ 200
Real property taxes	Indirect	2,700	10	270
Home mortgage interest	Indirect	15,800	10	1,580
Electricity	Indirect	2,600	10	260
Gas and other utilities	Indirect	2,500	10	250
Homeowner's insurance	Indirect	1,000	10	100
Depreciation	Indirect	9,829	10	983
Total expenses		**$34,629**		**$3,643**

What if: Suppose Courtney elects to use the simplified method for determining her home office expenses. What would be the amount of her home office expenses?

Answer: $1,500 (300 square feet × $5 per square foot). Even though Courtney's home office is 500 square feet, for purposes of the home office expense under the simplified method, the square footage is limited to 300 square feet.

What if: Suppose Courtney elects to use the simplified method for home office expenses. What amount of home mortgage interest expenses and real property taxes would she be able to deduct on Schedule A as itemized deductions?

Answer: Home mortgage interest expense, $15,800; real property taxes, $2,700. She is allowed to deduct all of these expenses as itemized deductions.

The expenses attributable to the home office are deductible subject to the limitations discussed below.

Limitations on Deductibility of Expenses The process for determining the home office expense deduction using the actual expense method is similar to the process used to determine deductions for vacation homes. When net business income (net Schedule C income) exceeds total home office expenses (before applying any limitations), the full amount of the expenses is deductible. However, when home office expenses exceed net Schedule C income (before the home office deduction), the deduction is potentially limited. In these situations, taxpayers first divide home office expenses into one of three categories or "tiers." Tier 1 expenses consist of mortgage interest and real property taxes allocated to the business use of the home. Tier 2 expenses consist of all other expenses allocated to the business use of the home except for depreciation. Tier 3 expense consists of depreciation. Taxpayers first deduct tier 1 expenses in full even when tier 1 expenses exceed net Schedule C income before the home office deduction.[29] Second, taxpayers deduct tier 2 expenses. However, deductible tier 2 expenses are limited to net Schedule C income before home office deductions minus tier 1 expenses (that is, deducting tier 2 expenses cannot create a net Schedule C loss). Any tier 2 expenses not deductible due to the income limitation are suspended and carried forward to the next year, subject to the same limitations. Finally, taxpayers deduct tier 3 expense. The deductible tier 3 expense is limited to net Schedule C income before the home office deduction minus tier 1 and deductible tier 2 expenses (tier 3 expense cannot create a net Schedule C loss). The nondeductible portion of tier 3 expense is carried forward to the next year, subject to the same limitations.

[29]§280A(c)(5).

Under the simplified method, the expense, as calculated by multiplying the square footage by the $5 application rate, is limited to net Schedule C income before home office deductions. Further, taxpayers using the simplified method in a particular year may not carry over expenses disallowed by the income limitation and they may not deduct expenses carried over to that year under the actual expense method. However, disallowed expenses under the actual expense method can be carried over to a subsequent year in which the taxpayer uses the actual expense method for determining the home office expense deduction.

Example 6-14

THE KEY FACTS

Home Office Deduction

- Deductibility limits on expenses allocated to office.
  - Employee home office expenses are not deductible.
  - If self-employed, deducted *for* AGI but deductions may be subject to income limitation.
  - If deduction is limited by income limitation, apply the same tiered system as used for rental property (tier 2 and tier 3 deductions are limited to gross rental income minus tier 1 expenses).
- Taxpayers can elect simplified method to report home office expenses.
  - Business use square footage (limited to 300 sq. feet) × $5 per square foot.
  - Deduction limited to gross business revenue minus business expenses unrelated to home.
  - Deduct all property taxes and mortgage interest as itemized deductions.
  - Do not deduct depreciation expense, so basis in home is unaffected.
- Depreciation expense
  - Reduces basis in home.
  - Gain on sale due to depreciation is ineligible for exclusion.
  - This gain is taxed at a maximum 25 percent rate as unrecaptured §1250 gain.

What if: In 2018, Courtney generated only $3,000 of net business income before the home office deduction from her business. Her home office expenses before limitation total $3,643 (see previous example). The expenses consist of painting the office, $200; real property taxes, $270; home mortgage interest, $1,580; electricity, $260; gas and other utilities, $250; homeowner's insurance, $100; and depreciation, $983. What is the total amount of tier 1, tier 2, and tier 3 expenses?

Answer: Tier 1 expenses, $1,850 (real property taxes $270 and home interest expense of $1,580); tier 2 expenses, $810 (painting office $200, electricity $260, gas and other utilities $250, and homeowner's insurance $100); and tier 3 expense, $983 (depreciation).

What is Courtney's net income from the business after claiming the home office deduction, and what expenses, if any, will she carry over to next year?

Answer: $0 net income and carryover of $643 of depreciation expense, determined as follows:

Net Income from Business	
Gross business receipts	$3,000
Less: Tier 1 expenses	(1,850)
Income after tier 1 expenses	1,150
Less: Tier 2 expenses	(810)
Income after tier 2 expenses	340
Less: Tier 3 expenses	(340)
Taxable business income	$ 0

Due to the taxable income limitation, Courtney would be allowed to deduct only $340 of the $983 depreciation expense. She would carry over the remaining $643 ($983 – $340) to next year to deduct as a home office expense subject to the same limitations.

What if: Suppose Courtney uses the simplified method of determining home office expenses. What amount of the $1,500 expense (300 square feet × $5 application rate) would she be allowed to deduct?

Answer: All $1,500, because the expense is less than the $3,000 net business income before the home office deduction.

What if: Assume the same facts as in the previous "what if" example except that net business income before the home office deduction is now $1,200. What amount of the $1,500 home office expense would Courtney be allowed to deduct?

Answer: $1,200. The home office expense deduction under the simplified method is limited to net business income before the home office deduction. Courtney is not allowed to carry over the $300 nondeductible portion of the expense to a subsequent year.

It is important to note that, when a taxpayer deducts depreciation as a home office expense using the actual expense method, the depreciation expense reduces the taxpayer's basis in the home. Consequently, when the taxpayer sells the home, the gain on the sale will be greater than it would have been had the taxpayer not deducted depreciation expense. Further, the gain on the sale of the home attributable to the depreciation deductions is *not* eligible to be excluded under the home sale exclusion provisions. Rather, this gain is treated as unrecaptured §1250 gain and is subject to a maximum 25 percent tax rate (see the Property Dispositions chapter for a detailed discussion of unrecaptured §1250 gain).

Taxpayers using the simplified method are not allowed to deduct depreciation expense. Consequently, the simplified method does not affect the taxpayer's basis in the home. However, if a taxpayer switches from the simplified method in one year to the actual expense method in a subsequent year, the taxpayer is required to use modified depreciation tables to compute depreciation expense under the actual expense method.

Allowing taxpayers to deduct part of their home-related expenses as business expenses creates temptations for taxpayers to deduct home-related expenses that don't meet the requirements. Not surprisingly, the IRS is very concerned about taxpayers inappropriately deducting expenses relating to their home. Consequently, expenses for business use of the home are some of the most highly scrutinized deductions available to taxpayers. Self-employed taxpayers claiming home office deductions must file a Form 8829 "Expenses for Business Use of Your Home" when deducting home office expenses on a tax return. Self-employed taxpayers who use the simplified method report their home office deduction directly on Schedule C. With the high level of scrutiny applied to home office expenses, taxpayers should be sure to have documentation available to support their deductions.

DEDUCTIONS INDIRECTLY RELATED TO BUSINESS ACTIVITIES

LO 6-3

Taxpayers can incur expenses in activities that are not directly related to making money but that they would not have incurred if they were not involved in a business activity. Taxpayers are allowed to deduct some of these expenses that are indirectly related to business activities as deductions *for* AGI. We describe these deductions below.

Individual Retirement Accounts

Taxpayers who meet certain eligibility requirements can contribute to **traditional IRAs,** to **Roth IRAs,** or to both. Just like traditional and Roth 401(k) plans, traditional IRAs and Roth IRAs have different tax characteristics. In fact, in most respects, the tax characteristics of traditional 401(k) plans mirror those of traditional IRAs, and the tax characteristics of Roth 401(k) plans mirror those of Roth IRA accounts.

Traditional IRAs   Deductible contributions to IRAs are *for* AGI deductions. The maximum deductible contribution for a taxpayer in 2018 depends on the taxpayer's age as follows:

- $5,500 deduction limit if the taxpayer is less than 50 years of age at year-end.[30,31]
- $6,500 deduction limit if the taxpayer is at least 50 years of age at year-end.[32]
- $0 deduction if the taxpayer is at least 70½ years of age at year-end.

The deductible contribution limit may be further restricted depending on the following factors:

- Whether the taxpayer is an active participant in an employer-sponsored retirement plan.
- The taxpayer's filing status.
- The amount of the taxpayer's earned income.
- The taxpayer's modified AGI (MAGI). For purposes of determining the deductible amount of traditional IRA contributions, MAGI is the taxpayer's AGI disregarding the IRA deduction itself and certain other items.[33]

---

[30]Lump-sum distributions from qualified plans other than Roth 401(k) plans received prior to retirement are frequently rolled over into traditional IRA accounts to avoid the 10 percent premature distribution penalty and current taxation. Rollover contributions are not subject to normal contribution limits for traditional IRAs.

[31]The IRA contribution limit is indexed for inflation.

[32]The $1,000 increase in the deduction limit for older taxpayers is granted to allow taxpayers nearing retirement age to "catch up" on contributions they may not have made in previous years.

[33]§219(g)(3).

Unmarried taxpayers not participating in an employer-sponsored retirement plan may deduct IRA contributions up to the *lesser* of

- $5,500 ($6,500 for taxpayers 50+ years of age) or
- Earned income.

As we discuss in the Gross Income and Exclusions chapter, earned income generally includes income actually earned through the taxpayer's efforts, such as wages, salaries, tips, and other employee compensation, plus the amount of the taxpayer's net earnings from self-employment. Alimony income is also considered as earned income for this purpose.

For *unmarried taxpayers* who actively participate in an employer-sponsored retirement plan, the deduction limits are the same as for those who do not participate except that the maximum deduction is phased out based on the taxpayer's MAGI as follows:

- No phase-out if MAGI is equal to or less than $63,000.
- Proportional phase-out of full limit for MAGI between $63,000 and $73,000. The phase-out percentage is computed as follows: (MAGI minus $63,000) divided by ($73,000 minus $63,000) (e.g., if MAGI is $67,000, taxpayer loses 40 percent of contribution limit).
- Full phase-out (no deduction) if MAGI is equal to or greater than $73,000.

Example 6-15

As discussed in the Gross Income and Exclusions chapter, Courtney participates in EWD's 401(k) plan. Assuming that she makes a $5,500 contribution in 2018 to a traditional IRA, how much of this contribution may Courtney deduct?

Answer: $0. Because Courtney participates in an employer-sponsored retirement plan during the current year and her MAGI ($187,000) exceeds $73,000, she may not deduct the $5,500 contribution.

What if: Assume the same facts as above, except that Courtney's MAGI is $69,000. How much of the IRA contribution may Courtney deduct?

Answer: $2,200. The deductible amount before considering MAGI limitations is $5,500. However, because Courtney is a participant in EWD's retirement plan, the $5,500 deduction limit is subject to phase-out. Because Courtney's MAGI is 60 percent of the way through the $63,000 – $73,000 phase-out range for a single taxpayer [($69,000 – $63,000)/($73,000 – $63,000)], the $5,500 deductible contribution limit is reduced by 60 percent, to $2,200 [$5,500 × (1 – .60)]. So, $2,200 is the maximum deductible contribution she can make to her traditional IRA.

What if: Assume that EWD does not offer a retirement plan, and Courtney makes a $5,500 contribution in 2018 to a traditional IRA. How much of this contribution may Courtney deduct?

Answer: $5,500. Because Courtney does not participate in an employer-sponsored retirement plan, she may deduct the entire $5,500 contribution.

Married taxpayers can make deductible contributions to separate IRAs (an IRA for each spouse), subject to limitations. If the married couple files jointly, before considering any AGI-based phase-out amounts (discussed below), the maximum deduction for the spouse with the *higher* amount of earned income is the same as it is for unmarried taxpayers ($5,500 [plus $1,000 if at least 50 years of age at year-end] or earned income if it is less). However, the maximum deduction for the spouse with the lesser amount of earned income is limited to the lesser of:

- $5,500 ($6,500 if this spouse is age 50+) or
- Total earned income of both spouses reduced by deductible and nondeductible contributions to the higher earning spouse's traditional IRA and by contributions to the higher earning spouse's Roth IRA.[34]

The contribution to the lesser earning spouse's IRA is called a *spousal* IRA. The money in the account belongs to the lesser earning spouse no matter where the funds for the contribution came from.

If either spouse is an active participant in an employer's retirement plan and the couple files jointly, the maximum deduction for each spouse is phased out based on the *couple's* MAGI as follows:

- No phase-out if the couple's MAGI is equal to or less than $101,000.
- Proportional phase-out of full limit for MAGI between $101,000 and $121,000 (e.g., if MAGI is $106,000, taxpayer loses 25 percent of deductible contribution limit).
- Full phase-out (no deduction) if MAGI is equal to or greater than $121,000.

If one spouse is an active participant in an employer's retirement plan and the other is not and the couple files jointly, the deduction for the spouse who is not an active participant is phased out based on the *couple's* MAGI as follows:

- No phase-out if the couple's MAGI is equal to or less than $189,000.
- Proportional phase-out of full limit for MAGI between $189,000 and $199,000.
- Full phase-out (no deduction) if MAGI is equal to or greater than $199,000.

Married taxpayers who file separately may also make deductible contributions to an IRA. The maximum deduction is the lesser of:

- $5,500 ($6,500 if taxpayer is 50+), or
- The taxpayer's earned income.

However, if either spouse is an active participant in an employer's retirement plan and they file separately, then each spouse's deductible contribution (including the nonactive participant spouse) is phased out over the spouse's MAGI as follows:

- No phase-out if the couple's MAGI is $0 (also no tax benefit of deducting).
- Proportional phase-out of full limit for MAGI between $0 and $10,000.
- Full phase-out (no deduction) if MAGI is equal to or greater than $10,000.

If the couple files separate tax returns and did not live with each other at any time during the year, both spouses will be treated as unmarried taxpayers for purposes of the IRA deduction limitations.

Nondeductible contributions.   To the extent the maximum deductible contribution is phased out based on MAGI, taxpayers can still make *nondeductible* contributions of up to $5,500 per year ($6,500 for taxpayers at least 55 years of age at year-end) subject to two limits. First, taxpayers who have reached age 70½ by year-end are not allowed to contribute to an IRA. Second, the earned income limitations (including the spousal IRA limits) that apply and limit deductible IRA contributions also apply and limit nondeductible contributions. That is, a taxpayer must have earned income in order to make nondeductible contributions to a traditional IRA (with the exception of a spouse who is contributing to a

---

[34]§219(c).

spousal IRA). Similar to the earnings on deductible contributions, the earnings on nondeductible contributions grow tax-free until the taxpayer receives distributions from the IRA. On distribution, the taxpayer is taxed on the earnings generated by the nondeductible contributions but not on the actual nondeductible contributions. When taxpayers take partial distributions from an IRA to which they have made deductible and nondeductible contributions, each distribution consists of a taxable and nontaxable component. The portion of the distribution that is nontaxable is the ratio of the nondeductible contributions to the total account balance at the time of the distribution. Most taxpayers exceeding the deductibility limits on traditional IRAs would likely do better by contributing to a Roth IRA, if eligible, instead of making nondeductible contributions to traditional IRAs.

Taxpayers who are eligible to contribute to an IRA may contribute to the IRA up to April 15 of the subsequent year (the unextended tax return due date). That is, as long as the taxpayer makes a contribution to the IRA by April 15 of year 2, the contribution counts as though it were made during year 1 (the prior calendar year).

Distributions. Just as with traditional 401(k) plans, distributions from traditional IRAs are taxed as ordinary income to the taxpayer. Also, taxpayers withdrawing funds from traditional IRAs before reaching the age of 59½ are subject to a 10 percent early distribution penalty on the amount of the withdrawal. The IRA rules exempt certain distributions from the 10 percent penalty for early withdrawal. Among others, these distributions include proceeds distributed in the form of a life annuity (fixed payment each month or year over the taxpayer's life) and proceeds used for qualifying medical expenses, health insurance premiums for the owner, qualified higher education expenses, or first-time home purchases.[35] Taxpayers are also subject to the same minimum distribution requirements applicable to traditional 401(k) and other qualified retirement plans. Because the distribution rules for traditional IRAs are so similar to the rules for traditional 401(k) accounts, taxpayers with traditional IRAs face virtually the same issues as participants in traditional 401(k) plans when planning for distributions. Thus, they should be careful to avoid the 10 percent penalty while at the same time taking similar steps to maximize the tax deferral on their traditional IRA account balances.

Roth IRAs As an alternative to traditional IRAs, taxpayers meeting certain requirements can contribute to Roth IRAs. Contributions to Roth IRAs are *not* deductible and *qualifying* distributions from Roth IRAs are *not* taxable.

Contributions. Roth IRAs are subject to the same annual contribution limits as traditional IRAs (the lesser of $5,500 [$6,500 if at least age 50 at year-end] or earned income). Further, the same spousal IRA rules that apply to traditional IRAs apply to Roth IRA contributions. These limits apply to the sum of a taxpayer's contributions to deductible IRAs, nondeductible IRAs, and Roth IRAs.

Whether or not they participate in an employer-sponsored retirement plan, the Roth IRA contribution limitation phases out based on modified AGI (MAGI) as follows:[36]

Unmarried taxpayers
- No phase-out if the taxpayer's MAGI is $120,000 or below.
- Proportional phase-out of full limit for MAGI between $120,000 and $135,000.
- Full phase-out (no contribution) if MAGI is $135,000 or higher.

Married taxpayer filing jointly
- No phase-out if the taxpayer's MAGI is $189,000 or below.
- Proportional phase-out of full limit for MAGI between $189,000 and $199,000.
- Full phase-out (no contribution) if MAGI is $199,000 or higher.

[35]§72(t).

[36]Modified AGI (MAGI) for this purpose is the same as it is for traditional IRA contributions but it excludes income from rolling over a traditional IRA to a Roth IRA. See §408A(c)(3)(B)(i).

Married taxpayers filing separately

- No phase-out if the taxpayer's MAGI is $0 (also no tax benefit of deducting).
- Proportional phase-out of full limit if taxpayer's MAGI is between $0 and $10,000.
- Full phase-out (no contribution) if taxpayer's MAGI is equal to or greater than $10,000.

Distributions. *Qualified* distributions from Roth IRAs are not taxable. A qualified distribution is a distribution from funds or earnings from funds in a Roth IRA *if the distribution is at least five years after the taxpayer opened the Roth IRA*[37] and the distribution meets one of the following requirements:

- Distribution is made on or after the date the taxpayer reaches 59½ years of age,
- Distribution is made to a beneficiary (or to the estate of the taxpayer) on or after the death of the taxpayer,
- Distribution is attributable to the taxpayer being disabled, or
- Distribution is used to pay qualified acquisition costs for first-time home buyers (limited to $10,000).[38]

All other distributions are considered to be *nonqualified* distributions.

Nonqualified distributions are not necessarily taxable, however. Because taxpayers do not deduct Roth IRA contributions, they are able to withdraw the contributions tax-free at any time. However, *nonqualified* distributions of the *earnings* of a Roth IRA are taxable as ordinary income. The distributed earnings are also subject to a 10 percent penalty unless the taxpayer is 59½ years of age at the time of the distribution. Nonqualified distributions are deemed to come:

- First from the taxpayer's contributions (nontaxable).
- Then from account earnings after the total contributions have been distributed (note that this is different from the equivalent rule for Roth 401[k] plans).

Thus, taxpayers can treat the Roth IRA as an emergency savings account to the extent of their contributions without incurring any penalties.

Example 6-16

What if: Assume that when Courtney started working she made a one-time contribution of $4,000 to a Roth IRA. Years later, she retired at the age of 65 when the value of her Roth account was $60,000. If Courtney receives a $10,000 distribution from her Roth IRA, what amount of taxes (and penalty, if applicable) must she pay on the distribution (assume her ordinary marginal tax rate is 32 percent)?

Answer: $0 taxes and $0 penalty. Qualified Roth IRA distributions are not taxable.

What if: Assume the same facts as above, except that Courtney received a $10,000 distribution when she was 57 years of age. What amount of taxes (and penalty, if applicable) is she required to pay on the distribution (assume a 32 percent ordinary marginal rate)?

Answer: $2,520 in total, consisting of $1,920 in taxes ($6,000 earnings distributed × 32 percent marginal tax rate) and $600 penalty ($6,000 earnings × 10 percent penalty rate). Because Courtney has not reached age 59½ at the time of the distribution, this is a nonqualified distribution. Consequently, she is taxed on the $6,000 distribution of earnings ($10,000 distribution minus $4,000 contribution). She is penalized on the distribution of earnings because she is not 59½ years of age at the time of the distribution.

(continued on page 6-28)

---

[37]The five-year period starts on January 1 of the year in which the contribution was made and ends on the last day of the fifth taxable year. See Reg §1.408A-6, Q&A2 and Q&A-5(b).

[38]§408A(d)(2). A first-time homebuyer is someone who did not own a principal residence in the two years before acquiring the new home [see §72(t)(2)(F)].

What if: Assume that when Courtney was 62 years old, she opened a Roth IRA, contributing $4,000. Three years later, Courtney withdrew the entire account balance of $5,000. What amount of taxes (and penalty, if applicable) must Courtney pay on the distribution (assume her marginal tax rate is 32 percent)?

Answer: $320 of taxes ($1,000 earnings × 32 percent marginal tax rate) but zero penalty. The distribution is a nonqualified distribution because Courtney did not have the Roth IRA open for five years before receiving the distribution. Consequently, she must pay tax on the $1,000 earnings portion of the distribution ($5,000 − $4,000) but she is not penalized on the distribution because she was over 59½ years of age at the time of the distribution.

In contrast to taxpayers with traditional IRAs, taxpayers are *not* required to take minimum distributions from Roth IRAs. Thus, taxpayers can minimize distributions from Roth IRAs to maintain a source of tax-free income for as long as they choose.

Rollover from traditional to Roth IRA.   Many taxpayers made contributions to traditional IRAs before Roth IRAs were available. Some taxpayers may have contributed to traditional IRAs and then later decided they should have contributed to Roth IRAs. The tax laws accommodate these taxpayers by allowing them to transfer funds from a traditional IRA (and other qualified defined contribution plans) to a Roth IRA.[39] This transfer of funds is called a **rollover.** When taxpayers do this, the entire amount taken out of the traditional IRA is taxed at ordinary rates. However, it is not subject to the 10 percent penalty tax as long as the taxpayer contributes the full amount to a Roth IRA within 60 days of the withdrawal from the traditional IRA.[40]

Example 6-17

What if: Let's assume that Courtney in prior years made fully deductible contributions of $4,000 to a traditional IRA. This year, when her marginal tax rate is 24 percent, she rolls over the entire $5,000 account balance into a Roth IRA. What amount of taxes is she required to pay on the rollover?

Answer: $1,200 ($5,000 × 24%). The entire $5,000 transferred from the IRA to the Roth IRA is taxed at 24 percent but is not subject to the 10 percent early withdrawal penalty. Even though Courtney pays $1,200 in taxes on the transfer, she is required to contribute $5,000 to the Roth IRA within 60 days from the time she withdraws the money from the traditional IRA.

What if: What are the tax consequences if Courtney pays the $1,200 tax bill and contributes only $3,800 to the Roth IRA account?

Answer: She must pay a $120 penalty. The penalty is 10 percent of the $1,200 that she withdrew from the IRA and did not contribute to the Roth IRA ($5,000 − $3,800).

Why would anyone be willing to pay taxes currently in order to avoid paying taxes later? Typically, a rollover from a traditional to a Roth IRA makes sense when a taxpayer's marginal tax rate is currently low (when the tax cost of the rollover is low) and expected to be significantly higher in the future (when the expected benefit of the rollover is high). Note that high-income taxpayers may not be allowed to contribute to Roth IRAs

---

[39]See Notice 2009-75, 2009-39 IRB.

[40]§408(d)(3). Taxpayers who roll over funds from a traditional IRA (or other traditional retirement account) to a Roth IRA must wait at least five years from the date of the rollover to withdraw the funds from the rollover in order to avoid a 10 percent penalty on the distribution [§408(d)(3)(F)].

due to the AGI restrictions on contribution limits. However, because currently there is no AGI restriction on who may roll over funds from a traditional IRA (or other qualified defined contribution plan) into a Roth IRA, high-income taxpayers who would like to fund a Roth IRA may do so through a rollover.[41]

Comparing Traditional and Roth IRAs   So, which type of IRA is better for taxpayers? In general, after-tax rates of return from traditional IRAs will exceed those from Roth IRAs when marginal tax rates decline. However, after-tax rates of return from Roth IRAs will exceed those from traditional IRAs when tax rates increase.

Unrelated to marginal tax rates, Roth IRAs have other advantages relative to traditional IRAs as follows:

- Taxpayers can contribute to Roth IRAs at any age. In contrast, taxpayers are not allowed to make deductible contributions to traditional IRAs once they have reached 70½ years of age.
- The minimum distribution requirements for traditional IRAs do not apply to Roth IRAs. This provision permits owners of Roth IRAs to use their accounts to generate tax-free returns long after retirement.
- Taxpayers can withdraw their Roth contributions tax-free at any time without paying tax or paying a penalty. Taxpayers who withdraw their traditional IRA contributions are taxed on the distribution and potentially penalized.

Exhibit 6-9 summarizes tax-related requirements for traditional and Roth IRAs.

Self-Employed Retirement Accounts   Individually managed retirement plans such as traditional and Roth IRAs are not particularly attractive to self-employed taxpayers due to the relatively low contribution limits on these plans. As such, Congress created a number of retirement savings plans targeted toward self-employed taxpayers. Two of the more popular plans for the self-employed are SEP IRAs[42] and individual (or "self-employed") 401(k) plans.[43] These are defined contribution plans that generally work the same as employer-provided plans. That is, amounts set aside in these plans are deducted from income, earnings are free from tax until distributed, and distributions from the plans are fully taxable.[44]

Moving Expenses

For years prior to 2018, moving expenses associated with changing a taxpayer's principal place of work were deductible subject to a distance test and a time employed test associated with the move. For years after 2017, moving expenses generally are not deductible

---

[41] §408A(c)(3).

[42] For 2018, the annual contribution to SEP IRAs is limited to the *lesser* of (a) $55,000 or (b) 20 percent of Schedule C net income (after reducing Schedule C net income by the deduction for the employer's portion of self-employment taxes paid). Contributions can be made up to the extended due date of the tax return. The Individual Income Tax Computation and Tax Credits chapter addresses self-employment taxes in more detail.

[43] For 2018, a sole proprietor can contribute the lesser of (a) $55,000 or (b) the sum of (i) 20 percent of Schedule C net income (after reducing Schedule C net income by the deduction of the employer's portion of self-employment taxes paid) (employer's contribution) and (ii) $18,500 (employee's contribution). Further, if the sole proprietor is at least 50 years of age by the end of the tax year, she may contribute an additional $6,000 (as a catch-up contribution). However, total contributions may not exceed the taxpayer's Schedule C net income minus the self-employment tax deduction.

[44] Savings Incentive Match Plans for Employees (SIMPLE) IRA or "Keogh" self-employed defined benefit plans are also options for the self-employed. For those earning lower amounts of self-employment income, the contribution limits for a SIMPLE IRA tend to be higher than contribution limits for SEP IRAs. Keogh plans are attractive to older, self-employed individuals with profitable businesses because they allow for greater deductible contributions. However, Keogh plans are usually more costly to maintain than the defined contribution plans.

EXHIBIT 6-9 Traditional IRA versus Roth IRA Summary

	Traditional IRA	Roth IRA
Contributions requirements	• Taxpayer must not be a participant in an employer-sponsored plan or, if participating in an employer-provided plan, must meet certain income thresholds. Those above the threshold will have deductible portion of contribution phased out.	• No deduction allowed for contributions. Must meet certain income requirements to be able to contribute to a Roth IRA.
Contributions	• Deductible unless participant in employer plan and high AGI. • Nondeductible contributions allowed.	• Not deductible. • May not contribute if high AGI.
Maximum contribution	• Lesser of $5,500 per taxpayer ($6,500 for taxpayers over 50 years old) or earned income.	• Same as traditional IRA.
	• The contribution limits apply to the sum of contributions to traditional deductible IRAs, nondeductible IRAs, and Roth IRAs for the year.	• Same as traditional IRA.
	• For married couples filing jointly, contributions for the lesser earning spouse may not exceed the total earned income of both spouses reduced by deductible and nondeductible contributions to the other spouse's traditional IRA and by contributions to the other spouse's Roth IRA.	• Same as traditional IRA.
Contribution dates	• Can contribute up to unextended tax return due date—generally April 15.	• Same as traditional IRA.
Distributions	• Generally taxed as ordinary income. • If made before 59½, generally subject to 10 percent penalty. • If nondeductible contribution made, allocate distribution between taxable and nontaxable amounts similar to annuity rules. • Minimum distributions required by April 1 of the later of (1) the year after the year in which the taxpayer reaches 70½ or (2) the year after the year in which the taxpayer retires. • Failure to meet minimum distribution timing and amount requirements triggers 50 percent penalty.	• Qualified distributions not taxed. • Generally, distributions are qualified after account has been open for five years and employee has reached the age of 59½. • Nonqualified distributions not taxed to extent of prior contributions. • Nonqualified distributions of earnings subject to tax at ordinary rates and also subject to a 10 percent penalty if the taxpayer is not at least 59½ years of age at the time of the distribution. • No minimum distribution requirements.

(and employer reimbursements of moving expenses are taxable). The lone exception is for members of the Armed Forces (or their spouse or dependents) on active duty that move pursuant to a military order and incident to a permanent change of station. Their moving costs are nontaxable if paid by their employer and deductible if the costs are not paid by their employer.[45]

[45]§217.

Example 6-18

This year, Courtney moved from Cincinnati to Kansas City, her new place of work with EWD. She incurred considerable expenses associated with the move (none were reimbursed). Can Courtney deduct the expenses of moving her residence to Kansas City?

Answer: No. Because Courtney does not meet the exception for members of the Armed Forces (or their spouse or dependents) on active duty, she cannot deduct the moving costs.

Health Insurance Deduction by Self-Employed Taxpayers

The cost of health insurance is essentially a personal expense. However, *employers* often pay a portion of health insurance premiums for employees as a qualified fringe benefit. Employers are allowed to deduct health insurance premiums as compensation expense, while employees are allowed to *exclude* these premiums from gross income. The health insurance fringe benefit does not apply to self-employed taxpayers because they are not "employees." So to provide equitable treatment, Congress allows self-employed taxpayers to claim personal health insurance premiums for the taxpayer, the taxpayer's spouse, the taxpayer's dependents, and the taxpayer's children under age 27 (regardless of whether the child is a dependent of the taxpayer) as deductions *for* AGI, but only to the extent of the self-employment income derived from the specific trade or business.[46]

This deduction is intended to help self-employed taxpayers who must pay their own insurance premiums. Consequently, self-employed taxpayers are *not* allowed to deduct health care insurance premiums if the taxpayer is *eligible* to participate in an employer-provided health plan. This restriction applies regardless of whether the health plan is sponsored by either an employer of the taxpayer or an employer of the taxpayer's spouse, and it is irrelevant whether the taxpayer actually participates in the plan.[47]

Self-Employment Tax Deduction

Employees and employers each pay Social Security and Medicare tax on employee salaries. Employers deduct the Social Security and Medicare taxes they pay on employee salaries. In contrast, because self-employed individuals do not have an employer, these individuals are required to pay self-employment tax. This tax represents both the employee's *and* the employer's share of the Social Security and Medicare taxes. Unfortunately for the self-employed, the self-employment tax is *not* considered a business expense. To put self-employed individuals on somewhat equal footing with other employers who are allowed to deduct the *employer's* share of the Social Security and Medicare taxes, however, self-employed taxpayers are allowed to deduct the employer portion of the self-employment tax they pay.

---

[46]§162(l). As we'll explain shortly, health insurance premiums also qualify as itemized deductions as medical expenses, but itemizing these deductions may not produce any tax benefits. To the extent that self-employed taxpayers do not have sufficient self-employment income to deduct all of their health insurance premiums as a *for* AGI deduction, they may deduct the remaining premiums as an itemized deduction. Finally, subject to certain restrictions, self-employed taxpayers who purchase health insurance through an exchange, have household incomes below 400 percent of the poverty line, and are not eligible for affordable coverage through an employer health plan that provides at least 60 percent of the expected costs for covered services can receive a premium tax credit under §36B. Any premiums offset by the tax credit cannot be deducted as either a *for* AGI or itemized deduction.

[47]§162(l)(2)(B).

Example 6-19

As we indicated in Example 6-2, Courtney reported $18,000 of net income from her self-employed consulting activities. She will pay $482 in self-employment taxes on this income, with $241 representing the employer portion of the self-employment tax.[48] What amount of self-employment tax can she deduct this year?

Answer: $241 (the employer portion of the self-employment tax).

Penalty for Early Withdrawal of Savings

Taxpayers are allowed a deduction *for* AGI for any interest income an individual forfeits to a bank as a penalty for prematurely withdrawing a certificate of deposit or similar deposit. This deduction reduces the taxpayer's net interest income to the amount she actually received. Otherwise, taxpayers would be required to report the full amount of interest income as taxable income and unfortunately, the forfeited interest would be a nondeductible investment expense.

Example 6-20

Gram invested $100,000 in a three-year certificate of deposit (CD). On December 31, she decides to cash out the certificate of deposit after holding it for less than a year. She receives the $4,100 of interest income the CD had generated up to the withdrawal date, less a $410 early withdrawal penalty. How will Gram report the interest and early withdrawal for tax purposes?

Answer: Gram reports $4,100 as interest income this year and deducts the $410 early withdrawal penalty as a deduction *for* AGI.

THE KEY FACTS

Interest on Education Loans

- Up to $2,500 of interest on education loans is deductible *for* AGI.
- A loan qualifies as an education loan if the proceeds are used to fund qualified education.
- The interest deduction is phased out for taxpayers with AGI exceeding $65,000 ($135,000 if married filing jointly).

DEDUCTIONS SUBSIDIZING SPECIFIC ACTIVITIES

To address specific policy objectives, Congress provides that certain expenditures are deductible *for* AGI. For example, alimony payments paid pursuant to divorce or separation agreements executed before 2019 are deductible for AGI to maintain equity given that these payments are taxable to the recipient. In contrast, contributions to retirement savings are deductible *for* AGI to encourage savings.[49] Further, Congress created a deduction *for* AGI to encourage and subsidize higher education. Taxpayers are allowed to deduct *for* AGI, subject to certain limitations, interest expense on **qualified educational loans.**[50] As we discuss throughout the text, Congress has also created a number of related provisions, including education tax credits, to encourage and subsidize higher education.

---

[48]In this case, Courtney uses the following equation to determine her total self-employment tax: $18,000 × .9235 × .029 (Courtney's business income is subject to the Medicare tax but not the Social Security tax due to the level of her salary). Of the total self-employment tax, the employer portion is calculated as $18,000 × .9235 × .0145 = $241. We discuss how to compute the self-employment tax in detail in the Individual Income Tax Computation and Tax Credits chapter.

[49]See the Gross Income and Exclusions chapter for a detailed discussion of alimony.

[50]See §221. For years prior to 2018, taxpayers could also deduct tuition and fees paid for the taxpayer or dependent at a postsecondary institution of higher education. The deduction was limited (maximum of $4,000) and subject to a phase-out based upon the taxpayer's AGI (with modification). At press time, this deduction has not been extended to years after 2017. See §222.

Deduction for Interest on Qualified Education Loans

Qualified education loans are loans whose proceeds are used to pay qualified education expenses. Qualified education expenses encompass expenses paid for the education of the taxpayer, the taxpayer's spouse, or a taxpayer's dependent to attend a postsecondary institution of higher education.[51] These expenses include tuition and fees, books and expenses required for enrollment, room and board, and other necessary supplies and expenses, including travel.

The deduction for interest expense on qualified education loans is the amount of interest paid up to $2,500. However, the deduction is reduced (phased out) for taxpayers depending on the taxpayer's filing status and modified AGI. Modified AGI for this purpose is AGI *before* deducting interest expense on the qualified education loans. Married individuals who file separately are not allowed to deduct this expense under any circumstance. The deduction limitations for other taxpayers are summarized in Exhibit 6-10 as follows:

EXHIBIT 6-10 **Summary of Limitations on Deduction of Interest on Education Loans**

Panel A: AGI Limitations	
Modified AGI Level	**Maximum Deduction**
Not over $65,000 ($135,000 for married filing jointly)	Amount paid up to $2,500.
Above $65,000 ($135,000 for married filing jointly) but below $80,000 ($165,000 for married filing jointly)	Amount paid up to $2,500 reduced by the phase-out amount. The phase-out amount is the amount paid up to $2,500 times the phase-out percentage (see Panel B for the phase-out percentage computation).
Equal to or above $80,000 ($165,000 for married filing jointly)	Zero

Panel B: Phase-Out Percentage*	
Filing Status	**Phase-Out Percentage**
Single or head of household	(Modified AGI − $65,000)/$15,000
Married filing jointly	(Modified AGI − $135,000)/$30,000

*Married taxpayers filing separately are ineligible for the deduction.

Example 6-21

What if: Assume that Courtney's brother Jason paid interest on a qualified education loan that he used to pay the tuition and fees for his three daughters to attend State University. In 2018, Jason was married and filed a joint return, paid $2,000 of interest expense on the loan, and reported modified AGI of $147,000. What amount of interest expense on the education loan is Jason allowed to deduct as a *for* AGI deduction?

(continued on page 6-34)

[51]Postsecondary education includes courses at a university, college, or vocational school, including internship programs leading to a degree or certificate.

Answer: $1,200, computed as follows:

Description	Amount	Explanation
(1) Modified AGI	$147,000	AGI before higher education deductions
(2) Amount of interest paid up to $2,500	2,000	Lesser of amount paid ($2,000) or $2,500
(3) Phase-out (reduction) percentage	40%	[(1) − $135,000]/$30,000
(4) Phase-out amount (reduction in maximum)	$ 800	(2) × (3)
Deductible interest expense	**$ 1,200**	(2) − (4)

Summary: Deductions *for* AGI

Business expenses and rental and royalty expenses are two of the most important deductions *for* AGI. There are other important deductions *for* AGI that are indirectly related to business or provided to subsidize certain activities. After we have determined the deductions *for* AGI, we can compute AGI. Exhibits 6-11 and 6-12 summarize the computation of AGI for Courtney and Gram. Exhibit 6-13 shows Courtney's AGI calculation as presented on the front page of her Form 1040.

EXHIBIT 6-11   **Courtney's Adjusted Gross Income**

Description	Amount	Reference
Gross income for current year	$197,741	Exhibit 5-5 and related discussion
Deductions *for* AGI:		
Business expenses	(1,500)	Example 6-2
Rental expenses	(9,000)	Example 6-3
Employer-portion of self-employment taxes	(241)	Example 6-19
Adjusted gross income	**$187,000**	

EXHIBIT 6-12   **Gram's Adjusted Gross Income**

Description	Amount	Reference
Gross income for current year	$ 16,000	Exhibit 5-7
Deduction *for* AGI:		
Penalty for early withdrawal of savings	(410)	Example 6-20
Adjusted gross income	**$15,590**	

CONCLUSION

We started this chapter with Courtney and Gram's gross incomes. In this chapter, we identified the duo's separate deductions *for* AGI and we computed their AGI. With this knowledge, we proceed to the next chapter and identify the *from* AGI deductions for Courtney and Gram. This will allow us to calculate their taxable income.

EXHIBIT 6-13   Courtney's AGI Computation on Form 1040, Page 1

Income	7	Wages, salaries, tips, etc. Attach Form(s) W-2		7	142,800
	8a	**Taxable** interest. Attach Schedule B if required		8a	321
	b	**Tax-exempt** interest. **Do not** include on line 8a . . .	**8b** 500		
Attach Form(s)	9a	Ordinary dividends. Attach Schedule B if required		9a	700
W-2 here. Also	b	Qualified dividends	**9b** 700		
attach Forms	10	Taxable refunds, credits, or offsets of state and local income taxes		10	420
W-2G and	11	Alimony received		11	20,000
1099-R if tax	12	Business income or (loss). Attach Schedule C or C-EZ		12	18,000
was withheld.	13	Capital gain or (loss). Attach Schedule D if required. If not required, check here ▶ ☐		13	
If you did not	14	Other gains or (losses). Attach Form 4797		14	
get a W-2,	15a	IRA distributions .	**15a**	b Taxable amount . . .	15b	
see instructions.	16a	Pensions and annuities	**16a**	b Taxable amount . . .	16b	
	17	Rental real estate, royalties, partnerships, S corporations, trusts, etc. Attach Schedule E		17	5,000
	18	Farm income or (loss). Attach Schedule F		18	
	19	Unemployment compensation		19	
	20a	Social security benefits	**20a**	b Taxable amount . . .	20b	
	21	Other income. List type and amount _____		21	
	22	Combine the amounts in the far right column for lines 7 through 21. This is your **total income** ▶		22	187,241
Adjusted	23	Educator expenses	**23**		
Gross	24	Certain business expenses of reservists, performing artists, and			
Income		fee-basis government officials. Attach Form 2106 or 2106-EZ	**24**		
	25	Health savings account deduction. Attach Form 8889 .	**25**		
	26	Moving expenses. Attach Form 3903	**26**		
	27	Deductible part of self-employment tax. Attach Schedule SE .	**27** 241		
	28	Self-employed SEP, SIMPLE, and qualified plans . .	**28**		
	29	Self-employed health insurance deduction	**29**		
	30	Penalty on early withdrawal of savings	**30**		
	31a	Alimony paid **b** Recipient's SSN ▶	**31a**		
	32	IRA deduction	**32**		
	33	Student loan interest deduction	**33**		
	34	Reserved for future use	**34**		
	35	Domestic production activities deduction. Attach Form 8903	**35**		
	36	Add lines 23 through 35		36	241
	37	Subtract line 36 from line 22. This is your **adjusted gross income** . . . . . ▶		37	187,000

Summary

Identify *for* AGI deductions directly related to business activities.   **LO 6-1**

- The deductions *for* AGI directly related to business activities include business expenses, rent and royalty expenses, losses from the disposition of business assets, and expenses and losses incurred by flow-through entities.
- Business deductions are reported with business revenues on Schedule C.
- Rent and royalty expenses and expenses and losses incurred by flow-through entities, which pass through to their owners, are reported on Schedule E.

Describe the loss limitation rules for passive activities, the rental use of a home, and home office   **LO 6-2**
deductions.

- A taxpayer's share of operating losses from flow-through entities and other trade or business activities are deductible to the extent they clear the tax-basis, at-risk, and passive activity loss hurdles. In addition, for losses that clear each of the three separate hurdles, taxpayers are not allowed to deduct excess business losses.
- A taxpayer's passive losses from an activity are limited to passive income from all other sources until disposition of the activity. On disposition, current and prior passive losses from an activity can be used without limitation.
- The tax treatment of the rental use of a home depends on amount of personal and rental use. The three categories are (1) residence with minimal rental use (personal residence with rental excluded and no deduction for rental expenses), (2) residence with significant rental use (vacation home with expenses allocated between personal use and rental use; rental deductions limited to rental revenue), and (3) nonresidence (rental property subject to passive loss rules).

- To deduct expenses relating to a home office, the taxpayer must use the home office exclusively and regularly for business purposes. The home office deduction cannot exceed the taxpayer's net Schedule C income (before home office expenses) minus the mortgage interest and real property taxes allocated to business use of the home. Special rules apply for taxpayers electing to claim home office expenses under the simplified method.

LO 6-3 Explain *for* AGI deductions indirectly related to business activities and *for* AGI deductions that subsidize specific activities.

- The *for* AGI deductions indirectly related to business activities include the deduction for IRA contributions, medical and health insurance by self-employed taxpayers, self-employment taxes, and forfeited interest.

- Other common deductions *for* AGI include the deductions for interest on student loans and the early withdrawal penalties.

KEY TERMS

active participant in a rental activity (6-10)
at-risk rules (6-7)
business activities (6-2)
excess business loss (6-11)

flow-through entity (6-6)
home office deductions (6-17)
investment activities (6-2)
ordinary and necessary (6-4)
passive activity loss (PAL) rules (6-8)

qualified educational loans (6-32)
rollover (6-28)
Roth IRAs (6-23)
trade or business (6-2)
traditional IRAs (6-23)

DISCUSSION QUESTIONS

Discussion Questions are available in Connect®.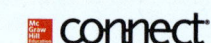

LO 6-1 1. It has been suggested that tax policy favors deductions *for* AGI compared to itemized deductions. Describe two ways in which deductions *for* AGI are treated more favorably than itemized deductions.

LO 6-1 2. How is a business activity distinguished from an investment activity? Why is this distinction important for the purpose of calculating federal income taxes?

LO 6-2 3. What types of losses may potentially be characterized as passive losses?

LO 6-2 4. What are the implications of treating losses as passive?

LO 6-2 5. What tests are applied to determine if losses should be characterized as passive?

planning **LO 6-2** 6. All else being equal, would a taxpayer with passive losses rather have wage income or passive income?

planning **LO 6-2** 7. Is it possible for a taxpayer to receive rental income that is not subject to taxation? Explain.

LO 6-2 8. Halle just acquired a vacation home. She plans on spending several months each year vacationing in the home and renting the property for the rest of the year. She is projecting tax losses on the rental portion of the property for the year. She is not too concerned about the losses because she is confident she will be able to use the losses to offset her income from other sources. Is her confidence misplaced? Explain.

planning **LO 6-2** 9. A taxpayer stays in a second home for the entire month of September. He would like the home to fall into the residence with significant rental use category for tax purposes. What is the maximum number of days he can rent out the home and have it qualify?

LO 6-2 10. Compare and contrast the IRS method and the Tax Court method for allocating expenses between personal use and rental use for vacation homes. Include the Tax Court's justification for departing from the IRS method in your answer.

11. In what circumstances is the IRS method for allocating expenses between personal use and rental use for second homes more beneficial to a taxpayer than the Tax Court method? `LO 6-2`

12. Under what circumstances would a taxpayer who generates a loss from renting a home that is not a residence be able to fully deduct the loss? What potential limitations apply? `LO 6-2`

13. Describe the circumstances in which a taxpayer acquires a home and rents it out and is not allowed to deduct a portion of the interest expense on the loan the taxpayer used to acquire the home. `LO 6-2`

14. Is it possible for a rental property to generate a positive annual cash flow and at the same time produce a loss for tax purposes? Explain. `LO 6-2`

15. How are the tax issues associated with home offices and vacation homes used as rentals similar? How are the tax issues or requirements dissimilar? `LO 6-2`

16. For taxpayers qualifying for home office deductions, what are considered to be indirect expenses of maintaining the home? How are these expenses allocated to personal and home office use? `LO 6-2`

17. What limitations exist for self-employed taxpayers in deducting home office expenses, and how does the taxpayer determine which expenses are deductible and which are not in situations when the overall amount of the home office deduction is limited? `LO 6-2`

18. What are the primary tax differences between traditional IRAs and Roth IRAs? `LO 6-3`

19. Describe the circumstances in which it would be more favorable for a taxpayer to contribute to a traditional IRA rather than a Roth IRA and vice versa. `LO 6-3`

20. What are the requirements for a taxpayer to make a deductible contribution to a traditional IRA? Why do the tax laws impose these restrictions? `LO 6-3`

21. What is the limitation on a deductible IRA contribution for 2018? `LO 6-3`

22. Compare the minimum distribution requirements for traditional IRAs to those of Roth IRAs. `LO 6-3`

23. How are qualified distributions from Roth IRAs taxed? How are nonqualified distributions taxed? `LO 6-3`

24. Explain when a taxpayer will be subject to the 10 percent penalty when receiving distributions from a Roth IRA. `LO 6-3`

25. Is a taxpayer who has contributed to a traditional IRA able to transfer or "roll over" the money into a Roth IRA? If yes, explain the tax consequences of the transfer. `LO 6-3`

26. Assume a taxpayer makes a nondeductible contribution to a traditional IRA. How does the taxpayer determine the taxability of distributions from the IRA on reaching retirement? `LO 6-3`

27. When a taxpayer takes a nonqualified distribution from a Roth IRA, is the entire amount of the distribution treated as taxable income? `LO 6-3`

28. Explain why Congress allows self-employed taxpayers to deduct the cost of health insurance above the line (*for* AGI) when employees can only itemize this cost as a medical expense. Would a self-employed taxpayer ever prefer to claim health insurance premiums as an itemized deduction rather than as a deduction *for* AGI? Explain. `LO 6-3`

29. Explain why Congress allows self-employed taxpayers to deduct the employer portion of their self-employment tax. `LO 6-3`

30. Using the Internal Revenue Code, describe two deductions *for* AGI that are not discussed in this chapter. `LO 6-3` **research**

31. Explain why Congress allows taxpayers to deduct interest forfeited as a penalty on the premature withdrawal from a certificate of deposit. `LO 6-3`

32. Describe the mechanical limitation on the deduction for interest on qualified educational loans. `LO 6-3`

PROBLEMS

Select problems are available in Connect®.

tax forms

LO 6-1

33. Betty operates a beauty salon as a sole proprietorship. Betty also owns and rents an apartment building. This year Betty had the following income and expenses. Determine Betty's AGI and complete page 1 of Form 1040 for Betty. You may assume that Betty will owe $2,502 in self-employment tax on her salon income, with $1,251 representing the employer portion of the self-employment tax. You may also assume that her divorce from Rocky was finalized in 2016.

Interest income	$11,255
Salon sales and revenue	86,360
Salaries paid to beauticians	45,250
Beauty salon supplies	23,400
Alimony paid to her ex-husband, Rocky	6,000
Rental revenue from apartment building	31,220
Depreciation on apartment building	12,900
Real estate taxes paid on apartment building	11,100
Real estate taxes paid on personal residence	6,241
Contributions to charity	4,237

LO 6-2

34. Larry recently invested $20,000 (tax basis) in purchasing a limited partnership interest in which he will have no management rights in the company. His at-risk amount is also $20,000. In addition, Larry's share of the limited partnership loss for the year is $2,000, his share of income from a different limited partnership is $1,000, and he has $3,000 of dividend income from the stock he owns. How much of Larry's $2,000 loss from the limited partnership can he deduct in the current year?

LO 6-2

35. Rubio recently invested $20,000 (tax basis) in purchasing a limited partnership interest in which he will have no management rights in the company. His at-risk amount is $15,000. In addition, Rubio's share of the limited partnership loss for the year is $22,000, his share of income from a different limited partnership is $5,000, and he has $40,000 in wage income and $10,000 in long-term capital gains.

a) How much of Rubio's $22,000 loss is allowed considering only the tax-basis loss limitations?

b) How much of the loss from part (a) is allowed under the at-risk limitations?

c) How much of Rubio's $22,000 loss from the limited partnership can he deduct in the current year considering all limitations?

LO 6-2

36. Anwar owns a rental home and is involved in maintaining it and approving renters. During the year he has a net loss of $8,000 from renting the home. His other sources of income during the year were a salary of $111,000 and $34,000 of long-term capital gains. How much of Anwar's $8,000 rental loss can he deduct currently if he has no sources of passive income?

LO 6-2

37. Dillon rented his personal residence at Lake Tahoe for 14 days while he was vacationing in Ireland. He resided in the home for the remainder of the year. Rental income from the property was $6,500. Expenses associated with use of the home for the entire year were as follows:

Real property taxes	$ 3,100
Mortgage interest	12,000
Repairs	1,500
Insurance	1,500
Utilities	3,900
Depreciation	13,000

a) What effect does the rental have on Dillon's AGI?

b) What effect does the rental have on Dillon's itemized deductions?

Use the following facts to answer problems 38 and 39.

Natalie owns a condominium near Cocoa Beach in Florida. This year, she incurs the following expenses in connection with her condo:

Insurance	$1,000
Advertising expense	500
Mortgage interest	3,500
Property taxes	900
Repairs and maintenance	650
Utilities	950
Depreciation	8,500

During the year, Natalie rented out the condo for 75 days, receiving $10,000 of gross income. She personally used the condo for 35 days during her vacation. Assume there are 365 days in the year.

38. Assume Natalie uses the IRS method of allocating expenses to rental use of the property.   `LO 6-2`

     a) What is the total amount of *for* AGI (rental) deductions Natalie may deduct in the current year related to the condo?

     b) What is the total amount of itemized deductions Natalie may deduct in the current year related to the condo?

     c) If Natalie's basis in the condo at the beginning of the year was $150,000, what is her basis in the condo at the end of the year?

     d) Assume that gross rental revenue was $1,000 (rather than $10,000). What amount of *for* AGI deductions may Natalie deduct in the current year related to the condo?

39. Assume Natalie uses the Tax Court method of allocating expenses to rental use of the property.   `LO 6-2`

     a) What is the total amount of *for* AGI (rental) deductions Natalie may deduct in the current year related to the condo?

     b) What is the total amount of itemized deductions Natalie may deduct in the current year related to the condo?

     c) If Natalie's basis in the condo at the beginning of the year was $150,000, what is her basis in the condo at the end of the year?

     d) Assume that gross rental revenue was $2,000 (rather than $10,000). What amount of *for* AGI deductions may Natalie deduct in the current year related to the condo?

Use the following facts to answer problems 40–42.

Alexa owns a condominium near Cocoa Beach in Florida. This year, she incurs the following expenses in connection with her condo:

Insurance	$ 2,000
Mortgage interest	6,500
Property taxes	2,000
Repairs and maintenance	1,400
Utilities	2,500
Depreciation	14,500

During the year, Alexa rented out the condo for 100 days. She did not use the condo at all for personal purposes during the year. Alexa's AGI from all sources other than the rental property is $200,000. Unless otherwise specified, Alexa has no sources of passive income. Assume there are 365 days in the year.

40. Assume Alexa receives $30,000 in gross rental receipts.   `LO 6-2`

     a) What effect do the expenses associated with the property have on her AGI?

     b) What effect do the expenses associated with the property have on her itemized deductions?

LO 6-2

41. Assuming Alexa receives $20,000 in gross rental receipts, answer the following questions:

    a) What effect does the rental activity have on her AGI for the year?

    b) Assuming that Alexa's AGI from other sources is $90,000, what effect does the rental activity have on Alexa's AGI? Alexa makes all decisions with respect to the property.

    c) Assuming that Alexa's AGI from other sources is $120,000, what effect does the rental activity have on Alexa's AGI? Alexa makes all decisions with respect to the property.

    d) Assume that Alexa's AGI from other sources is $200,000. This consists of $150,000 salary, $10,000 of dividends, $25,000 of long-term capital gain, and net rental income from another rental property in the amount of $15,000. What effect does the Cocoa Beach condo rental activity have on Alexa's AGI?

LO 6-2

42. Assume that in addition to renting the condo for 100 days, Alexa uses the condo for 8 days of personal use. Also assume that Alexa receives $30,000 of gross rental receipts. Answer the following questions:

    a) What is the total amount of *for* AGI deductions relating to the condo that Alexa may deduct in the current year? Assume she uses the IRS method of allocating expenses between rental and personal days.

    b) What is the total amount of *from* AGI deductions relating to the condo that Alexa may deduct in the current year? Assume she uses the IRS method of allocating expenses between rental and personal days.

    c) Would Alexa be better or worse off after taxes if she uses the Tax Court method of allocating expenses?

LO 6-2

tax forms

43. Brooke owns a sole proprietorship in which she works as a management consultant. She maintains an office in her home where she meets with clients, prepares bills, and performs other work-related tasks. The home office is 300 square feet and the entire house is 4,500 square feet. Brooke incurred the following home-related expenses during the year. Unless indicated otherwise, assume Brooke uses the actual expense method to compute home office expenses.

Real property taxes	$ 3,600
Interest on home mortgage	14,000
Operating expenses of home	5,000
Depreciation	12,000
Repairs to home theater room	1,000

    a) What amount of each of these expenses is allocated to the home office?

    b) What are the total amounts of tier 1, tier 2, and tier 3 expenses, respectively, allocated to the home office?

    c) If Brooke reported $2,000 of Schedule C income before the home office expense deduction, what is the amount of her home office expense deduction and what home office expenses, if any, would she carry over to next year?

    d) Assuming Brooke reported $2,000 of Schedule C income before the home office expense deduction, complete Form 8829 for Brooke's home office expense deduction. Also assume the value of the home is $500,000 and the adjusted basis of the home (exclusive of land) is $468,019.

    e) Assume that Brooke uses the simplified method for computing home office expenses. If Brooke reported $2,000 of Schedule C income before the home office expense deduction, what is the amount of her home office expense deduction and what home office expenses, if any, would she carry over to next year?

Use the following facts to answer problems 44 and 45.

Rita owns a sole proprietorship in which she works as a management consultant. She maintains an office in her home (500 square feet) where she meets with clients, prepares bills, and performs other work-related tasks. Her business expenses, other than home office expenses, total $5,600. The following home-related expenses have been allocated to her home office under the actual expense method for calculating home office expenses.

Real property taxes	$1,600
Interest on home mortgage	5,100
Operating expenses of home	800
Depreciation	1,600

Also, assume that not counting the sole proprietorship, Rita's AGI is $60,000.

44. Assume Rita's consulting business generated $15,000 in gross income.

    a) What is Rita's home office deduction for the current year? (Answer for both the actual expense method and the simplified method).

    b) What would Rita's home office deduction be if her business generated $10,000 of gross income instead of $15,000? (Answer for both the actual expense method and the simplified method.)

    c) Given the original facts, what is Rita's AGI for the year?

    d) Given the original facts, what types and amounts of expenses will she carry over to next year?

45. Assume Rita's consulting business generated $13,000 in gross income for the current year. Further, assume Rita uses the actual expense method for computing her home office expense deduction.

    a) What is Rita's home office deduction for the current year?

    b) What is Rita's AGI for the year?

46. Boodeesh is contemplating running a consulting business out of her home. She has a large garage apartment in her backyard that would be perfect for her business. Given that the garage apartment is separate from her house (about 30 feet behind her house) would the office be considered part of her home for purposes of the home office rules?

47. Don Juan, a single taxpayer, is the sole owner, of DJ's Inc., an S Corporation. This year, DJ's Inc. incurred a massive $600,000 business loss, all of which is allocable to Don Juan as the sole shareholder. Assume that the $600,000 loss is not limited by the basis, at-risk, or passive loss rules, and that Don Juan has no other business income or business losses. How much of the $600,000 loss will Don Juan be able to deduct this year? What happens to any loss not deducted this year?

48. Clem is married and is a skilled carpenter. Clem's wife, Wanda, works part-time as a substitute grade school teacher. Determine the amount of Clem's expenses that are deductible *for* AGI this year (if any) under the following circumstances:

    a) Clem is self-employed and this year he incurred $525 in expenses for tools and supplies related to his job. Since neither were covered by a qualified health plan, Wanda paid health insurance premiums of $3,600 to provide coverage for herself and Clem (not through an exchange).

    b) Clem and Wanda own a garage downtown that they rent to a local business for storage. This year they incurred expenses of $1,250 in utilities and $780 in depreciation.

    c) Clem paid self-employment tax of $15,300 (the employer portion is $7,650), and Wanda had $3,000 of Social Security taxes withheld from her pay.

    d) Clem paid $45 to rent a safe deposit box to store his coin collection. Clem has collected coins intermittently since he was a boy, and he expects to sell his collection when he retires.

LO 6-3   49. Smithers is a self-employed individual who earns $30,000 per year in self-employment income. Smithers pays $2,200 in annual health insurance premiums (not through an exchange) for his own medical care. In each of the following situations, determine the amount of the deductible health insurance premium for Smithers before any AGI limitation.

a) Smithers is single and the self-employment income is his only source of income.

b) Smithers is single, but besides being self-employed, Smithers is also employed part-time by SF Power Corporation. This year Smithers elected not to participate in SF's health plan.

c) Smithers is self-employed and he is also married. Smithers's spouse, Samantha, is employed full-time by SF Power Corporation and is covered by SF's health plan. Smithers is not eligible to participate in SF's health plan.

d) Smithers is self-employed and he is also married. Smithers' spouse, Samantha, is employed full-time by SF Power Corporation and is covered by SF's health plan. Smithers elected not to participate in SF's health plan.

LO 6-3   50. Hardaway earned $100,000 of compensation this year. He also paid (or had paid for him) $3,000 of health insurance (not through an exchange). What is Hardaway's AGI in each of the following situations (ignore the effects of Social Security and self-employment taxes)?

a) Hardaway is an employee and his employer paid Hardaway's $3,000 of health insurance for him as a nontaxable fringe benefit. Consequently, Hardaway received $97,000 of taxable compensation and $3,000 of nontaxable compensation.

b) Hardaway is a self-employed taxpayer, and he paid $3,000 of health insurance himself. He is not eligible to participate in an employer-sponsored plan.

LO 6-3   51. John (age 51 and single) has earned income of $3,000. He has $30,000 of unearned (capital gain) income.

a) If he does not participate in an employer-sponsored plan, what is the maximum deductible IRA contribution John can make in 2018?

b) If he does participate in an employer-sponsored plan, what is the maximum deductible IRA contribution John can make in 2018?

c) If he does not participate in an employer-sponsored plan, what is the maximum deductible IRA contribution John can make in 2018 if he has earned income of $10,000?

LO 6-3   52. William is a single writer (age 35) who recently decided that he needs to save more for retirement. His 2018 AGI is $67,000 (all earned income).

a) If he does not participate in an employer-sponsored plan, what is the maximum deductible IRA contribution William can make in 2018?

b) If he does participate in an employer-sponsored plan, what is the maximum deductible IRA contribution William can make in 2018?

c) Assuming the same facts as in part (b) except his AGI is $76,000, what is the maximum deductible IRA contribution William can make in 2018?

LO 6-3   53. In 2018, Susan (44 years old) is a highly successful architect and is covered by an employee-sponsored plan. Her husband, Dan (47 years old), however, is a PhD student and is unemployed. Compute the maximum deductible IRA contribution for each spouse in the following alternative situations.

a) Susan's salary and the couple's AGI is $200,000. The couple files a joint tax return.

b) Susan's salary and the couple's AGI is $122,000. The couple files a joint tax return.

c) Susan's salary and the couple's AGI is $80,000. The couple files a joint tax return.

d) Susan's salary and her AGI is $80,000. Dan reports $5,000 of AGI (earned income). The couple files separate tax returns.

54. In 2018, Rashaun (62 years old) retired and planned on immediately receiving distributions (making withdrawals) from his traditional IRA account. The current balance of his IRA account is $160,000. Over the years, Rashaun has contributed $40,000 to the IRA. Of his $40,000 contributions, $30,000 was *nondeductible* and $10,000 was *deductible*.

   LO 6-3

   tax forms

   a) If Rashaun currently withdraws $20,000 from the IRA, how much tax will he be required to pay on the withdrawal if his marginal tax rate is 22 percent?

   b) If Rashaun currently withdraws $70,000 from the IRA, how much tax will he be required to pay on the withdrawal if his marginal tax rate is 32 percent?

   c) Using the information provided in part (b), complete Form 8606, Part I, to report the taxable portion of the $70,000 distribution (withdrawal). Use the most recent form available.

55. Brooklyn has been contributing to a traditional IRA for seven years (all deductible contributions) and has a total of $30,000 in the account. In 2018, she is 39 years old and has decided that she wants to get a new car. She withdraws $20,000 from the IRA to help pay for the car. She is currently in the 24 percent marginal tax bracket. What amount of the withdrawal, after tax considerations, will Brooklyn have available to purchase the car?

   LO 6-3

56. Jackson and Ashley Turner (both 45 years old) are married and want to contribute to a Roth IRA for Ashley. In 2018, their AGI is $170,000. Jackson and Ashley each earned half of the income.

   LO 6-3

   a) How much can Ashley contribute to her Roth IRA if they file a joint return?

   b) How much can Ashley contribute if she files a separate return?

57. Harriet and Harry Combs (both 37 years old) are married and both want to contribute to a Roth IRA. In 2018, their AGI is $50,000. Harriet earned $46,000 and Harry earned $4,000.

   LO 6-3

   a) How much can Harriet contribute to her Roth IRA if they file a joint return?

   b) How much can Harriet contribute if she files a separate return?

   c) How much can Harry contribute to his Roth IRA if they file separately?

58. George (age 42 at year-end) has been contributing to a traditional IRA for years (all deductible contributions) and his IRA is now worth $25,000. He is planning on transferring (or rolling over) the entire balance into a Roth IRA account. George's marginal tax rate is 24 percent.

   LO 6-3

   a) What are the tax consequences to George if he takes $25,000 out of the traditional IRA and puts the entire amount into a Roth IRA?

   b) What are the tax consequences to George if he takes $25,000 out of the traditional IRA, pays the taxes due from the IRA distribution, and contributes the remaining distribution to the Roth IRA?

   c) What are the tax consequences to George if he takes $25,000 out of the traditional IRA, keeps $10,000 to pay taxes and to make a down payment on a new car, and contributes the remaining distribution to the Roth IRA?

59. Jimmer has contributed $15,000 to his Roth IRA and the balance in the account is $18,000. In the current year, Jimmer withdrew $17,000 from the Roth IRA to pay for a new car. If Jimmer's marginal ordinary income tax rate is 24 percent, what amount of tax and penalty, if any, is Jimmer required to pay on the withdrawal in each of the following alternative situations?

   LO 6-3

   a) Jimmer opened the Roth account 44 months before he withdrew the $17,000, and Jimmer is 62 years of age.

   b) Jimmer opened the Roth account 44 months before he withdrew the $17,000, and Jimmer is age 53.

c) Jimmer opened the Roth account 76 months before he withdrew the $17,000, and Jimmer is age 62.

d) Jimmer opened the Roth account 76 months before he withdrew the $17,000, and Jimmer is age 53.

LO 6-3 60. Over the past three years, Sherry has contributed a total of $12,000 to a Roth IRA account ($4,000 a year). The current value of the Roth IRA is $16,300. In the current year, Sherry withdraws $14,000 of the account balance to purchase a car. Assuming Sherry (currently age 52) is in the 24 percent marginal tax bracket, how much of the $14,000 withdrawal will she retain after taxes to fund her car purchase?

LO 6-3 61. Seven years ago, Halle (currently age 41) contributed $4,000 to a Roth IRA account. The current value of the Roth IRA is $9,000. In the current year, Halle withdraws $8,000 of the account balance to use as a down payment on her first home. Assuming Halle is in the 24 percent marginal tax bracket, how much of the $8,000 withdrawal will she retain after taxes to fund her house down payment?

LO 6-3 62. Sarah was contemplating making a contribution to her traditional individual retirement account for 2018. She determined that she would contribute $5,000 to her IRA and she deducted $5,000 for the contribution when she completed and filed her 2018 tax return on February 15, 2019. Two months later, on April 15, Sarah realized that she had not yet actually contributed the funds to her IRA. On April 15, she went to the post office and mailed a $5,000 check to the bank holding her IRA. The bank received the payment on April 20. In which year is Sarah's $5,000 contribution deductible?

research

LO 6-3 63. Lionel is an unmarried law student at State University Law School, a qualified educational institution. This year Lionel borrowed $24,000 from County Bank and paid interest of $1,440. Lionel used the loan proceeds to pay his law school tuition. Calculate the amounts Lionel can deduct for interest on higher education loans under the following circumstances:

a) Lionel's AGI before deducting interest on higher education loans is $50,000.

b) Lionel's AGI before deducting interest on higher education loans is $74,000.

c) Lionel's AGI before deducting interest on higher education loans is $90,000.

LO 6-3 64. This year Jack intends to file a married-joint return. Jack received $167,500 of salary and paid $5,000 of interest on loans used to pay qualified tuition costs for his dependent daughter, Deb. This year Jack has also paid moving expenses of $4,300 and $28,300 of alimony to his ex-wife, Diane, who divorced him in 2012.

planning

a) What is Jack's adjusted gross income?

b) Suppose that Jack also reported income of $8,800 from a half share of profits from a partnership. What AGI would Jack report under these circumstances?

COMPREHENSIVE PROBLEMS

Select problems are available in Connect®.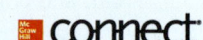

 65. Read the following letter and help Shady Slim with his tax situation. Assume that his gross income is $172,900 (which consists only of salary) for purposes of this problem.

tax forms

December 31, 2018

To the friendly student tax preparer:

Hi, it's Shady Slim again. I just got back from my 55th birthday party, and I'm told that you need some more information from me in order to complete my tax return. I'm an open book! I'll tell you whatever I think you need to know.

I had to move this year after getting my job at Roca Cola. I moved on February 3 of this year, and I worked my job at Roca Cola for the rest of the year. I still live in the same state, but I moved 500 miles away from my old house. I hired a moving company to move my stuff at a cost of $2,300, and I drove in my car. I got a hotel room along the way that cost $65 (I love Super 8!).

Can you believe I'm still paying off my student loans, even after 15 years? I paid a total of $900 in interest on my old student loans this year.

Since Roca Coca (my employer) never started a retirement plan, I decided I should probably start saving for my golden years. I contributed $3,000 to what the bank referred to as a regular IRA (or was it an REM?). Oh yeah. I also did a little investing this year. I bought a limited partnership interest in Duds Ltd. for $10,000. I thought it was going to be a real winner, but this year they took a bath. My portion of the loss was $8,000. Well, at least I did not actually do any work for Duds, and I get the tax deduction—right?

That should be all the information you need right now. Please calculate my adjusted gross income and complete page 1 of Form 1040. You're still doing this for free, right?

66. Jeremy and Alyssa Johnson have been married for five years and do not have any children. Jeremy was married previously and has one child from the prior marriage. He is self-employed and operates his own computer repair store. For the first two months of the year, Alyssa worked for Office Depot as an employee. In March, Alyssa accepted a new job with Super Toys Inc. (ST), where she worked for the remainder of the year. This year, the Johnsons received $255,000 of gross income. Determine the Johnsons' AGI given the following information :

a) Expenses associated with Jeremy's store include $40,000 in salary (and employment taxes) to employees, $45,000 of supplies, and $18,000 in rent and other administrative expenses.

b) Alyssa contributed $5,000 to a regular IRA. She did not participate in an employer-provided retirement plan. Jeremy currently is not saving for his retirement. As a salesperson, Alyssa incurred $2,000 in travel expenses related to her employment that were not reimbursed by her employer.

c) The Johnsons own a piece of raw land held as an investment. They paid $500 of real property taxes on the property and they incurred $200 of expenses in travel costs to see the property and to evaluate other similar potential investment properties.

d) The Johnsons own a rental home. They incurred $8,500 of expenses associated with the property.

e) Jeremy paid $4,500 for health insurance coverage for himself (not through an exchange). Alyssa was covered by health plans provided by her employer, but Jeremy is not eligible for the plan until next year.

f) Jeremy paid $2,500 in self-employment taxes ($1,250 represents the employer portion of the self-employment taxes).

g) Jeremy paid $5,000 in alimony and $3,000 in child support from his prior marriage (divorced in 2010).

67. Joe and Jessie are married and have one dependent child, Lizzie. Lizzie is currently in college at State University. Joe works as a design engineer for a manufacturing firm while Jessie runs a craft business from their home. Jessie's craft business consists of making craft items for sale at craft shows that are held periodically at various locations. Jessie spends considerable time and effort on her craft business and it has been consistently profitable over the years. Joe and Jessie pay interest on a personal loan to pay for Lizzie's college expenses (balance of $35,000). Based on their estimates, determine Joe and Jessie's AGI and complete page 1 of Form 1040. Assume that the employer portion of the self-employment tax on Jessie's income is

tax forms

$831. Joe and Jessie have summarized the income and expenses they expect to report this year as follows:

Income:	
Joe's salary	$124,100
Jessie's craft sales	18,400
Interest from certificate of deposit	1,650
Interest from Treasury bond funds	716
Interest from municipal bond funds	920
Income from renting out their personal residence for 10 days during local golf tournament	800
Expenditures:	
Social Security tax withheld from Joe's wages	7,482
Cost of Jessie's craft supplies	4,260
Postage for mailing crafts	145
Travel and lodging for craft shows	2,230
Self-employment tax on Jessie's craft income	1,662
College tuition paid for Lizzie	5,780
Interest on loans to pay Lizzie's tuition	3,200
Lizzie's room and board at college	12,620
Cleaning fees and advertising expense associated with renting their residence during local golf tournament	600

 **ROGER** | *CPA Review*

Sample CPA Exam questions from Roger CPA Review are available in Connect as support for the topics in this text. These Multiple Choice Questions and Task-Based Simulations include expert-written explanations and solutions and provide a starting point for students to become familiar with the content and functionality of the actual CPA Exam.

In the previous chapter, we determined the adjusted gross income (AGI) for both Courtney and Gram. To compute their taxable income, however, we need to identify their deductions *from* AGI. We begin our discussion of *from* AGI deductions by describing itemized deductions, and we conclude by briefly revisiting the standard deduction and tackling the deduction for qualified business income.

LO 7-1 **ITEMIZED DEDUCTIONS**

There are a variety of itemized deductions. Many itemized deductions are personal in nature but are allowed to subsidize desirable activities such as home ownership and charitable giving. Other itemized deductions, such as medical expenses, provide relief for taxpayers whose ability to pay taxes has been involuntarily reduced. We discuss itemized deductions in the order they appear on the individual tax return, Form 1040, Schedule A.

Medical Expenses

The medical-expense deduction is designed to provide relief for taxpayers whose ability to pay taxes is seriously hindered by health-related circumstances. Qualified medical expenses include any payments for the care, prevention, diagnosis, or cure of injury, disease, or bodily function that are not reimbursed by health insurance or are not paid for through a "flexible spending account."[1] Taxpayers may also deduct medical expenses incurred to treat their spouses and their dependents.[2] Common medical expenses include:

- Prescription medications, insulin, and medical aids such as eyeglasses, contact lenses, and wheelchairs. (Nonprescription medications are generally *not* deductible.)
- Payments to medical care *providers* such as doctors, dentists, and nurses and medical care *facilities* such as hospitals.
- Transportation for medical purposes.
- Long-term care facilities.
- Health insurance premiums (if not deducted *for* AGI by self-employed taxpayers) and insurance for long-term care services.[3,4]

Example 7-1

In April, Courtney broke her wrist in a mountain biking accident. She paid $2,000 for a visit to the hospital emergency room and follow-up visits with her doctor. While she recuperated, Courtney paid $300 for prescription medicine and $700 to a therapist for rehabilitation. Courtney's insurance reimbursed her $1,840 for these expenses. What is the amount of Courtney's qualified medical expenses?

---

[1]Taxpayers participating in flexible spending accounts are allowed to direct that a fixed amount of their salary be placed in an account to pay for medical expenses. The salary paid into these accounts is excluded from gross income and used to pay for medical expenses.

[2]For the purpose of deducting medical expenses, a dependent need not meet the gross income test [§213(a)], and a child of divorced parents is considered a dependent of both parents [§213(d)(5)]. We discuss the general requirements for dependency in the Individual Income Tax Overview, Dependents, and Filing Status chapter.

[3]This includes the annual cost of Medicare and prescription insurance withheld from a Social Security recipient's benefits checks.

[4]The portion of any premiums for health insurance purchased through an exchange and offset by a premium tax credit under §36B is not deductible as an itemized deduction.

Answer: $1,160, computed as follows:

Description	Deduction
Emergency room and doctor visits	$ 2,000
Prescription medication	300
Physical therapy	700
Total qualified medical expenses	$ 3,000
Less insurance reimbursement	−1,840
Qualified medical expenses from the accident	**$1,160**

Medical expenses for cosmetic surgery or other similar procedures are not deductible unless the surgery or procedure is necessary to ameliorate a deformity arising from, or directly related to, a congenital abnormality, a personal injury resulting from an accident or trauma, or a disfiguring disease.[5]

TAXES IN THE REAL WORLD Are Discretionary Medical Expenses Deductible?

While cosmetic surgery is generally not deductible, discretionary medical costs may be deducted where the procedure affects the structure or function of the body. Take, for example, procedures that facilitate pregnancy by overcoming infertility. In IRS Letter Ruling 200318017, the IRS ruled that egg donor fees and expenses related to obtaining a willing donor, paid by a taxpayer who could not conceive using her own eggs, qualified as deductible medical expenses because they were incurred in preparation of the taxpayer's medical procedure (the implantation of a donated egg). Deductible expenses included the donor's fee for her time and expense in following the procedures to ensure successful egg retrieval, the agency's fee for procuring the donor and coordinating the transaction, expenses for medical and psychological testing and assistance of the donor before and after the procedure, and legal fees for preparing a contract between the taxpayer and the donor.

What about the same type of expenses paid by a single male to father a child through a surrogate? Are those expenses deductible? No, because in that situation, the expenses are not related to an underlying medical condition or defect of the taxpayer, nor are they affecting any structure or function of his body. See *William Magdalin*, TC Memo 2008-293.

Transportation and Travel for Medical Purposes Taxpayers traveling for the primary purpose of receiving essential and deductible medical care may deduct the cost of lodging while away from home overnight (with certain restrictions) and transportation.[6] Taxpayers using personal automobiles for medical transportation purposes may deduct a standard mileage allowance in lieu of actual costs. For 2018, the mileage rate is 18 cents a mile.

Example 7-2

Gram drove Courtney, *in Courtney's car*, 110 miles back and forth from the doctor's office and the physical therapist's facility during the period Courtney was being treated for her broken wrist. What is the amount of Courtney's qualifying medical expense for her trips to the doctor's office?

Answer: $20 (110 × $0.18, rounded).

---

[5]§213(d)(9)(A).

[6]The cost of travel for and essential to medical care, including lodging (with certain limitations) is also deductible if the expense is not extravagant and the travel has no significant element of personal pleasure. However, under §213(d)(2) the deduction for the cost of lodging is limited to $50 per night per individual.

Hospitals and Long-Term Care Facilities   Taxpayers may deduct the cost of meals and lodging at hospitals. However, the cost of meals and lodging at other types of facilities such as nursing homes are deductible only when the principal purpose for the stay is medical care rather than convenience.[7] Of course, taxpayers may deduct the costs of actual medical care whether the care is provided at hospitals or other long-term care facilities.

Example 7-3

Gram considered moving into a long-term care facility before she decided she would move in with Courtney. The facility was not primarily for medical care and would have cost Gram $36,000 a year. During discussions with facility administrators, Gram learned that typically 20 percent of the total cost for the facility is allocable to medical care. If Gram were to stay in the facility for an entire year, what amount of the long-term care costs would qualify as a medical expense for Gram?

Answer: $7,200 ($36,000 × 20% allocable to medical care).

Medical Expense Deduction Limitation   The deduction for medical expenses is limited to the amount of unreimbursed qualified medical expenses paid during the year (no matter when the services were provided) *reduced* by 7.5 percent of the taxpayer's AGI for 2017 and 2018 (and 10 percent thereafter). This restriction is called a **floor limitation** because it eliminates any deduction for amounts below the floor. The purpose of a floor limitation is to restrict a deduction to taxpayers with substantial qualified expenses. Because this floor limitation is set at a high percentage of AGI, unreimbursed medical expenses rarely produce tax benefits, especially for high-income taxpayers.

Example 7-4

This year Courtney incurred $2,400 in unreimbursed qualified medical expenses (including the $1,160 of qualifying medical expenses associated with the accident and the $20 transportation deduction for mileage). Given that Courtney's AGI is $187,000 (see Exhibit 6-11), what is the amount of Courtney's itemized medical expense deduction?

Answer: $0, computed as follows:

Description	Expense
Total unreimbursed qualified medical expenses	$ 2,400
Minus: 7.5% of AGI ($187,000 × 7.5%)	(14,025)
Medical expense itemized deduction	$ 0

What if: What amount of medical expenses would Courtney be allowed to deduct if her AGI was $20,000?

Answer: $900, computed as follows:

Description	Expense
Total unreimbursed qualified medical expenses	$ 2,400
Minus: 7.5% of AGI ($20,000 × 7.5%)	(1,500)
Medical expense itemized deduction	$ 900

---

[7]§7702B. Taxpayers may deduct the cost of long-term care facilities if they are chronically ill under a prescribed plan of care. A taxpayer is deemed to be chronically ill, generally, if she or he cannot perform at least two daily living tasks (eating, bathing, dressing, toileting, transferring, continence) for 90 days or more. Taxpayers may also deduct long-term care insurance premiums, which are limited annually based on the age of the taxpayer.

Taxes

Individuals may deduct as itemized deductions the payments they made during the year for the following taxes:

- State, local, and foreign *income* taxes, including state and local taxes paid during the year through employer withholding, estimated tax payments, and overpayments on the prior year return that the taxpayer applies to the current year (the taxpayer asks the state to keep the overpayment rather than refund it).
- State and local real estate taxes on property held for personal or investment purposes.
- State and local personal property taxes that are assessed on the *value* of the specific property.[8]

Taxpayers may elect to deduct state and local sales taxes *instead of* deducting state and local income taxes. This election is particularly advantageous for taxpayers in states that don't have an individual state income tax.[9] For years after 2017, the total itemized deduction for taxes is limited to $10,000 ($5,000 for a taxpayer filing married separate).

Example 7-5

During the year, Courtney paid $6,700 of state income taxes through withholding from her paycheck. She also paid $2,700 of real estate taxes on her personal residence and $980 of real estate taxes on an investment property she owns in Oklahoma. Finally, Courtney paid $180 as a registration fee for her automobile (the fee is based on the year the automobile was manufactured, not its value). What amount of these payments can Courtney deduct as itemized deductions?

Answer: $10,000 ($6,700 state taxes + $2,700 real estate taxes on residence + $980 real estate taxes on investment property, limited to $10,000). Courtney is not allowed to deduct the registration fee for her car because the fee is not based on the value of the automobile.

What if: Suppose that on April 15, 2018, Courtney filed her 2017 state tax return and was due a refund from the state in the amount of $420. However, Courtney elected to have the state keep the overpayment and apply it to her 2018 tax payments. Assume that Courtney also had the $6,700 of state income tax withholding but only had $1,500 of real estate taxes in total. What amount of state income taxes is Courtney allowed to deduct as an itemized deduction in 2018?

Answer: $8,620 ($6,700 withholding + $420 overpayment applied to 2018 + $1,500 real estate taxes). The treatment of the overpayment is the same as if Courtney had received the refund in 2018 and then remitted it to the state as payment of 2018 taxes. Because she paid the tax in 2018, she is allowed to deduct the tax in 2018. Recall that under the tax benefit rule (see the Gross Income and Exclusions chapter), Courtney was required to include the $420 in her 2018 gross income.

Interest

There are two itemized deductions for interest expense.[10] First, subject to limitations, individuals can deduct interest paid on acquisition indebtedness secured by a qualified residence (the taxpayer's principal residence and one other residence).[11] Acquisition

---

[8]§164.

[9]The deduction can be based upon either the amount paid or the amount published in the IRS tables (IRS Publication 600) based upon the state of residence, income, and number of dependents. The states with no income tax are Alaska, Florida, Nevada, South Dakota, Texas, Washington, and Wyoming. Tennessee and New Hampshire have no state income tax on wages but do impose a tax on unearned income.

[10]Interest paid on loans where the proceeds are used in a trade or business is fully deductible as a business expense deduction *for* AGI.

[11]Prior to 2018, taxpayers could deduct mortgage interest on up to $100,000 of home-equity indebtedness ($50,000 if married filing separately). Prior to 2018, taxpayers could also deduct premiums paid or accrued on mortgage insurance (insurance premiums paid by the borrower to protect the lender against the borrower defaulting on the loan) as qualified residence interest expense. At press time, the deduction for mortgage insurance premiums has not been extended to 2018.

indebtedness is any debt secured by a qualified residence that is incurred in acquiring, constructing, or substantially improving the residence.[12]

The home mortgage interest deduction is limited by a cap on acquisition indebtedness that varies based upon when the indebtedness originated. For acquisition indebtedness incurred after December 15, 2017, taxpayers may only deduct mortgage interest on up to $750,000 of acquisition indebtedness ($375,000 if married filing separately). For acquisition indebtedness incurred before December 16, 2017, the limitation on acquisition indebtedness is $1,000,000 ($500,000 if filing married separate), even if the debt is refinanced after December 15, 2017. When a taxpayer has both acquisition indebtedness incurred before December 16, 2017 and after December 15, 2017, the $750,000 ($375,000) limit is reduced (not below zero) by the acquisition indebtedness incurred before December 16, 2017.

Individuals can also deduct interest paid on loans used to purchase investment assets such as stocks, bonds, or land (investment interest expense). The deduction of investment interest is limited to a taxpayer's net investment income.[13] Any investment interest in excess of the net investment income limitation carries forward to the subsequent year. Taxpayers are not allowed to deduct interest on personal credit card debt or on loans to acquire (and secured by) personal-use automobiles.

Example 7-6

Courtney acquired her home in Kansas City in January of this year for $300,000 (also its value throughout the year). She purchased it by paying $40,000 as a down payment and borrowing $260,000 from a credit union. Her home is the collateral for the loan. During the year, Courtney paid $15,800 in interest on the loan. How much of this interest may Courtney deduct?

Answer: $15,800. Because Courtney's home mortgage is secured by her home, she is allowed to deduct the interest expense on the home as an itemized deduction.

Example 7-7

What if: Suppose Courtney borrowed $2,000 from her bank to purchase stock in Delta Inc. During the year, she paid $130 of interest expense on the loan and realized $321 of investment income. What amount of the $130 in interest expense can Courtney deduct as an itemized deduction this year?

Answer: $130. Courtney can deduct investment interest expense as an itemized deduction to the extent of her net investment income. Courtney recognized $321 of investment income, but she had no deductible investment expenses (investment interest expense is not an investment expense). Hence, Courtney's net investment income is $321. Because net investment income exceeds the amount of Courtney's investment interest expense, she can deduct the entire $130 of investment interest expense on her return.[14]

What if: Suppose Courtney received net investment income of only $100 this year. How much of the $130 investment interest expense would she be allowed to deduct?

Answer: $100. Her deduction is limited to the net investment income of $100. Courtney would be allowed to carry over the $30 of interest expense that was not deductible to deduct in a future year when she has net investment income.

[12]Subject to certain restrictions, points paid on indebtedness incurred in acquiring a home are also generally deductible as mortgage interest expense in the year the loan originates, and points to refinance a home mortgage are typically amortized and deducted over the life of the loan (but see research memo in the Tax Compliance, the IRS, and Tax Authorities chapter for an exception).

[13]§163(d). Net investment income is defined as investment income minus investment expenses. Because investment expenses are no longer deductible as itemized deductions, the investment interest expense deduction is effectively limited to the taxpayer's investment income.

[14]Recall from the Gross Income and Exclusions chapter that Courtney also had $700 of investment income in the form of dividends on her 1,000 shares of GE stock. However, this income is subject to a preferential tax rate, and absent a special election to tax this income at ordinary tax rates, the dividends would not qualify as net investment income. The same rules apply to long-term capital gains as well.

Charitable Contributions

Congress encourages donations to charities by allowing taxpayers to deduct contributions of money and other property to *qualified* domestic charitable organizations. Qualified charitable organizations include organizations that engage in educational, religious, scientific, governmental, and other public activities.[15] Political and campaign contributions are not deductible even though they arguably indirectly support the government (contributions to which are generally deductible).

Example 7-8

This year Courtney donated $1,700 to the American Red Cross. She also gave $200 in cash to various homeless people she met on the street during the year. What amount of these donations is Courtney allowed to deduct as a charitable contribution?

Answer: $1,700. Because the American Red Cross is a public charity recognized by the IRS, Courtney may deduct her $1,700 charitable contribution to it as an itemized deduction. However, despite Courtney's charitable intent, her donations to the homeless are not deductible as charitable contributions because individuals do not qualify as charitable organizations.

What if: Suppose that instead of transferring cash to homeless people on the street, Courtney donated $200 cash to a local food bank that is listed in the IRS Exempt Organizations Select Check as a qualified charity. The food bank provides meals to those in need. Would Courtney be allowed to deduct this contribution?

Answer: Yes, because the food bank is a qualified charity.

The *amount* of the charitable contribution deduction depends on whether the taxpayer contributes money or other property to the charity. Note that in virtually all circumstances, donations are deductible only if the contribution is substantiated by written records.[16]

Contributions of Money   Cash contributions are deductible in the year paid, including donations of cash or by check, electronic funds transfers, credit card charges, and payroll deductions.[17] Taxpayers are also considered as making monetary contributions for the cost of transportation and travel for charitable purposes if there is no significant element of pleasure or entertainment in the travel. When taxpayers use their personal vehicles for charitable transportation purposes, they may deduct, as a cash contribution, a standard mileage allowance for each mile driven (14 cents a mile in 2018). While taxpayers are allowed to deduct their transportation costs and other out-of-pocket costs of providing services for charities, they are not allowed to deduct the value of the services they provide for charities.

---

[15]§170(c). The IRS Exempt Organizations Select Check (https://www.irs.gov/charities-non-profits/exempt-organizations-select-check) lists the organizations that the IRS has determined to be qualified charities.

[16]For example, to deduct monetary donations, taxpayers must keep a bank record or a written communication from the charity showing the name of the charity and the date and amount of the contribution. In addition, to deduct charitable contributions for cash or noncash contributions of $250 or more, a taxpayer must receive a written acknowledgment from the charity that shows the amount of cash and a description of any property contributed. The acknowledgement must also state whether the donee organization provided any goods or services to the donor for the contribution and if so, either include a description and estimate of the value of the goods or services provided by the donee organization or, if applicable, a statement that the goods or services provided by the donee organization consist entirely of intangible religious benefits. See Publication 526 for more information.

[17]When individual taxpayers mail a contribution, they are allowed to deduct the contribution when they place the payment in the mail. When they pay via credit card, they are allowed to deduct the contribution on the day of the charge. Rev. Rul. 78-38, 1978-1 CB 67.

Example 7-9

> Once a month, Courtney does volunteer work at a Goodwill Industries outlet about 20 miles from her home. Altogether, Courtney traveled 500 miles during the year driving to and from the Goodwill outlet. Courtney has determined that the services she provided during the year are reasonably valued at $1,500. What amount is Courtney allowed to deduct for her volunteer work with Goodwill Industries?
>
> **Answer:** $70. Courtney is *not* allowed to deduct the value of the services she provides to Goodwill. However, she is allowed to deduct the $70 cost of her transportation to and from the Goodwill outlet (500 miles × 14 cents per mile).

Taxpayers receiving goods or services from a charity in exchange for a contribution may only deduct the amount of the contribution *in excess of the fair market value of the goods or services they receive* in exchange for their contribution.[18]

Contributions of Property Other Than Money   When a taxpayer donates *property* to charity, the *amount* the taxpayer is allowed to deduct depends on whether the property is **capital gain property** or **ordinary income property.**

Capital gain property.   In general, taxpayers are allowed to deduct the *fair market value* of capital gain property on the date of the donation. Capital gain property is any appreciated asset that would have generated a *long-term* capital gain if the taxpayer had sold the property for its fair market value instead of contributing the asset to charity. To qualify as long-term, the taxpayer must have held the asset for more than a year. Capital assets include the following assets:

- Investment assets (stocks, bonds, land held for investment, paintings, etc.).
- Business assets (to the extent that gain on the sale of the business asset would *not* have been considered ordinary income).[19]
- Personal-use assets.

Contributing capital gain property is a particularly tax efficient way to make charitable contributions because taxpayers are allowed to deduct the fair market value of the property and they are *not* required to include the appreciation on the asset in gross income.

Example 7-10

> In December of the current year, Courtney donated 100 shares of stock in JBD Corp. to her church, a qualified charity. Courtney purchased the stock several years ago for $2,600, but the shares were worth $10,600 at the time of the donation. What is the amount of Courtney's charitable deduction for donating the stock?
>
> **Answer:** $10,600. Because the stock is an appreciated investment asset held for more than a year, it qualifies as capital gain property. Hence, Courtney is allowed to deduct the $10,600 fair market value of the stock, and she is *not* required to recognize any of the $8,000 realized gain ($10,600 − $2,600).

Certain contributions of capital gain property do not qualify for a fair market value deduction. The deduction for capital gain property that is *tangible personal property* is limited to the *adjusted basis* of the property if the charity uses the property for a purpose

[18]Reg. §1.170A-1(h). To help with this determination, a charity that provides goods or services in return for a contribution of more than $75 must provide contributors with a written statement estimating the value of goods and services that the charity has provided to the donor.

[19]These assets are considered to be §1231(b) assets. We discuss the tax treatment of dispositions of business assets in the Property Dispositions chapter.

that is *unrelated* to its charitable purpose.[20] That is, this restriction applies to capital gain property that is (1) tangible, (2) personal property (not realty), and (3) unrelated to the charity's operations. The third requirement does not apply if, at the time of the donation, the taxpayer reasonably anticipates that the charity will put the property to a related use.

Example 7-11

What if: Suppose Courtney donated a religious-themed painting to her church. Courtney purchased the painting several years ago for $2,600, but the painting was worth $10,600 at the time of the donation. When Courtney contributed the painting, she reasonably expected the church to hang the painting in the chapel. What would be the amount of Courtney's charitable contribution deduction?

Answer: $10,600. Because Courtney reasonably expected the church to use the painting in a manner related to its tax-exempt purpose, Courtney is allowed to deduct the full fair market value of the painting without recognizing the $8,000 realized gain.

What if: Suppose Courtney was told at the time she donated the painting that the church intended to sell it and use the cash to help fund expansion of the church building. What would be Courtney's charitable contribution deduction?

Answer: $2,600, the adjusted basis of the property. Because the church expects to sell it, the painting is being used for a purpose unrelated to the charitable purpose of the church. Thus, Courtney may deduct only the tax basis of the painting.

What if: Suppose Courtney donated stock to her church ($10,600 current fair market value, originally purchased several years ago for $2,600) and the church informed her that it intended to immediately sell the stock. What would be the amount of Courtney's charitable contribution deduction?

Answer: $10,600. Stock is intangible property, not tangible personal property. Hence, Courtney would deduct the fair market value of the stock.

Ordinary income property.   Taxpayers contributing ordinary income property can only deduct the *lesser* of (1) the property's fair market value or (2) the property's adjusted basis. Ordinary income property consists of all assets other than capital gain property. That is, ordinary income property is property that if sold would generate income taxed at ordinary rates. This includes the following types of assets:

- Assets the taxpayer has held for a year or less.
- Inventory the taxpayer sells in a trade or business.
- Business assets held for more than a year to the extent the taxpayer would recognize ordinary income under the depreciation recapture rules if the taxpayer had sold the property.[21]
- Assets, including investment assets and personal-use assets, with a value *less than* the taxpayer's basis in the assets (assets that have declined in value).

Example 7-12

Before her move from Cincinnati, Courtney decided to donate her excess possessions to Goodwill Industries. Courtney estimated that she paid over $900 for these items, including clothing, a table, and a couch. However, although the items were in excellent condition, they were worth only $160. What amount can Courtney deduct for her donation of these items?

Answer: $160. Because Courtney's possessions have declined in value, they are considered to be ordinary income property. Consequently, Courtney may deduct the lesser of (1) the fair market value of $160 or (2) her tax basis in the property of $900.

---

[20]Reg. §1.170A-4(b)(2). The taxpayer's deduction for donating capital gain property is also limited to basis if the taxpayer contributes capital gain property other than publicly traded stock to a private nonoperating foundation. There are also other exceptions in which capital gain property might not otherwise qualify for deduction at value, such as the subsequent sale of donated property by the charity. These exceptions are beyond the scope of this text.

[21]We discuss depreciation recapture in the Property Dispositions chapter.

Charitable Contribution Deduction Limitations   The amount of a taxpayer's charitable contribution deduction for the year is limited to a **ceiling** or maximum deduction. The ceiling depends upon the type of property the taxpayer donates and the nature of the charity receiving the donation; donations to public charities (charities that are publicly supported such as churches and schools) and **private operating foundations** (privately sponsored foundations that actually fund and conduct charitable activities) are subject to less stringent restrictions than other charities. In general, cash donations to public charities and private operating foundations are limited to 60 percent of the taxpayer's AGI, whereas property donations to public charities and private operating foundations are limited to 50 percent of the taxpayer's AGI. Deductions for contributions of capital gain property to public charities and private operating foundations are generally limited to 30 percent of the taxpayer's AGI. Deductions for cash and property contributions to **private nonoperating foundations** (privately sponsored foundations that disburse funds to other charities, such as the Bill and Melinda Gates Foundation) are limited to 30 percent of the taxpayer's AGI. Finally, deductions for contributions of capital gain property to private nonoperating foundations are limited to 20 percent of the taxpayer's AGI. Exhibit 7-1 summarizes the charitable contribution limitations for individual taxpayers.

When taxpayers make contributions that are subject to different percentage limitations, they apply the AGI limitations in the following sequence:

Step 1: Determine the limitation for the 60 percent contributions.

Step 2: Apply the limitations to the 50 percent contributions. The 50 percent contribution limit is AGI × 50 percent minus the contributions subject to the 60 percent limit.

Step 3: Apply the limitations to the 30 percent contributions. The 30 percent contribution limit is the *lesser* of (a) AGI × 30 percent or (b) AGI × 50 percent minus the contributions subject to the 50 percent limit and the contributions subject to the 60 percent limit.

Step 4: Apply the limitations to the 20 percent contributions. The 20 percent contribution limit is the *lesser* of (a) AGI × 20 percent, (b) AGI × 30 percent minus contributions subject to the 30 percent limit, or (c) AGI × 50 percent minus the contributions subject to the 50 percent limit, the contributions subject to the 60 percent limit, and the contributions subject to the 30 percent limit.

When a taxpayer's contributions exceed the AGI ceiling limitation for the year, the excess contribution is treated as though it were made in the subsequent tax year and is subject to the same AGI limitations in the next year. The excess contribution can be carried forward for five years before it expires. If a charitable contribution deduction is

EXHIBIT 7-1   **Summary of Charitable Contribution Limitation Rules**

Contribution Type	Public Charity and Private Operating Foundation	Private Nonoperating Foundation
Cash:		
Amount	Cash amount	Cash amount
AGI limit	60%	30%
Capital gain property:		
Amount	FMV	Basis*
AGI limit	30%	20%
Ordinary income property:		
Amount	Lesser of basis or FMV	Lesser of basis or FMV
AGI limit	50%	30%

*FMV if the stock is publicly traded [§170(e)(5)].

carried forward, the current year contributions must first be used when applying the AGI percentage limitations. However, because the ceiling limitations are fairly generous, tax-payers exceed the ceiling limitations only in unusual circumstances.

Example 7-13

This year Courtney made the following contributions to qualified charities:

Organization	Amount	Type	AGI Limitation	Reference
Red Cross	$ 1,700	Cash	60%	Example 7-8
Goodwill Industries	70	Cash-mileage	60	Example 7-9
Goodwill	160	Ordinary income property	50	Example 7-12
Church	10,600	Capital gain property	30	Example 7-10
Total contributions	$12,530			

After applying the AGI limitations, how much of the $12,530 in contributions is Courtney allowed to deduct if she itemizes her deductions?

Answer: $12,530, computed as follows:

Description	Amount	Explanation
(1) AGI	$187,000	Exhibit 6-11
(2) 60% contributions	1,770	($1,700 + 70)
(3) 60% AGI contribution limit	112,000	(1) × 60%
(4) Allowable 60% deductions	1,770	Lesser of (2) or (3)
(5) 50% contributions	160	
(6) 50% AGI contribution limit	91,730	(1) × 50% − (4)
(7) Allowable 50% deductions	160	Least of (5) or (6)
(8) 30% contributions	10,600	
(9) 30% AGI contribution limit	56,100	
(10) Remaining 50% contribution limit	91,570	(6) − (7)
(8) Allowable 30% deductions	10,600	Least of (8), (9), or (10)
Deductible charitable contributions	**$ 12,530**	(4) + (7) + (11)

What if: Suppose that Courtney's AGI was $30,000. After applying the AGI limitations, how much of the $12,530 in contributions would Courtney be allowed to deduct if she itemizes her deductions?

Answer: $10,930, computed as follows:

Description	Amount	Explanation
(1) AGI	$ 30,000	
(2) 60% contributions	1,770	
(3) 60% AGI contribution limit	18,000	(1) × 60%
(4) Allowable 60% deductions	1,770	Lesser of (2) and (3)
(5) 50% contributions	160	
(6) 50% AGI contribution limit	13,230	(1) × 50% − (4)
(7) Allowable 50% deductions	160	Least of (5) or (6)
(8) 30% contributions	10,600	
(9) 30% AGI contribution limit	9,000	
(10) Remaining 50% AGI contribution limit	$ 13,070	(6) − (7)
(11) Allowable 30% deductions	9,000	Least of (8), (9), or (10)
Deductible charitable contributions	**$10,930**	(4) + (7) + (11)

This year, Courtney would not be allowed to deduct $1,600 of her $10,600 capital gain property contribution to her church. However, she would carry forward the $1,600 to next year (and up to four years after that, if necessary) and treat it as though she made a $1,600 contribution next year subject to the 30 percent of AGI limitation.

Casualty and Theft Losses on Personal-Use Assets

Individuals cannot deduct losses they realize when they sell or dispose of assets used for personal purposes (personal-use assets as opposed to business or investment assets). Prior to 2018, taxpayers could deduct casualty losses (defined as losses arising from a sudden, unexpected, or unusual event such as a "fire, storm, or shipwreck" or from theft) on personal-use assets subject to a $100 floor for each casualty and 10 percent of AGI floor for all casualty losses in the year. After 2017, only casualty losses on personal-use assets attributable to a federally declared disaster are deductible (subject to the $100 floor and 10 percent of AGI floor).[22]

Miscellaneous Itemized Deductions

Prior to 2018, there were a number of expenses including unreimbursed employee business expenses, tax preparation fees, investment expenses (other than real estate tax or investment interest expense), and hobby expenses (limited to hobby income), among others, that were deductible as **miscellaneous itemized deductions** subject to 2 percent of AGI floor.[23] After 2017, these expenses are no longer deductible. The nondeductibility of these expenses is especially painful for taxpayers with hobbies, as hobby revenues are included in gross income but hobby expenses are no longer deductible (unless they are deductible as real estate taxes or mortgage interest expense).

Despite the nondeductibility of several expenses previously deductible as miscellaneous deductions subject to the 2 percent of AGI floor, there are a few expenses that remain deductible as miscellaneous itemized deductions not subject to the 2 percent of AGI floor. Perhaps because gambling includes a significant element of personal enjoyment (losers may think otherwise), individuals include all gambling winnings for the year in gross income, but they may also deduct gambling expenses and gambling losses *to the extent of gambling winnings* for the year.[24] The deductible gambling losses are miscellaneous itemized deductions; therefore, *losses don't directly offset*

---

[22]§165. As we discuss in more detail in the Business Income, Deductions, and Accounting Methods chapter, businesses may deduct casualty and theft losses of business property as a deduction *for* AGI. Further, casualty or theft losses on investment assets are deductible as a miscellaneous itemized deduction.

[23]Hobbies are revenue-generating activities for primarily personal enjoyment rather than profit. The IRS considers a list of factors (taxpayer's history of income or losses with the activity, taxpayer's expertise or his advisers, taxpayer's time and effort expended in the activity, activity's elements of personal pleasure or recreation, etc.) in determining whether an activity is a hobby or for profit.

[24]§165(d).

winnings.[25] Casualty and theft losses on property held for investment (not personal use property) and the unrecovered cost of a life annuity (if the taxpayer died before recovering the full cost of the annuity) also are deductible as miscellaneous itemized deductions.

Summary of Itemized Deductions

This part of the chapter examined the various itemized deductions. Some of these deductions are subject to limitations in the form of floor limitations or caps. All require good records and a good understanding to support and maximize your deductions.

Example 7-14

Given Courtney's current year AGI of $187,000, what is the amount of her total itemized deductions she may claim on her tax return?

Answer: Courtney's itemized deductions for the year are $38,330, calculated as follows:

Description	Amount	Reference
Taxes	$ 10,000	Example 7-5
Home mortgage interest	15,800	Example 7-6
Charitable contributions	12,530	Example 7-13
Total itemized deductions	**$38,330**	

Exhibit 7-2 presents Courtney's itemized deductions on Form 1040, Schedule A. As with other forms, we use the 2017 form since the 2018 form was not available at press time.

THE STANDARD DEDUCTION

LO 7-2

Standard Deduction

The **standard deduction** is a flat amount that most individuals can elect to deduct *instead* of deducting their itemized deductions (if any). That is, taxpayers generally deduct *the greater of their standard deduction or their itemized deductions.*

The amount of the standard deduction varies according to the taxpayer's filing status, age, and eyesight. The basic standard deduction is greater for married taxpayers filing jointly and those supporting a family (head of household) than it is for married taxpayers filing separately and unmarried taxpayers not supporting a family. Taxpayers who are at least 65 years of age on the last day of the year or are blind are entitled to additional standard deduction amounts above and beyond their basic standard deduction.[26] Exhibit 7-3 summarizes the standard deduction amounts.[27] With significantly larger standard deduction amounts in 2018, many more taxpayers are expected now to deduct the standard deduction instead of deducting itemized deductions.

---

[25]If gambling is deemed to be a business activity (see *Linda M. Myers,* TC Summary Opinion 2007-194), then the taxpayer reports gambling winnings, expenses, and losses on Schedule C (not as a miscellaneous itemized deduction). However, gambling expenses and losses remain only deductible to the extent of gambling winnings.

[26]Taxpayers are considered 65 on the day before their 65th birthday. Taxpayers are considered to be blind if they have a certified statement from their eye doctor or registered optometrist that their corrected vision of their better eye is no better than 20/200 or their field of vision is 20 degrees or less.

[27]The standard deduction amount is indexed for inflation.

EXHIBIT 7-2 **Courtney's Form 1040, Schedule A**

SCHEDULE A (Form 1040)	**Itemized Deductions**	OMB No. 1545-0074
Department of the Treasury Internal Revenue Service (99)	▶ Go to *www.irs.gov/ScheduleA* for instructions and the latest information. ▶ **Attach to Form 1040.** **Caution:** If you are claiming a net qualified disaster loss on Form 4684, see the instructions for line 28.	20**17** Attachment Sequence No. **07**

Name(s) shown on Form 1040

Courtney Wilson

Your social security number **123-45-6789**

Medical and Dental Expenses	**Caution:** Do not include expenses reimbursed or paid by others.		
	1 Medical and dental expenses (see instructions)	**1** 2,400	
	2 Enter amount from Form 1040, line 38 **2** 187,000		
	3 Multiply line 2 by 7.5% (0.075)	**3** 14,025	
	4 Subtract line 3 from line 1. If line 3 is more than line 1, enter -0-	**4** 0
Taxes You Paid	**5** State and local **(check only one box):**		
	a ☑ Income taxes, **or**	**5** 6,320	
	b ☐ General sales taxes		
	6 Real estate taxes (see instructions)	**6** 3,680	
	7 Personal property taxes	**7**	
	8 Other taxes. List type and amount ▶ _____		
	_____	**8**	
	9 Add lines 5 through 8	**9** 10,000
Interest You Paid **Note:** Your mortgage interest deduction may be limited (see instructions).	**10** Home mortgage interest and points reported to you on Form 1098	**10** 15,800	
	11 Home mortgage interest not reported to you on Form 1098. If paid to the person from whom you bought the home, see instructions and show that person's name, identifying no., and address ▶ _____ _____	**11**	
	12 Points not reported to you on Form 1098. See instructions for special rules	**12**	
	13 Reserved for future use	**13**	
	14 Investment interest. Attach Form 4952 if required. See instructions	**14**	
	15 Add lines 10 through 14	**15** 15,800
Gifts to Charity If you made a gift and got a benefit for it, see instructions.	**16** Gifts by cash or check. If you made any gift of $250 or more, see instructions.	**16** 1,770	
	17 Other than by cash or check. If any gift of $250 or more, see instructions. You **must** attach Form 8283 if over $500 . . .	**17** 10,760	
	18 Carryover from prior year	**18**	
	19 Add lines 16 through 18	**19** 12,530
Casualty and Theft Losses	**20** Casualty or theft loss(es) other than net qualified disaster losses. Attach Form 4684 and enter the amount from line 18 of that form. See instructions	**20**
Job Expenses and Certain Miscellaneous Deductions	**21** Unreimbursed employee expenses—job travel, union dues, job education, etc. Attach Form 2106 or 2106-EZ if required. See instructions. ▶ _____	**21**	
	22 Tax preparation fees	**22**	
	23 Other expenses—investment, safe deposit box, etc. List type and amount ▶ _____ _____	**23**	
	24 Add lines 21 through 23	**24**	
	25 Enter amount from Form 1040, line 38 **25**		
	26 Multiply line 25 by 2% (0.02)	**26**	
	27 Subtract line 26 from line 24. If line 26 is more than line 24, enter -0-	**27**
Other Miscellaneous Deductions	**28** Other—from list in instructions. List type and amount ▶ _____ _____		
		28
Total Itemized Deductions	**29** Is Form 1040, line 38, over $156,900?		
	☐ **No.** Your deduction is not limited. Add the amounts in the far right column for lines 4 through 28. Also, enter this amount on Form 1040, line 40.	**29** 38,330
	☐ **Yes.** Your deduction may be limited. See the Itemized Deductions Worksheet in the instructions to figure the amount to enter.	
	30 If you elect to itemize deductions even though they are less than your standard deduction, check here . . . . ▶ ☐	

For Paperwork Reduction Act Notice, see the Instructions for Form 1040.　　Cat. No. 17145C　　Schedule A (Form 1040) 2017

EXHIBIT 7-3   **Standard Deduction Amounts***

2017 Amounts		
Filing Status	**Basic Standard Deduction**	**Additional Standard Deduction for Age and/or Blindness at End of Year**
Married filing jointly	$12,700	$1,250
Head of household	9,350	1,550
Single	6,350	1,550
Married filing separately	6,350	1,250

2018 Amounts		
Filing Status	**Basic Standard Deduction**	**Additional Standard Deduction for Age and/or Blindness at End of Year**
Married filing jointly	$24,000	$1,300
Head of household	18,000	1,600
Single	12,000	1,600
Married filing separately	12,000	1,300

*For individuals claimed as a dependent on another return, the 2018 standard deduction is the greater of (1) $1,050 or (2) $350 plus earned income not to exceed the standard deduction amount of those who are not dependents.

For 2018, the additional standard deduction for either age and/or blindness is $1,300 for married taxpayers and $1,600 for taxpayers who are not married. Thus, a blind individual who is 65 years old and single is entitled to a standard deduction of $15,200 ($12,000 + $1,600 + $1,600). A married couple filing a joint return with one spouse over age 65 and one spouse considered legally blind is entitled to a standard deduction of $26,600 ($24,000 + $1,300 + $1,300). Finally, for an individual who is eligible to be claimed as a dependent on another's return, the standard deduction is the greater of (1) $1,050 or (2) $350 plus the individual's earned income limited to the regular standard deduction. The additional standard deduction amounts for age and blindness, if any, are not impacted by the preceding limitation for eligible dependents.

Example 7-15

What is Courtney's standard deduction for the year?

Answer: $18,000. Because Courtney is unmarried at the end of the year and she maintains a household for more than six months for Deron and Ellen, who both qualify as her dependents (as qualifying children), Courtney's filing status is head of household, which allows her to claim a standard deduction of $18,000.

Given that Courtney's itemized deductions are $38,330 (see Example 7-14), will Courtney deduct her itemized deductions or her standard deduction?

Answer: She will deduct her itemized deductions because they exceed her standard deduction.

What if: Suppose that Courtney's 10-year-old son, Deron, earned $600 this summer by mowing lawns for neighbors. If Deron is Courtney's dependent, what amount of standard deduction can Deron claim on his individual return?

Answer: Deron claims a minimum standard deduction of $1,050 because he is Courtney's dependent. Hence, Deron would not pay any income tax because his taxable income is reduced to zero by the standard deduction.[28]

(continued on page 7-16)

---

[28]Deron will need to file a tax return because his self-employment income exceeds $400 and, as explained in the Individual Income Tax Computation and Tax Credits chapter, he will likely owe self-employment tax.

> ***What if:*** What amount of standard deduction would Deron claim if he had earned $2,100?
>
> **Answer:** Because of the amount of his earnings, Deron would claim a standard deduction in the amount of his earned income plus $350. Hence, Deron would claim a standard deduction of $2,450 ($2,100 + $350) and he would not pay any income tax.[29]
>
> ***What if:*** Suppose Deron earned $14,000. What amount of standard deduction would he claim?
>
> **Answer:** Again, Deron would claim a standard deduction in the amount of his earned income plus $350. However, Deron's standard deduction would be limited to $12,000, the maximum allowable standard deduction for a taxpayer filing single.

From the government's standpoint, the standard deduction serves two purposes. First, to help taxpayers with lower income, it automatically provides a minimum amount of income that is not subject to taxation. Second, it eliminates the need for the IRS to verify and audit itemized deductions for those taxpayers who choose to deduct the standard deduction. From the taxpayers' perspective, the standard deduction allows them to avoid taxation on a portion of their income, and for those not planning to itemize deductions, it eliminates the need to substantiate and collect information about them. The standard deduction, however, is a double-edged sword. While it reduces taxes by offsetting income with an automatic deduction, it eliminates the tax benefits of itemized deductions up to the amount of the standard deduction. This is a very important point to consider when evaluating the tax benefits of itemized deductions.

Example 7-16

> In Example 7-14, we determined that Courtney is entitled to deduct $38,330 of itemized deductions this year. How much do Courtney's itemized deductions reduce her taxable income relative to a situation in which she has $0 of itemized deductions?
>
> **Answer:** $20,330. Because Courtney files as a head of household, she is able to deduct $18,000 as a standard deduction even if she does not incur any itemized deductions. Consequently, her itemized deductions reduce her taxable income by only $20,330 ($38,330 − $18,000) beyond what her taxable income would have been if she did not itemize deductions.

Bunching Itemized Deductions   Some taxpayers may deduct the standard deduction every year because their itemized deductions always fall just short of the standard deduction amount and thus never produce any tax benefit. They may gain some tax benefit from their itemized deductions by implementing a simple timing tax planning strategy called **bunching itemized deductions.** The basic strategy consists of shifting itemized deductions into one year such that the amount of itemized deductions exceeds the standard deduction for the year, and then deducting the standard deduction in the next year (or vice versa).

Because individuals are cash-method taxpayers, they may shift certain itemized deductions by accelerating payment into the current year. For example, a taxpayer could make charitable contributions at the end of December rather than at the beginning of January in the following year. Taxpayers' ability to shift itemized deductions is limited because the timing of these payments is not completely discretionary. For example, real estate taxes have due dates, state taxes are generally paid throughout the year via with-

---

[29]As mentioned previously, Deron will need to file a tax return because his self-employment income exceeds $400 and, as explained in the Individual Income Tax Computation and Tax Credits chapter, he will likely owe self-employment taxes.

holding, and employees may incur and be required to pay business expenses throughout the year. However, taxpayers who annually make a certain amount of charitable contributions, for example, may consider lumping contributions for two years into one year and not contributing in the next year.[30]

Example 7-17

What if: Gram is 70 years old and files as a single taxpayer. This year Gram paid deductible medical expenses (after the AGI floor limitation) of $4,000. She also contributed $7,500 to her local church. This year her total itemized deductions were $11,500 ($4,000 medical + $7,500 charitable). Assuming Gram will have similar expenditures next year, what amount of additional deductions would Gram have been able to deduct this year if she had bunched her deductions by making her 2018 and 2019 charitable contributions in 2018? Use the 2018 standard deduction amounts for both 2018 and 2019.

Answer: $5,400, computed as follows:

	No Bunching		Bunching	
	2018	**2019**	**2018**	**2019**
(1) Standard deduction*	$13,600	$13,600	$13,600	$13,600
(2) Itemized deductions	11,500	11,500	19,000	4,000
Greater of (1) and (2)	$13,600	$13,600	$19,000	$13,600
Total deductions (combined years)	$27,200 ($13,600 + $13,600)		$32,600 ($19,000 + $13,600)	
Deductions gained through bunching	**$5,400** ($32,600 bunching deductions – $27,200 nonbunching deductions)			

*For 2018, her standard deduction is the $12,000 standard deduction for single taxpayers plus an additional $1,600 standard amount for age (see Exhibit 7-3). For 2019, we assume she has the same standard deduction as 2018.

DEDUCTION FOR QUALIFIED BUSINESS INCOME

LO 7-3

Deduction for Qualified Business Income

The last *from* AGI deduction that we will cover is the **deduction for qualified business income.** If applicable, this deduction is allowed as a *from* AGI deduction in addition to the taxpayer's itemized deductions or standard deduction. The deduction applies to taxpayers with qualified business income from a partnership, S Corporation, or sole proprietorship. Specifically, a taxpayer may deduct the lesser of:

(a) 20 percent of the taxpayer's **qualified business income** from a **qualified trade or business** (after application of the wage limit), plus 20 percent of the taxpayer's qualified real estate investment trust dividends and qualified publicly traded partnership income, if any or

(b) 20 percent of the excess, if any, of taxable income over the taxpayer's net capital gains (including qualified dividends).[31]

> **THE KEY FACTS**
>
> **Deduction for Qualified Business Income**
>
> • The deduction for qualified business income is a *from* AGI deduction in addition to the taxpayer's itemized deduction or standard deduction.
>
> • The deduction is limited to qualified trades or businesses and is subject to a number of limitations.

---

[30]Of course, as we discuss in the Tax Planning Strategies and Related Limitations chapter, taxpayers adopting this strategy must also consider the time value of money for the contribution amounts they pay in advance to determine whether a tax planning strategy designed to save taxes makes economic sense.

[31]The rules are a little more complex if the taxpayer receives cooperative dividends (known as patronage dividends) paid from the cooperative's profits to its members. Subject to limitations, cooperative dividends are eligible for the deduction for qualified business income.

A qualified trade or business is any trade or business other than a **specified service trade or business** and other than the trade or business of being an employee. A specified service trade or business is any trade or business involving the performance of services in the fields of health, law, consulting, accounting, actuarial science, performing arts, athletics, financial services, brokerage services, or any trade or business where the principal asset of such trade or business is the reputation or skill of one or more of its employees or owners, or which involves the performance of services that consist of investing and investment management trading, or dealing in securities, partnership interests, or commodities. Architecture and engineering services (their services build things) are specifically excluded from the definition of specified service trade or business.

For any year in which the taxpayer's taxable income (before the deduction for qualified business income) is less than $157,500 ($315,000, if married filing jointly), the exclusion for specified service trades or business will not apply (the business will be deemed a qualified trade or business). This means that a taxpayer operating a business that is not a qualified trade or business still gets the deduction for qualified business income if his or her taxable income is low enough. For taxpayers with taxable income above $157,500 ($315,000, if married filing jointly), the exclusion from the definition of a qualified business for specified service trades or businesses phases in over a $50,000 range ($100,000, if married filing jointly). The exclusion from the definition of a qualified business for specified service trades or businesses is fully phased in for taxpayers with taxable income in excess of $207,500 ($415,000, if married filing jointly).

Example 7-18

As described in Example 5-7, Courtney performs architectural consulting services outside of her employment with EWD. Will her income from the architectural services be considered qualified business income?

Answer: Yes. Architecture services are not a specified service or trade business. Thus, her income from the architectural services would be qualified trade or business income.

What if: Assume Courtney decides to establish a sole proprietorship to perform investment advising services. This year, Courtney reports $250,000 of taxable income before the deduction for qualified business income. Will her income from investment advisory services be considered qualified business income?

Answer: No. Investment advisory services fall within the definition of a specified service or trade business. Because her taxable income exceeds $207,500 ($157,500 + $50,000 phase-in range), the exclusion from the specified service trades or business rules based on taxable income does not apply. Thus, her investment advisory service income would not be considered qualified trade or business income. Consequently, she is not eligible for the deduction for qualified business income on that income.

What if: Assume Courtney decides to establish a sole proprietorship to perform investment advising services. This year, Courtney reports $100,000 of taxable income before the deduction for qualified business income. Will her income from investment advisory services be considered qualified business income?

Answer: Yes. Because her taxable income falls below the $157,500, the exclusion for specified service trades or businesses will not apply (the business will be deemed a qualified trade or business). Consequently, she is eligible for the deduction for qualified business income on that income.

What if: Assume Courtney decides to establish a sole proprietorship to perform investment advising services. This year, Courtney reports $187,500 of taxable income before the deduction for qualified business income. Will her income from advisory services be considered qualified business income?

Answer: If Courtney had $187,500 of taxable income (before the deduction for qualified business income), 60 percent of her investment advising income would not be considered qualified business income [($187,500 taxable income − $157,500)/($50,000 phase-out range)=60%]. The remaining 40 percent of her investment advising income would be considered qualified business income.

Qualified business income is the net amount of qualified items of income, gain, deduction, and loss with respect to the taxpayer's qualified trade or business conducted within the United States. Qualified items do not include specified investment-related income, deductions, or loss (e.g., capital gains or losses, dividends, interest income not allocable to a trade or business, etc.).[32] If the net amount of qualified business income from all qualified trades or businesses during the taxable year is a loss, it is carried forward as a loss from a qualified trade or business in the next taxable year.[33]

Limitations   The deduction for qualified business income cannot exceed the greater of:

1. 50 percent of the wages paid with respect to the qualified trade or business, or
2. the sum of 25 of percent of the wages with respect to the qualified trade or business plus 2.5 percent of the unadjusted basis, immediately after acquisition, of all qualified property in the qualified trade or business.[34]

For purposes of the wage-based limit, each partner or S corporation shareholder is treated as having wages for the year equal to his or her allocable share of the wages from the partnership or S corporation. The wage-based limits only apply to taxpayers with taxable income in excess of $157,500 ($315,000, if married filing jointly). The wage limit is phased in ratably over $50,000 ($100,000, if married filing jointly) so that it fully applies to taxpayers with taxable income in excess of $207,500 ($415,000, if married filing jointly).

Example 7-19

Courtney reports taxable income this year of $148,670 ($187,000 AGI less $38,330 itemized deductions; see Exhibit 6-11 and Example 7-14) before the deduction for qualified business income, and she has no capital gains and $700 of qualified dividends included in her taxable income (see Exhibit 5-6). Her architectural consulting services generates $18,000 of qualified business income, and she paid no wages in this business. What is Courtney's deduction for qualified business income?

Answer: $3,600. Because her taxable income before the qualified business income deduction is less than $157,500, the wage limitation does not apply. Likewise, Courtney is not limited by the taxable income limitation because 20 percent of her qualified business income ($18,000 × 20% = $3,600) is less than 20 percent of her taxable income in excess of her qualified dividends and before the deduction [($148,670 taxable income − $700 qualified dividends) × 20% = $29,594]. Thus, Courtney's deduction for qualified business income is $3,600 ($18,000 qualified business income × 20%).

What if: Assume Courtney reports taxable income this year of $300,000 (before the deduction for qualified business income), has no qualified dividends or capital gains, and that her architectural consulting business generates $75,000 of qualified business income, has no qualified property, and pays $20,000 of wages. What is Courtney's deduction for qualified business income?

(continued on page 7-20)

---

[32]Qualified business income does not include any amount paid by an S corporation that is treated as reasonable compensation of the taxpayer or any guaranteed payment for services rendered with respect to the trade or business.

[33]Similar to a qualified trade or business that has a qualified business loss for the current taxable year, any deduction allowed in a subsequent year is reduced (but not below zero) by 20 percent of any carryover qualified business loss.

[34]Qualified property is tangible, depreciable property held and available for use at the end of the tax year, used in the production of qualified business income during the year, for which the depreciable period has not ended by the end of the tax year. The depreciable period with respect to qualified property of a taxpayer means the period beginning on the date the property is first placed in service by the taxpayer and ending on the later of (a) the date 10 years after that date, or (b) the last day of the last full year in the applicable recovery period that would apply to the property under §168 (without regard to §168(g)).

Answer: $10,000. Before limitation, 20 percent of Courtney's qualified business income is $15,000 ($75,000 × 20%), and the greater of:

1. 50 percent of the wages paid by the qualified business ($20,000 × 50% = $10,000) or
2. 25 percent of the wages paid by the qualified business ($20,000 × 25% = $5,000) plus 2.5 percent of the unadjusted basis of qualified property ($0 × 2.5% = $0),

is $10,000. Because her taxable income of $300,000 exceeds the $157,500 phase-in threshold by more than $50,000, the wage limit fully applies. Thus, Courtney's deduction for qualified business income is limited to $10,000. Courtney is not limited by the taxable income limitation because 20 percent of her qualified business income after application of the wage limitation ($10,000) is less than 20 percent of her taxable income before the deduction ($300,000 × 20% = $60,000).

What if: Assume that Courtney reports taxable income this year of $177,500 (before the deduction for qualified business income), has no qualified dividends or capital gains, and that her architectural consulting business generates $75,000 of qualified business income, has no qualified property, and has $20,000 of wages. What is Courtney's deduction for qualified business income?

Answer: $13,000. Before limitation, 20 percent of Courtney's qualified business income is $15,000 ($75,000 × 20 percent), and the greater of:

1. 50 percent of the wages paid by the qualified business ($20,000 × 50% = $10,000) or
2. 25 percent of the wages paid by the qualified business ($20,000 × 25% = $5,000) plus 2.5 percent of the unadjusted basis of qualified property ($0 × 2.5% = $0),

is $10,000. Because her taxable income of $177,500 exceeds the $157,500 phase-in threshold by $20,000, the wage limit is phased in by 40 percent [[($177,500 − $157,500)/$50,000] phase-in range = 40 percent]. Courtney's wage limit of $5,000 (the excess of (a) 20 percent of business income of $15,000 over (b) 50 percent of wages, $10,000 ($20,000 × 50%)) is phased in by 40 percent. Thus, her deduction for qualified business income is limited to $13,000 [$15,000 − ($5,000 × 40%)]. Courtney is not limited by the taxable income limitation because 20 percent of her qualified business income after application of the wage limitation ($13,000) is less than 20 percent of her taxable income before the deduction ($177,500 × 20% = $35,500).

Taxable Income Summary

We now have enough information to calculate Courtney's and Gram's taxable income. Exhibit 7-4 shows Courtney's taxable income calculation and Exhibit 7-5 illustrates how this information would be displayed on page 2 of Courtney's Form 1040.

EXHIBIT 7-4   Courtney's Taxable Income

Description	Amount	Reference
AGI	$187,000	Exhibit 6-11
Less: Greater of (1) itemized deductions ($38,330) or (2) standard deduction ($18,000)	(38,330)	Example 7-15
Less: Deduction for qualified business income	(3,600)	Example 7-19
Taxable income	$145,070	

EXHIBIT 7-5   Courtney's Taxable Income Computation as Presented on Form 1040, Page 2

Form 1040 (2017) — Page **2**

Tax and Credits	38	Amount from line 37 (adjusted gross income)	38		187,000
	39a	Check if: ☐ **You** were born before January 2, 1953, ☐ **Blind.** ☐ **Spouse** was born before January 2, 1953, ☐ **Blind.** } Total boxes checked ▶ 39a			
	b	If your spouse itemizes on a separate return or you were a dual-status alien, check here▶ 39b☐			
Standard Deduction for— • People who check any box on line	40	**Itemized deductions** (from Schedule A) **or** your **standard deduction** (see left margin) . .	40		38,330
	41	Subtract line 40 from line 38	41		148,670
	42	Deduction for qualified business income	42		3,600
	43	**Taxable income.** Subtract line 42 from line 41. If line 42 is more than line 41, enter -0- . .	43		145,070

Exhibit 7-6 provides Gram's taxable income calculation.

EXHIBIT 7-6   Gram's Taxable Income

Description	Amount	Reference
(1) AGI	$ 15,590	Exhibit 6-12
(2) Greater of (a) itemized deductions ($11,500) or (b) standard deduction ($13,600)	(13,600)	Example 7-17
Taxable income	$ 1,990	(1) + (2)

Note that because Gram's gross income of $16,000 (Exhibit 5-7) is more than her standard deduction amount ($13,600), she is required to file a tax return.

CONCLUSION

We started this chapter with Courtney's and Gram's adjusted gross incomes. In this chapter, we first identified the duo's separate itemized deductions. Courtney deducted her itemized deductions because they exceeded her standard deduction. Gram, on the other hand, deducted her standard deduction. Finally, Courtney was able to take advantage of the deduction for qualified business income, while Gram did not have any qualified business income. By subtracting their *from* AGI deductions from their AGI, we determined taxable income for both Courtney and Gram. With this knowledge, we proceed to the next chapter and address issues relating to determining the amount of tax Courtney and Gram are required to pay on their taxable income. As we'll discover, it's not always as simple as applying taxable income to a tax rate schedule to determine the tax liability.

Summary

Describe the different types of itemized deductions available to individuals and compute itemized deductions.   **LO 7-1**

- The medical expense deduction is designed to provide tax benefits to needy individuals but is subject to significant floor limitation.
- The itemized deduction for interest is limited to home mortgage interest and investment interest, and the latter is limited by net investment income.
- The deduction for charitable contributions extends to contributions of money and property to qualifying charities. The charitable deduction is subject to ceiling limitations, which are more restrictive for donations of property.
- The deduction for taxes is subject to a cap and includes state income and property taxes. Sales taxes can be deducted in lieu of deducting state and local income taxes.

Determine the standard deduction available to individuals.   **LO 7-2**

- Taxpayers generally deduct the greater of their standard deduction or their itemized deductions.
- The amount of the standard deduction varies according to the taxpayer's filing status, age, and eyesight.

Calculate the deduction for qualified business income.   **LO 7-3**

- The deduction for qualified business income is a *from* AGI deduction in addition to the taxpayer's itemized deduction or standard deduction.
- The deduction is limited to qualified trades or businesses and is subject to a number of limitations.

KEY TERMS

bunching itemized deductions (7-16)
capital gain property (7-8)
ceiling (7-10)
deduction for qualified business income (7-17)
floor limitation (7-4)

miscellaneous itemized deductions (7-12)
ordinary income property (7-8)
private nonoperating foundations (7-10)
private operating foundations (7-10)

qualified business income (7-17)
qualified trade or business (7-17)
specified service trade or business (7-18)
standard deduction (7-13)

DISCUSSION QUESTIONS

Discussion Questions are available in Connect®.

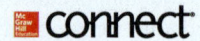

LO 7-1 1. Explain why the medical expense provisions are sometimes referred to as "wherewithal" deductions and how this rationale is reflected in the limits on these deductions.

LO 7-1 2. Describe the type of medical expenditures that qualify for the medical expense deduction. Does the cost of meals consumed while hospitalized qualify for the deduction? Do over-the-counter drugs and medicines qualify for the deduction?

LO 7-1 3. Under what circumstances can a taxpayer deduct medical expenses paid for a member of his family? Does it matter if the family member reports significant amounts of gross income and cannot be claimed as a dependent?

LO 7-1 4. What types of taxes qualify to be deducted as itemized deductions? Would a vehicle registration fee qualify as a deductible tax?

LO 7-1 5. Explain the argument that the deductions for charitable contributions and home mortgage interest represent indirect subsidies for these activities.

LO 7-1
research 6. Cash donations to charities are subject to a number of very specific substantiation requirements. Describe these requirements and how charitable gifts can be substantiated. Describe the substantiation requirements for property donations.

LO 7-1 7. Describe the conditions in which a donation of property to a charity will result in a charitable contribution deduction of fair market value and when it will result in a deduction of the tax basis of the property.

LO 7-1 8. Jake is a retired jockey who takes monthly trips to Las Vegas to gamble on horse races. So far this year, Jake has won almost $47,500 during his trips to Las Vegas while spending $27,250 on travel expenses and incurring $62,400 of gambling losses. Explain how Jake's gambling winnings and related costs will be treated for tax purposes.

LO 7-1
research 9. Frank paid $3,700 in fees for an accountant to tabulate business information (Frank operates as a self-employed contractor and files a Schedule C). The accountant also spent time tabulating Frank's income from his investments and determining Frank's personal itemized deductions. Explain to Frank whether or not he can deduct the $3,700 as a business expense or as an itemized deduction, and provide a citation to an authority that supports your conclusion.

LO 7-1 10. Contrast ceiling and floor limitations, and give an example of each.

LO 7-1 11. Identify which itemized deductions are subject to floor limitations, ceiling limitations, or some combination of these limits.

12. Describe the tax benefits from "bunching" itemized deductions in one year. Describe the characteristics of the taxpayers who are most likely to benefit from using bunching and explain why this is so.

`LO 7-2`

13. Explain how the standard deduction is rationalized and why the standard deduction might be viewed as a floor limit on itemized deductions.

`LO 7-2`

14. Determine whether a taxpayer can change his or her election to itemize deductions once a return is filed. (*Hint:* Read about itemization under Reg. §1.63-1.)

`LO 7-2` **research**

15. Determine whether a taxpayer who is claimed as a dependent on another return is entitled to an addition to the standard deduction for age or blindness. (*Hint:* Read the calculation of the standard deduction under IRC §63.)

`LO 7-2`

research

16. Describe what is meant by qualified business income for purposes of the deduction for qualified business income.

`LO 7-3`

17. Under what circumstances would business income from an accounting practice qualify for the deduction for qualified business income?

`LO 7-3`

18. For purposes of the deduction for qualified business income, what is a specified service trade or business and why is it important?

`LO 7-3`

PROBLEMS

Select problems are available in Connect®.

connect

19. In each of the following independent cases, indicate the amount (1) deductible *for* AGI, (2) deductible *from* AGI, and (3) neither deductible *for* nor *from* AGI before considering income limitations or the standard deduction.

`LO 7-1`

 a) Ted paid $8 rent on a safety deposit box at the bank. In this box he kept the few shares of stock that he owned.

 b) Tyler paid $85 for minor repairs to the fence at a rental house he owned.

 c) Timmy paid $545 for health insurance premiums this year (not through an exchange and not with pretax dollars). Timmy is employed full time and his employer paid the remaining premiums as a qualified fringe benefit.

 d) Tess paid $1,150 of state income taxes on her consulting income.

20. In each of the following independent cases, indicate the amount (1) deductible *for* AGI, (2) deductible *from* AGI, and (3) neither deductible *for* nor deductible *from* AGI before considering income limitations or the standard deduction.

`LO 7-1`

 a) Fran spent $90 for uniforms for use on her job. Her employer reimbursed her for $75 of this amount under an accountable plan (and did not report the reimbursement as wages).

 b) Timothy, a plumber employed by ACE Plumbing, spent $65 for small tools to be used on his job, but he was not reimbursed by ACE.

 c) Jake is a perfume salesperson. Because of his high pay, he receives no allowance or reimbursement from his employer for advertising expenses even though his position requires him to advertise frequently. During the year, he spent $2,200 on legitimate business advertisements.

 d) Trey is a self-employed, special-duty nurse. He spent $120 for uniforms.

 e) Mary, a professor at a community college, spent $340 for magazine subscriptions. The magazines were helpful for her research activities, but she was not reimbursed for the expenditures.

 f) Wayne lost $325 on the bets he made at the race track, but he won $57 playing slot machines.

LO 7-1

21. Penny, a full-time biochemist, loves stock car racing. To feed her passion, she bought a used dirt-track car and has started entering some local dirt-track races. The prize money is pretty small ($1,000 for the winner), but she really is not in it for the money. Penny reported the following income and expenses from her nights at the track:

Prize money	$2,500
Expenses:	
Transportation from her home to the races	1,000
Depreciation on the dirt-track car	4,000
Entry fees	3,500
Oil, gas, supplies, repairs for the dirt-track car	2,050

What are the tax effects of Penny's racing income and expenses assuming that the racing activity is a hobby for Penny?

LO 7-1

22. Simpson, age 45, is a single individual who is employed full time by Duff Corporation. This year Simpson reports AGI of $50,000 and has incurred the following medical expenses:

Dentist charges	$ 900
Physician's charges	1,800
Optical charges	500
Cost of eyeglasses	300
Hospital charges	2,100
Prescription drugs	250
Over-the-counter drugs	450
Medical insurance premiums (not through an exchange)	775

a) Calculate the amount of medical expenses that will be included with Simpson's itemized deductions after any applicable limitations.

b) Suppose that Simpson was reimbursed for $250 of the physician's charges and $1,200 for the hospital costs. Calculate the amount of medical expenses that will be included with Simpson's itemized deductions after any applicable limitations.

LO 7-1

 **research**

23. Tim is 45 years old and considering enrolling in an insurance program that provides for long-term care insurance. He is curious about whether the insurance premiums are deductible as a medical expense. If so, he wants to know the maximum amount that can be deducted in any year.

LO 7-1

research

24. Doctor Bones prescribed physical therapy in a pool to treat Jack's broken back. In response to this advice (and for no other reason), Jack built a swimming pool in his backyard and strictly limited use of the pool to physical therapy. Jack paid $25,000 to build the pool, but he wondered if this amount could be deducted as a medical expense. Determine if a capital expenditure such as the cost of a swimming pool qualifies for the medical expense deduction.

LO 7-1

25. Charles has AGI of $50,000 and has made the following payments related to (1) land he inherited from his deceased aunt and (2) a personal vacation taken last year. Calculate the amount of taxes Charles may include in his itemized deductions for the year under the following circumstances:

State inheritance tax on the land	$1,200
County real estate tax on the land	1,500
School district tax on the land	690
City special assessment on the land (replacing curbs and gutters)	700
State tax on airline tickets (paid on vacation)	125
Local hotel tax (paid during vacation)	195

a) Suppose that Charles holds the land for appreciation.

b) Suppose that Charles holds the land for rent.

c) Suppose that Charles holds the land for appreciation and that the vacation was actually a business trip.

26. Dan has AGI of $50,000 and paid the following taxes during this tax year. Calculate how much Dan can deduct for taxes as an itemized deduction this year. **LO 7-1**

State income tax withholding	$1,400
State income tax estimated payments	750
Federal income tax withholding	3,000
Social Security tax withheld from wages	2,100
State excise tax on liquor	400
Automobile license (based on the car's weight)	300
State sales tax paid	475

27. Tim is a single, cash-method taxpayer and an AGI of $50,000. In April of this year, Tim paid $1,020 with his state income tax return for the previous year. During the year, Tim had $5,400 of state income tax and $18,250 of federal income tax withheld from his salary. In addition, Tim made estimated payments of $1,360 and $1,900 of state and federal income taxes, respectively. Finally, Tim expects to receive a refund of $500 for state income taxes when he files his state tax return for this year in April next year. What is the amount of taxes that Tim can deduct as an itemized deduction? **LO 7-1**

28. Janyce, a single taxpayer, has AGI of $125,000 and paid the following taxes this year. Calculate how much Janyce can deduct for taxes as an itemized deduction this year. **LO 7-1**

State income tax withholding	$7,200
State income tax estimated payments	600
State income tax refund (applied to this year's tax)	800
State automobile tax (based on car's value)	1,900

29. Jack, who files married separate, has AGI of $45,000 and paid the following taxes this year. Calculate how much Jack can deduct for taxes as an itemized deduction this year. **LO 7-1**

State income tax withholding	$6,200
State income tax estimated payments	500
State income tax refund (applied to this year's tax)	1,000
State automobile tax (based on car's weight)	800

30. This year Randy paid $28,000 of interest. (Randy borrowed $450,000 to buy his residence, which is currently worth $500,000.) Randy also paid $2,500 of interest on his car loan and $4,200 of margin interest to his stockbroker (investment interest expense). How much of this interest expense can Randy deduct as an itemized deduction under the following circumstances? **LO 7-1**

a) Randy received $2,200 of interest this year and no other investment income or expenses. His AGI is $75,000.

b) Randy had no investment income this year, and his AGI is $75,000.

31. This year, Major Healy paid $40,000 of interest on a mortgage on his home (he borrowed $800,000 to buy the residence in 2015; $900,000 original purchase price and value at purchase), $6,000 of interest on a $120,000 home-equity loan on his home (loan proceeds were used to buy antique cars), and $10,000 of interest on a mortgage on his vacation home (borrowed $200,000 to purchase the home in 2010). Major Healy's AGI is $220,000. How much interest expense can Major Healy deduct as an itemized deduction? **LO 7-1**

LO 7-1 32. Juanita paid $50,000 of interest on a mortgage on her home (loan of $1,000,000 at 5% interest rate to buy the residence in 2018; $1,200,000 original purchase price and value at purchase) and $6,500 of interest on a $100,000 home-equity loan on her home (loan proceeds were used to buy furniture). Juanita's AGI is $600,000. How much interest expense can Juanita deduct as an itemized deduction?

LO 7-1 33. Ray Ray made the following contributions this year.

Charity	Property	Cost	FMV
Athens Academy School	Cash	$ 5,000	$ 5,000
United Way	Cash	4,000	4,000
American Heart Association	Antique painting	15,000	75,000
First Methodist Church	Coca-Cola stock	12,000	20,000

Determine the maximum amount of charitable deduction for each of these contributions *ignoring* the AGI ceiling on charitable contributions and assuming that the American Heart Association plans to sell the antique painting to fund its operations. Ray Ray has owned the painting and Coca-Cola stock since 1990.

LO 7-1 34. Calvin reviewed his cancelled checks and receipts this year for charitable contributions, which included a painting and IBM stock. He has owned the IBM stock and painting since 2005. Calculate Calvin's charitable contribution deduction and carryover (if any) under the following circumstances.

Donee	Item	Cost	FMV
Hobbs Medical Center	IBM stock	$5,000	$22,000
State Museum	Painting	5,000	3,000
A needy family	Food and clothes	400	250
United Way	Cash	8,000	8,000

a) Calvin's AGI is $100,000.

b) Calvin's AGI is $100,000 and the State Museum told Calvin that it plans to sell the painting.

c) Calvin's AGI is $50,000.

d) Calvin's AGI is $100,000 and Hobbs is a nonoperating private foundation.

e) Calvin's AGI is $100,000 and the painting is worth $10,000.

LO 7-1 35. In addition to cash contributions to charity, Dean decided to donate shares of stock and a portrait painted during the earlier part of the last century. Dean purchased the stock and portrait many years ago as investments. Dean reported the following recipients:

Charity	Property	Cost	FMV
State University	Cash	$15,000	$15,000
Red Cross	Cash	14,500	14,500
State History Museum	Antique painting	5,000	82,000
City Medical Center	Dell stock	28,000	17,000

a) Determine the maximum amount of charitable deduction for each of these contributions *ignoring* the AGI ceiling on charitable contributions.

b) Assume that Dean's AGI this year is $150,000. Determine Dean's itemized deduction for his charitable contributions this year and any carryover.

c) Suppose Dean is a dealer in antique paintings and had held the painting for sale before the contribution. What is Dean's charitable contribution deduction for the painting in this situation?

d) Suppose that Dean's objective with the donation to the museum was to finance expansion of the historical collection. Hence, Dean was not surprised when the museum announced the sale of the portrait because of its limited historical value. What is Dean's charitable contribution deduction for the painting in this situation (ignoring AGI limitations)?

36. Trevor is a single individual who is a cash-method, calendar-year taxpayer. For each of the next two years (year 1 and year 2), Trevor expects to report AGI of $80,000, contribute $8,000 to charity, and pay $2,800 in state income taxes.   **LO 7-1**   **planning**

    a) Estimate Trevor's taxable income for year 1 and year 2 using the 2018 amounts for the standard deduction for both years.

    b) Now assume that Trevor combines his anticipated charitable contributions for the next two years and makes the combined contribution in December of year 1. Estimate Trevor's taxable income for each of the next two years using the 2018 amounts for the standard deduction. Reconcile the total taxable income to your solution to part (a).

    c) Trevor plans to purchase a residence next year, and he estimates that additional property taxes and residential interest will cost $2,000 and $10,000, respectively, each year. Estimate Trevor's taxable income for each of the next two years (year 1 and year 2) using the 2018 amounts for the standard deduction and also assuming Trevor makes the charitable contribution of $8,000 and state tax payments of $2,800 in each year.

    d) Assume that Trevor makes the charitable contribution for year 2 and pays the real estate taxes for year 2 in December of year 1. Estimate Trevor's taxable income for year 1 and year 2 using the 2018 amounts for the standard deduction. Reconcile the total taxable income to your solution to part (c).

    e) Explain the conditions in which the bunching strategy in part (d) will generate tax savings for Trevor.

37. Simon lost $5,000 gambling this year on a trip to Las Vegas. In addition, he paid $2,000 to his broker for managing his $200,000 portfolio and $1,500 to his accountant for preparing his tax return. In addition, Simon incurred $2,500 in transportation costs commuting back and forth from his home to his employer's office, which were not reimbursed. Calculate the amount of these expenses that Simon is able to deduct (assuming he itemizes his deductions).   **LO 7-1**

38. Stephanie is 12 years old and often assists neighbors on weekends by babysitting their children. Calculate the 2018 standard deduction Stephanie will claim under the following independent circumstances (assume that Stephanie's parents will claim her as a dependent).   **LO 7-2**

    a) Stephanie reported $850 of earnings from her babysitting.

    b) Stephanie reported $1,500 of earnings from her babysitting.

    c) Stephanie reported $18,000 of earnings from her babysitting.

39. Jackson is 18 years old and has a dog-sitting business. Calculate the 2018 standard deduction Jackson will claim under the following independent circumstances.   **LO 7-2**

    a) Jackson reported $2,000 of earnings from his dog sitting, $300 in interest income from his savings account, and Jackson's parents claim him as a dependent.

    b) Jackson reported $500 of earnings from his dog sitting and $2,000 in interest income from his savings account, and Jackson's parents claim him as a dependent.

    c) Jackson reported $8,000 of earnings from his dog sitting, $3,000 in interest income, and Jackson's parents do not claim him as a dependent.

40. Amelie, a retired physician, is 66 years old. Determine her standard deduction under the following scenarios.   **LO 7-2**

    a) Amelie is married to Roget, age 52, and they file married joint.

    b) Amelie is single.

    c) Amelie is single and her 10-year-old granddaughter, Emma, lives with her. Amelie supports Emma and claims her as a dependent.

LO 7-3 41. Roquan, a single taxpayer, is an attorney and practices as a sole proprietor. This year, Roquan had net business income of $90,000 from his law practice. Assume that Roquan pays $40,000 wages to his employees, he has $10,000 of property (unadjusted basis of equipment he purchased last year), has no capital gains or qualified dividends, and his taxable income before the deduction for qualified business income is $100,000.

a) Calculate Roquan's deduction for qualified business income.

b) Assume the same facts as earlier, except Roquan's taxable income before the deduction for qualified business income is $300,000.

LO 7-3 42. Katie, a single taxpayer, is a shareholder in Engineers One, a civil engineering company. This year, Katie's share of net business income from Engineers One is $200,000. Assume that Katie's allocation of wages paid by Engineers One to its employees is $300,000 and her allocation of Engineers One's qualified property is $150,000 (unadjusted basis of equipment, all purchased within past three years). Assume Katie has no other business income, no capital gains or qualified dividends, and that her taxable income before the deduction for qualified business income is $400,000.

a) Calculate Katie's deduction for qualified business income.

b) Assume the same facts as earlier, except Katie's net business income from Engineers One is $400,000 and taxable income before the deduction for qualified business income is $350,000.

LO 7-3 43. Felipe, a single taxpayer, is a technology consultant, who operates as a sole proprietorship. Felipe's net business income is $600,000, he pays wages of $100,000 to his employees, and he has $200,000 of qualified property (unadjusted basis). Felipe's taxable income before the deduction for qualified business income is $500,000. Assume he has no capital gains or qualified dividends.

a) Calculate Felipe's deduction for qualified business income.

b) How would your answer to (a) change if Felipe was an investment broker.

COMPREHENSIVE PROBLEMS

Select problems are available in Connect®.

tax forms

44. Read the following letter and help Shady Slim with his tax situation. Assume that his gross income is $172,900 (which consists only of salary) for purposes of this problem.

December 31, 2018

To the friendly student tax preparer:

Hi, it's Shady Slim again. I just got back from my 55th birthday party, and I'm told that you need some more information from me in order to complete my tax return. I'm an open book! I'll tell you whatever I think you need to know.

Let me tell you a few more things about my life. As you may recall, I am divorced from my wife, Alice. I know that it's unusual, but I have custody of my son, Shady, Jr. The judge owed me a few favors and I really love the kid. He lives with me full-time and my ex-wife gets him every other weekend. I pay the vast majority of my son's expenses. I think Alice should have to pay some child support, but she doesn't have to pay a dime. The judge didn't owe me that much, I guess.

Remember when I told you about that guy that hit me with his car? I had a bunch of medical expenses that were not reimbursed by the lawsuit or by my insurance. I incurred a total of $20,000 in medical expenses, and I was only reimbursed for $11,000. Good thing I can write off medical expenses, right?

I contributed a lot of money to charity this year (and have receipt documentation for all contributions). I'm such a nice guy! I gave $1,000 in cash to the March of Dimes. I contributed some of my old furniture to the church. It was some good stuff! I contributed a red velvet couch and my old recliner. The furniture is considered vintage and is worth $5,000 today (the appraiser surprised me!), even though I only paid $1,000 for it back in the day. When I contributed the furniture, the pastor said he didn't like the fabric and was going to sell the furniture to pay for some more pews in the church. Oh well, some people just have no taste, right? Roca Cola had a charity drive for the United Way this year and I contributed $90. Turns out, I don't even miss it, because Roca Cola takes it right off my paycheck every month . . . $15 a month starting in July. My pay stub verifies that I contributed the $90 to the United Way. Oh, one other bit of charity from me this year. An old buddy of mine was down on his luck. He lost his job and his house. I gave him $500 to help him out.

I paid a lot of money in interest this year. I paid a total of $950 in personal credit card interest. I also paid $18,000 in interest on my $500,000 home mortgage that helped me buy my dream home. I also paid $2,000 in real estate taxes for my new house.

A few other things I want to tell you about this year. Someone broke into my house and stole my kid's brand new bicycle and my set of golf clubs. The total loss from theft was $900. I paid $125 in union dues this year. I had to pay $1,200 for new suits for my job. Roca Cola requires its managers to wear suits every day on the job. I spent a total of $1,300 to pay for gas to commute to my job this year.

Oh, this is pretty cool. I've always wanted to be a firefighter. I spent $1,400 in tuition to go to the local firefighter's school. I did this because someone told me that I can deduct the tuition as an itemized deduction, so the money would be coming back to me.

That should be all the information you need right now. Please calculate my taxable income and complete pages 1 and 2 of Form 1040 (through taxable income, line 43) and Schedule A. You're still doing this for free, right?

45. Shauna Coleman is single. She is employed as an architectural designer for Streamline Design (SD). Shauna wanted to determine her taxable income for this year. She correctly calculated her AGI. However, she wasn't sure how to compute the rest of her taxable income. She provided the following information with hopes that you could use it to determine her taxable income.

tax forms

a) Shauna paid $4,680 for medical expenses for care related to a broken ankle. Also, Shauna's boyfriend, Blake, drove Shauna (in her car) a total of 115 miles to the doctor's office so she could receive care for her broken ankle.

b) Shauna paid a total of $3,400 in health insurance premiums during the year (not through an exchange). SD did not reimburse any of this expense. Besides the health insurance premiums and the medical expenses for her broken ankle, Shauna had Lasik eye surgery last year and she paid $3,000 for the surgery (she received no insurance reimbursement). She also incurred $450 of other medical expenses for the year.

c) SD withheld $1,800 of state income tax, $7,495 of Social Security tax, and $14,500 of federal income tax from Shauna's paychecks throughout the year.

d) In 2018, Shauna was due a refund of $250 for overpaying her 2017 state taxes. On her 2017 state tax return that she filed in April 2018, she applied the overpayment toward her 2018 state tax liability. She estimated that her state tax liability for 2018 will be $2,300.

e) Shauna paid $3,200 of property taxes on her personal residence. She also paid $500 to the developer of her subdivision, because he had to replace the sidewalk in certain areas of the subdivision.

f) Shauna paid a $200 property tax based on the state's estimate of the value of her car.

g) Shauna has a home mortgage loan in the amount of $220,000 that she secured when she purchased her home. The home is worth about $400,000. Shauna paid interest of $12,300 on the loan this year.

h) Shauna made several charitable contributions throughout the year. She contributed stock in ZYX Corp. to the Red Cross. On the date of the contribution, the fair market value of the donated shares was $1,000 and her basis in the shares was $400. Shauna originally bought the ZYX Corp. stock in 2008. Shauna also contributed $300 cash to State University and religious artifacts she has held for several years to her church. The artifacts were valued at $500 and Shauna's basis in the items was $300. Shauna had every reason to believe the church would keep them on display indefinitely. Shauna also drove 200 miles doing church-related errands for her minister. Finally, Shauna contributed $1,200 of services to her church last year.

i) Shauna paid $250 in investment advisory fees and another $150 to have her tax return prepared (that is, she paid $150 in 2018 to have her 2017 tax return prepared).

j) Shauna is involved in horse racing as a hobby. During the year, she won $2,500 in prize money and incurred $10,000 in expenses. She has never had a profitable year with her horse-racing activities, so she acknowledges that this is a hobby for federal income tax purposes.

k) Shauna sustained $2,000 in gambling losses over the year (mostly horse-racing bets) and had only $200 in winnings.

Required:

A) Assume Shauna's AGI is $107,000. Determine Shauna's taxable income and complete page 2 of Form 1040 (through taxable income, line 43) and Schedule A.

B) Assume Shauna's AGI is $207,000. Determine Shauna's taxable income and complete page 2 of Form 1040 (through taxable income, line 43) and Schedule A.

tax forms

46. Joe and Jessie are married and have one dependent child, Lizzie. Lizzie is currently in college at State University. Joe works as a design engineer for a manufacturing firm while Jessie runs a craft business from their home. Jessie's craft business consists of making craft items for sale at craft shows that are held periodically at various locations. Jessie spends considerable time and effort on her craft business and it has been consistently profitable over the years. Joe and Jessie own a home and pay interest on their home loan (balance of $220,000) and a personal loan to pay for Lizzie's college expenses (balance of $35,000). Neither Joe nor Jessie is blind or over age 65, and they plan to file as married-joint. Based on their estimates, determine Joe and Jessie's AGI and taxable income for the year and complete pages 1 and 2 of Form 1040 (through taxable income, line 43) and Schedule A. Assume that the employer portion of the self-employment tax on Jessie's income is $831. Joe and Jessie have summarized the income and expenses they expect to report this year as follows:

Income:

Joe's salary	$124,100
Jessie's craft sales	18,400
Interest from certificate of deposit	1,650
Interest from Treasury bond funds	716
Interest from municipal bond funds	920

Expenditures:

Federal income tax withheld from Joe's wages	$ 13,700
State income tax withheld from Joe's wages	6,400
Social Security tax withheld from Joe's wages	7,482
Real estate taxes on residence	6,200

Automobile licenses (based on weight)	310
State sales tax paid	1,150
Home mortgage interest	14,000
Interest on Masterdebt credit card	2,300
Medical expenses (unreimbursed)	1,690
Joe's employee expenses (unreimbursed)	2,400
Cost of Jessie's craft supplies	4,260
Postage for mailing crafts	145
Travel and lodging for craft shows	2,230
Self-employment tax on Jessie's craft income	1,662
College tuition paid for Lizzie	5,780
Interest on loans to pay Lizzie's tuition	3,200
Lizzie's room and board at college	12,620
Cash contributions to the Red Cross	525

 **ROGER** | *CPA Review*

Sample CPA Exam questions from Roger CPA Review are available in Connect as support for the topics in this text. These Multiple Choice Questions and Task-Based Simulations include expert-written explanations and solutions and provide a starting point for students to become familiar with the content and functionality of the actual CPA Exam.

chapter

8

Individual Income Tax Computation and Tax Credits

Learning Objectives

Upon completing this chapter, you should be able to:

LO 8-1 Determine a taxpayer's regular tax liability.

LO 8-2 Compute a taxpayer's alternative minimum tax liability.

LO 8-3 Calculate a taxpayer's employment and self-employment taxes payable.

LO 8-4 Compute a taxpayer's allowable child tax credit, child and dependent care credit, American opportunity credit, lifetime learning credit, and earned income credit.

LO 8-5 Explain how to compute a taxpayer's underpayment, late filing, and late payment penalties.

©Image Source

Storyline Summary

Taxpayers:	Courtney Wilson, age 40, and Courtney's mother Dorothy "Gram" Weiss, age 70
Family description:	Courtney is divorced with a son, Deron, age 10, and a daughter, Ellen, age 20. Gram is currently residing with Courtney.
Location:	Kansas City, Missouri
Employment status:	Courtney works as an architect for EWD. Gram is retired.
Filing status:	Courtney is head of household. Gram is single.
Current situation:	Courtney and Gram have computed their taxable income. Now they are trying to determine their tax liability, tax refund, or additional taxes due and whether they owe any payment-related penalties.

Courtney has already determined her taxable income. Now she's working on computing her tax liability. She knows she owes a significant amount of regular income tax on her employment and business activities. However, she's not sure how to compute the tax on the qualified dividends she received from General Electric and is worried that she may be subject to the alternative minimum tax this year. Finally, Courtney knows she owes some self-employment taxes on her business income. Courtney would like to determine whether she is eligible to claim any tax credits, such as the child tax credit for her two children and education credits, because she paid for a portion of her daughter Ellen's tuition at the University of Missouri–Kansas City this year. Courtney is hoping that she has paid enough in taxes during the year to avoid underpayment penalties.

She's planning on filing her tax return and paying her taxes on time.

Gram's tax situation is much more straightforward. She needs to determine the regular income tax on her taxable income. Her income is so low she knows she need not worry about the alternative minimum tax, and she believes she doesn't owe any self-employment tax. Gram didn't prepay any taxes this year, so she is concerned that she might be required to pay an underpayment penalty. She also expects to file her tax return and pay her taxes by the looming due date.

to be continued . . .

In earlier chapters we've learned how to compute taxable income for taxpayers such as Courtney and Gram. This chapter describes how to determine a taxpayer's tax liability for the year. We discover that the process is not as easy as simply applying taxable income to the applicable tax rate schedule or tax table. Taxpayers may generate taxable income that is taxed at rates not provided in the tax rate schedules or tax tables. We will learn that they may also be required to pay taxes in addition to the regular income tax. We also describe tax credits taxpayers may use to reduce their gross taxes payable. We conclude the chapter by describing taxpayer filing requirements and identifying certain penalties taxpayers may be required to pay when they underpay or are late paying their taxes. We start our coverage by explaining how to compute one's regular tax liability.

LO 8-1 REGULAR FEDERAL INCOME TAX COMPUTATION

Once taxpayers have determined their taxable income, they are ready to compute their gross tax from a series of progressive tax rates called a **tax rate schedule.**

Tax Rate Schedules

Congress has constructed four different tax rate schedules for individuals. The applicable tax rate schedule is determined by the taxpayer's filing status, which we discussed in depth in the Individual Income Tax Overview, Dependents, and Filing Status chapter. Recall that a taxpayer's filing status is one of the following:

1. Married filing jointly.
2. Qualifying widow or widower, also referred to as surviving spouse.
3. Married filing separately.
4. Head of household.
5. Single.

As we described in the Introduction to Tax chapter, a tax rate schedule is composed of several ranges of income taxed at different (increasing) rates. Each separate range of income subject to a different tax rate is referred to as a **tax bracket.** While each filing status has its own tax rate schedule (married filing jointly and qualifying widow or widower use the same rate schedule), all tax rate schedules consist of tax brackets taxed at 10 percent, 12 percent, 22 percent, 24 percent, 32 percent, 35 percent, and 37 percent. However, the width or range of income within each bracket varies by filing status. In general, the tax brackets are widest and higher levels of income are taxed at the lowest rates for the married filing jointly filing status, followed by the head of household filing status, single filing status, and finally, the married filing separately filing status.

The tax rate schedule for each filing status is provided in Appendix D. Notice that the married filing separately schedule is the same as the married filing jointly schedule except that the taxable income levels listed in the schedule are exactly one-half the taxable income levels for married filing jointly.

Example 8-1

As we determined in the Individual Deductions chapter, Courtney files under the head of household filing status and her 2018 taxable income is $145,070 (see Exhibit 6-11).

What if: For now, let's *assume* that all of Courtney's income is taxed as ordinary income. That is, assume that none of her income is taxed at a preferential rate (some is, but we'll address this in a bit). What is the tax on her taxable income?

Answer: $27,715. Using the head of household tax rate schedule, her taxable income falls in the 24 percent marginal tax rate bracket, in between $82,500 and $157,500, so her tax is computed as follows:

Description	Amount	Explanation
(1) Base tax	$ 12,698	From head of household tax rate schedule for taxpayer with taxable income in 24% bracket.
(2) Income taxed at marginal tax rate	62,570	$145,070 – $82,500 from head of household tax rate schedule.
(3) Marginal tax rate	24%	From head of household tax rate schedule.
(4) Tax on income at marginal tax rate	15,017	(2) × (3)
Tax on taxable income	**$27,715**	(1) + (4), rounded

Example 8-2

As we determined in the Individual Deductions chapter, Gram files under the single filing status. In the Individual Deductions chapter we calculated her 2018 taxable income to be $1,990 (see Exhibit 6-13). None of her income is taxed at a preferential rate. What is the tax on her taxable income using the tax rate schedules?

Answer: $199 ($1,990 × 10%)

For administrative convenience and to prevent low- and middle-income taxpayers from making mathematical errors using a tax rate schedule, the IRS provides **tax tables** that present the gross tax for various amounts of taxable income under $100,000 and filing status (it's impractical to provide a table for essentially unlimited amounts of income). Taxpayers with taxable income less than $100,000 generally must use the tax tables to determine their tax liability.[1]

Because the tax tables generate nearly the same tax as calculated from the tax rate schedule, we use the tax rate schedules throughout this chapter.

Marriage Penalty or Benefit

An interesting artifact of the tax rate schedules is that they can impose what some refer to as a **marriage penalty,** but they may actually produce a **marriage benefit.** A marriage penalty (benefit) occurs when, for a given level of income, a married couple incurs a greater (lesser) tax liability by using the married filing jointly tax rate schedule to determine the tax on their joint income than they would have owed (in total) if each spouse had used the single tax rate schedule to compute the tax on their individual incomes. Exhibit 8-1 explores the marriage penalty in a scenario in which both spouses earn income and another in which only one spouse earns income. As the exhibit illustrates, the marriage penalty applies to couples with two wage earners with high incomes, but a marriage benefit applies to couples with single breadwinners. For couples with two wage earners with moderate to low incomes, there is typically not a marriage penalty.

Exceptions to the Basic Tax Computation

In certain circumstances, taxpayers cannot completely determine their final tax liability from their tax rate schedule or tax table. Taxpayers must perform additional computations to determine their tax liability (1) when they recognize long-term capital gains or receive dividends that are taxed at preferential (lower) rates, (2) when they receive investment income subject to the net investment income tax, or (3) when the taxpayer is a child and the child's unearned income is taxed using the trusts and estates tax rates. We describe these additional computations in detail below.

[1]Exceptions to this requirement include taxpayers subject to the kiddie tax, with qualified dividends or capital gains, or claiming the foreign-earned income exclusion. You may view the tax tables in the instructions for Form 1040 located at www.irs.gov/.

EXHIBIT 8-1 **2018 Marriage Penalty (Benefit): Two-Income vs. Single-Income Married Couple***

Married Couple	Taxable Income	Tax If Filing Jointly (1)	Tax If Filing Single[†] (2)	Marriage Penalty (Benefit) (1) − (2)
Scenario 1: *Two wage earners*				
Wife	$350,000		$ 98,189.50	
Husband	350,000		$ 98,189.50	
Combined	$700,000	$198,379	$196,379	$2,000
Scenario 2: *One wage earner*				
Wife	$700,000		$224,689.50	
Husband	0		0	
Combined	$700,000	$198,379	$224,689.50	$(26,310.50)

*This analysis assumes the taxpayers do not owe any alternative minimum tax (discussed below).
[†]Married couples do not actually have the option of filing as single. If they choose not to file jointly they must file as married filing separately.

Preferential Tax Rates for Capital Gains and Dividends   As we described in detail in the Investments chapter, certain capital gains and certain dividends are taxed at a lower or **preferential tax rate** relative to other types of income. In general, the preferential tax rate is 0 percent, 15 percent, or 20 percent.[2] The preferential tax rates vary with the taxpayer's taxable income. See Appendix D for the tax brackets by filing status that apply to preferentially taxed capital gains and dividends. Taxpayers with income subject to the preferential rate (long-term capital gains and qualified dividends) can use the following three-step process to determine their tax liability.

Step 1: Split taxable income into the portion that is subject to the preferential rate and the portion taxed at the ordinary rates.

Step 2: Compute the tax separately on each type of income. Note that the income that is not taxed at the preferential rate is taxed at the ordinary tax rates using the tax rate schedule for the taxpayer's filing status.

Step 3: Add the tax on the income subject to the preferential tax rates and the tax on the income subject to the ordinary rates. This is the taxpayer's regular tax liability.

Example 8-3

Courtney's taxable income of $145,070 includes $700 of qualified dividends from GE (Example 5-8). What is her tax liability on her taxable income?

Answer: $27,652, computed at head of household rates as follows:

Description	Amount	Explanation
(1) Taxable income	$145,070	Exhibit 6-11
(2) Preferentially taxed income	700	Exhibit 5-4
(3) Income taxed at ordinary rates	$144,370	(1) − (2)

[2]As we discovered in the Investments chapter, some types of income may be taxed at a preferential rate of 28 percent or 25 percent. In addition, as we discuss later in this chapter, dividends and capital gains for higher income taxpayers are subject to the 3.8 percent net investment income tax.

Description	Amount	Explanation
(4) Tax on income taxed at ordinary rates	$ 27,546.80	[$12,698 + ($144,370 − $82,500) × 24%]
(5) Tax on preferentially taxed income	105	(2) × 15% [Preferential tax rate for taxpayer filing head of household with income between $51,701 and $452,400]
Tax on taxable income	**$27,652**	(4) + (5), rounded

In this example, what is Courtney's tax savings from having the dividends taxed at the preferential rate rather than the ordinary rate?

Answer: $63. $700 × (24% − 15%). This is the amount of the dividend times the difference in the ordinary and preferential tax rates.

What if: Assume that Courtney's taxable income is $462,400, including $15,000 of qualified dividends taxed at the preferential rate. What would be Courtney's tax liability under these circumstances?

Answer: $133,638, computed using the head of household tax rate schedule as follows:

Description	Amount	Explanation
(1) Taxable income	$ 462,400	
(2) Preferentially taxed income	15,000	
(3) Income taxed at ordinary rates	447,400	(1) − (2)
(4) Tax on income at ordinary tax rates	$ 130,888	$44,298 + [($447,400 − $200,000) × 35%] (See tax rate schedule for head of household.)
(5) Tax on preferentially taxed income	2,750	[($5,000 × 15%) + ($10,000 × 20%)]*
Tax	**$133,638**	(4) + (5)

*Courtney had $15,000 of preferentially taxed income. $10,000 of her dividends fall in the 20 percent preferential tax bracket ($462,400 taxable income − $452,400 end of 20 percent preferential tax bracket; see preferential tax rate schedule for head of household). The remaining $5,000 is taxed at 15 percent (15 percent bracket for preferentially taxed income extends from $51,701 to $452,400 for head of household).

Net Investment Income Tax   Higher-income taxpayers are required to pay a 3.8 percent tax on net investment income. For purposes of the **net investment income tax,** net investment income equals the sum of:

1. Gross income from interest, dividends, annuities, royalties, and rents (unless these items are derived in a trade or business to which the net investment income tax does not apply).
2. Income from a trade or business that is a passive activity or a trade or business of trading financial instruments or commodities.
3. Net gain from disposing of property (other than property held in a trade or business in which the net investment income tax does not apply).[3]
4. Less the allowable deductions that are allocable to items 1, 2, and 3.

Tax-exempt interest, veterans' benefits, excluded gain from the sale of a principal residence, distributions from qualified retirement plans, and any amounts subject to self-employment tax are not subject to the net investment income tax.

The tax imposed is 3.8 percent of the lesser of (1) net investment income or (2) the excess of modified adjusted gross income over $250,000 for married joint filers and surviving spouses, $125,000 for married separate filers, and $200,000 for other taxpayers.

[3]However, the income, gain, or loss attributable to invested working capital of a trade or business is subject to the net investment income tax. §1411(c)(3).

Modified adjusted gross income equals adjusted gross income increased by income excluded under the foreign-earned income exclusion less any disallowed deductions associated with the foreign-earned income exclusion.[4]

Example 8-4

Courtney's AGI (and modified AGI) is $187,000, and her investment income consists of $321 of taxable interest, $700 of dividends, and $5,000 of rental income. How much net investment income tax will Courtney owe?

Answer: $0. Because Courtney's modified AGI ($187,000) is less than the $200,000 threshold for the net investment income tax for a taxpayer filing as head of household, she will not be subject to the tax.

What if: Assume that Courtney's AGI (and modified AGI) is $225,000. How much net investment income tax will Courtney owe?

Answer: $229, calculated as follows:

Description	Amount	Explanation
(1) Net investment income	$ 6,021	$321 interest + $700 dividends + $5,000 rental income
(2) Modified AGI	225,000	
(3) Modified AGI threshold	200,000	
(4) Excess modified AGI above threshold	25,000	(2) − (3)
(5) Net investment income tax base	6,021	Lesser of (1) or (4)
Net investment income tax	**$ 229**	(5) × 3.8%

Kiddie Tax Parents can reduce their family's income tax bill by shifting income that would otherwise be taxed at their higher tax rates to their children whose income is taxed at lower rates. However, as we described in the Gross Income and Exclusions chapter, under the assignment of income doctrine, taxpayers cannot simply assign or transfer income to other parties. Earned income, or income from services or labor, is taxed to the person who earns it. Thus, it's difficult for a parent to shift *earned* income to a child. However, unearned income or income from property such as dividends from stocks or interest from bonds is taxed to the *owner* of the property. Thus, a parent can shift unearned income to a child by transferring actual ownership of the income-producing property to the child. By transferring ownership, the parent runs the risk that the child will sell the asset or use it in a way unintended by the parent. However, this risk is relatively small for parents transferring property ownership to younger children.

The tax laws reduce parents' ability to shift unearned income to children through the so-called **kiddie tax.** The kiddie tax provisions apply (or potentially apply) to a child if (1) the child is under 18 years old at year-end, (2) the child is 18 at year-end but her earned income does *not* exceed half of her support, or (3) the child is over age 18 but under age 24 at year-end and is a full-time student during the year, and her earned income does not exceed half of her support (excluding scholarships).[5] The kiddie tax does not apply to a married child filing a joint tax return or to a child without living parents. In general terms, if the kiddie tax applies, children must pay tax on a

---

[4]Taxpayers compute the net investment income tax using Form 8960.

[5]§1(g)(2)(A).

certain amount of their **net unearned income** (discussed below) at tax rates that apply to trusts and estates (see Appendix D) rather than at their own marginal tax rate.[6]

The kiddie tax base is the child's net unearned income. Net unearned income is the *lesser* of (1) the child's gross *unearned income* minus $2,100[7] or (2) the child's taxable income (the child is not taxed on more than her taxable income).[8] Consequently, the kiddie tax does not apply unless the child has *unearned* income in *excess* of $2,100. Thus the kiddie tax limits, but does not eliminate, the tax benefit gained by a family unit when parents transfer income-producing assets to children.

Example 8-5

What if: Suppose that during 2018, Deron received $5,100 in interest from the IBM bond, and he received another $2,200 in interest income from a money market account that his parents have been contributing to over the years. Is Deron potentially subject to the kiddie tax?

Answer: Yes, Deron is younger than 18 years old at the end of the year and his net unearned income exceeds $2,100.

What is Deron's taxable income and corresponding tax liability?

Answer: $6,250 taxable income and $996 tax liability, calculated as follows:

Description	Amount	Explanation
(1) Gross income/AGI	$ 7,300	$5,100 interest from IBM bond + $2,200 interest. All unearned income.
(2) Standard deduction	1,050	Minimum for taxpayer claimed as a dependent on another return (no earned income, so must use minimum). See the Individual Deductions chapter.
(3) Taxable income	**$6,250**	(1) – (2)
(4) Gross unearned income minus $2,100	5,200	(1) – 2,100
(5) Net unearned income	$ 5,200	Lesser of (3) or (4)
(6) Kiddie tax	$ 891	[[$255 + ([((5) – $2,550) × 24%])]], see trust and estate tax rate schedule in Appendix D.
(7) Taxable income taxed at Deron's rate	1,050	(3) – (5)
(8) Tax on taxable income using Deron's tax rates	$ 105	(7) × 10% (See single filing status, $1,050 taxable income.)
Deron's total tax liability	**$ 996**	(6) + (8)

(continued on page 8-8)

THE KEY FACTS

Tax Rates

- Regular tax rates
  - Schedule depends on filing status.
  - Progressive tax rate schedules with tax rates ranging from 10 percent to 37 percent.
  - Marriage penalty (benefit) occurs because dual-earning spouses pay more (less) combined tax than if they each filed single.
- Preferential tax rates
  - Net long-term capital gains and qualified dividends generally taxed at 0 percent, 15 percent, or 20 percent.
- Net investment income tax
  - 3.8 percent tax on lesser of (a) net investment income or (b) excess of modified AGI over applicable threshold based on filing status.
- Kiddie tax
  - Unearned income in excess of $2,100 is taxed at trust and estate tax rates if child is (1) under age 18, (2) 18 but earned income does not exceed one-half of support, or (3) over 18 and under 24, full-time student, and earned income does not exceed one-half of support.

---

[6]§1(g). Both the ordinary tax rates and preferential tax rates for trusts and estates apply to taxpayers subject to the kiddie tax. Consequently, for preferentially taxed capital gains and dividends, the 0 percent rate applies to taxable income between $0 and $2,600, the 15 percent rate applies to taxable income between $2,601 and $12,700, and the 20 percent rate applies to taxable income over $12,700.

[7]The $2,100 consists of $1,050 of the child's standard deduction (even if the child is entitled to a larger standard deduction) plus an extra $1,050. See the Individual Deductions chapter for a discussion of the standard deduction for the dependent of another taxpayer. If the child itemizes deductions, then the calculation becomes more complex and is beyond the scope of this text.

[8]§1(g)(4).

What if: Assume Deron's only source of income is qualified dividends of $5,200 (unearned income). What is his taxable income and tax liability?

Answer: Taxable income is $4,150; tax liability is $75, computed as follows:

Description	Amount	Explanation
(1) Gross income/(AGI)	$ 5,200	Qualified dividends, all unearned income.
(2) Minimum standard	1,050	Minimum for taxpayer claimed as a dependent deduction on another return (all unearned income, so must use minimum). See the Individual Deductions chapter.
(3) Taxable income	**$4,150**	(1) – (2)
(4) Gross unearned income minus $2,100	3,100	(1) – $2,100
(5) Net unearned income	$ 3,100	Lesser of (3) or (4)
(6) Kiddie tax	$ 75	[($2,600 × 0%) + ((5) – $2,600) × 15%)], see trust and estate tax rate schedule for preferentially taxed dividends.
(7) Taxable income taxed at Deron's rate	1,050	(3) – (5)
(8) Tax on taxable income using Deron's tax rates	$ 0	(8) × 0%, see single tax rate schedule for preferentially taxed dividends.
Deron's total tax liability	**$ 75**	(6) + (8)

As we've just described, all individual taxpayers must pay federal income taxes on their federal taxable income. However, taxpayers may be liable for other federal taxes in addition to the regular tax liability. Many taxpayers are also required to pay the alternative minimum tax, and some working taxpayers are required to pay employment or self-employment taxes. We delve into these additional taxes below.

LO 8-2   ALTERNATIVE MINIMUM TAX

Each year, a number of taxpayers are required to pay the **alternative minimum tax (AMT)** in addition to their regular tax liability. The **alternative minimum tax system** was implemented in 1986 (earlier variations date back to the late 1960s) to ensure that taxpayers generating income pay some *minimum* amount of income tax each year. After several years in which a large number of taxpayers were subject to AMT, 2017 tax law changes were designed to reduce the number of taxpayers subject to AMT. The tax is targeted at higher-income taxpayers who are benefiting from or are perceived by the public to be benefiting from the excessive use (more than Congress intended) of tax preference items such as exclusions, deferrals, and deductions to reduce or even eliminate their tax liabilities.

In general terms, the alternative minimum tax is a tax on an *alternative* tax base meant to more closely reflect economic income than the regular income tax base. Thus the **alternative minimum tax (AMT) base** is more inclusive (or more broadly defined) than is the regular income tax base. To compute their AMT, taxpayers first compute their regular income tax liability. Then they compute the AMT base and multiply the base by the applicable alternative tax rate.[9] They must pay the AMT only when the tax on the AMT base exceeds their regular tax liability.

[9]The rate of the alternative minimum tax (AMT) is set below that of the income tax with the objective of avoiding the perception that the AMT is an additional assessment.

Alternative Minimum Tax Formula

Regular taxable income is the starting point for determining the alternative minimum tax. As the AMT formula in Exhibit 8-2 illustrates, taxpayers make several "plus" and "minus" adjustments to regular taxable income to compute alternative minimum taxable income (AMTI). They then arrive at the AMT base by subtracting an AMT exemption from AMTI. Taxpayers multiply the AMT base by the AMT rate to determine their **tentative minimum tax.** Finally, to determine their alternative minimum tax, taxpayers subtract their regular tax liability from the tentative minimum tax. The alternative minimum tax is the *excess* of the tentative minimum tax over the regular tax. If the regular tax liability equals or exceeds the tentative minimum tax, taxpayers need not pay any AMT. Individual taxpayers compute their AMT on Form 6251 (see Exhibit 8-4).

Alternative Minimum Taxable Income (AMTI) In order to compute alternative minimum taxable income (AMTI), taxpayers make several **alternative minimum tax adjustments** to regular taxable income. Many of these are plus adjustments that are added to regular taxable income to reach AMTI and some are minus adjustments that are subtracted from regular taxable income to determine AMTI. Consequently, these adjustments tend to expand the regular income tax base to more closely reflect economic income.

EXHIBIT 8-2   **Formula for Computing the Alternative Minimum Tax**

	Regular Taxable Income
Plus:	Standard deduction if taxpayer deducted the standard deduction in computing regular taxable income
Plus or *Minus:*	Other adjustments*
	Alternative minimum taxable income
Minus:	AMT exemption amount (if any)
Equals:	Tax base for AMT
Times:	AMT rate
Equals:	Tentative minimum tax
Minus:	Regular tax
Equals:	Alternative minimum tax

*Technically, some of these adjustments are referred to as preference items and some are referred to as adjustments. We refer to all of these items as *adjustments* for simplicity's sake.

Adjustments.   Taxpayers first add back to regular taxable income the standard deduction amount, but only if they deducted it in determining taxable income. Taxpayers add back the standard deduction because it is a deduction that does not reflect an actual economic outflow from the taxpayer.[10] Taxpayers are then required to make several adjustments to compute AMTI. Exhibit 8-3 describes the most common of these adjustments, and Exhibit 8-4 presents Form 6251, which taxpayers use to calculate the AMT. Because 2018 forms were not available at press time, we present the 2017 form as an example of the form.

The major itemized deductions that are deductible for both regular tax and AMT purposes using the *same limitations* are:

- Charitable contributions.
- Home mortgage interest expenses.
- Gambling losses.

Some deductions are deductible for regular tax and AMT purposes but have different limitations. For example, interest income that is tax exempt for regular tax purposes but included in the AMT base is included in investment income for determining the AMT investment interest expense deduction.

---

[10]The standard deduction is accomplished on Form 6251 by beginning with taxable income before the standard deduction if the taxpayer does not itemize.

EXHIBIT 8-3 **Common AMT Adjustments**

Adjustment	Description
Plus adjustments:	
Tax-exempt interest from private activity bonds	Taxpayers must add back interest income that was excluded for regular tax purposes if the bonds were used to fund private activities (privately owned baseball stadium or private business subsidies) and not for the public good (build or repair public roads). However, taxpayers do not add back interest income from private activity bonds if the bonds were issued in either 2009 or 2010. Taxpayers do not personally make the determination of whether a bond is a private activity bond. Instead, interest from private activity bonds is denoted as such on Form 1099 that taxpayers receive.
Real property and personal property taxes deducted as itemized deductions	Deductible for regular tax purposes (subject to $10,000 limitation for itemized tax deduction), but not for AMT purposes.
State income or sales taxes	Deductible for regular tax purposes (subject to $10,000 limitation for itemized tax deduction), but not for AMT purposes.
Plus or Minus adjustment:	
Depreciation	Taxpayers must compute their depreciation expense for AMT purposes. For certain types of assets, the regular tax method is more accelerated than the AMT method. In any event, if the regular tax depreciation exceeds the AMT depreciation, this is a plus adjustment. If the AMT depreciation exceeds the regular tax depreciation, this is a minus adjustment.
Minus adjustments:	
State income tax refunds included in regular taxable income	Because state income taxes paid are not deductible for AMT purposes, refunds are not taxable (they do not increase the AMT base).
Gain or loss on sale of depreciable assets	Due to differences in regular tax and AMT depreciation methods, taxpayers may have a different adjusted basis (cost minus accumulated depreciation) for regular tax and for AMT purposes. Thus, they may have a different gain or loss for regular tax purposes than they do for AMT purposes. If regular tax gain exceeds AMT gain, this is a minus adjustment. Because AMT accumulated depreciation will never exceed regular tax accumulated depreciation, this would never be a plus adjustment.

Example 8-6

Courtney continued to work on her AMT computation by determining the other adjustments she needs to make to determine her alternative minimum taxable income (AMTI). What is Courtney's AMTI?

Answer: $155,150, computed as follows:

Description	Amount	Explanation
(1) Taxable income	$ 145,070	Exhibit 6-11
Plus adjustments:		
(2) Tax-exempt interest on Cincinnati bond used to pay for renovations to major league baseball stadium (Private activity bond: issued in 2005)	500	Example 5-22
(3) Itemized deduction for taxes	10,000	Example 6-13
Minus adjustments:		
(4) State income tax refund	(420)	Example 5-3
Alternative minimum taxable income	**$155,150**	Sum of (1) through (4)

EXHIBIT 8-4   **2017 Form 6251 (Page 1 of 2)**

Form **6251**	**Alternative Minimum Tax—Individuals**	OMB No. 1545-0074
Department of the Treasury Internal Revenue Service (99)	▶ Go to *www.irs.gov/Form6251* for instructions and the latest information. ▶ **Attach to Form 1040 or Form 1040NR.**	**20**17 Attachment Sequence No. **32**

Name(s) shown on Form 1040 or Form 1040NR | Your social security number

Part I   Alternative Minimum Taxable Income (See instructions for how to complete each line.)

1	If filing Schedule A (Form 1040), enter the amount from Form 1040, line 41, and go to line 2. Otherwise, enter the amount from Form 1040, line 38, and go to line 7. (If less than zero, enter as a negative amount.)	**1**	
2	Reserved for future use	**2**	
3	Taxes from Schedule A (Form 1040), line 9	**3**	
4	Enter the home mortgage interest adjustment, if any, from line 6 of the worksheet in the instructions for this line	**4**	
5	Miscellaneous deductions from Schedule A (Form 1040), line 27.	**5**	
6	If Form 1040, line 38, is $156,900 or less, enter -0-. Otherwise, see instructions	**6**	( )
7	Tax refund from Form 1040, line 10 or line 21	**7**	( )
8	Investment interest expense (difference between regular tax and AMT).	**8**	
9	Depletion (difference between regular tax and AMT)	**9**	
10	Net operating loss deduction from Form 1040, line 21. Enter as a positive amount	**10**	
11	Alternative tax net operating loss deduction	**11**	( )
12	Interest from specified private activity bonds exempt from the regular tax	**12**	
13	Qualified small business stock, see instructions	**13**	
14	Exercise of incentive stock options (excess of AMT income over regular tax income)	**14**	
15	Estates and trusts (amount from Schedule K-1 (Form 1041), box 12, code A)	**15**	
16	Electing large partnerships (amount from Schedule K-1 (Form 1065-B), box 6)	**16**	
17	Disposition of property (difference between AMT and regular tax gain or loss)	**17**	
18	Depreciation on assets placed in service after 1986 (difference between regular tax and AMT)	**18**	
19	Passive activities (difference between AMT and regular tax income or loss)	**19**	
20	Loss limitations (difference between AMT and regular tax income or loss)	**20**	
21	Circulation costs (difference between regular tax and AMT)	**21**	
22	Long-term contracts (difference between AMT and regular tax income)	**22**	
23	Mining costs (difference between regular tax and AMT)	**23**	
24	Research and experimental costs (difference between regular tax and AMT)	**24**	
25	Income from certain installment sales before January 1, 1987	**25**	( )
26	Intangible drilling costs preference	**26**	
27	Other adjustments, including income-based related adjustments	**27**	
28	**Alternative minimum taxable income.** Combine lines 1 through 27. (If married filing separately and line 28 is more than $249,450, see instructions.)	**28**	

Part II   Alternative Minimum Tax (AMT)

29 Exemption. (If you were under age 24 at the end of 2017, see instructions.)

IF your filing status is . . .	AND line 28 is not over . . .	THEN enter on line 29 . . .	
Single or head of household	$120,700	$54,300	
Married filing jointly or qualifying widow(er)	160,900	84,500	
Married filing separately.	80,450	42,250	**29**

If line 28 is **over** the amount shown above for your filing status, see instructions.

30	Subtract line 29 from line 28. If more than zero, go to line 31. If zero or less, enter -0- here and on lines 31, 33, and 35, and go to line 34	**30**	
31	• If you are filing Form 2555 or 2555-EZ, see instructions for the amount to enter. • If you reported capital gain distributions directly on Form 1040, line 13; you reported qualified dividends on Form 1040, line 9b; **or** you had a gain on both lines 15 and 16 of Schedule D (Form 1040) (as refigured for the AMT, if necessary), complete Part III on the back and enter the amount from line 64 here. • **All others:** If line 30 is $187,800 or less ($93,900 or less if married filing separately), multiply line 30 by 26% (0.26). Otherwise, multiply line 30 by 28% (0.28) and subtract $3,756 ($1,878 if married filing separately) from the result.	**31**	
32	Alternative minimum tax foreign tax credit (see instructions)	**32**	
33	Tentative minimum tax. Subtract line 32 from line 31	**33**	
34	Add Form 1040, line 44 (minus any tax from Form 4972), and Form 1040, line 46. Subtract from the result any foreign tax credit from Form 1040, line 48. If you used Schedule J to figure your tax on Form 1040, line 44, refigure that tax without using Schedule J before completing this line (see instructions)	**34**	
35	**AMT.** Subtract line 34 from line 33. If zero or less, enter -0-. Enter here and on Form 1040, line 45	**35**	

For Paperwork Reduction Act Notice, see your tax return instructions. | Cat. No. 13600G | Form **6251** (2017)

Source: Form 6251

AMT Exemption   To help ensure that most taxpayers aren't required to pay the alternative minimum tax, Congress allows taxpayers to deduct an **alternative minimum tax (AMT) exemption** amount to determine their alternative minimum tax base.[11] The amount of the exemption depends on the taxpayer's filing status. The exemption is phased out (reduced) by 25 cents for every dollar the AMTI exceeds the threshold amount. Exhibit 8-5 identifies, by filing status, the base exemption amount, the phase-out threshold, and the range of AMTI over which the exemption is phased out for 2018. The exemption amounts and phase-out thresholds are considerably higher in 2018 than in prior years due to tax law changes enacted in 2017.

EXHIBIT 8-5   2018 AMT Exemptions

Filing Status	Exemption	Phase-Out Begins at This Level of AMTI	Phase-Out Complete for This Level of AMTI
Married filing jointly	$109,400	$1,000,000	$1,437,600
Married filing separately	54,700	500,000	718,800
Head of household and single	70,300	500,000	781,200

Example 8-7

THE KEY FACTS

Alternative Minimum Tax (AMT)

- Implemented to ensure taxpayers pay some minimum level of income tax.
- AMT base
  - More broad than regular income tax base.
  - No deductions for standard deduction, state income taxes, and property taxes in addition to other adjustments.
- AMT exemption amounts for 2018
  - $109,400 married filing jointly.
  - $54,700 married filing separately.
  - $70,300 single or head of household.
  - Phased out by 25 cents for each dollar of AMTI over threshold.
- AMT rates
  - 26 percent on first $191,100 of AMT base.
  - 28 percent on AMT base in excess of $191,100.
  - Net long-term capital gains and qualified dividends taxed at same preferential rates used for regular tax purposes.
- AMT is the excess of tentative minimum tax (tax on AMT base) over regular tax liability.

What is Courtney's AMT base?

Answer: $84,850, computed by subtracting her allowable exemption amount from her AMTI as follows:

Description	Amount	Explanation
(1) AMTI	$155,150	Example 8-6
(2) Full AMT exemption (head of household)	70,300	Exhibit 8-5
(3) Exemption phase-out threshold	500,000	
(4) AMTI in excess of exemption phase-out threshold	0	(1) − (3)
(5) Exemption phase-out percentage	25%	
(6) Exemption phase-out amount	0	(4) × (5), rounded
(7) Deductible exemption amount	70,300	(2) − (6)
AMT base	**$ 84,850**	(1) − (7)

What if: Suppose Courtney's AMTI is $700,000. What is Courtney's AMT base?

Answer: $679,700, computed as follows:

Description	Amount	Explanation
(1) AMTI	$ 700,000	
(2) Full AMT exemption (head of household	70,300	Exhibit 8-5
(3) Exemption phase-out threshold	500,000	
(4) AMTI in excess of exemption phase-out	200,000	(1) − (3)
(5) Exemption phase-out percentage	25%	
(6) Exemption phase-out amount	50,000	(4) × (5)
(7) Deductible exemption amount	20,300	(2) − (6)
AMT base	**$679,700**	(1) − (7)

Tentative Minimum Tax and AMT Computation   Taxpayers compute the tentative minimum tax by multiplying the AMT base by the applicable AMT rates. The 2018 AMT tax rate schedule consists of the following two brackets:

- 26 percent on the first $191,100 (indexed for inflation annually) of AMT base for all taxpayers other than married taxpayers filing separately ($95,550, indexed for inflation annually, for married taxpayers filing separately).

[11]Similar to standard deduction amounts, the AMT exemption is indexed for inflation. The phase-out threshold amounts are also indexed annually for inflation.

- 28 percent on AMT base in excess of $191,100 (indexed for inflation annually) for all taxpayers other than married taxpayers filing separately ($95,550, indexed for inflation annually, for married taxpayers filing separately).

However, for AMT purposes long-term capital gains and dividends are taxed at the same preferential rate as they were taxed for regular tax purposes (generally 0 percent, 15 percent, or 20 percent).

Example 8-8

Courtney's AMT base is $84,850. However, Courtney also received $700 in dividends that are included in the base but are subject to a tax rate of 15 percent even under the AMT system. The remaining $84,150 ($84,850 – $700) is taxed at the normal AMT rates. What is Courtney's tentative minimum tax?

Answer: $21,984, computed as follows:

Description	Amount	Explanation
(1) AMT base	$ 84,850	Example 8-7
(2) Dividends taxed at preferential rate	700	Example 8-3
(3) Tax rate applicable to dividends	15%	
(4) Tax on dividends	105	(2) × (3)
(5) AMT base taxed at regular AMT rates	84,150	(1) – (2)
(6) Regular AMT tax rate	26%	For AMT base below $191,100.
(7) Tax on AMT base taxed at regular AMT rates	21,879	(5) × (6), rounded
Tentative minimum tax	**$21,984**	(4) + (7)

Taxpayers subtract their regular tax liability from their tentative minimum tax to determine their AMT.[12] If the taxpayer's regular tax liability is equal to or exceeds the tentative minimum tax liability, the taxpayer does not owe any AMT.

Example 8-9

What is Courtney's alternative minimum tax liability?

Answer: $0, computed as follows:

Description	Amount	Reference
(1) Tentative minimum tax	$21,984	Example 8-8
(2) Regular tax liability	27,652	Example 8-3
Alternative minimum tax	**$ 0**	(1) – (2) ($0 if negative)

Courtney owes alternative minimum tax in addition to her regular tax liability.

In some situations, taxpayers who pay the AMT are entitled to a **minimum tax credit** to use when the regular tax exceeds the tentative minimum tax. They can use the credit to offset regular tax but not below the tentative minimum tax for that year.[13]

---

[12]As might be expected, self-employment taxes and the net investment income tax are not considered as part of a taxpayer's regular tax liability in determining whether a taxpayer owes AMT.

[13]The credit applies only when the taxpayer has positive adjustments that will reverse and become negative adjustments in the future. For example, depreciation, gain or loss on asset sales, and incentive stock option bargain element adjustments (see the Compensation chapter) fall into this category. Due to the nature of her adjustments, Courtney does not qualify for the minimum tax credit.

LO 8-3 EMPLOYMENT AND SELF-EMPLOYMENT TAXES

As we discussed in the Introduction to Tax chapter, employees and self-employed taxpayers must pay employment (or self-employment) taxes known as FICA taxes.[14] The FICA tax consists of a Social Security and a Medicare component that are payable by both employees and employers. The **Social Security tax** is intended to provide basic pension coverage for the retired and disabled. The **Medicare tax** helps pay medical costs for qualified individuals. Because Social Security and Medicare taxes are paid by working taxpayers but received by retired taxpayers, Social Security and Medicare taxes represent intergenerational transfers. The Social Security tax rate is 12.4 percent on the tax base (limited to $128,400 in 2018), and the Medicare tax rate is 2.9 percent on the tax base. An **additional Medicare tax** of .9 percent applies on the tax base in excess of $200,000 ($125,000 for married filing separately; $250,000 for married filing jointly). Below we discuss these taxes apply for employees, employers, and self-employed taxpayers.

Employee FICA Taxes Payable

Both employees and employers have to pay **FICA taxes** on employee salary, wages, and other compensation paid by employers. The Social Security tax rate for employees is 6.2 percent of their salary or wages (wage base limited to $128,400 in 2018), the Medicare tax rate for employees is 1.45 percent of their salary or wages, and the additional Medicare tax rate is .9 percent on salary or wages in excess of $200,000 ($125,000 for married filing separate; $250,000 of combined salary or wages for married filing joint).

Employers withhold the employees' FICA tax liabilities from the employees' paychecks for both the Social Security tax and the Medicare tax. For the additional Medicare tax, employers are required to withhold the tax at a rate of .9 percent for any salary or wages above $200,000, irrespective of the taxpayer's filing status (e.g., single, married filing separate, married filing joint, or head of household).[15] Taxpayers use Form 8959 to determine their liability for the additional Medicare tax and report all of the additional Medicare tax withheld as a tax payment on Form 1040.

Employers must also pay their portion of the Social Security tax (6.2 percent of employee salary or wages) and Medicare tax (1.45 percent of employee salary or wages, regardless of the amount of salary or wages). In contrast to employees, employers are not subject to the additional Medicare tax on employee salary or wages.

THE KEY FACTS

Employee FICA Tax

- Social Security tax
  - 6.2 percent rate on wage base.
  - 2018 wage base limit is $128,400.
- Medicare tax
  - 1.45 percent rate on wage base.
  - Wage base unlimited.
- Additional Medicare tax
  - .9 percent rate on wage base in excess of $200,000 ($125,000 for married filing separately; $250,000 married filing jointly).

Example 8-10

While she was attending school full-time, Ellen received $15,000 in wages working part-time for an off-campus employer during the year. How much in FICA taxes should Ellen's employer have withheld from her paychecks during the year?

Answer: $1,148, computed as follows:

Description	Amount	Reference
(1) Wages	$15,000	
(2) Social Security tax rate	6.2%	
(3) Social Security tax	930	(1) × (2)
(4) Medicare tax rate	1.45%	
(5) Medicare tax	218	(1) × (4)
FICA taxes withheld	**$ 1,148**	(3) + (5)

---

[14]FICA stands for Federal Insurance Contributions Act.

[15]To avoid potential underpayment penalty, taxpayers can request additional income tax withholding or make estimated tax payments to pay any Medicare tax that otherwise would have been owed upon filing their tax return.

Example 8-11

During 2018, Courtney received a total of $142,800 in employee compensation from EWD. Recall that the compensation consisted of $118,000 in wages, $4,800 performance bonus, $6,000 discount for architectural design services, $4,000 compensation for a below-market loan, and $10,000 forgiveness of debt (see Exhibit 5-4). What is her FICA tax liability on this income?

Answer: $10,032, computed as follows:

Description	Amount	Reference
(1) Compensation subject to FICA tax	$142,800	
(2) Social Security tax base limit for 2018	128,400	
(3) Compensation subject to Social Security tax	128,400	Lesser of (1) or (2)
(4) Social Security tax rate	6.2%	
(5) Social Security tax	7,961	(3) × (4), rounded
(6) Medicare tax rate	1.45%	
(7) Medicare tax	2,071	(1) × (6), rounded
FICA taxes	**$ 10,032**	(5) + (7)

What amount of FICA taxes for the year must EWD pay on Courtney's behalf?

Answer: $10,032, which includes $7,961 of Social Security tax ($128,400 × 6.2%) and $2,071 of Medicare tax ($142,800 × 1.45%).

What if: Suppose Courtney received a total of $220,000 in employee compensation. What would be her FICA tax liability on this income?

Answer: $11,331, computed as follows:

Description	Amount	Reference
(1) Compensation subject to FICA tax	$220,000	
(2) Social Security tax base limit for 2018	128,400	
(3) Compensation subject to Social Security tax	128,400	Lesser of (1) or (2)
(4) Social Security tax rate	6.2%	
(5) Social Security tax	7,961	(3) × (4), rounded
(6) Medicare tax rate	1.45%	
(7) Compensation subject to Medicare tax	220,000	(1)
(8) Additional Medicare tax rate on compensation in excess of $200,000	.9%	
(9) Compensation subject to additional Medicare tax	20,000	Greater of [(1) − $200,000] or $0
(10) Medicare tax and additional Medicare tax	3,370	[(6) × (7)] + [(8) × (9)]
FICA taxes	**$ 11,331**	(5) + (10)

What amount of FICA taxes for the year must EWD pay on Courtney's behalf?

Answer: $11,151, which includes $7,961 of Social Security tax ($128,400 × 6.2%) and $3,190 of Medicare tax ($220,000 × 1.45%).

Employees who work for multiple employers within a calendar year may receive aggregate compensation that exceeds the Social Security wage base. Because each employer is required to withhold Social Security taxes on the employee's wages until the employee has reached the wage base limit *with that employer,* the employee may end up paying Social Security tax in excess of the required maximum. As it does in situations in which excess Medicare tax has been withheld, the IRS treats the excess Social Security tax paid through withholding as an additional federal income tax payment (or credit) on Page 2 of

Form 1040. The government refunds the excess withholding to the employee through either lower taxes payable with the tax return or a larger tax refund. Employers, on the other hand, are not able to recover excess Social Security taxes paid on behalf of their employees.

Example 8-12

What if: Suppose Courtney worked for her former employer Landmark Architects Inc. (LA), in Cincinnati for two weeks in January 2018 before moving to Kansas City. During those two weeks, Courtney would have earned $4,000 in salary. LA would have withheld $306 in FICA taxes from her final paycheck consisting of $248 of Social Security taxes ($4,000 × 6.2%) and $58 of Medicare taxes ($4,000 × 1.45%). How much excess Social Security tax would have been withheld from Courtney's combined salaries from LA and EWD during 2018?

Answer: $248 ($4,000 wages earned with LA × 6.2% Social Security rate). Due to the $128,400 Social Security tax wage base for the year, Courtney's Social Security tax liability is limited to $7,961 ($128,400 × 6.2%). However, through employer withholding, she would have paid a total of $8,209 in Social Security taxes, consisting of $248 withheld by LA ($4,000 × 6.2%) and $7,961 withheld by EWD ($128,400 × 6.2%). Thus, given these facts, Courtney's *excess* Social Security tax withheld was $248 ($8,209 − $7,961). Courtney would get this amount back from the government through either lower taxes payable with her tax return or a larger tax refund.

Self-Employment Taxes

While employees share their FICA (Social Security and Medicare) tax burden with employers, self-employed taxpayers must pay the *entire* FICA tax burden on their self-employment earnings.[16] Like FICA taxes for employees, self-employment taxes consist of both Social Security and Medicare taxes. Because their FICA taxes are based on their self-employment earnings, FICA taxes for self-employed taxpayers are referred to as **self-employment taxes.** The base for the Social Security component of the self-employment tax is limited to $128,400. The base for the Medicare portion of the self-employment tax is unlimited. Taxpayers use Schedule SE to determine their Social Security tax and 2.9 percent Medicare tax on self-employment earnings, and they use Form 8959 to determine the additional Medicare tax on self-employment earnings. Although applied to self-employment earnings, the additional Medicare tax is not considered technically a part of the self-employment tax. The process for determining the taxpayer's self-employment taxes (and additional Medicare tax) payable requires the following steps:

Step 1: Compute the amount of the taxpayer's net income from self-employment activities that is subject to self-employment taxes. This is generally the taxpayer's net income from **Schedule C** of Form 1040. Schedule C reports the taxpayers self-employment–related income and expenses.

Step 2: Multiply the amount from Step 1 by 92.35 percent. The product is called **net earnings from self-employment.** Because self-employed taxpayers are responsible for paying the entire amount of their FICA taxes, they are allowed an implicit deduction for the 7.65 percent "employer's portion" of the taxes,

---

[16]As we discussed in the Gross Income and Exclusions and Individual Deductions chapters, self-employed taxpayers report their self-employment earnings on Schedule C of Form 1040. Individuals who are partners in partnerships and who are actively involved in the partnerships' business activities may be required to pay self-employment taxes on the income they are allocated from the partnerships. They would report these earnings on Schedule E of Form 1040.

leaving 92.35 percent (100% – 7.65%) of the full amount subject to self-employment taxes. Note that the 7.65 percent consists of the 6.2 percent Social Security tax and 1.45 percent Medicare tax. Net earnings from self-employment is the base for the self-employment tax. If net earnings from self-employment is less than $400, the taxpayer is not subject to self-employment tax (but is still subject to income tax on the earnings).

Step 3: Compute the Social Security tax. The Social Security tax component of the self-employment tax equals 12.4 percent [the combined Social Security tax rate for employer and employee (6.2% + 6.2% = 12.4%)] multiplied by the lesser of (a) the taxpayer's net earnings from self-employment (from Step 2) or (b) $128,400 (the maximum tax base for the Social Security tax).

Step 4: Compute the Medicare tax. The Medicare tax component of the self-employment tax equals 2.9 percent [the combined Medicare tax rate for employer and employee (1.45% + 1.45% = 2.9%)] multiplied by the net earnings from self-employment (from Step 2).

Step 5: Compute the additional Medicare tax. The additional Medicare tax due on net self-employment earnings equals .9 percent multiplied by the greater of (1) zero or (2) net earnings from self-employment (from Step 2) less $200,000 ($125,000 for married filing separately; $250,000 for married filing jointly). The additional Medicare tax is considered an "employee" tax (and not a "self-employment" tax).

Note that, as we discussed in the Individual Deductions chapter, taxpayers are allowed to deduct the employer portion of their self-employment taxes as a *for* AGI deduction.

Example 8-13

What if: Assume that Courtney's only income for the year is her $18,000 in net self-employment income from her weekend consulting business. What amount of self-employment taxes and additional Medicare tax would Courtney be required to pay on this income?

Answer: $2,543 self-employment taxes and $0 of additional Medicare tax, computed as follows:

Step 1: $18,000 of net self-employment income subject to self-employment taxes.

Step 2: $18,000 × .9235 = $16,623. This is net earnings from self-employment.

Step 3: $16,623 × 12.4% = $2,061. This is Courtney's Social Security tax payable for her self-employment income.

Step 4: $16,623 × 2.9% = $482. This is Courtney's Medicare tax payable for her self-employment income.

Step 5: $0. Since Courtney's net earnings from self-employment do not exceed $200,000, she is not subject to the additional Medicare tax.

Total $2,543 self-employment taxes [sum of Steps (3) and (4)] and **$0** of additional Medicare tax [Step (5)].

Under these circumstances, Courtney would be able to deduct $1,272 as a *for* AGI deduction for the employer portion of self-employment taxes she paid [i.e., $16,623 × (6.2% + 1.45%)].

When a taxpayer receives both employee compensation and self-employment earnings in the same year, the calculation of Social Security and additional Medicare taxes is a bit more complicated. For the Social Security tax component, the taxpayer's total earnings subject to the Social Security tax are capped at $128,400. In these situations, the taxpayer's Social Security tax liability on the employee compensation is determined as if the employee had no self-employment income. The taxpayer then computes her Social Security tax on her net self-employment earnings. This ordering is favorable for taxpayers because it allows them to use up all or a portion of the Social Security wage base limit with their employee income (taxed at 6.2 percent) before they determine the Social Security tax on their net earnings from self-employment (taxed at 12.4 percent). Consequently, if an employee's wages exceed the Social Security tax wage base limitation, she is not required to pay any Social Security tax on her self-employment earnings.

Likewise, the additional Medicare tax calculation is more complicated when (1) the taxpayer receives both employee compensation and self-employment earnings or (2) the taxpayer files married jointly with a spouse receiving employee compensation or net self-employment earnings. For taxpayers not filing married jointly, the additional Medicare tax equals .9 percent of the taxpayer's salary or wages and net self-employment earnings in excess of $200,000 ($125,000 for married filing separately). For married filing jointly taxpayers, the additional Medicare tax equals .9 percent of the taxpayer's and his or her spouse's salary or wages and net self-employment earnings in excess of $250,000.

The calculation of the taxpayer's Social Security and Medicare taxes on self-employment earnings in these settings can be determined as follows:[17]

Social Security Tax:

Step 1: Determine the limit on the Social Security portion of the self-employment tax base by subtracting the employee compensation from the Social Security wage base ($128,400 in 2018) (not below $0).

Step 2: Determine the net earnings from self-employment (self-employment earnings times 92.35 percent).

Step 3: Multiply the lesser of Steps 1 and 2 by 12.4 percent. This is the amount of Social Security taxes due on the self-employment income.

Medicare Tax:

Step 4: Multiply the amount from Step 2 by 2.9 percent, the combined Medicare tax rate for employer and employee.

Additional Medicare Tax:

Step 5: Add the amount from Step 2 and the taxpayer's compensation. If married filing jointly, also add the spouse's compensation and net earnings from self-employment (spouse's self-employment earnings times 92.35 percent).

Step 6: Multiply the greater of [(a) zero or (b) the amount from Step 5 minus $200,000 ($125,000 for married filing separately; $250,000 for married filing jointly)] by .9 percent.

Step 7: Take the amount from Step 6 and subtract the amount of the .9 percent additional Medicare tax withheld by the taxpayer's employer (and his or her spouse's employer if married filing jointly). This is the .9 percent additional Medicare tax due on the self-employment income.

---

[17]If net earnings from self-employment is less than $400, the taxpayer is *not* subject to self-employment tax (but the taxpayer is still subject to income tax on the earnings).

Example 8-14

In 2018, Courtney received $142,800 in taxable compensation from EWD (see Example 8-11) and $18,000 in self-employment income from her weekend consulting activities (see Example 6-2). What are Courtney's *self-employment taxes* and additional Medicare tax payable on her $18,000 of income from self-employment? Assume that Courtney's employer correctly withheld $7,961 of Social Security tax and $2,071 of Medicare tax.

Answer: $482 of self-employment taxes and $0 of additional Medicare tax, computed as follows:

Description	Amount	Explanation
(1) Social Security wage base limit less employee compensation subject to Social Security tax	$ 0	$128,400 − $128,400, limited to $0
(2) Net earnings from self-employment	16,623	$18,000 × 92.35%
(3) Social Security portion of self-employment tax	0	[Lesser of Step (1) or (2)] × 12.4%
(4) Medicare tax	482	Step (2) × 2.9%
(5) Sum of taxpayer's compensation and net earnings from self-employment	159,423	$142,800 + Step (2)
(6) [Greater of (a) zero or (b) the amount from Step (5) minus $200,000] × 0.9%	0	0 × 0.9%
(7) Step (6) less any additional Medicare tax withheld by Courtney's employer	0	0 − 0
Steps (3) + (4) + (7)	$ 482	$0 + $482 + $0. [**$482** of self-employment taxes (3) + (4) and **$0** of additional Medicare tax]

As we reported in Example 6-6, Courtney is entitled to a $241 *for* AGI deduction for the employer portion of the $482 self-employment taxes she incurred during the year ($16,623 × 1.45% employer portion of the Medicare tax rate = $241).

Example 8-15

What if: Let's change the facts and assume that Courtney received $100,000 of taxable compensation from EWD in 2018, and she received $180,000 in self-employment income from her consulting activities. What amount of self-employment taxes and additional Medicare tax is Courtney required to pay on her $180,000 of business income? Assume that Courtney's employer correctly withheld $6,200 of Social Security tax, $1,450 of Medicare tax, and $0 of additional Medicare tax.

Answer: $8,343 of self-employment taxes and $596 of additional Medicare tax, computed as follows:

Description	Amount	Explanation
(1) Social Security wage base limit less employee compensation subject to Social Security tax	$ 28,400	$128,400 − $100,000, limited to $0
(2) Net earnings from self-employment	166,230	$180,000 × 92.35%
(3) Social Security portion of self-employment tax	3,522	[Lesser of Step (1) or (2)] × 12.4%, rounded
(4) Medicare tax	4,821	Step (2) × 2.9%, rounded

(continued on page 8-20)

Description	Amount	Explanation
(5) Sum of taxpayer's compensation and net earnings from self-employment	266,230	$100,000 + Step (2)
(6) [Greater of (a) zero or (b) the amount from Step (5) minus $200,000] × 0.9%	596	$66,230 × 0.9%, rounded
(7) Step (6) less any additional Medicare tax withheld by Courtney's employer	596	$596 − $0
Steps (3) + (4) + (7)	$ 8,939	$3,522 + $4,821 + $596. [**$8,343** of self-employment taxes (3) + (4) and **$596** of additional Medicare tax]

What if: Now let's assume that Courtney is married and files jointly. Assume that Courtney received $100,000 of taxable compensation from EWD in 2018 and $180,000 in self-employment income from her weekend consulting activities. In addition, her husband received $75,000 of taxable compensation from his employer. What amount of self-employment taxes and additional Medicare tax is Courtney required to pay on her $180,000 of business income? Assume that Courtney's employer correctly withheld $6,200 of Social Security tax, $1,450 of Medicare tax, and $0 of additional Medicare tax, and that her husband's employer correctly withheld $4,650 of Social Security tax, $1,088 of Medicare tax, and $0 of additional Medicare tax.

Answer: $8,343 of self-employment taxes and $821 of additional Medicare tax, computed as follows:

Description	Amount	Explanation
(1) Social Security wage base limit less employee compensation subject to Social Security tax	$ 28,400	$128,400 − $100,000, limited to $0
(2) Net earnings from self-employment	166,230	$180,000 × 92.35%
(3) Social Security portion of self-employment tax	3,522	[Lesser of Step (1) or (2)] × 12.4%, rounded
(4) Medicare tax	4,821	Step (2) × 2.9%, rounded
(5) Sum of taxpayer's and spouse's compensation and net earnings from self-employment	341,230	$100,000 + $75,000 + Step (2)
(6) [Greater of (a) zero or (b) the amount from Step (5) minus $250,000] × 0.9%	821	$91,230 × 0.9%, rounded
(7) Step (6) less any additional Medicare tax withheld by Courtney's employer and her husband's employer	821	$821 − $0
Steps (3) + (4) + (7)	$ 9,164	$3,522 + $4,821 + $821. [**$8,343** of self-employment taxes (3) + (4) and **$821** of additional Medicare tax]

Unlike employees, whose employers withhold tax throughout the year on their behalf, self-employed taxpayers must satisfy their self-employment tax obligations through periodic, usually quarterly, estimated tax payments. Taxpayers who are employed and self-employed (an employee with a business on the side, like Courtney) may have their employers withhold enough taxes to cover both their income, self-employment, and additional Medicare tax obligations. Any self-employment or additional Medicare taxes not paid through these mechanisms must be paid with the self-employed taxpayer's individual tax return.

continued from page 8-1...

Courtney was enjoying her work with EWD, but she also really liked her weekend consulting work. A couple of months ago, after she had played an integral part in completing a successful project, her boss jokingly mentioned that, if Courtney ever decided to leave EWD to work for herself as a full-time consultant, EWD would love to hire her back for contract work. This caused Courtney to start thinking about the possibilities of starting her own consulting business. She always had some interest in working for herself, but she is not at a point in her life where she can take significant financial risks even if it might mean a more satisfying career. Courtney knows that before making such a move she would need to seriously consider the nontax issues associated with self-employment and learn more about the tax consequences of working as an independent contractor. She is particularly interested in the tax consequences of working for EWD as an independent contractor (contract worker) relative to working for EWD as an employee. ■

Employee vs. Self-Employed (Independent Contractor)

Determining whether an individual should be taxed as an **employee** or as an **independent contractor** can be straightforward or quite complex, depending on the specific arrangement between the parties. In its published guidance, the IRS stipulates that an employer/employee relationship exists when the party for whom services are performed has the right to direct or control the individual performing services.[18] To assist taxpayers in deciding whether the party receiving services has the requisite amount of control over the individual providing services, the IRS has published a list of 20 factors to consider.[19] A few of the factors suggesting independent contractor rather than employee status include the contractor's ability to:

1. Set her own working hours.
2. Work part-time.
3. Work for more than one firm.
4. Realize either a profit or a loss from the activities.
5. Perform work somewhere other than on an employer's premises.
6. Work without frequent oversight.

When these factors are absent, individuals are more likely to be classified as employees. Rather than simply summing the number of factors in favor of independent contractor status and those in favor of employee status, however, taxpayers and their advisers should use the factors as guides in determining the overall substance of the contractual relationship.

Whether a taxpayer is classified as an employee or as an independent contractor (self-employed) has both tax and nontax consequences to the employer and the taxpayer. The best classification for the taxpayer is situation-specific.

Employee vs. Independent Contractor Comparison   The two primary *tax* differences between independent contractors and employees relate to (1) the amount of FICA taxes payable and (2) the deductibility of business expenses.[20] However, there are several nontax factors to consider as well. In the previous section, we detailed how

---

[18]IRS Publication 1779. Independent Contractor or Employee brochure.

[19]Rev. Rul. 87-41, 1987-1 CB 296.

[20]Also, independent contractors generally receive a Form 1099 from each client reporting the gross income they received from the client during the year. Employees receive Form W-2 reporting the compensation the employee received from the employer during the year.

THE KEY FACTS

Employee vs. Independent Contractor

- Employees
  - Less control over how, when, and where to perform duties.
  - Pay 6.2 percent Social Security tax subject to limit.
  - Pay 1.45 percent Medicare tax.
  - Pay additional Medicare tax of .9 percent on salary or wages above $200,000 ($125,000 for married filing separate; $250,000 of combined salary or wages for married filing joint).
- Independent contractors
  - More control over how, when, and where to perform duties.
  - Report income and expenses on Form 1040, Schedule C.
  - Pay 12.4 percent Social Security tax subject to limit.
  - Pay Medicare tax of 2.9 percent.

(continued)

- Pay additional Medicare tax of .9 percent on net self-employment earnings above $200,000 ($125,000 for married filing separate; $250,000 of combined salary or wages for married filing joint).
- Self-employment tax base is 92.35 percent of net self-employment income.
- Deduct the employer portion of self-employment taxes paid *for* AGI.

to determine the FICA taxes payable for employees and independent contractors (self-employed taxpayers). In terms of the deductibility of business expenses, as we discussed in the Individual Deductions chapter, *employees* who incur unreimbursed business expenses relating to their employment cannot deduct these expenses. In contrast, as we also described in the Individual Deductions chapter, self-employed independent contractors are able to deduct expenses relating to their business activities as *for* AGI deductions, which they can deduct without restriction. While these factors appear to favor independent contractor status over employee status, note that employees generally don't incur many unreimbursed expenses relating to their employment. Thus, even though independent contractors may be able to deduct more expenses than employees, they typically incur more costs in doing business.

When taxpayers are classified as independent contractors rather than employees, they are not eligible for nontaxable fringe benefits available to employees, such as health care insurance, retirement plan benefits, and others. Further, independent contractors are responsible for paying their estimated tax liability throughout the year because the employer does not withhold taxes from an independent contractor's pay. However, as we mentioned above, taxpayers are allowed to deduct the employer portion of the self-employment taxes they pay.

From the employer's perspective, it is generally less costly to hire an independent contractor than an employee, because the employer need not provide these benefits or withhold or pay any FICA taxes on behalf of an independent contractor. As a result, an employer may be willing to offer an apparently higher level of taxable compensation to an independent contractor than to a similarly situated employee. However, after considering all relevant factors, the taxpayer may do better receiving less compensation as an employee than slightly higher compensation as an independent contractor.

ETHICS

Sudipta is an accounting major who works during the day and takes classes in the evening. He was excited to finally land his first accounting job doing the books for a local dry cleaners. In his new job, Sudipta works 30 hours a week at the dry cleaners' main office. His excitement quickly dampened when he realized that his new employer was not withholding any income taxes or FICA taxes from his paycheck. Apparently, Sudipta's employer is treating him as an independent contractor. Sudipta likes his job, appreciates the money he is earning, but recognizes that he should be treated as an employee instead of an independent contractor. What would you do if you were Sudipta?

Example 8-16

What if: Let's compare Courtney's compensation as an employee with EWD to her compensation if she were to work for EWD as an independent contractor. Assume Courtney works an average of 40 hours per week for 50 weeks per year to earn a salary of $100,000; in addition she receives fringe benefits including a 5 percent contribution to her retirement plan, life insurance coverage, and health insurance coverage. Would Courtney be "made whole" in terms of her hourly rate if EWD agreed to pay her $55 an hour for her contract work (10 percent more than her hourly rate as an employee)?

Answer: Not very likely. As an independent contractor, Courtney must pay more costly self-employment taxes (at nearly twice the rate of employment taxes) under the new arrangement. In addition, she will be ineligible for the nontaxable fringe benefits (retirement plan contributions, life insurance, and health coverage) she was receiving as an employee and will not receive as a contractor.

We've described how to calculate a taxpayer's regular tax liability, alternative minimum tax liability, Social Security and Medicare tax liability, additional Medicare tax liability, and self-employment tax liability. These tax liabilities sum to a taxpayer's gross tax liability. While Gram's gross tax is simply her regular income tax liability of $199 (see Example 8-2), Courtney's gross tax includes other taxes. Courtney's gross tax liability is calculated in Exhibit 8-6.

EXHIBIT 8-6   Courtney's Gross Tax

Description	Amount	Explanation
(1) Regular federal income tax	$ 27,652	Example 8-3
(2) Alternative minimum tax	0	Example 8-9
(3) Self-employment tax	482	Example 8-14
Gross tax	$ 28,134	(1) + (2) + (3)

Taxpayers reduce their gross tax by tax credits and tax prepayments (withholding and estimated tax payments) for the year. As indicated in Exhibit 8-7, if the gross tax exceeds the tax credits and prepayments, the taxpayer owes additional taxes when she files her tax

EXHIBIT 8-7   Formula for Computing Net Tax Due or Refund

Gross tax
Minus: Tax credits
Minus: Prepayments
Net tax due (refund)

return. In contrast, if the prepayments exceed the gross tax after applying tax credits, the taxpayer is entitled to a tax refund. We next explore available tax credits and conclude the chapter by dealing with taxpayer prepayments.

TAX CREDITS

Congress provides a considerable number of credits for taxpayers. **Tax credits** reduce a taxpayer's *tax liability* dollar for dollar. In contrast, deductions reduce *taxable income* dollar for dollar, but the tax savings deductions generated depend on the taxpayer's marginal tax rate. Because tax credits generate tax savings independent of a taxpayer's marginal tax rate, they are a popular tax policy tool for avoiding the perception that tax benefits for certain tax policies are distributed disproportionately to taxpayers with higher incomes and corresponding higher marginal tax rates. Further, tax credits are powerful tax policy tools because they directly affect taxes due. By using tax credits, policy makers can adjust the magnitude of the tax effects of tax policy without changing tax rates.

LO 8-4

Tax credits can be either nonrefundable or refundable. A **nonrefundable credit** may reduce a taxpayer's gross tax liability to zero, but if the amount of the credit exceeds the amount of the taxpayer's gross tax liability, the credit in excess of the gross tax liability is not refunded to the taxpayer. It expires without ever providing tax benefits, unless it can be carried over to a different year. Refundable credits in excess of a taxpayer's gross tax liability are refunded to the taxpayer.

Tax credits are generally classified into one of three categories: nonrefundable personal, refundable personal, or business credits, depending on the nature of the credit. The primary exception to this general rule is the foreign tax credit. The foreign tax credit is a hybrid between personal and business credits because, like nonrefundable personal credits, it reduces the taxpayer's liability before business credits but, like business credits, unused foreign tax credits can be carried over to use in other years.

Nonrefundable Personal Credits

Congress provides many nonrefundable personal tax credits to generate tax relief for certain groups of individuals. For example, the child tax credit (partially refundable) provides tax relief for taxpayers who provide a home for dependent children, and the child and dependent care credit provides tax relief for taxpayers who incur expenses to care for their children and other dependents in order to work. The American opportunity credit (partially refundable) and the lifetime learning credit help taxpayers pay for the cost of higher education. Because the child tax credit, the child and dependent care credit, and the American opportunity and lifetime learning credits are some of the most common nonrefundable personal credits, we discuss them in detail.

THE KEY FACTS

Child Tax Credit

- Taxpayers may claim a $2,000 credit for each qualifying child under age 17 or $500 credit for other qualifying dependents.
- Credit is phased out for taxpayers with AGI above threshold.
  - Lose $50 for every $1,000 or portion thereof that AGI exceeds threshold.

Child Tax Credit   Taxpayers may claim a $2,000 **child tax credit** for *each qualifying child* [same definition for dependency purposes—see §152(c) and the Individual Income Tax Overview, Dependents, and Filing Status chapter] who is under age 17 at the end of the year and who is claimed as their dependent.[21] To claim the credit for a qualifying child, the taxpayers must provide the qualifying child's Social Security number on the tax return. Taxpayers may also claim a $500 credit for qualifying dependents other than qualifying children for which the $2,000 credit is claimed. Social Security numbers are not required to be reported to claim the $500 child tax credit for these dependents. The credit is subject to phase-out based on the taxpayer's AGI. The phase-out threshold depends on the taxpayer's filing status and is provided in Exhibit 8-8.

EXHIBIT 8-8   Child Tax Credit Phase-Out Threshold

Filing Status	Phase-Out Threshold
Married filing jointly	$400,000
Married filing separately	200,000
Head of household and single	200,000

The total amount of the credit is phased out, but not below zero, by $50 for each $1,000 *or portion thereof* by which the taxpayer's AGI exceeds the applicable threshold. Taxpayers can determine their allowable child tax credit after the phase-out by using the following four steps:

Step 1: Determine the excess AGI by subtracting the threshold amount (see Exhibit 8-8) from the taxpayer's AGI.

Step 2: Divide the excess AGI from Step 1 by 1,000 and round up to the next whole number.

Step 3: Multiply the amount from Step 2 by $50. This is the amount of the total credit that is phased out or disallowed.

Step 4: Subtract the amount from Step 3 from the total credit before phase-out (limited to $0) to determine the allowable child tax credit.

Because the phase-out is based upon a fixed amount ($50) rather than a percentage, the phase-out range varies according to the amount of credit claimed.[22]

---

[21]§24(a).

[22]The child tax credit is partially refundable. The $500 child tax credit is nonrefundable. The refundable portion of the credit is the lesser of (1) $1,400 per each qualifying child for which the $2,000 credit is claimed, (2) the taxpayer's earned income in excess of $2,500 times 15 percent, or (3) the amount of the unclaimed portion of the otherwise nonrefundable credit. Thus, if a taxpayer has enough tax liability to absorb the nonrefundable portion of the credit, the refundable portion is reduced to zero. The computation is modified for taxpayers with three or more qualifying children. See IRS Publication 972 for more information relating to the child tax credit.

Example 8-17

Both Ellen and Deron are Courtney's qualifying children. Courtney may claim a $2,000 child tax credit for Deron because he is under age 17 at the end of the year. Courtney cannot claim the $2,000 child tax credit for Ellen because she is not under age 17 at the end of the year, but Courtney may claim the $500 credit for Ellen because she is a qualified dependent. What amount of child tax credit is Courtney allowed to claim for Deron and Ellen after accounting for the credit phase-out?

Answer: $2,500. Because Courtney's AGI of $187,000 (Exhibit 6-5) does not exceed the $200,000 phase-out threshold (Exhibit 8-8), she may claim full credit of $2,000 for Deron and $500 for Ellen.

What if: Suppose Courtney's AGI is $230,000. How much child tax credit may she claim for Deron and Ellen?

Answer: $1,000, computed as follows:

Description	Amount	Explanation
(1) AGI	$230,000	
(2) Phase-out threshold	200,000	Exhibit 8-8
(3) AGI in excess of threshold	30,000	(1) − (2)
(4) Credit phase-out increment	30	(3)/1,000
(5) Credit phase-out	1,500	(4) × 50
(6) Credit before phase-out	2,500	$2,000 for Deron; $500 for Ellen
Credit after phase-out	**$ 1,000**	(6) − (5)

Child and Dependent Care Credit The child and dependent care credit is a tax subsidy to help taxpayers pay the cost of providing care for their dependents to allow taxpayers to work or look for work. The amount of the credit is based on the amount of the taxpayer's expenditures to provide care for one or more qualifying persons. A qualifying person includes (1) a dependent under the age of 13, and (2) a dependent or spouse who is physically or mentally incapable of caring for herself or himself and who lives in the taxpayer's home for more than half the year.

The amount of expenditures eligible for the credit is the *least* of the following three amounts:

1. The total amount of dependent care expenditures for the year.
2. $3,000 for one qualifying person or $6,000 for two or more qualifying persons.
3. The taxpayer's earned income including wage, salary, or other taxable employee compensation, or net earnings from self-employment. Married taxpayers must file a joint tax return and the amount of earned income for purposes of the dependent care credit limitation is the earned income of the lesser-earning spouse.[23]

Expenditures for care qualify whether the care is provided outside or within the home. But they do *not* qualify if the caregiver is a dependent relative or child of the taxpayer.[24] The amount of the credit is calculated by multiplying qualifying expenditures by the appropriate credit percentage. The credit percentage is based upon the taxpayer's AGI level and begins at 35 percent for taxpayers with AGI of $15,000 or less. The maximum dependent care credit is 20 percent for taxpayers with AGI over $43,000. Exhibit 8-9 provides the dependent care credit percentage for different levels of AGI.

THE KEY FACTS

Child and Dependent Care Credit

- Designed to help taxpayers who work or seek work when they must provide care for dependents.
- Nonrefundable.
- Based on maximum qualifying expenditures multiplied by the rate based on AGI.
  - Maximum expenditures are $3,000 for one qualifying person or $6,000 for two or more qualifying persons.
  - Rate is 35 percent for the lowest AGI taxpayers and 20 percent for the highest.

[23]If the lesser-earning spouse cannot work due to a disability or is a full-time student, the lesser-earning spouse is *deemed* to have earned $250 a month if the couple is computing the credit for one qualifying person or $500 a month if the couple is computing the credit for more than one qualifying person.

[24]§21(e)(6). Also, the regulations indicate that the costs of summer school and tutoring programs are indistinguishable from general education and, therefore, do not qualify for the credit [see Reg. §1.21-1(b)].

EXHIBIT 8-9   **Child and Dependent Care Credit Percentage**

If AGI is over	but not over	then the percentage is
$ 0	15,000	35%
15,000	17,000	34
17,000	19,000	33
19,000	21,000	32
21,000	23,000	31
23,000	25,000	30
25,000	27,000	29
27,000	29,000	28
29,000	31,000	27
31,000	33,000	26
33,000	35,000	25
35,000	37,000	24
37,000	39,000	23
39,000	41,000	22
41,000	43,000	21
43,000	No limit	20

Example 8-18

What if: Suppose that this year, Courtney paid a neighbor $3,200 to care for her 10-year-old son, Deron, so Courtney could work. Would Courtney be allowed to claim the child and dependent care credit for the expenditures she made for Deron's care?

Answer: Yes. (1) Courtney paid for Deron's care to allow her to work, and (2) Deron is a qualifying person for purposes of the credit because (a) he is Courtney's dependent and (b) he is under 13 years of age at the end of the year.

What amount of child and dependent care credit, if any, would Courtney be allowed to claim for the $3,200 she spent to provide Deron's care given her AGI is $187,000?

Answer: $600, computed as follows:

Description	Amount	Explanation
(1) Dependent care expenditures	$ 3,200	
(2) Limit on qualifying expenditures for one dependent	3,000	
(3) Courtney's earned income	160,800	$142,800 compensation from EWD + $18,000 business income (see Example 8-14)
(4) Expenditures eligible for credit	3,000	Least of (1), (2), and (3)
(5) Credit percentage rate	20%	AGI over $43,000 (see Exhibit 8-9)
Dependent care credit	**$ 600**	(4) × (5)

What if: If Courtney's AGI (and her earned income) were only $31,500, what would be her child and dependent care credit?

Answer: $780, computed as follows:

Description	Amount	Explanation
(1) Dependent care expenditures	$ 3,200	
(2) Limit on qualifying expenditures for one dependent	3,000	
(3) Courtney's earned income	31,500	
(4) Expenditures eligible for credit	3,000	Least of (1), (2), and (3)
(5) Credit percentage rate	26%	AGI between $31,000 and $33,000 (see Exhibit 8-9)
Dependent care credit	**$ 780**	(4) × (5)

Education Credits Congress provides the American opportunity credit (AOC) and the lifetime learning credit to encourage taxpayers and their dependents to obtain higher education by reducing the costs of the education. Taxpayers may claim credits for eligible expenditures made for themselves, their dependents, and third parties on behalf of the taxpayers' dependents.[25] If a student is claimed as a dependent of another taxpayer, only that taxpayer may claim the education credits (even if the dependent or another third party actually pays the education expenses).[26] Married taxpayers filing separate returns are not eligible for the AOC or the lifetime learning credit.

The AOC is available for students in their first four years of postsecondary (post high school) education. To qualify, students must be enrolled in a qualified postsecondary educational institution at least half-time.[27] The amount of the credit is 100 percent of the first $2,000 of eligible expenses paid by the taxpayer (or another person) plus 25 percent of the next $2,000 of eligible expenses paid by the taxpayer (or another person). Thus, the maximum AOC for eligible expenses paid for any one person is $2,500 [$2,000 + (25% × $2,000)]. To be eligible for the 2018 credit, taxpayers must pay the eligible expenses in 2018 for any academic period beginning in 2018 or in the first three months of 2019.[28]

Eligible expenses for the AOC include tuition, fees, and course materials (cost of books and other materials) needed for courses of instruction at an eligible educational institution.[29] The AOC is applied on a *per student* basis. Consequently, a taxpayer with three eligible dependents can claim a maximum AOC of $2,500 for *each* dependent. The AOC is subject to phase-out based on the taxpayer's AGI. The credit is phased out pro rata for taxpayers with AGI between $80,000 and $90,000 ($160,000 – $180,000 for married taxpayers filing jointly).[30] Forty percent of a taxpayer's allowable AOC is refundable.[31]

Example 8-19

Courtney paid $2,000 of tuition and $300 for books for Ellen to attend the University of Missouri–Kansas City during the summer following the end of her first year. What is the maximum American opportunity credit (AOC) (before phase-out) Courtney may claim for these expenses?

Answer: $2,075. Because the cost of tuition and books is an eligible expense, Courtney may claim a maximum AOC before phase-out of $2,075 [($2,000 × 100%) + ($2,300 – $2,000) × 25%].

How much AOC is Courtney allowed to claim on her 2018 tax return (how much can she claim after applying the phase-out)?

Answer: $0. Because Courtney's AGI exceeds the head of household limit of $90,000, she is not allowed to claim any AOC.

THE KEY FACTS

Education Credits

- American opportunity credit
- Qualifying expenses include tuition for a qualifying student incurred during the first four years at a qualifying institution of higher education.
- Maximum credit of $2,500 per student calculated as percentage of maximum of $4,000 qualifying expenses.

(continued)

---

[25]§25A(g)(3).

[26]If a third party pays the education expenses of a student claimed as a dependent by another taxpayer, the dependent is deemed to have paid the education expenses and the taxpayer claiming the student as a dependent is allowed to claim the credit for the expenses.

[27]§25A(b). Generally, eligible institutions are those eligible to participate in the federal student loan program [§25A(f)(2)].

[28]Reg. §1.25A-3(e).

[29]§25A(i)(3). Eligible expenses for both the AOC and the lifetime learning credit must be reduced by scholarships received to pay for these expenses or other amounts received as reimbursements for the expenses (Pell grants, employer-sponsored reimbursement plans, Educational IRAs, 529 plans, and the like). The cost of room and board or other personal expenses do not qualify as eligible expenses for either the AOC or the lifetime learning credit.

[30]§25A(i)(4).

[31]§25A(i)(5). The refundability of the tax credit is not applicable to a taxpayer that is a child subject to the "kiddie tax" rules —i.e., a child (a) who does not file a joint return, (b) has at least one living parent, and who is either (1) under 18 years old at year-end, (2) 18 at year-end with earned income that does not exceed half of her support, or (3) over age 18 but under age 24 at year-end, is a full-time student during the year, and has earned income that does not exceed half of her support.

- Subject to phase-out for taxpayers with AGI in excess of $80,000 ($160,000 married filing jointly).
- Lifetime learning credit
  - Qualifying expenses include costs at a qualifying institution associated with acquiring or improving job skills.
  - Maximum credit of $2,000 per taxpayer calculated as percentage of maximum of $10,000 in annual expenses.
  - Subject to phase-out for taxpayers with AGI in excess of $57,000 ($114,000 married filing jointly).

What if: How much AOC would Courtney have been allowed to claim on her 2018 tax return if she were married and filed a joint return with her husband (assuming the couple's AGI is $162,000)?

Answer: $1,867, computed as follows:

Description	Amount	Explanation
(1) AOC before phase-out	$ 2,075	
(2) AGI	162,000	
(3) Phase-out threshold	160,000	
(4) Excess AGI	2,000	(2) − (3)
(5) Phase-out range for taxpayer filing for married filing jointly	20,000	$180,000 − $160,000
(6) Phase-out percentage	10%	(4)/(5)
(7) Phase-out amount	208	(1) × (6)
AOC after phase-out	**$ 1,867**	(1) − (7)

What if: Suppose Courtney could claim a $1,867 AOC in 2018 (after phase-out). How much of this credit would be refundable?

Answer: $747 ($1,867 × 40%).

The lifetime learning credit is a nonrefundable credit that applies to the cost of tuition and fees (but generally not books) for any course of instruction to acquire or improve a taxpayer's job skills.[32] This includes the cost of professional or graduate school tuition (expenses are not limited to those incurred in the first four years of postsecondary education). The credit is equal to 20 percent of eligible expenses up to an annual maximum of $10,000 of eligible expenses (maximum of $2,000). The credit for a year is based on the amount paid during that year for an academic period beginning in that year or the first three months of the following year.

In contrast to the American opportunity credit, the lifetime learning credit limit applies to the taxpayer (a married couple filing a joint return may claim only $2,000 of lifetime learning credit). Thus, a taxpayer with multiple eligible dependents can claim a maximum lifetime learning credit of only $2,000. Finally, the credit is phased out pro rata for taxpayers with AGI between $57,000 and $67,000 ($114,000 and $134,000 for married taxpayers filing jointly).[33]

Example 8-20

Courtney paid $1,550 to attend a class at the local university to help her improve her job skills. How much lifetime learning credit can Courtney claim before applying the phase-out?

Answer: $310 ($1,550 × 20%)

How much lifetime learning credit is Courtney allowed to claim on her 2018 tax return (how much can she claim after applying the phase-out)?

Answer: $0. Because Courtney's AGI exceeds the head of household limit of $67,000, she is not allowed to claim any lifetime learning credit.

[32] §25A(f)(1).
[33] §25A(d).

For expenses that qualify for both the AOC and lifetime learning credit (tuition and fees during the first four years of postsecondary education), taxpayers may choose which credit to use, but they may not claim both credits for the same student in the same year.

Example 8-21

What if: Suppose Courtney paid $5,000 of tuition for Ellen to attend the University of Missouri–Kansas City during the summer following the end of her first year. Further assume that Courtney's AGI is $45,000, so her education credits are not subject to phase-out. Courtney would be allowed to claim the maximum AOC of $2,500 on the first $4,000 of the qualifying educational expenditures. Assuming Courtney used $4,000 of the educational expenses to claim the maximum AOC, would she be allowed to claim the lifetime credit on the remaining $1,000 of tuition costs ($5,000 total expenses − $4,000 maximum AOC expenses)?

Answer: No. If Courtney claims any AOC for Ellen's expenditures, she is not allowed to claim a lifetime learning credit for Ellen's expenditures (even for the expenses not used in computing the AOC).

Refundable Personal Credits

Several personal credits are refundable, the most common of which is the earned income credit, which we discuss below.

Earned Income Credit   The **earned income credit** is a refundable credit that is designed to help offset the effect of employment taxes on compensation paid to low-income taxpayers and to encourage lower-income taxpayers to seek employment. Because it is refundable (if the credit exceeds the tax after considering nonrefundable credits, the taxpayer receives a refund for the excess), it is sometimes referred to as a *negative income tax*. The credit is available for qualified individuals who have earned income for the year.[34] Qualified individuals generally include (1) those who have at least one qualifying child (same definition of qualifying child for dependent purposes—see the Individual Income Tax Overview, Dependents, and Filing Status chapter) and (2) those who do not have a qualifying child for the taxable year but who live in the United States for more than half the year, are at least 25 years old but younger than 65 years old at the end of the year, and are not a dependent of another taxpayer. Earned income includes wages, salaries, tips, and other employee compensation included in gross income and net earnings from self-employment. Taxpayers with investment income such as interest, dividends, and capital gains in excess of $3,500 are ineligible for the credit.[35]

The amount of the credit depends on the taxpayer's filing status, the number of the taxpayer's qualifying children who live in the home for more than half of the year, and the amount of the taxpayer's earned income. To be eligible for the credit, married taxpayers must file a joint tax return. The credit is computed by multiplying the appropriate credit percentage times the taxpayer's earned income up to a maximum amount. The credit percentage depends upon the number of qualifying children in the home and is subject to a phase-out based upon AGI (or earned income if greater). As summarized in Exhibit 8-10, the earned income credit increases as taxpayers receive earned income up to the maximum amount of earned income eligible for the credit. However, as taxpayers earn more income, the credit begins to phase out and is completely eliminated once taxpayers' earned income reaches established levels.

---

[34]§32.
[35]§32(i).

EXHIBIT 8-10 **2018 Earned Income Credit Table**

Qualifying Children	(1) Maximum Earned Income Eligible for Credit	(2) Credit %	(3) Maximum Credit (1) × (2)	(4) Credit Phase-Out for AGI (or earned income if greater) Over This Amount	(5) Phase-Out Percentage	No Credit When AGI (or earned income if greater) Equals or Exceeds This Amount (4) + [(3)/(5)]
Married taxpayers filing joint returns						
0	$ 6,780	7.65%	$ 519	$14,170	7.65%	$20,950
1	10,180	34	3,461	24,350	15.98	46,010
2	14,290	40	5,716	24,350	21.06	51,492
3+	14,290	45	6,431	24,350	21.06	54,884
All taxpayers *except* married taxpayers filing joint returns						
0	$ 6,780	7.65%	$ 519	$ 8,490	7.65%	$15,270
1	10,180	34	3,461	18,660	15.98	40,320
2	14,290	40	5,716	18,660	21.06	45,802
3+	14,290	45	6,431	18,660	21.06	49,194

Example 8-22

Courtney's earned income for the year is $160,800 (Example 8-18) and her AGI is $187,000 (Exhibit 6-5). Deron and Ellen both qualify as Courtney's qualifying children. What amount of earned income credit is Courtney entitled to claim on her 2018 tax return?

Answer: $0. Courtney's AGI (which is greater than her earned income) exceeds the $45,802 limit for unmarried taxpayers with two qualifying children. Consequently, Courtney is not allowed to claim any earned income credit.

What if: Assume Courtney's only source of income for the year was $30,000 in salary. Also assume Courtney's AGI for the year was $30,000. What would be Courtney's earned income credit in these circumstances?

Answer: $3,328, computed as follows:

Description	Amount	Explanation
(1) Earned income	$30,000	
(2) Maximum earned income eligible for earned income credit for taxpayers filing as head of household with two qualifying children	14,290	Exhibit 8-10
(3) Earned income eligible for credit	14,290	Lesser of (1) and (2)
(4) Earned income credit percentage for taxpayer with two qualifying children	40%	
(5) Earned income credit before phase-out	5,716	(3) × (4)
(6) Phase-out threshold begins at this level of AGI (or earned income if greater)	18,660	See Exhibit 8-10 for head of household filing status and two qualifying children.
(7) Greater of (a) AGI or (b) earned income, less the phase-out threshold	11,340	(1) − (6) In this example, AGI equals earned income.
(8) Phase-out percentage	21.06%	See Exhibit 8-10.
(9) Credit phase-out amount	2,388	(7) × (8), rounded
Earned income credit after phase-out	**$ 3,328**	(5) − (9)

TAXES IN THE REAL WORLD	Taking a Bite Out of Earned Income Tax Credit Abuse

The IRS has special reporting requirements (Form 8867) for tax professionals filing tax returns that include an earned income tax credit. Form 8867, the Paid Preparer's Earned Income Credit Checklist, is intended to ensure that tax professionals use appropriate due diligence in determining the amount of, and a taxpayer's eligibility for, the earned income tax credit.

Why the extra concern with the earned income tax credit? Because the earned income tax credit is a refundable tax credit, the potential for abuse (fraudulent claim) is quite high. Only paid tax preparers are required to complete the form, and failure to do so can result in a $500 penalty for each failure. See Form 8867 and IRC Sec. 6695(g).

Source: See Form 8867 and IRC Sec. 6695(g).

Other Refundable Personal Credits   Other refundable personal tax credits include a portion of the child tax credit (discussed above), excess FICA withholdings (see discussion above under FICA taxes), and taxes withheld on wages and estimated tax payments. We address withholdings and estimated taxes below when we discuss tax prepayments.

Business Tax Credits

Business tax credits are designed to provide incentives for taxpayers to hire certain types of individuals or to participate in certain business activities. For example, Congress provides the employment tax credit to encourage businesses to hire certain unemployed individuals, and it provides the research and development credit to encourage businesses to expend funds to develop new technology. Business tax credits are *nonrefundable* credits. However, when business credits other than the foreign tax credit (discussed below) exceed the taxpayer's gross tax for the year, the credits are carried back one year and forward 20 years to use in years when the taxpayer has sufficient gross tax liability to use them.

Why discuss business credits in an individual tax chapter? We discuss business credits here because self-employed individuals may qualify for them. Also, individuals may be allocated business credits from flow-through entities (partnerships, LLCs, and S corporations). Finally, individuals working as employees overseas or receiving dividends from investments in foreign securities may qualify for the foreign tax credit.

Foreign Tax Credit   U.S. citizens must pay U.S. tax on their worldwide income. However, when they generate some or all of their income in other countries, they generally are required to pay income taxes to the foreign country where they earned their income. Without some form of tax relief, taxpayers earning income overseas would be double-taxed on this income. When taxpayers pay income taxes to foreign countries, for U.S. tax purposes they may treat the payment in one of three ways: (1) as we discussed in the Gross Income and Exclusions chapter when we introduced the foreign-earned income exclusion, taxpayers may exclude the foreign-earned income from U.S. taxation (in which case they would not deduct or receive a credit for any foreign taxes paid); (2) they may include the foreign income in their gross income and deduct the foreign taxes paid as itemized deductions (subject to $10,000 limitation on itemized tax deductions); or (3) they may include foreign income in gross income and claim a foreign tax credit for the foreign taxes paid. Here, we discuss the foreign tax credit.

The foreign tax credit helps reduce the double tax taxpayers may face when they pay income taxes on foreign-earned income to the United States and to foreign countries. Taxpayers are allowed to claim a foreign tax credit, against their U.S. tax liability, for the income taxes they pay to foreign countries.[36] In certain situations, taxpayers may not be able to claim the full amount of foreign tax paid as a credit. This restriction may apply when the taxpayer's foreign tax rate is higher than the U.S. tax rate on the foreign earnings. Taxpayers generally benefit from claiming credits rather than deductions for foreign taxes paid because credits reduce their liabilities dollar for dollar. However, when the foreign tax credit is restricted (see above), taxpayers may benefit by claiming deductions for the taxes paid (subject to $10,000 limitation on itemized tax deductions) instead of credits.

As we discussed above, the foreign tax credit may be limited in circumstances in which a taxpayer's effective foreign tax rate exceeds her U.S. tax rate. In addition, as a nonrefundable credit, it can reduce the taxpayer's tax liability only to zero (but not create a refund). When the use of a foreign tax credit is limited, taxpayers may carry back unused credits one year and carry forward the credits up to 10 years.[37]

Tax Credit Summary

Exhibit 8-11 identifies several tax credits and for each credit identifies the credit type, notes the IRC section allowing the credit, and describes the credit.

Credit Application Sequence

As we've discussed, credits are applied against a taxpayer's gross tax. However, we still must describe what happens when the taxpayer's allowable credits exceed the taxpayer's gross tax. Keep in mind that nonrefundable personal credits and business credits may be used to reduce a taxpayer's gross tax to zero, but not below zero.[38] In contrast, by definition, a refundable credit may reduce a taxpayer's gross tax below zero. This excess refundable credit generates a tax refund for the taxpayer.

When a nonrefundable personal credit exceeds the taxpayer's gross tax, it reduces the gross tax to zero, but the excess credit (credit in excess of the taxpayer's gross tax) disappears. That is, the taxpayer may not carry over any excess nonrefundable personal credits to use in other years. However, when a business credit or foreign tax credit exceeds the gross tax, it reduces the taxpayer's gross tax to zero, but the excess credit may be carried forward or back to be used in other years when the taxpayer has sufficient gross tax to use the credit (subject to certain time restrictions discussed above).

Because the tax treatment of excess credits depends on the type of credit, it is important to identify the sequence in which taxpayers apply the credits when they have more than one type of credit for the year. In this case, they apply the credits against their gross tax in the following order: (1) nonrefundable personal credits, (2) business credits, and (3) refundable credits. This sequence maximizes the chances that taxpayers will receive full benefit for their tax credits.

Because, as we discuss above, the foreign tax credit is a hybrid credit subject to a unique set of application rules, we exclude it from our general discussion on applying credits. Exhibit 8-12 summarizes the order in which the credits are applied against gross tax and indicates the tax treatment of any excess credits.

---

[36]§904.

[37]See IRS Publication 514, "Foreign Tax Credit for Individuals," for more information about the foreign tax credit.

[38]In general, nonrefundable personal credits can offset a taxpayer's regular tax and AMT (§26) but not self-employment tax. The limitation on business credits is more complex. We limit our discussion here to basic concepts. See §38(c) for the detailed limitations.

EXHIBIT 8-11   **Summary of Selected Tax Credits**

Credit	Type of Credit	IRC	Description
Child and dependent care credit	Nonrefundable personal	§21	Credit for taxpayers who pay dependent care expenses due to their employment activities.
Credit for elderly and disabled	Nonrefundable personal	§22	Credit for elderly low-income taxpayers who retire because of a disability.
Adoption expense credit	Nonrefundable personal	§23	Credit for qualified adoption-related expenses.
Child tax credit	Nonrefundable and refundable personal	§24	Credit for providing home for dependent children under the age of 17.
American opportunity credit	Nonrefundable and refundable personal	§25A	Credit for higher education expenses for the first four years of postsecondary education.
Lifetime learning credit	Nonrefundable personal	§25A	Credit for higher education expenses.
Saver's credit	Nonrefundable personal	§25B	Credit for contributing to qualified retirement plans.
Residential energy	Nonrefundable personal	§25D	Credit for qualified expenditures for solar electric property, solar water heating property, fuel cell property, wind energy property, and qualified geothermal heat pump property.
Earned income credit	Refundable personal	§32	Credit to encourage low-income taxpayers to work.
Premium tax credit	Refundable personal	§36B	Credit for health insurance purchased through an exchange for individuals and families with household incomes between 100% and 400% of the poverty line.
Credit for increasing research activities	Business	§41	Credit to encourage research and development.
Employer-provided child care credit	Business	§45F	Credit for providing child care for employees.
Small employer health insurance credit	Business	§45R	Credit to encourage employer-provided health insurance.
Rehabilitation credit	Business	§47	Credit for expenditures to renovate or restore older business buildings.
Energy credit	Business	§48	Credit for businesses that invest in energy conservation measures.
Work opportunity credit	Business	§51	Credit for hiring certain qualified veterans.
Foreign tax credit	Hybrid business and personal	§904	Credit to reduce effects of double taxation of foreign income.

EXHIBIT 8-12   **Credit Application**

Credit Type	Order Applied	Excess Credit
Nonrefundable personal	First	Lost
Business	Second	Carryback and carryover
Refundable personal	Last	Refunded

Example 8-23

What if: As we describe in Example 8-2, Gram's gross tax liability is $199. For illustrative purposes, let's assume Gram is entitled to an $800 nonrefundable personal tax credit, a $700 business tax credit, and a $600 refundable personal tax credit. What is the amount of Gram's refund or taxes due?

Answer: $600 refund. Gram would apply these credits as follows:

Description	Amount	Treatment of Excess Credit
Gross tax liability	$ 199	Example 8-2
Nonrefundable personal credits	(199)	$601 ($800 − $199) excess credit expires unused
Business credits	0	$700 carried back one year or forward 20 years (10 years for foreign tax credit)
Refundable personal credits	**(600)**	Generates $600 tax refund to Gram

LO 8-5

TAXPAYER PREPAYMENTS AND FILING REQUIREMENTS

After determining their tax liabilities, taxpayers must file a tax return and pay any additional tax due or receive a refund. When they don't pay enough taxes during the year or are late filing their tax return or paying their taxes due, they may be subject to certain penalties.

Prepayments

The income tax must be paid on a *pay-as-you-go* basis. This means it must be prepaid via **withholding** from salary or through periodic **estimated tax payments** during the tax year. Employees pay tax through withholding, and self-employed taxpayers generally pay taxes through estimated tax payments. Employers are required to withhold taxes from an employee's wages based upon the employee's marital status, exemptions, and estimated annual pay. Wages include both cash and noncash remuneration for services, and employers remit withholdings to the government on behalf of employees. At the end of the year, employers report the amounts withheld to each employee via Form W-2. Estimated tax payments are required of employees only if withholdings are insufficient to meet the taxpayer's tax liability. For calendar-year taxpayers, estimated tax payments are due on April 15, June 15, and September 15 of the current year and January 15 of the following year. If the due date falls on a Saturday, Sunday, or holiday, it is automatically extended to the next day that is not a Saturday, Sunday, or holiday.

Example 8-24

Courtney's gross tax liability for the year, including federal income tax, alternative minimum tax, and self-employment taxes is $28,134 (see Exhibit 8-6), and her net tax liability is $25,634 after the $2,500 child tax credit (see Example 8-17). However, because she had only $21,634 withheld from her paycheck by EWD (per her Form W-2 received from her employer), she underpaid $4,000 for the year ($25,634 − $21,634). Because Courtney did not pay her full tax liability, she may be subject to underpayment penalties discussed below. If she had been aware that her withholding would be insufficient, she could have increased her withholding at any time during the year (even in her December paycheck) or made estimated tax payments of $1,000 on April 17, June 15, and September 17 in 2018 and January 15, 2019 ($4,000/4).

What if: If Courtney were self-employed (instead of employed by EWD) and thus had no tax withholdings by an employer, she would be required to pay quarterly estimated tax payments. In this scenario, she would need to pay $6,408.50 ($25,634/4 = $6,408.50) by April 17, June 15, and September 17 of 2018 and $6,408.50 by January 15, 2019, to cover her gross tax liability of $25,634.

Underpayment Penalties   When taxpayers like Courtney fall behind on their tax prepayments, they may be subject to an **underpayment penalty.**[39] Taxpayers with unpredictable income streams may be particularly susceptible to this penalty because it is difficult for them to accurately estimate their tax liability for the year. To help taxpayers who may not be able to predict their earnings for the year and to provide some margin of error for those who can, the tax laws provide some **safe-harbor provisions.** Under these provisions taxpayers can avoid underpayment penalties if their withholdings and estimated tax payments equal or exceed one of the following two safe harbors: (1) 90 percent of their *current tax liability* or (2) 100 percent of their *previous-year tax liability* (110 percent for individuals with AGI greater than $150,000).

These two safe harbors determine on a quarterly basis the minimum tax prepayments that a taxpayer must have made to avoid the underpayment penalty. The first safe harbor requires that a taxpayer must have paid at least 22.5 percent (90 percent/4 = 22.5 percent) of the *current*-year liability via withholdings or estimated tax payments by April 15 to avoid the underpayment penalty for the first quarter. Similarly by June 15, September 15, and January 15, the taxpayer must have paid 45 percent (22.5 percent × 2), 67.5 percent (22.5 percent × 3), and 90 percent (22.5 percent × 4), respectively, of the current-year liability via withholding or estimated tax payments to avoid the underpayment penalty in the second, third, and fourth quarters.[40] In determining taxpayers' prepayments for a quarter, tax withholdings are generally treated as though they are withheld evenly throughout the year. In contrast, estimated tax payments are credited to the taxpayer's account when they are remitted.

Example 8-25

Because all Courtney's prepayments were made through withholding by EWD, the payments are treated as though they were made evenly throughout the year. What are Courtney's actual and required withholdings under the 90 percent safe-harbor provision throughout the year?

Answer: See the following table:

Dates	(1) Actual Withholding	(2) Required Withholding	(1) − (2) Over- (Under-) Withheld
April 17, 2018	$5,409	$5,768	$(359)
	($21,634 × .25)	($25,634 × .9 × .25)	
June 15, 2018	$10,817	$11,535	(718)
	($21,634 × .50)	($25,634 × .9 × .50)	
September 17, 2018	$16,226	$17,303	(1,077)
	($21,634 × .75)	($25,634 × .9 × .75)	
January 15, 2019	$21,634	$23,071	(1,437)
		($25,634 × .9 × 1)	

It looks like Courtney is underwithheld in each quarter.

The second safe harbor requires that by April 15, June 15, September 15, and January 15, the taxpayer must have paid 25 percent, 50 percent (25 percent × 2), 75 percent (25 percent × 3), and 100 percent (25 percent × 4), respectively, of the *previous*-year tax liability (110 percent of the previous-year tax liability for individuals with AGI greater than $150,000), via withholding or estimated tax payments, to avoid the underpayment penalty in the first, second, third, and fourth quarters.

---

[39]§6654.

[40]As an alternative method of estimating safe harbor, (1) taxpayers can compute 90 percent of the current liability using the seasonal method. This method allows taxpayers to estimate 90 percent of their current tax liability by annualizing their taxable income earned through the month prior to the payment date (e.g., through March for April 15, May for June 15, and August for September 15). Taxpayers with uneven taxable income throughout the year with smaller taxable income earlier in the year benefit from this method.

A taxpayer who does not satisfy either of the safe-harbor provisions can compute the underpayment penalty owed using Form 2210. The underpayment penalty is determined by multiplying the **federal short-term interest rate** plus 3 percentage points by the amount of tax underpayment per quarter. For purposes of this computation, the quarterly tax underpayment is the difference between the taxpayer's quarterly withholding and estimated tax payments and the required minimum tax payment under the first or second safe harbor (whichever is less). If the taxpayer does not complete Form 2210 and remit the underpayment penalty with the taxpayer's tax return, the IRS will compute and assess the penalty for the taxpayer.

Example 8-26

In the previous example, we discovered that Courtney was underwithheld in each quarter based on the first (90 percent of current year) safe-harbor provision. Assuming Courtney was underwithheld by even more under the second (100 percent of prior year) safe-harbor provision, she is required to pay an underpayment penalty based on the underpayments determined using the first safe-harbor provision. Assuming the federal short-term rate is 5 percent, what is Courtney's underpayment penalty for 2018?

Answer: $72, computed as follows:

Description	First Quarter	Second Quarter	Third Quarter	Fourth Quarter
Underpayment	$359	$718	$1,077	$1,437
Times: Federal rate + 3% (5% + 3%)	× 8%	× 8%	× 8%	× 8%
	$ 29	$ 57	$ 86	$ 115
Times one quarter of a year[41]	× 25%	× 25%	× 25%	× 25%
Underpayment penalty per quarter	$ 7	$ 14	$ 22	$ 29

That's a lot of work to figure out a $72 penalty: (7 + 14 + 22 + 29)

As a matter of administrative convenience, taxpayers are not subject to underpayment penalties if they had no tax liability in the previous year, or if their tax payable is less than $1,000 after subtracting their withholding amounts (but not estimated payments).

Example 8-27

Gram's tax liability for the year is $199 (Example 8-2), but she did not have any taxes withheld during the year, and she did not make any estimated tax payments. What is Gram's underpayment penalty?

Answer: $0. Because Gram's $199 tax payable after subtracting her withholding amounts ($199 tax – $0 withholding) is less than $1,000, she is not subject to an underpayment penalty.

Filing Requirements

Individual taxpayers are required to file a tax return only if their gross income exceeds certain thresholds, which vary based on the taxpayer's filing status and age. However, a taxpayer may prefer to file a tax return even when she is not required to do so. For example, a taxpayer with gross income less than the threshold may want to file a tax

---

[41]Form 2210 actually computes the penalty per quarter based on the number of days in the quarter divided by the number of days in the year. For simplicity, we assume this ratio is per quarter.

return to receive a refund of income taxes withheld. In general, the thresholds are simply the applicable standard deduction amount for the different filing statuses.[42] With the increased standard deduction amounts in 2018, fewer taxpayers are now required to file.

Individual tax returns are due on April 15 for calendar-year individuals (the fifteenth day of the fourth month following year-end). If the due date falls on a Saturday, Sunday, or holiday, it is automatically extended to the next day that is not a Saturday, Sunday, or holiday. Taxpayers unable to file a tax return by the original due date can request (by that same deadline) a six-month extension to file, which is granted automatically by the IRS. The extension gives the taxpayer additional time to file the tax return, but it does *not* extend the due date for paying the tax.

Late Filing Penalty

The tax law imposes a **late filing penalty** on taxpayers who do not file a tax return by the required date (the original due date plus extension).[43] The penalty equals 5 percent of the amount of tax owed for each month (or fraction of a month) that the tax return is late, with a maximum penalty of 25 percent. For fraudulent failure to file, the penalty is 15 percent of the amount of tax owed per month with a maximum penalty of 75 percent. If the taxpayer owes no tax as of the due date of the tax return (plus extension), the tax law does not impose a late filing penalty.

Late Payment Penalty

An extension allows the taxpayer to delay filing a tax return but does not extend the due date for tax payments. If a taxpayer fails to pay the entire balance of tax owed by the original due date of the tax return, the tax law imposes a **late payment penalty** from the due date of the return until the taxpayer pays the tax.[44] The late payment penalty equals .5 percent of the amount of tax owed for each month (or fraction of a month) that the tax is not paid.

The combined maximum penalty that may be imposed for late payment and late filing (nonfraudulent) is 5 percent per month (25 percent in total). For late payment and filing due to fraud, the combined maximum penalty for late payment and late filing is 15 percent per month (75 percent in total).

Example 8-28

Courtney filed her tax return on April 10 and included a check with the return for $4,072 made payable to the United States Treasury. The $4,072 consisted of her underpaid tax liability of $4,000 (Example 8-24) and her $72 underpayment penalty (Example 8-26).

What if: If Courtney had waited until May 1 to file her return and pay her taxes, what late filing and late payment penalties would she owe?

Answer: Her combined late filing penalty and late payment penalty would be $200 ($4,000 late payment × 5 percent × 1 month or portion thereof—the combined penalty is limited to 5 percent per month).

TAX SUMMARY

Courtney's and Gram's net taxes due, including an underpayment penalty for Courtney, are provided in Exhibits 8-13 and 8-15, respectively. Exhibit 8-14 illustrates how this information would be presented on Courtney's tax return by providing Courtney's Form 1040, page 2. We use 2017 forms as 2018 forms were not available at press time.

[42]§6012. Filing requirements for individuals who are dependents of other taxpayers are subject to special rules that consider the individual's unearned income, earned income, and gross income. See IRS Publication 17, "Your Federal Income Tax."

[43]§6651.

[44]§6651. As we discussed in the Tax Compliance, the IRS, and Tax Authorities chapter, the tax law also assesses interest on any tax underpayments until the tax is paid (§6601).

EXHIBIT 8-13   Courtney's Net Tax Payable

Description	Amount	Reference
(1) Regular federal income tax	$ 27,652	Example 8-3
(2) Alternative minimum tax	0	Example 8-9
(3) Self-employment tax	482	Example 8-14
(4) Gross tax	$ 28,134	(1) + (2) + (3)
(5) Tax credits	$ (2,500)	Examples 8-17, 8-19, 8-20, and 8-22
(6) Prepayments	$(21,634)	Example 8-24
(7) Underpayment penalties	72	Example 8-26
Tax and penalties due with tax return	$ 4,072	

EXHIBIT 8-14   Courtney's Net Tax Payable (as presented on her Form 1040, page 2)

Form 1040 (2017)   Page **2**

		Description		Line	Amount
Tax and Credits	38	Amount from line 37 (adjusted gross income)		38	187,000
	39a	Check if: ☐ You were born before January 2, 1953, ☐ Blind. ☐ Spouse was born before January 2, 1953, ☐ Blind. Total boxes checked ▶ 39a			
	b	If your spouse itemizes on a separate return or you were a dual-status alien, check here▶ 39b☐			
Standard Deduction for— • People who check any box on line 39a or 39b or who can be claimed as a dependent, see instructions. • All others: Single or Married filing separately, $6,350 Married filing jointly or Qualifying widow(er), $12,700 Head of household, $9,350	40	Itemized deductions (from Schedule A) or your standard deduction (see left margin)		40	38,330
	41	Subtract line 40 from line 38		41	148,670
	42	Deduction for qualified business income		42	3,600
	43	Taxable income. Subtract line 42 from line 41. If line 42 is more than line 41, enter -0-		43	145,070
	44	Tax (see instructions). Check if any from: a ☐ Form(s) 8814 b ☐ Form 4972 c ☐		44	27,652
	45	Alternative minimum tax (see instructions). Attach Form 6251		45	
	46	Excess advance premium tax credit repayment. Attach Form 8962		46	
	47	Add lines 44, 45, and 46 ▶		47	27,652
	48	Foreign tax credit. Attach Form 1116 if required	48		
	49	Credit for child and dependent care expenses. Attach Form 2441	49		
	50	Education credits from Form 8863, line 19	50		
	51	Retirement savings contributions credit. Attach Form 8880	51		
	52	Child tax credit. Attach Schedule 8812, if required	52	2,500	
	53	Residential energy credit. Attach Form 5695	53		
	54	Other credits from Form: a ☐ 3800 b ☐ 8801 c ☐	54		
	55	Add lines 48 through 54. These are your total credits		55	2,500
	56	Subtract line 55 from line 47. If line 55 is more than line 47, enter -0- ▶		56	25,152
Other Taxes	57	Self-employment tax. Attach Schedule SE		57	482
	58	Unreported social security and Medicare tax from Form: a ☐ 4137 b ☐ 8919		58	
	59	Additional tax on IRAs, other qualified retirement plans, etc. Attach Form 5329 if required		59	
	60a	Household employment taxes from Schedule H		60a	
	b	First-time homebuyer credit repayment. Attach Form 5405 if required		60b	
	61	Health care: individual responsibility (see instructions) Full-year coverage ☐		61	
	62	Taxes from: a ☐ Form 8959 b ☐ Form 8960 c ☐ Instructions; enter code(s)		62	
	63	Add lines 56 through 62. This is your total tax ▶		63	25,634
Payments If you have a qualifying child, attach Schedule EIC.	64	Federal income tax withheld from Forms W-2 and 1099	64	21,634	
	65	2017 estimated tax payments and amount applied from 2016 return	65		
	66a	Earned income credit (EIC)	66a		
	b	Nontaxable combat pay election	66b		
	67	Additional child tax credit. Attach Schedule 8812	67		
	68	American opportunity credit from Form 8863, line 8	68		
	69	Net premium tax credit. Attach Form 8962	69		
	70	Amount paid with request for extension to file	70		
	71	Excess social security and tier 1 RRTA tax withheld	71		
	72	Credit for federal tax on fuels. Attach Form 4136	72		
	73	Credits from Form: a ☐ 2439 b ☐ Reserved c ☐ 8885 d ☐	73		
	74	Add lines 64, 65, 66a, and 67 through 73. These are your total payments ▶		74	21,634
Refund Direct deposit? See instructions.	75	If line 74 is more than line 63, subtract line 63 from line 74. This is the amount you overpaid		75	
	76a	Amount of line 75 you want refunded to you. If Form 8888 is attached, check here ▶☐		76a	
	b	Routing number ▶c Type: ☐ Checking ☐ Savings			
	d	Account number			
	77	Amount of line 75 you want applied to your 2018 estimated tax ▶ 77			
Amount You Owe	78	Amount you owe. Subtract line 74 from line 63. For details on how to pay, see instructions ▶		78	4,072
	79	Estimated tax penalty (see instructions) 79	72		

Third Party Designee Do you want to allow another person to discuss this return with the IRS (see instructions)? ☐ Yes. Complete below. ☐ No
Designee's name ▶   Phone no. ▶   Personal identification number (PIN) ▶

Sign Here Under penalties of perjury, I declare that I have examined this return and accompanying schedules and statements, and to the best of my knowledge and belief, they are true, correct, and accurately list all amounts and sources of income I received during the tax year. Declaration of preparer (other than taxpayer) is based on all information of which preparer has any knowledge.
Joint return? See instructions. Keep a copy for your records.
Your signature   Date   Your occupation   Daytime phone number
Spouse's signature. If a joint return, both must sign.   Date   Spouse's occupation   If the IRS sent you an Identity Protection PIN, enter it here (see inst.)

Paid Preparer Use Only
Print/Type preparer's name   Preparer's signature   Date   Check ☐ if self-employed   PTIN
Firm's name ▶   Firm's EIN ▶
Firm's address ▶   Phone no.

Go to www.irs.gov/Form1040 for instructions and the latest information.   Form **1040** (2017)

Source: www.irs.gov/Form1040

EXHIBIT 8-15   Gram's Tax Payable

Description	Amount	Reference
(1) Gross tax	$199	Example 8-2
(2) Alternative minimum tax	0	
(3) Self-employment tax	0	
(4) Gross tax	$199	(1) + (2) + (3)
(5) Tax credits	0	
(6) Prepayments	0	
(7) Penalties	0	
Tax due with return	$199	(4) − (5) − (6) − (7)

CONCLUSION

This chapter reviewed the process for determining an individual's gross and net tax liability. We discovered that taxpayers may be required to pay regular federal income tax, alternative minimum tax, and employment-related tax. Taxpayers are able to offset their gross tax liability dollar for dollar with various types of tax credits and by the amount of tax they prepay during the year. Taxpayers must pay additional taxes with their tax return or they may receive a refund when they file their tax return depending on their gross tax liability and their available tax credits and tax prepayments. The previous chapters have covered the basic individual tax formula. The next three chapters address issues relevant for taxpayers involved in business activities.

Summary

Determine a taxpayer's regular tax liability.   **LO 8-1**

- Individual income is taxed using progressive tax rate schedules with rates ranging from 10 percent to 37 percent.
- Marginal tax rates depend on filing status and amount of taxable income.
- Progressive tax rate schedules may lead to either a marriage penalty or a marriage benefit for married taxpayers.
- Long-term capital gains and qualified dividends are taxed at either 0 percent, 15 percent, or 20 percent, depending on the amount of taxable income.
- A 3.8 percent tax is levied on net investment income for higher-income taxpayers.
- Strategies to shift investment income from parents to children are limited by the "kiddie tax" whereby children's investment income is taxed using the trust and estate tax rate schedule.

Compute a taxpayer's alternative minimum tax liability.   **LO 8-2**

- The AMT was designed to ensure that higher-income taxpayers pay some minimum level of income tax.
- The AMT base is broader than the regular income tax base. The AMT base is designed to more closely reflect economic income, as opposed to regular taxable income.
- The starting point for calculating AMT is regular taxable income. To compute AMTI, taxpayers add back items that are not deductible for AMT purposes (but were deducted for regular tax purposes) and items taxable for AMT purposes (but tax exempt or deferred for regular tax purposes). Taxpayers then subtract the allowable AMT exemption to generate the AMT base. They then apply the AMT rates and compare the product (the tentative minimum tax) to their regular tax liability. They owe AMT if the tentative minimum tax exceeds the regular tax liability.
- The AMT exemption depends on the taxpayer's filing status and is subject to phase-out of 25 cents for each dollar of AMTI over the specific thresholds based on filing status.

- The 2018 AMT tax rates are 26 percent up to $191,100 of AMT base ($95,550 of AMT base for married taxpayers filing separately) and 28 percent thereafter. However, long-term capital gains and qualified dividends are subject to the same preferential rate at which they are taxed for regular tax purposes.
- The amount of the AMT is the excess of the tentative minimum tax over the taxpayer's regular tax liability.

LO 8-3   Calculate a taxpayer's employment and self-employment taxes payable.

- Employees' wages are subject to FICA tax. For employees, the Social Security component is 6.2 percent, the Medicare component 1.45 percent, and the additional Medicare tax is .9 percent. For employers, the Social Security component is 6.2 percent and the Medicare component is 1.45 percent. The Social Security tax applies to the first $128,400 of salary or wages in 2018. The wage base on the Medicare tax is unlimited. The additional Medicare tax applies to employees (not employers) on salary or wages above $200,000 ($125,000 for married filing separate; $250,000 of combined salary or wages for married filing joint).
- Self-employed taxpayers pay self-employment tax on their net self-employment income (92.35 percent of their net Schedule C income). They pay Social Security tax of 12.4 percent and Medicare tax of 2.9 percent on their net self-employment income. The Social Security tax applies to the first $128,400 of net Schedule C income in 2018. The base for the Medicare tax is unlimited. Self-employed taxpayers are also subject to the additional Medicare tax of .9 percent on net self-employment earnings in excess of $200,000 ($200,000 ($125,000 for married filing separate; $250,000 of combined salary or wages for married filing joint).
- The determination as to whether to treat a worker as an independent contractor or as an employee for tax purposes is a subjective test based in large part on the extent of control the worker has over things such as the nature, timing, and location of work performed.
- Independent contractors are able to deduct ordinary and necessary business expenses as *for* AGI deductions. Employees cannot deduct unreimbursed employee business expenses.
- Independent contractors may deduct the employer portion of their self-employment taxes paid during the year. Employees may not deduct their FICA taxes.
- Independent contractors are required to pay self-employment tax, which represents the employer and employee portions of FICA taxes. Further, independent contractors must pay estimated taxes on their income because the employer does not withhold taxes from the independent contractor's paychecks.
- Hiring independent contractors is generally less costly for employers than is hiring employees. Employers do not pay FICA taxes, withhold taxes, or provide fringe benefits for independent contractors.

LO 8-4   Compute a taxpayer's allowable child tax credit, child and dependent care credit, American opportunity credit, lifetime learning credit, and earned income credit.

- Tax credits are generally classified into one of three categories: business, nonrefundable personal, or refundable personal credits.
- Nonrefundable personal tax credits provide tax relief to specified groups of individuals.
- The child tax credit is $2,000 for a qualifying child under the age of 17 and $500 for other qualified dependents.
- The child and dependent care credit is provided to help taxpayers pay the cost of providing care for their dependents and allow taxpayers to work or to look for work.
- The American opportunity credit provides a credit for a percentage of the costs of the first four years of a student's college education. Forty percent of the credit is refundable.
- The lifetime learning credit provides a credit for a percentage of the costs for instruction in a postsecondary degree program or the costs to acquire or improve a taxpayer's job skills.
- Nonrefundable credits are first used to reduce a taxpayer's gross tax but cannot reduce the gross tax below zero. Any excess credit is lost unless it is allowed to be carried to a different tax year.
- The earned income credit is refundable but subject to a very complex calculation.
- Business credits reduce the tax after applying nonrefundable credits. Any credit in excess of the remaining tax is generally allowed to be carried over or back to be used in other years.
- Refundable credits are the last credit applied to the tax after applying nonrefundable and business credits. Any refundable credit in excess of the remaining tax is treated as an overpayment and refunded to the taxpayer.

Explain how to compute a taxpayer's underpayment, late filing, and late payment penalties.   LO 8-5

- The income tax must be prepaid via withholding from salary or through periodic estimated tax payments during the tax year. Estimated tax payments are required only if withholdings are insufficient to meet the taxpayer's tax liability. For calendar-year taxpayers, estimated tax payments are due on April 15, June 15, and September 15 of the current year and January 15 of the following year.

- Taxpayers can avoid an underpayment penalty if their withholdings and estimated tax payments equal or exceed one of two safe harbors: (1) 90 percent of current-year tax or (2) 100 percent of previous-year tax (110 percent if AGI exceeds $150,000). If the taxpayer does not satisfy either of the safe-harbor provisions, the underpayment penalty is determined by multiplying the federal short-term interest rate plus 3 percentage points by the amount of tax underpayment per quarter.

- Individual taxpayers are required to file a tax return only if their *gross income* exceeds certain thresholds, which vary based on the taxpayer's filing status, age, and gross income.

- Individual tax returns are due on April 15 for calendar-year individuals. Taxpayers unable to file a tax return by the original due date can request a six-month extension to file.

- The tax law imposes penalties on taxpayers who do not file a tax return (by the original due date plus extension) or pay the tax owed (by the original due date). The failure-to-file penalty equals 5 percent of the amount of tax owed for each month (or fraction thereof) that the tax return is late with a maximum penalty of 25 percent. The late payment penalty equals .5 percent of the amount of tax owed for each month (or fraction thereof) that the tax is not paid. The combined maximum penalty that may be imposed for late filing and late payment is 5 percent per month (25 percent in total). The late filing and late payment penalties are higher if fraud is involved.

KEY TERMS

additional Medicare tax (8-14)	federal short-term interest rate (8-36)	nonrefundable credit (8-23)
alternative minimum tax (AMT) (8-8)	FICA taxes (8-14)	preferential tax rate (8-4)
alternative minimum tax adjustments (8-9)	independent contractor (8-21)	safe-harbor provisions (8-35)
	kiddie tax (8-6)	Schedule C (8-16)
alternative minimum tax (AMT) base (8-8)	late filing penalty (8-37)	self-employment taxes (8-16)
	late payment penalty (8-37)	Social Security tax (8-14)
alternative minimum tax (AMT) exemption (8-12)	marriage benefit (8-3)	tax bracket (8-2)
alternative minimum tax system (8-8)	marriage penalty (8-3)	tax credits (8-23)
business tax credits (8-31)	Medicare tax (8-14)	tax rate schedule (8-2)
child tax credits (8-24)	minimum tax credit (8-13)	tax tables (8-3)
earned income credit (8-29)	net earnings from self-employment (8-16)	tentative minimum tax (8-9)
employee (8-21)		underpayment penalty (8-35)
estimated tax payments (8-34)	net investment income tax (8-5)	withholding (8-34)
	net unearned income (8-7)	

DISCUSSION QUESTIONS

Discussion Questions are available in Connect®.   connect

1. What is a tax bracket? What is the relationship between filing status and the width of the tax brackets in the tax rate schedule?   LO 8-1

2. In 2018, for a taxpayer with $50,000 of taxable income, without doing any actual computations, which filing status do you expect to provide the lowest tax liability? Which filing status provides the highest tax liability?   LO 8-1

3. What is the tax marriage penalty and when does it apply? Under what circumstances would a couple experience a tax marriage benefit?   LO 8-1

LO 8-1 4. Once they've computed their taxable income, how do taxpayers determine their regular tax liability? What additional steps must taxpayers take to compute their tax liability when they have preferentially taxed income?

LO 8-1

research 5. Are there circumstances in which preferentially taxed income (long-term capital gains and qualified dividends) is taxed at the same rate as ordinary income? Explain.

LO 8-1 6. Augustana received $10,000 of qualified dividends this year. Under what circumstances might the entire $10,000 of income not be taxed at the same rate?

LO 8-1 7. What is the difference between earned and unearned income?

LO 8-1 8. Does the kiddie tax eliminate the tax benefits gained by a family when parents transfer income-producing assets to children? Explain.

LO 8-1 9. Does the kiddie tax apply to all children no matter their age? Explain.

LO 8-1 10. What is the kiddie tax? Explain.

LO 8-1 11. Lauren is 17 years old. She reports earned income of $3,000 and unearned income of $6,200. Is it likely that she is subject to the kiddie tax? Explain.

LO 8-2 12. In very general terms, how is the alternative minimum tax system different from the regular income tax system? How is it similar?

LO 8-2 13. Describe, in general terms, why Congress implemented the AMT.

LO 8-2 14. Do taxpayers always add back the standard deduction when computing alternative minimum taxable income? Explain.

LO 8-2 15. The starting point for computing alternative minimum taxable income is regular taxable income. What are some of the plus adjustments, plus or minus adjustments, and minus adjustments to regular taxable income to compute alternative minimum taxable income?

LO 8-2 16. Describe what the AMT exemption is and who is and isn't allowed to deduct the exemption. How is it similar to the standard deduction and how is it dissimilar?

LO 8-1 **LO 8-2** 17. How do the AMT tax rates compare to the regular income tax rates?

LO 8-2 18. Is it possible for a taxpayer who pays AMT to have a marginal tax rate higher than the stated AMT rate? Explain.

LO 8-2 19. What is the difference between the tentative minimum tax (TMT) and the AMT?

LO 8-3 20. Are an employee's entire wages subject to the FICA tax? Explain.

LO 8-3 21. Bobbie works as an employee for Altron Corp. for the first half of the year and for Betel Inc. for the rest of the year. She is relatively well paid. What FICA tax issues is she likely to encounter? What FICA tax issues do Altron Corp. and Betel Inc. need to consider?

LO 8-3 22. Compare and contrast an employee's FICA tax payment responsibilities with those of a self-employed taxpayer.

LO 8-3 23. When a taxpayer works as an employee and as a self-employed independent contractor during the year, how does the taxpayer determine her employment and self-employment taxes payable?

LO 8-3 24. What are the primary factors to consider when deciding whether a worker should be considered an employee or a self-employed taxpayer for tax purposes?

LO 8-3 25. How do the tax consequences of being an employee differ from those of being self-employed?

LO 8-3

planning 26. Mike wanted to work for a CPA firm but he also wanted to work on his father's farm in Montana. Because the CPA firm wanted Mike to be happy, they offered to let him work for them as an independent contractor during the fall and winter and let him return to Montana to work for his father during the spring and summer. He was very excited to hear that they were also going to give him a 5 percent higher "salary" for the six months he would be working for the firm over what he would have made over the same six-month period if he worked full-time as an employee (i.e., an increase from $30,000 to $31,500). Should Mike be excited about his 5 percent raise? Why or why not? What counteroffer could Mike reasonably suggest?

27. How are tax credits and tax deductions similar? How are they dissimilar? `LO 8-4`

28. What are the three types of tax credits? Explain why it is important to distinguish between the different types of tax credits. `LO 8-4`

29. Explain why there is such a large number and variety of tax credits. `LO 8-4`

30. What is the difference between a refundable and nonrefundable tax credit? `LO 8-4`

31. Is the child tax credit a refundable or nonrefundable credit? Explain. `LO 8-4`

32. Diane has a job working three-quarter time. She hired her mother to take care of her two small children so Diane could work. Do Diane's child care payments to her mother qualify for the child and dependent care credit? Explain. `LO 8-4`

33. The amount of the child and dependent care credit is based on the amount of the taxpayer's expenditures to provide care for one or more qualifying persons. Who is considered to be a qualifying person for this purpose? `LO 8-4`

34. Compare and contrast the lifetime learning credit with the American opportunity credit. `LO 8-4`

35. Jennie's grandfather paid her tuition this fall to State University (an eligible educational institution). Jennie is claimed as a dependent by her parents, but she also files her own tax return. Can Jennie claim an education credit for the tuition paid by her grandfather? What difference would it make, if any, if Jennie did not qualify as a dependent of her parents (or anyone else)? `LO 8-4`

research

36. Why is the earned income credit referred to as a negative income tax? `LO 8-4`

37. Under what circumstances can a college student qualify for the earned income credit? `LO 8-4`

38. How are business credits similar to personal credits? How are they dissimilar? `LO 8-4`

39. When a U.S. taxpayer pays income taxes to a foreign government, what options does the taxpayer have when determining how to treat the expenditure on her U.S. individual income tax return? `LO 8-4`

40. Describe the order in which different types of tax credits are applied to reduce a taxpayer's tax liability. `LO 8-4`

41. Describe the two methods that taxpayers use to prepay their taxes. `LO 8-5`

42. What are the consequences of a taxpayer underpaying his or her tax liability throughout the year? Explain the safe-harbor provisions that may apply in this situation. `LO 8-5`

43. Describe how the underpayment penalty is calculated. `LO 8-5`

44. What determines if a taxpayer is required to file a tax return? If a taxpayer is not required to file a tax return, does this mean that the taxpayer should not file a tax return? `LO 8-5`

45. What is the due date for individual tax returns? What extensions are available? `LO 8-5`

46. Describe the consequences for failure to file a tax return and late payment of taxes owed. `LO 8-5`

PROBLEMS

Select problems are available in Connect®.

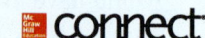

LO 8-1 47. Whitney received $75,000 of taxable income in 2018. All of the income was salary from her employer. What is her income tax liability in each of the following alternative situations?

a) She files under the single filing status.

b) She files a joint tax return with her spouse. Together their taxable income is $75,000.

c) She is married but files a separate tax return. Her taxable income is $75,000.

d) She files as a head of household.

LO 8-1 48. In 2018, Lisa and Fred, a married couple, had taxable income of $300,000. If they were to file separate tax returns, Lisa would have reported taxable income of $125,000 and Fred would have reported taxable income of $175,000. What is the couple's marriage penalty or benefit?

LO 8-1 49. In 2018, Jasmine and Thomas, a married couple, had taxable income of $150,000. If they were to file separate tax returns, Jasmine would have reported taxable income of $140,000 and Thomas would have reported taxable income of $10,000. What is the couple's marriage penalty or benefit?

LO 8-1 50. Lacy is a single taxpayer. In 2018, her taxable income is $40,000. What is her tax liability in each of the following alternative situations?

a) All of her income is salary from her employer.

b) Her $40,000 of taxable income includes $1,000 of qualified dividends.

c) Her $40,000 of taxable income includes $5,000 of qualified dividends.

LO 8-1 51. Henrich is a single taxpayer. In 2018, his taxable income is $450,000. What is his income tax and net investment income tax liability in each of the following alternative scenarios?

a) All of his income is salary from his employer.

b) His $450,000 of taxable income includes $2,000 of long-term capital gain that is taxed at preferential rates.

c) His $450,000 of taxable income includes $55,000 of long-term capital gain that is taxed at preferential rates.

d) Henrich has $195,000 of taxable income, which includes $50,000 of long-term capital gain that is taxed at preferential rates. Assume his modified AGI is $210,000.

LO 8-1 52. In 2018, Sheryl is claimed as a dependent on her parents' tax return. Sheryl did not provide more than half her own support. What is Sheryl's tax liability for the year in each of the following alternative circumstances?

a) She received $7,000 from a part-time job. This was her only source of income. She is 16 years old at year-end.

b) She received $7,000 of interest income from corporate bonds she received several years ago. This is her only source of income. She is 16 years old at year-end.

c) She received $7,000 of interest income from corporate bonds she received several years ago. This is her only source of income. She is 20 years old at year-end and is a full-time student.

d) She received $7,000 of qualified dividend income. This is her only source of income. She is 16 years old at year-end.

53. In 2018, Carson is claimed as a dependent on his parents' tax return. Carson's parents provided most of his support. What is Carson's tax liability for the year in each of the following alternative circumstances? **LO 8-1**

    a) Carson is 17 years old at year-end and earned $14,000 from his summer job and part-time job after school. This was his only source of income.

    b) Carson is 23 years old at year-end. He is a full-time student and earned $14,000 from his summer internship and part-time job. He also received $5,000 of qualified dividend income.

54. Brooklyn files as a head of household for 2018. She claimed the standard deduction of $18,000 for regular tax purposes. Her regular taxable income was $80,000. What is Brooklyn's AMTI? **LO 8-2**

55. Sylvester files as a single taxpayer during 2018. He itemizes deductions for regular tax purposes. He paid charitable contributions of $7,000, real estate taxes of $1,000, state income taxes of $4,000, and mortgage interest of $2,000 on $30,000 of acquisition indebtedness on his home. Sylvester's regular taxable income is $100,000. What is Sylvester's AMTI? **LO 8-2**

56. In 2018, Nadia has $100,000 of regular taxable income. She itemizes her deductions as follows: real property taxes of $1,500, state income taxes of $2,000, and mortgage interest expense of $10,000 (acquisition indebtedness of $200,000). In addition, she receives tax-exempt interest of $1,000 from a municipal bond (issued in 2006) that was used to fund a new business building for a (formerly) out-of-state employer. Finally, she received a state tax refund of $300 from the prior year. **LO 8-2**

    tax forms

    a) What is Nadia's AMTI this year if she deducted $15,000 of itemized deductions last year and did not owe any AMT last year? Complete Form 6251 (through line 28) for Nadia.

    b) What is Nadia's AMTI this year if she deducted the standard deduction last year and did not owe any AMT last year? Complete Form 6251 (through line 28) for Nadia.

57. In 2018, Sven is single and has $120,000 of regular taxable income. He itemizes his deductions as follows: real property tax of $2,000, state income tax of $4,000, and mortgage interest expense of $15,000 (acquisition debt of $300,000). He also has a positive AMT depreciation adjustment of $500. What is Sven's alternative minimum taxable income (AMTI)? Complete Form 6251 (through line 28) for Sven. **LO 8-2**

    tax forms

58. Olga is married and files a joint tax return with her husband. What amount of AMT exemption may she deduct under each of the following alternative circumstances? **LO 8-2**

    a) Her AMTI is $390,000.

    b) Her AMTI is $1,080,000.

    c) Her AMTI is $1,500,000.

59. Corbett's AMTI is $600,000. What is his AMT exemption under the following alternative circumstances? **LO 8-2**

    a) He is married and files a joint return.

    b) He is married and files a separate return.

    c) His filing status is single.

    d) His filing status is head of household.

60. In 2018, Juanita is married and files a joint tax return with her husband. What is her tentative minimum tax in each of the following alternative circumstances? **LO 8-2**

    a) Her AMT base is $100,000, all ordinary income.

    b) Her AMT base is $250,000, all ordinary income.

    c) Her AMT base is $100,000, which includes $10,000 of qualified dividends.

    d) Her AMT base is $250,000, which includes $10,000 of qualified dividends.

LO 8-2   61. Steve's tentative minimum tax for 2018 is $245,000. What is his AMT if

    a) His regular tax is $230,000?

    b) His regular tax is $250,000?

LO 8-2   62. In 2018, Janet and Ray are married filing jointly. They have five dependent children under 18 years of age. Janet and Ray's taxable income is $2,400,000 and they itemize their deductions as follows: state income taxes of $10,000, and mortgage interest expense of $25,000 (acquisition debt of $300,000). What is Janet and Ray's AMT? Complete Form 6251 for Janet and Ray.

tax forms

LO 8-2   63. In 2018, Deon and NeNe are married filing jointly. Deon and NeNe's taxable income is $1,090,000, and they itemize their deductions as follows: real property taxes of $10,000, charitable contributions of $30,000, and mortgage interest expense of $40,000 ($700,000 acquisition debt for home). What is Deon and NeNe's AMT? Complete Form 6251 for Deon and NeNe.

tax forms

LO 8-3   64. Brooke, a single taxpayer, works for Company A for all of 2018, earning a salary of $50,000.

    a) What is her FICA tax obligation for the year?

    b) Assume Brooke works for Company A for half of 2018, earning $50,000 in salary, and she works for Company B for the second half of 2018, earning $90,000 in salary. What is Brooke's FICA tax obligation for the year?

LO 8-3   65. Rasheed works for Company A, earning $350,000 in salary during 2018. Assuming he is single and has no other sources of income, what amount of FICA tax will Rasheed pay for the year?

LO 8-3   66. Alice is single and self-employed in 2018. Her net business profit on her Schedule C for the year is $140,000. What is her self-employment tax liability and additional Medicare tax liability for 2018?

LO 8-3   67. Kyle, a single taxpayer, worked as a free-lance software engineer for the first three months of 2018. During that time, he earned $44,000 of self-employment income. On April 1, 2018, Kyle took a job as a full-time software engineer with one of his former clients, Hoogle Inc. From April through the end of the year, Kyle earned $178,000 in salary. What amount of FICA taxes (self-employment and employment related) does Kyle owe for the year?

LO 8-3   68. Eva received $60,000 in compensation payments from JAZZ Corp. during 2018. Eva incurred $5,000 in business expenses relating to her work for JAZZ Corp. JAZZ did not reimburse Eva for any of these expenses. Eva is single and she deducts a standard deduction of $12,000. Based on these facts answer the following questions:

    a) Assume that Eva is considered to be an *employee*. What amount of FICA taxes is she required to pay for the year?

    b) Assume that Eva is considered to be an *employee*. What is her regular income tax liability for the year?

    c) Assume that Eva is considered to be a *self-employed contractor*. What is her self-employment tax liability and additional Medicare tax liability for the year?

    d) Assume that Eva is considered to be a *self-employed contractor*. What is her regular tax liability for the year?

69. Terry Hutchison worked as a self-employed lawyer until two years ago when he retired. He used the cash method of accounting in his business for tax purposes. Five years ago, Terry represented his client ABC Corporation in an antitrust lawsuit against XYZ Corporation. During that year, Terry paid self-employment taxes on all of his income. ABC won the lawsuit but Terry and ABC could not agree on the amount of his earnings. Finally, this year, the issue got resolved and ABC paid Terry $90,000 for the services he provided five years ago. Terry plans to include the payment in his gross income, but because he spends most of his time playing golf and absolutely no time working on legal matters, he does not intend to pay self-employment taxes on the income. Is Terry subject to self-employment taxes on this income?

LO 8-3
research

70. Trey has two dependents, his daughters, ages 14 and 17, at year-end. Trey files a joint return with his wife. What amount of child credit will Trey be able to claim for his daughters under each of the following alternative situations?

LO 8-4

a) His AGI is $100,000.
b) His AGI is $420,000.
c) His AGI is $420,100, and his daughters are ages 10 and 12.

71. Julie paid a day care center to watch her two-year-old son while she worked as a computer programmer for a local start-up company. What amount of child and dependent care credit can Julie claim in each of the following alternative scenarios?

LO 8-4

a) Julie paid $2,000 to the day care center and her AGI is $50,000 (all salary).
b) Julie paid $5,000 to the day care center and her AGI is $50,000 (all salary).
c) Julie paid $4,000 to the day care center and her AGI is $25,000 (all salary).
d) Julie paid $2,000 to the day care center and her AGI is $14,000 (all salary).
e) Julie paid $4,000 to the day care center and her AGI is $14,000 ($2,000 salary and $12,000 unearned income).

72. In 2018, Elaine paid $2,800 of tuition and $600 for books for her dependent son to attend State University this past fall as a freshman. Elaine files a joint return with her husband. What is the maximum American opportunity credit that Elaine can claim for the tuition payment and books in each of the following alternative situations?

LO 8-4

a) Elaine's AGI is $80,000.
b) Elaine's AGI is $168,000.
c) Elaine's AGI is $184,000.

73. In 2018, Laureen is currently single. She paid $2,800 of qualified tuition and related expenses for each of her twin daughters Sheri and Meri to attend State University as freshmen ($2,800 each for a total of $5,600). Sheri and Meri qualify as Laureen's dependents. Laureen also paid $1,900 for her son Ryan's (also Laureen's dependent) tuition and related expenses to attend his junior year at State University. Finally, Laureen paid $1,200 for herself to attend seminars at a community college to help her improve her job skills. What is the maximum amount of education credits Laureen can claim for these expenditures in each of the following alternative scenarios?

LO 8-4
planning

a) Laureen's AGI is $45,000.
b) Laureen's AGI is $95,000.
c) Laureen's AGI is $45,000 and Laureen paid $12,000 (not $1,900) for Ryan to attend graduate school (i.e., his fifth year, not his junior year).

LO 8-4   74. In 2018, Amanda and Jaxon Stuart have a daughter who is 1 year old. The Stuarts are full-time students and they are both 23 years old. Their only sources of income are gains from stock they held for three years before selling and wages from part-time jobs. What is their earned income credit in the following alternative scenarios if they file jointly?

a) Their AGI is $15,000, consisting of $5,000 of capital gains and $10,000 of wages.

b) Their AGI is $15,000, consisting of $10,000 of lottery winnings (unearned income) and $5,000 of wages.

c) Their AGI is $25,000, consisting of $20,000 of wages and $5,000 of lottery winnings (unearned income).

d) Their AGI is $25,000, consisting of $5,000 of wages and $20,000 of lottery winnings (unearned income).

e) Their AGI is $10,000, consisting of $10,000 of lottery winnings (unearned income).

LO 8-4   75. In 2018, Zach is single with no dependents. He is not claimed as a dependent on another's return. All of his income is from salary and he does not have any *for* AGI deductions. What is his earned income credit in the following alternative scenarios?

a) Zach is 29 years old and his AGI is $5,000.

b) Zach is 29 years old and his AGI is $10,000.

c) Zach is 29 years old and his AGI is $19,000.

d) Zach is 24 years old and his AGI is $5,000.

LO 8-4   76. This year Luke has calculated his gross tax liability at $1,800. Luke is entitled to a $2,400 nonrefundable personal tax credit, a $1,500 business tax credit, and a $600 refundable personal tax credit. In addition, Luke has had $2,300 of income taxes withheld from his salary. What is Luke's net tax due or refund?

LO 8-5
planning   77. This year Lloyd, a single taxpayer, estimates that his tax liability will be $10,000. Last year, his total tax liability was $15,000. He estimates that his tax withholding from his employer will be $7,800.

a) Is Lloyd required to increase his withholding or make estimated tax payments this year to avoid the underpayment penalty? If so, how much?

b) Assuming Lloyd does not make any additional payments, what is the amount of his underpayment penalty? Assume the federal short-term rate is 5 percent.

LO 8-5
planning   78. This year, Paula and Simon (married filing jointly) estimate that their tax liability will be $200,000. Last year, their total tax liability was $170,000. They estimate that their tax withholding from their employers will be $175,000. Are Paula and Simon required to increase their withholdings or make estimated tax payments this year to avoid the underpayment penalty? If so, how much?

LO 8-5
planning   79. This year, Santhosh, a single taxpayer, estimates that his tax liability will be $100,000. Last year, his total tax liability was $15,000. He estimates that his tax withholding from his employer will be $35,000. Is Santhosh required to increase his withholding or make estimated tax payments this year to avoid the underpayment penalty? If so, how much?

LO 8-5   80. For the following taxpayers, determine if they are required to file a tax return in 2018.

a) Ricko, single taxpayer, with gross income of $15,000.

b) Fantasia, head of household, with gross income of $17,500.

c) Ken and Barbie, married taxpayers with no dependents, with gross income of $20,000.

d) Dorothy and Rudolf, married taxpayers, both age 68, with gross income of $25,500.

e) Janyce, single taxpayer, age 73, with gross income of $13,500.

81. For the following taxpayers, determine the due date of their tax returns.

a) Jerome, a single taxpayer, is not requesting an extension this year. Assume the due date falls on a Tuesday.

b) Lashaunda, a single taxpayer, requests an extension this year. Assume the extended due date falls on a Wednesday.

c) Barney and Betty, married taxpayers, do not request an extension this year. Assume the due date falls on a Sunday.

d) Fred and Wilma, married taxpayers, request an extension this year. Assume the extended date falls on a Saturday.

82. Determine the amount of the late filing and late payment penalties that apply for the following taxpayers.

a) Jolene filed her tax return by its original due date but did not pay the $2,000 in taxes she owed with the return until one and a half months later.

b) Oscar filed his tax return and paid his $3,000 tax liability seven months late.

c) Wilfred, attempting to evade his taxes, did not file a tax return or pay his $10,000 in taxes for several years.

COMPREHENSIVE PROBLEMS

Select problems are available in Connect®.

83. In 2018, Jack is single and has two children, ages 10 and 12. Jack works full-time and earns an annual salary of $195,000 as a consultant. Jack files as a head of household and does not itemize his deductions. In the fall of this year, he was recently offered a position with another firm that would pay him an additional $35,000.

a) Calculate the marginal tax rate on the additional income, *excluding employment taxes,* to help Jack evaluate the offer.

b) Calculate the marginal tax rate on the additional income, *including employment taxes,* to help Jack evaluate the offer.

84. Reba Dixon is a fifth-grade schoolteacher who earned a salary of $38,000 in 2018. She is 45 years old and has been divorced for four years. She receives $1,200 of alimony payments each month from her former husband (divorced in 2016). Reba also rents out a small apartment building. This year Reba received $50,000 of rental payments from tenants and she incurred $19,500 of expenses associated with the rental.

Reba and her daughter Heather (20 years old at the end of the year) moved to Georgia in January of this year. Reba provides more than one-half of Heather's support. They had been living in Colorado for the past 15 years, but ever since her divorce, Reba has been wanting to move back to Georgia to be closer to her family. Luckily, last December, a teaching position opened up and Reba and Heather decided to make the move. Reba paid a moving company $2,010 to move their personal belongings, and she and Heather spent two days driving the 1,426 miles to Georgia.

Reba rented a home in Georgia. Heather decided to continue living at home with her mom, but she started attending school full-time in January at a nearby university. She was awarded a $3,000 partial tuition scholarship this year, and Reba helped out by paying the remaining $500 tuition cost. If possible, Reba thought it would be best to claim the education credit for these expenses.

Reba wasn't sure if she would have enough items to help her benefit from itemizing on her tax return. However, she kept track of several expenses this year that she thought might qualify if she was able to itemize. Reba paid $5,800 in state income taxes and $12,500 in charitable contributions during the year. She also paid the following medical-related expenses for herself and Heather:

Insurance premiums	$5,795
Medical care expenses	1,100
Prescription medicine	350
Nonprescription medicine	100
New contact lenses for Heather	200

Shortly after the move, Reba got distracted while driving and she ran into a street sign. The accident caused $900 in damage to the car and gave her whiplash. Because the repairs were less than her insurance deductible, she paid the entire cost of the repairs. Reba wasn't able to work for two months after the accident. Fortunately, she received $2,000 from her disability insurance. Her employer, the Central Georgia School District, paid 60 percent of the premiums on the policy as a nontaxable fringe benefit and Reba paid the remaining 40 percent portion.

A few years ago, Reba acquired several investments with her portion of the divorce settlement. This year she reported the following income from her investments: $2,200 of interest income from corporate bonds and $1,500 interest income from City of Denver municipal bonds. Overall, Reba's stock portfolio appreciated by $12,000 but she did not sell any of her stocks.

Heather reported $6,200 of interest income from corporate bonds she received as gifts from her father over the last several years. This was Heather's only source of income for the year.

Reba had $10,000 of federal income taxes withheld by her employer. Heather made $1,000 of estimated tax payments during the year. Reba did not make any estimated payments. Reba had qualifying insurance for purposes of the Affordable Care Act (ACA).

Required:

a) Determine Reba's federal income taxes due or taxes payable for the current year. Complete pages 1 and 2 of Form 1040 for Reba.
b) Is Reba allowed to file as a head of household or single?
c) Determine the amount of FICA taxes Reba was required to pay on her salary.
d) Determine Heather's federal income taxes due or payable.

tax forms

85. John and Sandy Ferguson got married eight years ago and have a seven-year-old daughter, Samantha. In 2018, John worked as a computer technician at a local university earning a salary of $152,000, and Sandy worked part-time as a receptionist for a law firm earning a salary of $29,000. John also does some Web design work on the side and reported revenues of $4,000 and associated expenses of $750. The Fergusons received $800 in qualified dividends and a $200 refund of their state income taxes. The Fergusons always itemize their deductions and their itemized deductions were well over the standard deduction amount last year. The Fergusons had qualifying insurance for purposes of the Affordable Care Act (ACA).

The Fergusons reported making the following payments during the year:

- State income taxes of $4,400. Federal tax withholding of $21,000
- Alimony payments to John's former wife of $10,000 (divorced in 2014).
- Child support payments for John's child with his former wife of $4,100.
- $12,200 of real property taxes.
- Sandy was reimbursed $600 for employee business expenses she incurred. She was required to provide documentation for her expenses to her employer.
- $3,600 to Kid Care day care center for Samantha's care while John and Sandy worked.
- $14,000 interest on their home mortgage ($400,000 acquisition debt).
- $3,000 interest on a $40,000 home-equity loan. They used the loan to pay for a family vacation and new car.
- $15,000 cash charitable contributions to qualified charities.
- Donation of used furniture to Goodwill. The furniture had a fair market value of $400 and cost $2,000.

Required:

What is the Fergusons' 2018 federal income taxes payable or refund, including any self-employment tax and AMT, if applicable? Complete pages 1 and 2 of Form 1040 and Form 6251 for John and Sandy.

 **ROGER** | *CPA Review*

Sample CPA Exam questions from Roger CPA Review are available in Connect as support for the topics in this text. These Multiple Choice Questions and Task-Based Simulations include expert-written explanations and solutions and provide a starting point for students to become familiar with the content and functionality of the actual CPA Exam.

Business Income, Deductions, and Accounting Methods

Upon completing this chapter, you should be able to:

LO 9-1 Identify common business deductions.

LO 9-2 Determine the limits on deducting business expenses.

LO 9-3 Identify special business deductions specifically permitted under the tax laws.

LO 9-4 Describe accounting periods available to businesses.

LO 9-5 Apply cash and accrual methods to determine business income and expense deductions.

©Tom Merton/Caiaimage/Getty Images

Storyline Summary

Taxpayer:	Rick Grime
Location:	San Antonio, Texas
Family description:	Unmarried
Employment status:	Rick quit his landscaping job in Dallas and moved to San Antonio to start a business as a self-employed landscaper.

Rick Grime graduated from Texas A&M University with a degree in agronomy, and for the past few years he has been employed by a landscape architect in Dallas. Nearly every day that Rick went to work, he shared ideas with his employer about improving the business. Rick finally decided to take his ideas and start his own landscaping business in his hometown of San Antonio, Texas. In mid-April, Rick left his job and moved his belongings to San Antonio. Once in town, Rick discovered he had to do a lot of things to start his business. First, he registered his new business name (Green Acres Landscaping, LLC) and established a bank account for the business. Next, he rented a used sport utility vehicle (SUV) and a shop for his place of business. Rick didn't know much about accounting for business activities, so he hired a CPA, Jane Bronson, to help him. Jane and Rick decided that Green Acres would operate as a sole proprietorship, but Jane suggested that as the business grew, he might want to consider organizing it as a different type of legal entity. Operating as a corporation, for instance, would allow him to invite new investors or business partners to help fund future expansion. Rick formally started his business on May 1. He spent a lot of time attracting new customers, and he figured he would hire employees as he needed them.

to be continued . . .

In previous chapters, we've emphasized the process of determining gross income and deductions for *individuals*. This chapter describes the process for determining income for *businesses*. Keep in mind that the concepts we discuss in this chapter generally apply to all types of tax entities, including sole proprietorships (such as Rick's company, Green Acres), partnerships, entities tax as partnerships (such as LLCs), S corporations, and C corporations.[1] Because Rick is a sole proprietor, our examples emphasize business income and deductions from his personal perspective. Proprietors report business income on Schedule C of their individual income tax returns. However, the choice of the organizational form is a complex decision that is described in the Entities Overview chapter.

Schedule C income is subject to both individual income and self-employment taxes. Entities other than sole proprietorships report income on tax forms separate from the owners' tax returns. For example, partnerships report taxable income on Form 1065, S corporations report taxable income on Form 1120S, and C corporations report taxable income on Form 1120. Of all these entity types, generally only C corporations pay taxes on their income.

BUSINESS GROSS INCOME

In most respects, the rules for determining business gross income are the same as for determining gross income for individuals. Gross income includes "all income from whatever source derived."[2] The tax laws specifically indicate that this definition includes gross income from "business." Generally speaking, income from business includes gross profit from inventory sales (sales minus cost of goods sold), income from services provided to customers, and income from renting property to customers. Just like individuals, businesses are allowed to exclude certain types of realized income from gross income, such as municipal bond interest.

LO 9-1

BUSINESS DEDUCTIONS

THE KEY FACTS

Business Expenses

- Business expenses must be incurred in pursuit of profits, not personal goals.
- A deduction must be ordinary and necessary (appropriate and helpful).
- Only reasonable amounts are allowed as deductions.

Because Congress intended for taxable income to reflect the *net* increase in wealth from a business, it is only fair that businesses be allowed to deduct expenses incurred to generate business income. Typically, Congress provides *specific* statutory rules authorizing deductions. However, as you can see from the following excerpt from IRC §162, the provision authorizing business deductions is relatively broad and ambiguous:

> There shall be allowed as a deduction all the ordinary and necessary expenses paid or incurred during the taxable year in carrying on any trade or business . . .

This provision authorizes taxpayers to deduct expenses for "trade or business" activities.[3] The tax code does not define the phrase "trade or business," but it's clear that the objective of business activities is to make a profit. Thus, the law requires that a business expense be made in the pursuit of profits rather than the pursuit of other, presumably personal, motives.

When a taxpayer's activity does not meet the "for profit" requirement, it is treated as a hobby, an activity motivated by personal objectives. A taxpayer engaged in a hobby cannot deduct expenses associated with that activity (commencing in 2018).

---

[1] S corporations are treated as flow-through entities (S corporation income is taxed to its owners) while C corporations are taxed as separate taxable entities.

[2] §61(a).

[3] §212 contains a sister provision to §162 allowing deductions for ordinary and necessary expenses incurred for the production of income ("investment expenses") and for the management and maintenance of property (including expenses incurred in renting property in situations when the rental activity is not considered to be a trade or business). A business activity, sometimes referred to as a trade or business, requires a relatively high level of involvement or effort from the taxpayer. Unlike business activities, investments are profit-motivated activities that don't require a high degree of taxpayer involvement or effort.

Ordinary and Necessary

Business expenditures must be both **ordinary and necessary** to be deductible. An *ordinary* expense is an expense that is normal or appropriate for the business under the circumstances.[4] An expense is *not* necessarily required to be typical or repetitive in nature to be considered ordinary. For example, a business could deduct the legal fees it expends to defend itself in an antitrust suit. Although an antitrust suit would be atypical and unusual for most businesses, defending the suit would probably be deemed ordinary because it would be expected under the circumstances. A *necessary* expense is an expense that is helpful or conducive to the business activity, but the expenditure need not be essential or indispensable. For example, a deduction for metric tools would qualify as ordinary and necessary even if there was only a small chance that a repairman might need these tools. The "ordinary and necessary" requirements are applied on a case-by-case basis, and while the deduction depends on individual circumstances, the IRS is often reluctant to second-guess business decisions. Exhibit 9-1 presents examples of expenditures that are ordinary and necessary for typical businesses.

EXHIBIT 9-1   **Examples of Typical Ordinary and Necessary Business Expenses**

• Advertising	• Office expenses
• Car and truck expenses	• Rent
• Depreciation	• Repairs
• Employee compensation and benefits	• Supplies
• Insurance	• Travel
• Interest	• Utilities
• Legal fees	• Wages

Example 9-1

Outside Rick's office is a small waiting room for clients. Rick paid $50 for several books to occupy clients while waiting for appointments. These are hardcover books with photographs and illustrations of landscape designs. Rick believes that the books will inspire new designs and alleviate boredom for potential clients, and he deducted the $50 cost as a business expense. Is he correct?

Answer: Under the law, expenses directly connected to a business are deductible if the expenditure is ordinary and necessary. The phrase *ordinary and necessary* is interpreted as *helpful or conducive to business activity.* In Rick's situation, it seems highly unlikely that the IRS or a court would conclude that the cost of these books is not ordinary and necessary. What do you think?

What if: Suppose that Rick's hobby was pre-Columbian Maya civilization. Do you think Rick would be able to deduct the cost of a new treatise on translating Maya script if he placed the book in his waiting room? Why or why not?

ETHICS

Sheri is an attorney who operates as a sole practitioner. Despite her busy schedule, in the past Sheri found time for her family. This year Sheri took on two new important clients, and she hired a personal assistant to help her manage her schedule and make timely court filings. Occasionally, Sheri asked her assistant to assist her with personal tasks such as having her car serviced or buying groceries. Do you think that Sheri should treat her assistant's entire salary as a business expense? Would your answer be any different if personal assistants were to commonly perform these tasks for other busy professionals, such as corporate executives and accountants?

---

[4]*Welch v. Helvering* (1933), 290 US 111.

Reasonable in Amount

Ordinary and necessary business expenses are deductible only *to the extent* they are also **reasonable in amount.** The courts have interpreted this requirement to mean that an expenditure is not reasonable when it is extravagant or exorbitant.[5] If the expenditure is extravagant in amount, the courts presume the excess amount is spent for personal rather than business reasons and is not deductible.

Determining whether an expenditure is reasonable is not an exact science, and not surprisingly, taxpayers and the IRS may have different opinions. Generally, the courts and the IRS test for extravagance by comparing the amount of the expense to a market price or an **arm's length amount.** If the amount of the expense is within the range of amounts typically charged in the market by unrelated persons, the amount is considered to be reasonable. The underlying issue is *why* a profit-motivated taxpayer would pay an extravagant amount. Hence, reasonableness is most likely to be an issue when a payment is made to an individual related to the taxpayer or when the taxpayer enjoys some incidental benefit from the expenditure.

Example 9-2

During the busy part of the year, Rick could not keep up with all the work. Therefore, he hired four part-time employees and paid them $10 an hour to mow lawns and pull weeds for an average of 20 hours a week. When things finally slowed down in late fall, Rick released his four part-time employees. Rick paid a total of $22,000 in compensation to the four employees. He still needed some extra help now and then, so he hired his brother, Tom, on a part-time basis. Tom performed the same duties as the prior part-time employees (his quality of work was about the same). However, Rick paid Tom $25 per hour because Tom is a college student and Rick wanted to provide some additional support for Tom's education. At year-end, Tom had worked a total of 100 hours and received $2,500 from Rick. What amount can Rick deduct for the compensation he paid to his employees?

Answer: $23,000. Rick can deduct the entire $22,000 paid to the four part-time employees. However, he can only deduct $10 an hour for Tom's compensation because the extra $15 per hour Rick paid Tom is unreasonable in amount.[6] The remaining $15 per hour is considered a personal (nondeductible) gift from Rick to Tom. Hence, Rick can deduct a total of $23,000 for compensation expense this year [$22,000 + ($10 × 100)].

LIMITATIONS ON BUSINESS DEDUCTIONS

For a variety of reasons, Congress specifically prohibits or limits a business's ability to deduct certain expenditures that appear to otherwise meet the general business expense deductibility requirements.

Expenditures against Public Policy

Businesses occasionally incur fines and penalties and may even pay illegal bribes and kickbacks. However, these payments are not deductible for tax purposes.[7] Congress disallows these expenditures under the rationale that allowing them would subsidize illegal activities and frustrate public policy. Interestingly enough, businesses conducting an illegal activity (selling stolen goods or conducting illegal gambling) are allowed

THE KEY FACTS

Limitations on Business Deductions

- No business deductions are allowable for expenditures that are against public policy (bribes) or are political contributions.
- Expenditures that benefit a period longer than 12 months generally must be capitalized.
- No deductions are allowable for expenditures associated with the production of tax-exempt income.
- Personal expenditures are not deductible.

---

[5]§162(a) and *Comm. v. Lincoln Electric Co.* (CA-6, 1949), 176 F.2d 815.

[6]In practice, this distinction is rarely cut and dried. Rick may be able to argue for various reasons that Tom's work is worth more than $10 an hour but perhaps not as much as $25 per hour. We use this example to illustrate the issue of reasonable expenses and not to discuss the merits of what actually is reasonable compensation to Tom.

[7]§162(c) and Reg. §1.162-21. This prohibition applies to fines and penalties imposed by a government or governmental unit unless the taxpayer establishes that the payment is either restitution, remediation, or required to come into compliance with the law. Fines and penalties imposed by other organizations, such as a fine levied by NASCAR or the NFL, would be fully deductible if the payment otherwise qualified as an ordinary and necessary business expense.

to offset gross income with the cost of the illegal goods (the cost of goods sold) and deduct other ordinary and necessary business expenses incurred in conducting the illegal business activity. However, they are not allowed to deduct fines, penalties, bribes, or illegal kickbacks.[8] Of course, the IRS is probably more concerned that many illegal businesses fail to report *any* income than that illegal businesses overstate deductions.[9]

Political Contributions and Lobbying Costs

Perhaps to avoid the perception that the federal government subsidizes taxpayer efforts to influence politics, the tax laws prohibit deductions for political contributions and most lobbying expenses.[10]

Example 9-3

In July, the city fined Rick $200 for violating the city's watering ban when he watered a newly installed landscape. Later, Rick donated $250 to the mayor's campaign for reelection. Can Rick deduct these expenditures?

Answer: No. Rick cannot deduct either the fine or the political contribution as a business expense because the tax laws specifically prohibit deductions for these expenditures.

Capital Expenditures

Whether a business uses the cash or the accrual method of accounting, it must capitalize expenditures for *tangible* assets such as buildings, machinery and equipment, furniture and fixtures, and similar property that have useful lives of more than one year (12 months).[11] For tax purposes, businesses recover the cost of capitalized tangible assets (other than land) through depreciation.

Businesses also capitalize the cost to create or acquire *intangible* assets such as patents, goodwill, start-up costs, and organizational expenditures.[12] They recover the costs of capitalized intangible assets either through amortization (when the tax laws allow them to do so) or upon disposition of the assets. Prepaid expenses are also subject to capitalization, but there is a special exception that we discuss under accounting methods later in this chapter.[13]

Expenses Associated with the Production of Tax-Exempt Income

Expenses that do not help businesses generate *taxable* income are not allowed to offset taxable income. For example, this restriction disallows interest expense deductions for businesses that borrow money and invest the loan proceeds in municipal (tax-exempt)

---

[8]*Comm. v. Sullivan* (1958), 356 US 27. In addition, beginning after December 22, 2017, no deduction is allowed for any settlement, payout, or attorney fees related to sexual harassment or abuse if the payments are subject to a nondisclosure agreement.

[9]§280E explicitly prohibits drug dealers from deducting any business expenses associated with this "business" activity. However, drug dealers are able to deduct cost of goods sold because cost of goods sold is technically a reduction in gross income and not a business expense. See Reg. §1.61-3(a).

[10]§162(e).

[11]Reg. §1.263(a)-2(d)(4). The act of recording the asset is sometimes referred to as *capitalizing* the expenditure.

[12]Reg. §1.263(a)-4(b). The extent to which expenditures for intangible assets must be capitalized is explored in *Indopco v. Comm.* (1992), 503 US 79.

[13]See §195, §197, and §248 for provisions that allow taxpayers to amortize the cost of certain intangible assets.

bonds. It also disallows deductions for life insurance premiums businesses pay on policies that cover the lives of officers or other key employees and compensate the business for the disruption and lost income they may experience due to a key employee's death. Because the death benefit from the life insurance policy is not taxable, the business is not allowed to deduct the insurance premium expense associated with this nontaxable income.

Example 9-4

Rick employs Joan, an arborist who specializes in trimming trees and treating local tree ailments. Joan generates a great deal of revenue for Rick's business, but she is in her mid-60s and suffers from diabetes. In November, Rick purchased a "key employee" term life-insurance policy on Joan's life. The policy cost Rick $720 and will pay Rick (Green Acres) a $20,000 death benefit if Joan passes away during the next 12 months. What amount of life insurance policy premium can Rick deduct?

Answer: $0. Rick cannot deduct the $720 premium on the life insurance policy because the life insurance proceeds from the policy are tax-exempt.

What if: Suppose Rick purchased the life insurance policy on Joan's life and allowed Joan to name the beneficiary. The policy cost Rick $720 and will pay the beneficiary a $20,000 death benefit if Joan passes away during the next 12 months. What amount of life insurance policy premium can Rick deduct?

Answer: $720. In this scenario, Rick can deduct the entire premium of $720 as a *compensation* expense because the benefit of the policy inures to Joan and not to Rick's business.

Personal Expenditures

Taxpayers are not allowed to deduct **personal expenses** unless the expenses are "expressly" authorized by a provision in the law.[14] While the tax laws do not define personal expenses, they imply the scope of personal expenses by stating that "personal, living, or family expenses" are not deductible. Therefore, at a minimum, the costs of food, clothing, and shelter are assumed to be personal and nondeductible. Of course, there are the inevitable exceptions when otherwise personal items are specially adapted to business use. For example, taxpayers may deduct the cost of uniforms or special clothing they purchase for use in their business, if the clothing is not appropriate to wear as ordinary clothing outside the place of business. However, when the clothing is adaptable as ordinary clothing, the cost of the clothing is a nondeductible personal expenditure.

Example 9-5

Rick spent $500 to purchase special coveralls that identify his landscaping service and provide a professional appearance. How much of the cost for the clothing can Rick deduct as a business expense?

Answer: All $500. While the cost of clothing is inherently personal, Rick can deduct the $500 cost of the coveralls because, due to the design and labeling on the coveralls, they are not suitable for ordinary use.

---

[14]§262(a).

Many business owners, particularly small business owners such as sole proprietors, may be in a position to use business funds to pay for items that are entirely personal in nature. For example, a sole proprietor could use the business checking account to pay for family groceries. These expenditures, even though funded by the business, are not deductible.

Expenditures made by a taxpayer for education, such as tuition and books, are often related to a taxpayer's business aspirations. However, educational expenditures are not deductible as business expenses unless the taxpayer is self employed and the education maintains or improves skills required by the individual in his existing trade or business. Education expenses necessary to meet minimum requirements for an occupation are not deductible. For example, tuition payments for courses to satisfy the education requirement to sit for the CPA exam are not deductible. This is an example of education that qualifies the taxpayer for a new trade or business rather than improving his skills in an existing trade or business. However, education expense necessary to maintain the skill of a self employed taxpayer would be a deductible business expense.

TAXES IN THE REAL WORLD Web Sales and the Cohan Rule

Thomas began collecting coins in 1958 and later inherited his father's coin collection. He wasn't employed during 2013, so he actively engaged in buying and selling coins and related items (such as silver ingots and items issued by the Franklin Mint) on eBay using PayPal. At year end, PayPal filed a Form 1099-K reporting sales of $37,013 by Thomas during 2013. However, Thomas failed to report these sales on his return, and because he didn't report these sales, Thomas also didn't claim the costs he incurred in making his eBay sales. The IRS subsequently assessed a tax deficiency of $12,905 based on unreported income of $37,013.

The law generally requires the Tax Court to presume that the deficiency determined by the IRS is correct, and hence, Thomas had the burden of proving them wrong. At trial the IRS conceded that Thomas was engaged in a "trade or business" with the intent to earn a profit. However, Thomas was still required to substantiate expenses for any deductions by producing records sufficient to enable the court to determine the correct tax liability. Unfortunately, Thomas maintained no records of any kind to establish his cost or other bases in the coins and related items that he sold on eBay.

Despite a continuance at trial, Thomas was unable to present any documentation to establish his cost of goods. Rather, he submitted eBay records of his sales and coin catalogs tracking the market prices during 2010–2013. Thomas testified that he turned over his inventory fairly quickly and the sales records provided some support for this contention. On the other hand, Thomas also sold some of the coins he had previously collected or inherited.

If a taxpayer with inadequate business records testifies credibly that he incurred certain expenses, under the Cohan rule the Court can estimate the amount of deductions. This rule originated with George M. Cohan who was a Broadway star in the early 1900s. He was audited by the IRS which disallowed many of his business- and entertainment-related expenses. The IRS argued that without receipts, the expenses were nondeductible despite Cohan's credible testimony in court. The 2nd Circuit Court of appeals agreed with Cohan and forced the IRS to accept estimates of his expenses. *Cohan v. Commissioner*, 39 F. 2d 540 (2d Cir. 1930)

Under the Cohan rule, the Court is not required to guess at a number but must have some basis for an estimate. In Thomas's case, the Tax Court evaluated his testimony and decided that Thomas substantiated a cost of goods sold of $12,000 (a nice round number) and expense deductions of $4,430 for PayPal fees, Internet charges, and postage. As a side note, Thomas was also assessed an accuracy-related penalty because he did not make a good-faith effort to determine his tax correctly.

Source: Thomas R. Huzella, TC Memo 2017-20.

Mixed-Motive Expenditures

Business owners in general, and owners of small or closely held businesses in particular, often make expenditures that are motivated by *both* business and personal concerns. These **mixed-motive expenditures** are of particular concern to lawmakers and the IRS because of the tax incentive to disguise nondeductible personal expenses as deductible business expenses. Thus, deductions for business expenditures with potentially personal motives are closely monitored and restricted. The rules for determining the amount of *deductible* mixed-motive expenditures depend on the type of expenditure. Here we review the rules for determining the deductible portion of mixed-motive expenditures for meals, travel and transportation, and the use of property for both business and personal purposes.

Meals   Because everyone needs to eat, even business meals contain a significant personal element. To allow for this personal element, taxpayers may deduct only 50 percent of actual business meals.[15] In addition, to deduct any portion of the cost of a meal as a business expense, (1) the amount must be reasonable under the circumstances, (2) the taxpayer (or an employee) must be present when the meal is furnished, and (3) the meal must be directly associated with the active conduct of the taxpayer's business.[16]

Example 9-6

Rick went out to dinner with prospective clients to discuss Rick's ideas for landscaping several business properties. After dinner, Rick and the prospective clients attended the theater. Rick paid $540 for the meal and $850 for the tickets, amounts that were reasonable under the circumstances. What amount of these expenditures can Rick deduct as a business expense?

Answer: Rick can deduct $270 [$540 × 50%], representing half the cost of the meal, as a business expense, as long as he can substantiate the business purpose and substantial nature of the dinner discussion. The cost of the tickets to the theater is a nondeductible entertainment expense.

What if: Suppose that Rick did not discuss business with the clients either before, during, or after the meal. What amount of the expenditures can Rick deduct as a business expense?

Answer: $0. In this scenario, Rick cannot deduct the cost of the meal because the activity was not directly related to or associated with a substantial business discussion.

Travel and Transportation   Under certain conditions, sole proprietors and self-employed taxpayers may deduct the cost of travel and transportation for business purposes. Transportation expenses include the direct cost of transporting the taxpayer to and from business sites. However, the cost of commuting between the taxpayer's home and regular place of business is personal and, therefore, not deductible. If the taxpayer uses a vehicle for business, the taxpayer can deduct the costs of operating the vehicle plus depreciation on the vehicle's tax basis. Alternatively, in lieu of deducting these costs, the taxpayer may simply deduct a standard amount for each business mile driven. The standard mileage rate represents the per-mile cost of operating an automobile (including depreciation or lease payments).[17] For 2018, the standard mileage rate has been set at 54.5 cents per mile. To be deductible, the transportation must be for business reasons. If the transportation is primarily for personal purposes, the cost is not deductible.

[15]§274 also provides some exceptions to the 50 percent reduction for meals, such as meals provided as employee compensation. Taxpayers can also use a *per diem* rate (an automatic, flat amount per meal) in lieu of actual expenditures to determine the amount of the deduction.

[16]Under §274, there are special limits placed on certain expenditures, such as those related to expenditures associated with conventions and travel.

[17]This mileage rate is updated periodically (sometimes two or three times within a year) to reflect changes in the cost of operating a vehicle.

Example 9-7

Rick decided to lease an SUV to drive between his shop and various work sites. Rick carefully documents the business use of the SUV (8,100 miles this year) and his operating expenses ($5,335 this year, including $3,935 for gas, oil, and repairs and $1,400 for lease payments). At no time does Rick use the SUV for personal purposes. What amount of these expenses may Rick deduct as business expenses?

Answer: $5,335. Since Rick uses the SUV in his business activities, he can deduct (1) the $5,335 cost of operating and leasing the SUV or (2) $4,414.50 for the 8,100 business miles driven this year (54.5 cents per mile × 8,100 miles). Assuming Rick chooses to deduct operating expenses and lease payments in lieu of using the mileage rate, he can deduct $5,335.

In contrast to transportation expenses, travel expenses are only deductible if the taxpayer is *away from home* overnight while traveling. This distinction is important because, besides the cost of transportation, the deduction for **travel expenses** includes meals (50 percent), lodging, and incidental expenses. A taxpayer is considered to be away from home overnight if the travel is away from the primary place of business and of sufficient duration to require sleep or rest (typically this will be overnight). When a taxpayer travels solely for business purposes, *all* of the costs of travel are deductible (but only 50 percent of meals). When the travel has both business and personal aspects, the deductibility of the transportation costs depends upon whether business is the *primary* purpose for the trip. If the primary purpose of a trip is business, the transportation costs are fully deductible, but meals (50 percent), lodging, and incidental expenditures are limited to those incurred during the business portion of the travel.[18] If the taxpayer's primary purpose for the trip is personal, the taxpayer may not deduct *any* transportation costs to arrive at the location but may deduct meals (50 percent), lodging, transportation, and incidental expenditures for the *business* portion of the trip. The primary purpose of a trip depends upon facts and circumstances and is often the subject of dispute.

The rule for business travel is modified somewhat if a trip abroad includes both business and personal activities. Like the rule for domestic travel, if foreign travel is primarily for personal purposes, then only those expenses directly associated with business activities are deductible. However, unlike the rule for domestic travel, when foreign travel is primarily for business purposes, a portion of the round-trip transportation costs is not deductible. The nondeductible portion is typically computed based on a time ratio such as the proportion of personal days to total days (travel days count as business days).[19]

Example 9-8

Rick paid a $300 registration fee for a three-day course in landscape design. The course was held in upstate New York (Rick paid $700 for airfare to attend) and he spent four days away from home. He spent the last day sightseeing. During the trip, Rick paid $150 a night for three nights' lodging, $50 a day for meals, and $70 a day for a rental car. What amount of these travel-related expenditures may Rick deduct as business expenses?

(continued on page 9-10)

[18]Note that travel days are considered business days. Also, special limitations apply to a number of travel expenses that are potentially abusive, such as luxury water travel, foreign conventions, conventions on cruise ships, and travel expenses associated with taking a companion.

[19]Foreign transportation expense is deductible without prorating under special circumstances authorized in §274(c). For example, the cost of getting abroad is fully deductible if the travel is for one week or less or if the personal activity constitutes less than one-fourth of the travel time.

Answer: $1,435 for business travel and $300 for business education. The primary purpose for the trip appears to be business because Rick spent three days on business activities versus one day on personal activities. He can deduct travel costs, computed as follows:

Deductible Travel Costs		
Description	**Amount**	**Explanation**
Airfare	$ 700	Primary purpose is business
Lodging	450	3 business days × $150 a day
Meals	75	3 business days × $50 a day × 50% limit
Rental car	210	3 business days × $70 a day
Total business travel expenses	**$1,435**	

What if: Assume Rick stayed in New York for 10 days, spending 3 days at the seminar and 7 days sightseeing. What amount could he deduct?

Answer: In this scenario Rick can deduct $735 for business travel and $300 for business education. Rick would not be able to deduct the $700 cost of airfare because the trip is primarily personal, as evidenced by the seven days of personal activities compared to only three days of business activities.

Deductible Travel Costs		
Description	**Amount**	**Explanation**
Airfare	$ 0	Primary purpose is personal
Lodging	450	3 business days × $150 a day
Meals	75	3 business days × $50 a day × 50% limit
Rental car	210	3 business days × $70 a day
Total business travel expenses	**$735**	

What if: Assume the original facts in the example except Rick traveled to London (rather than upstate New York) for 10 days, spending 6 days at the seminar and 4 days sightseeing. What amount could he deduct?

Answer: In this scenario Rick can deduct $1,890 for travel (computed below) and $300 for business education.

Deductible Travel Costs		
Description	**Amount**	**Explanation**
Airfare to London	$ 420	6 business days/10 total days × $700
Lodging in London	900	6 business days × $150 a day
Meals	150	6 business days × $50 a day × 50% limit
Rental car	420	6 business days × $70 a day
Total business travel expenses	**$1,890**	

Rick is allowed to deduct $420 of the $700 airfare (60 percent) because he spent 6 of the 10 days on the trip conducting business activities.

Property Use   Several types of property may be used for both business and personal purposes. For example, business owners often use automobiles, computers, or cell phones for both business and personal purposes.[20] However, because expenses relating to these assets

[20]These types of assets are referred to as "listed property." Note that cell phones and computers are specifically exempted from the definition of listed property [§280F(d)(4)(A)], as amended by the 2010 Small Business Act §2043(a).

are deductible only to the extent the assets are used for business purposes, taxpayers must allocate the expenses between the business and personal use portions. For example, if a full year's expense for a business asset is $1,000, but the asset is only used for business purposes 90 percent of the time, then only $900 of expense can be deducted ($1,000 × 90%). The calculation of depreciation on mixed-use assets is discussed in the Property Acquisition and Cost Recovery chapter.

Example 9-9

Rick occasionally uses his personal auto (a BMW) to drive to interviews with prospective clients and to drive back and forth between his shop and various work sites. This year Rick carefully recorded that the BMW was driven 562 miles for business activities and 10,500 miles in total. What expenses associated with the BMW may Rick deduct?

Answer: $306. Based on the standard mileage rate of 54.5 cents per mile, Rick can deduct $306 (562 × 54.5 cents) for business use of his BMW. Alternatively, Rick can track the operating expenses of the BMW (including depreciation) and deduct the business portion [based upon the percentage of business miles driven to total miles driven (562 business miles/10,500 total miles)]. Once Rick chooses his method of accounting for the business use of the BMW, he must use this same method in future periods.

Record Keeping and Other Requirements   Because distinguishing business purposes from personal purposes is a difficult and subjective task, the tax laws include provisions designed to help the courts and the IRS determine the business element of mixed-motive transactions. Under these provisions, taxpayers must maintain specific, written, contemporaneous records (of time, amount, and business purpose) for mixed-motive expenses. For example, as we discussed above, the tax laws prohibit any deductions for business meals unless substantial business discussions accompany the meal. Consequently, when taxpayers incur meal expenses, they must document the business purpose and the extent of the business discussion to deduct any of the expenditures.[21]

Limitation on Business Interest Deductions

The deduction for business interest expense is limited to the sum of (1) business interest income and (2) 30 percent of the adjusted taxable income of the taxpayer for the taxable year. Adjusted taxable income is taxable income of the taxpayer computed without regard to (1) any item of income, gain, deduction, or loss which is not properly allocable to a trade or business; (2) any business interest expense or business interest income; (3) the amount of any net operating loss deduction; and (4) deductions allowable for depreciation, amortization, or depletion.[22] Business interest expense is defined as interest paid or accrued on indebtedness allocable to a trade or business. Business interest income means the amount of interest includible in gross income which is also properly allocable to a trade or business. However, business interest expense does not include investment interest expense, and business interest income does not include investment income. For example, business interest expense would include interest paid on a loan used to purchase business equipment, but would not include interest paid on a loan to purchase stock for investment purposes. The amount of any business interest expense not allowed as a deduction for any taxable year is carried forward indefinitely. The limitation does not apply to any taxpayer with average annual gross receipts of $25 million or less for the prior three taxable years.

THE KEY FACTS

Business Interest Limitation

- The deduction of business interest expense is limited to business interest income plus 30 percent of the business's adjusted taxable income.

- Adjusted taxable income is taxable income allocable to the business computed without interest income and before depreciation and interest expense deductions.

- Disallowed business interest expense can be carried forward indefinitely.

---

[21]§274 requires substantiation of all elements of travel, including sufficient corroborating evidence. Although there are a few exceptions to this rule, approximations and estimates are generally not sufficient. Also, taxpayers must maintain records to deduct the business portion of mixed-use assets such as cars used for both business and personal purposes. Note that when the taxpayer is unable to substantiate other deductions, the court may estimate the deductible amount under the Cohan rule (*George Cohan v. Com.*, (1930, CA2), 39 F2d 540).

[22]Adjusted taxable income of the taxpayer cannot be less than zero. Under §163(j) the interest expense disallowance is determined at the filer level but special rules apply to pass-through entities. For years after 2021, adjusted taxable income is not reduced for depreciation, amortization, and depletion.

Example 9-10

What if: Suppose that at the beginning of the year Rick borrowed $300,000 to provide liquidity for starting up Green Acres. Suppose further that at year-end Rick had paid $9,000 in interest and that Green Acres reported $70,000 of revenue from services and incurred $47,000 of deductible expenses. The deductible expenses included $5,000 of depreciation but did not include the interest expense. What amount of interest can Rick deduct as a business expense for Green Acres?

Answer: $9,000. Green Acres is not subject to the business interest expense limitation because Rick's gross receipts do not exceed the $25 million average receipts test.

What if: Suppose the interest expense limitation applies to Green Acres. What amount of business interest expense could Rick deduct for Green Acres?

Answer: $8,400. Green Acres generated $28,000 of adjusted taxable income. Adjusted taxable income is the amount of revenue less expense before interest and depreciation ($70,000 – $42,000). The 2018 business interest limitation is 30 percent of the adjusted taxable income or $8,400. The $600 of disallowed interest from 2018 is carried over into 2019.

LO 9-3

SPECIFIC BUSINESS DEDUCTIONS

As we discussed above, the tax code provides general guidelines for determining whether business expenditures are deductible. We learned that to be deductible, business expenditures must be ordinary, necessary, and reasonable in amount. In some cases, however, the tax laws identify specific items businesses are allowed to deduct. We discuss several of these deductions below.

Losses on Dispositions of Business Property

Businesses are generally allowed to deduct losses incurred when selling or disposing of business assets.[23] The calculation of losses from business property dispositions can be complex, but the main idea is that businesses realize and recognize a loss when the asset's tax basis exceeds the sale proceeds. We will discuss the rules governing the tax treatment of gains and losses on asset disposition in more detail in the Property Dispositions chapter.

Example 9-11

What if: Assume that in late October, Rick purchased a used trailer to transport equipment to work sites. Rick bought the trailer for what he thought was a bargain price of $1,000. However, shortly after Rick acquired it, the axle snapped and was not repairable. Rick was forced to sell the trailer to a parts shop for $325. What amount can Rick deduct as a loss from the trailer sale?

Answer: $675, because the trailer was a business asset (amount realized of $325 minus adjusted basis of $1,000). (Note that Rick is not allowed to deduct depreciation on the trailer because he disposed of it in the same year he acquired it.)

Business Casualty Losses

Businesses can incur losses when their assets are stolen, damaged, or completely destroyed by a force outside the control of the business. These events are called casualties.[24] Businesses may deduct **casualty losses** in the year the casualty occurs or in the year the theft of an asset is discovered. The amount of the loss deduction depends on whether the asset is (1) completely destroyed or stolen or (2) only partially destroyed. When its asset

---

[23]In most circumstances businesses may *not* deduct losses on assets sold to related persons. We describe who qualifies as a related person later in this chapter.

[24]Casualties are unexpected events driven by forces outside the control of the taxpayer that damage or destroy a taxpayer's property. §165 lists "fire, storm, and shipwreck" as examples of casualties.

is *completely* destroyed or stolen, the business calculates the amount of the loss as though it sold the asset for the insurance proceeds, if any. That is, the loss is the amount of insurance proceeds minus the adjusted tax basis of the asset. If the asset is damaged but not completely destroyed, the amount of the loss is the amount of the insurance proceeds minus the *lesser* of (1) the asset's adjusted tax basis or (2) the decline in the value of the asset due to the casualty. For individuals, business casualty losses and casualty losses associated with rentals and royalties are deducted *for* AGI.

Example 9-12

What if: Suppose Rick acquired business equipment several years ago for $9,000 and had deducted $4,000 of depreciation expense against the asset. Hence, the equipment's adjusted tax basis was $5,000 ($9,000 – $4,000). Suppose further that a fire destroyed the asset, and at that time the asset was worth $1,000 and insured for $250. What would be the amount of his business casualty loss?

Answer: $4,750, computed as follows:

Insurance proceeds	$ 250
Minus adjusted tax basis	−5,000
Casualty loss deduction	**$(4,750)**

ACCOUNTING PERIODS

LO 9-4

So far we've discussed how to determine a business's income and how to determine its deductible business expenses. In this section, we discuss accounting periods, which affect when taxpayers determine their income and deductions. Businesses must report their income and deductions over a fixed **accounting period** or **tax year.** A full tax year consists of 12 full months. A tax year can consist of a period less than 12 months (a short tax year) in certain circumstances. For instance, a business may report income for such a short year in its first year of existence (for example, it reports income on a calendar year-end and starts business after January 1) or in its final year of existence (for example, a calendar-year business ends its business before December 31). Short tax years in a business's initial or final year are treated the same as full years. A business also may have a short year when it changes its tax year, and this can occur when the business is acquired by new owners. In these situations, special rules may apply for computing the tax liability of the business.[25]

There are three types of tax years, each with different year-ends:

1. A calendar year ends on December 31.
2. A **fiscal year** ends on the last day of a month other than December.
3. A 52/53-week year. This is a fiscal year that ends on the same day of the week that is the last such day in the month or on the same day of the week nearest the end of the month. For example, a business could adopt a 52/53-week fiscal year that (1) ends on the last Saturday in July each year or (2) ends on the Saturday closest to the end of July (although this Saturday might be in August rather than July).[26]

THE KEY FACTS

Accounting Periods

- Individuals and proprietorships generally account for income using a calendar year-end.
- Corporations are allowed to choose a fiscal year.
- Partnerships and other flow-through entities generally use a tax year consistent with their owners' tax years.

---

[25]§443. Discussion of tax consequences associated with these short years is beyond the scope of this text.

[26]Businesses with inventories, such as retailers, can benefit from 52/53-week year-ends. These year-ends can facilitate inventory counts (e.g., the store is closed, such as over a weekend) and financial reporting.

Not all types of tax years are available to all types of businesses. The rules for determining the tax years available to the business depend on whether the business is a sole proprietorship, a **flow-through entity,** or a C corporation. These rules are summarized as follows:

- *Sole proprietorships*: Because individual proprietors must report their business income on their individual returns, proprietorships use a calendar year-end to report their business income.[27]
- *Flow-through entities*: Partnerships and S corporations are flow-through entities (partners and S corporation owners report the entity's income directly on their own tax returns), and these entities generally must adopt tax years consistent with the owners' tax years.[28] Because owners are allocated income from flow-through entities on the last day of the entity's taxable year, the tax laws impose the tax year consistency requirement to minimize income tax deferral opportunities for the owners.
- *C corporations*: C corporations are generally allowed to select a calendar, fiscal, or 52/53-week year-end.

A business adopts a calendar year-end or fiscal year-end by filing its initial tax return. In contrast, a business adopts a 52/53-week year-end by filing a special election with the IRS. Once a business establishes its tax year, it generally must receive permission from the IRS to change.

Example 9-13

Rick is a calendar-year taxpayer. What tax year must Rick use to report income from Green Acres?

Answer: Calendar year. This is true even though Rick began his business in May of this year. He will calculate income and expense for his landscaping business over the calendar year and include business income and deductions from May through December of this year on Schedule C of his individual tax return.

What if: Suppose that Rick incorporated Green Acres at the time he began his business. What tax year could Green Acres adopt?

Answer: If Green Acres was operated as a C corporation, it could elect a calendar year-end, a fiscal year-end, or a 52/53-week year-end. If it were an S corporation, it likely would use a calendar year-end.

LO 9-5

ACCOUNTING METHODS

Once a business adopts a tax year, it must determine which items of income and deduction to recognize during a particular year. Generally speaking, the taxpayer's **accounting methods** determine the tax year in which a business recognizes a particular item of income or deduction. Because accounting methods affect the *timing* of when a taxpayer reports income and deductions, these methods are very important for taxpayers using a timing tax strategy to defer income or accelerate deductions.[29]

---

[27]Virtually all individual taxpayers use a calendar-year tax year.

[28]See §706 for the specific restrictions on year-ends for partnerships and §1378 for restrictions on S corporations. If they can show a business purpose (a difficult task), both partnerships and S corporations can adopt year-ends other than those used by their owners.

[29]Accounting methods do not determine whether an item of income is taxable or an expense is deductible. Accordingly, accounting methods generally do not affect the total income or deductions recognized over the lifetime of the business.

Financial and Tax Accounting Methods

Many businesses are required to generate financial statements for nontax reasons. For example, publicly traded corporations must file financial statements with the Securities and Exchange Commission (SEC) based on generally accepted accounting principles (GAAP). Also, privately owned businesses borrowing money from banks are often required to generate financial statements under GAAP, so that the lender can evaluate the business's creditworthiness. In reporting financial statement income, businesses have incentives to select accounting methods permissible under GAAP that *accelerate income* and *defer deductions*. In contrast, for tax planning purposes, businesses have incentives to choose accounting methods that *defer income* and *accelerate deductions*. This natural tension between financial reporting incentives and tax reporting incentives may be the reason the tax laws sometimes require businesses to use the same accounting methods for tax purposes that they use for financial accounting purposes. In other words, in many circumstances, if businesses want to defer taxable income, they must also defer book income.[30]

Sometimes the tax laws require businesses to use different, presumably more appropriate, accounting methods for tax purposes. Consequently, for policy and administrative reasons, the tax laws also identify several circumstances when businesses must use specific tax accounting methods to determine taxable income no matter what accounting method they use for financial reporting purposes. We will now turn our attention to accounting methods prescribed by the tax laws. With certain restrictions, businesses are able to select their *overall* accounting method and accounting methods for *specific* items or transactions. We will cover each of these in turn.

Overall Accounting Method

Businesses must choose an overall method of accounting to track and report their business activities for tax purposes. The overriding requirement for any tax accounting method is that the method must "clearly reflect income" and be applied consistently.[31] The two primary overall methods are the cash method and the accrual method. Businesses also may choose a hybrid method (some accounts on the cash method and others on the accrual method).

Cash Method   A taxpayer (or business) using the cash method of accounting recognizes revenue when property or services are actually or constructively received. This is generally true no matter when the business sells the goods or performs the service that generates the revenue. Likewise, a business adopting the cash method generally recognizes deductions when the expense is paid. Thus, the timing of the liability giving rise to the expense is usually irrelevant.

Keep in mind that a cash-method business receiving payments in *noncash* form (as property or services) must recognize the noncash payments as gross income when the goods or services are received. Also, in certain circumstances, a business expending cash on ordinary and necessary business expenses may not be allowed to *currently* deduct the expense at the time of the payment. For example, cash-method taxpayers (and accrual-method taxpayers) are not allowed to deduct prepaid interest expense and cannot usually deduct prepaid expenses or payments that create a tangible or intangible asset.[32] However, the regulations provide a **12-month rule** for prepaid business expenses to simplify the process of determining whether to capitalize or immediately expense payments that create benefits for a relatively brief period of time, such as insurance,

---

[30]§446(a). Businesses that use different accounting methods for book and tax income must typically file a Schedule M-1 or Schedule M-3 that reconciles the results from the two accounting methods.

[31]§446(b).

[32]263(a).

security, rent, and warranty service contracts. When a business prepays business expenses, it may *immediately* deduct the prepayment if (1) the contract period does not last more than a year *and* (2) the contract period does not extend beyond the end of the taxable year following the tax year in which the taxpayer makes the payment.[33] If the prepaid expense does not meet both these criteria, the business must capitalize the prepaid amount and amortize it over the length of the contract whether the business uses the cash or accrual method of accounting.[34]

Example 9-14

On July 1 of this year, Rick paid $1,200 for a 12-month insurance policy that covers his business property from accidents and casualties from July 1 of this year through June 30 of next year. How much of the $1,200 expenditure may Rick deduct this year if he uses the cash method of accounting for his business activities?

Answer: $1,200. Because the insurance coverage does not exceed 12 months and does not extend beyond the end of next year, Rick is allowed to deduct the entire premium payment under the 12-month rule.

What if: Suppose the insurance policy was for 12 months but the policy ran from February 1 of next year, through January 31 of the following year. How much of the expenditure may Rick deduct this year if he uses the cash method of accounting for his business activities?

Answer: $0. Even though the contract period is 12 months or less, Rick is required to capitalize the cost of the prepayment for the insurance policy because the contract period extends beyond the end of next year.

What if: Suppose Rick had paid $1,200 for an *18-month* policy beginning July 1 of this year and ending December 31 of next year. How much may he deduct this year if he uses the cash method of accounting for his business activities?

Answer: $400. In this scenario, because the policy exceeds 12 months, Rick is allowed to deduct the portion of the premium pertaining to this year. Hence, this year, he would deduct $400 [(6 months/18 months) × $1,200]. He would deduct the remaining $800 in the next year.

Accrual Method Businesses using the accrual method to determine taxable income follow rules similar to GAAP with two basic differences.[35] First, as we discuss below, requirements for recognizing taxable income tend to be structured to recognize income earlier than the recognition rules for financial accounting. Second, requirements for accruing tax deductions tend to be structured to recognize less accrued expenses than the recognition rules for financial reporting purposes. These differences reflect the underlying objectives of financial accounting income and taxable income. The objective of financial accounting is to provide useful information to stakeholders such as creditors, prospective investors, and shareholders. Because financial accounting methods are designed to guard against businesses overstating their profitability to these users, financial accounting tends to bias against *overstating* income. In contrast, the government's main objective for writing tax laws is to collect revenues. Thus, tax accounting rules for accrual-method businesses tend to bias against *understating* income. These differences will become apparent as we describe tax accounting rules for businesses.

---

[33]This 12-month rule applies to both cash-method and accrual-method taxpayers. However, for accrual-method taxpayers to deduct prepaid expenses, they must meet both the 12-month rule requirements and the economic performance requirements that we discuss in the next section.

[34]Reg. §1.263(a)-4(f).

[35]Prior to 2018, C corporations and partnerships with C corporation partners were generally required to use the accrual method. However, beginning in 2018, unless they are tax shelters, these entities can use the cash method if they report average gross receipts of $25 million or less for the three-tax-year period ending with the prior tax year.

continued from page 9-1...

Rick's CPA, Jane, informed him that he needs to select an overall method of accounting for Green Acres to compute its taxable income. Jane advised Rick to use the cash method. However, Rick wanted to prepare GAAP financial statements and use the accrual method of accounting. He decided that if Green Acres was going to become a big business, it needed to act like a big business. Finally, after much discussion, Rick and Jane reached a compromise. For the first year, they decided they would track Green Acres's business activities using both the cash *and* the accrual methods. In addition, they would also keep GAAP-based books for financial purposes. When filing time comes, Rick will need to decide which method to use in reporting taxable income. Jane told Rick that he could wait until he filed his tax return to select the overall accounting method for tax purposes. ∎

Accrual Income

Businesses using the accrual method of accounting generally recognize income when they meet the all-events test.

All-Events Test for Income   The all-events test requires that businesses recognize income when (1) all events have occurred that determine or fix their right to receive the income and (2) the amount of the income can be determined with reasonable accuracy.[36] Assuming the amount of income can be determined with reasonable accuracy, businesses meet the all-events requirement on the *earliest* of the following three dates:

1. When they complete the task required to earn the income. Businesses earn income for services as they provide the services, and they generally earn income from selling property when the title of the property passes to the buyer.
2. When the payment for the task is due from the customer.
3. When the business receives payment for the task.

Generally, beginning in 2018, the all-events test is satisfied no later than the tax year in which such income is recognized on their financial statements.

Example 9-15

In early fall, Rick contracted with a dozen homeowners to landscape their yards. Rick agreed to do the work for an aggregate of $11,000. Rick and his crew started in the fall and completed the jobs in December of this year. However, he didn't mail the bills until after the holidays and didn't receive any payments until the following January. When must Rick recognize the income from this work?

Answer: Under the accrual method, Rick would recognize the entire $11,000 as income this year because his right to the income is fixed at year-end, when Rick and his crew complete the work. Under the cash method, however, Rick would not recognize the $11,000 as income until next year, when he receives it.

Taxation of Advance Payments of Income (Unearned Income)

In some cases, businesses receive income payments *before* they actually earn the income (they receive a prepayment). When the business must recognize a prepayment as income depends on the type of income. The rule for interest and rental income is relatively strict. Businesses must recognize unearned rental and unearned interest income *immediately* upon receipt (the income is recognized before it is earned). However, businesses are not required to recognize security deposits received from rental customers because they incur

---

[36]Reg. §1.451-1(a).

a liability to return the deposits when they receive the payments.[37] The income recognition rules are less strict when businesses receive advance payments for services or goods.

Advance Payments for Goods and Services   For financial reporting purposes, a business does not immediately recognize income on payments it receives for services to be provided in the future. For financial reporting purposes, an advance payment for goods and services is recorded as a debit for cash received and a credit to a liability account (unearned income). The business then recognizes the *financial* income from the services or sales as it performs the services or provides the goods. In contrast, for tax purposes, the all-events test generally requires businesses receiving advance payments for goods and services to recognize the income when they receive the payment, rather than when they deliver the goods or perform the services. This rule is called the full inclusion method.

The law provides an exception to immediate recognition. Specifically, businesses receiving advance payments for goods and services may elect to defer recognizing the advance as income until the tax year following the year they receive the payment.[38] This one-year deferral method does *not* apply (1) if (or to the extent to which) the income is actually earned by the end of the year of receipt, (2) to the extent that the advance was included in financial reporting income, or (3) if the advance was for interest or rent (taxpayers must recognize unearned interest and rental income on receipt).

Example 9-16

In late November 2018, Rick received a $7,200 payment in advance from a client for monthly landscaping services from December 1, 2018, through November 30, 2020 ($300 a month for 24 months). When must Rick recognize the income from the advance payment for services?

Answer: Under the accrual method, if Rick elects the deferral method to account for advance payments, he would initially recognize the $300 income he earned in December 2018. In 2019, he would recognize the remaining $6,900 (rather than only the $3,600 related to 2019) because he is not allowed to defer the prepayments for more than a year. If Rick does not elect the deferral method, he would recognize the entire prepayment of $7,200 as income upon receipt in 2018. Under the cash method, Rick would recognize the entire prepayment, $7,200, as income upon receipt in 2018.

What if: Suppose that rather than receiving payment in advance for services, Rick's client paid $7,200 in 2018 for landscape supplies that Rick purchased and provided in 2019. When must Rick recognize the income from the advance payment for goods?

Answer: Using the accrual method, if Rick elects the deferral method to account for advance payments, he would not recognize any income in 2018 because none of the income had been earned in 2018. Rick would then recognize the entire $7,200 in 2019. If Rick did not elect the deferral method, he would recognize the entire $7,200 in 2018. Under the cash method, Rick would recognize the entire $7,200 in 2018.

Inventories

Many businesses generate income by selling products they acquire for resale or products they manufacture. When selling inventory is a material income-producing factor, larger businesses generally must account for gross profit (sales minus cost of goods sold) using the accrual method, even if the business is a cash-method taxpayer. However, beginning in 2018, taxpayers need not use the accrual method to account for inventory if they report average gross receipts of $25 million or less or less for the three-tax year period ending with the prior tax year. Instead, these taxpayers can generally treat purchases of goods for sale as either non-incidental materials or use an accounting method that conforms to the taxpayer's financial accounting treatment of inventory.

---

[37]*Comm. v. Indianapolis Power & Light Co.* (1990), 493 US 203. In this case, it was determined that customer deposits required by a public utility weren't taxable income because the right to keep the deposits depended on events outside of the taxpayer's control, such as the decision to have the deposit applied to future bills.

[38]IRC §451(c). Prior to 2018, this exception was provided under Rev. Proc. 2004-34, 2004-1 CB 991.

Businesses that account for inventory must determine their inventory costs to accurately compute taxable income. This requires businesses to maintain records of balances for finished goods inventory and, if applicable, for partially finished goods and raw materials. Inventory costs include the purchase price of raw materials (minus any discounts), shipping costs, and any indirect costs it allocates to the inventory under the **uniform cost capitalization (UNICAP) rules.**[39]

Uniform Capitalization   The tax laws require businesses that account for inventories to capitalize certain direct and indirect costs associated with inventories.[40] Congress enacted these rules primarily for two reasons. First, the rules accelerate tax revenues for the government by deferring deductions for the capitalized costs until the business sells the associated inventory. Thus, there is generally a one-year lag between when businesses initially capitalize the costs and when they deduct them. Second, Congress designed the "uniform" rules to reduce variation in the costs businesses include in inventory and Congress intended these provisions to apply to large manufacturers and resalers.[41]

Under these uniform cost capitalization rules, large businesses are generally required to capitalize more costs to inventory for tax purposes than they capitalize under financial accounting rules. Under GAAP, businesses generally include in inventory only those costs incurred within their production facility. In contrast, the UNICAP rules require businesses to allocate to inventory the costs they incur inside the production facility and the costs they incur outside the facility to support production (or inventory acquisition) activities. For example, under the UNICAP provisions, a business must capitalize at least a portion of the compensation paid to employees in its purchasing department, general and administrative department, and even its information technology department, to the extent these groups provide support for the production process. In contrast, businesses immediately expense these items as period costs for financial accounting purposes. The regulations provide guidance on the costs that must be allocated to inventory. Selling, advertising, and research are specifically identified as costs that do not have to be allocated to inventory under the UNICAP provisions.[42]

Example 9-17

What if: Green Acres sells trees but Rick anticipates selling flowers, shrubs, and other plants in future years. Ken is Rick's employee in charge of purchasing inventory. Ken's compensation this year is $30,000, and Rick estimates that Ken spends about 5 percent of his time acquiring inventory and the remaining time working on landscaping projects. Assuming Rick was required to apply the UNICAP rules, how would he allocate Ken's compensation under the UNICAP rules?

Answer: If the UNICAP rules applied to Green Acres, Rick would allocate $1,500 ($30,000 × 5%) of Ken's compensation to the cost of the inventory Green Acres acquired this year. In contrast, Ken's entire salary would be expensed as a period cost for financial accounting purposes. (Note, however, because Green Acres's gross receipts for the year are under $25 million, it is not *required* to apply the UNICAP rules.)

Inventory Cost-Flow Methods   Once a business determines the cost of its inventory, it must use an inventory cost-flow method to determine its cost of goods sold. Three primary cost-flow methods are (1) the **first-in, first-out (FIFO) method,** (2) the **last-in, first-out (LIFO) method,** and (3) the **specific identification method.** Businesses might

---

[39]Inventory valuation allowances are generally not allowed, but taxpayers can adopt the lower of cost or market method of inventory valuation. In addition, under certain conditions specific goods not salable at normal prices can be valued at bona fide selling prices less direct cost of disposition.

[40]§263A(a).

[41]Beginning in 2018, taxpayers need not employ UNICAP to adjust inventory costs if they report average gross receipts of $25 million or less or less for the three-tax year period ending with the prior tax year.

[42]Reg. §1.263A–1(e)(3)(iii).

be inclined to use FIFO or LIFO methods when they sell similar, relatively low-cost, high-volume products such as cans of soup or barrels of oil. These methods simplify inventory accounting because the business need not track the individual cost of each item it sells. In contrast, businesses that sell distinct, relatively high-cost, low-volume products might be more likely to adopt the specific identification method. For example, jewelry and used-car businesses would likely use the specific identification method to account for their cost of sales. In general terms, when costs are increasing, a business using the FIFO method will report a higher gross margin than if it used the LIFO method. The opposite is true if costs are decreasing.

Example 9-18

In late August, Rick purchased 10 oak saplings (immature trees) for a total purchase price of $3,000. In September, he purchased 12 more for a total price of $3,900, and in late October, he purchased 15 more for $5,000. The total cost of each lot of trees was determined as follows:

Purchase Date	Trees	Direct Cost	Other Costs	Total Cost
August 20	10	$ 3,000	$200	$ 3,200
September 15	12	3,900	300	4,200
October 22	15	5,000	400	5,400
Totals	37	$11,900	$900	$12,800

Before the end of the year, Green Acres sold 20 of the oak saplings (5 from the August lot, 5 from the September lot, and 10 from the October lot) for cash. To illustrate the effects of inventory accounting, assume that Rick prefers to keep inventory records (recall that taxpayers are not required to keep inventories for tax purposes if their average annual gross receipts are under $25 million). What is Green Acres's gross profit from sales of oak saplings if the sales revenue totaled $14,000 (all collected by year-end), and what is its ending oak sapling inventory under the accrual and cash methods of accounting?

Answer: Under the accrual method, Green Acres's gross profit from sapling sales and its ending inventory balance for the remaining oak saplings under the FIFO, LIFO, and specific identification cost-flow methods is as follows:

	FIFO	LIFO	Specific ID
Sales	$14,000	$14,000	$14,000
Cost of goods sold	−6,700	−7,150	−6,950
Gross profit	$ 7,300	$ 6,850	$ 7,050
Ending inventory:			
August 20 trees	$ 0	$ 3,200	$ 1,600
September 15 trees	700	2,450	2,450
October 22 trees	5,400	0	1,800
Total ending inventory	**$ 6,100**	**$ 5,650**	**$ 5,850**

Under both the accrual and cash methods, Rick is allowed to elect to deduct the cost of purchases as non-incidental materials and supplies. Hence, Rick could deduct the $12,800 currently. However, if Rick elects to keep an inventory of his trees, he would be entitled to choose his inventory method (LIFO, FIFO, or specific identification) and deduct the cost of goods sold under that method.

When costs are subject to inflation over time, a business would get the best of both worlds if it adopted the FIFO method for financial reporting purposes and the LIFO method for tax purposes. Not surprisingly, the tax laws require that a business can use

LIFO for tax purposes only if it also uses LIFO for financial reporting purposes.[43] While this "conformity" requirement may not matter to entities not required to generate financial reports, it can be very restrictive to publicly traded corporations.

Accrual Deductions

Generally, when accrual-method businesses incur a liability relating to a business expense, they account for it by crediting a liability account (or by crediting cash if they pay the liability at the time they incur it) and debiting an expense account. However, to claim a tax deduction for the expense, the expense must meet (1) an **all-events test** *and* (2) an **economic performance test.**[44] While the all-events test for recognizing deductions is similar to the all-events test for recognizing income, the additional economic performance requirement makes the deduction recognition rules more stringent than the income recognition rules. The deduction rules generally preclude businesses from deducting estimated expenses or reserves.

All-Events Test for Deductions

For a business to recognize a deduction, the events that establish the liability giving rise to the deduction must have occurred, and the amount of the liability must be determinable with reasonable accuracy.[45]

Example 9-19

On November of this year, Rick agreed to a one-year $6,000 contract with Ace Advertising to produce a radio ad campaign. Ace agreed that Rick would owe nothing under the contract unless his sales increase a minimum of 25 percent over the next six months. What amount, if any, may Rick deduct this year for this contract under the accrual and cash methods?

Answer: Under the accrual method, Green Acres is not allowed to recognize *any* deduction this year for the liability. Even though Ace will have completed two months of advertising for Green Acres by the end of the year, its guarantee means that Rick's liability is not fixed until and unless his sales increase by 25 percent. Under the cash method, Rick would not deduct any of the cost of the campaign this year because he has not paid anything to Ace.

Economic Performance

Even when businesses meet the all-events test, they still must clear the economic performance hurdle to recognize the tax deduction. Congress added the economic performance requirement because in some situations taxpayers claimed current deductions and delayed paying the associated cash expenditures for years. Thus, the delayed payment reduced the real (present value) cost of the deduction. This requirement specifies that businesses may not recognize a deduction for an expense until the underlying activity generating the associated liability has occurred. Thus, an accrual-method business is not allowed to deduct a prepaid business expense even if it qualifies to do so under the 12-month rule (discussed above) unless it also has met the economic performance test with respect to the liability associated with the expense.

The specific requirements for the economic performance test differ based on whether the liability has arisen from:

- Receiving goods or services *from* another person.
- Use of property.
- Providing goods or services *to* another person.
- Certain activities creating **payment liabilities.**

> **THE KEY FACTS**
>
> **Accrual of Business-Expense Deductions**
>
> - Both all-events and economic performance are required for deducting accrued business expenses.
> - The all-events test requires that the business be liable for the payment.
> - Economic performance generally requires that the underlying activity generating the liability has occurred in order for the associated expense to be deductible.

[43]§472(c).
[44]§461(h).
[45]§461.

Receiving goods and (or) services from another person.   When a business agrees to pay another person for goods or services, the business deducts the expense associated with the liability only when the other person provides the goods or services (assuming the all-events test is met for the liability). An exception to this general rule occurs when a business hires another person to provide goods or services and the business actually pays the liability before the other person provides the goods or services. In this circumstance, the business may treat the actual payment as economic performance as long as it reasonably expects the other person to provide the goods or all of the services within three and one-half months after the payment.[46]

Example 9-20

On December 15, 2018, Rick hires Your New Fence LLC (YNF) to install a concrete wall for one of his clients by paying $1,000 of the cost as a down payment and agreeing to pay the remaining $7,000 when YNF finishes the wall. YNF was not going to start building the wall until early 2019, so as of the end of the year Rick has not billed his client for the wall. Rick expects YNF to finish the wall by the end of April. What amount associated with his liability to YNF is Rick allowed to deduct in 2018 and 2019?

Answer: Under the accrual method, Rick is not entitled to a deduction in 2018. Rick will deduct his full $8,000 cost of the wall in 2019 when YNF builds the wall, because economic performance occurs as YNF provides the services, even though Rick paid for part of the goods and services in 2018. Under the cash method, Rick would deduct $1,000 (his down payment) in 2018 and the remainder in 2019 when he pays the remainder on the contract.

What if: Assume that Rick expected YNF to finish building the wall by the end of January 2019. What amount associated with this liability to YNF is Rick allowed to deduct in 2018 and 2019?

Answer: Under the accrual method, Rick is allowed to deduct $1,000 in 2018 because Rick actually paid this amount in 2018 and he reasonably expected YNF to finish its work on the wall within 3½ months after he made the payment to YNF on December 15. Rick would deduct the remaining $7,000 cost of the wall in 2019 when YNF builds the wall. Under the cash method, Rick deducts the $1,000 down payment in 2018 and the remaining $7,000 when he makes the payment in 2019.

Renting or leasing property from another person.   When a business enters into an agreement to rent or lease property from another person, economic performance occurs over the rental period. Thus, the business is allowed to deduct the rental expense over the lease.

Example 9-21

On May 1, 2018, Rick paid $7,200 in advance to rent his shop for 12 months ($600 per month). What amount may Rick deduct for rent in 2018 if he accounts for his business activities using the accrual method?

Answer: $4,800 ($600 × 8 months use). Even though the rent is a prepaid business expense under the 12-month rule (the contract period is for 12 months and the contract period does not extend beyond 2019), he must deduct the rent expense over the term of the lease because that is when economic performance occurs.

What if: Assuming the original facts, what amount of the $7,200 rental payment may Rick deduct in 2018 if he is using the cash method of accounting for his business?

Answer: $7,200. In this case, Rick may deduct the expense under the 12-month rule. He does not have to meet the economic performance requirement to deduct the expense because the economic performance requirements apply to accrual-method taxpayers, but not cash-method taxpayers.

---

[46]Reg. §1.461-4(d)(6).

Example 9-22

On November 1, 2018, Rick paid $2,400 to rent a trailer for 24 months. What amount of this payment may Rick deduct and when may he deduct it?

Answer: Under the accrual method, even though Rick paid the entire rental fee in advance, economic performance occurs over the 24-month rental period. Thus, Green Acres deducts $200 for the trailer rental in 2018, $1,200 in 2019, and $1,000 in 2020. Because the rental period exceeds 12 months, the amount and timing of the deductions are the same under the cash method.

Providing goods and services to another person. Businesses liable for providing goods and services to other persons meet the economic performance test as they provide the goods or services that satisfy the liability.

Example 9-23

In the summer, Rick landscaped a city park. As part of this service, Rick agreed to remove a fountain from the park at the option of the city parks committee. In December 2018, the committee decided to have Rick remove the fountain. Rick began the removal in December and paid an employee $850 on December 31. Rick completed the removal work in the spring of 2019 and paid an employee $685 on March 31. What amounts will Rick deduct for the removal project and when may he deduct them?

Answer: Under the accrual method, Rick is allowed to deduct his costs as he provides the services. Consequently, in 2018 Rick can deduct $850 for the cost of the services provided by his employee in 2018. In 2019, Rick can deduct the remaining $685 cost of the services provided by his employee in 2019. Under the cash method, the amount and timing of his deductions would be the same as under the accrual method.

Payment liabilities. Economic performance occurs for certain liabilities only when the business actually pays the liability. Thus, accrual-method businesses incurring payment liabilities are essentially on the cash method for deducting the associated expenses. Exhibit 9-2 describes different categories of these payment liabilities.

EXHIBIT 9-2   Categories of Payment Liabilities

Economic performance occurs when the taxpayer pays liabilities associated with:

- Workers' compensation, tort, breach of contract, or violation of law.
- Rebates and refunds.
- Awards, prizes, and jackpots.
- Insurance, warranties, and service contracts provided *to* the business. (*Note:* This relates to insurance, warranties, and product service contracts that cover the taxpayer and *not* a warranty that the taxpayer provides to others.)
- Taxes.[47]
- Other liabilities not provided for elsewhere.

Recurring item exception. One of the most common exceptions to economic performance is the **recurring item** exception. This exception is designed to minimize the cost of applying economic performance to expenses that occur on a regular basis. Under this exception, accrual method taxpayers can deduct certain accrued expenses even if economic performance has not occurred by year-end.[48] A recurring item is a liability

---

[47]While taxes are generally not deducted until they are paid, §461(c) allows businesses to elect to accrue the deduction for real property taxes ratably over the tax period instead of deducting them when they actually pay them.

[48]§461(h)(3).

that is expected to recur in future years and is either not material in amount or deducting the expense currently matches with revenue. Payment liabilities, such as insurance, rebates and refunds, are deemed to meet the matching requirement.[49] In addition, the all-events test must be satisfied at year-end and actual economic performance of the item must occur within a reasonable time after year-end (but prior to the filing of the tax return, which could be up to 8½ months with an extension). As a final note, the recurring item exception does not apply to workers' compensation or tort liabilities.

Example 9-24

If clients are not completely satisfied with Green Acres's landscaping work, Rick offers a $200 refund with no questions asked. Near the end of 2018, Rick had four clients request refunds. Rick incurred the liability for the refunds this year. However, Rick was busy during the holiday season, so he didn't pay the refunds until January 2019. When should Rick deduct the customer refunds?

Answer: Because refunds are payment liabilities, economic performance does not occur until Rick actually pays the refunds. Consequently, Rick deducts the $800 of refunds in 2019 even though the liability for the refunds met the all-events test in 2018. Under the cash method, Rick would not deduct the refunds until he paid them in 2019.

What if: Suppose that Rick expected that $800 of refunds would typically be accrued at year-end. Under what conditions could Rick deduct the refunds in 2018 if he elects to use accrual accounting?

Answer: To claim $800 of deductions for the refunds in 2018, either the accrued refunds must not be material in amount or a 2018 deduction must better match 2018 revenue than 2019 revenue. Fortunately, Rick doesn't need to worry about the matching requirement. Under the regulations refunds are deemed to meet the matching requirement for purposes of the recurring item exception. Rick must also expect actual economic performance (payment) within a reasonable time after year-end (but not longer than 8½ months or the filing of the tax return). Note also that Rick must elect to deduct the refunds in 2018 using the recurring item exception and then must follow this method in future periods.

Accrual-method taxpayers that prepay business expenses for payment liabilities (insurance contracts, warranties, and product service contracts provided to the taxpayer) that qualify as recurring items are allowed to immediately deduct the prepayments subject to the 12-month rule for prepaid expenses. Thus, the deductible amounts for Rick's prepaid insurance contracts in Example 9-14 are the same for both the cash method and accrual method of accounting. Exhibit 9-3 describes the requirements for economic performance for the different types of liabilities.

EXHIBIT 9-3   Economic Performance

Taxpayer incurs liability from	Economic performance occurs
Receiving goods and services *from* another person.	When the goods or services are provided to the taxpayer or with payment if the taxpayer reasonably expects actual performance within 3½ months.
Renting or leasing property *from* another person.	Ratably over the time period during which the taxpayer is entitled to use the property or money.
Providing goods and services *to* another person.	When the taxpayer incurs costs to satisfy the liability or provide the goods and services.
Activities creating "payment" liabilities.	When the business actually makes payment.
Interest expense.	As accrued. This technically does not fall within the economic performance rules but it is a similar concept.

Bad Debt Expense

When accrual method businesses sell a product or a service on credit, they debit accounts receivable and credit sales revenue for both financial and tax purposes. However, because businesses usually are unable to collect the full amount of their accounts receivable, they incur bad debt expense (a customer owes them a debt that the

---

[49]Reg §1.461-5(b)(5)(ii).

customer will not pay). For financial reporting purposes, the business estimates the amount of the bad debt, debits bad debt expense, and credits an allowance for doubtful accounts. However, for tax purposes, businesses are allowed to deduct bad debt expense only when the debt actually becomes worthless within the taxable year.[50] Consequently, for tax purposes, businesses determine which debts are uncollectible and write them off by debiting bad debt expense and directly crediting the actual account receivable account that is uncollectible. This required method of determining bad debt expense for tax purposes is called the **direct write-off method.** In contrast, the method used for financial reporting purposes is called the **allowance method.** Businesses reporting taxable income on the cash method of accounting are *not* allowed to deduct bad debt expenses, because they do not include receivables in taxable income (they do not credit revenue until they actually receive payment).

Example 9-25

At year-end, Rick estimates that about $900 of the receivables from his landscaping services will be uncollectible, but he has identified only one client, Jared, who will definitely not pay his bill. Jared, who has skipped town, owes Rick $280 for landscaping this fall. What amount of bad debt expense may Rick deduct for the year?

Answer: For financial reporting purposes, Rick recognizes a $900 bad debt expense. However, for tax purposes, under the accrual method, Rick can deduct only $280—the amount associated with specifically writing off Jared's receivable. Under the cash method, Rick would not be able to claim any deduction, because he did not receive a payment from Jared and thus did not recognize income on the amount Jared owed him.

Limitations on Accruals to Related Persons   To prevent businesses and related persons from working together to defer taxes, the tax laws prevent an accrual-method business from accruing (and deducting) an expense for a liability owed to a related person using the cash method until the related person recognizes the income associated with the payment.[51] For this purpose, related persons include:

- Family members, including parents, siblings, and spouses.
- Shareholders and C corporations when the shareholder owns more than 50 percent of the corporation's stock.[52]
- Owners of partnerships and S corporations no matter the ownership percentage.[53]

This issue frequently arises in situations in which a business employs the owner or a relative of an owner. The business is not allowed to deduct compensation expense owed to the related party until the year in which the related person includes the compensation in income. However, this related-person limit extends beyond compensation to any accrued expense the business owes to a related cash-method taxpayer.

Example 9-26

In December, Rick asked his retired father, Lee, to help him finish a landscaping job. By the end of 2018, Rick owed Lee $2,000 of (reasonable) compensation for his efforts, which he paid in January 2019. What amount of this compensation may Rick deduct and when may he deduct it?

Answer: If Rick uses the accrual method and Lee the cash method, Rick will not be able to deduct the $2,000 compensation expense until 2019. Rick is Lee's son, so Rick and Lee are "related" persons for tax purposes. Consequently, Rick can deduct the compensation only when Lee includes the payment in his taxable income in 2019. If Rick uses the cash method, he will deduct the expense when he pays it in January 2019.

---

[50]§166(a).

[51]§267(a).

[52]Certain constructive ownership rules apply in determining ownership percentages for this purpose. See §267(c).

[53]See §267(b) for related-person definitions.

Comparison of Accrual and Cash Methods

From a business perspective, the two primary advantages of adopting the cash method over the accrual method are that (1) the cash method provides the business with more flexibility to time income and deductions by accelerating or deferring payments (timing tax planning strategy) and (2) bookkeeping for the cash method is easier. For example, a cash-method taxpayer could defer revenue by waiting to bill clients for goods or services until after year-end, thereby increasing the likelihood that customers would send payment after year-end. There are some concerns with this tax strategy. For example, delaying the bills might increase the likelihood that the customers will not pay their bills at all.

The primary advantage of the accrual method over the cash method is that it better matches revenues and expenses. For that reason, external financial statement users who want to evaluate a business's financial performance prefer the accrual method. Consistent with this idea, the cash method is not allowed for financial reporting under GAAP.

Although the cash method is by far the predominate accounting method among sole proprietors, it is less common in other types of businesses. As we noted previously, tax laws generally prohibit large C corporations and partnerships with corporate partners from using the cash method of accounting.[54] Exhibit 9-4 details the basic differences in accounting for income and deductions under the accrual and cash methods of accounting.

EXHIBIT 9-4 Comparison of Cash and Accrual Methods

Income or Expense Item	Cash Method	Accrual Method
Income recognition.	Actually or constructively received.	Taxable once the all-events test is satisfied.
Unearned rent and interest income.	Taxable on receipt.	Taxable on receipt.
Advance payment for goods and services.	Taxable on receipt.	Taxed when received or taxpayers can elect to be taxed in the following year of receipt if not earned by end of year of receipt.
General deduction recognition.	Deduct when paid; economic performance does not apply.	Deduct once all-events test and economic performance test are both satisfied.
Expenditures for tangible assets with a useful life of more than one year.	Capitalize and apply cost recovery.	Same as the cash method.
Expenditures for intangible assets other than prepaid business expenses.	Capitalize and amortize if provision in code allows it.	Same as the cash method.
Prepaid business expenses.	Immediately deductible. However, amortize if contract period exceeds 12 months or extends beyond the end of the next taxable year.	Same as cash method for payment liabilities; otherwise, apply all-events and economic performance tests to ascertain when to capitalize and amortize.
Prepaid interest expense.	Not deductible until interest accrues.	Same as the cash method.
Bad debt expense.	Not deductible because sales on account not included in income.	Deduct under direct write-off method.

[54]Recall that these entities are able to adopt the cash method if their average annual gross receipts for the three tax years ending with the prior tax year do not exceed $25 million (see §448).

Example 9-27

At year-end, Rick determined that Green Acres had collected a total of $78,000 of service revenue and $12,575 in other expenses (not described elsewhere in examples but listed in Exhibit 9-5). Rick is debating whether to adopt the cash or accrual method. To help him resolve his dilemma, Jane calculates Green Acres's taxable income under the cash and accrual methods assuming that Rick elects not to maintain an inventory (summarized in Exhibit 9-5). What are the differences between the two calculations?

Answer: Jane provided the following summary of the differences between taxable income under the cash method and taxable income under the accrual method:

Description	(1) Accrual	(2) Cash	(1)–(2) Difference	Example
Revenue:				
Credit sales	11,000	0	+11,000	9-15
Prepaid revenue	300	7,200	−6,900	9-16
Expenses:				
Prepaid services	0	−1,000	+1,000	9-20
Prepaid rent expense	−4,800	−7,200	+2,400	9-21
Bad debts	−280	0	−280	9-25
Total difference (accrual income > cash income)			**+ 7,220**	

After comparing the revenue and expenses recognized under the two accounting methods, Jane explains that the selection of the accrual method for Green Acres means that Rick will be taxed on an additional $7,220 of income this year.

The business income for Green Acres under the accrual and cash methods is summarized in Exhibit 9-5. After reflecting on these numbers and realizing that he would recognize $7,220 more taxable income (and self-employment income subject to self-employment tax) this year under the accrual method, Rick determined that it made sense to instead adopt the cash method of accounting for Green Acres's first tax return. Meanwhile, he knew he had to include Green Acres's business income on Schedule C of his individual tax return. Exhibit 9-6 presents Rick's Schedule C for Green Acres using the cash method of accounting.

Adopting an Accounting Method

We've seen that businesses use overall accounting methods (cash, accrual, or hybrid) and many specific accounting methods (inventory cost-flow assumption, methods of accounting for prepaid income for goods and services, and methods for accounting for prepaid expenses, among other methods) to account for their business activities. For tax purposes, it's important to understand how and when a business technically adopts an accounting method, because once it does so, it must get the IRS's permission to change the method.

Businesses generally elect their accounting methods by using them on their tax returns. However, when the business technically adopts a method depends on whether it is a **permissible accounting method** or an **impermissible accounting method.** So far, our discussion has emphasized accounting methods permissible under the tax laws. A business adopts a permissible accounting method by using and reporting the tax results of the method for at least one year. However, businesses may unwittingly (or intentionally) use impermissible accounting methods. For example, a business using the allowance method for determining bad debt expense for tax purposes is using an impermissible accounting method because the tax laws prescribe the use of the direct write-off method for determining bad debt expense. A business adopts an impermissible method by using and reporting the results of the method for two consecutive years.

EXHIBIT 9-5 Green Acres's Net Business Income

Description	Cash	Accrual	Example
Income			
Service revenue:			
Landscaping revenue	$ 78,000	$ 78,000	9-27
December landscape service	0	11,000	9-15
Prepaid landscape services	7,200	300	9-16
Sales of inventory:			
Tree sales	14,000	14,000	9-18
Gross Profit	**$99,200**	**$103,300**	
Nonincidental materials and supplies	$ 12,800	$ 12,800	9-18
Car and truck expense:			
SUV operating expense	5,335	5,335	9-7
BMW operating expense	306	306	9-9
Insurance	1,200	1,200	9-14
Rent:			
Shop	7,200	4,800	9-21
Trailer	200	200	9-22
Travel and business meals:			
Travel to NY seminar	1,435	1,435	9-8
Business dinner with clients	270	270	9-6
Wages and subcontractor fees:			
Part-time employees	23,000	23,000	9-2
Full-time employee (Ken)	30,000	30,000	9-17
Fountain removal (part-time employee)	850	850	9-23
Fence installation (prepaid subcontractor)	1,000	0	9-20
Other expenses:			
Books for waiting room	50	50	9-1
Education—seminar	300	300	9-8
Uniforms	500	500	9-5
Bad debts	0	280	9-25
Other expenses not in examples:			
Advertising	1,160	1,160	
Depreciation	4,000	4,000	
Interest	300	300	
Legal and professional services	1,040	1,040	
Office expense	1,500	1,500	
Repairs and maintenance	1,975	1,975	
Taxes and licenses	400	400	
Utilities	2,200	2,200	
Total deductions	**$97,021**	**$ 93,901**	
Net Business Income	**$ 2,179**	**$ 9,399**	

Changing Accounting Methods

Once a business has adopted an accounting method, it must generally receive permission to change the method, regardless of whether it is a permissible or an impermissible method.[55] A taxpayer requests permission to change accounting methods by

---

[55]For tax years beginning after 2017, there is a special exception for taxpayers who change accounting methods under the $25 million gross receipts test either by switching to the cash method or who opt to treat purchases of goods for sale as noninventory. These changes in accounting method are treated as initiated by the taxpayer and no longer need the consent of the Secretary.

EXHIBIT 9-6   Green Acres Schedule C

SCHEDULE C (Form 1040) Department of the Treasury Internal Revenue Service (99)	**Profit or Loss From Business** (Sole Proprietorship) ▶ Go to *www.irs.gov/ScheduleC* for instructions and the latest information. ▶ Attach to Form 1040, 1040NR, or 1041; partnerships generally must file Form 1065.	OMB No. 1545-0074 20**17** Attachment Sequence No. **09**

Name of proprietor **RICK GRIME**		Social security number (SSN) **000-00-0000**

A	Principal business or profession, including product or service (see instructions) **LANDSCAPING**	**B** Enter code from instructions ▶	5	7	1	6	3	0

C	Business name. If no separate business name, leave blank. **GREEN ACRES LANDSCAPING**	**D** Employer ID number (EIN) (see instr.) 0 0 0 0 0 0 0 0 0

E Business address (including suite or room no.) ▶ **BUCKSNORT STREET**

City, town or post office, state, and ZIP code   **SAN ANTONIO, TX 78208**

F Accounting method: (1) ☑ Cash   (2) ☐ Accrual   (3) ☐ Other (specify) ▶ _____

G Did you "materially participate" in the operation of this business during 2017? If "No," see instructions for limit on losses   ☑ Yes   ☐ No

H If you started or acquired this business during 2017, check here   .   .   .   .   ▶ ☑

I Did you make any payments in 2017 that would require you to file Form(s) 1099? (see instructions)   .   .   .   .   .   ☐ Yes   ☑ No

J If "Yes," did you or will you file required Forms 1099?   .   .   .   .   ☐ Yes   ☐ No

Part I   Income

1	Gross receipts or sales. See instructions for line 1 and check the box if this income was reported to you on Form W-2 and the "Statutory employee" box on that form was checked . . . . ▶ ☐	**1**	99,200
2	Returns and allowances	**2**	
3	Subtract line 2 from line 1	**3**	99,200
4	Cost of goods sold (from line 42)	**4**	
5	**Gross profit.** Subtract line 4 from line 3	**5**	99,200
6	Other income, including federal and state gasoline or fuel tax credit or refund (see instructions) . . .	**6**	
7	**Gross income.** Add lines 5 and 6 . . . . ▶	**7**	99,200

Part II   Expenses. Enter expenses for business use of your home **only** on line 30.

8	Advertising	**8**	1,160	**18**	Office expense (see instructions)	**18**		1,500
9	Car and truck expenses (see instructions)	**9**	5,641	**19**	Pension and profit-sharing plans .	**19**		
10	Commissions and fees .	**10**		**20**	Rent or lease (see instructions):			
11	Contract labor (see instructions)	**11**	1,000	**a**	Vehicles, machinery, and equipment	**20a**		7,400
12	Depletion	**12**		**b**	Other business property . . .	**20b**		
13	Depreciation and section 179 expense deduction (not included in Part III) (see instructions)	**13**	4,000	**21**	Repairs and maintenance . . .	**21**		1,975
				22	Supplies (not included in Part III) .	**22**		12,800
				23	Taxes and licenses	**23**		400
				24	Travel, meals, and entertainment:			
14	Employee benefit programs (other than on line 19) . .	**14**		**a**	Travel	**24a**		1,435
15	Insurance (other than health)	**15**	1,200	**b**	Deductible meals and entertainment (see instructions) .	**24b**		270
16	Interest:			**25**	Utilities	**25**		2,200
a	Mortgage (paid to banks, etc.)	**16a**	300	**26**	Wages (less employment credits) .	**26**		53,850
b	Other	**16b**		**27a**	Other expenses (from line 48) . .	**27a**		850
17	Legal and professional services	**17**	1,040	**b**	**Reserved for future use** . . .	**27b**		

28	**Total expenses** before expenses for business use of home. Add lines 8 through 27a . . . . . . ▶	**28**	97,021
29	Tentative profit or (loss). Subtract line 28 from line 7	**29**	2,179
30	Expenses for business use of your home. Do not report these expenses elsewhere. Attach Form 8829 unless using the simplified method (see instructions). **Simplified method filers only:** enter the total square footage of: (a) your home: _____ and (b) the part of your home used for business: _____ . Use the Simplified Method Worksheet in the instructions to figure the amount to enter on line 30	**30**	
31	**Net profit or (loss).** Subtract line 30 from line 29. • If a profit, enter on both **Form 1040, line 12** (or **Form 1040NR, line 13**) and on **Schedule SE, line 2.** (If you checked the box on line 1, see instructions). Estates and trusts, enter on **Form 1041, line 3.** • If a loss, you **must** go to line 32.	**31**	2,179
32	If you have a loss, check the box that describes your investment in this activity (see instructions). • If you checked 32a, enter the loss on both **Form 1040, line 12,** (or **Form 1040NR, line 13**) and on **Schedule SE, line 2.** (If you checked the box on line 1, see the line 31 instructions). Estates and trusts, enter on **Form 1041, line 3.** • If you checked 32b, you **must** attach **Form 6198.** Your loss may be limited.	**32a** ☑ All investment is at risk. **32b** ☐ Some investment is not at risk.	

For Paperwork Reduction Act Notice, see the separate instructions.	Cat. No. 11334P	Schedule C (Form 1040) 2017

Source: Form 1040

filing Form 3115 with the IRS. The IRS automatically approves certain types of accounting method changes, but for others the business must provide a good business purpose for the change and pay a fee. The IRS also requires permission when a business must change from using an impermissible method; this requirement helps the IRS to certify that the business properly makes the transition to a permissible method. In essence, the IRS requires the business to report its own noncompliance. Why would a business do so? Besides complying with the tax laws, a business might report its own noncompliance to receive leniency from the IRS. Without getting into the details, the IRS is likely to assess fewer penalties and less interest expense for noncompliance when the business reports the noncompliance before the IRS discovers it on its own.

Tax Consequences of Changing Accounting Methods

When a business changes from one accounting method to another, the business determines its taxable income for the year of change using the new method. Furthermore, the business must make an adjustment to taxable income that effectively represents the cumulative difference, as of the beginning of the tax year, between the amount of income (or deductions) recognized under the old accounting method and the amount that would have been recognized for all prior years if the new method had been applied. This adjustment is called a **§481 adjustment.** The §481 adjustment prevents the duplication or omission of items of income or deduction due to a change in accounting method. If the §481 adjustment increases taxable income, the taxpayer recognizes the total adjustment spread evenly over four years beginning with the year of the change (25 percent of the full adjustment each year).[56] If the adjustment decreases taxable income, the taxpayer recognizes it entirely in the year of change.[57]

Example 9-28

What if: Suppose that at the end of 2018, Green Acres has $24,000 of accounts receivable. Assuming Green Acres uses the cash method of accounting in 2018, it would not include the $24,000 of receivables in income in determining its 2018 taxable income. Suppose further that Rick decides to switch Green Acres to the accrual method of accounting in 2019 by filing a Form 3115 and receiving permission from the IRS. What is Rick's §481 adjustment for his change in accounting method from the cash to the accrual method?

Answer: $24,000 increase to income and because this adjustment is income-increasing, the total is spread evenly over four years ($6,000 in 2019 and each of the subsequent three years). Since Rick would use the accrual method in 2019, he would *not* include payments he receives for the $24,000 receivables as income because he earned this income in 2018 (not 2019). Instead, Rick would be required to make a §481 adjustment to ensure that he does not *omit* these items from taxable income. His total §481 adjustment is to increase income by $24,000. Because this is an income-increasing adjustment, Rick includes $6,000 of the adjustment (25 percent) in Green Acres's taxable income in 2019. He would likewise include a $6,000 income-increasing §481 adjustment in each of the subsequent three years.

What if: Suppose that at the end of 2018, Green Acres has $4,000 of accounts payable instead of $24,000 of accounts receivable. What is Rick's §481 adjustment for his change in accounting method from the cash to the accrual method in 2019?

Answer: In this instance Green Acres would have a negative (income-decreasing) §481 adjustment of $4,000 because the $4,000 of expenses would have accrued in 2018 but would not have been deducted. Hence, Green Acres would be entitled to deduct the full $4,000 as a negative §481 adjustment amount in 2019.

---

[56]Taxpayers with positive §481 adjustments less than $25,000 can elect to recognize the entire amount in the year of change. Rev. Proc. 2002-19, 2002 IRB 696.

[57]Taxpayers changing accounting methods under the Tax Cuts and Jobs Act will need to make § 481 adjustments for those changes.

CONCLUSION

This chapter discusses issues relating to business income and deductions. We learned that the income rules for businesses are very similar to those for individuals and that businesses may deduct only ordinary and necessary business expenses and other business expenses specifically authorized by law. We also described several business expense limitations and discussed the accounting periods and methods businesses may use in reporting taxable income to the IRS. The issues described in this chapter are widely applicable to all types of business entities, including sole proprietorships, partnerships, S corporations, and C corporations.

Summary

Identify common business deductions.   **LO 9-1**

- Ordinary and necessary business expenses are allowed as deductions to calculate net income from activities entered into with a profit motive.
- Only reasonable amounts are allowed as business expense deductions. Extravagant or excessive amounts are likely to be characterized by personal motives and are disallowed.

Determine the limits on deducting business expenses.   **LO 9-2**

- The law specifically prohibits deducting expenses that are against public policy (such as fines or bribes) and expenses that produce tax-exempt income.
- Expenses benefiting more than 12 months must be capitalized and special limits and record-keeping requirements are applied to business expenses that may have personal benefits, such as meals.
- The deduction of business interest expense is limited to business interest income plus 30 percent of the business's adjusted taxable income. Adjusted taxable income is taxable income before depreciation and interest deductions allocable to the business activity. Disallowed business interest expense can be carried forward indefinitely.

Identify special business deductions specifically permitted under the tax laws.   **LO 9-3**

- Special calculations are necessary for deductions such as the deduction for casualty losses. The deduction when an asset is damaged (not destroyed) is limited to the lesser of the reduction in value or the adjusted tax basis of the asset.

Describe accounting periods available to businesses.   **LO 9-4**

- Accounting periods and methods are chosen at the time of filing the first tax return.
- There are three types of tax years—calendar year, fiscal year, and 52/53-week year—and each tax year is distinguished by year-end.

Apply cash and accrual methods to determine business income and expense deductions.   **LO 9-5**

- Under the cash method, taxpayers recognize revenue when they actually or constructively receive property or services and they recognize deductions when they actually pay the expense. Taxpayers, including C corporations and partnerships with C corporation partners but not tax shelters, can elect to use the cash method if their average annual gross receipts is $25 million or less. Under this rule, C corporations and partnerships with C corporation partners can elect to use the cash method.
- Under the accrual method, the all-events test requires that income be recognized when all the events have occurred that are necessary to fix the right to receive payments and the amount of the payments can be determined with reasonable accuracy.
- Except for taxpayers who meet the $25 million gross receipts test, the accrual method must be used to account for sales and purchases for businesses where inventories are an income-producing factor.

- Under the accrual method, accrued expenses can be deducted only when the all-events test and the economic performance test both have been met. The application of the economic performance test depends, in part, on the type of business expense.
- Changes in accounting method or accounting period typically require the consent of the IRS and a §481 adjustment to taxable income. A negative adjustment is included in income for the year of change, whereas a positive adjustment is spread over four years.

KEY TERMS

12-month rule (9-15)
accounting methods (9-14)
accounting period (9-13)
all-events test (9-21)
allowance method (9-25)
arm's length amount (9-4)
casualty losses (9-12)
direct write-off method (9-25)
economic performance
    test (9-21)

first-in, first-out (FIFO)
    method (9-19)
fiscal year (9-13)
flow-through entities (9-14)
impermissible accounting
    method (9-27)
last-in, first-out (LIFO) method (9-19)
mixed-motive expenditures (9-8)
ordinary and necessary (9-3)
payment liabilities (9-21)

permissible accounting method (9-27)
personal expenses (9-6)
reasonable in amount (9-4)
recurring item (9-23)
§481 adjustment (9-30)
specific identification method (9-19)
tax year (9-13)
travel expenses (9-9)
uniform cost capitalization
    (UNICAP) rules (9-19)

DISCUSSION QUESTIONS

Discussion Questions are available in Connect®.

LO 9-1 1. What is an "ordinary and necessary" business expenditure?

LO 9-1 2. Explain how cost of goods is treated when a business sells inventory.

LO 9-1 3. Whether a business expense is "reasonable in amount" is often a difficult question. Explain why determining reasonableness is difficult, and describe a circumstance where reasonableness is likely to be questioned by the IRS.

LO 9-1 4. Jake is a professional dog trainer who purchases and trains dogs for use by law enforcement agencies. Last year Jake purchased 500 bags of dog food from a large pet food company at an average cost of $30 per bag. This year, however, Jake purchased 500 bags of dog food from a local pet food company at an average cost of $45 per bag. Under what circumstances would the IRS likely challenge the cost of Jake's dog food as unreasonable?

LO 9-2 5. What kinds of deductions are prohibited as a matter of public policy? Why might Congress deem it important to disallow deductions for expenditures that are against public policy?

LO 9-2 6. Provide an example of an expense associated with the production of tax-exempt income, and explain what might happen if Congress repealed the prohibition against deducting expenses incurred to produce tax-exempt income.

LO 9-2 7. Peggy is a rodeo clown, and this year she expended $1,000 on special "funny" clothes and outfits. Peggy would like to deduct the cost of these clothes as work-related because she refuses to wear the clothes unless she is working. Under what circumstances can Peggy deduct the cost of her clown clothes?

LO 9-2 8. Jimmy is a sole proprietor of a small dry-cleaning business. This month Jimmy paid for his groceries by writing checks from the checking account dedicated to the dry-cleaning business. Why do you suppose Jimmy is using his business checking account rather than his personal checking account to pay for personal expenditures?

LO 9-2 9. Troy operates an editorial service that employs two editors. These editors often entertain authors to encourage them to use Troy's service. This year Troy reimbursed the editors $3,000 for the cost of meals and $6,200 for the cost of entertaining authors. Describe whether Troy can deduct the cost of the meals and entertainment.

10. Jenny uses her car for both business and personal purposes. She purchased the auto this year and drove 11,000 miles on business trips and 9,000 miles for personal transportation. Describe how Jenny will determine the amount of deductible expenses associated with the auto. `LO 9-2`

11. What expenses are deductible when a taxpayer combines both business and personal activities on a trip? How do the rules for international travel differ from the rules for domestic travel? `LO 9-1` `LO 9-2`

12. Clyde lives and operates a sole proprietorship in Dallas, Texas. This year Clyde found it necessary to travel to Fort Worth (about 25 miles away) for legitimate business reasons. Is Clyde's trip likely to qualify as "away from home"? Why would this designation matter? `LO 9-2`

13. Describe the record-keeping requirements for deducting business expenses, including mixed-motive expenditures. `LO 9-2`

14. Describe the computation of the limit placed on the business interest deduction. Is the disallowed interest ever deductible? `LO 9-2`

15. Explain the difference between calculating a loss deduction for a business asset that was partially damaged in an accident and calculating a loss deduction for a business asset that was stolen or completely destroyed in an accident. `LO 9-3`

16. How do casualty loss deductions differ when a business asset, as opposed to a personal-use asset, is completely destroyed? `LO 9-3`

17. What is the difference between a full tax year and a short tax year? Describe circumstances in which a business may have a short tax year. `LO 9-4`

18. Explain why a taxpayer might choose one tax year-end over another if given a choice. `LO 9-4`

19. Compare and contrast the different year-ends available to sole proprietorships, flow-through entities, and C corporations. `LO 9-4`

20. Why does the law generally require partnerships to adopt a tax year consistent with the year used by the partners? `LO 9-4`

21. How does an entity choose its tax year? Is it the same process no matter the type of tax year-end the taxpayer adopts? `LO 9-4`

22. Explain when an expenditure should be "capitalized" based upon accounting principles. From time to time, it is suggested that all business expenditures should be deducted when incurred for tax purposes. Do you agree with this proposition, and if so, why? `LO 9-5`

23. Describe the 12-month rule for determining whether and to what extent businesses should capitalize or immediately deduct prepaid expenses such as insurance or security contracts. Explain the apparent rationale for this rule. `LO 9-5`

24. Explain why Congress sometimes mandates that businesses use particular accounting methods while other times Congress is content to require businesses to use the same accounting methods for tax purposes that they use for financial accounting purposes. `LO 9-5`

25. Why is it not surprising that specific rules differ between tax accounting and financial accounting? `LO 9-5`

26. Fred is considering using the accrual method for his next business venture. Explain to Fred the conditions for recognizing income for tax purposes under the accrual method. `LO 9-5`

27. Describe the all-events test for determining income and describe how to determine the date on which the all-events test has been met. `LO 9-5`

LO 9-5 28. Compare and contrast the tax treatment for rental income received in advance and advance payments for goods and services.

LO 9-5 29. Compare and contrast the rules for determining the tax treatment of advance payments for services versus advance payments for goods.

LO 9-5 30. Jack operates a plumbing business as a sole proprietorship and uses the cash method. Besides providing plumbing services, Jack also sells plumbing supplies to homeowners and other plumbers. The sales of plumbing supplies constitute less than $20,000 per year, and this is such a small portion of Jack's income that he does not keep physical inventories for the supplies. Describe how Jack would account for sales and purchases of plumbing supplies using the accrual method.

LO 9-5 31. Explain why Congress enacted the UNICAP rules and describe the burdens these rules place on taxpayers.

LO 9-5 32. Compare and contrast financial accounting rules with the tax rules under UNICAP (§263A). Explain whether the UNICAP rules tend to accelerate or defer income relative to the financial accounting rules.

LO 9-5 33. Compare and contrast the tests for accruing income and those for accruing deductions for tax purposes.

LO 9-5 34. Compare and contrast when taxpayers are allowed to deduct the cost of warranties provided by others to the taxpayer (i.e., purchased by the taxpayer) and when taxpayers are allowed to deduct the costs associated with warranties they provide (sell) to others.

LO 9-5 35. Describe when economic performance occurs for the following expenses:
    a) Workers' compensation
    b) Rebates and refunds
    c) Insurance, warranties, and service contracts provided *to* the business
    d) Taxes

LO 9-5 36. On December 31 of the current year, a taxpayer prepays an advertising company to provide advertising services for the next 10 months. Using the 12-month rule and the economic performance rules, contrast when the taxpayer would be able to deduct the expenditure if the taxpayer uses the cash method of accounting versus if the taxpayer uses the accrual method of accounting.

LO 9-5 37. Compare and contrast how bad debt expense is determined for financial accounting purposes and how the deduction for bad debts is determined for accrual-method taxpayers. How do cash-method taxpayers determine their bad debt expense for accounts receivable?

LO 9-5 38. Describe the related-person limitation on accrued deductions. What tax savings strategy is this limitation designed to thwart?

LO 9-5 39. What are the relative advantages of the cash and accrual methods of accounting?

LO 9-5 40. Describe how a business adopts a permissible accounting method. Explain whether a taxpayer can adopt an impermissible accounting method.

LO 9-5 41. Describe why the IRS might be skeptical of permitting requests for changes in accounting method without a good business purpose.

LO 9-5 42. What is a §481 adjustment, and what is the purpose of this adjustment?

PROBLEMS

Select problems are available in Connect®.

LO 9-1 43. Manny hired his brother's firm to provide accounting services to his business. During the current year, Manny paid his brother's firm $82,000 for services even though other firms were willing to provide the same services for $40,000. How much of this expenditure, if any, is deductible as an ordinary and necessary business expenditure?

44. Michelle operates a food truck. Indicate the amount (if any) that she can deduct as an ordinary and necessary business deduction in each of the following situations and explain your solution.   `LO 9-1` `LO 9-2`

    a) Michelle moves her food truck between various locations on a daily rotation. Last week, Michelle was stopped for speeding. She paid a fine of $125 for speeding, including $80 for legal advice in connection with the ticket.

    b) Michelle paid $750 to reserve a parking place for her food truck for the fall football season outside the local football arena. Michelle also paid $95 for tickets to a game for her children.

    c) Michelle provided a candidate with free advertising painted on her truck during the candidate's campaign for city council. Michelle paid $500 to have the ad prepared and an additional $200 to have the ad removed from the truck after the candidate lost the election.

45. Indicate the amount (if any) that Josh can deduct as an ordinary and necessary business deduction in each of the following situations and explain your solution.   `LO 9-1` `LO 9-2`

    a) Josh borrowed $50,000 from First State Bank using his business assets as collateral. He used the money to buy City of Blanksville bonds. Over the course of a year, Josh paid interest of $4,200 on the borrowed funds, but he received $3,500 of interest on the bonds.

    b) Josh purchased a piece of land for $45,000 in order to get a location to expand his business. He also paid $3,200 to construct a new driveway for access to the property.

    c) This year Josh paid $15,000 to employ the mayor's son in the business. Josh would typically pay an employee with these responsibilities about $10,000 but the mayor assured Josh that after his son was hired, some city business would be coming his way.

    d) Josh paid his brother, a mechanic, $3,000 to install a robotic machine for Josh's business. The amount he paid to his brother is comparable to what he would have paid to an unrelated person to do the same work. Once the installation was completed by his brother, Josh began calibrating the machine for operation. However, by the end of the year, he had not started using the machine in his business.

46. Ralph operates a business that acts as a sales representative for a large firm that produces and sells precious metals to electronic manufacturers. Ralph contacts manufacturers and convinces them to sign contracts for delivery of metals. Ralph's company earns a commission on the sales. This year, Ralph contacted a jeweler to engrave small lapel buttons for each of his clients. Ralph paid $20 each for the lapel buttons and the jeweler charged Ralph an additional $12 for engraving. The electronic manufacturers, however, prohibit their employees from accepting gifts related to sales contracts. Can Ralph deduct the cost of the lapel buttons as business gifts?   `LO 9-2` `research`

47. Melissa recently paid $400 for round-trip airfare to San Francisco to attend a business conference for three days. Melissa also paid the following expenses: $250 fee to register for the conference, $300 per night for three nights lodging, $200 for meals, and $150 for cab fare.   `LO 9-2`

    a) What amount of the travel costs can Melissa deduct as business expenses?

    b) Suppose that while Melissa was on the coast, she also spent two days sightseeing the national parks in the area. To do the sightseeing, she paid $1,000 for transportation, $800 for lodging, and $450 for meals during this part of her trip, which she considers personal in nature. What amount of the travel costs can Melissa deduct as business expenses?

c) Suppose that Melissa made the trip to San Francisco primarily to visit the national parks and only attended the business conference as an incidental benefit of being present on the coast at that time. What amount of the airfare can Melissa deduct as a business expense?

d) Suppose that Melissa's permanent residence and business was located in San Francisco. She attended the conference in San Francisco and paid $250 for the registration fee. She drove 100 miles over the course of three days and paid $90 for parking at the conference hotel. In addition, she spent $150 for breakfast and dinner over the three days of the conference. She bought breakfast on the way to the conference hotel and she bought dinner on her way home each night from the conference. What amount of the travel costs can Melissa deduct as business expenses?

LO 9-2 48. Kimberly is a self-employed taxpayer. She recently spent $1,000 for airfare to travel to Italy. What amount of the airfare is deductible in each of the following alternative scenarios?

a) Her trip was entirely for personal purposes.

b) On the trip, she spent eight days on personal activities and two days on business activities.

c) On the trip, she spent seven days on business activities and three days on personal activities.

d) Her trip was entirely for business purposes.

LO 9-2 49. Ryan is self-employed. This year Ryan used his personal auto for several long business trips. Ryan paid $1,500 for gasoline on these trips. His depreciation on the car if he was using it fully for business purposes would be $3,000. During the year, he drove his car a total of 12,000 miles (a combination of business and personal travel).

a) Ryan can provide written documentation of the business purpose for trips totaling 3,000 miles. What business expense amount can Ryan deduct (if any) for these trips?

b) Ryan estimates that he drove approximately 1,300 miles on business trips, but he can only provide written documentation of the business purpose for trips totaling 820 miles. What business expense amount can Ryan deduct (if any) for these trips?

LO 9-1 **LO 9-2** 50. Christopher is a cash-method, calendar-year taxpayer, and he made the following cash payments related to his business this year. Calculate the after-tax cost of each payment assuming Christopher has a 37 percent marginal tax rate.

a) $500 fine for speeding while traveling to a client meeting.

b) $800 of interest on a short-term loan incurred in September and repaid in November. Half of the loan proceeds were used immediately to pay salaries and the other half was invested in municipal bonds until November.

c) $600 for office supplies in May of this year. He used half of the supplies this year and he will use the remaining half by February of next year.

d) $450 for several pairs of work boots. Christopher expects to use the boots about 80 percent of the time in his business and the remainder of the time for hiking. Consider the boots to be a form of clothing.

LO 9-2 51. Heather paid $15,000 to join a country club in order to meet potential clients. This year she paid $4,300 in greens fees when golfing with clients and paid an additional $5,700 for meals when Heather business meetings with clients in the clubhouse conference rooms. Under what circumstances, if any, can Heather deduct the $25,000 paid to the country club this year?

52. Assume Sarah is a cash-method, calendar-year taxpayer, and she is considering making the following cash payments related to her business. Calculate the after-tax cost of each payment assuming she is subject to 37 percent marginal tax rate.   **LO 9-1 LO 9-2**

   a) $2,000 payment for next year's property taxes on her place of business.

   b) $800 to reimburse the cost of meals incurred by employees while traveling for the business.

   c) $1,200 for football tickets to entertain out-of-town clients during contract negotiations.

   d) $500 contribution to the mayor's reelection campaign.

53. Renee operates a proprietorship selling collectibles over the web, and last year she purchased a building for $24 million for her business. This year, Renee's proprietorship reported revenue of $85 million and incurred total expenses of $78.1 million. Her expenses included cost of goods sold of $48.5 million, sales commissions paid of $16.9 million, $10.5 million of interest paid on the building mortgage, and $12.7 million of depreciation.   **LO 9-2**

   a. What is Renee's adjusted taxable income for purposes of calculating the limitation on business interest expense?

   b. What is the maximum amount of business interest expense that Renee can deduct this year, and how is the disallowed interest expense (if any) treated?

   c. Suppose that Renee's revenue includes $5 million of business interest income. What is the maximum amount of business interest expense that Renee can deduct this year?

54. This year Amy purchased $2,000 of equipment for use in her business. However, the machine was damaged in a traffic accident while Amy was transporting the equipment to her business. Note that because Amy did not place the equipment into service during the year, she does not claim any depreciation expense for the equipment.   **LO 9-3**

   a) After the accident, Amy had the choice of repairing the equipment for $1,800 or selling the equipment to a junk shop for $300. Amy sold the equipment. What amount can Amy deduct for the loss of the equipment?

   b) After the accident, Amy repaired the equipment for $800. What amount can Amy deduct for the loss of the equipment?

   c) After the accident, Amy could not replace the equipment so she had the equipment repaired for $2,300. What amount can Amy deduct for the loss of the equipment?

55. In July of this year, Stephen started a proprietorship called ECR (which stands for electric car repair). ECR uses the cash method of accounting and Stephen has produced the following financial information for this year: **LO 9-3**

   tax forms

   • ECR collected $81,000 in cash for repairs completed during the year and an additional $3,200 in cash for repairs that will commence after year-end.

   • Customers owe ECR $14,300 for repairs completed this year, and while Stephen isn't sure which bills will eventually be paid, he expects to collect all but about $1,900 of these revenues next year.

   ECR has made the following expenditures:

Interest expense	$ 1,250
Shop rent ($1,500 per month)	27,000
Utilities	1,075
Contract labor	8,250
Compensation	21,100
Liability insurance premiums ($350 per month)	4,200
Term life insurance premiums ($150 per month)	1,800

The interest paid relates to interest accrued on a $54,000 loan made to Stephen in July of this year. Stephen used half of the loan to pay for 18 months of shop rent, and the remainder he used to upgrade his personal wardrobe. In July, Stephen purchased 12 months of liability insurance to protect against liability should anyone be injured in the shop. ECR has only one employee (the remaining workers are contract labor), and this employee thoroughly understands how to repair an electric propulsion system. On November 1 of this year, Stephen purchased a 12-month term-life policy that insures the life of this "key" employee. Stephen paid Gecko Insurance Company $1,800; in return, Gecko promises to pay Stephen a $40,000 death benefit if this employee dies any time during the next 12 months.

Fill out a draft of the front page of Stephen's Schedule C.

LO 9-5

planning

56. Nicole is a calendar-year taxpayer who accounts for her business using the cash method. On average, Nicole sends out bills for about $12,000 of her services at the first of each month. The bills are due by the end of the month, and typically 70 percent of the bills are paid on time and 98 percent are paid within 60 days.

   a) Suppose that Nicole is expecting a 2 percent reduction in her marginal tax rate next year. Ignoring the time value of money, estimate the tax savings for Nicole if she postpones mailing the December bills until January 1 of next year.

   b) Describe how the time value of money affects your calculations.

   c) Would this tax savings strategy create any additional business risks? Explain.

LO 9-5

57. Jeremy is a calendar-year taxpayer who sometimes leases his business equipment to local organizations. He recorded the following receipts this year. Indicate the extent to which these payments are taxable income to Jeremy this year if Jeremy is (1) a cash-method taxpayer and (2) an accrual-method taxpayer.

   a) $1,000 deposit from the Ladies' Club, which wants to lease a trailer. The club will receive the entire deposit back when the trailer is returned undamaged.

   b) $800 from the Ladies' Club for leasing the trailer from December of this year through March of next year ($200 per month).

   c) $300 lease payment received from the Men's Club this year for renting Jeremy's trailer last year. Jeremy billed the club last year but recently he determined that the Men's Club would never pay him, so he was surprised when he received the check.

LO 9-5

58. Brown Thumb Landscaping is a calendar-year, accrual-method taxpayer. In September, Brown Thumb negotiated a $14,000 contract for services it would provide to the city in November of the current year. The contract specifies that Brown Thumb will receive $4,000 in October as a down payment for these services and it will receive the remaining $10,000 in January of next year.

   a) How much income from this $14,000 contract will Brown Thumb recognize in the current year? Explain.

   b) How much income from this $14,000 contract will Brown Thumb recognize in the current year if it uses the cash method of accounting?

   c) Suppose that the total amount to be paid under the contract with the city is estimated at $14,000 but may be adjusted to $12,000 next year during the review of the city budget. What amount from the contract, if any, should Brown Thumb recognize as income this year? Explain.

   d) Suppose that in addition to the basic contract, Brown Thumb will be paid an additional $3,000 if its city landscape design wins the annual design competition next year. Should Brown Thumb accrue $3,000 revenue this year? Why or why not?

LO 9-5

59. In January of year 0, Justin paid $4,800 for an insurance policy that covers his business property for accidents and casualties. Justin is a calendar-year taxpayer who

uses the cash method of accounting. What amount of the insurance premium may Justin deduct in year 0 in each of the following alternative scenarios?

a) The policy covers the business property from April 1 of year 0 through March 31 of year 1.

b) The policy begins on February 1 of year 1 and extends through January 31 of year 2.

c) Justin pays $6,000 for a 24-month policy that covers the business from April 1, year 0, through March 31, year 2.

d) Instead of paying an insurance premium, Justin pays $4,800 to rent his business property from April 1 of year 0 through March 31 of year 1.

60. Ben teaches golf lessons at a country club under a business called Ben's Pure Swings (BPS). He operates this business as a sole proprietorship on the accrual basis of accounting. Use the following accounting information for BPS to complete the firm's Schedule C:

LO 9-5

tax forms

This year BPS billed clients for $86,700 and collected $61,000 in cash for golf lessons completed during the year. In addition, BPS collected an additional $14,500 in cash for lessons that will commence after year-end. Ben hopes to collect about half of the outstanding billings next year but the rest will likely be written off.

Besides providing private golf lessons, BPS also contracted with the country club to staff the driving range. This year, BPS billed the country club $27,200 for the service. The club paid $17,000 of the amount but disputed the remainder. By year-end, the dispute had not been resolved, and while Ben believes he is entitled to the money, he has still not collected the remaining $10,200.

BPS has accrued the following expenses (explained below):

Advertising (in the clubhouse)	$13,150
Pro golf teachers' membership fees	860
Supplies (golf tees, balls, etc.)	4,720
Club rental	6,800
Malpractice insurance	2,400
Accounting fees	8,820

The expenditures were all paid for this calendar year with several exceptions. First, Ben initiated his golfer's malpractice insurance on June 1 of this year. The $2,400 insurance bill covers the last six months of this calendar year and the first six months of next year. At year-end, Ben had only paid $600, but he has assured the insurance agent he will pay the remaining $1,800 early next year. Second, the amount paid for club rental ($100 per week) represents rental charges for the last 6 weeks of the previous year, the 52 weeks in this calendar year, and the first 10 weeks of next year. Ben has also mentioned that BPS only pays for supplies that are used at the club. Although BPS could buy the supplies for half the cost elsewhere, Ben likes to "throw some business" to the golf pro shop because it is operated by his brother.

Fill out a draft of Parts I and II on the front page of a Schedule C for BPS.

61. On April 1 of year 0 Stephanie received a $9,000 payment for full payment on a three-year service contract (under the contract Stephanie is obligated to provide advisory services for the next three years).

LO 9-5

a) What amount of income should Stephanie recognize in year 0 if she uses the accrual method of accounting (she recognized $2,250 for financial accounting purposes)?

b) What amount of income will Stephanie recognize in year 1 if she uses the accrual method of accounting?

c) What amount of income will Stephanie recognize in year 2 if she uses the accrual method of accounting?

d) What amount of income will Stephanie recognize in year 0 if she recognizes $5,000 of income from the contract for financial statement purposes?

LO 9-5 62. In October of year 0, Janine received a $6,000 payment from a client for 25 months of security services she will provide starting on November 1 of year 0. This amounts to $240 per month.

a) When must Janine recognize the income from the $6,000 advance payment for services if she uses the cash method of accounting?

b) When must Janine recognize the income from the $6,000 advance payment for services if she uses the accrual method of accounting?

c) Suppose that instead of services, Janine received the payment for a security system (inventory) that she will deliver and install in year 2. When would Janine recognize the income from the advance payment for inventory sale if she uses the accrual method of accounting and she elects to use the deferral method for reporting income from advance payments? For financial accounting purposes, she reports the income when the inventory is delivered.

d) Suppose that instead of services, Janine received the payment for inventory to be delivered next year. When would Janine recognize the income from the advance payment for sale of goods if she uses the accrual method of accounting and she does not elect to use the deferral method for advance payments?

LO 9-5 63. Nicole's business uses the accrual method of accounting and accounts for inventory with specific identification. In year 0, Nicole received a $4,500 payment with an order for inventory to be delivered to the client early next year. Nicole has the inventory ready for delivery at the end of year 0 (she purchased the inventory in year 0 for $2,300).

a) When does Nicole recognize the $2,200 of gross profit ($4,500 revenue minus $2,300 cost of the inventory) if she does not elect to use the deferral method?

b) When does Nicole recognize the $2,200 of gross profit from the inventory sale if she elects to use the deferral method?

c) How would Nicole account for the inventory-related transactions if she uses the cash method of accounting and her annual sales are usually less than $100,000?

d) How would Nicole account for the inventory-related transactions if she uses the cash method of accounting and her annual sales are usually over 50 million per year?

LO 9-5 64. This year Amber purchased a factory to process and package landscape mulch. Approximately 20 percent of management time, space, and expenses are spent on this manufacturing process.

		Costs (in thousands)	Tax Inventory
Material:	Mulch and packaging	$ 5,000	?
	Administrative supplies	250	?
Salaries:	Factory labor	12,000	?
	Sales & advertising	3,500	?
	Administration	5,200	?
Property taxes:	Factory	4,600	?
	Offices	2,700	?
Depreciation:	Factory	8,000	?
	Offices	1,500	?

a) At the end of the year, Amber's accountant indicated that the business had processed 10 million bags of mulch but only 1 million bags remained in the ending inventory. What is Amber's tax basis in her ending inventory if the UNICAP rules are used to allocate indirect costs to inventory? (Assume direct costs are allocated to inventory according to the level of ending inventory. In contrast, indirect costs are first allocated by time spent and then according to level of ending inventory.)

b) Under what conditions could Amber's business avoid having to apply UNICAP rules to allocate indirect costs to inventory for tax purposes?

65. Suppose that David has elected to account for inventories and has adopted the last-in, first-out (LIFO) inventory-flow method for his business inventory of widgets (purchase prices below).

Widget	Purchase Date	Direct Cost	Other Costs	Total Cost
#1	August 15	$2,100	$100	$2,200
#2	October 30	2,200	150	2,350
#3	November 10	2,300	100	2,400

In late December, David sold widget #2 and next year David expects to purchase three more widgets at the following estimated prices:

Widget	Purchase Date	Estimated Cost
#4	Early spring	$2,600
#5	Summer	2,260
#6	Fall	2,400

a) What cost of goods sold and ending inventory would David record if he elects to use the LIFO method this year?

b) If David sells two widgets next year, what will be his cost of goods sold and ending inventory next year under the LIFO method?

c) How would you answer (a) and (b) if David had initially selected the first-in, first-out (FIFO) method instead of LIFO?

d) Suppose that David initially adopted the LIFO method, but wants to apply for a change to FIFO next year. What would be his §481 adjustment for this change, and in what year(s) would he make the adjustment?

66. On November 1 of year 0, Jaxon borrowed $50,000 from Bucksnort Savings and Loan for use in his business. In December, Jaxon paid interest of $4,500 relating to the 12-month period from November of year 0 through October of year 1.

a) How much interest, if any, can Jaxon deduct in year 0 if his business uses the cash method of accounting for tax purposes?

b) How much interest, if any, can Jaxon deduct in year 0 if his business uses the accrual method of accounting for tax purposes?

67. Matt hired Apex Services to repair his business equipment. On November 1 of year 0, Matt paid $2,000 for the repairs that he expects to begin in early March of year 1.

a) What amount of the cost of the repairs can Matt deduct in year 0 if he uses the cash method of accounting for his business?

b) What amount of the cost of the repairs can Matt deduct in year 0 if he uses the accrual method of accounting for his business?

c) What amount of the cost of the repairs can Matt deduct in year 0 if he uses the accrual method and he expects the repairs to be done by early February?

d) What amount of the cost of the repairs can Matt deduct in year 0 if he uses the cash method of accounting and he expects the repairs to be done by early February?

LO 9-5   68. Circuit Corporation (CC) is a calendar-year, accrual-method taxpayer. CC manufactures and sells electronic circuitry. On November 15, year 0, CC enters into a contract with Equip Corp (EC) that provides CC with exclusive use of EC's specialized manufacturing equipment for the five-year period beginning on January 1 of year 1. Pursuant to the contract, CC pays EC $100,000 on December 30, year 0. How much of this expenditure is CC allowed to deduct in year 0 and in year 1?

LO 9-5   69. This year (year 0) Elizabeth agreed to a three-year service contract with an engineering consulting firm to improve efficiency in her factory. The contract requires Elizabeth to pay the consulting firm $1,500 for each instance that Elizabeth requests its assistance. The contract also provides that Elizabeth only pays the consultants if their advice increases efficiency as measured 12 months from the date of service. This year Elizabeth requested advice on three occasions and she has not yet made any payments to the consultants.

a) How much should Elizabeth deduct in year 0 under this service contract if she uses the accrual method of accounting?

b) How much should Elizabeth deduct in year 0 under this service contract if she uses the cash method of accounting?

LO 9-5   70. Travis is a professional landscaper. He provides his clients with a one-year (12-month) warranty for retaining walls he installs. In June of year 1, Travis installed a wall for an important client, Sheila. In early November, Sheila informed Travis that the retaining wall had failed. To repair the wall, Travis paid $700 cash for additional stone that he delivered to Sheila's location. Travis also offered to pay a mason $800 to repair the wall on November 20 of year 1. Due to some bad weather and the mason's work backlog, the mason agreed to finish the work by the end of January of year 2. Even though Travis expected the mason to finish the project by the end of February, Travis informed the mason that he would pay the mason the $800 when he completed the job.

a) Assuming Travis is an accrual-method taxpayer, how much can he deduct in year 1 from these activities?

b) Assuming Travis is a cash-method taxpayer, how much can he deduct in year 1 from these activities?

LO 9-5

research

71. Adam elects the accrual method of accounting for his business. What amount of deductions does Adam recognize in year 0 for the following transactions?

a) Adam guarantees that he will refund the cost of any goods sold to a client if the goods fail within a year of delivery. In December of year 0, Adam agreed to refund $2,400 to clients, and he expects to make payment in January of year 1.

b) On December 1 of year 0, Adam paid $480 for a one-year contract with CleanUP Services to clean his store. The agreement calls for services to be provided on a weekly basis.

c) Adam was billed $240 for annual personal property taxes on his delivery van. Because this was the first time Adam was billed for these taxes, he did not make payment until January. However, he considers the amounts immaterial.

LO 9-5   72. Rebecca is a calendar-year taxpayer who operates a business. She made the following business-related expenditures in December of year 0. Indicate the amount of these payments that she may deduct in year 0 under both the cash method of accounting and the accrual method of accounting.

a) $2,000 for an accountant to evaluate the accounting system of Rebecca's business. The accountant spent three weeks in January of year 1 working on the evaluation.

b) $2,500 for new office furniture. The furniture was delivered on January 15, year 1.

c) $3,000 for property taxes payable on her factory.

d) $1,500 for interest on a short-term bank loan relating to the period from November 1, year 0, through March 31, year 1.

73. BCS Corporation is a calendar-year, accrual-method taxpayer. BCS was formed and started its business activities on January 1, year 0. It reported the following information for year 0. Indicate BCS's deductible amount for year 0 in each of the following alternative scenarios.   `LO 9-5`

a) BCS provides two-year warranties on products it sells to customers. For its year 0 sales, BCS estimated and accrued $200,000 in warranty expense for financial accounting purposes. During year 0, BCS actually spent $30,000 repairing its product under the warranty.

b) BCS accrued an expense for $50,000 for amounts it anticipated it would be required to pay under the workers' compensation act. During year 0, BCS actually paid $10,000 for workers' compensation–related liabilities.

c) In June of year 0, a display of BCS's product located in its showroom fell and injured a customer. The customer sued BCS for $500,000. The case is scheduled to go to trial next year. BCS anticipates that it will lose the case and accrued a $500,000 expense on its financial statements.

d) Assume the same facts as in (c) except that BCS was required to pay $500,000 to a court-appointed escrow fund in year 0. If BCS loses the case in year 1, the money from the escrow fund will be transferred to the customer suing BCS.

e) On December 1 of year 0, BCS acquired equipment from Equip Company. As part of the purchase, BCS signed a warranty agreement with Equip so that Equip would warranty the equipment for two years (from December 1 of year 0 through November 30 of year 2). The cost of the warranty was $12,000. BCS paid Equip for the warranty in January of year 1.

74. This year William provided $4,200 of services to a large client on credit. Unfortunately, this client has recently encountered financial difficulties and has been unable to pay William for the services. Moreover, William does not expect to collect for his services. William has "written off" the account and would like to claim a deduction for tax purposes.   `LO 9-5`

a) What amount of deduction for bad debt expense can William claim this year if he uses the accrual method?

b) What amount of deduction for bad debt expense can William claim this year if he uses the cash method?

75. Dustin has a contract to provide services to Dado Enterprises. In November of year 0, Dustin billed Dado $10,000 for the services he rendered during the year. Dado is an accrual-method proprietorship that is owned and operated by Dustin's father.   `LO 9-5`

a) What amount of revenue must Dustin recognize in year 0 if Dustin uses the cash method and Dado remits payment for the services in December of year 0? What amount can Dado deduct in year 0?

b) What amount of revenue must Dustin recognize in year 0 if Dustin uses the accrual method and Dado remits payment for the services in December of year 0? What amount can Dado deduct in year 0?

c) What amount of revenue must Dustin recognize in year 0 if Dustin uses the cash method and Dado remits payment for the services in January of year 1? What amount can Dado deduct in year 0?

d) What amount of revenue must Dustin recognize in year 0 if Dustin uses the accrual method and Dado remits payment for the services in January of year 1? What amount can Dado deduct in year 0?

LO 9-5 76. Nancy operates a business that uses the accrual method of accounting. In December, Nancy asked her brother, Hank, to provide her business with consulting advice. Hank billed Nancy for $5,000 of consulting services in year 0 (a reasonable amount), but Nancy was only able to pay $3,000 of the bill by the end of year 0. However, Nancy paid the remainder of the bill in year 1.

a) How much of the $5,000 consulting services will Hank include in his income in year 0 if he uses the cash method of accounting? What amount can Nancy deduct in year 0 for the consulting services?

b) How much of the $5,000 consulting services will Hank include in his income in year 0 if he uses the accrual method of accounting? What amount can Nancy deduct in year 0 for the consulting services?

LO 9-5 77. Erin is considering switching her business from the cash method to the accrual method at the beginning of next year (year 1). Determine the amount and timing of her §481 adjustment assuming the IRS grants Erin's request in the following alternative scenarios.

a) At the end of year 0/beginning of year 1, Erin's business has $15,000 of accounts receivable and $18,000 of accounts payable that have not been recorded for tax purposes.

b) At the end of year 0/beginning of year 1, Erin's business reports $25,000 of accounts receivable and $9,000 of accounts payable that have not been recorded for tax purposes.

COMPREHENSIVE PROBLEMS

Select problems are available in Connect®.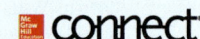

78. Joe operates a business that locates and purchases specialized assets for clients, among other activities. Joe uses the accrual method of accounting but he doesn't keep any significant inventories of the specialized assets that he sells. Joe reported the following financial information for his business activities during year 0. Determine the effect of each of the following transactions on the taxable business income.

a) Joe has signed a contract to sell gadgets to the city. The contract provides that sales of gadgets are dependent upon a test sample of gadgets operating successfully. In December, Joe delivers $12,000 worth of gadgets to the city that will be tested in March. Joe purchased the gadgets especially for this contract and paid $8,500.

b) Joe paid $180 for entertaining a visiting out-of-town client. The client didn't discuss business with Joe during this visit, but Joe wants to maintain good relations to encourage additional business next year.

c) On November 1, Joe paid $600 for premiums providing for $40,000 of "key man" insurance on the life of Joe's accountant over the next 12 months.

d) At the end of year 0, Joe's business reports $9,000 of accounts receivable. Based upon past experience, Joe believes that at least $2,000 of his new receivables will be uncollectible.

e) In December of year 0, Joe rented equipment to complete a large job. Joe paid $3,000 in December because the rental agency required a minimum rental of three months ($1,000 per month). Joe completed the job before year-end, but he returned the equipment at the end of the lease.

f) Joe hired a new sales representative as an employee and sent her to Dallas for a week to contact prospective out-of-state clients. Joe ended up reimbursing his employee $300 for airfare, $350 for lodging, and $250 for meals (Joe provided adequate documentation to substantiate the business purpose for the meals). Joe requires the employee to account for all expenditures in order to be reimbursed.

g) Joe uses his BMW (a personal auto) to travel to and from his residence to his factory. However, he switches to a business vehicle if he needs to travel after he reaches the factory. Last month, the business vehicle broke down and he was forced to use the BMW both to travel to and from the factory and to visit work sites. He drove 120 miles visiting work sites and 46 miles driving to and from the factory from his home. Joe uses the standard mileage rate to determine his auto-related business expenses.

h) Joe paid a visit to his parents in Dallas over the Christmas holidays. While he was in the city, Joe spent $50 to attend a half-day business symposium. Joe paid $200 for airfare, $50 for meals during the symposium, and $20 on cab fare to the symposium.

79. Jack, a geologist, had been debating for years whether or not to venture out on his own and operate his own business. He had developed a lot of solid relationships with clients and he believed that many of them would follow him if he were to leave his current employer. As part of a New Year's resolution, Jack decided he would finally do it. Jack put his business plan together and, on January 1 of this year, Jack opened his doors for business as a C corporation called Geo-Jack (GJ). Jack is the sole shareholder. Jack reported the following financial information for the year (assume GJ reports on a calendar year, uses the accrual method of accounting and elects to account for inventory).

a) In January, GJ rented a small business office about 12 miles from Jack's home. GJ paid $10,000, which represented a damage deposit of $4,000 and rent for two years ($3,000 annually).

b) GJ earned and collected $290,000 performing geological-related services and selling its specialized digging tool [see part (i)].

c) GJ received $50 interest from municipal bonds and $2,100 interest from other investments.

d) GJ purchased some new equipment in February for $42,500. It claimed depreciation on these assets during the year in the amount of $6,540.

e) GJ paid $7,000 to buy luxury season tickets for Jack's parents for State U football games.

f) GJ paid Jack's father $10,000 for services that would have cost no more than $6,000 if Jack had hired any other local business to perform the services. While Jack's dad was competent, he does not command such a premium from his other clients.

g) In an attempt to get his name and new business recognized, GJ paid $7,000 for a one-page ad in the *Geologic Survey*. It also paid $15,000 in radio ads to be run through the end of December.

h) GJ leased additional office space in a building downtown. GJ paid rent of $27,000 for the year.

i) In November, Jack's office was broken into and equipment valued at $5,000 was stolen. The tax basis of the equipment was $5,500. Jack received $2,000 of insurance proceeds from the theft.

j) GJ incurred a $4,000 fine from the state government for digging in an unauthorized digging zone.

k) GJ contributed $3,000 to lobbyists for their help in persuading the state government to authorize certain unauthorized digging zones.

l) On July 1, GJ paid $1,800 for an 18-month insurance policy for its business equipment. The policy covers the period July 1 of this year through December 31 of next year.

m) GJ borrowed $20,000 to help with the company's initial funding needs. GJ used $2,000 of funds to invest in municipal bonds. At the end of the year, GJ paid the $1,200 of interest expense that accrued on the loan during the year.

n) Jack lives 12 miles from the office. He carefully tracked his mileage and drove his truck 6,280 miles between the office and his home. He also drove an additional 7,200 miles between the office and traveling to client sites. Jack did not use the truck for any other purposes. He did not keep track of the specific expenses associated with the truck. However, while traveling to a client site, Jack received a $150 speeding ticket. GJ reimbursed Jack for business mileage and for the speeding ticket.

o) GJ purchased two season tickets (20 games) to attend State U baseball games for a total of $1,100. Jack took existing and prospective clients to the games to maintain contact and find further work. This was very successful for Jack as GJ gained many new projects through substantial discussions with the clients following the games.

p) GJ reimbursed employee-salespersons $3,500 for meals involving substantial business discussion.

q) GJ had a client who needed Jack to perform work in Florida. Because Jack had never been to Florida before, he booked an extra day and night for sightseeing. Jack spent $400 for airfare and booked a hotel for three nights ($120/night). (Jack stayed two days for business purposes and one day for personal purposes.) He also rented a car for $45 per day. The client arranged for Jack's meals while Jack was doing business. GJ reimbursed Jack for all expenses.

r) GJ paid a total of $10,000 of wages to employees during the year and cost of goods sold was $15,000.

Required:

a) What is GJ's net business income for tax purposes for the year?

b) As a C corporation, does GJ have a required tax year? If so, what would it be?

c) If GJ were a sole proprietorship, would it have a required tax year-end? If so, what would it be?

d) If GJ were an S corporation, would it have a required tax year-end? If so, what would it be?

80. Rex loves to work with his hands and is very good at making small figurines. Three years ago, Rex opened Bronze Age Miniatures (BAM) for business as a sole proprietorship. BAM produces miniature characters ranging from sci-fi characters (his favorite) to historical characters like George Washington (the most popular). Business has been going very well for him, and he has provided the following information relating to his business. Calculate the business taxable income for BAM assuming that BAM elects to account for their inventory of miniatures.

a) Rex received approval from the IRS to switch from the cash method of accounting to the accrual method of accounting effective January 1 of this year. At the end of last year, BAM reported accounts receivable that had not been included in income under the accrual method of $14,000 and accounts payable that had not been deducted under the accrual method of $5,000.

b) In March, BAM sold 5,000 miniature historical figures to History R Us Inc. (HRU), a retailer of historical artifacts and figurines, for $75,000.

c) HRU was so impressed with the figurines that it purchased in March that it wanted to contract with BAM to continue to produce the figurines for it for the next three years. HRU paid BAM $216,000 ($12 per figurine) on October 30 of this year, to produce 500 figurines per month for 36 months beginning on November 1 of this year. BAM delivered 500 figurines on November 30 and again on December 30. Rex elects to use the deferral method to account for the transaction.

d) Though the sci-fi figurines were not quite as popular, BAM sold 400 figurines at a sci-fi convention in April. Rex accepted cash only and received $11,000 for these sales.

e) In January, BAM determined that it would not be able to collect on $2,000 of its beginning-of-the-year receivables, so it wrote off $2,000 of specific receivables. BAM sold 100,000 other figurines on credit for $120,000. BAM estimates that it will be unable to collect 5 percent of the sales revenue from these sales but it has not been able to specifically identify any accounts to write off.

f) Assume that BAM correctly determined that its cost of goods sold using an appropriate inventory method is $54,000 this year.

g) The sci-fi convention in April was held in Chicago, Illinois. Rex attended the convention because he felt it was a good opportunity to gain new customers and to get new ideas for figurines. He paid $350 round-trip airfare, $100 for entrance to the convention, $210 for lodging, $65 for cab fare, and $110 for meals during the trip. He was busy with business activities the entire trip.

h) On August 1, BAM purchased a 12-month insurance policy that covers its business property for accidents and casualties through July 31 of next year. The policy cost BAM $3,600.

i) BAM reported depreciation expense of $8,200 for this year.

j) Rex had previously operated his business out of his garage, but in January he decided to rent a larger space. He entered into a lease agreement on February 1 and paid $14,400 ($1,200 per month) to possess the space for the next 12 months (February of this year through January of next year).

k) Before he opened his doors for business, Rex spent $30,000 investigating and otherwise getting ready to do business. He expensed $5,000 immediately and is amortizing the remainder using the straight-line method over 180 months.

l) In December, BAM agreed to a 12-month, $8,000 contract with Advertise-With-Us (AWU) to produce a radio ad campaign. BAM paid $3,000 up front (in December of this year) and AWU agreed that BAM would owe the remaining $5,000 only if BAM's sales increased by 15 percent over the 9-month period after the contract was signed.

m) In November of this year, BAM paid $2,500 in business property taxes (based on asset values) covering the period December 1 of this year through November 30 of next year. In November of last year, BAM paid $1,500 for business property taxes (based on asset values) covering the period December 1 of last year through November 30 of this year.

81. Bryan followed in his father's footsteps and entered into the carpet business. He owns and operates I Do Carpet (IDC). Bryan prefers to install carpet only, but in order to earn additional revenue, he also cleans carpets and sells carpet-cleaning supplies. Compute his taxable income for the current year considering the following items:

a) IDC contracted with a homebuilder in December of last year to install carpet in 10 new homes being built. The contract price of $80,000 includes $50,000 for materials (carpet). The remaining $30,000 is for IDC's service of installing the carpet. The contract also stated that all money was to be paid up front. The homebuilder paid IDC in full on December 28 of last year. The contract required IDC to complete the work by January 31 of this year. Bryan purchased the necessary carpet on January 2 and began working on the first home January 4. He completed the last home on January 27 of this year.

b) IDC entered into several other contracts this year and completed the work before year-end. The work cost $130,000 in materials and IDC elects to immediately deduct supplies. Bryan billed out $240,000 but only collected $220,000 by year-end. Of the $20,000 still owed to him, Bryan wrote off $3,000 he didn't expect to collect as a bad debt from a customer experiencing extreme financial difficulties.

c) IDC entered into a three-year contract to clean the carpets of an office building. The contract specified that IDC would clean the carpets monthly from July 1 of this year through June 30 three years hence. IDC received payment in full of $8,640 ($240 a month for 36 months) on June 30 of this year.

d) IDC sold 100 bottles of carpet stain remover this year for $5 per bottle (it collected $500). Rex sold 40 bottles on June 1 and 60 bottles on November 2. IDC had the following carpet-cleaning supplies on hand for this year, and IDC has elected to use the LIFO method of accounting for inventory under a perpetual inventory system:

Purchase Date	Bottles	Total Cost
November last year	40	$120
February this year	35	112
July this year	25	85
August this year	40	140
Totals	140	$457

e) On August 1 of this year, IDC needed more room for storage and paid $900 to rent a garage for 12 months.

f) On November 30 of this year, Bryan decided it was time to get his logo on the sides of his work van. IDC hired We Paint Anything Inc. (WPA) to do the job. It paid $500 down and agreed to pay the remaining $1,500 upon completion of the job. WPA indicated it wouldn't be able to begin the job until January 15 of next year, but the job would only take one week to complete. Due to circumstances beyond its control, WPA wasn't able to complete the job until April 1 of next year, at which time IDC paid the remaining $1,500.

g) In December, Bryan's son, Aiden, helped him finish some carpeting jobs. IDC owed Aiden $600 (reasonable) compensation for his work. However, Aiden did not receive the payment until January of next year.

h) IDC also paid $1,000 for interest on a short-term bank loan relating to the period from November 1 of this year through March 31 of next year.

82. Hank started a new business, Hank's Donut World (HW for short), in June of last year. He has requested your advice on the following specific tax matters associated with HW's first year of operations. Hank has estimated HW's income for the first year as follows:

Revenue:		
Donut sales	$252,000	
Catering revenues	71,550	$323,550
Expenditures:		
Donut supplies	$124,240	
Catering expense	27,910	
Salaries to shop employees	52,500	
Rent expense	40,050	
Accident insurance premiums	8,400	
Other business expenditures	6,850	−259,950
Net income		$ 63,600

HW operates as a sole proprietorship and Hank reports on a calendar year. Hank uses the cash method of accounting and plans to do the same with HW (HW has no inventory of donuts because unsold donuts are not salable). HW does not purchase donut supplies on credit nor does it generally make sales on credit. Hank has provided the following details for specific first-year transactions.

- A small minority of HW clients complained about the catering service. To mitigate these complaints, Hank's policy is to refund dissatisfied clients 50 percent of the catering fee. By the end of the first year, only two HW clients had complained but had not yet been paid refunds. The expected refunds amount to $1,700, and Hank reduced the reported catering fees for the first year to reflect the expected refund.

- In the first year, HW received a $6,750 payment from a client for catering a monthly breakfast for 30 consecutive months beginning in December. Because the payment didn't relate to last year, Hank excluded the entire amount when he calculated catering revenues.

- In July, HW paid $1,500 to ADMAN Co. for an advertising campaign to distribute fliers advertising HW's catering service. Unfortunately, this campaign violated a city code restricting advertising by fliers, and the city fined HW $250 for the violation. HW paid the fine, and Hank included the fine and the cost of the campaign in "other business" expenditures.

- In July, HW also paid $8,400 for a 24-month insurance policy that covers HW for accidents and casualties beginning on August 1 of the first year. Hank deducted the entire $8,400 as accident insurance premiums.

- In May of the first year, Hank signed a contract to lease the HW donut shop for 10 months. In conjunction with the contract, Hank paid $2,000 as a damage deposit and $8,050 for rent ($805 per month). Hank explained that the damage deposit was refundable at the end of the lease. At this time, Hank also paid $30,000 to lease kitchen equipment for 24 months ($1,250 per month). Both leases began on June 1 of the first year. In his estimate, Hank deducted these amounts ($40,050 in total) as rent expense.

- Hank signed a contract hiring WEGO Catering to help cater breakfasts. At year-end, WEGO asked Hank to hold the last catering payment for the year, $9,250, until after January 1 (apparently because WEGO didn't want to report the income on its tax return). The last check was delivered to WEGO in January after the end of the first year. However, because the payment related to the first year of operations, Hank included the $9,250 in last year's catering expense.

- Hank believes that the key to the success of HW has been hiring Jimbo Jones to supervise the donut production and manage the shop. Because Jimbo is such an important employee, HW purchased a "key-employee" term-life insurance policy on his life. HW paid a $5,100 premium for this policy and it will pay HW a $40,000 death benefit if Jimbo passes away any time during the next 12 months. The term of the policy began on September 1 of last year and this payment was included in "other business" expenditures.

- In the first year, HW catered a large breakfast event to celebrate the city's anniversary. The city agreed to pay $7,100 for the event, but Hank forgot to notify the city of the outstanding bill until January of this year. When he mailed the bill in January, Hank decided to discount the charge to $5,500. On the bill, Hank thanked the mayor and the city council for their patronage and asked them to "send a little more business our way." This bill is not reflected in Hank's estimate of HW's income for the first year of operations.

Required:

a) Hank files his personal tax return on a calendar year, but he has not yet filed last year's personal tax return nor has he filed a tax return reporting HW's results for the first year of operations. Explain when Hank should file the tax return for HW and calculate the amount of taxable income generated by HW last year.

b) Determine the taxable income that HW will generate if Hank chooses to account for the business under the accrual method.

c) Describe how your solution might change if Hank incorporated HW before he commenced business last year.

83. R.E.M., a calendar-year corporation and Athens, Georgia, band, recently sold tickets ($20,000,000) for concerts scheduled in the United States for next year and the following two years. For financial statement purposes, R.E.M. will recognize the income from the ticket sales when it performs the concerts, and R.E.M is obligated to return the ticket payments should a concert be cancelled. For tax purposes, R.E.M. uses the accrual method and would prefer to defer the income from the ticket sales until after the concerts are performed. This is the first time that it has sold tickets one or two years in advance. Michael Stipe has asked your advice. Write a memo to Michael explaining your findings.

Sample CPA Exam questions from Roger CPA Review are available in Connect as support for the topics in this text. These Multiple Choice Questions and Task-Based Simulations include expert-written explanations and solutions and provide a starting point for students to become familiar with the content and functionality of the actual CPA Exam.

chapter

10

Property Acquisition and Cost Recovery

Learning Objectives

Upon completing this chapter, you should be able to:

LO 10-1 Describe the cost recovery methods for recovering the cost of personal property, real property, intangible assets, and natural resources.

LO 10-2 Determine the applicable cost recovery (depreciation) life, method, and convention for tangible personal and real property and the deduction allowable under basic MACRS.

LO 10-3 Calculate the deduction allowable under the additional special cost recovery rules (§179, bonus, and listed property).

LO 10-4 Calculate the deduction for amortization.

LO 10-5 Explain cost recovery of natural resources and the allowable depletion methods.

©Brand X Pictures/Superstock

Storyline Summary

Taxpayer: Teton Mountaineering Technology, LLC (Teton)—a calendar-year single-member LLC (treated as a sole proprietorship for tax purposes)

Location: Cody, Wyoming

President/ Founder: Steve Dallimore

Current situation: Teton has acquired property for its manufacturing operations and wants to understand the tax consequences of property acquisitions.

S everal years ago while climbing the Black Ice Couloir (pronounced "cool-wahr") in Grand Teton National Park, Steve Dallimore and his buddy got into a desperate situation. The climbers planned to move fast and light and to be home before an approaching storm reached the Teton. But just shy of the summit, climbing conditions forced them to turn back. Huddled in a wet sleeping bag in a dark snow cave waiting for the tempest to pass, Steve had an epiphany—he conceived of a design for a better ice-climbing tool. Since that moment, Steve has been working toward making his dream—designing and selling his own line of climbing equipment—a reality. Steve spent the next few years planning his business while continuing his current sales career. In December 2016, Steve decided to exercise his stock options, leave his sales position, and start Teton Mountaineering Technology (Teton). At the beginning of 2017, Steve identified a location for his business in Cody, Wyoming, and purchased a building and some equipment to begin his business. He soon discovered the he needed help dealing with the tax issues related to his business assets.

to be continued . . .

Steve obviously has many issues to resolve and decisions to make. In this chapter, we focus on the tax issues relating to the assets Steve acquires for use in his new business. In particular, we explain how Teton determines its cost recovery (depreciation, amortization, and depletion) deductions for the assets in the year the business begins and in subsequent years.[1] These deductions can generate significant tax savings for companies in capital-intensive industries.

This chapter explores the tax consequences of acquiring new or used property, depreciation methods businesses may use to recover the cost of their assets, and other special cost recovery incentives. The Tax Cuts and Jobs Act made many changes to the way taxpayers will determine their depreciation deductions. Although these changes dramatically accelerate the depreciation deductions for many assets, they do not apply to all assets. Therefore, it is still important to understand the basic depreciation rules as we discuss in more detail later in the chapter. To begin, we discuss the amount that is subject to cost recovery. We then discuss the basic depreciation rules, followed by the special incentives. We also address the tax consequences of using intangible assets and natural resources in business activities.

LO 10-1

COST RECOVERY AND TAX BASIS FOR COST RECOVERY

Most businesses make a significant investment in property, plant, and equipment that is expected to provide benefits over a number of years. For both financial accounting and generally for tax accounting purposes, businesses must capitalize the cost of assets with a useful life of more than one year (on the balance sheet) rather than expense the cost immediately. Businesses are allowed to use various methods to allocate the cost of these assets over time because the assets are subject to wear, tear, and obsolescence.

The method of **cost recovery** depends on the nature of the underlying asset. **Depreciation** is the method of deducting the cost of *tangible* personal and real property (other than land) over time. **Amortization** is the method of deducting the cost of **intangible assets** over time. Finally, **depletion** is the method of deducting the cost of natural resources over time. Exhibit 10-1 summarizes these concepts.

Generally, a significant portion of a firm's assets consists of property, plant, equipment, intangibles, or even natural resources. In most cases, this holds true for small businesses like Teton and also for large publicly traded companies. For example, Exhibit 10-2 describes the assets held by Weyerhaeuser, a publicly traded timber company. As indicated in Exhibit 10-2, Weyerhaeuser has over $1.5 billion in property and equipment (net of depreciation) and $14.3 billion in timber (net of depletion), together comprising roughly 80 percent of its assets.

Businesses must choose accounting methods for the assets acquired during the year. Attention to detail is important because the **tax basis** of an asset must be reduced by the cost recovery deductions allowed or *allowable*.[2] This means that if a business fails to deduct (by mistake or error) the allowable amount of depreciation for the year, the business still must reduce the asset's tax basis by the depreciation the taxpayer could have deducted under the method the business is using to depreciate the asset. This means that the business will never receive a tax benefit for the amount of depreciation it failed to deduct.

EXHIBIT 10-1   Assets and Cost Recovery

Asset Type	Cost Recovery Method
Personal property comprises tangible assets such as automobiles, equipment, and machinery.	Depreciation
Real property comprises buildings and land (although land is nondepreciable).	Depreciation
Intangible assets are nonphysical assets such as goodwill and patents.	Amortization
Natural resources are commodities that are considered valuable in their natural form such as oil, coal, timber, and gold.	Depletion

---

[1]Cost recovery is the common term used to describe the process by which businesses allocate the cost of their fixed assets over the time period in which the assets are used.

[2]If a business discovers that it failed to claim allowable depreciation in a previous year, it can deduct the depreciation it failed to claim in prior years in the current year by filing an automatic consent to a change in accounting method using Form 3115 (Rev. Procs. 2002-9, 2004-11, and 2015-14).

EXHIBIT 10-2   Weyerhaeuser Assets

Assets (in millions) per 2016 10-K Statement	2016	2015
Total current assets	$ 1,622	$ 3,639
Property and equipment, net (Note 7)	1,562	1,233
Construction in progress	213	144
Timber and timberlands at cost, less depletion charged to disposals	14,299	6,552
Minerals and mineral rights, less depletion	319	14
Investments in and advances to equity affiliates (Note 8)	56	—
Goodwill	40	40
Deferred tax assets (Note 19)	293	254
Restricted assets held by special purpose entities (Note 8)	615	615
Other	224	229
Total assets	$19,243	$12,720

Basis for Cost Recovery

Businesses may begin recouping the cost of purchased business assets once they begin using the asset in their business (place it in service).[3] Once the business establishes its cost in an asset, the business recovers the cost of the asset through cost recovery deductions such as depreciation, amortization, or depletion. The amount of an asset's cost that has yet to be recovered through cost recovery deductions is called the asset's **adjusted basis** or **tax basis**.[4] An asset's adjusted basis can be computed by subtracting the accumulated depreciation (or amortization or depletion) from the asset's initial cost or historical basis.[5]

For most assets, the initial basis is the cost plus all the expenses to purchase, prepare for use, and begin using the asset. These expenses include sales tax, shipping costs, and installation costs. The financial accounting and tax rules for computing an asset's basis are very similar. Thus, a purchased asset's initial basis is generally the same for both tax and book purposes.[6] So how do taxpayers know whether they should immediately deduct the cost of an asset or capitalize and depreciate it? Taxpayers generally capitalize assets with useful lives over one year, but there are exceptions to this rule. The Treasury has issued regulations that are quite lengthy (over 200 pages) and complex to guide taxpayers in answering this question.[7] The regulations provide a *de minimis* safe harbor that allows taxpayers to

THE KEY FACTS

Cost Basis

- An asset's cost basis includes all costs needed to purchase the asset, prepare it for use, and begin using it.
- Cost basis is usually the same for book and tax purposes.
- Special basis rules apply when personal-use assets are converted to business use and when assets are acquired through nontaxable transactions, gifts, or inheritances.

---

[3]Basis is defined under §1012. The mere purchase of an asset does not trigger cost recovery deductions. A business must begin using the asset for business purposes (place it in service) in order to depreciate the asset. However, because businesses generally acquire and place assets in service at the same time, we refer to these terms interchangeably throughout the chapter.

[4]Throughout the chapter we use several different terms to refer to an asset's tax basis. The differences in these terms are somewhat subtle but can often be important. For example, an asset's initial basis refers to the tax basis of an asset at the time the taxpayer initially acquires the asset. If a taxpayer purchases the asset, the initial basis is the same as its cost. However, if a taxpayer acquires the asset through means other than purchase (e.g., gift, inheritance, nontaxable transaction, or conversion from personal use), the initial basis will typically differ from the asset's cost. We discuss some of these differences in the Property Dispositions chapter. The broad term, tax basis, refers to an asset's carrying value for tax purposes at a given point in time. When an asset's initial basis is recovered through depreciation, amortization, or depletion, the asset's tax basis is often referred to as the adjusted tax basis or sometimes simply the adjusted basis. It is not common to use the term adjusted tax basis for assets that are not subject to cost recovery. For example, the tax basis for a common stock investment would typically be referred to simply as its tax basis rather than its adjusted tax basis. Finally, the depreciable basis of an asset refers to the amount of the initial basis that can be depreciated over time using the regular depreciation rules. In many cases, the depreciable basis and the initial basis are the same—for example in the case of real property (i.e., buildings). However, the depreciable basis may differ from the initial basis when taxpayers take advantage of special incentives such as §179 expensing or bonus depreciation that accelerate an asset's cost recovery in the year it is placed in service.

[5]§1011.

[6]However, special basis rules apply when an asset is acquired through a nontaxable transaction. See discussion in the Property Dispositions chapter.

[7]Reg. §1.263(a)-1, -2, and -3.

immediately deduct low-cost personal property items used in their business. The definition of low-cost depends on whether the taxpayer has an applicable financial statement, which generally means a certified, audited financial statement. If taxpayers have an applicable financial statement, they may use the *de minimis* safe harbor to immediately deduct amounts paid for tangible property up to $5,000 per invoice or item.[8] If taxpayers don't have an applicable financial statement, they may use the safe harbor to deduct amounts up to $2,500 per invoice or item. Taxpayers generally use the invoice amount to determine whether they meet the safe harbor; however, if the total invoice amount exceeds the $5,000/$2,500 threshold and the invoice provides detailed cost information about each item, taxpayers may immediately deduct individual items that are less than the threshold amount. Taxpayers must capitalize the cost of personal property that does not fall under the *de minimis* safe harbor provision.[9]

When a business acquires multiple assets for one purchase price, the tax laws require the business to determine a cost basis for each separate asset. For example, for Teton's building purchase, Teton must treat the building and land as separate assets. In these types of acquisitions, businesses determine the cost basis of each asset by allocating a portion of the purchase price to each asset based on that asset's value relative to the total value of all the assets the business acquired in the same purchase. The asset values are generally determined by an appraisal.[10]

Example 10-1

Steve determined that he needed machinery and office furniture for a manufacturing facility and a design studio (located in Cody, Wyoming). During 2017, Steve purchased the following assets and incurred the following costs to prepare the assets for business use. His cost basis in each asset is determined as follows:

Asset	Date Acquired	(1) Purchase Price	(2) Business Preparation Costs	(1) + (2) Cost Basis
Office furniture	2/3/17	$ 20,000		$ 20,000
Warehouse	5/1/17	270,000*	$ 5,000 (minor modifications)	275,000
Land (10 acres)	5/1/17	75,000*		75,000
Machinery	7/22/17	600,000	$ 10,000 (delivery and setup)	610,000
Delivery truck (used)	8/17/17	25,000		25,000

*Note that the warehouse and the land were purchased together for $345,000. Steve and the seller determined that the value (and cost) of the warehouse was $270,000 and the value (and cost) of the land was $75,000.

What if: Assume Steve acquired a printer for $800 on July 9. Would he immediately deduct the cost of the printer or capitalize it?

Answer: Assuming that Steve has a policy to expense items costing $2,500 or less for nontax purposes, he would be able to immediately deduct the cost of the printer under the *de minimis* safe harbor.[11]

When a business incurs additional costs associated with an asset after the asset has been placed in service, are these costs immediately deducted or are they capitalized? In general, the answer depends on whether the expenditure constitutes routine maintenance on the asset or whether it results in a "betterment, restoration, or new or different

---

[8]Taxpayers must have accounting procedures in place at the beginning of the year treating items costing less than a specified dollar figure as an expense for nontax purposes.

[9]Separate rules apply when taxpayers purchase materials and supplies to be used in their business (Reg. §1.162-3).

[10]Reg. §1.167(a)-5.

[11] Later in this chapter, we discuss alternative ways to immediately deduct the cost of certain assets (§179 expensing and bonus depreciation). The first step however is to determine if it must be capitalized or immediately deducted under the Treasury regulations for §263.

use for the property."[12] Taxpayers can immediately deduct the costs if they meet the routine maintenance safe harbor rules provided in the Treasury regulations.[13] Routine maintenance is defined as preventative or cyclical maintenance that is an essential part of the ongoing care and upkeep of a building or building system. Costs related to the replacement of damaged or worn parts with comparable and commercially available replacement parts arising from inspecting, cleaning, and testing of the property are immediately deductible if two conditions are met. First, the taxpayer must fully expect to perform the activity more than once during a 10-year period (for buildings and structures related to buildings), or more than once during the property's class life (for property other than buildings). Second, the safe harbor cannot be used to deduct expenses incurred from major renovations, restorations, or improvements.

Example 10-2

What if: Suppose that Steve's business requires an annual safety certification on all its equipment and machinery. As a result of a required inspection of the machinery, Steve finds a defect in the engine of one of his machines and must replace the engine at a cost of $3,000. Can Steve immediately deduct the cost of the new engine?

Answer: Steve's business requires an annual safety certification inspection; thus Steve meets the requirement of reasonably expecting to perform the activity more than once during the machinery's class life. Assuming that Steve replaces the engine with a comparable, commercially available engine, he may immediately deduct the $3,000 cost of the new engine.

If the routine maintenance safe harbor rules do not apply, then taxpayers must determine whether the costs result in a betterment, restoration, or adaptation for a new or different use for the property.[14] If so, they must capitalize the costs; if not, they may immediately deduct the costs.[15] For example, if the roof of Teton's warehouse was completely replaced because it was leaking, Steve would be required to capitalize the costs to replace the roof as a restoration because a significant portion (100 percent) of a major component was replaced. If Teton needed to replace only 10 percent of the roof, Steve would most likely be able to immediately deduct the costs.[16]

Special rules apply when determining the tax basis of assets converted from personal to business use or assets acquired through a nontaxable exchange, gift, or inheritance. If an asset is used for personal purposes and is later converted to business (or rental) use, the basis for cost recovery purposes is the *lesser* of (1) the cost basis of the asset or (2) the fair market value of the asset on the date of conversion to business use.[17] This rule prevents taxpayers from converting a nondeductible personal loss into a deductible business loss. For example, if Steve had purchased a truck for $20,000 several years ago for personal use but decided to use it as a delivery truck when its value had declined to $15,000, his basis in the

---

[12]Reg. §1.263(a)-3.

[13]The routine maintenance safe harbor is discussed in Reg. §1.263(a)-3(i). In addition to the routine maintenance safe harbor, the regulations provide an additional safe harbor for small taxpayers. This safe harbor allows taxpayers with average annual gross receipts over the last three years of $10 million or less to immediately deduct amounts paid for maintenance and improvement on buildings with an unadjusted basis of $1 million or less if the amounts expended are less than the lesser of 2 percent of the building's unadjusted basis or $10,000 [Reg. §1.263(a)-3(h)].

[14]Reg. §1.263(a)-3.

[15]The regulations provide detailed guidelines for taxpayers to use to establish when they have expenditures related to these three distinct concepts. Coverage of these concepts is beyond the scope of this chapter. See Reg. §1.263(a)-3 for details.

[16]After 2017, Steve may have an opportunity to expense the cost of the roof under §179 (discussed later in the chapter) as the TCJA modified the definition of real property for purposes of the expensing provision.

[17]Reg. §§1.167(g)-1 and 1.168(i)-4(b). However, this rule creates an interesting situation when selling converted assets. The taxpayer uses the lower of the adjusted basis or the fair market value at the time of the conversion for computing loss but uses the adjusted basis to compute a gain when selling converted assets.

truck for cost recovery purposes would be $15,000. The $5,000 decline in the truck's value from $20,000 to $15,000 would be a nondeductible personal loss to Steve, and the reduction in basis ensures that he will not be allowed to deduct the loss as a business loss.

Assets acquired through a nontaxable exchange, such as a like-kind exchange (like-kind exchanges are discussed later in the Property Dispositions chapter), generally take the same basis the taxpayer had in the property that the taxpayer transferred in the transaction. Assets acquired by gift have a carryover basis. This means that the taxpayer's basis in property received through a gift is generally the same basis the transferor had in the property.[18] For example, if Steve's parents gave him equipment worth $45,000 to help him start his business and his parents had purchased the equipment 10 years earlier for $25,000, Steve's basis in the equipment would be $25,000 (the same basis his parents had in the equipment). Assets acquired through inheritance generally receive a basis equal to the fair market value on the transferor's date of death.[19] For example, if Steve inherited a building worth $90,000 from his grandfather who originally paid $35,000 for it, Steve's basis would be $90,000 (its fair market value at date of death) because Steve acquired it through an inheritance.

ETHICS

Catherine Travis is starting a new business. She has several assets that she wants to use in her business that she has been using personally. Since she plans to convert several assets from personal to business use, she will need to find out how much each asset is worth so she can determine her basis for depreciating the assets. Catherine has decided that getting an appraisal would be too costly so she simply uses her cost basis for the assets. What do you think of Catherine's strategy for determining her business asset bases?

LO 10-2

DEPRECIATION

THE KEY FACTS

Tax Depreciation

- To depreciate an asset, a business must determine:
  - Original basis
  - Depreciation method
  - Recovery period
  - Depreciation convention

As a preface to this section, the TCJA made many changes to how taxpayers will recover the cost of their assets for the next several years. In this chapter, we discuss the depreciation provisions both before and after the TCJA effective dates for several reasons. First, existing assets continue to follow the rules in place before the tax law change; therefore, for assets placed in service before the effective dates of the TCJA, taxpayers will need to understand the rules in effect at the time the assets were placed in service. Second, the new provisions provide very generous deductions for personal property; however, taxpayers may opt out of these provisions and instead can follow the pre-TCJA ruless. Taxpayers with large losses may opt to forgo the large depreciation deductions provided under the TCJA to reduce their losses, which may be subject to limitations (e.g., NOL limitations and excess business loss limitations). These taxpayers would then use the standard depreciation methods used prior to the TCJA. Third, for assets that do not qualify for the special provisions in the TCJA, taxpayers must fall back to the standard depreciation methods used under prior law. Finally, the TCJA expanded §179 expensing and extended bonus depreciation; however, bonus depreciation is temporary and is scheduled to begin phasing out for assets placed in service after December 31, 2022. Therefore, it is important to include discussions for the rules in effect before and after the TCJA.

With that in mind, we proceed by discussing the basic rules in effect prior to the enactment of the TCJA. These rules continue to apply to assets placed in service before the TCJA effective date. In this section, we consider how Steve could have depreciated the assets he acquired in 2017. We will then discuss the special rules (§179, bonus depreciation, and listed property), which were modified and expanded by the TCJA.

Since 1986, businesses calculate their tax depreciation using the **Modified Accelerated Cost Recovery System (MACRS)**—which is pronounced "makers" by tax accountants.[20] Compared to financial (book) depreciation, MACRS tax depreciation is quite simple. To

---

[18]§1015. The basis may be increased if the transferor is required to pay gift tax on the transfer [see §1015(d)]. In addition, special dual basis rules apply if the basis in the gifted property at the gift date is greater than its fair market value.

[19]§1014. In certain circumstances, the estate can elect an alternative valuation date six months after death.

[20]IRS Publication 946 provides a useful summary of MACRS depreciation.

compute MACRS depreciation for an asset, the business need only know the asset's *initial basis,* date placed in service, the applicable *depreciation method,* the asset's **recovery period** (or depreciable "life"), and the applicable depreciation *convention* (the amount of depreciation deductible in the year of acquisition and the year of disposition). The method, recovery period, and convention vary based on whether the asset is **personal property** or **real property.** Before we turn our attention to the determination of the depreciation deduction for personal property, it is important to emphasize that there may be a difference in when an asset is acquired and when it is placed in service. Being placed in service requires that the property is in a condition or state of readiness and availability for a specifically assigned function. This requirement is often met when an asset is acquired but may not be when additional installation is required or modifications must be made to ready the asset for its intended use.[21]

TAXES IN THE REAL WORLD   What a Difference a Day (or two) Makes

Taxpayers may begin taking depreciation deductions on their tax returns for business assets "placed in service" during the taxable year. As one taxpayer recently found out, determining when an asset is placed in service is not as simple as purchasing and using an asset. Michael Brown, a wealthy insurance salesman, purchased a $22 million Bombardier Challenger 604 airplane for use in his business. He took possession of the plane on December 30, 2003, and flew the plane across the country on business trips before the end of the year. Accordingly, Brown claimed about $11 million of bonus depreciation on his 2003 tax return. In January 2004, the plane was grounded for a period of time while a conference table and a display screen were added at an additional cost of $500,000. These improvements were "needed" and "required" for his insurance business, according to Brown.

The IRS challenged Brown's bonus depreciation deduction claiming that the plane was not "placed in service" in 2003. The issue is when the plane was regularly available for use in its specifically intended function. Per Brown's testimony, he insisted on having the conference table and display screen so he could conduct business on the plane. Because of this testimony that determined the plane's specifically intended function, the Tax Court denied the bonus depreciation deduction for 2003.

The outcome of this case illustrates the importance of determining the specific function for an asset and whether seemingly minor (2 percent) upgrades can make the asset substantially unavailable for its specifically intended function. It seems the taxpayer's own testimony of the plane's specifically intended function drove the Tax Court's decision to disallow the bonus depreciation deduction.

Source: Brown, T. C. Memo. 2013-275.

Personal Property Depreciation

Personal property includes all tangible property, such as computers, automobiles, furniture, machinery, and equipment, other than real property. Note that *personal* property and *personal-use* property are not the same thing. Personal property denotes any property that is not real property (e.g., building and land) while personal-use property is any property used for personal purposes (e.g., a personal residence is personal-use property even though it is real property). Personal property is relatively short-lived and subject to obsolescence as compared to real property.

Depreciation Method   MACRS provides three acceptable methods for depreciating personal property: 200 percent (double) declining balance (DB), 150 percent declining balance, and straight-line.[22] The 200 percent declining balance method is the default method. This method takes twice the straight-line amount of depreciation in the first year and continues to take twice the straight-line percentage on the asset's declining basis until switching to the straight-line method in the year that the straight-line method over the

---

[21]§1.167(a)-11(e)(1)(1) and Brown v Commissioner, TC Memo 2013-275.

[22]MACRS includes two depreciation systems: the general depreciation system (GDS) and the alternative depreciation system (ADS). MACRS provides three methods under GDS (200 percent DB, 150 percent DB, and straight-line) and one method under ADS (straight-line).

remaining life provides a greater depreciation expense. Fortunately, as we describe below, the IRS provides depreciation tables to simplify the calculations.

Profitable businesses with relatively high marginal tax rates generally choose to use the 200 percent declining balance method because it generates the largest depreciation deduction in the early years of the assets' lives and, thus, the highest current-year after-tax cash flows. For tax planning purposes, companies that currently have lower marginal tax rates but expect their marginal tax rates to increase in the near future may elect the straight-line method because that method generates less depreciation in the early years of the asset's life, relatively, and more depreciation in the later years when their marginal tax rates may increase.

Example 10-3

If Teton wants to accelerate its current depreciation deductions to the extent possible, what method should it use to depreciate its office furniture, machinery, and delivery truck?

Answer: The 200 percent declining balance method (default). Teton could elect to use either the 150 percent declining balance or the straight-line method, if it wants a less accelerated method for determining its depreciation deductions.

Each year, businesses elect the depreciation method for the assets placed in service during *that year*. Specifically, businesses elect one depreciation method for all similar assets they acquired that year.[23] Thus, if a business acquires several different machines during the year, it must use the same method to depreciate all of the machines. However, the methods may differ for machines acquired in different tax years.

Depreciation Recovery Period   For financial accounting purposes, an asset's recovery period (depreciable life) is based on its taxpayer-determined estimated useful life. In contrast, for tax purposes an asset's recovery period is predetermined by the IRS in Rev. Proc. 87-56. This revenue procedure helps taxpayers categorize each of their assets based upon the property's description. Once the business has determined the appropriate categories for its assets, it can use the revenue procedure to identify the recovery period for all assets in a particular category. For example, Teton placed office furniture in service during the year. By examining the excerpt from Rev. Proc. 87-56 provided in Exhibit 10-3, you can see that Category or Asset Class 00.11 includes office furniture and that assets in this category, including Teton's office furniture, have a recovery period of seven years (emphasis in excerpt added through bold text).[24]

While even this small excerpt from Rev. Proc. 87-56 may seem a bit intimidating, you can classify the vast majority of business assets acquired by knowing a few common recovery periods. Exhibit 10-4 lists the most commonly purchased assets and their recovery periods.

To this point, our discussion has emphasized computing regular MACRS depreciation for new assets. Does the process change when businesses acquire used assets? No, it is exactly the same. For example, Teton purchased a *used* delivery truck. The fact that the truck is used does not change its MACRS recovery period. No matter how long the previous owner used the truck, Teton will restart the five-year recovery period for light general-purpose trucks to depreciate the delivery truck (see Exhibit 10-4).

Under MACRS, the tax recovery period for machinery and equipment is seven years. Using Rev. Proc. 87-56, Teton has determined the cost recovery periods for the personal property it purchased and placed in service during 2017. Exhibit 10-5 summarizes this information.

---

[23]Technically, similar assets are assets in the same property class.

[24]The "alternative" recovery period in Rev. Proc. 87-56 refers to an asset's life under the alternative depreciation system referred to as ADS (which we discuss later in this chapter). The class life referred to in Rev. Proc. 87-56 refers to the midpoint of asset depreciation range (ADR) applicable under pre-ACRS and has little or no meaning under MACRS.

EXHIBIT 10-3   **Excerpt from Revenue Procedure 87-56**

Description of Assets Included			
Specific depreciable assets used in all business activities, except as noted:	Class Life	General Recovery Period	Alternative Recovery Period
00.11 Office Furniture, Fixtures, and Equipment: Includes furniture and fixtures that are not a structural component of a building. Includes such assets as desks, files, safes, and communications equipment. Does not include communications equipment that is included in other classes.	10	7	10
00.12 Information Systems: Includes computers and their peripheral equipment used in administering normal business transactions and the maintenance of business records.	6	5	5
00.241 Light General Purpose Trucks: Includes trucks for use over the road (actual unloaded weight less than 13,000 pounds) . . .	4	5	5
34.0 Manufacture of Fabricated Metal Products Special Tools: Includes assets used in the production of metal cans, tinware . . .	12	7	12

EXHIBIT 10-4   **Recovery Period for Most Common Business Assets**

Asset Description (Summary of Rev. Proc. 87-56)	Recovery Period
Cars, light general-purpose trucks, and computers and peripheral equipment	5 years
Office furniture, fixtures, and equipment	7 years

EXHIBIT 10-5   **Teton Personal Property Summary (Base Scenario)**

Asset	Date Acquired	Quarter Acquired	Cost Basis	Recovery Period	Reference
Office furniture	2/3/17	1st	$ 20,000	7	Example 10-1; Exhibit 10-3
Machinery	7/22/17	3rd	610,000	7	Example 10-1; Exhibit 10-3
Delivery truck	8/17/17	3rd	25,000	5	Example 10-1; Exhibit 10-3
Total personal property			$655,000		

Depreciation Conventions   Once a business has determined the depreciation methods and recovery periods for the assets it placed in service during the year, it then must determine the applicable depreciation conventions. The depreciation convention specifies the portion of a full year's depreciation the business can deduct for an asset in the year the asset is first placed in service *and* in the year the asset is sold. For *personal property*, taxpayers must use either the **half-year convention** or the **mid-quarter convention.** But, taxpayers are *not* free to choose between the two conventions. The half-year convention applies most of the time, particularly after the TCJA. However, under certain conditions taxpayers are required to use the mid-quarter convention (discussed below). The depreciation convention is determined annually. Once the convention is determined for the assets acquired during the year, the convention remains the same for the entire recovery period for those assets.

Before MACRS, taxpayers were required the use of the half-year convention for all personal property placed in service during the year. However, Congress believed that many businesses took unfair advantage of the half-year convention by purposely acquiring assets at the end of the year that they otherwise would have acquired at the beginning of the next taxable year. Thus, businesses received one-half of a year's worth of depreciation for assets that they used for only a small portion of the year. Even though the half-year convention is the default convention, policy makers introduced the *mid-quarter convention* under MACRS to limit or prevent this type of opportunistic behavior. Nevertheless, as we discuss below, the new tax laws allow taxpayers to accelerate their cost recovery deductions no matter when during the year the assets are placed in service. Consequently, the mid-quarter convention will likely have limited application to assets placed in service after December 31, 2017.

Half-year convention.   The half-year convention allows one-half of a full year's depreciation in the year the asset is placed in service (and in the year in which it is disposed), regardless of when it was actually placed in service. For example, when the half-year convention applies to a calendar-year business, an asset placed in service on either February 3 or August 17 is treated as though it was placed in service on July 1, which is the middle of the calendar year. Thus, under this convention, Teton would deduct one-half of a year's worth of depreciation for the machinery, office furniture, and delivery truck even though it acquired the machinery, delivery truck, and office furniture at various times during the year (see Exhibit 10-5). The half-year convention is built into the depreciation tables provided by the IRS, which simplifies the depreciation calculation for the year the asset is placed into service.

Mid-quarter convention.   Businesses must use the mid-quarter convention when *more than 40 percent* of their total *tangible personal property* that they place in service during the year is placed in service during the *fourth* quarter. Under the mid-quarter convention, businesses treat assets *as though* they were placed in service during the middle of the *quarter* in which the business actually placed the assets into service. For example, when the mid-quarter convention applies, if a business places an asset in service on December 1 (in the fourth quarter) it must treat the asset as though it was placed in service on November 15, which is the middle of the fourth quarter. Consequently, the business deducts only one-half of a quarter's worth of depreciation in the year the asset is placed in service (depreciation for the second half of November and the entire month of December). In addition, if the mid-quarter convention applies, businesses must use the convention for all tangible personal property placed in service during the year. The mid-quarter test is applied after the §179 expense but before bonus depreciation (discussed later in the chapter), meaning that any property expensed under §179 is not included in the mid-quarter test. The IRS depreciation tables have built in the mid-quarter convention to simplify the calculations.

For assets placed in service under the TCJA regime (effective for assets acquired after September 27, 2017), the mid-quarter convention will be largely irrelevant as businesses can use either §179 or 100 percent bonus depreciation to recover the cost in full in the year of acquisition. However, for assets placed in service before TCJA and assets that fail to qualify for §179 and bonus depreciation, the mid-quarter convention may apply.

Calculating Depreciation for Personal Property

Once a business has identified the applicable method, recovery period, and convention for personal property, tax depreciation is relatively easy to calculate because the Internal Revenue Service provides depreciation percentage tables in Rev. Proc. 87-57. The percentages in the depreciation tables for tangible personal property incorporate the method and convention. Accordingly, there are separate tables for each combination of depreciation method (200 percent declining balance, 150 percent declining balance, and straight-line) and convention (half-year and mid-quarter; each quarter has its own table). To determine the depreciation for an asset for the year, use the following steps:

Step 1:   Determine the appropriate convention (half-year or mid-quarter) by determining whether more than 40 percent of qualified property was placed in service in the last quarter of the tax year.

Step 2: Locate the applicable table provided in Rev. Proc. 87-57 also reproduced in Appendix A of this chapter.

Step 3: Select the column that corresponds with the asset's recovery period.

Step 4: Find the row identifying the year of the asset's recovery period.

The tables are constructed so that the intersection of the row and column provides the percentage of the asset's *initial basis* that is deductible as depreciation expense for the particular year. Thus, depreciation expense for a particular asset is the product of the percentage from the table and the asset's *initial basis*.

Applying the Half-Year Convention   Consider Table 1 in Appendix A at the end of the chapter that shows the depreciation percentages for MACRS 200 percent declining balance using the half-year convention. If a seven-year asset is placed into service during the current year, the depreciation percentage is 14.29 percent (the intersection of row 1 [year 1] and the seven-year property column).

Notice from Table 1 that the depreciation percentages for five-year property extend for six years and the percentages for seven-year property extend for eight years. Why does it take six years to fully depreciate an asset with a five-year recovery period and eight years for a seven-year asset? Because the business does not deduct a full year's depreciation in the first year, an entire year of depreciation is effectively split between the first and last year. For example, when the half-year convention applies to a five-year asset, the taxpayer deducts one-half of a year's depreciation in year 1 and one-half of a year's depreciation in year 6.

Example 10-4

Teton is using the 200 percent declining balance method and half-year convention to compute depreciation expense on its 2017 personal property additions. What is Teton's 2017 depreciation expense for these assets?

Answer: $95,027, computed as follows:

Asset	Date Placed in Service	(1) Original Basis	(2) Rate	(1) × (2) Depreciation
Office furniture	February 3	$ 20,000	14.29%	$ 2,858
Machinery	July 22	610,000	14.29	87,169
Used delivery truck	August 17	25,000	20.00	5,000
Total				**$95,027**

Because the office furniture and machinery have a seven-year recovery period and it is the first year for depreciation, the depreciation rate is 14.29 percent (see Table 1). The depreciation rate for the used delivery truck (five-year property) is 20 percent and is determined in a similar manner.

Calculating depreciation for assets in years after the year of acquisition is also relatively simple. Again, using Table 1 to compute depreciation for the second year, the taxpayer would multiply the asset's initial basis by the percentage in the *year 2* row; in the following year, the taxpayer would use the percentage in the *year 3* row; and so on.

Example 10-5

What if: Assume that Teton holds the tangible personal property it acquired and placed in service in 2017 until the assets are fully depreciated. Using the IRS provided tables (see Table 1), how would Teton determine its depreciation expense for 2017 through 2024?

Answer: See the following table:

(continued on page 10-12)

Depreciation Over Asset Recovery Period					
Recovery Period	Year	7-Year Office Furniture	7-Year Machinery	5-Year Delivery Truck	Yearly Total
1	2017	$ 2,858	$ 87,169	$ 5,000	$ 95,027
2	2018	4,898	149,389	8,000	162,287
3	2019	3,498	106,689	4,800	114,987
4	2020	2,498	76,189	2,880	81,567
5	2021	1,786	54,473	2,880	59,139
6	2022	1,784	54,412	1,440	57,636
7	2023	1,786	54,473	N/A	56,259
8	2024	892	27,206	N/A	28,098
Accumulated Depreciation		$20,000	$610,000	$25,000	$655,000

Half-year convention for year of disposition. Businesses often sell or dispose of assets before they fully depreciate them. Recall that the half-year convention applies in both the year of acquisition and the year of disposition. Note, however, that the tables can't anticipate when a business may dispose of an asset. Accordingly, the tables only provide depreciation percentages for assets assuming the asset won't be disposed of before it is fully depreciated. That is, for each year in the asset's recovery period, the tables provide a percentage for an entire year's worth of depreciation. So, to calculate the depreciation for the year of disposition, the business first calculates depreciation for the *entire year* as if the property had not been disposed of. Then the business applies the half-year convention by multiplying the full year's depreciation by 50 percent (one-half of a year's depreciation).[25] Note, however, that if a business acquires and disposes of an asset in the same tax year, it is not allowed to claim any depreciation on the asset.

Example 10-6

What if: Assume that Teton sells all of its office furniture in 2018 (the year after it buys it). What is Teton's depreciation for the office furniture in the year of disposition (2018)?

Answer: $2,449, calculated using the MACRS Half-Year Convention Table (Table 1) as follows:

Asset	Amount	Explanation
(1) Office furniture	$20,000	Original basis
(2) Depreciation percentage	24.49%	Seven-year property, year 2
(3) Full year of depreciation	$ 4,898	(1) × (2)
(4) Half-year convention percentage	50%	Depreciation limit in year of disposal
Depreciation in year of disposal	**$ 2,449**	(3) × (4)

What if: Assume that Teton sold all of its office furniture in year 1 (the year it bought it and placed it in service). How much depreciation expense can Teton deduct for the office furniture in year 1?

Answer: $0. A business is not allowed to claim any depreciation expense for assets it acquires and disposes of in the same tax year.

[25]Suppose Teton sells the 5-year delivery truck in year 6 on January 5. What depreciation percentage should Teton use for purposes of determining year 6 depreciation? Teton should take one-half year's depreciation on the truck. The percentage shown in Table 1 for the year of an asset's recovery period (in this case, year 6) already reflects the half-year convention, so Teton would take $1,440 of depreciation regardless of when during year 6 the truck was sold.

Applying the Mid-Quarter Convention When the mid-quarter convention applies, the process for computing depreciation is the same as it is when the half-year convention applies, except that businesses use a different set of depreciation tables (a separate table for each quarter). After categorizing the assets by recovery period and grouping them into quarters, businesses consult the Mid-Quarter Convention Tables (Tables 2a–d in Appendix A to this chapter) to determine the depreciation rate for each asset group.

The depreciation deduction for an asset is the product of the asset's original basis and the percentage from the table.

<table>
<tr><td colspan="2">

Example 10-7

</td></tr>
<tr><td>

What if: For this example, assume the machinery Teton placed in service in Exhibit 10-5 was placed in service on November 1, 2017 rather than July 22 (see table below). What is Teton's 2017 depreciation for its personal property additions?

Answer: $30,527, computed as follows:

Asset	Purchase Date	Quarter	Original Basis	Rate	Depreciation
Office furniture (7-year)	February 3	1st	$ 20,000	25.00%	$ 5,000
Delivery truck (5-year)	August 17	3rd	25,000	15.00%	3,750
Machinery (7-year)	November 1	4th	610,000	3.57%	21,777
					$30,527

The mid-quarter convention applies because more than 40 percent of the assets were placed in service during the last quarter of the year ($610,000/$655,000 = 93%). The office furniture rate of 25 percent is located in Table 2a. See the columns for property placed into service during the first quarter (first two columns); select the seven-year recovery period column (last column), and the year 1 row. The process for determining the rate for the delivery truck and machinery follows the same method using Tables 2c and 2d, respectively.

</td><td>

THE KEY FACTS

Mid Quarter Convention

- The mid-quarter convention is required when more than 40 percent of personal property is placed in service during the fourth quarter of the tax year.

- Each quarter has its own depreciation table. Once the mid-quarter convention applies, the taxpayer must continue to use it over the assets' entire recovery period.

- If an asset is disposed of before it is fully depreciated, use the formula given to determine the allowable depreciation in the year of disposition.

</td></tr>
</table>

The process for calculating depreciation for assets in years after acquisition is the same as the process we described for the half-year convention except the taxpayer uses the MACRS Mid-Quarter Convention Tables (Table 2 in Appendix A) for the appropriate quarter rather than the MACRS Half-Year Convention Table (Table 1).

Mid-quarter convention for year of disposition. Calculating depreciation expense in the year of sale or disposition is a bit more involved when the mid-quarter convention applies than when it does not. When the mid-quarter convention applies, the asset is treated as though it is sold in the middle of the quarter of which it was actually sold. The process for calculating mid-quarter convention depreciation for the year of sale is exactly the same as the process for using the half-year convention, except that instead of multiplying the full year's depreciation by 50 percent, the business multiplies the amount of depreciation it would have been able to claim on the asset if it had not sold the asset (a full year's depreciation) by the applicable percentage in Exhibit 10-6.

EXHIBIT 10-6 **Mid-Quarter Convention Percentage of Full Year's Depreciation in Year of Disposition**

Quarter of Disposition	Percentage	Calculation*
1st	12.5%	1.5/12
2nd	37.5	4.5/12
3rd	62.5	7.5/12
4th	87.5	10.5/12

*The calculation is the number of months the taxpayer held or is deemed to have held the asset in the year of disposition divided by 12 months in the year.

Example 10-8

What if: Assume that Teton depreciates its personal property under the mid-quarter convention (Example 10-7), and that it sells its office furniture in the third quarter of 2018. The office furniture ($20,000 original basis) was placed into service during the first quarter of 2017 and has a seven-year recovery period. What is Teton's 2018 depreciation for the office furniture?

Answer: $30,527, computed as follows:

Description	Amount	Explanation
(1) Original basis	$20,000	Example 10-7
(2) 2018 depreciation percentage	21.43%	Table 2a, mid-quarter, first quarter table, 7-year property, year 2
(3) Full year depreciation	$4,286	(1) × (2)
(4) Percentage of full year's depreciation in year of disposition if mid-quarter convention applies	62.5%	From Exhibit 10-6; asset disposed of in third quarter
Depreciation in year of disposition	**$2,679**	(3) × (4)

Real Property

The TCJA made no changes to the depreciation of real property except to reclassify certain improvements to be eligible for §179.[26] Therefore, for real property placed in service after TCJA, businesses will calculate their depreciation on real property as described below.

For depreciation purposes, real property is classified as land, *residential rental* property, or *nonresidential property*. Land is nondepreciable. Residential rental property consists of dwelling units such as houses, condominiums, and apartment complexes. Residential rental property has a 27.5-year recovery period. Nonresidential property consists of all other buildings (office buildings, manufacturing facilities, shopping malls, and the like). Nonresidential property placed in service on or after May 13, 1993, has a 39-year recovery period, and nonresidential property placed in service after December 31, 1986, and before May 13, 1993, has a 31.5-year recovery period. Exhibit 10-7 summarizes the recovery periods for real property.

If a building is substantially improved (i.e., expanded) at some point after the initial purchase, the building addition is treated as a new asset with the same recovery period of the original building. For example, if Teton expanded its warehouse 10 years after the building was placed in service, the expansion or building addition would be depreciated as a *new, separate* asset over 39 years because it is nonresidential property.

An important area of tax practice related to real property is cost segregation. This practice attempts to partition or divide the costs of a building into two or more categories. The first category is the building itself, which has a recovery period as noted in Exhibit 10-7. The second category is building components (tangible personal property

EXHIBIT 10-7   Recovery Period for Real Property

Asset Description (Summary from Rev. Proc. 87-57)	Recovery Period
Residential	27.5 years
Nonresidential property placed in service on or after May 13, 1993	39 years
Nonresidential property placed in service before May 13, 1993	31.5 years

[26]Section 179(f)(2) now classifies the following improvements to nonresidential real property as eligible for immediate expensing: roofs; heating, ventilation and air-conditioning systems; fire protection and alarm systems; and security systems. In addition, §179(f)(1) allows qualified improvements (any improvement to an interior portion of a nonresidential building placed in service after the date the building was placed in service) to be eligible for §179. Qualified improvements do not include expansions, additions of elevators/escalators, or improvements to the internal structural framework of the building; therefore, these items are not eligible to be immediately deducted under §179 [§168(e)(6)(B)].

associated with the building such as electrical and plumbing fixtures that have a shorter recovery period and accelerated depreciation method). Cost segregation utilizes engineers and construction experts who divide the costs between real and tangible personal property. This can generate significant tax savings due to the difference in the present value of the tax savings from the accelerated depreciation deductions associated with personal property relative to real property.

Applicable Method   All depreciable real property is depreciated for tax purposes using the straight-line method. This is generally consistent with depreciation methods used for financial accounting purposes.

Applicable Convention   All real property is depreciated using the mid-month convention. The **mid-month convention** allows the owner of real property to expense one-half of a month's depreciation for the month in which the property was placed in service (and in the month of the year it is sold as well). This is true regardless of whether the asset was placed in service at the beginning or at the end of the month. For example, if Teton placed its warehouse into service on May 1 (or on *any* other day in May), it would deduct *one-half* of a month's depreciation for May and then full depreciation for the months June through December.

Depreciation Tables   Just as it does for personal property, the IRS provides depreciation tables for real property. The depreciation tables for 27.5 years, 31.5 years, and 39 years real property are reproduced as Tables 3, 4, and 5, respectively, in Appendix A. The percentage of the asset's original basis that is depreciated in a particular year is located at the intersection of the month the asset was placed in service (column) and the year of depreciation (row).

Example 10-9

As indicated in Example 10-1, Teton's initial basis in the warehouse it purchased on May 1, 2017, is $275,000. What is Teton's 2017 and 2018 depreciation on its warehouse?

Answer: $4,414 in 2017 and $7,051 in 2018, calculated as follows:

Warehouse	Method	Recovery Period	Date Placed in Service	(1) Basis	(2) Rate	(1) × (2) Depreciation
2017	SL	39	5/1/2017	$275,000	1.605%	$4,414
2018	SL	39	5/1/2017	275,000	2.564%	7,051

What if: What would be Teton's 2017 and 2018 depreciation expense if, instead of a warehouse, the building was an apartment building that it rented to Teton's employees?

Answer: $6,251 in 2017 and $9,999 in 2018, calculated as follows:

Apartment Bldg	Method	Recovery Period	Date Placed in Service	(1) Basis	(2) Rate	(1) × (2) Depreciation
2017	SL	27.5	5/1/2017	$275,000	2.273%	$6,251
2018	SL	27.5	5/1/2017	275,000	3.636%	9,999

*The 1.605 percent for the year is found in the 39-year table (Table 5, in Appendix A) in the fifth column (fifth month) and first row (first year).

†The 2.273 percent for the year is found in the 27.5-year table (Table 3, in Appendix A) in the fifth column (fifth month) and first row (first year).

When using depreciation tables for real property, it is important to stay in the month column corresponding with the month the property was originally placed in service.[27] Thus, to calculate depreciation for real property placed in service in May (the fifth month), businesses will *always* (for each year of depreciation) find the current-year rate factor in the fifth column for that asset. This is true even if the asset is sold in a subsequent year in July (it's easy to make the mistake of using the seventh column to calculate the depreciation for the year of disposition in this situation).

---

[27]Failure to do so will result in the wrong depreciation expense and is technically a change in accounting method (which requires filing of Form 3115 with the IRS).

Mid-month convention for year of disposition. Businesses deduct one-half of a month's depreciation in the month they sell or otherwise dispose of real property. For example, if Teton sold its warehouse on March 5 of year 2, it would deduct two and one-half months of depreciation in that year for the warehouse (depreciation for January, February, and one-half of March). Calculating depreciation expense in the year of sale or disposition for mid-month convention assets is similar to the calculation under the mid-quarter convention. When the mid-month convention applies, the asset is treated as though it is sold in the *middle of the month* of which it was actually sold. The simplest process for calculating mid-month convention depreciation for the year of sale consists of the following four steps:

Step 1: Determine the amount of depreciation deduction for the asset as if the asset was held for the entire year.

Step 2: Subtract one-half of a month from the month in which the asset was sold (if sold in third month, subtract .5 from 3 to get 2.5). (Subtract half of a month because the business is treated as though the asset was disposed of in the middle of the third month—not the end.)

Step 3: Divide the amount determined in Step 2 by 12 months (2.5/12). This is the fraction of the full year's depreciation the business is eligible to deduct.

Step 4: Multiply the Step 3 outcome by the full depreciation determined in Step 1.

These steps are summarized in the following formula:

Mid-month depreciation for year of disposition

$$= \text{Full year's depreciation} \times \frac{(\text{Month in which asset was disposed of} - .5)}{12}$$

Example 10-10

What if: Assume that Teton sells its warehouse on March 5, 2018 (the year after Teton buys it). What is Teton's depreciation for the warehouse in the year of disposition?

Answer: $1,469, computed using the four-step procedure outlined above as follows.

Step 1: Determine full year's depreciation: $275,000 × 2.564%* = $7,051

Step 2: 3 (month sold) − .5 = 2.5

Step 3: 2.5/12

Step 4: $7,051 × 2.5/12 = $1,469 (see formula above)

*The 2.564 percent (full-year percentage) in Step 1 is obtained from the MACRS Mid-Month Table for 39-year property (Table 5) placed in service during the fifth month (year 2 row).

Storyline Summary

Taxpayer:	Teton Mountaineering Technology, LLC (Teton)—a calendar-year single-member LLC (treated as a sole proprietorship for tax purposes)
Location:	Cody, Wyoming
President/Founder	Steve Dallimore

continued from page 10-2 . . .

During 2017, Teton had huge success, generating a large profit. To continue to grow the business and increase Teton's production capacity, Steve acquired more assets in 2018. He has heard about ways to "write off" the costs of business assets and wants to learn more.

to be continued . . .

SPECIAL RULES RELATING TO COST RECOVERY

In addition to the basic MACRS rules, several additional provisions affect the depreciation of personal property. Congress often uses these special rules for economic stimulus or to curb perceived taxpayer abuses. The TCJA substantially modifies and extends these special rules (§179, bonus depreciation, and listed property). For many businesses, the calculation of MACRS depreciation for its personal property will become a thing of the past because of the expansion of these special rules. It is worth noting, however, that Congress did not make all of the changes permanent. For example, the changes to bonus depreciation are effective for property placed in service before January 1, 2023 with a subsequent four-year phase-out. We discuss these rules below.

Immediate Expensing (§179)   Policy makers created §179 as an incentive to help small businesses purchasing new or used tangible personal property. This incentive is commonly referred to as the **§179 expense** or *immediate expensing* election.[28] This provision will have limited application under TCJA because bonus depreciation discussed below allows taxpayers to immediately deduct assets' initial basis. As discussed earlier in the chapter, businesses must generally depreciate assets over the assets' recovery periods. However, under §179, businesses may elect to immediately expense up to $1,000,000 of tangible personal property placed in service during 2018.[29,30] Businesses can also use immediate expensing for off-the-shelf computer software and qualified real property.[31] They may also elect to deduct less than the maximum. When businesses elect to deduct a certain amount of §179 expense, they immediately expense all or a portion of an asset's basis or several assets' bases. To reflect this immediate depreciation, they must reduce the basis of the asset or assets (to which they applied the §179 amount) *before* they compute MACRS depreciation (from the tables).

Exhibit 10-8 shows the assets Teton acquires in 2018.

EXHIBIT 10-8   Teton's 2018 Asset Acquisitions

Asset	Cost	Date Placed in Service
Computers & information systems	$ 920,000	March 3
Delivery truck*	80,000	May 26
Machinery	1,200,000	August 15
Total	$2,200,000	

*Steve had used this truck personally and converted it to business use in May.

Example 10-11

What if: Assume Teton is eligible for and elects to immediately deduct $800,000 of §179 expense against the basis of the machinery acquired in 2018 (see Exhibit 10-8). (Note that Teton could have elected to deduct up to $1,000,000.) What is the amount of Teton's current-year depreciation deduction, including regular MACRS depreciation and the §179 expense on its machinery (assuming the half-year convention applies)?

(continued on page 10-18)

---

[28]Intangibles and tangible personal property that are used less than 50 percent for business and most real property are not eligible for immediate expensing.

[29]The maximum allowable expense under §179 is indexed for inflation beginning with years after 2018.

[30]These maximum amounts are per tax return. Thus, if an individual has multiple businesses with asset acquisitions, the taxpayer may only deduct up to these maximum amounts for the combined businesses.

[31]Qualified real property means improvements to nonresidential real property placed in service after the date the building was placed in service including roofs; heating, ventilation, and air-conditioning; fire protection and alarm systems; and security systems.

Answer: $857,160, computed as follows:

Description	Amount	Explanation
(1) Machinery	$1,200,000	Exhibit 10-8
(2) §179 expense	800,000	
(3) Remaining basis in machinery	$ 400,000	(1) − (2)
(4) MACRS depreciation rate for 7-year machinery	14.29%	Rate from Table 1
(5) MACRS depreciation expense on machinery	$ 57,160	(3) × (4)
Total depreciation on machinery	**$ 857,160**	(2) + (5)

What if: Assume that Teton was eligible for and elected to claim the maximum amount of §179 expense. What would be its total current-year depreciation deduction, including MACRS depreciation and §179 expense (assuming the half-year convention applies)?

Answer: $1,028,580, computed as follows:

Description	Amount	Explanation
(1) Machinery	$ 1,200,000	Exhibit 10-8
(2) §179 expense	1,000,000	Maximum expense in 2018
(3) Remaining basis in machinery	$ 200,000	(1) − (2)
(4) MACRS depreciation rate for 7-year machinery	14.29%	Rate from Table 1
(5) MACRS depreciation expense on machinery	$ 28,580	(3) × (4)
Total depreciation on machinery	**$1,028,580**	(2) + (5)

Limits on immediate expensing.   The maximum amount of §179 expense a business may elect to claim for the year is subject to a phase-out limitation. Under the phase-out limitation, businesses must reduce the $1,000,000 maximum available expense dollar for dollar for the amount of *tangible personal property* purchased and placed in service during 2018 over a $2,500,000 threshold.[32] Thus if a business places $3,500,000 ($2,500,000 threshold plus $1,000,000) or more of tangible personal property into service during 2018, its maximum available §179 expense for the year is $0. The phased-out portion of the maximum expense disappears and does *not* carry over to another year.

Example 10-12

What if: Let's assume that during 2018, Teton placed into service $2,400,000 of machinery (up from the Exhibit 10-8 amount of $1,200,000), $920,000 of computers, and an $80,000 delivery truck for a total of $3,400,000 tangible *personal* property placed in service for the year. What is Teton's maximum §179 expense after applying the phase-out limitation?

Answer: $100,000, computed as follows:

Description	Amount	Explanation
(1) Property placed in service in 2018	$3,400,000	Exhibit 10-8
(2) Threshold for §179 phase-out	2,500,000	2018 amount [§179(b)(2)]
(3) Phase-out of maximum §179 expense	900,000	(1) − (2)
(4) Maximum §179 expense before phase-out	1,000,000	§179(b)(1)
(5) Phase-out of maximum §179 expense	900,000	From (3)
Maximum §179 expense after phase-out*	**$ 100,000**	(4) − (5)

*Note that this is the maximum expense after phase-out but *before* the taxable income limitation we discuss next.

[32]The threshold under §179 is indexed for inflation beginning with years after 2018.

What if: Assume further that on November 13, Teton acquired and placed in service a storage building costing $400,000. Taking the building into account, what is Teton's maximum §179 amount after the phase-out?

Answer: $100,000, the same answer as above. The phase-out is based on the amount of tangible personal property placed in service during the year. Because the warehouse is *real property* (not qualified), its acquisition has no effect on Teton's maximum §179 expense.

Businesses may elect to claim the §179 expense for the year up to the maximum amount available (after computing the phase-out—see the previous example). When a business elects to claim a certain amount of §179 expense, it must reduce the basis of the asset(s) to which the expense is applied. It then computes regular depreciation on the remaining basis after reducing the basis of the asset(s) for the §179 expense.

A business's *deductible* §179 expense is limited to the taxpayer's business income after deducting all expenses (including regular and bonus depreciation) except the §179 expense. Consequently, the §179 expense cannot create or extend a business's net operating loss. Taxpayers' business income includes income from all businesses. For example, a sole-proprietor's business income for purposes of §179 would include the income not only from all Schedules C but also from regular wages. If a business claims more §179 expense than it is allowed to deduct due to the taxable income limitation, it carries the excess forward (indefinitely) and deducts it in a subsequent year, subject to the taxable income limitation (but not the phase-out limitation) in the subsequent year.[33]

Example 10-13

What if: Let's assume the facts of the previous example, where Teton's maximum §179 expense after applying the phase-out limitation is $100,000. Also assume that Teton elects to claim the entire $100,000 expense and it chooses to apply it against the machinery. Further assume that Teton reports $400,000 of taxable income before deducting any §179 expense and depreciation. What amount of total depreciation (including §179 expense) is Teton able to deduct on the machinery for the year?

Answer: $400,000, computed as follows:

Description	Amount	Explanation
(1) Machinery	$2,400,000	Example 10-11
(2) Elected §179 expense	100,000	
(3) Remaining basis	$2,300,000	(1) − (2)
(4) MACRS depreciation rate for 7-year machinery, year 1	14.29%	See Table 1
(5) MACRS depreciation expense on machinery	$ 328,670	(3) × (4)
(6) Deductible §179 expense	71,330	Taxable income limitation ($400,000 − $328,670)
(7) Total depreciation expense on machinery for the year	**$ 400,000**	(5) + (6)
(8) Excess §179 expense	$ 28,670	(2) − (6)

THE KEY FACTS

§179 Expenses

- $1,000,000 of tangible personal property can be immediately expensed in 2018.
- Businesses are eligible for the full amount of this expense when tangible personal property placed in service is less than $2,500,000. Beginning at $2,500,000, the §179 expense is phased out, dollar-for-dollar. When assets placed in service reach $3,500,000, no §179 expense can be taken.
- §179 expenses are also limited to a business's taxable income before the §179 expense. §179 expenses cannot create losses.

---

[33]Businesses typically elect only to expense the currently deductible amount since the taxable income limitation may also limit their §179 expense in future years just as it does for the current year. Electing the amount deductible after the taxable income limitation also maximizes the current year depreciation deduction.

What is the amount of Teton's excess §179 expense (elected expense in excess of the deductible amount due to the taxable income limitation), and what does Teton do with it for tax purposes?

Answer: $28,670. See the above table for the computation (line 8). Teton carries this $28,670 excess §179 expense forward to future years and may deduct it subject to the taxable income limitation. Note that the depreciable basis of the machinery remaining after the §179 expense is $2,300,000 because the depreciable basis is reduced by the full $100,000 of §179 expense elected even though the deductible §179 expense was limited to $71,330 in the current year.

Choosing the assets to immediately expense. Businesses qualifying for immediate expensing are allowed to choose the asset or assets (from tangible personal property placed in service during the year) they immediately expense under §179. If a business's objective is to maximize its current depreciation deduction, it should immediately expense the asset

---

Example 10-14

What if: Let's assume that on June 1, Teton placed into service five-year property costing $1,400,000 and seven-year property costing $1,400,000 and had no other fixed asset additions during the year. Further assume that Teton is not subject to the taxable income limitation for the §179 expense. What is Teton's depreciation deduction (including §179 expense) if it elects to apply the full §179 expense against the five-year property (Scenario A)? What is its depreciation deduction if it applies the full §179 expense against its seven-year property (Scenario B)?

Answer: $1,280,060 if it applies the full §179 expense to the five-year property (Scenario A) and $1,337,160 if it applies it to the seven-year property (Scenario B). See the computations below:

Description	(Scenario A) §179 Expense on 5-Year Property	(Scenario B) §179 Expense on 7-Year Property	Explanation
(1) Original basis	$1,400,000	$1,400,000	
(2) Elected §179 expense	1,000,000	1,000,000	Maximum expense
(3) Remaining basis	400,000	400,000	(1) − (2)
(4) MACRS depreciation rate	20%	14.29%	See Table 1
(5) MACRS depreciation expense	$ 80,000	$ 57,160	(3) × (4)
(6) Deductible §179 expense	1,000,000	1,000,000	Maximum §179 expense allowed this year.
(7) MACRS depreciation on other property	200,060	280,000	This is the depreciation on the $1,400,000 7-year property in the 5-year column ($1,400,000 × 14.29% = $200,060 and on the $1,400,000 5-year property in the 7-year column ($1,400,000 × 20% = $280,000).
Total depreciation expense	**$1,280,060**	**$1,337,160**	(5) + (6) + (7)

Note that Teton deducts $57,100 more in depreciation expense if it applies the §179 expense to the seven-year property.

with the lowest first-year cost recovery percentage including bonus depreciation (discussed in the next section).[34, 35]

Bonus Depreciation   Since 2001, businesses have had the ability to immediately deduct a percentage of the acquisition cost of qualifying assets under rules known as **bonus depreciation.**[36] The percentage allowable for each tax year during this period has changed many times ranging from 30 percent to 100 percent. Just prior to the TCJA, the bonus percentage was 50 percent. However, the TCJA increased the percentage to 100 percent for qualified property acquired after September 27, 2017. This provision (and the enhancement of §179) simplifies the depreciation calculation for many businesses because they can deduct the full amount of certain assets placed in service during the year.[37] There are several nuances of this provision that businesses need to consider. We discuss them in this section.

Bonus depreciation is mandatory for all taxpayers that qualify. However, taxpayers may elect out of bonus depreciation (on a property class basis) by attaching a statement to their tax return indicating they are electing not to claim bonus depreciation.[38] That is, taxpayers can elect out of bonus depreciation for all of their 5-year class property but still claim bonus for all of their 7-year property acquisitions. The election to opt out of bonus depreciation is made annually. Businesses in a loss position may want to elect out of bonus depreciation to reduce these losses, which may be limited under the NOL rules. In addition, businesses may want to elect out of bonus and use §179 instead because §179 allows taxpayers to pick and choose carefully which assets to expense whereas bonus is all-or-nothing based on property class. For taxpayers claiming the deduction, bonus depreciation is calculated after the §179 expense but before regular MACRS depreciation.[39] Bonus depreciation is a temporary provision and the percentage phases down after five years.[40] The bonus depreciation percentages by year are provided in Exhibit 10-9.

EXHIBIT 10-9   **Bonus Depreciation Percentages**[41]

Placed in Service	Bonus Depreciation Percentage
September 28, 2017 – December 31, 2022	100 percent
2023	80 percent
2024	60 percent
2025	40 percent
2026	20 percent
2027 and after	None

[34]Treasury Regulation §1.168(d)-1(b)(4)(i).

[35]Looking at Tables 2a and 2c in Appendix A, if a business has to choose between immediately expensing seven-year property placed in service in the first quarter or five-year property placed in service in the third quarter, which asset should it elect to expense under §179 if it wants to maximize its current-year depreciation expense? The answer is the five-year asset because its first-year depreciation percentage is 15 percent, while the seven-year asset's first-year depreciation percentage is 25 percent. Finally, note that businesses reduce the basis of the assets for the §179 expense before computing whether the mid-quarter convention applies.

[36]§168(k)(1).

[37]Many states do not allow bonus depreciation, so businesses will be required to calculate their depreciation using basic MACRS for those state tax returns.

[38]§168(k)(7). Property classes are broader categories of the asset classes discussed in Rev. Proc. 87-56. There are nine property classes of assets: 3-year, 5-year, 7-year, 10-year, 15-year, 20-year, 25-year, residential rental property, and nonresidential real property.

[39]Reg. §1.168(k)-1(a)(2)(iii) and Reg. §1.168(k)-1(d)(3) Example (2).

[40]§168(k)(6).

[41]A transition rule allows taxpayers to use a 50 percent bonus percentage for their first taxable year ending after September 27, 2017 [§168(k)(10)(A)].

Qualified property. Taxpayers must first determine whether the assets acquired during the year are eligible for bonus depreciation. To qualify, property must meet the following requirements:[42]

(1) New or used property (as long as the property had not previously been used by the taxpayer),[43]

(2) Have a regular depreciation life of 20 years or less,

(3) Computer software,[44]

(4) Water utility property, or

(5) Qualified film, television, and live theatrical productions.[45]

Example 10-15

What if: Assume that Teton claims bonus depreciation for the eligible personal property acquired in Exhibit 10-8.

Asset	Date acquired	Cost Basis	Recovery Period
Computers & information systems	3/3/2018	$ 920,000	5
Delivery truck*	5/26/2018	80,000	5
Machinery	8/15/2018	1,200,000	7
Total		$2,200,000	

*Steve had used this truck personally and converted it to business use in May.

Assuming Teton elects no §179 expense, what is Teton's bonus depreciation?

Answer: $2,120,000, computed as follows:

Description	Amount	Explanation
(1) Qualified property	$ 2,120,000	All but the delivery truck
(2) Bonus depreciation rate	100%	§168(k)(1)(A) and §168(k)(6)(i)
Bonus depreciation	**$2,120,000**	(1) × (2)

Note that the delivery truck is not eligible for bonus depreciation. Although used property usually qualifies, the truck is ineligible because Steve used the truck before converting it to business property. The delivery truck's cost will be recovered using basic MACRS rules.

---

[42]Under prior law, qualified improvements were considered eligible for bonus depreciation, and Congress likely intended for this property to be eligible. However, due to a technical error in the TCJA, qualified improvement property is currently considered 39-year property and is not eligible for bonus depreciation (although it is eligible for §179).

[43]§168(k)(2)((E)(ii). Taxpayers may not use bonus depreciation for assets received as a gift or inheritance, for like-kind property (unless the taxpayer pays money in addition to the exchanged property), for property received in nontaxable exchanges (reorganizations), or for property acquired from a related entity.

[44]For this purpose, computer software means any program designed to cause a computer to perform a desired function. This software has a basic MACRS cost recovery period of five years.

[45]Qualified film, television, and live theatrical productions are defined in §181.

What if: Assuming Teton elects the maximum §179 expense, what is Teton's bonus depreciation?

Answer: $1,200,000, computed as follows:

Description	Amount	Explanation
(1) §179 qualified property	$ 2,200,000	
(2) §179 expense	1,000,000	Maximum expense
(3) Remaining basis	$ 1,200,000	(1) – (2)
(4) Remaining amount eligible for bonus depreciation	1,200,000	Remaining amount relates to the computers and the machinery. Because the truck is not eligible for bonus depreciation, we apply the §179 expense first to the truck to maximize the current-year depreciation deduction. We next apply the §179 expense to the machinery (7-year), which reduces its basis to $280,000.
(5) Bonus depreciation rate	100%	§168(k)(1)(A) and §168(k)(6)(A)(i)
(6) Bonus depreciation	**$1,200,000**	(4) × (5)

What if: Assuming Teton elects the maximum §179 and bonus depreciation, what is Teton's total depreciation on its personal property?

Answer: $2,200,000. Teton is able to fully depreciate its tangible personal property placed in service in 2018 due to a combination of §179 ($1,000,000) and bonus depreciation ($1,200,000). Teton does not need to calculate regular MACRS depreciation on any of its tangible personal property. Alternatively, Teton could elect to take §179 on the delivery truck only and use bonus depreciation on the remaining assets. This option would produce $80,000 of §179 expense and $2,120,000 of bonus depreciation, for a total of $2,200,000.

Listed Property   Most business-owned assets are used for business rather than personal purposes. For example, Weyerhaeuser employees probably have little or no personal interest in using Weyerhaeuser's timber-harvesting equipment during their free time. In contrast, business owners and employees may find some business assets, such as company automobiles or laptop computers, conducive to personal use.

Business assets that tend to be used for both business and personal purposes are referred to as **listed property.** For example, automobiles, other means of transportation (planes, boats, and recreation vehicles), and even digital cameras are considered to be listed property. The tax law limits the allowable depreciation on listed property to the portion of the asset used for business purposes.

How do taxpayers compute depreciation for listed property? First, they must determine the percentage of business versus personal use of the asset for the year. If the business-use percentage for the year exceeds 50 percent, the deductible depreciation is limited to the full annual depreciation multiplied by the business-use percentage for the year. Listed property used in trade or business more than 50 percent of the time is eligible for the §179 expensing election and bonus depreciation (limited to the business-use percentage).

THE KEY FACTS

Listed Property
- When an asset is used for both personal and business use, calculate the business-use percentage.
- If the business-use percentage is above 50 percent, the allowable depreciation is limited to the business-use percentage.
- If a listed property's business-use percentage ever falls to or below 50 percent, depreciation for all previous years is retroactively restated using MACRS straight-line method.

Example 10-16

What if: Assume that, in addition to the assets Teton purchased in 2018 presented in Exhibit 10-8, it also purchased a new digital camera for $2,000 that its employees use for business on weekdays. On weekends, Steve uses the camera for his photography hobby. Since the camera is listed property, Teton must assess the business-use percentage to properly calculate its deductible depreciation for the camera. Assuming that Teton determines the business-use percentage to be 75 percent, what is Teton's depreciation deduction on the camera for the year (ignoring bonus depreciation and §179 expensing)?

Answer: $300, computed as follows:

Description	Amount	Explanation
(1) Original basis of camera	$2,000	
(2) MACRS depreciation rate	20%	5-year property, year 1, half-year convention
(3) Full MACRS depreciation expense	$ 400	(1) × (2)
(4) Business-use percentage	75%	
Depreciation deduction for year	**$ 300**	(3) × (4)

When the business-use percentage of an asset is 50 percent or less, the business must compute depreciation for the asset using the MACRS *straight-line* method over the MACRS ADS (alternative depreciation system) recovery period.[46] For five-year assets such as automobiles, the assets on which the personal-use limitation is most common, the MACRS ADS recovery period is also five years. However, for seven-year assets, the ADS recovery period is generally 10 years.[47]

If a business initially uses an asset more than 50 percent of the time for business (and appropriately adopts the 200 percent declining balance method, §179, or bonus depreciation) but subsequently its business use drops to 50 percent or below, the depreciation expense for all prior years must be recomputed as if the business had been using the straight-line depreciation over the ADS recovery period the entire time. The firm must then recapture any excess accelerated depreciation (including §179 and bonus depreciation) it deducted over the straight-line depreciation that it should have deducted by adjusting the current-year depreciation. In practical terms, the business can use the following five steps to determine its current depreciation expense for the asset:

Step 1: Compute depreciation for the year it drops to 50 percent or below using the straight-line method (this method also applies to all subsequent years).

Step 2: Compute the amount of depreciation the taxpayer would have deducted if the taxpayer had used the straight-line method over the ADS recovery period for all prior years (recall that depreciation is limited to the business-use percentage in those years).

Step 3: Compute the amount of depreciation (including §179 and bonus depreciation) the taxpayer actually deducted on the asset for all prior years.

Step 4: Subtract the amount from Step 2 from the amount in Step 3. The difference is the prior-year accelerated depreciation in excess of straight-line depreciation.

Step 5: Subtract the excess accelerated depreciation determined in Step 4 from the current-year straight-line depreciation in Step 1. This is the business's allowable depreciation expense on the asset for the year. If the prior-year excess depreciation from Step 4 exceeds the current-year straight-line depreciation in Step 1, the business is not allowed to deduct any depreciation on the asset for the year and must recognize additional ordinary income for the amount of the excess.

This five-step process is designed to place the business in the same position it would have been in if it had used straight-line depreciation during all years of the asset's life.

[46]This is the alternative recovery period listed in Rev. Proc. 87-56. See §168(g)(3)(C) and Reg. §1.280F-3T(d)(1).

[47]However, there are exceptions to this general rule. For example, the ADS recovery period for certain machinery for food and beverages is 12 years and the ADS recovery period for machinery for tobacco products is 15 years. Thus, it is important to check Rev. Proc. 87-56 to verify the ADS recovery period in these situations.

Example 10-17

What if: Assume that, consistent with the previous example, in 2018 Teton used the camera 75 percent of the time for business purposes and deducted $1,500 depreciation expense on the camera. However, in year 2, Teton's business-use percentage falls to 40 percent. What is Teton's depreciation deduction for the camera in year 2?

Answer: $10, computed using the five-step process described above as follows:

Description	Amount	Explanation*
(1) Straight-line depreciation in current year	$160	$2,000/5 years × 40 percent business-use percentage (Step 1)
(2) Prior-year straight-line depreciation	150	$2,000/5 × 50 percent (half-year convention) × 75 percent business-use percentage (Step 2)
(3) Prior-year accelerated depreciation	300	Example 10-14 (prior example) (Step 3)
(4) Excess accelerated depreciation	150	(3) − (2) (Step 4)
Allowable current-year depreciation	**$ 10**	(1) − (4) (Step 5)

*Note that the MACRS ADS recovery period (five years) for digital cameras (qualified technological equipment) is the same as the standard MACRS recovery period (five years).

What if: Now assume that, in 2018, Teton took bonus depreciation and deducted $1,500 depreciation expense ($2,000 × 100% × 75%) on the camera. However, in year 2, Teton's business-use percentage falls to 40 percent. What is Teton's depreciation deduction for the camera in year 2?

Answer: $0 depreciation deduction and $1,190 of ordinary income because excess accelerated depreciation exceeds current-year straight-line depreciation, computed as follows:

Description	Amount	Explanation
(1) Straight-line depreciation in current year	$160	$2,000/5 years × 40 percent business use
(2) Prior-year straight-line depreciation	150	$2,000/5 × 50 percent (half-year convention) × 75 percent business-use percentage from year 1
(3) Prior-year accelerated depreciation	1,500	Bonus depreciation
(4) Excess accelerated depreciation	1,350	(3) − (2)
Allowable current-year depreciation (income)	**($1,190)**	(1) − (4)

TAXES IN THE REAL WORLD   Cost Segregation

Consider a taxpayer that purchases a strip mall for $1 million, excluding land, in July. Typically, the taxpayer records the purchase as a 39-year asset and depreciates it using a straight-line method according to the MACRS rules for depreciating real property. After five years, the taxpayer would have claimed $114,330 of depreciation deductions on the property. Is it possible for the taxpayer to accelerate the depreciation deductions on the property to take advantage of the timing tax planning strategy? Yes, with the help of a cost segregation study! Cost segregation is the process of identifying personal property assets that are included in the purchase price of real property such as a strip mall. Cost segregation separates out the personal property from the real property for tax reporting purposes. Personal property includes a building's nonstructural elements, exterior land improvements, and indirect construction costs. Now suppose a cost segregation study on the strip mall identifies five-year property of $200,000, 15-year property of $250,000, and 39-year property of $550,000. The taxpayer would claim $345,562 of depreciation expense over the five-year period, even without considering bonus depreciation on the identified personal property. Taking bonus depreciation into consideration, the total depreciation over the five years would be $512,882, an increase of almost $398,552 in deductions over the five-year period!

Luxury Automobiles   As we discussed in the Business Income, Deductions, and Accounting Methods chapter, §162 limits business deductions to those considered to be "ordinary, necessary, and reasonable" to prevent subsidizing (giving a tax deduction for) unwarranted business expenses. Although these terms are subject to interpretation, most taxpayers agree that for purposes of simply transporting passengers for business-related purposes, the cost of acquiring and using a Ford Focus is more likely to be ordinary, necessary, and reasonable than the cost of acquiring and using a Ferrari California—although perhaps not as exhilarating. Since either vehicle should be able to transport an employee or business owner from the office to a business meeting, the Ford Focus should be just as effective at accomplishing the business purpose as the Ferrari.

If this is true, why should the government help taxpayers pay for expensive cars with tax savings from large depreciation deductions associated with automobiles? Congress decided it shouldn't. Therefore, with certain exceptions we discuss below, the tax laws generally limit the annual depreciation expense for automobiles. Each year, the IRS provides a maximum depreciation schedule for automobiles placed in service during that particular year.[48] In 2018, taxpayers are allowed to expense $8,000 of bonus depreciation above the otherwise allowable maximum depreciation (maximum depreciation of $18,000).[49] Exhibit 10-10 summarizes these schedules for automobiles placed in service for each year from 2018 back to 2015. The TCJA substantially increased the limitations in 2018 perhaps because the limitations had become severe relative to automobile prices. That is, a limit of $3,160 would apply for an automobile costing more than $15,800, which most would not consider a "luxury" car.

EXHIBIT 10-10   **Automobile Depreciation Limits**

Recovery Year	Year Placed in Service			
	2018	**2017**	**2016**	**2015**
1	10,000*	3,160*	3,160*	3,160*
2	16,000	5,100	5,100	5,100
3	9,600	3,050	3,050	3,050
4 and after	5,760	1,875	1,875	1,875

*$8,000 additional depreciation is allowed when bonus depreciation is claimed (§168(k)(2)(F)).

Ignoring bonus depreciation for a moment, businesses placing automobiles into service during the year determine depreciation for the automobiles by first computing regular MACRS depreciation (using the appropriate convention). They then compare it to the maximum depreciation amount for the first year of the recovery period based on the IRS-provided tables. Businesses are allowed to deduct the lesser of the two. Each subsequent year, businesses should compare the regular MACRS amount with the limitation amount and deduct the lesser of the basic MACRS depreciation or the limitation. In 2018, if the half-year convention applies, the table limits the depreciation on automobiles placed in service during the year costing more than $50,000.[50] Automobiles to which the depreciation limits apply are commonly referred to as **luxury automobiles**.[51] Comparing the lifetime depreciation for two cars—say, a 2019 Honda Civic and a 2019 Porsche 911—we can see that the annual depreciation deduction is lower and the recovery period much shorter for the Civic than for the Porsche. In fact, the Porsche will take 17 years to fully depreciate!

[48]These limitations are indexed for inflation and change annually. §280F(a)(1)(A) provides the 2018 limitations for automobiles.

[49]§168(k)(2)(F)(i).

[50]In 2018, the full first-year depreciation on an automobile costing $50,000 is $10,000 ($50,000 × 20 percent). This is the amount of the first-year limit for automobiles placed in service in 2018.

[51]Correspondingly, the depreciation limits on automobiles are commonly referred to as the *luxury auto depreciation limits.*

Example 10-18

What is the maximum annual depreciation deduction available for 2018 (year 1) on a 2019 Honda Civic costing $19,150 and a 2019 Porsche 911 costing $112,000 (ignoring bonus depreciation)?

Answer: $3,830 for the Honda and $10,000 for the Porsche. See the following depreciation schedules for each automobile.

Luxury Auto Depreciation		
Year/Make	**2019 Honda Civic**	**2019 Porsche 911**
Model	DX 2dr Coupe	Carrera 4S
Price	$19,150	$112,000
Depreciation		
Year 1	$ 3,830	$ 10,000
Year 2	6,128	16,000
Year 3	3,677	9,600
Year 4	2,206	5,760
Year 5	2,206	5,760
Year 6	1,103	5,760
Year 7		5,760
Year 8		5,760
Years 9-16		5,760
Year 17		1,520

The depreciation schedule for the Honda Civic follows the standard depreciation amounts calculated under MACRS because these annual amounts are lower than the limitations. The Honda is fully depreciated in year 6. The MACRS depreciation amounts for the Porsche, however, exceed the limitations so the schedule shows the limited amount of depreciation each year. The limitations extend the recovery period for the Porsche to 17 years—however, it is unlikely the business will actually hold the Porsche through year 17.

The luxury automobile limitations don't apply to vehicles weighing more than 6,000 pounds (for example, large SUVs) and those that charge for transportation such as taxi cabs, limousines, and hearses. It also excludes delivery trucks and vans. Thus, businesses owning these vehicles are allowed to claim §179, bonus, and regular MACRS depreciation expense for these vehicles.[52]

Just like businesses using other types of listed property, businesses using automobiles exceeding the automobile limitation for business and personal purposes may deduct depreciation on the asset only to the extent of business use. Business use is determined by miles driven for business purposes relative to total miles driven for the year.[53] Consequently, if a business places a luxury automobile into service in 2018 and uses the automobile 90 percent of the time for business purposes during the year (9,000 miles for business and 1,000 miles of personal use), the owner's depreciation (ignoring bonus depreciation) on the auto for the year is limited to $9,000 (year 1 full depreciation of $10,000 × 90 percent business use—see Exhibit 10-10).[54] Further, if the business use falls to 50 percent or less in any subsequent year, just as with other listed property, the taxpayer must use the straight-line method of depreciation and reduce depreciation expense by the amount of excess accelerated depreciation (see Example 10-17). However, because straight-line depreciation is also limited by the luxury auto depreciation limits, it may turn out that the business doesn't have any excess accelerated depreciation.

---

[52]§280F(d)(5)(A).

[53]As an alternative to deducting depreciation expense and other costs of operating an automobile, taxpayers using automobiles for both personal and business purposes may deduct a standard mileage rate for each mile of business use. In 2018 the business mileage rate is 54.5 cents per mile.

[54]Even if the business-use percentage multiplied by the MACRS depreciation is greater than the $10,000 maximum, the depreciation amount is limited to the maximum depreciation amount times the business-use percentage.

Automobiles and §179.   Are businesses allowed to deduct §179 expensing on luxury automobiles? The answer is yes, but . . . the luxury car limitation in 2018 is $10,000 and this limit applies regardless of whether the taxpayer claims regular MACRS depreciation or §179 expensing on the car. So, for cars that cost more than $50,000, the taxpayer doesn't benefit by electing §179 because the regular MACRS depreciation deduction would be greater than $10,000 but would be limited to $10,000 anyway. For cars that cost less than $50,000, taxpayers could benefit by electing to take $10,000 of §179 expense on the car to boost the depreciation deduction in first year. For instance, in Example 10-18, the regular MACRS depreciation amount for the Honda Civic was only $3,830. By electing §179, a taxpayer could increase the first-year depreciation deduction to $10,000.

Recall that large SUVs (those weighing more than 6,000 pounds) are not subject to the luxury car limitations. Therefore a business will calculate its regular MACRS depreciation each year without the limitations for passenger cars. For these vehicles, businesses may take a §179 expense amount of $25,000 in 2018 in the acquisition year in addition to their MACRS depreciation (calculated after the §179 expense).[55]

Automobiles and bonus depreciation.   But wait! Why don't businesses simply use bonus depreciation to fully recover the cost of their automobiles in the year they buy the vehicle? For passenger cars (automobiles weighing 6,000 pounds or less), the luxury car limitations still apply. With bonus depreciation taxpayers are allowed to increase the limitation in the first year by $8,000 making the first-year limit $18,000 in 2018.

Example 10-19

What if: Suppose Teton purchases a $62,000 car, which is used 100 percent of the time for business purposes. Teton would like to claim bonus depreciation. What is Teton's depreciation deduction for the car in 2018?

Answer: $18,000, calculated as follows:

Description	Amount	Explanation
(1) Automobile	$ 62,000	
(2) Bonus percentage	100%	§168(k)(1) and §168(k)(6)(A)(i)
(3) MACRS depreciation	$ 62,000	(1) × (2)
(4) Luxury car limitation	18,000	Luxury car limitation [[$10,000 [§280F(a)(1)] + $8,000 [§168(k)(2)(F)]]]
Year 1 depreciation	**$18,000**	Lesser of (3) or (4)

In year 1, Teton's regular depreciation on the car would have been $12,400 ($62,000 × 20 percent MACRS percentage). This amount is greater than the $10,000 automobile limitation, so without taking bonus Teton would be limited to $10,000 of depreciation on the car. By taking bonus depreciation, Teton is able to increase 2018 depreciation by $8,000.

However, in years 2–6 (recovery period for passenger cars), taxpayers must again compare the regular MACRS amount in each year to the car limitation in Exhibit 10-10 for the year. If the taxpayer claims bonus depreciation, then technically, all of the allowable depreciation was taken in year 1 (100 percent bonus depreciation) even though the taxpayer was limited by the automobile limitations. This means that there is no regular depreciation remaining for years 2–6. So, absent a special rule, taxpayers would not be allowed to take ANY depreciation for those years. The remaining cost to be recovered would occur beginning in year 7 using the limitation for year 4 and after. Fortunately the IRS provides a way for taxpayers to continue to take depreciation in years 2–6 when they claim bonus depreciation.[56] The entire calculation involves a 6-step process as follows:

---

[55]This amount is indexed for inflation beginning with years after 2018 (§179(b)(6)).
[56]Rev. Proc. 2011-26.

Year 1:

Step 1: Deduct the lower of the cost of the automobile or the first year limitation from Exhibit 10-10 plus the additional $8,000 bonus amount, which is $18,000 for 2018.

Step 2: Calculate depreciation "as if" the bonus amount in year 1 were 50 percent rather than 100 percent. This step requires taxpayers to take 50 percent of the basis as bonus then reduce the original basis by the 50 percent bonus amount to calculate the regular MACRS depreciation on the remaining basis.

Step 3: Subtract the actual depreciation taken in year 1 from Step 1 from the "as if" year 1 depreciation amount determined in Step 2. If positive, this unrecovered basis is not deductible until after the MACRS recovery period expires (year 7).

Step 4: Determine the "as if" remaining depreciable basis amount. The remaining basis for calculating years 2–6 depreciation is the original cost less the 50 percent bonus.

Years 2–6:

Step 5: The remaining depreciable basis calculated in Step 4 is depreciated by taking the lesser of 1) the MACRS depreciation on the remaining basis or 2) the automobile limitation from Exhibit 10-10 for each recovery year.

Years 7 and after:

Step 6: If any basis remains undepreciated after the end of year 6 (the end of the MACRS recovery period) because of the automobile limitations, it is recovered beginning in year 7 but is limited to the amount provided in Exhibit 10-10 for periods 4 and after.

Example 10-20

What if: Same facts as in Example 10-19. What is Teton's depreciation on the car in year 2?

Answer: $9,920, calculated as follows:

Step	Amount	Description
Step 1: Year 1 depreciation	$18,000	Calculated in Example 10-19
Step 2: "As if" year 1 depreciation	37,200	"As if" year 1 depreciation is 50% bonus depreciation of $31,000 ($62,000 × 50%) plus MACRS depreciation on the remaining $31,000 basis of $6,200 ($31,000 × 20%).
Step 3: Unrecovered basis	19,200	Step 2 - Step 1; This is the unrecovered basis, which will be deductible beginning in year 7.
Step 4: Remaining "as if" depreciable basis	31,000	Cost of $62,000 × 50%. This is the remaining depreciable basis.
Step 5: Year 2 depreciation	$ 9,920	Lesser of $9,920 [$31,000 (Step 4) x 32% (5-year property, year 2MACRS percentage)] or $16,000 (Year 2 limitation)
Step 6: Recovery of Step 3 amount	N/A	The unrecovered basis from step 3 will be recovered beginning in year 7 and has no impact on the year 2 depreciation amount.

Can taxpayers avoid this calculation? Yes! There are at least two ways to avoid having to calculate depreciation on cars in this way. First, taxpayers can elect out of bonus depreciation. By electing out of bonus, taxpayers would calculate the depreciation on automobiles as the lesser of the regular MACRS depreciation or the limitation amount for each year. The downside of electing out of bonus for automobiles is that the election must be done on a property class basis. Automobiles are in the 5-year property class, but so are computers and office machinery (calculators and copiers). So, if taxpayers elect out of bonus for automobiles, they also elect out for other assets included in the 5-year property class. The second way to avoid this calculation is to purchase SUVs that weigh more than

6,000 pounds instead of passenger cars. These large SUVs are not subject to the listed property automobile limitations. Taxpayers can deduct the full cost of these vehicles in the first year under the bonus depreciation rules.

Depreciation for the Alternative Minimum Tax

Individuals are subject to tax under the alternative minimum tax (AMT) system.[57] In determining their alternative minimum taxable income, individuals may be required to recalculate their depreciation expense. For AMT purposes, the allowable recovery period and conventions are the same for all depreciable assets as they are for regular tax purposes.[58] However, for AMT purposes, businesses are not allowed to use the 200 percent declining balance method to depreciate tangible personal property. Rather, they must choose from the 150 percent declining balance method or the straight-line method to depreciate the property for AMT purposes. The difference between regular tax depreciation and AMT depreciation is an adjustment that is either added to or subtracted from regular taxable income in computing the alternative minimum tax base.[59] In contrast, the §179 expense and bonus depreciation are equally deductible for both regular tax and AMT purposes. Depreciation of real property is the same for both regular tax and AMT purposes.

Depreciation Summary

Teton's depreciation for 2018 on all its assets is summarized in Exhibit 10-11 and Exhibit 10-12 presents Teton's depreciation as it would be reported on its tax return on Form 4562 (assuming Teton does not elect §179 and elects out of bonus depreciation for assets acquired in 2017).

EXHIBIT 10-11   Teton's 2018 Depreciation Expense

	Date Acquired	Original Basis	§179 Expense	Remaining Basis*	Bonus Depreciation	Remaining basis	Depreciation Expense	Reference
2017 Assets								
Machinery	7/22/2017	$ 610,000	—	$610,000	—	$ 610,000	$ 149,389	Example 10-5
Office furniture	2/3/2017	20,000	—	20,000	—	20,000	4,898	Example 10-5
Delivery truck	8/17/2017	25,000	—	25,000	—	25,000	8,000	Example 10-5
Warehouse	5/1/2017	275,000	—	275,000	—	275,000	7,051	Example 10-9
Land	5/1/2017	75,000	—	75,000	—	75,000	—	N/A
2018 Assets								
Computers & info systems	3/3/2018	920,000	—	920,000	920,000	—	—	Example 10-15 *What if* scenario
Delivery truck	5/26/2018	80,000	80,000	—	—	—	—	Example 10-15 *What if* scenario
Machinery	8/15/2018	1,200,000	920,000	280,000	280,000	—	—	Example 10-15 *What if* scenario
§179 expense							1,000,000	Example 10-15 *What if* scenario
Bonus depreciation							1,200,000	Example 10-15 *What if* scenario
Total 2018 Depreciation Expense							**$2,369,338**	

[57]Corporations are no longer subject to the alternative minimum tax for tax years after December 31, 2017.

[58]This is true for assets placed in service after 1998.

[59]If the taxpayer elected either the 150 percent declining balance or the straight-line method for regular tax depreciation of tangible personal property, then there is no AMT adjustment with respect to that property.

EXHIBIT 10-12 Teton's Form 4562 Parts I–IV for Depreciation (Assumes $1,500,000 of taxable income before the §179 expense)

Form **4562**

Department of the Treasury
Internal Revenue Service   (99)

Depreciation and Amortization
(Including Information on Listed Property)
▶ Attach to your tax return.
▶ Go to *www.irs.gov/Form4562* for instructions and the latest information.

OMB No. 1545-0172

20**17**

Attachment
Sequence No. **179**

Name(s) shown on return	Business or activity to which this form relates	Identifying number
Steve Dallimore	Teton Mountaineering Technologies, LLC	

Part I Election To Expense Certain Property Under Section 179
Note: If you have any listed property, complete Part V before you complete Part I.

1	Maximum amount (see instructions)	**1**	1,000,000
2	Total cost of section 179 property placed in service (see instructions)	**2**	1,200,000
3	Threshold cost of section 179 property before reduction in limitation (see instructions)	**3**	2,500,000
4	Reduction in limitation. Subtract line 3 from line 2. If zero or less, enter -0-	**4**	0
5	Dollar limitation for tax year. Subtract line 4 from line 1. If zero or less, enter -0-. If married filing separately, see instructions	**5**	1,000,000

6	(a) Description of property	(b) Cost (business use only)	(c) Elected cost	
	Machinery	1,200,000	920,000	
	Delivery Truck	80,000	80,000	

7	Listed property. Enter the amount from line 29 . . . . **7**		
8	Total elected cost of section 179 property. Add amounts in column (c), lines 6 and 7	**8**	1,000,000
9	Tentative deduction. Enter the **smaller** of line 5 or line 8	**9**	1,000,000
10	Carryover of disallowed deduction from line 13 of your 2016 Form 4562	**10**	
11	Business income limitation. Enter the smaller of business income (not less than zero) or line 5 (see instructions)	**11**	1.000,000
12	Section 179 expense deduction. Add lines 9 and 10, but don't enter more than line 11	**12**	1,000,000
13	Carryover of disallowed deduction to 2018. Add lines 9 and 10, less line 12 ▶ **13**		

Note: Don't use Part II or Part III below for listed property. Instead, use Part V.

Part II Special Depreciation Allowance and Other Depreciation (Don't include listed property.) (See instructions.)

14	Special depreciation allowance for qualified property (other than listed property) placed in service during the tax year (see instructions)	**14**	1,200,000
15	Property subject to section 168(f)(1) election	**15**	
16	Other depreciation (including ACRS)	**16**	

Part III MACRS Depreciation (Don't include listed property.) (See instructions.)
Section A

17	MACRS deductions for assets placed in service in tax years beginning before 2017	**17**	169,338
18	If you are electing to group any assets placed in service during the tax year into one or more general asset accounts, check here . . . . ▶ ☐		

Section B—Assets Placed in Service During 2017 Tax Year Using the General Depreciation System

(a) Classification of property	(b) Month and year placed in service	(c) Basis for depreciation (business/investment use only—see instructions)	(d) Recovery period	(e) Convention	(f) Method	(g) Depreciation deduction
19a 3-year property						
b 5-year property						
c 7-year property						
d 10-year property						
e 15-year property						
f 20-year property						
g 25-year property			25 yrs.		S/L	
h Residential rental property			27.5 yrs.	MM	S/L	
			27.5 yrs.	MM	S/L	
i Nonresidential real property			39 yrs.	MM	S/L	
				MM	S/L	

Section C—Assets Placed in Service During 2017 Tax Year Using the Alternative Depreciation System

20a Class life					S/L	
b 12-year			12 yrs.		S/L	
c 40-year			40 yrs.	MM	S/L	

Part IV Summary (See instructions.)

21	Listed property. Enter amount from line 28	**21**	
22	**Total.** Add amounts from line 12, lines 14 through 17, lines 19 and 20 in column (g), and line 21. Enter here and on the appropriate lines of your return. Partnerships and S corporations—see instructions	**22**	2,369,338
23	For assets shown above and placed in service during the current year, enter the portion of the basis attributable to section 263A costs **23**		

For Paperwork Reduction Act Notice, see separate instructions.   Cat. No. 12906N   Form **4562** (2017)

Source: IRS Form 4562, 2017

LO 10-4 # AMORTIZATION

Businesses recover the cost of intangible assets through amortization rather than depreciation. Intangible assets in the form of capitalized expenditures, such as capitalized **research and experimentation (R&E) costs** or **covenants not to compete,** do not have physical characteristics. Nonetheless, they may have determinable lives. While research and experimentation costs may have an indeterminate life, a covenant not to compete, for example, would have a life equal to the stated term of the contractual agreement. When the life of intangible assets cannot be determined, taxpayers recover the cost of the assets when they dispose of them—unless they are assigned a specific tax recovery period.

For tax purposes, an intangible asset can be placed into one of the following four general categories:

1. §197 purchased intangibles.
2. Start-up expenditures and organizational costs.
3. Research and experimentation costs.
4. Patents and copyrights.

Businesses amortize all intangible assets in these categories using the straight-line method for both financial accounting and tax purposes.

Section 197 Intangibles

THE KEY FACTS

§197 Intangible Assets

- Purchased intangibles are amortized over a period of 180 months, regardless of their explicitly stated lives.
- The full-month convention applies to amortizable assets.

When a business purchases the *assets* of another business for a single purchase price, the business must determine the initial basis of each of the assets it acquired in the transaction. To determine basis, the business must allocate a portion of the purchase price to each of the individual assets acquired in the transaction. Generally, under this approach, each asset acquired (cash, machinery, and real property, for example) takes a basis equal to its fair market value. However, some of the assets acquired in the transaction may not appear on the seller's balance sheet. In fact, a substantial portion of a business's value may exist in the form of intangible assets such as customer lists, patents, trademarks, trade names, goodwill, going-concern value, covenants not to compete, and so forth. Nearly all these assets are amortized according to §197 of the Internal Revenue Code— hence, they are often referred to as **§197 intangibles.**

According to §197, these assets have a recovery period of 180 months (15 years), *regardless of their actual life.*[60] For example, when a business buys an existing business, the owner selling the business often signs a covenant not to compete for a specified period such as five years.[61] Even though a five-year covenant not to compete clearly has a fixed and determinable life, it must be amortized over 180 months (15 years). The **full-month convention** applies to the amortization of purchased intangibles. This convention allows taxpayers to deduct an entire month's worth of amortization for the month of purchase and all subsequent months in the year. The full-month convention also applies in the month of sale or disposition.[62]

---

[60]§197 was Congress's response to taxpayers manipulating the valuation and recovery periods assigned to these purchased intangibles.

[61]A covenant not to compete is a contract between the seller of a business and its buyer that the seller will not operate a similar business that would compete with the previous business for a specified period of time.

[62]Reg. §1.197-2(g)(l)(i) illustrates the special rules that apply when a taxpayer sells a §197 intangible or the intangible becomes worthless and the taxpayer's basis in the asset exceeds the sale proceeds (if any). A business may recognize a loss on the sale or disposition only when the business does not hold any other §197 assets that the business acquired in the *same initial transaction.* Otherwise, the taxpayer may not deduct the loss on the sale or disposition until the business sells or disposes of *all* of the other §197 intangibles that it purchased in the same initial transaction. The same loss disallowance rule applies if a §197 intangible expires before it is fully amortized.

Example 10-21

What if: Assume that on January 30, 2017, Teton acquires a competitor's assets for $350,000.[63] Of the $350,000 purchase price, $125,000 is allocated to tangible assets and $225,000 is allocated to §197 intangible assets (patent, goodwill, and a customer list with a three-year life).[64] For each of the first three years, Teton would deduct one-fifteenth of the basis of each asset as amortization expense. What is Teton's accumulated amortization and remaining basis in each of these §197 intangibles after three years?

Answer: See the table below:

Description	Patent	Goodwill	Customer List
Basis	$25,000	$150,000	$50,000
Accumulated amortization (3/15 of original basis)	(5,000)	(30,000)	(10,000)
Remaining basis	$20,000	$120,000	$40,000

When a taxpayer sells a §197 intangible for more than its basis, the taxpayer recognizes gain. We describe how to characterize this type of gain in the next chapter.

Organizational Expenditures and Start-Up Costs

Organizational expenditures include expenditures to form and organize a business in the form of a corporation or a partnership.[65] Organizational expenditures typically include costs of organizational meetings, state fees, accounting service costs incident to organization, and legal service expenditures such as document drafting, taking minutes of organizational meetings, and creating terms of the original stock certificates. These costs are generally incurred prior to the starting of business (or shortly thereafter) but relate to creating the business entity. The costs of selling or marketing stock do *not* qualify as organizational expenditures and cannot be amortized.[66]

Example 10-22

What if: Suppose Teton was organized as a corporation rather than a sole proprietorship (sole proprietorships cannot expense organizational expenditures). Steve paid $35,000 of legal costs to Scott, Tang, and Malan to draft the corporate charter and articles of incorporation; $10,000 to Harvey and Stratford for accounting fees related to the organization; and $7,000 for organizational meetings, $5,000 for stock issuance costs, and $1,000 for state fees related to the incorporation. What amounts of these expenditures qualify as organizational costs?

Answer: $53,000, computed as follows (with the exception of the stock issuance costs, each of Teton's expenses qualify as amortizable organizational expenditures):

Description	Qualifying Organizational Expenditures
Legal drafting of corporate charter and articles of incorporation	$ 35,000
Accounting fees related to organization	10,000
Organizational meetings	7,000
Stock issuance costs	0
State incorporation fees	1,000
Total	**$53,000**

THE KEY FACTS

Organizational Expenditures and Start-Up Costs

- Taxpayers may immediately expense up to $5,000 of organizational expenditures and $5,000 of start-up costs.
- The immediate expense rule has a dollar-for-dollar phase-out that begins at $50,000 for organizational expenditures and for start-up costs. Thus, when organizational expenditures or start-up costs exceed $55,000 there is no immediate expensing.

[63]If a business acquires a corporation's stock (rather than assets) there is no goodwill assigned for tax purposes, and the purchase price simply becomes the basis of the stock purchased.

[64]A customer base is the value assigned to current customers (i.e., the lists that will allow the new owner to capture future benefits from the current customers).

[65]§248 for corporations and §709 for partnerships. Sole proprietorships cannot deduct organizational expenditures.

[66]These syndication costs are capitalized and deducted on the final tax return.

Businesses may *immediately expense* up to $5,000 of organizational expenditures.[67] However, corporations and partnerships incurring more than $50,000 in organizational expenditures must phase out (reduce) the $5,000 immediate expense amount dollar for dollar for expenditures exceeding $50,000. Thus, businesses incurring at least $55,000 of organizational expenditures are not allowed to immediately expense any of the expenditures.

Example 10-23

What if: Suppose Teton is a corporation and it wants to maximize its first-year organizational expenditure deduction. As described in Example 10-22, Teton incurred $53,000 of organizational expenditures in year 1. How much of the organizational expenditures can Teton immediately deduct in year 1?

Answer: $2,000, computed as follows:

Description	Amount	Explanation
(1) Maximum immediate expense	$ 5,000	§248(a)(1)
(2) Total organizational expenditures	53,000	Example 10-22
(3) Phase-out threshold	50,000	§248(a)(1)(B)
(4) Immediate expense phase-out	3,000	(2) − (3)
(5) Allowable immediate expense	**2,000**	(1) − (4), but not below zero
Remaining organizational expenditures	$51,000*	(2) − (5)

What if: Assuming that Teton is a corporation and that it incurred $41,000 of organizational expenditures in year 1, how much of the organizational expenditures could Teton immediately expense in year 1?

Answer: $5,000, computed as follows:

Description	Amount	Explanation
(1) Maximum immediate expense	$ 5,000	§248(a)(1)
(2) Total organizational expenditures	41,000	
(3) Phase-out threshold	50,000	§248(a)(1)(B)
(4) Immediate expense phase-out	0	(2) − (3), limit to zero
(5) Allowable immediate expense	**5,000**	(1) − (4)
Remaining organizational expenditures	$36,000*	(2) − (5)

What if: Assuming that Teton is a corporation and it incurred $60,000 of organizational expenditures in year 1, how much of the organizational expenditures could Teton immediately expense in year 1?

Answer: $0, computed as follows:

Description	Amount	Explanation
(1) Maximum immediate expense	$ 5,000	§248(a)(1)
(2) Total organizational expenditures	60,000	
(3) Phase-out threshold	50,000	§248(a)(1)(B)
(4) Immediate expense phase-out	10,000	(2) − (3)
(5) Allowable immediate expense	**0**	(1) − (4)
Remaining organizational expenditures	$60,000*	(2) − (5)

*As we discuss below, Teton amortizes the remaining organizational costs.

Businesses amortize organizational expenditures that they do not immediately expense using the straight-line method over a recovery period of 15 years (180 months).

[67]§248(a)(1) for corporations or §709 for partnerships.

Example 10-24

What if: Assume Teton is a corporation and it amortizes the $51,000 of organizational expenditures remaining after it immediately expenses $2,000 of the costs (see the first *what-if* scenario in Example 10-23). If Teton began business on February 1 of year 1, how much total cost recovery expense for the organizational expenditures is Teton able to deduct in year 1? How much cost recovery expense will Teton be able to deduct in year 2?

Answer: $5,117 in year 1 and $3,400 in year 2, computed as follows:

Description	Amount	Explanation
(1) Total organizational expenditures	$53,000	Example 10-22
(2) Amount immediately expensed	2,000	Example 10-23
(3) Expenditures subject to straight-line amortization	$51,000	(1) − (2)
(4) Recovery period in months	180	15 years §248(a)(2)
(5) Monthly straight-line amortization	283.33	(3)/(4)
(6) Teton business months during year 1	× 11	February through December
(7) Year 1 straight-line amortization	3,117	(5) × (6)
Total year 1 cost recovery expense for organizational expenditures	**$ 5,117**	(2) + (7)
Total year 2 cost recovery expense	**3,400**	(3)/15 years

Start-up costs are costs businesses incur to, not surprisingly, start up a business.[68] Start-up costs apply to all types of business forms.[69] These costs include costs associated with investigating the possibilities of and actually creating or acquiring a trade or business. For example, costs Teton incurs in deciding whether to locate the business in Cody, Wyoming, or Bozeman, Montana, are start-up costs. Start-up costs also include costs that would normally be deductible as ordinary business expenses except that they don't qualify as business expenses because they are incurred before the trade or business activity actually begins. For example, costs Teton incurs to train its employees before the business begins are start-up costs.

The rules for immediately expensing and amortizing start-up costs are the same as those for immediately expensing and amortizing organizational expenditures. Consequently, businesses incurring at least $55,000 of start-up costs are not allowed to immediately expense any of the costs. The limitations are computed separately for organizational expenditures and for start-up costs. Thus, a business could immediately expense $5,000 of organizational expenditures and $5,000 of start-up costs in its first year of business in addition to the 15-year amortization amount.

Example 10-25

What if: Assume that in January of year 1 (before it began business on February 1) Teton spent $4,500 investigating the climbing hardware market, creating company logos, and determining the locations for both the office and manufacturing facility. The $4,500 of expenditures qualify as start-up costs. How much of the $4,500 of start-up costs is Teton allowed to immediately expense?

Answer: All $4,500. Teton is allowed to immediately expense the entire $4,500 because its total start-up costs do not exceed $50,000. Teton could have immediately expensed up to $5,000 of start-up costs as long as its total start-up costs did not exceed $50,000.

---

[68]§195.
[69]Recall that rules for amortizing organizational expenditures apply only to corporations and partnerships.

Exhibit 10-13 illustrates the timing of organizational expenditures, start-up costs, and normal trade or business expenses.

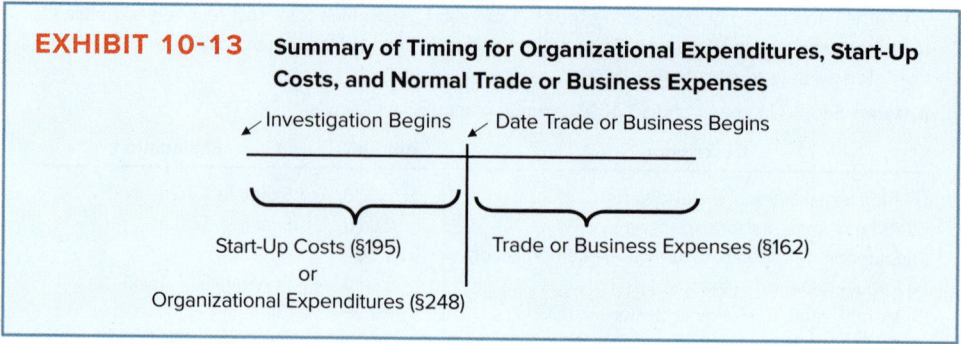

EXHIBIT 10-13   Summary of Timing for Organizational Expenditures, Start-Up Costs, and Normal Trade or Business Expenses

Research and Experimentation Expenditures

To stay competitive, businesses often invest in activities they believe will generate innovative products or significantly improve their current products or processes. These research and experimentation costs include expenditures for research laboratories, including salaries, materials, and other related expenses. Businesses may immediately expense these costs or they may *elect* to capitalize these costs and amortize them using the straight-line method over the determinable useful life or, if there is no determinable useful life, over a period of not less than 60 months, beginning in the month benefits are first derived from the research.[70] However, if a business elects to capitalize and amortize the costs, it must stop amortizing the costs if and when the business receives a patent relating to the expenditures. When the business obtains a patent, it adds any remaining basis in the costs to the basis of the patent and it amortizes the basis of the patent over the patent's life (see discussion below).

Patents and Copyrights

The manner in which a business amortizes a patent or copyright depends on whether the business directly purchases the patent or copyright or whether it self-creates the intangibles. Businesses directly purchasing patents or copyrights (not in an asset acquisition to which §197 applies) amortize the cost over the remaining life of the patents or copyrights.[71] Businesses receiving "self-created" patents or copyrights amortize the cost or basis of the self-created intangible assets over their legal lives. The costs included in the basis of a self-created patent or copyright include legal costs, fees, and, as we discussed above, unamortized research and experimentation expenditures associated with the creation of the patent or copyright. However, because the patent approval process is slow, the unamortized research and experimentation costs included in the patent's basis are likely to be relatively small because, with a five-year recovery period, the research and experimentation costs would likely be mostly or even fully amortized by the time the patent is approved.

---

[70]See §174. High-tax-rate taxpayers may choose to deduct these costs while low-tax-rate taxpayers may prefer to capitalize and amortize them so that they will have more future deductions when they generate more income. The research and experimentation credit is also available to some businesses. Beginning in tax years after December 31, 2021, taxpayers will no longer have the option of immediately expensing these costs. Rather, these costs will be capitalized and amortized ratably over five years beginning with the midpoint of the year in which the costs were incurred.

[71]§167(f).

In September of year 1, Teton purchased a patent with a remaining life of 10 years from Chouinard Equipment for $60,000. What amount of amortization expense is Teton allowed to deduct for the patent in year 1?

Answer: $2,000, computed as follows:

Description	Amount	Explanation
(1) Cost of patent	$60,000	
(2) Remaining life of patent in months	120	10 years
(3) Monthly amortization	$ 500	(1)/(2)
(4) Months in year 1 Teton held patent	× 4	September through December
(5) Monthly straight-line amortization	**$ 2,000**	(3) × (4)
Unamortized cost of patent at end of year 1	$58,000	(1) − (5)

Amortizable Intangible Asset Summary

Exhibit 10-14 summarizes the different types of amortizable intangible assets, identifies the recovery period of these assets, and describes the applicable amortization method for each asset. Exhibit 10-14 also identifies the applicable convention for each type of amortizable intangible asset and identifies the financial accounting treatment for recovering the cost of the intangible assets under GAAP.

EXHIBIT 10-14 **Summary of Amortizable Assets**

Asset Description	Recovery Period (months)	Applicable Method	Applicable Convention	Financial Accounting Treatment
§197 purchased intangibles, including goodwill, trademarks, patents, and covenants not to compete[72]	180	Straight-line	Full-month beginning with month of purchase	ASC 350 tests for annual impairment
Organizational expenditures and start-up costs that are required to be capitalized	180	Straight-line	Full-month in month business begins	AICPA SOP 98-5
Research and experimentation costs that are capitalized	Determinable useful life, or (not less than) 60; ceases when patent is issued.	Straight-line	Full-month in first month that benefits from research are obtained	Expensed
Self-created patents and copyrights	Actual life	Straight-line	Full-month in month intangible is obtained	Expensed
Purchased patents and copyrights	Remaining life	Straight-line	Full-month in month intangible is obtained	Expensed

[72]A patent or copyright that is part of a basket purchase (several assets together) is treated as a §197 intangible. A patent or copyright that is purchased separately is simply amortized over its remaining life (§167[f]).

Exhibit 10-15 presents Teton's amortization expense as it would be reported on its tax return on Form 4562 (the exhibit assumes that Teton is a corporation so it can amortize organizational expenditures). The amortization is reported on line 43 because it is Teton's second year in business. The amortization would be reported on line 42 (with more detail) had this been Teton's first year in business.

EXHIBIT 10-15   Teton Form 4562, Part VI Amortization of Organizational Expenditures and Patent

Part VI **Amortization**

(a) Description of costs	(b) Date amortization begins	(c) Amortizable amount	(d) Code section	(e) Amortization period or percentage	(f) Amortization for this year
42 Amortization of costs that begins during your 2017 tax year (see instructions):					

43 Amortization of costs that began before your 2017 tax year	**43**	9,400
44 Total. Add amounts in column (f). See the instructions for where to report	**44**	9,400

Form **4562** (2017)

Source: IRS Form 4562, 2017

---

continued from page 10-16...

Teton was developing some additional employee parking on a lot adjacent to the warehouse when the excavation crew discovered a small gold deposit. Steve called his friend Ken, who had some experience in mining precious metals, to see what Ken thought of the find. Ken was impressed and offered Steve $150,000 for the rights to the gold. Steve accepted the offer on Teton's behalf. ∎

LO 10-5   # DEPLETION

Depletion is the method taxpayers use to recover their capital investment in natural resources. Depletion is a particularly significant deduction for businesses in the mining, oil and gas, and forestry industries. These businesses generally incur depletion expense as they use the natural resource. Specifically, businesses compute annual depletion expense under both the cost and percentage depletion methods and deduct the larger of the two.[73]

Under **cost depletion,** taxpayers must estimate or determine the number of recoverable units or reserves (tons of coal, barrels of oil, or board feet of timber, for example) that remain at the beginning of the year and allocate a pro rata share of the property's adjusted basis to each unit. To determine the cost depletion amount, taxpayers then multiply the per-unit basis amount by the number of units sold during the year.[74]

---

[73]Depletion of timber and major integrated oil companies must be calculated using only the cost depletion method (no percentage depletion is available).

[74]§612.

Example 10-27

Ken's cost basis in the gold is the $150,000 he paid for it. Based on a mining engineer's estimate that the gold deposit probably holds 1,000 ounces of gold, Ken can determine his cost depletion. What is Ken's cost depletion for year 1 and year 2, assuming he extracts and sells 300 and 700 ounces of gold in year 1 and year 2, respectively?

Answer: $45,000 in year 1 and $105,000 in year 2, computed as follows:

Description	Amount	Explanation
(1) Cost basis in gold	$ 150,000	
(2) Estimated ounces of gold	1,000	
(3) Per-ounce cost depletion rate	150	(1)/(2)
(4) Year 1 ounces sold	300	
(5) Year 1 cost depletion	**$ 45,000**	(3) × (4)
(6) Basis remaining after year 1 depletion	105,000	(1) − (5)
(7) Year 2 ounces sold	700	
(8) Year 2 cost depletion	**$105,000**	(7) × (3)
Basis remaining after year 2 depletion	$ 0	(6) − (8)

Ken is not eligible for cost depletion after year 2 because as of the end of year 2, his cost basis has been reduced to $0.

THE KEY FACTS

Depletion

- Cost depletion involves estimating resource reserves and allocating a pro-rata share of basis based on the number of units extracted.
- Percentage depletion is determined by a statutory percentage of gross income that is permitted to be expensed each year. Different resources have different statutory percentages (i.e., gold, tin, coal).
- Taxpayers may expense the larger of cost or percentage depletion.

Because the cost depletion method requires businesses to estimate the number of units of the resource they will actually extract, it is possible that their estimate will prove to be inaccurate. If they underestimate the number of units, they will fully deplete the cost basis of the resource before they have fully extracted the resource. Once they have recovered the entire cost basis of the resource, businesses are not allowed to use cost depletion to determine depletion expense. They may, however, continue to use percentage depletion (see discussion below). If a business overestimates the number of units to be extracted, it will still have basis remaining after the resource has been fully extracted. In these situations, the business deducts the unrecovered basis once it has sold all the remaining units.

The amount of **percentage depletion** for a natural resource business activity is determined by multiplying the *gross income* from the resource extraction activity by a fixed percentage based on the type of natural resource, as indicated in Exhibit 10-16.[75]

EXHIBIT 10-16   **Applicable Percentage Depletion Rates**

Statutory Percentage	Natural Resources (partial list)
5 percent [§613(b)(6)]	Gravel, pumice, and stone
14 percent [§613(b)(3)]	Asphalt rock, clay, and other metals
15 percent [§613(b)(2)]	Gold, copper, oil shale, and silver
15 percent [§613A(c)(1)]	Domestic oil and gas
22 percent [§613(b)(1)]	Platinum, sulfur, uranium, and titanium

Source: §613.

In many cases, percentage depletion may generate *larger* depletion deductions than cost depletion. Recall that taxpayers are allowed to deduct the greater of cost or percentage depletion. Businesses reduce their initial basis in the resource when they deduct

[75]§613.

percentage depletion. However, once the initial basis is exhausted, they are allowed to continue to deduct percentage (but not cost) depletion. This provides a potentially significant governmental subsidy to extraction businesses that have completely recovered their costs in a natural resource.[76]

Note that businesses deduct percentage depletion when they *sell* the natural resource, and they deduct cost depletion in the year they *produce* or *extract* the natural resource. Also, percentage depletion cannot exceed 50 percent (100 percent in the case of oil and gas properties) of the taxable income from the natural resource business activity before considering the depletion expense, while cost depletion has no such limitation.

Example 10-28

In Example 10-27, Ken determined his cost depletion expense for the gold. However, because he is allowed to deduct the greater of cost or percentage depletion each year, he set out to determine his percentage depletion for year 2. Assuming that Ken has gross (taxable) income from the gold mining activity before depletion expense of $200,000 ($50,000), $600,000 ($450,000), and $600,000 ($500,000) in year 1, year 2, and year 3, respectively, what is his percentage depletion expense for each of these three years?

Answer: $25,000, $90,000, and $90,000 for years 1, 2, and 3, respectively, computed as follows:

	Year 1	Year 2	Year 3	Explanation
(1) Taxable income from activity (before depletion expense)	$ 50,000	$450,000	$500,000	
(2) Gross income	$200,000	$600,000	$600,000	
(3) Percentage	× 15%	× 15%	× 15%	Exhibit 10-16
(4) Percentage depletion expense before limit	$ 30,000	$ 90,000	$ 90,000	(2) × (3)
(5) 50 percent of taxable income limitation	$ 25,000	$225,000	$250,000	(1) × 50%
Allowable percentage depletion	**$ 25,000**	**$ 90,000**	**$ 90,000**	Lesser of (4) or (5)

Finally, as we discussed above, a business's depletion deduction is the greater of either the annual cost or percentage depletion.

Example 10-29

Based on his computations of cost depletion and percentage depletion, Ken was able to determine his deductible depletion expense. Using the cost and percentage depletion computations from Examples 10-27 and 10-28, what is Ken's deductible depletion expense for years 1, 2, and 3?

Answer: $45,000 for year 1, $105,000 for year 2, and $90,000 for year 3, computed as follows:

Tax Depletion Expense	Year 1	Year 2	Year 3	Explanation
(1) Cost depletion	$ 45,000	$ 105,000	$ 0	Example 10-27
(2) Percentage depletion	25,000	90,000	90,000	Example 10-28
Allowable expense	**$45,000**	**$105,000**	**$90,000**	Greater of (1) or (2)

[76]Percentage depletion in excess of basis is an AMT preference item.

CONCLUSION

This chapter describes and discusses how businesses recover the costs of their tangible and intangible assets. Cost recovery is important because it represents a significant tax deduction for many businesses. Businesses must routinely make choices that affect the amount and timing of these deductions. Further understanding cost recovery basics helps businesses determine how to compute and characterize the gain and loss they recognize when they sell or otherwise dispose of business assets. We address the interaction between cost recovery deductions and gain and loss on property dispositions in the next chapter.

Appendix A MACRS Tables

TABLE 1   **MACRS Half-Year Convention**

Year	Depreciation Rate for Recovery Period					
	3-Year	5-Year	7-Year	10-Year	15-Year	20-Year
1	33.33%	20.00%	14.29%	10.00%	5.00%	3.750%
2	44.45	32.00	24.49	18.00	9.50	7.219
3	14.81	19.20	17.49	14.40	8.55	6.677
4	7.41	11.52	12.49	11.52	7.70	6.177
5		11.52	8.93	9.22	6.93	5.713
6		5.76	8.92	7.37	6.23	5.285
7			8.93	6.55	5.90	4.888
8			4.46	6.55	5.90	4.522
9				6.56	5.91	4.462
10				6.55	5.90	4.461
11				3.28	5.91	4.462
12					5.90	4.461
13					5.91	4.462
14					5.90	4.461
15					5.91	4.462
16					2.95	4.461
17						4.462
18						4.461
19						4.462
20						4.461
21						2.231

TABLE 2a   **MACRS Mid-Quarter Convention:** *For property placed in service during the first quarter*

Year	Depreciation Rate for Recovery Period	
	5-Year	7-Year
1	35.00%	25.00%
2	26.00	21.43
3	15.60	15.31
4	11.01	10.93
5	11.01	8.75
6	1.38	8.74
7		8.75
8		1.09

TABLE 2b   **MACRS Mid-Quarter Convention:** *For property placed in service during the second quarter*

Depreciation Rate for Recovery Period		
Year	5-Year	7-Year
1	25.00%	17.85%
2	30.00	23.47
3	18.00	16.76
4	11.37	11.97
5	11.37	8.87
6	4.26	8.87
7		8.87
8		3.34

TABLE 2c   **MACRS Mid-Quarter Convention:** *For property placed in service during the third quarter*

Depreciation Rate for Recovery Period		
Year	5-Year	7-Year
1	15.00%	10.71%
2	34.00	25.51
3	20.40	18.22
4	12.24	13.02
5	11.30	9.30
6	7.06	8.85
7		8.86
8		5.53

TABLE 2d   **MACRS-Mid Quarter Convention:** *For property placed in service during the fourth quarter*

Depreciation Rate for Recovery Period		
Year	5-Year	7-Year
1	5.00%	3.57%
2	38.00	27.55
3	22.80	19.68
4	13.68	14.06
5	10.94	10.04
6	9.58	8.73
7		8.73
8		7.64

TABLE 3   Residential Rental Property Mid-Month Convention Straight Line—27.5 Years

Year					Month Property Placed in Service							
	1	2	3	4	5	6	7	8	9	10	11	12
1	3.485%	3.182%	2.879%	2.576%	2.273%	1.970%	1.667%	1.364%	1.061%	0.758%	0.455%	0.152%
2–9	3.636	3.636	3.636	3.636	3.636	3.636	3.636	3.636	3.636	3.636	3.636	3.636
10	3.637	3.637	3.637	3.637	3.637	3.637	3.636	3.636	3.636	3.636	3.636	3.636
11	3.636	3.636	3.636	3.636	3.636	3.636	3.637	3.637	3.637	3.637	3.637	3.637
12	3.637	3.637	3.637	3.637	3.637	3.637	3.636	3.636	3.636	3.636	3.636	3.636
13	3.636	3.636	3.636	3.636	3.636	3.636	3.637	3.637	3.637	3.637	3.637	3.637
14	3.637	3.637	3.637	3.637	3.637	3.637	3.636	3.636	3.636	3.636	3.636	3.636
15	3.636	3.636	3.636	3.636	3.636	3.636	3.637	3.637	3.637	3.637	3.637	3.637
16	3.637	3.637	3.637	3.637	3.637	3.637	3.636	3.636	3.636	3.636	3.636	3.636
17	3.636	3.636	3.636	3.636	3.636	3.636	3.637	3.637	3.637	3.637	3.637	3.637
18	3.637	3.637	3.637	3.637	3.637	3.637	3.636	3.636	3.636	3.636	3.636	3.636
19	3.636	3.636	3.636	3.636	3.636	3.636	3.637	3.637	3.637	3.637	3.637	3.637
20	3.637	3.637	3.637	3.637	3.637	3.637	3.636	3.636	3.636	3.636	3.636	3.636
21	3.636	3.636	3.636	3.636	3.636	3.636	3.637	3.637	3.637	3.637	3.637	3.637
22	3.637	3.637	3.637	3.637	3.637	3.637	3.636	3.636	3.636	3.636	3.636	3.636
23	3.636	3.636	3.636	3.636	3.636	3.636	3.637	3.637	3.637	3.637	3.637	3.637
24	3.637	3.637	3.637	3.637	3.637	3.637	3.636	3.636	3.636	3.636	3.636	3.636
25	3.636	3.636	3.636	3.636	3.636	3.636	3.637	3.637	3.637	3.637	3.637	3.637
26	3.637	3.637	3.637	3.637	3.637	3.637	3.636	3.636	3.636	3.636	3.636	3.636
27	3.636	3.636	3.636	3.636	3.636	3.636	3.637	3.637	3.637	3.637	3.637	3.637
28	1.97	2.273	2.576	2.879	3.182	3.485	3.636	3.636	3.636	3.636	3.636	3.636
29							0.152	0.455	0.758	1.061	1.364	1.667

TABLE 4   Nonresidential Real Property Mid-Month Convention Straight Line—31.5 Years (for assets placed in service before May 13, 1993)

Year	\multicolumn{12}{c}{Month Property Placed in Service}											
	1	2	3	4	5	6	7	8	9	10	11	12
1	3.042%	2.778%	2.513%	2.249%	1.984%	1.720%	1.455%	1.190%	0.926%	0.661%	0.397%	0.132%
2–7	3.175	3.175	3.175	3.175	3.175	3.175	3.175	3.175	3.175	3.175	3.175	3.175
8	3.175	3.174	3.175	3.174	3.175	3.174	3.175	3.175	3.175	3.175	3.175	3.175
9	3.174	3.175	3.174	3.175	3.174	3.175	3.174	3.175	3.175	3.175	3.175	3.175
10	3.175	3.174	3.175	3.174	3.175	3.174	3.175	3.174	3.175	3.175	3.175	3.175
11	3.174	3.175	3.174	3.175	3.174	3.175	3.174	3.175	3.174	3.175	3.175	3.175
12	3.175	3.174	3.175	3.174	3.175	3.174	3.175	3.174	3.175	3.174	3.175	3.175
13	3.174	3.175	3.174	3.175	3.174	3.175	3.174	3.175	3.174	3.175	3.174	3.175
14	3.175	3.174	3.175	3.174	3.175	3.174	3.175	3.174	3.175	3.174	3.175	3.174
15	3.174	3.175	3.174	3.175	3.174	3.175	3.174	3.175	3.174	3.175	3.174	3.175
16	3.175	3.174	3.175	3.174	3.175	3.174	3.175	3.174	3.175	3.174	3.175	3.174
17	3.174	3.175	3.174	3.175	3.174	3.175	3.174	3.175	3.174	3.175	3.174	3.175
18	3.175	3.174	3.175	3.174	3.175	3.174	3.175	3.174	3.175	3.174	3.175	3.174
19	3.174	3.175	3.174	3.175	3.174	3.175	3.174	3.175	3.174	3.175	3.174	3.175
20	3.175	3.174	3.175	3.174	3.175	3.174	3.175	3.174	3.175	3.174	3.175	3.174
21	3.174	3.175	3.174	3.175	3.174	3.175	3.174	3.175	3.174	3.175	3.174	3.175
22	3.175	3.174	3.175	3.174	3.175	3.174	3.175	3.174	3.175	3.174	3.175	3.174
23	3.174	3.175	3.174	3.175	3.174	3.175	3.174	3.175	3.174	3.175	3.174	3.175
24	3.175	3.174	3.175	3.174	3.175	3.174	3.175	3.174	3.175	3.174	3.175	3.174
25	3.174	3.175	3.174	3.175	3.174	3.175	3.174	3.175	3.174	3.175	3.174	3.175
26	3.175	3.174	3.175	3.174	3.175	3.174	3.175	3.174	3.175	3.174	3.175	3.174
27	3.174	3.175	3.174	3.175	3.174	3.175	3.174	3.175	3.174	3.175	3.174	3.175
28	3.175	3.174	3.175	3.174	3.175	3.174	3.175	3.174	3.175	3.174	3.175	3.174
29	3.174	3.175	3.174	3.175	3.174	3.175	3.174	3.175	3.174	3.175	3.174	3.175
30	3.175	3.174	3.175	3.174	3.175	3.174	3.175	3.174	3.175	3.174	3.175	3.174
31	3.174	3.175	3.174	3.175	3.174	3.175	3.174	3.175	3.174	3.175	3.174	3.175
32	1.720	1.984	2.249	2.513	2.778	3.042	3.175	3.174	3.175	3.174	3.175	3.174
33							0.132	0.397	0.661	0.926	1.190	1.455

TABLE 5   Nonresidential Real Property Mid-Month Convention Straight Line—39 Years (for assets placed in service on or after May 13, 1993)

Year	\multicolumn{12}{c}{Month Property Placed in Service}											
	1	2	3	4	5	6	7	8	9	10	11	12
1	2.461%	2.247%	2.033%	1.819%	1.605%	1.391%	1.177%	0.963%	0.749%	0.535%	0.321%	0.107%
2–39	2.564	2.564	2.564	2.564	2.564	2.564	2.564	2.564	2.564	2.564	2.564	2.564
40	0.107	0.321	0.535	0.749	0.963	1.177	1.391	1.605	1.819	2.033	2.247	2.461

Summary

Describe the cost recovery methods for recovering the cost of personal property, real property, intangible assets, and natural resources.   **LO 10-1**

- Tangible personal and real property (depreciation), intangibles (amortization), and natural resources (depletion) are all subject to cost recovery.
- An asset's initial basis is the amount that is subject to cost recovery. Generally, an asset's initial basis is its purchase price, plus the cost of any other expenses incurred to get the asset in working condition.
- The taxpayer's basis of assets acquired in a nontaxable exchange is the same basis the taxpayer transferred to acquire the property received.
- Expenditures on an asset are either expensed currently or capitalized as a new asset. Expenditures for routine or general maintenance of the asset are expensed currently. Expenditures that better, restore, or adapt an asset to a new use are capitalized.
- When acquiring a business and purchasing a bundle of property, the basis of each asset is determined as the fair market value of the asset.

Determine the applicable cost recovery (depreciation) life, method, and convention for tangible personal and real property and the deduction allowable under basic MACRS.   **LO 10-2**

- Tax depreciation is calculated under the Modified Accelerated Cost Recovery System (MACRS).
- MACRS for tangible personal property is based upon recovery period (Rev. Proc. 87-56), method (200 percent declining balance, 150 percent declining balance, and straight-line), and convention (half-year or mid-quarter).
- Real property is divided into two groups for tax purposes: residential rental and nonresidential. The recovery period is 27.5 years for residential property and 31.5 years or 39 years for nonresidential property, depending on when the property was placed in service. The depreciation method is straight-line and the convention is mid-month.

Calculate the deduction allowable under the additional special cost recovery rules (§179, bonus, and listed property).   **LO 10-3**

- §179 allows taxpayers to expense tangible personal property. The deduction is limited by the amount of property placed in service and taxable income.
- Bonus depreciation allows taxpayers to immediately deduct 100 percent of qualified property in the year of acquisition.
- Listed property includes automobiles, other means of transportation, and assets that tend to be used for both business and personal purposes. Depreciation is limited to the expense multiplied by business-use percentage. Special rules apply if business use is less than or equal to 50 percent.
- Additional limitations apply to luxury automobiles.

Calculate the deduction for amortization.   **LO 10-4**

- Intangible assets (such as patents, goodwill, and trademarks) have their costs recovered through amortization.
- Intangible assets are amortized (straight-line method) using the full-month convention.
- Intangibles are divided into four types (§197 purchased intangibles, start-up costs and organizational expenditures, research and experimentation, and self-created intangibles).

Explain cost recovery of natural resources and the allowable depletion methods.   **LO 10-5**

- Depletion allows a taxpayer to recover his or her capital investment in natural resources.
- Two methods of depletion are available, and the taxpayer must calculate both and take the one that results in the larger depletion deduction each year.
- Cost depletion allows taxpayers to estimate number of units and then allocate a pro rata share of the basis to each unit extracted during the year.
- Percentage depletion allows the taxpayer to take a statutory determined percentage of gross income as an expense. Deductions are not limited to basis.

KEY TERMS

adjusted basis (10-3)
amortization (10-2)
bonus depreciation (10-21)
cost depletion (10-38)
cost recovery (10-2)
covenant not to compete (10-32)
depletion (10-2)
depreciation (10-2)
full-month convention (10-32)
half-year convention (10-9)

intangible assets (10-2)
listed property (10-23)
luxury automobile (10-26)
mid-month convention (10-15)
mid-quarter convention (10-9)
Modified Accelerated Cost Recovery System (MACRS) (10-6)
organizational expenditures (10-33)
percentage depletion (10-39)
personal property (10-7)

real property (10-7)
recovery period (10-7)
research and experimentation (R&E) costs (10-32)
§179 expense (10-17)
§197 intangibles (10-32)
start-up costs (10-35)
tax basis (10-2)

DISCUSSION QUESTIONS

Discussion Questions are available in Connect®.

LO 10-1 1. Explain why certain long-lived assets are capitalized and recovered over time rather than immediately expensed.

LO 10-1 2. Explain the differences and similarities between personal property, real property, intangible property, and natural resources. Also, provide an example of each type of asset.

LO 10-1 3. Explain the similarities and dissimilarities between depreciation, amortization, and depletion. Describe the cost recovery method used for each of the four asset types (personal property, real property, intangible property, and natural resources).

LO 10-1 4. Is an asset's initial or cost basis simply its purchase price? Explain.

LO 10-1 5. Compare and contrast the basis of property acquired via purchase, conversion from personal use to business or rental use, nontaxable exchange, gift, and inheritance.

LO 10-1 6. Explain why the expenses incurred to get an asset in place and operable should be included in the asset's basis.

LO 10-1 7. Graber Corporation runs a long-haul trucking business. Graber incurs the following expenses: replacement tires, oil changes, and a transmission overhaul. Which of these expenditures may be deducted currently and which must be capitalized? Explain.

LO 10-2 8. MACRS depreciation requires the use of a recovery period, method, and convention to depreciate tangible personal property assets. Briefly explain why each is important to the calculation.

LO 10-2 9. Can a taxpayer with very little current-year income choose to not claim any depreciation deduction for the current year and thus save depreciation deductions for the future when the taxpayer expects to be more profitable?

planning **LO 10-2** 10. What depreciation methods are available for tangible personal property? Explain the characteristics of a business likely to adopt each method.

LO 10-2 11. If a business places several different assets in service during the year, must it use the same depreciation method for all assets? If not, what restrictions apply to the business's choices of depreciation methods?

LO 10-2 12. Describe how you would determine the MACRS recovery period for an asset if you did not already know it.

13. Compare and contrast the recovery periods used by MACRS and those used under generally accepted accounting principles (GAAP).   `LO 10-2` **research**

14. What are the two depreciation conventions that apply to tangible personal property under MACRS? Explain why Congress provides two methods.   `LO 10-2`

15. A business buys two identical tangible personal property assets for the same price. It buys one at the beginning of the year and one at the end of the year. Under what conditions would the taxpayer's depreciation on each asset be exactly the same? Under what conditions would it be different?   `LO 10-2`

16. AAA Inc. acquired a machine in year 1. In May of year 3, it sold the asset. Can AAA find its year 3 depreciation percentage for the machine on the MACRS table? If not, what adjustment must AAA make to its full-year depreciation percentage to determine its year 3 depreciation?   `LO 10-2`

17. There are two recovery period classifications for real property. What reasons might Congress have to allow residential real estate a shorter recovery period than nonresidential real property?   `LO 10-2`

18. Discuss why Congress has instructed taxpayers to depreciate real property using the mid-month convention as opposed to the half-year convention used for tangible personal property.   `LO 10-2`

19. If a taxpayer has owned a building for 10 years and decides that it should make significant improvements to the building, what is the recovery period for the improvements?   `LO 10-2` **research**

20. Compare and contrast the differences between computing depreciation deduction for tangible personal property and computing depreciation deduction for real property under both the regular tax and alternative tax systems.   `LO 10-2`

21. Discuss how the property limitation restricts large businesses from taking the §179 expense.   `LO 10-3`

22. Explain the two limitations placed on the §179 deduction. How are they similar? How are they different?   `LO 10-3`

23. Compare and contrast the types of businesses that would and would not benefit from the §179 expense.   `LO 10-3`

24. What strategies will help a business maximize its current depreciation deductions (including §179)? Why might a taxpayer choose *not* to maximize its current depreciation deductions?   `LO 10-3`

25. Why might a business claim a reduced §179 expense amount in the current year rather than claiming the maximum amount available?   `LO 10-3`

26. Describe assets that are considered to be listed property. Why do you think Congress requires them to be "listed"?   `LO 10-3`

27. Are taxpayers allowed to claim depreciation deduction on assets they use for both business and personal purposes? What are the tax consequences if the business use drops from above 50 percent in one year to below 50 percent in the next?   `LO 10-3`

28. Discuss why Congress limits the amount of depreciation deduction businesses may claim on certain automobiles.   `LO 10-3`

29. Compare and contrast how a Land Rover SUV and a Mercedes Benz sedan are treated under the luxury auto rules. Also include a discussion of the similarities and differences in available §179 expense.   `LO 10-3`

30. What is a §197 intangible? How do taxpayers recover the costs of these intangibles? How do taxpayers recover the cost of a §197 intangible that expires (such as a covenant not to compete)?   `LO 10-4`

LO 10-4 31. Compare and contrast the tax and financial accounting treatment of goodwill. Are taxpayers allowed to deduct amounts associated with self-created goodwill?

LO 10-4 32. Compare and contrast the similarities and differences between organizational expenditures and start-up costs for tax purposes.

LO 10-4 33. Discuss the method used to determine the amount of organizational expenditures or start-up costs that may be immediately expensed in the year a taxpayer begins business.

LO 10-4 34. Explain the amortization convention applicable to intangible assets.

LO 10-4 35. Compare and contrast the recovery periods of §197 intangibles, organizational expenditures, start-up costs, and research and experimentation expenses.

LO 10-5 36. Compare and contrast the cost and percentage depletion methods for recovering the costs of natural resources. What are the similarities and differences between the two methods?

LO 10-5 37. Explain why percentage depletion has been referred to as a government subsidy.

PROBLEMS

Select problems are available in Connect®.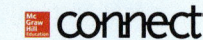

LO 10-1 38. Jose purchased a delivery van for his business through an online auction. His winning bid for the van was $24,500. In addition, Jose incurred the following expenses before using the van: shipping costs of $650; paint to match the other fleet vehicles at a cost of $1,000; registration costs of $3,200, which included $3,000 of sales tax and a registration fee of $200; wash and detailing for $50; and an engine tune-up for $250. What is Jose's cost basis for the delivery van?

LO 10-1
research 39. Emily purchased a building to store inventory for her business. The purchase price was $760,000. Emily also paid legal fees of $300 to acquire the building. In March, Emily incurred $2,000 to repair minor leaks in the roof (from storm damage earlier in the month) and $5,000 to make the interior suitable for her finished goods. What is Emily's cost basis in the new building?

LO 10-1
research 40. In January, Prahbu purchases a new machine for use in an existing production line of his manufacturing business for $90,000. Assume that the machine is a unit of property and is not a material or supply. Prahbu pays $2,500 to install the machine, and after the machine is installed, he pays $1,300 to perform a critical test on the machine to ensure that it will operate in accordance with quality standards. On November 1, the critical test is complete, and Prahbu places the machine in service on the production line. On December 3, Prahbu pays another $3,300 to perform periodic quality control testing after the machine is placed in service. How much will Prahbu be required to capitalize as the cost of the machine?

LO 10-1 41. Dennis contributed business assets to a new business in exchange for stock in the company. The exchange did not qualify as a nontaxable exchange. The fair market value of these assets was $287,000 on the contribution date. Dennis's original basis in the assets he contributed was $143,000, and the accumulated depreciation on the assets was $78,000.

a) What is the business's basis in the assets it received from Dennis?

b) What would be the business's basis if the transaction qualified as a nontaxable exchange?

LO 10-1 42. Brittany started a law practice as a sole proprietor. She owned a computer, printer, desk, and file cabinet she purchased during law school (several years ago) that she is planning to use in her business. What is the depreciable basis that Brittany should use in her business for each asset, given the following information?

Asset	Purchase Price	FMV at Time Converted to Business Use
Computer	$5,500	$3,800
Printer	3,300	3,150
Desk	4,200	4,000
File cabinet	3,200	3,225

43. Meg O'Brien received a gift of some small-scale jewelry manufacturing equipment that her father had used for personal purposes for many years. Her father originally purchased the equipment for $1,500. Because the equipment is out of production and no longer available, the property is currently worth $4,000. Meg has decided to begin a new jewelry manufacturing trade or business. What is her depreciable basis for depreciating the equipment?   **LO 10-1**

44. Gary inherited a Maine summer cabin on 10 acres from his grandmother. His grand-parents originally purchased the property for $500 in 1950 and built the cabin at a cost of $10,000 in 1965. His grandfather died in 1980 and when his grandmother recently passed away, the property was appraised at $500,000 for the land and $700,000 for the cabin. Since Gary doesn't currently live in New England, he decided that it would be best to put the property to use as a rental. What is Gary's basis in the land and in the cabin?   **LO 10-1**

45. Wanting to finalize a sale before year-end, on December 29, WR Outfitters sold to Bob a warehouse and the land for $125,000. The appraised fair market value of the warehouse was $75,000, and the appraised value of the land was $100,000.   **LO 10-1**
   a) What is Bob's basis in the warehouse and in the land?
   b) What would be Bob's basis in the warehouse and in the land if the appraised value of the warehouse was $50,000 and the appraised value of the land was $125,000?
   c) Which appraisal would Bob likely prefer?

46. At the beginning of the year, Poplock began a calendar-year dog boarding business called Griff's Palace. Poplock bought and placed in service the following assets dur-ing the year: **LO 10-2**

Asset	Date Acquired	Cost Basis
Computer equipment	3/23	$ 5,000
Dog-grooming furniture	5/12	7,000
Pickup truck	9/17	10,000
Commercial building	10/11	270,000
Land (one acre)	10/11	80,000

Assuming Poplock does not elect §179 expensing and elects not to use bonus depre-ciation, answer the following questions:
   a) What is Poplock's year 1 depreciation deduction for each asset?
   b) What is Poplock's year 2 depreciation deduction for each asset?

47. DLW Corporation acquired and placed in service the following assets during the year: **LO 10-2**

Asset	Date Acquired	Cost Basis
Computer equipment	2/17	$ 10,000
Furniture	5/12	17,000
Commercial building	11/1	270,000

Assuming DLW does not elect §179 expensing and elects not to use bonus depreciation, answer the following questions:

a) What is DLW's year 1 cost recovery for each asset?

b) What is DLW's year 3 cost recovery for each asset if DLW sells all of these assets on 1/23 of year 3?

LO 10-2

48. At the beginning of the year, Dee began a calendar-year business and placed in service the following assets during the year:

Asset	Date Acquired	Cost Basis
Computer equipment	3/23	$ 5,000
Furniture	5/12	7,000
Pickup truck	9/15	10,000
Commercial building	10/11	270,000

Assuming Dee does not elect §179 expensing and elects not to use bonus depreciation, answer the following questions:

a) What is Dee's year 1 cost recovery for each asset?

b) What is Dee's year 2 cost recovery for each asset?

LO 10-2

planning

49. Parley needs a new truck to help him expand Parley's Plumbing Palace. Business has been booming and Parley would like to accelerate his tax deductions as much as possible (ignore §179 expense and bonus depreciation for this problem). On April 1, Parley purchased a new delivery van for $25,000. It is now September 26 and Parley, already in need of another vehicle, has found a deal on buying a truck for $22,000 (all fees included). The dealer tells him if he doesn't buy the truck (Option 1), it will be gone tomorrow. There is an auction (Option 2) scheduled for October 5 where Parley believes he can get a similar truck for $21,500, but there is also a $500 auction fee. Parley makes no other asset acquisitions during the year.

a) Which option allows Parley to generate more depreciation deductions this year (the vehicles are not considered to be luxury autos)?

b) Assume the original facts, except that the delivery van was placed in service one day earlier on March 31 rather than April 1. Which option generates more depreciation deduction?

LO 10-2

50. Way Corporation disposed of the following tangible personal property assets in the current year. Assume that the delivery truck is not a luxury auto. Calculate Way Corporation's 2018 depreciation deduction (ignore §179 expense and bonus depreciation for this problem).

Asset	Date Acquired	Date Sold	Convention	Original Basis
Furniture (7-year)	5/12/14	7/15/18	HY	$ 55,000
Machinery (7-year)	3/23/15	3/15/18	MQ	72,000
Delivery truck* (5-year)	9/17/16	3/13/18	HY	20,000
Machinery (7-year)	10/11/17	8/11/18	MQ	270,000
Computer (5-year)	10/11/18	12/15/18	HY	80,000

*Used 100 percent for business.

LO 10-2

51. On November 10 of year 1 Javier purchased a building, including the land it was on, to assemble his new equipment. The total cost of the purchase was $1,200,000; $300,000 was allocated to the basis of the land and the remaining $900,000 was allocated to the basis of the building.

a) Using MACRS, what is Javier's depreciation deduction on the building for years 1 through 3?

b) What would be the year 3 depreciation deduction if the building was sold on August 1 of year 3?

c) Answer the question in part (a), except assume the building was purchased and placed in service on March 3 instead of November 10.

d) Answer the question in part (a), except assume that the building is residential property.

e) What would be the depreciation for 2018, 2019, and 2020 if the property were nonresidential property purchased and placed in service November 10, 2001 (assume the same original basis)?

52. Carl purchased an apartment complex for $1.1 million on March 17 of year 1. Of the purchase price, $300,000 was attributable to the land the complex sits on. He also installed new furniture into half of the units at a cost of $60,000.

    a) What is Carl's allowable depreciation deduction for his real property for years 1 and 2?

    b) What is Carl's allowable depreciation deduction for year 3 if the real property is sold on January 2 of year 3?

`LO 10-2`

53. Evergreen Corporation (calendar-year-end) acquired the following assets during the current year:

`LO 10-2` `LO 10-3`

Asset	Date Placed in Service	Original Basis
Machinery	October 25	$ 70,000
Computer equipment	February 3	10,000
Used delivery truck*	August 17	23,000
Furniture	April 22	150,000

*The delivery truck is not a luxury automobile.

a) What is the allowable MACRS depreciation on Evergreen's property in the current year assuming Evergreen does not elect §179 expense and elects out of bonus depreciation?

b) What would be the allowable MACRS depreciation on Evergreen's property in the current year if Evergreen does not elect out of bonus depreciation?

54. Convers Corporation (calendar-year-end) acquired the following assets during the current tax year:

`LO 10-2` `LO 10-3`

Asset	Date Placed in Service	Original Basis
Machinery	October 25	$ 70,000
Computer equipment	February 3	10,000
Delivery truck*	March 17	23,000
Furniture	April 22	150,000
Total		$253,000

*The delivery truck is not a luxury automobile.

In addition to these assets, Convers installed new flooring (qualified improvement property) to its office building on May 12 at a cost of $300,000.

a) What is the allowable MACRS depreciation on Convers's property in the current year assuming Convers does not elect §179 expense and elects out of bonus depreciation?

b) What is the allowable MACRS depreciation on Convers's property in the current year assuming Convers does not elect out of bonus depreciation (but does not take §179 expense)?

LO 10-2 LO 10-3 55. Harris Corp. is a technology start-up and is in its second year of operations. The company didn't purchase any assets this year but purchased the following assets in the prior year:

Asset	Placed in Service	Basis
Office equipment	August 14	$10,000
Manufacturing equipment	April 15	68,000
Computer system	June 1	16,000
Total		$94,000

Harris did not know depreciation was tax deductible until it hired an accountant this year and didn't claim any depreciation deduction in its first year of operation.

a) What is the maximum amount of depreciation deduction Harris Corp. can deduct in its second year of operation?

b) What is the basis of the office equipment at the end of the second year?

LO 10-2 LO 10-3 56. AMP Corporation (calendar-year-end) has 2018 taxable income of $900,000 for purposes of computing the §179 expense. During 2018, AMP acquired the following assets:

Asset	Placed in Service	Basis
Machinery	September 12	$1,550,000
Computer equipment	February 10	365,000
Office building	April 2	480,000
Total		$2,395,000

a) What is the maximum amount of §179 expense AMP may deduct for 2018?

b) What is the maximum total depreciation including §179 expense, that AMP may deduct in 2018 on the assets it placed in service in 2018 assuming no bonus depreciation?

LO 10-2 LO 10-3 57. Assume that TDW Corporation (calendar-year-end) has 2018 taxable income of $650,000 for purposes of computing the §179 expense. The company acquired the following assets during 2018:

Asset	Placed in Service	Basis
Machinery	September 12	$1,270,000
Computer equipment	February 10	263,000
Furniture	April 2	880,000
Total		$2,413,000

a) What is the maximum amount of §179 expense TDW may deduct for 2018?

b) What is the maximum total depreciation including §179 expense, that TDW may deduct in 2018 on the assets it placed in service in 2018 assuming no bonus depreciation?

LO 10-2 LO 10-3 58. Assume that Timberline Corporation has 2018 taxable income of $240,000 for purposes of computing the §179 expense. It acquired the following assets in 2018:

Asset	Purchase Date	Basis
Furniture (7-year)	December 1	$ 450,000
Computer equipment (5-year)	February 28	90,000
Copier (5-year)	July 15	30,000
Machinery (7-year)	May 22	480,000
Total		$1,050,000

a) What is the maximum amount of §179 expense Timberline may deduct for 2018? What is Timberline's §179 carryforward to 2019, if any?

b) What would Timberline's maximum depreciation deduction be for 2018 assuming no bonus depreciation?

c) What would Timberline's maximum depreciation deduction be for 2018 if the machinery cost $3,000,000 instead of $480,000 and assuming no bonus depreciation?

59. Dain's Diamond Bit Drilling purchased the following assets this year. Assume its taxable income for the year was $53,000 for purposes of computing the §179 expense (assume no bonus depreciation).

LO 10-2 LO 10-3

planning

Asset	Purchase Date	Original Basis
Drill bits (5-year)	January 25	$ 90,000
Drill bits (5-year)	July 25	95,000
Commercial building	April 22	220,000

a) What is the maximum amount of §179 expense Dain may deduct for the year?

b) What is Dain's maximum depreciation deduction for the year (including §179 expense)?

c) If the January drill bits' original basis was $2,875,000, what is the maximum amount of §179 expense Dain may deduct for the year?

d) If the January drill bits' original basis was $3,875,000, what is the maximum amount of §179 expense Dain may deduct for the year?

60. Assume that ACW Corporation has 2018 taxable income of $1,000,000 for purposes of computing the §179 expense. The company acquired the following assets during 2018 (assume no bonus depreciation):

LO 10-2 LO 10-3

research

Asset	Placed in Service	Basis
Machinery	September 12	$ 470,000
Computer equipment	February 10	70,000
Delivery truck	August 21	93,000
Qualified improvement property	April 2	$1,380,000
Total		$2,013,000

a) What is the maximum amount of §179 expense ACW may deduct for 2018?

b) What is the maximum *total* depreciation that ACW may deduct in 2018 on the assets it placed in service in 2018?

61. Chaz Corporation has taxable income in 2018 of $312,000 for purposes of computing the §179 expense and acquired the following assets during the year:

LO 10-2 LO 10-3

Asset	Placed in Service	Basis
Office furniture	September 12	$1,280,000
Computer equipment	February 10	930,000
Delivery truck	August 21	68,000
Total		$2,278,000

What is the maximum *total* depreciation deduction that Chaz may deduct in 2018?

62. Woolard Supplies (a sole proprietorship) has taxable income in 2018 of $240,000 before any depreciation deductions (§179, bonus, or MACRS) and placed some office furniture into service during the year. The furniture had been used previously by Liz Woolard (the owner of the business) before it was placed in service by the business.

LO 10-2 LO 10-3

planning

research

Asset	Placed in Service	Basis
Office furniture (used)	March 20	$1,200,000

a) If Woolard elects $50,000 of §179, what is Woolard's total depreciation deduction for the year?

b) If Woolard elects the maximum amount of §179 for the year, what is the amount of deductible §179 expense for the year? What is the *total* depreciation that Woolard may deduct in 2018? What is Woolard's §179 carryforward amount to next year, if any?

c) Woolard is concerned about future limitations on its §179 expense. How much §179 expense should Woolard expense this year if it wants to maximize its depreciation this year and avoid any carryover to future years?

63. Assume that Sivart Corporation has 2018 taxable income of $1,750,000 for purposes of computing the §179 expense and acquired several assets during the year. The delivery truck was acquired in a nontaxable transaction.

Asset	Placed in Service	Basis
Machinery	June 12	$1,440,000
Computer equipment	February 10	70,000
Delivery truck—used	August 21	93,000
Furniture	April 2	310,000
Total		$1,913,000

a) What is the maximum amount of §179 expense Sivart may deduct for 2018?

b) What is the maximum *total* depreciation (§179, bonus, MACRS) that Sivart may deduct in 2018 on the assets it placed in service in 2018?

64. Acorn Construction (calendar-year-end C corporation) has had rapid expansion during the last half of the current year due to the housing market's recovery. The company has record income and would like to maximize its cost recovery deduction for the current year. Acorn provided you with the following information:

Asset	Placed in Service	Basis
New equipment and tools	August 20	$1,800,000
Used light duty trucks	October 17	1,500,000
Used machinery	November 6	525,000
Total		$3,825,000

The used assets had been contributed to the business by its owner in a nontaxable transaction.

a) What is Acorn's maximum cost recovery deduction in the current year?

b) What planning strategies would you advise Acorn to consider?

LO 10-3 65. Phil owns a ranch business and uses four-wheelers to do much of his work. Occasionally, though, he and his boys will go for a ride together as a family activity. During year 1, Phil put 765 miles on the four-wheeler that he bought on January 15 for $6,500. Of the miles driven, only 175 miles were for personal use. Assume four-wheelers qualify to be depreciated according to the five-year MACRS schedule and the four-wheeler was the only asset Phil purchased this year.

a) Calculate the allowable depreciation for year 1 (ignore the §179 expense and bonus depreciation).

b) Calculate the allowable depreciation for year 2 if total miles were 930 and personal use miles were 400 (ignore the §179 expense and bonus depreciation).

66. Assume that Ernesto purchased a digital camera on July 10 of year 1 for $3,000. In   LO 10-3
    year 1, 80 percent of his computer usage was for his business and 20 percent was for
    personal photography activities. This was the only asset he placed in service during
    year 1. Ignoring any potential §179 expense and bonus depreciation, answer the
    questions for each of the following alternative scenarios:

    a) What is Ernesto's depreciation deduction for the camera in year 1?

    b) What would be Ernesto's depreciation deduction for the camera in year 2 if his
       year 2 usage was 75 percent business and 25 percent for personal use?

    c) What would be Ernesto's depreciation deduction for the camera in year 2 if his
       year 2 usage was 45 percent business and 55 percent for personal use?

    d) What would be Ernesto's depreciation deduction for the camera in year 2 if his
       year 2 usage was 30 percent business and 70 percent for personal use?

67. Lina purchased a new car for use in her business during 2018. The auto was the   LO 10-3
    only business asset she purchased during the year and her business was extremely
    profitable. Calculate her maximum depreciation deductions (including §179
    expense unless stated otherwise) for the automobile in 2018 and 2019 (Lina doesn't
    want to take bonus depreciation for 2018 or 2019) in the following alternative
    scenarios (assuming half-year convention for all):

    a) The vehicle cost $35,000 and business use is 100 percent (ignore §179
       expense).

    b) The vehicle cost $80,000, and business use is 100 percent.

    c) The vehicle cost $80,000, and she used it 80 percent for business.

    d) The vehicle cost $80,000, and she used it 80 percent for business. She sold it
       on March 1 of year 2.

    e) The vehicle cost $80,000, and she used it 20 percent for business.

    f) The vehicle cost $80,000 and is an SUV that weighs 6,500 pounds. Business
       use was 100 percent.

68. Tater Meer purchased a new car for use in her business during 2018 for $75,000.   LO 10-2   LO 10-3
    The auto was the only business asset she purchased during the year and her business
    was very profitable. Calculate Tater's maximum depreciation deductions for the
    automobile in 2018 and 2019 under the following scenarios:

    a) Tater does not want to take §179 expense and she elects out of bonus
       depreciation.

    b) Tater wants to maximize her 2018 depreciation using bonus depreciation.

69. Burbank Corporation (calendar-year-end) acquired the following property this year: LO 10-2   LO 10-3

Asset	Placed in Service	Basis
Used copier	November 12	$ 7,800
New computer equipment	June 6	14,000
Furniture	July 15	32,000
New delivery truck	October 28	19,000
Luxury auto	January 31	70,000
Total		$142,800

    Burbank acquired the copier in a nontaxable transaction when the shareholder
    contributed the copier to the business in exchange for stock.

    a) Assuming no bonus or §179 expense, what is Burbank's maximum cost recovery
       deduction for this year?

    b) Assuming Burbank would like to maximize its cost recovery deductions by
       claiming bonus and §179 expense, which assets should Burbank immediately
       expense?

c) What is Burbank's maximum cost recovery deduction this year assuming it elects §179 expense and claims bonus depreciation?

LO 10-3

 research

70. Paul Vote purchased the following assets this year (ignore §179 expensing and bonus depreciation when answering the questions below):

Asset	Purchase Date	Basis
Machinery	May 12	$ 23,500
Computers	August 13	20,000
Warehouse	December 13	180,000

a) What is Paul's allowable MACRS depreciation for the property?

b) What is Paul's allowable alternative minimum tax (AMT) depreciation for the property? You will need to find the AMT depreciation tables to compute the depreciation.

LO 10-4

research

71. After several profitable years running her business, Ingrid decided to acquire the assets of a small competing business. On May 1 of year 1, Ingrid acquired the competing business for $300,000. Ingrid allocated $50,000 of the purchase price to goodwill. Ingrid's business reports its taxable income on a calendar-year basis.

a) How much amortization expense on the goodwill can Ingrid deduct in year 1, year 2, and year 3?

b) In lieu of the original facts, assume that Ingrid purchased only a phone list with a useful life of 5 years for $10,000. How much amortization expense on the phone list can Ingrid deduct in year 1, year 2, and year 3?

LO 10-4

72. Juliette formed a new business to sell sporting goods this year. The business opened its doors to customers on June 1. Determine the amount of start-up costs Juliette can immediately expense (not including the portion of the expenditures that are amortized over 180 months) this year in the following alternative scenarios:

a) She incurred start-up costs of $2,000.

b) She incurred start-up costs of $45,000.

c) She incurred start-up costs of $53,500.

d) She incurred start-up costs of $63,000.

e) How would you answer parts (a) through (d) if she formed a partnership or a corporation and she incurred the same amount of organizational expenditures rather than start-up costs (how much of the organizational expenditures would be immediately deductible)?

LO 10-4

73. Nicole organized a new corporation. The corporation began business on April 1 of year 1. She made the following expenditures associated with getting the corporation started:

Expense	Date	Amount
Attorney fees for articles of incorporation	February 10	$32,000
March 1–March 30 wages	March 30	4,500
March 1–March 30 rent	March 30	2,000
Stock issuance costs	April 1	20,000
April 1–May 30 wages	May 30	12,000

a) What is the total amount of the start-up costs and organizational expenditures for Nicole's corporation?

b) What amount of the start-up costs and organizational expenditures may the corporation immediately expense in year 1 (excluding the portion of the expenditures that are amortized over 180 months)?

c) What amount can the corporation deduct as amortization expense for the organizational expenditures and for the start-up costs for year 1 [not including the amount determined in part (b)]?

d) What would be the total allowable organizational expenditures if Nicole started a sole proprietorship instead of a corporation?

74. Bethany incurred $20,000 in research and experimental costs for developing a specialized product during July of year 1. Bethany went through a lot of trouble and spent $10,000 in legal fees to receive a patent for the product in August of year 3. Bethany expects the patent to have a remaining useful life of 10 years.

a) What amount of research and experimental expenses for year 1, year 2, and year 3 may Bethany deduct if she elects to amortize the expenses over 60 months?

b) How much *patent* amortization expense would Bethany deduct in year 3, assuming she elected to amortize the research and experimental costs over 60 months?

c) If Bethany chose to capitalize but *not* amortize the research and experimental expenses she incurred in year 1, how much patent amortization expense would Bethany deduct in year 3?

75. Last Chance Mine (LC) purchased a coal deposit for $750,000. It estimated it would extract 12,000 tons of coal from the deposit. LC mined the coal and sold it, reporting gross receipts of $1 million, $3 million, and $2 million for years 1 through 3, respectively. During years 1–3, LC reported net income (loss) from the coal deposit activity in the amount of ($20,000), $500,000, and $450,000, respectively. In years 1–3, LC actually extracted 13,000 tons of coal as follows:

(1) Tons of Coal	(2) Basis	Depletion (2)/(1) Rate	Tons Extracted per Year		
			Year 1	Year 2	Year 3
12,000	$750,000	$62.50	2,000	7,200	3,800

a) What is Last Chance's cost depletion for years 1, 2, and 3?

b) What is Last Chance's percentage depletion for each year (the applicable percentage for coal is 10 percent)?

c) Using the cost and percentage depletion computations from parts (a) and (b), what is Last Chance's actual depletion expense for each year?

COMPREHENSIVE PROBLEMS

Select problems are available with Connect®.

76. Karane Enterprises, a calendar-year manufacturer based in College Station, Texas, began business in 2017. In the process of setting up the business, Karane has acquired various types of assets. Below is a list of assets acquired during 2017:

tax forms

Asset	Cost	Date Placed in Service
Office furniture	$ 150,000	02/03/2017
Machinery	1,560,000	07/22/2017
Used delivery truck*	40,000	08/17/2017

*Not considered a luxury automobile.

During 2017, Karane was very successful (and had no §179 limitations) and decided to acquire more assets this next year to increase its production capacity. These are the assets acquired during 2018:

Asset	Cost	Date Placed in Service
Computers & info. system	$ 400,000	03/31/2018
Luxury auto†	80,000	05/26/2018
Assembly equipment	1,200,000	08/15/2018
Storage building	700,000	11/13/2018

†Used 100% for business purposes.

Karane generated taxable income in 2018 of $1,732,500 for purposes of computing the §179 expense.

Required:

a) Compute the maximum 2017 depreciation deductions including §179 expense (ignoring bonus depreciation).

b) Compute the maximum 2018 depreciation deductions including §179 expense (ignoring bonus depreciation).

c) Compute the maximum 2018 depreciation deductions including §179 expense, but now assume that Karane would like to take bonus depreciation.

d) Now assume that during 2018, Karane decides to buy a competitor's assets for a purchase price of $1,350,000. Compute the maximum 2018 cost recovery including §179 expense and bonus depreciation. Karane purchased the following assets for the lump-sum purchase price.

Asset	Cost	Date Placed in Service
Inventory	$220,000	09/15/2018
Office furniture	230,000	09/15/2018
Machinery	250,000	09/15/2018
Patent	198,000	09/15/2018
Goodwill	2,000	09/15/2018
Building	430,000	09/15/2018
Land	20,000	09/15/2018

e) Complete Part I of Form 4562 for part (b) (use the most current form available).

tax forms

77. While completing undergraduate school work in information systems, Dallin Bourne and Michael Banks decided to start a technology support company called eSys Answers. During year 1, they bought the following assets and incurred the following start-up fees:

Year 1 Assets	Purchase Date	Basis
Computers (5-year)	October 30, Y1	$15,000
Office equipment (7-year)	October 30, Y1	10,000
Furniture (7-year)	October 30, Y1	3,000
Start-up costs	October 30, Y1	17,000

In April of year 2, they decided to purchase a customer list from a company providing virtually the same services, started by fellow information systems students preparing to graduate. The customer list cost $10,000 and the sale was completed on April 30. During their summer break, Dallin and Michael passed on internship opportunities in an attempt to really grow their business into something they could do full-time after graduation. In the summer, they purchased a small van (for transportation, not considered a luxury auto) and a pinball machine (to help attract new employees). They bought the van on June 15, Y2, for $15,000 and spent $3,000 getting it ready to put into service. The pinball machine cost $4,000 and was placed in service on July 1, Y2.

Year 2 Assets	Purchase Date	Basis
Van	June 15, Y2	$18,000
Pinball machine (7-year)	July 1, Y2	4,000
Customer list	April 30, Y2	10,000

Assume that eSys Answers does not claim any §179 expense or bonus depreciation.

a) What are the maximum cost recovery deductions for eSys Answers for Y1 and Y2?

b) Complete eSys Answers's Form 4562 for Y1 (use the most current form available).

c) What is eSys Answers's basis in each of its assets at the end of Y2?

78. Diamond Mountain was originally thought to be one of the few places in North America to contain diamonds, so Diamond Mountain Inc. (DM) purchased the land for $1,000,000. Later, DM discovered that the only diamonds on the mountain had been planted there and the land was worthless for mining. DM engineers discovered a new survey technology and discovered a silver deposit estimated at 5,000 pounds on Diamond Mountain. DM immediately bought new drilling equipment and began mining the silver.

In years 1–3 following the opening of the mine, DM had net (gross) income of $200,000 ($700,000), $400,000 ($1,100,000), and $600,000 ($1,450,000), respectively. Mining amounts for each year were as follows: 750 pounds (year 1), 1,450 pounds (year 2), and 1,800 pounds (year 3). At the end of year 2, engineers used the new technology (which had been improving over time) and estimated there was still an estimated 6,000 pounds of silver deposits.

DM also began a research and experimentation project with the hopes of gaining a patent for its new survey technology. Diamond Mountain Inc. chose to capitalize research and experimentation expenditures and to amortize the costs over 60 months or until it obtained a patent on its technology. In March of year 1, DM spent $95,000 on research and experimentation. DM spent another $75,000 in February of year 2 for research and experimentation. In September of year 2, DM paid $20,000 of legal fees and was granted the patent in October of year 2 (the entire process of obtaining a patent was unusually fast).

Answer the following questions regarding DM's activities (assume that DM tries to maximize its deductions if given a choice).

a) What is DM's depletion expense for years 1–3?

b) What is DM's research and experimentation amortization for years 1 and 2?

c) What is DM's basis in its patent and what is its amortization for the patent in year 2?

 **ROGER** | *CPA Review*

Sample CPA Exam questions from Roger CPA Review are available in Connect as support for the topics in this text. These Multiple Choice Questions and Task-Based Simulations include expert-written explanations and solutions and provide a starting point for students to become familiar with the content and functionality of the actual CPA Exam.

chapter

11 Property Dispositions

Learning Objectives

Upon completing this chapter, you should be able to:

LO 11-1 Calculate the amount of gain or loss recognized on the disposition of assets used in a trade or business.

LO 11-2 Describe the general character types of gain or loss recognized on property dispositions.

LO 11-3 Calculate depreciation recapture.

LO 11-4 Describe the tax treatment of unrecaptured §1250 gains.

LO 11-5 Describe the tax treatment of §1231 gains or losses, including the §1231 netting process.

LO 11-6 Explain common exceptions to the general rule that realized gains and losses are recognized currently.

Storyline Summary

Taxpayer:	Teton Mountaineering Technology, LLC (Teton)—a calendar-year, single-member LLC (treated as a sole proprietorship for tax purposes)
President:	Steve Dallimore
Location:	Cody, Wyoming

By most measures, Teton Mountaineering Technology, LLC (Teton), has become a success, with sponsored climbers summiting the world's highest peaks, satisfied customers creating brand loyalty, and profitability improving steadily. However, after several years of operation, some of Teton's machinery is wearing out and must be replaced. Further, because Teton has outgrown its manufacturing capacity, Steve is considering whether to expand the company's current facility or sell it and build a new one in a different location. Steve would like to know how any asset dispositions will affect Steve's tax bill.

Steve has found a willing buyer for some of Teton's land, and he has options for trading the land. For tax purposes, does it matter whether he sells or trades the land? Steve also has questions about how to best manage Teton's acquisitions and dispositions of real property. It all seems a bit overwhelming. . . . He picks up the phone and dials his tax accountant's number. ∎

You can imagine why Steve might be eager to reach out to his accountant. Tax accounting widely impacts business decisions: What are the tax consequences of selling, trading, or even abandoning business assets? Are the tax consequences the same whether taxpayers sell machinery, inventory, or investment assets? Does it matter for tax purposes whether Teton is structured as a sole proprietorship or a corporation when it sells its warehouse? If Steve sells his personal sailboat, car, or furniture, what are the tax consequences?

In the previous chapter we explained the tax consequences associated with purchasing assets and recovering the cost of the assets through depreciation, amortization, or depletion. This chapter explores fundamental tax issues associated with property dispositions (sales, trades, or other dispositions). We focus on the disposition of tangible assets, but the same principles apply to the sale of intangible assets and natural resources.

LO 11-1 DISPOSITIONS

Taxpayers can dispose of assets in many ways. For example, a taxpayer could sell an asset, donate it to charity, trade it for a similar asset, take it to the landfill, or have it destroyed in a natural disaster. No matter how it is accomplished, every asset disposition triggers a realization event for tax purposes. To calculate the amount of gain or loss taxpayers realize when they sell assets, they must determine the amount realized on the sale and the *adjusted basis* of each asset they are selling.

Amount Realized

Simply put, the **amount realized** by a taxpayer from the sale or other disposition of an asset is everything of *value* received from the buyer *less* any selling costs.[1] Although taxpayers typically receive cash when they sell property, they may also accept marketable securities, notes receivable, similar assets, or any combination of these items as payment. Additionally, taxpayers selling assets such as real property subject to loans or mortgages may receive some debt relief. In this case, they would increase their amount realized by the amount of debt relief (the buyer's assumption of the seller's liability increases the seller's amount realized). The amount realized computation is captured in the following formula:

$$\text{Amount realized} = \text{Cash received} + \text{Fair market value of other property} + \text{Buyer's assumption of liabilities} - \text{Seller's expenses}$$

Example 11-1

Teton wants to upgrade its old manufacturing machinery that is wearing out. On November 1 of the current year, Teton sells the machinery for $230,000 cash and marketable securities valued at $70,500. Teton paid a broker $500 to find a buyer. What is Teton's amount realized on the sale of the machinery?

Answer: $300,000, computed as follows:

Description	Amount	Explanation
(1) Cash received	$230,000	
(2) Marketable securities received	70,500	
(3) Broker commission paid	(500)	
Amount realized	**$300,000**	(1) + (2) + (3)

Determination of Adjusted Basis

In the previous chapter, we discussed the basis for cost recovery and focused on purchased assets in which the initial basis is the asset's cost. However, taxpayers may acquire assets

[1]*S.C. Chapin*, CA-8, 50-1 USTC ¶9171.

without purchasing them. For example, a taxpayer may acquire an asset as a gift or as an inheritance. In either case, the taxpayer does not purchase the asset, so the taxpayer's initial basis in the asset must be computed as something other than purchase price. Although there are many situations when an asset's initial basis is not the asset's cost, we focus on three cases: gifts, inherited assets, and property converted from personal use to business use.

Gifts A gift is defined as a transfer of property proceeding from a detached and disinterested generosity, out of affection, respect, admiration, charity, or like impulses.[2] The initial basis of gift property to a recipient (donee) depends on whether the value of the asset exceeds the donor's basis on the date of the gift. If the fair market value of the asset on the date of the gift is greater than the donor's basis, then the asset's initial basis to the recipient of the gift will be the same as the donor's basis.[3] That is, the donor's basis carries over to the donee.

If the asset has declined in value since the donor acquired it (fair market value at the date of the gift is less than the donor's basis), then special dual basis rules apply. A dual basis means that the gift property has one basis to the donee if the donee sells the property at a price above the donor's basis and a different basis if the donee sells the property at a price below the fair market value at the date of the gift. Interestingly, the donee will not know the basis for calculating gain or loss until the donee sells the property. Thus, the basis of gifted property that has declined in value depends on the sales price of the asset subsequent to the gift. The donee uses the carryover basis if the asset is sold for a gain (sales price > donor's basis), whereas the donee uses the fair market value at the date of the gift if the asset is sold for a loss (sales price < FMV at date of gift). If the asset sells at a price between the donor's basis and the fair market value at the date of the gift, then the donee's basis at the time of the sale is set equal to the selling price and the donee does not recognize gain or loss on the sale. The dual basis rule prevents the transfer of unrealized losses from one taxpayer to another by gift.

When the dual basis rules apply, the donee's holding period of the asset depends on whether the gift property subsequently sells for a gain or loss. If the donor's basis is used to determine the gain, the holding period includes that of the donor. If the fair market value at the date of the gift is used to figure the loss, the holding period starts on the date of the gift. If the asset subsequently sells at a price between the donor's basis and the fair market value at the date of the gift, the holding period is irrelevant because there is no recognized gain or loss.

Inherited Property For inherited property, the general rule is that the heir's basis in property passing from a decedent to the heir is the fair market value on the date of the decedent's death.[4] The holding period of inherited property is deemed to be long-term regardless of how long the heir owns the property.[5]

Property Converted from Personal Use to Business Use The basis for determining the gain or loss on the sale of converted property depends on whether the property appreciated or declined in value during the time the property was used personally. For appreciated property (the fair market value at the date of the conversion is greater than the taxpayer's basis in the property), the taxpayer will use the taxpayer basis to calculate depreciation and gain or loss at disposition.

For property that has declined in value, taxpayers may try to convert nondeductible personal losses to business losses by converting the property into business property and then selling it. In order to prevent this from occurring, the dual basis rules apply. If the fair market value at the date of conversion is below the taxpayer's basis, the taxpayer will use the fair market value at the date of conversion as the basis for calculating loss and will use the basis at date of conversion to calculate gain. The fair market value at the date of conversion is also the basis used to calculate depreciation on property that has declined in

---

[2]*Comr. v. Duberstein*, 363 U.S. 278 (1960), rev'g 265 F.2d 28 (6th Cir. 1959), rev'g T. C. Memo 1958–4.

[3]§1015(a). The basis to the donee may be increased if the donor is required to pay gift tax on the gift.

[4]§1014(a)(1). An alternate valuation date may be used to determine the basis to the heirs if elected by the estate.

[5]§1223(9).

value prior to the conversion regardless of whether the taxpayer subsequently sells the property for a gain or a loss. After conversion, the taxpayer adjusts the basis (whether gain or loss) for depreciation deductions from the date of conversion to the date of disposition. If the property later sells for an amount that falls between the adjusted basis for gain and the adjusted basis for loss, the basis for the sale is treated as the sales price so that the taxpayer does not recognize gain or loss on the sale.[6]

Example 11-2

Assume that Steve received 100 shares of FZL stock from his grandfather on January 8. On the date of the gift, the stock was worth $15,000. Steve's grandfather originally purchased the stock 10 years earlier for $10,000. What is Steve's initial basis in the stock?

Answer: Since the stock had appreciated in value while Steve's grandfather owned it, Steve's initial basis is a carryover basis of $10,000.

What if: Assume that on the date of the gift, the fair market value of the stock was $8,000. What is Steve's initial basis in the stock?

Answer: Steve's initial basis depends on the price for which he later sells the stock. If Steve sells the stock six months later at a price greater than $10,000, his basis is the $10,000 carryover basis. He will recognize a long-term capital gain because his holding period is 10½ years (i.e., it includes the time his grandfather owned the stock). If he sells the stock six months later at a price less than $8,000, his basis is $8,000, the fair market value at the date of the gift. He will recognize a short-term capital loss because his holding period is only six months (i.e., it begins on the date of the gift). If he sells the stock for a price that is between $10,000 and $8,000, his basis is the sales price and he recognizes no gain or loss (his holding period does not matter).

What if: Assume that Steve inherited the stock from his grandfather on January 8. What is Steve's initial basis if the fair market value is (a) $15,000 and (b) $8,000 at the time of his grandfather's death?

Answer: Steve's initial basis is the fair market value at the date of his grandfather's death regardless of whether the value is greater or less than his grandfather's original cost. If the fair market value is $15,000, Steve's initial basis is $15,000. If the fair market value is $8,000, Steve's initial basis is $8,000. Steve's holding period is long-term regardless of how long he actually holds the stock because it is inherited property.

What if: Assume Steve owns some mountaineering equipment that he uses personally and purchased two years ago for $4,000. On March 20, he converts the equipment into business-use property when the fair market value of the equipment is $5,000. What is Steve's initial basis in the equipment for business purposes?

Answer: Because the equipment appreciated in value before Steve converted it to business use, his basis is his original cost of $4,000. Steve will use the $4,000 as his initial basis for calculating cost recovery and determining his adjusted basis when he sells or otherwise disposes of the equipment.

What if: Assume that the equipment that Steve converts from personal to business use has a fair market value of $3,000 at the date of conversion. What is Steve's initial basis in the equipment for business purposes?

Answer: The equipment declined in value before Steve converted it to business use. In order to prevent Steve from converting his $1,000 personal loss into a business loss, his initial basis for business purposes will depend on whether he subsequently sells the equipment at a gain or loss. His initial basis for loss (and cost recovery) is the $3,000 fair market value at the conversion date. His initial basis for gain is his $4,000 original cost.

What if: Assume that the equipment that Steve converts from personal to business use has a fair market value of $3,000 at the date of conversion. Two years later, after taking $500 of depreciation deductions, he sells the equipment for $3,300. What is Steve's adjusted basis in the equipment for purposes of determining the gain or loss on the disposition?

Answer: Steve's initial basis for loss was the $3,000 fair market value at the conversion date, and his initial basis for gain was the $4,000 original cost. At the time of the sale, the adjusted basis for loss is $2,500, and the adjusted basis for gain is $3,500. Because the sales price falls between the adjusted basis for gain and the adjusted basis for loss, the adjusted basis is assumed to be equal to the sales price of $3,300.

---

[6]Reg. §1.165-9(b)(2) and Reg. §1.167(g)-1.

The **adjusted basis** for determining the gain or loss on the sale of an asset is the initial basis (however determined) reduced by depreciation or other types of cost recovery deductions allowed (or allowable) on the property. The adjusted basis of an asset can be determined using the following formula:

Adjusted basis = Initial basis − Cost recovery allowed (or allowable)

Example 11-3

To determine its realized gain or loss on the sale, Teton must calculate the adjusted basis of the machinery it sold in Example 11-1 for $300,000. Teton originally purchased the machinery for $610,000 three years ago. For tax purposes, Teton depreciated the machinery using MACRS (seven-year recovery period, 200 percent declining balance method, and half-year convention).

The machinery's adjusted basis at the time of the sale is $228,658, computed as follows:

Description	Tax	Explanation
(1) Initial basis	$ 610,000	Example 10-1
(2) Year 1	(87,169)	Example 10-5
(3) Year 2	(149,389)	Example 10-5
(4) Year 3	(106,689)	Example 10-5
(5) Year 4	(38,095)	$76,189 (Example 10-5) × 50% (half-year convention)
(6) Accumulated depreciation	(381,342)	(2) + (3) + (4) + (5)
Adjusted basis	**$228,658**	(1) + (6)

Because businesses generally use more highly accelerated depreciation methods for tax purposes than they do for book purposes, the tax-adjusted basis of a particular asset is likely to be lower than the book-adjusted basis.

Realized Gain or Loss on Disposition

The amount of gain or loss taxpayers realize on a sale or other disposition of assets is simply the amount they realize minus their adjusted basis in the disposed assets.[7] The formula for computing **realized gain or loss** is as follows:

Gain or (loss) realized = Amount realized − Adjusted basis

Example 11-4

In Example 11-1 we learned that Teton sold machinery for a total amount realized of $300,000, and in Example 11-3 we learned that its basis in the machinery was $228,658. What is Teton's realized gain or loss on the sale of the machinery?

Answer: $71,342, computed as follows:

Description	Amount	Explanation
(1) Amount realized	$300,000	Example 11-1
(2) Adjusted basis	(228,658)	Example 11-3
Gain realized	**$ 71,342**	(1) + (2)

Exhibit 11-1 details the important formulas necessary to determine realized tax gains and losses.

[7]§1001(a).

EXHIBIT 11-1   **Summary of Formulas for Computing Gain or Loss Realized on an Asset Disposition**

- Gain (loss) realized = Amount realized − Adjusted basis; where
  - Amount realized = Cash received + Fair market value of other property + Buyer's assumption of seller's liabilities − Seller's expenses
  - Adjusted basis = Initial basis − Cost recovery deductions

So far, our examples have used one of Teton's asset sales to demonstrate how to compute gain or loss realized when property is sold. However, as we describe in Exhibit 11-2, Teton disposed of several assets during the year. We refer to this exhibit throughout the chapter as a reference point for discussing the tax issues associated with property dispositions.

EXHIBIT 11-2   **Teton's Asset Dispositions:* Realized Gain (Loss) for Tax Purposes**

Asset	(1) Amount Realized	(2) Initial Basis	(3) Accumulated Depreciation	(4) [(2) − (3)] Adjusted Basis	(5) [(1) − (4)] Gain (Loss) Realized
Machinery	$300,000	$610,000	$381,342	$228,658	$ 71,342
Office furniture	23,000	20,000	14,000	6,000	17,000
Delivery truck	2,000	25,000	17,500	7,500	(5,500)
Warehouse	350,000	275,000	15,000	260,000	90,000
Land	175,000	75,000	0	75,000	100,000
Total gain realized					$272,842

*These are the assets initially purchased by Teton in Example 10-1. This chapter generally assumes that Teton has been in business for four years. For simplicity, this chapter assumes Teton did not previously elect any §179 immediate expensing and opted out of bonus depreciation.

Recognized Gain or Loss on Disposition

As a general rule, taxpayers realizing gains and losses during a year must recognize the gains or losses. **Recognized gains or losses** are gains (losses) that increase (decrease) taxpayers' gross income.[8] Thus, taxpayers must report recognized gains and losses on their tax returns. Although taxpayers must immediately recognize the vast majority of realized gains and losses, in certain circumstances they may be allowed to defer recognizing gains to subsequent periods, or they may be allowed to permanently exclude the gains from taxable income. However, taxpayers may also be required to defer losses to later periods and, in more extreme cases, they may have their realized losses permanently disallowed. We address certain nonrecognition provisions later in the chapter.

LO 11-2   CHARACTER OF GAIN OR LOSS

In order to determine how a recognized gain or loss affects a taxpayer's income tax liability, the taxpayer must determine the *character* or type of gain or loss recognized. Ultimately, every gain or loss is characterized as either ordinary or capital (long-term or short-term). As described below, businesses may recognize certain gains or losses (known as §1231) on property dispositions that require some intermediary steps, but even the §1231 gains or losses are eventually characterized as ordinary or capital (long-term).

[8]Recall under the return of capital principle we discussed in the Gross Income and Exclusions chapter, when a taxpayer sells an asset, the taxpayer's adjusted basis is a return of capital and not a deductible expense.

The character of a gain or loss is important because gains and losses of different characters are treated differently for tax purposes. For example, ordinary income (loss) is generally taxed at ordinary rates (fully deductible against ordinary income). However, capital gains may be taxed at preferential (lower) rates, while deductions for capital losses are subject to certain restrictions. The character of the gains or losses taxpayers recognize when they sell assets depend on the character of the assets they are selling. The character of an asset depends on how the taxpayer used the asset and how long the taxpayer owned the asset (the holding period) before selling it.

In general terms, property can be used in a trade or business, treated as inventory or accounts receivable of a business, held for investment, or used for personal purposes. The holding period may be short-term (one year or less) or long-term (more than a year). Exhibit 11-3 provides a table showing the character of assets (ordinary, capital, or §1231) depending on how taxpayers used the assets and the length of time they held the property before selling it.

EXHIBIT 11-3 Character of Assets Depending on Property Use and Holding Period

Holding Period	Property Use		
	Trade or Business	Investment or Personal-Use Assets*	Inventory and Accounts Receivable
Short-term (one year or less)	Ordinary	Short-term capital	Ordinary
Long-term (more than one year)	§1231†	Long-term capital	Ordinary

*Gains on the sale of personal-use assets are taxable, but losses on the sale of personal-use assets are not deductible.
†As we describe later in the chapter, gain or loss is eventually characterized as ordinary or capital (long-term).

Ordinary Assets

Ordinary assets are generally assets created or used in a taxpayer's trade or business. For example, inventory is an **ordinary asset** because it is held for sale to customers in the ordinary course of business. Accounts receivable are ordinary assets because receivables are generated from the sale of inventory or business services. Other assets used in a trade or business such as machinery and equipment are also considered to be ordinary assets if they have been used in a business for *one year or less*. For example, if Teton purchased a forklift for the warehouse but sold it six months later, the gain or loss would be ordinary. When taxpayers sell ordinary assets at a gain, they recognize an ordinary gain that is taxed at ordinary rates. When taxpayers sell ordinary assets at a loss, they deduct the loss against other ordinary income.

Capital Assets

A **capital asset** is generally something held for investment (stocks and bonds) for the **production of income** (a for-profit activity that doesn't rise to the level of a trade or business) or for personal use (your car, house, or personal computer).[9] Whether an asset qualifies as a capital asset depends on the purpose for which the taxpayer uses the asset. Thus, the same asset may be considered a capital asset to one taxpayer and an ordinary asset to another taxpayer. For example, a piece of land held as an investment because it is expected to appreciate in value over time is a capital asset to that taxpayer. However, the same piece of land held as inventory by a real estate developer would be an ordinary asset. Finally, the same piece of land would be a §1231 asset if the taxpayer held it for more than one year and used it in a trade or business (e.g., as a parking lot).

[9]§1221 defines what is not a capital asset. Broadly speaking, a *capital asset* is any property *other than* property used in a trade or business (e.g., inventory, manufacturing equipment) or accounts (or notes) receivable acquired in a business from the sale of services or property.

Individual taxpayers generally prefer capital gains to ordinary income because certain capital gains are taxed at lower rates and capital gains may offset capital losses that cannot be deducted against ordinary income. Individuals also prefer ordinary losses to capital losses because ordinary losses are deductible without limit, while individuals may deduct only $3,000 of net capital losses against ordinary income each year. Corporate taxpayers may prefer capital gains to ordinary income because capital gains may offset capital losses that they would not be allowed to offset otherwise. Corporations are not allowed to deduct net capital losses, but they are allowed to carry net capital losses back three years and forward five years to offset net capital gains in those years. Exhibit 11-4 reviews the treatment of capital gains and losses for individuals and corporations.

EXHIBIT 11-4   **Review of Capital Gains and Losses**

Taxpayer Type	Preferential Rates	Loss Limitations
Individuals	• Net capital gains on assets held more than one year are taxed at 15 percent (0 percent to the extent taxable income including the gain is below the maximum zero percent threshold and 20 percent to the extent taxable income including capital gains is above the maximum 15 percent threshold). When determining which capital gains tax rate applies, capital gains that fall within the range of taxable income specified in Appendix D are included in taxable income last. • Unrecaptured §1250 gains on real property held more than one year remaining after the netting process are taxed at a maximum rate of 25 percent. • Net gains on collectibles held for more than a year are taxed at a maximum rate of 28 percent. • Net capital gains on assets held one year or less are taxed at ordinary rates.	• Individuals may annually deduct up to $3,000 of net capital losses against ordinary income. • Losses can be carried forward indefinitely but not carried back.
Corporations	• No preferential rates; taxed at ordinary rates	• No offset against ordinary income. • Net capital losses can generally be carried back three years and forward five years to offset net capital gains in those years.

Section 1231 Assets

Section 1231 assets are depreciable assets and land used in a trade or business (including rental property) held by taxpayers for *more* than one year.[10] At a general level, when a taxpayer sells a §1231 asset, the taxpayer recognizes a §1231 gain or loss. As discussed above, however, ultimately §1231 gains or losses are characterized as ordinary or capital on a taxpayer's return. When taxpayers sell multiple §1231 assets during the year, they combine or "net" their §1231 gains and §1231 losses together. If the netting results in a net §1231 gain, the net gain is treated as a long-term capital gain. If the netting results in a net §1231 loss, the net loss is treated as an ordinary loss. Because net §1231 gains are treated as capital gains and §1231 losses are treated as ordinary losses, §1231 assets are tax favored relative to other types of assets.

---

[10]As noted above, property used in a trade or business and held for *one year or less* is ordinary income property.

As we discuss below, §1231 gains on individual depreciable assets may be recharacterized as ordinary income under the depreciation recapture rules. However, because land is not depreciable, when taxpayers sell or otherwise dispose of land that qualifies as §1231 property, the gain or loss from the sale is always characterized as a §1231 gain or loss. Thus, we refer to land as a pure §1231 asset.

Example 11-5

In order to acquire another parcel of land to expand its manufacturing capabilities, Teton sold five acres of land that it had been using in its trade or business for $175,000. Teton purchased the land several years ago for $75,000. What is the amount and character of Teton's gain recognized on the land?

Answer: $100,000 §1231 gain, calculated as follows:

Description	Amount	Explanation
(1) Amount realized	$ 175,000	
(2) Original basis and current adjusted basis	75,000	
Gain (loss) realized and recognized	**$100,000**	(1) – (2) §1231 gain

What if: Assume that Teton sold the land for $50,000. What would be the character of the ($25,000) loss it would recognize?

Answer: §1231 loss.

What if: Assume that the land was the only asset Teton sold during the year. How would the §1231 gain or §1231 loss on the sale ultimately be characterized on its tax return?

Answer: If Teton recognized a §1231 gain on the sale, it would be characterized as a long-term capital gain on its return. If Teton recognized a §1231 loss on the sale, it would be characterized as an ordinary loss.

DEPRECIATION RECAPTURE

LO 11-3

Although Congress intended for businesses to receive favorable treatment on economic gains from the economic *appreciation* of §1231 assets, it did not intend for this favorable treatment to apply to gains that were created artificially through depreciation deductions that offset ordinary income. For example, if a taxpayer purchases an asset for $100 and sells it three years later for the same amount, we would generally agree that there is no economic gain on the disposition of the asset. However, if the taxpayer claimed depreciation deductions of $70 during the three years of ownership, the taxpayer would recognize a $70 gain on the disposition simply because the depreciation deductions reduced the asset's adjusted basis. Depreciation is an ordinary deduction that offsets income that would otherwise be taxed at ordinary rates.

Absent tax rules to the contrary, the gain recognized by the taxpayer upon the sale of the asset would be treated as long-term capital gain and would be taxed at a preferential rate (for individuals). Thus, depreciation deductions save taxes at the ordinary rate but the gains created by depreciation generate income taxed at a preferential rate. This potential asymmetrical treatment led Congress to implement the concept of **depreciation recapture.** Depreciation recapture potentially applies to gains (but not losses) on the sale of depreciable or amortizable business property. When depreciation recapture applies, it changes the character of the gain on the sale of a §1231 asset (all or a portion of the gain) from §1231 gain into ordinary income. Note, however, that depreciation recapture does not affect losses recognized on the disposition of §1231 assets.

The method for computing the amount of depreciation recapture depends on the type of §1231 asset the taxpayer is selling (personal property or real property). As presented in

Exhibit 11-5, §1231 assets can be categorized as pure §1231 assets (land), §1245 assets (personal property), or §1250 assets (real property). Whether personal or real property is sold, it is important to understand that depreciation recapture changes only the *character* but not the *amount* of gain recognized.

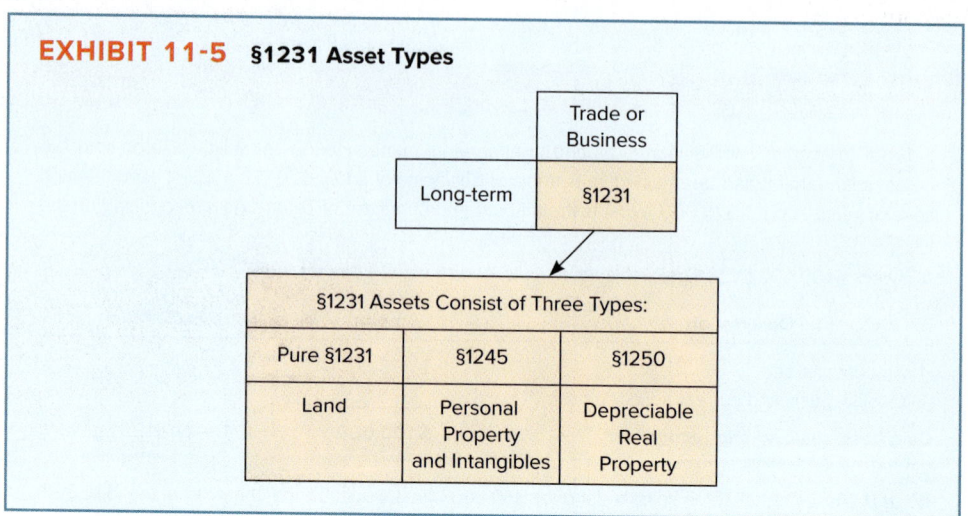

EXHIBIT 11-5 **§1231 Asset Types**

§1245 Property

Tangible personal property (machinery, equipment, and automobiles) and amortizable intangible property (patents, copyrights, and purchased goodwill) are a subset of §1231 property known as **§1245 property.**[11] The gain from the sale of §1245 property is characterized as ordinary income to the extent the gain was created by depreciation or amortization deductions. The amount of *ordinary income* (§1245 depreciation recapture) taxpayers recognize when they sell §1245 property is the lesser of (1) recognized gain on the sale *or* (2) total accumulated depreciation (or amortization) on the asset.[12] The remainder of any recognized gain is characterized as §1231 gain.[13] The sum of the ordinary income (due to depreciation recapture) and the §1231 gain on the sale equals the *total* gain recognized because depreciation recapture changes only the character of the gain, not the amount.

When taxpayers sell or dispose of §1245 property, they encounter one of the following three scenarios involving gain or loss:

Scenario 1: They recognize a gain created solely through depreciation deductions.

Scenario 2: They recognize a gain created through both depreciation deductions and actual asset appreciation.

Scenario 3: They recognize a loss.

The following discussion considers each of these scenarios.

---

[11]An exception in the law is that §1245 property also includes nonresidential real property placed in service between 1981 and 1986 (ACRS) for which the taxpayer elected accelerated depreciation.

[12]§1245 recapture is commonly referred to as "full" depreciation recapture because it may cause a taxpayer to recapture the entire accumulated depreciation amount as ordinary income. §1245 recapture applies notwithstanding any other provision of the Internal Revenue Code (depreciation recapture trumps all other tax rules (e.g., installment sales)).

[13]As a practical matter, taxpayers are unlikely to recognize any §1231 gain on the disposition of personal property because the real economic value of most tangible personal property does not increase over time as the property is used.

Scenario 1: Gain Created Solely through Cost Recovery Deductions   Most §1231 assets that experience wear and tear or obsolescence generally do not appreciate in value. Thus, when a taxpayer sells these types of assets at a gain, the gain is usually created because the taxpayer's depreciation deductions associated with the asset reduced the asset's adjusted basis faster than the real decline in the asset's economic value. That is, the entire gain is artificially generated through depreciation and absent these deductions, the taxpayer would recognize a loss on the sale of the asset. Therefore, the entire gain on the disposition is recaptured (or characterized) as ordinary income under §1245 (recall that without depreciation recapture the gain would be §1231 gain, which can generate long-term capital gain and could create a double benefit for the taxpayer: ordinary depreciation deductions and preferentially-taxed capital gain upon disposition).

Example 11-6

As indicated in Exhibit 11-2, Teton sold machinery for $300,000. What is the amount and character of the gain Teton recognizes on the sale?

Answer: $71,342 of ordinary income under the §1245 depreciation recapture rules and $0 of §1231 gain, computed as follows:

Machinery Sale: Scenario 1 (Original scenario sales price = $300,000)		
Description	**Amount**	**Explanation**
(1) Amount realized	$300,000	Exhibit 11-2
(2) Original basis	610,000	Exhibit 11-2
(3) Accumulated depreciation	381,342	Exhibit 11-2
(4) Adjusted basis	228,658	(2) − (3)
(5) Gain (loss) recognized	71,342	(1) − (4)
(6) Ordinary income **(§1245 depreciation recapture)**	**$ 71,342**	Lesser of (3) or (5)
§1231 gain	0	(5) − (6)

Note that in this situation, because Teton's entire gain is created through depreciation deductions reducing the basis, the entire gain is treated as ordinary income under §1245.

What if: What would be the amount and character of Teton's gain without the depreciation recapture rules?

Answer: $71,342 of §1231 gain. Note that the recapture rules change the character of the gain but not the amount of the gain.

Both §179 expensing and bonus depreciation allow taxpayers to accelerate the depreciation taken on assets in the year of acquisition. After the Tax Jobs and Cuts Act (TCJA), many taxpayers will fully deduct the cost of acquired assets. These provisions, however, require that taxpayers reduce the basis of the assets by the amount of depreciation taken. When taxpayers deduct the full cost of an asset under these rules, the asset's basis is reduced to zero. As a result, taxpayers will have larger gains post-TCJA and the gains will typically be ordinary in character.

Scenario 2: Gain Due to Both Cost Recovery Deductions and Asset Appreciation   Assets subject to cost recovery deductions may actually *appreciate* in value over time. When these assets are sold, the recognized gain must be divided into ordinary gain from depreciation recapture and §1231 gain. The portion of the gain created through cost recovery deductions is recaptured as ordinary income. The remaining gain (the gain due to economic appreciation) is §1231 gain.

Example 11-7

What if: Let's assume the same facts as in Example 11-6 and Exhibit 11-2, except that Teton sells the machinery for $620,000. What is the amount and character of the gain Teton would recognize on this sale?

Answer: $381,342 of ordinary income under the §1245 depreciation recapture rules and $10,000 of §1231 gain due to the asset's economic appreciation, computed as follows:

Machinery Sale: Scenario 2 (Assumed sales price = $620,000)		
Description	**Amount**	**Explanation**
(1) Amount realized	$ 620,000	
(2) Original basis	610,000	Exhibit 11-2
(3) Accumulated depreciation	$ 381,342	Exhibit 11-2
(4) Adjusted basis	228,658	(2) – (3)
(5) Gain (loss) recognized	391,342	(1) – (4)
(6) Ordinary income **(§1245 depreciation recapture)**	**$381,342**	Lesser of (3) or (5)
§1231 gain	**$ 10,000**	(5) – (6)

Note that taxpayers can quickly determine their §1231 gain (if any) when they sell §1245 property by subtracting the asset's *initial* basis from the amount realized. For example, in Example 11-7, the §1231 gain is $10,000 ($620,000 amount realized less the $610,000 original basis).

Scenario 3: Asset Sold at a Loss
Many §1231 assets, such as computer equipment or automobiles, tend to decline in value faster than the corresponding depreciation deductions reduce the asset's adjusted basis. When taxpayers sell or dispose of these assets before the assets are fully depreciated, they recognize a loss on the disposition. Because the depreciation recapture rules don't apply to losses, taxpayers selling §1245 property at a loss recognize a §1231 loss.

Example 11-8

What if: Let's assume the same facts as in Example 11-6 and Exhibit 11-2, except that Teton sells the machinery for $180,000. What is the amount and character of the gain or loss Teton would recognize on this sale?

Answer: A $48,658 §1231 loss, computed as follows:

Machinery Sale: Scenario 3 (Assumed sales price = $180,000)		
Description	**Amount**	**Explanation**
(1) Amount realized	$180,000	
(2) Original basis	610,000	Exhibit 11-2
(3) Accumulated depreciation	381,342	Exhibit 11-2
(4) Adjusted basis	228,658	(2) – (3)
(5) Gain (loss) recognized	(48,658)	(1) – (4)
(6) Ordinary income (§1245 depreciation recapture)	$ 0	Lesser of (3) or (5) (limited to $0)
§1231 (loss)	**$(48,658)**	(5) – (6)

Exhibit 11-6 graphically illustrates the §1245 depreciation recapture computations for the machinery sold in Scenarios 1, 2, and 3, presented in Examples 11-6, 11-7, and 11-8, respectively.[14]

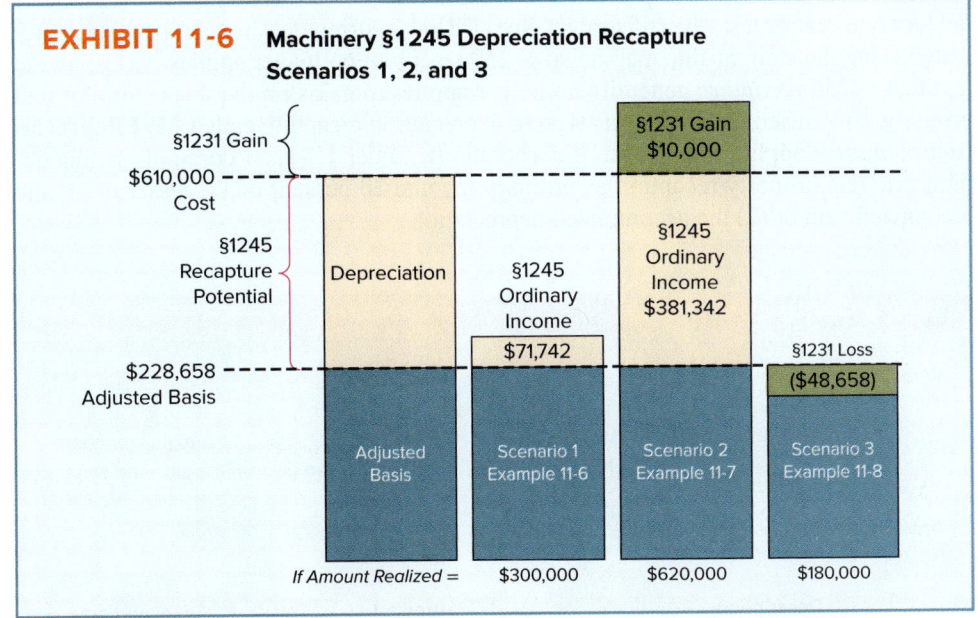

EXHIBIT 11-6   Machinery §1245 Depreciation Recapture Scenarios 1, 2, and 3

Example 11-9

In Example 11-6 (Scenario 1), we characterized the gain Teton recognized when it sold its machinery. For completeness, let's characterize the gain or loss Teton recognized on the other two §1245 assets it sold during the year (see Exhibit 11-2). Teton sold its office furniture for $23,000 and its delivery truck for $2,000. What is the amount and character of gain or loss Teton recognizes on the sale of the office furniture and the delivery truck?

Answer: Office furniture: $14,000 ordinary income and $3,000 §1231 gain. Delivery truck: $5,500 §1231 loss. The computations supporting the answers are as follows:

Description	Office Furniture	Delivery Truck	Explanation
(1) Amount realized	$ 23,000	$ 2,000	Exhibit 11-2
(2) Initial basis	20,000	25,000	Exhibit 11-2
(3) Accumulated depreciation	14,000	17,500	Exhibit 11-2
(4) Adjusted basis	6,000	7,500	(2) − (3)
(5) Gain (loss) recognized	17,000	(5,500)	(1) − (4)
(6) Ordinary income	**$14,000**	**$ 0**	Lesser of (3) or (5),
(§1245 depreciation recapture)			limited to $0
§1231 gain (loss)	**$ 3,000**	**$(5,500)**	(5) − (6)

§1250 Depreciation Recapture for Real Property

Depreciable real property, such as an office building or a warehouse, sold at a gain is *not* subject to §1245 depreciation recapture. Rather, it is subject to a different type of recapture called §1250 depreciation recapture. Thus, depreciable real property is frequently

---

[14]The authors thank PwC for allowing us to use this exhibit.

referred to as **§1250 property.** Under §1250, when depreciable real property is sold at a gain, the amount of gain recaptured as ordinary income is limited to *additional* depreciation, defined as the excess of *accelerated* depreciation deductions on the property over the amount that would have been deducted if the taxpayer had used the straight-line method of depreciation to depreciate the asset and depreciation was taken on property held for one year or less (even if straight-line).[15] Under current law, real property is depreciated using the straight-line method so §1250 recapture no longer applies.[16] Despite the fact that *§1250 recapture* generally no longer applies to gains on the disposition of real property, a modified version of this type of depreciation recapture called **§291 depreciation recapture** applies, but only to C corporations. Under §291, corporations selling depreciable real property recapture as ordinary income 20 percent of the lesser of (1) the recognized gain or (2) the accumulated depreciation.

Example 11-10

What if: Suppose that Teton was organized as a C corporation and that, as described in Exhibit 11-2, it sold its existing warehouse. Let's assume the same facts: Teton sold the warehouse for $350,000, it initially purchased the warehouse for $275,000, and it has deducted $15,000 of straight-line depreciation deductions as of the date of the sale. What is Teton's recognized gain on the sale and what is the character of its gain on the sale?

Answer: $90,000 gain recognized; $3,000 ordinary income and $87,000 §1231 gain, computed as follows:

Description	Amount	Explanation
(1) Amount realized	$350,000	Exhibit 11-2
(2) Initial basis	275,000	Exhibit 11-2
(3) Accumulated depreciation	15,000	Exhibit 11-2
(4) Adjusted basis	260,000	(2) − (3)
(5) Gain (loss) recognized	90,000	(1) − (4)
(6) Lesser of accumulated depreciation or recognized gain	15,000	Lesser of (3) or (5)
(7) §291 recapture (ordinary income)	**$ 3,000**	20% × (6)
§1231 gain	**$ 87,000**	(5) − (7)

LO 11-4

OTHER PROVISIONS AFFECTING THE RATE AT WHICH GAINS ARE TAXED

Other provisions, other than depreciation recapture, may affect the rate at which gains are taxed. The first potentially applies when individuals sell §1250 property at a gain, and the second potentially applies when taxpayers sell property to related persons at a gain.

Unrecaptured §1250 Gain for Individuals

Except for assets held 12 months or less, neither corporations nor individuals recognize §1250 recapture on the sale of §1250 property when it is sold at a gain. Instead, corporations recognize §291 recapture as ordinary income on the sale of these assets. Individuals,

---

[15]§1250 recapture is commonly referred to as *partial depreciation recapture.*

[16]Accelerated depreciation was allowed for real property placed in service before 1987. Such property had a maximum recovery period of 19 years, which means that as of 2005 all of this property is now fully depreciated under both the accelerated and straight-line depreciation methods.

however, do not recognize ordinary income from the sale of §1250 property when it is held long term. Rather, individual taxpayers treat a gain resulting from the disposition of §1250 property as a §1231 gain and combine it with other §1231 gains and losses to determine whether a net §1231 gain or a net §1231 loss results for the year.

After the §1231 netting process (described below), if the gain on the sale of the §1250 property is ultimately determined to be a long-term capital gain, the taxpayer must determine the rate at which the gain will be taxed. Tax policy makers have determined that the portion of the gain caused by depreciation deductions reducing the basis, called **unrecaptured §1250 gain,** should be taxed at a maximum rate of 25 percent (taxed at the ordinary rate if the ordinary rate is lower than 25 percent) and not the 0/15/20 percent rate generally applicable to other types of long-term capital gains. Consequently, when an individual sells §1250 property at a gain, the amount of the gain taxed at a maximum rate of 25 percent is the *lesser* of (1) the recognized gain or (2) the accumulated depreciation on the asset.[17] The remainder of the gain is taxed at a maximum rate of 0/15/20 percent.[18]

Example 11-11

Teton bought its warehouse for $275,000, depreciated it $15,000, and sold it for $350,000. What is the amount and character of the gain Teton (and thus Steve) reports on the sale? (Recall that income of sole proprietorships is taxed directly to the owner of the business.)

Answer: $90,000 of §1231 gain, which includes $15,000 of unrecaptured §1250 gain, computed as follows:

Description	Amount	Explanation
(1) Amount realized	$350,000	Exhibit 11-2
(2) Original basis	275,000	Exhibit 11-2
(3) Accumulated depreciation	15,000	Exhibit 11-2
(4) Adjusted basis	260,000	(2) − (3)
(5) Gain (loss) recognized	90,000	(1) − (4)
(6) Unrecaptured §1250 gain	$ 15,000	Lesser of (3) or (5)
(7) Remaining §1231 gain	$ 75,000	(5) − (6)
Total §1231 gain	**$ 90,000**	(6) + (7)

What if: Suppose Steve's marginal ordinary tax rate is 32 percent. What amount of tax will he pay on the gain (assuming no other asset dispositions)?

Answer: $15,000, computed as follows:

Description	(1) Gain	(2) Rate	(1) × (2) Tax	Explanation
Long-term capital gain (unrecaptured §1250 gain portion)	$15,000	25%	$ 3,750	This is the gain due to depreciation deductions.
Long-term capital gain (15 percent portion)	75,000	15%	11,250	Taxed at 15 percent because Steve's taxable income including the capital gain is below the maximum 15 percent rate threshold.
Totals	$90,000		$15,000	

Because Steve did not sell any other §1231 assets during the year, the entire §1231 gain is treated as a long-term capital gain that is split into a portion taxed at 25 percent and a portion taxed at 15 percent.

THE KEY FACTS

Unrecaptured §1250 Gains

- Depreciable real property sold at a gain is §1250 property but is no longer subject to §1250 recapture unless it is held 12 months or less.
- The lesser of the (1) recognized gain or (2) accumulated depreciation on the assets is called *unrecaptured* §1250 gain.
- Unrecaptured §1250 gain is §1231 gain that, if ultimately characterized as a long-term capital gain, is taxed at a maximum rate of 25 percent.

[17]The amount taxed at a maximum rate of 25 percent cannot exceed the amount of the taxpayer's net §1231 gain.

[18]These rates (25 or 0/15/20 percent) apply to net §1231 gains after a netting process for capital gains, which we discuss in the Gross Income and Exclusions chapter.

Characterizing Gains on the Sale of Depreciable Property to Related Persons

Under §1239, when a taxpayer sells property to a *related person* and the property is depreciable property to the *buyer*, the entire gain on the sale is characterized as ordinary income to the *seller*.[19] Without this provision, related taxpayers could create tax savings by currently generating capital or §1231 gains through selling appreciated assets to related persons who would receive future ordinary deductions through depreciation expense on the basis of the property (stepped up to fair market value through the sale) acquired in the transaction.

The §1239 recapture provision is different from depreciation recapture in the sense that the seller is required to recognize ordinary income for depreciation deductions the buyer will receive *in the future*, while depreciation recapture requires taxpayers to recognize ordinary income for depreciation deductions they have received *in the past*. In both cases, however, the tax laws are designed to provide symmetry between the character of deductions an asset generates and the character of income the asset generates when it is sold. When depreciation recapture and the §1239 recapture provision apply to the same gain, the depreciation recapture rule applies first.

For purposes of §1239, a related person includes an individual and his or her controlled (more than 50 percent owned) corporation or partnership or a taxpayer and any trust in which the taxpayer (or spouse) is a beneficiary.[20]

Example 11-12

What if: Suppose that Teton is organized as a C corporation and Steve is the sole shareholder. Steve sells equipment that he was using for personal purposes to Teton for $90,000 (he originally purchased the equipment for $80,000). The equipment was a capital asset to Steve because he had been using it for personal purposes (he did not depreciate it). What is the amount and character of the gain Steve would recognize on the sale?

Answer: $10,000 of ordinary income (amount realized $90,000 − $80,000 adjusted basis). Even though Steve is selling what is a capital asset to him, because it is a depreciable asset to Teton and because Steve and Teton are considered to be related persons, Steve is required to characterize the entire amount of gain as ordinary under §1239. Without the §1239 provision, Steve would have recognized a capital gain.

Exhibit 11-7 provides a flowchart for determining the character of gains and losses on the taxable sale of assets used in a trade or business.

LO 11-5 CALCULATING NET §1231 GAINS OR LOSSES

Once taxpayers determine the amount and character of gain or loss they recognize on *each* §1231 asset they sell during the year, they still have work to do to determine whether the gains or losses will be treated as ordinary or capital. After recharacterizing §1231 gain as ordinary income under the §1245 and §291 (if applicable) depreciation recapture rules and the §1239 related-person rules, the remaining §1231 gains and losses are netted together.[21] Recall that a portion of the §1231 gains may include unrecaptured §1250 gains that are taxed at a maximum of 25 percent. When netting the §1231 losses against §1231 gains,

---

[19]§1239. §707(b)(2) contains a similar provision for partnerships.

[20]Additional related persons for purposes of §1239 include two corporations that are members of the same controlled group, a corporation and a partnership if the same person owns more than 50 percent of both entities, two S corporations controlled by the same person, and an S corporation and a C corporation controlled by the same person.

[21]If any of the §1231 gains and losses result from casualty or theft, these gains and losses are netted together first. If a net loss results, the net loss from §1231 casualty and theft events are treated as ordinary loss. Net gains from casualty and theft are treated as other §1231 gains and continue through the normal §1231 netting process.

EXHIBIT 11-7

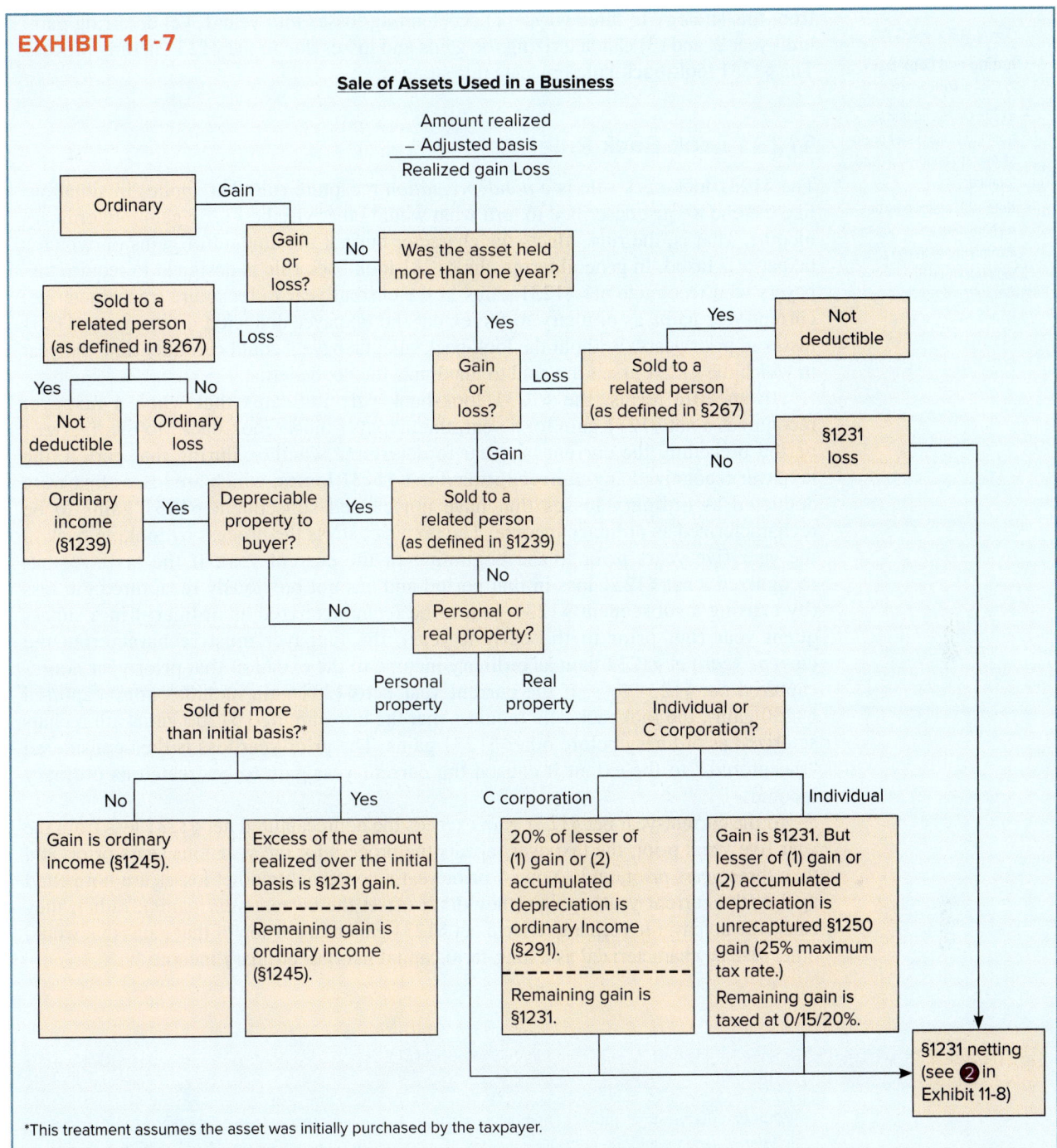

Sale of Assets Used in a Business

*This treatment assumes the asset was initially purchased by the taxpayer.

the losses first offset regular §1231 gains before offsetting unrecaptured §1250 gains. If the gains exceed the losses, the net gain becomes a long-term capital gain (a portion of which may be taxed at the maximum rate of 25 percent). If the losses exceed the gains, the net loss is treated as an ordinary loss.

A taxpayer could obtain significant tax benefits by discovering a way to have all §1231 gains treated as long-term capital gains and all §1231 losses treated as ordinary losses. The *annual* netting process makes this task impossible for a *particular* year. However, a taxpayer who owns multiple §1231 assets could sell the §1231 loss assets at the end of year 1 and the §1231 gain assets at the beginning of year 2. The taxpayer could benefit from this strategy in three ways: (1) accelerating losses into year 1, (2) deferring gains until year 2, and (3) characterizing the gains and losses due to the §1231 netting process. The **§1231 look-back rule** prevents this strategy.

§1231 Look-Back Rule

The §1231 look-back rule is a *nondepreciation* recapture rule that applies in situations like the one we just described to turn what would otherwise be §1231 gain into ordinary income. That is, the rule affects the character but not the amount of gains on which a taxpayer is taxed. In general terms, the §1231 look-back rule is designed to require taxpayers who recognize net §1231 gains in the current year to recapture (recharacterize) current-year gains as ordinary to the extent the taxpayer deducted ordinary net §1231 losses in prior years. Without the look-back rule, taxpayers could carefully time the year in which the §1231 assets are sold to maximize the tax benefits.

In specific terms, the §1231 look-back rule indicates that when a taxpayer recognizes a net §1231 gain for a year, the taxpayer must "look-back" to the *five-year* period preceding the current tax year to determine whether, during that period, the taxpayer recognized any **nonrecaptured net §1231 losses,** which are losses that were deducted as ordinary losses that have not caused subsequent §1231 gains to be recharacterized as ordinary income. The taxpayer starts the process by looking back to the year five years prior to the beginning of the current year. If the taxpayer has recognized a net §1231 loss in that period and has not previously recaptured the loss (by causing a subsequent §1231 gain to be recharacterized as ordinary) in a subsequent year (but prior to the current year), the taxpayer must recharacterize the *current-year* net §1231 gain as ordinary income to the extent of that prior-year nonrecaptured net §1231 loss. If the current year net §1231 gain includes nonrecaptured §1250 gains, the lookback rule requires that the unrecaptured §1250 gains are recharacterized as ordinary before other §1231 gains. The prior-year loss is then considered "recaptured," to the extent it caused the current-year gain to be treated as ordinary income.

If the current-year net §1231 gain exceeds the nonrecaptured net §1231 loss from the year five years prior, the taxpayer repeats the process for the year four years prior, and then three years prior, and so on. A prior year's nonrecaptured net losses are not netted against the current year's gains (they don't offset the current-year gains); rather, they cause the taxpayer to recharacterize a net §1231 gain or a portion of that gain (that would otherwise be characterized as a long-term capital gain) as ordinary income.

Example 11-13

What if: Suppose that Teton began business in year 1 and that it recognized a $7,000 net §1231 loss in year 1. Assume that the current year is year 6 and that Teton reports a *net* §1231 gain of $25,000 for the year. Teton did not recognize any §1231 gains or losses in years 2–5. For year 6, what would be the ultimate character of the $25,000 net §1231 gain?

Answer: $7,000 ordinary income and $18,000 long-term capital gain. Because it recognized a net §1231 loss in year 1, it must recharacterize $7,000 of its net §1231 gain in year 6 as ordinary income. The remaining $18,000 §1231 gain is taxed as long-term capital gain.

What if: Assume the same facts as above, except that Teton also recognized a $2,000 net §1231 loss in year 5. For year 6, what would be the ultimate character of the $25,000 net §1231 gain?

Answer: $9,000 ordinary income and $16,000 long-term capital gain. Note that the overall gain is still $25,000, but to the extent of the $7,000 loss in year 1 and the $2,000 loss in year 5, the §1231 gain is recharacterized as ordinary income under the §1231 look-back rule.

Emma Bean operates a yoga studio and wants to sell some of her business equipment and a piece of land that is used as a parking lot. She expects to realize a $10,000 loss on the equipment and a $15,000 gain on the land. Emma has talked to her accountant and has learned about the look-back rule for §1231 property. To avoid any negative effects, she has decided to game the system and sell the land this year and then sell the equipment early next year. What do you think about her strategy to avoid the look-back rule?

As we've mentioned before, ultimately, all of a taxpayer's §1231 gains and losses must be characterized as ordinary or capital for purposes of determining the taxpayer's tax liability. Exhibit 11-8 summarizes the process of characterizing §1231 gains and losses as ordinary or capital.

EXHIBIT 11-8   §1231 Netting Process

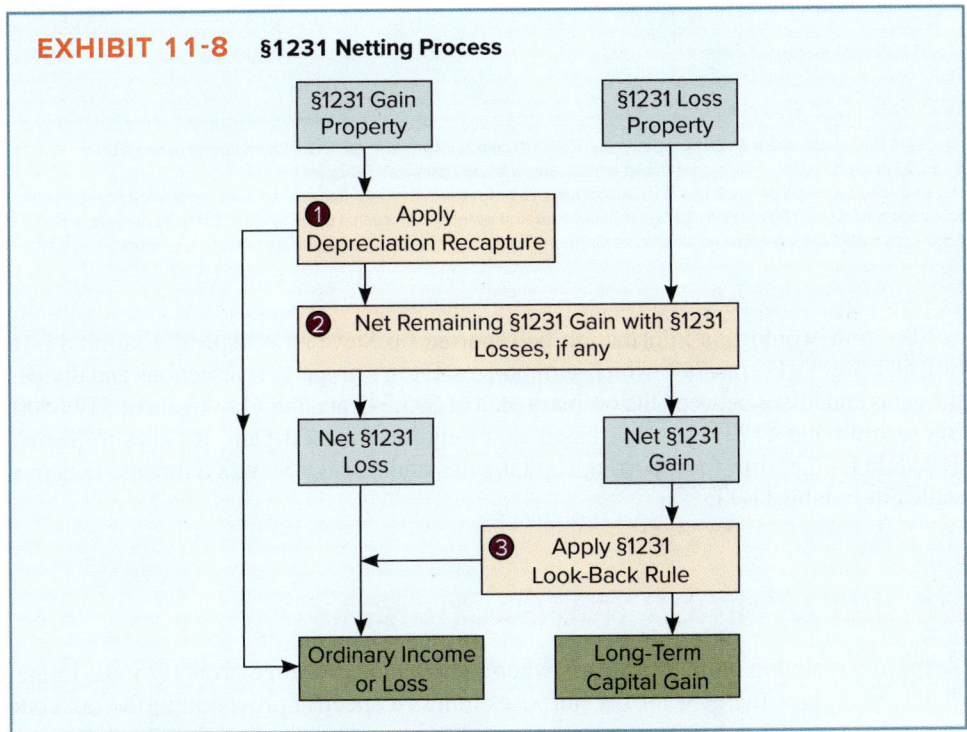

The following provides details on Steps 1–3 from Exhibit 11-8:

Step 1: Apply the *depreciation* recapture rules (and the §1239 recapture rules) to §1231 assets sold at a gain (any recaptured amounts become ordinary).

Step 2: Net the remaining §1231 gains with the §1231 losses. The §1231 losses offset regular §1231 gains before the unrecaptured §1250 gains. If the netting process yields a §1231 loss, the net §1231 loss becomes an ordinary loss.

Step 3: If the netting process produces a net §1231 gain, the taxpayer applies the §1231 look-back rule to determine if any of the remaining §1231 gain should be recharacterized as ordinary gain. Under the lookback rule, the unrecaptured §1250 gains will be recharacterized before the regular §1231 gains. Any gain remaining after applying the look-back rule is treated as long-term capital gain (including unrecaptured §1250 gain). This gain is included in the capital gains netting process, which is discussed in the Gross Income and Exclusions chapter.

GAIN OR LOSS SUMMARY

As indicated in Exhibit 11-2, Teton sold several assets during the year. Exhibit 11-9 summarizes the character of the gain or loss Teton (and thus Steve) recognized on each asset sale.

EXHIBIT 11-9   Summary of Teton Gains and Losses on Property Dispositions

Asset	(1) §1245 Ordinary Gain	(2) Total Ordinary Gain	(3) §1231 Gain (Loss)	(2) + (3) Total Gain
Machinery	$71,342	$71,342	$ 0	$ 71,342
Office furniture	14,000	14,000	3,000	17,000
Delivery truck	0	0	(5,500)	(5,500)
Warehouse	0	0	90,000*	90,000
Land	0	0	100,000	100,000
§1231 look-back		10,000	(10,000)†	0
Totals	$85,342	$95,342	$177,500*	$272,842

*Because the warehouse is §1231 property, the $90,000 gain is included in the §1231 gain (loss) column. Further, $15,000 of the $90,000 gain is considered unrecaptured §1250 gain (see Example 11-11).
†This exhibit assumes that Teton had $10,000 of net §1231 losses in the prior five years. Following the application of the lookback rule, $172,500 of the §1231 gains will be treated as long-term capital gains taxed at 0/15/20 percent and $5,000 of the §1231 gains will be treated as long-term capital gains taxed at a maximum rate of 25 percent.

So, how would this information be reported on Steve's tax return? Exhibit 11-10 provides Steve's Form 4797, which summarizes Teton's property transactions and divides the gains and losses between the ordinary gain of $95,342 and the §1231 gain of $177,500. Because the net §1231 gain is treated as a long-term capital gain, it flows to Steve's Schedule D (the form for reporting capital gains and losses). Steve's Schedule D is presented in Exhibit 11-11.

LO 11-6 ## NONRECOGNITION TRANSACTIONS

Taxpayers realizing gains and losses when they sell or exchange property must immediately recognize the gain for tax purposes unless a specific provision in the tax code says otherwise. Under certain tax provisions, taxpayers defer or delay recognizing a gain or loss until a subsequent period. We first explore tax provisions that allow taxpayers to defer recognizing realized gains. Congress allows taxpayers to defer recognizing gains in certain types of exchanges because the exchange itself does not provide the taxpayers with the wherewithal (cash) to pay taxes on the realized gain if the taxpayers were required to immediately recognize the gain. In particular, we discuss common **nonrecognition transactions** such as like-kind exchanges, involuntary conversions, installment sales, and other business-related transactions such as business formations and reorganizations.

Like-Kind Exchanges

Taxpayers involved in a business may have valid reasons to trade business assets to others for similar business assets. For example, a taxpayer may want to trade land used in its business for a different parcel of land in a better location. As we discussed earlier in this chapter, taxpayers exchanging property *realize* gains (or losses) on exchanges just as

EXHIBIT 11-10 Teton's (on Steve's return) Form 4797

Form **4797**	**Sales of Business Property** (Also Involuntary Conversions and Recapture Amounts Under Sections 179 and 280F(b)(2)) ► Attach to your tax return. ► Go to www.irs.gov/Form4797 for instructions and the latest information.	OMB No. 1545-0184 2017
Department of the Treasury Internal Revenue Service		Attachment Sequence No. **27**

Name(s) shown on return	Identifying number
Steve Dallimore (Teton Mountaineering Technology, LLC)	

1 Enter the gross proceeds from sales or exchanges reported to you for 2017 on Form(s) 1099-B or 1099-S (or substitute statement) that you are including on line 2, 10, or 20. See instructions . . . . | **1** |

Part I — Sales or Exchanges of Property Used in a Trade or Business and Involuntary Conversions From Other Than Casualty or Theft—Most Property Held More Than 1 Year (see instructions)

2	(a) Description of property	(b) Date acquired (mo., day, yr.)	(c) Date sold (mo., day, yr.)	(d) Gross sales price	(e) Depreciation allowed or allowable since acquisition	(f) Cost or other basis, plus improvements and expense of sale	(g) Gain or (loss) Subtract (f) from the sum of (d) and (e)
	Delivery truck	Yr0	Yr4	2,000	17,500	25,000	(5,500)
	Land	Yr0	Yr4	175,000	0	75,000	100,000

3	Gain, if any, from Form 4684, line 39	**3**	
4	Section 1231 gain from installment sales from Form 6252, line 26 or 37	**4**	
5	Section 1231 gain or (loss) from like-kind exchanges from Form 8824	**5**	
6	Gain, if any, from line 32, from other than casualty or theft	**6**	93,000
7	Combine lines 2 through 6. Enter the gain or (loss) here and on the appropriate line as follows:	**7**	187,500

Partnerships (except electing large partnerships) and S corporations. Report the gain or (loss) following the instructions for Form 1065, Schedule K, line 10, or Form 1120S, Schedule K, line 9. Skip lines 8, 9, 11, and 12 below.

Individuals, partners, S corporation shareholders, and all others. If line 7 is zero or a loss, enter the amount from line 7 on line 11 below and skip lines 8 and 9. If line 7 is a gain and you didn't have any prior year section 1231 losses, or they were recaptured in an earlier year, enter the gain from line 7 as a long-term capital gain on the Schedule D filed with your return and skip lines 8, 9, 11, and 12 below.

8	Nonrecaptured net section 1231 losses from prior years. See instructions	**8**	10,000
9	Subtract line 8 from line 7. If zero or less, enter -0-. If line 9 is zero, enter the gain from line 7 on line 12 below. If line 9 is more than zero, enter the amount from line 8 on line 12 below and enter the gain from line 9 as a long-term capital gain on the Schedule D filed with your return. See instructions	**9**	177,500

Part II — Ordinary Gains and Losses (see instructions)

10	Ordinary gains and losses not included on lines 11 through 16 (include property held 1 year or less):		

11	Loss, if any, from line 7	**11** ( )	
12	Gain, if any, from line 7 or amount from line 8, if applicable	**12**	10,000
13	Gain, if any, from line 31	**13**	85,342
14	Net gain or (loss) from Form 4684, lines 31 and 38a	**14**	
15	Ordinary gain from installment sales from Form 6252, line 25 or 36	**15**	
16	Ordinary gain or (loss) from like-kind exchanges from Form 8824.	**16**	
17	Combine lines 10 through 16	**17**	95,342

18 For all except individual returns, enter the amount from line 17 on the appropriate line of your return and skip lines a and b below. For individual returns, complete lines a and b below:

a If the loss on line 11 includes a loss from Form 4684, line 35, column (b)(ii), enter that part of the loss here. Enter the part of the loss from income-producing property on Schedule A (Form 1040), line 28, and the part of the loss from property used as an employee on Schedule A (Form 1040), line 23. Identify as from "Form 4797, line 18a." See instructions . . | **18a** | |

b Redetermine the gain or (loss) on line 17 excluding the loss, if any, on line 18a. Enter here and on Form 1040, line 14 | **18b** | 95,342 |

For Paperwork Reduction Act Notice, see separate instructions.   Cat. No. 13086I   Form **4797** (2017)

EXHIBIT 11-10   Teton's (On Steve's return) Form 4797 (*continued*)

Form 4797 (2017)   Page **2**

Part III   Gain From Disposition of Property Under Sections 1245, 1250, 1252, 1254, and 1255
(see instructions)

19	(a) Description of section 1245, 1250, 1252, 1254, or 1255 property:	(b) Date acquired (mo., day, yr.)	(c) Date sold (mo., day, yr.)
A	Machinery	Yr0	Yr4
B	Office furniture	Yr0	Yr4
C	Warehouse	Yr0	Yr4
D			

	These columns relate to the properties on lines 19A through 19D. ▶		Property A	Property B	Property C	Property D
20	Gross sales price (**Note:** *See line 1 before completing.*) .	20	300,000	23,000	350,000	
21	Cost or other basis plus expense of sale	21	610,000	20,000	275,000	
22	Depreciation (or depletion) allowed or allowable. . .	22	381,342	14,000	15,000	
23	Adjusted basis. Subtract line 22 from line 21. . . .	23	228,658	6,000	260,000	
24	Total gain. Subtract line 23 from line 20	24	71,342	17,000	90,000	
25	If section 1245 property:					
a	Depreciation allowed or allowable from line 22 . . .	25a	381,342	14,000		
b	Enter the **smaller** of line 24 or 25a	25b	71,342	14,000		
26	If section 1250 property: If straight line depreciation was used, enter -0- on line 26g, except for a corporation subject to section 291.					
a	Additional depreciation after 1975. See instructions .	26a				
b	Applicable percentage multiplied by the **smaller** of line 24 or line 26a. See instructions	26b				
c	Subtract line 26a from line 24. If residential rental property **or** line 24 isn't more than line 26a, skip lines 26d and 26e	26c				
d	Additional depreciation after 1969 and before 1976. .	26d				
e	Enter the **smaller** of line 26c or 26d	26e				
f	Section 291 amount (corporations only)	26f				
g	Add lines 26b, 26e, and 26f.	26g			0	
27	If section 1252 property: Skip this section if you didn't dispose of farmland or if this form is being completed for a partnership (other than an electing large partnership).					
a	Soil, water, and land clearing expenses	27a				
b	Line 27a multiplied by applicable percentage. See instructions	27b				
c	Enter the **smaller** of line 24 or 27b	27c				
28	If section 1254 property:					
a	Intangible drilling and development costs, expenditures for development of mines and other natural deposits, mining exploration costs, and depletion. See instructions	28a				
b	Enter the **smaller** of line 24 or 28a	28b				
29	If section 1255 property:					
a	Applicable percentage of payments excluded from income under section 126. See instructions	29a				
b	Enter the **smaller** of line 24 or 29a. See instructions .	29b				

Summary of Part III Gains. Complete property columns A through D through line 29b before going to line 30.

30	Total gains for all properties. Add property columns A through D, line 24	30	178,342
31	Add property columns A through D, lines 25b, 26g, 27c, 28b, and 29b. Enter here and on line 13	31	85,342
32	Subtract line 31 from line 30. Enter the portion from casualty or theft on Form 4684, line 33. Enter the portion from other than casualty or theft on Form 4797, line 6	32	93,000

Part IV   Recapture Amounts Under Sections 179 and 280F(b)(2) When Business Use Drops to 50% or Less
(see instructions)

			(a) Section 179	(b) Section 280F(b)(2)
33	Section 179 expense deduction or depreciation allowable in prior years.	33		
34	Recomputed depreciation. See instructions	34		
35	Recapture amount. Subtract line 34 from line 33. See the instructions for where to report . .	35		

Form **4797** (2017)

EXHIBIT 11-11 Steve's Schedule D (Assumes Steve had no other capital gains and losses other than those incurred by Teton)

**SCHEDULE D
(Form 1040)**

Department of the Treasury
Internal Revenue Service (99)

Capital Gains and Losses

▶ Attach to Form 1040 or Form 1040NR.
▶ Go to *www.irs.gov/ScheduleD* for instructions and the latest information.
▶ Use Form 8949 to list your transactions for lines 1b, 2, 3, 8b, 9, and 10.

OMB No. 1545-0074

20**17**

Attachment
Sequence No. **12**

Name(s) shown on return

Steve Dallimore

Your social security number

Part I Short-Term Capital Gains and Losses—Assets Held One Year or Less

See instructions for how to figure the amounts to enter on the lines below.

This form may be easier to complete if you round off cents to whole dollars.

	(d) Proceeds (sales price)	(e) Cost (or other basis)	(g) Adjustments to gain or loss from Form(s) 8949, Part I, line 2, column (g)	(h) Gain or (loss) Subtract column (e) from column (d) and combine the result with column (g)
1a Totals for all short-term transactions reported on Form 1099-B for which basis was reported to the IRS and for which you have no adjustments (see instructions). However, if you choose to report all these transactions on Form 8949, leave this line blank and go to line 1b .				
1b Totals for all transactions reported on Form(s) 8949 with **Box A** checked				
2 Totals for all transactions reported on Form(s) 8949 with **Box B** checked				
3 Totals for all transactions reported on Form(s) 8949 with **Box C** checked				

4 Short-term gain from Form 6252 and short-term gain or (loss) from Forms 4684, 6781, and 8824 .	**4**	
5 Net short-term gain or (loss) from partnerships, S corporations, estates, and trusts from Schedule(s) K-1	**5**	
6 Short-term capital loss carryover. Enter the amount, if any, from line 8 of your **Capital Loss Carryover Worksheet** in the instructions	**6**	( )
7 **Net short-term capital gain or (loss).** Combine lines 1a through 6 in column (h). If you have any long-term capital gains or losses, go to Part II below. Otherwise, go to Part III on the back	**7**	

Part II Long-Term Capital Gains and Losses—Assets Held More Than One Year

See instructions for how to figure the amounts to enter on the lines below.

This form may be easier to complete if you round off cents to whole dollars.

	(d) Proceeds (sales price)	(e) Cost (or other basis)	(g) Adjustments to gain or loss from Form(s) 8949, Part II, line 2, column (g)	(h) Gain or (loss) Subtract column (e) from column (d) and combine the result with column (g)
8a Totals for all long-term transactions reported on Form 1099-B for which basis was reported to the IRS and for which you have no adjustments (see instructions). However, if you choose to report all these transactions on Form 8949, leave this line blank and go to line 8b .				
8b Totals for all transactions reported on Form(s) 8949 with **Box D** checked				
9 Totals for all transactions reported on Form(s) 8949 with **Box E** checked				
10 Totals for all transactions reported on Form(s) 8949 with **Box F** checked.				

11 Gain from Form 4797, Part I; long-term gain from Forms 2439 and 6252; and long-term gain or (loss) from Forms 4684, 6781, and 8824	**11**	177,500
12 Net long-term gain or (loss) from partnerships, S corporations, estates, and trusts from Schedule(s) K-1	**12**	
13 Capital gain distributions. See the instructions	**13**	
14 Long-term capital loss carryover. Enter the amount, if any, from line 13 of your **Capital Loss Carryover Worksheet** in the instructions	**14**	( )
15 **Net long-term capital gain or (loss).** Combine lines 8a through 14 in column (h). Then go to Part III on the back	**15**	177,500

For Paperwork Reduction Act Notice, see your tax return instructions.   Cat. No. 11338H   Schedule D (Form 1040) 2017

taxpayers do by selling property for cash. However, taxpayers exchanging property for property are in a different situation than taxpayers selling the same property for cash. Taxpayers exchanging one piece of business property for another haven't changed their relative economic position, since both before and after the exchange they hold similar assets for use in their business. Further, exchanges of property do not generate the wherewithal (cash) for the taxpayers to pay taxes on the gain they realize and recognize on the exchanges. While taxpayers selling property for cash must immediately recognize gain on the sale, taxpayers exchanging property for assets other than cash must defer recognizing gain (or loss) realized on the exchange if they meet certain requirements. This type of deferred gain (or loss) transaction is commonly referred to as a **like-kind exchange** or §1031 exchange.[22]

Like-kind exchange treatment can provide taxpayers with significant tax advantages by allowing them to defer gain (and current taxes payable) that would otherwise be recognized immediately.[23] For an exchange to qualify as a like-kind exchange for tax purposes, the transaction must meet the following three criteria:

1. Real property is exchanged "solely for like-kind" property.
2. Both the real property given up and the real property received in the exchange by the taxpayer are either "used in a trade or business" or "held for investment" by the taxpayer.
3. The "exchange" must meet certain time restrictions.

Below, we discuss each of these requirements in detail.

Definition of Like-Kind Property

Real property is eligible for like-kind treatment while personal property is not.[24] Real property is considered to be "like-kind" with any other type of real property as long as the real property is used in a trade or business or held for investment. For example, from Teton's perspective, its warehouse on 10 acres is considered to be like-kind with a nearby condominium, a 20-acre parcel of raw land across town, or even a Manhattan skyscraper. Real property held for sale is not eligible for like-kind treatment, so taxpayers whose business is to buy and sell real property cannot do so using the like-kind exchange rules.[25] In addition, real property located in the United States and real property located outside the United States are not like-kind.

Property Use

Even when property meets the definition of like-kind property, taxpayers can exchange the property in a qualifying like-kind exchange only if they used the transferred property in a trade or business or for investment *and* they will use the property received in the exchange in a trade or business or for investment. For example, Teton could exchange its warehouse on 10 acres for a 200-acre parcel of land it intends to hold as an investment in a qualifying like-kind exchange, because Teton was using the warehouse in its business and it will hold the land as an investment. However, if Steve exchanged his cabin in Maine for a personal residence in Wyoming, the exchange would not qualify because Steve used the Maine residence for personal purposes, and he would be using the Wyoming property for personal rather than business or investment purposes. In fact, even if Steve were renting his Maine cabin (meaning it qualifies as investment property) when he exchanged it for his principal residence in Wyoming, the exchange

---

THE KEY FACTS

Like-Kind Property

- Real property
  - All real property used in a trade or business or held for investment is considered "like kind" with other real property used in a trade or business or held for investment.
- Ineligible property
  - Domestic property exchanged for property used in a foreign country and all property used in a foreign country.
  - Real property held for sale.

---

[22]Prior to the TCJA, personal property could be exchanged under the like-kind exchange rules. The TCJA eliminated this benefit for property other than real property.

[23]Like-kind exchanges are defined in §1031 of the Internal Revenue Code.

[24]In contrast, financial accounting rules require businesses to recognize (for financial accounting purposes) any gain they realize in a like-kind exchange transaction.

[25]§1031(a)(2).

would not qualify for like-kind exchange treatment because *both* properties must meet the use test for Steve (the personal residence does not qualify as business or investment property).

Timing Requirements for a Like-Kind Exchange

The like-kind rules require an exchange of real property for real property; however, a simultaneous exhange may not be practical or possible. For example, taxpayers may not always be able to immediately (or even eventually) find another party who is willing to exchange properties with them. In these situations taxpayers often use **third-party intermediaries** to facilitate like-kind exchanges.

When a third party is involved, the taxpayer transfers the like-kind property to the intermediary, who then sells the property and uses the proceeds to acquire the new property for the taxpayer.[26] Because the third party must sell the taxpayer's old property and locate and purchase suitable replacement property, this process is subject to delay. Does a delay in the completion of the exchange disqualify an otherwise allowable like-kind exchange? Not necessarily. The tax laws do not require a simultaneous exchange of assets, but they do impose some timing requirements to ensure that a transaction is completed within a reasonable time in order to qualify as a **deferred like-kind exchange** (not simultaneous)—often referred to as a *Starker exchange*.[27]

The two timing rules applicable to like-kind exchanges are that (1) the taxpayer must *identify* the like-kind replacement property within 45 days after transferring the property given up in the exchange, and (2) the taxpayer must receive the replacement like-kind property within 180 days (or the due date of the tax return including extensions) after the taxpayer initially transfers property in the exchange.[28] The time limits force the taxpayer to close the transaction within a specified time period in order to be able to report the tax consequences of the transaction. Exhibit 11-12 provides a diagram of a like-kind exchange involving a third-party intermediary.

THE KEY FACTS

Timing Requirements

- Like-kind property exchanges may involve intermediaries.
- Taxpayers must identify replacement like-kind property within 45 days of giving up their real property.
- Like-kind property must be received within 180 days of when the taxpayer transfers real property in a like-kind exchange.

EXHIBIT 11-12 Diagram of Deferred or Starker Exchange

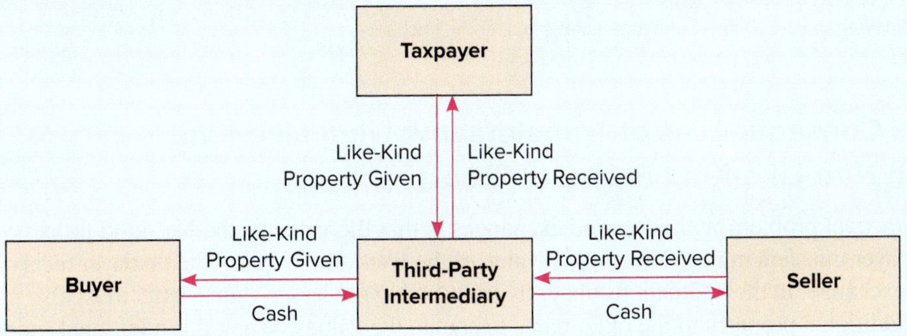

[26]Exchanges involving third-party intermediaries are very common with real estate exchanges. For real estate, taxpayers must use a "qualified exchange intermediary," such as a title company, and cannot use a personal attorney (because attorneys are considered to be the taxpayer's agent).

[27]The term *Starker exchange* refers to a landmark court case that first allowed deferred exchanges (*T.J. Starker, Appellant v. United States of America,* 79-2 USTC ¶9541). The rules for deferred exchanges are found in §1031(a)(3). The tax laws also allow for reverse like-kind exchanges where replacement property is acquired before the taxpayer transfers the like-kind property.

[28]The taxpayer must identify at least one like-kind asset; however, since failure to obtain the asset disqualifies the transaction from having deferred like-kind exchange status, the taxpayer may identify up to three alternatives to hedge against the inability to obtain the first identified asset. Generally, a taxpayer must obtain only one to facilitate the exchange [see Reg. §1.1031(k)-1(c)(4)].

When a taxpayer fails to meet the timing requirements, the exchange fails to qualify for like-kind treatment and is fully taxable.

Example 11-14

What if: Suppose that on November 16 of year 1 Steve transferred a parcel of real property that he was holding as an investment to a third-party intermediary with the intention of exchanging the property for another suitable investment property. By what date does Steve need to identify the replacement property?

Answer: December 31 of year 1, which is 45 days after Steve transferred the property to the intermediary.[29]

Assuming Steve identifies the replacement property within the 45-day time period, by what date does he need to receive the replacement property in order to qualify for like-kind exchange treatment?

Answer: May 15 of year 2, which is 180 days from November 16, the date he transferred the property to the intermediary (assuming Steve extends his tax return and that it is not a leap year).

Tax Consequences When Like-Kind Property Is Exchanged Solely for Like-Kind Property

As we've discussed, when taxpayers exchanging property meet the like-kind exchange requirements, they do not recognize gain or loss on the exchange. They also establish or receive an **exchanged basis** in the like-kind property they receive. That is, they exchange the basis they had in the property given up and transfer it to the basis of the property received.[30]

Example 11-15

Teton would like to trade land worth $29,500 (adjusted basis of $18,000) for land in a different location that is also worth $29,500. How much gain does Teton recognize on this exchange?

Answer: $0. Teton's exchange qualifies as a like-kind exchange and the $11,500 realized gain ($29,500 amount realized minus $18,000) adjusted basis) is deferred.

What is Teton's basis in the new land?

Answer: $18,000, the basis it had in the old land it exchanged.

> **THE KEY FACTS**
>
> **Like-Kind Exchanges Involving Boot**
>
> - Non-like-kind property is known as *boot*.
> - When boot is given as part of a like-kind transaction:
>   - The asset received is recorded in two parts: (1) property received in exchange for like-kind property and (2) property received in a sale (bought by the boot).
> - When boot is received:
>   - Boot received usually creates recognized gain.
>   - Gain recognized is lesser of gain realized or boot received.

Tax Consequences of Transfers Involving Like-Kind and Non-Like-Kind Property (Boot)

A practical problem with like-kind exchanges is that the value of the like-kind property the taxpayer transfers may differ from the value of the like-kind property the taxpayer receives in the exchange. In these situations the party transferring the lesser-valued asset must also transfer additional property to the other party to equate the values. When this additional property or **boot** (non-like-kind property) is transferred, the party receiving it apparently fails the first like-kind exchange requirement that like-kind property be exchanged solely for like-kind property. Nevertheless, if a taxpayer receives boot in addition to like-kind property, the transaction can still qualify for like-kind exchange treatment, but the taxpayer is required to recognize realized gain *to the extent of the boot received.*[31] As a practical matter, this means the taxpayer's recognized gain is the *lesser of* (1) gain realized or (2) boot received.

---

[29]The identification period begins on the date the taxpayer transfers the property and ends at midnight on the 45th day after the transfer. Similarly, the exchange period begins on the date of the transfer and ends at midnight on the earlier of the 180th day after the transfer or the due date (including extensions) for the taxpayer's return. Reg. §1.1031(k)-1(b)(2).

[30]If the asset is a depreciable asset, the taxpayer continues to depreciate the new asset as if it were the old asset.

[31]§1031(b).

The reason a taxpayer must recognize gain is that the taxpayer is essentially selling a portion of the like-kind property for the boot in a taxable exchange. The receipt of boot triggers taxable gain (but not a taxable loss) in an otherwise qualifying like-kind exchange. If the taxpayer transfers loss property (adjusted basis is greater than fair market value) in a qualifying like-kind exchange, the taxpayer defers recognition of the loss until the taxpayer sells or disposes of the loss property in a taxable transaction—so it may be important for tax planning purposes to avoid the like-kind exchange rules if the taxpayer wishes to currently recognize the loss.[32] When a taxpayer recognizes gain in a like-kind exchange, the character of the gain depends on the character of the asset transferred by the taxpayer (the depreciation recapture rules apply when characterizing gains).

Example 11-16

What if: Suppose that Teton trades land with a value of $29,500 and an adjusted basis of $18,000 for land in a different location valued at $27,500. To equate the value of the property exchanged, the other party also pays Teton $2,000. What gain or loss does Teton realize on the exchange and what gain or loss does Teton recognize on the exchange?

Answer: $11,500 realized gain and $2,000 recognized gain, calculated as follows:

Description	Amount	Explanation
(1) Amount realized from machine	$ 27,500	
(2) Amount realized from boot (cash)	2,000	
(3) Total amount realized	29,500	(1) + (2)
(4) Adjusted basis	18,000	
(5) Gain realized	**$11,500**	(3) − (4)
Gain recognized	**$ 2,000**	Lesser of (2) or (5)

What is the character of Teton's $2,000 gain?

Answer: §1231 gain. Teton will include the gain in its §1231 netting process when it eventually recognizes the gain in a taxable transaction.

What if: Suppose the same facts as above, except that Teton's adjusted basis in the land was $29,000. What amount of gain would Teton recognize on the exchange?

Answer: $500. Teton recognizes the lesser of (1) $500 gain realized ($29,500 minus $29,000) or (2) $2,000 boot received.

When taxpayers receive like-kind property and boot in a like-kind exchange, their basis in the like-kind property can be computed in two ways as shown in Exhibit 11-13:

EXHIBIT 11-13   Like-kind Basis Calculation

Simplified Method	Method under §1031(d)
Fair market value of like-kind property received	Adjusted basis of like-kind property surrendered
− Deferred gain, or	+ Adjusted basis of boot given
+ Deferred loss	+ Gain recognized
= Basis of like-kind property received	− Fair market value of boot received
	− Loss recognized
	= Basis of like-kind property received

---

[32]§1031(a) states that no gain or loss is recognized in a qualifying like-kind exchange.

The basis of boot received in the exchange is always the boot's fair market value. The formula for computing basis ensures that the taxpayer's deferred gain or loss on the exchange (the gain or loss realized that is not recognized) is captured in the difference between the value and the basis of the new property received. Consequently, taxpayers defer realized gains or losses on qualifying like-kind exchanges; they do not exclude them. Taxpayers will ultimately recognize the gain or loss when they dispose of the new asset in a taxable transaction.[33]

Example 11-17

What if: Assume the facts in Example 11-16, where Teton exchanged land with a value of $29,500 and an adjusted basis of $18,000 for land valued at $27,500 and $2,000 cash. Teton recognized $2,000 on the exchange. What is Teton's basis in the new land it received from the dealer?

Answer: $18,000, computed using the simplified method, as follows:

Description	Amount	Explanation
(1) Amount realized from land	$ 27,500	Fair market value of new land
(2) Amount realized from boot (cash)	2,000	
(3) Total amount realized	29,500	(1) + (2)
(4) Adjusted basis of land	18,000	
(5) Gain realized	11,500	(3) − (4)
(6) Gain recognized	$ 2,000	Lesser of (2) or (5)
(7) Deferred gain	9,500	(5) − (6)
Adjusted basis in new land	**$18,000**	(1) − (7)

Anything a taxpayer receives in an exchange other than like-kind property is considered boot. This includes cash, other property, or even the amount of a taxpayer's liability transferred to (assumed by) the other party in the exchange. Let's return to the previous example. If, instead of paying Teton $2,000 of cash, the buyer had assumed Teton's $2,000 liability secured by Teton's old land, the tax consequences would have been identical. The buyer relieved Teton of $2,000 of debt, and the debt relief is treated the same as if the buyer had paid Teton cash and Teton had paid off its $2,000 liability. Generally, when a taxpayer both transfers and receives boot in an otherwise qualifying like-kind exchange, the taxpayer must recognize any realized gain to the extent of the boot received. That is, the taxpayer is not allowed to offset boot received with boot paid.[34] However, when the taxpayer receives boot in the form of liabilities, the taxpayer is allowed to net any boot paid against the (liability) boot received.[35]

Reporting Like-Kind Exchanges

Like-kind exchange transactions are reported on Form 8824. Exhibit 11-14 presents the computations from Form 8824 reflecting the like-kind exchange of the land in Example 11-15.

---

[33]Additionally, the deferred gain is subject to depreciation recapture when the asset is eventually disposed of in a taxable disposition.

[34]However, Reg. §1.1031(j)-1 provides an exception where multiple like-kind exchanges are made in a single exchange.

[35]Further details of this important exception are beyond the scope of our discussion. See the examples provided in Reg. §1.1031(d)-2 for further guidance.

EXHIBIT 11-14   Form 8824, Part III (From exchange in Example 11-15)

Form 8824 (2017)   Page **2**

Name(s) shown on tax return. Do not enter name and social security number if shown on other side.	Your social security number

Steve Dallimore (Teton Mountaineering Technology LLC)

Part III   **Realized Gain or (Loss), Recognized Gain, and Basis of Like-Kind Property Received**

Caution: If you transferred **and** received **(a)** more than one group of like-kind properties or **(b)** cash or other (not like-kind) property, see **Reporting of multi-asset exchanges** in the instructions.

Note: Complete lines 12 through 14 **only** if you gave up property that was not like-kind. Otherwise, go to line 15.

12	Fair market value (FMV) of other property given up	12	
13	Adjusted basis of other property given up	13	
14	Gain or (loss) recognized on other property given up. Subtract line 13 from line 12. Report the gain or (loss) in the same manner as if the exchange had been a sale	14	
	Caution: If the property given up was used previously or partly as a home, see **Property used as home** in the instructions.		
15	Cash received, FMV of other property received, plus net liabilities assumed by other party, reduced (but not below zero) by any exchange expenses you incurred. See instructions	15	0
16	FMV of like-kind property you received	16	29,500
17	Add lines 15 and 16	17	29,500
18	Adjusted basis of like-kind property you gave up, net amounts paid to other party, plus any exchange expenses **not** used on line 15. See instructions	18	18,000
19	**Realized gain or (loss).** Subtract line 18 from line 17	19	11,500
20	Enter the smaller of line 15 or line 19, but not less than zero	20	0
21	Ordinary income under recapture rules. Enter here and on Form 4797, line 16. See instructions	21	
22	Subtract line 21 from line 20. If zero or less, enter -0-. If more than zero, enter here and on Schedule D or Form 4797, unless the installment method applies. See instructions	22	0
23	**Recognized gain.** Add lines 21 and 22	23	0
24	Deferred gain or (loss). Subtract line 23 from line 19. If a related party exchange, see instructions	24	11,500
25	**Basis of like-kind property received.** Subtract line 15 from the sum of lines 18 and 23	25	18,000

Involuntary Conversions

Usually, when taxpayers sell, exchange, or abandon property they intend to do so. However, sometimes taxpayers may involuntarily dispose of property due to circumstances beyond their control. The tax law refers to these types of property dispositions as **involuntary conversions.**[36] Involuntary conversions occur when property is partially or wholly destroyed by a natural disaster or accident, stolen, condemned, or seized via eminent domain by a governmental agency. Tragic examples of this include the results of Hurricanes Harvey, Irma, and Maria in 2017. Even in situations when taxpayers experience a loss of property due to theft, disaster, or other circumstances, they might realize a gain for tax purposes if they receive replacement property or insurance proceeds in excess of their basis in the property that was stolen or destroyed.

Taxpayers may experience a tremendous financial hardship if they are required to recognize the realized gain in these circumstances. For example, let's consider a business that acquired a building for $100,000. The building appreciates in value, and when it is worth $150,000 it is destroyed by fire. The building is fully insured at its replacement cost, so the business receives a check from the insurance company for $150,000. The problem for the business is that it realizes a $50,000 gain on this involuntary conversion ($150,000 insurance proceeds minus $100,000 basis in property without considering depreciation). Assuming the business's income is taxed at a 32 percent marginal rate, it must pay $16,000 of tax on the insurance money it receives. That leaves it with only $134,000 to replace property worth $150,000. This hardly seems equitable. Congress provides special tax laws to allow taxpayers to defer the gains on such *involuntary* conversions.

Taxpayers may defer realized gains on both direct and indirect involuntary conversions. **Direct conversions** occur when taxpayers receive a direct property replacement for the involuntarily converted property. For example, a municipality that is widening its

THE KEY FACTS

Involuntary Conversions

- Gain is deferred when appreciated property is involuntarily converted in an accident or natural disaster.
- Basis of property directly converted is carried over from the old property to the new property.
- In an indirect conversion, gain recognized is the lesser of:
  - Gain realized, or
  - Amount of reimbursement the taxpayer does not reinvest in qualified property.
- Qualified replacement property must be of a similar or related use to the original property.

[36]§1033.

streets may seize land from a taxpayer through its eminent domain and compensate the taxpayer with another parcel of similar value. In this case, the taxpayer would not recognize gain on the exchange of property and would take an adjusted basis in the new parcel of land equal to the taxpayer's basis in the land that was claimed by the municipality. Just as with like-kind exchanges, an exchanged basis (basis of old property exchanged for basis of new property) ensures that the gain built into the new property (fair market value minus adjusted basis) includes the same gain that was built into the old property.

Indirect conversions occur when taxpayers receive money for the involuntarily converted property through insurance reimbursement or some other type of settlement. Taxpayers meeting the involuntary conversion requirements may *elect* to either recognize or defer realized gain on the conversions. Indirect conversions are more common than direct conversions. Taxpayers can defer realized gains on indirect conversions *if* they acquire **qualified replacement property** within a prescribed time limit, which is generally two years (three years in case of condemnation) after the close of the tax year in which they receive the proceeds.[37]

In contrast to the like-kind exchange rules, both personal and real property can qualify for the tax treatment under the involuntary conversion rules. Qualified replacement property is defined somewhat narrowly to be similar *and* related in service or use to qualify.[38] For example, a bowling alley is not qualified replacement property for a pool hall, even though both are real properties used for entertainment purposes. This definition is stricter than the like-kind exchange rules that would allow the bowling alley to be exchanged for any other real property, including a pool hall. In addition, the involuntary conversion rules allow a taxpayer's personal residence (personal-use property) to qualify for gain deferral; however, qualified replacement property of a personal residence is restricted to another residence. Taxpayers recognize realized gain to the extent that they do not reinvest the reimbursement proceeds in qualified property. However, just as in like-kind exchanges, taxpayers do not recognize more gain than they realize on involuntary conversions. That is, a taxpayer's recognized gain on an involuntary conversion can be determined by the following formula: Recognized gain on involuntary conversion is equal to the *lesser of* (1) the gain realized on the conversion or (2) the amount of reimbursement the taxpayer does *not reinvest* in qualified property.

The character of any gain recognized in an involuntary conversion depends on the nature of the asset that was converted—including depreciation recapture, if applicable. The basis of the replacement property in an involuntary conversion is calculated in the same way it is for like-kind exchange property (see Exhibit 11-13 Simplified Method). That is, the basis of the replacement property is the fair market value of the new property minus the deferred gain on the conversion.

Example 11-18

What if: Assume that one of Teton's employees was in a traffic accident while driving a delivery van. The employee escaped without serious injury but the van was totally destroyed. Before the accident, Teton's delivery van had a fair market value of $15,000 and an adjusted basis of $11,000 (the cost basis was $15,000 and accumulated depreciation on the van was $4,000). Teton received $15,000 of insurance proceeds to cover the loss. Teton was considering two alternatives for replacing the van: Alternative 1 was to purchase a new delivery van for $20,000 and Alternative 2 was to purchase a used delivery van for $14,000. What gain or loss does Teton recognize under Alternative 1 and Alternative 2?

Answer: $0 gain recognized under Alternative 1 and $1,000 gain recognized under Alternative 2 (see computations below). Teton qualifies for a deferral because the new property (delivery van) has a similar and related use to the old property (delivery van). But it must recognize gain under Alternative 2 because it did not reinvest all of the insurance proceeds in a replacement van.

What is Teton's basis in the replacement property it acquired under Alternative 1 and Alternative 2?

---

[37]§1033(a)(2)(B). The time period varies depending on the type of property converted. Additionally, the IRS may consent to an extension of the time period for replacement.

[38]The similar and related-use test has been developed through a variety of administrative pronouncements and judicial law.

Answer: $16,000 in Alternative 1 and $11,000 in Alternative 2, computed as follows:

Description	Alternative 1 Amount	Alternative 2 Amount	Explanation
(1) Amount realized	$15,000	$15,000	
(2) Adjusted basis	11,000	11,000	
(3) Gain realized	4,000	4,000	(1) − (2)
(4) Insurance proceeds	15,000	15,000	
(5) Proceeds reinvested	15,000	14,000	
(6) Amount not reinvested	0	1,000	(4) − (5)
(7) Gain recognized	**0**	**1,000**	Lesser of (3) or (6)*
(8) Deferred gain	4,000	3,000	(3) − (7)
(9) Value of replacement property	20,000	14,000	
Basis of replacement property	**16,000**	**11,000**	(9) − (8)

*The character of the $1,000 recognized gain is ordinary income under §1245 (lesser of gain recognized or accumulated depreciation).

Involuntary conversions share several characteristics with like-kind exchanges, such as the concept of qualified property, time period restrictions, the method of computing gain recognized (lesser of realized gain or cash received in addition to qualifying property), and basis calculation (gain or loss from old property remains built into new property). However, there are two important differences between like-kind exchanges and involuntary conversions. First, involuntary conversion rules allow taxpayers to defer gains on both personal and real property (business, investment, or personal-use property); whereas, the like-kind exchange rules limit the deferral treatment to only real property (business or investment use). Second, taxpayers experiencing a loss from involuntary conversion may immediately deduct the loss as a casualty loss either as a business loss or as a personal loss, if qualified (federally-declared disaster area), depending on the nature of the loss.

TAXES IN THE REAL WORLD   Weather Break

Weather conditions across the country have caused hardship to many cattle farmers. Drought in the Southwest or floods in the Plains could cause cattle farmers to sell more of their herds than normal because they may not have enough crops to feed the livestock. To aid these farmers, the IRS offers relief in the form of an election to postpone recognizing gain from the sale of livestock sold due to weather-related conditions. What's the catch? The livestock must be replaced within a two-year period. In essence, the IRS allows cattle farmers to take advantage of the §1033 (involuntary conversion) rules.

As an alternative, if a taxpayer sells livestock because of weather-related conditions, he or she may be able to defer reporting the sale of the livestock for a one-year period. As a result of these two possibilities, cattle farmers may need to consider whether they will replace the livestock to take advantage of the involuntary conversion provision or whether the one-year deferral will better suit their plans.

Installment Sales

In general, when taxpayers sell property for cash and collect the entire sale proceeds in one lump-sum payment, they immediately recognize gain or loss for tax purposes. However, taxpayers selling property don't always collect the sale proceeds in one lump sum from the buyer. For example, the buyer may make a down payment in the year of sale and then agree to pay the remainder of the sale proceeds over a period of time. This type of arrangement is termed an **installment sale.** Technically, an installment sale is any sale of property where the seller receives at least one payment in a taxable year subsequent to the year of disposition of the property.[39]

Taxpayers selling property via an installment sale realize gains to the extent the selling price (the amount realized) exceeds their adjusted basis in the property sold. The

[39]§453(b)(1).

THE KEY FACTS

Installment Sales

- Sale of property where the seller receives at least one payment in a taxable year subsequent to the year of disposition of the property.
- Must recognize a portion of gain on each installment payment received.
- Gains from installment sales are calculated as follows:

  Gross profit percentage = Gross profit/Contract price

  Gain recognized = Gross profit percentage × Principal payment received in the year

- Inventory, marketable securities, and depreciation recapture cannot be accounted for under installment sale rules.
- Installment sale rules do not apply to losses.

installment sale rules stay true to the wherewithal-to-pay concept and allow taxpayers selling property in this manner to use the installment method of recognizing *gain* on the sale over time.[40] The installment method does not apply to property sold at a loss. Under the installment method, taxpayers determine the amount of realized gain on the transaction, and they recognize the gain pro rata as they receive the installment payments. So, by the time they have received all the installment payments, they will have recognized all the initial realized gain.[41] For financial accounting purposes, businesses selling property on an installment basis generally immediately recognize the realized gain on their financial statements.[42]

To calculate the amount of gain the taxpayer (seller) must recognize on each installment payment received, the seller must compute the gross profit percentage on the transaction. The gross profit percentage is calculated as follows:

$$\text{Gross profit percentage} = \frac{\text{Gross profit}}{\text{Contract price}}$$

The gross profit percentage indicates the percentage of the contract price that will ultimately be recognized as gain. Gross profit is calculated as the sales price minus the adjusted basis of the property being sold. The contract price is the sales price less the seller's liabilities that are assumed by the buyer. To calculate the portion of a particular payment that is currently recognized as gain, the seller multiplies the amount of the payments received during the year (including the year of sale) by the gross profit percentage (note that once established, the gross profit percentage does not change). As in fully taxable transactions, the character of gain taxpayers recognize using the installment method is determined by the character of the asset sold.

Example 11-19

What if: Suppose Teton decides to sell five acres of land adjacent to the warehouse for $100,000. The basis for the land is $37,500. Teton agrees to sell the property for four equal payments of $25,000—one now (in year 1) and the other three on January 1 of the next three years—plus interest. What amount of gain does Teton realize on the sale and what amount of gain does it recognize in year 1?

Answer: The realized gain on the transaction is $62,500 ($100,000 amount realized less $37,500 adjusted basis), and the year 1 recognized gain is $15,625, computed as follows:

Description	Amount	Explanation
(1) Sales price	$100,000	
(2) Adjusted basis	37,500	
(3) Gross profit	$ 62,500	(1) − (2)
(4) Contract price	$100,000	(1) − assumed liabilities (-0-)
(5) Gross profit percentage	62.5%	(3)/(4)
(6) Payment received in year 1	$ 25,000	
Gain recognized in year 1	**$ 15,625**	(5) × (4)

Because Teton used the land in its trade or business and it held the land for more than a year, the character of the gain is §1231 gain.

---

[40]Technically, a taxpayer selling property on an installment basis at a gain is required to use the installment method of reporting the recognized gain from the transaction. However, taxpayers are allowed to *elect* out of using the installment method §453(d).

[41]Because the seller in an installment sale is essentially lending money to the buyer, the buyer makes the required installment payments to the seller and the buyer pays interest to the seller for the money the buyer is borrowing. Any interest income received by the seller is immediately taxable as ordinary income. Special rules apply regarding interest for installment sales of more than $150,000 (see §453A).

[42]One exception is that the installment sale method, similar to the tax installment method, is used for financial accounting purposes when there is doubt that the business will collect the receivable.

The formula for determining the basis of an installment note receivable is (1 − gross profit percentage) × remaining payments on note. Because the gross profit percentage reflects the percentage of the installment payments that will be recognized as gain, (1 − gross profit percentage) is the percentage that is not recognized as gain because it reflects a return of capital (basis).

Gains Ineligible for Installment Reporting

Not all gains are eligible for installment sale reporting. Taxpayers selling marketable securities or inventory on an installment basis may not use the installment method to report gain on the sales. Similarly, any depreciation recapture (including §1245, §1250, and §291 depreciation recapture) is not eligible for installment reporting and must be recognized in the year of sale.[43] However, the §1231 gain remaining after the depreciation recapture can be recognized using the installment method. To ensure that any depreciation recapture is not taxed twice (once immediately and then a second time as payments are received), immediately taxable recapture-related gains are *added to* the adjusted basis of the property sold to determine the gross profit percentage. The increase in basis reduces the gain realized, which also reduces the gross profit percentage and the amount of future gain that will ultimately be recognized as the taxpayer receives the installment payments.

Example 11-20

What if: Assume that Teton agrees to sell some of its machinery for $90,000 for two equal payments of $45,000 plus interest. Teton's original basis was $80,000 and accumulated depreciation on the machinery was $30,000. Teton will receive one payment in year 1 (the current year) and the other payment in year 2. What is the amount and character of the gain Teton recognizes on the sale in year 1?

Answer: $30,000 ordinary income and $5,000 of §1231 gain, computed as follows:

Description	Amount	Explanation
(1) Sales price	$ 90,000	
(2) Initial basis	80,000	
(3) Accumulated depreciation	(30,000)	
(4) Adjusted basis	50,000	(2) + (3)
(5) Realized gain (loss)	$ 40,000	(1) − (4)
(6) Ordinary income from depreciation recapture (not eligible for installment reporting)	**$30,000**	Ordinary income; lesser of (3) or (5)
(7) Gain eligible for installment reporting	$ 10,000	(5) − (6)
(8) Contract price	$ 90,000	(1) − assumed liabilities (-0-)
(9) Gross profit percentage	11.11%	(7)/(8)
(10) Payment received in year 1	$ 45,000	
Installment gain recognized in year 1	**$ 5,000**	(10) × (9) §1231 gain

What is the amount and character of the gain Teton recognized upon receipt of the payment in year 2?

Answer: $5,000 of §1231 gain ($45,000 payment received times the gross profit percentage of 11.11 percent).

Other Nonrecognition Provisions

Several tax law provisions allow businesses to change the form or organization of their business while deferring the realized gains for tax purposes. For example, a sole

[43] §453(i).

proprietor can form his business as a corporation or contribute assets to an existing corporation and defer the gain realized on the exchange of assets for an ownership interest in the business entity.[44] Without the nonrecognition provision, the tax cost of forming a corporation may be large enough to deter taxpayers from doing so. Nonrecognition rules also apply to taxpayers forming partnerships or contributing assets to partnerships.[45] In still other corporate transactions, such as mergers, divisions (spin-offs or split-offs), or reorganizations, corporations can often do so in tax-deferred transactions.[46] While these transactions generally result in deferred gain or loss for the involved parties, the specific details of these topics can easily fill entire chapters. Further coverage is beyond the scope of this text.

Related-Person Loss Disallowance Rules

Taxpayers selling business or investment property at a loss to unrelated persons are generally able to deduct the loss.[47] This makes sense in most situations because taxpayers are selling the property for less than their remaining investment (adjusted basis) in the property, and after the sale, the taxpayer's investment in the property is completely terminated. In contrast, when a taxpayer sells property at a loss to a related person, she effectively retains some element of control over the property through the related person. Consistent with this idea, §267(a) disallows recognition of losses on sales to related persons. Under §267, related persons include individuals with family relationships, including siblings, spouses, ancestors, and lineal descendants. Related persons also include an individual and a corporation if the individual owns more than 50 percent of the value of the stock of the corporation.[48]

Example 11-21

What if: Suppose Teton is formed as a corporation and Steve is its sole shareholder. Teton is looking to make some long-term investments to fund its anticipated purchase of a new manufacturing facility. Steve currently owns 1,000 shares of stock in his previous company, Northeastern Corp., which he intends to sell in the near future. Steve initially paid $40 a share for the stock but the stock is currently valued at $30 a share. While Steve believes the stock has good long-term potential, he needs cash now to purchase a personal residence in Cody, Wyoming. Steve believes selling the shares to Teton makes good sense because he can deduct the loss and save taxes now and Teton can benefit from the expected long-term appreciation of the stock. If Steve sells 1,000 shares of Northeastern Corp. stock to Teton for $30 per share, what amount of loss will he realize and what amount of loss will he recognize for tax purposes?

Answer: $10,000 loss realized and $0 loss recognized, determined as follows:

Description	Amount	Explanation
(1) Amount realized on sale	$30,000	(1,000 × $30)
(2) Adjusted basis in stock	40,000	(1,000 × $40)
(3) Loss realized on sale	**(10,000)**	(1) − (2)
Loss recognized on sale	**$ 0**	Losses on sales to related persons are disallowed.

Because Steve owns more than 50 percent of Teton (he owns 100 percent), Steve and Teton are considered to be related persons. Consequently, Steve is not allowed to recognize any loss on the sale.

---

[44]§351.

[45]§721.

[46]§368(a) contains the numerous variations and requirements of these tax-deferred reorganizations.

[47]Capital losses are subject to certain limitations for individuals and corporate taxpayers (§1211).

[48]§267(a). The related-person rules include both direct ownership as well as indirect ownership (ownership attributed to the taxpayer from related persons). See §267(c) for a description of the indirect ownership rules.

Although taxpayers are not allowed to immediately deduct losses when they sell property to the related person, the related-person buyer may be able to subsequently deduct the disallowed loss by selling the property to an *unrelated* third party at a gain. The rules follow:

- If the related buyer sells the property at a gain (the related-person buyer sells it for more than she purchased it for) greater than the disallowed loss, the entire loss that was disallowed for the related-person seller is deductible by the buyer.
- If the related-person buyer subsequently sells the property and the related-person seller's disallowed loss exceeds the related person's gain on the subsequent sale, the related-person buyer may only deduct or offset the previously disallowed loss *to the extent of the gain* on the sale to the unrelated third party—the remaining disallowed loss expires unused.
- If the related-person buyer sells the property for less than her purchase price from the related seller, the disallowed loss expires unused.
- The holding period for the related-person buyer begins on the date of the sale between the related persons.[49]

Example 11-22

What if: Let's return to Example 11-21, where Steve sold 1,000 shares of Northeastern Corp. stock to Teton (a corporation) for $30,000. As we discovered in that example, Steve realized a $10,000 loss on the sale, but he was not allowed to deduct it because Steve and Teton are related persons. Let's assume that a few years after Teton purchased the stock from Steve, Teton sells the Northeastern Corp. stock to an unrelated third party. What gain or loss does *Teton* recognize when it sells the stock in each of three scenarios, assuming it sells the stock for $37,000 in Scenario 1, $55,000 in Scenario 2, and $25,000 in Scenario 3?

Answer: $0 gain or loss in Scenario 1, $15,000 gain in Scenario 2, and $5,000 loss in Scenario 3, computed as follows:

Description	Scenario 1	Scenario 2	Scenario 3	Explanation
(1) Amount realized	$ 37,000	$ 55,000	$25,000	
(2) Adjusted basis	30,000	30,000	30,000	Example 11-21 (Teton's purchase price)
(3) Realized gain (loss)	7,000	25,000	(5,000)	(1) − (2)
(4) Benefit of Steve's ($10,000) disallowed loss	(7,000)	(10,000)	0	Loss benefit limited to realized gain.
Recognized gain (loss)	**$ 0**	**$ 15,000**	**$(5,000)**	(3) + (4)

In Scenario 1, $3,000 of Steve's $10,000 remaining disallowed loss expires unused. In Scenario 3, Steve's entire $10,000 disallowed loss expires unused.

CONCLUSION

This chapter describes and discusses the tax consequences associated with sales and other types of property dispositions. We've learned how to determine the amount of gain or loss taxpayers recognize when they sell or otherwise dispose of property, and we've learned how to determine the character of these gains and losses. Tax accountants who understand the rules and concepts of property dispositions are able to comply with the tax law and advise clients of potential tax planning opportunities and avoid pitfalls associated with various nonrecognition provisions.

---

[49]Reg. §1.267(d)-1(c)(3).

Summary

LO 11-1 Calculate the amount of gain or loss recognized on the disposition of assets used in a trade or business.

- Dispositions occur in the form of sales, trades, or other realization events.
- Gain realized is the amount realized less the adjusted basis of an asset.
- Amount realized is everything of value received in the transaction less any selling costs.
- Adjusted basis is the historical cost or initial basis of an asset less any cost recovery deductions applied against the asset.
- Gain realized on asset dispositions is not always recognized.

LO 11-2 Describe the general character types of gain or loss recognized on property dispositions.

- Recognized gains must be characterized as ordinary, capital, or §1231. An asset's character is a function of the asset's use and holding period.
- Ordinary assets are derived from normal transactions of the business (revenues and accounts receivable), the sale of short-term trade or business assets, and depreciation recapture.
- Capital assets are assets that are held either for investment or for personal use (a taxpayer's principal residence).
- §1231 assets consist of property used in a taxpayer's trade or business that has been held for more than one year.
- Net §1231 gains are treated as long-term capital gains and net §1231 losses are treated as ordinary losses.

LO 11-3 Calculate depreciation recapture.

- §1231 assets, other than land, are subject to cost recovery deductions (depreciation), which generate ordinary deductions.
- Gains that are created through depreciation deductions are subject to depreciation recapture. Any remaining gain is §1231 gain.
- Depreciation recapture does not change the amount of the gain but simply converts or recharacterizes the gain from §1231 to ordinary.
- Different recapture rules apply to tangible personal property (§1245) and real property (§291 for C corporations only and §1250).

LO 11-4 Describe the tax treatment of unrecaptured §1250 gains.

- When individuals sell §1250 property at a gain, the portion of the gain generated by depreciation deductions is called unrecaptured §1250 gain.
- This gain is a §1231 gain that, when treated as a capital gain after the §1231 netting process, flows into the capital gain/loss process and is taxed at a maximum rate of 25 percent.
- If a taxpayer sells an asset at a gain to a related person and the asset is a depreciable asset to the related person, the seller must characterize the entire gain as ordinary income.

LO 11-5 Describe the tax treatment of §1231 gains or losses, including the §1231 netting process.

- After applying the depreciation recapture rules, taxpayers calculate the net §1231 gain or loss.
- If a net §1231 loss results, the loss will become ordinary and offset ordinary income.
- If a net §1231 gain results, the §1231 look-back rule must be applied.
- After applying the look-back rule, any remaining net §1231 gain is a long-term capital gain.

LO 11-6 Explain common exceptions to the general rule that realized gains and losses are recognized currently.

- Like-kind exchanges involve trading or exchanging real property used in a business or held for investment for similar real property. The gain is deferred unless boot or non-like-kind property is received.

- Involuntary conversions are the losses on property through circumstances beyond taxpayers' control. Reasons include natural disasters, accidents, theft, or condemnation.
- Installment sales occur when any portion of the amount realized is received in a year subsequent to the disposition. A portion of the gain is initially deferred, but then recognized over time as payments are received.
- §267 related-person losses are disallowed but the related-person buyer may be able to deduct the disallowed loss if she subsequently sells the property at a gain.

KEY TERMS

adjusted basis (11-5)	installment sale (11-31)	recognized gain or loss (11-6)
amount realized (11-2)	involuntary conversion (11-29)	§291 depreciation recapture (11-14)
boot (11-26)	like-kind exchange (11-24)	§1231 assets (11-8)
capital asset (11-7)	nonrecaptured net §1231 losses (11-18)	§1231 look-back rule (11-18)
deferred like-kind exchange (11-25)	nonrecognition transaction (11-20)	§1245 property (11-10)
depreciation recapture (11-9)	ordinary asset (11-7)	§1250 property (11-14)
direct conversion (11-29)	production of income (11-7)	third-party intermediaries (11-25)
exchanged basis (11-26)	qualified replacement property (11-30)	unrecaptured §1250 gain (11-15)
indirect conversion (11-30)	realized gain or loss (11-5)	

DISCUSSION QUESTIONS

Discussion Questions are available in Connect®.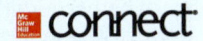

1. Compare and contrast different ways in which a taxpayer triggers a realization event by disposing of an asset. `LO 11-1`

2. Potomac Corporation wants to sell a warehouse that it has used in its business for 10 years. Potomac is asking $450,000 for the property. The warehouse is subject to a mortgage of $125,000. If Potomac accepts Wyden Inc.'s offer to give Potomac $325,000 in cash and assume full responsibility for the mortgage on the property, what amount does Potomac realize on the sale? `LO 11-1`

3. Montana Max sells a 2,500-acre ranch for $1,000,000 in cash, a note receivable of $1,000,000, and debt relief of $2,400,000. He also pays selling commissions of $60,000. In addition, Max agrees to build a new barn on the property (cost $250,000) and spend $100,000 upgrading the fence on the property before the sale. What is Max's amount realized on the sale? `LO 11-1`

4. Hawkeye sold farming equipment for $55,000. It bought the equipment four years ago for $75,000, and it has since claimed a total of $42,000 in depreciation deductions against the asset. Explain how to calculate Hawkeye's adjusted basis in the farming equipment. `LO 11-1`

5. When a taxpayer sells an asset, what is the difference between realized and recognized gain or loss on the sale? `LO 11-1`

6. What does it mean to characterize a gain or loss? Why is characterizing a gain or loss important? `LO 11-2`

7. Explain the difference between ordinary, capital, and §1231 assets. `LO 11-2`

8. Discuss the reasons why individuals generally prefer capital gains over ordinary gains. Explain why corporate taxpayers might prefer capital gains over ordinary gains. `LO 11-2`

9. Dakota Conrad owns a parcel of land he would like to sell. Describe the circumstances in which the sale of the land would generate §1231 gain or loss, ordinary gain or loss, or capital gain or loss. Also, describe the circumstances under which Dakota would not be allowed to deduct a loss on the sale. `LO 11-2`

LO 11-2   10. Lincoln has used a piece of land in her business for the past five years. The land qualifies as §1231 property. It is unclear whether Lincoln will have to recognize a gain or loss when she eventually sells the asset. She asks her accountant how the gain or loss would be characterized if she decides to sell. Her accountant says that selling §1231 assets gives sellers "the best of both worlds." Explain what her accountant means by this.

LO 11-3   11. Explain Congress's rationale for depreciation recapture.

LO 11-3   12. Compare and contrast §1245 recapture and §1250 recapture.

LO 11-3   13. Why is depreciation recapture not required when assets are sold at a loss?

LO 11-3   14. What are the similarities and differences between the tax benefit rule and depreciation recapture?

LO 11-3 LO 11-4   15. Are both corporations and individuals subject to depreciation recapture when they sell depreciable real property at a gain? Explain.

LO 11-4   16. How is unrecaptured §1250 gain for individuals similar to depreciation recapture? How is it different?

LO 11-4   17. Explain why gains from depreciable property sold to a related taxpayer are treated as ordinary income under §1239.

LO 11-5   18. Bingaman Resources sold two depreciable §1231 assets during the year. One asset resulted in a large gain (the asset was sold for more than it was purchased for) and the other in a small loss. Describe the §1231 netting process for Bingaman.

LO 11-5   19. Jeraldine believes that when the §1231 look-back rule applies, the taxpayer deducts a §1231 loss in a previous year against §1231 gains in the current year. Explain whether Jeraldine's description is correct.

LO 11-5   20. Explain the purpose behind the §1231 look-back rule.

LO 11-5   21. Does a taxpayer apply the §1231 look-back rule in a year when the taxpayer recognizes a net §1231 loss? Explain.

LO 11-4 LO 11-5   22. Describe the circumstances in which an individual taxpayer with a net §1231 gain will have different portions of the gain taxed at different rates.

LO 11-6   23. Rocky and Bullwinkle Partnership sold a parcel of land during the current year and realized a gain of $250,000. Rocky and Bullwinkle did not recognize gain related to the sale of the land on its tax return. Is this possible? Explain how a taxpayer could realize a gain but not recognize it.

LO 11-6   24. Why does the tax code allow taxpayers to defer gains on like-kind exchanges? How do the tax laws ensure that the gains (or losses) are deferred and not permanently excluded from a taxpayer's income?

LO 11-6   25. Describe the like-kind property requirements for real property for purposes of qualifying for a like-kind exchange. Explain whether land held for investment by a corporation will qualify as like-kind property with land held by an individual for personal use.

LO 11-6   26. Salazar Inc., a Colorado company, is relocating to a nearby town. It would like to trade its real property for some real property in the new location. While Salazar has found several prospective buyers for its real property and has also located several properties that are acceptable in the new location, it cannot find anyone willing to trade Salazar Inc. for its property in a like-kind exchange. Explain how a third-party intermediary could facilitate Salazar's like-kind exchange.

LO 11-6   27. Minuteman wants to enter into a like-kind exchange by exchanging its old New England manufacturing facility for a ranch in Wyoming. Minuteman is using a third-party intermediary to facilitate the exchange. The purchaser of the manufacturing facility wants to complete the transaction immediately but, for various reasons, the ranch transaction will not be completed for three to four months. Will this delay cause a problem for Minuteman's desire to accomplish this through a like-kind exchange? Explain.

28. Olympia Corporation, of Kittery, Maine, wants to exchange its manufacturing facility for Bangor Company's warehouse. Both parties agree that that Olympia's building is worth $100,000 and that Bangor's building is worth $95,000. Olympia would like the transaction to qualify as a like-kind exchange. What could the parties do to equalize the value exchanged but still allow the exchange to qualify as a like-kind exchange? How would the necessary change affect the tax consequences of the transaction?   **LO 11-6**

29. Compare and contrast the similarities and differences between like-kind exchanges and involuntary conversions for tax purposes.   **LO 11-6**

30. What is an installment sale? How do the tax laws ensure that taxpayers recognize all the gain they realize on an installment sale? How is depreciation recapture treated in an installment sale? Explain the gross profit ratio and how it relates to gains recognized under installment method sales.   **LO 11-6**

31. Mr. Kyle owns stock in a local publicly traded company. Although the stock price has declined since he purchased it two years ago, he likes the long-term prospects for the company. If Kyle sells the stock to his sister because he needs some cash for a down payment on a new home, is the loss deductible? If Kyle is right and the stock price increases in the future, how is his sister's gain computed if she sells the stock?   **LO 11-6**

PROBLEMS

Select problems are available in Connect®.

32. Rafael sold an asset to Jamal. What is Rafael's amount realized on the sale in each of the following alternative scenarios?   **LO 11-1**
    a) Rafael received $80,000 cash and a vehicle worth $10,000. Rafael also paid $5,000 in selling expenses.
    b) Rafael received $80,000 cash and was relieved of a $30,000 mortgage on the asset he sold to Jamal. Rafael also paid a commission of $5,000 on the transaction.
    c) Rafael received $20,000 cash, a parcel of land worth $50,000, and marketable securities of $10,000. Rafael also paid a commission of $8,000 on the transaction.

33. Alan Meer inherits a hotel from his grandmother, Mary, on February 11 of the current year. Mary bought the hotel for $730,000 three years ago. Mary deducted $27,000 of cost recovery on the hotel before her death. The fair market value of the hotel in February is $725,000. (Assume that the alternative valuation date is not used.)   **LO 11-1**
    a) What is Alan's adjusted basis in the hotel?
    b) If the fair market value of the hotel at the time of Mary's death was $500,000, what is Alan's basis?

34. Shasta Corporation sold a piece of land to Bill for $45,000. Shasta bought the land two years ago for $30,600. What gain or loss does Shasta realize on the transaction?   **LO 11-1**

35. Lassen Corporation sold a machine to a machine dealer for $25,000. Lassen bought the machine for $55,000 and has claimed $15,000 of depreciation expense on the machine. What gain or loss does Lassen realize on the transaction?   **LO 11-1**

36. Hannah Tywin owns 100 shares of MM Inc. stock. She sells the stock on December 11 for $25 per share. She received the stock as a gift from her Aunt Pam on March 20 of this year when the fair market value of the stock was $18 per share. Aunt Pam originally purchased the stock seven years ago at a price of $12 per share. What is the amount and character of Hannah's recognized gain on the stock?   **LO 11-1** **LO 11-2**

LO 11-1 LO 11-2 37. On September 30 of last year, Rex received some investment land from Holly as a gift. Holly's adjusted basis was $50,000 and the land was valued at $40,000 at the time of the gift. Holly acquired the land five years ago. What is the amount and character of Rex's recognized gain (loss) if he sells the land on May 12 this year at the following prices?

   a) $32,000

   b) $70,000

   c) $45,000

LO 11-1 LO 11-2 38. Franco converted a building from personal to business use in May 2016 when the fair market value was $55,000. He purchased the building in July 2013 for $80,000. On December 15 of this year, Franco sells the building for $40,000. On the date of sale, the accumulated depreciation on the building is $5,565. What is Franco's recognized gain or loss on the sale?

LO 11-2 39. Identify each of White Corporation's following assets as an ordinary, capital, or §1231 asset.

   a) Two years ago, White used its excess cash to purchase a piece of land as an investment.

   b) Two years ago, White purchased land and a warehouse. It uses these assets in its business.

   c) Manufacturing machinery White purchased earlier this year.

   d) Inventory White purchased 13 months ago that is ready to be shipped to a customer.

   e) Office equipment White has used in its business for the past three years.

   f) 1,000 shares of stock in Black Corporation that White purchased two years ago because it was a good investment.

   g) Account receivable from a customer with terms 2/10, net 30.

   h) Machinery White held for three years and then sold at a loss of $10,000.

LO 11-3 LO 11-4 40. In year 0, Canon purchased a machine to use in its business for $56,000. In year 3, Canon sold the machine for $42,000. Between the date of the purchase and the date of the sale, Canon depreciated the machine by $32,000.

   a) What is the amount and character of the gain Canon will recognize on the sale, assuming that it is a partnership?

   b) What is the amount and character of the gain Canon will recognize on the sale, assuming that it is a corporation?

   c) What is the amount and character of the gain Canon will recognize on the sale, assuming that it is a corporation and the sale proceeds were increased to $60,000?

   d) What is the amount and character of the gain Canon will recognize on the sale, assuming that it is a corporation and the sale proceeds were decreased to $20,000?

LO 11-3 LO 11-4 41. In year 0, Longworth Partnership purchased a machine for $40,000 to use in its business. In year 3, Longworth sold the machine for $35,000. Between the date of the purchase and the date of the sale, Longworth depreciated the machine by $22,000.

   a) What is the amount and character of the gain (loss) Longworth will recognize on the sale?

   b) What is the amount and character of the gain (loss) Longworth will recognize on the sale if the sale proceeds are increased to $45,000?

   c) What is the amount and character of the gain (loss) Longworth will recognize on the sale if the sale proceeds are decreased to $15,000?

42. On August 1 of year 0, Dirksen purchased a machine for $20,000 to use in its business. On December 4 of year 0, Dirksen sold the machine for $18,000.

    a) What is the amount and character of the gain or loss Dirksen will recognize on the sale?

    b) What is the amount and character of the gain or loss Dirksen will recognize on the sale if the machine is sold on January 15 of year 1 instead?

   LO 11-3 LO 11-4

43. Rayburn Corporation has a building that it bought during year 0 for $850,000. It sold the building in year 5. During the time it held the building Rayburn depreciated it by $100,000. What is the amount and character of the gain or loss Rayburn will recognize on the sale in each of the following alternative situations?

    a) Rayburn receives $840,000.

    b) Rayburn receives $900,000.

    c) Rayburn receives $700,000.

   LO 11-3 LO 11-4

44. Moran owns a building he bought during year 0 for $150,000. He sold the building in year 6. During the time he held the building he depreciated it by $32,000. What is the amount and character of the gain or loss Moran will recognize on the sale in each of the following alternative situations?

    a) Moran received $145,000.

    b) Moran received $170,000.

    c) Moran received $110,000.

   LO 11-3 LO 11-4

45. Hart, an individual, bought an asset for $500,000 and has claimed $100,000 of depreciation deductions against the asset. Hart has a marginal tax rate of 32 percent. Answer the questions presented in the following alternative scenarios (assume Hart had no property transactions other than those described in the problem):

    a) What is the amount and character of Hart's recognized gain if the asset is tangible personal property sold for $450,000? What effect does the sale have on Hart's tax liability for the year?

    b) What is the amount and character of Hart's recognized gain if the asset is tangible personal property sold for $550,000? What effect does the sale have on Hart's tax liability for the year?

    c) What is the amount and character of Hart's recognized gain if the asset is tangible personal property sold for $350,000? What effect does the sale have on Hart's tax liability for the year?

    d) What is the amount and character of Hart's recognized gain if the asset is a nonresidential building sold for $450,000? What effect does the sale have on Hart's tax liability for the year?

    e) Now assume that Hart is a C corporation. What is the amount and character of its recognized gain if the asset is a nonresidential building sold for $450,000? What effect does the sale have on Hart's tax liability for the year (assume a 21 percent tax rate)?

    f) Assuming that the asset is real property, which entity type should be used to minimize the taxes paid on real estate gains?

   LO 11-3 LO 11-4
LO 11-5
planning

46. Luke sold a building and the land on which the building sits to his wholly owned corporation, Studemont Corp., at fair market value. The fair market value of the building was determined to be $325,000; Luke built the building several years ago at a cost of $200,000. Luke had claimed $45,000 of depreciation expense on the building. The fair market value of the land was determined to be $210,000 at the time of the sale; Luke purchased the land many years ago for $130,000.

    a) What is the amount and character of Luke's recognized gain or loss on the building?

    b) What is the amount and character of Luke's recognized gain or loss on the land?

   LO 11-4

LO 11-5 47. Buckley, an individual, began business two years ago and has never sold a §1231 asset. Buckley has owned each of the assets since he began the business. In the current year, Buckley sold the following business assets:

Asset	Original Cost	Accumulated Depreciation	Gain/Loss
Computers	$ 6,000	$ 2,000	$(3,000)
Machinery	10,000	4,000	(2,000)
Furniture	20,000	12,000	7,000
Building	100,000	10,000	(1,000)

Assuming Buckley's marginal ordinary income tax rate is 32 percent, answer the questions for the following alternative scenarios:

a) What is the character of Buckley's gains or losses for the current year? What effect do the gains and losses have on Buckley's tax liability?

b) Assume that the amount realized increased so that the building was sold at a $6,000 gain instead. What is the character of Buckley's gains or losses for the current year? What effect do the gains and losses have on Buckley's tax liability?

c) Assume that the amount realized increased so that the building was sold at a $15,000 gain instead. What is the character of Buckley's gains or losses for the current year? What effect do the gains and losses have on Buckley's tax liability?

LO 11-3 **LO 11-4** 48. Lily Tucker (single) owns and operates a bike shop as a sole proprietorship. **LO 11-5** In 2018, she sells the following long-term assets used in her business:

Asset	Sales Price	Cost	Accumulated Depreciation
Building	$230,000	$200,000	$52,000
Equipment	80,000	148,000	23,000

Lily's taxable income before these transactions is $160,500. What are Lily's taxable income and tax liability for the year?

LO 11-3 **LO 11-4** 49. Shimmer Inc. is a calendar-year-end, accrual-method corporation. This year, it sells **LO 11-5** the following long-term assets:

Asset	Sales Price	Cost	Accumulated Depreciation
Building	$650,000	$642,000	$37,000
Sparkle Corporation stock	130,000	175,000	n/a

Shimmer does not sell any other assets during the year, and its taxable income before these transactions is $800,000. What are Shimmer's taxable income and tax liability for the year?

LO 11-5 50. Aruna, a sole proprietor, wants to sell two assets that she no longer needs for
planning her business. Both assets qualify as §1231 assets. The first is machinery and will generate a $10,000 §1231 loss on the sale. The second is land that will generate a $7,000 §1231 gain on the sale. Aruna's ordinary marginal tax rate is 32 percent.

a) Assuming she sells both assets in December of year 1 (the current year), what effect will the sales have on Aruna's tax liability?

b) Assuming that Aruna sells the land in December of year 1 and the machinery in January of year 2, what effect will the sales have on Aruna's tax liability for each year?

c) Explain why selling the assets in separate years will result in greater tax savings for Aruna.

51. Bourne Guitars, a corporation, reported a $157,000 net §1231 gain for year 6.   `LO 11-5`

    a) Assuming Bourne reported $50,000 of nonrecaptured net §1231 losses during years 1–5, what amount of Bourne's net §1231 gain for year 6, if any, is treated as ordinary income?

    b) Assuming Bourne's nonrecaptured net §1231 losses from years 1–5 were $200,000, what amount of Bourne's net §1231 gain for year 6, if any, is treated as ordinary income?

52. Tonya Jefferson (single), a sole proprietor, runs a successful lobbying business in Washington, DC. She doesn't sell many business assets, but she is planning on retiring and selling her historic townhouse, from which she runs her business, to buy a place somewhere sunny and warm. Tonya's townhouse is worth $1,000,000 and the land is worth another $1,000,000. The original basis in the townhouse was $600,000, and she has claimed $250,000 of depreciation deductions against the asset over the years. The original basis in the land was $500,000. Tonya has located a buyer that would like to finalize the transaction in December of the current year. Tonya's marginal ordinary income tax rate is 35 percent and her capital gains tax rate is 20 percent.   `LO 11-5` `planning`

    a) What amount of gain or loss does Tonya recognize on the sale? What is the character of the gain or loss? What effect does the gain or loss have on her tax liability?

    b) In addition to the original facts, assume that Tonya reports the following nonrecaptured net §1231 loss:

Year	Net §1231 Gains/(Losses)
Year 1	$(200,000)
Year 2	0
Year 3	0
Year 4	0
Year 5	0
Year 6 (current year)	?

    What amount of gain or loss does Tonya recognize on the sale? What is the character of the gain or loss? What effect does the gain or loss have on her year 6 (the current year) tax liability?

    c) As Tonya's tax adviser, you suggest that Tonya sell the townhouse in year 7 in order to reduce her taxes. What amount of gain or loss does Tonya recognize on the sale in year 7?

53. Morgan's Water World (MWW), an LLC, opened several years ago. MWW has reported the following net §1231 gains and losses since it began business. Net §1231 gains shown are before the lookback rule.   `LO 11-5`

Year	Net §1231 Gains/(Losses)
Year 1	$ (11,000)
Year 2	5,000
Year 3	(21,000)
Year 4	(4,000)
Year 5	17,000
Year 6	(43,000)
Year 7 (current year)	113,000

    What amount, if any, of the current year (year 7) $113,000 net §1231 gain is treated as ordinary income?

LO 11-5 54. Hans runs a sole proprietorship. Hans has reported the following net §1231 gains and losses since he began business. Net §1231 gains shown are before the lookback rule.

Year	Net §1231 Gains/(Losses)
Year 1	$(65,000)
Year 2	15,000
Year 3	0
Year 4	0
Year 5	10,000
Year 6	0
Year 7 (current year)	50,000

a) What amount, if any, of the year 7 (current year) $50,000 net §1231 gain is treated as ordinary income?

b) Assume that the $50,000 net §1231 gain occurs in year 6 instead of year 7. What amount of the gain would be treated as ordinary income in year 6?

LO 11-6 55. Independence Corporation needs to replace some of the assets used in its trade or business and is contemplating the following exchanges:

Exchange	Asset Given Up by Independence	Asset Received by Independence
A	Office building in Chicago, IL	Piece of land in Toronto, Canada
B	Large warehouse on two acres	Small warehouse on 22 acres
C	Office building in Green Bay, WI, used in the business	Apartment complex in Newport Beach, CA, that will be held as an investment

Determine whether each exchange qualifies as a like-kind exchange. Also, explain the rationale for why each qualifies or does not qualify as a like-kind exchange.

LO 11-6 56. Kase, an individual, purchased some property in Potomac, Maryland, for $150,000 approximately 10 years ago. Kase is approached by a real estate agent representing a client who would like to exchange a parcel of land in North Carolina for Kase's Maryland property. Kase agrees to the exchange. What is Kase's realized gain or loss, recognized gain or loss, and basis in the North Carolina property in each of the following alternative scenarios?

a) The transaction qualifies as a like-kind exchange and the fair market value of each property is $675,000.

b) The transaction qualifies as a like-kind exchange and the fair market value of each property is $100,000.

LO 11-6
 **research**
57. Longhaul Real Estate exchanged a parcel of land it held for sale in Bryan, Texas, for a warehouse in College Station, Texas. Will the exchange qualify for like-kind treatment?

LO 11-6
 **research**
58. Twinbrook Corporation needed to upgrade to a larger manufacturing facility. Twinbrook first acquired a new manufacturing facility for $2,100,000 cash and then transferred the facility it was using (building and land) to White Flint Corporation for $2,000,000 three months later. Does the exchange qualify for like-kind exchange treatment? (*Hint:* Examine Revenue Procedures 2000-37 and 2004-51.) If not, can you propose a change in the transaction that will allow it to qualify?

LO 11-6
 **research**
59. Woodley Park Corporation currently owns two parcels of land (parcel 1 and parcel 2). It owns a warehouse facility on parcel 1. Woodley needs to acquire a new and larger manufacturing facility. Woodley was approached by Blazing Fast Construction (which specializes in prefabricated warehouses) about acquiring Woodley's existing warehouse on parcel 1. Woodley indicated that it would prefer to exchange its

existing facility for a new and larger facility in a qualifying like-kind exchange. Blazing Fast indicated that it could construct a new manufacturing facility on parcel 2 to Woodley's specification within four months. Woodley and Blazing Fast agreed to the following arrangement. First, Blazing Fast would construct the new warehouse on parcel 2 and then relinquish the property to Woodley within four months. Woodley would then transfer the warehouse facility and land parcel 1 to Blazing Fast. All of the property exchanged in the deal was identified immediately and the construction was completed within 180 days. Does the exchange of the new building for the old building and parcel 1 qualify as a like-kind exchange? (*Hint*: See *DeCleene v. Commissioner,* 115 TC 457.)

60. Metro Corp. traded Land A for Land B. Metro originally purchased Land A for $50,000 and Land A's adjusted basis was $25,000 at the time of the exchange. What is Metro's realized gain or loss, recognized gain or loss, and adjusted basis in Land B in each of the following alternative scenarios?   `LO 11-6`

    a) The fair market value of Land A and of Land B is $40,000 at the time of the exchange. The exchange does not qualify as a like-kind exchange.

    b) The fair market value of Land A and of Land B is $40,000. The exchange qualifies as a like-kind exchange.

    c) The fair market value of Land A is $35,000 and Land B is valued at $40,000. Metro exchanges Land A and $5,000 cash for Land B. Land A and Land B are like-kind property.

    d) The fair market value of Land A is $45,000 and Metro trades Land A for Land B valued at $40,000 and $5,000 cash. Land A and Land B are like-kind property.

61. Prater Inc. enters into an exchange in which it gives up its warehouse on 10 acres of land and receives a tract of land. A summary of the exchange is as follows: `LO 11-6`

Transferred	FMV	Original Basis	Accumulated Depreciation
Warehouse	$300,000	$225,000	$45,000
Land	50,000	50,000	
Mortgage on warehouse	30,000		
Cash	20,000	20,000	

Assets received	FMV
Land	$340,000

    What is Prater's realized and recognized gain on the exchange and its basis in the assets it received in the exchange?

62. Baker Corporation owned a building located in Kansas. Baker used the building for its business operations. Last year a tornado hit the property and completely destroyed it. This year, Baker received an insurance settlement. Baker had originally purchased the building for $350,000 and had claimed a total of $100,000 of depreciation deductions against the property. What is Baker's realized and recognized gain or (loss) on this transaction and what is its basis in the new building in the following alternative scenarios?   `LO 11-6`

    a) Baker received $450,000 in insurance proceeds and spent $450,000 rebuilding the building during the current year.

    b) Baker received $450,000 in insurance proceeds and spent $500,000 rebuilding the building during the current year.

    c) Baker received $450,000 in insurance proceeds and spent $400,000 rebuilding the building during the current year.

    d) Baker received $450,000 in insurance proceeds and spent $450,000 rebuilding the building during the next three years.

LO 11-6 63. Russell Corporation sold a parcel of land valued at $400,000. Its basis in the land was $275,000. For the land, Russell received $50,000 in cash in year 0 and a note providing that Russell will receive $175,000 in year 1 and $175,000 in year 2 from the buyer.

a) What is Russell's realized gain on the transaction?

b) What is Russell's recognized gain in year 0, year 1, and year 2?

LO 11-6 64. In year 0, Javens Inc. sold machinery with a fair market value of $400,000 to Chris. The machinery's original basis was $317,000 and Javens's accumulated depreciation on the machinery was $50,000, so its adjusted basis to Javens was $267,000. Chris paid Javens $40,000 immediately (in year 0) and provided a note to Javens indicating that Chris would pay Javens $60,000 a year for six years beginning in year 1. What is the amount and character of the gain that Javens will recognize in year 0? What amount and character of the gain will Javens recognize in years 1 through 6?

LO 11-6

65. Ken sold a rental property for $500,000. He received $100,000 in the current year and $100,000 each year for the next four years. Of the sales price, $400,000 was allocated to the building and the remaining $100,000 was allocated to the land. Ken purchased the property several years ago for $300,000. When he initially purchased the property, he allocated $225,000 of the purchase price to the building and $75,000 to the land. Ken has claimed $25,000 of depreciation deductions over the years against the building. Ken had no other sales of §1231 or capital assets in the current year. For the year of the sale, determine Ken's recognized gain or loss and the character of Ken's gain, and calculate Ken's tax due because of the sale (assuming his marginal ordinary tax rate is 32 percent). (*Hint:* See the examples in Reg. §1.453-12.)

LO 11-6

planning

66. Hill Corporation is in the leasing business and faces a marginal tax rate of 21 percent. It has leased a building to Whitewater Corporation for several years. Hill bought the building for $150,000 and claimed $20,000 of depreciation deductions against the asset. The lease term is about to expire and Whitewater would like to acquire the building. Hill has been offered two options to choose from:

Option	Details
Like-kind exchange	Whitewater would provide Hill with a like-kind building. The like-kind building has a fair market value of $135,000.
Installment sale	Whitewater would provide Hill with two payments of $69,000. It would use the proceeds to purchase another building that it could also lease.

Ignoring time value of money, which option provides the greatest after-tax value for Hill, assuming it is indifferent between the proposals based on nontax factors?

LO 11-6 67. Deirdre sold 100 shares of stock to her brother, James, for $2,400. Deirdre purchased the stock several years ago for $3,000.

a) What gain or loss does Deirdre recognize on the sale?

b) What amount of gain or loss does James recognize if he sells the stock for $3,200?

c) What amount of gain or loss does James recognize if he sells the stock for $2,600?

d) What amount of gain or loss does James recognize if he sells the stock for $2,000?

COMPREHENSIVE PROBLEMS

Select problems are available in Connect®.

68. Two years ago, Bethesda Corporation bought a delivery truck for $30,000 (not subject to the luxury auto depreciation limits). Bethesda used MACRS 200 percent declining balance and the half-year convention to recover the cost of the truck, but it did not elect §179 expensing and opted out of bonus depreciation. Answer the questions for the following alternative scenarios.

    a) Assuming Bethesda used the truck until it sold it in March of year 3, what depreciation expense can it claim on the truck for years 1 through 3?

    b) Assume that Bethesda claimed $18,500 of depreciation expense on the truck before it sold it in year 3. What is the amount and character of the gain or loss if Bethesda sold the truck in year 3 for $17,000 and incurred $2,000 of selling expenses on the sale?

    c) Assume that Bethesda claimed $18,500 of depreciation expense on the truck before it sold it in year 3. What is the amount and character of the gain or loss if Bethesda sold the truck in year 3 for $35,000 and incurred $3,000 of selling expenses on the sale?

69. Hauswirth Corporation sold (or exchanged) a warehouse in year 0. Hauswirth bought the warehouse several years ago for $65,000 and it has claimed $23,000 of depreciation expense against the building.

    a) Assuming that Hauswirth receives $50,000 in cash for the warehouse, compute the amount and character of Hauswirth's recognized gain or loss on the sale.

    b) Assuming that Hauswirth exchanges the warehouse in a like-kind exchange for some land with a fair market value of $50,000, compute Hauswirth's gain realized, gain recognized, deferred gain, and basis in the new land.

    c) Assuming that Hauswirth receives $20,000 in cash in year 0 and a $50,000 note receivable that is payable in year 1, compute the amount and character of Hauswirth's gain in year 0 and in year 1.

70. Fontenot Corporation sold some machinery to its majority owner Gray (an individual who owns 60 percent of Fontenot). Fontenot purchased the machinery for $100,000 and has claimed a total of $40,000 of depreciation expense deductions against the property. Gray will provide Fontenot with $10,000 cash today and provide a $100,000 note that will pay Fontenot $50,000 one year from now and $50,000 two years from now.

    a) What gain does Fontenot realize on the sale?

    b) What is the amount and character of the gain that Fontenot must recognize in the year of sale (if any) and each of the two subsequent years? (*Hint:* Use the Internal Revenue Code and start with §453; please give appropriate citations.)

71. Moab Inc. manufactures and distributes high-tech biking gadgets. It has decided to streamline some of its operations so that it will be able to be more productive and efficient. Because of this decision it has entered into several transactions during the year.

    Part (1): Determine the gain/loss realized and recognized in the current year for each of these events. Also determine whether the gain/loss recognized will be §1231, capital, or ordinary.

    a) Moab Inc. sold a machine that it used to make computerized gadgets for $27,300 cash. It originally bought the machine for $19,200 three years ago and has taken $8,000 depreciation.

    b) Moab Inc. held stock in ABC Corp., which had a value of $12,000 at the beginning of the year. That same stock had a value of $15,230 at the end of the year.

    c) Moab Inc. sold some of its inventory for $7,000 cash. This inventory had a basis of $5,000.

d) Moab Inc. disposed of an office building with a fair market value of $75,000 for another office building with a fair market value of $55,000 and $20,000 in cash. It originally bought the office building seven years ago for $62,000 and has taken $15,000 in depreciation.

e) Moab Inc. sold some land held for investment for $28,000. It originally bought the land for $32,000 two years ago.

f) Moab Inc. sold another machine for a note payable in four annual installments of $12,000. The first payment was received in the current year. It originally bought the machine two years ago for $32,000 and has claimed $9,000 in depreciation expense against the machine.

g) Moab Inc. sold stock it held for eight years for $2,750. It originally purchased the stock for $2,100.

h) Moab Inc. sold another machine for $7,300. It originally purchased this machine six months ago for $9,000 and has claimed $830 in depreciation expense against the asset.

Part (2): From the recognized gains/losses determined in part (1), determine the net §1231 gain/loss and the net ordinary gain/loss Moab will recognize on its tax return. Moab Inc. also has $2,000 of nonrecaptured net §1231 losses from previous years.

Part (3): Complete Moab Inc.'s Form 4797 for the year. Use the most current form available.

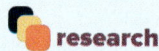

72. Vertovec Inc., a large local consulting firm in Utah, hired several new consultants from out of state last year to help service its expanding list of clients. To aid in relocating the consultants, Vertovec Inc. purchased the consultants' homes in their prior location if the consultants were unable to sell their homes within 30 days of listing them for sale. Vertovec Inc. bought the homes from the consultants for 5 percent less than the list price and then continued to list the homes for sale. Each home Vertovec Inc. purchased was sold at a loss. By the end of last year, Vertovec had suffered a loss totaling $250,000 from the homes. How should Vertovec treat the loss for tax purposes? Write a memo to Vertovec Inc. explaining your findings and any planning suggestions that you may have if Vertovec Inc. continues to offer this type of relocation benefit to newly hired consultants.

73. WAR (We Are Rich) has been in business since 1985. WAR is an accrual method sole proprietorship that deals in the manufacturing and wholesaling of various types of golf equipment. Hack & Hack CPAs has filed accurate tax returns for WAR's owner since WAR opened its doors. The managing partner of Hack & Hack (Jack) has gotten along very well with the owner of WAR—Mr. Someday Woods (single). However, in early 2018, Jack Hack and Someday Woods played a round of golf and Jack, for the first time ever, actually beat Mr. Woods. Mr. Woods was so upset that he fired Hack & Hack and has hired you to compute his 2018 taxable income. Mr. Woods was able to provide you with the following information from prior tax returns. The taxable income numbers reflect the results from all of Mr. Wood's activities *except for the items separately stated*. You will need to consider how to handle the separately stated items for tax purposes. Also, note that the 2013–2017 numbers do not reflect capital loss carryovers.

	2013	2014	2015	2016	2017
Ordinary taxable income	$ 4,000	$ 2,000	$94,000	$170,000	$250,000
Other items not included in ordinary taxable income					
Net gain (loss) on disposition of §1231 assets	3,000	10,000		(6,000)	
Net long-term capital gain (loss) on disposition of capital assets	(15,000)	1,000	(7,000)		(7,000)

In 2018, Mr. Woods had taxable income in the amount of $480,000 before considering the following events and transactions that transpired in 2018:

a) On January 1, 2018, WAR purchased a plot of land for $100,000 with the intention of creating a driving range where patrons could test their new golf equipment. WAR never got around to building the driving range; instead, WAR sold the land on October 1, 2018, for $40,000.

b) On August 17, 2018, WAR sold its golf testing machine, "Iron Byron" and replaced it with a new machine "Iron Tiger." "Iron Byron" was purchased and installed for a total cost of $22,000 on February 5, 2014. At the time of sale, "Iron Byron" had an adjusted tax basis of $4,000. WAR sold "Iron Byron" for $25,000.

c) In the months October through December 2018, WAR sold various assets to come up with the funds necessary to invest in WAR's latest and greatest invention—the three-dimple golf ball. Data on these assets are provided below:

Asset	Placed in Service (or Purchased)	Sold	Initial Basis	Accumulated Depreciation	Selling Price
Someday's black leather sofa (used in office)	4/4/17	10/16/18	$ 3,000	$ 540	$ 2,900
Someday's office chair	3/1/16	11/8/18	8,000	3,000	4,000
Marketable securities	2/1/15	12/1/18	12,000	0	20,000
Land held for investment	7/1/17	11/29/18	45,000	0	48,000
Other investment property	11/30/16	10/15/18	10,000	0	8,000

d) Finally, on May 7, 2018, WAR decided to sell the building where it tested its plutonium shaft, lignite head drivers. WAR purchased the building on January 5, 2006, for $190,000 ($170,000 for the building, $20,000 for the land). At the time of the sale, the accumulated depreciation on the building was $50,000. WAR sold the building (with the land) for $300,000. The fair market value of the land at the time of sale was $45,000.

Part (1): Compute Mr. Woods's taxable income *after* taking into account the transactions described above.

Part (2): Compute Mr. Woods's tax liability for the year. (Ignore any net investment income tax for the year and assume the 20 percent qualified business income deduction is included in taxable income before these transactions.)

Part (3): Complete Mr. Woods's Form 8949, Schedule D, and Form 4797 (use the most current version of these schedules) to be attached to his Form 1040. Assume that asset bases are not reported to the IRS.

74. Fizbo Corporation is in the business of breeding and racing horses. Fizbo has taxable income of $5,000,000 other than from these transactions. It has nonrecaptured §1231 losses of $10,000 from 2014 and $13,000 from 2012.

Consider the following transactions that occur during 2018:

a) A building with an adjusted basis of $300,000 is totally destroyed by fire. Fizbo receives insurance proceeds of $400,000, but does not plan to replace the building. The building was built 12 years ago at a cost of $420,000 and was used to provide lodging for employees.

b) Fizbo sells four acres of undeveloped farmland (used for grazing) for $50,000. Fizbo purchased the land 15 years ago for $15,000.

c) Fizbo sells a racehorse for $250,000. The racehorse was purchased four years ago for $200,000. Total depreciation taken on the racehorse was $160,000.

d) Fizbo exchanges equipment that was purchased three years ago for $300,000 for $100,000 of IBM common stock. The adjusted basis of the equipment is $220,000. If straight-line depreciation had been used, the adjusted basis would be $252,000.

e) On November 1, Fizbo sold XCON stock for $50,000. Fizbo had purchased the stock on December 12, 2017, for $112,000.

Part (1): After *all* netting is complete, what is Fizbo's total amount of income from these transactions to be treated as ordinary income or loss? What is its capital gain or loss?

Part (2): What is Fizbo's taxable income for the year after including the effects of these transactions?

 **ROGER** | *CPA Review*

Sample CPA Exam questions from Roger CPA Review are available in Connect as support for the topics in this text. These Multiple Choice Questions and Task-Based Simulations include expert-written explanations and solutions and provide a starting point for students to become familiar with the content and functionality of the actual CPA Exam.

12 Entities Overview

Learning Objectives

Upon completing this chapter, you should be able to:

LO 12-1 Discuss the legal and nontax characteristics of different types of legal entities.

LO 12-2 Describe the different types of entities for tax purposes.

LO 12-3 Identify fundamental differences in tax characteristics across entity types.

©PhotoAlto/MediaBakery

Nicole Johnson is currently employed by the Utah Chamber of Commerce in Salt Lake City, Utah. While she enjoys the relatively short workweeks, she eventually would like to work for herself. In her current position, she deals with a lot of successful entrepreneurs who have become role models for her. Nicole has also developed an extensive list of contacts that should serve her well when she starts her own business. It has taken a while, but Nicole believes she has finally developed a viable new business idea. Her idea is to design and manufacture bed sheets that have various colored patterns and are made of unique fabric blends. The sheets look great and are extremely comfortable whether the bedroom is warm or cool. She has had several friends try out her prototype sheets and they have consistently given the sheets rave reviews. With this encouragement, Nicole started giving serious thought to making "Color Comfort Sheets" a money-making enterprise.

Nicole has enough business background to realize that she is embarking on a risky path, but one, she hopes, with significant potential rewards. After creating some initial income projections, Nicole realized that it will take a few years for the business to become profitable.

While Nicole's original plan was to start the business by herself, she is considering seeking out another equity owner so that she can add financial resources and business experience to the venture. Nicole feels like she has a grasp on her business plan, but she still needs to determine how to organize the business for tax purposes. After doing some research, Nicole learned that she should consider many factors in order to determine the "best" entity type for her business. Each type of entity has advantages and disadvantages from both tax and nontax perspectives, and the best entity for a business depends on the goals, outlook, and strategy for that particular business and its owners. She understands that she has more work to do to make an informed decision.

to be continued . . .

This chapter explores various types of legal entities and then discusses entities available for tax purposes. We outline some of the pros and cons of each entity type from both nontax and tax perspectives, as we help Nicole determine how she will organize her business to best accomplish her goals. Subsequent chapters provide additional detail concerning the tax characteristics of each entity type.

LO 12-1 ENTITY LEGAL CLASSIFICATION AND NONTAX CHARACTERISTICS

When forming new business ventures, entrepreneurs can choose to house their operations under one of several basic entity types. These entities differ in terms of their legal and tax considerations. In fact, as we discuss in more depth below, the legal classification of a business may be different from its tax classification. These entities differ in terms of the formalities that entrepreneurs must follow to create them, the legal rights and responsibilities conferred on the entities and their owners, and the tax rules that determine how the entities and owners will be taxed on income generated by the entities. CPAs are frequently asked to help clients choose the best entity choice for their businesses. CPAs can help clients navigate recent tax legislation that has significantly changed the tax landscape for entity choice.

Legal Classification

Generally, a business entity may be classified as a **corporation,** a **limited liability company (LLC),** a **general partnership (GP),** a **limited partnership (LP),** or a **sole proprietorship** (not formed as an LLC).[1] Under state law, corporations are recognized as legal entities separate from their owners (shareholders). Business owners legally form corporations by filing **articles of incorporation** with the state in which they organize the business. State laws also recognize limited liability companies (LLCs) as legal entities separate from their owners (members). Business owners create limited liability companies by filing either a **certificate of organization** or **articles of organization** with the state in which they are organizing the business (depending on the state).

Partnerships are formed under state partnership statutes and the degree of formality required depends on the type of partnership being formed. General partnerships may be formed by written agreement among the partners, called a **partnership agreement,** or they may be formed informally without a written agreement when two or more owners join together in an activity to generate profits. Although general partners are not required to file partnership agreements with the state, general partnerships are still considered to be legal entities separate from their owners under state laws. Unlike general partnerships, limited partnerships are usually organized by written agreement and typically must file a **certificate of limited partnership** to be recognized by the state.[2]

Finally, for state law purposes, sole proprietorships are *not* treated as legal entities separate from their individual owners. As a result, sole proprietors are not required to formally organize their businesses with the state, and they hold title to business assets in their own names rather than in the name of their businesses.

Nontax Characteristics

Rather than identify and discuss all possible nontax entity characteristics, we compare and contrast several prominent characteristics across the different legal entity types.

[1]Variations of these entities include limited liability partnerships (LLPs), limited liability limited partnerships (LLLPs), professional limited liability companies (PLLCs), and professional corporations (PCs).

[2]Similar to limited partnerships, LLPs, LLLPs, PLLCs, and PCs must register with the state to receive formal recognition.

Responsibility for Liabilities Whether the entity or the owner(s) is ultimately responsible for paying the liabilities of the business depends on the type of entity. Under state law, a corporation is solely responsible for its liabilities.[3] Similarly, LLCs and not their members are responsible for the liabilities of the business.[4] For entities formed as partnerships, all general partners are ultimately responsible for the liabilities of the partnership. In contrast, limited partners are not responsible for the partnership's liabilities.[5] However, limited partners are not allowed to actively participate in the activities of the business.

Finally, if a business is conducted as a sole proprietorship, the individual owner is responsible for the liabilities of the business. However, individual business owners may organize their businesses as single-member LLCs. In exchange for observing the formalities of organizing as an LLC, they receive the liability protection afforded LLC members.[6]

Rights, Responsibilities, and Legal Arrangements among Owners State corporation laws specify the rights and responsibilities of corporations and their shareholders. For example, to retain limited liability protection for shareholders, corporations must create, regularly update, and comply with a set of bylaws (internal rules governing how the corporation is run). They must have a board of directors. They must have regular board meetings and regular (at least annual) shareholder meetings, and they must keep minutes of these meetings. They must also issue shares of stock to owners (shareholders) and maintain a stock ledger reflecting stock ownership. They must comply with annual filing requirements specified by the state of incorporation, pay required filing fees, and pay required corporate taxes, if any. Consequently, shareholders have no flexibility to alter their legal treatment with respect to one another (rights are determined solely by stock ownership not by agreements), with respect to the corporation, or with respect to outsiders. In contrast, while state laws provide default provisions specifying rights and responsibilities of LLCs and their members, members have the flexibility to alter their arrangement by spelling out, through an operating agreement, the management practices of the entity and the rights and responsibilities of the members consistent with their wishes. Thus, LLCs allow more flexible business arrangements than do corporations.

Like LLC statutes, state partnership laws provide default provisions specifying the partners' legal rights and responsibilities for dealing with each other absent an agreement to the contrary. Because partners have the flexibility to depart from the default provisions, they frequently craft partnership agreements that are consistent with their preferences.

Although in many instances having the flexibility to customize business arrangements is desirable, sometimes inflexible governance rules mandated by state statute are needed to limit the participation of owners in management when their participation becomes impractical. For example, when businesses decide to "go public" with an **initial public offering (IPO)** on one of the public securities exchanges, they usually solicit a

---

[3]Payroll tax liabilities are an important exception to this general rule. Shareholders of closely held corporations may be held responsible for these liabilities.

[4]When closely held corporations and LLCs borrow from banks or other lenders, shareholders or members are commonly asked to personally guarantee the debt. To the extent they do this, they become personally liable to repay the loan in the event the corporation or LLC is unable to repay it.

[5]Limited liability limited partnerships (LLLPs) are limited partnerships in which general and limited partners are protected from the liabilities of the entity. Also, professional service businesses such as accounting firms and law firms are generally not allowed to operate as corporations, LLCs, or limited partnerships. These businesses are frequently organized as limited liability partnerships (LLPs), professional limited liability companies (PLLCs), or professional corporations (PCs). Owners of a PLLC or a PC are protected from liabilities of the entity other than liabilities stemming from their own negligence. LLPs do not provide protection against liabilities stemming from a partner's own negligence or from the LLP's contractual liabilities.

[6]Shareholders of corporations and LLC members are responsible for liabilities stemming from their own negligence.

vast pool of potential investors to become corporate shareholders.[7] State corporation laws prohibit shareholders from directly amending corporate governance rules and from directly participating in management—they have only the right to vote for corporate directors or officers. In comparison, LLC members generally have the right to amend the LLC operating agreement, provide input, and manage LLCs. Obviously, managing a publicly traded business would be next to impossible if thousands of owners had the legal right to change operating rules and directly participate in managing the enterprise.

Exhibit 12-1 summarizes several nontax characteristics of different types of legal entities.

EXHIBIT 12-1   Business Types: Legal Entities and Nontax Characteristics

Nontax Characteristics	Corporation	LLC	General Partnership	Limited Partnership	Sole Proprietorship
Must formally organize with state	Yes	Yes	No	Yes	No*
Responsibility for liabilities of business	Entity	Entity	General partner(s)	General partner(s)	Owner†
Legal arrangement among owners	Not flexible	Flexible	Flexible	Flexible	Not applicable
Suitable for initial public offering	Yes	No	No	No^	No

*A sole proprietor must organize with the state if she forms a single-member LLC.
†The owner is not responsible for the liabilities of the business if the sole proprietorship is organized as an LLC. However, the owner is responsible for liabilities stemming from her own negligence and for any liabilities the owner personally guarantees.
^While it is uncommon, certain limited partnerships are eligible for IPOs.

As summarized in Exhibit 12-1, corporations and LLCs have the advantage in liability protection, LLCs and partnerships have an advantage over other entities in terms of legal flexibility, and corporations have the advantage when owners want to take a business public.

continued from page 12-1 . . .
As an initial step in the process of selecting the type of legal entity to house Color Comfort Sheets (CCS), Nicole began to research nontax issues that might be relevant to her decision. Early in her research she realized that the nontax benefits unique to traditional corporations were relevant primarily to large, publicly traded corporations. Although Nicole was very optimistic about CCS's prospects, she knew it would likely be a long time, if ever, before it went public. However, she remained interested in limiting her own and other potential investors' liability in the new venture, so she began to dig a little deeper. As she perused the Utah state website, she learned that corporations and LLCs are the only legal entities that can completely shield investors from liabilities. Although Nicole doesn't anticipate any trouble from her future creditors, she decides to limit her choice of legal entity to either a corporation or LLC.

At this point in her information-gathering process, Nicole is leaning toward the LLC option because she is not sure she wants to deal with board meetings and all the other formalities of operating a corporation; however, she decides to assemble a five-year forecast of CCS's expected operating results and to learn a little more about the way corporations and LLCs are taxed before making a final decision.

to be continued . . .

[7]The vast majority of IPOs involve corporate shares; however, limited partnership interests are occasionally sold in IPOs. Like shareholders, limited partners are typically not allowed to participate in management. Limited partnerships are used for public offerings in lieu of corporations when they qualify for favorable partnership tax treatment available to some publicly traded partnerships.

ENTITY TAX CLASSIFICATION

LO 12-2

A business's legal form may be different from its tax form. We discussed the legal form of business entities above. We now discuss the tax form of business entities. In general terms, for tax purposes business entities can be classified as either separate taxpaying entities or **flow-through entities.** Separate taxpaying entities pay tax on their own income. In contrast, flow-through entities generally don't pay taxes because income from these entities flows through to their business owners, who are responsible for paying tax on the income.

How do we determine whether a particular business entity is treated as a separate tax-paying entity or as a flow-through entity for tax purposes? According to Treasury Regulations, commonly referred to as the "check-the-box" regulations, entities that are legal corporations under state law are, by default, treated as **C corporations** for tax purposes. These corporations and their shareholders are subject to tax provisions in Subchapter C (and not Subchapter S) of the Internal Revenue Code.[8] C corporations report their taxable income to the IRS on Form 1120. However, shareholders of *legal* corporations may qualify to make a special tax election known as an "S" election, thus permitting the corporation to be taxed as a flow-through entity called an **S corporation.**[9] S corporations and their shareholders are subject to tax provisions in Subchapter S of the Internal Revenue Code. S corporations report the results of their operations to the IRS on Form 1120S.

Also under the check-the-box regulations, unincorporated entities are, by default, treated as flow-through entities.[10] However, owners of an unincorporated entity can still elect to have their business taxed as a C corporation instead of as the default flow-through entity.[11] In fact, the owner(s) of an unincorporated entity could elect to have the business taxed as a C corporation and then make a second election to have the "C corporation" taxed as an S corporation (provided that it meets the S corporation eligibility requirements).[12] Before making such elections, however, the business owner(s) would need to be convinced that the move makes sense from a tax perspective.[13] The nontax considerations do not change because these elections do not affect the legal classification of the entity.

Finally, unincorporated flow-through entities (all flow-through entities except S corporations) are treated for tax purposes as either partnerships, sole proprietorships, or **disregarded entities** (considered to be the same entity as the owner).[14] Unincorporated entities (including LLCs) with more than one owner are treated as partnerships.[15] Partnerships report their operating results to the IRS on Form 1065. Unincorporated entities (including LLCs) with only one *individual* owner such as sole proprietorships and **single-member LLCs** are treated as sole proprietorships.[16] Income from businesses taxed as sole proprietorships is reported on Schedule C of Form 1040. Similarly, unincorporated entities with only one *corporate* owner, typically a single-member LLC, are disregarded for tax purposes. Thus, income and losses from this single, corporate-member LLC is reported as if it had originated from a division of the corporation and is reported directly on the single-member corporation's return. Exhibit 12-2 provides a flowchart for determining the tax form of a business entity under the check-the-box regulations. Taxpayers check the box by filing Form 8832.

THE KEY FACTS

Tax Classification of Legal Entities

- Corporations are C corporations unless they make a valid S election.
- Unincorporated entities are taxed as partnerships if they have more than one owner.
- Unincorporated entities are taxed as sole proprietorships if held by a single individual or as disregarded entities if held by a single entity.
- Unincorporated entities may elect to be treated as C corporations. They then may make an S election if eligible.

---

[8]Reg. §301.7701-3(a).

[9]§1362(a). Because §1361 limits the number and type of shareholders of corporations qualifying to make an S election, some corporations are ineligible to become S corporations.

[10]Reg. §301.7701-3(b). However, §7704 mandates that unincorporated publicly traded entities be taxed as corporations unless their income predominately consists of certain types of passive income.

[11]Reg. §301.7701-3(a).

[12]In general, a noncorporate entity that is eligible to elect to be treated as a corporation can elect to be treated as a corporation for tax purposes and as an S corporation in one step by filing a timely S corporation election.

[13]As presented in Exhibit 12-3, compared to corporations, unincorporated entities taxed as partnerships have more favorable ownership requirements and more favorable tax treatment on nonliquidating and liquidating distributions of noncash property.

[14]Reg. §301.7701-3(a).

[15]Reg. §301.7701-3(b)(i).

[16]Reg. §301.7701-3(b)(ii).

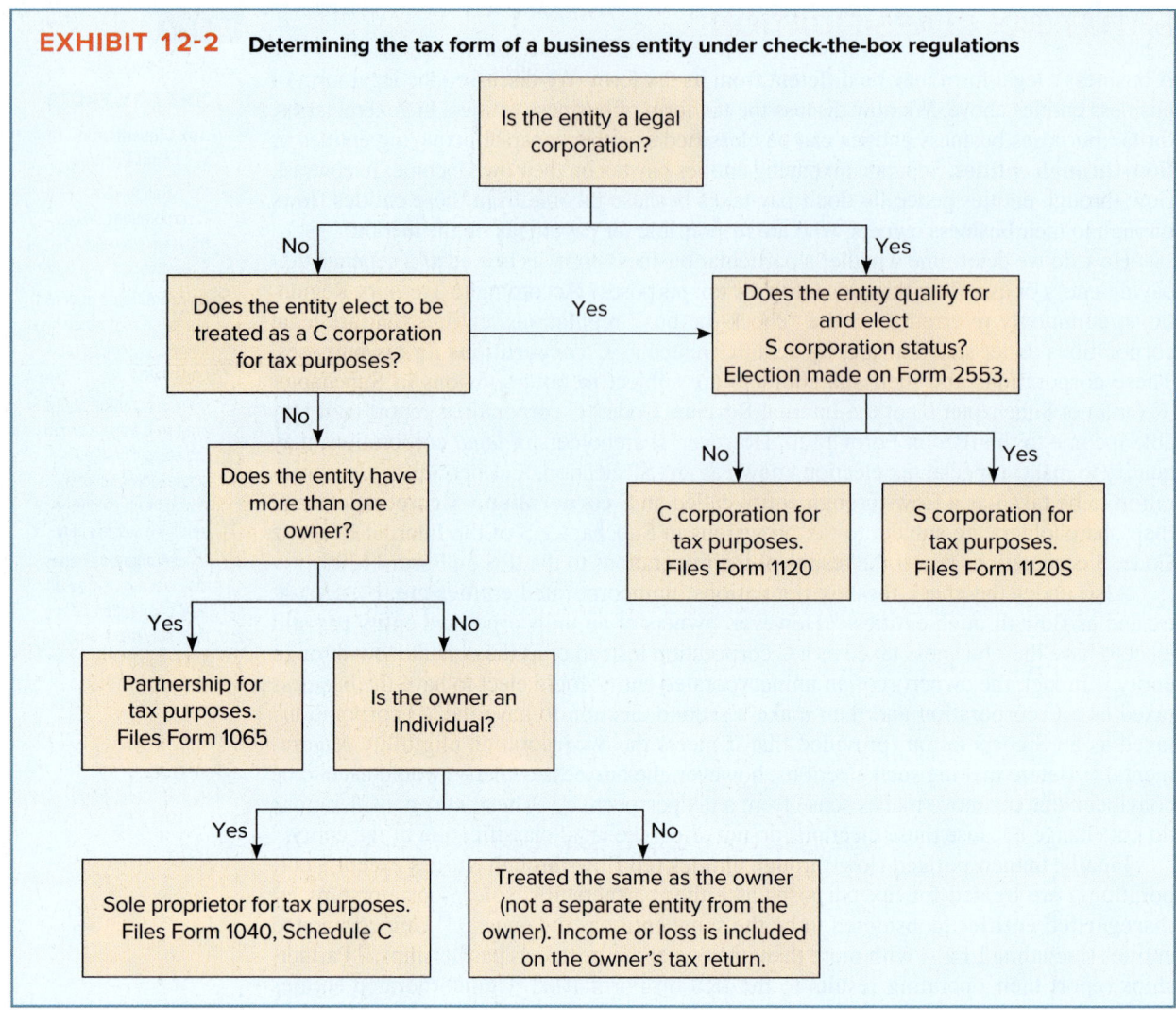

EXHIBIT 12-2   **Determining the tax form of a business entity under check-the-box regulations**

To summarize, although there are other types of legal entities, there are really only four categories of business entities recognized by the U.S. tax system, as follows:

1. C corporation (separate taxpaying entity; income reported on Form 1120).
2. S corporation (flow-through entity; income reported on Form 1120S).
3. Partnership (flow-through entity; income reported on Form 1065).
4. Sole proprietorship (flow-through entity; income reported on Form 1040, Schedule C).

Example 12-1

What if: Assume Nicole legally forms CCS as a corporation (with only common stock) by filing articles of incorporation with the state. What are her options for classifying CCS for tax purposes if she is the only shareholder of CCS?

Answer: Nicole may treat CCS as either a C corporation or an S corporation. The default tax classification is a C corporation for tax purposes. However, given the facts provided, CCS is eligible to make an election to be taxed as an S corporation.[17]

[17]§1361(b).

> **What if:** Assume Nicole legally forms CCS as an LLC (with only one class of ownership rights) by filing articles of organization with the state. What are her options for classifying CCS for tax purposes if she is the only member of CCS?
>
> **Answer:** The default classification for CCS is a sole proprietorship because CCS is unincorporated with one individual member. However, Nicole may elect to have CCS taxed as a C corporation or as an S corporation. CCS can be treated as a C corporation because unincorporated entities may elect to be taxed as corporations. Further, eligible entities taxed as corporations can elect to be treated as S corporations. Given the facts provided, CCS is eligible to elect to be treated as a corporation and to be treated as an S corporation.
>
> **What if:** Assume Nicole legally forms CCS as an LLC and allows other individuals or business entities to become members in return for contributing their cash, property, or services to CCS. What is the default tax classification of CCS under these assumptions?
>
> **Answer:** Partnership. The default tax classification for unincorporated entities with more than one owner is a partnership.

It might seem at this point that owners of businesses classified as flow-through entities would be treated the same for tax purposes; however, that is true only in a general sense. We see in this and other chapters that there are subtle and not-so-subtle differences in ways the owners of ventures classified as S corporations, partnerships, and sole proprietorships are taxed.[18]

ENTITY TAX CHARACTERISTICS

`LO 12-3`

In choosing among the available options for the tax form of business entities, owners and their advisers must carefully consider whether tax rules that apply to a particular tax classification would be either more or less favorable than tax rules under other alternative tax classifications. The specific tax rules they must compare and contrast are unique to their situations; however, certain key differences in the tax rules tend to be relevant in many scenarios. We turn our attention to the taxation of business entity income, owner compensation, and the tax treatment of entity losses, because these are a few of the most important tax characteristics to consider when selecting the tax form of the entity. Later in the chapter we preview other tax factors that differ between entities, and we identify the chapter where each factor is discussed in detail.

Taxation of Business Entity Income

The taxation of a business entity's income depends on whether the entity is a flow-through entity or a C corporation. Flow-through entity income is taxed once to the owner when the income "flows through" or is allocated (on paper) to entity owners at the end of the year, whether or not the income is distributed to them. The income is included on the owners' tax returns as if they had earned the income themselves. Flow-through entity owners are not, however, taxed when the income is actually distributed to them. C corporation income is taxed twice. The income is first taxed to the corporation at the corporate tax rate. A C corporation's income is taxed again to the shareholders when the corporation distributes the income as a dividend or when the shareholders sell their stock.[19]

The Taxation of Flow-Through Entity Business Income
The tax that flow-through entity owners pay on the entity's business income depends in large part on the owner's marginal income tax rate. For 2017, the maximum marginal tax rate was 39.6 percent.

---

[18]The Business Income, Deductions, and Accounting Methods chapter explains how sole proprietors are taxed, and the Forming and Operating Partnerships, Dispositions of Partnership Interests and Partnership Distributions, and the S Corporations chapters explain how partners and S corporation shareholders are taxed.

[19]Distributions to C corporation shareholders are taxed as dividends to the extent they come from the "earnings and profits" (similar to economic income) of corporations.

For 2018, the top rate declined to 37 percent. Nevertheless, flow-through entity owners' tax burden on the flow through income also depends on whether the income is eligible for the qualified business income deduction, whether it is subject to the net investment income tax, and whether it is subject to self-employment tax and the additional Medicare tax. Below, we discuss the deduction for qualified business income, the net investment income tax, the self-employment tax, the additional Medicare tax, and the overall tax rate on flow-through entity income (assuming the owners are individuals).

Deduction for qualified business income. This deduction applies to individuals with **qualified business income (QBI)** from flow-through entities, including partnerships, S corporations, or sole proprietorships.[20] That is, this is a deduction for individuals not for business entities. In general, a taxpayer can deduct 20 percent of the amount of qualified business income allocated to them from the entity, subject to certain limitations.[21] Qualified business income is the net business income from a qualified trade or business conducted in the United States. To qualify, the business income must be from a business other than a **specified service trade or business.** In general, a specified service trade or business includes all service businesses other than architecture and engineering.[22] Business income does not include income earned as an employee or investment type income such as capital gains, dividends, and investment interest income. The deduction is a *from* AGI deduction but is not an itemized deduction. Therefore, individuals can claim the deduction even though they claim the standard deduction instead of itemized deductions.

Net investment income tax. When an owner of an entity taxed as a partnership or a shareholder of an S corporation does not work for the entity (that is, the owner is a passive owner or investor in the entity), the business income allocated to the taxpayer is considered to be "passive" income.[23] Because passive income is considered to be investment income for purposes of the net investment income tax, passive owners of flow-through entities may be required to pay net investment income tax on income allocated to them from the business. The net investment income tax rate is 3.8 percent and it applies only when a taxpayer's (modified) AGI exceeds certain thresholds. The threshold amount is $250,000 for married taxpayers filing jointly and surviving spouses, $125,000 for married taxpayers filing separately, and $200,000 for all other taxpayers.[24]

Self-employment tax and the additional Medicare tax. Self-employment income is subject to self-employment tax and the additional Medicare tax. Whether a flow-through entity's business income is considered to be self-employment income to an owner depends on the type of entity and the owner's involvement in the entity's business activities.

---

[20]§199A.

[21]Under §199A(b)(2)(B), the deduction cannot exceed the greater of 50 percent of the wages paid with respect to the qualified trade or business, or the sum of 25 percent of the wages with respect to the qualified trade or business plus 2.5 percent of the unadjusted basis, immediately after acquisition, of all qualified property in the qualified trade or business. This limit does not apply to taxpayers with taxable income (before the deduction) below a certain threshold and the limitation phases in over a range of taxable income above the threshold [see §199A(b)(3)]. The limit is applied at the individual owner level and is beyond the scope of this chapter.

[22]§199A(d)(2) defines specified service trade or businesses as any trade or business involving the performance of services in the fields of health, law, accounting, actuarial science, performing arts, consulting, athletics, financial services, brokerage services, or any trade or business where the principal asset of such trade or business is the reputation or skill of one or more of its employees or which involves the performance of services that consist of investing and investment management trading, or dealing in securities, partnership interests, or commodities. The specified service trade or business requirement does not apply to taxpayers with taxable income (before the deduction) below a certain threshold and the requirement phases in over a range of taxable income above the threshold [see §199A(d)(3)].

[23]See §469. We discuss specific tests for determining when an owner is a passive investor in the Forming and Operating Partnerships chapter.

[24]See §1411.

An S corporation's business income allocated to a shareholder is not self-employment income to the shareholder. In contrast, a sole proprietorship's income is self-employment income to the sole proprietor. The determination isn't as clear for the business income allocated to owners of entities taxed as a partnership. For these entities, whether business income is self-employment income to an owner depends on the owner's involvement in the entity's business activities.[25]

When an owner's allocation of business income is determined to be self-employment income, the owner must pay self-employment tax and potentially the additional Medicare tax on the income. Both the self-employment tax and additional Medicare tax are based on the taxpayer's **net earnings from self-employment.** Net earnings from self-employment is 92.35 percent of a taxpayer's self-employment income.[26] For 2018, the self-employment tax is 15.3 percent of the first $128,400 (reduced by compensation received as an employee) of net earnings from self-employment plus 2.9 percent of net earnings from self-employment above $128,400 (reduced by compensation received as an employee). Taxpayers can deduct 50 percent of the self-employment taxes they pay as a *for* AGI deduction. The additional Medicare tax is .9 percent of the earned income (employee compensation plus net earnings from self-employment) in excess of a threshold amount. The threshold amount is $250,000 for married taxpayers filing jointly and surviving spouses, $125,000 for married taxpayers filing separately, and $200,000 for all other taxpayers.[27] Taxpayers are not allowed to deduct any of the additional Medicare tax they pay.

EXAMPLE 12-2

What if: Assume that Nicole chooses to form CCS as an S corporation. She makes the following assumptions:

- CCS's taxable income is $500,000 and all of the income is business income.
- Her marginal ordinary tax rate is 37 percent.
- Nicole is eligible for the full deduction for qualified business income on the flow-through income from CCS.
- The income is not passive income and is therefore not subject to the net investment income tax.
- Because CCS is an S corporation, the flow-through business income from CCS is not self-employment income to Nicole.

What is the overall tax rate on CCS's business income?

Answer: 29.6 percent, computed as follows:

Description	Amount	Explanation
(1) Business income allocated to Nicole	$500,000	
(2) Deduction for qualified business income	(100,000)	(1) × 20 percent
(3) Net taxable income to Nicole from CCS	400,000	(1) + (2)
(4) Earnings after-entity-level tax	37%	Marginal tax rate
(5) Owner-level income tax	148,000	(3) × (4)
Overall tax rate on business income allocation	29.6%	(5)/(1)

(continued on page 12-10)

---

[25]We discuss more details of determining whether business income allocated to partners is self-employment income in the Forming and Operating Partnerships chapter.

[26]See §1402. Taxing 92.35 percent of self-employment income for self-employment tax and additional Medicare tax purposes provides the taxpayer with an implicit 7.65 percent deduction for the employer's portion of the 15.3 percent self-employment tax.

[27]The self-employment tax is assessed on an individual by individual basis. The additional Medicare tax applies to combined earned income of both spouses if married filing jointly.

What if: Assume the original facts except that the income from CCS is not eligible for the deduction for qualified business income. What is the overall tax rate on CCS's business income?

Answer: 37 percent. The entire $500,000 business income is taxed to Nicole at her marginal ordinary tax rate of 37%.

What if: Assume the original facts except the income from CCS is not eligible for the deduction for qualified business income and that Nicole is a passive investor in CCS and Nicole must pay the 3.8 percent net investment income tax on the income. What is the overall tax rate on the income of CCS?

Answer: 40.8 percent. The full $500,000 of business income is taxed to Nicole at her marginal ordinary tax rate of 37 percent plus the net investment income tax rate of 3.8 percent.

EXAMPLE 12-3

What if: Assume that Nicole forms CCS as an LLC with another investor so that CCS is taxed as a partnership. Nicole makes the following assumptions:
- CCS earns business income of $1,000,000 and her share of the business income is $500,000.
- Her marginal ordinary tax rate is 37 percent.
- Nicole is entitled to the full deduction for qualified business income on the flow-through income from CCS.
- Because Nicole works full-time for the entity, the business income allocated to her is self-employment income.
- Nicole's marginal self-employment tax rate is 2.9 percent (other sources of income put her over the $128,400 threshold).
- The income allocation is subject to the additional Medicare tax.

What is the overall tax rate on the CCS business income allocated to Nicole?

Answer: 32.61 percent, computed as follows:

Description	Amount	Explanation
(1) Business income allocated to Nicole	$500,000	
(2) Deduction for qualified business income	(100,000)	(1) × 20 percent
(3) Deduction for 50 percent of self-employment tax	(6,695)	(1) × .9235 × .029 × .5
(4) Income net of Nicole's deductions	393,305	
(5) Owner-level income tax	145,523	(4) × 37 percent
(6) Self-employment tax	13,391	(1) × .9235 × .029
(7) Additional Medicare tax	4,156	(1) × .9235 × .009
(8) Total tax paid on CCS business income allocations	$163,070	(6) + (7) + (8)
Overall tax rate on business income allocation	32.61%	(9)/(1)

What if: Assume the original facts except that the business income allocation is not qualified business income (QBI). What is the overall tax rate on the CCS business income allocated to Nicole?

Answer: 40.01 percent. The only difference between the original and the new facts in this what-if example is that Nicole would pay an additional $37,000 in income tax ($100,000 QBI deduction × 37 percent tax rate). Consequently, the overall taxes due on the business income allocation would be $200,070 ($163,070 + $37,000) and the overall tax rate would be 40.01 percent ($200,070/$500,000).

What if: Assume the original facts except the income from CCS is not eligible for the QBI deduction and that Nicole is a passive investor in CCS so that Nicole must pay the net investment income tax on the income but not the self-employment tax or the additional Medicare tax. What is the overall tax rate on the CCS business income allocated to Nicole?

Answer: 40.8 percent. The entire $500,000 business income allocation is taxed to Nicole at her marginal ordinary tax rate of 37 percent plus the percent net investment income tax rate of 3.8 percent.

In summary, while income from a flow-through entity is taxed only once, the overall tax rate on the entity's business income depends on whether the income (and the owner) qualifies for the deduction for qualified business income and whether the income is subject to the net investment tax or is considered to be self-employment income.

Overall Tax Rate of C Corporation Income

C corporations are taxed on their taxable income at corporate rates. For tax years beginning before 2018, the tax rate depended on where the corporation's taxable income fell in the corporate tax rate schedule. The lowest marginal tax rate for corporations was 15 percent and the top marginal rate was 39 percent. The most profitable corporations were taxed at a flat 35 percent rate. For tax years beginning after 2017, the corporate tax rate has been cut to a flat 21 percent. Thus, for most corporations, corporate tax rates have decreased significantly. The tax rate on the second level of tax on a C corporation's income depends on whether the shareholder is an individual, a C corporation, an **institutional shareholder,** a tax exempt entity, or a foreign entity.

Individual shareholders.   The tax rate on dividends to individual taxpayers depends on the individual's taxable income. High-income taxpayers are taxed on dividends at a 20 percent rate, low-income taxpayers are taxed at a 0 percent rate, and others are taxed on dividends at a 15 percent rate.[28] Also, as discussed above, taxpayers with (modified) AGI in excess of a threshold amount pay an additional 3.8 percent net investment income tax on dividends.

Example 12-4

What if: Assume that Nicole forms CCS as a C corporation and she makes the following assumptions:
- CCS earns taxable income of $500,000.
- CCS will distribute all of its after-tax earnings annually as a dividend.
- Nicole's marginal ordinary tax rate is 37 percent and her dividend tax rate is 23.8 percent (including the net investment income tax).

What is the overall tax rate on CCS's taxable income??

Answer: 39.8 percent, computed as follows:

Description	Amount	Explanation
(1) Taxable income	$ 500,000	
(2) Corporate tax rate	21%	Flat corporate tax rate
(3) Corporate-level tax	**$105,000**	(1) × (2) [first level of tax]
(4) Income remaining after taxes and amount distributed as a dividend	$ 395,000	(1) − (3)
(5) Dividend tax rate	23.8%	20% dividend rate + 3.8% net investment income tax rate
(6) Shareholder-level tax on dividend	**$ 94,010**	(4) × (5) [second level of tax]
(7) Total tax paid on corporate taxable income	**$199,010**	(3) + (6)
Overall tax rate on corporate taxable income	**39.8%**	(7)/(1)

Note that the overall rate is not 44.8 percent (21 percent corporate rate + 23.8 percent shareholder rate) because the amount of corporate-level tax ($105,000) is income that is not taxed twice (it is paid to the government, not to the shareholders).

(continued on page 12-12)

---

[28]To the extent the dividend income increases a taxpayer's taxable income beyond specific "breakpoints" the dividend is taxed at a higher rate. For 2018, the breakpoint between the 0 and 15 percent rate is $77,200 for married taxpayers filing jointly, $51,700 for head of household filers, and $38,600 for all other taxpayers. The breakpoint between the 15 percent and 20 percent rate is $479,000 for married taxpayers filing jointly, $239,500 for married taxpayers filing separately, $425,800 for single taxpayers, and $452,400 for head of household filers.

What if: Assume that Nicole forms CCS as a C corporation and she makes the following assumptions:
- CCS earns taxable income of $500,000.
- CCS distributes 25 percent of its after-tax earnings as a dividend and retains the rest to grow the business.
- Nicole's marginal ordinary tax rate is 37 percent and her dividend tax rate is 23.8 percent (including the net investment income tax).

Answer: 25.7 percent, computed as follows:

Description	Amount	Explanation
(1) Taxable income	$ 500,000	
(2) Corporate tax rate	21%	Flat corporate tax rate
(3) Corporate-level tax	**$105,000**	(1) × (2) [first level of tax]
(4) Income remaining after taxes and amount distributed as a dividend	$ 395,000	(1) − (3)
(5) Dividend	$98,750	(4) × 25% distributed
(6) Dividend tax rate	23.8%	20% dividend rate + 3.8% net investment income tax rate
(7) Shareholder-level tax on dividend	**$ 23,503**	(5) × (6) [second level of tax]
(8) Total tax paid on corporate taxable income	**$128,503**	(3) + (7)
Overall tax rate on corporate taxable income	**25.7%**	(8)/(1)

The overall tax rate is lower in this situation because CCS retains most of its after-tax income and thus protects that portion of its income from immediate double taxation. If CCS retained all of its after-tax earnings, the current overall tax rate on its income would have been 21 percent (the corporate tax rate). Also, while the overall tax rate is lower when CCS distributes less of its income, Nicole also receives less cash from the business ends up with less cash from the business.

Shareholders that are C corporations. Shareholders that are C corporations are taxed on dividends at 21 percent, the same rate as they are taxed on ordinary income. In addition, dividends received by a corporation are potentially subject to another (third) level of tax when the corporation receiving the dividend distributes its earnings as dividends to its shareholders. This potential for more than two levels of tax on the same before-tax earnings prompted Congress to allow corporations to claim the **dividends received deduction** (DRD). In the next chapter, we discuss the DRD in detail, but the underlying concept is that a corporation *receiving* a dividend is allowed to deduct a certain percentage of the dividend from its taxable income to offset the potential for additional layers of taxation on the dividend when it distributes the dividend to its shareholders. For tax years beginning before 2018, the dividends received deduction percentage was 70, 80, or 100 percent of the dividend received, depending on the level of the recipient corporation's ownership in the dividend-paying corporation's stock. For tax years beginning after 2017, the dividends received deduction is reduced to 50, 65, or 100 percent. Thus, for tax years beginning after 2017, a corporation's net tax rate on a dividend received is 10.5 percent if it claims a 50 percent DRD [.21 tax rate × (1 minus .5 DRD)], 7.35 percent if it claims a 65 percent DRD [.21 tax rate × (1 minus .65 DRD)], and 0 percent if it claims a 100 percent DRD [.21 × (1 minus 1.0 DRD)].

Example 12-5

What if: Assume that Nicole invites a corporation to invest in CCS in exchange for a 10 percent share in the company. Nicole makes the following assumptions as part of her calculations:
- CCS is a C corporation.
- CCS earns taxable income of $500,000.
- CCS will pay out all of its after-tax earnings annually as a dividend.

Given these assumptions, what would be the overall tax rate on the corporate investor's share of CCS's income given that the corporation would be eligible for the 50 percent dividends received deduction?

CHAPTER 12   Entities Overview   **12-13**

Answer: 29.3 percent, computed as follows:

Description	Amount	Explanation
(1) Taxable income	$500,000	
(2) Corporate tax rate	21%	
(3) Entity-level tax	$105,000	(1) × (2) [first level of tax]
(4) After-tax income	$395,000	(1) − (3)
(5) Corporate investor's dividend	$39,500	(4) × 10%
(6) Taxable dividend	$19,750	(5) × (1 − 50% DRD)
(7) Corporate investor's share of entity-level tax	$10,500	(3) × 10% investor's share
(8) Corporate investor's tax on dividend	$4,148	(6) × 21% corporate tax rate
(9) Total tax paid on corporate taxable income	$14,648	(7) + (8)
Overall tax rate on corporate taxable income	**29.3%**	(9)/[(1) × 10% investor's share]

Note: The income of the corporate shareholder will be taxed again when the corporate shareholder distributes it to its own shareholders.

Institutional shareholders.   Pension and retirement funds are some of the largest institutional shareholders of corporations. However, these entities do not pay shareholder-level tax on the dividends they receive. Ultimately, retirees pay the second tax on this income when they receive retirement distributions from these funds. While retirees pay the second tax at ordinary rates, not the reduced dividend rates, they are able to defer the tax until they receive fund distributions.

Tax-exempt and foreign shareholders.   Tax-exempt organizations such as churches and universities are exempt from tax on their investment income, including dividend income from investments in corporate stock. Similarly, foreign investors may be eligible for reduced rates on dividend income depending on the tax treaty, if any, their country of residence has signed with the United States.

As we discuss and illustrate above, C corporation income is subject to **double taxation.** The first tax is paid by the corporation when it earns the income and the second tax is paid by the shareholder when the corporation distributes its earnings as dividends to shareholders. Can C corporations avoid the second level of tax entirely by not paying dividends? The answer is generally no because even when corporations retain after-tax income, their shareholders pay the second level of tax at capital gains rates on the undistributed income when they sell their stock because the undistributed income indirectly increases the value of their stock and thus increases their gain when they sell the stock. Assuming the shareholder is an individual and the shareholder owns stock in a corporation for more than a year, the gain is taxed at the same rates as the tax rates on qualified dividends we discussed above (0, 15, or 20 plus 3.8 percent net investment income tax for higher income taxpayers). Because this second level of tax is deferred until taxpayers sell their stock, the longer they hold the stock, the less the tax cost on a present value basis. In the extreme, taxpayers can avoid the second level of income tax completely on their stock appreciation by holding the stock until death. At death, gain built into the stock is eliminated because the stock takes basis equal to the value of the stock on the date of death.[29] Shareholders other than individuals will face different tax consequences when they sell their shares. When shareholders that

[29]See §1014.

are C corporations eventually sell the stock they are taxed on capital gains at a flat 21 percent tax rate. Consequently, income from stock appreciation may expose income to *more* than two levels of taxation because capital gains from selling stock doesn't qualify for the dividends received deduction. Also, institutional shareholders don't pay tax when they sell their stock and recognize capital gains. However, retirees generally pay tax on the gains at ordinary rates when they receive distributions from their retirement accounts. Finally, tax-exempt shareholders do not pay tax on capital gains from selling stock, and foreign investors are generally not subject to U.S. tax on their capital gains from selling corporate stock.

Finally, the tax law provides incentives for C corporations to distribute income rather than to retain it for the purpose of avoiding the second level of tax. First, **personal holding companies** (closely held corporations generating primarily investment income) are subject to a 20 percent **personal holding company tax** on their undistributed income.[30] Second, corporations that retain earnings for the purpose of avoiding the second level of tax are subject to a 20 percent **accumulated earnings tax** on the retained earnings.[31] Corporations are not considered to be retaining earnings for tax avoidance purposes, and are not subject to the accumulated earnings tax to the extent they reinvest the earnings in assets necessary for their business or to the extent they retain liquid assets for reasonable planned needs of the business.

Under the tax rate system prior to 2018, flow-through entities were generally considered to be superior to corporations for tax purposes because they generated income that was taxed only once while corporations produced income that was taxed twice, with the first level of tax imposed at a rate comparable to the individual tax rate. However, for years after 2017, under new tax law, the corporate tax rate is significantly lower than the maximum individual tax rate. Further, new tax law provides a deduction for qualified business income (QBI) for individuals who are owners of flow-through entities. This tax legislation makes the optimal choice of entity based on overall tax rates of the entity's business income less clear than it was under prior law. It is important to note, however, that the corporate tax rate reduction is a permanent change while the QBI deduction is scheduled to expire in 2026. The overall tax rate on a flow-through entity's business income depends on whether the flow-through entity's business income is eligible for the QBI deduction and whether the income is subject to the net investment income tax or the self-employment tax and the additional Medicare tax. For C corporations, the overall tax rate depends in large part on the extent to which the corporation distributes its after-tax earnings as a dividend to its shareholders. As we saw in Example 12-2, the overall tax rate on CCS's taxable income as a flow-through entity ranged from 29.6 percent to 40.8 percent depending on whether the QBI deduction and the net investment income tax applied. In Example 12-4, the overall tax rate on CCS's taxable income as a C corporation ranged from 21 percent when CCS retained all of its after-tax income to 39.8 percent when it distributed all of its after-tax income.

Owner Compensation

Entity owners who work for the entity are compensated in different ways, depending on the entity type. Owners of S corporations and C corporations receive compensation as employees. Owners of flow-through entities taxed as partnerships receive compensation in the form of guaranteed payments. Sole proprietors don't receive a separate compensation payment because a sole proprietorship is the same entity as the individual sole proprietor.

S corporations and C corporations deduct the wages paid to shareholders/employees to calculate the entity's business income. They also pay (and deduct) the employer's portion of the FICA tax (social security tax plus Medicare tax) on the employee's behalf. The employer's portion of the tax is 7.65 percent of the employee's first $128,400 of

---

[30]§541.

[31]See §§531–533.

employee compensation and 1.45 percent of employee compensation above $128,400. The shareholder/employee is taxed on the wages received at ordinary rates and is required to pay the employee's portion of the FICA tax, which is generally the same as the employer's portion. When considering both the employer's and employee's portions of the FICA tax, the overall FICA rate is 15.3 percent of the first $128,400 of wages and 2.9 percent of the rest. This is the same rate as the self-employment tax rate. Also, similar to self-employment income, employee compensation is subject to the additional Medicare tax when the taxpayer's AGI is over the threshold amount (discussed above).

Entities taxed as partnerships deduct guaranteed payments made to owners working for the entity. However, the entity is not required to pay FICA tax on the owner-worker's behalf because guaranteed payments are self-employment income and self-employment taxes are the sole responsibility of the owner-worker.[32] The owner-worker is taxed on the amount of the guaranteed payment at ordinary rates and is required to pay self-employment tax and potentially additional Medicare tax on the income, depending on their income level (see prior discussion on computing the self-employment tax). A sole proprietorship does not pay deductible compensation to the sole proprietor. All of the income of a sole proprietorship is self-employment income and, consequently, is subject to self-employment tax and the additional Medicare tax.

Owner compensation provides potential tax planning opportunities, depending on the type of entity. For S corporations, business income allocations to owners are not subject to FICA or self-employment tax. However, wages paid to owner/employees are subject to FICA tax. (Recall that the combined employer/employee FICA rate is the same as the self-employment tax rate.) Consequently, as we discuss in the S corporations chapter, S corporations have a tax incentive to pay lower salary/wages to shareholders/employees that is subject to FICA tax so there is more business income to allocate to shareholders/employees that is not subject to FICA or self-employment tax (lower deductible wages means higher business income allocations). Further, S corporations have an incentive to reduce wages to shareholder/employees in order to increase business income because employee compensation is not eligible for the deduction for qualified business income, but business income allocations to shareholders are eligible. In the extreme, S corporations may prefer to pay zero wages to shareholders/employees in order to maximize business income allocations to them. However, to the extent an S corporation shareholder receives an unreasonably low salary for the services provided, the IRS may reclassify some of the shareholder's business income allocation as salary.

In contrast to S corporations, entities taxed as partnerships don't have an incentive to decrease guaranteed payments in order to increase business income allocations in an attempt to save self-employment taxes to owners. This is because both guaranteed payments and business income allocations are self-employment income to the owner-worker. However, similar to S corporations, entities taxed as partnerships have an incentive to reduce guaranteed payments to owner-workers in order to increase business income allocations to them because guaranteed payments are not eligible for the qualified business income but allocations of business income are eligible. Finally, relative to both S corporations and entities taxed as partnerships, sole proprietorships may be the most advantageous for purposes of maximizing the qualified business income deduction in certain situations. This is because the sole proprietorship's qualifying business income is not reduced by a deduction for compensation paid to the owner/ sole proprietor.

For C corporations, tax planning opportunities have potentially shifted with the steep reduction in the corporate tax rate relative to individual rates. Prior to the rate reduction, corporations could avoid double taxation of their income by paying deductible salaries to shareholders/employees. This income would be taxed once to the employee at ordinary

---

[32]Taxpayers pay self-employment tax on self-employment income and FICA taxes on employee compensation.

rates that are similar to the corporate rate. The IRS could evaluate compensation to employee/shareholders to determine if the compensation was unreasonably high for the work the employee/shareholder was doing and, to the extent it was, reclassify the excess compensation as nondeductible dividends. Currently, however, with the corporate rate significantly lower than the maximum individual rate, corporations have an incentive to pay lower salaries to shareholders/employees in order to have more of their income taxed at the lower corporate rate. By reducing deductible salaries, more of the corporate income is subject to tax at the lower 21 percent tax rate. If the income is paid as salaries, it will be subject to the individual rate (top rate is 37 percent) and subject to both the employer and employee's portion of the FICA tax. This type of strategy is more likely to be useful for closely held corporations where all of the owners work for the corporation. It remains to be seen how the IRS will respond to such strategies.

While the overall tax rate of an entity's income and the tax treatment of owner compensation are important entity choice factors, it is important to consider the tax treatment of the entity's losses and other tax characteristics when choosing a tax entity for a new business.

Deductibility of Entity Losses

When a C corporation's tax deductions exceed its income for the year, the excess is called a **net operating loss (NOL).** While NOLs provide no tax benefit to C corporations for the year they incur them, corporations may use NOLs to offset corporate taxable income and reduce corporate taxes in other years. The specific tax treatment for a NOL depends on when the NOL was generated. For NOLs generated in tax years ending before 2018, corporations could carry the NOLs back and offset up to 100 percent of taxable income (before the NOL deduction) reported in the two preceding years and carry it forward to offset up to 100 percent of taxable income for up to 20 years. Under new tax law, corporations can carry NOLs generated in tax years ending after 2017 forward indefinitely but they are not allowed to carry them back. Further, the deduction for post 2017 NOLs is limited to 80 percent of taxable income (before the NOL deduction) for a given year.[33] In any event, losses from C corporations are *not* available to offset shareholders' personal income.

In contrast to losses generated by C corporations, losses generated by sole proprietorships and other flow-through entities are generally available to offset the owners' personal income, subject to certain restrictions. For example, the owner of an entity taxed as a partnership or an S corporation shareholder may deduct losses from the entity only to the extent of the owner's basis in her ownership interest in the flow-through entity. In addition, deductibility of losses from flow-through entities may be further limited by the at-risk and passive activity loss limitation. The at-risk limitation is similar to the basis limitation but slightly more restrictive. The passive activity loss limitation typically applies to individual investors who are passive investors in the flow-through entity. For passive investors, the business activities of the entity are called passive activities. In these circumstances, taxpayers can deduct losses from passive activities only to the extent they have income from other passive activities. Due to the complex nature of these limitations, we defer a detailed discussion of these limitations until the Forming and Operating Partnerships chapter.

For tax years beginning after 2017, individual taxpayers are not allowed to deduct an **"excess business loss"** for the year. An excess business loss is the excess of aggregate business deductions for the year over the sum of aggregate business gross income or gain of the taxpayer plus a threshold amount. The threshold amount for a tax year is $500,000 for married taxpayers filing jointly and $250,000 for other taxpayers. The amounts are indexed for inflation. Excess business losses include business losses from sole proprietorships, entities taxed as partnerships, and S corporations. In the case of an S corporation or of an entity

---

[33]We discuss the net operating loss deduction in more detail in the Corporate Operations chapter.

taxed as a partnership, the provision applies at the owner level. Excess business losses are carried forward and used in subsequent years. The excess business loss limitation applies to losses that are otherwise deductible after applying the basis, at-risk, and passive loss rules. See the Forming and Operating Partnerships chapter for more details.

The ability to deduct flow-through losses against other sources of income can be a significant issue for owners of new businesses because new businesses tend to report losses early on as the businesses get established. If owners form a new business as a C corporation, the corporate-level losses provide no current tax benefit to the shareholders. The fact that C corporation losses are trapped at the corporate level can impose a higher tax cost for shareholders initially doing business as a C corporation relative to a flow-through entity such as an S corporation or an entity taxed as a partnership.

TAXES IN THE REAL WORLD Will Entity Selection Be Affected by the New Tax Law?

In its Statistics of Income Tax Report, the Internal Revenue Service reported the following information relating to tax entity selection by business owners as of 2013 (the most recent year reported). Sole proprietorships were the most common followed by S corporations, entities taxed as partnerships, and then C corporations. Nevertheless, C corporations by far generated the most business entity receipts and net income. Under recent tax legislation, the C corporation tax rate was reduced from 35 percent to 21 percent and owners of flow-through entities are allowed a new deduction for qualified business income generated by the entity. Going forward, how do you expect the percentage of each entity type to change, if at all, under the new tax system? It is likely we will see a shift toward C corporations as the entity of choice?

	Number of Entities	Business Receipts	Net Income (including deficits)
Totals for all entities	33,423,187	$33,260,092,484	$3,065,208,464
Entity Type	**Percentage**	**Percentage**	**Percentage**
C corporations	4.82	61.24	46.64
S corporations	12.74	20.55	17.93
General partnerships	1.69	1.22	3.56
Limited partnerships	1.25	3.89	10.00
LLCs (taxed as partnerships)	6.84	9.02	9.72
Sole proprietorships (nonfarm)	72.03	4.09	12.15
Other*	.63	0	0

*Other includes Real Estate Investment Trusts (REITs) and Regulated Investment Companies (RICs). Neither type of entity has business receipts or net income.

Source: https://www.irs.gov/statistics/soi-tax-stats-integrated-business-data Tax Year 2013.

ETHICS

Troy is the sole shareholder and CEO of BQT. BQT is a very profitable S corporation. Until recently, Troy's salary was in line with the salaries of comparable CEOs. However, Troy recently learned that he could reduce his tax burden if he were to reduce his salary. In particular, by lowering his salary Troy would receive less employee compensation that is subject to FICA tax and is not eligible for the qualified business income deduction, and he would be allocated more business income that is not subject to FICA tax and qualifies for the qualified business income deduction. After considering the potential benefits, Troy decided to cut his salary in half. Do you think Troy's decision is ethical? Why or why not?

THE KEY FACTS

Taxation of Entity Income

- Flow-through entity income is taxed at the owner's tax rate. Individuals are taxed at a top marginal income rate of 37 percent on business income allocated to them from a flow-through entity.
- Flow-through entity owners who receive qualified business income from a flow-through entity are allowed to claim a qualified business income deduction equal to 20 percent of the qualified business income allocated to them (subject to certain limitations).
- Business income allocations to passive owners of flow-through entities may be subject to the 3.8 percent net investment income tax.
- Business income allocated to S corporation shareholders is not subject to self-employment tax.
- Owners of entities taxed as a partnership may be subject to self-employment tax on business income allocations, depending on the owner's involvement in the business activities.
- Sole proprietors are subject to self-employment tax on the sole proprietorship's income.
- C corporation taxable income is subject to a flat 21 percent tax rate.
- Individuals who are C corporation shareholders are generally taxed at a maximum rate of 20 percent on dividends received. Further, certain taxpayers may be charged a 3.8 percent net investment income tax on dividends and capital gains.
- C corporation shareholders that are themselves C corporations are generally eligible to receive a 50 percent or greater dividends received deduction (DRD).

(continued)

> ### Example 12-6
>
> - C corporation shareholders who are individuals generally pay capital gains taxes when shares are sold at a gain.
> - S corporation and C corporation shareholders receive employee compensation for work they do for the entity.
> - Owner-workers for entities taxed as a partnership receive compensation in the form of guaranteed payments. Guaranteed payments are self-employment income.
>
> **What if:** Assume that Nicole organizes CCS as a C corporation and that, in spite of her best efforts as CEO of the company, CCS reports a tax loss of $50,000 in its first year of operation (year 1). Also assume that Nicole's marginal tax rate is 37 percent and her husband's salary for year 1 is $200,000. Nicole files a joint tax return with her husband. How much tax will CCS pay in year 1 and how much tax will Nicole (and her husband) pay on the $200,000 of other taxable income if CCS is organized as a C corporation?
>
> **Answer:** CCS will pay $0 in taxes because it reports a loss for tax purposes. However, CCS can carry the loss forward to future years and can use the loss to offset up to 80 percent of its taxable income in a given year. Because Nicole may not use the CCS loss to offset her husband's salary, she (and her husband) must pay $74,000 in taxes. See the computations in the table below.
>
> **What if:** Suppose CCS is organized as an S corporation and Nicole's stock basis in CCS before the year 1 loss is $100,000. How much tax will CCS pay in year 1, and how much tax will Nicole (and her husband) pay on the $200,000 salary?
>
> **Answer:** CCS will pay $0 taxes (S corporations are not taxpaying entities) and Nicole will pay $55,500 in taxes. See the computations in the table below.
>
> | Description | C Corporation | S Corporation (flow-through) | Explanation |
> |---|---|---|---|
> | (1) Taxable income (loss) | $ (50,000) | $ (50,000) | |
> | **(2) CCS corporate-level tax** | $ 0 | $ 0 | No taxable income |
> | (3) Nicole's other income | $200,000 | $200,000 | |
> | (4) CCS loss available to offset Nicole's other income | $ 0 | $ (50,000) | $0 if C corp. (1) if S corporation (flow-through entity) |
> | (5) Nicole's other income reduced by entity loss | $200,000 | $150,000 | (3) + (4) |
> | (6) Nicole's marginal ordinary tax rate | 37% | 37% | |
> | **Nicole's tax on other income** | **$ 74,000** | **$ 55,500** | (5) × (6) |
>
> **What if:** Suppose CCS is organized as an S corporation and Nicole's stock basis before the $50,000 year 1 loss is $100,000. Further, assume that Nicole does not participate in CCS's business activities; that is, assume she is a passive investor in the business entity. How much tax will Nicole (and her husband) pay on the $200,000 of other income?
>
> **Answer:** $74,000. Because Nicole is a passive investor, she is not allowed to deduct the loss allocated to her this year. She must carry it over and use it in future years (this assumes neither Nicole nor her husband have income from other investments in which they are passive investors).

As the example above illustrates, owners' ability to immediately use start-up losses from flow-through entities to offset income from other sources is a tax advantage of flow-through entities over C corporations.

OTHER TAX CHARACTERISTICS

There are many tax factors that differ across entities and can influence the entity selection decision. Exhibit 12-3 provides an overview of these tax characteristics. The exhibit describes the general rules for each tax characteristic as it relates to C corporations, S corporations, entities taxed as partnerships, and sole proprietorships, and it ranks the entities on each characteristic (1 is most tax favorable). Finally, it identifies the chapters where detail on these tax characteristics can be found.

EXHIBIT 12-3   Comparison of Tax Characteristics across Entities

Tax Characteristic	C Corporation	Entity Taxed as Partnership	S Corporation	Sole Proprietorship	Summary
Owner limits	At least one shareholder.	At least two owners.	Not more than 100; no corporations, partnerships, nonresident aliens, or certain trusts.	N/A	Limitations are least strict for C corporations and most strict for S corporations. S corporations are the only entity with significant owner limitations. More detail for this factor is discussed in the S Corporations chapter.
Rank[1]	1	2	3	N/A	
Owner contributions of appreciated property to entity	Tax deferred to shareholder if certain requirements are met.	Tax deferred to owner.	Tax deferred to shareholder if certain requirements are met.	N/A	This factor favors entities taxed as partnerships because partners are not required to meet special requirements in order to avoid recognizing gain on the contribution of appreciated property to the partnership, but shareholders of both C and S corporations are required to meet certain requirements to avoid recognizing gain on such contributions to the corporation. More detail for this factor is provided in the Corporate Formation, Reorganization, and Liquidation, the Forming and Operating Partnerships, and the S Corporations chapters.
Rank	2	1	2	N/A	
Accounting periods	Generally, any tax year that ends on the last day of any month.[2]	Generally, must use tax year that matches tax year of owners (special rules when not all owners have same tax year-end).	Calendar year.	Generally a calendar year.	C corporations generally have the most flexibility to select their year-end. But because C corporations are not flow-through entities, this is not a real advantage or disadvantage from a tax perspective. Partnerships generally are not free to choose their year-end but they can have a year-end that is a different year-end from some of the owners. Because this allows some partners to defer reporting income, this factor favors partnerships over S corporations. S corporations generally have the same calendar year-end as their shareholders. More detail for this factor is provided in the Business Income, Deductions, and Accounting Methods, the Forming and Operating Partnerships, and the S Corporations chapters.
Rank	2	1	2	N/A	
Overall accounting method	Generally, must use accrual method unless smaller corporation.[3]	Generally, allowed to use cash or accrual method.	Generally, allowed to use cash or accrual method.	Cash or accrual method.	Entities taxed as partnerships, S corporations, and sole proprietorships generally have more flexibility to choose their overall accounting method than do C corporations. The cash method makes it easier for these entities to plan the timing of income and expenses than does the accrual method. More detail for this factor is provided in the Business Income, Deductions, and Accounting Methods, the Corporate Operations, the Forming and Operating Partnerships, and the S Corporations chapters.
Rank	4	1	1	1	
Allocation of income or loss items to owners	N/A	Allocations based on partnership agreement (can differ from ownership percentages).	Allocations based on stock ownership percentages.	N/A	This factor applies to partnerships and S corporations only. Partnerships have more flexibility than S corporations to determine how to allocate income and loss items to entity owners. More detail for this factor is provided in the Forming and Operating Partnerships and the S Corporations chapters.
Rank	N/A	1	2	N/A	

(continued on page 12-20)

Tax Characteristic	C Corporation	Entity Taxed as Partnership	S Corporation	Sole Proprietorship	Summary
Share of flow-through entity debt included in basis of owner's equity interest	N/A	Increase basis in ownership interest by owner's share of entity's debt.	No increase in stock basis for debt of entity (special rules if shareholder lends money to S corporation).	N/A	Partners are allowed to increase the basis in their ownership interest by their share of the partnership's debt; S corporation shareholders generally are not. This factor favors partnerships over S corporations. More detail for this factor is provided in the the Forming and Operating Partnerships and the S Corporations chapters.
Rank	N/A	1	2	N/A	
Nonliquidating distributions of noncash property	Gains recognized on distributions of appreciated property and losses disallowed on distributions of appreciated property.	Generally no gain or loss recognized on noncash property distributions.	Same as C corporation.	N/A	This factor favors partnerships for distributions of appreciated and depreciated property. More detail for this factor is provided in the Corporate Taxation: Nonliquidating Distributions, the Dispositions of Partnership Interests and Partnership Distributions, and the S Corporations chapters.
Rank	2	1	1	N/A	
Liquidating distributions	Gain and loss (certain losses disallowed).	Generally no gain or loss.	Gain and loss (certain losses disallowed).	N/A	This factor tends to favor partnerships if the liquidating entities have gain assets, and it tends to favor corporations if the entities have loss assets. More detail for this factor is provided in the Corporate Formation, Reorganization, and Liquidation, the Dispositions of Partnership Interests and Partnership Distributions, and the S Corporations chapters.
Rank	1	1	1	N/A	

[1]"Rank" orders the entities based on the particular characteristic (1 is most favorable).

[2]C corporations that qualify as personal service corporations (PSCs) are generally required to use a calendar year. In general, a personal service corporation is a corporation whose shareholders perform professional services such as law, engineering, and accounting. See §448(d)(2) for more detail.

[3]For tax years before 2018, corporations with average gross receipts in excess of $5 million over the three prior years could not use the cash method. For tax years beginning after 2017, the gross receipts test limit for the cash method was increased to $25 million.

[4]C corporations that are qualified personal service corporations are required to use the cash method.

Converting to Other Entity Types

With the significant reduction in corporate tax rates for tax years beginning after 2017, owners of existing flow-through entities may reevaluate their entity status and determine whether they prefer to have their entity taxed as a C corporation rather than as a flow-through entity. Fortunately for flow-through entity owners wanting to change entity type, it is easy and inexpensive to convert flow-through entities, including sole proprietorships, into C corporations. Owners of S corporations can revoke their election to be taxed as an S corporation and be taxed as a C corporation (see the S Corporations chapter for details on this process). As we discussed in the Entity Tax Classification section of this chapter, owners of entities taxed as partnerships and sole proprietors doing business as an LLC can retain the same legal entity type but make a check-the-box election to be taxed as a C corporation. Alternatively, owners of partnerships and sole proprietors can contribute the assets of the business entity to a newly formed corporation in a tax-deferred transaction without any special tax elections.[34] However, because this alternative involves creating a new legal entity, nontax factors (e.g., cost of creating a new entity, changing asset title to new entity, etc.) may make this option less desirable than the check-the-box election to be taxed as a C corporation.

Conversely, with the new tax law providing a deduction for qualified business income and slightly lower individual tax rates, C corporation shareholders may prefer to have their business taxed as a flow-through entity rather than as a C corporation. Shareholders of existing corporations really have only two options for converting into flow-through entities. First, shareholders of C corporations could make an election to treat the corporation as an S corporation (flow-through entity), if they are eligible to do so. This option is not available for many corporations due to the tax rule restrictions prohibiting certain corporations from operating as S corporations.[35] The only other option is for the shareholders to liquidate the corporation and form the business as an entity taxed as a partnership or sole proprietorship for tax purposes. This may not be a viable option, however, because the taxes imposed on liquidating corporations with appreciated assets can be punitive, even with the significantly lower corporate tax rate under the new law. As described in Exhibit 12-3, liquidating corporations are taxed on the appreciation in the assets they distribute to their shareholders in liquidation. Further, shareholders of liquidating corporations are also taxed on the difference between the fair market value of the assets they receive from the liquidating corporation and the tax basis in their stock. Effectively, the total double-tax cost of liquidating a corporation can swamp expected tax savings from operating as a flow-through entity. The tax cost of liquidating an entity is a factor to consider when making the tax entity choice for a business.

Example 12-7

What if: Assume we are years down the road and that Nicole is the sole shareholder of CCS (a C corporation). CCS's assets have a fair market value of $10 million and adjusted tax basis of $6 million ($4 million built-in gain). Further assume that the corporate tax rate is 21 percent, Nicole's stock basis in CCS is $2 million, and her marginal tax rate on long-term capital gains is 23.8 percent (20 percent capital gains rate + 3.8 percent net investment income tax). How much tax would CCS and Nicole be required to pay if CCS were to liquidate in order to form an LLC?

Answer: $2,544,080. This would be a steep tax price to pay for changing from a C corporation to an LLC.

Description	Amount	Explanation
(1) FMV of CCS assets	$10,000,000	
(2) Adjusted basis of CCS assets	6,000,000	
(3) CCS taxable income on liquidation	4,000,000	(1) − (2)
(4) Corporate tax rate	21%	
(5) Entity-level tax	840,000	(3) × (4)

(continued on page 12-22)

---

[34]§351 and Rev. Rul. 84-111 1984-2 CB 88.

[35]See the S Corporations chapter for details on making the S corporation election.

Description	Amount	Explanation
(6) After-tax assets distributed to Nicole	$ 9,160,000	(1) − (5)
(7) Nicole's stock basis	2,000,000	
(8) Nicole's long-term capital gain on distribution	7,160,000	(6) − (7)
(9) Nicole's marginal tax rate on gain	23.8%	
(10) Shareholder-level tax	1,704,080	(8) × (9)
Total entity and shareholder-level tax on liquidation	**$ 2,544,080**	(5) + (10)

continued from page 12-4 . . .

Nicole quickly determined she would legally form CCS as an LLC in Utah. This would provide her with limited liability and allow her complete flexibility for determining the tax entity type of CCS. If at some point she wanted to convert CCS into a corporation in Utah, she was advised that she could make the conversion simply by filing some paperwork. Nicole's five-year forecast of CCS's expected operating results showed that CCS would generate losses for the first three years and then become very profitable thereafter. With these projections in hand, Nicole first considered forming CCS as a partnership for tax purposes (she was planning on bringing in another investor) or electing to become an S corporation. Nicole determined that income allocated to her from CCS would be eligible for the deduction for qualified business income whether she operated CCS as a partnership or an S corporation. She then compared the specific tax rules applicable to partnerships and S corporations before deciding her preference between the two tax entity types. She identified some differences that could sway her decision one way or the other. Supporting a decision to select a partnership, Nicole learned she would likely be able to deduct the projected start-up losses from CCS more quickly with a partnership compared with an S corporation because she could include a share of the partnership's debt in her tax basis in her ownership interest (whereas she would not be able to include a share of the S corporation's debt in the tax basis of her ownership interest). Nicole also hoped to attract corporate investors, and she discovered that a partnership can have corporate partners but that S corporations are not permitted to have corporate shareholders. Supporting a decision to select an S corporation, Nicole learned that S corporations appear to have a compelling advantage over partnerships in reducing the self-employment tax of owners active in managing their businesses. Nicole decided that she preferred a partnership over an S corporation because she would be willing to potentially incur additional self-employment taxes with a partnership in exchange for the ability to deduct her losses sooner and for the freedom to solicit corporate investors. Nicole then turned her attention to whether she preferred to operate CCS as a C corporation rather than a partnership. Favoring the partnership tax entity choice was the fact that Nicole would be able to immediately deduct initial losses of the business against her personal income. Favoring the C corporation choice was the overall tax rate on the CCS income when it becomes profitable. She reasoned that the corporate tax rate is significantly lower than her marginal individual tax rate and she planned to grow CCS by having CCS retain rather than distribute its income and subject it to a second level of tax. Consequently, Nicole determined that the overall tax rate to CCS income would be significantly lower if she operated CCS as a C corporation. Further, as a C corporation she would be able to solicit corporate owners and eventually take CCS public if her projections went as planned. After much thought and analysis, Nicole chose to make the election necessary to have CCS taxed as a C corporation. With this big decision out of the way, Nicole could focus on applying for a small business loan from her local bank and on having her attorney take the necessary steps to formally organize CCS as a limited liability company. ■

CONCLUSION

Any time a new business is formed, and periodically thereafter as circumstances change (such as relevant tax law), business owners must carefully evaluate what type of business entity will maximize the after-tax profits from their business ventures. Many of the key factors to consider in the entity selection decision-making process are outlined in this chapter. When making the entity selection decision, owners must carefully balance the tax and nontax characteristics unique to the entities available to them. This chapter explains how various legal entities are treated for tax purposes and how certain tax characteristics differ between entity types. Moreover, it also identifies some of the more important nontax issues that come to bear on the choice of entity decision. With this understanding, taxpayers and their advisers will be better prepared to face this frequently encountered business decision. In the Forming and Operating Partnerships chapter, we return to Nicole and Color Comfort Sheets LLC to examine the tax rules that apply to Nicole and other members in CCS as they form the entity for tax purposes and begin business operations.

Summary

Discuss the legal and nontax characteristics of different types of legal entities.   **LO 12-1**

- Entities that differ in terms of their legal characteristics include corporations, limited liability companies, general partnerships, limited partnerships, and sole proprietorships.
- Corporations are formally organized by filing articles of incorporation with the state. They are legally separate entities and protect their shareholders from the liabilities of the corporation. State corporation laws dictate interactions between corporations and shareholders. As a result, shareholders have limited flexibility to customize their business arrangements with the corporation and other shareholders. State corporate governance rules do, however, facilitate initial public offerings.
- Limited liability companies are formally organized by filing articles of organization with the state. Like corporations, they are separate legal entities that shield their members from liabilities. In contrast to corporations, state LLC statutes give members a great deal of latitude in customizing their business arrangements with the LLC and other members.
- General partnerships may be organized informally without state approval, but limited partnerships must file a certificate of limited partnership with the state to organize. Although they are considered to be legally separate entities, they provide either limited or no liability protection for partners. While limited partners in limited partnerships have liability protection, general partners are fully exposed to the liabilities of the partnership. General and limited partnerships are given a great deal of latitude in customizing their partnership agreements.
- Sole proprietorships are businesses legally indistinguishable from their sole individual owners. As such, they are very flexible but provide no liability protection. Sole proprietors can obtain liability protection by converting to a single-member LLC.

Describe the different types of entities for tax purposes.   **LO 12-2**

- The four categories of business entities recognized by our tax system include: C corporations, S corporations, partnerships, and sole proprietorships.
- Legal corporations that don't make the S election are treated as C corporations and therefore pay taxes. All other entities recognized for tax purposes are flow-through entities.
- Legal corporations that qualify for and make the S election are treated as S corporations.
- Unincorporated entities with more than one owner are treated as partnerships.
- Unincorporated entities with one owner are treated as sole proprietorships, where the sole owner is an individual, or as disregarded entities otherwise.

LO 12-3 Identify fundamental differences in tax characteristics across entity types.

- Flow-through entity income is taxed once at the owner level. For individual owners, the top rate is 37 percent. Flow-through income may also be subject to the net investment income tax for passive investors or the self-employment tax for those involved in the business activities of a partnership or sole proprietorship.

- Flow-through business owners are eligible to deduct 20 percent of their qualified business income as a *from* AGI deduction that is not an itemized deduction. The deduction is subject to certain limitations determined at the individual level.

- Qualified business income is generally nonservice business income generated in the United States.

- Flow-through entity business income allocated to passive owners is subject to the 3.8 percent net investment income tax for taxpayers with AGI over a threshold dependent on filing status.

- Self-employment income is subject to self-employment tax and additional Medicare tax.

- S corporation business income allocated to shareholders is not self-employment income.

- Sole proprietorship income is self-employment income to the sole proprietor.

- Whether business income of entities taxed as a partnership is self-employment income to an owner depends on the owner's involvement in the entity's business activities.

- Corporate taxable income is taxed at the corporate level and again at the shareholder level. For tax years beginning after 2017, the corporate tax rate is reduced to 21 percent. This significantly reduces the first level of tax on corporate income. The second level of tax is paid at the shareholder level when the corporation distributes after-tax earnings as a dividend or when the shareholder sells the stock. The tax rate for the second level of tax depends on the type of shareholder.

- Dividends and long-term capital gains are taxed at a top rate of 23.8 percent (20 percent dividend plus 3.8 percent net investment income tax). Corporate shareholders are taxed on dividends and capital gains at the corporate tax rate. However, corporations are entitled to deduct 50, 65, or 100 percent of dividends received based on the extent of their ownership in the distributing corporation.

- Corporations can defer the second level of tax by not distributing their after-tax income. However, corporations that retain earnings for tax avoidance rather than business purposes may be subject to the accumulated earnings tax or the personal holding company tax. These taxes reduce the incentive for corporations to retain earnings in order to avoid the second level of tax. Corporations are allowed to retain earnings to invest in their business.

- Business entity owners who work for the entity are compensated in different ways, depending on the type of entity.

- S corporation and C corporation shareholders who work for the entity receive employee compensation.

- Owners who work for entities taxed as partnerships receive guaranteed payments that are self-employment income to the owner-worker.

- Sole proprietors don't receive compensation from the business because the sole proprietorship and the sole proprietor are the same entity for tax purposes.

- Operating losses from S corporations and entities taxed as partnerships flow through to the owners. Owners may deduct these losses only to the extent of the basis in their ownership interest. The losses must also clear "at-risk" limitations and passive activity loss limitations in order for the owners to deduct the loss.

- The at-risk limitation is similar to the basis limitation. The passive activity loss limitations typically apply to individual investors who do little, if any, work relating to the business activities of the flow-through entity (referred to as passive activities to the individual investors). In these circumstances, taxpayers can deduct such losses only to the extent they have income from other passive activities.

- Flow-through entity individual owners are not allowed to deduct an excess business loss for the year. This provision potentially limits losses that would otherwise be deductible after applying the at-risk and passive activity loss limitations.

- Shareholders can mitigate the double tax by increasing the time they hold shares before selling.

- C corporation losses are referred to as net operating losses (NOLs).

- C corporations incurring NOLs before 2018 can carry the losses back two years and forward up to 20 years to offset up to 100 percent of taxable income in those years. C corporations incurring losses after 2017 can carry the losses forward indefinitely but may not carry the losses back. Further, the NOL deduction is limited to 80 percent of taxable income without the deduction in those years.

- C corporations may have one or many shareholders. S corporations may have one shareholder and as many as 100 unrelated shareholders; but corporations, nonresident aliens, partnerships, and certain trusts may not be S corporation shareholders. Partnerships must have at least two partners but are not restricted to a maximum number of partners. Sole proprietorships may have only one owner.

- Gains and income from contributing appreciated property to business entities are more easily deferred with partnerships compared to C and S corporations.

- S corporations, partnerships, and sole proprietorships are generally required to use tax year-ends conforming to the tax year-ends of their owners. C corporations may use any tax year-end.

- C corporations generally must use the accrual method unless they are a smaller corporation (average gross receipts of $25 million or less in the prior three years). S corporations may use either the cash or accrual method of accounting. Partnerships generally may use either the cash or accrual method. Sole proprietorships may use either the cash or accrual method.

- Income and losses may be specially allocated to partners based on the partnership agreement. This gives partnerships a great deal of flexibility in determining how the risks and rewards of the enterprise are shared among partners. In contrast, income and losses must be allocated pro rata to S corporation shareholders consistent with their ownership percentages.

- Partners, but not S corporation shareholders, may add their share of entity debt to the basis in their ownership interest.

- Generally, distributions of appreciated property trigger gain at both the corporate and shareholder level when made to shareholders of C corporations; trigger gain at the corporate level when made to S corporation shareholders; and don't trigger any gain at all when made to partners.

- On liquidation, C and S corporations will generally recognize gains and losses on distributed assets. In contrast, partnerships and their partners generally do not recognize gains or losses on liquidating distributions.

- Converting a flow-through entity into a C corporation for tax purposes is generally fairly easy and inexpensive to do. S corporation shareholders can revoke the S corporation election and partnerships (and sole proprietorships formed as LLCs) can check the box to be taxed as a corporation or partnerships, and sole proprietors can contribute assets to a corporate entity in tax-deferred transactions.

- C corporations wanting to convert to a flow-through entity have two options. They may elect to become an S corporation if eligible, or they may liquidate the corporation and organize as a new entity. Taxes from liquidating C corporations can be significant when C corporations have appreciated assets.

KEY TERMS

accumulated earnings tax (12-14)

articles of incorporation (12-2)

articles of organization (12-2)

C corporation (12-5)

certificate of limited partnership (12-2)

certificate of organization (12-2)

corporation (12-2)

disregarded entities (12-5)

dividends received deduction (12-12)

double taxation (12-13)

excess business loss (12-16)

flow-through entities (12-5)

general partnership (GP) (12-2)

initial public offering (IPO) (12-3)

institutional shareholders (12-11)

limited liability company (LLC) (12-2)

limited partnership (LP) (12-2)

net earnings from
        self-employment (12-9)

net operating loss (NOL) (12-16)

partnership agreement (12-2)

personal holding companies (12-14)

personal holding company tax (12-14)

qualified business income (QBI) (12-8)

S corporation (12-5)

single-member LLCs (12-5)

sole proprietorship (12-2)

specified service trade or
        business (12-8)

DISCUSSION QUESTIONS

Discussion Questions are available in Connect®.

LO 12-1 1. What are the most common legal entities used for operating a business? How are these entities treated similarly and differently for state law purposes?

LO 12-1 2. How do business owners create legal entities? Is the process the same for all entities? If not, what are the differences?

LO 12-1 3. What is an operating agreement for an LLC? Are operating agreements required for limited liability companies? If not, why might it be important to have one?

LO 12-1 4. Explain how legal entities differ in terms of the liability protection they afford their owners.

LO 12-1 5. Why are C corporations still popular despite the double tax on their income?

LO 12-1 6. Why is it a nontax advantage for corporations to be able to trade their stock on the stock market?

LO 12-1 7. How do corporations protect shareholders from liability? If you formed a small corporation, would you be able to avoid repaying a bank loan from your community bank if the corporation went bankrupt? Explain.

LO 12-1 **LO 12-2** 8. Other than corporations, are there other legal entities that offer liability protection? Are any of them taxed as flow-through entities? Explain.

LO 12-2 9. In general, how are unincorporated entities classified for tax purposes?

LO 12-2 10. Can unincorporated legal entities ever be treated as corporations for tax purposes? Can corporations ever be treated as flow-through entities for tax purposes? Explain.

LO 12-2 11. What are the differences, if any, between the legal and tax classifications of business entities?

LO 12-2 12. What types of business entities does the U.S. tax system recognize?

LO 12-3 13. For flow-through entities with individual owners, how many times is flow-through entity income taxed, who pays the tax, and what is the tax rate?

LO 12-3 14. What is the qualified business income deduction and how does it affect the tax rate on flow-through entity income?

LO 12-3 15. Doug is considering investing in one of two partnerships that will build, own, and operate a hotel. One is located in Canada and one is located in Arizona. Assuming both investments will generate the same before-tax rate of return, which entity should Doug invest in when considering the after-tax consequences of the investment? Assume Doug's marginal rate is 37 percent, he will be a passive investor in the business, and he will report the flow-through income from either entity on his tax return. Explain (ignore any foreign tax credit issues).

LO 12-3 16. Is business income allocated from a flow-through entity to its owner's self-employment income? Explain.

LO 12-3 17. Who pays the first level of tax on a C corporation's income? What is the tax rate applicable to the first level of tax? Did recent tax law changes increase or decrease the corporate tax rate?

LO 12-3 18. Who pays the second level of tax on a C corporation's income? What is the tax rate applicable to the second level of tax and when is it levied?

LO 12-3 19. Is it possible for shareholders to defer or avoid the second level of tax on corporate income? Briefly explain.

LO 12-3 20. How does a corporation's decision to pay dividends affect its overall tax rate?

21. Is it possible for the overall tax rate on corporate taxable income to be lower than the tax rate on flow-through entity taxable income? If so, under what conditions would you expect the overall corporate tax rate to be lower?   **LO 12-3**

22. Assume Congress increases individual tax rates on ordinary income while leaving all other tax rates unchanged. How would this change affect the overall tax rate on corporate taxable income? How would this change affect overall tax rates for owners of flow-through entities?   **LO 12-3**

23. Assume Congress increases the dividend tax rate to the ordinary tax rate while leaving all other tax rates unchanged. How would this change affect the overall tax rate on corporate taxable income?   **LO 12-3**

24. Evaluate the following statement: "When dividends and long-term capital gains are taxed at the same rate, the present value of the taxes paid on corporate income is the same whether the corporation distributes its after-tax earnings as a dividend or whether it reinvests the after-tax earnings to increase the value of the corporation."   **LO 12-3**

25. If XYZ Corporation is a shareholder of BCD Corporation, how many levels of tax is BCD's before-tax income potentially subject to? Has Congress provided any tax relief for this result? Explain.   **LO 12-3**

26. How many times is income from a C corporation taxed if a retirement fund is the owner of the corporation's stock? Explain.   **LO 12-3**

27. For tax purposes, how is the compensation paid to an S corporation shareholder similar to compensation paid to an owner of an entity taxed as a partnership? How is it different?   **LO 12-3**

28. Why might it be a good tax planning strategy for an S corporation with one shareholder to pay a salary to the shareholder on the low end of what the services are potentially worth?   **LO 12-3**

29. When a C corporation reports a loss for the year, can shareholders use the loss to offset their personal income? Why or why not?   **LO 12-3**

30. Is a current-year net operating loss of a C corporation available to offset income from the corporation in other years? Explain.   **LO 12-3**

31. Would a corporation with a small amount of current-year taxable income (before the net operating loss deduction) and a large net operating loss carryover have a tax liability for the current year? Explain.   **LO 12-3**

32. In its first year of existence, SMS, an S corporation, reported a business loss of $10,000. Michelle, SMS's sole shareholder, reports $50,000 of taxable income from sources other than SMS. What must you know to determine whether she can deduct the $10,000 loss against her other income? Explain.   **LO 12-3**

33. ELS, an S corporation, reported a business loss of $1,000,000. Ethan, ELS's sole shareholder, is involved in ELS's daily business activities and he reports $1,200,000 of taxable income from sources other than ELS. What must you know in order to determine how much, if any, of the $1,000,000 loss Ethan may deduct in the current year? Explain.   **LO 12-3**

34. Why are S corporations less favorable than C corporations and entities taxed as partnerships in terms of owner-related limitations?   **LO 12-3**

35. Are C corporations or flow-through entities (S corporations and entities taxed as partnerships) more flexible in terms of selecting a tax year-end? Why are the tax rules in this area different for C corporations and flow-through entities?   **LO 12-3**

36. Which entity types are generally allowed to use the cash method of accounting?   **LO 12-3**

37. According to the tax rules, how are profits and losses allocated to owners of entities taxed as partnerships (partners or LLC members)? How are they allocated to S corporation shareholders? Which entity permits greater flexibility in allocating profits and losses?   **LO 12-3**

LO 12-3 38. Compare and contrast the FICA tax burden of S corporation shareholder-employees and LLC members (assume an LLC taxed as a partnership) receiving compensation for working for the entity (guaranteed payments) and business income allocations to S corporation shareholders and LLC members assuming the owners are actively involved in the entity's business activities. How does your analysis change if the owners are not actively involved in the entity's business activities?

LO 12-3 39. Explain how liabilities of an LLC (taxed as a partnership) or an S corporation affect the amount of tax losses from the entity that limited liability company members and S corporation shareholders may deduct. Do the tax rules favor LLCs or S corporations?

LO 12-3 40. Compare the entity-level tax consequences for C corporations, S corporations, and entities taxed as partnerships for both nonliquidating and liquidating distributions of noncash property. Do the tax rules tend to favor one entity type more than the others? Explain.

LO 12-3 41. If entities taxed as partnerships and S corporations are both flow-through entities for tax purposes, why might an owner prefer one form over the other for tax purposes? List separately the tax factors supporting the decision to operate as either an entity taxed as a partnership or as an S corporation.

LO 12-3 42. What are the tax advantages and disadvantages of converting a C corporation into an LLC (taxed as a partnership)?

PROBLEMS

Select problems are available in Connect®.

LO 12-1 43. Visit your state's official website and review the information there related to forming and operating business entities in your state. Write a short report explaining the steps for organizing a business in your state and summarizing any tax-related information you found.

research

LO 12-3 44. Andrea would like to organize SHO as either an LLC (taxed as a sole proprietorship) or a C corporation. In either form, the entity is expected to generate an 11 percent annual before-tax return on a $200,000 investment. Andrea's marginal income tax rate is 35 percent and her tax rate on dividends and capital gains is 15 percent. Andrea will also pay a 3.8 percent net investment income tax on dividends and capital gains she recognizes. If Andrea organizes SHO as an LLC, Andrea will be required to pay an additional 2.9 percent for self-employment tax and an additional .9 percent for the additional Medicare tax. Further, she is eligible to claim the full deduction for qualified business income. Assume that SHO will pay out all of its after-tax earnings every year as a dividend if it is formed as a C corporation.

a) How much cash after taxes would Andrea receive from her investment in the first year if SHO is organized as either an LLC or a C corporation?

b) What is the overall tax rate on SHO's income in the first year if SHO is organized as an LLC or as a C corporation?

LO 12-3 45. Jacob is a member of WCC (an LLC taxed as a partnership). Jacob was allocated $100,000 of business income from WCC for the year. Jacob's marginal income tax rate is 37 percent. The business allocation is subject to 2.9 percent of self-employment tax and .9 percent additional Medicare tax.

a) What is the amount of tax Jacob will owe on the income allocation if the income is not qualified business income?

b) What is the amount of tax Jacob will owe on the income allocation if the income is qualified business income (QBI) and Jacob qualifies for the full QBI deduction?

46. Amanda would like to organize BAL as either an LLC (taxed as a sole proprietorship) or a C corporation. In either form, the entity is expected to generate an 8 percent annual before-tax return on a $500,000 investment. Amanda's marginal income tax rate is 37 percent and her tax rate on dividends and capital gains is 23.8 percent (including the 3.8 percent net investment income tax). If Amanda organizes BAL as an LLC, she will be required to pay an additional 2.9 percent for self-employment tax and an additional .9 percent for the additional Medicare tax. Also, she is eligible to claim a full deduction for qualified business income on BAL's income. Assume that BAL will distribute half of its after-tax earnings every year as a dividend if it is formed as a C corporation.

    `LO 12-3`

    a) How much cash after taxes would Amanda receive from her investment in the first year if BAL is organized as either an LLC or a C corporation?

    b) What is the overall tax rate on BAL's income in the first year if BAL is organized as an LLC or as a C corporation?

47. Sandra would like to organize BAL as either an LLC (taxed as a sole proprietorship) or a C corporation. In either form, the entity is expected to generate an 8 percent annual before-tax return on a $500,000 investment. Sandra's marginal income tax rate is 37 percent and her tax rate on dividends and capital gains is 23.8 percent (including the 3.8 percent net investment income tax). If Sandra organizes BAL as an LLC, she will be required to pay an additional 2.9 percent for self-employment tax and an additional .9 percent for the additional Medicare tax. BAL's income is not qualified business income (QBI) so Sandra is not allowed to claim the QBI deduction. Assume that BAL will distribute all of its after-tax earnings every year as a dividend if it is formed as a C corporation.

    `LO 12-3`

    a) How much cash after taxes would Sandra receive from her investment in the first year if BAL is organized as either an LLC or a C corporation?

    b) What is the overall tax rate on BAL's income in the first year if BAL is organized as an LLC or as a C corporation?

48. Tremaine would like to organize UTA as either an S Corporation or a C corporation. In either form, the entity will generate a 9 percent annual before-tax return on a $1,000,000 investment. Tremaine's marginal income tax rate is 37 percent and his tax rate on dividends and capital gains is 23.8 percent (including the net investment income tax). If Tremaine organizes UTA as an S corporation he will be allowed to claim the deduction for qualified business income. Also, because Tremaine will participate in UTA's business activities, the income from UTA will not be subject to the net investment income tax. Assume that UTA will pay out 25 percent of its after-tax earnings every year as a dividend if it is formed as a C corporation.

    `LO 12-3`

    research

    a) How much cash after taxes would Tremaine receive from his investment in the first year if UTA is organized as either an S corporation or a C corporation?

    b) What is the overall tax rate on UTA's income in the first year if UTA is organized as an S corporation or as a C corporation?

    c) What is the overall tax rate on UTA's income in the first year if it is organized as an S corporation but UTA's income is not qualified business income?

    d) What is the overall tax rate on UTA's income if UTA's income is not qualified business income and Tremaine is a passive investor in UTA?

49. Marathon Inc. (a C corporation) reported $1,000,000 of taxable income in the current year. During the year, it distributed $100,000 as dividends to its shareholders as follows:

    `LO 12-3`

    tax forms

    - $5,000 to Guy, a 5 percent individual shareholder.
    - $15,000 to Little Rock Corp., a 15 percent shareholder (C corporation).
    - $80,000 to other shareholders.

a) How much of the dividend payment did Marathon deduct in determining its taxable income?

b) Assuming Guy's marginal ordinary tax rate is 37 percent, how much tax will he pay on the $5,000 dividend he received from Marathon Inc. (including the net investment income tax)?

c) What amount of tax will Little Rock Corp. pay on the $15,000 dividend it received from Marathon Inc. (50 percent dividends received deduction)?

d) Complete Form 1120 Schedule C for Little Rock Corp. to reflect its dividends received deduction. (Note that the 2017 form is not updated for DRD percentages effective in 2018. If using 2017 form, report the DRD on line 1).

e) On what line on page 1 of Little Rock Corp.'s Form 1120 is the dividend from Marathon Inc. reported, and on what line of Little Rock Corp.'s Form 1120 is its dividends received deduction reported?

LO 12-3

research

50. After several years of profitable operations, Javell, the sole shareholder of JBD Inc., a C corporation, sold 22 percent of her JBD stock to ZNO Inc., a C corporation in a similar industry. During the current year JBD reports $1,000,000 of after-tax income. JBD distributes all of its after-tax earnings to its two shareholders in proportion to their shareholdings. How much tax will ZNO pay on the dividend it receives from JBD? What is ZNO's tax rate on the dividend income (after considering the DRD)? [*Hint:* See IRC §243.]

LO 12-3

51. Mackenzie is considering conducting her business, Mac561, as either a single-member LLC or as an S corporation. Determine Mackenzie's after-tax cash flow from the entity's business income and any compensation she receives from the business assuming her marginal ordinary income tax rate is 37 percent, her marginal FICA rate on employee compensation is 1.45 percent, her marginal self-employment tax rate is 2.9 percent, and any employee compensation or self-employment income she receives is subject to the .9 percent additional Medicare tax. Finally, Mac561 generated $200,000 of business income before considering the deduction for compensation Mac561 pays to Mackenzie and Mackenzie can claim the full qualified business income deduction on Mac561's business income.

a) Mackenzie conducted Mac561 as a single-member LLC.

b) Mackenzie conducted Mac561 as an S corporation and she received a salary of $100,000. All business income allocated to her is also distributed to her.

c) Mackenzie conducted Mac561 as an S corporation and she received a salary of $20,000. All business income allocated to her is also distributed to her.

d) Which entity/compensation combination generated the most after-cash flow for Mackenzie? What are the primary contributing factors favoring this combination?

LO 12-3

52. In its first year of existence (year 1), SCC corporation (a C corporation) reported a loss for tax purposes of $30,000. How much tax will SCC pay in year 2 if it reports taxable income from operations of $20,000 before considering loss carryovers under the following assumptions?

a) Year 1 is 2017.

b) Year 1 is 2018.

LO 12-3

53. In its first year of existence (year 1), Willow Corp. (a C corporation) reports a loss for tax purposes of $50,000. In year 2 it reports a $40,000 loss. For year 3, it reports taxable income from operations of $100,000 before any loss carryovers. How much tax will Willow Corp. pay in year 3, what is its NOL carryover to year 4, and when will the NOL expire under the following assumptions?

a) Year 1 is 2017.

b) Year 1 is 2018.

54. Damarcus is a 50 percent owner of Hoop (a business entity). In the current year, Hoop reported a $100,000 business loss. Answer the following questions associated with each of the following alternative scenarios. **LO 12-3**

   a) Hoop is organized as a C corporation and Damarcus works full-time as an employee for Hoop. Damarcus has a $20,000 basis in his Hoop stock. How much of Hoop's loss is Damarcus allowed to deduct against his other income?

   b) Hoop is organized as an LLC taxed as a partnership. Fifty percent of Hoop's loss is allocated to Damarcus. Damarcus works full-time for Hoop (he is not considered to be a passive investor in Hoop). Damarcus has a $20,000 basis in his Hoop ownership interest and he also has a $20,000 at-risk amount in his investment in Hoop. Damarcus does not report income or loss from any other business activity investments. How much of the $50,000 loss allocated to him by Hoop is Damarcus allowed to deduct this year?

   c) Hoop is organized as an LLC taxed as a partnership. Fifty percent of Hoop's loss is allocated to Damarcus. Damarcus does not work for Hoop at all (he is a passive investor in Hoop). Damarcus has a $20,000 basis in his Hoop ownership interest and he also has a $20,000 at-risk amount in his investment in Hoop. Damarcus does not report income or loss from any other business activity investments. How much of the $50,000 loss allocated to him by Hoop is Damarcus allowed to deduct this year?

   d) Hoop is organized as an LLC taxed as a partnership. Fifty percent of Hoop's loss is allocated to Damarcus. Damarcus works full-time for Hoop (he is not considered to be a passive investor in Hoop). Damarcus has a $70,000 basis in his Hoop ownership interest and he also has a $70,000 at-risk amount in his investment in Hoop. Damarcus does not report income or loss from any other business activity investments. How much of the $50,000 loss allocated to him by Hoop is Damarcus allowed to deduct this year?

   e) Hoop is organized as an LLC taxed as a partnership. Fifty percent of Hoop's loss is allocated to Damarcus. Damarcus does not work for Hoop at all (he is a passive investor in Hoop). Damarcus has a $20,000 basis in his Hoop ownership interest and he also has a $20,000 at-risk amount in his investment in Hoop. Damarcus reports $10,000 of income from a business activity in which he is a passive investor. How much of the $50,000 loss allocated to him by Hoop is Damarcus allowed to deduct this year?

55. Danni is a single 30 percent owner of Kolt (a business entity). In the current year, Kolt reported a $1,000,000 business loss. Answer the following questions associated with each of the following alternative scenarios: **LO 12-3**

   a) Kolt is organized as a C corporation and Danni works 20 hours a week as an employee for Kolt. Danni has a $200,000 basis in her Kolt stock. How much of Kolt's loss is Danni allowed to deduct this year against her other income?

   b) Kolt is organized as an LLC taxed as a partnership. Thirty percent of Kolt's loss is allocated to Danni. Danni works 20 hours a week on Kolt business activities (she is not considered to be a passive investor in Kolt). Danni has a $400,000 basis in her Kolt ownership interest and she also has a $400,000 at-risk amount in her investment in Kolt. Danni does not report income or loss from any other business activity investments. How much of the $300,000 loss allocated to her from Kolt is Danni allowed to deduct this year?

   c) Kolt is organized as an LLC taxed as a partnership. Thirty percent of Kolt's loss is allocated to Danni. Danni is not involved in Kolt business activities. Consequently, she is considered to be a passive investor in Kolt. Danni has a $400,000 basis in her Kolt ownership interest and she also has a $400,000 at-risk amount in her investment in Kolt. Danni does not report income or loss from any other business activity investments. How much of the $300,000 loss allocated to her from Kolt is Danni allowed to deduct this year?

LO 12-3

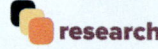 **research**

56. Mickey, Mickayla, and Taylor are starting a new business (MMT). To get the business started, Mickey is contributing $200,000 for a 40 percent ownership interest, Mickayla is contributing a building with a value of $200,000 and a tax basis of $150,000 for a 40 percent ownership interest, and Taylor is contributing legal services for a 20 percent ownership interest. What amount of gain is each owner required to recognize under each of the following alternative situations? [*Hint:* Look at §351 and §721.]

a) MMT is formed as a C corporation.

b) MMT is formed as an S corporation.

c) MMT is formed as an LLC.

LO 12-3

research

57. Dave and his friend Stewart each own 50 percent of KBS. During the year, Dave receives $75,000 compensation for services he performs for KBS during the year. He performed a significant amount of work for the entity and he was heavily involved in management decisions (he was not a passive investor in KBS). After deducting Dave's compensation, KBS reports taxable income of $30,000. How much FICA and/or self-employment tax is Dave required to pay on his compensation and his share of the KBS income if KBS is formed as a C corporation, an S corporation, or a limited liability company (ignore the .9 percent additional Medicare tax)?

LO 12-3

research

58. Rondo and his business associate, Larry, are considering forming a business entity called R&L but they are unsure about whether to form it as a C corporation, an S corporation, or an LLC taxed as a partnership. Rondo and Larry would each invest $50,000 in the business. Thus, each owner would take an initial basis in his ownership interest of $50,000 no matter which entity type is formed. Shortly after the formation of the entity, the business borrowed $30,000 from the bank. If applicable, this debt will be shared equally between the two owners.

a) After taking the loan into account, what is Rondo's tax basis in his R&L stock if R&L is formed as a C corporation?

b) After taking the loan into account, what is Rondo's tax basis in his R&L stock if R&L is formed as an S corporation?

c) After taking the loan into account, what is Rondo's tax basis in his R&L ownership interest if R&L is formed and taxed as a partnership?

LO 12-3

research

59. Kevin and Bob have owned and operated SOA as a C corporation for a number of years. When they formed the entity, Kevin and Bob each contributed $100,000 to SOA. They each have a current basis of $100,000 in their SOA ownership interest. Information on SOA's assets at the end of year 5 is as follows (SOA does not have any liabilities):

Assets	FMV	Adjusted Basis	Built-in Gain
Cash	$200,000	$200,000	$ 0
Inventory	80,000	40,000	40,000
Land and building	220,000	170,000	50,000
Total	$500,000		

At the end of year 5, SOA liquidated and distributed half of the land, half of the inventory, and half of the cash remaining after paying taxes (if any) to each owner.

Assume that, excluding the effects of the liquidating distribution, SOA's taxable income for year 5 is $0.

a) What is the amount and character of gain or loss SOA will recognize on the liquidating distribution?

b) What is the amount and character of gain or loss Kevin will recognize when he receives the liquidating distribution of cash and property? Recall that his stock basis is $100,000 and he is treated as having sold his stock for the liquidation proceeds.

COMPREHENSIVE PROBLEMS

Select problems are available with Connect®.

60. Daisy Taylor has developed a viable new business idea. Her idea is to design and manufacture cookware that remains cool to the touch when in use. She has had several friends try out her prototype cookware and they have consistently given the cookware rave reviews. With this encouragement, Daisy started giving serious thought to starting up a business called "Cool Touch Cookware" (CTC).

Daisy understands that it will take a few years for the business to become profitable. She would like to grow her business and perhaps at some point "go public" or sell the business to a large retailer.

Daisy, who is single, decided to quit her full-time job so that she could focus all of her efforts on the new business. Daisy had some savings to support her for a while but she did not have any other source of income. She was able to recruit Kesha and Aryan to join her as initial equity investors in CTC. Kesha has an MBA and a law degree. Kesha was employed as a business consultant when she decided to leave that job and work with Daisy and Aryan. Kesha's husband earns close to $300,000 a year as an engineer (employee). Aryan owns a *very* profitable used car business. Because buying and selling used cars takes all his time, he is interested in becoming only a passive investor in CTC. He wanted to get in on the ground floor because he really likes the product and believes CTC will be wildly successful. While CTC originally has three investors, Daisy and Kesha have plans to grow the business and seek more owners and capital in the future.

The three owners agreed that Daisy would contribute land and cash for a 30 percent interest in CTC, Kesha would contribute services (legal and business advisory) for the first two years for a 30 percent interest, and Aryan would contribute cash for a 40 percent interest. The plan called for Daisy and Kesha to be actively involved in managing the business while Aryan would not be. The three equity owners' contributions are summarized as follows:

Daisy Contributed	FMV	Adjusted Basis	Ownership Interest
Land (held as investment)	$120,000	$70,000	30%
Cash	30,000		
Kesha Contributed			
Services	150,000		30
Aryan Contributed			
Cash	200,000		40

Working together, Daisy and Kesha made the following five-year income and loss projections for CTC. They anticipate the business will be profitable and that it will continue to grow after the first five years.

Cool Touch Cookware 5-Year Income and Loss Projections	
Year	Income (Loss)
1	$(200,000)
2	(80,000)
3	(20,000)
4	60,000
5	180,000

With plans for Daisy and Kesha to spend a considerable amount of their time working for and managing CTC, the owners would like to develop a compensation plan that works for all parties. Down the road, they plan to have two business locations (in different cities). Daisy would take responsibility for the activities of one location and Kesha would take responsibility for the other. Finally, they would like to arrange for some performance-based financial incentives for each location.

To get the business activities started, Daisy and Kesha determined CTC would need to borrow $800,000 to purchase a building to house its manufacturing facilities and its administrative offices (at least for now). Also, in need of additional cash, Daisy and Kesha arranged to have CTC borrow $300,000 from a local bank and to borrow $200,000 cash from Aryan. CTC would pay Aryan a market rate of interest on the loan but there was no fixed date for principal repayment.

Required:

Identify significant tax and nontax issues or concerns that may differ across entity types and discuss how they are relevant to the choice of entity decision for CTC.

61. Cool Touch Cookware (CTC) has been in business for about 10 years now. Daisy and Kesha are each 50 percent owners of the business. They initially established the business with cash contributions. CTC manufactures unique cookware that remains cool to the touch when in use. CTC has been fairly profitable over the years. Daisy and Kesha have both been actively involved in managing the business. They have developed very good personal relationships with many customers (both wholesale and retail) that, Daisy and Kesha believe, keep the customers coming back.

On September 30 of the current year, CTC had all of its assets appraised. Below is CTC's balance sheet, as of September 30, with the corresponding appraisals of the fair market value of all of its assets. Note that CTC has several depreciated assets. CTC uses the hybrid method of accounting. It accounts for its gross margin-related items under the accrual method and it accounts for everything else using the cash method of accounting.

Assets	Adjusted Tax Basis	FMV
Cash	$150,000	$150,000
Accounts receivable	20,000	15,000
Inventory*	90,000	300,000
Equipment	120,000	100,000
Investment in XYZ stock	40,000	120,000
Land (used in the business)	80,000	70,000
Building	200,000	180,000
Total assets	$700,000	$935,000

Liabilities

Accounts payable	$ 40,000
Bank loan	60,000
Mortgage on building	100,000
Equity	500,000
Total liabilities and equity	$700,000

*CTC uses the LIFO method for determining the adjusted basis of its inventory. Its basis in the inventory under the FIFO method would have been $110,000.

'In addition, Daisy and Kesha had the entire business appraised at $1,135,000, which is $200,000 more than the value of the identifiable assets.

From January 1 of the current year through September 30, CTC reported the following income:

Ordinary business income	$530,000
Dividends from XYZ stock	12,000
Long-term capital losses	15,000
Interest income	3,000

Daisy and Kesha are considering changing the business form of CTC.

Required:

a) Assume CTC is organized as a C corporation. Identify significant tax and nontax issues associated with converting CTC from a C corporation to an S corporation. [*Hint:* See IRC §1374 and §1363(d).]

b) Assume CTC is organized as a C corporation. Identify significant tax and nontax issues associated with converting CTC from a C corporation to an LLC. Assume CTC converts to an LLC (taxed as a partnership) by distributing its assets to its shareholders, who then contribute the assets to a new LLC. [*Hint:* See IRC §§331, 336, and 721(a).]

c) Assume that CTC is a C corporation with a net operating loss carryforward as of the beginning of the year in the amount of $2,000,000. Identify significant tax and nontax issues associated with converting CTC from a C corporation to an LLC (taxed as a partnership). Assume CTC converts to an LLC by distributing its assets to its shareholders, who then contribute the assets to a new LLC. [*Hint:* See IRC §§172(a), 331, 336, and 721(a).]

ROGER | *CPA Review*

Sample CPA Exam questions from Roger CPA Review are available in Connect as support for the topics in this text. These Multiple Choice Questions and Task-Based Simulations include expert-written explanations and solutions and provide a starting point for students to become familiar with the content and functionality of the actual CPA Exam.

Corporate Formations and Operations

Learning Objectives

Upon completing this chapter, you should be able to:

LO 13-1 Compute the tax consequences of transactions in which shareholders transfer property or services to corporations in exchange for stock of the corporation.

LO 13-2 Describe the corporate income tax formula, compare and contrast the corporate tax formula to the individual tax formula, and discuss tax considerations relating to corporations' accounting periods and accounting methods.

LO 13-3 Identify common book–tax differences, distinguish between permanent and temporary differences, and compute a corporation's taxable income and income tax liability.

LO 13-4 Describe a corporation's tax return reporting and estimated tax payment obligations.

Storyline Summary

Taxpayers:	Nicole Johnson, Sarah Walker, and Chanzz Inc. (calendar year-end)
Location:	Salt Lake City, Utah
Status:	Shareholders of Color Comfort Sheets Inc. (CCS)
Situation:	Form and operate CCS as a C corporation.

In the Entities Overview chapter, we introduced you to Nicole Johnson, who started a full-time business called Color Comfort Sheets (CCS). In this chapter, we assume that Nicole (and others) formed CCS as a C corporation with a calendar year-end. Nicole realized she needed to raise capital to get the business started. She was willing to contribute a parcel of land that she had inherited five years ago from her grandfather and was currently holding as an investment. Her friend and mentor, Sarah Walker, offered to contribute both her time and money to help CCS get started. With Sarah on board, things seemed to be coming together nicely for Nicole. Hoping to obtain the additional funding they needed, Nicole and Sarah visited Chance Armstrong, a successful local sports-team owner who had a reputation for his willingness to take chances on new ventures. After listening to Nicole and Sarah's proposal, Chance agreed to invest the additional cash needed to fully fund CCS. Rather than use his personal funds, however, Chance planned to have his closely held corporation, Chanzz Inc., invest in CCS. Soon CCS had cash, land on which to build its manufacturing facility and offices, and owners who were excited and willing to work hard to make it a successful company.

to be continued . . .

This chapter introduces the shareholder and corporate-level tax consequences when shareholders transfer property to corporations to form the corporations and when they transfer property to existing corporations. Once we understand the tax consequences of these transactions, we address issues in computing and reporting corporate taxable income for C corporations (we consider similar issues for S corporations in the S Corporations chapter).

LO 13-1

TRANSFERS OF PROPERTY TO A CORPORATION

Whether shareholders transfer property to a newly formed corporation or to an existing corporation in exchange for the transferee corporation's stock, the tax consequences to the shareholders are the same. Unless the transfer meets certain requirements, the transaction is treated as a taxable sale or exchange of the shareholder's property to the corporation. That is, the taxpayer is treated as selling the property to the corporation for the corporation's stock. We discussed the tax consequences of a sale or exchange of property in depth in the Property Dispositions chapter. Applying concepts from that chapter in this context, shareholders recognize gain to the extent the value of the stock they receive exceeds the basis of the property they transfer to the corporation. They (generally) recognize loss to the extent the basis of the property they transfer to the corporation exceeds the value of the stock they receive from the corporation. The shareholders take a fair market value basis in the stock they receive in the exchange.

Taxpayers who meet certain requirements, however, defer (not exclude) gain or loss on the transfer of property to a corporation in exchange for stock.[1] Justification for tax deferral is based on the concept that when taxpayers transfer property to a corporation, they are simply trading direct ownership in the property for indirect ownership in the property (through stock ownership). For qualifying taxpayers, the deferral minimizes tax consequences as an impediment to forming a corporation (or to contributing property to an existing corporation) and thus provides taxpayers with increased flexibility in choosing their preferred form of doing business.

Transactions Subject to Tax Deferral

For shareholders to defer gain (or loss) on transfers of property to a corporation, either at formation or later, the shareholders who transfer property to the corporation in the exchange (called the transferors) must meet the following requirements provided in IRC §351:

- One or more shareholders must transfer *property* to a corporation;
- Shareholders who transfer property to the corporation (transferors) must receive *stock* of the transferee corporation in exchange for the property they transfer; and
- After the transfer, the transferors, together, must *control* the corporation to which they transferred the property.

Each of these requirements is discussed below. When all three requirements are met, deferral of gain or loss is mandatory. This tax provision applies to transfers to both C corporations and S corporations.

Shareholders Must Transfer Property
Shareholders must transfer property to the corporation to be eligible to qualify for deferral under §351. The definition of property for §351 purposes is very broad and includes tangible and intangible assets (e.g., company name, patents, customer lists, trademarks, and logos). However, services are excluded from the definition of property. Thus, a person performing services for a corporation in exchange for stock in that corporation must recognize (compensation) income equal to the fair market value of the stock received for services. The shareholder's basis in the stock received for services is the fair market value of the stock.

[1]§351(a).

THE KEY FACTS

Requirements for Tax Deferral in a Corporate Formation

- Tax deferral applies only to transfers of property to a corporation.
- The persons transferring property to a corporation (transferors) must receive stock in the corporation in return.
- The transferors must together control the corporation after the transaction.
- Control is defined as ownership of 80 percent or more of the corporation's voting stock and 80 percent or more of each class of nonvoting stock.

Example 13-1

What if: Suppose Sarah received 10 percent of the stock in CCS valued at $20,000 in exchange for her services in setting up the corporation. Is Sarah eligible to defer the $20,000 of gain she realized on the exchange? What is Sarah's basis in the CCS stock she received in the transaction?

Answer: No. Sarah must recognize compensation income of $20,000 on the exchange because services are not considered property under §351. Sarah will take a $20,000 fair market value basis in the stock she received.

What if: Suppose Sarah received 10 percent of the stock in CCS valued at $20,000 in exchange for a slogan she created to provide the company with a distinctive logo. Assume her tax basis in the slogan is $0 because she created it. Nicole and Chanzz Inc. transferred property to CCS in exchange for the other 90 percent of the CCS stock. How much of the $20,000 realized gain does Sarah recognize on the transfer of the slogan?

Answer: $0. Because the slogan (an intangible asset) is considered to be property for purposes of §351, Sarah meets the property, stock, and control requirements for deferral of the gain she realized on the transfer. She meets the control requirement because the transferors of property (Nicole, Chanzz Inc., and Sarah) together own 100 percent of the CCS stock after the exchange.

Shareholders Who Transfer Property Must Receive Stock of the Transferee Corporation in the Exchange

To qualify for deferral, the transferors of property must receive stock in the transferee corporation in exchange for the property they transfer to the corporation. The type of stock a transferor can receive in a §351 exchange is flexible and includes both voting and nonvoting stock and both common and preferred stock. However, stock for this purpose does not include stock warrants, rights, or options.[2] As we discuss in more detail below, transferors who receive stock and something in addition to stock (referred to as **boot**) recognize gain but not loss realized on the exchange.[3]

Shareholders Who Transfer Property Must Together Control the Corporation Immediately after the Transfer

For purposes of this requirement, control is defined as ownership of 80 percent or more of the total combined *voting power* of all voting stock that is issued and outstanding, and 80 percent or more of the total number of shares of *each class* of nonvoting stock.[4]

Whether the control test is met is based on the transferors' combined ownership in the corporation after the transaction (even if they also transferred services in addition to property) immediately after the transfer and does not depend on the ownership before the transfer.[5,6]

---

[2]§351(g) precludes nonqualified preferred stock from qualifying as equity eligible for deferral. Nonqualified preferred stock generally has characteristics that cause it to more resemble debt than equity.

[3]§351(b). The term *boot* derives from a trading expression where a party to an exchange might throw in additional property "to boot" to equalize values in an exchange.

[4]§368(c). Voting power is generally defined as the ability of the shareholders to elect members of the corporation's board of directors.

[5]Reg. §1.351-1(a)(1)(ii). Transferors who transfer both property and services are counted as transferors of property (included in control test) unless the value of stock they receive for property is of "relatively small value" compared to the stock they receive for services (but only if the primary purpose of the transfer is to qualify under §351 the exchanges of property by other persons transferring property). In Rev. Proc. 77-37, 1977-2 C.B. 568, the IRS determined for ruling purposes the value of the stock received for property must be at least 10 percent of the value of the stock received for services in order for the transferor's stock to count for control test purposes.

[6]Reg. §1.351-1(a)(1)(ii). For an existing shareholder to be considered a transferor of property and thus have the existing shareholder's ownership included in the control computation, the value of the stock the shareholder is receiving for property transferred must not be of "relatively small value" compared to the value of the stock the shareholder already owns (but only if the primary purpose of the transfer is to qualify under §351 the exchanges of property by other persons transferring property). In Rev. Proc. 77-37, 1977-2 C.B. 568, the IRS determined for ruling purposes the value of the stock received for property must be at least 10 percent of the value of the stock the shareholder already owns in order for the transferor's (existing shareholder's) stock to count for control test purposes.

Example 13-2

What if: Suppose Sarah received 25 percent of the CCS stock in exchange for services, Nicole received 50 percent of the CCS stock in exchange for appreciated land, and Chanzz Inc. received 25 percent of the CCS stock in exchange for cash. Must Nicole recognize the gain she realized on her transfer of appreciated land?

Answer: Yes. Because Nicole and Chanzz Inc. are the only transferors of property to CCS, only their stock counts for purposes of the 80 percent control test. Because Nicole and Chanzz Inc. together own less than 80 percent of the CCS stock (they own 75 percent) immediately after the transfer, Nicole's transfer does not qualify under §351, and she must recognize the gain on the appreciated land.

What if: Suppose Sarah received 10 percent of the CCS stock in exchange for services, and she received 15 percent of the CCS stock in exchange for cash (i.e., she transferred both services and property to CCS). Also, Nicole received 50 percent of the CCS stock in exchange for appreciated land and Chanzz Inc. received 25 percent of the CCS stock in exchange for cash. Must Nicole recognize gain on her transfer of appreciated land?

Answer: No. Because Sarah transferred property to CCS, all 25 percent of the CCS stock she received counts for purposes of the control test. Thus, shareholders transferring property to CCS in exchange for stock own 100 percent of CCS after the exchange, and Nicole defers her realized gain on the exchange (this is a qualifying §351 transfer).

Example 13-3

What if: Assume Sarah was initially hesitant to join with Nicole and Chanzz Inc. in forming CCS. After six months, she changed her mind and exchanged appreciated property to CCS for 10 percent of the CCS stock. Is Sarah required to recognize her realized gain on the transaction?

Answer: Yes, she must recognize all of her realized gain. In this transaction, Sarah is the only shareholder transferring property to CCS in exchange for stock. Because Sarah does not control CCS immediately after the exchange (she does not own 80 percent or more of the CCS stock), she is not eligible to defer her realized gain under §351.

Tax Consequences to Shareholders in a Qualifying §351 Exchange with No Boot

In a qualifying §351 transaction with no boot (the corporation transfers only its stock to shareholders), the shareholders do not recognize any gain or loss realized on the exchange. The tax basis of the stock shareholders receive in the transfer equals the tax basis of the property they transferred to the corporation. Most practitioners refer to the stock as having a **substituted basis** (i.e., the basis of the property transferred is substituted for the basis of the stock received). Finally, the shareholders' holding period in the stock they receive includes the holding period of the property they transfer if they transfer a capital asset or a §1231 asset to the corporation.[7] The holding period for the stock received starts on the day of the exchange for shareholders transferring assets that are neither capital nor §1231 assets.

Example 13-4

When incorporating CCS, Nicole transferred a parcel of land (held as an investment for five years) to CCS in exchange for 50 percent of the corporation's stock (50 shares valued at $100,000). The land's fair market value was $100,000, and its tax basis to Nicole was $40,000. Assuming the transfer qualifies under §351, what gain or loss does Nicole recognize on the transfer? What is her basis in the stock she received on the exchange? What is her holding period in the stock?

[7] §1223(1).

Answer: $0 gain recognized and $40,000 basis in the stock with a five-year holding period. Nicole realizes a $60,000 gain on the exchange ($100,000 stock received minus $40,000 basis in property transferred) but does not recognize any gain because she meets the §351 requirements and she did not receive boot. Her basis in the stock is the same as the basis she had in the land she transferred to CCS. Finally, Nicole's holding period in the stock includes the five years she owned the land because the land was a capital asset to Nicole.

Tax Consequences to Shareholders in a Qualifying §351 Exchange with Boot

Shareholders can still qualify for deferral treatment under §351 when they receive stock in the transferee corporation and they also receive something in addition to stock (boot). However, when a shareholder receives boot in an otherwise qualifying §351 exchange, the shareholder must recognize gain (but not loss) equal to the *lesser of* (1) the gain realized or (2) the fair market value of the boot received. That is, the shareholder must recognize realized gain to the extent of boot received (the shareholder does not recognize more than the realized gain). When a shareholder transfers more than one asset to the corporation, the amount of gain recognized when boot is received is determined by allocating the stock and the boot received pro rata to each property transferred to the corporation, using the relative fair market values of the properties.[8] The character of gain recognized (capital gain, §1231 gain, or ordinary income) on each asset is determined by the type of property to which the boot is allocated. Boot received in a §351 transaction receives a tax basis equal to its fair market value. We discuss computing a shareholder's tax basis in the stock received in the exchange below.

Example 13-5

What if: Suppose Nicole contributed land she held as an investment (fair market value $120,000; basis $40,000) in exchange for 50 percent of the CCS stock (50 shares valued at $100,000) and $20,000 cash in a qualifying §351 exchange. What would be the amount and character of gain Nicole recognizes on the transfer?

Answer: $20,000 capital gain. Nicole realized a gain of $80,000 on the transfer of the land ($120,000 fair market value of stock and cash received minus $40,000 basis in land). She also received $20,000 of boot in the exchange (the cash). Her recognized gain is the lesser of the $80,000 gain realized and the $20,000 boot received. The gain is capital because the land was a capital asset to Nicole.

What if: Suppose Nicole contributed land she held as an investment (fair market value $90,000; basis of $40,000) and inventory (fair market value $30,000; basis of $26,000) to CCS in exchange for 50 percent of the CCS stock (50 shares valued at $100,000) and $20,000 cash in a qualifying §351 exchange. What percentage of the $120,000 value received by Nicole was received for the land and the inventory, respectively?

(continued on page 13-6)

---

[8]Rev. Rul. 68-55, 1968-1 C.B. 140 and Rev. Rul. 85-164, 1985-2 C.B. 117.

Answer: 75 percent for the land and 25 percent for the inventory, computed as follows:

Description	Amount	Explanation
(1) Stock received	$100,000	
(2) Cash (boot) received	20,000	
(3) Total amount realized	$120,000	
(4) Amount realized for land	75%	$90,000 fair market value of land/ $120,000 (total amount realized)
(5) Amount realized for inventory	25%	$30,000 fair market value of inventory/ $120,000 (total amount realized)

What amount of gain does Nicole recognize on the exchange? What is the character of the gain?

Answer: Nicole recognizes $15,000 of capital gain on the land and $4,000 of ordinary income on the inventory transfer, computed as follows:

Description	Land	Inventory	Explanation
(6) Amount realized from stock	$75,000	$25,000	(1) × (4) for land; (1) × (5) for inventory
(7) Amount realized from boot	15,000	5,000	(2) × (4) for land; (2) × (5) for inventory
(8) Total amount realized	90,000	30,000	(6) + (7)
(9) Adjusted basis	40,000	26,000	
(10) Gain realized	50,000	4,000	(8) − (9)
(11) Boot received	15,000	5,000	(7)
(12) Gain recognized	**15,000**	**4,000**	Lesser of (10) or (11)
Gain character	**Capital**	**Ordinary**	The land (held for investment) is a capital asset; inventory is an ordinary asset

What if: Assume the same facts except that Nicole received $20,000 of equipment from CCS instead of $20,000 cash. What is the amount and character of gain Nicole would recognize on the exchange?

Answer: $15,000 capital gain and $4,000 ordinary income. The form of the boot (equipment vs. cash in this case) does not change the computation for Nicole.

What if: Assume the original facts in this example except that the inventory had an adjusted basis of $35,000 so that Nicole realized a $5,000 loss on the inventory (she still realized a $50,000 gain on the land). How much gain or loss would she recognize on the exchange?

Answer: Nicole would recognize a $15,000 capital gain on the land but would not recognize any loss on the inventory. Taxpayers recognize gain but not loss (even when they receive boot) in qualifying §351 exchanges.

Assumption of Shareholder Liabilities by the Transferee Corporation

When a sole proprietor chooses to turn her business into a corporation, the proprietor contributes the assets and liabilities of the business to the newly formed corporation in exchange for the corporation's stock. In these situations, the new (transferee) corporation assumes the liabilities (such as accounts payable or mortgages) of the proprietor.[9] An

---

[9]Similarly, when a corporation creates a subsidiary by transferring assets and liabilities to the subsidiary in exchange for stock in the subsidiary, the (transferee) subsidiary assumes liabilities of the (transferor) corporation.

important tax issue is whether the assumption of these liabilities by the newly created corporation constitutes boot received by the shareholder transferring the liabilities to the corporation. After all, the shareholder does receive something other than stock in the transaction—that is, the shareholder is relieved of debt.

Under the general rule, the corporation's assumption of a shareholder's liability (such as accounts payable or a mortgage attached to contributed land) is *not* treated as boot received by the shareholder.[10] However, as we discuss below, there is an exception to the general rule when the taxpayer is involved in a tax-avoidance transaction.

Tax-Avoidance Transactions   Under the exception to the general rule, if *any* of the liabilities of a shareholder assumed by the corporation are assumed with the purpose of avoiding federal income tax or if there is no corporate business purpose for the assumption, *all* of the liabilities assumed from the shareholder are treated as boot to that shareholder.[11] This "avoidance" motive may be present when shareholders borrow against their appreciated assets prior to contributing them to the corporation and then have the corporation assume the liabilities on the transfer (the end result is the same as if the corporation had paid cash to the shareholder and the shareholder had paid off the liability). The "no business purpose" motive can be present when shareholders have the corporation assume the shareholder's personal liabilities (e.g., grocery bills or alimony).

Example 13-6

What if: Suppose that when incorporating CCS, Nicole transferred a parcel of land to CCS in exchange for 50 percent of the corporation's stock (50 shares valued at $100,000). The land's fair market value was $120,000, and its adjusted tax basis to Nicole was $40,000. The land was subject to a $20,000 mortgage that CCS assumed on the transfer (Nicole transferred $100,000 of net value to CCS). Nicole borrowed the $20,000 from a bank (using the land as collateral) shortly before transferring the land to CCS and she used the mortgage proceeds to pay for a new family car. Assuming the transfer qualifies under §351 and that the mortgage has a tax-avoidance purpose, what gain or loss does Nicole recognize on the transfer?

Answer: $20,000 gain recognized. Nicole realized an $80,000 gain on the land transfer ($120,000 fair market value minus $40,000 basis). Because the mortgage has a tax-avoidance purpose, the $20,000 relief of debt is treated as boot received by Nicole on the exchange. Consequently, she must recognize gain in the amount of the lesser of (1) the $80,000 realized gain or (2) the $20,000 boot received.

What if: If the liability did not have a tax-avoidance purpose, what gain would Nicole recognize on the exchange?

Answer: $0. Because the liability is not considered to be boot, Nicole is allowed to defer her entire gain realized on the exchange.

ETHICS

Lisa is the sole proprietor of a business that manufactures solar panels. This week Lisa was approached to exchange her business assets for shares in Burns Power Corporation. As part of the exchange, Lisa is requiring Burns Power Corporation to assume the home-equity loan on her home. Do you think that Lisa should argue that there is no tax-avoidance motive in this arrangement? Suppose that Lisa established her business five years ago by investing funds from a home-equity loan on her home. Does this make a difference?

---

[10]§357(a).
[11]§357(b).

Liabilities in Excess of Basis   Even when liabilities are not treated as boot, the shareholder is required to recognize gain on the exchange to the extent the liabilities assumed by the corporation exceed the aggregate tax basis of the properties transferred by that shareholder.[12] The character of the gain depends on the character of the assets transferred to the corporation.

Example 13-7

What if: Suppose that when forming CCS, Nicole transferred a parcel of land (held as an investment) to CCS in exchange for 50 percent of the CCS stock (50 shares valued at $100,000). The land's fair market value was $150,000 and its adjusted tax basis to Nicole was $40,000. The land was subject to a $50,000 mortgage that CCS assumed on the transfer (not treated as boot). Assuming the transfer qualifies under §351, what is the amount and character of the gain Nicole recognizes on the exchange?

Answer: $10,000 capital gain. Even though Nicole did not receive boot on the exchange she still must recognize a $10,000 gain because the $50,000 mortgage assumed by CCS on the exchange exceeds the $40,000 basis of the property Nicole transferred by $10,000 ($50,000 liabilities minus $40,000 adjusted basis transferred = $10,000 recognized gain). The gain is a capital gain because the land was a capital asset to her.

What if: Assume the same facts as above except that in addition to the land, Nicole also transferred inventory with a fair market value of $15,000 and an adjusted basis of $10,000 for additional CCS stock. What is the amount and character of gain Nicole would recognize on the exchange of the land and inventory for stock?

Answer: $0. Nicole did not receive any boot, and the $50,000 mortgage assumed by CCS does not exceed the $50,000 aggregate basis of the assets Nicole transferred to CCS ($40,000 basis of land + $10,000 basis of inventory).

Under an exception to the general rule, the assumption of liabilities is disregarded in determining whether the liabilities assumed exceed basis if payment of the liabilities would give rise to a deduction. Examples include when a corporation assumes the accounts payable of a cash-method sole proprietorship or when a subsidiary assumes the "payment liabilities" (for example, accrued vacation pay) of an accrual-method corporation.[13]

Example 13-8

What if: Suppose that when incorporating CCS, Nicole transferred accounts receivable (fair market value $20,000 and $0 tax basis) and $15,000 of accounts payable from accounting fees from her cash-method sole proprietorship to CCS in exchange for CCS stock valued at $5,000. Assuming the transfer qualifies under §351, what is the amount and character of the gain Nicole must recognize on the exchange?

Answer: $0 gain recognized. Because Nicole did not receive boot in the exchange and because the accounts payable do not count as liabilities for purposes of the liabilities-in-excess-of-basis test (the accounts payable would give rise to a deduction when paid because they had not been previously deducted), she does not recognize any gain. (Note that if the accounts payable did not meet the special exception, Nicole would have had to recognize $15,000 of gain for liabilities in excess of the $0 basis from the accounts receivable she contributed to CCS.)

Shareholders' Basis in Stock Received in a Qualifying §351 Exchange

Shareholders are allowed to defer but not exclude gain realized on qualifying §351 exchanges. The deferred gain in the exchange is reflected in the difference between the fair market value of the stock the shareholder receives and the shareholder's adjusted basis in

---

[12]§357(c).

[13]§357(c)(3). Note that this exception is not available when the liabilities create basis in assets.

that stock. Thus, shareholders generally defer gain until they sell the stock they received in the exchange. The starting point for computing the shareholders' basis in the stock they receive is the basis of the property they contribute to the corporation (including cash). To this, they add gain they recognize on the transfer, subtract the fair market value of boot they receive (boot is subtracted because shareholders take basis in the boot equal to its fair market value), and subtract liabilities assumed by the corporation on the exchange (however, assumed liabilities that would give rise to a deduction do not reduce stock basis).[14] When liabilities are treated as boot they are subtracted as either boot or as liabilities but not both. Exhibit 13-1 provides a comprehensive template for computing stock basis in a §351 exchange.

EXHIBIT 13-1   **Computing the Tax Basis of Stock Received in a §351 Exchange**

		Cash contributed
+		Tax basis of other property contributed
+		Gain recognized on the transfer
−		Fair market value of boot received for stock
−		Liabilities assumed by the corporation on property contributed*
		Tax basis of stock received

*Does not include assumed liabilities that give rise to a deduction or that create tax basis.[15]

Example 13-9

What if: Let's return to the second set of *What if* facts in Example 13-5, in which Nicole exchanged land (fair market value $90,000; basis $40,000) and inventory (fair market value $30,000; basis $26,000) in exchange for stock valued at $100,000 and boot valued at $20,000 (assume the boot is equipment). She recognized $15,000 of capital gain and $4,000 of ordinary income on the exchange. What is Nicole's basis in her CCS stock? What is her basis in the equipment she received from CCS?

Answer: Nicole's basis in the stock is $65,000, computed as follows:

Description	Amount	Explanation
(1) Tax basis of land contributed	$ 40,000	
(2) Tax basis of inventory contributed	26,000	
(3) Gain recognized on the exchange	19,000	
(4) Fair market value of boot (equipment) received	(20,000)	
Tax basis of stock received	**$ 65,000**	Sum of (1) through (4)

Nicole's basis in the equipment received is $20,000, which is its fair market value.

Note that if Nicole subsequently sells her CCS stock for its current fair market value of $100,000, she would recognize gain of $35,000. This is the amount of gain she deferred on the exchange (realized gain of $54,000 minus recognized gain of $19,000).

Example 13-10

What if: Assume the same facts in Example 13-6, in which Nicole transferred a parcel of land (held as an investment) to CCS in exchange for 50 percent of the CCS stock (50 shares valued at $100,000). The land's fair market value was $120,000, and its adjusted tax basis to Nicole was $40,000. The land was subject to a $20,000 mortgage that CCS assumed on the transfer, which was treated as boot

(*continued on page 13-10*)

---

[14]§358(a) and §358(d).
[15]Source: §358(d)(2).

because the liability was assumed for tax-avoidance purposes. Nicole recognized $20,000 of gain on the exchange. What is Nicole's basis in the CCS stock she received in the exchange?

Answer: $40,000 computed as follows:

+	$40,000	Tax basis of land contributed
+	20,000	Gain recognized on the transfer
−	20,000	Fair market value of boot received
−	0	Liability is treated as boot so it is not subtracted twice
	$40,000	**Tax basis of stock received**

What if: Assume the same facts as above except that the liability was not for tax-avoidance purposes. What would be Nicole's basis in her CCS stock after the exchange?

Answer: $20,000, computed as follows:

+	$40,000	Tax basis of land contributed
+	0	No gain recognized because no boot received
−	0	Fair market value of boot received
−	20,000	Liability assumed by CCS
	$20,000	**Tax basis of stock received**

Example 13-11

What if: Assume the same facts in Example 13-7, in which Nicole transferred a parcel of land (held as an investment) to CCS in exchange for 50 percent of the CCS stock (50 shares valued at $100,000). The land's fair market value was $150,000 and its adjusted tax basis to Nicole was $40,000. The land was subject to a $50,000 mortgage that CCS assumed on the transfer (not treated as boot). Nicole recognized $10,000 of gain on the exchange because the liabilities assumed by CCS exceeded the basis of the property Nicole transferred to CCS by $10,000. What is Nicole's basis in her CCS stock after the exchange?

Answer: $0, computed as follows:

+	$40,000	Tax basis of land contributed
+	10,000	Gain recognized on the transfer
−	0	Fair market value of boot received
−	50,000	Liabilities assumed by the corporation on property contributed
	$ 0	**Tax basis of stock received**

Note that Nicole has stock valued at $100,000 with a basis of $0. This $100,000 built-in gain is equal to her deferred gain on the transaction. She realized gain of $110,000 ($150,000 minus $40,000) and recognized gain of $10,000.

What if: Assume the same facts except that the $50,000 liability was for accounts payable from accounting fees from Nicole's cash-method sole proprietorship. What would be Nicole's basis in her CCS stock?

Answer: $40,000, computed as follows:

+	$ 40,000	Tax basis of land contributed
+	0	Gain recognized on the transfer*
−	0	Fair market value of boot received
−	0	Liabilities assumed by the corporation on property contributed*
	$40,000	**Tax basis of stock received**

*Because the liabilities would give rise to a deduction if paid, they do not count for purposes of liabilities in excess of basis and they do not reduce Nicole's stock basis.

Note that Nicole deferred the $110,000 gain realized on the transaction. But, her built-in gain on the stock is only $60,000 ($100,000 fair market value minus $40,000 adjusted basis). The $50,000 difference is the built-in $50,000 deduction CCS will claim when it pays the accounts payable. That is, Nicole's $110,000 deferred gain minus the $50,000 deferred deduction equals the $60,000 deferred gain built in to her stock.

Tax Consequences to the Transferee Corporation in a Qualifying §351 Exchange

The corporation receiving property in exchange for its stock in a §351 exchange does not recognize gain or loss on the transfer.[16] The tax basis of property received by the corporation equals the property's tax basis in the transferor's (shareholder's) hands.[17] This is referred to as a **carryover basis** because the shareholder's basis in the property "carries over" to the corporation.[18] The shareholder's holding period in the property also carries over to the corporation (it *tacks* to the property received by the corporation).[19] This could be important in determining if subsequent gain or loss recognized on the disposition of the property qualifies as a §1231 gain or loss or whether it qualifies as a long-term rather than short-term capital gain or loss (the long-term vs. short-term distinction is more important for S corporations than C corporations). For ordinary assets, the corporation's holding period always starts when it receives the assets.

If the shareholder recognizes gain as a result of the property transfer (e.g., because boot is received), the corporation increases its tax basis in the property by the gain recognized by the shareholder on that property. This addition to basis is treated as a newly acquired asset by the corporation.[20]

Example 13-12

What if: Let's return to the second set of *What if* facts in Example 13-5. In that example, Nicole contributed land (fair market value $90,000; basis of $40,000) and inventory (fair market value $30,000; basis of $26,000) to CCS in exchange for 50 percent of the stock of CCS (50 shares valued at $100,000) and $20,000 cash in a qualifying §351 exchange. In the exchange, Nicole recognized $15,000 of capital gain on the land and $4,000 of ordinary income on the inventory. What is CCS's tax basis in the land and inventory it received from Nicole? What is its holding period in the land and inventory?

Answer: CCS's basis in the land is $55,000 ($40,000 original basis + $15,000 gain recognized by Nicole on the exchange) and its basis in the inventory is $30,000 ($26,000 original basis + $4,000 gain recognized by Nicole on the exchange). CCS's holding period in the land includes Nicole's holding period in the land because the land was a capital asset to Nicole. The holding period of the inventory begins on the day CCS received the inventory from Nicole because the inventory was an ordinary asset to Nicole.

The tax law limits the ability of a shareholder to transfer a "built-in loss" to a corporation in a §351 exchange. In particular, if the *aggregate* adjusted tax basis of property transferred to a corporation by a shareholder in a §351 exchange exceeds the aggregate fair market value of the assets, the aggregate tax basis of the assets in the hands of the transferee corporation cannot exceed their aggregate fair market value.[21]

---

[16]§1032.

[17]§362(a).

[18]§7701(a)(43) refers to this type of property as *transferred basis property.*

[19]§1223(2).

[20]If the asset is a depreciable asset, the corporation would start a new depreciation schedule for additional basis created by the gain recognized by the shareholder on that asset in the exchange.

[21]§362(e)(2). The aggregate reduction in tax basis is allocated among the assets transferred in proportion to their respective built-in losses immediately before the transfer. As an alternative, the transferor and transferee (corporation) can elect to have the transferor (shareholder) reduce her stock basis to fair market value (after the transfer, the duplicate loss is eliminated at either the corporate or shareholder level).

Issues Related to Incorporating an Ongoing Business

Practitioners often advise against transferring appreciated property to a closely held corporation. By transferring the property to the corporation, the shareholder creates two assets with the same built-in gain as the original property (the stock received in the hands of the shareholder and the property now owned by the corporation). The federal government can now tax the same gain twice: once when the corporation sells the property received and a second time when the shareholder sells the stock. Notice that Congress is not concerned about duplicating gains (when transferring appreciated property to a corporation) but it is concerned about duplicating losses (when transferring loss property to a corporation). By retaining the property outside the corporation, the shareholder can lease the property to the corporation, thereby reducing the corporation's taxable income through rent deductions. Note, however, that there may be valid state tax reasons to own the property inside a corporation, such as lower property taxes.

Contributions to Capital

A **contribution to capital** is a transfer of property to a corporation by a shareholder for which no stock or other property is received in return. The corporation receiving the property does not recognize income on the receipt of the property[22] and the corporation takes a carryover tax basis in the property.[23] Contributions by nonshareholders (e.g., a city contributes land to induce a corporation to locate its operations there) generally do not qualify as contributions to capital and therefore taxable to the corporation.[24]

A capital contribution generally is not a taxable event to the shareholder because the shareholder does not receive any additional consideration in return for the transfer. A shareholder making a capital contribution gets to increase the tax basis in her existing stock in an amount equal to the tax basis of the property contributed.

continued from page 13-1...

After a few rough years, CCS is now on solid footing and generating a profit. To maintain necessary capital in the early years, CCS borrowed from its bank. The bank agreed to lend money to CCS but required CCS to maintain and submit GAAP financial statements each year. Because it is a C corporation, CCS also must file tax returns each year and make estimated tax payments each quarter. When filing its tax return, CCS must reconcile its financial statement income to its taxable income. ■

  ## CORPORATE TAXABLE INCOME FORMULA

The formula for computing taxable income for C corporations and taxable income for individuals is similar in some respects and different in others. Exhibit 13-2 presents the corporate income tax formula along with the individual tax formula for comparison purposes.

Corporations compute gross income in the same manner as other types of business entities and individual taxpayers. However, in contrast to individual taxpayers,

---

[22]§118.
[23]§362(a)(2).
[24]§118(b).

EXHIBIT 13-2   **Corporate and Individual Tax Formulas**

	Corporate Tax Formula	Individual Tax Formula
Equals	Gross income	Gross income
Minus	Deductions	*For* AGI deductions
Equals		Adjusted gross income
Minus		*From* AGI deductions
		(1) Deduction for qualified business income and
		(2) *Greater* of:
		(a) Standard deduction or (b) Itemized deductions
Equals	Taxable income	Taxable income
Times	Tax rates	Tax rates
Equals	Income tax liability	Income tax liability
Add	Other taxes	Other taxes
Equals	Total tax	Total tax
Minus	Credits	Credits
Minus	Prepayments	Prepayments
Equals	Taxes due or (refund)	Taxes due or (refund)

corporations treat all deductions as related to a trade or business and do not compute adjusted gross income. Corporations do not claim a deduction for qualified business income and they do not itemize deductions or receive a standard deduction. Consequently, the "formula" to compute a corporation's taxable income is relatively straightforward.

Accounting Periods and Methods

In the Business Income, Deductions, and Accounting Methods chapter, we discussed accounting periods and methods for all forms of business entities. We learned that corporations measure their taxable income over a tax year and that their tax year must be the same as their financial accounting year. Corporations generally elect their tax year when they file their first income tax returns.

The timing of when corporations recognize income and deductions depends on their accounting methods. As we discussed in the Business Income, Deductions, and Accounting Methods chapter, accounting methods include overall methods of accounting (accrual method, cash method, or hybrid method) and accounting methods for individual items such as inventory (e.g., LIFO vs. FIFO) or depreciation (e.g., accelerated vs. straight-line). For tax purposes, corporations have some flexibility in choosing methods of accounting for individual items or transactions. However, corporations generally are required to use the accrual method of accounting.[25] Nonetheless, corporations with average annual gross receipts of $25 million or less for the three years prior to the current tax year may use the cash method of accounting.[26] Corporations that have not been in existence for at least three years compute their average annual gross receipts over the prior periods they have been in existence to determine if they are allowed to use the cash method of accounting.

THE KEY FACTS

Corporate Taxable Income Formula and Accounting Periods and Methods

- The corporate tax formula is similar to the individual tax formula, but corporations don't claim the deduction for qualified business income and they don't itemize or deduct the standard deduction.
- Corporations with average annual gross receipts of $25 million or less over the three prior tax years (or a shorter period for new corporations) may use the cash method of accounting.

[25]See the Business Income, Deductions, and Accounting Methods chapter for a detailed discussion of determining the timing of taxable income and tax deductions under the accrual method.

[26]§448. Qualified personal service corporations may use the cash method of accounting.

LO 13-3 # COMPUTING CORPORATE TAXABLE INCOME

To compute taxable income, most corporations start with **book (financial reporting) income** and then make adjustments for book–tax differences to reconcile to the tax numbers.[27]

Book–Tax Differences

Many income and expense items are accounted for differently for book and tax purposes. The following discussion describes several common **book–tax differences** applicable to corporations. Each book–tax difference can be considered to be either "unfavorable" or "favorable" depending on its effect on taxable income relative to book income. Any book–tax difference that requires an add back to book income to compute taxable income is an **unfavorable book–tax difference** because it requires an adjustment that increases taxable income (and taxes payable) relative to book income. Any book–tax difference that requires corporations to subtract the difference from book income in computing taxable income is a **favorable book–tax difference** because it decreases taxable income (and taxes payable) relative to book income.

In addition to the favorable/unfavorable distinction, book–tax differences also can be categorized as either permanent or temporary. **Permanent book–tax differences** arise from items that are income or deductions during the year for either book purposes or for tax purposes but not both. Permanent differences *do not reverse* over time, so over the long term the *total* amount of income or deductions for the items is different for book and tax purposes. In contrast, **temporary book–tax differences** are those book–tax differences that reverse over time such that over the long term, corporations recognize the same amount of income or deductions for the items on their financial statements as they recognize on their tax returns. Temporary book–tax differences arise because the income or deduction items are included in financial accounting income in one year and in taxable income in a different year. It also is important to note that temporary book–tax differences that *initially* are favorable (unfavorable) subsequently will become unfavorable (favorable) in future years when they reverse.

Distinguishing between permanent and temporary book–tax differences is important for at least two reasons. First, as we discuss later in the chapter, large corporations are *required to disclose* their permanent and temporary book–tax differences on their tax returns. Second, the distinction is useful for those responsible for computing and tracking book–tax differences. For temporary book–tax differences, it is important to understand how the items were accounted for in previous years to appropriately account for current-year reversals. In contrast, for permanent book–tax differences, corporations need only consider current-year amounts to determine book–tax differences. Below we describe some of the most common book–tax differences.

Common Permanent Book–Tax Differences
As we described in the Business Income, Deductions, and Accounting Methods chapter, businesses, including corporations, are allowed to exclude certain income items from gross income, and they are not allowed to deduct certain expenditures for tax purposes. Because these income items are included in book income, and the expenditures are deductible for financial reporting purposes, they generate permanent book–tax differences. Exhibit 13-3 identifies several permanent book–tax differences, explains their tax treatment, and identifies whether the items create favorable or unfavorable book–tax differences.

---

[27]This chapter generally assumes that GAAP is used to determine book income numbers.

EXHIBIT 13-3   Common Permanent Book–Tax Differences

Description	Explanation	Difference
Federal income tax expense	Expensed for books but not for tax.	Unfavorable
Interest income from municipal bonds	Income included in book income, excluded from taxable income.	Favorable
Death benefit from life insurance on key employees	Income included in book income, excluded from taxable income.	Favorable
Interest expense on loans to acquire investments generating tax-exempt income	Deductible for books, but expenses incurred to generate tax-exempt income are not deductible for tax.	Unfavorable
Life insurance premiums for which corporation is beneficiary	Deductible for books, but expenses incurred to generate tax-exempt income (life insurance death benefit) are not deductible for tax.	Unfavorable
Meals expense	Fully deductible for books, but generally only 50 percent deductible for tax.	Unfavorable
Entertainment expense	Deductible for books, but not for tax.	Unfavorable
Fines and penalties and political contribution	Deductible for books, but not for tax.	Unfavorable

---

Example 13-13

A review of CCS's current-year trial balance indicated that CCS earned $300 of interest income on Salt Lake City municipal bonds, expensed $1,200 for premiums on key employee life insurance policies (for Nicole and Sarah), $2,800 for meals, and $1,200 for entertainment. CCS also reported $20,000 in federal income tax expense. What amount of permanent book–tax differences will CCS report from these transactions? Are the differences favorable or unfavorable?

Answer: See summary below:

Item	Adjustment (Favorable) Unfavorable	Notes
Interest on Salt Lake City municipal bonds	($300)	Income excluded from gross income.
Premiums paid for key employee life insurance policies	1,200	Premiums paid to insure lives of key company executives are not deductible for tax purposes.
Meals expense	1,400	$2,800 expense for book purposes, but only 50 percent deductible for tax purposes.
Entertainment expense	1,200	Not deductible for tax purposes.
Federal income tax expense	20,000	Federal income expense is not deductible for tax purposes.

THE KEY FACTS

Computing Corporate Taxable Income

- Corporations reconcile from book income to taxable income.
  - Favorable (unfavorable) book–tax differences decrease (increase) book income relative to taxable income.
  - Permanent book–tax differences arise in one year and never reverse.
  - Temporary book–tax differences arise in one year and reverse in a subsequent year.

Common Temporary Book–Tax Differences   Corporations experience temporary book–tax differences because the accounting methods they apply to determine certain items of income and expense for financial reporting purposes differ from the accounting methods they use for tax purposes. Unlike permanent book–tax differences, temporary book–tax differences balance out so that over time corporations recognize the same amount of income or deduction for the particular item. Exhibit 13-4 identifies common temporary book–tax differences and identifies where they are discussed in other chapters. Exhibit 13-5 summarizes CCS's temporary book–tax differences described in Exhibit 13-4.

EXHIBIT 13-4 **Common Temporary Book–Tax Differences Associated with Items Discussed in Other Chapters**

Description	Explanation	Initial Difference*
Depreciation expense (Property Acquisition and Cost Recovery chapter)	Difference between depreciation expense for tax purposes and depreciation expense for book purposes.	Favorable
Gain or loss on disposition of depreciable assets (Property Dispositions chapter)	Difference between gain or loss for tax and book purposes when corporation sells or disposes of depreciable property. Difference generally arises because depreciation expense, and thus the adjusted basis of the asset, is different for tax and book purposes. This difference is essentially the reversal of the book–tax difference for the depreciation expense on the asset sold or disposed of.	Unfavorable
Bad debt expense (Business Income, Deductions, and Accounting Methods chapter)	Direct write-off method for tax purposes, allowance method for book purposes.	Unfavorable
Unearned rent revenue (Business Income, Deductions, and Accounting Methods chapter)	Taxable on receipt but recognized when earned for book purposes.	Unfavorable
Deferred compensation (Business Income, Deductions, and Accounting Methods chapter)	Deductible when accrued for book purposes, but deductible when paid for tax purposes if accrued but not paid within 2.5 months after year-end. Also, accrued compensation to shareholders owning more than 50 percent of the corporation is not deductible until paid.	Unfavorable
Organizational expenses and start-up costs (Property Acquisition and Cost Recovery chapter)	Immediately deducted for book purposes but capitalized and amortized for tax purposes (limited immediate expensing allowed for tax).	Unfavorable
Warranty expense and other estimated expenses (Business Income, Deductions, and Accounting Methods chapter)	Estimated expenses deducted for book purposes, but actual expenses deducted for tax purposes.	Unfavorable
UNICAP (§263A) (Business Income, Deductions, and Accounting Methods chapter)	Certain expenditures deducted for book purposes, but capitalized to inventory for tax purposes. Difference reverses when inventory is sold.	Unfavorable
Purchased (not self-created) goodwill (Business Income, Deductions, and Accounting Methods chapter)	For tax purposes, amortized over 180 months (straight line). For book purposes, expensed as impaired)	Favorable (unless impaired in the first year by more than the first year amortization)

*Note that each of the initial book–tax differences will reverse over time [the initially favorable (unfavorable) book–tax differences will reverse to become unfavorable (favorable) book–tax differences in the future].

EXHIBIT 13-5   CCS's Temporary Book–Tax Differences Associated
with Items Discussed in Other Chapters

Item	(1) Book (Dr.) Cr.	(2) Tax (Dr.) Cr.	(2) – (1) Difference (Favorable) Unfavorable
Depreciation expense	$(24,000)	$(39,000)	$(15,000)
Gain on fixed asset disposition	540	700	160
Bad debt expense	(25,600)	(24,900)	700
Warranty expense	(5,800)	(4,100)	1,700

Corporate-Specific Deductions and Associated Book–Tax Differences

Certain deductions and corresponding limitations apply specifically to corporations. In this section, we introduce these deductions and identify corresponding book–tax differences.

Stock Options   As we discussed in the Gross Income and Exclusions chapter, corporations often compensate executives and other employees with stock options. Stock options allow recipients to acquire stock in corporations issuing the options. To acquire the stock, employees exercise the options and pay the **exercise price.** The exercise price is usually the stock price on the day the options are issued to the employee. For example, at a time when a corporation's stock is trading for $10 per share, a corporation might issue (or grant) 100 stock options to an employee that allow the employee to purchase up to 100 shares of the corporation's stock for $10 a share (one share per option in this case). Employees usually must wait a certain amount of time between when they receive the options and when they are able to exercise them (i.e., they must wait until the options **vest** before they can exercise them). If employees quit working for the corporation before the options vest, they forfeit the options.

The tax treatment of the option-related transactions to the corporation (and the employee[28]) depends on whether the options are **incentive stock options (ISOs)** (less common, more administrative requirements for the corporation to qualify) or **nonqualified stock options (NQOs)** (more common, options that don't qualify as ISOs).[29] For tax purposes, corporations issuing incentive stock options generally do not deduct any compensation expense associated with the options. Consequently, when a corporation reports book compensation expense for incentive stock options, it generates an unfavorable, permanent book–tax difference.

For nonqualified options, corporations deduct the difference between the fair market value of the stock and the exercise price of the option (the **bargain element**) as compensation expense in the year in which employees exercise the stock options. Nonqualified options may generate permanent and/or temporary book–tax differences. The amount of the permanent difference is the difference between the total amount of the book expense for the options (the estimated value of the options expensed over the vesting period) and the amount of the tax deduction for the options (the bargain element). The permanent book–tax difference is favorable if the bargain element exceeds the estimated value of the

---

[28]Employees do not recognize any income for regular tax purposes when they exercise incentive stock options. However, for nonqualified options, they recognize ordinary income for the difference between the value of the stock and the exercise price on the date of exercise. This chapter emphasizes the tax treatment of the options from the corporation's perspective.

[29]Requirements for options to qualify as incentive stock options are more restrictive than for nonqualified stock options. The formal requirements for incentive stock options are beyond the scope of this chapter.

applied after the current-year contribution deduction. Corporations may deduct the carryover in future years to the extent the 10 percent limitation does not restrict deductions for charitable contributions they actually make in those years. Unused carryovers expire after five years.

Example 13-19

What if: Assume that CCS's 2018 taxable income before considering the charitable contribution limitation was $40,000. The taxable income computation includes a $5,000 charitable contribution deduction, a $1,000 DRD, a $2,000 net capital loss carryover deduction, and $12,000 depreciation deduction. Under these circumstances, what would be CCS's 2018 deductible charitable contribution? What would be its charitable contribution carryover? When would the carryover expire?

Answer: $4,600 deductible charitable contribution and $400 charitable contribution carryover (expires at end of 2023), computed as follows:

Description	Amount	Explanation
(1) Taxable income before charitable contribution limitation	$40,000	
(2) Charitable contribution deduction before limitation	$ 5,000	Added back to taxable income in computing limitation.
(3) Dividends received deduction (DRD)	$ 1,000	Added back to taxable income in computing limitation.
(4) Charitable contribution limit modified taxable income	$46,000	Sum of (1) through (3)
(5) Tax deduction limitation percentage	10%	§170(b)(2)(A)
(6) Charitable contribution deduction limitation	$ 4,600	(5) × (6)
(7) **Charitable contribution deduction for year**	**$ 4,600**	Lesser of (2) or (6)
Charitable contribution carryover	**$ 400**	(2) – (7)

Corporations report *unfavorable, temporary* book–tax differences to the extent the 10 percent modified taxable income limitation restricts the amount of their tax charitable contribution deduction. That is, they recognize unfavorable, temporary book–tax differences in the amount of the charitable contribution *carryover* they generate for the year. Conversely, corporations report *favorable, temporary* book–tax differences when they deduct charitable contribution carryovers because they deduct the carryovers for tax purposes, but not book purposes.

Example 13-20

What if: Assume the same facts as in Example 13-19, where CCS reported a $4,600 charitable contribution deduction and a $400 charitable contribution carryover. What would be CCS's book–tax difference associated with the charitable contribution? Would it be favorable or unfavorable? Would it be permanent or temporary?

Answer: $400 unfavorable, temporary difference. The amount of the carryover was not deductible for tax in the current year but it was expensed for books. When CCS uses the charitable contribution carryover, it will report a $400 favorable, temporary book–tax difference.

Dividends Received Deduction   When corporations receive dividends from other corporations they are taxed on the dividends at 21 percent, not the 15 or 20 percent preferential rate available to individual taxpayers. This isn't all bad news, however, because corporations are allowed a dividends received deduction (DRD) that reduces the actual tax they pay on the dividends. The DRD is designed to mitigate the extent to which corporate earnings are subject to three (or perhaps even more) levels of taxation. Corporate taxable income is subject to triple taxation when a corporation pays tax on its income and then distributes its after-tax income to shareholders that are corporations. Corporate shareholders are taxed on the dividends, creating the second tax. When corporate shareholders distribute their after-tax earnings from the dividends to their shareholders the income is taxed for a third time. The dividends received deduction reduces the amount of the second-level tax and thus reduces the impact of triple taxation (or more) of earnings that corporations distribute as dividends.

Corporations generally compute their dividends received deduction by multiplying the dividend amount by 50 percent, 65 percent, or 100 percent, depending on their level of ownership in the distributing corporation's stock. Exhibit 13-6 summarizes the stock ownership thresholds and the corresponding dividends received deduction percentage. Generally, only dividends received from domestic corporations are eligible for the DRD.[37]

EXHIBIT 13-6   **Stock Ownership and Dividends Received Deduction Percentage**

Receiving Corporation's Stock Ownership in Distributing Corporation's Stock	Dividends Received Deduction Percentage
Less than 20 percent	50
At least 20 percent but less than 80 percent	65
80 percent or more	100

Example 13-21

During the year, CCS received a $3,000 dividend from IBM. CCS owns less than 1 percent of the IBM stock. What is CCS's DRD associated with the dividend?

Answer: $1,500 ($3,000 × 50%).

What if: What is CCS's tax rate on the IBM dividend income *after* considering the dividends received deduction?

Answer: 10.5 percent marginal tax rate on dividend income, computed as follows:

Description	Amount	Explanation
(1) Dividend from IBM	$ 3,000	
(2) DRD percentage	50%	Less than 20 percent ownership in IBM.
(3) **Dividends received deduction**	**$1,500**	(1) × (2)
(4) Dividend subject to taxation after DRD	$ 1,500	(1) − (3)
(5) Corporate tax rate	21%	
(6) Taxes payable on dividend *after* DRD	$ 315	(4) × (5)
Marginal tax rate on dividend *after* DRD	**10.50%**	(6)/(1)

---

[37]Domestic corporations that own at least 10 percent of certain foreign corporations are eligible for a 100 percent DRD for the foreign-source portion of dividends received from the foreign corporation.

Deduction limitation. The dividends received deduction is limited to the product of the applicable dividends received deduction percentage (see Exhibit 13-6) and **DRD modified taxable income.**[38] DRD modified taxable income is the dividend-receiving corporation's taxable income *before* deducting the following:

- The DRD.
- The NOL deduction.
- Capital loss *carrybacks.*[39]

Thus, to the extent these items were deducted in determining taxable income, they would have to be added back to determine the DRD modified taxable income. Because the dividends received deduction is strictly a tax deduction and not a book deduction, *any* dividends received deduction creates a *favorable, permanent* book–tax difference.

Example 13-22

What if: Suppose that CCS received a $3,000 dividend from IBM and that CCS owns less than 1 percent of the IBM stock. Further assume that CCS's taxable income before the dividends received deduction was $5,000 in Scenario A and $1,500 in Scenario B. To arrive at the taxable income under both scenarios (before the DRD), CCS deducted a $1,000 NOL carryover. What is CCS's dividends received deduction associated with the dividend in Scenario A and in Scenario B?

Answer: $1,500 in Scenario A and $1,250 in Scenario B, computed as follows:

Description	Scenario A	Scenario B	Explanation
(1) Taxable income before the dividends received deduction (includes dividend income)	$5,000	$1,500	
(2) NOL carryover (add back)	1,000	1,000	
(3) DRD modified taxable income	$6,000	$2,500	(1) + (2)
(4) Dividend income	$3,000	$3,000	
(5) Dividends received deduction percentage based on ownership	50%	50%	§243(a)
(6) Dividends received deduction before limitation	$1,500	$1,500	(4) × (5)
(7) Dividends received deduction income limitation	3,000	1,250	(3) × (5)
Deductible DRD	**1,500***	**1,250***	Lesser of (6) or (7)

*The DRD creates a favorable, permanent book–tax difference.

The modified taxable income limitation *does not apply* if after deducting the *full* dividends received deduction (dividend × DRD percentage) a corporation reports a current-year net operating loss (negative taxable income). That is, if after deducting the full dividends received deduction, the corporation has a net operating loss, the corporation is allowed to deduct the *full* dividends received deduction no matter the amount of modified taxable income.[40] As illustrated in the following example, this rule can cause some strange results.

---

[38]When corporations receive dividends from multiple corporations with different deduction percentages, according to §246(b)(3), the limitations first apply to the 65 percent dividends received deduction and then the 50 percent dividends received deduction.

[39]§246(b)(1).

[40]§246(b)(2).

Example 13-23

What if: Assume the same facts as in Scenario B of Example 13-22, except that taxable income before the dividends received deduction is $1,490 instead of $1,500. What is CCS's DRD modified taxable income? What is CCS's dividends received deduction?

Answer: $2,490 modified taxable income; and $1,500 DRD, computed as follows:

Description	Amount	Explanation
(1) Taxable income before the DRD (includes dividend income)	$ 1,490	
(2) NOL carryover (add back)	$ 1,000	
(3) **DRD modified taxable income**	**$2,490**	(1) + (2)
(4) Dividend income	$ 3,000	
(5) DRD percentage based on ownership	50%	
(6) DRD before limitation	$ 1,500	(4) × (5)
(7) DRD income limitation	$ 1,245	(3) × (5)
(8) Taxable income (loss) after deducting full DRD	(10)	(1) − (6)
Deductible DRD	**$1,500**	Lesser of (6) or (7) unless (8) is negative, then (6).

In this example, CCS was able to deduct the entire $1,500 DRD because in deducting the full DRD it had a net operating loss of $10. If CCS's taxable income before the DRD had been $10 more as it was in Example 13-22, line (1), Scenario B, its DRD would have been $250 less (it would be limited to $1,250).

Taxable Income Summary

Exhibit 13-7 presents a template for reconciling book and taxable income. Note that the template does not follow the typical financial accounting format because it organizes the information to facilitate the taxable income computation. In particular, it puts the deductions in the *sequence in which they are deducted for tax purposes.*

Tax Liability

After corporations determine their taxable income, they compute their tax liability by multiplying taxable income by a flat 21 percent rate. This rate is effective for tax years ending after 2017.[41]

Example 13-24

CCS's taxable income is $130,700. What is its income tax liability?

Answer: $27,447, ($130,700 × 21 percent).

The corporate alternative minimum tax (AMT) was recently repealed for taxable years beginning after 2017. Corporations that paid the AMT received a minimum tax credit (MTC) that could be carried forward indefinitely to offset the excess of regular tax over the AMT in future years. In essence, the AMT acted as a prepayment of the regular tax. Under the new tax law, existing MTCs can offset the tax liability for any taxable year following 2017, after deducting certain credits. For tax years beginning in 2018, 2019, and 2020, 50 percent of the MTC in excess of the tax liability is refundable. Any remaining MTC is fully refundable in 2021.

[41]For tax years ending before 2018, the corporate tax rates ranged from 15 percent to 39 percent, depending on level of taxable income. The most profitable corporations were taxed at a flat 35 percent rate.

EXHIBIT 13-7 **CCS Book–Tax Reconciliation Template**

CCS Inc.		Book to Tax		
Income Statement for Current Year	**Book Income**	**Adjustments (Dr.)***	**Cr.***	**Taxable Income**
Revenue from sales	$ 900,000			$ 900,000
Cost of goods sold	(300,000)			(300,000)
Gross profit	$ 600,000			$ 600,000
Other income:				
Dividend income	$ 3,000			$ 3,000
Interest income	700	(300)[ex. 13]		400
Capital gains (losses)	(9,000)		9,000[ex. 15]	0
Gain on fixed asset dispositions	540		160[exh. 5]	700
Gross income	$ 595,240			$ 604,100
Expenses:				
Compensation	$(350,000)			$(350,000)
Repairs and maintenance	(6,000)			(6,000)
Bad debts	(25,600)		700[exh. 5]	(24,900)
Taxes and licenses	(14,000)			(14,000)
Interest expense	(4,000)			(4,000)
Charitable donations	Moved below			
Depreciation	(24,000)	(15,000)[exh. 5]		(39,000)
Advertising	(16,000)			(16,000)
Warranty expense	(5,800)		1,700[exh. 5]	(4,100)
Insurance premiums	(4,200)		1,200[ex. 13]	(3,000)
Meals expense	(2,800)		1,400[ex. 13]	(1,400)
Entertainment expense	(1,300)		1,300[ex. 13]	0
Other expenses	(4,500)			(4,500)
Federal income tax expense	(25,000)		25,000[ex. 13]	0
Total expenses before charitable contribution and DRD	$(483,200)			$(466,900)
Taxable income before CC and DRD (taxable income limit for charitable contribution)	$ 112,040			$ 137,200
Charitable contribution	(5,000)			(5,000)
Taxable income before DRD				$ 132,200
Dividends received deduction		(1,500)[ex. 22]		(1,500)
Book/taxable income	**$107,040**	**(16,800)**	**40,460**	**$130,700**

*Note that the superscript by each book–tax difference identifies the example (ex.) or exhibit (exh.) where the adjustment is calculated. Also note that the numbers in the debit column are favorable book–tax adjustments while numbers in the credit column are unfavorable book–tax adjustments.

LO 13-4 **COMPLIANCE**

Corporations report their taxable income on Form 1120.[42] Exhibit 13-8 presents the front page of CCS's current-year Form 1120 through the tax liability. Form 1120 includes a schedule for corporations to report their book–tax differences and reconcile

---

[42]Corporations with gross receipts, total income, and total assets under $500,000 may complete Form 1120A, which is a short version of Form 1120.

EXHIBIT 13-8   **CCS Form 1120 page 1, through Tax Refund**

U.S. Corporation Income Tax Return

Form **1120**

Department of the Treasury
Internal Revenue Service

For calendar year 2017 or tax year beginning _____ , 2017, ending _____ , 20 _____

▶ Go to *www.irs.gov/Form1120* for instructions and the latest information.

OMB No. 1545-0123

2017

A Check if:			Name	B Employer identification number
1a Consolidated return (attach Form 851) .	☐	**TYPE OR PRINT**	**Color Comfort Sheets**	12-3456789
b Life/nonlife consolidated return . .	☐		Number, street, and room or suite no. If a P.O. box, see instructions.	C Date incorporated
2 Personal holding co. (attach Sch. PH) .	☐		**123 East Town Avenue**	
3 Personal service corp. (see instructions) . .	☐		City or town, state, or province, country, and ZIP or foreign postal code	D Total assets (see instructions) $ 145,000
4 Schedule M-3 attached	☐	E Check if: **(1)** ☐ Initial return **(2)** ☐ Final return **(3)** ☐ Name change **(4)** ☐ Address change		

Income

1a	Gross receipts or sales	1a	900,000		
b	Returns and allowances	1b			
c	Balance. Subtract line 1b from line 1a			1c	900,000
2	Cost of goods sold (attach Form 1125-A)			2	300,000
3	Gross profit. Subtract line 2 from line 1c			3	600,000
4	Dividends (Schedule C, line 19)			4	3,000
5	Interest			5	400
6	Gross rents			6	
7	Gross royalties			7	
8	Capital gain net income (attach Schedule D (Form 1120))			8	
9	Net gain or (loss) from Form 4797, Part II, line 17 (attach Form 4797)			9	700
10	Other income (see instructions—attach statement)			10	
11	**Total income.** Add lines 3 through 10 . . . . ▶			11	604,100

Deductions (See instructions for limitations on deductions.)

12	Compensation of officers (see instructions—attach Form 1125-E) . . . ▶			12	100,000
13	Salaries and wages (less employment credits)			13	250,000
14	Repairs and maintenance			14	6,000
15	Bad debts			15	24,900
16	Rents			16	
17	Taxes and licenses			17	14,000
18	Interest			18	4,000
19	Charitable contributions			19	5,000
20	Depreciation from Form 4562 not claimed on Form 1125-A or elsewhere on return (attach Form 4562) . .			20	39,000
21	Depletion			21	
22	Advertising			22	16,000
23	Pension, profit-sharing, etc., plans			23	
24	Employee benefit programs			24	
25	Domestic production activities deduction (attach Form 8903)			25	
26	Other deductions (attach statement)			26	13,000
27	**Total deductions.** Add lines 12 through 26 . . . . ▶			27	471,900
28	Taxable income before net operating loss deduction and special deductions. Subtract line 27 from line 11.			28	132,200
29a	Net operating loss deduction (see instructions)	29a			
b	Special deductions (Schedule C, line 20)	29b	1,500		
c	Add lines 29a and 29b			29c	1,500

Tax, Refundable Credits, and Payments

30	**Taxable income.** Subtract line 29c from line 28. See instructions			30	130,700
31	Total tax (Schedule J, Part I, line 11)			31	27,447
32	Total payments and refundable credits (Schedule J, Part II, line 21)			32	
33	Estimated tax penalty. See instructions. Check if Form 2220 is attached . . . ▶ ☐			33	
34	**Amount owed.** If line 32 is smaller than the total of lines 31 and 33, enter amount owed			34	
35	**Overpayment.** If line 32 is larger than the total of lines 31 and 33, enter amount overpaid			35	
36	Enter amount from line 35 you want: **Credited to 2018 estimated tax** ▶		Refunded ▶	36	

Sign Here

Under penalties of perjury, I declare that I have examined this return, including accompanying schedules and statements, and to the best of my knowledge and belief, it is true, correct, and complete. Declaration of preparer (other than taxpayer) is based on all information of which preparer has any knowledge.

▶ _____   _____   ▶ _____
  Signature of officer   Date   Title

May the IRS discuss this return with the preparer shown below? See instructions. ☐ **Yes** ☐ **No**

Paid Preparer Use Only

Print/Type preparer's name	Preparer's signature	Date	Check ☐ if self-employed	PTIN
Firm's name ▶			Firm's EIN ▶	
Firm's address ▶			Phone no.	

For Paperwork Reduction Act Notice, see separate instructions.   Cat. No. 11450Q   Form **1120** (2017)

EXHIBIT 13-9   Form 1120, Schedule M-1

Schedule M-1	Reconciliation of Income (Loss) per Books With Income per Return			
	Note: The corporation may be required to file Schedule M-3. See instructions.			

1	Net income (loss) per books	107,040	7	Income recorded on books this year	
2	Federal income tax per books	25,000		not included on this return (itemize):	
3	Excess of capital losses over capital gains .	9,000		Tax-exempt interest $ 300	
4	Income subject to tax not recorded on books				
	this year (itemize):				300
	_____ gain on fixed asset disposition	160	8	Deductions on this return not charged	
5	Expenses recorded on books this year not			against book income this year (itemize):	
	deducted on this return (itemize):		a	Depreciation . . $ 15,000	
a	Depreciation . . . . $ _____		b	Charitable contributions $ _____	
b	Charitable contributions . $ _____				
c	Travel and entertainment . $ _____				15,000
	Other: See statement 1	6,300	9	Add lines 7 and 8	15,300
6	Add lines 1 through 5	147,500	10	Income (page 1, line 28)—line 6 less line 9	132,200

Statement 1
Other Expenses Recorded on Books Not
Deducted on Return
Form 1120, Schedule M-1, line 5

Warranty Expense	$1,700
Bad Debts	700
Insurance Premiums	1,200
Meals Expense	1,400
Entertainment Expense	1,300
Total Other Expenses	$6,300

their book and taxable income. Corporations with total assets of less than $10,000,000 report their book–tax differences on Schedule M-1. Corporations with total assets of $10,000,000 or more are required to report their book–tax differences on Schedule M-3.[43] Because corporations report book–tax differences as adjustments to book income to compute taxable income on either Schedule M-1 or M-3, these book-to-tax adjustments are often referred to as **Schedule M adjustments, M adjustments,** and even "Ms" (plural version of M).

Because CCS's total assets are $145,000 (see Exhibit 13-8, line D), it may complete a Schedule M-1 rather than a Schedule M-3. Exhibit 13-9 presents CCS's completed Schedule M-1 based on the information provided in Exhibit 13-7. Schedule M-1 is a relatively short schedule, and it does not require corporations to provide much detail about the nature of their book–tax differences.

The schedule begins on line 1 with book income after taxes. The left-hand column includes all unfavorable book–tax differences (add-backs to book income to arrive at taxable income). In general, the top part of the left column is for income items and the bottom part is for expense items. The right-hand column consists of all favorable book–tax differences. The top part of the right column is for income items and the bottom part includes expense items.

[43]Corporations with at least $10 million but less than $50 million in total assets at tax year-end are permitted to file Schedule M-1 in place of Schedule M-3, Parts II and III. Schedule M-3, Part I, lines 1–12 are still required for these taxpayers. Corporations with $10 million to $50 million in total assets may voluntarily file Schedule M-3, Parts II and III, rather than Schedule M-1.

Finally, it is important to note that Schedule M-1 (and Schedule M-3) reconcile to taxable income *before* the net operating loss deduction and the dividends received deduction.[44] Consequently, to fully reconcile book and taxable income, corporations must deduct net operating loss carryovers and dividends received deductions from line 10 on Schedule M-1 (or the amount on line 30d on Schedule M-3).

Example 13-25

The bottom line (line 10) of CCS's Schedule M-1 is $132,200. How would one reconcile from the $132,200 on CCS's Schedule M-1 line 10 to CCS's taxable income of $130,700?

Answer: Start with the amount on line 10 and subtract CCS's DRD, as illustrated below:

Description	Amount	Explanation
(1) Schedule M-1 taxable income	$ 132,200	Form 1120, Schedule M-1, line 10
(2) Dividends received deduction	(1,500)	Exhibit 13-7
Taxable income	**$130,700**	(1) + (2)

Schedule M-3 requires corporations to report significantly more information than Schedule M-1 does. For example, Schedule M-3 includes more than 60 specific types of book–tax differences, while Schedule M-1 includes only 10 summary lines. Furthermore, Schedule M-3 requires corporations to identify each book–tax difference as either temporary or permanent. The IRS created Schedule M-3 in hopes of providing a better and more efficient starting point for agents to identify and scrutinize large dollar compliance issues.

Form 1120 also requires corporations to complete Schedule M-2, which provides a reconciliation of the corporation's beginning and ending balance in its unappropriated retained earnings from its financial accounting balance sheet (reported on Schedule L). Corporations with total receipts and total assets less than $250,000 are not required to complete Schedules L, M-1, or M-2.

Consolidated Tax Returns

An affiliated group of corporations may elect to file a **consolidated tax return** in which the group files a tax return as if it were one entity for tax purposes. An **affiliated group** exists when one corporation owns at least 80 percent of (1) the total voting power and (2) the total stock value of another corporation.[45] Filing a consolidated tax return allows the losses of one group member to offset the income of other members. Further, income from certain intercompany transactions is deferred until realized through a transaction outside of the affiliated group. However, losses from certain intercompany transactions are also deferred until realized through a transaction outside of the affiliated group.

Affiliated groups cannot file consolidated tax returns unless they elect to do so. Because the election is binding on subsequent years, it should be made with care. Consolidated tax returns may impose additional administrative and compliance costs on the

---

[44]Schedule M-1 (and the Schedule M-3) reconciles to line 28 on Form 1120. Line 28 is taxable income before the net operating loss and special deductions (the dividends received deduction).

[45]§1504(a).

taxpayers. The consolidated tax return laws are very complex and beyond the scope of this text.[46] Further, the rules for consolidated reporting for financial statement purposes are different from the tax rules.

Corporate Tax Return Due Dates and Estimated Taxes

The tax return due date for a C corporation is three and one-half months after the corporation's year-end (two and one-half months after year-end for June 30 year-end corporations). Thus, a calendar-year corporation's unextended tax return due date is April 15. Corporations requesting an extension can extend the due date for filing their tax returns (not for paying the taxes) for six months (seven months for a June 30 year-end corporation). Consequently, a calendar-year corporation's extended tax return due date is October 15.

Corporations with a federal income tax liability of $500 or more are required to pay their tax liability for the year in quarterly estimated installments.[47] The installments are due on the 15th day of the 4th, 6th, 9th, and 12th months of their respective tax years.[48] When corporations file their tax returns, they determine whether they must pay estimated tax underpayment penalties. Generally, corporations are subject to underpayment penalties if they did not pay in 25 percent, 50 percent, 75 percent, and 100 percent of their *required annual payment* by the due date of their first, second, third, and fourth installment payments, respectively.[49] The required annual payment is the *lowest* of:

1. 100 percent of the tax liability on the prior year's return, but only if there was a positive tax liability on the return and the prior-year return covered a 12-month period (however, see discussion of "large" corporations below).
2. 100 percent of the current-year tax liability (corporations usually don't rely on this method to determine the required payment because they won't know what this is until they complete their tax returns—after the estimated tax due dates).
3. 100 percent of the estimated current-year tax liability using the annualized income method (discussed below).[50]

From a cash management (time value of money) perspective, it generally makes sense for corporations to make the *minimum* required estimated payment installments for each quarter. Thus, as each estimated tax due date approaches, corporations will generally compute the required estimated payment under the prior-year tax method (if available) and under the annualized method and pay the lesser of the two.

The **annualized income method** is perhaps the most popular method of determining estimated tax payments (particularly for corporations that can't use the prior-year tax liability to determine their current-year estimated tax payment obligations). Under this method, corporations determine their taxable income as of the end of each quarter and then annualize (project) the amounts to determine their estimated taxable income and tax liability for the year. Corporations multiply the first quarter taxable income by 4 (12/3) to project their annual tax liability for the *first and second quarter* estimated tax payments. They multiply their taxable income at the end of the second quarter by 2 (12/6) to determine the third quarter estimated tax payment requirement. Finally, they multiply their taxable income at the end of the third quarter by 1.333 (12/9) to determine their fourth quarter payment requirement.

---

[46]The tax rules for consolidated tax returns are provided primarily in the Regulations under §1502.

[47]§6655; §6655(e).

[48]§6655(c).

[49]§6655(d).

[50]Source: §6655(e). Corporations may also use the adjusted seasonal income method of determining their required estimated tax payments. This method is similar in concept to the annualized method but is less common and is beyond the scope of this text.

Example 13-26

CCS determined its taxable income at the close of the first, second, and third quarters as follows:

Quarter-End	Cumulative Taxable Income
First	$20,000
Second	55,000
Third	96,000

What is CCS's annual estimated taxable income for estimated tax purposes as of the end of the first, second, third, and fourth quarters, respectively?

Answer: $80,000 for the first and second quarters, $110,000 for the third quarter, and $128,000 for the fourth quarter, computed as follows:

Installment	(1) Taxable Income	(2) Annualization Factor	(1) × (2) Annual Estimated Taxable Income
First quarter	$20,000	12/3 = 4	**$ 80,000**
Second quarter	20,000	12/3 = 4	**80,000**
Third quarter	55,000	12/6 = 2	**110,000**
Fourth quarter	96,000	12/9 =1.333	**128,000**

Once corporations have determined their annual estimated taxable income for each quarter, they can compute the required estimated tax installments for each quarter under the annualized income method.

Example 13-27

Based on the estimated taxable income in Example 13-26, what are CCS's required estimated tax payments for the year under the annualized income method?

Answer: $4,200 for the first and second quarters, $8,925 for the third quarter, and $9,555 for the fourth quarter, computed as follows:

Installment	(1) Annual Estimated Taxable Income	(2) (1) × 21% Tax on Estimated Taxable Income	(3) Percentage of Tax Required to Be Paid	(4) (2) × (3) Required Cumulative Payment	(5) Prior Cumulative Payments	(4) − (5) Required Estimated Tax Payment
First quarter	$ 80,000	$ 16,800	25%	$ 4,200	$ 0	**$4,200**
Second quarter	80,000	16,800	50%	8,400	4,200	**4,200**
Third quarter	110,000	23,100	75%	17,325	8,400	**8,925**
Fourth quarter	128,000	26,880	100%	26,880	17,325	**9,555**

What if: Assuming CCS reported a net operating loss last year, can it use its prior-year tax liability of $0 to determine its current-year estimated tax payments?

Answer: No. Because under this scenario CCS did not pay tax last year, it may not use its prior-year tax liability to determine its current-year estimated tax payments.

Would the current-year tax liability method result in lower total required estimated tax payments for CCS than the annualized income method?

Answer: No. As we determined in Example 13-24, CCS's actual tax liability for the year is $27,447. So, CCS could have avoided estimated tax penalties by paying in $27,447 ($6,861.75 each quarter) which is more than the $26,880 it was required to pay under the annualized method. Also, note that CCS did not know its final tax liability when it was required to make its estimated tax payments. Consequently, even if the annualized method required CCS to pay more in tax than paying in the 100 percent of the current tax liability, it likely would likely have used the annualized income method of determining its estimated tax payments to protect itself from penalties.

"Large" corporations, defined as corporations with over $1,000,000 of taxable income in *any* of the three years prior to the current year,[51] may use the prior-year tax liability to determine their *first quarter* estimated tax payments only. If they use the prior-year tax liability to determine their first quarter payment, their second quarter payment must "catch up" their estimated payments. That is, the second quarter payment must be large enough for the sum of their first and second quarter payments to equal or exceed 50 percent of their actual current-year tax liability or estimated current-year tax liability using the annualized income method.[52]

Example 13-28

What if: Assume that CCS is considered to be a large corporation and that last year (2017) CCS reported taxable income of $50,000 and a tax liability of $7,500. Further, CCS determined its required estimated tax payments under the annualized income method as described in the prior example. What would be CCS's required minimum estimated tax payments for each quarter for the current year (ignore the current year tax requirement)?

Answer: $1,875 for the first quarter, $6,525 for the second quarter, $8,925 for the third quarter, and $9,555 for the fourth quarter, computed as follows:

Installment	(1) Estimated Tax Payment under Prior-Year Tax Exception	(2) Estimated Tax Payment under Annualized Income Method	(3) Required Cumulative Payment for Quarter × [sum of the lesser of (1) or (2) through quarter x]	(4) Prior Cumulative Payments	(5) (3) − (4) Required Estimated Tax Payment
First quarter	$1,875*	$ 4,200	$ 1,875	$ 0	**$1,875**
Second quarter	Not applicable*	8,400	8,400	1,875	**6,525**
Third quarter	Not applicable*	17,325	17,325	8,400	**8,925**
Fourth quarter	Not applicable*	26,880	26,880	17,325	**9,555**

*Because CCS is a large corporation in this example, it may determine its first quarter estimated tax payment using its prior-year liability ($7,500 × 25% = $1,875). However, it must use the annualized income method to determine its second, third, and fourth quarter required payments.

With its second installment, CCS must have paid in $8,400. Because it only paid in $1,875 with the first quarter installment, it must pay $6,525 with its second quarter payment.

What if: Assume the same facts as above, except that last year CCS paid $10,000 in tax and CCS is *not* a large corporation. What would be CCS's required minimum estimated tax payments for each quarter (ignore the current-year tax liability requirement)?

Answer: $2,500 for the first quarter, $2,500 for the second quarter, $2,500 for the third quarter, and $2,500 for the fourth quarter, computed as follows:

Installment	(1) Estimated Tax Payment under Prior-Year Tax Exception ($10,000/4)	(2) Estimated Tax Payment under Annualized Income Method	(3) Required Cumulative Payment for Quarter × [sum of the lesser of (1) or (2) through quarter x]	(4) Prior Cumulative Payments	(5) (3) − (4) Required Prior Estimated Tax Payment
First quarter	$2,500	$ 4,200	$ 2,500	$ 0	**$2,500**
Second quarter	2,500	8,400	5,000	2,500	**2,500**
Third quarter	2,500	17,325	7,500	5,000	**2,500**
Fourth quarter	2,500	26,880	10,000	7,500	**2,500**

CCS can use the prior-year tax to determine its minimum required estimated tax payments.

[51]§6655(g)(2).
[52]§6655(d).

Corporations that have underpaid their estimated taxes for any quarter must pay an underpayment penalty determined on Form 2220. The amount of the penalty is based on the underpayment rate (or interest rate), the amount of the underpayment, and the period of the underpayment. The interest rate is generally the federal short-term interest rate plus 3 percent. The period of the underpayment is the due date for the installment through the earlier of (1) the date the payment is made or (2) the unextended due date of the tax return. The penalties are not deductible.[53]

TAXES IN THE REAL WORLD   Government Used to Get More Corporate Profits Than Shareholders. Will That Change with the New Tax Law?

IRS-provided data from corporate income tax returns filed for the years 1994 through 2008 indicate that in all but three of those years, total taxes paid by corporations exceeded after-tax profits. That means the government generally gets more of corporate income than the corporations (and, consequently, the corporations' shareholders). Corporations got to keep more than half of their earnings in 2005 through 2007. This analysis includes federal corporate income taxes, foreign corporate income taxes, and other taxes (such as state income taxes, property taxes, and sales taxes). The Tax Cuts and Jobs Act (TCJA) reduced corporate tax rates from 34-35 percent for most corporations to 21 percent for all corporations. It could be that the trend of the government getting more corporate profits than shareholders will change with the new tax law.

Source: http://taxfoundation.org/blog/government-takes-greater-share-shareholders.

CONCLUSION

In this chapter we discussed some important tax rules that apply during the life cycle of a C corporation. We learned that forming a corporation generally does not create any taxable income to any of the parties to the transaction. Gain or loss realized by shareholders on the transfer of property is deferred. We also learned that a C corporation is a separate legal and taxpaying entity from its stockholders. Consequently, it must determine and report its own taxable income to the IRS. This chapter discussed and described the process of computing a corporation's taxable income and the associated tax liability for C corporations. We learned that book income is the starting point for determining taxable income. Corporations adjust their book income for book–tax differences that arise because they account for many items of income and deduction differently for book purposes than they do for tax purposes. Some of these book–tax differences are temporary (the differences balance out over time) and some are permanent in nature (they don't balance out over the long term).

Summary

Compute the tax consequences of transactions in which shareholders transfer property or services to corporations in exchange for stock of the corporation.   **LO 13-1**

- Section 351 applies to exchanges in which one or more persons transfer property to a corporation in return for stock and, immediately after the transfer, these same persons control the corporation to which they transferred the property.

[53]§6655(b)(2).

- If an exchange meets these requirements, shareholders who transfer property to the corporation in exchange for stock defer gain or loss realized (they do not recognize it) on the exchange.
- Shareholders contributing property to a corporation in a §351 exchange compute gain or loss realized by subtracting the tax-adjusted basis of the property they contribute to the corporation from the fair market value of the consideration they receive in return (amount realized).
- Gain, but not loss, is recognized when shareholders receive stock and property other than the corporation's stock (boot) in the exchange.
- Shareholders recognize gain in an amount equal to the *lesser of* the gain realized or the fair market value of boot received.
- The tax basis of stock received in the exchange equals the tax basis of the property transferred, plus any gain recognized, minus boot received, minus liabilities assumed by the corporation on the property contributed (substituted basis).
- Shareholders take a fair market value in boot received.
- The corporation receiving property for its stock in a §351 exchange does not recognize (excludes) gain or loss on the exchange.
- The tax basis of the property received by the corporation equals the property's tax basis in the transferor's hands (carryover basis).
- The asset's tax basis is increased by any gain recognized by the shareholder on the transfer of the property to the corporation.

LO 13-2   Describe the corporate income tax formula, compare and contrast the corporate tax formula to the individual tax formula, and discuss tax considerations relating to corporations' accounting periods and accounting methods.

- The corporate tax formula is similar to the individual formula except that corporations can't claim the deduction for qualified business income and they don't itemize deductions or deduct standard deductions.
- Corporations may generally elect any tax year for reporting their taxable income, but the year must coincide with their financial accounting year.
- The timing of a corporation's income and deductions depends on the corporation's overall accounting method and its methods for specific transactions.
- Corporations are generally required to use the accrual overall method of accounting. However, smaller corporations may be allowed to use the cash method.

LO 13-3   Identify common book–tax differences, distinguish between permanent and temporary differences, and compute a corporation's taxable income and tax liability.

- Corporations typically compute taxable income by starting with book income and adjusting for book–tax differences.
- Book–tax differences are favorable when they reduce taxable income relative to book income and unfavorable when they increase it.
- Book–tax differences are permanent when the amount of income or deduction items is different for book and tax purposes and the amount will not reverse in the future.
- Book–tax differences are temporary when the amount of income or deduction items is different for book and tax purposes in the current year but the same for book and tax purposes over the long term. That is, temporary book–tax differences reverse over time.
- Common permanent book–tax differences include interest from municipal bonds (favorable), life insurance premiums on policies covering key employees (unfavorable), one-half of meals expense (unfavorable) and entertainment expense (unfavorable), among others.
- Incentive stock options typically generate unfavorable permanent book–tax differences.
- Nonqualified stock options generate permanent book–tax differences for the difference between the bargain element and the estimated value of the options for book purposes.
- Common temporary book–tax differences include depreciation expense, gain or loss on sale of depreciable assets, bad debt expense, purchased goodwill amortization, and warranty expense, among others.

- Corporations may not deduct net capital losses for tax purposes. However, they may carry them back three years and forward five years to offset capital gains in those other years.
- Corporations with NOLs originating in years before 2018 can carry the NOLs forward up to 20 years to offset up to 100 percent of a corporation's taxable income in any given year (they also could have carried them back two years).
- Corporations with NOLs originating in years after 2017 can carry the NOLs forward indefinitely offset up to 80 percent of the corporation's taxable income in any given year. These losses may not, however, be carried back.
- When corporations have NOL carryovers from multiple years, they apply the oldest first to offset taxable income in a given year.
- When computing their net operating losses for the year, corporations may not deduct net operating losses from other years.
- Subject to limitation, corporations can deduct the amount of money, the fair market value of capital gain property, and the adjusted basis of ordinary income property they donate to charity.
- The charitable contribution deduction for the year is limited to 10 percent of taxable income before deducting the charitable contribution, the dividends received deduction, and capital loss carrybacks. Amounts in excess of the limitation can be carried forward for up to five years.
- Corporations are allowed a deduction for dividends received to help mitigate potential triple taxation of the income distributed as a dividend. The amount of the deduction depends on the corporation's ownership in the distributing corporation. The deduction is 50 percent if the ownership is less than 20 percent; 65 percent if the ownership is at least 20 percent but less than 80 percent; and 100 percent if the ownership is 80 percent or more.
- The dividends received deduction (DRD) is subject to a taxable income limitation. This limitation does not apply if the full DRD extends or creates a net operating loss for the corporation in the current year.
- Corporate taxable income is taxed at a flat 21 percent rate.

Describe a corporation's tax return reporting and estimated tax payment obligations. **LO 13-4**

- Corporations file their tax returns on Form 1120, which are due three and one-half months after the corporation's year-end. Corporations can apply for an extension of the due date for filing the return for six months.
- Small corporations report their book–tax differences on Schedule M-1 of Form 1120. Large corporations (assets of $10 million or more) report them on Schedule M-3. Schedule M-3 requires much more detail than Schedule M-1.
- Corporations pay income taxes through estimated tax payments. Each payment should be 25 percent of their required annual payment. The installments are due on the 15th day of the 4th, 6th, 9th, and 12th months of the corporation's taxable year.
- Corporations' required annual payment is the least of (1) 100 percent of their current-year tax liability, (2) 100 percent of their prior-year tax liability (but only if they had a positive tax liability in the prior year), or (3) 100 percent of the estimated current-year tax liability using the annualized income method. Large corporations may rely on (2) only to compute their first quarter estimated payment requirement.

KEY TERMS

affiliated group (13-29)
annualized income method (13-30)
bargain element (13-17)
book (financial reporting) income (13-14)
book–tax differences (13-14)
boot (13-3)
capital gain property (13-20)
carryover basis (13-11)

charitable contribution limit modified taxable income (13-21)
consolidated tax return (13-29)
contribution to capital (13-12)
DRD modified taxable income (13-24)
exercise price (13-17)
favorable book–tax difference (13-14)

incentive stock options (ISOs) (13-17)
M adjustments (13-28)
net capital loss carryback (13-18)
net capital loss carryover (13-18)
net operating loss (NOL) (13-19)
net operating loss carryover (13-19)
nonqualified stock options (NQOs) (13-17)
ordinary income property (13-20)

permanent book–tax
   differences (13-14)
Schedule M adjustments (13-28)

substituted basis (13-4)
temporary book–tax
   differences (13-14)

unfavorable book–tax
   difference (13-14)
vest (13-17)

DISCUSSION QUESTIONS

Discussion Questions are available in Connect®.

LO 13-1   1. Why does Congress allow tax deferral on the formation of a corporation?

LO 13-1   2. List the key statutory requirements that must be met before a corporate formation is tax-deferred under §351.

LO 13-1   3. What is the definition of *control* for purposes of §351? Why does Congress require the shareholders to control a corporation to receive tax deferral?

LO 13-1   4. What is a *substituted basis* as it relates to stock received in exchange for property in a §351 transaction? What is the purpose of attaching a substituted basis to stock received in a §351 transaction?

LO 13-1   5. True or False. The receipt of boot by a shareholder in a §351 transaction causes the transaction to be fully taxable. Explain.

LO 13-1   6. True or False. A corporation's assumption of shareholder liabilities will always constitute boot in a §351 transaction. Explain.

LO 13-1   7. How does the tax treatment differ in cases where liabilities are assumed with a tax-avoidance purpose versus where liabilities assumed exceed basis? When would this distinction cause a difference in the tax consequences of the transactions?

LO 13-1   8. What is a *carryover basis* as it relates to property received by a corporation in a §351 transaction? What is the purpose of attaching a carryover basis to property received in a §351 transaction?

LO 13-1   9. Under what circumstances does property received by a corporation in a §351 transaction *not* receive a carryover basis? What is the reason for this rule?

LO 13-1   10. True or False. The tax consequences to a corporation receiving property are the same whether the property is received in a §351 exchange (with no boot) or as a capital contribution. Explain.

LO 13-2   11. In general terms, identify the similarities and differences between the corporate taxable income formula and the individual taxable income formula.

LO 13-2   12. Is a corporation's choice of its tax year independent from its year-end for financial accounting purposes?

LO 13-2   13. Can C corporations use the cash method of accounting? Explain.

LO 13-3   14. Briefly describe the process of computing a corporation's taxable income assuming the corporation must use GAAP to determine its book income. How might the process differ for corporations not required to use GAAP for book purposes?

LO 13-3   15. What role does a corporation's audited income statement play in determining its taxable income?

LO 13-3   16. What is the difference between favorable and unfavorable book–tax differences?

LO 13-3   17. What is the difference between permanent and temporary book–tax differences?

LO 13-3   18. Why is it important to be able to determine whether a particular book–tax difference is permanent or temporary?

LO 13-3   19. Describe the relation between the book–tax differences associated with depreciation expense and with gain or loss on disposition of depreciable assets.

LO 13-3   20. Describe how purchased goodwill leads to temporary book–tax differences.

LO 13-3   21. Describe the book–tax differences that arise from incentive stock options.

LO 13-3   22. Describe the book–tax differences that arise from nonqualified stock options.

23. How do corporations account for capital gains and losses for tax purposes? How is this different from the way individuals account for capital gains and losses? `LO 13-3`

24. What are the common book–tax differences relating to accounting for capital gains and losses? Do these differences create favorable or unfavorable book-to-tax adjustments? `LO 13-3`

25. What is the carryover period for a net operating loss? Explain. `LO 13-3`

26. Is a net operating loss incurred in 2017 treated the same as a net operating loss incurred in 2018? Explain. `LO 13-3`

27. When a corporation has NOL carryovers arising in different years, how does the corporation apply the NOLs to reduce taxable income in a given year? `LO 13-3` **planning**

28. A corporation commissioned an accounting firm to recalculate the way it accounted for leasing transactions. With the new calculations, the corporation was able to file amended tax returns for the past few years that increased the corporation's net operating loss carryover from $3,000,000 to $5,000,000. Was the corporation wise to pay the accountants for their work that led to the increase in the NOL carryover? What factors should be considered in making this determination? `LO 13-3`

29. Compare and contrast the general rule for determining the amount of the charitable contribution if the corporation contributes capital gain property versus ordinary income property. `LO 13-3`

30. Which limitations might restrict a corporation's deduction for a cash charitable contribution? Explain how to determine the amount of the limitation. `LO 13-3`

31. For tax purposes, what happens to a corporation's charitable contributions that are not deducted in the current year because of the taxable income limitation? `LO 13-3`

32. What are common book–tax differences relating to corporate charitable contributions? Are these differences favorable or unfavorable? `LO 13-3`

33. Why does Congress provide the dividends received deduction for corporations receiving dividends? `LO 13-3`

34. How does a corporation determine the percentage for its dividends received deduction? Explain. `LO 13-3`

35. What limitations apply to the amount of the allowable dividends received deduction? `LO 13-3`

36. How many tax brackets are there in the corporate tax rate schedule? `LO 13-3`

37. How is the Schedule M-1 similar to and different from a Schedule M-3? How does a corporation determine whether it must complete Schedule M-1 or Schedule M-3 when it completes its tax return? `LO 13-4`

38. What is the due date for the corporation tax return Form 1120? Is it possible to extend the due date? Explain. `LO 13-4`

39. How does a corporation determine the minimum amount of estimated tax payments it must make to avoid underpayment penalties? How are these rules different for large corporations? `LO 13-4`

40. Describe the annualized income method for determining a corporation's required estimated tax payments. What advantages does this method have over other methods? `LO 13-4`

PROBLEMS

Select problems are available in Connect®.

41. Betty joined Jim in forming DBJ Corp. Betty contributed appreciated land for 90 percent of the stock in DBJ. Jim received 10 percent of the DBJ stock valued at $15,000. Determine Jim's tax consequences in each of the following alternative scenarios. `LO 13-1`

a) Jim received the stock in exchange for providing computer-related services for the corporation. What amount of income or gain does Jim recognize on the exchange? What is Jim's basis in the stock he received in the exchange?

b) Jim contributed the rights to a patent he owned to DBJ in exchange for the DBJ stock. The patent was worth $15,000 and Jim's basis in the patent was $8,000. How much gain does Jim recognize on the exchange? What is Jim's basis in the DBJ stock?

LO 13-1   42. Carole, Karmen, and Charles formed ABC Corporation. Carole received 60 percent of the stock in ABC Corporation in exchange for appreciated property, Karmen received 30 percent of the stock in ABC Corporation in exchange for legal services, and Charles received 10 percent of the stock in ABC Corporation in exchange for cash.

a) Must Carole recognize the gain she realized on her transfer of the appreciated property?

b) Suppose that, instead of receiving the entire 30 percent of the ABC Corporation stock in exchange for legal services, Karmen received 10 percent of the ABC Corporation stock in exchange for her legal services and she received 20 percent of the ABC Corporation stock in exchange for cash (i.e., she transferred both services and property to ABC Corporation). Must Carole recognize gain on her transfer of appreciated property?

LO 13-1   43. Ramon incorporated his sole proprietorship by transferring inventory, a building, and land to the corporation in return for 100 percent of the corporation's stock. The property transferred to the corporation had the following fair market values and tax bases:

	FMV	Tax Basis
Inventory	$ 10,000	$ 4,000
Building	50,000	30,000
Land	100,000	50,000
Total	$160,000	$84,000

The fair market value of the corporation's stock received in the exchange equaled the fair market value of the assets transferred to the corporation by Ramon.

a) What amount of gain or loss does Ramon *realize* on the transfer of the property to his corporation?

b) What amount of gain or loss does Ramon *recognize* on the transfer of the property to his corporation?

c) What is Ramon's basis in the stock he receives in his corporation?

LO 13-1   44. Carla incorporated her sole proprietorship by transferring inventory, a building, and land to the corporation in return for 100 percent of the corporation's stock. The property transferred to the corporation had the following fair market values and tax bases:

	FMV	Tax Basis
Inventory	$ 20,000	$ 10,000
Building	150,000	100,000
Land	250,000	300,000
Total	$420,000	$410,000

The corporation also assumed a mortgage of $120,000 attached to the building and land. The fair market value of the corporation's stock received in the exchange was $300,000.

a) What amount of gain or loss does Carla *realize* on the transfer of the property to her corporation?

b) What amount of gain or loss does Carla *recognize* on the transfer of the property to her corporation?

c) What is Carla's basis in the stock she receives in her corporation?

45. Ivan incorporated his sole proprietorship by transferring inventory, a building, and land to the corporation in return for 100 percent of the corporation's stock. The property transferred to the corporation had the following fair market values and tax bases:

LO 13-1

	FMV	Tax Basis
Inventory	$ 10,000	$15,000
Building	50,000	40,000
Land	60,000	30,000
Total	$120,000	$85,000

The fair market value of the corporation's stock received in the exchange equaled the fair market value of the assets transferred to the corporation by Ivan. The transaction met the requirements to be tax-deferred under §351.

a) What amount of gain or loss does Ivan *realize* on the transfer of the property to his corporation?

b) What amount of gain or loss does Ivan *recognize* on the transfer of the property to his corporation?

c) What is Ivan's basis in the stock he receives in his corporation?

d) What is the corporation's tax basis in each of the assets received in the exchange?

46. Zhang incorporated her sole proprietorship by transferring inventory, a building, and land to the corporation in return for 100 percent of the corporation's stock. The property transferred to the corporation had the following fair market values and tax bases:

LO 13-1

	FMV	Tax Basis
Inventory	$ 20,000	$ 10,000
Building	150,000	100,000
Land	230,000	70,000
Total	$400,000	$180,000

The corporation also assumed a mortgage of $200,000 attached to the building and land. The fair market value of the corporation's stock received in the exchange was $220,000. The exchange met the requirements to be tax-deferred under §351.

a) What amount of gain or loss does Zhang *recognize* on the transfer of the property to her corporation?

b) What is Zhang's tax basis in the stock she receives in the exchange?

47. Sam and Devon agree to go into business together selling college-licensed clothing. According to the agreement, Sam will contribute inventory valued at $100,000 in return for 80 percent of the stock in the corporation. Sam's tax basis in the inventory is $60,000. Devon will receive 20 percent of the stock in return for providing

LO 13-1

 planning

accounting services to the corporation (these qualified as organizational expenditures). The accounting services are valued at $25,000.

a) What amount of income gain or loss does Sam *realize* on the formation of the corporation? What amount, if any, does he *recognize*?

b) What is Sam's tax basis in the stock he receives in return for his contribution of property to the corporation?

c) What amount of income gain or loss does Devon *realize* on the formation of the corporation? What amount, if any, does he *recognize*?

d) What is Devon's tax basis in the stock he receives in return for his contribution of services to the corporation?

Assume Devon received 25 percent of the stock in the corporation in return for his services for parts (e) through (i).

e) What amount of gain or loss does Sam *recognize* on the formation of the corporation?

f) What is Sam's tax basis in the stock he receives in return for his contribution of property to the corporation?

g) What amount of income gain or loss does Devon *recognize* on the formation of the corporation?

h) What is Devon's tax basis in the stock he receives in return for his contribution of services to the corporation?

i) What tax advice would you give Sam and Devon to improve the tax consequences?

LO 13-1   48. Robert and Kelly invited Ben to join them in forming Aero, a plane-chartering company, as a corporation. Ben did not want to join at the time and declined their invitation. More than a year later, Ben changed his mind and transferred appreciated property to Aero in exchange for 45 percent of Aero stock. Is Ben required to recognize his realized gain on the transaction?

LO 13-1   49. Kristine transferred investment property she has owned for six years to XYZ Corporation in exchange for 40 percent of the corporation's stock (40 shares valued at $160,000) at the time XYZ was incorporated. The property's adjusted tax basis was $90,000 and its fair market value was $160,000. Assume the transfer qualifies under §351.

a) What gain or loss does Kristine recognize on the transfer?

b) What is her basis in the stock she received in the exchange?

c) What is her holding period in the stock?

LO 13-1   50. Jasmine transferred land she held as an investment (fair market value $140,000; basis $110,000) in exchange for 50 percent of Kandy Corporation stock (40 shares valued at 100,000) and $40,000 cash in a qualifying §351 exchange. What is the amount and character of gain Jasmine recognizes on the transfer?

LO 13-1   51. Jorge contributed land he held as an investment (fair market value $120,000; basis $55,000) and inventory (fair market value $80,000; basis $75,000) to ABC Corporation in exchange for 50 percent of the ABC stock (50 shares valued at $160,000) and $40,000 cash in a qualifying §351 exchange.

a) What amount of gain does Jorge recognize on the exchange? What is the character of the gain? What would be Jorge's basis in his ABC stock after the exchange?

b) Assume the same facts except that Jorge received $40,000 of business property from ABC instead of $40,000 cash. What is the amount and character of gain Jorge would recognize on the exchange?

c) Assume the original facts in this example except that the inventory had an adjusted basis of $90,000 so that Jorge realized a $10,000 loss on the inventory (he still realized a $65,000 gain on the land). How much gain or loss would he recognize on the exchange?

52. In forming Parts Inc. as a corporation, Candice transferred inventory to Parts Inc. in exchange for 30 percent of the corporation's stock (60 shares valued at $130,000). The inventory's fair market value was $147,000 and its adjusted tax basis to Candice was $75,000. The inventory was subject to a $17,000 liability that Parts Inc. assumed on the transfer. Candice borrowed the $17,000 from the bank (using the inventory as collateral) shortly before transferring the inventory to Parts Inc. and she used the loan proceeds to pay for a family vacation to Europe.   **LO 13-1**

    a) Assuming the transfer qualifies under §351 and that the liability has a tax-avoidance purpose, what gain or loss will Candice recognize on the transfer?

    b) Assuming the original facts, what is Candice's basis in the stock she received in the exchange?

    c) Suppose the liability does not have a tax-avoidance purpose. What gain will Candice recognize on the transfer?

    d) Assuming the facts in part (c), what is Candice's basis in the stock she received in the exchange?

53. Johanne transferred investment property to S&J Corporation in exchange for 60 percent of the S&J Corporation stock (60 shares valued at $115,000). The property's fair market value was $190,000 and its adjusted basis to Johanne was $60,000. The investment property was subject to a $75,000 mortgage that S&J Corporation assumed on the transfer (not treated as boot).   **LO 13-1**

    a) Assuming the transfer qualifies under §351, what is the amount and character of the gain Johanne must recognize on the exchange?

    b) What is Johanne's basis in the S&J stock he received in the exchange?

    c) Assume that in addition to the investment property, Johanne transferred inventory with a fair market value of $30,000 and an adjusted basis of $20,000 for additional S&J Corporation stock. What is the amount and character of gain Johanne must recognize on the exchange of the land and inventory for stock?

    d) Assuming the facts in part (c), what is Johanne's basis in the S&J stock he received in the exchange?

    e) Assume the original facts except that the liability assumed by S&J corporation would give rise to a deduction when paid. What is the amount and character of gain Johanne must recognize on the exchange?

    f) Assuming the facts in part (e), what is Johanne's basis in the S&J stock he received in the exchange?

54. When incorporating Spotfree, a cleaning company, Jayne transferred accounts receivable (fair market value $20,000 and $0 tax basis) and $12,000 of accounts payable from her cash-method sole proprietorship to Spotfree in exchange for Spotfree stock valued at $8,000. Assume the transfer qualifies under §351.   **LO 13-1**

    a) What is the amount and character of the gain Jayne must recognize on the exchange?

    b) What is Jayne's basis in the Spotfree stock she received in the exchange?

55. Jekyll and Hyde formed a corporation (Halloween Inc.) on October 31 to develop a drug to address split personalities. Jekyll will contribute a patented formula valued at $200,000 in return for 50 percent of the stock in the corporation. Hyde will contribute an experimental formula worth $120,000 and medical services in exchange for the remaining stock. Jekyll's tax basis in the patented formula is $125,000, whereas Hyde has a basis of $15,000 in his experimental formula.   **LO 13-1**

tax forms

research

    a) Describe the tax consequences of the transaction.

    b) Identify and prepare the §351 statement that must be included with the return.

LO 13-1 56. Ron and Hermione formed Wizard Corporation on January 2. Ron contributed cash of $200,000 in return for 50 percent of the corporation's stock. Hermione contributed a building and land with the following fair market values and tax bases in return for 50 percent of the corporation's stock:

	FMV	Tax Basis
Building	$ 75,000	$ 20,000
Land	175,000	80,000
Total	$250,000	$100,000

To equalize the exchange, Wizard Corporation paid Hermione $50,000 in addition to her stock.

a) What amount of gain or loss does Ron *recognize* on the formation of the corporation?

b) What is Ron's tax basis in the stock he receives in return for his contribution of property to the corporation?

c) What amount of gain or loss does Hermione *recognize* on the formation of the corporation?

d) What is Hermione's tax basis in the stock she receives in return for her contribution of property to the corporation?

e) What tax basis does Wizard Corporation take in the land and building received from Hermione?

For parts (f) and (g), assume Hermione's tax basis in the land is $200,000.

f) What amount of gain or loss does Hermione *realize* on the formation of the corporation? What amount, if any, does she *recognize*?

g) What tax basis does Wizard Corporation take in the land and building received from Hermione?

LO 13-1 57. Breslin Inc. made a capital contribution of investment property to its 100 percent–owned subsidiary, Crisler Company. The investment property had a fair market value of $3,000,000 and a tax basis to Breslin of $2,225,000.

a) What are the tax consequences to Breslin Inc. on the contribution of the investment property to Crisler Company?

b) What is the tax basis of the investment property to Crisler Company after the contribution to capital?

LO 13-2 58. LNS corporation reports book income of $2,000,000. Included in the $2,000,000 is $15,000 of tax-exempt interest income. LNS reports $1,345,000 in ordinary and necessary business expenses. What is LNS corporation's taxable income for the year?

LO 13-2 59. ELS corporation is about to begin its sixth year of existence. Assume that ELS reported gross receipts for each of its first five years of existence for Scenarios A, B, and C as follows:

Year of Existence	Scenario A	Scenario B	Scenario C
1	$24,000,000	$23,000,000	$25,500,000
2	25,000,000	25,000,000	25,000,000
3	25,900,000	27,500,000	24,750,000
4	26,000,000	26,000,000	25,000,000
5	24,500,000	24,500,000	25,250,000

a) In what years is ELS allowed to use the cash method of accounting under Scenario A?

b) In what years is ELS allowed to use the cash method of accounting under Scenario B?

c) In what years is ELS allowed to use the cash method of accounting under Scenario C?

60. On its year 1 financial statements, Seatax Corporation, an accrual-method taxpayer, reported federal income tax expense of $570,000. On its year 1 tax return, it reported a tax liability of $650,000. During year 1, Seatax made estimated tax payments of $700,000. What book-tax difference, if any, associated with its federal income tax expense should Seatax have reported when computing its year 1 taxable income? Is the difference favorable or unfavorable? Is it temporary or permanent?   **LO 13-3**

61. On July 1 of year 1, Riverside Corp. (RC), a calendar-year taxpayer, acquired the assets of another business in a taxable acquisition. When the purchase price was allocated to the assets purchased, RC determined it had purchased $1,200,000 of goodwill for both book and tax purposes. At the end of year 1, the auditors for RC determined that the goodwill had not been impaired during the year. In year 2, however, the auditors concluded that $200,000 of the goodwill had been impaired, and they required RC to write down the goodwill by $200,000 for book purposes.   **LO 13-3**

    a) What book–tax difference associated with its goodwill should RC report in year 1? Is it favorable or unfavorable? Is it permanent or temporary?

    b) What book–tax difference associated with its goodwill should RC report in year 2? Is it favorable or unfavorable? Is it permanent or temporary?

62. On December 31, year 1, ABC Inc. issued 5,000 stock options with an estimated value of $10 per option. Each option entitles the owner to purchase one share of ABC stock for $25 a share (the per share price of ABC stock on December 31, year 1). Assume the options vest on December 31, year 2, and that all 5,000 stock options were exercised on the vesting date when the stock was valued at $31 per share. Identify ABC's tax deduction and book–tax difference associated with the stock options under the following alternative scenarios: **LO 13-3**

    a) The stock options are incentive stock options.

    b) The stock options are nonqualified stock options.

63. What book–tax differences in year 1 and year 2 associated with its capital gains and losses would ABD Inc. report in the following alternative scenarios? Identify each book–tax difference as favorable or unfavorable and as permanent or temporary.   **LO 13-3**

a)

	Year 1	Year 2
Capital gains	$20,000	$5,000
Capital losses	8,000	0

b)

	Year 1	Year 2
Capital gains	$ 8,000	$5,000
Capital losses	20,000	0

c)

	Year 1	Year 2
Capital gains	$ 0	$50,000
Capital losses	25,000	30,000

d)

	Year 1	Year 2
Capital gains	$ 0	$40,000
Capital losses	25,000	0

e) Answer for year 6 only.

	Year 1	Years 2–5	Year 6
Capital gains	$ 0	$0	$15,000
Capital losses	10,000	0	0

f) Answer for year 7 only.

	Year 1	Years 2–6	Year 7
Capital gains	$ 0	$0	$15,000
Capital losses	10,000	0	0

LO 13-3 64. What book–tax differences in year 1 and year 2 associated with its capital gains and losses would DEF Inc. report in the following alternative scenarios? Identify each book–tax difference as favorable or unfavorable and as permanent or temporary.

a) In year 1, DEF recognized a loss of $15,000 on land that it had held for investment. In year 1, it also recognized a $30,000 gain on equipment it had purchased a few years ago. The equipment sold for $50,000 and had an adjusted basis of $20,000. DEF had deducted $40,000 of tax depreciation on the equipment. In year 2, DEF recognized a capital loss of $2,000.

b) In year 1, DEF recognized a loss of $15,000 on land that it had held for investment. It also recognized a $20,000 gain on equipment it had purchased a few years ago. The equipment sold for $50,000 and had an adjusted basis of $30,000. DEF had deducted $15,000 of tax depreciation on the equipment.

LO 13-3 65. WCC Corp. has a $100,000 net operating loss carryover into 2019. Assume that it reported $75,000 of taxable income in 2019 (before the net operating loss deduction) and $30,000 of taxable income in 2020 (before the net operating loss deduction).

a) What is WCC's taxable income in 2019 and 2020 (after the net operating loss deduction), assuming the $100,000 NOL carryover originated in 2016?

b) What is WCC's taxable income in 2019 and 2020 (after the net operating loss deduction), assuming the $100,000 NOL carryover originated in 2018?

c) Assume the same facts as in part (b), what is WCC's book-tax difference associated with the NOL in 2019 and in 2020 and identify the book tax difference for each year as permanent or temporary?

LO 13-3 66. In 2019, SML Corp. reported taxable income of $100,000 before any NOL deductions. SML has a $170,000 NOL carryover from 2017 and a $90,000 NOL carryover from 2018. What is SML's 2019 taxable income after the NOL deduction? What NOLs can SML carry over to 2020?

LO 13-3 67. Golf Corp. (GC), a calendar-year accrual-method corporation, held its directors' meeting on December 15 of year 1. During the meeting, the board of directors authorized GC to pay a $75,000 charitable contribution to the Tiger Woods Foundation, a qualifying charity.

a) If GC actually pays $50,000 of this contribution on January 15 of year 2 and the remaining $25,000 on March 15 of year 2, what book–tax difference will it report associated with the contribution in year 1 (assume the 10 percent limitation does not apply)? Is it favorable or unfavorable? Is it permanent or temporary?

b) Assuming the same facts as in part (a), what book–tax difference will GC report in year 2 (assuming the 10 percent limitation does not apply)? Is it favorable or unfavorable?

c) If GC actually pays $50,000 of this contribution on January 15 of year 2 and the remaining $25,000 on April 30 of year 2, what book–tax difference will it report associated with the contribution in year 1 (assume the 10 percent limitation does not apply)? Is it favorable or unfavorable? Is it permanent or temporary?

d) Assuming the same facts as in part (c), what book–tax difference will GC report in year 2 (assuming the 10 percent limitation does not apply)? Is it favorable or unfavorable?

68. In year 1 (the current year), OCC Corp. made a charitable donation of $200,000 to the Phil and Amy Mickelson Foundation (a qualifying charity). For the year, OCC reported taxable income of $1,500,000 before deducting any charitable contributions, before deducting its $20,000 dividends received deduction, and before deducting its $40,000 NOL carryover from last year.   **LO 13-3**

a) What amount of the $200,000 donation is OCC allowed to deduct for tax purposes in year 1?

b) In year 2, OCC did not make any charitable contributions. It reported taxable income of $300,000 before any charitable contribution deductions and before a $15,000 dividends received deduction. What book–tax difference associated with the charitable contributions will OCC report in year 2? Is the difference favorable or unfavorable? Is it permanent or temporary?

c) Assume the original facts and those provided in part (b). In years 3, 4, and 5, OCC reported taxable losses of $50,000. Finally, in year 6 it reported $1,000,000 in taxable income before any charitable contribution deductions. It did not have any dividends received deduction. OCC did not actually make any charitable donations in year 6. What book–tax difference associated with charitable contributions will OCC report in year 6?

69. In year 1 (the current year), LAA Inc. made a charitable donation of $100,000 to the American Red Cross (a qualifying charity). For the year, LAA reported taxable income of $550,000, which included a $100,000 charitable contribution deduction (before limitation), and a $50,000 dividends received deduction. What is LAA Inc.'s charitable contribution deduction for year 1?   **LO 13-3**

70. Maple Corp. owns several highly valued paintings that are on display in the corporation's headquarters. This year, it donated one of the paintings valued at $100,000 (adjusted basis of $25,000) to a local museum for the museum to display. What is the amount of Maple Corp.'s charitable contribution deduction for the painting (assuming income limitations do not apply)? What would be Maple's deduction if the museum sold the painting one month after it received it from Maple? (Assume Maple Corp. had prior knowledge of the museum's intention to sell the painting after it received it.)   **LO 13-3** **research**

71. Riverbend Inc. received a $200,000 dividend from stock it held in Hobble Corporation. Riverbend's taxable income is $2,100,000 before deducting the dividends received deduction (DRD), a $100,000 charitable contribution.   **LO 13-3**

a) What is Riverbend's deductible DRD assuming it owns 10 percent of Hobble Corporation?

b) Assuming the facts in part (a), what is Riverbend's tax rate on the dividend, taking into account the DRD?

c) What is Riverbend's DRD assuming it owns 60 percent of Hobble Corporation?

d) Assuming the facts in part (c), what is Riverbend's tax rate on the dividend, taking into account the DRD?

e) What is Riverbend's DRD assuming it owns 85 percent of Hobble Corporation (and is part of the same affiliated group)?

f) Assuming the facts in part (e), what is Riverbend's tax rate on the dividend, taking into account the DRD?

LO 13-3 72. Wasatch Corp. (WC) received a $200,000 dividend from Tager Corporation (TC). WC owns 15 percent of the TC stock. Compute WC's deductible DRD in each of the following situations:

    a) WC's taxable income (loss) without the dividend income or the DRD is $10,000.

    b) WC's taxable income (loss) without the dividend income or the DRD is $(10,000).

    c) WC's taxable income (loss) without the dividend income or the DRD is $(99,000).

    d) WC's taxable income (loss) without the dividend income or the DRD is $(101,000).

    e) WC's taxable income (loss) without the dividend income or the DRD is $(500,000).

    f) What is WC's book–tax difference associated with its DRD in part (a)? Is the difference favorable or unfavorable? Is it permanent or temporary?

LO 13-3 73. Compute SWK Inc.'s tax liability for each of the following scenarios:

    a) SWK's taxable income is $60,000.

    b) SWK's taxable income is $275,000.

    c) SWK's taxable income is $50,000,000.

LO 13-4 74. Last year, TBA Corporation, a calendar-year taxpayer, reported a tax liability of $100,000. TBA confidently anticipates a current-year tax liability of $240,000. Compute the minimum estimated tax payments TBA should make for the first, second, third, and fourth quarters, respectively (ignore the annualized income method), assuming the following:

    a) TBA is not considered to be a large corporation for estimated tax purposes.

    b) TBA is considered to be a large corporation for estimated tax purposes.

LO 13-4 75. Last year, BTA Corporation, a calendar-year taxpayer, reported a net operating loss of $10,000 and a $0 tax liability. BTA confidently anticipates a current-year tax liability of $240,000. Determine the minimum estimated tax payments BTA should make for the first, second, third, and fourth quarters, respectively (ignore the annualized income method), assuming the following:

    a) BTA is not considered to be a large corporation for estimated tax purposes.

    b) BTA is considered to be a large corporation for estimated tax purposes.

LO 13-4 76. For the current year, LNS Corporation reported the following taxable income at the end of its first, second, and third quarters. What are LNS's minimum first, second, third, and fourth quarter estimated tax payments, using the annualized income method?

Quarter-End	Cumulative Taxable Income
First	$1,000,000
Second	1,600,000
Third	2,400,000

LO 13-4

planning

77. Last year, JL Corporation's tax liability was $500,000. For the current year, JL Corporation reported the following taxable income at the end of its first, second, and third quarters (see table below). What are JL's minimum required first, second, third, and fourth quarter estimated tax payments (ignore the actual current-year tax safe harbor)?

Quarter-End	Cumulative Taxable Income
First	$ 500,000
Second	1,250,000
Third	2,250,000

78. Last year, Cougar Corp. (CC) reported a net operating loss of $25,000. In the current year, CC expected its current-year tax liability to be $300,000, so it made four equal estimated tax payments of $75,000 each. Cougar closed its books at the end of each quarter. The following schedule reports CC's taxable income at the end of each quarter:

Quarter-End	Cumulative Taxable Income
First	$ 300,000
Second	700,000
Third	1,000,000
Fourth	1,470,588

CC's current-year tax liability on $1,470,588 of taxable income is $308,823. Does CC owe underpayment penalties on its estimated tax payments? If so, for which quarters does it owe the penalty?

COMPREHENSIVE PROBLEMS

Select problems are available in Connect®.

79. Several years ago, your client, Brooks Robinson, started an office-cleaning service. His business was very successful, owing much to his legacy as the greatest defensive third baseman in major league history and his nickname, "The Human Vacuum Cleaner." Brooks operated his business as a sole proprietorship and used the cash-basis method of accounting. Brooks was advised by his attorney that it is too risky to operate his business as a sole proprietorship and that he should incorporate to limit his liability. Brooks has come to you for advice on the tax implications of incorporation. His balance sheet is presented below. Under the terms of the incorporation, Brooks would transfer the assets to the corporation in return for 100 percent of the company's common stock. The corporation would also assume the company's liabilities (payables and mortgage).

Balance Sheet		
	Tax Basis	**FMV**
Accounts receivable	$ 0	$ 5,000
Cleaning equipment (net)	25,000	20,000
Building	50,000	75,000
Land	25,000	50,000
Total assets	$100,000	$150,000
Accounts payable	0	10,000
Salaries payable	0	5,000
Mortgage on land and building	35,000	35,000
Total liabilities	$ 35,000	$ 50,000

a) How much gain or loss (on a per asset basis) does Brooks *realize* on the transfer of the assets to the corporation?

b) How much, if any, gain or loss (on a per asset basis) does Brooks *recognize*?

c) How much gain or loss, if any, must the corporation recognize on the receipt of the assets of the sole proprietorship in exchange for the corporation's stock?

d) What tax basis does Brooks have in the corporation's stock?

e) What is the corporation's tax basis in each asset it receives from Brooks?

f) How would you answer the question in part (b) if Brooks had taken back a 10-year note worth $25,000 plus stock worth $75,000 plus the liability assumption?

80. Compute MV Corp.'s current-year taxable income given the following information relating to its current-year activities. Also, compute MV's Schedule M-1 assuming that MV's federal income tax expense for book purposes is $100,000.

- Gross profit from inventory sales of $500,000 (no book–tax differences).
- Dividends MV received from 25 percent–owned corporation of $100,000 (assume this is also MV's pro rata share of the distributing corporation's earnings).
- Expenses *other than* DRD, charitable contribution (CC), and net operating loss (NOL) are $350,000 (no book–tax differences).
- NOL carryover from prior year of $10,000.
- Cash charitable contribution of $120,000.

81. Compute HC Inc.'s current-year taxable income given the following information relating to its current-year activities. Also, compute HC's Schedule M-1 assuming that HC's federal income tax expense for book purposes is $30,000.

- Gross profit from inventory sales of $310,000 (no book–tax differences).
- Dividends HC received from 28 percent–owned corporation of $120,000 (this is also HC's pro rata share of the corporation's earnings).
- Expenses *other than* DRD, charitable contribution (CC), and net operating loss (NOL) are $300,000 (no book–tax differences).
- NOL carryover from prior year of $12,000.
- Cash charitable contribution of $50,000.

82. Timpanogos Inc. is an accrual-method calendar-year corporation. For 2018, it reported financial statement income after taxes of $1,552,000. Timpanogos provided the following information relating to its 2018 activities:

Life insurance proceeds as a result of CEO's death	$ 200,000
Revenue from sales (for both book and tax purposes)	2,000,000
Premiums paid on the key-person life insurance policies (the policies have no cash surrender value)	21,000
Charitable contributions	180,000
Interest income on tax-exempt bonds	40,000
Interest paid on loan obtained to purchase tax-exempt bonds	45,000
Rental income payments received and earned in 2018	15,000
Rental income payments received in 2017 but earned in 2018	10,000
Rental income payments received in 2018 but not earned by year-end	30,000
MACRS depreciation	55,000
Book depreciation	25,000
Net capital loss	42,000
Federal income tax expense for books in 2018	400,000

Required:

a) Reconcile book income to taxable income for Timpanogos Inc. Be sure to start with book income and identify all of the adjustments necessary to arrive at taxable income.

b) Identify each book–tax difference as either permanent or temporary.

c) Complete Schedule M-1 for Timpanogos.

d) Compute Timpanogos Inc.'s tax liability.

83. XYZ is a calendar-year corporation that began business on January 1, 2018. For the year, it reported the following information in its current-year audited income statement. Notes with important tax information are provided below.

Required:

Identify the book-to-tax adjustments for XYZ.

a) Reconcile book income to taxable income and identify each book–tax difference as temporary or permanent.

b) Compute XYZ's income tax liability.

c) Complete XYZ's Schedule M-1.

d) Complete XYZ's Form 1120, page 1 (use the most current form available). Ignore estimated tax penalties when completing this form.

e) Determine the quarters for which XYZ is subject to underpayment of estimated taxes penalties (see assumptions and estimated tax information below).

XYZ Corp. Income Statement for Current Year	Book Income	Book to Tax Adjustments (Dr.)	Cr.	Taxable Income
Revenue from sales	$ 40,000,000			
Cost of goods sold	(27,000,000)			
Gross profit	$ 13,000,000			
Other income:				
Income from investment in corporate stock	300,000[1]			
Interest income	20,000[2]			
Capital gains (losses)	(4,000)			
Gain or loss from disposition of fixed assets	3,000[3]			
Miscellaneous income	50,000			
Gross income	$ 13,369,000			
Expenses:				
Compensation	(7,500,000)[4]			
Stock option compensation	(200,000)[5]			
Advertising	(1,350,000)			
Repairs and maintenance	(75,000)			
Rent	(22,000)			
Bad debt expense	(41,000)[6]			
Depreciation	(1,400,000)[7]			
Warranty expenses	(70,000)[8]			
Charitable donations	(500,000)[9]			
Meals expense	(18,000)			
Goodwill impairment	(30,000)[10]			
Organizational expenditures	(44,000)[11]			
Other expenses	(140,000)[12]			
Total expenses	$ (11,390,000)			
Income before taxes	1,979,000			
Provision for income taxes	(400,000)[13]			
Net income after taxes	$ 1,579,000			

Notes:

1. XYZ owns 30 percent of the outstanding Hobble Corp. (HC) stock. Hobble Corp. reported $1,000,000 of income for the year. XYZ accounted for its investment in HC under the equity method and it recorded its pro rata share of HC's earnings for the year ($1,000,000 × 30%). HC also distributed a $200,000 dividend to XYZ. For tax purposes, HC reports the actual dividend received as income, not the pro rata share of HC's earnings.

2. Of the $20,000 interest income, $5,000 was from a City of Seattle bond, $7,000 was from a Tacoma City bond, $6,000 was from a fully taxable corporate bond, and the remaining $2,000 was from a money market account.

3. This gain is from equipment that XYZ purchased in February and sold in December (that is, it does not qualify as §1231 gain).

4. This includes total officer compensation of $2,500,000 (no one officer received more than $1,000,000 compensation).

5. This amount is the portion of incentive stock option compensation that was expensed during the year (recipients are officers).

6. XYZ actually wrote off $27,000 of its accounts receivable as uncollectible.

7. Tax depreciation was $1,900,000.

8. In the current year, XYZ did not make any actual payments on warranties it provided to customers.

9. XYZ made $500,000 of cash contributions to qualified charities during the year.

10. On July 1 of this year XYZ acquired the assets of another business. In the process it acquired $300,000 of goodwill. At the end of the year, XYZ wrote off $30,000 of the goodwill as impaired.

11. XYZ expensed all of its organizational expenditures for book purposes. It expensed the maximum amount of organizational expenditures allowed for tax purposes.

12. The other expenses do not contain any items with book–tax differences.

13. This is an estimated tax provision (federal tax expense) for the year. Assume that XYZ is not subject to state income taxes.

Estimated Tax Information:

XYZ made four equal estimated tax payments totaling $360,000. For purposes of estimated tax liabilities, assume XYZ was in existence in 2017 and that in 2017 it reported a tax liability of $500,000. During 2018, XYZ determined its taxable income at the end of each of the four quarters as follows:

Quarter-End	Cumulative Taxable Income (loss)
First	$ 400,000
Second	1,100,000
Third	1,400,000

Finally, assume that XYZ is not a large corporation for purposes of estimated tax calculations.

 **ROGER** | CPA Review

Sample CPA Exam questions from Roger CPA Review are available in Connect as support for the topics in this text. These Multiple Choice Questions and Task-Based Simulations include expert-written explanations and solutions and provide a starting point for students to become familiar with the content and functionality of the actual CPA Exam.

Corporate Nonliquidating and Liquidating Distributions

Learning Objectives

Upon completing this chapter, you should be able to:

LO 14-1 Explain the basic tax law framework that applies to property distributions from a corporation to a shareholder.

LO 14-2 Compute a corporation's earnings and profits and calculate a shareholder's dividend income.

LO 14-3 Explain the taxation of stock distributions.

LO 14-4 Understand the tax consequences of stock redemptions, including partial liquidations.

LO 14-5 Calculate the tax consequences of a complete liquidation of a corporation.

Storyline Summary

Taxpayers:	Nicole Johnson and Sarah Walker
Location:	Salt Lake City, Utah
Status:	Shareholders of Color Comfort Sheets Inc. (CCS)
Situation:	Determining the tax consequences of nonliquidating and liquidating distributions to shareholders.

After a few difficult years, Color Comfort Sheets Inc. (CCS) has become reasonably profitable. A few years ago, Nicole increased her stock ownership in CCS from 60 to 75 percent and Sarah increased her stock ownership in CCS from 20 to 25 percent by purchasing CCS shares from Chanzz Inc. Nicole and Sarah both work full time for CCS. Nicole primarily spends her time in marketing, earning an annual $80,000 salary, and Sarah primarily spends her time in accounting, earning an annual $70,000 salary.

Since the company has become profitable, the shareholders have put the profits back into the business to expand the store's inventory and marketing activities. By the end of the year, CCS had accumulated $300,000 in its bank accounts. Nicole and Sarah had made many sacrifices, both financially and personally, to make the business successful. While out on a morning run, Nicole and Sarah decided it was time to think about withdrawing some of the company's profits as a reward for their hard work. Nicole really wanted to make a significant dent in her home mortgage balance. She determined $96,000 would let her cut her existing mortgage in half. Sarah had her eye on a dark blue Acura TL that sold for approximately $32,000. Nicole and Sarah considered several options for receiving cash distributions from CCS. One option was to have the company pay each of them a dividend at year-end ($96,000 to Nicole and $32,000 to Sarah). Nicole's ordinary marginal tax rate is 32 percent and Sarah's is 24 percent.

to be continued . . .

As the storyline indicates, at some point during the life of a company, especially in the case of a closely held business, the owners (shareholders) will likely want to withdraw some of the company's accumulated after-tax profits. If the business is operated as a C corporation, the company can distribute its after-tax profits to its shareholders in the form of a nonliquidating distribution such as a **dividend, stock redemption,** or, in rare cases, a **partial liquidation.** When the corporation winds up its affairs and stops doing business, it makes liquidating distributions to its shareholders.

This chapter addresses the tax consequences to the corporation and its shareholders of both nonliquidating and liquidating distributions. As we discuss in the Entities Overview chapter, because Nicole and Sarah have chosen to operate their business entity as a C corporation for tax purposes, the corporation's income is taxed at the entity level when it is earned and at the shareholder level when the earnings are distributed or the shareholders sell their stock.

LO 14-1 THE BASIC TAX LAW FRAMEWORK THAT APPLIES TO PROPERTY DISTRIBUTIONS

The characterization of a distribution from a corporation to a shareholder has important tax consequences to both parties to the transaction. If the tax law characterizes the distribution as a dividend, the corporation may not deduct the amount paid in computing its taxable income. In addition, the shareholder is subject to tax on the gross amount of the dividend received. The nondeductibility of the distribution by the corporation, coupled with the taxation of the distribution to the shareholder, creates *double taxation* of the corporation's income, first at the corporate level and then at the shareholder level. The double taxation of distributed corporate income has been a fundamental principle of the U.S. income tax since 1913. Historically, much tax planning has gone into eliminating or mitigating the second level of taxation on C corporation earnings. However, due to recent tax legislation, the corporate tax rate (21 percent) is now significantly lower than the maximum individual tax rate (37 percent). Consequently, as we discuss in the Entities Overview chapter, some business owners may actually save taxes by choosing to have the business entity taxed as a C corporation and subjecting the business income to double tax rather than operating as a flow-through entity and subjecting the income to one tax at the higher individual tax rates.

The Internal Revenue Code (IRC), Subchapter C (§§301–385) provides guidelines and rules for determining the tax status of distributions from a C corporation to its shareholders. The recipient of a dividend or payment in exchange for corporate stock (stock redemption) generally receives preferential tax treatment on the distribution in the form of a reduced tax rate or as a nontaxable return of capital or both.[1]

LO 14-2 COMPUTING EARNINGS AND PROFITS AND CALCULATING A SHAREHOLDER'S DIVIDEND INCOME

Overview of the Shareholder Taxation of Corporate Distrbutions

When a corporation distributes property to shareholders *in their capacity as shareholders,* the tax consequences of the distribution to the *shareholder* can be summarized as follows:

- The portion of the distribution that is a dividend is included in gross income.
- The portion of the distribution that is not a dividend reduces the shareholder's tax basis in the corporation's stock (i.e., it is a nontaxable return of capital).

---

[1]The maximum tax rate for dividends and capital gains is generally 15 percent (20 percent for high income taxpayers). Further, §1411 imposes an additional 3.8 percent tax on net investment income (including dividends and capital gains) of high income taxpayers (defined differently than for purposes of the 20 percent rate). Thus, a taxpayer's tax rate on dividends or capital gains could be as high as 23.8 percent. However, the taxpayers described in this chapter do not qualify as high-income taxpayers under either definition. Consequently, the taxpayers in this chapter are taxed at 15 percent on dividends and capital gains.

- The portion of the distribution that is not a dividend and is in excess of the shareholder's stock basis is treated as gain from sale or exchange of the stock (i.e., it is capital gain).[2]

Corporate distributions of "property" usually take the form of cash, but they can include debt and other tangible or intangible assets. Special rules apply when a corporation distributes its own stock to its shareholders.[3]

Definition of a Dividend

The tax law defines a dividend as any distribution of property made by a corporation to its shareholders out of its earnings and profits (E&P) account. While earnings and profits is similar in concept to financial accounting retained earnings, its computation can be very different. Congress intended earnings and profits to be a measure of the corporation's *economic earnings* available for distribution to its shareholders.

Corporations keep two separate E&P accounts: One for the current year (**current earnings and profits**) and one for undistributed earnings and profits accumulated in all prior years (**accumulated earnings and profits**). Distributions are designated as dividends as follows:

1. Distributions are dividends up to the amount of current E&P.
2. Distributions in excess of current E&P are dividends up to the balance in accumulated E&P.

Current E&P plus beginning of the year accumulated E&P minus the E&P distributed during the year equals accumulated E&P at the beginning of the next year. Distributions reduce E&P but cannot produce (or extend) a deficit (negative balance) in E&P. However, E&P can have a deficit balance if losses exceed income. In other words, a corporation cannot distribute E&P if there is a deficit in E&P, and only losses can create a deficit in E&P. A corporation that makes a distribution in excess of its E&P (the distribution is a return of capital) must report the distribution on Form 5452, "Corporate Report of Nondividend Distributions," and include a calculation of its E&P balance to support the tax treatment.

Example 14-1

Nicole has a tax basis in her Color Comfort Sheets (CCS) stock of $48,000. Sarah's tax basis in her CCS stock is $20,000.

Assume CCS has current earnings and profits (CE&P) of $60,000, and no accumulated earnings and profits. At year-end, CCS distributes $96,000 to Nicole and $32,000 to Sarah. Recall that Nicole owns 75 percent of the CCS stock, while Sarah owns the remaining 25 percent.

What is the tax treatment of the distribution to Nicole and Sarah?

Answer: Nicole treats the $96,000 distribution for tax purposes as follows:

- $45,000 is treated as a dividend (to the extent of the 75 percent of current E&P allocated to her distribution)
- $48,000 is a nontaxable reduction in her stock tax basis (return of capital).
- $3,000 is treated as gain from the deemed sale of her stock (capital gain).

Note that a distribution cannot reduce a shareholder's stock basis below zero.

Sarah treats the $32,000 distribution for tax purposes as follows:

- $15,000 is treated as a dividend (to the extent of the 25 percent of current E&P allocated to her distribution).
- $17,000 is a nontaxable reduction in her stock tax basis (return of capital).

What is Nicole and Sarah's tax basis in their CCS stock after the distribution?

Answer: Nicole has a remaining tax basis in her CCS stock of $0, while Sarah has a remaining tax basis of $3,000 ($20,000 − $17,000) in her CCS stock.

---

[2]§301(c).
[3]§305.

Computing Earnings and Profits

Earnings and profits has been part of the tax law since 1916. Nevertheless, Congress has never provided a precise definition of E&P. The tax laws do, however, provide adjustments that should be made to taxable income to compute E&P. Earnings and profits includes taxable and nontaxable income, indicating that Congress intended E&P to represent a corporation's economic income. As a result, shareholders may be taxed on distributions of income not subject to tax at the corporate level.

Example 14-2

What if: Suppose CCS reported current E&P from its taxable income of $100,000 in its first year of operations. The company also earned $5,000 of tax-exempt interest from its investment in Salt Lake City municipal bonds. What is CCS's current E&P? If CCS distributes all of its current year E&P (all of its E&P in this case) to Nicole and Sarah, what amount will they report as dividend income in the current year?

Answer: Current E&P is $105,000. This includes the $100,000 of taxable income plus the $5,000 of tax-exempt interest in the computation of current E&P. Nicole and Sarah will report $105,000 of dividend income. The portion of the E&P that represents the tax-exempt interest will be treated as a taxable dividend even though Nicole and Sarah would not have included the interest in gross income had they earned it directly.

A corporation begins its computation of current E&P with taxable income or loss. It then makes adjustments required by the Internal Revenue Code (IRC) or accompanying regulations and IRS rulings. These adjustments fall into four broad categories:

- Increase current E&P for income that is excluded from taxable income.
- Increase current E&P for certain expenses that are deducted in computing taxable income but do not require an economic outflow.
- Decrease current E&P for certain expenses that are excluded from the computation of taxable income but require an economic outflow.
- Increase or decrease current E&P for amounts that differ due to different accounting methods used for taxable income and E&P purposes.[4]

Current E&P is computed as of the end of the year without reductions for distributions made during the year.

Increase Current E&P for Income That Is Excluded from Taxable Income   The regulations state that "all income exempted by statute" must be added back to taxable income in computing current E&P. However, most commentators do not interpret this phrase to mean that all statutory exclusions are included in E&P. Common examples of tax-exempt income included in E&P are tax-exempt interest and tax-exempt life insurance proceeds. Other types of exempt income such as gifts, bequests, and contributions to capital by shareholders are not included in E&P.

Increase Current E&P for Certain Expenses That Are Deducted in Computing Taxable Income but Do Not Require an Economic Outflow   Deductions that are allowed in computing taxable income but do not require an economic outflow of resources from a corporation generally are not deductible in computing current E&P. For example, the dividends received deduction falls into this category. Note that corporations are not required to add back the deduction for employee exercises of nonqualified stock options because, while the exercise does not require a cash outflow from the corporation, it requires an economic outflow equal to the amount of the bargain ele-

---

[4]Source: §312 and the related regulations describe these adjustments.

ment (i.e., the corporation is essentially selling its stock for less than the value of the stock). This category also includes carryovers from other tax years because the items are not subject to limitation for purposes of computing current E&P (see next category). Examples of carryovers include the net operating loss carryover, the net capital loss carryover, the disallowed business interest expense carryover, and the excess charitable contribution carryover.

Decrease Current E&P for Certain Expenses That Are Excluded from the Computation of Taxable Income but Require an Economic Outflow

A corporation reduces its current E&P for certain items that are not deductible in computing its taxable income but require an economic outflow from the corporation. Examples of such expenses include:

- Federal income taxes paid or accrued (depending on the corporation's method of accounting).
- Expenses incurred in earning tax-exempt income (such income is included in E&P).
- Current-year charitable contributions in excess of 10 percent of taxable income (there is no 10 percent limitation for E&P purposes).
- Business interest expense in excess of the 30 percent of adjusted taxable income limitation (the limitation does not apply E&P purposes).
- Premiums on life insurance contracts in excess of the increase in the policy's cash surrender value.
- Current-year net capital loss (there is no limit on net capital loss deductions).
- Nondeductible meals expense (generally 50 percent of the total).
- Entertainment expense (nondeductible for tax purposes).
- Nondeductible lobbying expense and political contributions.
- Penalties and fines.

Increase or Decrease Current E&P for Differences Relating to Differences in Accounting Methods Used for Taxable Income and for E&P Purposes

A corporation must use the same accounting method for computing E&P and taxable income unless otherwise specified. For example, a gain or loss deferred for tax purposes under the like-kind exchange rules or the involuntary conversion rules is also deferred for E&P purposes. A corporation using the accrual method for tax purposes generally must use the accrual method for E&P purposes.

However, some types of income or expenses deferred from current-year taxable income must be included in the computation of current E&P in the year in which the transaction occurs. For example, if a corporation uses the installment method for tax purposes, the deferred gain from current-year sales must be included in current E&P. This difference reverses in future years when the installment payments are received and increase taxable income but not current E&P in the year of receipt. In other cases, gain deferred from taxation is not added back in the E&P computation. Deferred gain from a §1031 (like-kind) exchange and a §351 exchange (discussed in the Corporate Formations and Operations chapter) falls into this category. In addition, certain expenses currently deductible in the computation of taxable income are deferred in computing E&P.[5] Organizational expenditures, which can be deducted currently or amortized for income tax purposes, must be capitalized for E&P purposes. Depreciation must be computed using the prescribed E&P method. For property acquired after 1986, the alternative depreciation system must be used. This system requires that assets be depreciated using a straight-line method over the asset's "mid-point class life" (40 years in the case of realty).[6]

---

[5]§312(n). Section 312(n) was added in 1984 to "ensure that a corporation's earnings and profits more closely conform to its economic income."

[6]§168(g)(2).

This generally results in more accelerated depreciation for taxable income purposes than for E&P purposes (bonus depreciation is not allowed for E&P purposes). Further, amounts expensed under §179 (first year expensing) must be amortized over five years for E&P purposes.[7] For any given year, adjustments in this category may increase or decrease current E&P because these adjustments are timing differences that reverse over time.

Example 14-3

This year, CCS reported taxable income of $500,000 and paid federal income tax of $105,000. The following deductions were included in the computation of taxable income:

- $90,000 of depreciation.
- $8,000 dividends received deduction.
- $10,000 net operating loss from the prior year

Not included in the computation of taxable income were the following items:

- $1,000 of tax-exempt interest.
- $4,500 meals expense.
- $1,500 entertainment expense.
- $4,000 net capital loss from the current year.

For E&P purposes, depreciation computed under the alternative depreciation method is $30,000.

What is CCS's current E&P?

Answer: $474,000, computed as follows:

Taxable income	$ 500,000
Add:	
Tax-exempt interest	1,000
Dividends received deduction	8,000
NOL carryover	10,000
Excess of income tax depreciation over E&P depreciation	70,000
Subtract:	
Federal income taxes	(105,000)
Nondeductible meals expense	(4,500)
Entertainment expense	(1,500)
Net capital loss for the current year	(4,000)
Current E&P	**$474,000**

What if: Assume CCS also reported a tax-deferred gain of $100,000 as the result of a §1031 exchange and deferred $75,000 of gain from an installment sale during the year. What is CCS's current E&P under these circumstances?

Answer: Current E&P would equal $549,000 ($474,000 + $75,000). Deferred gains from §1031 (like-kind) exchanges are not included in the computation of current E&P, but all gain from current-year installment sales is included in current E&P. In future years, as installment payments are received, CCS would subtract from current E&P the gain recognized for taxable income purposes.

The IRC does not impose a statute of limitations on the computation of earnings and profits. Exhibit 14-1 provides a summary of common adjustments made to taxable income to compute current E&P.

---

[7]§312(k)(3)(B).

EXHIBIT 14-1   **Template for Computing Current Earnings and Profits**

Taxable Income (Net Operating Loss)

Add:	**Exclusions from Taxable Income**

- Tax-exempt bond interest.
- Life insurance proceeds.
- Federal tax refunds (if a cash-method taxpayer).
- Increase in cash surrender value of corporate-owned life insurance policy.

Add:	**Deductions Allowed for Tax Purposes but Not for E&P**

- Dividends received deduction.
- NOL deduction carryovers.
- Net capital loss carrybacks and carryovers.
- Charitable contribution carryovers.
- Disallowed business interest expense carryover.

Subtract:	**Deductions Allowed for E&P Purposes but Not for Tax**

- Federal income taxes paid or accrued.
- Expenses of earning tax-exempt income.
- Current-year charitable contributions in excess of the 10 percent limitation.
- Disallowed business interest expense.
- Nondeductible premiums on life insurance policies.
- Current-year net capital loss.
- Penalties and fines.
- Disallowed meals expense.
- Entertainment expense.
- Disallowed lobbying expenses, dues, and political contributions.

Add or Subtract:	**Timing Differences Due to Separate Accounting Methods for Taxable Income and E&P for These Items**

- Installment method. Add back gain deferred under installment method in year of sale. Subtract original deferred gain when it is recognized in subsequent years.
- Depreciation. Compute depreciation (other than §179 expense but including bonus depreciation) under regular tax rules and compare to E&P depreciation (bonus depreciation is not allowed). Add back difference if tax depreciation exceeds E&P depreciation. Subtract difference if E&P depreciation exceeds tax depreciation for the year.
- §179 expense. Immediately deductible for income tax purposes. Deductible over five years for E&P purposes. Add back in year of §179 expense but subtract in subsequent years.
- Gain or loss on sale of depreciable assets. Subtract greater taxable gain (lesser taxable loss) due to lower asset basis for taxable income purposes than for E&P purposes. This is a reversal of the depreciation adjustment.
- Inventory cost flow. FIFO required for E&P purposes. If using LIFO for taxable income purposes, add back excess of LIFO over FIFO COGS for the year or subtract excess of FIFO over LIFO COGS for the year.
- Long-term contracts. Must use percentage completion method for E&P. Compare the income recognized under both methods. Add back if more income under the completed contract method and subtract if more income under the percentage completion method.
- Depletion. Must use the cost depletion method for E&P purposes. If using percentage depletion for taxable income, add back the difference if percentage depletion exceeds cost depletion for the year. Otherwise, subtract the excess of cost depletion over percentage depletion for the year.

Equals:	**Current Earnings & Profits**

THE KEY FACTS

Adjustments to Taxable Income (Loss) to Compute Current E&P

- A corporation makes the following adjustments to taxable income to compute current E&P:
  - Add certain income that is excluded from taxable income.
  - Add certain expenses that are deducted in computing taxable income.
  - Subtract certain expenses that are excluded from the computation of taxable income.
  - Add or subtract items that are accounted for differently for taxable income and E&P purposes.
- The amount distributed as a dividend equals:
  - Cash received.
  - Fair market value of noncash property received.
  - Less: Any liabilities assumed by the shareholder on property received.
- E&P is reduced by distributions as follows:
  - Cash distributed.
  - E&P basis of noncash property with a fair market value less than its E&P basis.
  - Fair market value of noncash appreciated property reduced by any liabilities assumed by the shareholder on property received.
  - E&P reductions for distributions cannot cause E&P to drop below zero. If accumulated E&P is negative, downward adjustments are not allowed.

Ordering of E&P Distributions

As we noted above, a corporation must maintain two separate E&P accounts: current E&P and accumulated E&P. Whether a distribution is characterized as a dividend depends on whether the balances in these accounts are positive or negative. There are four possible scenarios:

1. Positive current E&P, positive accumulated E&P.
2. Positive current E&P, negative accumulated E&P.
3. Negative current E&P, positive accumulated E&P.
4. Negative current E&P, negative accumulated E&P.

Positive Current E&P and Positive Accumulated E&P   Corporate distributions are deemed to be paid out of current E&P first. If there are multiple distributions during the year and the distributions (in total) exceed current E&P, the amount distributed out of current E&P is allocated to each distribution pro rata (based on relative fair market value of each distribution to total distributions). After current E&P has been fully allocated to distributions made during the year, accumulated E&P is allocated to the distributions in the chronological order in which the distributions were made.[8] This ordering of distributions is particularly important when distributions exceed current E&P and either the identity of the shareholders receiving the distributions changes or a shareholder's percentage ownership changes during the year.

Example 14-4

What if: Assume CCS reported current E&P of $120,000. The balance in accumulated E&P was $100,000. On December 31, CCS distributed $96,000 to Nicole and $32,000 to Sarah. What amount of dividend income will Nicole and Sarah report from the distribution, and what is CCS's remaining balance in E&P at year-end?

Answer: $96,000 to Nicole and $32,000 to Sarah. The distribution is first deemed to be paid from current E&P to each shareholder in proportion to the total distribution paid, $90,000 to Nicole (equal to $120,000 times $96,000/$128,000) and $30,000 to Sarah (equal to $120,000 times $32,000/$128,000). The additional amount is deemed to be paid from accumulated E&P ($6,000 to Nicole and $2,000 to Sarah). E&P exceeds the distribution, which makes the entire amount paid to Nicole and Sarah a taxable dividend. CCS has a remaining balance in accumulated E&P of $92,000 ($100,000 − $8,000) at year-end.

What if: Assume that CCS's current E&P is $80,000 and its accumulated E&P is $30,000. Also, assume that Nicole owned 100 percent the CCS stock and she received a $90,000 distribution on June 1. In July, Nicole sold all of her CCS stock to Sarah. On December 1, Sarah received a $30,000 distribution. What is the amount and the character of each distribution, and what is CCS's remaining balance in E&P at year-end?

Answer: Nicole has a $90,000 dividend. Sarah has a $20,000 dividend and a $10,000 nontaxable return of capital. Of the $80,000 of current E&P, $60,000 is allocated to Nicole's distribution and $20,000 is allocated to Sarah's distribution (pro rata to each distribution). However, because Nicole's distribution took place before Sarah's distribution, the accumulated E&P is allocated to Nicole's distribution ($30,000), leaving $0 in remaining accumulated E&P to be allocated to Sarah's distribution. Sarah is allocated only $20,000 of E&P, leaving her with an excess distribution of $10,000 ($30,000 − $20,000). This excess distribution is treated as a nontaxable reduction of her basis in the CCS stock. Note that current E&P is determined on the last day of the tax year before reduction for current year distributions.

Positive Current E&P and Negative Accumulated E&P   Distributions deemed paid out of current E&P are taxable as dividends even when the accumulated E&P is negative. Distributions in excess of current E&P in this scenario would first be treated as nontaxable reductions in the shareholders' tax basis in their stock. Any excess received over their stock basis would be treated as capital gain from the sale of stock.

Example 14-5

What if: Assume CCS reported current E&P of $120,000. The balance in accumulated E&P at the beginning of the year was negative $140,000. On December 31, CCS distributed $96,000 to Nicole and $32,000 to Sarah. Nicole has a tax basis in her CCS stock of $48,000. Sarah's tax basis in her CCS stock is $20,000. What amount of dividend income will Nicole and Sarah report?

---

[8]Reg. §1.316-2(b) and Rev. Rul. 74-164, 1974-1 C.B. 74.

Answer: $90,000 for Nicole and $30,000 for Sarah. The distribution is first deemed to be paid from current E&P ($90,000 to Nicole and $30,000 to Sarah). No additional amount is treated as a dividend because CCS has negative accumulated E&P.

What tax basis will Nicole and Sarah have in their CCS stock after the distribution?

Answer: The amount in excess of current E&P ($6,000 to Nicole, $2,000 to Sarah) would be treated as a nontaxable return of capital because Nicole and Sarah have enough tax basis in their CCS stock to absorb the amount paid in excess of E&P. Nicole's tax basis in her CCS stock after the distribution would be $42,000 ($48,000 − $6,000), and Sarah's tax basis in her CCS stock after the distribution would be $18,000 ($20,000 − $2,000).

What is CCS's remaining balance in accumulated E&P at the end of the year?

Answer: CCS has a negative (deficit) $140,000 balance in accumulated E&P. This is the same as the deficit at the beginning of the year.

TAXES IN THE REAL WORLD   Tax Planning for Distributions

Visteon Corporation is a global automotive supplier that manufactures vehicle information and controls. During 2008 and 2009, weakened economic conditions triggered a global economic recession that severely impacted the automotive sector. Visteon filed voluntary petitions for reorganization relief in 2009, and the company has been profitable since it emerged from bankruptcy in 2010.

Visteon currently has two technology-focused core businesses: vehicle cockpit electronics and thermal energy management. The company's vehicle cockpit electronics product line includes audio systems, infotainment systems, driver information systems, and electronic control modules. In order to focus its operations on automotive cockpit electronics, Visteon sold a subsidiary that generated a pretax gain of approximately $2.3 billion. The sale was completed on June 9, 2015, and Visteon received net cash proceeds of approximately $2.7 billion. The company then announced a plan to return $2.5 billion–$2.75 billion of cash to shareholders through a series of actions including a special distribution.

Based on the tax disclosures in Visteon's annual report, it appears that the company had about a $1 billion deficit in accumulated E&P entering 2015. If Visteon's operations and gain on the sale of the subsidiary generated current (2015) E&P of $1.5 billion, then a distribution of $2.5 billion in 2015 would generate a taxable dividend of $1.5 billion. Despite the deficit in accumulated E&P, the distribution would come from current E&P. The distribution in excess of current E&P ($1 billion) would be a return of capital to shareholders.

In contrast, if Visteon waited until 2016 to distribute the $2.5 billion, the distribution would generate a dividend of only $500 million. Assuming Visteon doesn't generate any additional E&P in 2016, the current E&P from 2015 would be offset by the deficit in accumulated E&P ($1.5 billion minus $1 billion equals $500 million).

Epilog: Visteon distributed approximately $1.75 billion on January 22, 2016, and authorized a share repurchase program to repurchase up to $500 million of its shares of common stock through December 31, 2016.

Sources: Visteon Corporation 2014 and 2015 Forms 10-K filed February 26, 2015, and Form 8-K filed September 11, 2015.

Negative Current E&P and Positive Accumulated E&P   When current E&P is negative, the tax status of a dividend is determined by accumulated E&P on the *date of the distribution*. This requires the corporation to prorate the negative current E&P to the distribution date and combine it with accumulated E&P at the beginning of the year to determine accumulated E&P at the distribution date. Distributions in excess of accumulated E&P on the date of the distribution in this scenario are treated as a return of capital that reduces shareholders' tax basis in their stock. Any excess over their stock basis is treated as a capital gain.

Example 14-6

What if: Assume CCS reported current E&P of negative $40,000. The balance in accumulated E&P at the beginning of the year was $120,000. On June 30, CCS distributed $96,000 to Nicole and $32,000 to Sarah. Nicole has a tax basis in her CCS stock of $48,000. Sarah's tax basis in her CCS stock is $20,000. What amount of dividend income will Nicole and Sarah report?

Answer: $75,000 for Nicole and $25,000 for Sarah. Because current E&P is negative, CCS must determine its accumulated E&P on the distribution date. CCS prorates the full-year negative current E&P to June 30 [6 months/12 months × $(40,000) = $(20,000)]. The negative current E&P of $20,000 is combined with the beginning balance in accumulated E&P of $120,000 to get accumulated E&P as of July 1 of $100,000. Because their distributions were made at the same time, Nicole is allocated 75 percent of the accumulated E&P and Sarah is allocated the remaining 25 percent.

What tax basis will Nicole and Sarah have in their CCS stock after the distribution?

Answer: The amount in excess of accumulated E&P ($21,000 to Nicole, $7,000 to Sarah) is treated first as a nontaxable return of capital. Nicole reduces the basis in her CCS stock to $27,000 ($48,000 − $21,000). Sarah reduces the basis in her CCS stock to $13,000 ($20,000 − $7,000).

What is CCS's remaining balance in accumulated E&P at the end of the year?

Answer: Negative $20,000, computed as follows:

Beginning balance	$120,000
Prorated negative current E&P, 1/1–6/30	(20,000)
Dividends	(100,000)
Prorated negative current E&P, 7/1–12/31	(20,000)
Ending balance	**$(20,000)**

Negative Current E&P and Negative Accumulated E&P When current E&P and accumulated E&P are both negative, none of the distribution is treated as a dividend. Distributions in this scenario would first be treated as reductions in the shareholders' tax basis in their stock. Any excess over their stock basis would be treated as a capital gain.

Example 14-7

What if: Assume CCS reported current E&P of negative $100,000. The balance in accumulated E&P at the beginning of the year was negative $120,000. Nicole has a tax basis in her CCS stock of $48,000. Sarah's tax basis in her CCS stock is $20,000. On December 31 of this year, CCS distributed $96,000 to Nicole and $32,000 to Sarah. What amount of dividend income will Nicole and Sarah report this year?

Answer: $0 for Nicole and $0 for Sarah. Because current E&P and accumulated E&P are negative, the entire distribution would be treated as either a return of capital or capital gain.

What are Nicole and Sarah's tax bases in their CCS stock after the distribution?

Answer: The amount in excess of E&P ($96,000 to Nicole, $32,000 to Sarah) is treated first as a nontaxable return of capital. Nicole reduces the basis in her CCS stock to $0 ($48,000 − $96,000, limited to $0). Sarah reduces the basis in her CCS stock to $0 ($20,000 − $32,000, limited to $0).

What amounts of capital gain do Nicole and Sarah report as a result of the distribution?

Answer: Nicole has a capital gain of $48,000, the amount by which the distribution exceeds the tax basis in her CCS stock ($96,000 − $48,000). Sarah has a capital gain of $12,000, the amount by which the distribution exceeds the tax basis in her CCS stock ($32,000 − $20,000).

What is CCS's remaining balance in accumulated E&P at the end of the year?

Answer: Negative $220,000, the sum of accumulated E&P of negative $120,000 plus current E&P of negative $100,000.

Distributions of Noncash Property to Shareholders

When corporations distribute noncash property to shareholders, the amount distributed is computed as follows:

> Money received
> + Fair market value of other property received
> − Liabilities assumed by the shareholder on property received
> = Amount distributed[9]

Example 14-8

What if: Assume Sarah received a distribution of $31,000 in cash and a sewing machine that had a fair market value of $1,000. CCS has current E&P of $200,000 and no accumulated E&P. What amount of dividend income will Sarah report on these distributions?

Answer: $32,000. Sarah would include the $31,000 plus the $1,000 fair market value of the sewing machine in her gross income as a dividend.

As a general rule, a shareholder's tax basis in noncash property received as a dividend equals the property's fair market value.[10] No adjustment is made for liabilities assumed by the shareholder (these are considered part of the property's cost). The shareholder determines fair market value as of the date of the distribution.

Example 14-9

What is Sarah's tax basis in the sewing machine (FMV = $1,000) she received as a dividend in the previous example?

Answer: $1,000. Sarah has a tax basis in the sewing machine of $1,000, the machine's fair market value. Sarah would pay income tax of $150 on receipt of the sewing machine (assuming the dividend qualifies for the preferential 15 percent tax rate).

Example 14-10

What if: Assume Nicole received a parcel of land the company had previously purchased for possible expansion instead of cash. The land has a fair market value of $120,000 and a remaining mortgage of $24,000 attached to it. CCS has a tax basis in the land of $40,000. Nicole will assume the mortgage on the land. CCS has current E&P of $200,000 and no accumulated E&P. How much dividend income does Nicole recognize on the distribution?

Answer: $96,000. Nicole recognizes dividend income in an amount equal to the land's fair market value of $120,000 less the mortgage she assumes on the land in the amount of $24,000.

What is Nicole's tax basis in the land she receives?

Answer: $120,000. Nicole receives a tax basis equal to the land's fair market value. The basis consists of the $96,000 taxable dividend plus the $24,000 liability Nicole assumes.

Tax Consequences to a Corporation Paying Noncash Property as a Dividend   The IRC provides that realized *gains* (but not losses) are recognized by a corporation on the distribution of noncash property.[11] Specifically, the corporation recognizes

[9]§301(b).
[10]§301(d).
[11]§311.

a taxable gain on the distribution to the extent the fair market value of property distributed exceeds the corporation's tax basis in the property. In contrast, if the fair market value of the property distributed is less than the corporation's tax basis in the property, the corporation does not recognize a deductible loss on the distribution.

Example 14-11

What if: Assume CCS's tax basis in the sewing machine it distributed to Sarah (see Example 14-8) was $650 and the sewing machine's fair market value was $1,000. How much gain, if any, does CCS recognize when it distributes the sewing machine to Sarah?

Answer: $350. CCS recognizes a taxable gain of $350 on the distribution of the sewing machine to Sarah ($1,000 – $650). Assuming depreciation recapture applies, CCS would characterize the gain as ordinary income. CCS would pay a corporate level tax of $74 on the distribution (21% × $350). The total tax paid by CCS and Sarah would be $224 ($150 + $74) [see Example 14-9 for the computation of Sarah's $150 tax].

What if: Assume CCS's tax basis in the sewing machine it distributed to Sarah was $1,200. The machine's fair market value declined to $1,000 because it was an outdated model. How much loss, if any, does CCS recognize when it distributes the machine to Sarah?

Answer: $0. CCS is not permitted to recognize a loss on the distribution of the sewing machine to Sarah.

What if: Assume CCS's tax basis in the sewing machine was $1,200 and that CCS *sold* the sewing machine to Sarah for $1,000. How much loss, if any, could CCS recognize if it sold the machine to Sarah?

Answer: $200. CCS is permitted to recognize a loss on the sale of the sewing machine to Sarah provided it does not run afoul of the related-person loss rules found in §267 (discussed in the Property Dispositions chapter). To be a related person, Sarah must own *more than* 50 percent of CCS, which she does not in this scenario.

Liabilities If the liability assumed by the shareholder receiving the distribution is greater than the property's fair market value, the property's fair market value is deemed to be the amount of the liability assumed by the shareholder. If the liability assumed is less than the property's fair market value, the gain recognized on the distribution is the excess of the property's fair market value over its tax basis, if any (i.e., the liability is ignored by the distributing corporation).

Example 14-12

What if: Assume CCS distributed to Nicole land that it had previously purchased for possible expansion. The land has a fair market value of $120,000 and a remaining mortgage of $24,000 attached to it. CCS has a tax basis in the land of $40,000. Nicole will assume the mortgage on the land. CCS has current E&P of $200,000 and no accumulated E&P. How much gain, if any, does CCS recognize when it distributes the land to Nicole?

Answer: $80,000 ($120,000 – $40,000). Because the mortgage assumed by Nicole is less than the land's fair market value, CCS recognizes gain in an amount equal to the excess of the land's actual fair market value of $120,000 over its tax basis of $40,000.

What if: Assume the mortgage assumed by Nicole was $150,000 instead of $24,000. The land has a fair market value of $120,000. CCS has a tax basis in the land of $40,000. Nicole will assume the mortgage on the land. CCS has current E&P of $200,000. How much gain, if any, does CCS recognize when it distributes the land to Nicole?

Answer: $110,000 ($150,000 – $40,000). Because the mortgage assumed by Nicole exceeds the land's fair market value, CCS treats the land's fair market value as $150,000 and recognizes gain in an amount equal to the excess of the mortgage assumed of $150,000 over its tax basis of $40,000.

When a corporation distributes appreciated noncash property (fair market value in excess of income tax basis), it must recognize the gain and pay income tax on the gain. If the E&P basis of the property is the same as the income tax basis of the property, the gain recognized increases current E&P (just as it increases taxable income) and the taxes paid (or payable) on the gain reduce current E&P. If, however, the property's income tax basis is different from its E&P basis (e.g., LIFO tax basis versus FIFO E&P basis), or when the accumulated depreciation for income tax is different from accumulated depreciation for E&P purposes, current E&P is increased by the E&P gain (fair market value in excess of E&P basis) and it is reduced by the income taxes paid (or payable) on the income tax gain. When a corporation distributes depreciated noncash property (income tax basis in excess of fair market value of property), it is not allowed to deduct the loss for income tax purposes. If the E&P basis exceeds the fair market value of the property, the corporation is not allowed to deduct the loss in determining current E&P. Consequently, the distribution of depreciated property (income tax and E&P basis in excess of fair market value) does not affect current E&P.

Effect of Noncash Property Distributions on Accumulated E&P When a corporation distributes appreciated property (fair market value in excess of E&P basis), it reduces accumulated E&P by the fair market value of the property distributed. When it distributes depreciated property (E&P basis in excess of fair market value of the property), it reduces accumulated E&P by the E&P basis of the property. When a corporation distributes property subject to a liability, it increases accumulated E&P by the amount of the liability assumed by the shareholder(s) on distribution. Downward adjustments for distributions cannot cause accumulated E&P to drop below zero. Finally, if accumulated E&P is negative, downward adjustments are not allowed.

Example 14-13

What if: Assume the same facts as in Example 14-12. CCS distributed land to Nicole that has a fair market value of $120,000 and a remaining mortgage of $24,000 attached to it. CCS has a tax and E&P basis in the land of $40,000. Nicole assumed the mortgage on the land. CCS has current E&P of $200,000, which includes the net gain of $63,200 from land distribution ($80,000 gain less a related tax liability of $16,800), and accumulated E&P at the beginning of the year of $500,000. What is CCS's beginning balance in accumulated E&P at January 1 of next year, as a result of the distribution of the land to Nicole?

Answer: $604,000, computed as follows:

Accumulated E&P, beginning of this year	$ 500,000
Current E&P	200,000
Fair market value of land distributed	(120,000)
Liability assumed by Nicole	24,000
Beginning balance, AE&P, next year	**$ 604,000**

(continued on page 14-14)

What if: Assume the land distributed to Nicole had a tax and E&P basis to CCS of $150,000 instead of $40,000 and that the land is subject to a $24,000 mortgage that Nicole assumes. CCS has current E&P of $136,800, which does not include the disallowed loss of $30,000 on the distribution ($120,000 fair market value less $150,000 tax basis). CCS has accumulated E&P at the beginning of the year of $500,000. What is CCS's beginning balance in accumulated E&P at January 1 of next year, as a result of the distribution of the land to Nicole?

Answer: $510,800, computed as follows:

Accumulated E&P, beginning of this year	$ 500,000
Current E&P	136,800
E&P basis of land distributed	(150,000)
Liability assumed by Nicole	24,000
Beginning balance, AE&P, next year	**$510,800**

LO 14-3 # STOCK DISTRIBUTIONS

Rather than distribute cash or other property to its shareholders, a corporation may instead distribute additional shares of its own stock or rights to acquire additional shares. Publicly held corporations are likely to distribute shares to promote shareholder goodwill (i.e., a stock distribution allows the corporation to retain cash and still provide shareholders with tangible evidence of their interest in corporate earnings) or reduce the market price of its outstanding shares. Stock distributions (often called stock dividends whether taxable as a dividend or not) are used by many firms to keep stock prices accessible to a diverse group of investors.

Tax Consequences to Shareholders Receiving a Stock Distribution

Nontaxable Stock Distributions
Stock distributions generally do not provide shareholders with any increase in value. Rather, after the stock distribution the shareholders' interest in the corporation remains unchanged except that they now own more pieces of paper (stock) than before. As a result, a stock distribution generally is not included in a shareholder's gross income.[12]

For the nontaxable general rule to apply, the stock distribution must meet two conditions: (1) it must be made with respect to the corporation's common stock, and (2) it must be pro rata with respect to all shareholders (i.e., the shareholders' relative equity positions do not change as a result of the distribution).

The recipient of a nontaxable stock distribution allocates a portion of the tax basis from the stock on which the stock distribution was issued to the newly issued stock based on the relative fair market value (FMV) of the stock.[13] The tax basis of the newly issued stock can be determined using the following formula:

$$\text{Adjusted basis of "old stock"} \times \frac{\text{FMV of stock received}}{\text{Total FMV of new and old stock}} = \text{Adjusted basis of "new stock"}$$

The holding period of the new stock includes the holding period for which the shareholder held the old stock.[14]

---

[12] §305(a).

[13] §307.

[14] §1223(4).

The shareholder reduces the adjusted tax basis of the "old stock" by the tax basis allocated to the "new stock." For example, assume a shareholder owns 100 shares of McDonald's Corporation stock, for which she paid $30,000. McDonald's declares a 2-for-1 stock distribution and sends the shareholder an additional 100 shares of stock. The shareholder will now own 200 shares of stock with the same total tax basis of $30,000. The basis of each share of stock decreases from its original $300 per share ($30,000/100) to $150 per share ($30,000/200).

Example 14-14

Nicole has a tax basis in her CCS stock of $48,000. Sarah's tax basis in her CCS stock is $20,000. Nicole owns 75 of the 100 shares of outstanding CCS stock, while Sarah owns the remaining 25 shares.

What if: Assume CCS declared a 2-for-1 stock distribution. As a result of the distribution, Nicole would own 150 shares of CCS stock, and Sarah would own the remaining 50 shares. Based on a recent valuation, Nicole and Sarah learned that each share of CCS stock was worth $10,000 prior to the distribution ($5,000 after the distribution). The total fair market value of Nicole's CCS stock prior to and after the distribution is $750,000 (75 shares × $10,000 before and 150 × $5,000 after). The total fair market value of Sarah's CCS stock is $250,000 (25 shares × $10,000 before and 50 × $5,000 after).

Is the stock distribution taxable to Nicole and Sarah?

Answer: No. The stock distribution to Nicole and Sarah is nontaxable because it is made pro rata to the shareholders.

What is the tax basis of each share of CCS stock now held by Nicole and Sarah?

Answer:

Nicole computes her tax basis in the new CCS stock received as follows:

$$\frac{\$375,000 \text{ (75 shares} \times \$5,000 \text{ FMV of new stock received)}}{\$750,000 \text{ (total FMV of old and new stock)}} \times \$48,000 = \$24,000$$

Her tax basis in the original shares of CCS stock is $48,000 − $24,000 = $24,000.

Sarah computes her tax basis in the new CCS stock received as follows:

$$\frac{\$125,000 \text{ (25 shares} \times \$5,000 \text{ FMV of new stock received)}}{\$250,000 \text{ (total FMV of old and new stock)}} \times \$20,000 = \$10,000$$

Her tax basis in the original shares of CCS stock is $20,000 − $10,000 = $10,000.

Taxable Stock Distributions   Non-pro rata stock distributions usually are included in the shareholder's gross income as taxable dividends to the extent of the distributing corporation's E&P.[15] This makes sense because the recipient has now received something of value: an increase in the shareholder's claim on the corporation's income and assets. For example, a corporation may give its shareholders the choice between a cash distribution or a stock distribution. In this case, shareholders who elect the stock distribution in lieu of money will have a taxable dividend equal to the fair market value of the stock received. Because the stock distribution is taxable, the recipient will have a tax basis in the stock equal to its fair market value. A technical discussion of all of the rules that apply to determine if a stock distribution is taxable is beyond the scope of this text.

THE KEY FACTS

Tax Consequences of Stock Distributions

- Pro rata distributions generally are nontaxable.
- Shareholders allocate basis from the "old" stock to the "new" stock based on relative fair market value.
- Non-pro rata stock distributions usually are taxable as dividends.

---

[15]§305(b).

LO 14-4   STOCK REDEMPTIONS

continued from page 14-1...

For purposes of the storyline for this section, assume that several years ago Nicole and Sarah owned 75 percent (75 shares) and 25 percent (25 shares) of the CCS stock, respectively. At that time, they needed additional capital to expand CCS's operations. To raise the necessary capital, CCS issued 25 additional shares of CCS stock to Diane (Nicole's mother) in exchange for $100,000. After issuing the shares, Nicole's ownership in CCS was 60 percent (75 shares/125 shares), Sarah's ownership was 20 percent (25 shares/125 shares), and Diane's CCS ownership was 20 percent (25/125 shares). Diane does not participate in the management of the company.

This year, Diane is hoping to cash out of CCS and use the money to put a down payment on a condominium in The Villages, a retirement community near Scottsdale, Arizona. With the CCS stock valued at $10,000 per share (Diane's stock value is $250,000 in total), Diane sees this as an opportunity to realize her retirement dream. Nicole and Sarah see this as an opportunity to own all of the company's stock, eliminating a potential source of discord should Diane disapprove of the way Nicole and Sarah are running the company. By the end of the year, the company expects to have sufficient cash to buy back some or all of Diane's shares of CCS stock. Nicole and Sarah are wondering about the potential tax consequences to CCS and to Diane under various redemption plans. Diane would like to know if there is a tax difference between (1) CCS buying back 5 of her shares this year, and the remaining 20 shares equally over the next four years (five shares per year), or (2) CCS buying back all 25 shares this year using an installment note that would pay her 20 percent of the purchase price in each of the next five years plus interest.

to be continued...

Publicly held corporations buy back (redeem) their stock from existing shareholders for many and varied reasons. For example, a corporation may have excess cash and limited investment opportunities, or management may feel the stock is undervalued. Management may see a large redemption as a way to get analysts to take a closer look at their company (this action sometimes is referred to as *signaling*). Reducing the number of outstanding shares also increases earnings per share (by reducing the number of shares in the denominator of the calculation) and potentially increases the stock's market price. Moreover, corporations are not taxed on gains or losses resulting from transactions in their own stock.[16] Stock redemptions also can be used to selectively buy out dissenting shareholders who have become disruptive to the company.

Privately held corporations engage in stock redemptions for reasons that are different from publicly traded corporations. These corporations often use stock redemptions to shift ownership control between family members (usually the older generation to the younger generation) when the acquiring family members do not have the resources to purchase shares directly from the other family members. They also use redemptions to buy out dissatisfied, disinterested, or deceased shareholders (e.g., a child who does not want to continue in the family business or a family member who has become disruptive in the management of the company). Finally, privately held corporations use redemptions to provide liquidity to shareholders for their nonpublicly traded shares. For example, redemptions of an ex-spouse's stock can provide liquidity in a divorce settlement and eliminate the ex-spouse from management or ownership in the company and

---

[16]§1032.

redemptions can be used to provide cash to satisfy estate taxes imposed on the estate of a deceased shareholder of the company.

Closely held corporations and their shareholders frequently have buy-sell agreements in which either the corporation or the other shareholders are obligated or given an option to purchase the shares of another shareholder when a "trigger event" occurs (usually the death or retirement of a shareholder). A buy-sell agreement in which the corporation is required or has the option to repurchase the shares is called a *redemption agreement*. A buy-sell agreement in which the shareholders are required or have the option to purchase the shares is called a *cross-purchase agreement*. Buy-sell agreements provide for the liquidation of a shareholder's stock for estate tax purposes and protect the remaining shareholders from a sale of the stock to an undesirable shareholder.

The Form of a Stock Redemption

A stock redemption is an acquisition by a corporation of its stock from a shareholder in exchange for property, whether or not the stock so acquired is cancelled, retired, or held as treasury stock.[17] The term *property* has the same meaning as it did for dividend transactions (i.e., cash and noncash property, not including the stock of the distributing corporation).

Stock redemptions take the form of an *exchange* where the shareholders exchange their stock in the corporation for property, usually cash. If the *form* of the transaction is respected, shareholders compute gain or loss (usually capital) by comparing the amount realized (money and the fair market value of other property received) with their tax basis in the stock exchanged.

Without any tax law restrictions, a sole shareholder of a corporation could circumvent the dividend rules by structuring distributions to have the form of an exchange (i.e., a stock redemption). For example, rather than have the corporation make a $100,000 dividend distribution, the shareholder could have the corporation buy back $100,000 of stock from the shareholder. If the shareholder had a tax basis of $60,000 in the stock redeemed, the amount of income reported on the shareholder's tax return would decrease from $100,000 (dividend) to $40,000 (capital gain). At present, both amounts would be taxed at the same preferential tax rate (generally 15 percent but potentially as high as 23.8 percent (including the net investment income tax), assuming the shareholder held the stock for more than a year. Similar to a dividend, however, the sole shareholder would continue to own 100 percent of the corporation before and after the stock redemption.

Form is not always respected in a redemption, however. The tax law may determine (or the IRS may argue that) the transaction is, in substance, a property distribution, the tax consequences of which should be determined under the previously discussed dividend rules.

The Internal Revenue Code (IRC) provides both objective ("bright line") and subjective tests to distinguish when a redemption should be treated as an exchange or a potential dividend.[18] The result is an intricate set of rules that must be navigated carefully by the corporation and its shareholders to ensure that the shareholders receive the tax treatment they desire.[19] This is especially true in closely held, family corporations, where the majority of stock is held by people related to each other through birth or marriage.

While individual shareholders usually prefer sale treatment, corporate shareholders generally have more incentive for dividend treatment. Dividends from domestic corporations are eligible for the dividends received deduction (usually 50 or 65 percent), whereas

---

[17]§317(b).

[18]§302.

[19]Not all taxpayers have the same tax incentives in a redemption. Corporate shareholders may desire dividend treatment to capture the dividends received deduction. Individuals, on the other hand, may desire exchange treatment to lessen the amount of gain recognized (by reducing the amount received by the basis of the stock exchanged) or to report a capital loss.

the full amount of capital gain is taxed at the 21 percent corporate tax rate. A corporate shareholder might prefer exchange treatment if the redemption results in a loss, its stock tax basis as a percentage of the redemption price exceeds the dividends received deduction ratio, or the corporation has capital loss carryovers.

Redemptions That Reduce a Shareholder's Ownership Interest

The IRC allows a shareholder to treat a redemption as an exchange if the transaction meets one of three change-in-stock-ownership tests.[20] These stock ownership tests look at the redemption from the shareholder's perspective.

Redemptions That Are Substantially Disproportionate with Respect to the Shareholder

In §302(b)(2), the IRC states that a redemption will be treated as an exchange if the redemption is "*substantially disproportionate with respect to the shareholder.*" A shareholder meets this requirement by satisfying three mechanical ("bright line") *stock ownership tests:*

- Immediately after the exchange, the shareholder owns less than 50 percent of the total combined voting power of all classes of stock entitled to vote.
- The shareholder's percentage ownership of voting stock after the redemption is less than 80 percent of his or her percentage ownership before the redemption.
- The shareholder's percentage ownership of the aggregate fair market value of the corporation's common stock (voting and nonvoting) after the redemption is less than 80 percent of his or her percentage ownership before the redemption.

For example, if a shareholder owns 60 percent of a corporation's stock before the redemption, she must own less than 48 percent of the stock after a stock redemption to have the redemption treated as an exchange (60 percent × 80 percent = 48 percent, which is also less than 50 percent). If the shareholder owns 70 percent of the stock before the redemption, she must own less than 50 percent of the stock after the redemption in order to meet both the 80 percent test and the 50 percent test. Even if the redemption meets the 80 percent test by decreasing ownership to less than 56 percent (70 percent × 80 percent = 56 percent), the shareholder would still not qualify for sale or exchange treatment unless the ownership after the redemption decreases to below 50 percent.

The determination as to whether a shareholder meets the 50 percent and 80 percent tests is evaluated on a shareholder-by-shareholder basis. As a result, for the same redemption, some shareholders satisfy the test while others do not. If a shareholder owns multiple classes (voting and nonvoting) of common stock, the less-than-80-percent of fair market value test is applied to the shareholder's aggregate ownership of the common stock rather than on a class-by-class basis.

Example 14-15

What if: Assume Diane is unrelated to both Nicole and Sarah (recall that Diane owns 25 of the 125 outstanding shares of CCS stock). This year, CCS redeemed five shares of her CCS stock in exchange for $50,000. Diane has a tax basis in the five shares of $20,000 ($4,000 per share). What is the tax treatment of the stock redemption to Diane under §302(b)(2)?

Answer: $50,000 dividend, assuming CCS has at least $50,000 of E&P. Prior to the redemption, Diane owns 20 percent of CCS (25/125 shares). After the redemption, her ownership percentage in CCS drops to 16.67 percent (20/120 shares). This redemption does not satisfy the substantially disproportionate test, which would treat the redemption as an exchange. After the redemption, Diane owns less than 50 percent of the CCS stock, but her ownership percentage after the redemption

---

[20]§302(b)(1), (b)(2), and (b)(3).

(16.67 percent) does not fall below 80 percent of her ownership percentage prior to the redemption (20% × 80% = 16%). Diane will not be able to treat the redemption as an exchange under this change-in-ownership test. Unless she can satisfy one of the other change-in-ownership tests, Diane will have a $50,000 distribution which will be treated as a dividend, assuming CCS has sufficient E&P, rather than a $30,000 capital gain ($50,000 − $20,000).

How many shares of stock would CCS have to redeem from Diane to guarantee her exchange treatment under the substantially disproportionate test?

Answer: Six shares. For Diane to meet the 80 percent test, CCS must redeem six shares of stock. The computation is made as follows:

$$\frac{25 - x}{125 - x} < 16\%, \text{ where } x \text{ is the number of shares to be redeemed}$$

Using some algebra, we can compute x to be 5.95, which we must round up to six shares.[21] If CCS redeems six shares from Diane, her ownership percentage after the redemption will be 15.97 percent (19/119 shares), which now meets the 80 percent test. In addition to providing $10,000 more in cash to Diane, the redemption of this one additional share transforms the transaction from a $50,000 dividend (5 shares × $10,000) to a $36,000 capital gain ($60,000 − $24,000).

In determining whether Diane meets the 50 percent and 80 percent tests, she must take into account the **constructive ownership** (stock attribution) rules found in IRC §318. These rules force stock owned by other persons (individuals and entities) to be treated as owned by (attributed to) the shareholder for purposes of determining whether the shareholder has met the change-in-stock-ownership tests. The purpose of the attribution rules is to prevent shareholders from dispersing stock ownership to either family members who have similar economic interests or entities controlled by the shareholder to avoid having stock redemptions recharacterized as dividends.

Family attribution. Individuals are treated as owning the shares of stock owned by their spouse, children, grandchildren, and parents. Stock owned constructively through the family attribution rule cannot be reattributed to another family member through the family attribution rule (this is known as *double family attribution*).

Example 14-16

Return to the original storyline facts, where Diane is Nicole's mother. This year, CCS redeemed six shares of stock from Diane in exchange for $60,000. Diane has a tax basis in the six shares of stock redeemed of $24,000 ($4,000 per share). What is the tax treatment of the stock redemption to Diane under §302(b)(2)?

Answer: $60,000 dividend (assuming CCS has at least $60,000 of E&P).

Prior to the redemption, Diane owned 20 percent of CCS (25/125 shares) directly. Under the family attribution rules, she is treated as constructively owning the shares of CCS stock owned by her daughter Nicole (75 shares). In applying the substantially disproportionate change-in-stock-ownership tests, Diane is treated as owning 100 shares of CCS stock (25 + 75), or 80 percent of the CCS stock (100/125 shares). After the redemption, her ownership percentage in CCS drops to 79 percent (94/119 shares). This redemption does not satisfy the substantially disproportionate test because Diane is deemed to own more than 50 percent of the CCS stock after the redemption. As a result, she will have a $60,000 dividend, assuming CCS has sufficient E&P, rather than a $36,000 capital gain ($60,000 − $24,000).

---

[21]Multiply both sides by $(125 - x)$ to get $25 - x = 20 - .16x$. Moving x to the right side of the equation and the integers to the left side of the equation simplifies to $5 = .84x$. Solving for x yields 5.95.

An interesting question arises as to what happens to the tax basis of stock redeemed that is not used in determining the shareholder's tax consequences. This occurs in a redemption treated as a dividend, where the tax basis of the stock redeemed is not subtracted from the amount received from the corporation. Under the current rules, the tax basis of the stock redeemed is added back to the tax basis of any shares still held by the shareholder.[22] If the shareholder no longer holds any shares, the tax basis transfers to the stock held by those persons who caused the shareholder to have dividend treatment under the attribution rules.

Example 14-17

In the prior example, CCS redeemed six shares of stock from Diane for $60,000, and the transaction was treated as a dividend because of the application of the family attribution rules. Diane had a tax basis in the six shares of stock redeemed of $24,000 ($4,000 per share), but this tax basis was not used in determining her taxable income from the transaction.

What is Diane's tax basis in her remaining 19 shares of CCS stock?

Answer: $100,000. Diane adds back the unused $24,000 tax basis in the six shares redeemed to the $76,000 tax basis of her remaining 19 shares (19 shares × $4,000 = $76,000). Her tax basis in these remaining shares increases to $100,000, the original tax basis of her 25 shares.

Attribution from entities to owners or beneficiaries. Owners or beneficiaries of entities can be deemed to own shares of stock owned by the entity itself. Under these rules, partners are deemed to own a pro rata share of their partnership's stock holdings (i.e., a partner who has a 10 percent interest in a partnership is deemed to own 10 percent of any stock owned by the partnership). Beneficiaries are deemed to own a pro rata share of the stock owned by the trust or estate of which they are a beneficiary. Shareholders are deemed to own a pro rata share of their corporation's stock holdings, but only if they own at least 50 percent of the value of the corporation's stock. The stock attribution rules apply in determining if this 50 percent test is met.

Example 14-18

What if: Assume that Diane is unrelated to Nicole, and that she is a 40 percent partner in a partnership that owns 25 shares in CCS. The other 60 percent of the partnership is owned by Diane's neighbors, Fred and Ethel, who are unrelated to Diane. How many shares of CCS is Diane treated as constructively owning through the partnership?

Answer: 10 shares. Diane is treated as owning her pro rata share of stock owned by the partnership; in this example, 40 percent times 25 shares.

What if: Assume the same facts as the previous what-if except that Diane is a 40 percent shareholder in XYZ Corporation and that XYZ owns 25 shares in CCS. The other 60 percent of the XZY is owned by Diane's neighbors, Fred and Ethel, who are unrelated to Diane. How many shares of CCS is Diane treated as constructively owning through the XYZ?

Answer: 0 shares. Because Diane does not own at least 50 percent of XYZ Corporation, there is no attribution of CCS shares from XYZ to Diane.

What if: Assume the same facts as the previous what-if except that Diane is a 50 percent shareholder in XYZ Corporation and that XYZ owns 25 shares in CCS. The other 50 percent of the XZY is owned by Diane's neighbors, Fred and Ethel, who are unrelated to Diane. How many shares of CCS is Diane treated as constructively owning through the XYZ?

Answer: 12.5 shares. Diane is treated as owning her pro rata share of stock owned by XYZ; in this example, 50 percent times 25 shares.

---

[22]Reg. §1.302-2.

Attribution from owners or beneficiaries to entities.   Entities can be deemed to own stock owned by their owners or beneficiaries. Under these rules, a partnership is deemed to own 100 percent of the shares owned by its partners. A trust or estate is deemed to own 100 percent of the shares owned by its beneficiaries. A corporation is deemed to own 100 percent of the shares owned by its shareholders, but only if the shareholder owns at least 50 percent of the value of the corporation's stock (after applying the stock attribution rules). Stock that is deemed owned by an entity cannot be reattributed to the other owners in the entity under the entity-to-owner rules previously discussed (this is known as *sideways attribution*).

For example, assume an individual owns 100 shares of a corporation's stock directly. In addition, she is a 50 percent partner in a partnership that owns 100 shares of stock in the same corporation. Under the owner-to-entity attribution rules, the partnership is deemed to own 100 percent of the partner's 100 shares in the corporation. The partnership is treated as owning 200 shares of stock in the corporation (100 + 100) for purposes of applying any of the change-in-stock-ownership tests in a stock redemption.

Option attribution.   A person having an option to purchase stock is deemed to own the stock that the option entitles the person to purchase.

Redemptions in Complete Redemption of All of a Shareholder's Stock in a Corporation

In §302(b)(3), the IRC indicates that a redemption will be treated as an exchange if the redemption is in "*complete redemption of all of the stock of the corporation owned by the shareholder.*" This test seems redundant with the substantially disproportionate test discussed previously; after all, a complete redemption automatically satisfies the 50 percent and 80 percent tests. The difference relates to the application of the stock attribution rules that apply to this form of redemption.

The stock attribution rules previously discussed also apply to a complete redemption. This presents a potential problem in family-owned corporations in which the only (or majority) shareholders are parents, children, and grandchildren. Parents who have all of their stock redeemed will be treated as having received a dividend if their children or grandchildren continue to own the remaining stock in the corporation because of the operation of the family attribution rules. To provide family members with relief in these situations, the IRC allows shareholders to waive (ignore) the family attribution rules in a complete redemption of their stock.[23] As you might expect, there are some strings attached.

The first requirement is that the shareholder has no interest in the corporation immediately after the exchange as a "*shareholder, employee, director, officer or consultant.*"[24] These relations to the corporation are referred to as prohibited interests. The second requirement is that the shareholder does not acquire a prohibited interest within 10 years after the redemption, unless by inheritance (this is known as the *10-year look-forward rule*). Finally, the shareholder must agree to notify the IRS district director within 30 days if he or she acquires a prohibited interest within 10 years after the redemption. These agreements are referred to as **triple i agreements.**[25] The shareholder can still be a creditor of the corporation (i.e., the parents can receive a corporate note in return for their stock if the corporation does not have the cash on hand to finance the redemption).

---

[23] §302(c)(2).

[24] §302(c).

[25] The agreement gets its name from the clause in which it is described [§302(c)(2)(A)(*iii*)].

Example 14-19

Return to the storyline facts, where Diane is Nicole's mother. Assume CCS redeemed all of Diane's 25 shares this year for $250,000. Her tax basis in the CCS shares is $100,000 (25 × $4,000). Under the family attribution rules, Diane would still be treated as constructively owning 75 percent of the CCS stock (Nicole would own 75 of the remaining 100 shares in CCS). The $250,000 payment would be treated as a taxable dividend.

What happens to Diane's unused $100,000 tax basis in the CCS stock redeemed?

Answer: Her tax basis transfers to Nicole's stock, giving Nicole a new tax basis in her CCS stock of $148,000 ($48,000 + $100,000).

How can Diane change the tax treatment of the complete redemption?

Answer: Because Diane has all of her shares redeemed, she can waive the family attribution rules provided she files a triple i agreement with the IRS and does not retain a prohibited interest in CCS (e.g., as an employee or consultant). By waiving the family attribution rules, Diane will be able to treat the redemption as an exchange and report a capital gain of $150,000 ($250,000 − $100,000).

Redemptions That Are Not Essentially Equivalent to a Dividend   In §302(b)(1), the IRC states that a redemption will be treated as an exchange if the redemption is *"not essentially equivalent to a dividend"* determined at the shareholder level. This is a subjective determination that depends on the facts and circumstances of each case. The IRS does not provide any mechanical tests to make this determination. As a result, shareholder reliance on this test usually is one of last resort. The Supreme Court has held that the only way for a shareholder to qualify under this test is for the redemption to "result in a meaningful reduction of the shareholder's proportionate interest in the corporation."[26]

Although the courts have held that a shareholder's interest can include the right to vote and exercise control, participate in current and accumulated earnings, or share in net assets on liquidation, the IRS generally looks at the change in voting power as the key factor. The shareholder's voting power generally must decrease as a result of the exchange and the shareholder's voting power must be below 50 percent after the redemption before this test can be considered.[27] As before, the stock attribution rules apply to these types of redemptions. Shareholders generally turn to this test to provide exchange treatment for redemptions when they cannot meet the "bright line" tests discussed previously.

Example 14-20

What if: Assume Diane is unrelated to Nicole. This year, CCS redeemed five shares of Diane's stock in exchange for $50,000. Diane has a tax basis in the five shares of CCS stock of $20,000 ($4,000 per share).

---

[26]*United States v. Davis,* 397 U.S. 301, at 313 (1970).

[27]In Rev. Rul. 76-385, 1976-2 C.B. 92, the IRS held that in the case of a "small, minority shareholder, whose relative stock interest is minimal and who exercises no control over the affairs of the corporation," any reduction in proportionate interest is "meaningful." In this ruling, the shareholder's ownership percentage decreased from .0001118 percent to .0001081 percent, which would not be considered a "meaningful" reduction by most standards. Because the reduction in stock ownership did not meet the substantially disproportionate tests of §302(b)(2), the shareholder's only hope for exchange treatment was to qualify under §302(b)(1).

What is the tax treatment of the stock redemption to Diane under the *not essentially equivalent to a dividend* test?

Answer: Most likely $30,000 capital gain ($50,000 – $20,000).

Prior to the redemption, Diane owned 20 percent of CCS (25/125 shares). After the redemption, her ownership percentage in CCS drops to 16.67 percent (20/120 shares). This redemption does not satisfy the substantially disproportionate test, which would treat the redemption as an exchange. Diane likely has a case that the redemption should be treated as an exchange because it was "not essentially equal to a dividend." After all, her ownership percentage decreased (20 percent to 16.67 percent) and is below 50 percent after the redemption, so she does not have control of the corporation. She likely has a case, although the result she seeks (exchange treatment) is not guaranteed. For peace of mind, Diane might prefer having CCS redeem one additional share and therefore have the certainty that the redemption will be treated as an exchange under the bright line test of §302(b)(2).

Example 14-21

What if: Assume Diane is Nicole's mother and CCS redeemed five shares of Diane's stock in exchange for $50,000. Diane has a tax basis in the five shares of CCS stock of $20,000 ($4,000 per share). What is the tax treatment of the stock redemption to Diane under the *not essentially equivalent to a dividend* test?

Answer: $50,000 dividend.

Prior to the redemption, Diane is treated as owning 80 percent of CCS (25 shares directly and 75 shares through Nicole). After the redemption, her ownership percentage in CCS drops to 79 percent (95/120 shares). This redemption does not satisfy the *not essentially equal to a dividend* test because she is treated as owning more than 50 percent of the CCS stock.

Tax Consequences to the Distributing Corporation

The corporation distributing property to shareholders in a redemption generally recognizes gain on distributions of appreciated property, but it is not permitted to recognize loss on distributions of property with tax basis greater than fair market value.[28]

If the shareholder treats the redemption as a *dividend,* the corporation reduces its current E&P by the cash distributed and the fair market value of other property distributed.[29] If the shareholder treats the redemption as an *exchange,* the corporation reduces E&P at the date of distribution by the percentage of stock redeemed (i.e., if 50 percent of the stock is redeemed, E&P is reduced by 50 percent), not to exceed the fair market value of the property distributed.[30] The distributing corporation reduces its current E&P by any dividend distributions made during the year before reducing its E&P for redemptions treated as exchanges.[31]

The distributing corporation cannot deduct expenses incurred in a stock redemption.[32] However, it can deduct interest on debt incurred to finance a redemption.

THE KEY FACTS

Stock Redemptions Treated as Exchanges

- A stock redemption is treated as an exchange if it meets one of the following three tests:
  - Not essentially equivalent to a dividend.
  - Substantially disproportionate with respect to the shareholders.
  - In complete termination of the shareholder's interest.
- The following attribution rules are used to determine if one of the three tests is met:
  - Family attribution.
  - Entity-to-owner attribution (pro rata).
  - Owner-to-entity attribution (100 percent).
  - Options.
- A corporation reduces its E&P as a result of a stock redemption as follows:
  - If the distribution is treated as an exchange, E&P is reduced by the lesser of (1) the amount distributed or (2) the percentage of stock redeemed times AE&P at the redemption date.
  - If the distribution is treated as a dividend, E&P is reduced using the dividend rules.

---

[28]§311(a) and (b).

[29]§312(a), and note that E&P cannot be reduced by more than the pro rata percentage of E&P allocated to the redeemed shares.

[30]§312(n)(7).

[31]Rev. Rul. 74-338, 1974-2 C.B. 101 and Rev. Rul. 74-339, 1974-2 C.B. 103.

[32]§162(k).

Example 14-22

What if: Assume CCS redeemed all of the 25 shares owned by Diane in exchange for $250,000. The stock redeemed represents 20 percent of the total stock outstanding. Diane has a tax basis in her CCS shares of $100,000. Further assume that Diane treated the redemption as an exchange because she waived the family attribution rules and filed a triple i agreement with the IRS.[33] As a result, Diane recognized a capital gain of $150,000 ($250,000 − $100,000). The redemption took place on December 31, on which date CCS had E&P of $500,000. CCS did not make any dividend payments during the year.

By what amount does CCS reduce its E&P as a result of this redemption?

Answer: $100,000. CCS reduces E&P by the lesser of (1) $100,000 (20% of stock redeemed × $500,000 E&P) or (2) $250,000, the amount paid to Diane in the redemption.

What if: Assume E&P was $2,000,000 at the end of the year. By what amount does CCS reduce its E&P as a result of this redemption?

Answer: $250,000. CCS reduces E&P by the lesser of (1) $400,000 (20% of stock redeemed × $2,000,000 E&P) or (2) $250,000, the amount paid to Diane in the redemption.

What if: Assume CCS paid a dividend of $100,000 to its shareholders on June 1. E&P was $500,000 at the end of the year, before taking into account the dividend and redemption. By what amount does CCS reduce its E&P as a result of this redemption?

Answer: $80,000. CCS first reduces E&P by the dividend paid during the year to $400,000 ($500,000 − $100,000). CCS then reduces its E&P for the redemption by the lesser of (1) $80,000 (20% of stock redeemed × $400,000 E&P) or (2) $250,000, the amount paid to Diane in the redemption.

LO 14-4   ## PARTIAL LIQUIDATIONS

Corporations can contract their operations either by distributing the stock of a subsidiary to their shareholders or by selling the business. In the case of a sale, the corporation may distribute the proceeds from the sale to its shareholders in partial liquidation of their ownership interests. The distribution may require the shareholders to tender shares of stock back to the corporation or may be pro rata to all the shareholders without an actual exchange of stock.

The tax treatment of a distribution received in a partial liquidation depends on the identity of the shareholder receiving the distribution.[34] All *noncorporate* shareholders receive exchange treatment. This entitles the individual to capital gain treatment with respect to gain or loss recognized on the actual or deemed exchange. If the shareholder is not required to tender stock to the corporation in return for the property received, the shareholder computes gain or loss recognized on the exchange by calculating the tax basis of the shares that would have been transferred to the corporation had the transaction been a stock redemption.

Because the partial liquidation provisions do not apply to corporate shareholders, corporate shareholders apply the other stock redemption tests to determine if they should treat the distribution from the partial liquidation as a sale or as a dividend. This usually results in dividend treatment to the corporate shareholder because partial liquidations almost always involve pro rata distributions. Corporate shareholders generally prefer dividend treatment because of the availability of the dividends received deduction.[35]

---

[33]The requirements for filing the triple i agreement are found in Reg. §1.302-4T.

[34]§302(b)(4).

[35]Note, however, that when a corporation receives a dividend distribution as part of a partial liquidation, the extraordinary dividend rules may mitigate the tax benefit of the dividends received deduction. See §1059.

For a distribution to be in partial liquidation of the corporation, it must either be *"not essentially equivalent to a dividend"* (determined at the corporate level) or the result of the termination of a *"qualified trade or business."*[36] The technical requirements to meet these requirements are beyond the scope of this text.

Partial liquidations can be a tax-efficient way for a corporation to satisfy both its corporate and individual shareholders. For example, in the 1990s, General Dynamics Corporation sold off several of its divisions and distributed the proceeds ($20 per share) to its shareholders in partial liquidation of the corporation. As a result, the company's largest corporate shareholder treated the distribution as a dividend and received a 70 percent dividends received deduction. The company's largest individual shareholders treated the redemption as an exchange and received preferential taxation at the capital gain tax rate. The corporation was able to distribute cash from the sale of its assets in a manner that was tax-efficient to its diverse set of shareholders. Despite their potentially beneficial tax results, partial liquidations are rare in practice.

COMPLETE LIQUIDATION OF A CORPORATION

LO 14-5

continued from page 14-16...

After many successful years, CCS has experienced an extended period of mediocre performance. Nicole and Sarah attribute CCS's declining profitability to increasing costs and stiffer competition. After considerable thought, Nicole and Sarah have reluctantly decided to wind up the business and liquidate the corporation. To help them determine the tax consequences of the liquidation, their accountant has constructed CCS's **tax accounting balance sheet,** which is reproduced below.

	FMV	Tax Basis	Built-in Gain (Loss)
Cash	$138,000	$138,000	
Receivables	2,000	2,000	$ 0
Inventory	10,000	12,000	(2,000)
Equipment	50,000	50,000	0
Building	120,000	98,000	22,000
Land	180,000	100,000	80,000
Total	$500,000	$400,000	$100,000

Nicole and Sarah agreed that CCS would sell off the remaining inventory, land, building, and equipment and collect the receivables. After the sale, CCS would pay taxes of $21,000 on the gains and divide the remaining $479,000 in cash pro rata between Nicole (75 percent) and Sarah (25 percent). ■

As the storyline indicates, the owners of a corporation may decide at some point to discontinue the corporation's business activities. This decision may be made because the corporation is not profitable, the officers and shareholders wish to change the organizational form of the business (e.g., to a flow-through entity), or the owners want to consolidate operations (e.g., a subsidiary is liquidated into the parent corporation).

A complete liquidation occurs when a corporation acquires all of its stock from its shareholders in exchange for "all" of its net assets, after which time the corporation ceases to do business. For tax purposes, a corporation files Form 966, "Corporate Dissolution or Liquidation," to inform the IRS of its intention to liquidate its tax existence.

[36]§302(e).

The form should be filed within 30 days after the owners (board of directors) resolve to liquidate the corporation. Depending on the type of shareholders and the ownership percentage of any corporate shareholders, the tax consequences of the liquidation can be categorized as either fully taxable, nontaxable, or partially taxable.

Fully Taxable Complete Liquidation

A liquidation is fully taxable unless a corporate shareholder owns at least 80 percent of the liquidating corporation. The tax consequences of a fully taxable liquidation are described below.

Tax Consequences to Shareholders

A shareholder receiving a liquidating distribution treats the property received as "full payment in exchange for the stock" transferred.[37] The shareholder computes capital gain or loss by subtracting the stock's tax basis from the money received plus the fair market value of property received in return for the stock. Whether the capital gain or loss is long-term or short-term depends on how long the shareholder has owned the stock in the liquidating corporation before the distribution. If a shareholder assumes the corporation's liabilities on property received in a liquidating distribution, the amount realized by the shareholder in the computation of gain or loss is reduced by the amount of the liabilities assumed. The shareholder's tax basis in noncash property received in the liquidating distribution equals the property's fair market value.

Example 14-23

Sarah received cash of $119,750 ($479,000 × 25 percent), representing her 25 percent ownership in the company after all debts were paid. Sarah's tax basis in her CCS stock is $40,000.

What is the amount and character of the gain or loss Sarah will recognize on the liquidating distribution?

Answer: $79,750 long-term capital gain ($119,750 − $40,000). Sarah owned the CCS stock for more than a year before receiving the distribution, so the gain is long-term capital gain.

What if: Suppose that Chanzz Inc. rather than Sarah was a 25 percent shareholder of CCS. Chanzz Inc. received a $119,750 distribution representing its 25 percent ownership in the company. Chanzz Inc.'s tax basis in its CCS stock is $40,000. What amount of gain does Chanzz Inc. recognize on the distribution?

Answer: $79,750 gain. The tax consequences to Chanzz Inc. are the same as the tax consequences are to Sarah even though Chanzz Inc. is a corporation.

What if: Suppose that rather than sell the land and building, CCS distributed the land, building, and $59,250 cash to Nicole, representing her 75 percent interest in the net fair market value of the company. Nicole's tax basis in her CCS stock is $100,000.

What is the amount and character of gain or loss Nicole will recognize on the liquidating distribution?

Answer: $259,250 capital gain [($180,000 (land) + $120,000 (building) + $59,250) − $100,000].

What is Nicole's tax basis in the land and in the building she receives in the liquidating distribution?

Answer: $180,000 in the land and $120,000 in the building. Nicole takes a fair market value basis in the assets received in the distribution.

Tax Consequences to Liquidating Corporation

In general, a liquidating corporation recognizes gain or loss on each of its assets as if it had sold each asset at its fair market value on the date of the distribution.[38] However, the liquidating corporation does not recognize *loss on property* if the property is distributed to a *related person* and either (1) the distribution is non-pro rata (i.e., the related person does not receive a percentage of the loss property equal to the related person's ownership interest in the

[37]§331(a).
[38]§336(a).

liquidating corporation), or (2) the asset distributed is *disqualified property*.[39] A *related person* generally is defined as a shareholder who owns more than 50 percent of the value of the stock of the liquidating corporation. *Disqualified property* is property acquired within five years of the date of distribution in a tax-deferred §351 transaction or as a contribution to capital.

Example 14-24

CCS made liquidating distributions to Nicole (75 percent owner) and Sarah (25 percent owner) during the current year.

What if: Suppose that CCS made a pro rata distribution of all its assets to its shareholders. The company's tax accounting balance sheet at the time of the distribution is reproduced below:

	FMV	Tax Basis	Built-in Gain (Loss)
Cash	$138,000	$138,000	
Receivables	2,000	2,000	$ 0
Inventory	10,000	12,000	(2,000)
Equipment	50,000	50,000	0
Building	120,000	98,000	22,000
Land	180,000	100,000	80,000
Total	$500,000	$400,000	$100,000

What amount of gain or loss does CCS recognize as a result of the distribution?

Answer: $100,000. CCS recognizes all gains and losses on the distribution of its assets in the following amounts and character:

	Gain (Loss) Recognized	Character
Inventory	$ (2,000)	Ordinary
Building	22,000	Ordinary (§291) and §1231
Land	80,000	§1231
Net gain	**$100,000**	

Note that the gain or loss on the complete liquidation is identical to gains and losses that would result if CCS had sold all of its assets at fair market value.

Example 14-25

What if: Assume that as part of its complete liquidating distribution, CCS distributed all of the inventory to Nicole (75 percent owner) in a non-pro rata distribution (the distribution of inventory is non-pro rata because Nicole did not receive exactly 75 percent of the inventory). The company's tax accounting balance sheet at the time of the distribution is reproduced below:

	FMV	Tax Basis	Difference
Cash	$138,000	$138,000	
Receivables	2,000	2,000	
Inventory	10,000	12,000	$ (2,000)
Equipment	50,000	50,000	0
Building	120,000	98,000	22,000
Land	180,000	100,000	80,000
Total	$500,000	$400,000	$100,000

(continued on page 14-28)

---

[39]§336(d)(1).

What amount of gain or loss does CCS recognize as a result of the liquidating distribution?

Answer: $102,000 gain. CCS recognizes all gains but does not recognize the inventory loss because the distribution of the loss property is non-pro rata and the loss property is distributed to a related person (Nicole owns more than 50 percent of the stock).

	Gain (Loss) Recognized	Character
Inventory	$ 0	
Building	22,000	Ordinary (§291) and §1231
Land	80,000	§1231
Net gain	**$102,000**	

What if: Suppose that as part of its complete liquidating distribution CCS distributed all of the inventory to Sarah in a non-pro rata distribution. What amount of gain or loss does CCS recognize as a result of the distribution?

Answer: $100,000. CCS recognizes all of the gain, and it can also recognize the $2,000 loss on the distribution of the inventory because the property was not distributed to a related person (note that if Sarah were related to Nicole, Sarah would be considered to be a related person to CCS).

What if: Assume that as part of its complete liquidating distribution, CCS distributed the inventory to Nicole and Sarah pro rata (i.e., Nicole got 75 percent of the inventory and Sarah got 25 percent). What amount of gain or loss does CCS recognize on the liquidating distribution?

Answer: $100,000. CCS recognizes the gain on the land and building, and it recognizes the loss on the inventory. It is allowed to recognize the loss on the inventory distributed to Nicole (related person) because it was distributed pro rata, and it can recognize loss on the inventory distributed to Sarah because she is not a related person (and it was distributed pro rata).

What if: Assume that as part of its complete liquidating distribution, CCS distributed the inventory to Nicole and Sarah pro rata (i.e., Nicole got 75 percent of the inventory and Sarah got 25 percent). Assume the inventory is disqualified property. What amount of gain or loss does CCS recognize on the liquidating distribution?

Answer: $101,500 ($22,000 + $80,000 − $500). CCS recognizes the gain on the land and building, and it recognizes the $500 loss on the inventory it distributed to Sarah (25 percent of all the inventory) who is not a related person. CCS is not allowed to deduct the $1,500 loss on the inventory it distributed to Nicole (75 percent of all the inventory) even though it was distributed pro rata because the inventory is disqualified property and Nicole is a related person.

A second loss disallowance rule applies to built-in loss that arises with respect to property acquired in a §351 transaction or as a contribution to capital. A loss on the complete liquidation of such property (whether distributed to a shareholder or sold to an outside third party) is not recognized if the property that is sold or distributed was acquired in a §351 transaction or as a contribution to capital, and a *principal purpose* of the contribution was to recognize a loss by the liquidating corporation.[40] This rule prevents a built-in loss existing at the time of the distribution (basis in excess of fair market value) from being recognized by treating the basis of the property sold or distributed as being its fair market value at the time it was contributed to the corporation. A prohibited tax avoidance purpose is presumed if the property transfer occurs within two years of the liquidation. This presumption can be overcome if the corporation can show that there was a corporate business purpose for contributing the property to the corporation.

This provision is designed as an *anti-stuffing* provision to prevent shareholders from contributing property with built-in losses to a corporation shortly before a liquidation to offset gains on property distributed in the liquidation. In the Corporate Formations and Operations chapter, you learned that Congress added a similar built-in loss disallowance rule that applies to §351 transfers.[41] Under that provision, if the *aggregate* adjusted tax

[40]§336(d)(2).
[41]§362(e)(2).

basis of property transferred to a corporation by a shareholder in a §351 transfer exceeds the aggregate fair market value of the assets, the aggregate tax basis of the assets in the hands of the transferee corporation cannot exceed their aggregate fair market value. The loss disallowance rule relating to liquidating sales or distributions of built-in loss property received in a §351 transaction applies on an asset-by-asset basis to those assets that retain their built-in loss when contributed to the corporation.

Example 14-26

What if: Suppose Nicole transferred a building and land to CCS in return for 75 percent of the corporation's stock in a transaction that qualified under §351. The property transferred to the corporation had the following fair market values and tax bases at the time of the transfer:

	FMV	Tax Basis
Building	$ 75,000	$100,000
Land	300,000	250,000
Total	$375,000	$350,000

In this case, the aggregate fair market value of the property transferred to the corporation exceeds the aggregate tax basis of the property. As a result, the building will retain its carryover basis of $100,000 and subsequent built-in loss of $25,000.

If the building and land are distributed to Nicole in complete liquidation of CCS within two years of the §351 transaction, will CCS be able to deduct the $25,000 loss on the distribution of the building?

Answer: It depends. Because the liquidating distribution is made within two years of the §351 transaction, the presumption is that Nicole contributed the property to CCS for tax avoidance purposes (i.e., to allow the corporation to deduct the loss). The corporation can rebut this presumption by demonstrating that the contribution of the property by Nicole had a corporate business purpose at the time of the §351 transaction. It may also be able to rebut the presumption due to the fact that Nicole contributed an aggregate built-in gain of $25,000 in the §351 transaction and not a built-in loss.

Would the answer be any different if CCS sold the building to an outside third party instead of distributing it to Nicole?

Answer: No. The answer would be exactly the same. It doesn't matter whether CCS sells the building to an outside third party or whether it distributes (or sells) the property to a shareholder.

When a corporation liquidates, its liquidation-related expenses—including the cost of preparing and implementing a plan of complete liquidation—are deductible by the liquidating corporation on its final Form 1120. This is true for the liquidating corporation no matter whether the complete liquidation is fully taxable, nontaxable, or partially taxable.

Nontaxable and Partially Taxable Complete Liquidations

A complete liquidation only qualifies as nontaxable or partially taxable when the liquidating corporation has a corporate shareholder that owns *at least* 80 percent of the liquidating corporation's stock.[42] Below, we describe the tax consequences of nontaxable and partially taxable complete liquidations to the shareholders and to the liquidating corporation.

Tax Consequences to Shareholders   When a corporate shareholder owns at least 80 percent of the liquidating corporation, that corporate shareholder does not recognize gain or loss on receipt of the liquidating distribution (nonrecognition treatment is

---

[42]§337(a) and §332(b).

mandatory). The shareholder's basis in the liquidating corporation's stock disappears and the shareholder's tax basis in the property (and liabilities) received from the liquidating corporation is the same basis the liquidating corporation had in the property (and liabilities). That is, the basis carries over to the shareholder.[43] This deferral provision allows a group of corporations under common control to reorganize their organizational structure without tax consequences.

Example 14-27

What if: Suppose CCS is a 100 percent owned subsidiary of Chanzz Inc. and that CCS liquidated by distributing all its assets and liabilities to Chanzz Inc. (net value transferred is $500,000). Chanzz Inc. has a tax basis in its CCS stock of $300,000.

What amount of gain or loss will Chanzz Inc. *realize* on the complete liquidation of CCS?

Answer: $200,000 gain ($500,000 – $300,000).

What amount of gain will Chanzz Inc. *recognize* on the exchange?

Answer: $0. Chanzz Inc. does not recognize any gain on the liquidating distribution because it owns 100 percent of CCS.

What is Chanzz Inc.'s tax basis in the assets and liabilities it receives in the liquidation?

Answer: Chanzz Inc. will take the same basis that CCS had in each of the assets and each of the liabilities it received from CCS.

What if: Suppose Chanzz Inc. owned 80 percent of CCS rather than 100 percent. Would it recognize any gain on receipt of the liquidating distribution from CCS?

Answer: No. Because Chanzz Inc. owns at least 80 percent of CCS, it does not recognize any gain or loss on receipt of the liquidating distribution, and it takes a carryover basis in property (and liabilities) received from CCS. If Chanzz Inc. owned less than 80 percent of CCS, the distribution would be fully taxable to Chanzz Inc. and Chanzz Inc. would take a fair market value basis in property received in the liquidating distribution.

While a liquidating distribution to a corporate shareholder that owns at least 80 percent of the liquidating corporation is nontaxable to that corporate shareholder, liquidating distributions to the minority interest shareholders (shareholders who own the remaining stock in the liquidating corporation) are fully taxable to those shareholders. That is, the minority interest shareholders recognize capital gain or loss on the difference between the net value of the liquidating distribution they receive and their stock basis in the liquidating corporation. The minority shareholders take a fair market value basis in any noncash property they receive in the distribution.

Example 14-28

What if: Suppose Chanzz Inc. owned 80 percent of CCS and Nicole owned the remaining 20 percent. In a complete liquidating distribution, CCS distributed to Nicole land with a fair market value of $100,000 and tax basis of $110,000 in exchange for Nicole's CCS shares. Assuming Nicole's basis in her CCS stock is $70,000, what is the amount and character of gain or loss Nicole would recognize on the distribution?

Answer: $30,000 long-term capital gain ($100,000 value of land minus $70,000 basis in stock). The gain is long-term capital gain because Nicole owned her CCS stock for more than a year before she received the liquidating distribution.

What is Nicole's basis in the land she received in the liquidating distribution?

Answer: $100,000. Nicole takes a fair market value basis in the land because the distribution was taxable to her.

[43]§334(b).

Tax Consequences to Liquidating Corporation   When a corporate shareholder owns at least 80 percent of the stock of the liquidating corporation, the liquidating corporation does not recognize gain or loss on any assets distributed to that corporate shareholder. However, when the corporate shareholder owns at least 80 percent but less than 100 percent of the liquidating corporation, the liquidating corporation recognizes gain on appreciated assets it distributes to minority interest shareholders. The gain and character of the gain is determined on an asset-by-asset basis. The liquidating corporation does not, however, recognize loss on assets distributed to the minority shareholders.[44]

Example 14-29

What if: Suppose Chanzz Inc. owns 80 percent of the CCS stock and Nicole owns the remaining 20 percent. As part of a liquidating distribution, CCS distributed the land to Nicole and the cash, building, and inventory to Chanzz Inc. CCS's tax accounting balance sheet at the time of the distribution is reproduced below:

	FMV	Tax Basis	Difference
Cash	$ 75,000	$ 75,000	
Inventory	55,000	65,000	$(10,000)
Building	270,000	200,000	70,000
Land	100,000	90,000	10,000
Total	$500,000	$430,000	$ 70,000

What amount of gain or loss does CCS recognize as a result of the liquidation?

Answer: $10,000 gain. CCS does not recognize gain or loss on the assets distributed to Chanzz Inc. (80 percent corporate shareholder), but it recognizes a $10,000 gain on the land distributed to Nicole (minority interest shareholder).

What if: Assume the same facts except that, in liquidation, CCS distributed the inventory and $45,000 cash to Nicole and the remaining assets to Chanzz Inc. What gain or loss does CCS recognize on the distribution?

Answer: $0 gain or loss. CCS does not recognize gain on the distribution of appreciated assets to Chanzz Inc. because Chanzz Inc. owns at least 80 percent of the stock of CCS. Further, CCS is not allowed to recognize the loss on distribution of inventory to Nicole even though Nicole is not a related person and is taxed on the distribution. When the liquidating corporation has a corporate shareholder that owns at least 80 percent of the liquidating corporation's stock, the liquidating corporation is not allowed to recognize losses on the distribution of property to minority shareholders.

What if: Assume the same facts except that CCS distributed each asset pro rata to Chanzz Inc. (80 percent) and Nicole (20 percent).[45] What gain or loss would CCS recognize on the liquidating distribution?

Answer: $16,000 gain ($14,000 gain on building and $2,000 gain on land). CCS would recognize 20 percent of the realized gain on the building and 20 percent of the realized gain on the land because it distributed 20 percent of each asset to Nicole, who is a minority interest shareholder. Also, CCS would not be able to deduct any loss on the inventory distributed to Nicole because CCS has a corporate shareholder that owns at least 80 percent of its stock (Chanzz Inc.).

CONCLUSION

In this chapter we learned that a corporation can distribute cash and other property to its shareholders in alternative ways. The most common forms are dividend distributions and stock buybacks (redemptions). The form chosen to make such a distribution affects the tax consequences to the recipients (shareholders) as well as the corporation itself. In some cases, the tax laws or the tax administrators can ignore the form of the transaction

---

[44]§336(d)(3).

[45]In the case of the building and the land, CCS assigned title of each piece of property such that Chanzz Inc. owned 80 percent of the building and 80 percent of the land and Nicole owned 20 percent of each property.

and assess tax based on the substance of the transaction. This is common in the case of stock redemptions that can be taxed as dividend payments. The tax rules that apply to make this distinction often are complex and must be evaluated carefully by taxpayers and their tax advisers prior to making a decision. Finally, we learned that when a corporation winds up its affairs and liquidates for tax purposes, the liquidation is generally fully taxable to the liquidating corporation and to the shareholders. However, when a subsidiary liquidates into its parent corporation, the liquidation is nontaxable or partially taxable, depending on whether there are minority interest shareholders.

Summary

LO 14-1 Explain the basic tax law framework that applies to property distributions from a corporation to a shareholder.

- Subchapter C of the Internal Revenue Code (IRC) provides guidelines and rules for determining the tax status of distributions from a C corporation to its shareholders.
- When a corporation distributes property to persons in their capacity as shareholders without receiving any property or services in return, the shareholder must determine if the amount received is a dividend.
- For noncash property distributions, the distributing corporation recognizes gain but not loss on the distribution.

LO 14-2 Compute a corporation's earnings and profits and calculate a shareholder's dividend income.

- The IRC defines a dividend as any distribution of property made by a corporation to its shareholders out of its current or accumulated earnings and profits (E&P).
- Earnings and profits is the tax equivalent of financial accounting retained earnings, although the computations can be significantly different.
- A corporation must keep two E&P accounts: current E&P and accumulated E&P.
- Current E&P is a measure of the corporation's economic earnings for the year.
- The IRC and the related regulations list four basic types of adjustments that a corporation must make to its taxable income to compute current E&P.
  - Add back economic income that is excluded from taxable income.
  - Add back certain expenses that are deducted in computing taxable income but require no economic outflow.
  - Subtract certain expenses that are excluded from the computation of taxable income but require an economic outflow.
  - Add or subtract amounts relating to different taxable income and E&P accounting methods.
- The shareholder computes the dividend amount to include in gross income as the sum of cash received plus the fair market value of property received less any liabilities assumed.
- The distributing corporation recognizes gain, but not loss, on the distribution of noncash property in a dividend distribution.
- A corporation reduces its E&P by the amount of cash distributed, the E&P basis of unappreciated property distributed, and the fair market value of appreciated property distributed, net of any liability assumed by the shareholders.

LO 14-3 Explain the taxation of stock distributions.

- The general rule is that a stock distribution is not taxable.
- The basis of the "new" stock received is computed by allocating basis from the existing stock based on relative fair market value.
- The holding period of the new stock includes the holding period of the existing stock on which the new stock was distributed.
- Non-pro rata stock distributions usually are treated as taxable dividends to the recipients.

Understand the tax consequences of stock redemptions, including partial liquidations

- If a redemption is treated as an exchange, the shareholder computes gain or loss by comparing the amount realized (money and property received) with the tax basis of the stock surrendered.
  - The character of the gain or loss is capital.
  - The basis of noncash property received is its fair market value.
  - The holding period of the property received begins at the date of receipt.
- If the transaction is treated as a distribution, the shareholder has gross (dividend) income in an amount equal to the cash and fair market value of other property received to the extent of the corporation's E&P.
  - The basis of the property received is its fair market value.
- The IRC treats redemptions as exchanges in transactions in which the shareholder's ownership interest in the corporation has been "meaningfully" reduced relative to other shareholders as a result of the redemption.
- There are three change-in-stock-ownership tests that entitle the shareholder to exchange treatment in a redemption:
  - The IRC states that a redemption will be treated as an exchange if the redemption is "not essentially equivalent to a dividend."
    - This is a facts and circumstances determination (subjective).
    - To satisfy this requirement, the courts or IRS must conclude that there has been a "meaningful" reduction in the shareholder's ownership interest in the corporation as a result of the redemption (usually below 50 percent stock ownership).
  - The IRC states that a redemption will be treated as an exchange if the redemption is "substantially disproportionate with respect to the shareholder," defined as follows:
    - Immediately after the exchange the shareholder owns less than 50 percent of the total combined voting power of all classes of stock entitled to vote.
    - The shareholder's percentage ownership of voting stock after the redemption is less than 80 percent of his or her percentage ownership before the redemption.
    - The shareholder's percentage ownership of the aggregate fair market value of the corporation's common stock (voting and nonvoting) after the redemption is less than 80 percent of his or her percentage ownership before the redemption.
  - The IRC holds that a redemption will be treated as an exchange if the redemption is in "complete redemption of all of the stock of the corporation owned by the shareholder."
- In determining whether the change-in-stock-ownership tests are met, each shareholder's percentage change in ownership in the corporation before and after a redemption must take into account constructive ownership (attribution) rules.
- The attribution rules cause stock owned by other persons to be treated as owned by (attributed to) the shareholder for purposes of determining whether the shareholder has met any of the change-in-stock-ownership tests to receive exchange treatment.
  - Family attribution. Individuals are treated as owning the shares of stock owned by their spouse, children, grandchildren, and parents.
  - Attribution from entities to owners or beneficiaries.
    - Partners are deemed to own a pro rata share of their partnership's stock holdings (i.e., a partner who has a 10 percent interest in a partnership is deemed to own 10 percent of any stock owned by the partnership).
    - Shareholders are deemed to own a pro rata share of their corporation's stock holdings, but only if they own at least 50 percent of the value of the corporation's stock.
  - Attribution from owners or beneficiaries to entities.
    - Partnerships are deemed to own 100 percent of stock owned by partners (i.e., a partnership is deemed to own 100 percent of stock owned by a 10 percent partner).
    - Attribution to a corporation only applies to shareholders owning 50 percent or more of the value of the corporation's stock.
  - Option attribution. A person having an option to purchase stock is deemed to own the stock that the option entitles the person to purchase.

- Shareholders can waive the family attribution rules in a complete redemption of their stock if the following conditions are met:
  - The shareholder has not retained a prohibited interest in the corporation immediately after the exchange (e.g., as a shareholder, employee, director, officer, or consultant).
  - The shareholder does not acquire a prohibited interest within 10 years after the redemption, unless by inheritance (the 10-year look-forward rule).
  - The shareholder agrees to notify the IRS district director within 30 days if she acquires a prohibited interest within 10 years (by signing a triple i agreement).
- If the redemption is treated as a dividend by the shareholder, the corporation generally reduces its E&P by the cash distributed and the fair market value of other property distributed.
- If the redemption is treated as an exchange by the shareholder, the corporation reduces E&P at the date of distribution by the percentage of stock redeemed (i.e., if 50 percent of the stock is redeemed, E&P is reduced by 50 percent), not to exceed the fair market value of the property distributed.
- For a distribution to be a partial liquidation, it must either be "not essentially equivalent to a dividend" (as determined at the corporate level, not the shareholder level) or the result of the termination of a "qualified trade or business."
- The tax treatment of a distribution received in partial liquidation of a corporation depends on the identity of the shareholder receiving it.
  - All noncorporate shareholders get exchange treatment.
  - All corporate shareholders are subject to the stock redemption change-in-ownership rules, which usually result in dividend treatment because partial liquidations are almost always pro rata distributions.

LO 14-5 Calculate the tax consequences of a complete liquidation of a corporation.

- Shareholders receiving a distribution in complete liquidation of their corporation generally recognize gain and loss in the exchange.
- Tax deferral is extended to corporate shareholders owning 80 percent or more of the liquidating corporation.
- The liquidating corporation recognizes gain and (usually) loss on the distribution of property to those shareholders other than corporate shareholders owning 80 percent or more of the liquidating corporation.
- The liquidating corporation cannot deduct losses on property distributed in the following three situations:
  - The loss property is distributed to a related person and is non-pro rata.
  - The loss property is contributed to the corporation in a §351 transaction and the principal purpose of the contribution is tax avoidance.
  - The loss property is distributed to a minority interest shareholder when a corporate shareholder owns 80 percent or more of the liquidating corporation.
- The liquidating corporation does not recognize gain or loss on the distribution of property to a corporate shareholder that owns 80 percent or more of the liquidating corporation.
- The tax basis of each asset received by the shareholder generally equals the asset's fair market value on the date of the distribution.
- The tax basis of each asset received by an 80 percent or more corporate shareholder in a tax-deferred complete liquidation carries over from the liquidating corporation.

KEY TERMS

accumulated earnings and
    profits (14-3)
constructive ownership (14-19)
current earnings and profits (14-3)

dividend (14-2)
partial liquidation (14-2)
stock redemption (14-2)

tax accounting balance
    sheet (14-25)
triple i agreement (14-21)

DISCUSSION QUESTIONS

Discussion Questions are available in Connect®.

1. What is meant by the phrase *double taxation of corporate income*? **LO 14-1**

2. Historically, taxpayers have implemented strategies to mitigate or eliminate the effects of double taxation. Why might taxpayers think twice before implementing such strategies today? Explain. **LO 14-1**

3. What are the three potential tax treatments of a cash distribution to a shareholder? Are these potential tax treatments elective by the shareholder? **LO 14-2**

4. In general, what is the concept of earnings and profits designed to represent? **LO 14-2**

5. How does *current earnings and profits* differ from *accumulated earnings and profits*? Is there any congressional logic for keeping the two accounts separate? **LO 14-2**

6. True or False. A calendar-year corporation has positive current E&P of $100 and accumulated negative E&P of $200. A cash distribution of $100 to the corporation's sole shareholder at year-end will not be treated as a dividend. Explain. **LO 14-2**

7. True or False. A calendar-year corporation has negative current E&P of $100 and accumulated E&P of $100. A cash distribution of $100 to the corporation's sole shareholder on June 30 will not be treated as a dividend. Explain. **LO 14-2**

8. List the four general categories of adjustments that a corporation makes to taxable income or net loss to compute current E&P. What is the rationale for making these adjustments? **LO 14-2**

9. When a shareholder receives a noncash distribution of property that is encumbered by a liability (the shareholder assumes the liability on the distribution), how does the shareholder determine the amount of the distribution? **LO 14-2**

10. What income tax issues must a corporation consider before it makes a noncash distribution to a shareholder? **LO 14-2**

11. Will the shareholder's tax basis in noncash property received equal the amount she includes in gross income as a dividend? Under what circumstances will the amounts be different, if any? **LO 14-2**

12. A shareholder receives appreciated noncash property from his corporation and assumes a liability attached to the property. How does the assumption affect the amount of dividend he reports in gross income? **LO 14-2**

13. A shareholder receives appreciated noncash property from his corporation and assumes a liability attached to the property. How does this assumption affect the amount of gain the corporation recognizes? From the corporation's perspective, does it matter if the liability assumed by the shareholder exceeds the property's gross fair market value? **LO 14-2**

14. A corporation distributes appreciated noncash property to a shareholder as a dividend. What impact does the distribution have on the corporation's earnings and profits? **LO 14-2**

15. Why might a corporation issue a stock distribution to its shareholders? **LO 14-3**

16. What tax issue arises when a shareholder receives a nontaxable stock distribution? **LO 14-3**

17. In general, what causes a stock distribution to be taxable to the recipient? **LO 14-3**

18. What are the potential tax consequences to a shareholder who participates in a stock redemption? **LO 14-3**

19. What stock ownership tests must be met before a shareholder receives exchange treatment under the substantially disproportionate change-in-stock-ownership test in a stock redemption? Why is a change-in-stock-ownership test used to determine the tax status of a stock redemption? **LO 14-4**

20. What are the criteria to meet the "not essentially equivalent to a dividend" change-in-stock-ownership test in a stock redemption? **LO 14-4**

LO 14-4 21. When might a shareholder have to rely on the "not essentially equivalent to a dividend" test in arguing that her stock redemption should be treated as an exchange for tax purposes?

LO 14-4 22. Why does the tax law impose constructive stock ownership rules on stock redemptions?

LO 14-4 23. Which members of a family are included in the family attribution rules? Is there any rationale for the family members included in the test?

LO 14-4 24. Ilya and Olga are brother and sister. Ilya owns 200 shares of stock in Parker Corporation. Is Olga deemed to own Ilya's 200 shares under the family attribution rules that apply to stock redemptions?

LO 14-4 25. Maria has all of her stock in Mayan Corporation redeemed. Under what conditions will Maria treat the redemption as an exchange and recognize capital gain or loss?

LO 14-4 26. What must a shareholder do to waive the family attribution rules in a complete redemption of stock?

LO 14-4 27. How does a corporation's computation of earnings and profits differ based on the tax treatment of a stock redemption to the shareholder (i.e., as either a dividend or exchange)?

LO 14-4 28. How does the tax treatment of a partial liquidation differ from a stock redemption?

LO 14-4 29. Bevo Corporation experienced a complete loss of its mill as the result of a fire. The company received $2 million from the insurance company. Rather than rebuild, Bevo decided to distribute the $2 million to its two shareholders. No stock was exchanged in return. Under what conditions will the distribution meet the requirements to be a partial liquidation and not a dividend? Why does it matter to the shareholders?

LO 14-5 30. True or False. All shareholders receive the same tax treatment in a complete liquidation of a corporation. Explain.

LO 14-5 31. True or False. A corporation recognizes all gains and losses on liquidating distributions of property to noncorporate shareholders. Explain.

LO 14-5 32. Under what circumstances does a corporate shareholder receive tax deferral in a complete liquidation?

LO 14-5 33. Under what circumstances will a liquidating corporation be allowed to recognize a loss in a non-pro rata distribution?

LO 14-5 34. Compare and contrast the built-in loss duplication rule as it relates to §351 with the built-in loss disallowance rule as it applies to a complete liquidation.

PROBLEMS

Select problems are available in Connect®.

LO 14-1 35. Gopher Corporation reported taxable income of $500,000 this year. Gopher paid a dividend of $100,000 to its sole shareholder, Sven Anderson. The dividend meets the requirements to be a qualified dividend, and Sven is subject to a tax rate of 15 percent on the dividend. What is the income tax imposed on the corporate income earned by Gopher and the dividend distributed to Sven?

LO 14-2 36. Hawkeye Company reports current E&P of $300,000 this year and accumulated E&P at the beginning of the year of $200,000. Hawkeye distributed $400,000 to its sole shareholder, Ray Kinsella, on December 31 of this year. Ray's tax basis in his Hawkeye stock is $75,000.

a) How much of the $400,000 distribution is treated as a dividend to Ray?

b) What is Ray's tax basis in his Hawkeye stock after the distribution?

c) What is Hawkeye's balance in accumulated E&P as of January 1 of next year?

37. Jayhawk Company reports current E&P of $300,000 and accumulated E&P of negative $200,000. Jayhawk distributed $400,000 to its sole shareholder, Christine Rock, on the last day of the year. Christine's tax basis in her Jayhawk stock is $75,000.   `LO 14-2`

    a) How much of the $400,000 distribution is treated as a dividend to Christine?

    b) What is Christine's tax basis in her Jayhawk stock after the distribution?

    c) What is Jayhawk's balance in accumulated E&P on the first day of next year?

38. This year, Sooner Company reports current E&P of negative $300,000. Its accumulated E&P at the beginning of the year was $200,000. Sooner distributed $400,000 to its sole shareholder, Boomer Wells, on June 30 of this year. Boomer's tax basis in his Sooner stock is $75,000.   `LO 14-2`

    a) How much of the $400,000 distribution is treated as a dividend to Boomer?

    b) What is Boomer's tax basis in his Sooner stock after the distribution?

    c) What is Sooner's balance in accumulated E&P on the first day of next year?

39. Blackhawk Company reports current E&P of negative $300,000. Its accumulated E&P at the beginning of the year was negative $200,000. Blackhawk distributed $400,000 to its sole shareholder, Melanie Rushmore, on June 30 of this year. Melanie's tax basis in her Blackhawk stock is $75,000.   `LO 14-2`

    a) How much of the $400,000 distribution is treated as a dividend to Melanie?

    b) What is Melanie's tax basis in her Blackhawk stock after the distribution?

    c) What is Blackhawk's balance in accumulated E&P on the first day of next year?

40. This year, Jolt Inc. reported $40,000 of taxable income before any charitable contribution deduction. Jolt contributed $10,000 this year to Goodwill Industries, a public charity. Compute the company's current E&P.   `LO 14-2`

41. Boilermaker Inc. reported taxable income of $500,000 this year and paid federal income taxes of $105,000. Not included in the company's computation of taxable income is tax-exempt income of $20,000, disallowed meals expense of $18,000, entertainment expenses of $12,000, and disallowed expenses related to the tax-exempt income of $1,000. Boilermaker deducted depreciation of $100,000 on its tax return. Under the alternative (E&P) depreciation method, the deduction would have been $60,000. Compute the company's current E&P.   `LO 14-2`

42. Gator Inc. reported taxable income of $1,000,000 this year and paid federal income taxes of $210,000. Included in the company's computation of taxable income is gain from the sale of a depreciable asset of $50,000. The income tax basis of the asset was $100,000. The E&P basis of the asset using the alternative depreciation system was $175,000. Compute the company's current E&P.   `LO 14-2`

43. Paladin Inc. reported taxable income of $1,000,000 this year and paid federal income taxes of $210,000. The company reported a capital gain from the sale of investments of $150,000, which was partially offset by a $100,000 net capital loss carryover from last year, resulting in a net capital gain of $50,000 included in taxable income. Compute the company's current E&P.   `LO 14-2`

44. Volunteer Corporation reported taxable income of $500,000 from operations this year. The company paid federal income taxes of $105,000 on this taxable income. During the year, the company made a distribution of land to its sole shareholder, Rocky Topp. The land's fair market value was $75,000 and its tax and E&P basis to Volunteer was $25,000. Rocky assumed a mortgage attached to the land of $15,000. The company had accumulated E&P of $750,000 at the beginning of the year.   `LO 14-2`

    a) Compute Volunteer's total taxable income and federal income tax.

    b) Compute Volunteer's current E&P.

    c) Compute Volunteer's accumulated E&P at the beginning of next year.

    d) What amount of dividend income does Rocky report as a result of the distribution?

    e) What is Rocky's income tax basis in the land received from Volunteer?

LO 14-2   45. Spieth Corporation reported taxable income of $500,000 from operations this year. The company paid federal income taxes of $105,000 on this taxable income. During the year, the company made a distribution of land to its sole shareholder, Jordan Day. The land's fair market value was $75,000 and its tax and E&P basis to Spieth was $125,000. Jordan assumed a mortgage attached to the land of $15,000. The company had accumulated E&P of $750,000 at the beginning of the year.

   a) Compute Spieth's total taxable income and federal income tax.

   b) Compute Spieth's current E&P.

   c) Compute Spieth's accumulated E&P at the beginning of next year.

   d) What amount of dividend income does Jordan report as a result of the distribution?

   e) What is Jordan's tax basis in the land he received from Spieth?

LO 14-2   46. Illini Corporation reported taxable income of $500,000 from operations for this year. The company paid federal income taxes of $105,000 on this taxable income. During the year, the company made a distribution of an automobile to its sole shareholder, Carly Urbana. The auto's fair market value was $30,000 and its tax basis to Illini was $0. The auto's E&P basis was $15,000. Illini had accumulated E&P of $1,500,000.

   a) Compute Illini's total taxable income and federal income tax.

   b) Compute Illini's current E&P.

   c) Compute Illini's accumulated E&P at the beginning of next year.

   d) What amount of dividend income does Carly report as a result of the distribution?

   e) What is Carly's tax basis in the auto she received from Illini?

LO 14-2   47. Beaver Corporation reported taxable income of $500,000 from operations this year. The company paid federal income taxes of $105,000 on this taxable income. During the year, the company made a distribution of land to its sole shareholder, Eugenia VanDam. The land's fair market value was $20,000 and its tax and E&P basis to Beaver was $50,000. Eugenia assumed a mortgage on the land of $25,000. Beaver Corporation had accumulated E&P of $1,500,000.

   a) Compute Beaver's taxable income and federal income tax.

   b) Compute Beaver's current E&P.

   c) Compute Beaver's accumulated E&P at the beginning of next year.

   d) What amount of dividend income does Eugenia report as a result of the distribution?

LO 14-2
research
tax forms   48. Tiny and Tim each own half of the 100 outstanding shares of Flower Corporation. This year, Flower reported taxable income of $10,000. In addition, Flower received $20,000 of life insurance proceeds due to the death of an employee (Flower paid $900 in life insurance premiums this year). Flower had $5,000 of accumulated E&P at the beginning of the year.

   a) What is Flower's current E&P?

   b) Flower distributed $6,000 on February 14 and $30,000 on August 1. What total amount of dividends will Tiny and Tim report?

   c) What amount of capital gain (if any) would Tiny and Tim report on the distributions in part (b) if their stock basis is $1,500 and $10,000, respectively?

   d) What form would Flower use to report nondividend distributions?

   e) On what tax form (and line) would Tiny and Tim report nondividend distributions?

LO 14-3   49. Hoosier Corporation declared a stock distribution to all shareholders of record on March 25 of this year. Shareholders will receive one share of Hoosier Corporation stock for each share of stock they already own. Hoosier reported current E&P of $600,000 and accumulated E&P of $3,000,000. The total fair market value of the stock distributed was $1,500,000. Barbara Bloomington owned 1,000 shares of Hoosier stock with a tax basis of $100 per share.

   a) What amount of taxable dividend income, if any, does Barbara recognize this year? Assume the fair market value of the stock was $150 per share on March 25 of this year.

b) What is Barbara's income tax basis in the new and existing stock she owns in Hoosier Corporation, assuming the distribution is nontaxable?

c) How does the stock distribution affect Hoosier's accumulated E&P at the beginning of next year?

50. Badger Corporation declared a stock distribution to all shareholders of record on March 25 of this year. Shareholders will receive one share of Badger stock for every 10 shares of stock they already own. Madison Cheesehead owns 1,000 shares of Badger stock with a tax basis of $100 per share. The fair market value of the Badger stock was $110 per share on March 25 of this year.

   LO 14-3

   a) What amount of taxable dividend income, if any, does Madison recognize this year?

   b) What is Madison's income tax basis in her new and existing stock in Badger Corporation, assuming the distribution is nontaxable?

   c) How would you answer parts (a) and (b) if Madison was offered the choice between (i) 1 share of stock in Badger for every 10 shares she owns, or (ii) $100 cash for every 10 shares of Badger stock she owns?

51. Wildcat Company is owned equally by Evan Stone and his sister Sara, each of whom hold 1,000 shares in the company. Sara wants to reduce her ownership in the company, and it is decided that the company will redeem 500 of her shares for $25,000 per share on December 31 of this year. Sara's income tax basis in each share is $5,000. Wildcat has current E&P of $10,000,000 and accumulated E&P of $50,000,000.

    LO 14-4

    a) What is the amount and character (capital gain or dividend) recognized by Sara as a result of the stock redemption?

    b) What is Sara's income tax basis in the remaining 500 shares she owns in the company?

    c) Assuming the company did not make any dividend distributions during this year, by what amount does Wildcat reduce its E&P as a result of the redemption?

52. Flintstone Company is owned equally by Fred Stone and his sister Wilma, each of whom hold 1,000 shares in the company. Wilma wants to reduce her ownership in the company, and it is decided that the company will redeem 250 of her shares for $25,000 per share on December 31 of this year. Wilma's income tax basis in each share is $5,000. Flintstone has current E&P of $10,000,000 and accumulated E&P of $50,000,000.

    LO 14-4

    a) What is the amount and character (capital gain or dividend) recognized by Wilma as a result of the stock redemption, assuming only the "substantially disproportionate with respect to the shareholder" test is applied?

    b) Given your answer to part (a), what is Wilma's income tax basis in the remaining 750 shares she owns in the company?

    c) Assuming the company did not make any dividend distributions this year, by what amount does Flintstone reduce its E&P as a result of the redemption?

    d) What other argument might Wilma make to treat the redemption as an exchange?

53. Acme Corporation has 1,000 shares outstanding. Joan and Bill are married, and they each own 20 shares of Acme. Joan's daughter, Shirley, also owns 20 shares of Acme. Joan is an equal partner with Jeri in the J&J partnership, and this partnership owns 60 shares of Acme. Jeri is not related to Joan or Bill. How many shares of Acme is Shirley deemed to own under the stock attribution rules?

    LO 14-4

54. Bedrock Inc. is owned equally by Barney Rubble and his wife Betty, each of whom hold 1,000 shares in the company. Betty wants to reduce her ownership in the company, and it is decided that the company will redeem 500 of her shares for $25,000 per share on December 31 of this year. Betty's income tax basis in each

    LO 14-4

share is $5,000. Bedrock has current E&P of $10,000,000 and accumulated E&P of $50,000,000.

a) What is the amount and character (capital gain or dividend) recognized by Betty as a result of the stock redemption, assuming only the "substantially disproportionate with respect to the shareholder" test is applied?

b) Given your answer to part (a), what is Betty's income tax basis in the remaining 500 shares she owns in the company?

c) Assuming the company did not make any dividend distributions this year, by what amount does Bedrock reduce its E&P as a result of the redemption?

d) Can Betty argue that the redemption is "not essentially equivalent to a dividend" and should be treated as an exchange?

LO 14-4

research

55. Assume the same facts as the previous problem but that Betty and Barney are not getting along and have separated due to marital discord (although they are not legally separated). In fact, they cannot even stand to talk to each other anymore and communicate only through their accountant. Betty wants to argue that she should not be treated as owning any of Barney's stock in Bedrock because of their hostility toward each other. Can family hostility be used as an argument to void the family attribution rules? Consult Rev. Rul. 80-26, 1980-1 C.B. 66, *Robin Haft Trust v. Comm.,* 510 F.2d 43 (CA-1 1975), *Metzger Trust v. Comm.,* 693 F.2d 459 (CA-5) 1982, and *Cerone v. Comm.,* 87 TC 1 (1986).

LO 14-4

56. Boots Inc. is owned equally by Frank Albert and his daughter Nancy, each of whom hold 1,000 shares in the company. Frank wants to retire from the company, and it is decided that the company will redeem all 1,000 of his shares for $25,000 per share on December 31 of this year. Frank's income tax basis in each share is $500. Boots Inc. has current E&P of $1,000,000 and accumulated E&P of $5,000,000.

a) What must Frank do to ensure that the redemption will be treated as an exchange?

b) If Frank remains as the chairman of the board after the redemption, what is the amount and character (capital gain or dividend) of income that Frank will recognize this year?

c) If Frank treats the redemption as a dividend, what happens to his stock basis in the 1,000 shares redeemed?

LO 14-4

research

57. Assume the same facts as in the previous problem, and that Nancy would like to have Frank stay on as a consultant after all of his shares are redeemed. She would pay him a modest amount of $500 per month. Nancy wants to know if there is any *de minimus* rule such that Frank would not be treated as having retained a prohibited interest in the company because he is receiving such a small amount of money. Consult *Lynch v. Comm.,* 801 F.2d 1176 (CA-9 1986), *reversing* 83 T.C. 597 (1984), *Seda,* 82 T.C. 484 (1984), and *Cerone,* 87 T.C. 1 (1986).

LO 14-4

planning

58. Limited Brands recently repurchased 68,965,000 of its shares, paying $29 per share. The total number of shares outstanding before the redemption was 473,223,066. The total number of shares outstanding after the redemption was 404,258,066. Assume your client owned 20,000 shares of stock in Limited Brands. What is the minimum number of shares she must tender to receive exchange treatment under the "substantially disproportionate with respect to the shareholder" change-in-ownership rules?

LO 14-4

59. Cougar Company is owned equally by Cat Stevens and a partnership that is owned equally by his father and two unrelated individuals. Cat and the partnership each own 3,000 shares in the company. Cat wants to reduce his ownership in the company, and it is decided that the company will redeem 1,500 of his shares for $25,000 per share. Cat's income tax basis in each share is $5,000. What are the income tax consequences to Cat as a result of the stock redemption, assuming the company has earnings and profits of $10 million?

60. Oriole Corporation, a privately held company, has one class of voting common stock, of which 1,000 shares are issued and outstanding. The shares are owned as follows:

Larry Byrd	400
Paul Byrd (Larry's son)	200
Lady Byrd (Larry's daughter)	200
Cal Rifkin (unrelated)	200
Total	1,000

Larry is considering retirement and would like to have the corporation redeem all of his shares for $400,000.

a) What must Larry do or consider if he wants to guarantee that the redemption will be treated as an exchange?

b) Could Larry act as a consultant to the company and still have the redemption treated as an exchange?

61. Using the facts from the previous problem, Oriole Corporation proposes to pay Larry $100,000 and give him an installment note that will pay him $30,000 per year for the next 10 years plus a market rate of interest. Will this arrangement allow Larry to treat the redemption as an exchange? Consult §453(k)(2)(A).

62. EG Corporation redeemed 200 shares of stock from one of its shareholders in exchange for $200,000. The redemption represented 20 percent of the corporation's outstanding stock. The redemption was treated as an exchange by the shareholder. By what amount does EG reduce its E&P as a result of the redemption under the following E&P assumptions?

a) EG's E&P at the time of the distribution was $2,000,000.

b) EG's E&P at the time of the distribution was $500,000.

63. Spartan Corporation redeemed 25 percent of its shares for $2,000 on July 1 of this year, in a transaction that qualified as an exchange under §302(a). Spartan's accumulated E&P at the beginning of the year was $2,000. Its current E&P is $12,000. Spartan made dividend distributions of $1,000 on June 1 and $4,000 on August 31. Determine the beginning balance in Spartan's accumulated E&P at the beginning of next year. See Rev. Rul. 74-338, 1974-2 C.B. 101, and Rev. Rul. 74-339, 1974-2 C.B. 103, for help in making this calculation.

64. Bonnie and Clyde are the only two shareholders in Getaway Corporation. Bonnie owns 60 shares with a basis of $3,000, and Clyde owns the remaining 40 shares with a basis of $12,000. At year-end, Getaway is considering different alternatives for redeeming some shares of stock. Evaluate whether each of the following stock redemption transactions will qualify for sale and exchange treatment.

a) Getaway redeems 10 of Bonnie's shares for $2,000. Getaway has $20,000 of E&P at year-end and Bonnie is unrelated to Clyde.

b) Getaway redeems 25 of Bonnie's shares for $4,000. Getaway has $20,000 of E&P at year-end and Bonnie is unrelated to Clyde.

c) Getaway redeems 10 of Clyde's shares for $2,500. Getaway has $20,000 of E&P at year-end and Clyde is unrelated to Bonnie.

65. Spartan Corporation made a distribution of $500,000 to Rusty Cedar in partial liquidation of the company on December 31 of this year. Rusty, an individual, owns 100 percent of Spartan Corporation. The distribution was in exchange for 50 percent of Rusty's stock in the company. At the time of the distribution, the shares had a fair market value of $200 per share. Rusty's income tax basis in the shares was $50 per share. Spartan had E&P of $8,000,000 at the time of the distribution.

a) What is the per share amount and character (capital gain or dividend) of any income or gain recognized by Rusty as a result of the partial liquidation?

b) Assuming Spartan made no other distributions to Rusty during the year, by what amount does Spartan reduce its E&P as a result of the partial liquidation?

LO 14-4

66. Wolverine Corporation made a distribution of $500,000 to Jim Harb Inc. in partial liquidation of the company on December 31 of this year. Jim Harb Inc. owns 100 percent of Wolverine Corporation. The distribution was in exchange for 50 percent of Jim Harb Inc.'s stock in the company. At the time of the distribution, the shares had a fair market value of $200 per share. Jim Harb Inc.'s income tax basis in the shares was $50 per share. Wolverine had E&P of $8,000,000 at the time of the distribution.

a) What is the amount and character (capital gain or dividend) of any income or gain recognized by Jim Harb Inc. as a result of the partial liquidation?

b) Assuming Wolverine made no other distributions to Jim Harb Inc. during the year, by what amount does Wolverine reduce its E&P as a result of the partial liquidation?

LO 14-5

67. Shauna and Danielle decided to liquidate their jointly owned corporation, Woodward Fashions Inc. (WFI). After liquidating its remaining inventory and paying off its remaining liabilities, WFI had the following tax accounting balance sheet:

	FMV	Tax Basis	Appreciation
Cash	$200,000	$200,000	
Building	50,000	10,000	$ 40,000
Land	150,000	90,000	60,000
Total	$400,000	$300,000	$100,000

Under the terms of the agreement, Shauna will receive the $200,000 cash in exchange for her 50 percent interest in WFI. Shauna's tax basis in her WFI stock is $50,000. Danielle will receive the building and land in exchange for her 50 percent interest in WFI. Danielle's tax basis in her WFI stock is $100,000. Assume for purposes of this problem that the cash available to distribute to the shareholders has been reduced by any tax paid by the corporation on gain recognized as a result of the liquidation.

a) What amount of gain or loss does WFI recognize in the complete liquidation?

b) What amount of gain or loss does Shauna recognize in the complete liquidation?

c) What amount of gain or loss does Danielle recognize in the complete liquidation?

d) What is Danielle's tax basis in the building and land after the complete liquidation?

LO 14-5

68. Tiffany and Carlos decided to liquidate their jointly owned corporation, Royal Oak Furniture (ROF). After liquidating its remaining inventory and paying off its remaining liabilities, ROF had the following tax accounting balance sheet:

	FMV	Tax Basis	Appreciation (Depreciation)
Cash	$200,000	$200,000	
Building	50,000	10,000	$ 40,000
Land	150,000	200,000	(50,000)
Total	$400,000	$410,000	$(10,000)

Under the terms of the agreement, Tiffany will receive the $200,000 cash in exchange for her 50 percent interest in ROF. Tiffany's tax basis in her ROF stock is $50,000. Carlos will receive the building and land in exchange for his 50 percent interest in ROF. His tax basis in the ROF stock is $100,000. Assume for purposes of this problem that the cash available to distribute to the shareholders has been reduced by any tax paid by the corporation on gain recognized as a result of the liquidation.

a) What amount of gain or loss does ROF recognize in the complete liquidation?

b) What amount of gain or loss does Tiffany recognize in the complete liquidation?

c) What amount of gain or loss does Carlos recognize in the complete liquidation?

d) What is Carlos's tax basis of the building and land after the complete liquidation?

Assume Tiffany owns 40 percent of the ROF stock and Carlos owns 60 percent. Tiffany will receive $160,000 in the liquidation and Carlos will receive the land and building plus $40,000.

e) What amount of gain or loss does ROF recognize in the complete liquidation?

f) What amount of gain or loss does Tiffany recognize in the complete liquidation?

g) What amount of gain or loss does Carlos recognize in the complete liquidation?

h) What is Carlos's tax basis in the building and land after the complete liquidation?

69. Jefferson Millinery Inc. (JMI) decided to liquidate its wholly owned subsidiary, 8 Miles High Inc. (8MH). 8MH had the following tax accounting balance sheet:

LO 14-5

	FMV	Tax Basis	Appreciation
Cash	$200,000	$200,000	
Building	50,000	10,000	$ 40,000
Land	150,000	90,000	60,000
Total	$400,000	$300,000	$100,000

a) What amount of gain or loss does 8MH recognize in the complete liquidation?

b) What amount of gain or loss does JMI recognize in the complete liquidation?

c) What is JMI's tax basis in the building and land after the complete liquidation?

70. Jefferson Millinery Inc. (JMI) decided to liquidate its wholly owned subsidiary, 8 Miles High Inc. (8MH). 8MH had the following tax accounting balance sheet:

LO 14-5

	FMV	Tax Basis	Appreciation
Cash	$200,000	$200,000	
Building	50,000	10,000	$ 40,000
Land	150,000	200,000	(50,000)
Total	$400,000	$410,000	$(10,000)

a) What amount of gain or loss does 8MH recognize in the complete liquidation?

b) What amount of gain or loss does JMI recognize in the complete liquidation?

c) What is JMI's tax basis in the building and land after the complete liquidation?

71. Cartman Corporation owns 90 shares of SP Corporation. The remaining 10 shares are owned by Kenny (an individual). After several years of operations, Cartman decided to liquidate SP Corporation by distributing the assets to Cartman and Kenny.

LO 14-5

SP reported the following balance sheet at the date of liquidation:

	FMV	Tax Basis
Cash	$ 10,000	$10,000
Accounts receivable	5,000	5,000
Land	65,000	15,000
Goodwill	25,000	0
Total assets	$105,000	$30,000
Accounts payable		$ 5,000
Common stock—Cartman (90%)	$ 90,000	$10,000
Common stock—Kenny (10%)	10,000	7,000
Total shareholder equity	$100,000	$17,000

a) Compute the gain or loss recognized by SP, Cartman, and Kenny on a complete liquidation of the corporation, where SP distributes $10,000 of cash to Kenny and the remaining assets to Cartman.

b) Compute the gain or loss recognized by SP and Kenny on a complete liquidation of the corporation, where SP distributes land to Kenny and the remaining assets to Cartman. Assume that the land has a fair market value of $10,000 and a basis of $2,000. Also assume that the land is not subject to any debt and that Kenny's distribution amount is not affected by any tax paid by SP (Cartman agrees to bear any SP tax costs).

c) What form needs to be filed with the liquidation of SP?

COMPREHENSIVE PROBLEMS

Select problems are available in Connect®.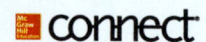

72. Lanco Corporation, an accrual-method corporation, reported taxable income of $1,460,000 this year. Included in the computation of taxable income were the following items:

- MACRS depreciation of $200,000. Depreciation for earnings and profits purposes is $120,000.
- A net capital loss carryover of $10,000 from last year.
- A net operating loss carryover of $25,000 from last year.
- $65,000 capital gain from the distribution of land to the company's sole shareholder (see below).

Not included in the computation of taxable income were the following items:

- Tax-exempt income of $5,000.
- Life insurance proceeds of $250,000.
- Excess current-year charitable contribution of $2,500 (to be carried over to next year).
- Tax-deferred gain of $20,000 on a like-kind exchange.
- Nondeductible life insurance premium of $3,500.
- Nondeductible interest expense of $1,000 on a loan used to buy tax-exempt bonds.

Lanco paid federal income taxes this year of $306,600. The company's accumulated E&P at the beginning of the year was $2,400,000.

During the year, Lanco made the following distributions to its sole shareholder, Luigi (Lug) Nutt:

- June 30: $50,000.
- September 30: Parcel of land with a fair market value of $75,000. Lanco's tax basis in the land was $10,000. Lug assumed an existing mortgage on the property of $15,000.

Required:

a) Compute Lanco's current E&P for this year.

b) Compute the amount of dividend income reported by Lug Nutt this year as a result of the distributions.

c) Compute Lanco's accumulated E&P at the beginning of next year.

73. Petoskey Stone Quarry Inc. (PSQ), a calendar-year, accrual-method C corporation, provides landscaping supplies to local builders in northern Michigan. PSQ has

always been a family-owned business and has a single class of voting common stock outstanding. The 500 outstanding shares are owned as follows:

Nick Adams	150
Amy Adams (Nick's sister)	150
Abigail Adams (Nick's daughter)	50
Charlie Adams (Nick's son)	50
Sandler Adams (Nick's father)	100
Total shares	500

Nick Adams serves as president of PSQ, and his father Sandler serves as chairman of the board. Amy is the company's CFO, and Abigail and Charlie work as employees of the company. Sandler would like to retire and sell his shares back to the company. The fair market value of the shares is $500,000. Sandler's tax basis is $10,000.

The redemption is tentatively scheduled to take place on December 31 of this year. At the beginning of the year, PSQ had accumulated earnings and profits of $2,500,000. The company projects current E&P of $200,000. The company intends to pay a pro rata cash distribution of $300 per share to its shareholders on December 1 of this year.

Required:

a) Assume the redemption takes place as planned on December 31 and no elections are made by the shareholders.

  I. What amount of dividend or capital gain will Sandler recognize as a result of the stock redemption?

  II. How will the tax basis of Sandler's stock be allocated to the remaining shareholders?

b) What must Sandler and the other shareholders do to change the tax results you calculated in part (a)?

c) Compute PSQ's accumulated earnings and profits on January 1 of next year, assuming the redemption is treated as an exchange.

74. Thriller Corporation has one class of voting common stock, of which 1,000 shares are issued and outstanding. The shares are owned as follows:

Joe Jackson	400
Mike Jackson (Joe's son)	200
Jane Jackson (Joe's daughter)	200
Vinnie Price (unrelated)	200
Total	1,000

Thriller Corporation has current E&P of $300,000 for this year and accumulated E&P at January 1 of this year of $500,000.

During this year, the corporation made the following distributions to its shareholders:

  03/31: Paid a distribution of $10 per share to each shareholder ($10,000 in total).

  06/30: Redeemed 200 shares of Joe's stock for $200,000. Joe's basis in the 200 shares redeemed was $100,000.

  09/30: Redeemed 60 shares of Vinnie's stock for $60,000. His basis in the 60 shares was $36,000.

  12/31: Paid a distribution of $10/share to each shareholder ($7,400 in total).

Required:

a) Determine the tax status of each distribution made this year. (*Hint:* First, consider if the redemptions are treated as dividend distributions or exchanges.)

b) Compute the corporation's accumulated E&P at January 1 next year.

c) Joe is considering retirement and would like to have the corporation redeem all of his shares for $100,000 plus a 10-year note with a fair market value of $300,000.

  I. What must Joe do or consider if he wants to ensure that the redemption will be treated as an exchange?

  II. Could Joe still act as a consultant to the company?

d) Thriller Corporation must pay attorney's fees of $5,000 to facilitate the stock redemptions. Is this fee deductible?

75. Rex and Felix are the sole shareholders of the Dogs and Cats Corporation (DCC). After several years of operations, they chose to liquidate the corporation and operate the business as a partnership. Rex and Felix hired a lawyer to draw up the legal papers to dissolve the corporation, but they need some tax advice from you, their trusted accountant.

    DCC's tax accounting balance sheet at the date of liquidation is as follows:

	FMV	Tax Basis
Assets		
Cash	$ 30,000	$ 30,000
Accounts receivable	10,000	10,000
Inventory	20,000	10,000
Equipment	20,000	30,000
Building	30,000	15,000
Land	40,000	5,000
Total assets	$150,000	$100,000
Liabilities		
Accounts payable	$ 5,000	
Mortgage payable—Building	10,000	
Mortgage payable—Land	10,000	
Total liabilities	$ 25,000	
Shareholders' Equity		
Common stock—Rex (80%)	$100,000	$ 60,000
Common stock—Felix (20%)	25,000	20,000
Total shareholders' equity	$125,000	$ 80,000

a) Compute the gain or loss recognized by DCC, Rex, and Felix on a complete liquidation of the corporation, assuming each shareholder receives a pro rata distribution of the corporation's assets and assumes a pro rata amount of the liabilities.

b) Compute the gain or loss recognized by DCC, Rex, and Felix on a complete liquidation of the corporation, assuming Felix receives $25,000 in cash and Rex receives the remainder of the assets and assumes all of the liabilities.

Assume Felix received the accounts receivable and equipment and assumed the accounts payable.

c) Will Felix recognize any income when he collects the accounts receivable?

d) Will Felix be able to take a deduction when he pays the accounts payable?

Assume Rex is a corporate shareholder of DCC.

e) Compute the gain or loss recognized by DCC, Rex, and Felix on a complete liquidation of the corporation, assuming each shareholder receives a pro rata distribution of the corporation's assets and assumes a pro rata amount of the liabilities.

f) Compute the gain or loss recognized by DCC, Rex, and Felix on a complete liquidation of the corporation, assuming Felix receives all cash and Rex receives the remainder of the assets and assumes all of the liabilities.

Assume the equipment was contributed by Rex to DCC in a §351 transaction two months prior to the liquidation. At the time of the contribution, the property's fair market value was $25,000.

g) Would the tax result change if the property was contributed one year ago? Two years ago? Three years ago?

ROGER | *CPA Review*

Sample CPA Exam questions from Roger CPA Review are available in Connect as support for the topics in this text. These Multiple Choice Questions and Task-Based Simulations include expert-written explanations and solutions and provide a starting point for students to become familiar with the content and functionality of the actual CPA Exam.

Forming and Operating Partnerships

Learning Objectives

Upon completing this chapter, you should be able to:

LO 15-1 Determine whether a flow-through entity is taxed as a partnership or S corporation.

LO 15-2 Resolve tax issues applicable to partnership formations and other acquisitions of partnership interests, including gain recognition to partners and tax basis for partners and partnerships.

LO 15-3 Determine the appropriate accounting periods and methods for partnerships.

LO 15-4 Calculate and characterize a partnership's ordinary business income or loss and its separately stated items, and demonstrate how to report these items to partners.

LO 15-5 Explain the importance of a partner's tax basis in their partnership interest and the adjustments that affect it.

LO 15-6 Apply the basis, at-risk, and passive activity loss limits to losses from partnerships.

©PhotoAlto/MediaBakery

Storyline Summary

Nicole Johnson

Location:	Salt Lake City, Utah
Status:	Managing member of Color Comfort Sheets LLC
Filing status:	Married to Tom Johnson
Marginal tax rate:	35 percent unless otherwise stated

Sarah Walker

Location:	Salt Lake City, Utah
Status:	Managing member of Color Comfort Sheets LLC
Filing status:	Married to Blaine Walker
Marginal tax rate:	24 percent unless otherwise stated

Chanzz Inc.

Location:	Salt Lake City, Utah
Business:	Managing sports franchises
Status:	Nonmanaging member of Color Comfort Sheets LLC
Filing status:	C Corporation with a June 30 year-end
Marginal tax rate:	28 (blended rate) percent

I n the Entities Overview chapter, we introduced you to Nicole Johnson, who decided to turn her sheet-making hobby into a full-time business called Color Comfort Sheets (CCS). Early in 2017, after deciding to organize her new enterprise as a limited liability company (LLC), Nicole turned her attention to raising capital for the business from other investors and a bank loan. Although her limited savings would clearly not be enough to get CCS started, she was willing to contribute a parcel of land in the industrial section of town that she had inherited five years ago from her grandfather. Her friend and mentor, Sarah Walker, offered to contribute time and money to help CCS get off the ground.

With Sarah on board, things seemed to be coming together nicely for Nicole. However, the amount her bank was willing to loan was not enough to fully capitalize CCS, and Nicole and Sarah were unable to invest any more cash into the business to make up the shortfall. Hoping to obtain the additional funding they needed, Nicole and Sarah visited Chance Armstrong, a successful local sports-team owner who had a reputation for being willing to take a chance on new ventures. After listening to Nicole and Sarah's proposal, Chance agreed to invest the additional cash needed to fully fund CCS. Rather than use his personal funds, however, Chance planned to have his closely held corporation, Chanzz Inc., invest in CCS. Unlike Nicole and Sarah, who would take an active role in managing CCS, Chanzz Inc., with everyone's agreement, would not play a part in running the company. By the end of March, CCS had cash, land on which to build its manufacturing facility and offices, and owners who were excited and willing to work hard to make it a successful company.

to be continued . . .

In this chapter, we review the options for operating a business with multiple owners as a **flow-through entity.** In addition, we explain the basic tax consequences of forming and operating business entities taxed as partnerships by examining the specific tax consequences of forming and operating Color Comfort Sheets as a limited liability company (LLC) taxed as a partnership. In the Entities Overview chapter, we learn that Color Comfort Sheets, LLC actually elected to be treated as a C corporation. In this chapter, we assume it did not make this election leaving it to be treated as a partnership for tax purposes.

LO 15-1

FLOW-THROUGH ENTITIES OVERVIEW

Income earned by flow-through entities is usually not taxed at the entity level. Instead, the *owners* of flow-through entities are taxed on the share of entity-level income allocated to them. Thus, unlike income earned by **C corporations,** income from flow-through entities is taxed only once—when it "flows through" to owners of these entities.[1]

Flow-through entities with multiple owners are governed by two somewhat different sets of rules in our tax system.[2] Unincorporated business entities such as **general partnerships, limited partnerships,** and **limited liability companies (LLCs)** are generally treated as partnerships under the rules provided in **Subchapter K** of the Internal Revenue Code.[3] In contrast, corporations whose owners elect to treat them as flow-through entities are classified as such under the rules in **Subchapter S.** These corporations are called **S corporations.** See the Entities Overview chapter for further detail regarding the tax treatment of different entity types.

There are many similarities and a few important differences between the tax rules for partnerships and S corporations. Our focus in this chapter and the next is on the tax rules for partnerships. Then, in the S Corporations chapter, we turn our attention to the tax treatment of S corporations and their shareholders.

TAXES IN THE REAL WORLD Hedge Funds

We can scarcely read the financial press these days without encountering some reference to hedge funds. Hedge funds are private investment funds that have grown in popularity in recent years; they were estimated to have over $7 trillion in assets under management at the end of 2016.[4] According to a study by the Joint Committee on Taxation, most hedge funds are organized as partnerships and their investors are taxed as limited partners.[5]

Aggregate and Entity Concepts

When Congress adopted Subchapter K in 1954, it had to decide whether to follow an **entity approach** and treat tax partnerships as entities separate from their partners or to apply an **aggregate approach** and treat partnerships simply as an aggregation of the partners' separate interests in the assets and liabilities of the partnership. In the end, Congress decided to apply both concepts in formulating partnership tax law. For instance, one of

---

[1]The "check the box" rules determine how various legal entities should be classified for tax purposes. See the discussion in the Entities Overview chapter for a more detailed explanation of these rules.

[2]Unincorporated entities with one individual owner are taxed as *sole proprietorships.* The tax rules relevant to sole proprietorships are discussed in the Business Income, Deductions, and Accounting Methods chapter. In addition to sole proprietorships, other specialized forms of flow-through entities such as real estate investment trusts and regulated investment companies are authorized by the Code. A discussion of these entities is beyond the scope of this chapter.

[3]Publicly traded partnerships may be taxed as corporations. The tax treatment of publicly traded partnerships is more fully developed in the Entities Overview chapter.

[4]*"Private Fund Statistics, Fourth Calendar Quarter 2016,"* SEC Division of Investment Management (sec.gov), July 7, 2017.

[5]*"Present Law and Analysis Relating to Tax Treatment of Partnership Carried Interests and Related Issues, Part I"* (JCX-62-07), September 4, 2007.

the most basic tenets of partnership tax law—that partnerships don't pay taxes—reflects the aggregate approach. However, Congress also adopted other partnership tax rules that fall more squarely on the side of the entity approach. For example, the requirement that partnerships, rather than partners, make most tax elections represents the entity concept. Throughout this and the following chapter, we highlight examples where one or the other basic approach underlies a specific partnership tax rule.

PARTNERSHIP FORMATIONS AND ACQUISITIONS OF PARTNERSHIP INTERESTS

LO 15-2

Acquiring Partnership Interests When Partnerships Are Formed

When a partnership is formed, and afterwards, partners may transfer cash, other tangible or intangible property, and services to the partnership in exchange for an equity interest called a **partnership interest.** Partnership interests represent the bundle of economic rights granted to partners under the partnership agreement (or operating agreement for an LLC).[6] These rights include the right to receive a share of the partnership net assets if the partnership is liquidated, called a **capital interest,** and the right or obligation to receive a share of *future* profits or *future* losses, called a **profits interest.**[7] It is quite common for partners contributing property to receive both capital and profits interests in the exchange. Partners who contribute services instead of property frequently receive only profits interests. The distinction between capital and profits interests is important because the tax rules for partnerships are sometimes applied to them differently.

Contributions of Property
Partnership formations are similar to other tax-deferred transactions, such as like-kind exchanges and corporate formations, because realized gains and losses from the exchange of contributed property for partnership interests are either fully or partially deferred for tax purposes, depending on the specifics of the transaction. The rationale for permitting taxpayers to defer realized gains or losses on property contributed to partnerships is identical to the rationale for permitting tax deferral when corporations are formed.[8] From a practical perspective, the tax rules in this area allow entrepreneurs to organize their businesses without having to pay taxes. In addition, these rules follow the aggregate theory of partnership taxation because they recognize that partners contributing property to a partnership still own the contributed property, albeit a smaller percentage, since other partners will also indirectly own the contributed property through their partnership interests.

Gain and loss recognition.   As a general rule, neither partnerships nor partners recognize gain or loss when they contribute property to partnerships.[9] This applies to property contributions when a partnership is initially formed and to subsequent property contributions. In this context, the term *property* is defined broadly to include a wide variety of both tangible and intangible assets but not services. The general rule facilitates contributions of property with **built-in gains,** meaning the fair market value is greater than the tax basis, but it discourages contributions of property with **built-in losses,** meaning the fair market value is less than the tax basis. In fact, partners holding property with built-in losses are usually better off selling the property, recognizing the related tax loss, and contributing the cash from the sale to the partnership so it can acquire property elsewhere.

THE KEY FACTS
Property Contributions
- Partners don't generally recognize gain or loss when they contribute property to partnerships.
- Initial tax basis for partners contributing property = Basis of contributed property − Debt securing contributed property + Partnership debt allocated to contributing partner + Gain recognized.
- Contributing partner's holding period in a partnership interest depends on the type of property contributed.

---

[6]The partnership books reflect partners' shares of the partnership's net assets in their individual capital accounts.

[7]An interest in the future profits or losses of a partnership is customarily referred to as a profits interest rather than a profits/loss interest.

[8]The Corporate Formation, Reorganization, and Liquidation chapter discusses the tax rules related to corporate formations.

[9]§721.

What if: Assume Nicole contributes land to CCS with a fair market value of $120,000 and an adjusted basis of $20,000. What amount of gain or loss would she recognize on the contribution?

Answer: None. Under the general rule for contributions of appreciated property, Nicole will not recognize any of the $100,000 built-in gain from her land.

What if: Suppose Chanzz Inc. contributed equipment with a fair market value of $120,000 and a tax basis of $220,000 to CCS. What amount of the gain or loss would Chanzz Inc. recognize on the contribution?

Answer: None. Chanzz Inc. would not recognize any of the $100,000 built-in loss on the equipment. However, if Chanzz Inc. sold the property to an unrelated party and contributed $120,000 in cash instead of the equipment, it could recognize the $100,000 built-in tax loss. If, for some reason, the equipment Chanzz planned to contribute was uniquely suited to CCS's operations, Chanzz could obtain the same result by selling the equipment to Sarah, who would then contribute the equipment to CCS.

Partner's initial tax basis. Among other things, partners need to determine the tax basis in their partnership interest to properly compute their taxable gains and losses when they sell their partnership interest. A partner's tax basis in her partnership interest is called her **outside basis.** In contrast, the partnership's basis in its assets is its **inside basis.** As we progress through this and the next chapter, you'll see other important reasons for calculating a partner's outside tax basis.

Calculating a partner's initial tax basis in a partnership interest acquired by contributing property and/or cash is relatively straightforward if the partnership doesn't have any debt. The partner will simply have a basis in her partnership interest equivalent to the tax basis of the property and cash she contributed.[10] This rule ensures that realized gains and losses on contributed property are merely deferred until either the contributing partner sells her partnership interest or the partnership sells the contributed property.

What if: Assume that Sarah contributed $120,000 in cash to CCS in exchange for her partnership interest and that CCS had no liabilities. What is Sarah's outside basis in her partnership interest after the contribution?

Answer: Sarah's basis is $120,000, the amount of cash she contributed to CCS.

What if: Assume Nicole contributed land with a fair market value of $120,000 and an adjusted basis of $20,000 and CCS had no liabilities. What is Nicole's initial tax basis in CCS?

Answer: Nicole's outside basis in CCS is $20,000, the basis of the property she contributed to CCS. If Nicole immediately sold her interest in CCS for $120,000 (the value of the land she contributed), she would recognize gain of $100,000—exactly the amount she would have recognized if she had sold the land instead of contributing it to CCS.

When partnerships have debt, a few additional steps are required to determine a partner's tax basis in her partnership interest. First, each partner must include her share of the partnership's debt in calculating the tax basis in her partnership interest, because partnership tax law treats each partner as borrowing her proportionate share of the partnership's debt and then contributing the borrowed cash to acquire her partnership interest.[11] You can understand the necessity for this basis increase by recalling that the basis of any purchased asset increases by the amount of any borrowed funds used to purchase it.

[10]§722.
[11]§752(a).

Partnerships may have either **recourse debt** or **nonrecourse debt** or both, and the specific approach to allocating partnership debt to individual partners differs for each. The fundamental difference between the two types of debt lies in the legal responsibility partners assume for ultimately paying the debt. Recourse debts are those for which at least one partner has economic risk of loss—that is, they may have to legally satisfy the debt with their own funds. For example, the unsecured debts of general partnerships, such as payables, are recourse debt because general partners are legally responsible for the debts of the partnership. Recourse debt is usually allocated to the partners who will ultimately be responsible for paying it.[12] The partners must consider their partner guarantees, other agreements, and state partnership or LLC statutes in making this determination.

Nonrecourse debts, in contrast, don't provide creditors the same level of legal recourse against partners. Nonrecourse debts such as mortgages are typically secured by real property and only give lenders the right to obtain the secured property in the event the partnership defaults on the debt. Because partners are responsible for paying nonrecourse debts only to the extent the partnership generates sufficient profits, such debts are generally allocated according to partners' profit-sharing ratios. (We discuss an exception to this general rule later in the chapter.[13]) The basic rules for allocating recourse and nonrecourse debt are summarized in Exhibit 15-1.

EXHIBIT 15-1   **Basic Rules for Allocating Partnership Debt to Partners**

Type of Debt	Allocation Method
Recourse	Allocated to partners with ultimate responsibility for paying debt
Nonrecourse	Allocated according to partners' profit-sharing ratios

The legal structure of entities taxed as partnerships also influences the way partners characterize and allocate partnership debt. Recourse debts in limited partnerships are typically allocated only to general partners, because, as we discuss in the Entities Overview chapter, limited partners are legally protected from a limited partnership's recourse debt holders.[14] Limited partners, however, may be allocated recourse debt if they forgo their legal protection by guaranteeing some or all of the recourse debt. Similarly, LLC members generally treat LLC debt as nonrecourse debt because they, like corporate shareholders, are shielded from the LLC's creditors. However, like limited partners, LLC members may treat debt as recourse debt to the extent they contractually assume risk of loss by agreeing to be legally responsible for paying the debt.[15]

Example 15-3

Sarah and Chanzz Inc. initially each contributed $120,000 and CCS borrowed $60,000 from a bank when CCS was formed. The bank required Nicole, Sarah, and Chanzz Inc. to personally guarantee the bank loan. The terms were structured so each of the members would (1) be responsible for a portion of the debt equal to the percentage of CCS losses allocated to each member (one-third each) and

(continued on page 15-6)

[12]Reg. §1.752-2. Under the regulations, partners' obligations for paying recourse debt are determined by assuming a hypothetical, worst-case scenario where partnership assets (including cash) become worthless, and the resulting losses are then allocated to partners. The partners who legally would be responsible for partnership recourse debts under this scenario must be allocated the recourse debt. A detailed description of this approach for allocating recourse debt is beyond the scope of this book.

[13]Reg. §1.752-3 provides the rules for allocating nonrecourse debt, some of which are beyond the scope of this text.

[14]Recall from the Entities Overview chapter that, in limited partnerships, general partners' liability is unlimited, whereas limited partners' liability is usually limited to the amount they have invested.

[15]It's actually quite common for banks and other lenders to require LLC members to personally guarantee loans made to LLCs.

(2) have no right of reimbursement from either CCS or the other members of CCS. How much of the $60,000 bank debt was allocated to each member?

Answer: Each member was allocated $20,000. The debt is treated as recourse debt because the members are personally guaranteeing it. Because each guarantees one-third of the debt, the $60,000 debt is allocated equally among them.

What if: Assuming the $60,000 bank loan is CCS's only debt, what is Sarah's initial basis in her CCS interest after taking her share of CCS's bank debt into account?

Answer: Sarah's basis is $140,000 ($120,000 + $20,000) and consists of her cash contribution plus her share of CCS's $60,000 bank loan.

Another step is needed to determine a partner's outside basis when the partnership assumes *debt of the partner* secured by property the partner contributes to the partnership. Essentially, the contributing partner must treat her debt relief as a deemed cash distribution from the partnership that reduces her outside basis.[16] If the debt securing the contributed property is *nonrecourse debt*, the amount of the debt in excess of the basis of the contributed property is allocated solely to the contributing partner, and the remaining debt is allocated to all partners according to their profit-sharing ratios.[17]

Example 15-4

What if: Nicole contributed $10,000 of cash and land with a fair market value of $150,000 and adjusted basis of $20,000 to CCS when it was formed. The land was encumbered by a $40,000 nonrecourse mortgage executed three years before. Recalling that CCS already had $60,000 in bank debt before Nicole's contribution, what tax bases do Nicole, Sarah, and Chanzz Inc. *initially* have in their CCS interests?

Answer: Their bases are $36,666, $146,666, and $146,666, respectively. Nicole, Sarah, and Chanzz Inc. would determine their initial tax bases as illustrated in the table below:

Description	Nicole	Sarah	Chanzz Inc.	Explanation
(1) Basis in contributed land	$ 20,000			
(2) Cash contributed	10,000	$ 120,000	$ 120,000	Example 15-3
(3) Members' share of $60,000 recourse bank loan	20,000	20,000	20,000	Example 15-3
(4) Nonrecourse mortgage in excess of basis in contributed land	20,000			Nonrecourse debt > basis is allocated only to Nicole
(5) Remaining nonrecourse mortgage	6,666	6,666	6,666	33.33% × [$40,000 − (4)]
(6) Relief from mortgage debt	(40,000)			
Members' initial tax basis in CCS	**$36,666**	**$146,666**	**$146,666**	Sum of (1) through (6)

Although in many instances partners don't recognize gains on property contributions, there is an important exception to the general rule that may apply when property secured by debt is contributed to a partnership. In these situations, the contributing partner recognizes gain *only if* the cash deemed to have been received from a partnership distribution

---

[16]§752(b).
[17]Reg. §1.752-3(a)(2).

exceeds the contributing partner's tax basis in her partnership interest prior to the deemed distribution.[18] Any gain recognized is generally treated as capital gain.[19]

Example 15-5

What if: Assume Sarah and Chanzz Inc., but *not* Nicole, personally guarantee all $100,000 of CCS's debt ($60,000 bank loan + $40,000 mortgage on land). How much gain, if any, would Nicole recognize on her contribution to CCS and what would be the basis in her CCS interest?

Answer: Nicole would recognize $10,000 gain and have a $0 basis, computed as follows:

Description	Amount	Explanation
(1) Basis in contributed land	$20,000	Example 15-4
(2) Cash contributed	10,000	Example 15-4
(3) Nicole's share of debt	0	Sarah and Chanzz guaranteed all of CCS's liabilities, including the mortgage on land, thereby turning them into recourse liabilities that should only be allocated to Sarah and Chanzz.
(4) Debt relief	(40,000)	Nicole was relieved of mortgage on land.
(5) Debt relief in excess of basis in contributed land and cash	(10,000)	Sum of (1) through (4)
(6) Capital gain recognized	**10,000**	(5) with opposite sign
Nicole's initial tax basis in CCS	**0**	(5) + (6)

Partner's holding period in partnership interest. Because a partnership interest is a capital asset, its holding period determines whether gains or losses from the disposition of the partnership interest are short-term or long-term capital gains or losses. The length of a partner's holding period for a partnership interest acquired by contributing property depends on the nature of the assets the partner contributed. When partners contribute capital assets or §1231 assets (assets used in a trade or business and held for more than one year), the holding period of the contributed property "tacks on" to the holding period of the partnership interest.[20] Otherwise, it begins on the day the partnership interest is acquired.

Example 15-6

What if: Assume Nicole contributed land held for investment (no cash) that she had held for five years in exchange for her partnership interest. One month after contributing the property, she sold her partnership interest and recognized a capital gain. Is the gain long-term or short-term?

Answer: The gain is long-term because the five-year holding period of the land is tacked on to Nicole's holding period for her partnership interest. She is treated as though she held the partnership interest for five years and one month at the time she sold it.

Partnership's tax basis and holding period in contributed property. Just as partners must determine their initial basis in their partnership interests after contributing property,

---

[18]§731(a). However, §707(a)(2)(B) provides that deemed cash received from the relief of debt should be considered as sale proceeds rather than a distribution when circumstances indicate the relief of debt constitutes a disguised sale. Further discussion of disguised sale transactions is beyond the scope of this book.

[19]§731(a). This is equivalent to increasing what would have been a negative basis by the recognized gain to arrive at a zero basis. This mechanism ensures that partners will be left with an initial tax basis of zero any time they recognize gain from a property contribution.

[20]Reg. §1.1223-1(a).

partnerships must establish their inside basis in the contributed property. Measuring both the partner's outside basis and the partnership's inside basis is consistent with the entity theory of partnership taxation. To ensure built-in gains and losses on contributed property are ultimately recognized if partnerships sell contributed property, partnerships generally take a basis in the property equal to the contributing partner's basis in the property at the time of the contribution.[21] Like the adjusted basis of contributed property, the holding period of contributed assets also carries over to the partnership.[22] In fact, the only tax attribute of contributed property that *doesn't* carry over to the partnership is the character of contributed property. Whether gains or losses on dispositions of contributed property are capital or ordinary usually depends on the manner in which the partnership uses contributed property.[23]

Example 15-7

What if: Assume CCS used the land Nicole contributed in its business for one month and then sold it for its fair market value of $150,000. What is the amount and character of the gain CCS would recognize on the sale? (See Example 15-4.)

Answer: CCS recognizes $130,000 of §1231 gain. Nicole's basis in the land prior to the formation of CCS was $20,000. Because CCS receives a carryover basis in the land of $20,000, it recognizes $130,000 of gain when the land is sold for $150,000 ($110,000 in cash and $40,000 of debt relief minus $20,000 basis in land). Also, because CCS used the land in its business and because Nicole's five-year holding period carries over to CCS, the land qualifies as a §1231 asset to CCS, and CCS recognizes §1231 gain when the land is sold. Note that $130,000 of gain is recognized regardless of whether Nicole sells the land, recognizes the gain, and contributes cash to CCS, or CCS sells the land shortly after it is contributed and recognizes the gain.

Unlike corporations, entities taxed as partnerships track the equity of their owners using a capital account for each owner. The methodology for maintaining owners' **capital accounts** depends on the approach these entities use to prepare their financial statements. For example, an entity preparing GAAP financial statements would track each owner's share of the equity using **GAAP capital accounts** maintained using generally accepted accounting principles.

In addition to tracking the inside basis of its assets for tax purposes, partnerships not required to produce GAAP financial statements may decide to use inside tax basis, as well as tax income and expense recognition rules, to maintain their books. Under this approach, a new partnership would prepare its initial balance sheet using the tax basis for its assets. In addition, it would create a **tax capital account** for each new partner, reflecting the tax basis of any property contributed (net of any debt securing the property) and cash contributions. Because each new partner's tax capital account measures that partner's equity in the partnership using tax accounting rules, it will later be adjusted to include the partner's share of earnings and losses, contributions, and distributions.

Besides satisfying bookkeeping requirements, a partnership's tax basis balance sheet can provide useful tax-related information. For example, we can calculate each partner's share of the inside basis of partnership assets by adding the partner's share of debt to her **tax capital account.** Interestingly, partners who acquire their interests by contributing property (without having to recognize any gain) will have an *outside basis* equal to their share of the partnership's total inside basis. However, as we discuss more fully in the next chapter, partners' inside and outside bases will likely be different when they purchase existing partnership interests.

As another alternative to maintaining GAAP capital accounts, partnerships may also maintain their partners' capital accounts using accounting rules prescribed in the §704(b) tax regulations.[24] In fact, many partnership agreements require the partnership to maintain **§704(b) capital accounts** for the partners in addition to tax basis capital accounts. Partnerships set up §704(b) capital accounts in much the same way as tax capital accounts, except that §704(b) capital accounts reflect the fair market value rather

[21]§723.
[22]§1223(2).
[23]§702(b). However, §724 provides some important exceptions to this general rule for certain receivables, inventory, and capital loss property.
[24]Reg. §1.704-1(b)(2)(iv).

than the tax basis of contributed assets. Once a partnership begins operations, it can adjust §704(b) capital accounts so they continue to reflect the fair market value of partners' capital interests as accurately as possible. Partnerships may prefer this approach over simply maintaining tax capital accounts because §704(b) capital accounts may be a better measure of the true value of partners' capital interests.

continued from page 15-1...

Before forming CCS, its members agreed to keep its books using the tax basis of contributed assets and tax income and expense recognition rules. After receiving the cash and property contributions from its members and borrowing $60,000 from Nicole's bank, CCS prepared the tax basis balance sheet in Exhibit 15-2.

to be continued...

EXHIBIT 15-2   Color Comfort Sheets LLC

Balance Sheet March 31, 2017		
	Tax Basis	**§704(b)/FMV***
Assets:		
Cash	$310,000	$310,000
Land	20,000	150,000
Totals	$330,000	$460,000
Liabilities and Capital:		
Long-term debt	$100,000	$100,000
Capital—Nicole	(10,000)	120,000
Capital—Sarah	120,000	120,000
Capital—Chanzz Inc.	120,000	120,000
Totals	$330,000	$460,000

*The §704(b)/FMV balance sheet is also provided to illustrate the difference in the two approaches to maintaining partners' capital accounts.

Contribution of Services   So far we've assumed partners receive their partnership interests in exchange for contributed property. They may also receive partnership interests in exchange for services they provide to the partnership. For example, an attorney or other service provider might accept a partnership interest in lieu of cash payment for services provided as part of a partnership formation. Similarly, ongoing partnerships may compensate their employees with partnership interests to reduce compensation-related cash payments and motivate employees to behave more like owners. Unlike property contributions, services contributed in exchange for partnership interests may create immediate tax consequences to both the contributing partner *and* the partnership, depending on the nature of the partnership interest received.[25]

Capital interests.   Partners who receive unrestricted capital interests in exchange for services have the right to receive a share of the partnership's capital if it liquidates.[26] Because capital interests represent a current economic entitlement amenable to measurement, partners receiving capital interests for services must treat the amount they would receive if the partnership were to liquidate, or the **liquidation value**[27] of the capital interest, as ordinary

[25]Rev. Proc. 93-27, 1993-2 CB 343 and Rev. Proc. 2001-43, 2001-2 CB 191. In 2005, the IRS issued Prop. Reg. §1.704-1, which will change certain elements of current tax law when it is adopted as a final regulation. The concepts and examples discussed here are consistent with both current law and the proposed regulation.

[26]Certain restrictions, such as vesting requirements, may be placed on partnership interests received for services. We limit our discussion here to unrestricted partnership interests.

[27]Proposed regulations in this area also allow the parties in this transaction to use the fair market value of partnership interests as a measure of value rather than liquidation value.

continued from page 15-9...

Once CCS was organized in March 2017, it built a small production facility on the commercial land Nicole had contributed, purchased and installed the equipment needed to produce sheets, and hired and trained workers—all before the actual production and marketing of the sheets. After production began on July 1, 2017, CCS started selling its sheets to local specialty bedding stores, but this local market was limited. To create additional demand for their product, the members of CCS decided to draw on Sarah's marketing expertise to develop an advertising campaign targeted at home and garden magazines. All members of CCS agreed Sarah would receive, on December 31, 2017, an additional *capital interest* in CCS with a liquidation value of $20,000 *and* an increase in her profit-and-loss-sharing ratio from 33.33 percent to 40 percent (leaving the other members each with a 30 percent share of profits and losses), to compensate her for the time she would spend on this additional project. At this point, CCS's debt remained at $100,000.

to be continued...

income.[28] In addition, the tax basis in the capital interest received by the **service partner** will equal the amount of ordinary income he recognizes, and his holding period will begin on the date he receives the capital interest. The partnership either deducts or capitalizes the value of the capital interest, depending on the nature of the services the partner provides. For example, a real estate partnership would capitalize the value of a capital interest compensating a partner for architectural drawings used for a real estate development project.[29] Conversely, the same partnership would deduct the value of a capital interest compensating a partner for providing property management services. When the partnership deducts the value of capital interests used to compensate partners for services provided, it allocates the deduction only to the partners *not* providing services, or **nonservice partners,** because the deduction is related to the segment of the partnership tax year ending immediately before the admission of the new service partner.[30]

Example 15-8

What if: What are the tax consequences to Sarah and CCS if Sarah receives a capital interest (no profits interest) with a $20,000 liquidation value for her marketing services?

Answer: As summarized below, Sarah has $20,000 of ordinary income, and CCS receives a $20,000 ordinary deduction. However, this deduction must be split equally between Nicole and Chanzz Inc. because, in effect, they transferred a portion of their capital to Sarah.

Description	Sarah	Nicole	Chanzz Inc.	Explanation
(1) Ordinary income	$20,000			Liquidation value of capital interest
Ordinary deduction		$(10,000)	$(10,000)	Capital shift from nonservice partners (1) × .5

---

[28]The ordinary income recognized by the service partner is treated as a "guaranteed payment" by the service partner. Guaranteed payments are discussed more fully later in this chapter.

[29]§263(a).

[30]The preamble to Prop. Reg. §1.721-1(b) applies the varying interest rule of §706(d)(1) to the admission of a service partner.

Profits interests. It's fairly common for partnerships to compensate service partners with profits rather than capital interests. Profits interests are fundamentally different from capital interests, because the only economic benefit they provide is the right to share in the future profits of the partnership. Unlike capital interests, profits interests have no liquidation value at the time they are received. Nonservice partners generally prefer to compensate service partners with profits interests because they don't have to forgo their current share of capital in the partnership and may not ever have to give up anything if the partnership is ultimately unprofitable. Thus, a profits interest is more risky than a capital interest from the perspective of the service partner.

The tax rules applicable to profits interests differ from those pertaining to capital interests due to the fundamental economic differences between them. Because there is no immediate liquidation value associated with a profits interest, the service partner typically will not recognize income and the nonservice partners will not receive deductions.[31] However, future profits and losses attributable to the profits interest are allocated to the service partner (and away from the nonservice partners) as they are generated. In addition, the partnership must adjust debt allocations based on profit-and-loss-sharing ratios to reflect the service partner's new or increased share of profits and losses.

Example 15-9

What if: Assuming Sarah received only a profits interest for her marketing services instead of the capital interest she received in Example 15-8, what are the tax consequences to Sarah, Nicole, Chanzz Inc., and CCS?[32]

Answer: Sarah would not be required to recognize any income, and CCS would not deduct or capitalize any costs. As CCS generates future profits, Sarah will receive a greater share of the profits than she would have otherwise received, and the other two members will receive a correspondingly smaller share. In addition, with the increase in Sarah's profit-and-loss-sharing ratios from 33.33 percent to 40 percent, debt allocations among the partners will change to reflect Sarah's additional entitlement. Note that the debt allocations affect each partner's outside basis. The change in debt allocations is reflected in the table below:

Description	Sarah	Nicole	Chanzz Inc.	Explanation
(1) Increase in debt allocation	$5,334			Loss-sharing ratio increases from 33.33 percent to 40 percent or 6.67 percent ($60,000 recourse bank loan × 6.67% increase in loss-sharing ratio) + ($20,000 nonrecourse mortgage not allocated solely to Nicole × 6.67% increase in profit-sharing ratio).
Decrease in debt allocation		$(2,666)	$(2,666)	(1) × .5

---

[31]Rev. Proc. 93-27 indicates that income is recognized by the service partner "if the profits interest relates to a substantially certain and predictable stream of income," if the partner disposes of the profits interest within two years, or "the profits interest is a limited partnership interest in a publicly traded partnership."

[32]It is common for partnerships to grant a profits interest without an accompanying capital interest.

Example 15-10

What are the tax consequences to Sarah, Nicole, and Chanzz Inc. associated with the capital interest (liquidation value of $20,000) and profits interest Sarah receives for her marketing services?

Answer: The tax consequences associated with giving Sarah *both* a capital and profits interest are summarized in the table below:

Description	Sarah	Nicole	Chanzz Inc.	Explanation
(1) Ordinary income	$20,000			Liquidation value of capital interest
Ordinary deduction		$(10,000)	$(10,000)	Capital shift from nonservice partners, (1) × .5
(2) Increase in debt allocation	5,334			Loss-sharing ratio increases from 33.33 percent to 40 percent or 6.67 percent ($60,000 recourse bank loan × 6.67% increase in loss-sharing ratio) + ($20,000 nonrecourse mortgage not allocated solely to Nicole × 6.67% increase in profit-sharing ratio).
Decrease in debt allocation		$(2,666)	$(2,666)	(2) × .5

TAXES IN THE REAL WORLD   Carried Interests

In debates over tax policy, politicians in the news have frequently discussed carried interests as if everyone within earshot understands the term. However, judging from the public's confusion over the issue, not everyone does.

Carried interests are nothing more than profits interests granted to managing partners and key employees of private equity and other similar investment partnerships. Industry norms suggest that typical carried interests provide managing partners with a 20 percent (and sometimes greater) share of profits when partnership investments are eventually sold. Because these investments are typically corporate shares that have been held more than one year,

any income from their sale is treated as long-term capital gain.

The benefits of these types of carried interest arrangements are twofold: Any income managing partners receive is deferred until partnership investments are sold, and, when the income is finally recognized, it is taxed at favorable, long-term capital gains rates. To some politicians and their supporters, this result seems unfair given that carried interests are economically equivalent to deferred salary that is taxed at higher ordinary rates.

Source: For a more detailed description of carried interests, see: "Business Taxation: What Is Carried Interest and How Should It Be Taxed?" in *The Tax Policy Briefing Book* at www.taxpolicycenter.org.

Organizational, Start-Up, and Syndication Costs   When partnerships are formed, they typically incur some costs that must be capitalized rather than expensed for tax purposes because they will benefit the partnership over its entire lifespan. This category of expenses includes **organization expenses** associated with legally forming a partnership (such as attorneys' and accountants' fees), **syndication costs** to promote and sell partnership interests, and **start-up costs** that would normally be deducted as operating expenses except that they are incurred before the start of active trade or business. However, with the exception of syndication costs,[33] which are not deductible, the partnership may elect to amortize these

---

[33]Syndication costs are typically incurred by partnerships whose interests are marketed to the public. Thus, syndication expenses are unusual in closely held partnerships.

costs. The Property Acquisition and Cost Recovery chapter provides additional detail about immediately expensing or amortizing business organizational expenses and start-up costs.

Acquisitions of Partnership Interests

After a partnership has been formed and begins operating, new or existing partners can acquire partnership interests in exchange for contributing property and/or services, in which case the tax rules discussed above in the context of forming a partnership still apply. Or new partners may purchase partnership interests from existing partners. Partners who purchase their partnership interests don't have to be concerned with recognizing taxable income when they receive their interests. However, in each of these scenarios they must still determine the initial tax basis and holding period in their partnership interests. Exhibit 15-3 summarizes the rules for determining the tax basis of partnership interests when they are received in exchange for contributed property or services or when they are purchased.

EXHIBIT 15-3   Summary of Partner's Outside Basis and Holding Period by Acquisition Method

Acquisition Method	Outside Basis	Holding Period
Contribute Property	Equals basis of contributed property − debt relief + debt allocation + gain recognized.	If property contributed is a capital or §1231 asset, holding period includes holding period of contributed property; otherwise begins on date interest received.
Contribute Services	Equals liquidation value of capital interest + debt allocation. Equals debt allocation if only profits interest received.	Begins on date interest received.
Purchase	Equals cost basis[34] + debt allocation.	Begins on date interest purchased.

Example 15-11

CCS had overall operating losses from July 1, 2017 (when it began operating), through June 30, 2018. Because of the losses, Chanzz Inc. decided to sell its 30 percent interest in CCS (Chanzz Inc.'s original 33.33 percent interest in CCS was reduced to 30 percent at the end of 2017 when Sarah's interest was increased to compensate her for services provided) on June 30, 2018, to Greg Randall. Like Chanzz Inc., Greg will be a nonmanaging member and guarantee a portion of CCS debt. Greg paid Chanzz Inc. $100,000 for his interest in CCS and was allocated a 30 percent share of CCS debt (CCS's debt remained at $100,000 on June 30, 2018). What is Greg's basis and holding period in CCS?

Answer: Greg's basis of $124,000 in CCS includes the $100,000 amount he paid to purchase the interest plus his $24,000 share of CCS's total $80,000 debt available to be allocated to all members ($60,000 recourse bank loan and $20,000 of nonrecourse mortgage remaining after allocating the first $20,000 to Nicole). Greg's holding period in his CCS interest begins on June 30, 2018.

PARTNERSHIP ACCOUNTING: TAX ELECTIONS, ACCOUNTING PERIODS, AND ACCOUNTING METHODS

LO 15-3

A newly formed partnership must adopt its required tax year-end and decide whether it intends to use either the cash or accrual method as its overall method of accounting. As discussed in the Business Income, Deductions, and Accounting Methods chapter, an entity's tax

---

[34]§742.

year-end determines the cutoff date for including income and deductions in a particular return, and its overall accounting method determines when income and deductions are recognized for tax purposes. Partnerships must frequently make other tax-related elections as well.

Tax Elections

New partnerships determine their accounting periods and make tax elections, including the election of overall accounting method, the election to expense a portion of organizational expenses and start-up costs, and the election to expense tangible personal property. Who formally makes all these elections? In theory, either the partnership or the partners themselves could do so. With just a few exceptions, the partnership tax rules rely on the entity theory of partnership taxation and make the partnership responsible for tax elections.[35] In many instances, the partnership does so in conjunction with filing its annual tax return. For example, it selects an accounting method and determines whether to elect to amortize organizational expenses or start-up costs by simply applying its elections in calculating ordinary business income on its first return. The partnership makes other tax elections by filing a separate document with the IRS, such as Form 3115 when it elects to change an accounting method.

Example 15-12

How will CCS elect its overall accounting method after it begins operations?

Answer: Nicole, Sarah, and Chanzz Inc. may jointly decide on an overall accounting method or, in their LLC operating agreement, they may appoint one of the members to be responsible for making this and other tax elections. Once they have made this decision, CCS makes the election by simply using the chosen accounting method when preparing its first return.

THE KEY FACTS

Partnership Accounting: Tax Elections, Accounting Periods, and Methods

- Partnerships are responsible for making most tax elections.
- A partnership's taxable year is the majority interest taxable year, the common taxable year of the principal partners, or the taxable year providing the least aggregate deferral to the partners.
- Partnerships are generally eligible to use the cash method unless they have average gross receipts over the three prior years of greater than $25 million and have corporate partners.

Accounting Periods

Required Year-Ends   Because partners include their share of partnership income or loss in their taxable year ending with the partnership taxable year, or within which the partnership taxable year falls, any partnership tax year other than that of the partners will result in some degree of tax deferral for some or all of the partners.[36] Exhibit 15-4 reflects the tax deferral a partner with a calendar year-end would receive if the corresponding partnership had a January 31 year-end.

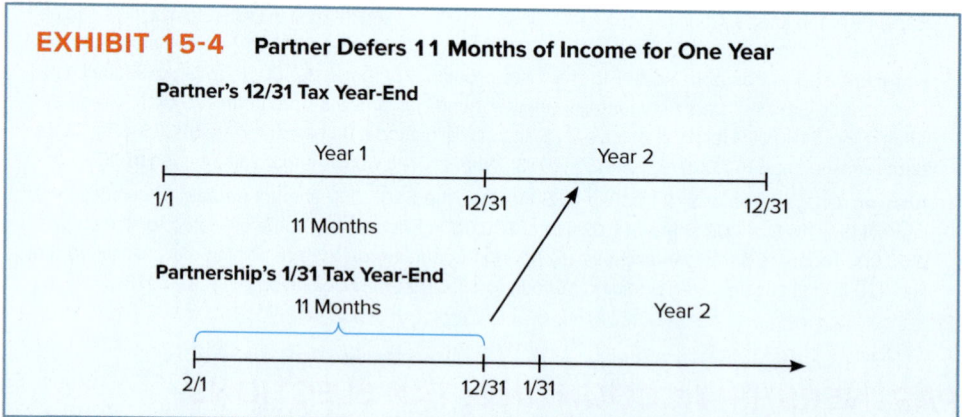

EXHIBIT 15-4 **Partner Defers 11 Months of Income for One Year**

Because the partner reports the partnership's year 1 income earned from February 1 until January 31 in the partner's second calendar year (the year within which the partnership's January 31 year-end falls), the partner defers reporting for one year the

---

[35]§703(b). Certain elections are made at the partner level.
[36]§706(a).

11 months of income she was allocated from February 1 through December 31 of her first calendar year.

The government's desire to reduce the aggregate tax deferral of partners (the sum of the deferrals for each individual partner) provides the underlying rationale behind the rules requiring certain partnership taxable year-ends. Partnerships are generally required to use one of three possible tax year-ends.[37] As illustrated in Exhibit 15-5, they must follow a series of steps to determine the appropriate year-end.

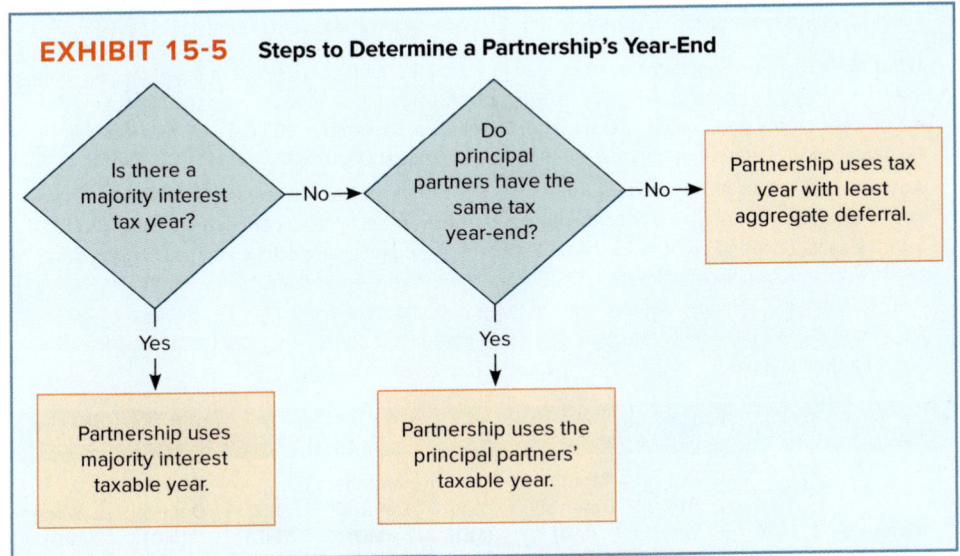

EXHIBIT 15-5   Steps to Determine a Partnership's Year-End

The first potential required tax year is the **majority interest taxable year,** the taxable year of one or more partners who together own more than 50 percent of the capital and profits interests in the partnership.[38] However, there may not be a majority interest taxable year when several partners have different year-ends. For example, if a partnership has two partners with 50 percent capital and profits interests and each has a different tax year, there will be no majority interest taxable year. In that case, the partnership next applies the principal partners test to determine its year-end.

Under the **principal partners** test, the required tax year is the taxable year the principal partners *all* have in common. For this purpose, principal partners are those who have 5 percent or more interest in the partnership profits and capital.[39] Consider a partnership with two calendar-year partners, each with a 20 percent capital and profits interest, and 30 additional fiscal year-end partners, each with less than a 5 percent capital and profits interest. In this scenario, the required taxable year of the partnership is a calendar year corresponding with the taxable year of the partnership's only two principal partners. If, as in the earlier example, the partnership had two 50 percent capital and profits partners with different tax years, it would then use the tax year providing the "least aggregate deferral" to the partners, unless it is eligible to elect an alternative year-end.[40]

The tax year with the **least aggregate deferral** is the one among the tax years of the partners that provides the partner group as a whole with the smallest amount of aggregate tax deferral. Under this approach, the total tax deferral is measured under each potential tax year mathematically by weighting each partner's months of deferral under the potential tax year by each partner's *profits* percentage and then summing the weighted months of deferral for all the partners.

---

[37]Under certain circumstances, other alternative taxable years may be available to partnerships. See Rev. Proc. 2002-38, 2002-1 CB 1037 and §444 for additional information concerning these options.

[38]§706(b)(1)(B)(i).

[39]§706(b)(3).

[40]Reg. §1.706-1(b)(3).

Example 15-13

When CCS began operating in 2017, it had two calendar year-end members, Nicole and Sarah, and one member with a June 30 year-end, Chanzz Inc. What tax year-end must CCS use for 2017?

Answer: CCS was required to use the calendar year as its taxable year unless it was eligible for an alternative year-end. Although Chanzz Inc. had a June 30 taxable year, Nicole and Sarah both had calendar year-ends. Because Nicole and Sarah each initially own 33.33 percent of the capital and profits of CCS, and together they own greater than 50 percent of the profits and capital of CCS, the calendar year is the required taxable year for CCS because it is the majority interest taxable year.

What if: Assume CCS initially began operating with three members: Nicole, a calendar year-end member with a 20 percent profits and capital interest; Chanzz Inc., a June 30 year-end member with a 40 percent profits and capital interest; and Telle Inc., a September 30 year-end member with a 40 percent profits and capital interest. What tax year-end must CCS use for 2017?

Answer: CCS would be required to use a June 30 year-end unless it was eligible for an alternative year-end. CCS does not have a majority interest taxable year because no partner or group of partners with the same year-end owns more than 50 percent of the profits and capital interests in CCS. Also, because all three principal partners in CCS have different year-ends, the principal partner test is not met. As a result, CCS must decide which of three potential year-ends, June 30, September 30, or December 31, will provide its members the least aggregate deferral. The table below illustrates the required computations:

Possible Year-Ends			12/31 Year-End		6/30 Year-End		9/30 Year-End	
Members	%	Tax Year	Months Deferral* (MD)	% × (MD)	Months Deferral* (MD)	% × (MD)	Months Deferral* (MD)	% × (MD)
Nicole	20	12/31	0	0	6	1.2	3	.6
Chanzz Inc.	40	6/30	6	2.4	0	0	9	3.6
Telle Inc.	40	9/30	9	3.6	3	1.2	0	0
Total aggregate deferral				6		2.4		4.2

*Months deferral equals number of months between the proposed year-end and partner's year-end.

June 30 is the required taxable year-end because it provides members with the least aggregate tax deferral (2.4 is less than 6 and 4.2).

Accounting Methods

Although partnerships may use the accrual method freely, they may not use the cash method under certain conditions because it facilitates the deferral of income and acceleration of deductions. For example, partnerships with C corporation partners are generally not eligible to use the cash method[41] unless their average annual gross receipts for the three prior taxable years do not exceed $25 million and they otherwise qualify.[42] Entities generally eligible to use the overall cash method of accounting must nevertheless use the accrual method to account for the purchase and sale of inventory unless they unless they have average annual gross receipts over the prior three years of $25 million or less.

[41]§448(a)(2). In addition, §448(a)(3) prohibits partnerships classified as "tax shelters" from electing the cash method.

[42]§448(b)(3). If a partnership has not been in existence for at least three years, this test is applied based on the number of years it has been in existence.

When CCS began operations, its members decided it should elect the cash method of accounting if eligible to do so. Would having a corporate member—Chanzz Inc.—prevent it from electing the cash method?

Answer: No. Although Chanzz Inc. was a founding member of CCS, its ownership share didn't affect the partnership's eligibility to use the cash method since CCS's average annual gross receipts were less than $25 million. If Chanzz Inc. had remained a member of CCS, the cash method might have been unavailable in future years if average annual gross receipts for a three year period exceeded $25 million.

REPORTING THE RESULTS OF PARTNERSHIP OPERATIONS   `LO 15-4`

The first section in the Internal Revenue Code dealing with partnerships states emphatically that partnerships are flow-through entities: "A partnership as such shall not be subject to the income tax imposed by this chapter. Persons carrying on business as partners shall be liable for income tax only in their separate or individual capacities."[43] This feature of partnership taxation explains why partnerships are sometimes favored over corporations, whose shareholders are subject to a double tax—once when the income is earned and again when it is distributed to shareholders as a dividend or when the shares are sold.

TAXES IN THE REAL WORLD   Publicly Traded Partnerships

Would it surprise you to know that many private equity firms are organized as partnerships for tax purposes? Even more surprising may be the fact that several well-known private equity funds—including Fortress, KKR, and Blackstone—are publicly traded. Publicly traded firms are typically taxed as corporations even if they are legally structured as partnerships or, in the case of these private equity firms, as limited partnerships. However, relying on a provision in the tax code, these private equity funds were able to maintain their tax status as partnerships after their public offerings.[44] Thus, investors purchasing shares in these funds are buying investments that are subject to only one level of taxation but, like shares in a corporation, can be readily traded in a public securities market.

Ordinary Business Income (Loss) and Separately Stated Items

Although partnerships are not taxpaying entities, they are required to file information returns annually. They also distribute information to each partner detailing the amount *and* character of items of income and loss flowing through the partnership.[45] Partners must report these income and loss items on their tax returns even if they don't receive cash distributions from the partnership during the year.

When gathering this information for their partners, partnerships must determine each partner's share of **ordinary business income (loss)** and **separately stated items.** Partnership ordinary business income (loss) is all partnership income (loss) exclusive of any separately stated items of income (loss). Separately stated items share one common characteristic—they are treated differently from a partner's share of ordinary business income (loss) for tax purposes. To better understand why certain items must be separately disclosed to partners, consider how two particular separately stated items, dividend income and capital losses, might affect an individual partner's tax liability. Qualified dividend income allocated to individual partners is taxed at either a 0 percent, 15 percent, or 20 percent rate, depending on individual partners' tax brackets.[46] In a similar vein, individual partners

> **THE KEY FACTS**
>
> **Reporting the Results of Partnership Operations**
> - Partnerships file annual information returns reporting their ordinary business income (loss) and separately stated items.
> - Ordinary business income (loss) = Partnership overall income or loss exclusive of separately stated items.
> - Separately stated items change partners' tax liabilities when they are separately stated.

---

[43]§701.

[44]§7704.

[45]Other items, such as tax credits, may also flow through the partnership to partners.

[46]§1(h).

without capital gains during the year may deduct up to $3,000 in capital losses against their ordinary income, while other individual partners with capital gains may deduct more.[47] If a partnership's dividends and capital losses were simply buried in the computation of its overall income or loss for the year, the partner would be unable to apply these specific tax rules to her unique situation and determine her correct tax liability.

The tax code specifically enumerates several common separately stated items, including short-term capital gains and losses, long-term capital gains and losses, §1231 gains and losses, charitable contributions, and dividends.[48] Many more items are considered under regulations issued by the IRS.[49] Exhibit 15-6 lists several other common separately stated items.

EXHIBIT 15-6   Common Separately Stated Items

• Interest income	• Net rental real estate income
• Guaranteed payments	• Investment interest expense
• Net earnings (loss) from self-employment	• Royalties
• Tax-exempt income	• §179 deduction

Example 15-15

After constructing a building and purchasing equipment in its first year of operations ending on December 31, 2017, CCS invested $15,000 of its remaining idle cash in stocks and bonds. CCS's books reflected an overall loss for the year of $80,000. Included in the $80,000 loss were $2,100 of dividend income, $1,200 of short-term capital gains, and a $20,000 deduction for the capital interest transferred to Sarah at the end of 2017 (see Example 15-10). How much ordinary business loss and what separately stated items are allocated to the CCS members for the taxable year ended December 31, 2017?

Answer: As reflected in the table below, CCS has $63,300 of ordinary business loss. In addition, it has $2,100 of dividend income, $1,200 in short-term capital gains, and $20,000 of ordinary deduction (related to the capital interest Sarah received) that are separately stated items. To Nicole, Sarah, and Chanzz Inc., CCS would report $21,100 of ordinary business loss, $700 of dividend income, and $400 of short-term capital gain. In addition, CCS would report $20,000 of ordinary income to Sarah for the capital interest she received, and a $10,000 deduction to Nicole and Chanzz Inc. reflecting the amount of partnership capital they relinquished.

Description	CCS	Nicole $\left(\frac{1}{3}\right)$	Sarah $\left(\frac{1}{3}\right)$	Chanzz Inc. $\left(\frac{1}{3}\right)$
2017 overall net loss	$(80,000)			
Less:				
Dividends	2,100			
Short-term capital gains	1,200			
Ordinary deduction for Sarah's capital interest	(20,000)			
Ordinary business loss	(63,300)	$(21,100)	$(21,100)	$(21,100)
Separately stated Items:				
Dividends	2,100	700	700	700
Short-term capital gains	1,200	400	400	400
Ordinary income for capital interest to Sarah	20,000		20,000	
Ordinary deduction for capital interest to Sarah	(20,000)	(10,000)		(10,000)

[47]§1211.

[48]§702.

[49]Reg. §1.702-1(a).

Nicole and Sarah will treat their shares of CCS's ordinary business loss as an *ordinary* loss and include it along with their shares of dividend income and short-term capital gain in their individual tax returns for the year.[50] Chanzz Inc. will also include its share of these items in its annual tax return. But because Chanzz is a corporation, different tax rules apply to its share of dividend income and short-term capital gains. For example, Chanzz will be entitled to the dividends received deduction, while Nicole and Sarah will pay tax on their share of dividend income at individual capital gains rates.

Notice that the character of separately stated items is determined at the partnership level rather than at the partner level.[51] This treatment reflects the entity theory.

Example 15-16

What if: Assume Chanzz Inc. is an investments dealer rather than a sports franchise operator. How would Chanzz Inc. classify its share of the $1,200 gain from the securities sold by CCS during 2017?

Answer: Chanzz Inc. would classify the $1,200 as short-term capital gains. Because the securities CCS sold were capital assets to it, the gain on the sale is a capital gain even though the securities are inventory (an ordinary asset) to Chanzz Inc. That is, we determine the character of the income at the partnership level, not the partner level.

Guaranteed Payments   In addition to dividends, capital gains, and other routine separately stated items, **guaranteed payments** are also a very common separately stated item for partners who receive them. As their name suggests, guaranteed payments are fixed amounts paid to partners regardless of whether the partnership shows a profit or loss for the year.[52] We can think of them—and some partnerships treat them—as economically equivalent to cash salary payments made to partners for services provided.[53] Specifically, they are typically deducted in computing a partnership's ordinary income or loss for the year. Though included in a partnership's ordinary business income (loss) computation, guaranteed payments must, nevertheless, be separately stated to the partners who receive them. This separate reporting serves the same purpose as providing W-2 forms to employees. Because guaranteed payments are similar to salary payments, partners treat them as ordinary income.

continued from page 15-10...

Because Sarah received an additional capital interest for marketing services she provided at the end of 2017, she held a 40 percent capital and profits interest, and Nicole and Chanzz Inc. each held a 30 percent capital and profits interest at the beginning of 2018. After Sarah's initial work in formulating a marketing strategy in 2017, Nicole suggested they hire a permanent employee to oversee product marketing. However, because they were unable to find a suitable candidate, Sarah continued to shoulder the product marketing responsibilities in addition to her normal role as a managing member of CCS. To compensate Sarah for her additional workload, all members of CCS agreed to give Sarah a $10,000 guaranteed payment for her marketing efforts in 2018. Exhibit 15-7 provides CCS's income statement for 2018. ∎

---

[50]Nicole and Sarah would report their share of ordinary business loss on Schedule E, their share of dividend income on Schedule B, and their share of short-term capital gain on Schedule D of Form 1040.

[51]§702(b).

[52]§707(c).

[53]Fringe benefits that partners receive for services provided such as medical insurance and group-term life insurance are also treated as guaranteed payments. In addition to compensating partners for services provided, guaranteed payments are also made to partners for the use of capital.

EXHIBIT 15-7 **Color Comfort Sheets LLC**

Income Statement December 31, 2018	
Sales revenue	$ 40,000
Cost of goods sold	(20,000)
Employee wages	(50,000)
Depreciation expense	(18,000)
Guaranteed payments	(10,000)
Miscellaneous expenses	(2,800)
Dividend income	500
Long-term capital gains	300
Overall net loss	$(60,000)

Example 15-17

Given CCS's operating results for 2018 presented in Exhibit 15-7, how much ordinary business loss and what separately stated items will it report on its return for the year? How will it allocate these amounts to its members?

Answer: The table below displays CCS's ordinary business loss and separately stated items and the allocation of these amounts to CCS's members:

Description	CCS	Nicole 30%	Sarah 40%	Chanzz Inc. 30% × 6/12*	Greg 30% × 6/12*
Sales revenue	$40,000				
Cost of goods sold	(20,000)				
Employee wages	(50,000)				
Depreciation expense	(18,000)				
Guaranteed payment to Sarah	(10,000)				
Miscellaneous expenses	(2,800)				
Ordinary business loss	(60,800)	$(18,240)	$(24,320)	$(9,120)	$(9,120)
Separately stated to partners					
Dividends	500	150	200	75	75
Long-term capital gains	300	90	120	45	45
Guaranteed payment			10,000		

*As we noted in Example 15-11, Chanzz Inc. sold out to Greg Randall on June 30, 2018. Therefore, the items related to Chanzz Inc.'s original 30 percent interest must be allocated between Chanzz Inc. and Greg Randall.[54]

THE KEY FACTS

Guaranteed Payments and Self-Employment Income

- Guaranteed payments are separately stated items, are treated as ordinary income by partners receiving them, and are either capitalized or expensed by partnerships.

- Guaranteed payments for services are always treated as self-employment income.

- Shares of ordinary business income (loss) are always treated as self-employment income (loss) by general partners and never treated as self-employment income (loss) by limited partners.

- Shares of ordinary business income (loss) may or may not be treated by LLC members as self-employment income (loss), depending on the extent of their involvement with the LLC.

Self-Employment Tax   Individual partners, like sole proprietors, may be responsible for paying **self-employment taxes** in addition to income taxes on their share of earned income from partnerships.[55] The degree to which partners are responsible for self-employment taxes depends on their legal status as general partners, limited partners, or LLC members and their business activities. General partners report guaranteed payments for services they provide and their share of ordinary business income (loss) as self-employment income (loss) because they are actively involved in managing the partnership. Limited partners, on the other hand, are generally not allowed under state law to participate in the management of limited partnerships. Therefore, their share of ordinary business income (loss) is conceptually more like investment income than trade or business income. As a result, ordinary business income (loss) allocated to limited partners is not subject to self-employment tax. However, if limited partners receive guaranteed payments for services provided to the partnership, they treat those payments as self-employment income.

[54]We assume here that the items are allocated based on the number of months the interest was held. See the Dispositions of Partnership Interests and Partnership Distributions chapter for additional detail regarding methods to account for partners' varying interests in a partnership when a partnership interest is sold.

[55]The Individual Income Tax Computation and Tax Credits chapter and the Entities Overview chapter more fully discuss earned income and related self-employment taxes.

Because LLC members may be either managing or nonmanaging members, the approach to taxing their share of ordinary business income (loss) for self-employment tax purposes does depend to some degree on their level of involvement in the LLC.[56] Tax rules in this area were developed before LLCs became popular, however, so the IRS has not issued any authoritative rules to help LLCs decide whether to characterize their members' shares of ordinary business income (loss) as self-employment income (loss). However, a proposed regulation issued by the IRS and later withdrawn can assist partnerships in drawing the line between aggressive and conservative positions in this area.[57] It provides that LLC members who have personal liability for the debts of the LLC by reason of being an LLC member, who have authority to contract on behalf of the LLC, *or* who participate more than 500 hours in the LLC's trade or business during the taxable year should be classified as general partners when applying the self-employment tax rules.

Historically, the lack of authoritative guidance from the IRS in this area has resulted in a predictable diversity of practice. Indeed, some aggressive taxpayers and their advisers have ignored the proposed regulation entirely and claimed that managing members of LLCs or members providing significant services to their LLCs are similar to limited partners and shouldn't have to pay self-employment taxes at all. This approach has been invalidated by a string of recent court decisions.[58] These decisions follow the spirit of the proposed regulation in that they provide that LLC members with either management control or that actively participate in the trade or business of an LLC should be treated as general partners for self-employment tax purposes and be subject to self-employment tax on their share of ordinary business income (loss).[59]

Example 15-18

For *2018*, should CCS classify Sarah's $10,000 guaranteed payment as self-employment income?

Answer: Yes. The law is clear with respect to guaranteed payments to LLC members—they are always treated as self-employment income.

Using the proposed regulation, will CCS classify Sarah's $24,320 (see Example 15-17) share of ordinary business loss for *2018* as a self-employment loss?

Answer: Yes. Under the proposed regulations, an LLC member who has personal liability for LLC debts or the ability to contract on behalf of the LLC, or who spends more than 500 hours participating in the business of the LLC, is classified as a general partner when applying the self-employment tax rules. Given Sarah's status as a managing member of CCS, at least one but probably all three criteria for classifying her share of CCS's ordinary business loss as self-employment loss will apply. Although these rules have not been finalized and are therefore not authoritative, the IRS would likely follow them because they represent its current thinking on the matter. Applying the law this way, CCS will report a $14,320 self-employment loss ($24,320 share of ordinary business loss + $10,000 guaranteed payment) as a separately stated item to Sarah so she can properly compute her self-employment tax liability on her individual return.

Example 15-19

Using the proposed regulation, will CCS classify Nicole's $18,240 (see Example 15-17) share of ordinary business loss for *2018* as self-employment loss?

Answer: Yes. Because Nicole, like Sarah, is involved in the day-to-day management of CCS, it will classify her entire share of ordinary business loss as self-employment loss, consistent with its classification of Sarah's share of ordinary business loss, and report the amount as a separately stated item to Nicole.

(*continued on page 15-22*)

---

[56]Guaranteed payments to LLC members are clearly subject to self-employment tax because they are similar to salary payments.

[57]Proposed Reg. §1.1402(a)-2.

[58]See *Renkemeyer, Campbell & Weaver, LLP, et al. v. Commissioner,* 136 TC 137 (2011), Riether, 919 F. Supp.2d 1140 (D. N.M. 2012), and *Castigliola* T.C. Memo. 2017-62.

[59]Of course, these cases also suggest that the opposite should also be true: LLC members without management control or that don't provide significant services should be treated as limited partners for self-employment tax purposes.

Under the proposed regulation, will CCS treat Greg's $9,120 share of ordinary business loss for *2018* as self-employment loss?

Answer: Yes. CCS will treat Greg's share of ordinary business loss as self-employment loss because he has guaranteed a portion of CCS's debt. CCS's total self-employment loss is $41,680, consisting of Sarah's $14,320 self-employment loss (an amount that includes Sarah's share of ordinary business loss offset by her guaranteed payment), Nicole's $18,240 self-employment loss, and Greg's $9,120 self-employment loss.

Limitation on Business Interest Expense   As explained in the Business Income, Deductions, and Accounting Methods chapter, the deduction for business interest expense is limited to the sum of (1) business interest income and (2) 30 percent of the adjusted taxable income of the taxpayer for the taxable year.[60] For entities taxed as partnerships, this limitation is applied at the partnership level first. Under this approach, any business interest expense of a partnership that is not disallowed due to the limitation is taken into account in determining the partnership's ordinary business income or loss for the year.

In contrast, disallowed business interest expense is allocated and separately stated to partners, reducing the basis in their partnership interests.[61] Subsequently, the disallowed business interest expense is carried forward indefinitely at the partner level until the partnership has excess business interest expense limitation to allocate to the partners. This will occur whenever the partnership's business interest expense limitation (partnership business interest income plus 30 percent of adjusted taxable income) exceeds the partnership's business interest expense in a given year. Partners may deduct their carried forward disallowed interest expense from a given partnership in any future year to the extent they are allocated excess business interest expense limitation (the adjusted taxable income equivalent is separately stated to partners[62]) from the same partnership.

The limitation on business interest expense does not apply to partnerships with average annual gross receipts for the prior three years that do not exceed $25 million. As a result, the limitation on business interest expense will only apply to a relatively small number of partnerships.

Deduction for Qualified Business Income   As we more fully discuss in the Entities Overview chapter, noncorporate owners of flow-through entities, including partnerships, may generally deduct 20 percent of the qualified business income allocated to them from the entity. Qualified business income is the net business income from a qualified trade or business conducted in the United States. In a partnership setting, qualified business income would typically not include a partnership's ordinary business income from most service-related businesses and would also not include a partnership's investment income such as capital gains, dividends, and investment interest income.[63] Further,

---

[60]§163(j).

[61]§163(j)(4).

[62]Under §163(j)(4)(A)(ii), a partner's share of adjusted taxable income is increased by their distributive share of the partnership's "excess taxable income." Per §163(j)(4)(C), excess taxable income is mathematically equivalent to the amount of a partnership's excess business interest expense limitation divided by 30 percent.

[63]§199A(d)(2) excludes income from certain specified service trade or businesses from the definition of qualified business income. Specified service trade or businesses are defined as any trade or business involving the performance of services in the fields of health, law, accounting, actuarial science, performing arts, consulting, athletics, financial services, brokerage services, or any trade or business where the principal asset of such trade or business is the reputation or skill of one or more of its employees or which involves the performance of services that consist of investing and investment management trading, or dealing in securities, partnership interests, or commodities. The definition specifically excludes architecture and engineering from the definition. The specified service trade or business requirement does not apply to taxpayers with taxable income (before the deduction) below a certain threshold and the requirement phases in over a range of taxable income above the threshold [see §199A(d)(3)].

guaranteed payments received by partners for services provided to the partnership are, by definition, not considered be qualified business income.

To facilitate the partner's calculation of the 20 percent deduction, partnerships must separately state certain items to the partners. First, the partnership must separately state the partners' share of qualified business income for each separate qualified trade or business within the partnership. Further, the partnership must also separately state for each qualified trade or business within the partnership any additional information required for the partners to calculate the limitations on the deduction applied at the partner level.[64]

Net Investment Income Tax

An individual partner's share of gross income from interest, dividends, annuities, royalties, or rents is included in the partner's net investment income when calculating the net investment income tax.[65] In addition, the partner's share of income from a trade or business that is a passive activity, income from a trade or business of trading financial instruments or commodities, and any net gain from disposing of property (other than property used in a trade or business that is not a passive activity) is also included in the partner's net investment income.[66]

Allocating Partners' Shares of Income and Loss

Partnership tax rules provide partners with tremendous flexibility in allocating overall profit and loss as well as specific items of profit and loss to partners, as long as partners agree to the allocations and they have "substantial economic effect." Partnership allocations designed to accomplish business objectives other than reducing taxes will generally have substantial economic effect.[67] If they are not defined in the partnership agreement or do not have substantial economic effect, allocations to partners must be made in accordance with the "partners' interests in the partnership."[68] According to tax regulations, the partners' interests in the partnership are a measure of the partners' economic arrangement and should be determined by considering factors such as their capital contributions, distribution rights, and interests in economic profits and losses (if different from their interests in taxable income and loss). Partnership allocations inconsistent with partners' capital interests or overall profit-and-loss-sharing ratios are called **special allocations.**

Although special allocations are made largely at the discretion of partners, certain special allocations of gains and losses from the sale of partnership property are mandatory. Specifically, when property contributed to a partnership with built-in gains (fair market value greater than tax basis) or built-in losses (tax basis greater than fair market value) is subsequently sold, the partnership must allocate, to the extent possible, the built-in gain or built-in loss (at the time of the contribution) solely to the contributing partner and then allocate any remaining gain or loss to all the partners in accordance with their

[64]Under §199A(b)(2)(B), the deduction cannot exceed the greater of 50 percent of the wages paid with respect to the qualified trade or business, or the sum of 25 percent of the wages with respect to the qualified trade or business plus 2.5 percent of the unadjusted basis, immediately after acquisition, of all qualified property in the qualified trade or business. These limitations do not apply to taxpayers with taxable income (before the deduction) below a certain threshold and the limitations phase in over a range of taxable income above the threshold [see §199A(b)(3)].

[65]§1411. The tax imposed is 3.8 percent of the lesser of (a) net investment income or (b) the excess of modified adjusted gross income over $250,000 for married-joint filers and surviving spouses, $125,000 for married separate filers, and $200,000 for other taxpayers. Modified adjusted gross income equals adjusted gross income increased by income excluded under the foreign-earned income exclusion less any disallowed deductions associated with the foreign-earned income exclusion.

[66]§1411(c)(2)(A). For purposes of computing the net investment income tax, a partner's status as either active or passive with respect to an activity is determined according to the §469 passive activity loss rules explained later in this chapter.

[67]Reg. §1.704-1 defines the requirements allocations must satisfy to have substantial economic effect.

[68]§704(b).

profit-and-loss-sharing ratios.[69] This rule prevents contributing partners from shifting their built-in gains and built-in losses to other partners.

Example 15-20

What if: Assume that at the beginning of 2018, Nicole and Sarah decide to organize CCS's marketing efforts by region. Nicole will take responsibility for marketing in the western United States, and Sarah will take responsibility for marketing in the eastern United States. All members agree that CCS's provision for allocating profits and losses in the operating agreement should be amended to provide Nicole and Sarah with better incentives. Specifically, CCS would like to allocate the first 20 percent of profits or losses from each region to Nicole and Sarah. Then, it will allocate any remaining profits or losses from each region among the members in proportion to their capital and profits interests at the end of 2018—40 percent to Sarah and 30 percent each to Nicole and Greg. Will CCS's proposed special allocation of profits and losses be accepted by the IRS?

Answer: Yes. Since CCS is a partnership for federal income tax purposes, it can make special allocations to members, and because the allocations are designed to accomplish a business objective other than tax reduction, the IRS will accept them.[70]

What if: Assume that the land Nicole contributed to CCS had a fair market value of $150,000 and tax basis of $20,000 (see original facts in Example 15-1) and was sold by CCS for $150,000 of consideration almost immediately after it was contributed. How would the resulting $130,000 gain be allocated among the members of CCS?

Answer: Nicole's built-in gain of $130,000 at the time of contribution must be allocated exclusively to her to prevent it from being shifted to other CCS members. Shifting the gain to other members could lower the overall tax liability of the CCS members if Sarah and Greg's marginal tax rates are lower than Nicole's marginal tax rate or it could increase it if their marginal rates are higher.

What if: Suppose CCS held the land Nicole contributed for one year and then sold it on March 31, 2018, for $180,000 instead of $150,000. How should the resulting $160,000 gain be allocated to Nicole, Sarah, and Chanzz Inc.?

Answer: The allocations are $139,000 to Nicole, $12,000 to Sarah, and $9,000 to Chanzz Inc., as reflected in the table below:

Description	CCS	Nicole 30%	Sarah 40%	Chanzz Inc. 30%
Total gain from sale of land	$160,000			
Less:				
Special allocation to Nicole of built-in gain	(130,000)	$ 130,000		
Post-contribution appreciation in land	30,000	9,000	$ 12,000	$ 9,000
Total gain allocations		**$139,000**	**$12,000**	**$9,000**

Partnership Compliance Issues

Although partnerships don't pay taxes, they are required to file **Form 1065,** U.S. Return of Partnership Income (shown in Exhibit 15-8), with the IRS by the 15th day of the 3rd month after their year-end (March 15th for a calendar year-end partnership). Partnerships may receive an automatic six-month extension to file by filing **Form 7004** with the IRS before the original due date of the return.[71] Page 1 of Form 1065

---

[69]§704(c). In addition to requiring built-in gains and losses to be specially allocated to contributing partners, §704(c) also requires depreciation to be specially allocated to noncontributing partners. Tax regulations permit partners to choose among several methods for making these required special allocations. Further discussion of these methods is beyond the scope of this book.

[70]Reg. §1.704-1(b)(5), Example 10, suggests that this type of special allocation would not violate the substantial economic effect rules.

[71]Under §6698, late filing penalties apply if the partnership fails to file by the normal or extended due date for the return. The penalty is $195 times the number of partners in the partnership times the number of months (or fraction thereof) the return is late up to a maximum of 12 months.

details the calculation of the partnership's ordinary business income (loss) for the year, and page 3, **Schedule K,** lists the partnership's ordinary business income (loss) and separately stated items. In addition to preparing Form 1065, the partnership is also responsible for preparing a Schedule K-1 for each partner detailing her individual share of the partnership's ordinary business income (loss) and separately stated items for the year. Once prepared, Schedule K-1s are included with Form 1065 when it is filed, and they are also separately provided to all partners (each partner receives a

EXHIBIT 15-8 (PART I) Page 1 Form 1065

CCS's 2018 Ordinary Business Loss (on 2017 forms)

Form **1065**

Department of the Treasury
Internal Revenue Service

U.S. Return of Partnership Income

OMB No. 1545-0123

For calendar year 2017, or tax year beginning _____, 2017, ending _____, 20 _____.

▶ Go to *www.irs.gov/Form1065* for instructions and the latest information.

2017

A Principal business activity		Name of partnership	D Employer identification number
Manufacturing	Type or Print	Color Comfort Sheets	00072359
B Principal product or service		Number, street, and room or suite no. If a P.O. box, see the instructions.	E Date business started
Textile Products		375 East 450 South	April 1, 2017
C Business code number		City or town, state or province, country, and ZIP or foreign postal code	F Total assets (see the instructions)
31400		Salt Lake City, UT 84608	$ 370,000

G Check applicable boxes: **(1)** ☐ Initial return **(2)** ☐ Final return **(3)** ☐ Name change **(4)** ☐ Address change **(5)** ☐ Amended return
    (6) ☐ Technical termination - also check (1) or (2)

H Check accounting method: **(1)** ☑ Cash **(2)** ☐ Accrual **(3)** ☐ Other (specify) ▶ _____

I Number of Schedules K-1. Attach one for each person who was a partner at any time during the tax year ▶4

J Check if Schedules C and M-3 are attached . . . . ☐

Caution. *Include **only** trade or business income and expenses on lines 1a through 22 below. See the instructions for more information.*

		Income				
1a	Gross receipts or sales	1a	40,000			
b	Returns and allowances	1b				
c	Balance. Subtract line 1b from line 1a			1c	40,000	
2	Cost of goods sold (attach Form 1125-A)			2	20,000	
3	Gross profit. Subtract line 2 from line 1c			3	20,000	
4	Ordinary income (loss) from other partnerships, estates, and trusts (attach statement) . .			4		
5	Net farm profit (loss) (attach Schedule F (Form 1040))			5		
6	Net gain (loss) from Form 4797, Part II, line 17 (attach Form 4797)			6		
7	Other income (loss) (attach statement)			7		
8	**Total income (loss).** Combine lines 3 through 7			8	20,000	

		Deductions (see the instructions for limitations)				
9	Salaries and wages (other than to partners) (less employment credits)			9	50,000	
10	Guaranteed payments to partners			10	10,000	
11	Repairs and maintenance			11		
12	Bad debts			12		
13	Rent			13		
14	Taxes and licenses			14		
15	Interest			15		
16a	Depreciation (if required, attach Form 4562)	16a	18,000			
b	Less depreciation reported on Form 1125-A and elsewhere on return	16b		16c	18,000	
17	Depletion **(Do not deduct oil and gas depletion.)**			17		
18	Retirement plans, etc.			18		
19	Employee benefit programs			19		
20	Other deductions (attach statement)			20	2,800	
21	**Total deductions.** Add the amounts shown in the far right column for lines 9 through 20 .			21	80,000	
22	**Ordinary business income (loss).** Subtract line 21 from line 8			22	(60,800)	

Sign Here

Under penalties of perjury, I declare that I have examined this return, including accompanying schedules and statements, and to the best of my knowledge and belief, it is true, correct, and complete. Declaration of preparer (other than partner or limited liability company member) is based on all information of which preparer has any knowledge.

▶ _____   ▶ _____

Signature of partner or limited liability company member   Date

May the IRS discuss this return with the preparer shown below (see instructions)? ☐ Yes ☐ No

Paid Preparer Use Only

Print/Type preparer's name	Preparer's signature	Date	Check ☐ if self-employed	PTIN
Firm's name ▶			Firm's EIN ▶	
Firm's address ▶			Phone no.	

For Paperwork Reduction Act Notice, see separate instructions. Cat. No. 11390Z Form **1065** (2017)

Source: Form 1065 Department of the Treasury, Internal Revenue Service

EXHIBIT 15-8 (PART II)   Page 3 Form 1065
CCS's 2018 Schedule K (on 2017 forms

Form 1065 (2017)   Page **4**

Schedule K		Partners' Distributive Share Items				Total amount
Income (Loss)	**1**	Ordinary business income (loss) (page 1, line 22)			**1**	60,800
	2	Net rental real estate income (loss) (attach Form 8825)			**2**	
	3a	Other gross rental income (loss)	**3a**			
	b	Expenses from other rental activities (attach statement)	**3b**			
	c	Other net rental income (loss). Subtract line 3b from line 3a			**3c**	
	4	Guaranteed payments			**4**	10,000
	5	Interest income			**5**	
	6	Dividends: **a** Ordinary dividends			**6a**	500
		b Qualified dividends	**6b**	500		
	7	Royalties			**7**	
	8	Net short-term capital gain (loss) (attach Schedule D (Form 1065))			**8**	
	9a	Net long-term capital gain (loss) (attach Schedule D (Form 1065))			**9a**	300
	b	Collectibles (28%) gain (loss)	**9b**			
	c	Unrecaptured section 1250 gain (attach statement) . .	**9c**			
	10	Net section 1231 gain (loss) (attach Form 4797)			**10**	
	11	Other income (loss) (see instructions) Type ▶			**11**	
Deductions	**12**	Section 179 deduction (attach Form 4562)			**12**	
	13a	Contributions			**13a**	
	b	Investment interest expense			**13b**	
	c	Section 59(e)(2) expenditures: **(1)** Type ▶ _____ **(2)** Amount ▶			**13c(2)**	
	d	Other deductions (see instructions) Type ▶			**13d**	
Self-Employ-ment	**14a**	Net earnings (loss) from self-employment			**14a**	41,680
	b	Gross farming or fishing income			**14b**	
	c	Gross nonfarm income			**14c**	20,000
Credits	**15a**	Low-income housing credit (section 42(j)(5))			**15a**	
	b	Low-income housing credit (other)			**15b**	
	c	Qualified rehabilitation expenditures (rental real estate) (attach Form 3468, if applicable)			**15c**	
	d	Other rental real estate credits (see instructions) Type ▶ _____			**15d**	
	e	Other rental credits (see instructions) Type ▶ _____			**15e**	
	f	Other credits (see instructions) Type ▶ _____			**15f**	
Foreign Transactions	**16a**	Name of country or U.S. possession ▶ _____				
	b	Gross income from all sources			**16b**	
	c	Gross income sourced at partner level			**16c**	
		Foreign gross income sourced at partnership level				
	d	Passive category ▶ _____ **e** General category ▶ _____ **f** Other ▶			**16f**	
		Deductions allocated and apportioned at partner level				
	g	Interest expense ▶ _____ **h** Other . . . . ▶			**16h**	
		Deductions allocated and apportioned at partnership level to foreign source income				
	i	Passive category ▶ _____ **j** General category ▶ _____ **k** Other ▶			**16k**	
	l	Total foreign taxes (check one): ▶ Paid ☐ Accrued ☐			**16l**	
	m	Reduction in taxes available for credit (attach statement)			**16m**	
	n	Other foreign tax information (attach statement)				
Alternative Minimum Tax (AMT) Items	**17a**	Post-1986 depreciation adjustment			**17a**	
	b	Adjusted gain or loss			**17b**	
	c	Depletion (other than oil and gas)			**17c**	
	d	Oil, gas, and geothermal properties—gross income			**17d**	
	e	Oil, gas, and geothermal properties—deductions			**17e**	
	f	Other AMT items (attach statement)			**17f**	
Other Information	**18a**	Tax-exempt interest income			**18a**	
	b	Other tax-exempt income			**18b**	
	c	Nondeductible expenses			**18c**	
	19a	Distributions of cash and marketable securities			**19a**	
	b	Distributions of other property			**19b**	
	20a	Investment income			**20a**	500
	b	Investment expenses			**20b**	
	c	Other items and amounts (attach statement)				

Form **1065** (2017)

Source: Form 1065 Department of the Treasury, Internal Revenue Service

EXHIBIT 15-8 (PART III)   2018 Schedule K-1 for Sarah Walker (on 2017 forms)
CCS Operates as an LLC

651117

☒ Final K-1   ☐ Amended K-1   OMB No. 1545-0123

Schedule K-1
(Form 1065)

20**17**

Department of the Treasury
Internal Revenue Service

For calendar year 2017, or tax year

beginning ___ / ___ / 2017   ending ___ / ___ / ___

Partner's Share of Income, Deductions,
Credits, etc.   ► See back of form and separate instructions.

Part I	Information About the Partnership

A   Partnership's employer identification number
00072359

B   Partnership's name, address, city, state, and ZIP code

Color Comfort Sheets
375 East 450 South
Salt Lake City UT 84608

C   IRS Center where partnership filed return

D   ☐ Check if this is a publicly traded partnership (PTP)

Part II	Information About the Partner

E   Partner's identifying number
429-88-3426

F   Partner's name, address, city, state, and ZIP code

Sarah Walker
549 Laurel Lane
Holladay, UT 84609

G   ☒ General partner or LLC member-manager   ☐ Limited partner or other LLC member

H   ☒ Domestic partner   ☐ Foreign partner

I1   What type of entity is this partner?   Individual

I2   If this partner is a retirement plan (IRA/SEP/Keogh/etc.), check here   ☐

J   Partner's share of profit, loss, and capital (see instructions):

	Beginning	Ending
Profit	40 %	40 %
Loss	40 %	40 %
Capital	40 %	40 %

K   Partner's share of liabilities at year end:

Nonrecourse	$	12,000
Qualified nonrecourse financing	$	8,000
Recourse	$	24,000

L   Partner's capital account analysis:

Beginning capital account	$	100,000
Capital contributed during the year	$	20,000
Current year increase (decrease)	$	(24,000)
Withdrawals & distributions	$ (	)
Ending capital account	$	96,000

☒ Tax basis   ☐ GAAP   ☐ Section 704(b) book
☐ Other (explain)

M   Did the partner contribute property with a built-in gain or loss?
☐ Yes   ☐ No
If "Yes," attach statement (see instructions)

Part III	Partner's Share of Current Year Income, Deductions, Credits, and Other Items

#	Item	#	Item
1	Ordinary business income (loss) (24,320)	15	Credits
2	Net rental real estate income (loss)		
3	Other net rental income (loss)	16	Foreign transactions
4	Guaranteed payments 10,000		
5	Interest income		
6a	Ordinary dividends 200		
6b	Qualified dividends 200		
7	Royalties		
8	Net short-term capital gain (loss)		
9a	Net long-term capital gain (loss) 120	17	Alternative minimum tax (AMT) items
9b	Collectibles (28%) gain (loss)		
9c	Unrecaptured section 1250 gain		
10	Net section 1231 gain (loss)	18	Tax-exempt income and nondeductible expenses
11	Other income (loss)		
		19	Distributions
12	Section 179 deduction		
13	Other deductions		
		20	Other information
		A	200
14	Self-employment earnings (loss)		
A	(14,320)		
C	8,000		

*See attached statement for additional information.

For IRS Use Only

For Paperwork Reduction Act Notice, see Instructions for Form 1065.   www.irs.gov/Form1065   Cat. No. 11394R   **Schedule K-1 (Form 1065) 2017**

Source: Form 1065 Department of the Treasury, Internal Revenue Service

Schedule K-1 with her income and loss allocations). Exhibit 15-8, parts I through III, displays CCS's return, showing the operating results we summarized in Example 15-17 and Sarah's actual Schedule K-1, reflecting the facts and conclusions in Examples 15-17 and 15-18.[72]

LO 15-5   ## PARTNER'S ADJUSTED TAX BASIS IN PARTNERSHIP INTEREST

Earlier in this chapter, we discussed how partners measure their initial tax basis in their partnership interests when they contribute property or services to partnerships in exchange for their partnership interests, or when they purchase partnership interests from an existing partner. Unlike the basis in a stock or other similar investment, which is usually fixed, the basis in a partnership interest is dynamic and must be *adjusted* as the partnership generates income and losses, changes its debt levels, and makes distributions to partners. These annual adjustments to a partner's tax basis are required to ensure partners don't double-count taxable income/gains and deductible expenses/ losses, either when they sell their partnership interests or when they receive partnership distributions. They also ensure tax-exempt income and nondeductible expenses are not ultimately taxed or deducted.

Partners make the following adjustments to the basis in their partnership interests, annually:

- Increase for actual and deemed cash contributions to the partnership during the year.[73]
- Increase for partner's share of ordinary business income and separately stated income/gain items.
- Increase for partner's share of tax-exempt income.
- Decrease for actual and deemed[74] cash distributions[75] during the year.
- Decrease for partner's share of nondeductible expenses (fines, penalties, etc.).
- Decrease for partner's share of disallowed business interest expense.[76]
- Decrease for partner's share of ordinary business loss and separately stated expense/ loss items.

Partners first adjust their bases for items that increase basis, then for distributions, then by nondeductible expenses, and then by deductible expenses and losses to the extent any basis remains after prior adjustments.[77] Basis adjustments that decrease basis may never reduce a partner's tax basis below zero.[78]

Example 15-21

Given the events that affected CCS and its members during *2017*, what tax basis did Nicole, Sarah, and Chanzz Inc. have in their ownership interests at the end of 2017?

[72]We use 2017 forms because 2018 forms were unavailable at the time the book was published.

[73]Recall that partners are deemed to have made a cash contribution to the partnership when they are allocated an additional share of partnership debt.

[74]Recall that partners are deemed to have received a cash distribution from the partnership when they are relieved of partnership debt.

[75]Property distributions to partners are also treated as basis reductions. We discuss property distributions at length in the Dispositions of Partnership Interests and Partnership Distributions chapter.

[76]§163(j)(4)(B)(iii).

[77]Reg. §1.704-1(d)(2).

[78]§705(a)(2).

Answer: Their bases in CCS were $4,000, $152,000, and $114,000, respectively. Their individual tax basis calculations at the end of 2017 are illustrated in the table below:

Description	Nicole	Sarah	Chanzz Inc.	Explanation
(1) Initial tax basis (including debt)	$36,666	$146,666	$146,666	Example 15-4
(2) Dividends	700	700	700	Example 15-15
(3) Short-term capital gains	400	400	400	Example 15-15
(4) Debt reallocation (deemed cash contribution/distribution)	(2,666)	5,334	(2,666)	Example 15-10
(5) Sarah's capital interest	(10,000)	20,000	(10,000)	Examples 15-10, 15-15
(6) CCS's ordinary business loss	(21,100)	(21,100)	(21,100)	Example 15-15
Tax basis on 12/31/17	**$ 4,000**	**$152,000**	**$114,000**	Sum of (1) through (6)

What if: Suppose Sarah sold her LLC interest but forgot to include her share of short-term capital gains when computing her basis to determine her gain on the sale. What are the tax consequences of Sarah's mistake?

Answer: Sarah would be double-taxed on the amount of the short-term capital gain. She was initially taxed on her share of the short-term capital gain allocation, and she will be taxed a second time when she recognizes $400 more gain on the sale than she would have had she included her share of the gain in her basis.

What if: Assume Sarah was allocated $700 of tax-exempt municipal bond income instead of dividend income. What will happen if she neglects to increase her basis in CCS by the $700 tax-exempt income?

Answer: If Sarah were to sell her interest in CCS for a price reflecting the tax-exempt income received, she would, in effect, be converting tax-exempt income into taxable income.

> **THE KEY FACTS**
>
> **Partner's Basis Adjustments**
>
> - A partner will increase the tax basis in her partnership interest for:
>   - Contributions.
>   - Share of ordinary business income.
>   - Separately stated income/gain items.
>   - Tax-exempt income.
> - A partner will decrease the tax basis in her partnership interest for:
>   - Cash distributions.
>   - Share of nondeductible expenses.
>   - Share of ordinary business loss.
>   - Separately stated expense/loss items.
> - A partner's tax basis may not be negative.

Example 15-22

In addition to the other events of *2018*, CCS increased its debt from $100,000 to $130,000 in the second half of the year. The $30,000 increase was attributable to accounts payable owed to suppliers. Unlike the case of the $60,000 bank loan, the members did not guarantee any of the accounts payable. Therefore, the accounts payable are considered nonrecourse debt because CCS is an LLC. Given this information, what are Nicole's, Sarah's, and Greg's tax bases in CCS at the end of *2018*?

Answer: Their bases are $0, $140,000, and $124,000, respectively. Nicole, Sarah, and Greg would determine their tax basis in CCS at the end of *2018* as illustrated in the table below:

Description	Nicole 30%	Sarah[79] 40%	Greg 30%	Explanation
(1) Tax basis on 1/1/18	$ 4,000	$152,000		Example 15-21
(1) Greg's purchase of Chanzz Inc.'s interest			$124,000	Example 15-11
(2) Dividends	150	200	75	Example 15-17
(3) Long-term capital gains	90	120	45	Example 15-17
(4) Increase in nonrecourse debt from accounts payable (deemed cash contribution)	9,000	12,000	9,000	$30,000 × member's profit-sharing ratio
(5) CCS's ordinary business loss	(18,240)	(24,320)	(9,120)	Example 15-17
Preliminary tax basis	(5,000)	140,000	124,000	Sum of (1) through (5)
Tax basis on 12/31/18	**$ 0***	**$140,000**	**$124,000**	*Nicole's basis can't go below zero.

---

[79]Recall that Sarah received a $10,000 cash guaranteed payment for services she performed in 2018. Cash guaranteed payments generally don't have a direct impact on the recipient partner's tax basis because they are similar to salary payments.

Cash Distributions in Operating Partnerships

Even after a partnership has been formed, partners are likely to continue to receive actual and deemed cash distributions. For example, excess cash may be distributed to partners to provide them with cash flow to pay their taxes or simply for consumption, and deemed cash distributions occur as partnerships pay down their debts. The principles underlying the calculation of a partner's tax basis in her partnership interest highlight the fact that partners are taxed on income as the partnership earns it instead of when it distributes it. If cash is distributed when partners have a positive tax basis in their partnership interests, the distribution effectively represents a distribution of profits that have been previously taxed, a return of capital previously contributed by the partner to the partnership, a distribution of cash the partnership has borrowed, or some combination of the three. Thus, as long as a cash distribution does not exceed a partner's outside basis basis before the distribution, it reduces the partner's tax basis but is not taxed. However, as we highlighted in our discussion of property contributions earlier in this chapter, cash distributions (deemed or actual) in excess of a partner's basis are taxable gains and are generally treated as capital gains.[80]

Example 15-23

What if: In Example 15-22, we determined that Sarah's basis in her partnership interest was $140,000. Assume that in addition to the facts provided in that example, Sarah received a $10,000 distribution in *2018*. What will her basis in CCS or her outside basis be at the end of the year?

Answer: Sarah's tax basis will be $130,000. After making only her positive adjustments for the year (positive adjustments come before negative adjustments such as distributions), she has a basis of $164,320, which is greater than the $10,000 distribution. Thus, the distribution is not taxable because it does not exceed her basis. Sarah will also reduce her basis by the $10,000 distribution in addition to the $24,320 reduction for her share of the ordinary business loss, leaving her with an ending basis of $130,000 ($164,320 − $10,000 − $24,320).

What problem will be created if Sarah does not reduce her basis by the $10,000 distribution?

Answer: After she receives the $10,000 distribution, the value of Sarah's interest will decrease by $10,000. If she doesn't reduce her tax basis by the distribution, selling her interest will produce a $10,000 artificial tax loss.

LO 15-6   ## LOSS LIMITATIONS

While partners generally prefer not to invest in partnerships with operating losses, these losses generate current tax benefits when partners can deduct them against other sources of taxable income. Unlike capital losses, which are of limited usefulness if taxpayers don't also have capital gains, ordinary losses from partnerships are deductible against any type of taxable income. However, they are deductible on the partner's tax return only when they clear three separate hurdles: (1) tax-basis, (2) at-risk, (3) passive activity, and (4) excess business loss limitations. We discuss each of these hurdles below.

Tax-Basis Limitation

A partner's basis limits the amount of partnership losses the partner can use to offset other sources of income. In theory, a partner's basis represents the amount a partner has invested in a partnership (or may have to invest to satisfy her debt obligations). As a result, partners may not utilize partnership losses in excess of their investment or outside basis in their partnership interests. Any losses allocated in excess of their basis must be suspended and carried forward indefinitely until they have sufficient basis to utilize the losses.[81] Any suspended losses remaining when partners sell or otherwise dispose of their

---

[80]§731.

[81]§704(d).

interests are lost forever. Among other things, partners may create additional tax basis in the future by making capital contributions, by guaranteeing more partnership debt, and by helping their partnership to become profitable.

Example 15-24

In Example 15-22 we discovered Nicole was allocated $5,000 of ordinary loss in excess of her tax basis for 2018, leaving her with a basis of $0 at the end of 2018. What does Nicole do with this loss?

Answer: Nicole will carry forward all $5,000 of ordinary loss in excess of her tax basis indefinitely until her tax basis in CCS becomes positive. To the extent her tax basis increases in the future, the tax-basis limitation will no longer apply to her ordinary loss. Even then, however, the at-risk and/or passive activity loss hurdles may ultimately apply to constrain her ability to deduct the loss on her future tax returns.

What if: Assuming Nicole is allocated $4,000 of income from CCS in 2019, how much of her $5,000 suspended loss will clear the tax basis hurdle in *2019*?

Answer: Nicole's basis will initially increase by $4,000. Then she can apply $4,000 of her suspended loss against this basis increase, leaving her tax basis at $0 and holding a remaining suspended loss of $1,000. The $4,000 loss clearing the tax-basis hurdle must still clear the at-risk and passive activity loss hurdles before Nicole can deduct it on her return.

At-Risk Limitation

The at-risk hurdle or limitation is more restrictive than the tax-basis limitation, because it excludes a type of debt normally included in a partner's tax basis. We have already highlighted the distinction between recourse and nonrecourse debt and noted that partners allocated recourse debt have economic risk of loss, while partners allocated nonrecourse debt have no risk of loss. Instead, the risk of loss on nonrecourse debt is borne by lenders. The **at-risk rules** in §465 were adopted to limit the ability of partners to use nonrecourse debt as a means of creating tax basis to use losses from tax shelter partnerships expressly designed to generate losses for the partners. The at-risk rules limit partners' losses to their amount "at risk" in the partnership—their **at-risk amount.** Generally, a partner's at-risk amount is the same as her tax basis except that, with one exception, the partner's share of certain nonrecourse debts is not included in the at-risk amount. Specifically, the only nonrecourse debts considered to be at risk are nonrecourse real estate mortgages from commercial lenders that are unrelated to borrowers. This type of debt is called **qualified nonrecourse financing.**[82] In addition to qualified nonrecourse financing, partners are considered to be at risk to the extent of cash and the tax basis of property contributed to the partnership. Further, partners are at risk for any partnership recourse debt allocated to them.

Partners apply the at-risk limitation after the tax-basis limitation. Any partnership losses that would otherwise have been allowed under the tax-basis limitation are further limited to the extent they exceed a partner's at-risk amount. Losses limited under the at-risk rules are carried forward indefinitely until the partner generates additional at-risk amounts to utilize the losses, or until they are applied to reduce any gain from selling the partnership interest.

THE KEY FACTS

Loss Limitations

- Partnership losses in excess of a partner's tax basis are suspended and carried forward until additional basis is created.
- Remaining partnership losses are further suspended by the at-risk rules to the extent a partner is allocated nonrecourse debt not secured by real property.
- If a partner is not a material participant or the partnership is involved in rental activities, losses remaining after application of the tax-basis and at-risk limitations may be used only against other passive income or when the partnership interest is sold.
- Losses remaining after applying the tax basis, at-risk, and passive active loss limitations are only deductible to the extent they do not add to or create an excess business loss at the partner level.

Example 15-25

In Example 15-22, we discovered Nicole was allocated an ordinary business loss of $18,240. There we also learned that of this loss, $13,240 cleared the tax basis hurdle and $5,000 did not. How much of the $13,240 ordinary business loss that clears the tax basis hurdle will clear the at-risk hurdle?

(continued on page 15-32)

[82]§465(b)(6).

Answer: $4,240. The table below summarizes and compares Nicole's calculations to determine her tax basis and at-risk limitations for *2018*:

Example	Description	Tax Basis	At-Risk Amount	Explanation
20-22	(1) Nicole's tax basis on 1/1/18	$ 4,000	$ 4,000	Nicole's tax basis and at-risk amount are the same because she was only allocated recourse debt and qualified nonrecourse financing.
20-22	(2) Dividends	150	150	
20-22	(3) Long-term capital gains	90	90	
20-22	(4) Nonrecourse accounts payable	9,000	0	
	(5) Tax basis and at-risk amount before ordinary business loss	13,240	4,240	Sum of (1) through (4)
20-22	(6) Ordinary business loss	(18,240)		
	(7) Loss clearing the tax-basis hurdle	(13,240)		Loss limited to (5)
	Loss suspended by tax-basis hurdle	(5,000)		(6) – (7)
	(8) Loss clearing tax-basis hurdle		(13,240)	(7)
	(9) Loss clearing at-risk hurdle		**(4,240)**	Loss limited to (5)
	Loss suspended by at-risk hurdle		$(9,000)	(8) – (9)

Although Nicole's $9,000 share of the nonrecourse accounts payable added in *2018* and her investment income of $240 allow her to create enough tax basis in *2018* to get $13,240 of her $18,240 ordinary business loss past the tax-basis limitation, she is not at risk with respect to her $9,000 share of accounts payable because LLC's accounts payable are general nonrecourse debt. Therefore, $9,000 of the $13,240 ordinary business loss clearing the tax-basis hurdle is suspended under the at-risk limitation. As a result, Nicole has two separate losses to carry forward: a $5,000 ordinary loss limited by her tax basis and a $9,000 ordinary loss limited by the at-risk rules, leaving $4,240 of ordinary loss that may be deducted on her *2018* return.

Passive Activity Loss Limitation

Prior to 1986, partners with sufficient tax basis and at-risk amounts were able to utilize ordinary losses from their partnerships to offset portfolio income (i.e., interest, dividends, and capital gains), salary income, and self-employment income from partnerships and other trades or businesses. During this time, a partnership tax shelter industry thrived by marketing to wealthy investors partnership interests designed primarily to generate ordinary losses they could use to shield other income from tax. To combat this practice, Congress introduced the **passive activity loss (PAL) rules.**[83] These rules were enacted as a backstop to the at-risk rules and are applied after the tax-basis and at-risk limitations. Thus, depending on their situation, partners may have to overcome *three separate hurdles* before finally reporting partnership ordinary losses on their returns. In a nutshell, the passive activity loss rules limit the ability of partners in rental real estate partnerships and other partnerships they don't actively manage (passive activities) from using their ordinary losses from these activities (remaining after the application of the tax-basis and at-risk limitations) to reduce other sources of taxable income.

[83]§469. The passive activity loss rules apply primarily to individuals but also to estates, trusts, closely held C corporations, and personal service corporations.

Passive Activity Defined   The passive activity rules define a passive activity as "any activity which involves the conduct of a trade or business,[84] and in which the taxpayer does not materially participate." According to the Code and Treasury regulations, participants in rental activities, including rental real estate,[85] and limited partners without management rights are automatically deemed to be passive participants. In addition, participants in all other activities are passive unless their involvement in an activity is "regular, continuous, and substantial." Clearly, these terms are quite subjective and difficult to apply. Fortunately, regulations provide more certainty in this area by enumerating seven separate tests for material participation.[86] An individual, other than a limited partner, can be classified as a material participant in activities, other than rental activities, by meeting any *one* of the seven tests in Exhibit 15-9.

EXHIBIT 15-9   Tests for Material Participation

1. The individual participates in the activity more than 500 hours during the year.
2. The individual's activity constitutes substantially all the participation in such activity by individuals.
3. The individual participates more than 100 hours during the year and the individual's participation is not less than any other individual's participation in the activity.
4. The activity qualifies as a "significant participation activity" (individual participates for more than 100 hours during the year) and the aggregate of all other "significant participation activities" is greater than 500 hours for the year.
5. The individual materially participated in the activity for any 5 of the preceding 10 taxable years.
6. The activity involves personal services in health, law, accounting, architecture, and so on, and the individual materially participated for any three preceding years.
7. Taking into account all the facts and circumstances, the individual participates on a regular, continuous, and substantial basis during the year.

TAXES IN THE REAL WORLD   Donald Trump's Tax Losses

During his run for the presidency in the fall of 2016, the first page of Donald Trump's New York State resident tax return for 1995 was mailed anonymously to the *New York Times*. When the *Times* subsequently published the first page of President Trump's New York State return, it showed that he reported a loss for the year of nearly $16 million from "rental real estate, royalties, partnerships, S corporations, trusts, etc." Given President Trump's status as a real estate developer and owner, it is likely that a significant portion of this loss originated from rental real estate activities held in partnership form. These partnerships frequently generate losses because they are able to deduct depreciation, interest, and other operating costs in determining their taxable income.

President Trump's return also showed that he used the $16 million loss to offset business income of $3.4 million, $6,000 in wages, and $7.4 million in interest he reported earning the same year. For many taxpayers, losses from rental real estate are presumed to be passive losses and therefore may not be used to offset active and portfolio income. So, how was Donald Trump able to use the portion of his $16 million loss attributable to rental real estate to legally shelter his other sources of income? President Trump was likely able to take advantage of the "real estate professional" exception found in §469(c)(6) of the Code. This exception permits individuals that are heavily involved in real property trades or businesses to overcome the presumption that their losses from rental real estate are passive and then go on to establish that their losses are active under one of the material participation tests found in the tax regulations.

---

[84]The term *trade or business* is also deemed to include property held for the production of income, such as rental property.

[85]§469(b)(7) provides an important exception to the general rule that all real estate activities are passive. To overcome this presumption, taxpayers must spend more than half their time working in trades or businesses materially participating in real estate activities and more than 750 hours materially participating in real estate activities during the year. This exception benefits partners that spend a substantial amount of time in partnership activities like real estate development and construction. Moreover, §469(i) permits individual taxpayers to treat up to $25,000 of losses from rental real estate as active losses each year.

[86]26 CFR 1.469-5T.

Income and Loss Baskets Under the passive activity loss rules, each item of a partner's income or loss from all sources for the year is placed in one of three categories or "baskets." Losses from the *passive basket* are not allowed to offset income from other baskets. The three baskets are (see Exhibit 15-10):

1. *Passive activity income or loss*—income or loss from an activity, including partnerships, in which the taxpayer is not a material participant.
2. *Portfolio income*—income from investments, including capital gains and losses, dividends, interest, annuities, and royalties.
3. *Active business income*—income from sources, including partnerships, in which the taxpayer is a material participant. For individuals, this includes salary and self-employment income.

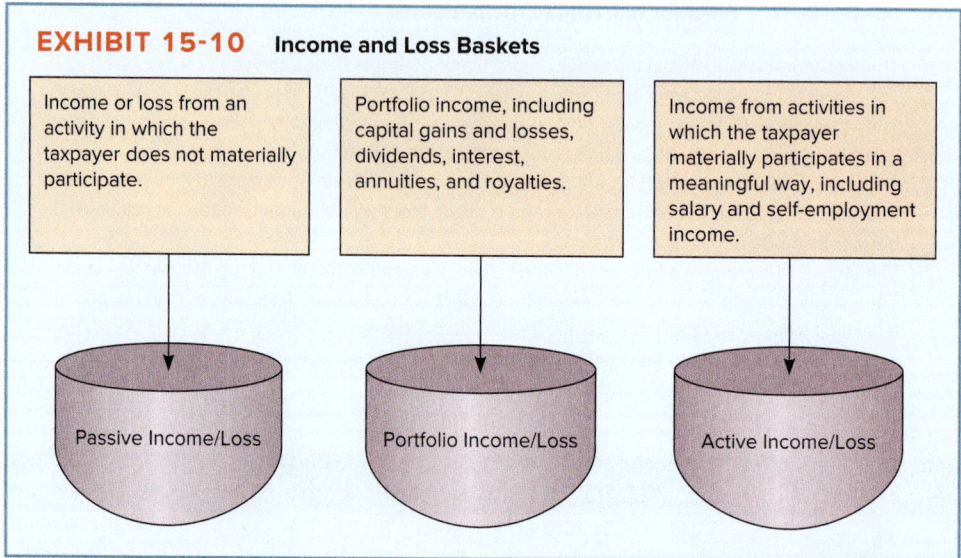

EXHIBIT 15-10 Income and Loss Baskets

Income or loss from an activity in which the taxpayer does not materially participate.

Portfolio income, including capital gains and losses, dividends, interest, annuities, and royalties.

Income from activities in which the taxpayer materially participates in a meaningful way, including salary and self-employment income.

Passive Income/Loss

Portfolio Income/Loss

Active Income/Loss

The impact of segregating a partner's income in these baskets is to limit her ability to apply passive activity losses against income in the other two baskets. In effect, passive activity losses are suspended and remain in the passive income or loss basket until the taxpayer generates current-year passive income, either from the passive activity producing the loss or from some other passive activity, or until the taxpayer sells the activity that generated the passive loss.[87] On the sale, in addition to reporting gain or loss from the sale of the property, the taxpayer will be allowed to deduct suspended passive losses as ordinary losses.

ETHICS

Several years ago, Lou, together with his friend Carlo, opened an Italian restaurant in their neighborhood. The venture was formed as an LLC, with Lou receiving a 75 percent ownership interest and Carlo receiving the remaining 25 percent ownership interest. While Lou was primarily responsible for operating the restaurant, Carlo came in only on weekends because he held a full-time job elsewhere. To document the time he spent in the restaurant, Carlo recorded the number of hours he had worked in a logbook at the end of every shift. This year, because of a downturn in the local economy, the restaurant showed a loss for the first time. To be able to deduct his share of this loss when he files his tax return, Carlo would like to establish that he worked more than 500 hours during the year and is therefore a material participant in the restaurant. His logbook shows that he worked for 502 hours during the year; however, he rounded up to the nearest hour at the end of every shift to simplify his record keeping. For example, if he worked 4 hours and 25 minutes during a shift, he wrote 5 hours in the logbook. Should Carlo claim that he is a material participant on the basis of the hours recorded in his logbook and deduct his share of the loss? What would you do?

[87]Under §469(k), this rule is even more restrictive for publicly traded partnerships. Passive activity losses from these partnerships may only be utilized to offset future passive income from the same partnership generating the passive activity loss.

Example 15-26

As indicated in Example 15-22, Greg was allocated a $9,120 ordinary loss for *2018* and had a $124,000 tax basis at year-end *after* adjusting his tax basis in his CCS interest for the loss. Given that Greg was allocated $9,000 of nonrecourse debt from accounts payable during *2018*, what is Greg's at-risk amount at the end of the year?

Answer: $115,000. Greg's at-risk amount is calculated by subtracting his $9,000 share of nonrecourse debt from his $124,000 tax basis.

Given Greg's status as a silent or nonmanaging member of CCS, how much of his $9,120 ordinary loss can he deduct in *2018* if he has no other sources of passive income?

Answer: None. Because Greg's tax basis and at-risk amount are large relative to his $9,120 ordinary loss, the tax basis and at-risk hurdles don't limit his loss. However, Greg's $9,120 loss would be classified as a passive loss and suspended until Greg receives passive income from another source—hopefully CCS—or until he disposes of his interest in CCS.

What could Greg do to deduct any losses from CCS in the future?

Answer: He could satisfy one of the seven tests in Exhibit 15-9 to be classified as a material participant in CCS, thereby converting his future CCS losses from passive to active losses. Or he could become a passive participant in some other activity, producing trade or business income that could be offset by any future passive losses from CCS.

Excess Business Loss Limitation

For years beginning after 2017, noncorporate taxpayers are not allowed to deduct an "**excess business loss**" for the year including business losses from entities taxed as partnerships.[88] Rather, excess business losses are carried forward and used in subsequent years. The excess business loss limitation applies to losses that are otherwise deductible under the basis, at-risk, and passive loss rules. An excess business loss for the year is the excess of aggregate business deductions for the year over the sum of aggregate business gross income or gain of the taxpayer plus a threshold amount. The threshold amount for a tax year is $500,000 for married taxpayers filing jointly and $250,000 for other taxpayers. The amounts are indexed for inflation. In the case of partnership business losses, the provision applies at the partner level.

Example 15-27

From Example 15-25 we learned that Nicole would report $150 of dividend income and $90 of long-term capital gains from CCS on her *2018* tax return. Further, we learned that $4,240 of her $18,240 *2018* ordinary loss allocation from CCS cleared both the tax-basis and at-risk hurdles, leaving a total of $14,000 ordinary loss suspended and carried forward. How much of the $4,240 of ordinary loss can Nicole actually deduct on her tax return, given her status as a managing member of CCS?

Answer: Because Nicole is a managing member of CCS, it is likely she will satisfy at least one of the seven tests for material participation in Exhibit 15-9. As a result, she will treat the $4,240 ordinary loss clearing the tax-basis and at-risk hurdles as an active loss. Because Nicole's $4,240 active business loss is less than the $500,000 threshold amount for married taxpayers filing jointly, she does not have an excess business loss and may fully deduct this loss on her tax return.

What if: Suppose that Nicole's share of the 2018 ordinary loss from CCS remaining after applying the tax basis, and at-risk limitation had been $510,000 rather than $4,240. How much of the loss would be deductible on her return?

Answer: $500,000. Deductible net business losses are limited to $500,000 for taxpayers married filing jointly. The $10,000 excess business loss would be carried forward and used in subsequent years.

What if: Assume Nicole was not a managing member of CCS during *2018* and could not satisfy one of the seven material participation tests in Exhibit 15-9. How much of the $4,240 ordinary loss could she deduct on her tax return, assuming she has no other sources of passive income?

Answer: None. Under this assumption, the $4,240 is a passive activity loss and suspended until Nicole either receives some passive income from CCS (or some other source) or sells her interest in CCS. In the end, her entire $18,240 loss from *2018* would be suspended: $5,000 due to the tax-basis limitation, $9,000 due to the at-risk limitation, and $4,240 due to the passive activity loss limitation.

[88]§461(l).

CONCLUSION

This chapter explained the relevant tax rules pertaining to forming and operating partnerships. Specifically, we introduced important tax issues arising from partnership formations, including partner gain or loss recognition and the calculation of inside and outside basis. In addition, we explained accounting periods and methods, allocations of partners' ordinary income (loss) and separately stated items, basis adjustments, and loss limitation rules in the context of an operating partnership. Although it would seem that partnership tax law should be relatively straightforward given that partnerships don't pay taxes, by now you may have come to realize quite the opposite is true. The next chapter continues our discussion of partnership tax law with a focus on dispositions of partnership interests and partnership distributions.

Summary

LO 15-1 Determine whether a flow-through entity is taxed as a partnership or S corporation.

- Unincorporated business entities with more than one owner are taxed as partnerships.
- Shareholders of certain corporations may elect to have them treated as flow-through entities by filing an S election with the IRS.
- Though partnerships and S corporations are both flow-through entities, the tax rules that apply to them differ.
- Partnership tax rules reflect both the aggregate and entity concepts.

LO 15-2 Resolve tax issues applicable to partnership formations and other acquisitions of partnership interests, including gain recognition to partners and tax basis for partners and partnerships.

- As a general rule, partners don't recognize gain or loss when they contribute property to partnerships in exchange for a partnership interest.
- Partnership recourse debt is allocated to partners with ultimate responsibility for paying the debt, and nonrecourse debt is allocated to partners using profit-sharing ratios.
- Partners contributing property encumbered by debt may have to recognize gain, depending on the basis of the property and the amount of the debt.
- Partners contributing property to a partnership will have an initial tax basis in their partnership interest equal to the basis of contributed property less any debt relief plus their share of any partnership debt and any gain they recognize.
- Partners receiving partnership interests by contributing capital assets or §1231 assets have a holding period in their partnership interest that includes the holding period of the contributed property. If they contribute any other type of property instead, their holding period begins on the date the partnership interest is received.
- Partnerships with contributed property have a tax basis and holding period in the property equal to the contributing partner's tax basis and holding period.
- Partners who receive capital interests in exchange for services must report the liquidation value of the capital interest as ordinary income, and the partnership either deducts or capitalizes an equivalent amount depending on the nature of the services provided.
- Partners who receive profits interest in exchange for services don't report any income. However, they share in any subsequent partnership profits and losses.
- Partners who purchase partnership interests have a tax basis in their interests equal to the purchase price plus their shares of partnership debt, and their holding periods begin on the date of purchase.

LO 15-3 Determine the appropriate accounting periods and methods for partnerships.

- Partnerships, rather than individual partners, are responsible for making most tax elections.
- The Code mandates that partners include their share of income (loss) or other partnership items for "any taxable year of the partnership ending within or with the taxable year of the partner."
- Partnerships must use a tax year-end consistent with the majority interest taxable year, the taxable year of the principal partners, or the year-end providing the least aggregate deferral for the partners.

- Partnerships with average annual gross receipts over $25 million that have corporate partners may not use the cash method of accounting. Partnerships eligible to use the overall cash method of accounting must still use the accrual method to account for the purchase and sale of inventory unless they have average annual gross receipts over the prior three years of $25 million or less. Otherwise, partnerships may use either the cash or accrual method of accounting.

Calculate and characterize a partnership's ordinary business income or loss and its separately stated items, and demonstrate how to report these items to partners.

- Partnerships must file Form 1065, U.S. Return of Partnership Income, with the IRS annually and must provide each partner with a Schedule K-1 detailing the partner's share of ordinary business income (loss) and separately stated items.
- Separately stated items include short-term and long-term capital gains and losses, dividends, §1231 gains and losses, and other partnership items that may be treated differently at the partner level.
- The character of separately stated items is determined at the partnership rather than at the partner level.
- Guaranteed payments are typically fixed payments made to partners for services provided to the partnership. They are treated as ordinary income by partners who receive them and are either deducted or capitalized by the partnership depending on the nature of services provided.
- Guaranteed payments to any type of partner (or LLC member) and general partners' shares of ordinary business income (loss) are treated as self-employment income (loss).
- Limited partners' shares of ordinary business income (loss) are not treated as self-employment income (loss).
- Though the tax law is uncertain in this area, all or a portion of LLC members' shares of ordinary business income (loss) should be classified as self-employment income (loss) if members are significantly involved in managing the LLC.
- Partnerships provide a great deal of flexibility because they may specially allocate their income, gains, expenses, losses, and other partnership items, as long as the allocations have "substantial economic effect" or are consistent with partners' interests in the partnership. Special allocations of built-in gain or loss on contributed property to contributing partners are mandatory.

Explain the importance of a partner's tax basis in her partnership interest and the adjustments that affect it.

- Partners must make specified annual adjustments to the tax basis in their partnership interests to ensure that partnership taxable income/gain or deductible expense/loss items are not double taxed or deducted twice and to ensure that partnership tax-exempt income or nondeductible expense is not taxed or deducted.
- Partners increase the tax basis in their interests by their actual or deemed cash contributions, shares of ordinary business income, separately stated income/gain items, and shares of tax-exempt income.
- Partners decrease the tax basis in their interests by their actual or deemed cash distributions, shares of ordinary business loss, separately stated expense/loss items, and shares of nondeductible expenses.
- A partner's tax basis in their partnership interest may never be reduced below zero.
- Cash distributions that are less than a partner's tax basis in their partnership interest immediately before the distribution are not taxable. However, cash distributions in excess of a partner's tax basis in their partnership interest immediately before the distribution are generally taxable as capital gain.

Apply the basis, at-risk, and passive activity loss limits to losses from partnerships.

- In order for losses to provide tax benefits to partners, partnership losses must clear the tax-basis, at-risk, and passive activity loss hurdles (in that order).
- Partnership losses in excess of a partner's tax basis are suspended and may be utilized only when additional tax basis is created.

- Losses clearing the tax-basis hurdle may be utilized only to the extent of the partner's at-risk amount. A partner's at-risk amount generally equals her tax basis (before any reduction for current year losses) less her share of nonrecourse debt that is not secured by real estate.
- If a partner is not a material participant in the partnership or if the partnership is involved in rental activities, losses clearing the tax-basis and at-risk hurdles may be reported on the partner's tax return only when she has passive income from the partnership (or other sources) or when she sells her partnership interest.
- If an individual partner is a material participant in the partnership, losses clearing the tax-basis and at-risk hurdles may be reported on the partner's tax return to the extent she has business income from other sources plus a threshold amount of $500,000 for married tax-payers filing jointly and $250,000 for other taxpayers.

KEY TERMS

aggregate approach (15-2)
at-risk amount (15-31)
at-risk rules (15-31)
built-in gain (15-3)
built-in loss (15-3)
C corporation (15-2)
capital account (15-8)
capital interest (15-3)
entity approach (15-2)
excess business loss (15-35)
flow-through entities (15-2)
Form 1065 (15-24)
Form 7004 (15-24)
GAAP capital accounts (15-8)
general partnership (GP) (15-2)
guaranteed payments (15-19)

inside basis (15-4)
least aggregate deferral (15-15)
limited liability company (LLC) (15-2)
limited partnership (15-2)
liquidation value (15-10)
majority interest taxable year (15-15)
nonrecourse debt (15-5)
nonservice partner (15-10)
ordinary business income (loss) (15-17)
organization costs (15-12)
outside basis (15-4)
partnership interest (15-3)
passive activity loss (PAL) rules (15-32)
principal partner (15-15)
profits interest (15-3)

qualified nonrecourse financing (15-31)
recourse debt (15-5)
S corporation (15-2)
Schedule K (15-25)
§704(b) capital accounts (15-8)
self-employment taxes (15-20)
separately stated items (15-17)
service partner (15-10)
special allocations (15-23)
start-up costs (15-12)
Subchapter K (15-2)
Subchapter S (15-2)
syndication costs (15-12)
tax capital accounts (15-8)

DISCUSSION QUESTIONS

Discussion Questions are available in Connect®.

LO 15-1 1. What is a *flow-through entity*, and what effect does this designation have on how business entities and their owners are taxed?

LO 15-1 2. What types of business entities are taxed as flow-through entities?

LO 15-1 3. Compare and contrast the aggregate and entity concepts for taxing partnerships and their partners.

LO 15-2 4. What is a partnership interest, and what specific economic rights or entitlements are included with it?

LO 15-2 5. What is the rationale for requiring partners to defer most gains and all losses when they contribute property to a partnership?

LO 15-2 6. Under what circumstances is it possible for partners to recognize gain when contributing property to partnerships?

LO 15-2 7. What is *inside basis* and *outside basis*, and why are they relevant for taxing partnerships and partners?

LO 15-2 8. What is *recourse* and *nonrecourse debt*, and how is each generally allocated to partners?

LO 15-2 9. How does the amount of debt allocated to a partner affect the amount of gain a partner recognizes when contributing property secured by debt?

10. What is a tax basis capital account, and what type of tax-related information does it provide? `LO 15-2`

11. Distinguish between a capital interest and a profits interest, and explain how partners and partnerships treat each when exchanging them for services provided. `LO 15-2`

12. How do partners who purchase a partnership interest determine the tax basis and holding period of their partnership interests? `LO 15-2`

13. Why do you think partnerships, rather than the individual partners, are responsible for making most of the tax elections related to the operation of the partnership? `LO 15-3`

14. If a partner with a taxable year-end of December 31 is in a partnership with a March 31 taxable year-end, how many months of deferral will the partner receive? Why? `LO 15-3`

15. In what situation will there be a common year-end for the principal partners when there is no majority interest taxable year? `LO 15-3`

16. Explain the least aggregate deferral test for determining a partnership's year-end and discuss when it applies. `LO 15-3`

17. When are partnerships eligible to use the cash method of accounting? `LO 15-3`

18. What is a partnership's ordinary business income (loss) and how is it calculated? `LO 15-4`

19. What are some common separately stated items, and why must they be separately stated to the partners? `LO 15-4`

20. Is the character of partnership income/gains and expenses/losses determined at the partnership or partner level? Why? `LO 15-4`

21. What are guaranteed payments and how do partnerships and partners treat them for income and self-employment tax purposes? `LO 15-4`

22. How do general and limited partners treat their share of ordinary business income for self-employment tax purposes? `LO 15-4`

23. What challenges do LLCs face when deciding whether to treat their members' shares of ordinary business income as self-employment income? `LO 15-4`

24. How much flexibility do partnerships have in allocating partnership items to partners? `LO 15-4`

25. What are the basic tax-filing requirements imposed on partnerships? `LO 15-4`

26. In what situations do partners need to know the tax basis in their partnership interests? `LO 15-5`

27. Why does a partner's tax basis in her partnership interest need to be adjusted annually? `LO 15-5`

28. What items will increase a partner's basis in her partnership interest? `LO 15-5`

29. What items will decrease a partner's basis in her partnership interest? `LO 15-5`

30. What hurdles (or limitations) must partners overcome before they can ultimately deduct partnership losses on their tax returns? `LO 15-6`

31. What happens to partnership losses allocated to partners in excess of the tax basis in their partnership interests? `LO 15-6`

32. In what sense is the at-risk loss limitation rule more restrictive than the tax-basis loss limitation rule? `LO 15-6`

33. How do partners measure the amount they have at risk in the partnership? `LO 15-6`

34. In what order are the loss limitation rules applied to limit partners' losses from partnerships? `LO 15-6`

35. How do partners determine whether they are passive participants in partnerships when applying the passive activity loss limitation rules? `LO 15-6`

36. Under what circumstances can partners with passive losses from partnerships deduct their passive losses? `LO 15-6`

PROBLEMS

Select problems are available in Connect®.

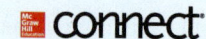

LO 15-2 37. Joseph contributed $22,000 in cash and equipment with a tax basis of $5,000 and a fair market value of $11,000 to Berry Hill Partnership in exchange for a partnership interest.

a) What is Joseph's tax basis in his partnership interest?

b) What is Berry Hill's basis in the equipment?

LO 15-2 38. Lance contributed investment property worth $500,000, purchased three years ago for $200,000 cash, to Cloud Peak LLC in exchange for an 85 percent profits and capital interest in the LLC. Cloud Peak owes $300,000 to its suppliers but has no other debts.

a) What is Lance's tax basis in his LLC interest?

b) What is Lance's holding period in his interest?

c) What is Cloud Peak's basis in the contributed property?

d) What is Cloud Peak's holding period in the contributed property?

LO 15-2 39. Laurel contributed equipment worth $200,000, purchased 10 months ago for $250,000 cash and used in her sole proprietorship, to Sand Creek LLC in exchange for a 15 percent profits and capital interest in the LLC. Laurel agreed to guarantee all $15,000 of Sand Creek's accounts payable, but she did not guarantee any portion of the $100,000 nonrecourse mortgage securing Sand Creek's office building. Other than the accounts payable and mortgage, Sand Creek does not owe any debts to other creditors.

a) What is Laurel's initial tax basis in her LLC interest?

b) What is Laurel's holding period in her interest?

c) What is Sand Creek's initial basis in the contributed property?

d) What is Sand Creek's holding period in the contributed property?

LO 15-2
planning 40. Harry and Sally formed the Evergreen Partnership by contributing the following assets in exchange for a 50 percent capital and profits interest in the partnership:

	Basis	Fair Market Value
Harry:		
Cash	$ 30,000	$ 30,000
Land	100,000	120,000
Totals	$130,000	$150,000
Sally:		
Equipment used in a business	200,000	150,000
Totals	$200,000	$150,000

a) How much gain or loss will Harry recognize on the contribution?

b) How much gain or loss will Sally recognize on the contribution?

c) How could the transaction be structured in a different way to get a better result for Sally?

d) What is Harry's tax basis in his partnership interest?

e) What is Sally's tax basis in her partnership interest?

f) What is Evergreen's tax basis in its assets?

g) Following the format in Exhibit 15-2, prepare a tax basis balance sheet for the Evergreen partnership showing the tax capital accounts for the partners.

LO 15-2 41. Cosmo contributed land with a fair market value of $400,000 and a tax basis of $90,000 to the Y Mountain Partnership in exchange for a 25 percent profits and capital interest in the partnership. The land is secured by $120,000 of nonrecourse debt. Other than this nonrecourse debt, Y Mountain Partnership does not have any debt.

a) How much gain will Cosmo recognize from the contribution?

b) What is Cosmo's tax basis in his partnership interest?

42. When High Horizon LLC was formed, Maude contributed the following assets in exchange for a 25 percent capital and profits interest in the LLC: LO 15-2

	Basis	Fair Market Value
Maude:		
Cash	$ 20,000	$ 20,000
Land*	100,000	360,000
Totals	$ 120,000	$380,000

*Nonrecourse debt secured by the land equals $160,000.

James, Harold, and Jenny each contributed $220,000 in cash for a 25 percent profits and capital interest.

a) How much gain or loss will Maude and the other members recognize?

b) What is Maude's tax basis in her LLC interest?

c) What tax basis do James, Harold, and Jenny have in their LLC interests?

d) What is High Horizon's tax basis in its assets?

e) Following the format in Exhibit 15-2, prepare a tax basis balance sheet for High Horizon LLC showing the tax capital accounts for the members.

43. Kevan, Jerry, and Dave formed Albee LLC. Jerry and Dave each contributed $245,000 in cash. Kevan contributed the following assets: LO 15-2

	Basis	Fair Market Value
Kevan:		
Cash	$ 15,000	$ 15,000
Land*	120,000	440,000
Totals	$135,000	$455,000

*Nonrecourse debt secured by the land equals $210,000.

Each member received a one-third capital and profits interest in the LLC.

a) How much gain or loss will Jerry, Dave, and Kevan recognize on the contributions?

b) What is Kevan's tax basis in his LLC interest?

c) What tax basis do Jerry and Dave have in their LLC interests?

d) What is Albee LLC's tax basis in its assets?

e) Following the format in Exhibit 15-2, prepare a tax basis balance sheet for Albee LLC showing the tax capital accounts for the members. What is Kevan's share of the LLC's inside basis?

f) If the lender holding the nonrecourse debt secured by Kevan's land required Kevan to guarantee 33.33 percent of the debt and Jerry to guarantee the remaining 66.67 percent of the debt when Albee LLC was formed, how much gain or loss will Kevan recognize?

g) If the lender holding the nonrecourse debt secured by Kevan's land required Kevan to guarantee 33.33 percent of the debt and Jerry to guarantee the remaining 66.67 percent of the debt when Albee LLC was formed, what are the members' tax bases in their LLC interests?

44. Jim has decided to contribute some equipment he previously used in his sole proprietorship in exchange for a 10 percent profits and capital interest in Fast Choppers LLC. Jim originally paid $200,000 cash for the equipment. Since then, the tax basis in the equipment has been reduced to $100,000 because of tax depreciation, and the fair market value of the equipment is now $150,000. LO 15-2

 research

a) Must Jim recognize any of the potential §1245 recapture when he contributes the machinery to Fast Choppers? [*Hint:* See §1245(b)(3).]

    b) What cost recovery method will Fast Choppers use to depreciate the machinery? [*Hint:* See §168(i)(7).]

    c) If Fast Choppers were to immediately sell the equipment Jim contributed for $150,000, how much gain would Jim recognize and what is its character? [*Hint:* See §1245 and 704(c).]

LO 15-2

research

45. Ansel purchased raw land three years ago for $200,000 to hold as an investment. After watching the value of the land drop to $150,000, he decided to contribute it to Mountainside Developers LLC in exchange for a 5 percent capital and profits interest. Mountainside plans to develop the property and will treat it as inventory, like all the other real estate it holds.

    a) If Mountainside sells the property for $150,000 after holding it for one year, how much gain or loss does it recognize and what is the character of the gain or loss? [*Hint:* See §724.]

    b) If Mountainside sells the property for $125,000 after holding it for two years, how much gain or loss does it recognize and what is the character of the gain or loss?

    c) If Mountainside sells the property for $150,000 after holding it for six years, how much gain or loss does it recognize and what is the character of the gain or loss?

LO 15-2

research

46. Claude purchased raw land three years ago for $1,500,000 to develop into lots and sell to individuals planning to build their dream homes. Claude intended to treat this property as inventory, like his other development properties. Before completing the development of the property, however, he decided to contribute it to South Peak Investors LLC when it was worth $2,500,000, in exchange for a 10 percent capital and profits interest. South Peak's strategy is to hold land for investment purposes only and then sell it later at a gain.

    a) If South Peak sells the property for $3,000,000 four years after Claude's contribution, how much gain or loss is recognized and what is its character? [*Hint:* See §724.]

    b) If South Peak sells the property for $3,000,000 five and one-half years after Claude's contribution, how much gain or loss is recognized and what is its character?

LO 15-2

research

47. Reggie contributed $10,000 in cash and a capital asset he had held for three years with a fair market value of $20,000 and tax basis of $10,000 for a 5 percent capital and profits interest in Green Valley LLC.

    a) If Reggie sells his LLC interest 13 months later for $30,000 when the tax basis in his partnership interest is still $20,000, how much gain does he report and what is its character?

    b) If Reggie sells his LLC interest two months later for $30,000 when the tax basis in his partnership interest is still $20,000, how much gain does he report and what is its character? [*Hint:* See Reg. §1.1223-3.]

LO 15-2

48. Connie recently provided legal services to the Winterhaven LLC and received a 5 percent interest in the LLC as compensation. Winterhaven currently has $50,000 of accounts payable and no other debt. The current fair market value of Winterhaven's capital is $200,000.

    a) If Connie receives a 5 percent capital interest only, how much income must she report and what is her tax basis in the LLC interest?

    b) If Connie receives a 5 percent profits interest only, how much income must she report and what is her tax basis in the LLC interest?

    c) If Connie receives a 5 percent capital and profits interest, how much income must she report and what is her tax basis in the LLC interest?

49. Mary and Scott formed a partnership that maintains its records on a calendar-year basis. The balance sheet of the MS Partnership at year-end is as follows:

LO 15-2

	Basis	Fair Market Value
Cash	$ 60	$ 60
Land	60	180
Inventory	72	60
	$192	$300
Mary	$ 96	$150
Scott	96	150
	$192	$300

At the end of the current year, Kari will receive a one-third capital interest only in exchange for services rendered. Kari's interest will not be subject to a substantial risk of forfeiture and the costs for the type of services she provided are typically not capitalized by the partnership. For the current year, the income and expenses from operations are equal. Consequently, the only tax consequences for the year are those relating to the admission of Kari to the partnership.

a) Compute and characterize any gain or loss Kari may have to recognize as a result of her admission to the partnership.

b) Compute Kari's basis in her partnership interest.

c) Prepare a balance sheet of the partnership immediately after Kari's admission showing the partners' tax capital accounts and capital accounts stated at fair market value.

d) Calculate how much gain or loss Kari would have to recognize if, instead of a capital interest, she received a profits interest.

50. Dave LaCroix recently received a 10 percent capital and profits interest in Cirque Capital LLC in exchange for consulting services he provided. If Cirque Capital had paid an outsider to provide the advice, it would have deducted the payment as compensation expense. Cirque Capital's balance sheet on the day Dave received his capital interest appears below:

LO 15-2

	Basis	Fair Market Value
Assets:		
Cash	$150,000	$ 150,000
Investments	200,000	700,000
Land	150,000	250,000
Totals	$500,000	$1,100,000
Liabilities and capital:		
Nonrecourse debt	$100,000	$ 100,000
Lance*	200,000	500,000
Robert*	200,000	500,000
Totals	$500,000	$1,100,000

*Assume that Lance's basis and Robert's basis in their LLC interests equal their tax basis capital accounts plus their respective shares of nonrecourse debt.

a) Compute and characterize any gain or loss Dave may have to recognize as a result of his admission to Cirque Capital.

b) Compute each member's tax basis in his LLC interest immediately after Dave's receipt of his interest.

c) Prepare a balance sheet for Cirque Capital immediately after Dave's admission showing the members' tax capital accounts and their capital accounts stated at fair market value.

d) Compute and characterize any gain or loss Dave may have to recognize as a result of his admission to Cirque Capital if he receives only a profits interest.

e) Compute each member's tax basis in his LLC interest immediately after Dave's receipt of his interest if Dave receives only a profits interest.

LO 15-2 51. Last December 31, Ramon sold the 10 percent interest in the Del Sol Partnership that he had held for two years to Garrett for $400,000. Prior to selling his interest, Ramon's basis in Del Sol was $200,000, which included a $100,000 share of nonrecourse debt allocated to him.

a) What is Garrett's tax basis in his partnership interest?

b) If Garrett sells his partnership interest three months after receiving it and recognizes a gain, what is the character of his gain?

LO 15-3 52. Broken Rock LLC was recently formed with the following members:

Name	Tax Year-End	Capital/Profits %
George Allen	December 31	33.33%
Elanax Corp.	June 30	33.33
Ray Kirk	December 31	33.34

What is the required taxable year-end for Broken Rock LLC?

LO 15-3 53. Granite Slab LLC was recently formed with the following members:

Name	Tax Year-End	Capital/Profits %
Nelson Black	December 31	22.0%
Brittany Jones	December 31	24.0
Lone Pine LLC	June 30	4.5
Red Spot Inc.	October 31	4.5
Pale Rock Inc.	September 30	4.5
Thunder Ridge LLC	July 31	4.5
Alpensee LLC	March 31	4.5
Lakewood Inc.	June 30	4.5
Streamside LLC	October 31	4.5
Burnt Fork Inc.	October 31	4.5
Snowy Ridge LP	June 30	4.5
Whitewater LP	October 31	4.5
Straw Hat LLC	January 31	4.5
Wildfire Inc.	September 30	4.5

What is the required taxable year-end for Granite Slab LLC?

LO 15-3 54. Tall Tree LLC was recently formed with the following members:

Name	Tax Year-End	Capital/Profits %
Eddie Robinson	December 31	40%
Pitcher Lenders LLC	June 30	25
Perry Homes Inc.	October 31	35

What is the required taxable year-end for Tall Tree LLC?

LO 15-3 55. Rock Creek LLC was recently formed with the following members:

Name	Tax Year-End	Capital/Profits %
Mark Banks	December 31	35%
Highball Properties LLC	March 31	25
Chavez Builders Inc.	November 30	40

What is the required taxable year-end for Rock Creek LLC?

56. Ryan, Dahir, and Bill have operated Broken Feather LLC for the last four years using a calendar year-end. Each has a one-third interest. Since they began operating, their busy season has run from June through August, with 35 percent of their gross receipts coming in July and August. The members would like to change their tax year-end and have asked you to address the following questions:

a) Can they change to an August 31 year-end and, if so, how do they make the change? [*Hint:* See Rev. Proc. 2002-38, 2002-1 CB 1037.]

b) Can they change to a September 30 year-end and, if so, how do they make the change? [*Hint:* See §444.]

57. Ashlee, Hiroki, Kate, and Albee LLC each own a 25 percent interest in Tally Industries LLC, which generates annual gross receipts of over $10 million. Ashlee, Hiroki, and Kate manage the business, but Albee LLC is a nonmanaging member. Although Tally Industries has historically been profitable, for the last three years losses have been allocated to the members. Given these facts, the members want to know whether Tally Industries can use the cash method of accounting. Why or why not? [*Hint:* See §448(b)(3).]

58. Turtle Creek Partnership had the following revenues, expenses, gains, losses, and distributions:

Sales revenue	$ 40,000
Long-term capital gains	2,000
Cost of goods sold	(13,000)
Depreciation—MACRS	(3,000)
Amortization of organization costs	(1,000)
Guaranteed payments to partners for general management	(10,000)
Cash distributions to partners	(2,000)

a) Given these items, what is Turtle Creek's ordinary business income (loss) for the year?

b) What are Turtle Creek's separately stated items for the year?

59. Georgio owns a 20 percent profits and capital interest in Rain Tree LLC. For the current year, Rain Tree had the following revenues, expenses, gains, and losses:

Sales revenue	$ 70,000
Gain on sale of land (§1231)	11,000
Cost of goods sold	(26,000)
Depreciation—MACRS	(3,000)
§179 deduction*	(10,000)
Employee wages	(11,000)
Fines and penalties	(3,000)
Municipal bond interest	6,000
Short-term capital gains	4,000
Guaranteed payment to Sandra	(3,000)

*Assume the §179 property placed in service limitation does not apply.

a) How much ordinary business income (loss) is allocated to Georgio for the year?

b) What are Georgio's separately stated items for the year?

60. Richard Meyer and two friends from law school recently formed Meyer and Associates as a limited liability partnership (LLP). Income from the partnership will be split equally among the partners. The partnership will generate fee income primarily from representing clients in bankruptcy and foreclosure matters. While some attorney friends have suggested that partners' earnings will be self-employment income, other attorneys they know from their local bar association meetings claim just the opposite. After examining relevant authority, explain how you would advise Meyer and Associates on this matter. [*Hint:* See §1402(a)(13) and *Renkemeyer, Campbell & Weaver LLP v. Commissioner,* 136 T.C. 137 (2011).]

LO 15-4   61. The partnership agreement of the G&P general partnership states that Gary will receive a guaranteed payment of $13,000, and that Gary and Prudence will share the remaining profits or losses in a 45/55 ratio. For year 1, the G&P partnership reports the following results:

Sales revenue	$ 70,000
Gain on sale of land (§1231)	8,000
Cost of goods sold	(38,000)
Depreciation—MACRS	(9,000)
Employee wages	(14,000)
Cash charitable contributions	(3,000)
Municipal bond interest	2,000
Other expenses	(2,000)

a) Compute Gary's share of ordinary income (loss) and separately stated items to be reported on his year 1 Schedule K-1, including his self-employment income (loss).

b) Compute Gary's share of self-employment income (loss) to be reported on his year 1 Schedule K-1, assuming G&P is a limited partnership and Gary is a limited partner.

c) What do you believe Gary's share of self-employment income (loss) to be reported on his year 1 Schedule K-1 should be, assuming G&P is an LLC and Gary spends 2,000 hours per year working there full time?

LO 15-4

62. Hoki Poki, a cash-method general partnership, recorded the following items for its current tax year:

Rental real estate income	$ 2,000
Sales revenue	70,000
§1245 recapture income	8,000
Interest income	2,000
Cost of goods sold	(38,000)
Depreciation—MACRS	(9,000)
Supplies expense	(1,000)
Employee wages	(14,000)
Investment interest expense	(1,000)
Partner's medical insurance premiums paid by Hoki Poki	(3,000)

As part of preparing Hoki Poki's current year return, identify the items that should be included in computing its ordinary business income (loss) and those that should be separately stated. [*Hint:* See Schedule K-1 and related preparer's instructions at www.irs.gov.]

LO 15-4

63. On the last day of its current tax year, Buy Rite LLC received $300,000 when it sold a machine it had purchased for $200,000 three years ago to use in its business. At the time of the sale, the basis in the equipment had been reduced to $100,000 due to tax depreciation taken. How much did the members' self-employment earnings from Buy Rite increase when the equipment was sold? [*Hint:* See §1402(a)(3).]

LO 15-4

64. Jhumpa, Stewart, and Kelly are all one-third partners in the capital and profits of Firewalker General Partnership. In addition to their normal share of the partnership's annual income, Jhumpa and Stewart receive an annual guaranteed payment of $10,000 to compensate them for additional services they provide. Firewalker's income statement for the current year reflects the following revenues and expenses:

Sales revenue	$ 340,000
Interest income	3,300
Long-term capital gains	1,200
Cost of goods sold	(120,000)
Employee wages	(75,000)
Depreciation expense	(28,000)
Guaranteed payments	(20,000)
Miscellaneous expenses	(4,500)
Overall net income	$ 97,000

a) Given Firewalker's operating results, how much ordinary business income (loss) and what separately stated items (including the partners' self-employment earnings [loss]) will it report on its return for the year?

b) How will it allocate these amounts to its partners?

c) How much self-employment tax will each partner pay assuming none has any other source of income or loss?

65. This year, Darrel's distributive share from Alcove Partnership includes $6,000 of interest income, $3,000 of dividend income, and $70,000 ordinary business income.   LO 15-4

a) Assume that Darrel materially participates in the partnership. How much of his distributive share from Alcove Partnership is potentially subject to the net investment income tax?

b) Assume that Darrel does not materially participate in the partnership. How much of his distributive share from Alcove Partnership is potentially subject to the net investment income tax?

66. This year, Alex's distributive share from Eden Lakes Partnership includes $8,000 of interest income, $4,000 of net long-term capital gains, $2,000 net §1231 gain from the sale of property used in the partnership's trade or business, and $83,000 of ordinary business income.   LO 15-4

a) Assume that Alex materially participates in the partnership. How much of his distributive share from Eden Lakes Partnership is potentially subject to the net investment income tax?

b) Assume that Alex does not materially participate in the partnership. How much of his distributive share from Eden Lakes Partnership is potentially subject to the net investment income tax?

67. Lane and Cal each own 50 percent of the profits and capital of HighYield LLC. HighYield owns a portfolio of taxable bonds and municipal bonds, and each year the portfolio generates approximately $10,000 of taxable interest and $10,000 of tax-exempt interest. Lane's marginal tax rate is 35 percent while Cal's marginal tax rate is 12 percent. To take advantage of the difference in their marginal tax rates, Lane and Cal want to modify their operating agreement to specially allocate all of the taxable interest to Cal and all of the tax-exempt interest to Lane. Until now, Lane and Cal had been allocated 50 percent of each type of interest income.   LO 15-4

a) Is HighYield's proposed special allocation acceptable under current tax rules? Why or why not? [*Hint:* See Reg. §1.704-1(b)(2)(iii)(b) and §1.704-1(b)(5) Example (5).]

b) If the IRS ultimately disagrees with HighYield's special allocation, how will it likely reallocate the taxable and tax-exempt interest among the members? [*Hint:* See Reg. §1.704-1(b)(5) Example (5)(ii).]

68. Larry's tax basis in his partnership interest at the beginning of the year was $10,000. If his share of the partnership debt increased by $10,000 during the year and his share of partnership income for the year is $3,000, what is his tax basis in his partnership interest at the end of the year?   LO 15-5

69. Carmine was allocated the following items from Piccolo LLC for last year: LO 15-5

Ordinary business loss
Nondeductible penalties
Tax-exempt interest income
Short-term capital gain
Cash distributions

Rank these items in terms of the order they should be applied to adjust Carmine's tax basis in Piccolo for the year (some items may be of equal rank).

LO 15-5

70. Oscar, Felix, and Marv are all one-third partners in the capital and profits of Eastside General Partnership. In addition to their normal share of the partnership's annual income, Oscar and Felix receive annual guaranteed payments of $7,000 to compensate them for additional services they provide. Eastside's income statement for the current year reflects the following revenues and expenses:

Sales revenue	$ 420,000
Dividend income	5,700
Short-term capital gains	2,800
Cost of goods sold	(210,000)
Employee wages	(115,000)
Depreciation expense	(28,000)
Guaranteed payments	(14,000)
Miscellaneous expenses	(9,500)
Overall net income	$ 52,000

In addition, Eastside owed creditors $120,000 at the beginning of the year but managed to pay down its debts to $90,000 by the end of the year. All partnership debt is allocated equally among the partners. Finally, Oscar, Felix, and Marv had a tax basis of $80,000 in their interests at the beginning of the year.

a) What tax basis do the partners have in their partnership interests at the end of the year?

b) Assume the partners began the year with a tax basis of $10,000 and all the debt was paid off on the last day of the year. How much gain will the partners recognize when the debt is paid off? What tax basis do the partners have in their partnership interests at the end of the year?

LO 15-5

71. Pam, Sergei, and Mercedes are all one-third partners in the capital and profits of Oak Grove General Partnership. Partnership debt is allocated among the partners in accordance with their capital and profits interests. In addition to their normal share of the partnership's annual income, Pam and Sergei receive annual guaranteed payments of $20,000 to compensate them for additional services they provide. Oak Grove's income statement for the current year reflects the following revenues and expenses:

Sales revenue	$ 476,700
Dividend income	6,600
§1231 losses	(3,800)
Cost of goods sold	(245,000)
Employee wages	(92,000)
Depreciation expense	(31,000)
Guaranteed payments	(40,000)
Miscellaneous expenses	(11,500)
Overall net income	$ 60,000

In addition, Oak Grove owed creditors $90,000 at the beginning of the year and $150,000 at the end, and Pam, Sergei, and Mercedes had a tax basis of $50,000 in their interests at the beginning of the year. Also, on December 31 of the current year, Sergei and Mercedes agreed to increase Pam's capital and profits interests from 33.33 percent to 40 percent in exchange for additional services she provided to the partnership. The current liquidation value of the additional capital interest Pam received is $40,000.

a) What tax basis do the partners have in their partnership interests at the end of the year?

b) If, in addition to the expenses listed above, the partnership donated $12,000 to a political campaign, what tax basis do the partners have in their partnership interests at the end of the year assuming the liquidation value of the additional capital interest Pam received at the end of the year remains at $40,000?

72. Laura Davis is a member in a limited liability company that has historically been profitable but is expecting to generate losses in the near future because of a weak local economy. In addition to the hours she works as an employee of a local business, she currently spends approximately 150 hours per year helping to manage the LLC. Other LLC members each work approximately 175 hours per year in the LLC, and the time Laura and other members spend managing the LLC has remained constant since she joined the company three years ago. Laura's tax basis and amount at-risk are large compared to her share of projected losses; however, she is concerned that her ability to deduct her share of the projected losses will be limited by the passive activity loss rules.

a) As an LLC member, will Laura's share of losses be presumed to be passive as they are for limited partners? Why or why not? [*Hint:* See §469(h)(2), *Garnett v. Commissioner,* 132 T.C. 368 (2009), and Prop. Reg. § 1.469-5(e)(3)(i).]

b) Assuming Laura's losses are not presumed to be passive, is she devoting sufficient time to the LLC to be considered a material participant? Why or why not?

c) What would you recommend to Laura to help her achieve a more favorable tax outcome?

73. Alfonso began the year with a tax basis in his partnership interest of $30,000. His share of partnership debt at the beginning and end of the year consists of $4,000 of recourse debt and $6,000 of nonrecourse debt. During the year, he was allocated $40,000 of partnership ordinary business loss. Alfonso does not materially participate in this partnership and he has $1,000 of passive income from other sources.

LO 15-6

a) How much of Alfonso's loss is limited by his tax basis?

b) How much of Alfonso's loss is limited by his at-risk amount?

c) How much of Alfonso's loss is limited by the passive activity loss rules?

74. Jenna began the year with a tax basis of $45,000 in her partnership interest. Her share of partnership debt consists of $6,000 of recourse debt and $10,000 of nonrecourse debt at the beginning of the year and $6,000 of recourse debt and $13,000 of nonrecourse debt at the end of the year. During the year, she was allocated $65,000 of partnership ordinary business loss. Jenna does not materially participate in this partnership and she has $4,000 of passive income from other sources.

LO 15-6

a) How much of Jenna's loss is limited by her tax basis?

b) How much of Jenna's loss is limited by her at-risk amount?

c) How much of Jenna's loss is limited by the passive activity loss rules?

75. Juan Diego began the year with a tax basis in his partnership interest of $50,000. During the year, he was allocated $20,000 of partnership ordinary business income, $70,000 of §1231 losses, and $30,000 of short-term capital losses and received a cash distribution of $50,000.

LO 15-5   LO 15-6

a) What items related to these allocations does Juan Diego actually report on his tax return for the year? [*Hint:* See Reg. §1.704-1(d)(2) and Rev. Rul. 66-94.]

b) If any deductions or losses are limited, what are the carryover amounts and what is their character? [*Hint:* See Reg. §1.704-1(d).]

76. Farell is a member of Sierra Vista LLC. Although Sierra Vista is involved in a number of different business ventures, it is not currently involved in real estate either as an investor or as a developer. On January 1, year 1, Farell has a $100,000 tax basis in his LLC interest that includes his $90,000 share of Sierra Vista's general debt obligations. By the end of the year, Farell's share of Sierra Vista's general debt obligations has increased to $100,000. Because of the time he spends in other endeavors, Farell does not materially participate in Sierra Vista. His share

LO 15-6

of the Sierra Vista losses for year 1 is $120,000. As a partner in the Riverwoods Partnership, he also has year 1, Schedule K-1 passive income of $5,000. Farrell is single and has no other sources of business income or loss.

a) Determine how much of the Sierra Vista loss Farell will currently be able to deduct on his tax return for year 1, and list the losses suspended due to tax-basis, at-risk, and passive activity loss limitations.

b) Assuming Farell's Riverwoods K-1 indicates passive income of $30,000, determine how much of the Sierra Vista loss he will ultimately be able to deduct on his tax return for year 1, and list the losses suspended due to tax-basis, at-risk, and passive activity loss limitations.

c) Assuming Farell is deemed to be an active participant in Sierra Vista, determine how much of the Sierra Vista loss he will ultimately be able to deduct on his tax return for year 1, and list the losses suspended due to tax-basis, at-risk, and passive activity loss limitations.

77. Jenkins has a one-third capital and profits interest in the Maverick General Partnership. On January 1, year 1, Maverick has $120,000 of general debt obligations and Jenkins has a $50,000 tax basis (including his share of Maverick's debt) in his partnership interest. During the year, Maverick incurred a $30,000 nonrecourse debt that is not secured by real estate. Because Maverick is a rental real estate partnership, Jenkins is deemed to be a passive participant in Maverick. His share of the Maverick losses for year 1 is $75,000. Jenkins is not involved in any other passive activities, and this is the first year he has been allocated losses from Maverick.

a) Determine how much of the Maverick loss Jenkins will currently be able to deduct on his tax return for year 1, and list the losses suspended due to tax-basis, at-risk, and passive activity loss limitations.

b) If Jenkins sells his interest on January 1, year 2, what happens to his suspended losses from year 1? [*Hint:* See §706(c)(2)(A), Reg. §1.704-1(d)(1), Prop. Reg. §1.465-66(a), and *Sennett v. Commissioner* 80 TC 825 (1983).]

78. Suki and Steve own 50 percent capital and profits interests in Lorinda LLC. Lorinda operates the local minor league baseball team and owns the stadium where the team plays. Although the debt incurred to build the stadium was paid off several years ago, Lorinda owes its general creditors $300,000 (at the beginning of the year) that is not secured by firm property or guaranteed by any of the members. At the beginning of the current year, Suki and Steve had a tax basis of $170,000 in their LLC interests, including their share of debt owed to the general creditors. Shortly before the end of the year they each received a $10,000 cash distribution, even though Lorinda's ordinary business loss for the year was $400,000. Because of the time commitment to operate a baseball team, both Suki and Steve spent more than 1,500 hours during the year operating Lorinda. Both Suki and Steve are single and neither of them have any business income or losses from other sources.

a) Determine how much of the Lorinda loss Suki and Steve will each be able to deduct on their current tax returns, and list their losses suspended by the tax-basis, at-risk, and passive activity loss limitations.

b) Assume that some time before receiving the $10,000 cash distribution, Steve is advised by his tax adviser that his marginal tax rate will be abnormally high during the current year because of an unexpected windfall. To help Steve utilize more of the losses allocated from Lorinda in the current year, his adviser recommends refusing the cash distribution and personally guaranteeing $100,000 of Lorinda's debt, without the right to be reimbursed by Suki. If Steve follows his adviser's recommendations, how much additional Lorinda loss can he deduct on his current tax return? How does Steve's decision affect the amount of loss Suki can deduct on her current return and the amount and type of her suspended losses?

79. Ray and Chuck own 50 percent capital and profits interests in Alpine Properties LLC. Alpine builds and manages rental real estate, and Ray and Chuck each work full time (over 1,000 hours per year) managing Alpine. Alpine's debt (both at the beginning and end of the year) consists of $1,500,000 in nonrecourse mortgages obtained from an unrelated bank and secured by various rental properties. At the beginning of the current year, Ray and Chuck each had a tax basis of $250,000 in their respective LLC interest, including their share of the nonrecourse mortgage debt. Alpine's ordinary business losses for the current year totaled $600,000, and neither member is involved in other activities that generate passive income.

a) How much of each member's loss is suspended because of the tax-basis limitation?

b) How much of each member's loss is suspended because of the at-risk limitation?

c) How much of each member's loss is suspended because of the passive activity loss limitation? [*Hint:* See §469(b)(7).]

d) If both Ray and Chuck are single and Ray has a current-year loss of $50,000 from a sole proprietorship, how much trade or business loss can each deduct on their tax returns?

COMPREHENSIVE PROBLEMS

Select problems are available in Connect®.

80. Aaron, Deanne, and Keon formed the Blue Bell General Partnership at the beginning of the current year. Aaron and Deanne each contributed $110,000 and Keon transferred an acre of undeveloped land to the partnership. The land had a tax basis of $70,000 and was appraised at $180,000. The land was also encumbered with a $70,000 nonrecourse mortgage for which no one was personally liable. All three partners agreed to split profits and losses equally. At the end of the first year, Blue Bell made a $7,000 principal payment on the mortgage. For the first year of operations, the partnership records disclosed the following information:

Sales revenue	$470,000
Cost of goods sold	410,000
Operating expenses	70,000
Long-term capital gains	2,400
§1231 gains	900
Charitable contributions	300
Municipal bond interest	300
Salary paid as a guaranteed payment to Deanne (not included in expenses)	3,000

a) Compute the adjusted basis of each partner's interest in the partnership immediately after the formation of the partnership.

b) List the separate items of partnership income, gains, losses, and deductions that the partners must show on their individual income tax returns that include the results of the partnership's first year of operations.

c) Using the information generated in answering parts (a) and (b), prepare Blue Bell's page 1 and Schedule K to be included with its Form 1065 for its first year of operations, along with Schedule K-1 for Deanne.

d) What are the partners' adjusted bases in their partnership interests at the end of the first year of operations?

tax forms

81. The TimpRiders LP has operated a motorcycle dealership for a number of years. Lance is the limited partner, Francesca is the general partner, and they share capital and profits equally. Francesca works full-time managing the partnership. Both the partnership and the partners report on a calendar-year basis. At the start of the current year, Lance and Francesca had bases of $10,000 and $3,000, respectively, and the partnership did not carry any debt. During the current year, the partnership reported the following results from operations:

Net sales	$650,000
Cost of goods sold	500,000
Operating expenses	160,000
Short-term capital loss	2,000
Tax-exempt interest	2,000
§1231 gain	6,000

On the last day of the year, the partnership distributed $3,000 each to Lance and Francesca.

a) What outside basis do Lance and Francesca have in their partnership interests at the end of the year?

b) How much of their losses are currently not deductible by Lance and Francesca because of the tax-basis limitation?

c) To what extent does the passive activity loss limitation apply in restricting their deductible losses for the year?

d) Using the information provided, prepare TimpRiders's page 1 and Schedule K to be included with its Form 1065 for the current year. Also, prepare a Schedule K-1 for Lance and Francesca.

82. LeBron, Dennis, and Susan formed the Bar T LLC at the beginning of the current year. LeBron and Dennis each contributed $200,000 and Susan transferred several acres of agricultural land she had purchased two years earlier to the LLC. The land had a tax basis of $50,000 and was appraised at $300,000. The land was also encumbered with a $100,000 nonrecourse mortgage (i.e., qualified nonrecourse financing) for which no one was personally liable. The members plan to use the land and cash to begin a cattle-feeding operation. Susan will work full time operating the business, but LeBron and Dennis will devote less than two days per year to the operation.

All three members agree to split profits and losses equally. At the end of the first year, Bar T had accumulated $40,000 of accounts payable jointly guaranteed by LeBron and Dennis and had made a $9,000 principal payment on the mortgage. None of the members have passive income from other sources or business income from other sources. LeBron and Dennis are married, while Susan is single.

For the first year of operations, the partnership records disclosed the following information:

Sales revenue	$620,000
Cost of goods sold	380,000
Operating expenses	670,000
Dividends	1,200
Municipal bond interest	300
Salary paid as a guaranteed payment to Susan (not included in expenses)	10,000
Cash distributions split equally among the members at year-end	3,000

a) Compute the adjusted basis of each member's interest immediately after the formation of the LLC.

b) When does each member's holding period for his or her LLC interest begin?

c) What is Bar T's tax basis and holding period in its land?

d) What is Bar T's required tax year-end?

e) What overall methods of accounting were initially available to Bar T?

f) List the separate items of partnership income, gains, losses, deductions, and other items that will be included in each member's Schedule K-1 for the first year of operations. Use the proposed self-employment tax regulations to determine each member's self-employment income or loss.

g) What are the members' adjusted bases in their LLC interests at the end of the first year of operations?

h) What are the members' at-risk amounts in their LLC interests at the end of the first year of operations?

i) How much loss from Bar T, if any, will the members be able to deduct on their individual returns from the first year of operations?

ROGER | *CPA Review*

Sample CPA Exam questions from Roger CPA Review are available in Connect as support for the topics in this text. These Multiple Choice Questions and Task-Based Simulations include expert-written explanations and solutions and provide a starting point for students to become familiar with the content and functionality of the actual CPA Exam.

says she will contribute $30,000 and Sarah antes up another $40,000.

The following couple of weeks fly by in a whirlwind of work—phone calls, meetings with bankers, and production scheduling. Oscar's special guest for the show is the popular film star Tom Hughes, promoting his soon-to-be-released movie *Global Warfare*. Tom is good-natured and expresses interest in the sheets. During the show, he announces he will order a set as soon as the broadcast is over. Nicole and Sarah anticipate orders will roll in. Sure enough, before Oscar has even said goodbye to his studio audience, CCS's website traffic has picked up and the phone lines are hopping with new orders.

By the end of 2019, CCS's financial situation has completely turned around; business is booming, the accounting records show a healthy profit, and the partners feel comfortable the trend will continue. Greg decides it is time to talk to Nicole and Sarah about cashing out his investment.

to be continued . . .

This chapter explores the tax consequences associated with selling partnership interests and distributing partnership assets to partners. In the Entities Overview chapter, we learned that Color Comfort Sheets, LLC actually elected to be taxed as a C corporation. In this chapter, we assume it did not make this election leaving it to be treated as a partnership for tax purposes.

LO 16-1 BASICS OF SALES OF PARTNERSHIP INTERESTS

As we've seen in preceding chapters, owners of various business entities receive returns on their investments, either when the business makes distributions or upon the sale of their business interest. Corporate shareholders may sell their stock to other investors or back to the corporation. Likewise, partners may dispose of their interest in several ways: sell to a third party, sell to another partner, or transfer the interest back to the partnership. The payments in a disposition (sale) can come from either another owner of the partnership or a new investor; in either case, the sale proceeds come from outside the partnership.

Selling a **partnership interest** raises unique issues because of the flow-through nature of the entity. For example, is the interest a separate asset, or does the disposition represent the sale of the partner's share of each of the partnership's assets? (See the Forming and Operating Partnerships chapter for a discussion of the entity and aggregate approaches to taxation of flow-through entities.) To the extent the tax rules follow an entity approach, the interest is considered a separate asset and a sale of the partnership interest is very similar to the sale of corporate stock. That is, the partner simply recognizes capital gain or loss on the sale, based on the difference between the sales price and the partner's tax basis in the partnership interest.

Alternately, to the extent the tax rules use the aggregate approach, the disposition represents a sale of the partner's share of each of the partnership's assets. This approach adds some complexity because of the differing character and holding periods of the partnership assets—ordinary, capital, and §1231. The selling partner also has the additional task of allocating the sales proceeds among the underlying assets in order to determine the gain or loss on each.

Rather than strictly following one approach, the tax rules end up being a mixture of the two approaches. When feasible, the entity approach controls; however, if the result distorts the amount or character of income, then the aggregate approach dominates. We discuss the tax consequences of sales of partnership interests by first taking the perspective of the seller (partner), followed by a discussion from the perspective of the buyer (new investor).

Seller Issues

The seller's primary tax concern in a partnership interest sale is calculating the amount and character of gain or loss on the sale. The selling partner calculates the gain or loss as the difference between the amount realized and her **outside basis** in the partnership.[1] Because the selling partner is no longer responsible for her share of the partnership liabilities, any debt relief increases the amount the partner *realizes* from the sale under general tax principles.

Example 16-1

Last year, Chanzz Inc. sold its 30 percent interest in CCS on June 30 to Greg Randall, a wealthy local businessman, to limit its exposure to any further losses. Greg anticipated that CCS would become profitable in the near future and paid Chanzz Inc. $100,000 for its interest in CCS. Chanzz's share of CCS liabilities as of June 30 was $24,000. Chanzz Inc.'s basis in its CCS interest at the sale date was $105,000 (including its share of CCS's liabilities). What amount of gain did Chanzz recognize on the sale?

Answer: $19,000 gain, computed as follows:

Description	Amount	Explanation
(1) Cash and fair market value of property received	$100,000	
(2) Debt relief	24,000	
(3) Amount realized	$124,000	(1) + (2)
(4) Basis in CCS interest	105,000	
Recognized gain	**$ 19,000**	(3) − (4)

The character of the gain or loss from a sale of a partnership interest is generally capital, because partnership interests are capital assets.[2] However, a portion of the gain or loss will be ordinary if a seller realizes any gain or loss attributable to **unrealized receivables** or **inventory items**.[3] Practitioners often refer to these assets that give rise to ordinary gains and losses as **hot assets**.[4] Let's discuss that term further, because these assets are central to determining the tax treatment of many transactions in this chapter.

Hot Assets   As you might expect, unrealized receivables include the right to receive payment for (1) "goods delivered, or to be delivered"[5] or (2) "services rendered, or to be rendered."[6] For cash-method taxpayers, unrealized receivables include amounts earned but not yet received (accounts receivable). Accrual-method taxpayers, however, do not

---

[1]Partners determine their outside basis as discussed in the previous chapter. Importantly, the outside basis includes the selling partner's share of distributive income for the year to the date of the sale.

[2]§731 and §741.

[3]§751(a). Partnerships are required to provide Form 8308 to all the parties to the sale as well as to the IRS. Selling partners include with their tax returns this form as well as a statement detailing the calculation of any ordinary gain from the sale of their interest.

[4]There are actually two definitions of *inventory items* in §751. Section 751(a) inventory items are defined in §751(d) to include *all* inventory items. However, under §751(b), the definition includes only *substantially appreciated* inventory. For purposes of determining the character of gain or loss from the sale of partnership interests, the term *inventory items* includes all inventory as in §751(a). However, these two definitions have created some confusion when using the term *hot assets*. In this chapter, we use the term *hot assets* to refer to unrealized receivables and all inventory items as in §751(a). The definition under §751(b) becomes more relevant when determining the tax treatment in a disproportionate distribution (discussed only briefly later in the chapter).

[5]§751(c)(1).

[6]§751(c)(2).

consider accounts receivable as unrealized receivables because they have already realized and recognized these items as ordinary income. Unrealized receivables also include items the partnership would treat as ordinary income if it sold the asset for its fair market value, such as depreciation recapture under §1245.[7]

Inventory items include classic inventory, defined as property held for sale to customers in the ordinary course of business, but also, more broadly, any assets that are *not* capital assets or §1231 assets.[8] Under this definition, assets such as equipment or real estate used in the business but not held for more than a year and all accounts receivable are considered inventory. This broad definition means cash, capital assets, and §1231 assets are the only properties not considered inventory.[9]

Example 16-2

CCS's balance sheet as of the date of Chanzz's sale of its CCS interest to Greg follows:

Color Comfort Sheets LLC June 30, 2018		
	Tax Basis	**FMV**
Assets		
Cash	$ 27,000	$ 27,000
Accounts receivable	0	13,000
Investments	15,000	12,000
Inventory	1,000	1,000
Equipment (acc. depr. = $20,000)	80,000	86,000
Building	97,000	97,000
Land	20,000	150,000
Totals	$240,000	$386,000
Liabilities and capital		
Long-term debt	$100,000*	
Capital—Nicole	(49,000)	
—Sarah	108,000	
—Chanzz	81,000	
Totals	$240,000	

*Of the $100,000 of long-term debt, $20,000 is allocated solely to Nicole. The remaining $80,000 is allocated to all three owners according to their profit-sharing ratios.

Which of CCS's assets are considered hot assets under §751(a)?

Answer: The hot assets are accounts receivable of $13,000 and $6,000 depreciation recapture (§1245) potential ($86,000 − $80,000) in the equipment. The accounts receivable is an unrealized receivable because CCS has not included it in income for tax purposes under CCS's cash accounting method. The depreciation recapture is also considered an unrealized receivable under §751(a). Inventory would be considered a hot asset; however, because the tax basis and fair market value are equal, it will not affect the character of any gain recognized on the sale.

---

[7]§751(c).

[8]§751(d)(1).

[9]This broad definition of inventory includes all unrealized receivables except for recapture. Recapture items are excluded from the definition of inventory items simply because recapture is not technically an asset; rather, it is merely a portion of gain that results from the sale of property. Recapture is, however, considered an unrealized receivable (i.e., hot asset) under §751(a). This idea is important in determining whether inventory is substantially appreciated for purposes of determining the §751 assets for distributions, as we discuss later in the chapter.

Example 16-3

Review CCS's balance sheet as of the end of 2019.

Color Comfort Sheets LLC December 31, 2019	Tax Basis	FMV
Assets		
Cash	$390,000	$ 390,000
Accounts receivable	0	40,000
Inventory	90,000	200,000
Investments	60,000	105,000
Equipment (acc. depr. = $50,000)	150,000	200,000
Building (acc. depr. = $10,000)	90,000	100,000
Land—original	20,000	160,000
Land—investment	140,000	270,000
Totals	$940,000	$1,465,000
Liabilities and capital		
Accounts payable	$ 80,000	
Long-term debt		
Mortgage on original land	40,000	
Mortgage on investment land	120,000	
Capital—Nicole	119,000	
—Sarah	332,000	
—Greg	249,000	
Totals	$940,000	

What amount of CCS's assets are considered to be hot assets as of December 31, 2019?

Answer: The hot assets include inventory with a fair market value of $200,000, and unrealized receivables consisting of $50,000 of depreciation recapture potential on the equipment, and $40,000 of accounts receivable.

When a partner sells her interest in a partnership that holds hot assets, she modifies her calculation of the gain or loss to ensure the portion that relates to hot assets is properly characterized as ordinary income. The process for determining the gain or loss follows:

Step 1: Calculate the total gain or loss recognized by subtracting outside basis from the amount realized.

Step 2: Calculate the partner's share of gain or loss from hot assets as if the partnership sold these assets at their fair market value. This represents the ordinary portion of the gain or loss.

Step 3: Finally, subtract the ordinary portion of the gain or loss obtained in Step 2 from the total gain or loss from Step 1. This remaining amount is the capital gain or loss from the sale.[10,11]

[10]The partner must also determine if any portion of the capital gain or loss relates to collectibles (28 percent capital gain property) or to unrecaptured §1250 gains. This is typically referred to as the *look-through rule.*

[11]Any capital gain from the sale of a partnership interest is potentially subject to the 3.8 percent net investment income tax unless the gain is allocable to trade or business assets held by the partnership that generate trade or business income not subject to the tax. See Prop. Reg. §1.1411-7 for a detailed discussion of this concept.

Example 16-4

In Example 16-1, we are reminded that Chanzz Inc. sold its interest in CCS to Greg Randall for $100,000 cash on June 30, 2018. As a result, Chanzz recognized a gain of $19,000 on the sale. What was the character of Chanzz's gain?

Answer: $5,700 of ordinary income and $13,300 of capital gain, determined as follows:

Step 1: Determine the total gain or loss: $19,000 gain (from Example 16-1).

Step 2: Determine the ordinary gain or loss recognized from hot assets:

Asset	(1) Basis	(2) FMV	(3) Gain/Loss (2) − (1)	Chanzz's Share 30% × (3)
Accounts receivable	$ 0	$13,000	$13,000	$ 3,900
Equipment	80,000	86,000	6,000	1,800
Total ordinary income				**$5,700**

Step 3: Determine the capital gain or loss:

Description	Amount	Explanation
(1) Total gain	$ 19,000	From Step 1
(2) Ordinary income from §751(a)	5,700	From Step 2
Capital gain	**$13,300**	(1) − (2)

Example 16-5

What if: Assume the same facts as in Example 16-1, except Greg only paid Chanzz $82,800 cash for its interest in CCS. What would be the amount and character of Chanzz's gain or loss?

Answer: $5,700 of ordinary income and capital loss of $3,900, determined as follows:

Step 1: Determine the total gain or loss recognized:

Description	Amount	Explanation
(1) Cash and fair market value of property received	$ 82,800	
(2) Debt relief	24,000	Chanzz's share of CCS's allocable debt (30% × $80,000)
(3) Amount realized	$106,800	(1) + (2)
(4) Basis in CCS interest	105,000	
Gain recognized	$ 1,800	(3) − (4)

Step 2: Determine the ordinary gain or loss from hot assets:

Asset	(1) Basis	(2) FMV	(3) Gain/Loss (2) − (1)	Chanzz's Share 30% × (3)
Accounts receivable	$ 0	$13,000	$13,000	$ 3,900
Equipment	80,000	86,000	6,000	1,800
Total ordinary income				**$5,700**

Step 3: Determine the capital gain or loss:

Description	Amount	Explanation
(1) Total gain	$ 1,800	From Step 1
(2) Ordinary income from §751(a)	5,700	From Step 2
Capital loss	**$(3,900)**	(1) − (2)

ETHICS

Sarah recently sold her partnership interest for significantly more than her outside basis in the interest. Two separate appraisals were commissioned at the time of the sale to estimate the value of the partnership's hot assets and other assets. The first appraisal estimates the value of the hot assets at approximately $750,000, while the second appraisal estimates the value of these assets at approximately $500,000. Given that the partnership's inside basis for its hot assets is $455,000, Sarah intends to use the second appraisal to determine the character of the gain from the sale of her partnership interest. Is it appropriate for Sarah to ignore the first appraisal when determining her tax liability from the sale of her partnership interest?

Buyer and Partnership Issues

A new investor in a partnership is of course concerned with determining how much to pay for the partnership interest. However, his primary tax concerns are about his outside basis and his share of the inside basis of the partnerships assets. In general, for a sale transaction, the new investor's outside basis will be equal to his cost of the partnership interest.[12] To the extent that the new investor shares in the partnership liabilities, his share of partnership liabilities increases his outside basis.

Example 16-6

When Greg Randall acquired Chanzz's 30 percent interest in CCS for $100,000 on June 30, 2018 (see Example 16-1), he guaranteed his share of CCS's debts just as Chanzz had done. As a result, Greg will be allocated his share of CCS's allocable debt in accordance with his 30 percent profit-sharing ratio. What is the outside basis of Greg's acquired interest?

Answer: $124,000, determined as follows:

Description	Amount	Explanation
(1) Initial tax basis	$ 100,000	Cash paid to Chanzz Inc.
(2) Share of CCS's liabilities	24,000	30% × CCS's allocable debt of $80,000
Outside basis	**$124,000**	(1) + (2)

The partnership experiences very few tax consequences when a partner sells her interest.[13] The sale does not generally affect a partnership's **inside basis** in its assets.[14] The new investor typically "steps into the shoes" of the selling partner to determine her share of the partnership's inside basis of the partnership assets. Consequently, the new investor's

---

[12]§1012. The outside basis will depend, in part, on how the new investor obtains the interest. For example, a gift generally results in a carryover basis whereas an inherited interest typically results in a basis equal to the fair market value as of the date of the decedent's death.

[13]Later in the chapter, we discuss situations in which the new investor's share of the partnership's asset bases is adjusted after a sale of a partnership interest under §754. Throughout this section, we assume that the partnership does not have a §754 election in effect.

[14]§743.

share of inside basis is equal to the selling partner's share of inside basis at the sale date. Recall from the preceding chapter that each partner has a tax capital account that reflects the tax basis of property and cash contributed by the partner, the partner's share of profits and losses, and distributions to the partner. In a sale of a partnership interest, the selling partner's tax capital account carries over to the new investor.[15]

Example 16-7

Refer to Example 16-2 for CCS's balance sheet as of June 30, 2018. What is Greg's share of CCS's inside basis in its assets immediately after purchasing Chanzz's 30 percent interest in CCS?

Answer: Greg's share is $105,000: the sum of Chanzz's tax capital account of $81,000 and its share of CCS's liabilities of $24,000. Greg simply steps into Chanzz's place after the acquisition. In Example 16-6, we determined Greg's outside basis to be $124,000. A sale of a partnership interest often results in a difference between the new investor's inside and outside bases because the outside basis is the price paid based on fair market value and the inside basis is the seller's share of tax basis in the partnership assets.

Varying Interest Rule   If a partner's interest in a partnership increases or decreases during the partnership's tax year, the partnership income or loss allocated to the partner for the year must be adjusted to reflect her *varying interest* in the partnership.[16] Partners' interests increase when they contribute property or cash to a partnership[17] or purchase a partnership interest. Conversely, partners' interests decrease when they receive partnership distributions[18] or sell all or a portion of their partnership interests. Upon the sale of a partnership interest, the partnership tax year closes for the *selling* partner only. Regulations allow partners to choose between two possible methods for allocating income or loss to partners when their interests change during the year.[19] The first method allows the partnership to prorate income or loss to partners with varying interests, while the second method sanctions an interim closing of the partnership's books.

Example 16-8

CCS had a $60,000 overall operating loss for the 2018 calendar year. The issue of how to allocate the 2018 loss between Chanzz Inc. and Greg was easily resolved because CCS's operating agreement specifies the proration method to allocate income or loss when members' interests in CCS change during the year. How much of CCS's 2018 loss will Chanzz be allocated under the proration method?

Answer: Chanzz is allocated a loss of $9,000, which includes its share of CCS's loss but for only one-half the year ($60,000 × 30% share × 6/12 months).[20] On the sale date, Chanzz decreases its outside basis in CCS by the $9,000 loss to determine its adjusted basis to use in calculating its gain or loss on the sale of its interest.

[15]An exception occurs when the selling partner contributes property with a built-in loss to the partnership. Only the contributing partner is entitled to that loss [see the Forming and Operating Partnerships chapter and §704(c) (1)(C)]. Therefore, when a new investor buys a partnership interest from a partner that contributed built-in loss property, the new investor reduces his inside basis by the amount of the built-in loss at the contribution date.

[16]§706(d)(1).

[17]If all partners simultaneously contribute property or cash with a value proportionate to their interests, their relative interests will not change.

[18]If all partners receive distributions with a value proportionate to their interests, their relative interests will not change.

[19]Reg. §1.706-1(c).

[20]Reg. §1.706-4(c)(3) requires the calendar-day convention when using the proration method. For the sake of mathematical simplicity, we use number of months here and elsewhere in the chapter when applying the proration method.

Example 16-9

What if: If CCS's overall loss through June 30 was $20,000, how much of the $60,000 overall loss for 2018 will Chanzz and Greg Randall be allocated under an interim closing of the books?

Answer: CCS will allocate $6,000 of loss (30% × $20,000) to Chanzz and $12,000 of loss (30% × $40,000) to Greg.

TAXES IN THE REAL WORLD Changing the Way Companies Dispose of a Business

Corporate takeovers seemed to be the transaction du jour during the 1990s, but many practitioners are predicting joint ventures will be the defining deal for the current decade. We regularly see articles in *The Wall Street Journal* describing how firms are starting up joint ventures or strategic alliances—or exiting them. For example, McGraw-Hill and the CME Group recently brought the S&P 500 index and the Dow Jones Industrial Average under the same roof by forming a new LLC called S&P/Dow Jones Indices. To form the new joint venture, McGraw-Hill contributed its Standard & Poor's index business and

CME Group contributed its Dow Jones index business. In the end, McGraw-Hill owned 73 percent and the CME Group owned 27 percent of the new venture.

The increase in the number of joint ventures and their possible dissolution or disposition brings an increasing need to understand the partnership tax rules and regulations. More than ever before, corporate tax executives find they must advise senior management on the opportunities and pitfalls of structuring joint ventures and investments as partnerships or LLCs under Subchapter K of the Internal Revenue Code.

BASICS OF PARTNERSHIP DISTRIBUTIONS

LO 16-2

Like shareholders receiving corporate dividend distributions, partners often receive distributions of the partnership profits, known as **operating distributions.** Recall that owners of flow-through entities are taxed currently on their business income regardless of whether the business distributes it. As a result, partners may require cash distributions in order to make quarterly estimated tax payments on their shares of business income. Usually, the general partners (or managing members of LLCs) determine the amount and timing of distributions; however, the partnership (operating) agreement may stipulate some distributions.

Partners may also receive **liquidating distributions.** Because the market for partnership interests is much smaller than for publicly traded stock, partners may have a difficult time finding buyers for their interests. Partnership agreements also often limit purchasers of an interest to the current partner group, to avoid adding an unwanted partner. If the current partner group either cannot or does not want to purchase the interest, the partnership can instead distribute assets to terminate a partner's interest. These liquidating distributions are similar to corporate redemptions of a shareholder's stock. They can also terminate the partnership. We first explore the tax consequences of operating distributions, and then examine the tax treatment for liquidating distributions.

LO 16-3

Operating Distributions

A distribution from a partnership is an operating distribution when the partners continue their interests afterwards. Operating distributions are usually made to distribute the business profits to the partners but can also reduce a partner's ownership. The partnership may distribute money or other assets. Let's look at the tax consequences of distributions of money, and then at the tax consequences of distributing property other than money.

Operating Distributions of Money Only The general rule for operating distributions states that the partnership does not recognize gain or loss on the distribution of

THE KEY FACTS

Operating Distributions

- **Gain or loss recognition:** Partners generally do not recognize gain or loss. One exception occurs when the partnership distributes money only and the amount is greater than the partner's outside basis.

(continued)

property or money.[21,22] Nor do the general tax rules require a partner to recognize gain or loss when she receives distributed property or money.[23] The partner simply reduces her (outside) basis in the partnership interest by the amount of cash distributed and the inside basis of any property distributed. In general, the partnership's basis in its remaining assets remains unchanged.[24]

Example 16-10

- **Basis of distributed assets:** Partners generally take a carryover basis in the distributed assets. If the partnership distribution includes other property and the combined inside basis is greater than the partner's outside basis, the bases of the other property distributed will be reduced.

- **Remaining outside basis:** In general, partners reduce outside basis by money and other property distributed.

What if: Suppose CCS makes its first distribution to the owners on December 31, 2019: $250,000 each to Nicole and Greg and $333,333 to Sarah. After taking into account their distributive share of CCS's income for the year, the owners have the following predistribution bases in their CCS interests:

Owner	Outside Basis
Nicole	$205,000
Sarah	420,000
Greg	334,000

What are the tax consequences (gain or loss and basis in CCS interest) of the distribution to Sarah?

Answer: Sarah does not recognize any gain or loss on the distribution. She reduces her outside basis from $420,000 to $86,667 ($420,000 − $333,333) after the distribution.

The general rule of no gain is impractical when the partner receives a greater amount of money than her outside basis. She cannot defer gain to the extent of the excess amount because the outside basis is insufficient for a full reduction. Therefore, the partner reduces her outside basis to zero[25] and recognizes gain (generally capital) to the extent the amount of money distributed is greater than her outside basis.[26] A partner *never* recognizes a loss from an *operating* distribution.

Example 16-11

What if: Suppose that in the December 31, 2019, distribution Nicole's distribution consists of $250,000 cash. Her outside basis is $205,000 before the distribution. What are Nicole's gain or loss and basis in her CCS interest after the distribution?

Answer: Nicole has $45,000 capital gain and $0 basis in CCS. Because she receives only money in the distribution, she decreases her outside basis to $0 and must recognize a $45,000 capital gain ($250,000 distribution less $205,000 basis). She recognizes gain because she receives a cash distribution in excess of her outside basis.

Operating Distributions That Include Property Other Than Money If a partnership makes a distribution that includes property *other than money*, the partners face the problem of determining how much outside basis to allocate to the distributed

---

[21]For distribution purposes, money includes cash, deemed cash from reductions in a partner's share of liabilities, and the fair market value of marketable securities.

[22]§731(b).

[23]§731.

[24]However, if the partnership has a §754 election in effect or if there is a substantial basis reduction, the partnership basis of its remaining assets must be adjusted following a distribution according to §734(b) and §755.

[25]§733.

[26]§731(a)(1).

property.[27] Under the general rule, the partner takes a basis in the distributed property equal to the partnership's basis in the property. This is called a **carryover basis.**[28] The tax rules define the order in which to allocate outside basis to the bases of distributed assets. First, the partner allocates the outside basis to any money received and then to other property as a carryover basis. The remainder is the partner's outside basis after the distribution.

Example 16-12

What if: Suppose CCS's December 31, 2019, distribution to Sarah consists of $133,333 cash and investments (other than marketable securities), with a fair market value of $200,000 and an adjusted basis of $115,000. Sarah has a predistribution outside basis of $420,000. What are the tax consequences (Sarah's gain or loss, basis of distributed assets, outside basis of CCS interest, and CCS's gain or loss) of the distribution?

Answer: Sarah recognizes no gain or loss on the distribution. To determine her bases in the distributed assets, she first allocates $133,333 to the cash and then takes a carryover basis in the investments so her basis in the investments is $115,000. Sarah reduces her outside basis by $248,333 ($133,333 cash + $115,000 basis of investments). Her outside basis after the distribution is $171,667 ($420,000 − $248,333). CCS does not recognize any gain or loss on the distribution.

When the partnership distributes property (other than money) with a basis that exceeds the remaining outside basis (after the allocation to any money distributed), the partner assigns the remaining outside basis to the distributed assets,[29] and the partner's outside basis is reduced to zero.[30] The first allocation of outside basis goes to money, then to hot assets, and finally to other property.[31] In this case, the partner's basis in the property received in the distribution will be less than the property's basis in the hands of the partnership.

Example 16-13

What if: Suppose Nicole's December 31, 2019, distribution consists of $150,000 cash and investments (other than marketable securities) with a fair market value of $100,000 and an adjusted basis of $90,000 to CCS. Her outside basis is $205,000 before the distribution. What are Nicole's tax consequences (gain or loss, basis of distributed assets, and outside basis in CCS interest) of the distribution?

Answer: Nicole recognizes no gain or loss and takes a basis of $55,000 in the investments. Her outside basis in CCS is $0, computed as follows:

Description	Amount	Explanation
(1) Nicole's outside basis	$205,000	
(2) Cash distribution	150,000	
(3) Remaining basis	55,000	(1) − (2); remaining outside basis to be allocated to the distributed investments
(4) Inside basis of investments	90,000	
(5) Basis in investments	55,000	Lesser of (3) or (4)
Nicole's outside basis in CCS	$ 0	(3) − (5)

---

[27]In this context, money includes marketable securities [§731(c)(1)(A)]. The special rules in §731(c) for the treatment of distributed marketable securities are beyond the scope of this book.

[28]§732(a).

[29]§732(a)(2).

[30]§733.

[31]If multiple assets are distributed, then the outside basis will be allocated in accordance with §732(c). We discuss these rules later in conjunction with liquidating distributions.

Because a partner's outside basis includes her share of the partnership liabilities, the outside basis must reflect any changes in a partner's share of partnership debt resulting from a distribution. In essence, a partner treats a reduction of her share of debt as a distribution of cash.[32] If the partner increases her share of debt, the increase is treated as a cash contribution to the partnership.

Example 16-14

What if: Suppose Greg receives land held for investment with a fair market value of $250,000 (adjusted inside basis is $140,000) as his distribution from CCS on December 31, 2019. He agrees to assume the $120,000 mortgage on the land after the distribution. His outside basis is $334,000 before considering the distribution. What are the tax consequences (gain or loss, basis of distributed assets, and outside basis in his CCS interest) of the distribution to Greg?

Answer: Greg does not recognize any gain or loss on the distribution. His basis in the land is $140,000 and his outside basis in CCS is $278,000, determined as follows:

Description	Amount	Explanation
(1) Greg's predistribution outside basis	$ 334,000	
(2) Mortgage assumed by Greg	120,000	
(3) Greg's predistribution share of mortgage	36,000	(2) × 30% ownership
(4) Deemed cash contribution from debt assumption	84,000	(2) − (3)
(5) Greg's outside basis after debt changes	418,000	(1) + (4)
(6) Greg's basis in distributed land	**140,000**	Carryover basis from CCS
Greg's post-distribution outside basis	**$278,000**	(5) − (6)

Greg must first consider the effects of changes in debt before determining the effects of the distribution. The tax rules treat him as making a net contribution of $84,000 cash to the partnership, the difference between the full mortgage he assumes and his predistribution share of the debt. Greg then allocates $140,000 of his outside basis to the land and reduces his outside basis accordingly.

LO 16-4   Liquidating Distributions

In contrast to operating distributions in which the partners retain a continuing interest in the partnership, liquidating distributions terminate a partner's interest in the partnership. If the current partners do not have sufficient cash or inclination to buy out the terminating partner, the partnership agreement usually allows the partnership to close out the partner's interest. At some point, all the partners may agree to terminate the partnership, either because they have lost interest in continuing it or because it has not been profitable. In such cases, the partnership may distribute all its assets to the partners in complete partnership liquidation. This latter process is analogous to a complete corporate liquidation.

The tax issues in liquidating distributions for partnerships are basically twofold: (1) to determine whether the terminating partner recognizes gain or loss and (2) to allocate his or her outside basis to the distributed assets. The rationale behind the rules for liquidating distributions is simply to replace the partner's outside basis with the underlying partnership assets distributed to the terminating partner. Ideally, there will be no gain or loss on the distribution, and the asset bases will be the same in the partner's hands as they were inside the partnership. Of course, this case rarely occurs. The rules therefore are designed to determine when gain or loss must be recognized and to allocate the partner's outside basis to the distributed assets.

[32]§752(b).

Gain or Loss Recognition in Liquidating Distributions   In general, neither partnerships nor partners recognize gain or loss from liquidating distributions. However, there are exceptions. For example, when a terminating partner receives more money in the distribution than her outside basis, she will recognize gain.[33] See Example 16-11 for an illustration in the context of operating distributions.

In contrast to operating distributions, a partner may recognize a *loss* from a liquidating distribution, but only when two conditions are met. These conditions are (1) the distribution includes only cash, unrealized receivables, and/or inventory; *and* (2) the partner's outside basis is greater than the sum of the *inside bases* of the distributed assets.[34] The loss on the distribution is a capital loss to the partner.

Commonly, the terminating partner's share of partnership debt decreases after a liquidating distribution. Any reduction in the partner's share of liabilities is considered a distribution of money to the partner and reduces the outside basis available for allocation of basis to other assets, including inventory and unrealized receivables.

		Example 16-15

What if: Suppose on January 1, 2020, CCS liquidates Greg's interest in the LLC by distributing to him cash of $206,000 and inventory with a fair market value of $103,000 (adjusted basis is $43,000). Greg's share of CCS's liabilities as of the liquidation is $66,000. On January 1, 2020, Greg's outside basis in CCS is $334,000, including his share of CCS's liabilities. What is Greg's gain or loss on the liquidation of his CCS interest?

Answer: Greg recognizes a capital loss of $19,000 from the liquidating distribution, computed as follows:

Description	Amount	Explanation
(1) Outside basis before distribution	$334,000	
(2) Debt relief	66,000	Deemed cash distribution
(3) Outside basis after considering debt relief	$268,000	(1) − (2)
(4) Basis of property distributed (cash + inventory)	249,000	
Gain (loss) on distribution	**$(19,000)**	(4) − (3)

Greg recognizes a loss because he meets the two necessary conditions: (1) he receives only cash and inventory in the distribution *and* (2) the sum of the adjusted inside bases of the distributed assets is less than his basis in his CCS interest ($249,000 inside basis in assets versus $268,000 CCS outside basis).

THE KEY FACTS

Gain or Loss Recognition in Liquidating Distributions

- **Generally:** Partners and partnerships do not recognize gain or loss.
- **Exceptions:**
  - **Gain:** Partner recognizes gain when partnership distributes money and the amount exceeds the partner's outside basis in the partnership interest.
  - **Loss:** Partner recognizes loss when two conditions are met: (1) Distribution consists of only cash and hot assets, and (2) the partner's outside basis exceeds the sum of the bases of the distributed assets.

Basis in Distributed Property   A key theme of the partnership tax rules is the idea that the partnership acts merely as a conduit for the partners' business activities. Thus, the rules attempt to keep the basis of the assets the same regardless of whether the partner or the partnership has possession of them. Moving assets in and out of the partnership should therefore have few tax consequences. The primary objective of the basis rules in liquidating distributions is to allocate the partner's entire outside basis in the partnership to the assets the partner receives in the liquidating distribution. The allocation essentially depends on two things: (1) the partnership's bases in distributed assets relative to the partner's outside basis and (2) the type of property distributed—whether it is money, hot assets, or other property. For purposes of distributions, hot assets include unrealized receivables and inventory, as we've defined above. We discuss each of the possible scenarios in Exhibit 16-1 in turn.

---

[33]These rules are very similar to those for operating distributions. When a partner receives money only in complete termination of the partnership interest, any gain on distribution cannot be deferred through a basis adjustment. Therefore, the partner recognizes the gain.

[34]§731(a)(2).

EXHIBIT 16-1   **Alternative Scenarios for Determining Basis in Distributed Property**

Type of Property Distributed	Partner's outside basis is *greater* than inside bases of distributed assets	Partner's outside basis is *less* than inside bases of distributed assets
Money only	Scenario 1	Scenario 3
Money and hot assets	Scenario 1	Scenario 4
Other property included in distribution[35]	Scenario 2	Scenario 5

Partner's Outside Basis Is Greater Than Inside Bases of Distributed Assets

Scenario 1: Distributions of money, inventory, and/or unrealized receivables.   If the partnership distributes only money, inventory, and/or unrealized receivables (ordinary income property) and the partner's outside basis is greater than the sum of the inside bases of the distributed assets, the partner recognizes a capital loss.[36] The partner assigns a basis to the distributed assets equal to the partnership's inside basis in the assets and the remaining outside basis is equal to the recognized loss. To prevent a partner from converting a capital loss from her investment into an ordinary loss, the tax law prohibits increasing her basis in unrealized receivables and inventory and requires the partner to recognize a capital loss.[37]

Example 16-16

What if: Suppose Greg has an outside basis in CCS of $334,000, including his share of liabilities of $66,000. In a liquidating distribution, he receives $159,000 cash and inventory with a fair market value and basis of $49,000. Will Greg recognize a gain or loss? Why or why not?

Answer: Greg will recognize a capital loss of $60,000 on the liquidation, computed as follows:

Description	Amount	Explanation
(1) Outside basis before distribution	$334,000	
(2) Debt relief	66,000	Deemed cash distribution
(3) Outside basis after considering debt relief	$268,000	(1) − (2)
(4) Basis of property distributed (cash + inventory)	208,000	
Gain (loss) on distribution	**$(60,000)**	(4) − (3)

In this case, Greg is unable to defer his loss without changing its character. Greg clearly cannot adjust the basis in the cash to defer the loss. *If* he were able to increase his basis in the distributed inventory, he could defer the loss. However, this would produce an ordinary loss of $60,000 when Greg sells the inventory.[38] To prevent the conversion of a capital loss to an ordinary loss, Greg must recognize a $60,000 capital loss.

Scenario 2: Other property included in distributions.   Recall that in this scenario the liquidating partner must allocate all her outside basis to the distributed assets. We determined in Scenario 1 that when the partnership distributes only money and/or hot assets

---

[35]This category includes distributions that include other property in addition to or instead of either money or unrealized receivables or inventory. For example, the distributions in this category can include any combination of money, unrealized receivables, and inventory as long as other property is also distributed.

[36]§731(a)(2).

[37]§732(c)(1) and §731(a)(2).

[38]If the inventory distributed to Greg is also considered inventory in his hands, the eventual sale of the inventory will generate ordinary income. If the inventory is a capital asset to Greg, a sale of the asset within five years of the distribution will generate ordinary income. After five years, the gain or loss will be capital.

and the total inside basis of the distributed assets is less than the partner's outside basis, it is impossible to allocate the entire outside basis to the distributed assets without changing the character of a resulting loss. Thus, a partner never increases the bases of hot assets. However, when the partnership distributes other property, in addition to money and/or hot assets, the partner can adjust the basis of the *other* property without converting ordinary gains and losses to capital, and the liquidating partner will not recognize any gain or loss from the distribution.

Example 16-17

What if: Suppose CCS has no liabilities or hot assets and distributes $50,000 in cash and land with a fair market value of $160,000 and an adjusted basis of $20,000 to Greg in complete liquidation of his CCS interest. Greg has an outside basis of $268,000 prior to the distribution. What is Greg's recognized gain or loss on the distribution?

Answer: Greg does not recognize any gain or loss. He receives money and other property with a total basis of $70,000, which is less than his outside basis of $268,000. Greg first reduces his outside basis by the amount of money he receives, and he assigns his remaining outside basis to the land as follows:

Description	Amount	Explanation
(1) Outside basis before distribution	$268,000	
(2) Basis allocated to money distributed	50,000	
Remaining outside basis assigned to land	$218,000	(1) − (2)

Note that Greg increases the basis of the other property received in liquidation (land) from $20,000 to $218,000 in order to allocate his entire outside basis to the distributed assets. In some cases, "other" property might include personal use assets for which the partner may never be able to recover the basis increase.

Example 16-17 illustrates the required basis increase in a very simple situation. In reality, liquidating distributions may include several types of assets. In these situations, to allocate the outside basis to the distributed assets, the partner completes the following, more detailed process:[39]

Step 1: The partner first determines their outside basis net of any debt relief, and then allocates that amount to any money, inventory, and unrealized receivables equal to the partnership's basis in these assets. The partner also assigns a basis to the other distributed property in an amount equal to the partnership's basis in those assets.

Step 2: The partner then allocates the remaining outside basis (full outside basis less the amounts assigned in Step (1) to the other distributed property that has unrealized appreciation to the extent of that appreciation. Thus, if an asset has an adjusted basis to the partnership of $500 and a fair market value of $700, the partner will allocate the first $200 of remaining basis to that asset.[40]

Step 3: The partner allocates any remaining basis to all other property in proportion to the relative *fair market values* of the other property.

$$\text{Basis allocation} = \text{Remaining basis} \times \frac{\text{FMV}_{asset}}{\text{Sum of FMV}_{distributed\ other\ property}}$$

---

[39]§732(c)(2).

[40]If the remaining outside basis is insufficient to allocate the full amount of appreciation to the distributed assets in this step, then the partner will allocate the remaining basis in this step to the appreciated assets based on their relative appreciation.

Example 16-18

What if: Suppose CCS makes the following distribution to Greg in liquidation of his CCS interest:

Asset	CCS Tax Basis	Fair Market Value
Cash	$181,000	$181,000
Investment A	5,000	12,000
Investment B	10,000	13,000
Inventory	43,000	103,000

Greg's basis in his CCS interest as of the liquidation is $334,000, including his $66,000 share of CCS's liabilities. What is Greg's recognized gain or loss on the distribution? What are Greg's bases in the distributed assets following the liquidation?

Answer: Greg recognizes no gain or loss on the distribution. Greg's bases in the distributed assets are:

Cash	$181,000
Investment A*	21,120
Investment B*	22,880
Inventory	43,000
Total	$268,000

Because Greg receives other property in the distribution and the distributed asset bases are less than Greg's outside basis (Scenario 2), he will allocate his outside basis as follows:

First, Greg determines his allocable basis:

Description	Amount	Explanation
(1) Basis in CCS before distribution	$334,000	
(2) Debt relief	66,000	Greg's 30 percent share of CCS's debt
Allocable basis	$268,000	(1) − (2)

Next, Greg allocates his remaining outside basis in CCS of $268,000 to the distributed assets by following the allocation process.

Description	Amount	Explanation
Step 1:		
(1) Allocable basis	$268,000	See above
(2) Basis assigned to cash	181,000	
(3) Basis assigned to inventory	43,000	
(4) Initial basis assigned to Investment A	5,000	
(5) Initial basis assigned to Investment B	10,000	
(6) Remaining allocable CCS basis	$ 29,000	(1) − (2) − (3) − (4) − (5)
Step 2:		
(7) Additional basis assigned to Investment A	$ 7,000	Unrealized appreciation on Investment A (FMV of $12,000 less basis of $5,000)
(8) Additional basis assigned to Investment B	3,000	Unrealized appreciation on Investment B (FMV of $13,000 less basis of $10,000)
(9) Remaining allocable CCS basis after Step 2	$ 19,000	(6) − (7) − (8)

Step 3:

(10) Additional basis allocated to other property: Investment A	$ 9,120	Basis allocation = $19,000 × ($12,000/$25,000) = $9,120
(11) Additional basis allocated to other property: Investment B	$ 9,880	Basis allocation = $19,000 × ($13,000/$25,000) = $9,880

In Step 3, Greg allocates the remaining basis to the distributed investments based on their relative fair market values using:

$$\text{Basis allocation} = \text{Remaining basis} \times \frac{\text{FMV}_{asset}}{\text{Sum of FMV}_{distributed\ other\ property}}$$

Thus, Greg's bases in the investments are $21,120 (Investment A) and $22,880 (Investment B):

Description	Inv. A	Explanation	Inv. B	Explanation
(12) Initial basis assignment	$ 5,000	From (4) above	$ 10,000	From (5) above
(13) Basis assigned in Step 2	7,000	From (7) above	3,000	From (8) above
(14) Basis assigned in Step 3	9,120	From (10) above	9,880	From (11) above
Greg's bases in investments	**$21,120**	(12) + (13) + (14)	**$22,880**	(12) + (13) + (14)

Partner's Outside Basis Is Less Than Inside Bases of Distributed Assets

Scenario 3: Distributions of money only.   A partner recognizes a gain (generally capital) if the partnership distributes money (only) that exceeds the partner's outside basis. The gain equals the excess amount received over the outside basis. Example 16-11 illustrates the tax consequences for this scenario in the context of an operating distribution.

Scenario 4: Distributions of money, inventory, and/or unrealized receivables.   In liquidating distributions when the partner's outside basis is less than the inside bases of the distributed assets and the partnership distributes money and any property other than money, the partner reduces the basis in the distributed assets other than money but does not recognize gain or loss. Because the tax law does not restrict *reducing* bases of ordinary income assets, distributions of hot assets and other property will cause reductions in basis. However, the tax law does prescribe a particular sequence for the required reductions.

   If the partnership distributes only money, inventory, and unrealized receivables, the partner reduces the basis of the hot assets distributed (assuming money doesn't exceed basis). The required decrease in the basis of the distributed assets is equal to the difference between the partner's outside basis and the partnership's inside basis in the distributed assets. The partner first assigns her outside basis to the assets received in an amount equal to the assets' inside bases (allocating to money first). Then the partner allocates the required *decrease* to the assets with unrealized depreciation, to eliminate any existing losses built into the distributed assets.[41] Finally, the partner allocates any remaining required decrease to the distributed assets in proportion to their *adjusted bases* (AB), after considering the preceding steps and using the following equation:

$$\text{Basis allocation} = \text{Required decrease} \times \frac{\text{AB}_{asset}}{\text{Sum of AB}_{distributed\ assets}}$$

[41]If the required decrease is insufficient to allocate the full amount of depreciation to the distributed assets in this step, then the partner will allocate the remaining required decrease in this step to the depreciated assets based on their relative unrealized depreciation.

Example 16-19

What if: Suppose CCS makes the following distribution to Greg in liquidation of his CCS interest:

Asset	CCS Tax Basis	Fair Market Value
Cash	$256,000	$256,000
Inventory A	50,000	129,000
Inventory B	25,000	6,000
Total	$331,000	

Greg's basis in his CCS interest as of the liquidation is $334,000, including his $66,000 share of CCS's liabilities. What is Greg's recognized gain or loss on the distribution? What is Greg's basis in the distributed assets following the liquidation?

Answer: Greg does not recognize any gain or loss. His basis in the cash is $256,000; his basis in Inventory A is $10,714; and his basis in Inventory B is $1,286, computed as follows:

First, Greg reduces his outside basis in CCS by his $66,000 debt relief, such that his outside basis allocable to distributed assets is $268,000 ($334,000 − $66,000). He must allocate this remaining basis to the distributed assets using the following steps:

Description	Amount	Explanation
Step 1:		
(1) Allocable basis	$268,000	Basis in CCS of $334,000 − debt relief of $66,000
(2) **Basis assigned to cash**	**256,000**	
(3) Initial basis assigned to Inventory A	50,000	
(4) Initial basis assigned to Inventory B	25,000	
(5) Required decrease	63,000	(2) + (3) + (4) − (1): Initial assignment of basis exceeds Greg's allocable CCS basis
Step 2:		
(6) Required decrease to Inventory B	19,000	Unrealized depreciation on Inventory B (FMV of $6,000 less basis of $25,000)
(7) Remaining required decrease	44,000	(5) − (6)
(8) Interim adjusted basis of Inventory B	6,000	(4) − (6)

Step 3: In Step 3, Greg decreases the basis of the inventory in proportion to its relative adjusted bases determined in Step 2 using the following allocation:

$$\text{Basis allocation} = \text{Required decrease} \times \frac{AB_{asset}}{\text{Sum of } AB_{distributed\ assets}}$$

(9) Required decrease to Inventory A	39,286	Basis reduction = $44,000 × ($50,000/$56,000)
(10) Required decrease to Inventory B	4,714	Basis reduction = $44,000 × ($6,000/$56,000)
Final basis of Inventory A	**10,714**	(3) − (9)
Final basis of Inventory B	**1,286**	(8) − (10)

Example 16-20

What if: Suppose CCS makes the following distribution to Greg in liquidation of his CCS interest:

Asset	CCS Tax Basis	Fair Market Value
Cash	$242,000	$242,000
Accounts receivable	0	12,000
Inventory	72,000	120,000
Total	$314,000	

Greg's basis in his CCS interest as of the liquidation is $334,000, including his share ($66,000) of CCS's liabilities. What is Greg's recognized gain or loss on the distribution? What is Greg's basis in the assets he receives in the liquidating distribution?

Answer: Greg does not recognize any gain or loss on the liquidation. His asset bases are:

Cash	$242,000
Accounts receivable	0
Inventory*	26,000
Total	$268,000

Greg computes the basis as follows:

As a preliminary step to the allocation, he reduces his outside basis in CCS by his $66,000 debt relief, leaving an allocable outside basis of $268,000 ($334,000 − $66,000). He allocates this basis to the distributed assets using the following steps:

Description	Amount	Explanation
Step 1:		
(1) Allocable basis	$268,000	Basis in CCS of $334,000 − debt relief of $66,000
(2) Basis assigned to cash	242,000	
(3) Initial basis assigned to accounts receivable	0	
(4) Initial basis assigned to inventory	72,000	
(5) Required decrease	46,000	(2) + (3) + (4) − (1): Initial assignment of basis exceeds Greg's allocable CCS basis

Step 2: N/A because no assets have unrealized depreciation.

Step 3: In Step 3, Greg decreases the basis of the accounts receivable and inventory in proportion to their relative adjusted bases using the following reduction:

$$\text{Basis allocation} = \text{Required decrease} \times \frac{AB_{asset}}{\text{Sum of } AB_{distributed\ assets}}$$

(6) Required decrease to accounts receivable	0	Basis reduction = $46,000 × ($–0–/$72,000)
(7) Required decrease to inventory	46,000	Basis reduction = $46,000 × ($72,000/$72,000)
Final basis of accounts receivable	0	(3) − (6)
Final basis of inventory	26,000	(4) − (7)

Note that in this scenario, the tax rules recharacterize a portion ($46,000) of Greg's ultimate gain from capital gain to ordinary income. The sum of the bases of the distributed assets ($314,000) exceeds Greg's allocable outside basis ($268,000) by $46,000. Absent the allocation rules illustrated in Example 16-20, this would have been a capital gain to Greg. Instead, as we discuss below, the basis decrease to the hot assets will cause Greg to recognize any gain as ordinary upon sale of these assets.

Scenario 5: Other property included in distributions.   In our final scenario, the partnership distributes other property in addition to or instead of money and/or inventory and unrealized receivables, and the partner's outside basis is less than the combined inside bases of the distributed property. The terminating partner does not recognize gain or loss; rather, he decreases the basis in the other property distributed. The process for assigning basis to the distributed assets is similar to the method we described above, although the required basis decrease is focused on the other property rather than the hot assets.[42] The procedure is as follows:

Step 1:   The partner first determines their outside basis net of any debt relief, and then allocates that amount to any money, inventory, and unrealized receivables equal to the partnership's basis in these assets. The partner also assigns a basis to any other property equal to the partnership's basis in the other property distributed.

Step 2:   The partner then allocates the required decrease (outside basis less partnership adjusted basis in distributed assets) to the other property that has unrealized depreciation to the extent of that depreciation to eliminate inherent losses. Thus, if an asset has an adjusted basis to the partnership of $700 and a fair market value of $600, the asset's basis is first reduced by $100 (unrealized depreciation).

Step 3:   If any required decrease remains after accounting for the inherent losses in the distributed assets, the partner then allocates it to all other property in proportion to their adjusted bases. The *adjusted bases* used in this step are the bases from Step 2. We can determine the allocation as follows:

$$\text{Basis reduction} = \text{Required decrease} \times \frac{AB_{\text{asset}}}{\text{Sum of } AB_{\text{all distributed other property}}}$$

Example 16-21

What if: Suppose CCS makes the following distribution to Greg in liquidation of his CCS interest:

Asset	CCS Tax Basis	Fair Market Value
Cash	$187,000	$187,000
Investment A	10,000	7,000
Investment B	10,000	18,000
Inventory	70,000	162,000
Total	$277,000	

Greg's basis in his CCS interest as of the liquidation is $334,000, including his $66,000 share of CCS's liabilities. What is Greg's recognized gain or loss on the distribution? What is Greg's basis in the distributed assets following the liquidation?

[42]§732(c)(3).

Answer: Greg does not recognize any gain or loss. His asset bases are as follows:

Cash	$187,000
Investment A	4,530
Investment B	6,470
Inventory	70,000
Total	$268,000

Greg's basis in these assets is determined as follows:

Greg first determines his allocable basis of $268,000 by reducing his CCS basis ($334,000) for the deemed cash distribution relating to his $66,000 share of the reduction in CCS's debt.

Description	Amount	Explanation
Step 1:		
(1) Allocable basis	$268,000	Basis in CCS of $334,000 – debt relief of $66,000
(2) Basis assigned to cash	187,000	
(3) Initial basis assigned to Investment A	10,000	
(4) Initial basis assigned to Investment B	10,000	
(5) Initial basis assigned to inventory	70,000	
(6) Required decrease	9,000	(2) + (3) + (4) + (5) − (1): Initial assignment of basis exceeds Greg's allocable CCS basis
Step 2:		
(7) Required decrease to Investment A	3,000	Unrealized depreciation on Investment A (FMV of $7,000 less basis of $10,000)
(8) Remaining required decrease	6,000	(6) − (7)
(9) Interim basis of Investment A	7,000	(3) − (7)

Step 3: In Step 3, Greg decreases the basis of the other property (Investments A and B) in proportion to their relative adjusted bases using the following allocation:

$$\text{Basis reduction} = \text{Required decrease} \times \frac{AB_{asset}}{\text{Sum of } AB_{all \ distributed \ other \ property}}$$

	Amount	Explanation
(10) Required decrease to Investment A	2,470	Basis reduction = $6,000 × ($7,000/$17,000)
(11) Required decrease to Investment B	3,530	Basis reduction = $6,000 × ($10,000/$17,000)
Final basis of Investment A	4,530	(9) − (10)
Final basis of Investment B	6,470	(4) − (11)

Character and Holding Period of Distributed Assets   For both operating and liquidating distributions, the character of the distributed assets usually stays the same for the partner as it was in the partnership, in order to prevent conversion of ordinary income to capital gain for both operating and liquidating distributions. Thus, if a partner sells certain assets with ordinary character after the distribution, the partner will recognize ordinary income from the sale.[43] These assets include inventory [§751(d)] and unrealized receivables [§751(c)]. For inventory items, the ordinary income "taint" will remain for five years after the distribution. For unrealized receivables, a subsequent sale at any time after the distribution will result in ordinary income. The reverse is not true, however. If a partnership distributes a capital asset that will be inventory to a terminating partner, the partner will have ordinary income from an eventual sale, not capital gain or loss. To ensure the character of any distributed long-term capital gain property retains its character to the partner, the partner's holding period generally includes the partnership's holding period.[44]

Example 16-22

Greg has decided to cash out his investment in CCS in order to invest in another project in which he can more actively participate. After he speaks to Nicole and Sarah about the options, the three owners decide Greg can cash out using one of two options.

Option 1: CCS will liquidate Greg's interest by distributing cash of $242,000; accounts receivable worth $12,000 (adjusted basis is $0); and inventory worth $120,000 (adjusted basis is $72,000).

Option 2: Nicole and Sarah will purchase Greg's interest in CCS. Nicole agrees to purchase two-thirds of Greg's interest for $249,333 cash and Sarah agrees to purchase the remaining one-third for $124,667 cash.

Greg's basis in his 30 percent CCS interest is $334,000, including his share of CCS's liabilities of $66,000. Either event would occur on January 1, 2020, when CCS's balance sheet is as follows:

Color Comfort Sheets LLC January 1, 2020		
	Tax Basis	**FMV**
Assets		
Cash	$390,000	$ 390,000
Accounts receivable	0	40,000
Inventory	90,000	200,000
Investments	60,000	105,000
Equipment (cost = $200,000)	150,000	200,000
Building (cost = $100,000)	90,000	100,000
Land—original	20,000	160,000
Land—investment	140,000	270,000
Totals	$940,000	$1,465,000
Liabilities and capital		
Accounts payable	$ 80,000	
Long-term debt	0	
Mortgage on original land	40,000	
Mortgage on investment land	120,000	
Capital—Nicole	119,000	
—Sarah	332,000	
—Greg	249,000	
Totals	$940,000	

---

[43]§735(a).
[44]§735(b).

What are the tax consequences (amount and character of recognized gain or loss, basis in assets) for Greg under each option?

Answer: *Option 1:* Greg recognizes no gain or loss on the liquidating distribution. His bases in the distributed assets are:

Cash	$242,000
Accounts receivable	0
Inventory	26,000
Total	$268,000

Option 2: Greg recognizes ordinary income of $60,000 and a capital gain of $46,000.

The tax consequences of both options are determined as follows:

Option 1: The distribution allows Greg to defer recognizing any gain or loss on the liquidation. Example 16-20 provides the details of the analysis. Greg has debt relief in an amount equal to his share of CCS's liabilities ($66,000). The debt relief is treated as a distribution of cash, so Greg reduces his outside basis by this amount from $334,000 to $268,000. The difference between the sum of the inside bases of the distributed property and his outside basis is $46,000 ($314,000 − $268,000) and represents a required *decrease* to the bases of assets distributed in liquidation. Greg follows the prescribed method illustrated in Example 16-20 to compute his asset bases.

The basis reduction for these assets allows Greg to defer recognizing a $46,000 gain on the liquidation. The cost to accomplish the deferral is that if Greg sells the inventory and the accounts receivable immediately after the distribution, he will recognize ordinary income of $106,000 as follows:

Amount realized:		
Cash (equal to FMV of accounts receivable and inventory)	$ 12,000 120,000	$132,000
Less: Adjusted basis		
Accounts receivable	0	
Inventory	26,000	26,000
Ordinary income		$106,000

The $106,000 ordinary income is $46,000 greater than the inherent gain on these assets of $60,000 ($132,000 − $72,000) had the partnership sold the assets. If Greg selects Option 1, he will not recognize income on the liquidation until he sells the inventory and collects (or sells) the accounts receivable, thereby leaving himself flexibility on the timing of gain recognition.

Option 2: In this option, Greg sells his CCS interest to Nicole and Sarah and receives cash of $374,000 ($249,333 from Nicole and $124,667 from Sarah). Greg computes his total gain or loss as follows:

Amount realized:		
Cash	$374,000	
Debt relief	66,000	$440,000
Less: Basis in CCS interest		334,000
Realized and recognized gain		$106,000

Next, Greg determines the character of the gain from the sale by first identifying the gain related to hot assets.

Hot Asset − CCS	(1) Basis	(2) FMV	(3) Gain/Loss (2) − (1)	Greg's Share 30% × (3)
Accounts receivable	$ 0	$ 40,000	$ 40,000	$12,000
Inventory	90,000	200,000	110,000	33,000
Equipment	150,000	200,000	50,000	15,000
Total ordinary income				$60,000

(*continued on page 16-24*)

The final step for Greg is to determine the capital gain or loss by subtracting the ordinary portion from the total gain.

Total gain	$106,000
Less: ordinary income from §751(a)	(60,000)
Capital gain	$ 46,000

If he chooses Option 2, Greg will recognize $60,000 of ordinary income and $46,000 of capital gain in 2020.

Example 16-23

Given the tax consequences to Greg in the previous example, should he have CCS liquidate his interest (Option 1) or sell his interest (Option 2)?

Answer: Under Option 1 (the liquidation), Greg is able to defer all recognition of gain until he later sells the distributed assets. This provides him flexibility in when he pays tax on the liquidating distribution. However, when he recognizes any income upon subsequent sales, the character of the income will be ordinary and taxed at ordinary rates. Under Option 2, Greg must recognize income immediately upon the sale: $60,000 of ordinary income and $46,000 of capital gain. He has no future tax liability related to the liquidating distribution. The capital gain could be taxed at a rate as high as 23.8 percent (including the net investment income tax). An additional consideration is that under Option 2 Greg receives cash, rather than a mix of cash and other assets. If he wants to immediately invest the proceeds in another venture, he may prefer a pure cash payment.

continued from page 16-2...

Greg takes the liquidating distribution option (Option 1) offered by CCS to avoid recognizing a gain currently. Although this option doesn't give him as much cash as a sale would have, Greg figures it is enough for another investment and he can avoid paying tax on the distribution this year.

For the first time, CCS has only two owners—Nicole and Sarah. After liquidating Greg's interest, Nicole's interest has increased to 43 percent and Sarah's to 57 percent. Both women are happy with that outcome, although they are sorry to lose Greg's investment in the business. ■

LO 16-5   DISPROPORTIONATE DISTRIBUTIONS

Up to this point in the chapter, our distribution examples have either assumed or represented that each partner received a pro rata share of the partnership's unrealized appreciation in its ordinary assets, as specified in the partnership agreement based on the partner's capital interests. In practice, distributions may not always reflect each partner's proportionate share.[45] Both operating and liquidating distributions can be **disproportionate distributions.** Without going into all the details of these complex rules, let's briefly discuss the implications of distributions in which partners receive either more or less of their share of the unrealized appreciation or losses in so-called hot assets [assets defined in IRC §751(b)

---

[45]A thorough discussion of these issues is beyond the scope of this chapter. Therefore, we will abbreviate our discussion just to give a flavor for the issues and consequences of these disproportionate distributions.

as **substantially appreciated inventory** and unrealized receivables].[46] Note that the definition of hot assets for purposes of disproportionate distributions includes only *substantially appreciated* inventory, not *all* inventory [as is the case under §751(a), the definition we used to characterize the gain in dispositions of partnership interests]. Inventory is considered substantially appreciated if its fair market value is more than 120 percent of its basis.

Suppose a partner receives less than her share of the appreciation in hot assets in a liquidating distribution. This may occur, for example, if a partner receives only cash in a liquidating distribution from a partnership with hot assets. Rather than only applying the rules we discussed above, the partner must treat part of the distribution as a sale or exchange.[47] Basically, the disproportionate distribution rules treat the partner as having sold her share of hot assets to the partnership in exchange for "cold" [non-§751(b)] assets. This deemed sale generates an ordinary gain or loss to the partner on the deemed sale, essentially equal to her share of the appreciation or depreciation in the portion of hot assets not distributed to her. From the partnership's perspective, the partnership is deemed to have purchased the hot assets from the partner in exchange for cold assets. Therefore, the *partnership* recognizes a capital or §1231 gain or loss equal to the remaining partners' inherent gain or loss in the distributed cold assets. The effects are reversed if a partner receives more than her share of the appreciation in a partnership's hot assets.[48] The rules are meant to ensure that partners cannot convert ordinary income into capital gain through distributions. Thus, they require that partners will ultimately recognize their share of the partnership ordinary income regardless of the form of their distributions.

Example 16-24

What if: Suppose CCS distributes $328,000 in cash to Greg Randall on January 1, 2020, in complete liquidation of Greg's 30 percent interest in CCS. Greg's basis in his CCS interest before the distribution is $334,000. Assume CCS's balance sheet is as follows:

Color Comfort Sheets LLC December 31, 2019	Tax Basis	FMV
Assets		
Cash	$700,000	$ 700,000
Inventory	240,000	440,000
Totals	$940,000	$1,140,000
Liabilities and capital		
Liabilities	$240,000	
Capital—Nicole	119,000	
—Sarah	332,000	
—Greg	249,000	
Totals	$940,000	

(continued on page 16-26)

[46]Unrealized receivables include the accounts receivable of a cash-method taxpayer, the excess of the fair market value over basis of accounts receivable for accrual-method taxpayers, and depreciation recapture under §1245. The definition of substantially appreciated inventory is broader than simply goods primarily held for sale to customers. It also includes property that would not be classified as capital assets or §1231 assets if sold by the partnership. As a result, receivables are included as "inventory."

[47]§751(b).

[48]The partner would generally recognize capital gain on the deemed sale and the partnership would recognize ordinary income.

Is this distribution disproportionate? What are the implications of the distribution?

Answer: The CCS balance sheet as of December 31, 2019 indicates that CCS's inventory is a hot asset given that its fair market value is more than 120 percent of its basis. Further, the CCS balance sheet indicates that the fair market value of Greg's share of the unrealized appreciation in CCS's hot assets for purposes of disproportionate distributions [§751(b)] is $60,000, or 30 percent of the $200,000 unrealized appreciation in inventory ($440,000 FMV less $240,000 adjusted basis). Since Greg receives only cash in the distribution, he has not received a proportionate share of the unrealized appreciation in CCS's hot assets. Thus, the distribution will be disproportionate.

The tax law treats Greg as having sold his share of the hot assets for cold assets, and he will recognize ordinary income equal to his share of the appreciation on the hot assets not distributed, or $60,000. Absent this provision in the tax law, all of Greg's gains from the distribution would have been treated as capital gains. CCS does not recognize any gain or loss because it has no appreciation in the assets (cash) used to "purchase" the hot assets.

LO 16-6 SPECIAL BASIS ADJUSTMENTS

Recall that when a partner sells her partnership interest, the partnership's inside basis is generally unaffected by the sale. This creates a discrepancy between the new investor's outside basis (cost) and her share of the partnership's inside basis, which artificially changes the potential income or loss at the partnership level. For example, earlier in the chapter Greg Randall purchased Chanzz's 30 percent interest in CCS for $82,800 (see the *what-if* scenario in Example 16-5). Greg's outside basis after the acquisition is $106,800, reflecting the cash payment of $82,800 and his share of CCS's debt at the time of the acquisition, $24,000. However, Greg's share of CCS's inside basis in its assets is $105,000 (see Example 16-7). This is the outcome because the sale does not affect CCS's inside basis and Greg simply steps into Chanzz's shoes for determining his share of the inside basis. The discrepancy reflects Chanzz's unrecognized share of appreciation of CCS's assets (which Greg paid full value for) as of the sale date and causes Greg to be temporarily overtaxed when CCS sells these appreciated assets.

Example 16-25

What if: Assume that Greg acquires his 30% interest in CCS for $82,800 (see Example 16-5). If under this assumption, CCS sells its accounts receivable for their fair market value of $13,000 (adjusted basis is $0) (see Example 16-2 for CCS's balance sheet as of June 30, 2018, the acquisition date), what is the amount and character of gain that Greg recognizes on the sale?

Answer: When CCS sells the accounts receivable, it recognizes $13,000 of ordinary income, of which $3,900 (30 percent) is allocated to Greg. However, when Chanzz sold its interest to Greg, Chanzz was already taxed on the $3,900 allocated portion of that ordinary income under §751(a), and Greg paid full value for his interest in the receivables when he acquired his 30 percent interest in CCS. This means Greg will be taxed on the $3,900 again in 2018, and his outside basis increases by $3,900. Because Greg paid fair market value for his share of the receivables, he should not have any income when they are sold at fair market value. Eventually, when Greg disposes of his CCS interest, his ultimate gain (or loss) on the disposition will be $3,900 less, because of the increase to his outside basis from this additional income; meanwhile, he is overtaxed on the receivables. Greg must report ordinary income today for an offsetting capital loss (or reduced capital gain) in the future when he disposes of his interest.

The tax rules allow the partnership to make an election for a **special basis adjustment** to eliminate discrepancies between the inside and outside bases and to correct the artificial income or loss at the partnership level.[49] For the most part, basis discrepancies arise in two situations: following *sales* of partnership interests, and following *distributions* when a partner receives an asset that takes more or less basis outside the partnership

---

[49]§754. The election is made by including a written statement declaring that the partnership is making the §754 election with the partnership return when filed for the year the election is to take effect.

than it had on the inside and when the partner recognizes a gain or loss on the distribution. Once a partnership makes a §754 election, the partnership is required to make the special basis adjustment for all subsequent sales of partnership interests and partnership distributions. The election can be revoked only with permission from the IRS.

Even without a §754 election in effect, the partnership must adjust its bases if the partnership has a **substantial built-in loss** at the time a partner sells her partnership interest. A substantial built-in loss exists if the partnership's aggregate inside basis in its property exceeds the property's fair market value by more than $250,000 when a transfer of an interest occurs or when the purchasing partner would be allocated a loss of more than $250,000 if the partnership assets were sold for fair market value immediately after the sale.[50] An analogous event—a **substantial basis reduction**—may occur for distributions, which also triggers a mandatory basis adjustment.

Although the election is made under §754, the actual authorization of the special basis adjustment is governed by two separate code sections, depending on which situation gives rise to the adjustment: (1) sale of partnership interest [§743(b)], or (2) distributions [§734(b)]. These two sections determine how much of an adjustment will be made, and §755 then stipulates how the adjustment is allocated among the partnership assets. The relationships among these code sections are depicted in Exhibit 16-2 below.

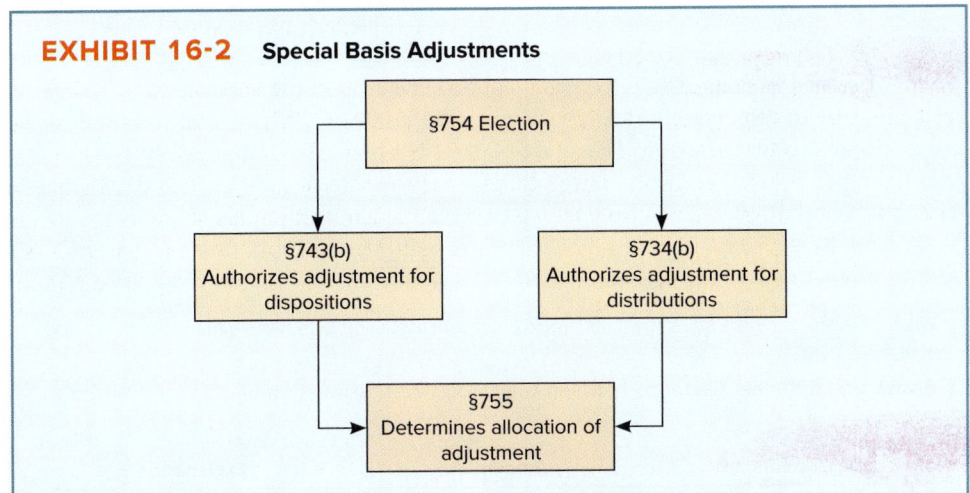

EXHIBIT 16-2 **Special Basis Adjustments**

Special Basis Adjustments for Dispositions

The special basis adjustment the partnership makes when a partner sells his partnership interest is designed to give the new investor an inside basis in the partnership assets equal to his outside basis. The basis adjustment in these cases applies *only* to the new investor. The inside bases of the continuing partners remain unchanged, so their income and losses will continue to be accurately allocated. The adjustment is equal to the difference between the new investor's outside basis and his share of inside basis.[51] The new investor's outside basis is generally equal to the cost of his partnership interest plus his share of partnership liabilities.[52] The

[50]§743(d). In this context, a transfer generally refers to sales, exchanges, or transfers at death, not gift transfers.

[51]§743(b).

[52]A partner's share of inside basis is also labeled *previously taxed capital* [§1.743-1(d)]. The technical calculation is determined as follows (but generally equals the partner's tax capital account):

(1) the amount of cash the partner would receive on liquidation after a hypothetical sale of all the partnership assets for their fair market value after the sale of the partnership interest, plus

(2) the amount of taxable loss allocated to the partner from the hypothetical sale, less

(3) the amount of taxable gain allocated to the partner from the hypothetical sale.

special basis adjustment must then be allocated to the assets under allocation rules in §755, which are beyond the scope of this text.

Example 16-26

What if: Suppose Greg acquired Chanzz's 30 percent interest in CCS on June 30, 2018, for $82,800. CCS's balance sheet as of the sale date is assumed to be as follows:

Color Comfort Sheets LLC June 30, 2018	Tax Basis	FMV
Assets		
Cash	$ 27,000	$ 27,000
Accounts receivable	0	13,000
Investments	15,000	12,000
Inventory	1,000	1,000
Equipment (cost = $100,000)	80,000	86,000
Building	97,000	97,000
Land	20,000	150,000
Totals	$240,000	$386,000
Liabilities and capital		
Long-term debt	$100,000	
Capital—Nicole	(49,000)	
—Sarah	108,000	
—Chanzz	81,000	
Totals	$240,000	

What is the special basis adjustment for Greg's purchase, assuming CCS has a §754 election in effect at the sale date?

Answer: $1,800, the difference between Greg's outside basis and inside basis, calculated as follows:

Description	Amount	Explanation
(1) Cash purchase price	$ 82,800	
(2) Greg's share of CCS debt	24,000	$80,000 × 30%
(3) Initial basis in CCS	$106,800	(1) + (2)
(4) Greg's inside basis	105,000	Chanzz's tax capital ($81,000) plus share of CCS debt ($24,000) (See Example 16-7)
Special basis adjustment	$ 1,800	(3) − (4)

When a new investor's special basis adjustment is allocated to depreciable or amortizable assets, the new investor will benefit from additional depreciation or amortization. In some cases, the amounts can be quite substantial, and a new investor may be willing to pay more for a partnership interest with a §754 election in place than he would for a partnership interest without it.

Special Basis Adjustments for Distributions

A similar potential problem exists when the partnership distributes assets to the partners that represent more (or, in some cases, less) than their share of the inside basis in the partnership assets. This usually occurs when a partner recognizes a gain or loss on a distribution or when a partner's basis in the distributed property is different from the partnership's basis in the property. In contrast to the special basis adjustment for sales of partnership interests, the special basis adjustment for distributions affects the common basis of *partnership* property and not merely one partner's basis.

The special basis adjustment can either increase or decrease the basis in the partnership assets. A **positive basis adjustment** will *increase* the basis in the partnership assets (1) when a partner receiving distributed property recognizes a gain on the distribution (for instance, in operating distributions where the partner receives money in excess of her outside basis), and (2) when a partner receiving distributed property takes a basis in the property less than the partnership's basis in the property. The positive adjustment will equal the sum of the gain recognized by the partners receiving distributed property and the amount of the basis reduction.

In Example 16-11, CCS distributed $250,000 cash to Nicole on December 31, 2019, as part of an operating distribution. Because Nicole's outside basis before the distribution was $205,000 and she received only money in the distribution, Nicole was required to recognize a $45,000 gain on the distribution. If CCS had a §754 election in effect, it would have a positive special basis adjustment from the distribution of $45,000.

A **negative basis adjustment** will *decrease* the basis in partnership assets (1) when a partner receiving distributed property in a liquidating distribution recognizes a loss on the distribution, and (2) when a partner receiving distributed property takes a basis in the property greater than the partnership's basis in the property.

The negative adjustment will equal the sum of the recognized loss and the amount of the basis increase made by the partners receiving the distribution. Recall from our previous discussion of distributions that negative adjustments can occur only in liquidating distributions. Only then does a partner recognize a loss or increase the distributed property's basis over its basis prior to the distribution.

In Example 16-15, CCS liquidated Greg's 30 percent interest by distributing cash of $206,000 and inventory with a fair market value of $103,000 (adjusted basis is $43,000). Because Greg's outside basis after considering his debt relief ($268,000) was greater than the sum of the bases of the property distributed ($249,000), Greg recognized a loss of $19,000 on the liquidation. If CCS had a §754 election in effect at the time of this liquidation, CCS would have a negative basis adjustment of $19,000.

As in the case of partnership dispositions, the allocation of the special basis adjustment among the partnership's remaining assets after a distribution is intended to offset any gain or loss the partners would have recognized twice absent the adjustment. The process of allocating the adjustment for distributions is prescribed in §755, and these procedures are beyond the scope of this text.

CONCLUSION

The tax rules for partnership dispositions and distributions are among the most complex in the Internal Revenue Code. This chapter provided an overview of these rules and in some cases plunged into the complexity. We discussed the calculation of gains and losses from the sale of a partnership interest, as well as the basis implications of the purchase to a new investor. In doing so, we discussed how *hot assets* might affect the gain or loss. The chapter also explained the basic rules for determining the tax treatment of partnership distributions.

We illustrated how partnership elections might affect the partnership's basis in assets following partnership interest dispositions or distributions. In general, the tax rules are designed to avoid having business owners make decisions based on tax rules rather than on business principles; however, making this goal a reality provides for some challenging applications.

Summary

LO 16-1 Determine the tax consequences to the buyer and seller of the disposition of a partnership interest, including the amount and character of gain or loss recognized.

- Sellers are primarily concerned about their realized and recognized gain or loss on the sale of their partnership interest.
- Sellers' debt relief is included in the amount realized from the sale.
- Buyers' main tax concerns are determining their basis in the partnership interest they acquire and their inside bases of the partnership assets.
- A buyer's outside basis after an acquisition is generally his cost plus his share of partnership liabilities. A buyer's inside basis is generally the same as the seller's inside basis at the sale date.
- The sale of a partnership interest does not generally affect a partnership's inside basis in its assets.
- A partnership's tax year closes for the selling partner upon the sale of a partnership interest.
- Hot assets include unrealized receivables and inventory items.
- Unrealized receivables include the rights to receive payment for goods delivered or to be delivered, or services rendered or to be rendered, as well as items that would generate ordinary income if the partnership sold the asset for its fair market value, such as depreciation recapture.
- There are actually two definitions of inventory items. The first under §751(a) applies to sales of partnership interests and includes all classic inventory items and assets that are *not* capital or §1231 assets. The second definition of inventory [§751(b)] applies primarily to distributions and includes only substantially appreciated inventory.
- Sellers classify gains and losses from the sale of partnership interests as ordinary to the extent the gain relates to hot assets.
- Hot assets are also important to determine whether a distribution is proportionate or disproportionate.

LO 16-2 Compare operating and liquidating distributions.

- Distributions from a flow-through entity are one mechanism to return business profits or capital to the owners of the entity.
- Distributions may also be used to liquidate an owner's interest in the business or to completely terminate the business.
- Operating distributions include distributions in which the owner retains an interest in the business.

LO 16-3 Determine the tax consequences of proportionate operating distributions.

- Partnerships do not generally recognize gain or loss on the distribution of property.
- Most operating distributions do not result in gain or loss to the partner receiving the distribution. Gains and losses are deferred through basis adjustments to the distributed assets and basis of the partnership interest.
- A partner recognizes a gain from an operating distribution if she receives a distribution of money that exceeds the basis in her partnership interest.
- Partners never recognize losses from operating distributions.

LO 16-4 Determine the tax consequences of proportionate liquidating distributions.

- The tax issues in liquidating distributions are primarily twofold: (1) determining whether the liquidating partner recognizes a gain or loss, and (2) allocating the liquidating partner's basis in her partnership interest to the distributed assets.
- A partner recognizes a gain only when the partner receives more money than her basis in the partnership interest.
- A partner recognizes a loss only when the partnership distributes cash and hot assets and the partner's basis in the partnership interest is greater than the sum of the bases of the assets the partner received in the distribution.

- In all other cases, a partner does not recognize gains or losses from a liquidating distribution; rather, she will simply allocate her basis in the partnership interest to the distributed assets.
- The key to the allocation process is to focus on two factors: (1) the type of property distributed, and (2) whether the total basis in distributed assets is larger or smaller than the partner's basis in the partnership interest.
- The character of the distributed assets usually stays the same to the partner as in the partnership.

Explain the significance of disproportionate distributions.   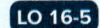 **LO 16-5**

- Disproportionate distributions occur when the assets distributed in either operating or liquidating distributions do not represent the partner's proportionate share of the partnership's unrealized appreciation in its hot and cold assets.
- A disproportionate distribution causes a shift in the proportion of ordinary income and capital gain income from the partnership. Therefore, the rules require the partner to treat the disproportionate portion of a distribution as a sale or exchange.
- If a partner receives more cold assets than her proportionate share in a distribution, she will generally recognize ordinary income in an amount equal to her share of the appreciation of hot assets not distributed to her. If a partner receives more hot assets than her proportionate share, she will recognize capital gain equal to her share of the appreciation in cold assets not distributed to her.
- The disproportionate distribution rules ensure that partners cannot convert ordinary income into capital gain through distributions.

Explain the rationale for special basis adjustments and the method for calculating them.   **LO 16-6**

- Discrepancies between a partner's inside and outside basis may cause a partner to be overtaxed or undertaxed, at least temporarily. Special basis adjustment rules allow the partnership to eliminate discrepancies between inside and outside bases to correct any artificial income or loss at the partnership level.
- Basis discrepancies may occur following the acquisition of a partnership interest and following distributions where a partner receives more or less than her share of the inside basis in the partnership property.
- When a new investor purchases a partnership interest, she may receive a special basis adjustment equal to the difference between her outside basis and her share of inside basis if the partnership has a §754 election in effect.
- A special basis adjustment is mandatory even without a §754 election in effect when a partnership has a substantial built-in loss at the time a partnership interest is transferred.
- When a partner recognizes a gain from a distribution or takes a basis in distributed property less than the partnership's basis in the property, the partnership will have a positive special basis adjustment to increase the basis in the partnership's assets.
- When a partner recognizes a loss from a liquidating distribution or takes a basis in distributed property greater than the partnership's basis in the property, the partnership will have a negative special basis adjustment to decrease the basis in partnership assets.

KEY TERMS

DISCUSSION QUESTIONS

Discussion Questions are available in Connect®.

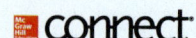

LO 16-1   1. Joey is a 25 percent owner of Loopy LLC. He no longer wants to be involved in the business. What options does Joey have to exit the business?

LO 16-1   2. Compare and contrast the aggregate and entity approaches for a sale of a partnership interest.

LO 16-1   3. What restrictions might prevent a partner from selling his partnership interest to a third party?

LO 16-1   4. Explain how a partner's debt relief affects his amount realized in a sale of partnership interest.

LO 16-1   5. Under what circumstances will the gain or loss on the sale of a partnership interest be characterized as ordinary rather than capital?

LO 16-1   6. What are *hot assets* and why are they important in the sale of a partnership interest?

LO 16-1   7. For an accrual-method partnership, are accounts receivable considered unrealized receivables? Explain.

LO 16-1   8. Can a partnership have unrealized receivables if it has no accounts receivable?

LO 16-1   9. How do hot assets affect the character of gain or loss on the sale of a partnership interest?

LO 16-1   10. Under what circumstances can a partner recognize both gain and loss on the sale of a partnership interest?

LO 16-1   11. Absent any special elections, what effect does a sale of partnership interest have on the partnership?

LO 16-1   12. Generally, a selling partner's capital account carries over to the purchaser of the partnership interest. Under what circumstances will this not be the case?

LO 16-2   13. What distinguishes operating from liquidating distributions?

LO 16-3   14. Under what circumstances will a partner recognize a gain from an operating distribution?

LO 16-3   15. Under what circumstances will a partner recognize a loss from an operating distribution?

LO 16-3   16. In general, what effect does an operating distribution have on the partnership?

LO 16-3   17. If a partner's outside basis is less than the partnership's inside basis in distributed assets, how does the partner determine his basis of the distributed assets in an operating distribution?

LO 16-4   18. Under what conditions will a partner recognize gain in a liquidating distribution?

LO 16-4   19. Under what conditions will a partner recognize loss in a liquidating distribution?

LO 16-4   20. Describe how a partner determines his basis in distributed assets in cases in which a partnership distributes only money, inventory, and/or unrealized receivables in a liquidating distribution.

LO 16-4   21. How does a partner determine his basis in distributed assets when the partnership distributes other property in addition to money and hot assets?

LO 16-5   22. SBT partnership distributes $5,000 cash and a parcel of land with a fair market value of $40,000 and a $25,000 basis to the partnership to Sam (30 percent partner). What factors must Sam and SBT consider in determining the tax treatment of this distribution?

LO 16-5   23. Discuss the underlying concern to tax policy makers in distributions in which a partner receives more or less than his share of the partnership's hot assets.

LO 16-5   24. In general, how do the disproportionate distribution rules ensure that partners recognize their share of partnership ordinary income?

LO 16-6   25. Why would a new partner who pays more for a partnership interest than the selling partner's outside basis want the partnership to elect a special basis adjustment?

26. List two common situations that will cause a partner's inside and outside basis to differ. `LO 16-6`

27. Explain why a partnership might not want to make a §754 election to allow special basis adjustments. `LO 16-6`

28. When might a new partner have an upward basis adjustment following the acquisition of a partnership interest? `LO 16-6`

29. When are partnerships mandated to adjust the basis of their assets (inside basis) when a partner sells a partnership interest or receives a partnership distribution? `LO 16-6`

PROBLEMS

Select problems are available in Connect®.   connect

30. Jerry is a 30 percent partner in the JJM Partnership when he sells his entire interest to Lucia for $56,000 cash. At the time of the sale, Jerry's basis in JJM is $32,000. JJM does not have any debt or hot assets. What is Jerry's gain or loss on the sale of his interest? `LO 16-1`

31. Joy is a 30 percent partner in the JOM Partnership when she sells her entire interest to Hope for $72,000 cash. At the time of the sale, Joy's basis in JOM is $44,000 (which includes her $6,000 share of JOM liabilities). JOM does not have any hot assets. What is Joy's gain or loss on the sale of her interest? `LO 16-1`

32. Allison, Keesha, and Steven each own equal interests in KAS Partnership, a calendar year-end, cash-method entity. On January 1 of the current year, Steven's basis in his partnership interest is $27,000. During January and February, the partnership generates $30,000 of ordinary income and $4,500 of tax-exempt income. On March 1, Steven sells his partnership interest to Juan for a cash payment of $45,000. The partnership has the following assets and no liabilities at the sale date: `LO 16-1`

	Tax Basis	FMV
Cash	$30,000	$30,000
Land held for investment	30,000	60,000
Totals	$60,000	$90,000

a) Assuming KAS's operating agreement provides for an interim closing of the books when partners' interests change during the year, what is Steven's basis in his partnership interest on March 1 just prior to the sale?

b) What is the amount and character of Steven's recognized gain or loss on the sale?

c) What is Juan's initial basis in the partnership interest?

d) What is the partnership's basis in the assets following the sale?

33. Grace, James, Helen, and Charles each own equal interests in GJHC Partnership, a calendar year-end, cash-method entity. On January 1 of the current year, James's basis in his partnership interest is $62,000. For the taxable year, the partnership generates $80,000 of ordinary income and $30,000 of dividend income. For the first five months of the year, GJHC generates $25,000 of ordinary income and no dividend income. On June 1, James sells his partnership interest to Robert for a cash payment of $70,000. The partnership has the following assets and no liabilities at the sale date: `LO 16-1`

	Tax Basis	FMV
Cash	$ 27,000	$ 27,000
Land held for investment	80,000	100,000
Totals	$107,000	$127,000

a) Assuming GJHC's operating agreement provides that the proration method will be used to allocate income or loss when partners' interests change during the year, what is James's basis in his partnership interest on June 1 just prior to the sale?

b) What is the amount and character of James's recognized gain or loss on the sale?

c) If GJHC uses an interim closing of the books, what is the amount and character of James's recognized gain or loss on the sale?

LO 16-1   34. At the end of last year, Lisa, a 35 percent partner in the five-person LAMEC Partnership, has an outside basis of $60,000, including her $30,000 share of LAMEC debt. On January 1 of the current year, Lisa sells her partnership interest to MaryLynn for a cash payment of $45,000 and the assumption of her share of LAMEC's debt.

a) What is the amount and character of Lisa's recognized gain or loss on the sale?

b) If LAMEC has $100,000 of unrealized receivables as of the sale date, what is the amount and character of Lisa's recognized gain or loss?

c) What is MaryLynn's initial basis in the partnership interest?

LO 16-1   35. Marco, Jaclyn, and Carrie formed Daxing Partnership (a calendar year-end entity) by contributing cash 10 years ago. Each partner owns an equal interest in the partnership and has an outside basis in his/her partnership interest of $104,000. On January 1 of the current year, Marco sells his partnership interest to Ryan for a cash payment of $137,000. The partnership has the following assets and no liabilities as of the sale date:

	Tax Basis	FMV
Cash	$ 18,000	$ 18,000
Accounts receivable	0	12,000
Inventory	69,000	81,000
Equipment	180,000	225,000
Stock investment	45,000	75,000
Totals	$312,000	$411,000

The equipment was purchased for $240,000, and the partnership has taken $60,000 of depreciation. The stock was purchased seven years ago.

a) What are the *hot assets* [§751(a)] for this sale?

b) What is Marco's gain or loss on the sale of his partnership interest?

c) What is the character of Marco's gain or loss?

d) What are Ryan's inside and outside bases in the partnership on the date of the sale?

LO 16-1   36. Franklin, Jefferson, and Washington formed the Independence Partnership (a calendar year-end entity) by contributing cash 10 years ago. Each partner owns an equal interest in the partnership and has an outside basis in his partnership interest of $104,000. On January 1 of the current year, Franklin sells his partnership interest to Adams for a cash payment of $122,000. The partnership has the following assets and no liabilities as of the sale date:

	Tax Basis	FMV
Cash	$ 18,000	$ 18,000
Accounts receivable	0	12,000
Inventory	69,000	81,000
Equipment	180,000	225,000
Stock investment	45,000	30,000
Totals	$312,000	$366,000

The equipment was purchased for $240,000, and the partnership has taken $60,000 of depreciation. The stock was purchased seven years ago.

a) What is Franklin's overall gain or loss on the sale of his partnership interest?

b) What is the character of Franklin's gain or loss?

37. Travis and Alix Weber are equal partners in the Tralix Partnership, which does not have a §754 election in place. Alix sells one-half of her interest (25 percent) to Michael Tomei for $30,000 cash. Just before the sale, Alix's basis in her entire partnership interest is $75,000, including her $30,000 share of the partnership liabilities. Tralix's assets on the sale date are as follows: `LO 16-1`

	Tax Basis	FMV
Cash	$ 40,000	$ 40,000
Inventory	30,000	90,000
Land held for investment	80,000	50,000
Totals	$150,000	$180,000

a) What is the amount and character of Alix's recognized gain or loss on the sale?

b) What is Alix's basis in her remaining partnership interest?

c) What is Michael's basis in his partnership interest?

d) What is the effect of the sale on the partnership's basis in the assets?

38. Newton is a one-third owner of ProRite Partnership. Newton has decided to sell his interest in the business to Betty for $50,000 cash plus the assumption of his share of ProRite's liabilities. Assume Newton's inside and outside bases in ProRite are equal. ProRite shows the following balance sheet as of the sale date: `LO 16-1`

	Tax Basis	FMV
Assets		
Cash	$ 80,000	$ 80,000
Receivables	25,000	25,000
Inventory	40,000	85,000
Land	30,000	20,000
Totals	$175,000	$210,000
Liabilities and capital		
Liabilities	$ 60,000	
Capital—Newton	38,333	
—Barbara	38,334	
—Liz	38,333	
Totals	$175,000	

What is the amount and character of Newton's recognized gain or loss?

39. Coy and Matt are equal partners in the Matcoy Partnership. Each partner has a basis in his partnership interest of $28,000 at the end of the current year, prior to any distribution. On December 31 they each receive an operating distribution. Coy receives $10,000 cash. Matt receives $3,000 cash and a parcel of land with a $7,000 fair market value and a $4,000 basis to the partnership. Matcoy has no debt or hot assets. `LO 16-3`

a) What is Coy's recognized gain or loss? What is the character of any gain or loss?

b) What is Coy's ending basis in his partnership interest?

c) What is Matt's recognized gain or loss? What is the character of any gain or loss?

d) What is Matt's basis in the distributed property?

e) What is Matt's ending basis in his partnership interest?

LO 16-3   40. Justin and Lauren are equal partners in the PJenn Partnership. The partners formed the partnership seven years ago by contributing cash. Prior to any distributions, the partners have the following bases in their partnership interests:

Partner	Outside Basis
Justin	$22,000
Lauren	22,000

On December 31 of the current year, the partnership makes a pro rata operating distribution of:

Partner	Distribution
Justin	Cash $25,000
Lauren	Cash $18,000
	Property $7,000 (FMV)
	($2,000 basis to partnership)

a) What is the amount and character of Justin's recognized gain or loss?
b) What is Justin's remaining basis in his partnership interest?
c) What is the amount and character of Lauren's recognized gain or loss?
d) What is Lauren's basis in the distributed assets?
e) What is Lauren's remaining basis in her partnership interest?

LO 16-3   41. Adam and Alyssa are equal partners in the PartiPilo Partnership. The partners formed the partnership three years ago by contributing cash. Prior to any distributions, the partners have the following bases in their partnership interests:

Partner	Outside Basis
Adam	$12,000
Alyssa	12,000

On December 31 of the current year, the partnership makes a pro rata operating distribution of:

Partner	Distribution
Adam	Cash $16,000
Alyssa	Cash $8,000
	Property $8,000 (FMV)
	($6,000 basis to partnership)

a) What is the amount and character of Adam's recognized gain or loss?
b) What is Adam's remaining basis in his partnership interest?
c) What is the amount and character of Alyssa's recognized gain or loss?
d) What is Alyssa's basis in the distributed assets?
e) What is Alyssa's remaining basis in her partnership interest?

LO 16-3   42. Karen has a $68,000 basis in her 50 percent partnership interest in the KD Partnership before receiving a current distribution of $6,000 cash and land with a fair market value of $35,000 and a basis to the partnership of $18,000.

a) What is the amount and character of Karen's recognized gain or loss?
b) What is Karen's basis in the land?
c) What is Karen's remaining basis in her partnership interest?

LO 16-3   43. Pam has a $27,000 basis (including her share of debt) in her 50 percent partnership interest in the Meddoc Partnership before receiving any distributions. This year Meddoc makes a current distribution to Pam of a parcel of land with a $40,000 fair market value and a $32,000 basis to the partnership. The land is encumbered with a $15,000 mortgage (the partnership's only liability).

a) What is the amount and character of Pam's recognized gain or loss?

b) What is Pam's basis in the land?

c) What is Pam's remaining basis in her partnership interest?

44. Two years ago, Kimberly became a 30 percent partner in the KST Partnership with a contribution of investment land with a $10,000 basis and a $16,000 fair market value. On January 2 of this year, Kimberly has a $15,000 basis in her partnership interest and none of her pre-contribution gain has been recognized. On January 2 Kimberly receives an operating distribution of a tract of land (not the contributed land) with a $12,000 basis and an $18,000 fair market value.   **LO 16-3**   **research**

   a) What is the amount and character of Kimberly's recognized gain or loss on the distribution?

   b) What is Kimberly's remaining basis in KST after the distribution?

   c) What is KST's basis in the land Kimberly contributed after Kimberly receives this distribution?

45. Rufus is a one-quarter partner in the Adventure Partnership. On January 1 of the current year, Adventure distributes $13,000 cash to Rufus in complete liquidation of his interest. Adventure has only capital assets and no liabilities at the date of the distribution. Rufus's basis in his partnership interest is $18,500.   **LO 16-4**

   a) What is the amount and character of Rufus's recognized gain or loss?

   b) What is the amount and character of Adventure's recognized gain or loss?

   c) If Rufus's basis is $10,000 at the distribution date rather than $18,500, what is the amount and character of Rufus's recognized gain or loss?

46. The Taurin Partnership (calendar year-end) has the following assets as of December 31 of the current year: **LO 16-4**

	Tax Basis	FMV
Cash	$ 45,000	$ 45,000
Accounts receivable	15,000	30,000
Inventory	81,000	120,000
Totals	$141,000	$195,000

On December 31, Taurin distributes $15,000 of cash, $10,000 (FMV) of accounts receivable, and $40,000 (FMV) of inventory to Emma (a one-third partner) in termination of her partnership interest. Emma's basis in her partnership interest immediately prior to the distribution is $40,000.

   a) What is the amount and character of Emma's recognized gain or loss on the distribution?

   b) What is Emma's basis in the distributed assets?

   c) If Emma's basis before the distribution was $55,000 rather than $40,000, what is Emma's recognized gain or loss and what is her basis in the distributed assets?

47. Melissa, Nicole, and Ben are equal partners in the Opto Partnership (calendar year-end). Melissa decides she wants to exit the partnership and receives a proportionate distribution to liquidate her partnership interest on January 1. The partnership has no liabilities and holds the following assets as of January 1:   **LO 16-4**

	Tax Basis	FMV
Cash	$18,000	$18,000
Accounts receivable	0	24,000
Stock investment	7,500	12,000
Land	30,000	36,000
Totals	$55,500	$90,000

Melissa receives one-third of each of the partnership assets. She has a basis in her partnership interest of $25,000.

a) What is the amount and character of any recognized gain or loss to Melissa?

b) What is Melissa's basis in the distributed assets?

c) What are the tax implications (amount and character of gain or loss and basis of assets) to Melissa if her outside basis is $11,000 rather than $25,000?

d) What is the amount and character of any recognized gain or loss from the distribution to Opto?

LO 16-4

 planning

48. Lonnie Davis has been a general partner in the Highland Partnership for many years and is also a sole proprietor in a separate business. To spend more time focusing on his sole proprietorship, he plans to leave Highland and will receive a liquidating distribution of $50,000 in cash and land with a fair market value of $100,000 (tax basis of $120,000). Immediately before the distribution, Lonnie's basis in his partnership interest is $350,000, which includes his $50,000 share of partnership debt. The Highland Partnership does not hold any hot assets.

a) What is the amount and character of any gain or loss to Lonnie?

b) What is Lonnie's basis in the land?

c) What is the amount and character of Lonnie's gain or loss if he holds the land for 13 months as investment property and then sells it for $100,000?

d) What is the amount and character of Lonnie's gain or loss if he places the land into service in his sole proprietorship and then sells it 13 months later for $100,000?

e) Do your answers to parts (c) and (d) suggest a course of action that would help Lonnie to achieve a more favorable tax outcome?

LO 16-4

49. AJ is a 30 percent partner in the Trane Partnership, a calendar year-end entity. On January 1, AJ has an outside basis in his interest in Trane of $73,000, which includes his share of the $50,000 of partnership liabilities. Trane generates $42,000 of income during the year and does not make any changes to its liabilities. On December 31, Trane makes a proportionate distribution of the following assets to AJ to terminate his partnership interest:

	Tax Basis	FMV
Inventory	$55,000	$65,000
Land	30,000	25,000
Totals	$85,000	$90,000

a) What are the tax consequences (gain or loss, basis adjustments) of the distribution to Trane?

b) What is the amount and character of any recognized gain or loss to AJ?

c) What is AJ's basis in the distributed assets?

d) If AJ sells the inventory four years after the distribution for $70,000, what is the amount and character of his recognized gain or loss?

LO 16-4

50. David's basis in the Jimsoo Partnership is $53,000. In a proportionate liquidating distribution, David receives cash of $7,000 and two capital assets: (1) land 1 with a fair market value of $20,000 and a basis to Jimsoo of $16,000, and (2) land 2 with a fair market value of $10,000 and a basis to Jimsoo of $16,000. Jimsoo has no liabilities.

a) How much gain or loss will David recognize on the distribution? What is the character of any recognized gain or loss?

b) What is David's basis in the distributed assets?

c) If the two parcels of land had been inventory to Jimsoo, what are the tax consequences to David (amount and character of gain or loss and basis in distributed assets)?

51. Megan and Matthew are equal partners in the J & J Partnership (calendar year-end entity). On January 1 of the current year, they decide to liquidate the partnership. Megan's basis in her partnership interest is $100,000 and Matthew's is $35,000. The two partners receive identical distributions, with each receiving the following assets:

LO 16-4

	Tax Basis	FMV
Cash	$30,000	$30,000
Inventory	5,000	6,000
Land	500	1,000
Totals	$35,500	$37,000

a) What is the amount and character of Megan's recognized gain or loss?

b) What is Megan's basis in the distributed assets?

c) What is the amount and character of Matthew's recognized gain or loss?

d) What is Matthew's basis in the distributed assets?

52. Bryce's basis in the Markit Partnership is $58,000. In a proportionate liquidating distribution, Bryce receives the following assets:

LO 16-4

	Tax Basis	FMV
Cash	$ 8,000	$ 8,000
Land A	20,000	45,000
Land B	20,000	25,000

a) How much gain or loss will Bryce recognize on the distribution? What is the character of any recognized gain or loss?

b) What is Bryce's basis in the distributed assets?

53. Danner Inc. has a $395,000 capital loss carryover that will expire at the end of the current tax year if it is not used. Also, Danner Inc. has been a general partner in the Talisman Partnership for three years and plans to end its involvement with the partnership by receiving a liquidating distribution. Initially, all parties agreed that Danner Inc.'s liquidating distribution would include $50,000 in cash and land with a fair market value of $400,000 (tax basis of $120,000). Immediately before the distribution, Danner's basis in its partnership interest is $150,000, which includes its $100,000 share of partnership debt. The Talisman Partnership does not hold any hot assets.

LO 16-4

planning

a) What is the amount and character of any gain or loss to Danner Inc.?

b) What is Danner Inc.'s basis in the land?

c) Can you suggest a course of action that would help Danner Inc. avoid the expiration of its capital loss carryover?

54. Bella Partnership is an equal partnership in which each of the partners has a basis in his partnership interest of $10,000. Bella reports the following balance sheet:

LO 16-1 LO 16-5

planning

	Tax Basis	FMV
Assets		
Inventory	$20,000	$30,000
Land	10,000	15,000
Totals	$30,000	$45,000
Liabilities and capital		
Capital—Toby	$10,000	
—Kaelin	10,000	
—Andrew	10,000	
Totals	$30,000	

a) Identify the *hot assets* if Toby decides to sell his partnership interest. Are these assets "hot" for purposes of distributions?

b) If Bella distributes the land to Toby in complete liquidation of his partnership interest, what tax issues should be considered?

LO 16-1 LO 16-6   55. Michelle pays $120,000 cash for Brittany's one-third interest in the Westlake Partnership. Just prior to the sale, Brittany's basis in Westlake is $96,000. Westlake reports the following balance sheet:

	Tax Basis	FMV
Assets		
Cash	$ 96,000	$ 96,000
Land	192,000	264,000
Totals	$288,000	$360,000
Liabilities and capital		
Capital—Amy	$ 96,000	
—Brittany	96,000	
—Ben	96,000	
Totals	$288,000	

a) What is the amount and character of Brittany's recognized gain or loss on the sale?

b) What is Michelle's basis in her partnership interest? What is Michelle's inside basis?

c) If Westlake were to sell the land for $264,000 shortly after the sale of Brittany's partnership interest, how much gain or loss would the partnership recognize?

d) How much gain or loss would Michelle recognize?

e) Suppose Westlake has a §754 election in place. What is Michelle's special basis adjustment? How much gain or loss would Michelle recognize on a subsequent sale of the land in this situation?

LO 16-4 LO 16-6   56. Cliff's basis in his Aero Partnership interest is $11,000. Cliff receives a distribution of $22,000 cash from Aero in complete liquidation of his interest. Aero is an equal partnership with the following balance sheet:

	Tax Basis	FMV
Assets		
Cash	$22,000	$22,000
Investment	8,800	8,800
Land	2,200	35,200
Totals	$33,000	$66,000
Liabilities and capital		
Capital—Chris	$11,000	
—Cliff	11,000	
—Cooper	11,000	
Totals	$33,000	

a) What is the amount and character of Cliff's recognized gain or loss? What is the effect on the partnership assets?

b) If Aero has a §754 election in place, what is the amount of the special basis adjustment?

57. Erin's basis in her Kiybron Partnership interest is $3,300. Erin receives a distribution of $2,200 cash from Kiybron in complete liquidation of her interest. Kiybron is an equal partnership with the following balance sheet: **LO 16-4** **LO 16-6**

	Tax Basis	FMV
Assets		
Cash	$2,200	$2,200
Stock (investment)	1,100	2,200
Land	6,600	2,200
Totals	$9,900	$6,600
Liabilities and capital		
Capital—Erin	$3,300	
—Carl	3,300	
—Grace	3,300	
Totals	$9,900	

a) What is the amount and character of Erin's recognized gain or loss? What is the effect on the partnership assets?

b) If Kiybron has a §754 election in place, what is the amount of the special basis adjustment?

58. Helen's basis in Haywood Partnership is $270,000. Haywood distributes all the land to Helen in complete liquidation of her partnership interest. The partnership reports the following balance sheet just before the distribution: **LO 16-4** **LO 16-6**

	Tax Basis	FMV
Assets		
Cash	$220,000	$220,000
Stock (investment)	480,000	220,000
Land	110,000	220,000
Totals	$810,000	$660,000
Liabilities and capital		
Capital—Charles	$270,000	
—Esther	270,000	
—Helen	270,000	
Totals	$810,000	

a) What is the amount and character of Helen's recognized gain or loss? What is the effect on the partnership assets?

b) If Haywood has a §754 election in place, what is the amount of the special basis adjustment?

COMPREHENSIVE PROBLEMS

Select problems are available in Connect®.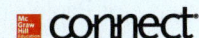

59. Simon is a 30 percent partner in the SBD Partnership, a calendar year-end entity. As of the end of this year, Simon has an outside basis in his interest in SBD of $188,000, which includes his share of the $60,000 of partnership liabilities. On December 31, SBD makes a proportionate distribution of the following assets to Simon:

	Tax Basis	FMV
Cash	$ 40,000	$ 40,000
Inventory	55,000	65,000
Land	30,000	45,000
Totals	$125,000	$150,000

a) What are the tax consequences (amount and character of recognized gain or loss, basis in distributed assets) of the distribution to Simon if the distribution is an operating distribution?

b) What are the tax consequences (amount and character of recognized gain or loss, basis in distributed assets) of the distribution to Simon if the distribution is a liquidating distribution?

c) Compare and contrast the results from parts (a) and (b).

planning 60. Paolo is a 50 percent partner in the Capri Partnership and has decided to terminate his partnership interest. Paolo is considering two options as potential exit strategies. The first is to sell his partnership interest to the two remaining 25 percent partners, Giuseppe and Isabella, for $105,000 cash and the assumption of Paolo's share of Capri's liabilities. Under this option, Giuseppe and Isabella would each pay $52,500 for half of Paolo's interest. The second option is to have Capri liquidate Paolo's partnership interest with a proportionate distribution of the partnership assets. Paolo's basis in his partnership interest is $110,000, including Paolo's share of Capri's liabilities. Capri reports the following balance sheet as of the termination date:

	Tax Basis	FMV
Assets		
Cash	$ 80,000	$ 80,000
Receivables	40,000	40,000
Inventory	50,000	80,000
Land	50,000	60,000
Totals	$220,000	$260,000
Liabilities and capital		
Liabilities	$ 50,000	
Capital—Paolo	85,000	
—Giuseppe	42,500	
—Isabella	42,500	
Totals	$220,000	

a) If Paolo sells his partnership interest to Giuseppe and Isabella for $105,000, what is the amount and character of Paolo's recognized gain or loss?

b) Giuseppe and Isabella each have a basis in Capri of $55,000 before any purchase of Paolo's interest. What are Giuseppe's and Isabella's bases in their partnership interests following the purchase of Paolo's interest?

c) If Capri liquidates Paolo's partnership interest with a proportionate distribution of the partnership assets ($25,000 deemed cash from debt relief, $15,000 of actual cash, and half of the remaining assets), what is the amount and character of Paolo's recognized gain or loss?

d) If Capri liquidates Paolo's interest, what is Paolo's basis in the distributed assets?

e) Compare and contrast Paolo's options for terminating his partnership interest. Assume Paolo's marginal tax rate is 35 percent and his capital gains rate is 15 percent.

 **tax forms** 61. Carrie D'Lake, Reed A. Green, and Doug A. Divot share a passion for golf and decide to go into the golf club manufacturing business together. On January 2, 2018, D'Lake, Green, and Divot form the Slicenhook Partnership, a general partnership. Slicenhook's main product will be a perimeter-weighted titanium driver with a patented graphite shaft. All three partners plan to actively participate in the business. The partners contribute the following property to form Slicenhook:

Partner	Contribution
Carrie D'Lake	Land, FMV $460,000
	Basis $460,000, Mortgage $60,000
Reed A. Green	$400,000
Doug A. Divot	$400,000

Carrie had recently acquired the land with the idea that she would contribute it to the newly formed partnership. The partners agree to share in profits and losses equally. Slicenhook elects a calendar year-end and the accrual method of accounting.

In addition, Slicenhook received a $1,500,000 recourse loan from Big Bank at the time the contributions were made. Slicenhook uses the proceeds from the loan and the cash contributions to build a state-of-the-art manufacturing facility ($1,200,000), purchase equipment ($600,000), and produce inventory ($400,000). With the remaining cash, Slicenhook invests $45,000 in the stock of a privately owned graphite research company and retains $55,000 as working cash.

Slicenhook operates on a just-in-time inventory system so it sells all inventory and collects all sales immediately. That means that at the end of the year, Slicenhook does not carry any inventory or accounts receivable balances. During 2018, Slicenhook has the following operating results:

Sales		$1,126,000
Cost of goods sold		400,000
Interest income from tax-exempt bonds		900
Qualified dividend income from stock		1,500
Operating expenses		126,000
Depreciation (tax)		
§179 on equipment	$39,000	
Equipment	81,000	
Building	24,000	144,000
Interest expense on debt		120,000

The partnership is very successful in its first year. The success allows Slicenhook to use excess cash from operations to purchase $15,000 of tax-exempt bonds (you can see the interest income already reflected in the operating results). The partnership also makes a principal payment on its loan from Big Bank in the amount of $300,000 and a distribution of $100,000 to each of the partners on December 31, 2018.

The partnership continues its success in 2019 with the following operating results:

Sales		$1,200,000
Cost of goods sold		420,000
Interest income from tax-exempt bonds		900
Qualified dividend income from stock		1,500
Operating expenses		132,000
Depreciation (tax)		
Equipment	$147,000	
Building	30,000	177,000
Interest expense on debt		96,000

The operating expenses include a $1,800 trucking fine that one of its drivers incurred for reckless driving and speeding and meals expense of $6,000.

By the end of 2019, Reed has had a falling out with Carrie and Doug and has decided to leave the partnership. He has located a potential buyer for his partnership interest, Indie Ruff. Indie has agreed to purchase Reed's interest in Slicenhook for $730,000 in cash and the assumption of Reed's share of Slicenhook's debt. Carrie and Doug, however, are not certain that admitting Indie to the partnership is such a good idea. They want to consider having Slicenhook liquidate Reed's interest on January 1, 2020. As of January 1, 2020, Slicenhook has the following assets:

	Tax Basis	FMV
Cash	$ 876,800	$ 876,800
Investment—tax exempts	15,000	18,000
Investment stock	45,000	45,000
Equipment—net of dep.	333,000	600,000
Building—net of dep.	1,146,000	1,440,000
Land	460,000	510,000
Total	$2,875,800	$3,489,800

Carrie and Doug propose that Slicenhook distribute the following to Reed in complete liquidation of his partnership interest:

	Tax Basis	FMV
Cash	$485,000	$485,000
Investment stock	45,000	45,000
Equipment—$200,000 cost, net of dep.	111,000	200,000
Total	$641,000	$730,000

Slicenhook has not purchased or sold any equipment since its original purchase just after formation.

a) Determine each partner's recognized gain or loss upon formation of Slicenhook.
b) What is each partner's initial tax basis in Slicenhook on January 2, 2018?
c) Prepare Slicenhook's opening tax basis balance sheet as of January 2, 2018.
d) Using the operating results, what are Slicenhook's ordinary income and separately stated items for 2018 and 2019? What amount of Slicenhook's income for each period would each of the partners receive?
e) Using the information provided, prepare Slicenhook's page 1 and Schedule K to be included with its Form 1065 for 2018. Also, prepare a Schedule K-1 for Carrie.
f) What are Carrie's, Reed's, and Doug's bases in their partnership interest at the end of 2018 and 2019?
g) If Reed sells his interest in Slicenhook to Indie Ruff, what is the amount and character of his recognized gain or loss? What is Indie's basis in the partnership interest?
h) What is Indie's inside basis in Slicenhook? What effect would a §754 election have on Indie's inside basis?
i) If Slicenhook distributes the assets proposed by Carrie and Doug in complete liquidation of Reed's partnership interest, what is the amount and character of Reed's recognized gain or loss? What is Reed's basis in the distributed assets?
j) Compare and contrast Reed's options for terminating his partnership interest. Assume Reed's marginal ordinary rate is 35 percent and his capital gains rate is 15 percent.

Sample CPA Exam questions from Roger CPA Review are available in Connect as support for the topics in this text. These Multiple Choice Questions and Task-Based Simulations include expert-written explanations and solutions and provide a starting point for students to become familiar with the content and functionality of the actual CPA Exam.

17 S Corporations

Learning Objectives

Upon completing this chapter, you should be able to:

LO 17-1 Describe the requirements and process to elect S corporation status.

LO 17-2 Explain the events that terminate the S corporation election.

LO 17-3 Describe operating issues relating to S corporation accounting periods and methods, and explain income and loss allocations and separately stated items.

LO 17-4 Explain stock-basis calculations, loss limitations, determination of self-employment income, and fringe benefit rules that apply to S corporation shareholders.

LO 17-5 Apply the tax rules for S corporation operating distributions and liquidating distributions.

LO 17-6 Describe the taxes that apply to S corporations, estimated tax requirements, and tax return filing requirements.

©PhotoAlto/MediaBakery

Storyline Summary

Taxpayers: Nicole Johnson, Sarah Walker, and Chance Armstrong

Location: Salt Lake City, Utah

Status: Shareholders of newly formed Color Comfort Sheets Inc. (CCS)

Situation: Formed CCS as a corporation and have elected to have the entity taxed as an S corporation.

In the Entities Overview chapter, we met Nicole Johnson, who turned her sheet-making hobby into a full-time business called Color Comfort Sheets (CCS). In this chapter, we assume Nicole formed CCS as a corporation, intending to elect S corporation tax status.

When starting the business, Nicole had cash to contribute to CCS but not enough to meet initial needs. She convinced her friend Sarah Walker to invest in CCS and fortunately, after listening to Nicole and Sarah's proposal, local sports team owner Chance Armstrong also agreed to invest.

Nicole and Sarah would take an active role in managing CCS; Chance would not. Nicole contributed a parcel of land and cash in exchange for one-third of CCS's stock. Sarah and Chance each contributed cash for one-third of the stock. With funding in place, CCS began operating on January 1, 2017. However, with the excitement (and turmoil) of starting the new business, it took Nicole, Sarah, and Chance a while to talk with their accountant about electing S corporation status. After several discussions, they filed their S election on May 1, 2017. ■

In this chapter, we discuss the tax and nontax characteristics of an **S corporation,** a hybrid entity that shares some characteristics with C corporations and some with partnerships.[1] S corporations are incorporated under state law and thus have the same legal protections as C corporations. They are governed by the same corporate tax rules that apply in the organization, liquidation, and reorganization of C corporations. However, unlike a C corporation, an S corporation is a flow-through entity and shares many tax similarities with partnerships. For example, basis calculations for S corporation shareholders and partners are similar, the income or loss of an S corporation flows through to its owners, and distributions are generally not taxed to the extent of the owner's basis.

Throughout this chapter, we highlight the tax similarities between S corporations and C corporations and between S corporations and partnerships, while focusing on the unique rules that apply to S corporations. These rules are more complex for S corporations that were once C corporations with previously undistributed **earnings and profits (E&P).**

LO 17-1 S CORPORATION ELECTIONS

Formations

The same rules for forming and contributing property govern S and C corporations. Section 351 and related provisions apply when one or more persons transfer property to a corporation (C or S) in return for stock, and immediately after the transfer, these persons control the corporation. These rules allow shareholders meeting the requirements to defer gains they realize when they transfer appreciated property to the corporation in exchange for stock. Note that similar rules apply to formations and property contributions to partnerships under §721. One important difference, however, is that partnership tax rules do not impose a control requirement to defer gains (see the Forming and Operating Partnerships chapter for partnership contributions).

S Corporation Qualification Requirements

Unlike C corporations and partnerships, S corporations are limited as to type and number of owners (shareholders).[2] Only U.S. citizens or residents, estates, certain trusts, and certain tax-exempt organizations may be shareholders. No corporations or partnerships can be shareholders.[3] S corporations may have no more than 100 shareholders; family members and their estates count as one shareholder. Family members include a common ancestor (not more than six generations removed) and her lineal descendants and their spouses (or former spouses).[4] Under this broad definition, great-grandparents, grandparents, parents, children, brothers and sisters, grandchildren, great-grandchildren, aunts, uncles, cousins, and the respective spouses are family members for this purpose. A practical implication of these limits is that large, publicly traded corporations cannot elect to be treated as S corporations.

---

[1]S Corporations get their name from Subchapter S of the Internal Revenue Code, which includes code sections 1361–1379.

[2]§1361.

[3]Grantor trusts, qualified Subchapter S trusts, electing small business trusts, certain testamentary trusts, and voting trusts can own S corporation stock. A discussion of these trusts is beyond the scope of this chapter. Eligible tax-exempt shareholders include qualified retirement plan trusts or charitable, religious, educational, etc., organizations that are tax-exempt under §501.

[4]The common ancestor (living or not, owning shares or not) must not be more than six generations removed from the youngest generation of shareholder family members determined at the later of the S corporation election date or the date the first member of the respective family holds the S corporation's stock.

Example 17-1

What if: Suppose CCS was formed with Nicole Johnson, Sarah Walker, and Chanzz Inc., a corporation owned by Chance Armstrong, as shareholders. Would CCS be eligible to elect S corporation status?

Answer: No. Because one of its shareholders is a corporation (Chanzz Inc.), CCS would not be eligible to elect S corporation status.

What if: Suppose Nicole, Sarah, and Chance recruited 97 U.S. residents to become shareholders of CCS. Meanwhile, Nicole gave several of her CCS shares to her grandfather and his bride as a wedding gift and to her first cousin as an MBA graduation gift. After the transfer, CCS had 103 shareholders. Can CCS elect S corporation status?

Answer: Yes. Nicole (descendant of common ancestor), her first cousin (descendant of common ancestor), her grandfather (common ancestor), and her grandfather's wife (spouse of common ancestor) are treated as *one* shareholder for purposes of the 100-shareholder limit.

S Corporation Election

An eligible corporation must make an affirmative election to be treated as an S corporation.[5] In addition to meeting the shareholder requirements above, it must:

- Be a domestic corporation (created or organized in the United States or under U.S. law or the law of any state in the United States).
- Not be a specifically identified ineligible corporation.[6]
- Have only one class of stock.

A corporation is considered to have only one class of stock if all its outstanding shares provide identical distribution and liquidation rights. Differences in voting powers are permissible. In general, debt instruments do not violate the single class of stock requirement unless they are treated as equity elsewhere under the tax law.[7] In addition, §1361 provides safe-harbor rules to ensure that debt obligations are not recharacterized as a second class of stock.[8]

> **THE KEY FACTS**
>
> **S Corporation Election**
>
> - An eligible corporation must make an affirmative election to be treated as an S corporation.
> - Eligible corporations meet the type and number of shareholder requirements, are domestic corporations, are not specifically identified as ineligible corporations, and have only one class of stock.
> - To elect S corporation status, the corporation makes a formal election using Form 2553.

Example 17-2

What if: Suppose Nicole were a resident of Toronto, Canada, and while she formed CCS in Canada under Canadian law, she still planned to do business in the United States. Is CCS eligible to elect S corporation status in the United States?

Answer: No. CCS would not be eligible for S corporation treatment because it was neither organized in the United States nor formed under U.S. laws.

What if: Suppose Nicole resided in Seattle and formed CCS under the state laws of Washington but planned to do a significant amount of business in Canada. Would CCS be eligible to elect S corporation status?

Answer: Yes, because CCS was formed under the laws of a U.S. state.

---

[5]§1362(a).

[6]Ineligible corporations include financial institutions using the reserve method of accounting under §585, insurance companies, corporations allowed a tax credit for income from Puerto Rico and from U.S. possessions under §936, corporations previously electing Domestic International Sales Corporation status, and corporations treated as a taxable mortgage pool.

[7]See §385 for factors considered in determining whether debt should be considered as equity for tax purposes.

[8]§1361(c)(5)(A) provides that straight debt issued during an S corporation year (i.e., not during a C corporation year) will not be treated as a second class of stock. §1361(c)(5)(A) defines straight debt as debt characterized by a written unconditional promise to pay on demand or on a specified date a sum certain in money if (1) the interest rate and interest payment dates are not contingent on profits, the borrower's discretion, or similar factors; (2) the debt is not convertible into stock; and (3) the creditor is an individual (other than a nonresident alien), an estate, a qualified trust, or a person who is actively and regularly engaged in the business of lending money.

To formally elect S corporation status effective as of the beginning of the current tax year, the corporation uses **Form 2553,** either in the prior tax year or on or before the 15th day of the third month of the current tax year.[9] Elections made after the 15th day of the third month of a year are effective at the beginning of the following year. All shareholders on the date of the election must consent to the election.

Example 17-3

What if: Suppose Nicole formed CCS as a C corporation in 2017 with a calendar tax year and finally got around to electing S corporation status on February 20, 2018. What is the earliest effective date of the S election?

Answer: January 1, 2018.

What if: Suppose Nicole formed CCS as a C corporation in 2017 with a calendar tax year and made the S election on March 20, 2018. When is the S election effective?

Answer: It is effective January 1, 2019, because Nicole made the election after March 15, 2018.

Even when the corporation makes the election on or before the 15th day of the third month of its tax year, the election will not be effective until the subsequent year if (1) the corporation did not meet the S corporation requirements for each day of the current tax year before it made the S election, or (2) one or more shareholders who held the stock in the corporation during the current year and before the S corporation election was made did not consent to the election (e.g., a shareholder disposes of his stock in the corporation in the election year before the election is made and fails to consent to the S election).[10]

Example 17-4

What if: Suppose in 2017 Nicole formed CCS as a C corporation (calendar tax year) with Nicole, Sarah, and Chanzz Inc. (a corporation) as shareholders. On January 2, 2018, Chanzz Inc. sold all its shares to Chance Armstrong. On January 31, 2018, CCS filed an S corporation election, with Nicole, Sarah, and Chance all consenting to the election. What is the earliest effective date of the S election?

Answer: January 1, 2019. Because CCS had an ineligible shareholder (Chanzz Inc.) during 2018, the election is not effective until the beginning of 2019.

What if: Suppose in 2017 Nicole formed CCS as a C corporation (calendar tax year) with Nicole, Sarah, and Chance as shareholders. On January 30, 2018, Chance sold his shares to Nicole. On February 15, 2018, CCS filed an S election, with Nicole and Sarah consenting to the election. Chance, however, did not consent to the election. What is the earliest effective date of the S election?

Answer: January 1, 2019. Because Chance was a shareholder until January 30, 2018, and he did not consent to the S election in 2018, the S election is not effective until the beginning of 2019, the year after the election.

The timing of the election may be especially important for C corporations with net operating losses. The reason: Net operating losses attributable to C corporation years generally cannot be carried over to the S corporation. Thus, it may be beneficial to delay the S election until the corporation has utilized its net operating losses.[11]

---

[9]§1362(b). When the IRS determines that taxpayers have reasonable cause for making late elections, it has the authority to treat late elections as timely [§1362(b)(5)]. Rev. Proc. 2013-30 provides a simplified method to provide relief for late elections by submitting Form 2553 to the IRS with a statement that explains (a) that there was either reasonable cause for the late election or the late election was inadvertent and (b) that the taxpayer acted diligently to correct the mistake upon discovery.

[10]Source: §1362(b)(2). Requiring all shareholders who own stock in an S corporation during the year to consent to the election ensures that shareholders who dispose of their stock before the election do not suffer adverse tax consequences from an election to which they did not consent.

[11]Later in this chapter we discuss one exception to the rule that disallows net operating loss carryovers from C corporation to S corporation years. See the discussion of the S corporation built-in gains tax.

S CORPORATION TERMINATIONS

Once the S election becomes effective, the corporation remains an S corporation until the election is terminated. The termination may be voluntary or involuntary.

Voluntary Terminations

The corporation can make a *voluntary revocation* of the S election if shareholders holding more than 50 percent of the S corporation stock (including nonvoting shares) agree.[12] The corporation files a statement with the IRS revoking the election made under §1362(a) and stating the effective date of the revocation and the number of shares issued and outstanding. In general, voluntary revocations made on or before the 15th day of the third month of the year are effective as of the beginning of the year. A revocation after this period is effective the first day of the following tax year. Alternatively, a corporation may specify the termination date as long as the date specified is on or after the date the revocation is made.[13]

> **THE KEY FACTS**
>
> **S Corporation Qualification Requirements**
>
> - Only U.S. citizens or residents, estates, certain trusts, and certain tax-exempt organizations may be S corporation shareholders.
> - S corporations may have no more than 100 shareholders.
> - For purposes of the 100-shareholder limit, family members and their estates count as only one shareholder.

Example 17-5

What if: Suppose CCS had been initially formed as an S corporation with a calendar year-end. After a couple of years, things were going so well that Nicole and Sarah (each one-third shareholders) wanted to terminate the S election and take CCS public. However, Chance (also a one-third shareholder) was opposed to the S election termination. Can Nicole and Sarah terminate the S election without Chance's consent?

Answer: Yes. To revoke the election, Nicole and Sarah need to own more than 50 percent of the shares, and together they own 66.7 percent.

What if: If Nicole and Sarah file the revocation on February 15, 2019, what is the effective date of the S corporation termination (assuming they do not specify one)?

Answer: January 1, 2019. If they file the S corporation revocation after March 15, 2019, it becomes effective January 1, 2020. Alternatively, CCS could have specified an effective date of the S corporation's termination (in 2019 or after) as long as it was on or after the date the revocation was made.

ETHICS

Suppose Chance Armstrong is a U.S. resident but a French citizen. His mother has recently been diagnosed with a terminal illness, and Chance has decided to move back to France to take care of his mother and her affairs. He anticipates that he will live in France for several years and that he will no longer be considered a U.S. resident. If you were Sarah or Nicole, how would you react to Chance's decision to move? Would you ignore the impact it may have on CCS's S corporation status? Would you pressure Chance to sell his CCS stock to you?

Involuntary Terminations

Involuntary terminations can result from failure to meet requirements (by far the most common reason) or from an excess of passive investment income.

Failure to Meet Requirements   A corporation's S election is automatically terminated if the corporation fails to meet the requirements. The termination is effective on the date it fails the S corporation requirements. If the IRS deems the termination inadvertent, it may allow the corporation to continue to be treated as an S corporation if, within a reasonable period after the inadvertent termination, the corporation takes the necessary steps to meet the S corporation requirements.[14]

---

[12]§1362(d)(1)(B).

[13]§1362(d)(1)(D).

[14]§1362(f). Because the restrictions on S corporation ownership are so specific and exact, many S corporations require their shareholders, as a condition of stock ownership, to enter into a shareholder's agreement. These agreements generally restrict the ability of a shareholder to transfer her stock ownership to any disqualified shareholder.

Example 17-6

What if: Suppose CCS was formed as a calendar-year S corporation with Nicole Johnson, Sarah Walker, and Chance Armstrong as equal shareholders. On June 15, 2018, Chance sold his CCS shares to his solely owned C corporation, Chanzz Inc. Is CCS's S election still in effect at the beginning of 2019? If not, when was it terminated?

Answer: No, the election was automatically terminated on June 15, 2018, when Chanzz Inc. became a shareholder because S corporations may not have corporate shareholders.

Excess of Passive Investment Income   If an S corporation has *earnings and profits* from a previous C corporation year (or through a reorganization with a corporation that has earnings and profits), its election is terminated if the S corporation has passive investment income in excess of 25 percent of gross receipts for three consecutive years. If the S corporation never operated as a C corporation or does not have C corporation earnings and profits (either by prior distribution of C corporation earnings and profits, or simply by not having earnings and profits at the effective date of the S election), this provision does not apply.

For purposes of the passive investment income test, **gross receipts** is the total amount of revenues received [including net capital gains from the sale of capital assets and gain (not offset by losses) from the sale of stock and securities] or accrued under the corporation's accounting method, *not* reduced by returns, allowances, cost of goods sold, or deductions. **Passive investment income (PII)** includes gross receipts from royalties, rents, dividends, interest (including tax-exempt interest), and annuities.[15] While net capital gain income is included in gross receipts, it is *not* considered passive investment income. S corporation election terminations due to excess passive investment income are effective on the first day of the year following the third consecutive tax year with excess passive investment income.

Example 17-7

What if: Suppose CCS was initially formed as an S corporation with a calendar year-end. During its first three years, it reported passive investment income in excess of 25 percent of its gross receipts. Is CCS's S election terminated under the excess passive investment income test? If so, what is the effective date of the termination?

Answer: No, the excess passive investment income test does not apply to CCS in this situation because CCS has never operated as a C corporation; consequently, it does not have C corporation earnings and profits.

What if: Suppose CCS was initially formed as a C corporation with a calendar year-end. After its first year of operations (very profitable), CCS elected S corporation status, effective January 1, 2018. During 2019, 2020, and 2021, it reported passive investment income in excess of 25 percent of its gross receipts and had undistributed earnings and profits from its C corporation year. Is CCS's S election terminated under the excess passive investment income test? If so, what is the effective date of the termination?

Answer: Yes, it is terminated. Because CCS has C corporation earnings and profits from 2017 and excess passive investment income for three consecutive years as an S corporation, its S election is terminated, effective January 1, 2022.

Short Tax Years

S corporation election terminations frequently create an S corporation *short tax year* (a reporting year less than 12 months) and a C corporation short tax year. The corporation must then allocate its income for the full year between the S and the C corporation years, using the number of days in each short year (the daily method). Or it may use the

[15]PII excludes certain rents (e.g., rents derived from the active trade or business of renting property, produced film rents, income from leasing self-produced tangible property, temporary parking fees, etc.).

corporation's normal accounting rules to allocate income to the actual period in which it was earned (the specific identification method).[16] Both short tax year returns are due on the corporation's customary tax return due date (with normal extensions available).

Example 17-8

What if: Suppose CCS was formed as a calendar-year S corporation with Nicole Johnson, Sarah Walker, and Chance Armstrong as equal shareholders. On June 15, 2018, Chance sold his CCS shares (one-third of all shares) to his solely owned C corporation, Chanzz Inc., terminating CCS's S election on June 15, 2018. Assume CCS reported the following business income for 2018:

Period	Income
January 1 through June 14 (165 days)	$100,000
June 15 through December 31 (200 days)	265,000
January 1 through December 31, 2018 (365 days)	$365,000

If CCS uses the daily method of allocating income between the S corporation short tax year (January 1–June 14) and the C corporation short tax year (June 15–December 31), how much income will it report on its S corporation short tax year return and its C corporation short tax year return for 2018?

Answer: S corporation short tax year = $165,000 ($365,000/365 days × 165 days); C corporation short tax year = $200,000 ($365,000/365 days × 200 days).

What if: If CCS uses the specific identification method to allocate income, how much will it allocate to the S corporation short tax year and how much will it allocate to the C corporation short tax year?

Answer: S corporation short tax year, $100,000; C corporation short tax year, $265,000.

Note that if the entity wanted to minimize the income subject to taxation as a C corporation, it would use the daily method of allocating income.

S Corporation Reelections

After terminating or voluntarily revoking S corporation status, the corporation may elect it again, but it generally must wait until the beginning of the fifth tax year *after* the tax year in which it terminated the election.[17] Thus, if the election was terminated effective the first day of the tax year, the corporation must wait five full years to again become an S corporation.

THE KEY FACTS

S Corporation Terminations and Reelections

- The S election may be revoked by shareholders holding more than 50 percent of the S corporation's stock (including nonvoting shares).

- A corporation's S election is automatically terminated if (1) the S corporation fails to meet the S corporation requirements, or (2) the S corporation has earnings and profits from a previous C corporation year and has passive investment income in excess of 25 percent of gross receipts for three consecutive years.

- A corporation losing its S corporation status must wait until the beginning of the fifth year after the election is terminated to elect S corporation status again.

Example 17-9

What if: Let's return to the facts of the previous example. CCS was formed as a calendar-year S corporation with Nicole Johnson, Sarah Walker, and Chance Armstrong as equal shareholders. On June 15, 2018, Chance sold his CCS shares (one-third of all shares) to his solely owned C corporation, Chanzz Inc., terminating CCS's S election on June 15, 2018. Absent permission from the IRS (see text below), what is the earliest date CCS may again elect to be taxed as an S corporation?

Answer: January 1, 2023. This is the fifth tax year after the year in which the termination became effective.

What if: Assume on February 1, 2018, CCS voluntarily elected to revoke its S corporation status effective January 1, 2019. Absent IRS permission, what is the earliest CCS may again elect to be taxed as an S corporation?

Answer: January 1, 2024. This is the fifth year after the year in which the termination became effective.

---

[16]Use of the specific identification method requires that all shareholders at any time during the S corporation short year and the shareholders on the first day of the C corporation short year consent to the election using the specific identification method [§1362(e)(3)(A)]. However, an S corporation must use the specific identification method to allocate income between the short years (the per day allocation method is not allowed) if there is a sale or exchange of 50 percent or more of the corporation's stock during the year [§1362(e)(6)(D)].

[17]§1362(g).

The IRS may consent to an earlier election under a couple of conditions: (1) if the corporation is now more than 50 percent owned by shareholders who were not owners at the time of termination, or (2) if the termination was not reasonably within the control of the corporation or shareholders with a substantial interest in the corporation and was not part of a planned termination by the corporation or shareholders. Given the potential adverse consequences of an S election termination, the corporation should carefully monitor compliance with the S corporation requirements.

LO 17-3 OPERATING ISSUES

Accounting Methods and Periods

<aside>
THE KEY FACTS

Operating Issues

- S corporations are generally required to adopt a calendar tax year.
- S corporations allocate profits and losses to shareholders pro rata, based on the number of outstanding shares each shareholder owns on each day of the tax year.
- S corporations determine each shareholder's share of ordinary business income (loss) and separately stated items.
- Ordinary business income (loss) is all income (loss) exclusive of any separately stated items of income (loss). Separately stated items are tax items that are treated differently than a shareholder's share of ordinary business income (loss) for tax purposes.
</aside>

Like partnerships, S corporations determine their accounting periods and make accounting method elections at the entity level. An S corporation makes most of its elections (like electing out of bonus depreciation) in conjunction with the filing of its annual tax return and some by filing a separate request with the IRS. (For example, an application to change accounting methods is filed on Form 3115, separate from the S corporation's tax return.) For an S corporation previously operating as a C corporation, all prior accounting methods carry over to the S corporation.

Recall that both C corporations and partnerships face restrictions on using the cash method. S corporations do not. They may choose the cash, accrual, or hybrid method unless selling inventory is a material income-producing factor for them. In that case they must account for gross profit (sales minus cost of goods sold) using the accrual method, even if they are otherwise cash-method taxpayers. Hence, they would use the hybrid method.

Tax laws also specify permissible tax years for S corporations, but they are a little less cumbersome than for partnerships. S corporations must use a calendar year-end unless they can establish a business purpose for an alternative year-end or a natural business year-end. (For example, a business that receives 25 percent or more of gross receipts for the previous three years in the last two months of the year-end requested would qualify for a noncalendar year-end.)[18]

Income and Loss Allocations

S corporations, like partnerships, are flow-through entities, and thus their profits and losses flow through to their shareholders annually for tax purposes. As we discussed in the Forming and Operating Partnerships chapter, partnerships have considerable flexibility in making special profit and loss allocations to their partners. In contrast, S corporations must allocate profits and losses pro rata, based on the number of outstanding shares each shareholder owns on each day of the tax year.[19]

An S corporation generally allocates income or loss items to shareholders on the last day of its tax year.[20] If a shareholder sells her shares during the year, she will report her share of S corporation income and loss allocated to the days she owned the stock (including the day of sale) using a pro rata allocation. If *all shareholders with changing ownership percentages* during the year agree, the S corporation can instead use its normal accounting rules to allocate income and loss (and other separately stated items, discussed below) to the specific periods in which it realized income and losses.

Example 17-10

What if: Assume CCS was formed as a calendar-year S corporation with Nicole Johnson, Sarah Walker, and Chance Armstrong as equal (one-third) shareholders. On June 14, 2018, Chance sold his CCS shares to Nicole. CCS reported the following business income for 2018:

---

[18]§1378(b). In addition, S corporations, like partnerships, have the option of electing an alternative taxable year under §444.

[19]§1366(a), §1377(a).

[20]§1366(a).

Period	Income
January 1 through June 14 (165 days)	$100,000
June 15 through December 31 (200 days)	265,000
January 1 through December 31, 2018 (365 days)	$365,000

How much 2018 income is allocated to each shareholder if CCS uses the daily method of allocating income?

Answer: Nicole's allocation is $188,333; Sarah's is $121,667; and Chance's is $55,000, calculated as follows.

	(1) **January 1–June 14**	**(2)** **June 15–December 31**	**(1) + (2)** **Total 2018** **Allocation**
Nicole	$55,000 ($365,000/365 × 165 × 1/3)	$133,333 ($365,000/365 × 200 × 2/3)	$188,333
Sarah	$55,000 ($365,000/365 × 165 × 1/3)	$66,667 ($365,000/365 × 200 × 1/3)	121,667
Chance	$55,000 ($365,000/365 × 165 × 1/3)	$0	55,000
Totals	$165,000	$200,000	$365,000

How much 2018 income is allocated to each shareholder if CCS uses its normal accounting rules to allocate income to the specific periods in which it was actually earned?

Answer: Nicole's allocation is $210,000 ($100,000 × 1/3 + $265,000 × 2/3); Sarah's is $121,667 ($365,000 × 1/3); and Chance's is $33,333 ($100,000 × 1/3).

Separately Stated Items

Like partnerships, S corporations are required to file tax returns (Form 1120S) annually. In addition, on Form 1120S, Schedule K-1, they supply information to each shareholder detailing the amount *and* character of items of income and loss flowing through the S corporation.[21] Shareholders must report these income and loss items on their tax returns even if they do not receive cash distributions during the year.

    S corporations determine each shareholder's share of ordinary business income (loss) and separately stated items. Like partnerships, **ordinary business income (loss)** (also referred to as *nonseparately stated income or loss*) is all income (loss) exclusive of any separately stated items of income (loss). **Separately stated items** are tax items that are treated differently from a shareholder's share of ordinary business income (loss) for tax purposes. The character of each separately stated item is determined at the S corporation level rather than at the shareholder level. The list of common separately stated items for S corporations is similar to that for partnerships, with a couple of exceptions. (For example, S corporations do not report self-employment income and do not have guaranteed payments.) Exhibit 17-1 lists several common separately stated items. See Form 1120S, Schedule K-1 (and related instructions) for a comprehensive list of separately stated items.[22] Similar to partners in a partnership, S corporation shareholders are allowed a 20 percent deduction for qualified business income, calculated and subject to limitations at the shareholder level. See the Entities Overview chapter for a discussion of the deduction. Informational items related

---

[21]Other items, such as tax credits and informational items such as AMT adjustments, also flow through from the S corporation to its shareholders and are reported to shareholders on Form 1120S, Schedule K-1.

[22]Similar to partnerships, S corporations with average annual gross receipts for the prior three years that exceed $25 million are subject to the 30 percent of taxable income limitation on the deduction for business interest expense. The limitation applies at the S corporation level. In years where the adjusted taxable income limitation is binding, the S corporation's excess business interest is allocated to its shareholders as a separately stated item. Shareholders then carry forward their share of excess business interest expense and deduct it when they are allocated a share of the S corportion's excess adjusted taxable income limitation in later years when the adjusted taxable income imitation is not binding.

EXHIBIT 17-1 **Common Separately Stated Items**

- Short-term capital gains and losses
- Long-term capital gains and losses
- Section 1231 gains and losses
- Dividends
- Interest income
- Charitable contributions
- Tax-exempt income
- Net rental real estate income
- Investment interest expense
- Section 179 deduction
- Foreign taxes
- Qualified business income, allocated wages, and unadjusted basis of qualified property

to the deduction calculation [e.g., qualified business income, W-2 wages paid by the S corporation (including owner's compensation), and unadjusted basis of qualified property] are reported to shareholders on Form 1120S, Schedule K-1.

S corporations may hold stock in C corporations, and any dividends S corporations receive will flow through to their shareholders. However, S corporations are not entitled to claim the dividends received deduction.

Assuming CCS operated as a C corporation in 2017 and an S corporation in 2018, Exhibit 17-2 presents the results of operations. CCS's S election was not effective until January 1, 2018, because the shareholders filed the S election after the required date for it to be effective in 2017.

EXHIBIT 17-2

Color Comfort Sheets Income Statement December 31, 2017 and 2018		
	2017, C Corporation	**2018, S Corporation**
Sales revenue	$220,000	$ 520,000
Cost of goods sold	(50,000)	(115,000)
Salary to owners Nicole and Sarah	(70,000)	(90,000)
Employee wages	(45,000)	(50,000)
Depreciation expense	(15,000)	(20,000)
Miscellaneous expenses	(4,000)	(5,000)
Interest income (from investments)	3,000	6,000
Dividend income	1,000	3,000
Overall net income	$ 40,000	$ 249,000

Example 17-11

Assume CCS was a C corporation for tax purposes in 2017 and an S corporation in 2018. Based on its operating results in Exhibit 17-2, what amounts of ordinary business income and separately stated items are allocated to CCS's shareholders for 2017?

Answer: $0 ordinary business income and $0 separately stated items. Because CCS is a C corporation in 2017, its income does *not* flow through to its shareholders.

Based on the information in Exhibit 17-2, what amounts of ordinary business income and separately stated items are allocated to CCS's shareholders for 2018? Assume CCS has qualified property with an unadjusted basis of $300,000 for purposes of the deduction for qualified business income.

Answer: See the following table for the allocations:

Description	CCS	Nicole 1/3	Sarah 1/3	Chance 1/3
		Allocations		
2018 overall net income Less:	$249,000			
Dividends	3,000			
Interest income	6,000			
Ordinary business income	240,000	**$80,000**	**$80,000**	**$80,000**
Separately Stated Items:				
Interest income	6,000	**2,000**	**2,000**	**2,000**
Dividends	3,000	**1,000**	**1,000**	**1,000**
Qualified Business Income				
Informational Items:				
Qualified business income	240,000	80,000	80,000	80,000
Allocated wages	140,000	46,667	46,667	46,666
Unadjusted basis of qualified property	300,000	100,000	100,000	100,000

Nicole, Sarah, and Chance will treat their shares of CCS's ordinary business income as *ordinary* income and include it, along with their shares of interest and dividend income, in their individual tax returns for the year.[23] Qualified business income does not include interest income because it was not allocable to the trade or business. Allocated wages include the $50,000 wages paid to employees and $90,000 wages paid to owners.

SHAREHOLDER'S BASIS

LO 17-4

Just as partners must determine their bases in their partnership interests, S corporation shareholders must determine their bases in the S corporation stock to determine the gain or loss they recognize when they sell the stock, the taxability of distributions, and the deductibility of losses.

Initial Basis An S corporation shareholder calculates his or her *initial basis* upon formation of the corporation, like a C corporation shareholder. Specifically, the shareholder's basis in stock received in the exchange equals the tax basis of the property transferred, less any liabilities assumed by the corporation on the property contributed (*substituted basis*). The shareholder's stock basis is increased by any gain recognized; it is reduced by the fair market value of any property received other than stock.[24] If, on the other hand, the shareholder purchased the S corporation stock from another shareholder or the corporation, the new shareholder's basis is simply the purchase price of the stock.[25]

Example 17-12

At the beginning of 2017, Nicole contributed $30,000 of cash and land with a fair market value of $130,000 and an adjusted basis of $125,000 to CCS. The land was encumbered by a $40,000 mortgage executed three years before. Sarah and Chance each contributed $120,000 of cash to CCS. What tax bases do Nicole, Sarah, and Chance have in their CCS stock at the beginning of 2017?

Answer: Nicole's basis is $115,000 ($30,000 cash + $125,000 adjusted basis of land − $40,000 mortgage assumed); Sarah's basis is $120,000; and Chance's basis is $120,000.

---

[23]Nicole, Sarah, and Chance would report their share of ordinary business income on Schedule E and their share of interest and dividend income on Schedule B of Form 1040.

[24]§358. This assumes the shareholder meets the §351 requirements. If the shareholder's exchange with the corporation does not meet these requirements, the shareholder's basis in the stock is its fair market value.

[25]If the shareholder acquires the stock by gift, her basis in the stock is the lesser of the donor's basis (increased for any gift taxes paid on the stock's appreciation) or the fair market value of the stock. In contrast, if the shareholder acquires the stock by bequest, her basis in the stock is the stock's fair market value on the date of the decedent's death adjusted to reflect any income in respect of the decedent.

Annual Basis Adjustments   While C corporation rules govern the initial stock basis of an S corporation shareholder, subsequent calculations more closely resemble the partnership rules. Specifically, an S corporation shareholder's stock basis is dynamic and must be *adjusted* annually to ensure that (1) taxable income/gains and deductible expenses/losses are *not* double-counted by shareholders either when they sell their shares or when they receive S corporation distributions (for example, because shareholders are taxed on the S corporation's income annually, they should not be taxed again when they receive distributions of the income) and (2) tax-exempt income and nondeductible expenses are not ultimately taxed or deducted.

S corporation shareholders make the following adjustments to their stock basis annually, in the order listed:

- Increase for any contributions to the S corporation during the year.
- Increase for shareholder's share of ordinary business income and separately stated income/gain items (including tax-exempt income).
- Decrease for distributions during the year.
- Decrease for shareholder's share of nondeductible expenses (fines, penalties).
- Decrease for shareholder's share of ordinary business loss and separately stated expense/loss items.[26]

As with a partnership, adjustments that decrease basis may never reduce an S corporation shareholder's tax basis below zero.[27]

S corporation shareholders are not allowed to include any S corporation debt in their stock basis. Recall that partners *are* allowed to include their share of partnership debt in their basis. One implication of this difference is that, everything else equal, an S corporation shareholder's basis will be lower than a partner's basis, due to the exclusion of debt (however, see the discussion of *debt basis* for S corporation shareholders below).

THE KEY FACTS

S Corporation Shareholder's Basis Adjustments

- A shareholder will *increase* the tax basis in his or her stock for:
  - Contributions.
  - Share of ordinary business income.
  - Separately stated income/gain items.
  - Tax-exempt income.
- A shareholder will *decrease* the tax basis in his or her stock for:
  - Cash distributions.
  - Share of nondeductible expenses.
  - Share of ordinary business loss.
  - Separately stated expense/loss items.
  - A shareholder's tax basis may not be negative.

Example 17-13

Given the shareholders' 2017 bases in their CCS stock from the previous example (Nicole, $115,000; Sarah, $120,000; and Chance, $120,000), what basis does each have at the end of 2018, after taking into account the information in Exhibit 17-2 (but before taking into account any distributions, which are discussed below)?

Answer: Nicole, $198,000; Sarah, $203,000; and Chance, $203,000, computed as follows:

Description	Nicole	Sarah	Chance	Explanation
(1) Initial tax basis	$115,000	$120,000	$120,000	Example 17-12
(2) Ordinary business income	80,000	80,000	80,000	Example 17-11
(3) Interest income	2,000	2,000	2,000	Example 17-11
(4) Dividends	1,000	1,000	1,000	Example 17-11
Tax basis in stock at end of 2018	**$198,000**	**$203,000**	**$203,000**	(1) + (2) + (3) + (4)

Note the shareholders do not include any portion of CCS's debt in their stock basis.

What if: Suppose that, in addition to the amounts in Exhibit 17-2, CCS also recognized $1,200 of tax-exempt interest income in 2018. Nicole's share of this separately stated item is $400. Taking this allocation into account, what is Nicole's stock basis at the end of 2018?

Answer: It is $198,400 ($198,000 + $400). The tax-exempt income allocated to Nicole as a separately stated item increases her tax basis to ensure that she is never taxed on her share of the tax-exempt income.

---

[26]Reg. §1.1367-1(g) allows a shareholder to elect to decrease basis by ordinary business losses and separately stated expense/loss items before decreasing basis by nondeductible expenses by attaching a statement to the shareholder's tax return. This election is advantageous because loss/expense deductions are limited to a shareholder's basis, and this election results in a higher basis limitation for deductible loss/expense items.

[27]§1367(a)(2).

Loss Limitations

S corporations have loss-limitation rules similar to those for partnerships. For an S corporation shareholder to deduct it, a loss must clear three separate hurdles: (1) tax-basis, (2) at-risk amount, and (3) passive activity.[28] In addition, for losses that clear each of the three hurdles, S corporation shareholders are not allowed to deduct excess business losses as described below.

Tax-Basis Limitation   S corporation shareholders may not deduct losses in excess of their stock basis. Recall they are not allowed to include debt in their basis; partners are. This restriction makes it more likely that the tax-basis limitation will apply to S corporation shareholders than to similarly situated partners. Losses not deductible due to the tax-basis limitation are not necessarily lost. Rather, they are suspended until the shareholder generates additional basis. The carryover period for the suspended loss is indefinite. However, if the shareholder sells the stock before creating additional basis, the suspended loss disappears unused.

Example 17-14

What if: Suppose at the beginning of 2019, Nicole's basis in her CCS stock was $14,000. During 2019, CCS reported a $60,000 ordinary business loss and no separately stated items. How much of the ordinary loss is allocated to Nicole?

Answer: The loss allocation is $20,000 ($60,000 × 1/3).

How much of the $20,000 loss clears the tax-basis hurdle for deductibility in 2019?

Answer: The amount of Nicole's basis in her CCS stock, or $14,000. The remaining $6,000 of loss does not clear the tax-basis hurdle; it is suspended until Nicole generates additional basis.

Shareholders can mitigate the disadvantage of not including S corporation debt in their stock basis by loaning money directly to their S corporations. These loans create **debt basis,** separate from the stock basis. Losses are limited first to the shareholders' tax bases in their shares and *then* to their bases in any direct loans made to their S corporations.[29] Specifically, if the total amount of items (besides distributions) that decrease the shareholder's basis for the year exceeds the shareholder's stock basis, the excess amount decreases the shareholder's debt basis. Like stock basis, debt basis cannot be decreased below zero. In subsequent years, any net increase in basis for the year restores first the shareholder's debt basis (up to the outstanding debt amount) and then the shareholder's stock basis. If the S corporation repays the debt owed to the shareholder before the shareholder's debt basis is restored, any loan repayment in excess of the shareholder's debt basis will trigger a taxable gain to the shareholder.

Example 17-15

What if: Suppose at the beginning of 2019, Nicole's basis in her CCS stock was $14,000. During 2019, Nicole loaned $8,000 to CCS, and CCS reported a $60,000 ordinary business loss and no separately stated items. How much of the $20,000 ordinary loss allocated to Nicole clears the tax-basis hurdle for deductibility in 2019?

Answer: All $20,000. The first $14,000 of the loss reduces her stock basis to $0, and the remaining $6,000 reduces her debt basis to $2,000 ($8,000 − $6,000).

What if: Suppose in 2020, CCS allocated $9,000 of ordinary business income to Nicole and no separately stated items. What are Nicole's CCS stock basis and debt basis at the end of 2020?

Answer: Her stock basis is $3,000; her debt basis is $8,000. The income first restores debt basis to the outstanding debt amount and then increases her stock basis.

---

[28]S corporations are also subject to the hobby loss rules in §183 that limit loss deductions for activities not engaged in for profit.

[29]§1366(d)(1)(B). These must be direct loans to the corporation. Thus, shareholders do not get debt basis when they guarantee a loan of the S corporation, although they would to the extent they had to "make good" on their guarantee obligation.

At-Risk Limitation   Like partners in partnerships, S corporation shareholders are subject to the *at-risk* rules. They may deduct S corporation losses only to the extent of their **at-risk amount** in the S corporation, as defined in §465. With one notable exception, an S corporation shareholder's at-risk amount is the sum of her stock and debt basis. The primary exception relates to nonrecourse loans and is designed to ensure that shareholders are deemed at risk only when they have an actual risk of loss. Specifically, an S corporation shareholder taking out a nonrecourse loan to make a capital contribution (either cash or other property) to the S corporation generally creates stock basis (equal to the basis of property contributed) in the S corporation but increases her amount at risk by only the net fair market value of her property, if any, used as collateral to secure the non-recourse loan.[30] The collateral's net fair market value is determined at the loan date.

Likewise, if the shareholder takes out a nonrecourse loan to make a direct loan to the S corporation, the loan creates debt basis but increases her amount at risk only by the net fair market value of her property, if any, used as collateral to secure the nonrecourse loan. When the stock basis plus debt basis is different from the at-risk amount, S corporation shareholders apply the tax-basis loss limitation first, and then the at-risk limitation. Losses limited under the at-risk rules are carried forward indefinitely until the shareholder generates additional at-risk amounts to utilize them or sells the S corporation stock.

Post-Termination Transition Period Loss Limitation   The voluntary or involuntary termination of a corporation's S election creates a problem for shareholders with suspended losses due to the basis and at-risk rules. The reason: These losses are generally not deductible after the S termination date. Shareholders can obtain some relief provided by §1366(d)(3), which allows them to treat any suspended losses existing at the S termination date as occurring on the last day of the **post-termination transition period (PTTP).** In general, the PTTP begins on the day after the last day of the corporation's last taxable year as an S corporation and ends on the later of (a) one year after the last S corporation day or (b) the due date for filing the return for the last year as an S corporation (including extensions).[31]

This rule allows the shareholder to create additional stock basis (by making additional capital contributions) during the PTTP and to utilize suspended losses based on his or her *stock* basis (not debt basis) at the end of the period. Any suspended losses utilized at the end of the PTTP reduce the shareholder's basis in the stock. Any losses not utilized at the end of the period are lost forever.

Example 17-16

What if: Suppose CCS terminated its S election on July 17, 2019. At the end of the S corporation's short tax year ending on July 17, Nicole's stock basis and at-risk amounts were both zero (she has never had debt basis), and she had a suspended loss of $15,000. In 2020, Nicole made additional capital contributions of $10,000 on February 20, 2020, and $7,000 on September 6, 2020. When does the PTTP end for CCS? How much loss may Nicole deduct, and what is her basis in the CCS stock at the end of the PTTP?

Answer: For loss deduction purposes, CCS's PTTP ends on September 15, 2020. That date represents (b) in the "later of (a) or (b) alternative—(a) one year after the last S corporation day, which would be July 17, 2020, or (b) the due date for filing the return for the last year as an S corporation, including extensions, which would be September 15, 2020, assuming CCS extends its tax return. (Note the short tax year S corporation return is due the same time as the short tax year C corporation return.) Nicole may deduct the entire $15,000 suspended loss because her basis at the end of the PTTP and before the loss deduction is $17,000. (That amount is calculated as a carryover basis of $0 on the last S corporation day plus $17,000 capital contributions during the PTTP.) Nicole's basis in CCS stock after the loss deduction is $2,000 ($17,000 basis at the end of the PTTP less the $15,000 loss deduction).

What if: Suppose Nicole made her second capital contribution on October 22, 2020, instead of September 6, 2020. How much loss can Nicole deduct, and what is her basis in CCS stock at the end of the PTTP?

---

[30]§465(b)(2)(B). In some circumstances (beyond the scope of this text), shareholders do not create stock basis (or debt basis) for contributions (or shareholder loans to the S corporation) that are funded by nonrecourse loans.

[31]§1377(b)(1)(A). §1377(b) indicates that the PTTP also includes the 120-day period beginning on the date of a determination (not the date of the actual termination) that the corporation's S election had terminated for a previous taxable year.

Answer: The loss deduction is $10,000: Nicole's stock basis at the end of the PTTP and before her loss deduction is only $10,000 because the $7,000 contribution occurred after the end of the PTTP. Nicole's basis in the CCS stock at the end of the PTTP and after the loss deduction is zero ($10,000 basis less $10,000 loss deduction). Her basis then increases to $7,000 on October 22, but the $5,000 suspended loss is lost forever.

Passive Activity Loss Limitation   S corporation shareholders, just like partners, are subject to the **passive activity loss rules.** There are no differences in the application of these rules for S corporations; the definition of a passive activity, the tests for material participation, the income and loss baskets, and the passive activity loss carryover rules described in the Forming and Operating Partnerships chapter are exactly the same. Thus, as in partnerships, the passive activity loss rules limit the ability of S corporation shareholders to deduct losses unless they are involved in actively managing the business.[32]

Example 17-17

What if: Suppose in 2020, CCS incurred an ordinary business loss and allocated the loss equally to its shareholders. Assuming Nicole, Sarah, and Chance all had adequate stock basis and at-risk amounts to absorb the losses, which of the three shareholders would be least likely to deduct the loss due to the passive activity limitation rules?

Answer: Chance. Because he is not actively involved in managing CCS's business activities, any loss allocated to him is a passive activity loss.

Excess Business Loss Limitation   For years beginning after 2017, taxpayers are not allowed to deduct an **"excess business loss"** for the year. Rather, excess business losses are carried forward to subsequent years as a net operating loss carryforward. The excess business loss limitation applies to losses that are otherwise deductible under the basis, at-risk, and passive loss rules. An excess business loss for the year is the excess of aggregate business deductions for the year over the sum of aggregate business gross income or gain of the taxpayer plus a threshold amount. The threshold amount for a tax year is $500,000 for married taxpayers filing jointly and $250,000 for other taxpayers. The amounts are indexed for inflation. In the case of partnership or S corporation business losses, the provision applies at the shareholder level.

Self-Employment Income

You might wonder whether an S corporation shareholder's allocable share of ordinary business income (loss) is classified as self-employment income for tax purposes. The answer is no, even when the shareholder actively works for the S corporation.[33]

When a shareholder does work as an employee of and receives a salary from an S corporation, the S corporation treats this salary payment like that made to any other employee: For Social Security taxes, it withholds 6.2 percent of the shareholder's salary or wages subject to the wage limitation ($128,400 in 2018), for Medicare taxes, it withholds 1.45 percent of the shareholder's salary or wages, and for the additional Medicare tax, it withholds .9 percent on any shareholder salary or wages above $200,000.[34] In addition, the S corporation must pay its portion of the Social Security tax (6.2 percent of the shareholder's salary or wages subject to the $128,400 wage limitation in 2018) and Medicare tax (1.45 percent of the shareholder's salary or wages, regardless of the amount of salary or wages). In contrast to shareholder-employees, S corporations are not subject to the additional Medicare tax on employee salary or wages.

[32]§469.
[33]Rev. Rul. 59-221, 1955-1 CB 225.
[34]Although employee liability for the additional Medicare tax varies based on filing status ($250,000 combined salary or wages for married filing jointly; $125,000 salary or wages for married filing separate; $200,000 salary or wages for all other taxpayers), employers are required to withhold the additional Medicare tax on salary or wages above $200,000 irrespective of the taxpayer's filing status.

Because of this stark contrast between the treatment of ordinary business income and that of shareholder salaries, S corporation shareholders may desire to avoid payroll taxes by limiting or even eliminating their salary payments. However, if they work as employees, they are required to pay themselves a reasonable salary for the services they perform. If they pay themselves an unreasonably low salary, the IRS may attempt to reclassify some or all of the S corporation's ordinary business income as shareholder salary!

TAXES IN THE REAL WORLD — S Corporation Salary in Question

In 2011, *The Wall Street Journal* reported that over the past 15 years when executive pay skyrocketed, the salaries of S corporation owners declined from 52 percent of the corporation's income in 1995 to 39 percent of the corporation's income in 2007. Over the same period, S corporation income doubled, while S corporation owner salary increased only 26 percent to an average salary of $38,400. Why the low pay? To avoid payroll taxes on salary, of course. The IRS, however, is wise to this strategy and has made this issue a top priority in auditing S corporations. In a recent 8th Circuit Court case, *Watson, P.C. v. U.S.*, the IRS argued that the $24,000 salary to a 20-year CPA/S corporation owner was far too low. In this case, Mr. Watson received a $24,000 salary for his work for his CPA firm while receiving profit distributions of $203,651 and $175,470 from his

S corporation in 2003 and 2004, respectively. The IRS contended that Mr. Watson's true pay was $91,044 for each year—and the 8th Circuit Court agreed with the IRS and district court, ruling that Mr. Watson owed extra tax plus interest and penalties. Factors indicating that Mr. Watson's salary was too low included the following: He was an exceedingly qualified accountant with an advanced degree and 20 years of experience; he worked 35 to 45 hours per week as a primary earner in a reputable firm, which had earnings much greater than comparable firms; the firm had significant gross earnings; and his salary was unreasonably low compared to those of other accountants and to the distributions he received.

Source: Watson, P.C. v. U.S. (8 Cir., 2012) 109 AFTR 2d 2012–1059; Laura Saunders, "The IRS Targets Income Tricks," *WSJ.com*, January 22, 2011.

Net Investment Income Tax

Just like partners in a partnership, S corporation shareholders are subject to a 3.8 percent net investment income tax on their share of an S corporation's gross income from interest, dividends, annuities, royalties, rents, a trade or business that is a passive activity or a trade or business of trading financial instruments or commodities, and any net gain from disposing of property (other than property held in a trade or business in which the net investment income tax does not apply), less any allowable deductions from these items.[35,36] Likewise, any gain from the sale of S corporation stock (or distributions in excess of basis) is subject to the net investment income tax to the extent it is allocable to assets held by the S corporation that would have generated a net gain subject to the net investment income tax if all S corporation assets were sold at fair market value.[37]

Fringe Benefits

True to their hybrid status, S corporations are treated in part like C corporations and in part like partnerships with respect to tax deductions for qualifying employee fringe benefits.[38] For shareholder-employees who own 2 percent or less of the entity, the S corporation receives C corporation tax treatment. That is, it gets a tax deduction for qualifying fringe benefits, and the benefits are nontaxable to *all* employees. For shareholder-employees who

---

[35]Interest, dividend, annuity, royalty, and rent income derived in the *ordinary* course of a trade or business that is not passive and does not involve financial instrument or commodity trading is exempt from the net investment income tax.

[36]The tax imposed is 3.8 percent of the lesser of (a) net investment income or (b) the excess of modified adjusted gross income over $250,000 for married-joint filers and surviving spouses, $125,000 for married separate filers, and $200,000 for other taxpayers. Modified adjusted gross income equals adjusted gross income increased by income excluded under the foreign earned income exclusion less any disallowed deductions associated with the foreign earned income exclusion.

[37]See Prop. Reg. §1.1411-7.

[38]Qualifying fringe benefits are nontaxable to the employee. Other fringe benefits (nonqualifying) are taxed as compensation to employees.

own more than 2 percent of the S corporation, it receives partnership treatment.[39] That is, it gets a tax deduction, but the otherwise qualifying fringe benefits are taxable to the shareholder-employees who own more than 2 percent.[40]

Fringe benefits taxable to this group include employer-provided health insurance[41] (§106), group-term life insurance (§79), meals and lodging provided for the convenience of the employer (§119), and benefits provided under a cafeteria plan (§125). Examples of benefits that are nontaxable to more than 2 percent shareholder-employees (and partners in a partnership) include employee achievement awards (§74), qualified group legal services plans (§120), educational assistance programs (§127), dependent care assistance programs (§129), no-additional-cost services (§132), qualified employee discounts (§132), working condition fringe benefits (§132), *de minimis* fringe benefits (§132), on-premises athletic facilities (§132), and medical savings accounts (§220).

DISTRIBUTIONS

LO 17-5

S corporations face special rules when accounting for distributions (operating distributions of cash or other property and liquidating distributions).[42]

Operating Distributions

The rules for determining the shareholder-level tax consequences of operating distributions depend on the S corporation's history; specifically whether, at the time of the distribution, it has accumulated *earnings and profits* from a previous year as a C corporation. We consider both situations—with and without accumulated earnings and profits.

S Corporation with No C Corporation Accumulated Earnings and Profits

Two sets of historical circumstances could apply here: (1) An entity may have been an S corporation since inception, or (2) it may have been converted from a C corporation but not have C corporation accumulated earnings and profits at the time of the distribution. In both cases, as long as there are no C corporation accumulated earnings and profits, the rules for accounting for the distribution are very similar to those applicable to distributions to partners. That is, shareholder distributions are tax-free to the extent of the shareholders' stock basis (determined after increasing the stock basis for income allocations for the year[43]). If a distribution exceeds the shareholder's stock basis, the shareholder has a capital gain equal to the excess distribution amount.

Example 17-18

What if: Suppose CCS has been an S corporation since its inception. On June 1, 2020, CCS distributed $30,000 to Nicole. Her basis in her CCS stock on January 1, 2020, was $20,000. For 2020, Nicole was allocated $15,000 of ordinary income from CCS and no separately stated items. What is the amount and character of income Nicole recognizes on the distribution, and what is her basis in her CCS stock after the distribution?

Answer: Nicole has $0 income from the distribution and $5,000 basis in stock after the distribution ($35,000 − $30,000). Her stock basis for determining the taxability of the distribution is $35,000, or her beginning basis of $20,000 plus the $15,000 income allocation for the year (which is taxable to Nicole).

(continued on page 17-18)

---

[39]§1372(a).

[40]The §318 attribution rules apply for purposes of determining which shareholders own more than 2 percent.

[41]Note, however, that shareholders who own more than 2 percent are allowed to deduct their insurance costs as *for* AGI deductions [§162(l)].

[42]The §302 stock redemption rules that determine whether a distribution in redemption of a shareholder's stock should be treated as a distribution or a sale or exchange apply to both C corporations and S corporations.

[43]§1368(d).

THE KEY FACTS

Cash Operating Distributions for S Corporations

- For S corporations without E&P: Distributions are tax-free to the extent of the shareholder's stock basis. If a distribution exceeds the shareholder's stock basis, the shareholder has a capital gain equal to the excess distribution amount.

- For S corporations with E&P: Distributions are deemed to be paid from (1) the AAA account (tax-free to the extent of basis and taxed as capital gain thereafter), (2) existing accumulated E&P (taxable as dividends), and (3) the shareholder's remaining basis in the S corporation stock, if any (tax-free to the extent of basis and taxed as capital gain thereafter).

What if: Assume the same facts except that CCS distributed $40,000 to Nicole rather than $30,000. What is the amount and character of income Nicole recognizes on the distribution, and what is her basis in her CCS stock after the distribution?

Answer: Nicole has a $5,000 long-term capital gain (she has held her CCS stock more than one year) and $0 basis in her stock (the distribution reduced her stock basis to $0).

What if: Suppose CCS began in 2017 as a C corporation and elected to be taxed as an S corporation in its second year of operations. In 2017, it distributed all its earnings and profits as a dividend, so it did not have any earnings and profits at the end of 2017. In 2018, it distributed $30,000 to Nicole when her basis in her stock was $35,000. What is the amount and character of income she recognizes on the distribution, and what is her basis in her CCS stock after the distribution?

Answer: Nicole has $0 income on the distribution and $5,000 basis in stock after the distribution ($35,000 − $30,000). Because CCS did not have C corporation earnings and profits at the time of the distribution, her outcome is the same as if CCS had been taxed as an S corporation since inception.

S Corporation with C Corporation Accumulated Earnings and Profits When an S corporation has accumulated earnings and profits (E&P) from prior C corporation years, the distribution rules are a bit more complex. These rules are designed to ensure that shareholders cannot avoid the dividend tax on dividend distributions out of C corporation accumulated E&P by simply electing S corporation status and then distributing the accumulated E&P. For S corporations in this situation, the tax laws require the corporation to maintain an **accumulated adjustments account (AAA)** to determine the taxability of S corporate distributions. The AAA represents the cumulative income or losses for the period the corporation has been an S corporation. It is calculated as:

The beginning of year AAA balance

+ Separately stated income/gain items (excluding tax-exempt income)

+ Ordinary income

− Separately stated losses and deductions

− Ordinary losses

− Nondeductible expenses that are not capital expenditures (except deductions related to generating tax-exempt income)

− Distributions out of AAA[44]

= End of year AAA balance

Unlike a shareholder's stock basis, the AAA may have a negative balance. However, the reduction for distributions may not cause the AAA to go negative or to become more negative. Also, unlike stock basis, the AAA is a corporate-level account rather than a shareholder-specific account.

Example 17-19

CCS was originally formed as a C corporation and reported 2017 taxable income (and earnings and profits) of $40,000 (see Exhibit 17-2). Effective the beginning of 2018, it elected to be taxed as an S corporation. In 2018, CCS reported $249,000 of overall income (including separately stated items—see Exhibit 17-2). What is the amount of CCS's AAA for 2018 before considering the effects of distributions?

---

[44]§1368(e)(1)(C). If the current-year income and loss items net to make a negative adjustment to the AAA, the net negative adjustment from these items is made to the AAA *after* any AAA reductions for distributions (i.e., the reduction in AAA for distributions is made before the net negative adjustment for current-year income and loss items).

Answer: $249,000, computed as follows:

Description	Amount	Explanation
(1) Separately stated income	$ 9,000	$6,000 interest income + $3,000 dividend income (see Exhibit 17-2)
(2) Ordinary business income	240,000	Example 17-11
AAA before distributions	**$249,000**	(1) + (2)

What if: Assume that during 2018, CCS distributed $300,000 to its shareholders. What is CCS's AAA at the end of 2018?

Answer: AAA is $0, because the distribution cannot cause AAA to be negative.

What if: Instead of reporting $249,000 of income during 2018, assume that during 2018 CCS reported an ordinary business loss of $45,000, a separately stated charitable contribution of $5,000, and a $6,000 distribution to its shareholders. What is CCS's AAA at the end of 2018?

Answer: AAA is −$50,000. CCS decreases its AAA by the $45,000 business loss and the $5,000 charitable contribution. AAA before distributions is −$50,000. CCS does not decrease AAA by the $6,000 distribution because the distribution cannot cause AAA to be negative or make it more negative.

S corporation distributions are deemed to be paid from the following sources in the order listed:[45]

1. The AAA account (to the extent it has a positive balance).[46]
2. Existing accumulated earnings and profits from years when the corporation operated as a C corporation.
3. The shareholder's stock basis.[47]

S corporation distributions from the AAA (the most common distributions) are treated the same as distributions when the S corporation does not have E&P. They are nontaxable to the extent of the shareholder's basis, and they create capital gains if they exceed the shareholder's stock basis. If an S corporation makes a distribution from accumulated E&P, the distribution is taxable to shareholders as a dividend. Once an S corporation's accumulated E&P is fully distributed, the remaining distributions reduce the shareholder's remaining basis in the S corporation stock (if any) and are nontaxable. Any excess distributions are treated as capital gain.

---

[45]S corporations may elect to have distributions treated as being first paid out of existing accumulated earnings and profits from C corporation years to avoid the excess net passive income tax. We discuss the excess net passive income tax later in the chapter.

[46]Prior to 1983, S corporations' shareholders were taxed on undistributed taxable income as a deemed distribution. This undistributed income is referred to as *previously taxable income (PTI)*. For S corporations with PTI, distributions are considered to be paid out of PTI (if there is any remaining that has not been distributed) after any distributions out of their AAA. These distributions are also nontaxable to the extent of basis and reduce both the shareholder's basis and PTI.

[47]Technically, the distributions come from the Other Adjustments Account (OAA) and then any remaining shareholder equity accounts (e.g., common stock, paid-in capital). The OAA starts at zero at the S corporation's inception; is increased for tax-exempt income; and is decreased by expenses related to tax-exempt income, any federal taxes paid that are attributable to a C corporation tax year, and any S corporate distributions after the AAA and accumulated E&P have been reduced to zero. As with the AAA, the reduction for distributions may not cause the OAA to go negative or to increase a negative balance. Because from the shareholder's perspective distributions out of the OAA and equity accounts both reduce the shareholder's stock basis, we do not discuss the OAA or other equity accounts in detail.

Example 17-20

What if: Assume at the end of 2018, before considering distributions, CCS's AAA was $24,000 and its accumulated E&P from 2017 was $40,000. Also assume Nicole's basis in her CCS stock is $80,000. If CCS distributes $60,000 on July 1 ($20,000 to each shareholder), what is the amount and character of income Nicole must recognize on her $20,000 distribution, and what is her stock basis in CCS after the distribution?

Answer: $12,000 dividend income and $72,000 stock basis after the distribution, computed as follows:

Description	Amount	Explanation
(1) Total distribution	$60,000	
(2) CCS's AAA beginning balance	24,000	
(3) Distribution from AAA	24,000	Lesser of (1) or (2)
(4) Distribution in excess of AAA	36,000	(1) − (3)
(5) Nicole's share of AAA distribution	8,000	(3) × 1/3 (nontaxable reduction of stock basis)
(6) Nicole's beginning stock basis	80,000	
(7) Nicole's ending stock basis	**72,000**	(6) − (5)
(8) CCS's E&P balance	40,000	
(9) Dividend distribution (from E&P)	36,000	Lesser of (4) or (8)
Nicole's share of dividend	**12,000**	(9) × 1/3

Property Distributions   At times, S corporations distribute appreciated property to their shareholders. When they do so, S corporations recognize gain as though they had sold the appreciated property for its fair market value just prior to the distribution.[48] (This rule contrasts with the partnership provisions for property distributions but is consistent with the C corporation rules.) Shareholders who receive the distributed property recognize their distributive share of the deemed gain and increase their stock basis accordingly. On the other hand, S corporations do not recognize losses on distributions of property whose value has declined.

For the shareholder, the amount of a property distribution is the fair market value of the property received (minus any liabilities the shareholder assumes on the distribution). The rules we described above apply in determining the extent to which the amount of the distribution is a tax-free reduction of basis, a capital gain for a distribution in excess of basis, or a taxable dividend to the shareholder.[49] (See the rules for the taxability of distributions for S corporations with and without C corporation accumulated earnings and profits.) Shareholders take a fair market value basis in the property received in the distribution.

Example 17-21

What if: Assume that at the end of 2019, CCS distributes long-term capital gain property (fair market value of $24,000, basis of $15,000) to each shareholder (aggregate property distribution of $72,000 with an aggregate basis of $45,000). At the time of the distribution, CCS has no corporate E&P and Nicole has a basis of $10,000 in her CCS stock. How much gain, if any, does CCS recognize on the distribution? How much income does Nicole recognize as a result of the distribution?

---

[48]§311(b). In addition, the S corporation may incur entity-level tax if the distributed property had built-in gains related to when the corporation converted to an S corporation. We discuss the built-in gains tax later in the chapter.

[49]Note that while S corporation shareholders reduce their stock basis by the fair market value of the property received, partners receiving property distributions from partnerships generally reduce the basis in their partnership interests by the adjusted basis of the distributed property.

Answer: CCS recognizes $27,000 of long-term capital gain and Nicole recognizes $14,000 of long-term capital gain, computed as follows:

Description	Amount	Explanation
(1) FMV of distributed property	$72,000	
(2) CCS's basis in distributed property	45,000	
(3) CCS's LTCG gain on distribution	**27,000**	(1) − (2)
(4) Nicole's share of LTCG from CCS	9,000	(3) × 1/3
(5) Nicole's stock basis after gain allocation	19,000	$10,000 beginning basis + (4)
(6) Distribution to Nicole	24,000	(1) × 1/3
(7) Nicole's stock basis after distribution	0	(5) − (6) limited to $0
(8) LTCG to Nicole on distribution in excess of stock basis	5,000	(6) in excess of (5)
Nicole's total LTCG on distribution	**14,000**	(4) + (8)

Post-Termination Transition Period Distributions

Recall the special tax rules relating to suspended losses at the S corporation termination date. Similarly, §1371(e) provides for special treatment of any S corporation distribution *in cash* after an S election termination and during the post-termination transition period (PTTP). Such cash distributions are tax-free to the extent they do not exceed the corporation's AAA balance and the individual shareholder's basis in the stock.

The PTTP for post-termination distributions is generally the same as the PTTP for deducting suspended losses, discussed above. For determining the taxability of distributions, the PTTP generally begins on the day after the last day of the corporation's last taxable year as an S corporation; it ends on the later of (a) one year after the last S corporation day or (b) the due date for filing the return for the last year as an S corporation (including extensions).[50,51]

Liquidating Distributions

Liquidating distributions of a shareholder interest in an S corporation follow corporate tax rules rather than partnership rules. For a complete liquidation of the S corporation, the rules under §§331 and 336 govern the tax consequences. S corporations generally recognize gain *or* loss on each asset they distribute in liquidation (recall that S corporations recognize gain but not loss on operating distributions of noncash property). These gains and losses are allocated to the S corporation shareholders, increasing or decreasing their stock basis. In general, shareholders recognize gain on the distribution if the value of the property exceeds their stock basis; they recognize loss if their stock basis exceeds the value of the property.

Example 17-22

What if: Assume that at the end of 2020, CCS liquidates by distributing long-term capital gain property (fair market value of $20,000, basis of $12,000) to each shareholder (aggregate property distribution of $60,000 with an aggregate basis of $36,000). At the time of the distribution, CCS has no corporate E&P

(continued on page 17-22)

---

[50]§1377(b)(1)(A). For purposes of the taxability of distributions, the PTTP also includes: (1) the 120-day period that begins on the date of any determination (court decision, closing agreement, and so on) from an IRS audit that occurs after the S election has been terminated and adjusts the corporation's income, loss, or deduction during the S period; and (2) the 120-day period beginning on the date of a determination (not the date of the actual termination) that the corporation's S election had terminated for a previous taxable year [§1377(b)(1)(B) and (C)].

[51]In addition to the general rules that apply to PTTP distributions, there is a special rule that applies to distributions from an "eligible terminated S corporation" that occur *after* the PTTP. Specifically, distributions from an eligible terminated S corporation that occur after the PTTP are treated as paid *pro rata* from its accumulated adjustments account and from its earnings and profits. An eligible terminated S corporation is any C corporation which (i) was an S corporation on December 21, 2017, (ii) revoked its S corporation election during the two-year period beginning on December 22, 2017, and (iii) had the same owners on December 22, 2017, and on the revocation date (in identical proportions).

and Nicole has a basis of $25,000 in her CCS stock. How much gain or loss, if any, does CCS recognize on the distribution? How much gain or loss does Nicole recognize as a result of the distribution?

Answer: CCS recognizes $24,000 of long-term capital gain and Nicole recognizes $5,000 of net long-term capital loss, computed as follows:

Description	Amount	Explanation
(1) FMV of distributed property	$60,000	
(2) CCS's basis in distributed property	36,000	
(3) CCS's LTCG gain on distribution	**24,000**	(1) − (2)
(4) Nicole's share of LTCG from CCS	8,000	(3) × 1/3
(5) Nicole's stock basis after gain allocation	33,000	$25,000 beginning basis + (4)
(6) Distribution to Nicole	20,000	(1) × 1/3
(7) Nicole's LTCL on liquidating distribution	(13,000)	(6) − (5)
Nicole's net LTCL on distribution	**(5,000)**	(4) + (7)

LO 17-6

THE KEY FACTS

Built-in Gains Tax

- The built-in gains tax applies only to S corporations that have a net unrealized built-in gain at the time they convert from C corporations and that recognize net built-in gains during the built-in gains tax recognition period.

- The net unrealized built-in gain represents the net gain (if any) that the corporation would recognize if it sold each asset at its fair market value.

- Recognized built-in gains (losses) include the gain (loss) for any asset sold during the year [limited to the unrealized gain (loss) for the specific asset at the S conversion date].

- The net recognized built-in gain is limited to the lowest of (a) the net recognized built-in gain less any net operating loss (NOL) and capital loss carryovers, (b) the net unrealized built-in gain not yet recognized, and (c) the corporation's taxable income for the year using the C corporation tax rules.

S CORPORATION TAXES AND FILING REQUIREMENTS

Although S corporations are flow-through entities generally not subject to tax, three potential taxes apply to S corporations that previously operated as C corporations: the **built-in gains tax, excess net passive income tax,** and **LIFO recapture tax.** The built-in gains tax is the most common of the three and will be our starting point.

Built-in Gains Tax

Congress enacted the built-in gains tax to prevent C corporations from avoiding corporate taxes on sales of appreciated property by electing S corporation status. The built-in gains tax applies only to an S corporation that has a *net unrealized built-in gain* at the time it converts from a C corporation. Further, for the built-in gains tax to apply, the S corporation must subsequently recognize net built-in gains during the **built-in gains tax recognition period.**[52] The built-in gains tax recognition period is the first five years a corporation operates as an S corporation.

What exactly is a **net unrealized built-in gain?** Measured on the first day of the corporation's first year as an S corporation, it represents the net gain (if any) the corporation would recognize if it sold each asset at its fair market value. For this purpose, we net gains and losses to determine whether indeed there is a net unrealized gain at the conversion date. The corporation's accounts receivable and accounts payable are also part of the computation: Under the cash method, accounts receivable are gain items and accounts payable are loss items. If the S corporation has a net unrealized gain at conversion, it must compute its net recognized built-in gains for each tax year during the applicable built-in gain recognition period to determine whether it is liable for the built-in gains tax.

Example 17-23

CCS uses the accrual method of accounting. At the beginning of 2018, it owned the following assets (but leased its manufacturing facility and its equipment):

Asset	Fair Market Value (FMV)	Adjusted Basis (AB)	Built-in Gain (Loss)
Cash	$ 80,000	$ 80,000	$ 0
Accounts receivable	20,000	20,000	0
Inventory (FIFO)	130,000	110,000	20,000
Land	100,000	125,000	(25,000)
Totals	$330,000	$335,000	$ (5,000)

[52]§1374.

What is CCS's net unrealized built-in gain when it converts to an S corporation on January 1, 2018?

Answer: CCS has $0 net unrealized built-in gain. It has a net unrealized built-in loss, so it is not subject to the built-in gains tax.

What if: Suppose CCS's inventory is valued at $155,000 instead of $130,000. What is its net unrealized built-in gain?

Answer: $20,000. The $45,000 built-in gain on the inventory is netted against the $25,000 built-in loss on the land.

Recognized built-in gains for an S corporation year include (1) the gain for any asset sold during the year (limited to the unrealized gain for the specific asset at the S conversion date) and (2) any income received during the current year attributable to pre-S corporation years (such as collection on accounts receivable for cash-method S corporations). Likewise, recognized built-in losses for a year include (1) the loss for any asset sold during the year (limited to the unrealized loss for the specific asset at the S conversion date) and (2) any deduction during the current year attributable to pre-S corporation years (such as deductions for accounts payable for cash-method S corporations). The net recognized built-in gain for any year is limited to *the least of:*

1. The net of the recognized built-in gains and losses for the year.
2. The net unrealized built-in gains as of the S election date less the net recognized built-in gains in previous years. (This restriction ensures the net recognized built-in gains during the recognition period do not exceed the net unrealized gain at the S conversion date.)
3. The corporation's taxable income for the year, using the C corporation tax rules exclusive of the dividends received deduction and net operating loss deduction.

If taxable income limits the net recognized built-in gain for any year [item (3) above], we treat the excess gain as a recognized built-in gain in the next tax year, *but only if* the next tax year is in the built-in gains tax recognition period. After the net recognized built-in gain to be taxed has been determined using the limitations above, it should be reduced by any net operating loss (NOL) or capital loss carryovers from prior C corporation years.[53] This base is then multiplied by the highest corporate tax rate (currently 21 percent) to determine the built-in gains tax. The built-in gains tax paid by the S corporation is allocated to the shareholders as a loss. The character of the allocated loss (ordinary, capital, §1231) depends on the nature of assets that give rise to the built-in gains tax. Specifically, the loss is allocated proportionately among the character of the recognized built-in gains resulting in the tax.[54] For planning purposes, the S corporation should consider when to recognize built-in losses to reduce its exposure to the built-in gains tax. That is, the company could seek to recognize built-in losses in years with recognized built-in gains, in order to avoid the built-in gains tax.

Example 17-24

What if: Suppose CCS had a net unrealized built-in gain of $20,000. In addition to other transactions in 2018, CCS sold inventory it owned at the beginning of the year; that inventory had built-in gain at the beginning of the year of $40,000 (FMV $150,000; cost basis $110,000). If CCS had been a C corporation in 2018, its taxable income would have been $200,000. How much built-in gains tax must CCS pay in 2018?

Answer: It must pay $4,200 ($20,000 × 21%) in built-in gains tax. CCS must pay a 21 percent tax on the least of (a) $40,000 (recognized built-in gain on inventory), (b) $20,000 (initial net unrealized gain), and (c) $200,000 (taxable income computed as if CCS were a C corporation for 2017). It will reduce the amount of ordinary business income it would otherwise allocate to its shareholders by $4,200—the amount of the built-in gains tax—because the entire amount of the tax is due to inventory sales.

What if: Assume the same facts as above (an initial net unrealized gain of $20,000) except CCS sold two assets that had built-in gains at the time CCS became an S corporation. CCS sold a capital asset

(continued on page 17-24)

---

[53]Capital loss carryovers only reduce built-in gains that are capital gains.

[54]§1366(f)(2).

with a built-in gain of $10,000 and inventory with a built-in gain of $40,000. CCS will still pay a $4,200 built-in gains tax. This tax will be allocated as a loss to its shareholders. What is the character of the $4,200 loss?

Answer: It is an $840 capital loss [$4,200 × (10,000 capital gain/$50,000 total recognized built-in gain)] and a $3,360 ordinary loss [$4,200 × ($40,000 ordinary income from inventory sale/$50,000 total recognized built-in gain)].

What if: Assume that in addition to the initial facts in the example, CCS also had a net operating loss from 2017 (the year it operated as a C corporation) of $15,000. How much built-in gains tax will CCS have to pay in 2018?

Answer: It will pay $1,050 ($5,000 × 21%). CCS is allowed to offset $15,000 of the $20,000 recognized portion of the initial net unrealized gain by its $15,000 net operating loss carryover from 2017.

What if: Suppose CCS had a net unrealized built-in gain of $20,000. In addition to other transactions in 2018, CCS sold inventory it owned at the beginning of the year; that inventory had built-in gain at the beginning of the year of $40,000 (FMV $150,000; AB $110,000). If CCS had been a C corporation in 2018, its taxable income would have been $4,000. How much built-in gains tax would CCS have to pay in 2018?

Answer: $840 ($4,000 × 21%). CCS must pay a 21 percent tax on the least of (a) $40,000 (recognized built-in gain on inventory), (b) $20,000 (initial net unrealized gain), and (c) $4,000 (taxable income computed as if CCS were a C corporation for 2018). Because the tax was limited due to the taxable income limitation, the excess gain of $16,000 ($20,000 recognized built-in gain minus $4,000 gain on which CCS paid tax) is treated as a recognized built-in gain in 2019.

Excess Net Passive Income Tax

If an S corporation previously operated as a C corporation *and* has accumulated earnings and profits at the end of the year from a prior C corporation year, it may be subject to the *excess net passive income tax.*[55] Congress created this tax to encourage S corporations to distribute their accumulated earnings and profits from prior C corporation years. It does not apply to S corporations that never operated as a C corporation, or to S corporations without earnings and profits from prior C corporation years.

The tax is levied on the S corporation's **excess net passive income,** computed as follows:

$$\text{Excess net passive income} = \text{Net passive investment income} \times \frac{\text{Passive investment income} - (25\% \times \text{Gross receipts})}{\text{Passive investment income}}$$

Note that an S corporation has excess net passive income only when (1) it has net passive investment income and (2) its passive investment income exceeds 25 percent of its gross receipts. For purposes of determining excess net passive income, *gross receipts* is the total amount of revenues (including passive investment income) received or accrued under the corporation's accounting method, and not reduced by returns, allowances, cost of goods sold, or deductions. Gross receipts include net capital gains from the sales or exchanges of capital assets and gains from the sales or exchanges of stock or securities (losses do not offset gains). As defined previously in the chapter, passive investment income includes gross receipts from royalties, rents, dividends, interest (including tax-exempt interest), and annuities. **Net passive investment income** is passive investment income decreased by any expenses connected with producing that income.

The excess net passive income tax is imposed on excess net passive income at the highest corporate tax rate (currently 21 percent). For purposes of computing the tax, excess net passive income is limited to taxable income computed as if the corporation were a C corporation (excluding net operating losses). The formula for determining the tax is:

$$\text{Excess net passive income tax} = 21\% \times \text{Excess net passive income}$$

[55]§1375.

Each item of passive investment income that flows through to shareholders is reduced by an allocable share of the excess net passive income tax. The portion of the tax allocated to each item of passive investment income is the amount of the item divided by the total amount of passive investment income.

The IRS may waive the excess net passive income tax in some circumstances—for example, if the S corporation determined in good faith it did not have accumulated earnings and profits at the end of the tax year and within a reasonable period distributed earnings and profits it identified later.[56]

Example 17-25

During 2018 CCS reported the following income (see Exhibit 17-2):

	2018 (S Corporation)
Sales revenue	$520,000
Cost of goods sold	(115,000)
Salary to owners Nicole and Sarah	(90,000)
Employee wages	(50,000)
Depreciation expense	(20,000)
Miscellaneous expenses	(5,000)
Interest income	6,000
Dividend income	3,000
Overall net income	$249,000

What are CCS's passive investment income, net passive investment income, and gross receipts for 2018?

Answer: The amounts are $9,000 passive income ($6,000 interest income + $3,000 dividends); $9,000 net passive investment income (because CCS has $0 expenses in producing passive investment income); and $529,000 gross receipts ($520,000 sales revenue + $3,000 dividends + $6,000 interest income).

What is CCS's excess net passive income tax in 2018, if any?

Answer: Zero. CCS has accumulated earnings and profits from 2017 (see Exhibit 17-2), but it owes zero excess net passive income tax because its passive investment income is less than 25 percent of its gross receipts [$9,000 < $132,250 ($529,000 × 25%)].

What if: Suppose CCS has passive investment income of $180,000 ($120,000 interest + $60,000 dividends), expenses associated with the passive investment income of $20,000, and gross receipts of $700,000 ($520,000 + $180,000). Also, if CCS were a C corporation, its taxable income would have been $249,000; assume it had accumulated earnings and profits of $40,000. What is CCS's excess net passive income tax, if any? What effect, if any, would the excess net passive income tax have on interest and dividends allocated to the shareholders?

Answer: The base for the tax is limited to the lesser of (a) excess net passive income of $4,444 [($180,000 passive investment income minus $20,000 expenses associated with passive investment income) × ($180,000 − 25% × $700,000)/$180,000] or $249,000 (CCS's taxable income if it had been a C corporation). Thus, the base for the tax is limited to $4,444, and the tax is $933 (21% × $4,444).

Interest and dividends allocated to the shareholders will be reduced by the excess net passive income tax. The interest income allocated to shareholders will be reduced by $622 [$933 tax × ($120,000 interest/$180,000 total passive investment income)], and dividend income will be reduced by $311 [$933 × ($60,000 dividend/$180,000)].

What if: Suppose CCS has passive investment income of $180,000, expenses associated with the passive investment income of $20,000, and gross receipts of $700,000 ($520,000 + $180,000). Also, if CCS were a C corporation, its taxable income would have been $2,000; assume it had accumulated earnings and profits of $40,000. What is CCS's excess net passive income tax, if any?

(continued on page 17-26)

[56]§1375(d).

> **Answer:** The base for the tax is limited to the lesser of (a) excess net passive investment income of $4,444 [$160,000 × ($180,000 − 25% × $700,000)/$180,000] or (b) $2,000 (taxable income if CCS had been a C corporation). So the tax is $420 (21% × $2,000).

Remember, if an S corporation pays the net excess passive income tax for three years in a row, its S election will be terminated by the excess passive income test.

LIFO Recapture Tax

C corporations that elect S corporation status and use the LIFO inventory method are subject to the *LIFO recapture tax*. The purpose of this tax is to prevent former C corporations from avoiding built-in gains tax by using the LIFO method of accounting for their inventories. Specifically, a LIFO method corporation would not recognize built-in gains unless the corporation invaded its LIFO layers during the built-in gains tax recognition period.

The LIFO recapture tax requires the C corporation to include the **LIFO recapture amount** in its gross income in the last year it operates as a C corporation.[57] That amount equals the excess of the inventory basis computed using the FIFO method over the inventory basis computed using the LIFO method at the end of the corporation's last tax year as a C corporation. In addition to being included in gross income (and taxed at the C corporation's marginal tax rate), the LIFO recapture amount also increases the corporation's adjusted basis in its inventory at the time it converts to an S corporation. The basis increase reduces the amount of net unrealized gain subject to the built-in gains tax.

The corporation pays the LIFO recapture tax (technically a C corporation tax) in four annual installments. The first installment is due on or before the due date (not including extensions) of the corporation's last *C corporation* tax return. The final three annual installments are due each year on or before the due date (not including extensions) of the *S corporation*'s tax return.

The LIFO recapture tax does not preclude the S corporation from using the LIFO method, but it obviously does accelerate the gain attributable to differences between LIFO and FIFO for inventory existing at the time of the S corporation election.

Example 17-26

What if: Suppose CCS uses the LIFO method of accounting for its inventory and elected S corporation status effective January 1, 2019. Assume that at the end of 2018, the basis of the inventory under the LIFO method was $90,000. Under the FIFO method, the basis of the inventory would have been $100,000. Finally, regular taxable income in 2018 was $40,000. What amount of LIFO recapture tax must CCS pay?

Answer: CCS must pay $2,100 [($100,000 FIFO inventory basis − $90,000 LIFO inventory basis) × 21 percent]. The 21 percent tax rate is the marginal rate at which the additional $10,000 of income would have been taxed in 2018 under the corporate tax rate schedule. CCS would increase its basis in its inventory by $10,000 to $100,000 as of the end of 2018, its last year as a C corporation. This would reduce the unrealized net built-in gain on the inventory.

When is CCS required to pay the tax?

Answer: CCS must pay $525 by April 15, 2019 (the unextended due date of the C corporation tax return); March 16, 2020 (March 15 falls on a Sunday); March 15, 2021 ; and March 15, 2022. March 15 is the annual tax return due date for calendar year-end S corporation returns without extensions (see discussion below).

---

[57]§1363(d).

EXHIBIT 17-3, PART I   CCS's Form 1120S, page 1

Form **1120S**

Department of the Treasury
Internal Revenue Service

U.S. Income Tax Return for an S Corporation

▶ Do not file this form unless the corporation has filed or is
attaching Form 2553 to elect to be an S corporation.
▶ Go to *www.irs.gov/Form1120S* for instructions and the latest information.

OMB No. 1545-0123

20**17**

For calendar year 2017 or tax year beginning _____ , 2017, ending _____ , 20_____

A S election effective date		Name	**D** Employer identification number
January 1, 2018	**TYPE**	**Color Comfort Sheets**	24-4681012
B Business activity code number (see instructions)	**OR**	Number, street, and room or suite no. If a P.O. box, see instructions.	**E** Date incorporated
		375 East 459 South	**January 1, 2017**
314000	**PRINT**	City or town, state or province, country, and ZIP or foreign postal code	**F** Total assets (see instructions)
C Check if Sch. M-3 attached ☐		**Salt Lake City, UT 84103**	$ 370,000

G Is the corporation electing to be an S corporation beginning with this tax year? ☑ Yes ☐ No If "Yes," attach Form 2553 if not already filed
H Check if: **(1)** ☐ Final return **(2)** ☐ Name change **(3)** ☐ Address change **(4)** ☐ Amended return **(5)** ☐ S election termination or revocation
I Enter the number of shareholders who were shareholders during any part of the tax year . . . . ▶

Caution: Include **only** trade or business income and expenses on lines 1a through 21. See the instructions for more information.

Income

1a	Gross receipts or sales	**1a**	520,000	
b	Returns and allowances	**1b**		
c	Balance. Subtract line 1b from line 1a	**1c**		520,000
2	Cost of goods sold (attach Form 1125-A)	**2**		115,000
3	Gross profit. Subtract line 2 from line 1c	**3**		405,000
4	Net gain (loss) from Form 4797, line 17 (attach Form 4797)	**4**		
5	Other income (loss) (see instructions—attach statement)	**5**		
6	**Total income (loss).** Add lines 3 through 5 . . . . ▶	**6**		405,000

Deductions (see instructions for limitations)

7	Compensation of officers (see instructions—attach Form 1125-E)	**7**	90,000
8	Salaries and wages (less employment credits)	**8**	50,000
9	Repairs and maintenance	**9**	
10	Bad debts	**10**	
11	Rents	**11**	
12	Taxes and licenses	**12**	
13	Interest	**13**	
14	Depreciation not claimed on Form 1125-A or elsewhere on return (attach Form 4562) . . .	**14**	20,000
15	Depletion **(Do not deduct oil and gas depletion.)**	**15**	
16	Advertising	**16**	
17	Pension, profit-sharing, etc., plans	**17**	
18	Employee benefit programs	**18**	
19	Other deductions (attach statement)	**19**	5,000
20	**Total deductions.** Add lines 7 through 19 . . . . ▶	**20**	165,000
21	**Ordinary business income (loss).** Subtract line 20 from line 6	**21**	240,000

Tax and Payments

22a	Excess net passive income or LIFO recapture tax (see instructions) . .	**22a**		
b	Tax from Schedule D (Form 1120S)	**22b**		
c	Add lines 22a and 22b (see instructions for additional taxes)		**22c**	
23a	2017 estimated tax payments and 2016 overpayment credited to 2017	**23a**		
b	Tax deposited with Form 7004	**23b**		
c	Credit for federal tax paid on fuels (attach Form 4136)	**23c**		
d	Add lines 23a through 23c		**23d**	
24	Estimated tax penalty (see instructions). Check if Form 2220 is attached . . . . . ▶ ☐		**24**	
25	**Amount owed.** If line 23d is smaller than the total of lines 22c and 24, enter amount owed . .		**25**	
26	**Overpayment.** If line 23d is larger than the total of lines 22c and 24, enter amount overpaid .		**26**	
27	Enter amount from line 26 **Credited to 2018 estimated tax** ▶ _____ Refunded ▶		**27**	

Sign Here

Under penalties of perjury, I declare that I have examined this return, including accompanying schedules and statements, and to the best of my knowledge and belief, it is true, correct, and complete. Declaration of preparer (other than taxpayer) is based on all information of which preparer has any knowledge.

▶ _____   _____   ▶ _____
Signature of officer   Date   Title

May the IRS discuss this return with the preparer shown below (see instructions)? ☐ Yes ☐ No

Paid Preparer Use Only

Print/Type preparer's name	Preparer's signature	Date	Check ☐ if self-employed	PTIN
Firm's name ▶			Firm's EIN ▶	
Firm's address ▶			Phone no.	

For Paperwork Reduction Act Notice, see separate instructions.   Cat. No. 11510H   Form **1120S** (2017)

EXHIBIT 17-3, PART II **CCS's 2018 partial Schedule K (on 2017 forms)**

Schedule K		Shareholders' Pro Rata Share Items			Total amount
Income (Loss)	1	Ordinary business income (loss) (page 1, line 21)	**1**		240,000
	2	Net rental real estate income (loss) (attach Form 8825)	**2**		
	3a	Other gross rental income (loss)	**3a**		
	b	Expenses from other rental activities (attach statement) . .	**3b**		
	c	Other net rental income (loss). Subtract line 3b from line 3a	**3c**		
	4	Interest income	**4**		6,000
	5	Dividends: a Ordinary dividends	**5a**		3,000
		b Qualified dividends	**5b**	3,000	
	6	Royalties	**6**		
	7	Net short-term capital gain (loss) (attach Schedule D (Form 1120S))	**7**		
	8a	Net long-term capital gain (loss) (attach Schedule D (Form 1120S))	**8a**		
	b	Collectibles (28%) gain (loss)	**8b**		
	c	Unrecaptured section 1250 gain (attach statement)	**8c**		
	9	Net section 1231 gain (loss) (attach Form 4797)	**9**		
	10	Other income (loss) (see instructions) . . Type ▶	**10**		

Source: Form 1120S Department of the Treasury, Internal Revenue Service
Note: In the revised 2018 Form 1120S, Schedule K, Color Comfort Sheets would also report qualified business income ($240,000), allocable S corporation wages paid to employees ($140,000), and the unadjusted basis of qualified property ($300,000) for purposes of the deduction for qualified business income (as detailed in Example 17-11).

Estimated Taxes

The estimated tax rules for S corporations generally follow the rules for C corporations: S corporations with a federal income tax liability of $500 or more due to the built-in gains tax or excess net passive income tax must estimate their tax liability for the year and pay it in four quarterly estimated installments. However, an S corporation is not required to make estimated tax payments for the LIFO recapture tax.[58]

Filing Requirements

S corporations are required to file **Form 1120S,** U.S. Income Tax Return for an S Corporation, with the IRS by the 15th day of the third month after the S corporation's year-end (e.g., March 15 for a calendar-year-end S corporation). S corporations may receive an automatic, six-month extension by filing **Form 7004** with the IRS prior to the original due date of the return.[59] Thus, the extended due date of an S corporation tax return is generally September 15.

Exhibit 17-3 presents page 1 of CCS's Form 1120S (for its 2018 activities), CCS's partial Schedule K, and Nicole's K-1 (we use 2017 forms because 2018 forms were unavailable at the time this book went to press). Note the K-1 of the 1120S is different from the K-1 of the 1065. In contrast to the 1065 Schedule K-1, the 1120S Schedule K-1 does not report self-employment income, does not allocate entity-level debt to shareholders, and does not allow for shareholders to have profit-and-loss-sharing ratios that are different from shareholders' percentage of stock ownership.

[58]Rev. Proc. 94-61, IRB 1994-38,56.

[59]Under §6698, late-filing penalties apply if the S corporation fails to file by the normal or extended due date for the return.

EXHIBIT 17-3, PART III   Nicole's 2018 Schedule K-1 (on 2017 forms)

671117

☐ Final K-1 ☐ Amended K-1	OMB No. 1545-0123

Schedule K-1
(Form 1120S)
Department of the Treasury
Internal Revenue Service

2017

For calendar year 2017, or tax year

beginning   /   / 2017   ending   /   /

Shareholder's Share of Income, Deductions, Credits, etc.   ▶ See back of form and separate instructions.

Part I   **Information About the Corporation**

A   Corporation's employer identification number
24-4681012

B   Corporation's name, address, city, state, and ZIP code

Color Comfort Sheets
375 East 450 South
Salt Lake City, UT 84103

C   IRS Center where corporation filed return
Ogden, UT

Part II   **Information About the Shareholder**

D   Shareholder's identifying number
123-45-8976

E   Shareholder's name, address, city, state, and ZIP code

Nicole Johnson
811 East 8320 South
Sandy, UT 84094

F   Shareholder's percentage of stock
ownership for tax year . . . . 33.333333 %

For IRS Use Only

Part III   **Shareholder's Share of Current Year Income, Deductions, Credits, and Other Items**

1	Ordinary business income (loss) 80,000	**13**	Credits
2	Net rental real estate income (loss)		
3	Other net rental income (loss)		
4	Interest income 2,000		
5a	Ordinary dividends 1,000		
5b	Qualified dividends 1,000	**14**	Foreign transactions
6	Royalties		
7	Net short-term capital gain (loss)		
8a	Net long-term capital gain (loss)		
8b	Collectibles (28%) gain (loss)		
8c	Unrecaptured section 1250 gain		
9	Net section 1231 gain (loss)		
10	Other income (loss)	**15**	Alternative minimum tax (AMT) items
11	Section 179 deduction	**16**	Items affecting shareholder basis
12	Other deductions		
		17	Other information
		A	3,000

* See attached statement for additional information.

For Paperwork Reduction Act Notice, see the Instructions for Form 1120S.   www.irs.gov/Form1120S   Cat. No. 11520D   **Schedule K-1 (Form 1120S) 2017**

Source: Form 1120S Department of the Treasury, Internal Revenue Service
Note: In the revised 2018 Form 1120S, Schedule K-1, Color Comfort Sheets would also report Nicole's share of qualified business income ($80,000), allocable S corporation wages paid to employees ($46,667), and the unadjusted basis of qualified property ($100,000) for purposes of the deduction for qualified business income (as detailed in Example 17-11).

COMPARING C AND S CORPORATIONS AND PARTNERSHIPS

Exhibit 17-4 compares tax consequences for C corporations, S corporations, and partnerships discussed in this chapter.

EXHIBIT 17-4   Comparison of Tax Consequences for C and S Corporations and Partnerships

Tax Characteristic	C Corporation	S Corporation	Partnership/LLC
Forming or contributing property to an entity	No gain or loss on contribution of appreciated or depreciated property if transferors of property have control (as defined in §351) after transfer.	Same as C corporation.	Same as C and S corporations except no control requirement (§721 applies to partnerships).
Type of owner restrictions	No restrictions	Only individuals who are U.S. citizens or residents, certain trusts, and tax-exempt organizations.	No restrictions
Number of owner restrictions	No restrictions	Limited to 100 shareholders. (Family members and their estates count as one shareholder.)	Must have more than one owner.
Election	Default status if corporation under state law.	Must formally elect to have corporation taxed as S corporation.	Default status if unincorporated and have more than one owner.
Income and loss allocations	Not allocated to shareholders.	Income and loss flow through to owners based on ownership percentages.	Income and loss flow through to owners but may be allocated based on something other than ownership percentages (special allocations).
Entity debt included in stock (or partnership interest) basis	No	Generally no. However, loans made from shareholder to corporation create debt basis. Losses may be deducted to extent of stock basis and then debt basis.	Yes. All entity liabilities are allocated to basis of partners.
Loss limitations	Losses remain at corporate level.	Losses flow through but subject to basis limitation, at-risk limitation, passive activity limitations, and excess business loss limitation.	Same as S corporations.
Self-employment income status of ordinary income allocations	Not applicable	Not self-employment income.	May be self-employment income depending on partner's status.

EXHIBIT 17-4 (concluded)

Tax Characteristic	C Corporation	S Corporation	Partnership/LLC
Salary to owners permitted	Yes	Yes	Generally no. Salary-type payments are guaranteed payments subject to self-employment tax.
Fringe benefits	Can pay nontaxable fringe benefits to owners.	Can pay nontaxable fringe benefits to owners who own 2 percent or less of stock.	May not pay nontaxable fringe benefits to owners.
Operating distributions: Owner tax consequences	Taxable as dividends to extent of earnings and profits.	Generally not taxable to extent of owner's basis.	Same as S corporations.
Operating distributions: Entity tax consequences	Gain on distribution of appreciated property; no loss on distribution of depreciated property.	Same as C corporations.	Generally no gain or loss on distribution of property.
Liquidating distributions	Corporation and shareholders generally recognize gain or loss on distributions.	Same as C corporations.	Partnership and partners generally do not recognize gain or loss on liquidating distributions.
Entity-level taxes	Yes, based on corporate tax rate schedule.	Generally no, but may be required to pay built-in gains tax, excess passive investment income tax, or LIFO recapture tax if converting from C to S corporation.	No
Tax year	Last day of any month or 52/53-week year.	Generally calendar year.	Based on tax year of owners.

CONCLUSION

This chapter highlighted the rules specific to S corporations and compared S corporations to C corporations and partnerships. S corporations are a true hybrid entity: They share characteristics with C corporations (the legal protection of a corporation and the tax rules that apply in organizing and liquidating a corporation). They also share characteristics with partnerships (the flow through of the entity's income and loss to its owners, ability to make tax-free distributions to the extent of the owner's basis, and basis calculations for owners).

Although many S corporation attributes follow from the C corporation or partnership rules, several specific attributes unique to S corporations may be particularly important in choosing an entity form or operating an S corporation in a tax-efficient manner. These attributes include unique S corporation taxes, the rules for how debt enters into the basis calculations and loss limitation rules for S corporations, and the rules for how distributions are taxed for S corporations previously operating as C corporations.

c) The termination seems to be the first thing all three could agree on. They file the election to terminate on March 28, 2018.

d) The termination seems to be the first thing all three could agree on. They file the election to terminate on February 28, 2018.

e) Knowing the other two disagree with the termination, on March 16, 2018, Heathcliff sells one of his 50 shares to his maid, who recently moved back to Bulgaria, her home country.

LO 17-2 47. Assume the following S corporations and gross receipts, passive investment income, and corporate E&P. Will any of these corporations have its S election terminated due to excessive passive income? If so, in what year? All became S corporations at the beginning of year 1.

a) Clarion Corp.

Year	Gross Receipts	Passive Investment Income	Corporate Earnings and Profits
1	$1,353,458	$250,000	$321,300
2	1,230,389	100,000	321,300
3	1,139,394	300,000	230,000
4	1,347,039	350,000	100,000
5	1,500,340	400,000	0

b) Hanson Corp.

Year	Gross Receipts	Passive Investment Income	Corporate Earnings and Profits
1	$1,430,000	$247,000	$138,039
2	700,380	200,000	100,000
3	849,000	190,000	100,000
4	830,000	210,000	80,000
5	1,000,385	257,390	80,000

c) Tiffany Corp.

Year	Gross Receipts	Passive Investment Income	Corporate Earnings and Profits
1	$1,000,458	$250,000	$0
2	703,000	300,480	0
3	800,375	400,370	0
4	900,370	350,470	0
5	670,000	290,377	0

d) Jonas Corp.

Year	Gross Receipts	Passive Investment Income	Corporate Earnings and Profits
1	$1,100,370	$250,000	$500
2	998,000	240,000	400
3	800,350	230,000	300
4	803,000	214,570	200
5	750,000	200,000	100

48. Hughie, Dewey, and Louie are equal shareholders in HDL, an S corporation. HDL's   LO 17-2
    S election terminates under each of the following alternative scenarios. When is the
    earliest it can again operate as an S corporation?

    a) The S election terminates on August 1, year 2, because Louie sells half his shares
       to his uncle Walt, a citizen and resident of Scotland.

    b) The S election terminates effective January 1, year 3, because on August 1, year 2,
       Hughie and Dewey vote (2 to 1) to terminate the election.

49. Winkin, Blinkin, and Nod are equal shareholders in SleepEZ, an S corporation. In   LO 17-3
    the conditions listed below, how much income should each report from SleepEZ for
    2018 under both the daily allocation and the specific identification allocation
    method? Refer to the following table for the timing of SleepEZ's income.

Period	Income
January 1 through March 15 (74 days)	$125,000
March 16 through December 31 (291 days)	345,500
January 1 through December 31, 2018 (365 days)	$470,500

    a) There are no sales of SleepEZ stock during the year.

    b) On March 15, 2018, Blinkin sells his shares to Nod.

    c) On March 15, 2018, Winkin and Nod each sell their shares to Blinkin.

Use the following information to complete problems 50 and 51:

UpAHill Corporation (an S Corporation) Income Statement December 31, Year 1 and Year 2		
	Year 1	Year 2
Sales revenue	$175,000	$310,000
Cost of goods sold	(60,000)	(85,000)
Salary to owners Jack and Jill	(40,000)	(50,000)
Employee wages	(15,000)	(20,000)
Depreciation expense	(10,000)	(15,000)
Miscellaneous expenses	(7,500)	(9,000)
Interest income (related to business)	2,000	2,500
Qualified dividend income	500	1,000
Overall net income	$ 45,000	$134,500

50. Jack and Jill are owners of UpAHill, an S corporation. They own 25 and 75 percent,   LO 17-3
    respectively.

    tax forms

    a) What amount of ordinary income and separately stated items are allocated to
       them for years 1 and 2 based on the information above? Assume that UpAHill
       Corporation has $100,000 of qualified property (unadjusted basis) in both years.

    b) Complete UpAHill's Form 1120S, Schedule K, for year 1.

    c) Complete Jill's 1120S, Schedule K-1, for year 1.

51. Assume Jack and Jill, 25 and 75 percent shareholders, respectively, in UpAHill Cor-   LO 17-3 LO 17-4
    poration, have tax bases in their shares at the beginning of year 1 of $24,000 and
    $56,000, respectively. Also assume no distributions were made. Given the income
    statement above, what are their tax bases in their shares at the end of year 1?

Use the following information to complete problems 52 and 53:

Falcons Corporation (an S Corporation) Income Statement December 31, Year 1 and Year 2		
	Year 1	**Year 2**
Sales revenue	$300,000	$430,000
Cost of goods sold	(40,000)	(60,000)
Salary to owners Julio and Milania	(40,000)	(80,000)
Employee wages	(25,000)	(50,000)
Depreciation expense	(20,000)	(40,000)
Section 179 expense	(30,000)	(50,000)
Interest income (related to business)	12,000	22,500
Municipal bond income	1,500	4,000
Government fines	0	(2,000)
Overall net income	$158,500	$174,500
Distributions	$ 30,000	$ 50,000

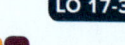

52. Julio and Milania are owners of Falcons Corporation, an S corporation. They each own 50 percent of Falcons Corporation. In year 1, Julio and Milania each received distributions of $15,000 from Falcons Corporation.

 a) What amount of ordinary income and separately stated items are allocated to them for year 1 based on the information above? Assume that Falcons Corporation has $200,000 of qualified property (unadjusted basis).

 b) Complete Falcons's Form 1120S, Schedule K for year 1.

 c) Complete Julio's 1120S, Schedule K-1 for year 1.

53. In year 2, Julio and Milania each received distributions of $25,000 from Falcons Corporation.

 a) What amount of ordinary income and separately stated items are allocated to them for year 2 based on the information above? Assume that Falcons Corporation has $200,000 of qualified property (unadjusted basis).

 b) Complete Falcons's Form 1120S, Schedule K for year 2.

 c) Complete Milania's 1120S, Schedule K-1 for year 2.

54. Harry, Hermione, and Ron formed an S corporation called Bumblebore. Harry and Hermione both contributed cash of $25,000 to get things started. Ron was a bit short on cash but had a parcel of land valued at $60,000 (basis of $50,000) that he decided to contribute. The land was encumbered by a $35,000 mortgage. What tax bases will each of the three have in his or her stock of Bumblebore?

55. Jessica is a one-third owner in Bikes-R-Us, an S corporation that experienced a $45,000 loss this year (year 1). If her stock basis is $10,000 at the beginning of the year, how much of this loss clears the hurdle for deductibility (assume the at-risk limitation equals the tax-basis limitation)? If she cannot deduct the whole loss, what happens to the remainder? Is she able to deduct her entire loss if she sells her stock at year-end?

56. Assume the same facts as in the previous problem, except that at the beginning of year 1 Jessica loaned Bikes-R-Us $3,000. In year 2, Bikes-R-Us reported ordinary income of $12,000. What amount is Jessica allowed to deduct in year 1? What are her stock and debt bases in the corporation at the end of year 1? What are her stock and debt bases in the corporation at the end of year 2?

57. Birch Corp., a calendar-year corporation, was formed three years ago by its sole shareholder, James, who has operated it as an S corporation since its inception. Last year, James made a direct loan to Birch Corp. in the amount of $5,000. Birch Corp. has paid the interest on the loan but has not yet paid any principal. (Assume the loan qualifies as debt for tax purposes.) For the year, Birch experienced a $25,000 business loss. What amount of the loss clears the tax-basis limitation, and what is James's basis in his Birch Corp. stock and Birch Corp. debt in each of the following alternative scenarios?

LO 17-4

a) At the beginning of the year, James's basis in his Birch Corp. stock was $45,000 and his basis in his Birch Corp. debt was $5,000.

b) At the beginning of the year, James's basis in his Birch Corp. stock was $8,000 and his basis in his Birch Corp. debt was $5,000.

c) At the beginning of the year, James's basis in his Birch Corp. stock was $0 and his basis in his Birch Corp. debt was $5,000.

58. Timo is the sole owner of Jazz Inc., an S corporation. On October 31, 2018, Timo executed an unsecured demand promissory note of $15,000 and transferred the note to Jazz (Jazz could require Timo to pay it $15,000 on demand). When Timo transferred the note to Jazz, his tax basis in his Jazz stock was $0. On January 31, 2019, Timo paid the $15,000 to Jazz as required by the promissory note. For the taxable year ending December 31, 2018, Jazz incurred a business loss of $12,000. How much of the loss clears the stock and debt basis hurdles for deductibility?

LO 17-4

research

59. Chandra was the sole shareholder of Pet Emporium that was originally formed as an S corporation. When Pet Emporium terminated its S election on August 31, 2017, Chandra had a stock basis and an at-risk amount of $0. Chandra also had a suspended loss from Pet Emporium of $9,000. What amount of the suspended loss is Chandra allowed to deduct, and what is her basis in her Pet Emporium stock at the end of the post-termination transition period under the following alternative scenarios (assume Pet Emporium files for an extension to file its tax returns)?

LO 17-4

a) Chandra makes capital contributions of $7,000 on August 30, 2018, and $4,000 on September 14, 2018.

b) Chandra makes capital contributions of $5,000 on September 1, 2018, and $5,000 on September 30, 2018.

c) Chandra makes a capital contribution of $10,000 on August 31, 2018.

d) Chandra makes a capital contribution of $10,000 on October 1, 2018.

60. Neil owns stock in two S corporations, Blue and Green. He actively participates in the management of Blue but maintains ownership in Green only as a passive investor. Neil has no other business investments. Both Blue and Green anticipate a loss this year, and Neil's basis in his stock of both corporations is $0. All else equal, if Neil plans on making a capital contribution to at least one of the corporations this year, to which firm should he contribute in order to increase his chances of deducting the loss allocated to him from the entity? Why?

LO 17-4

planning

61. In the past several years, Shakira had loaned money to Shakira Inc. (an S corporation) to help the corporation keep afloat in a downturn. Her stock basis in the S corporation is now $0, and she had deducted $40,000 in losses that reduced her debt basis from $100,000 to $60,000. Things appear to be turning around this year, and Shakira Inc. repaid Shakira $20,000 of the $100,000 outstanding loan. What is Shakira's income, if any, on the partial loan repayment?

LO 17-4

planning

LO 17-4   62. Adam Fleeman, a skilled carpenter, started a home improvement business with Tom Collins, a master plumber. Adam and Tom are concerned about the payroll taxes they will have to pay. Assume they form an S corporation and each earns a salary of $80,000 from the corporation; in addition, they expect their share of business profits to be $60,000 each. How much Social Security tax and Medicare tax (or self-employment tax) will Adam, Tom, and their corporation have to pay on their salary and profits?

planning **LO 17-4**   63. Using the facts in problem 62, could Adam and Tom lower their payroll tax exposure if they operated their business as a partnership? Why or why not?

LO 17-4   64. This year, Justin B.'s share of S corporation income includes $4,000 of interest income, $5,000 of dividend income, and $40,000 of net income from the corporation's professional service business activity.

a) Assume that Justin B. materially participates in the S corporation. How much of his S corporation income is potentially subject to the net investment income tax?

b) Assume that Justin B. does not materially participate in the S corporation. How much of his S corporation income is potentially subject to the net investment income tax?

LO 17-4   65. Friends Jackie (0.5 percent owner), Jermaine (1 percent owner), Marlon (2 percent owner), Janet (86 percent owner), and Tito (10.5 percent owner) are shareholders in Jackson 5 Inc. (an S corporation). As employees of the company, they each receive health insurance ($10,000 per year benefit), dental insurance ($2,000 per year benefit), and free access to a workout facility located at company headquarters ($500 per year benefit). What are the tax consequences of these benefits for each shareholder and for Jackson 5 Inc.?

LO 17-5   66. Maple Corp., a calendar-year corporation, was formed three years ago by its sole shareholder, Brady, who immediately elected S corporation status. On December 31 of the current year, Maple distributed $30,000 cash to Brady. What is the amount and character of gain Brady must recognize on the distribution in each of the following alternative scenarios?

a) At the time of the distribution, Brady's basis in his Maple Corp. stock was $35,000.

b) At the time of the distribution, Brady's basis in his Maple Corp. stock was $8,000.

c) At the time of the distribution, Brady's basis in his Maple Corp. stock was $0.

LO 17-5   67. Oak Corp., a calendar-year corporation, was formed three years ago by its sole shareholder, Glover, and has always operated as a C corporation. However, at the beginning of this year, Glover made a qualifying S election for Oak Corp., effective January 1. Oak Corp. did not have any C corporation earnings and profits on that date. On June 1, Oak Corp. distributed $15,000 to Glover. What is the amount and character of gain Glover must recognize on the distribution, and what is his basis in his Oak Corp. stock in each of the following alternative scenarios?

a) At the time of the distribution, Glover's basis in his Oak Corp. stock was $35,000.

b) At the time of the distribution, Glover's basis in his Oak Corp. stock was $8,000.

c) At the time of the distribution, Glover's basis in his Oak Corp. stock was $0.

68. Janna has a tax basis of $15,000 in her Mimikaki stock (Mimikaki has been an S corporation since inception). In 2018, Janna was allocated $20,000 of ordinary income from Mimikaki. What is the amount and character of gain she recognizes from end-of-the-year distributions in each of the following alternative scenarios, and what is her stock basis following each distribution?

    LO 17-5

    a) Mimikaki distributes $10,000 to Janna.
    b) Mimikaki distributes $20,000 to Janna.
    c) Mimikaki distributes $30,000 to Janna.
    d) Mimikaki distributes $40,000 to Janna.

69. Assume the following year 2 income statement for Johnstone Corporation, which was a C corporation in year 1 and elected to be taxed as an S corporation beginning in year 2. Johnstone's earnings and profits at the end of year 1 were $10,000. Marcus is Johnstone's sole shareholder, and he has a stock basis of $40,000 at the end of year 1. What is Johnstone's accumulated adjustments account at the end of year 2, and what amount of dividend income does Marcus recognize on the year 2 distribution in each of the following alternative scenarios?

    LO 17-5

Johnstone Corporation Income Statement December 31, Year 2	
	Year 2 (S Corporation)
Sales revenue	$150,000
Cost of goods sold	(35,000)
Salary to owners	(60,000)
Employee wages	(50,000)
Depreciation expense	(4,000)
Miscellaneous expenses	(4,000)
Interest income	10,000
Overall net income	$ 7,000

    a) Johnstone distributed $6,000 to Marcus in year 2.
    b) Johnstone distributed $10,000 to Marcus in year 2.
    c) Johnstone distributed $16,000 to Marcus in year 2.
    d) Johnstone distributed $26,000 to Marcus in year 2.

70. At the end of the year, before distributions, Bombay (an S corporation) has an accumulated adjustments account balance of $15,000 and accumulated E&P of $20,000 from a previous year as a C corporation. During the year, Nicolette (a 40 percent shareholder) received a $20,000 distribution (the remaining shareholders received $30,000 in distributions). What is the amount and character of gain Nicolette must recognize from the distribution? What is her basis in her Bombay stock at the end of the year? (Assume her stock basis is $40,000 after considering her share of Bombay's income for the year but before considering the effects of the distribution.)

    LO 17-5

71. Pine Corp., a calendar-year corporation, was formed three years ago by its sole shareholder, Connor, who has always operated it as a C corporation. However, at the beginning of this year, Connor made a qualifying S election for Pine Corp., effective January 1. Pine Corp. reported $70,000 of C corporation earnings and profits on the effective date of the S election. This year (its first S corporation year), Pine

    LO 17-5

Corp. reported business income of $50,000. Connor's basis in his Pine Corp. stock at the beginning of the year was $15,000. What is the amount and character of gain Connor must recognize on the following alternative distributions, and what is his basis in his Pine Corp. stock at the end of the year?

a) Connor received a $40,000 distribution from Pine Corp. at the end of the year.

b) Connor received a $60,000 distribution from Pine Corp. at the end of the year.

c) Connor received a $130,000 distribution from Pine Corp. at the end of the year.

d) Connor received a $150,000 distribution from Pine Corp. at the end of the year.

LO 17-5 72. Carolina Corporation, an S corporation, has no corporate E&P from its years as a C corporation. At the end of the year, it distributes a small parcel of land to its sole shareholder, Shadiya. The fair market value of the parcel is $70,000 and its tax basis is $40,000. Shadiya's basis in her stock is $14,000. Assume Carolina Corporation reported $0 taxable income before considering the tax consequences of the distribution.

a) What amount of gain or loss, if any, does Carolina Corporation recognize on the distribution?

b) How much gain must Shadiya recognize (if any) as a result of the distribution, what is her basis in her Carolina Corporation stock after the distribution, and what is her basis in the land?

c) What is your answer to part (a) if the fair market value of the land is $25,000 rather than $70,000?

d) What is your answer to part (b) if the fair market value of the land is $25,000 rather than $70,000?

LO 17-5 73. Last year, Miley decided to terminate the S corporation election of her solely owned corporation on October 17, 2017 (effective immediately), in preparation for taking it public. At the time of the election, the corporation had an accumulated adjustments account balance of $150,000 and $450,000 of accumulated E&P from prior C corporation years, and Miley had a basis in her S corporation stock of $135,000. During 2018, Miley's corporation reported $0 taxable income or loss. Also, during 2018 the corporation made distributions to Miley of $80,000 and $60,000. How are these distributions taxed to Miley assuming the following?

a) Both distributions are in cash, and the first was paid on June 15, 2018, and the second on November 15, 2018.

b) Both distributions are in cash, and the first was paid on June 15, 2018, and the second on September 30, 2018.

c) Assume the same facts as in part (b), except the June 15 distribution was a property (noncash) distribution (fair market value of distributed property equal to basis).

LO 17-6 74. Alabama Corporation, an S corporation, liquidates this year by distributing a parcel of land to its sole shareholder, Mark Ingram. The fair market value of the parcel is $50,000 and its tax basis is $30,000. Mark's basis in his stock is $25,000.

a) What amount of gain or loss, if any, does Alabama Corporation recognize on the distribution?

b) How much gain must Mark recognize (if any) as a result of the distribution and what is his basis in the land?

c) What is your answer to part (a) if the fair market value of the land is $20,000 rather than $50,000?

d) What is your answer to part (b) if the fair market value of the land is $20,000 rather than $50,000?

75. Rivendell Corporation uses the accrual method of accounting and has the following assets as of the end of 2017. Rivendell converted to an S corporation on
January 1, 2018.

LO 17-6

Asset	Adjusted Basis	FMV
Cash	$ 40,000	$ 40,000
Accounts receivable	30,000	30,000
Inventory	130,000	60,000
Land	100,000	125,000
Totals	$300,000	$255,000

a) What is Rivendell's net unrealized built-in gain at the time it converted to an
S corporation?

b) Assuming the land was valued at $200,000, what would be Rivendell's net unre-
alized gain at the time it converted to an S corporation?

c) Assuming the land was valued at $125,000 but that the inventory was valued at
$85,000, what would be Rivendell's net unrealized gain at the time it converted
to an S corporation?

76. Virginia Corporation is a calendar-year corporation. At the beginning of 2018, its
election to be taxed as an S corporation became effective. Virginia Corp.'s balance
sheet at the end of 2017 reflected the following assets (it did not have any earnings
and profits from its prior years as a C corporation).

LO 17-6

Asset	Adjusted Basis	FMV
Cash	$ 20,000	$ 20,000
Accounts receivable	40,000	40,000
Inventory	90,000	200,000
Land	150,000	175,000
Totals	$300,000	$435,000

In 2018, Virginia reported business income of $50,000 (this would have been its
taxable income if it were still a C corporation). What is Virginia's built-in gains tax
in each of the following alternative scenarios?

a) During 2018, Virginia sold inventory it owned at the beginning of the year for
$100,000. The basis of the inventory sold was $55,000.

b) Assume the same facts as part (a), except Virginia had a net operating loss carryover of $24,000 from its time as a C corporation.

c) Assume the same facts as part (a), except that if Virginia were a C corporation,
its taxable income would have been $1,500.

77. Tempe Corporation is a calendar-year corporation. At the beginning of 2018, its
election to be taxed as an S corporation became effective. Tempe Corp.'s balance
sheet at the end of 2017 reflected the following assets (it did not have any earnings
and profits from its prior years as a C corporation):

LO 17-6

Asset	Adjusted Basis	FMV
Cash	$ 20,000	$ 20,000
Accounts receivable	40,000	40,000
Inventory	160,000	200,000
Land	150,000	120,000
Totals	$370,000	$380,000

Tempe's business income for the year was $40,000 (this would have been its taxable income if it were a C corporation).

a) During 2018, Tempe sold all of the inventory it owned at the beginning of the year for $210,000. What is its built-in gains tax in 2018?

b) Assume the same facts as in part (a), except that if Tempe were a C corporation, its taxable income would have been $7,000. What is its built-in gains tax in 2018?

c) Assume the original facts except the land was valued at $140,000 instead of $120,000. What is Tempe's built-in gains tax in 2018?

LO 17-6 78. Wood Corporation was a C corporation in 2017 but elected to be taxed as an S corporation in 2018. At the end of 2017, its earnings and profits were $15,500. The following table reports Wood's (taxable) income for 2018 (its first year as an S corporation).

Wood Corporation Income Statement December 31, 2018	
Sales revenue	$150,000
Cost of goods sold	(35,000)
Salary to owners	(60,000)
Employee wages	(50,000)
Depreciation expense	(4,000)
Miscellaneous expenses	(4,000)
Interest income	8,000
Qualified dividend income	2,000
Overall net income	$ 7,000

What is Wood Corporation's excess net passive income tax for 2018?

LO 17-6 79. Calculate Anaheim Corporation's excess net passive income tax in each of the following alternative scenarios:

a) Passive investment income, $100,000; expenses associated with passive investment income, $40,000; gross receipts, $120,000; taxable income if C corporation, $40,000; corporate E&P, $30,000.

b) Passive investment income, $100,000; expenses associated with passive investment income, $70,000; gross receipts, $120,000; taxable income if C corporation, $1,200; corporate E&P, $30,000.

c) Passive investment income, $100,000; expenses associated with passive investment income, $40,000; gross receipts, $120,000; taxable income if C corporation, $40,000; corporate E&P, $0.

LO 17-5 **LO 17-6**

80. Mark is the sole shareholder of Tex Corporation. Mark first formed Tex as a C corporation. However, in an attempt to avoid having Tex's income double taxed, Mark elected S corporation status for Tex several years ago. On December 31, 2018, Tex reports $5,000 of earnings and profits from its years as a C corporation and $50,000 in its accumulated adjustments account from its activities as an S corporation (including its 2018 activities). Mark discovered that for the first time Tex was going to have to pay the excess net passive income tax. Mark wanted to avoid having to pay the tax but he determined the only way to avoid the tax was to eliminate Tex's E&P by the end of 2018. He determined that, because of the distribution ordering rules (AAA first), he would need to have Tex immediately (in 2018) distribute $55,000 to

him. This would clear out Tex's accumulated adjustments account first and then eliminate Tex's C corporation earnings and profits in time to avoid the excess net passive income tax. Mark was not sure Tex could come up with $55,000 of cash or property in time to accomplish his objective. Does Mark have any other options to eliminate Tex's earnings and profits without first distributing the balance in Tex's accumulated adjustments account?

81. Farve Inc. recently elected S corporation status. At the time of the election, the company had $10,000 of accumulated earnings and profits and a net unrealized gain of $1,000,000 associated with land it had invested in (although some parcels had an unrealized loss). In the next couple of years, most of the income the company expects to generate will be in the form of interest and dividends (approximately $200,000 per year). However, in the future, the company will want to liquidate some of its current holdings in land and possibly reinvest in other parcels. What strategies can you recommend for Farve Inc. to help reduce its potential tax liability as an S corporation?

LO 17-6

 **planning**

82. Until the end of year 0, Magic Carpets (MC) was a C corporation with a calendar year. At the beginning of year 1 it elected to be taxed as an S corporation. MC uses the LIFO method to value its inventory. At the end of year 0, under the LIFO method, its inventory of rugs was valued at $150,000. Under the FIFO method, the rugs would have been valued at $170,000. How much LIFO recapture tax must MC pay, and what is the due date of the first payment under the following alternative scenarios?

LO 17-6

a) Magic Carpets's regular taxable income in year 0 was $65,000.

b) Magic Carpets's regular taxable income in year 0 was $200,000.

COMPREHENSIVE PROBLEMS

Select problems are available in Connect®.

connect

83. Knowshon, sole owner of Moreno Inc., is contemplating electing S status for the corporation (Moreno Inc. is currently taxed as a C corporation). Provide recommendations related to Knowshon's election under the following alternative scenarios:

 **planning**

a) At the end of the current year, Moreno Inc. has a net operating loss of $800,000 carryover. Beginning next year, the company expects to return to profitability. Knowshon projects that Moreno will report profits of $400,000, $500,000, and $600,000 over the next three years. What suggestions do you have regarding the timing of the S election? Explain.

b) How would you answer part (a) if Moreno Inc. had been operating profitably for several years and thus had no net operating loss?

c) While several of Moreno Inc.'s assets have appreciated in value (to the tune of $2,000,000), the corporation has one property—some land in a newly identified flood zone—that has declined in value by $1,500,000. Knowshon plans on selling the loss property in the next year or two. Assume that Moreno does not have a net operating loss. What suggestions do you have for timing the sale of the flood zone property and why?

84. Barry Potter and Winnie Weasley are considering making an S election on March 1, 2019, for their C corporation, Omniocular. However, first they want to consider the implications of the following information:

planning

- Winnie is a U.S. citizen and resident.
- Barry is a citizen of the United Kingdom, but a resident of the United States.

- Barry and Winnie each own 50 percent of the voting power in Omniocular. However, Barry's stock provides him with a claim on 60 percent of the Omniocular assets in liquidation.
- Omniocular was formed under Arizona state law, but it plans on eventually conducting some business in Mexico.

a) Is Omniocular eligible to elect S corporation status? If so, when is the election effective?

For the remainder of the problem, assume Omniocular made a valid S election effective January 1, 2019. Barry and Winnie each own 50 percent of the voting power and have equal claim on Omniocular's assets in liquidation. In addition, consider the following information:

- Omniocular reports on a calendar tax year.
- Omniocular's earnings and profits as of December 31, 2018, were $55,000.
- Omniocular's 2018 taxable income was $15,000.
- Omniocular's assets at the end of 2018 are as follows:

Omniocular Assets December 31, 2018		
Asset	**Adjusted Basis**	**FMV**
Cash	$ 50,000	$ 50,000
Accounts receivable	20,000	20,000
Investments in stocks and bonds	700,000	700,000
Investment in land	90,000	100,000
Inventory (LIFO)	80,000*	125,000
Equipment	40,000	35,000
Totals	$980,000	$1,030,000

*$110,000 under FIFO accounting.

- On March 31, 2019, Omniocular sold the land for $42,000.
- In 2019, Omniocular sold all the inventory it had on hand at the beginning of the year. This was the only inventory it sold during the year.

Other Income/Expense Items for 2019	
Sales revenue	$155,000
Salary to owners	(50,000)
Employee wages	(10,000)
Depreciation expense	(5,000)
Miscellaneous expenses	(1,000)
Interest income	40,000
Qualified dividend income	65,000

- Assume that if Omniocular were a C corporation for 2019, its taxable income would have been $88,500.

b) How much LIFO recapture tax is Omniocular required to pay and when is it due?

c) How much built-in gains tax, if any, is Omniocular required to pay?

d) How much excess net passive income tax, if any, is Omniocular required to pay?

e) Assume Barry's basis in his Omniocular stock was $40,000 on January 1, 2019. What is his stock basis on December 31, 2019?

For the following questions, assume that after electing S corporation status Barry and Winnie had a change of heart and filed an election to terminate Omniocular's S election, effective August 1, 2020.

- In 2020, Omniocular reported the following income/expense items:

	January 1—July 31, 2020 (213 days)	August 1—December 31, 2020 (153 days)	January 1—December 31, 2020
Sales revenue	$ 80,000	$185,000	$ 265,000
Cost of goods sold	(40,000)	(20,000)	(60,000)
Salaries to Barry and Winnie	(60,000)	(40,000)	(100,000)
Depreciation expense	(7,000)	(2,000)	(9,000)
Miscellaneous expenses	(4,000)	(3,000)	(7,000)
Interest income	6,000	5,250	11,250
Overall net income (loss)	$(25,000)	$125,250	$ 100,250

f) For tax purposes, how would you recommend Barry and Winnie allocate income between the short S corporation year and the short C corporation year if they would like to minimize double taxation of Omniocular's income?

g) Assume in part (f) that Omniocular allocates income between the short S and C corporation years in a way that minimizes the double taxation of its income. If Barry's stock basis in his Omniocular stock on January 1, 2020, is $50,000, what is his stock basis on December 31, 2020?

h) When is the earliest tax year in which Omniocular can be taxed as an S corporation again?

85. Abigail, Bobby, and Claudia are equal owners in Lafter, an S corporation that was a C corporation several years ago. While Abigail and Bobby actively participate in running the company, Claudia has a separate day job and is a passive owner. Consider the following information for 2018:

- As of January 1, 2018, Abigail, Bobby, and Claudia each have a basis in Lafter stock of $15,000 and a debt basis of $0. On January 1, the stock basis is also the at-risk amount for each shareholder.
- Bobby and Claudia also are passive owners in Aggressive LLC, which allocated business income of $14,000 to each of them in 2018. Neither has any other source of passive income (besides Lafter, for Claudia).
- On March 31, 2018, Abigail lends $5,000 of her own money to Lafter.
- Anticipating the need for basis to deduct a loss, on April 4, 2018, Bobby takes out a $10,000 loan to make a $10,000 contribution to Lafter. Bobby uses his automobile ($12,000 fair market value) as the sole collateral for his loan (nonrecourse).
- Lafter has an accumulated adjustments account balance of $45,000 as of January 1, 2018.
- Lafter has C corporation earnings and profits of $15,000 as of January 1, 2018.
- During 2018, Lafter reports a business loss of $75,000, computed as follows:

Sales revenue	$ 90,000
Cost of goods sold	(85,000)
Salary to Abigail	(40,000)
Salary to Bobby	(40,000)
Business (loss)	$(75,000)

- Lafter also reported $12,000 of tax-exempt interest income.

  a) What amount of Lafter's 2018 business loss of $75,000 are Abigail, Bobby, and Claudia allowed to deduct on their individual tax returns? What are each owner's stock basis and debt basis (if applicable) and each owner's at-risk amount with respect to the investment in Lafter at the end of 2018?

- During 2019, Lafter made several changes to its business approach and reported $18,000 of business income, computed as follows:

Sales revenue	$208,000
Cost of goods sold	(90,000)
Salary to Abigail	(45,000)
Salary to Bobby	(45,000)
Marketing expense	(10,000)
Business income	$ 18,000

- Lafter also reported a long-term capital gain of $24,000 in 2019.
- Lafter made a cash distribution on July 1, 2019, of $20,000 to each shareholder.

  b) What amount of gain/income does each shareholder recognize from the cash distribution on July 1, 2019?

tax forms

86. While James Craig and his former classmate Paul Dolittle both studied accounting at school, they ended up pursuing careers in professional cake decorating. Their company, Good to Eat (GTE), specializes in custom-sculpted cakes for weddings, birthdays, and other celebrations. James and Paul formed the business at the beginning of 2018, and each contributed $50,000 in exchange for a 50 percent ownership interest. GTE also borrowed $200,000 from a local bank. Both James and Paul had to personally guarantee the loan. Both owners provide significant services for the business. The following information pertains to GTE's 2018 activities:

- GTE uses the cash method of accounting (for both book and tax purposes) and reports income on a calendar-year basis.
- GTE received $450,000 of sales revenue and reported $210,000 of cost of goods sold (it did not have any ending inventory).
- GTE paid $30,000 compensation to James, $30,000 compensation to Paul, and $40,000 of compensation to other employees (assume these amounts include applicable payroll taxes if any).
- GTE paid $15,000 of rent for a building and equipment, $20,000 for advertising, $14,000 in interest expense, $4,000 for utilities, and $2,000 for supplies.
- GTE contributed $5,000 to charity.
- GTE received a $1,000 qualified dividend from a great stock investment (it owned 2 percent of the corporation distributing the dividend), and it recognized $1,500 in short-term capital gain when it sold some of the stock.
- On December 1, 2018, GTE distributed $20,000 to James and $20,000 to Paul.
- GTE has qualified property of $300,000 (unadjusted basis).

Required:

a) Assume James and Paul formed GTE as an S corporation.
   - Complete GTE's Form 1120S, page 1; Form 1120 S, Schedule K; and Paul's Form 1120S, Schedule K-1 (note that you should use 2017 tax forms).
   - Compute the tax basis of Paul's stock in GTE at the end of 2018.
   - What amount of Paul's income from GTE is subject to FICA or self-employment taxes?

- What amount of income, including its character, will Paul recognize on the $20,000 distribution he receives on December 1?
- What amount of tax does GTE pay on the $1,000 qualified dividend it received?

b) Assume James and Paul formed GTE as an LLC.

- Complete GTE's Form 1065, page 1; Form 1065, Schedule K; and Paul's Form 1065, Schedule K-1 (note that you should use 2017 tax forms).
- Compute the tax basis of Paul's ownership interest in GTE at the end of 2018.
- What amount of Paul's income from GTE is subject to FICA or self-employment taxes?
- What amount of income, including its character, will Paul recognize on the $20,000 distribution he receives on December 1?
- What amount of tax does GTE pay on the $1,000 qualified dividend it received?

c) Assume James and Paul formed GTE as a C corporation.

- Complete GTE's Form 1120, page 1 (note that you should use the 2017 tax form).
- Compute the tax basis of Paul's stock in GTE at the end of 2018.
- What amount of Paul's income from GTE is subject to FICA or self-employment taxes?
- What amount of income, including its character, will Paul recognize on the $20,000 distribution he receives on December 1?
- What amount of tax does GTE pay on the $1,000 qualified dividend it received?

ROGER | *CPA Review*

Sample CPA Exam questions from Roger CPA Review are available in Connect as support for the topics in this text. These Multiple Choice Questions and Task-Based Simulations include expert-written explanations and solutions and provide a starting point for students to become familiar with the content and functionality of the actual CPA Exam.

Appendix A

Tax Forms

All tax forms can be obtained from the IRS website: www.irs.gov. These forms do not reflect tax law changes effective in 2018 under the Tax Cuts and Jobs Act. 2018 forms were not available at the time we went to press.

Form **1040**

Department of the Treasury—Internal Revenue Service   (99)

U.S. Individual Income Tax Return   2017   OMB No. 1545-0074   IRS Use Only—Do not write or staple in this space.

For the year Jan. 1–Dec. 31, 2017, or other tax year beginning _____, 2017, ending _____, 20___   See separate instructions.

Your first name and initial   Last name   Your social security number

If a joint return, spouse's first name and initial   Last name   Spouse's social security number

Home address (number and street). If you have a P.O. box, see instructions.   Apt. no.

▲ Make sure the SSN(s) above and on line 6c are correct.

City, town or post office, state, and ZIP code. If you have a foreign address, also complete spaces below (see instructions).

Presidential Election Campaign
Check here if you, or your spouse if filing jointly, want $3 to go to this fund. Checking a box below will not change your tax or refund.   ☐ You   ☐ Spouse

Foreign country name   Foreign province/state/county   Foreign postal code

Filing Status

Check only one box.

1 ☐ Single
2 ☐ Married filing jointly (even if only one had income)
3 ☐ Married filing separately. Enter spouse's SSN above and full name here. ▶
4 ☐ Head of household (with qualifying person). (See instructions.) If the qualifying person is a child but not your dependent, enter this child's name here. ▶
5 ☐ Qualifying widow(er) (see instructions)

Exemptions

6a ☐ **Yourself.** If someone can claim you as a dependent, **do not** check box 6a . . . . .
b ☐ **Spouse** . . . .

Boxes checked on 6a and 6b _____

c Dependents:

(1) First name Last name	(2) Dependent's social security number	(3) Dependent's relationship to you	(4) ✓ if child under age 17 qualifying for child tax credit (see instructions)
			☐
			☐
			☐
			☐

If more than four dependents, see instructions and check here ▶ ☐

No. of children on 6c who:
• lived with you _____
• did not live with you due to divorce or separation (see instructions) _____

Dependents on 6c not entered above _____

Add numbers on lines above ▶ _____

d Total number of exemptions claimed . . . .

Income

Attach Form(s) W-2 here. Also attach Forms W-2G and 1099-R if tax was withheld.

If you did not get a W-2, see instructions.

7	Wages, salaries, tips, etc. Attach Form(s) W-2	7
8a	**Taxable** interest. Attach Schedule B if required	8a
b	**Tax-exempt** interest. **Do not** include on line 8a 8b	
9a	Ordinary dividends. Attach Schedule B if required	9a
b	Qualified dividends 9b	
10	Taxable refunds, credits, or offsets of state and local income taxes	10
11	Alimony received	11
12	Business income or (loss). Attach Schedule C or C-EZ	12
13	Capital gain or (loss). Attach Schedule D if required. If not required, check here ▶ ☐	13
14	Other gains or (losses). Attach Form 4797	14
15a	IRA distributions 15a	b Taxable amount 15b
16a	Pensions and annuities 16a	b Taxable amount 16b
17	Rental real estate, royalties, partnerships, S corporations, trusts, etc. Attach Schedule E	17
18	Farm income or (loss). Attach Schedule F	18
19	Unemployment compensation	19
20a	Social security benefits 20a	b Taxable amount 20b
21	Other income. List type and amount _____	21
22	Combine the amounts in the far right column for lines 7 through 21. This is your **total income** ▶	22

Adjusted Gross Income

23	Educator expenses	23
24	Certain business expenses of reservists, performing artists, and fee-basis government officials. Attach Form 2106 or 2106-EZ	24
25	Health savings account deduction. Attach Form 8889	25
26	Moving expenses. Attach Form 3903	26
27	Deductible part of self-employment tax. Attach Schedule SE	27
28	Self-employed SEP, SIMPLE, and qualified plans	28
29	Self-employed health insurance deduction	29
30	Penalty on early withdrawal of savings	30
31a	Alimony paid b Recipient's SSN ▶	31a
32	IRA deduction	32
33	Student loan interest deduction	33
34	Reserved for future use	34
35	Domestic production activities deduction. Attach Form 8903	35
36	Add lines 23 through 35	36
37	Subtract line 36 from line 22. This is your **adjusted gross income** ▶	37

For Disclosure, Privacy Act, and Paperwork Reduction Act Notice, see separate instructions.   Cat. No. 11320B   Form **1040** (2017)

Tax and Credits	38	Amount from line 37 (adjusted gross income)		38	
	39a	Check if: ☐ **You** were born before January 2, 1953, ☐ Blind. ☐ **Spouse** was born before January 2, 1953, ☐ Blind. } Total boxes checked ▶ 39a		
	b	If your spouse itemizes on a separate return or you were a dual-status alien, check here▶ 39b☐		

Standard Deduction for—

• People who check any box on line 39a or 39b **or** who can be claimed as a dependent, see instructions.

• All others:

Single or Married filing separately, $6,350

Married filing jointly or Qualifying widow(er), $12,700

Head of household, $9,350

40	**Itemized deductions** (from Schedule A) **or** your **standard deduction** (see left margin) . .	40	
41	Subtract line 40 from line 38	41	
42	**Exemptions.** If line 38 is $156,900 or less, multiply $4,050 by the number on line 6d. Otherwise, see instructions	42	
43	**Taxable income.** Subtract line 42 from line 41. If line 42 is more than line 41, enter -0- . .	43	
44	**Tax** (see instructions). Check if any from: **a** ☐ Form(s) 8814 **b** ☐ Form 4972 **c** ☐ _____	44	
45	**Alternative minimum tax** (see instructions). Attach Form 6251	45	
46	Excess advance premium tax credit repayment. Attach Form 8962	46	
47	Add lines 44, 45, and 46 . . . . ▶	47	
48	Foreign tax credit. Attach Form 1116 if required	48	
49	Credit for child and dependent care expenses. Attach Form 2441	49	
50	Education credits from Form 8863, line 19	50	
51	Retirement savings contributions credit. Attach Form 8880	51	
52	Child tax credit. Attach Schedule 8812, if required . .	52	
53	Residential energy credit. Attach Form 5695	53	
54	Other credits from Form: **a** ☐ 3800 **b** ☐ 8801 **c** ☐	54	
55	Add lines 48 through 54. These are your **total credits**	55	
56	Subtract line 55 from line 47. If line 55 is more than line 47, enter -0- . . . . . ▶	56	

Other Taxes	57	Self-employment tax. Attach Schedule SE	57	
	58	Unreported social security and Medicare tax from Form: **a** ☐ 4137 **b** ☐ 8919 . .	58	
	59	Additional tax on IRAs, other qualified retirement plans, etc. Attach Form 5329 if required . .	59	
	60a	Household employment taxes from Schedule H	60a	
	b	First-time homebuyer credit repayment. Attach Form 5405 if required	60b	
	61	Health care: individual responsibility (see instructions) Full-year coverage ☐	61	
	62	Taxes from: **a** ☐ Form 8959 **b** ☐ Form 8960 **c** ☐ Instructions; enter code(s)	62	
	63	Add lines 56 through 62. This is your **total tax** . . . . ▶	63	

Payments	64	Federal income tax withheld from Forms W-2 and 1099 . .	64	
If you have a qualifying child, attach Schedule EIC.	65	2017 estimated tax payments and amount applied from 2016 return	65	
	66a	**Earned income credit (EIC)**	66a	
	b	Nontaxable combat pay election	66b	
	67	Additional child tax credit. Attach Schedule 8812	67	
	68	American opportunity credit from Form 8863, line 8 . . .	68	
	69	Net premium tax credit. Attach Form 8962	69	
	70	Amount paid with request for extension to file	70	
	71	Excess social security and tier 1 RRTA tax withheld	71	
	72	Credit for federal tax on fuels. Attach Form 4136	72	
	73	Credits from Form: **a** ☐ 2439 **b** ☐ Reserved **c** ☐ 8885 **d** ☐	73	
	74	Add lines 64, 65, 66a, and 67 through 73. These are your **total payments** . . . . . ▶	74	

Refund	75	If line 74 is more than line 63, subtract line 63 from line 74. This is the amount you **overpaid**	75	
Direct deposit? See instructions.	76a	Amount of line 75 you want **refunded to you.** If Form 8888 is attached, check here . ▶☐	76a	
	▶ b	Routing number	▶ c Type: ☐ Checking ☐ Savings	
	▶ d	Account number		
	77	Amount of line 75 you want **applied to your 2018 estimated tax** ▶	77	

Amount You Owe	78	**Amount you owe.** Subtract line 74 from line 63. For details on how to pay, see instructions ▶	78	
	79	Estimated tax penalty (see instructions)	79	

Third Party Designee	Do you want to allow another person to discuss this return with the IRS (see instructions)? ☐ **Yes.** Complete below. ☐ **No**	
	Designee's name ▶	Phone no. ▶	Personal identification number (PIN) ▶	

Sign Here

Joint return? See instructions. Keep a copy for your records.

Under penalties of perjury, I declare that I have examined this return and accompanying schedules and statements, and to the best of my knowledge and belief, they are true, correct, and accurately list all amounts and sources of income I received during the tax year. Declaration of preparer (other than taxpayer) is based on all information of which preparer has any knowledge.

Your signature	Date	Your occupation	Daytime phone number
Spouse's signature. If a joint return, **both** must sign.	Date	Spouse's occupation	If the IRS sent you an Identity Protection PIN, enter it here (see inst.)

Paid Preparer Use Only

Print/Type preparer's name	Preparer's signature	Date	Check ☐ if self-employed	PTIN
Firm's name ▶			Firm's EIN ▶	
Firm's address ▶			Phone no.	

Go to *www.irs.gov/Form1040* for instructions and the latest information.   Form **1040** (2017)

Source: Form 1040, Department of the Treasury—Internal Revenue Service, 2017

SCHEDULE A
(Form 1040)

Department of the Treasury
Internal Revenue Service (99)

Itemized Deductions

▶ Go to *www.irs.gov/ScheduleA* for instructions and the latest information.
▶ **Attach to Form 1040.**

Caution: If you are claiming a net qualified disaster loss on Form 4684, see the instructions for line 28.

OMB No. 1545-0074

2017

Attachment
Sequence No. **07**

Name(s) shown on Form 1040

Your social security number

Medical and Dental Expenses

Caution: Do not include expenses reimbursed or paid by others.

1. Medical and dental expenses (see instructions) . . . . . | 1 |
2. Enter amount from Form 1040, line 38 | **2** |
3. Multiply line 2 by 7.5% (0.075) . . . . . . | 3 |
4. Subtract line 3 from line 1. If line 3 is more than line 1, enter -0- . . . . | **4** |

Taxes You Paid

5. State and local **(check only one box):**
   a. ☐ Income taxes, **or**
   b. ☐ General sales taxes . . . . . . | 5 |
6. Real estate taxes (see instructions) . . . . . . | 6 |
7. Personal property taxes . . . . | 7 |
8. Other taxes. List type and amount ▶ _____
   _____ | 8 |
9. Add lines 5 through 8 . . . . | **9** |

Interest You Paid

Note:
Your mortgage interest deduction may be limited (see instructions).

10. Home mortgage interest and points reported to you on Form 1098 | 10 |
11. Home mortgage interest not reported to you on Form 1098. If paid to the person from whom you bought the home, see instructions and show that person's name, identifying no., and address ▶
    _____
    _____ | 11 |
12. Points not reported to you on Form 1098. See instructions for special rules . . . . | 12 |
13. Reserved for future use . . . . . . | 13 |
14. Investment interest. Attach Form 4952 if required. See instructions | 14 |
15. Add lines 10 through 14 . . . . | **15** |

Gifts to Charity

If you made a gift and got a benefit for it, see instructions.

16. Gifts by cash or check. If you made any gift of $250 or more, see instructions . . . . | 16 |
17. Other than by cash or check. If any gift of $250 or more, see instructions. You **must** attach Form 8283 if over $500 . . . | 17 |
18. Carryover from prior year . . . . . . | 18 |
19. Add lines 16 through 18 . . . . | **19** |

Casualty and Theft Losses

20. Casualty or theft loss(es) other than net qualified disaster losses. Attach Form 4684 and enter the amount from line 18 of that form. See instructions . . . . | **20** |

Job Expenses and Certain Miscellaneous Deductions

21. Unreimbursed employee expenses—job travel, union dues, job education, etc. Attach Form 2106 or 2106-EZ if required. See instructions. ▶ _____ | 21 |
22. Tax preparation fees . . . . . . | 22 |
23. Other expenses—investment, safe deposit box, etc. List type and amount ▶ _____
    _____ | 23 |
24. Add lines 21 through 23 . . . . . . | 24 |
25. Enter amount from Form 1040, line 38 | **25** |
26. Multiply line 25 by 2% (0.02) . . . . . | 26 |
27. Subtract line 26 from line 24. If line 26 is more than line 24, enter -0- . . . . | **27** |

Other Miscellaneous Deductions

28. Other—from list in instructions. List type and amount ▶ _____
    _____ | **28** |

Total Itemized Deductions

29. Is Form 1040, line 38, over $156,900?

☐ **No.** Your deduction is not limited. Add the amounts in the far right column for lines 4 through 28. Also, enter this amount on Form 1040, line 40. }

☐ **Yes.** Your deduction may be limited. See the Itemized Deductions Worksheet in the instructions to figure the amount to enter. | **29** |

30. If you elect to itemize deductions even though they are less than your standard deduction, check here . . . . ▶ ☐

For Paperwork Reduction Act Notice, see the Instructions for Form 1040.   Cat. No. 17145C   **Schedule A (Form 1040) 2017**

Source: Schedule A, Form 1040, Department of the Treasury—Internal Revenue Service, 2017

SCHEDULE B
(Form 1040A or 1040)

Department of the Treasury
Internal Revenue Service (99)

Interest and Ordinary Dividends

▶ Attach to Form 1040A or 1040.
▶ Go to *www.irs.gov/ScheduleB* for instructions and the latest information.

OMB No. 1545-0074

20**17**

Attachment
Sequence No. **08**

Name(s) shown on return

Your social security number

Part I **Interest** (See instructions and the instructions for Form 1040A, or Form 1040, line 8a.) **Note:** If you received a Form 1099-INT, Form 1099-OID, or substitute statement from a brokerage firm, list the firm's name as the payer and enter the total interest shown on that form.	**1**	List name of payer. If any interest is from a seller-financed mortgage and the buyer used the property as a personal residence, see the instructions and list this interest first. Also, show that buyer's social security number and address ▶		**Amount**
			1	
	2	Add the amounts on line 1	**2**	
	3	Excludable interest on series EE and I U.S. savings bonds issued after 1989. Attach Form 8815	**3**	
	4	Subtract line 3 from line 2. Enter the result here and on Form 1040A, or Form 1040, line 8a . . . . ▶	**4**	

Note: If line 4 is over $1,500, you must complete Part III.

Part II **Ordinary Dividends** (See instructions and the instructions for Form 1040A, or Form 1040, line 9a.) **Note:** If you received a Form 1099-DIV or substitute statement from a brokerage firm, list the firm's name as the payer and enter the ordinary dividends shown on that form.	**5**	List name of payer ▶		**Amount**
			5	
	6	Add the amounts on line 5. Enter the total here and on Form 1040A, or Form 1040, line 9a . . . . ▶	**6**	

Note: If line 6 is over $1,500, you must complete Part III.

Part III **Foreign Accounts and Trusts** (See instructions.)		You must complete this part if you **(a)** had over $1,500 of taxable interest or ordinary dividends; **(b)** had a foreign account; or **(c)** received a distribution from, or were a grantor of, or a transferor to, a foreign trust.	Yes	No
	7a	At any time during 2017, did you have a financial interest in or signature authority over a financial account (such as a bank account, securities account, or brokerage account) located in a foreign country? See instructions		
		If "Yes," are you required to file FinCEN Form 114, Report of Foreign Bank and Financial Accounts (FBAR), to report that financial interest or signature authority? See FinCEN Form 114 and its instructions for filing requirements and exceptions to those requirements		
	b	If you are required to file FinCEN Form 114, enter the name of the foreign country where the financial account is located ▶		
	8	During 2017, did you receive a distribution from, or were you the grantor of, or transferor to, a foreign trust? If "Yes," you may have to file Form 3520. See instructions		

For Paperwork Reduction Act Notice, see your tax return instructions.   Cat. No. 17146N   **Schedule B (Form 1040A or 1040) 2017**

Source: Schedule B, Form 1040, Department of the Treasury—Internal Revenue Service, 2017

SCHEDULE C
(Form 1040)

Department of the Treasury
Internal Revenue Service (99)

Profit or Loss From Business
(Sole Proprietorship)

▶ Go to *www.irs.gov/ScheduleC* for instructions and the latest information.
▶ **Attach to Form 1040, 1040NR, or 1041; partnerships generally must file Form 1065.**

OMB No. 1545-0074

2017

Attachment
Sequence No. **09**

Name of proprietor	Social security number (SSN)

A	Principal business or profession, including product or service (see instructions)	**B** Enter code from instructions ▶
C	Business name. If no separate business name, leave blank.	**D** Employer ID number (EIN) (see instr.)
E	Business address (including suite or room no.) ▶	
	City, town or post office, state, and ZIP code	

F Accounting method: **(1)** ☐ Cash **(2)** ☐ Accrual **(3)** ☐ Other (specify) ▶

G Did you "materially participate" in the operation of this business during 2017? If "No," see instructions for limit on losses . ☐ Yes ☐ No

H If you started or acquired this business during 2017, check here . . . . ▶ ☐

I Did you make any payments in 2017 that would require you to file Form(s) 1099? (see instructions) . . . . ☐ Yes ☐ No

J If "Yes," did you or will you file required Forms 1099? . . . . ☐ Yes ☐ No

Part I Income

1	Gross receipts or sales. See instructions for line 1 and check the box if this income was reported to you on Form W-2 and the "Statutory employee" box on that form was checked . . . . ▶ ☐	**1**	
2	Returns and allowances	**2**	
3	Subtract line 2 from line 1	**3**	
4	Cost of goods sold (from line 42)	**4**	
5	**Gross profit.** Subtract line 4 from line 3	**5**	
6	Other income, including federal and state gasoline or fuel tax credit or refund (see instructions) . . .	**6**	
7	**Gross income.** Add lines 5 and 6 . . . . ▶	**7**	

Part II Expenses. Enter expenses for business use of your home **only** on line 30.

8	Advertising	**8**		**18**	Office expense (see instructions)	**18**	
9	Car and truck expenses (see instructions).	**9**		**19**	Pension and profit-sharing plans .	**19**	
10	Commissions and fees .	**10**		**20**	Rent or lease (see instructions):		
11	Contract labor (see instructions)	**11**		**a**	Vehicles, machinery, and equipment	**20a**	
12	Depletion	**12**		**b**	Other business property . .	**20b**	
13	Depreciation and section 179 expense deduction (not included in Part III) (see instructions). . . .	**13**		**21**	Repairs and maintenance . .	**21**	
				22	Supplies (not included in Part III) .	**22**	
				23	Taxes and licenses	**23**	
				24	Travel, meals, and entertainment:		
14	Employee benefit programs (other than on line 19) . .	**14**		**a**	Travel	**24a**	
15	Insurance (other than health)	**15**		**b**	Deductible meals and entertainment (see instructions)	**24b**	
16	Interest:			**25**	Utilities	**25**	
a	Mortgage (paid to banks, etc.)	**16a**		**26**	Wages (less employment credits).	**26**	
b	Other	**16b**		**27a**	Other expenses (from line 48) . .	**27a**	
17	Legal and professional services	**17**		**b**	**Reserved for future use** . . .	**27b**	

28	**Total expenses** before expenses for business use of home. Add lines 8 through 27a . . . . . . ▶	**28**	
29	Tentative profit or (loss). Subtract line 28 from line 7	**29**	
30	Expenses for business use of your home. Do not report these expenses elsewhere. Attach Form 8829 unless using the simplified method (see instructions). **Simplified method filers only:** enter the total square footage of: (a) your home: _____ and (b) the part of your home used for business: _____. Use the Simplified Method Worksheet in the instructions to figure the amount to enter on line 30	**30**	
31	**Net profit or (loss).** Subtract line 30 from line 29. • If a profit, enter on both **Form 1040, line 12** (or Form 1040NR, line 13) and on **Schedule SE, line 2.** (If you checked the box on line 1, see instructions). Estates and trusts, enter on **Form 1041, line 3.** • If a loss, you **must** go to line 32.	**31**	
32	If you have a loss, check the box that describes your investment in this activity (see instructions). • If you checked 32a, enter the loss on both **Form 1040, line 12,** (or **Form 1040NR, line 13**) and on **Schedule SE, line 2.** (If you checked the box on line 1, see the line 31 instructions). Estates and trusts, enter on **Form 1041, line 3.** • If you checked 32b, you **must** attach Form 6198. Your loss may be limited.	**32a** ☐ All investment is at risk. **32b** ☐ Some investment is not at risk.

For Paperwork Reduction Act Notice, see the separate instructions.   Cat. No. 11334P   Schedule C (Form 1040) 2017

| Part III | Cost of Goods Sold (see instructions) |

33 Method(s) used to value closing inventory: **a** ☐ Cost   **b** ☐ Lower of cost or market   **c** ☐ Other (attach explanation)

34 Was there any change in determining quantities, costs, or valuations between opening and closing inventory?
If "Yes," attach explanation . . . .   ☐ Yes   ☐ No

35 Inventory at beginning of year. If different from last year's closing inventory, attach explanation . . .	**35**	
36 Purchases less cost of items withdrawn for personal use	**36**	
37 Cost of labor. Do not include any amounts paid to yourself	**37**	
38 Materials and supplies	**38**	
39 Other costs	**39**	
40 Add lines 35 through 39	**40**	
41 Inventory at end of year	**41**	
42 **Cost of goods sold.** Subtract line 41 from line 40. Enter the result here and on line 4	**42**	

| Part IV | Information on Your Vehicle. Complete this part **only** if you are claiming car or truck expenses on line 9 and are not required to file Form 4562 for this business. See the instructions for line 13 to find out if you must file Form 4562. |

43 When did you place your vehicle in service for business purposes? (month, day, year) ▶ _____ / _____ / _____

44 Of the total number of miles you drove your vehicle during 2017, enter the number of miles you used your vehicle for:

a Business _____   **b** Commuting (see instructions) _____   **c** Other _____

45 Was your vehicle available for personal use during off-duty hours? . . . .   ☐ Yes   ☐ No

46 Do you (or your spouse) have another vehicle available for personal use?. . . . .   ☐ Yes   ☐ No

47a Do you have evidence to support your deduction? . . . .   ☐ Yes   ☐ No

b If "Yes," is the evidence written? . . . .   ☐ Yes   ☐ No

| Part V | Other Expenses. List below business expenses not included on lines 8–26 or line 30. |

----------------------------------		
48 **Total other expenses.** Enter here and on line 27a	**48**	

Source: Schedule C, Form 1040, Department of the Treasury—Internal Revenue Service, 2017

SCHEDULE D
(Form 1040)

Department of the Treasury
Internal Revenue Service (99)

Capital Gains and Losses

▶ Attach to Form 1040 or Form 1040NR.
▶ Go to *www.irs.gov/ScheduleD* for instructions and the latest information.
▶ Use Form 8949 to list your transactions for lines 1b, 2, 3, 8b, 9, and 10.

OMB No. 1545-0074

20**17**

Attachment
Sequence No. **12**

Name(s) shown on return

Your social security number

Part I   Short-Term Capital Gains and Losses—Assets Held One Year or Less

See instructions for how to figure the amounts to enter on the lines below. This form may be easier to complete if you round off cents to whole dollars.	**(d)** Proceeds (sales price)	**(e)** Cost (or other basis)	**(g)** Adjustments to gain or loss from Form(s) 8949, Part I, line 2, column (g)	**(h) Gain or (loss)** Subtract column (e) from column (d) and combine the result with column (g)
1a Totals for all short-term transactions reported on Form 1099-B for which basis was reported to the IRS and for which you have no adjustments (see instructions). However, if you choose to report all these transactions on Form 8949, leave this line blank and go to line 1b .				
1b Totals for all transactions reported on Form(s) 8949 with **Box A** checked				
2 Totals for all transactions reported on Form(s) 8949 with **Box B** checked				
3 Totals for all transactions reported on Form(s) 8949 with **Box C** checked				

4 Short-term gain from Form 6252 and short-term gain or (loss) from Forms 4684, 6781, and 8824 .	**4**	
5 Net short-term gain or (loss) from partnerships, S corporations, estates, and trusts from Schedule(s) K-1	**5**	
6 Short-term capital loss carryover. Enter the amount, if any, from line 8 of your **Capital Loss Carryover Worksheet** in the instructions	**6**	( )
7 **Net short-term capital gain or (loss).** Combine lines 1a through 6 in column (h). If you have any long-term capital gains or losses, go to Part II below. Otherwise, go to Part III on the back	**7**	

Part II   Long-Term Capital Gains and Losses—Assets Held More Than One Year

See instructions for how to figure the amounts to enter on the lines below. This form may be easier to complete if you round off cents to whole dollars.	**(d)** Proceeds (sales price)	**(e)** Cost (or other basis)	**(g)** Adjustments to gain or loss from Form(s) 8949, Part II, line 2, column (g)	**(h) Gain or (loss)** Subtract column (e) from column (d) and combine the result with column (g)
8a Totals for all long-term transactions reported on Form 1099-B for which basis was reported to the IRS and for which you have no adjustments (see instructions). However, if you choose to report all these transactions on Form 8949, leave this line blank and go to line 8b .				
8b Totals for all transactions reported on Form(s) 8949 with **Box D** checked				
9 Totals for all transactions reported on Form(s) 8949 with **Box E** checked				
10 Totals for all transactions reported on Form(s) 8949 with **Box F** checked.				

11 Gain from Form 4797, Part I; long-term gain from Forms 2439 and 6252; and long-term gain or (loss) from Forms 4684, 6781, and 8824	**11**	
12 Net long-term gain or (loss) from partnerships, S corporations, estates, and trusts from Schedule(s) K-1	**12**	
13 Capital gain distributions. See the instructions	**13**	
14 Long-term capital loss carryover. Enter the amount, if any, from line 13 of your **Capital Loss Carryover Worksheet** in the instructions	**14**	( )
15 **Net long-term capital gain or (loss).** Combine lines 8a through 14 in column (h). Then go to Part III on the back	**15**	

For Paperwork Reduction Act Notice, see your tax return instructions.   Cat. No. 11338H   **Schedule D (Form 1040) 2017**

Source: Schedule D, Form 1040, Department of the Treasury—Internal Revenue Service, 2017

Part III   **Summary**

16   Combine lines 7 and 15 and enter the result . . . . | **16** |

   - If line 16 is a **gain,** enter the amount from line 16 on Form 1040, line 13, or Form 1040NR, line 14. Then go to line 17 below.
   - If line 16 is a **loss,** skip lines 17 through 20 below. Then go to line 21. Also be sure to complete line 22.
   - If line 16 is **zero,** skip lines 17 through 21 below and enter -0- on Form 1040, line 13, or Form 1040NR, line 14. Then go to line 22.

17   Are lines 15 and 16 **both** gains?
   ☐ **Yes.** Go to line 18.
   ☐ **No.** Skip lines 18 through 21, and go to line 22.

18   If you are required to complete the **28% Rate Gain Worksheet** (see instructions), enter the amount, if any, from line 7 of that worksheet . . . . ▶ | **18** |

19   If you are required to complete the **Unrecaptured Section 1250 Gain Worksheet** (see instructions), enter the amount, if any, from line 18 of that worksheet . . . . ▶ | **19** |

20   Are lines 18 and 19 **both** zero or blank?
   ☐ **Yes.** Complete the **Qualified Dividends and Capital Gain Tax Worksheet** in the instructions for Form 1040, line 44 (or in the instructions for Form 1040NR, line 42). **Don't** complete lines 21 and 22 below.

   ☐ **No.** Complete the **Schedule D Tax Worksheet** in the instructions. **Don't** complete lines 21 and 22 below.

21   If line 16 is a loss, enter here and on Form 1040, line 13, or Form 1040NR, line 14, the **smaller** of:

   - The loss on line 16 or
   - ($3,000), or if married filing separately, ($1,500)   } . . . . | **21** |( )

   Note: When figuring which amount is smaller, treat both amounts as positive numbers.

22   Do you have qualified dividends on Form 1040, line 9b, or Form 1040NR, line 10b?

   ☐ **Yes.** Complete the **Qualified Dividends and Capital Gain Tax Worksheet** in the instructions for Form 1040, line 44 (or in the instructions for Form 1040NR, line 42).

   ☐ **No.** Complete the rest of Form 1040 or Form 1040NR.

Form **8949**

Department of the Treasury
Internal Revenue Service

Sales and Other Dispositions of Capital Assets

▶ Go to *www.irs.gov/Form8949* for instructions and the latest information.

▶ File with your Schedule D to list your transactions for lines 1b, 2, 3, 8b, 9, and 10 of Schedule D.

OMB No. 1545-0074

2017

Attachment
Sequence No. **12A**

Name(s) shown on return

Social security number or taxpayer identification number

Before you check Box A, B, or C below, see whether you received any Form(s) 1099-B or substitute statement(s) from your broker. A substitute statement will have the same information as Form 1099-B. Either will show whether your basis (usually your cost) was reported to the IRS by your broker and may even tell you which box to check.

Part I   **Short-Term.** Transactions involving capital assets you held 1 year or less are short term. For long-term transactions, see page 2.

Note: You may aggregate all short-term transactions reported on Form(s) 1099-B showing basis was reported to the IRS and for which no adjustments or codes are required. Enter the totals directly on Schedule D, line 1a; you aren't required to report these transactions on Form 8949 (see instructions).

You **must** check Box A, B, *or* C below. **Check only one box.** If more than one box applies for your short-term transactions, complete a separate Form 8949, page 1, for each applicable box. If you have more short-term transactions than will fit on this page for one or more of the boxes, complete as many forms with the same box checked as you need.

- ☐ **(A)** Short-term transactions reported on Form(s) 1099-B showing basis was reported to the IRS (see **Note** above)
- ☐ **(B)** Short-term transactions reported on Form(s) 1099-B showing basis **wasn't** reported to the IRS
- ☐ **(C)** Short-term transactions not reported to you on Form 1099-B

1 (a) Description of property (Example: 100 sh. XYZ Co.)	(b) Date acquired (Mo., day, yr.)	(c) Date sold or disposed of (Mo., day, yr.)	(d) Proceeds (sales price) (see instructions)	(e) Cost or other basis. See the **Note** below and see *Column (e)* in the separate instructions	(f) Code(s) from instructions	(g) Amount of adjustment	(h) Gain or (loss). Subtract column (e) from column (d) and combine the result with column (g)

2 Totals. Add the amounts in columns (d), (e), (g), and (h) (subtract negative amounts). Enter each total here and include on your Schedule D, **line 1b** (if **Box A** above is checked), **line 2** (if **Box B** above is checked), or **line 3** (if **Box C** above is checked) ▶

Note: If you checked Box A above but the basis reported to the IRS was incorrect, enter in column (e) the basis as reported to the IRS, and enter an adjustment in column (g) to correct the basis. See *Column (g)* in the separate instructions for how to figure the amount of the adjustment.

For Paperwork Reduction Act Notice, see your tax return instructions.   Cat. No. 37768Z   Form **8949** (2017)

Form 8949 (2017)   Attachment Sequence No. **12A**   Page **2**

Name(s) shown on return. Name and SSN or taxpayer identification no. not required if shown on other side	Social security number or taxpayer identification number

Before you check Box D, E, or F below, see whether you received any Form(s) 1099-B or substitute statement(s) from your broker. A substitute statement will have the same information as Form 1099-B. Either will show whether your basis (usually your cost) was reported to the IRS by your broker and may even tell you which box to check.

Part II **Long-Term.** Transactions involving capital assets you held more than 1 year are long term. For short-term transactions, see page 1.

Note: You may aggregate all long-term transactions reported on Form(s) 1099-B showing basis was reported to the IRS and for which no adjustments or codes are required. Enter the totals directly on Schedule D, line 8a; you aren't required to report these transactions on Form 8949 (see instructions).

You *must* check Box D, E, *or* F below. Check only one box. If more than one box applies for your long-term transactions, complete a separate Form 8949, page 2, for each applicable box. If you have more long-term transactions than will fit on this page for one or more of the boxes, complete as many forms with the same box checked as you need.

☐ **(D)** Long-term transactions reported on Form(s) 1099-B showing basis was reported to the IRS (see **Note** above)

☐ **(E)** Long-term transactions reported on Form(s) 1099-B showing basis **wasn't** reported to the IRS

☐ **(F)** Long-term transactions not reported to you on Form 1099-B

1 (a) Description of property (Example: 100 sh. XYZ Co.)	(b) Date acquired (Mo., day, yr.)	(c) Date sold or disposed of (Mo., day, yr.)	(d) Proceeds (sales price) (see instructions)	(e) Cost or other basis. See the **Note** below and see *Column (e)* in the separate instructions	Adjustment, if any, to gain or loss. If you enter an amount in column (g), enter a code in column (f). See the separate instructions.		(h) Gain or (loss). Subtract column (e) from column (d) and combine the result with column (g)
					(f) Code(s) from instructions	(g) Amount of adjustment	

2 Totals. Add the amounts in columns (d), (e), (g), and (h) (subtract negative amounts). Enter each total here and include on your Schedule D, **line 8b** (if **Box D** above is checked), **line 9** (if **Box E** above is checked), or **line 10** (if **Box F** above is checked) ▶

Note: If you checked Box D above but the basis reported to the IRS was incorrect, enter in column (e) the basis as reported to the IRS, and enter an adjustment in column (g) to correct the basis. See *Column (g)* in the separate instructions for how to figure the amount of the adjustment.

Form **8949** (2017)

Source: Form 8949, Department of the Treasury - Internal Revenue Service, 2017

SCHEDULE E (Form 1040) Department of the Treasury Internal Revenue Service (99)	**Supplemental Income and Loss** (From rental real estate, royalties, partnerships, S corporations, estates, trusts, REMICs, etc.) ▶ Attach to Form 1040, 1040NR, or Form 1041. ▶ Go to *www.irs.gov/ScheduleE* for instructions and the latest information.	OMB No. 1545-0074 20**17** Attachment Sequence No. **13**

Name(s) shown on return | | Your social security number

Part I   **Income or Loss From Rental Real Estate and Royalties**   Note: If you are in the business of renting personal property, use **Schedule C** or **C-EZ** (see instructions). If you are an individual, report farm rental income or loss from **Form 4835** on page 2, line 40.

A Did you make any payments in 2017 that would require you to file Form(s) 1099? (see instructions) . . . . . ☐ Yes ☐ No
B If "Yes," did you or will you file required Forms 1099? . . . . ☐ Yes ☐ No

1a Physical address of each property (street, city, state, ZIP code)

A	
B	
C	

1b	Type of Property (from list below)	**2**	For each rental real estate property listed above, report the number of fair rental and personal use days. Check the **QJV** box only if you meet the requirements to file as a qualified joint venture. See instructions.		Fair Rental Days	Personal Use Days	QJV
A				**A**			☐
B				**B**			☐
C				**C**			☐

Type of Property:

1 Single Family Residence   3 Vacation/Short-Term Rental   5 Land   7 Self-Rental
2 Multi-Family Residence   4 Commercial   6 Royalties   8 Other (describe)

Income:	Properties:		A	B	C
3 Rents received	**3**				
4 Royalties received	**4**				
Expenses:					
5 Advertising	**5**				
6 Auto and travel (see instructions)	**6**				
7 Cleaning and maintenance	**7**				
8 Commissions.	**8**				
9 Insurance	**9**				
10 Legal and other professional fees	**10**				
11 Management fees	**11**				
12 Mortgage interest paid to banks, etc. (see instructions)	**12**				
13 Other interest.	**13**				
14 Repairs.	**14**				
15 Supplies	**15**				
16 Taxes	**16**				
17 Utilities	**17**				
18 Depreciation expense or depletion	**18**				
19 Other (list) ▶ _____	**19**				
20 Total expenses. Add lines 5 through 19 . .	**20**				
21 Subtract line 20 from line 3 (rents) and/or 4 (royalties). If result is a (loss), see instructions to find out if you must file **Form 6198**	**21**				
22 Deductible rental real estate loss after limitation, if any, on **Form 8582** (see instructions)	**22**	(	)(	)(	)

23a	Total of all amounts reported on line 3 for all rental properties	**23a**	
b	Total of all amounts reported on line 4 for all royalty properties	**23b**	
c	Total of all amounts reported on line 12 for all properties	**23c**	
d	Total of all amounts reported on line 18 for all properties	**23d**	
e	Total of all amounts reported on line 20 for all properties	**23e**	
24	**Income.** Add positive amounts shown on line 21. **Do not** include any losses	**24**	
25	**Losses.** Add royalty losses from line 21 and rental real estate losses from line 22. Enter total losses here .	**25**	( )
26	**Total rental real estate and royalty income or (loss).** Combine lines 24 and 25. Enter the result here. If Parts II, III, IV, and line 40 on page 2 do not apply to you, also enter this amount on Form 1040, line 17, or Form 1040NR, line 18. Otherwise, include this amount in the total on line 41 on page 2 . . .	**26**	

For Paperwork Reduction Act Notice, see the separate instructions.   Cat. No. 11344L   Schedule E (Form 1040) 2017

Schedule E (Form 1040) 2017 | Attachment Sequence No. **13** | Page **2**

Name(s) shown on return. Do not enter name and social security number if shown on other side.	Your social security number

Caution: The IRS compares amounts reported on your tax return with amounts shown on Schedule(s) K-1.

Part II   **Income or Loss From Partnerships and S Corporations**   **Note:** If you report a loss from an at-risk activity for which **any** amount is **not** at risk, you **must** check the box in column (e) on line 28 and attach **Form 6198.** See instructions.

27   Are you reporting any loss not allowed in a prior year due to the at-risk, excess farm loss, or basis limitations, a prior year unallowed loss from a passive activity (if that loss was not reported on Form 8582), or unreimbursed partnership expenses? If you answered "Yes," see instructions before completing this section . . . . ☐ **Yes**   ☐ **No**

28

(a) Name	(b) Enter **P** for partnership; **S** for S corporation	(c) Check if foreign partnership	(d) Employer identification number	(e) Check if any amount is not at risk
A		☐		☐
B		☐		☐
C		☐		☐
D		☐		☐

	Passive Income and Loss		Nonpassive Income and Loss		
	(f) Passive loss allowed (attach **Form 8582** if required)	(g) Passive income from **Schedule K-1**	(h) Nonpassive loss from **Schedule K-1**	(i) Section 179 expense deduction from **Form 4562**	(j) Nonpassive income from **Schedule K-1**
A					
B					
C					
D					
29a Totals					
b Totals					

30   Add columns (g) and (j) of line 29a . . . . **30** |

31   Add columns (f), (h), and (i) of line 29b . . . . **31** (   )

32   **Total partnership and S corporation income or (loss).** Combine lines 30 and 31. Enter the result here and include in the total on line 41 below **32**

Part III   **Income or Loss From Estates and Trusts**

33

(a) Name	(b) Employer identification number
A	
B	

	Passive Income and Loss		Nonpassive Income and Loss	
	(c) Passive deduction or loss allowed (attach **Form 8582** if required)	(d) Passive income from **Schedule K-1**	(e) Deduction or loss from **Schedule K-1**	(f) Other income from **Schedule K-1**
A				
B				
34a Totals				
b Totals				

35   Add columns (d) and (f) of line 34a **35**

36   Add columns (c) and (e) of line 34b . . . . **36** (   )

37   **Total estate and trust income or (loss).** Combine lines 35 and 36. Enter the result here and include in the total on line 41 below **37**

Part IV   **Income or Loss From Real Estate Mortgage Investment Conduits (REMICs)—Residual Holder**

38

(a) Name	(b) Employer identification number	(c) Excess inclusion from **Schedules Q,** line 2c (see instructions)	(d) Taxable income (net loss) from **Schedules Q,** line 1b	(e) Income from **Schedules Q,** line 3b

39   Combine columns (d) and (e) only. Enter the result here and include in the total on line 41 below   **39**

Part V   **Summary**

40   Net farm rental income or (loss) from **Form 4835.** Also, complete line 42 below **40**

41   Total income or (loss). Combine lines 26, 32, 37, 39, and 40. Enter the result here and on Form 1040, line 17, or Form 1040NR, line 18 ▶   **41**

42   **Reconciliation of farming and fishing income.** Enter your **gross** farming and fishing income reported on Form 4835, line 7; Schedule K-1 (Form 1065), box 14, code B; Schedule K-1 (Form 1120S), box 17, code V; and Schedule K-1 (Form 1041), box 14, code F (see instructions) . .   **42**

43   **Reconciliation for real estate professionals.** If you were a real estate professional (see instructions), enter the net income or (loss) you reported anywhere on Form 1040 or Form 1040NR from all rental real estate activities in which you materially participated under the passive activity loss rules . .   **43**

Schedule E (Form 1040) 2017

Source: Schedule E, Form 1040, Department of the Treasury—Internal Revenue Service, 2017

SCHEDULE SE (Form 1040) Department of the Treasury Internal Revenue Service (99)	**Self-Employment Tax** ▶ Go to *www.irs.gov/ScheduleSE* for instructions and the latest information. ▶ **Attach to Form 1040 or Form 1040NR.**	OMB No. 1545-0074 20**17** Attachment Sequence No. **17**
Name of person with **self-employment** income (as shown on Form 1040 or Form 1040NR)		Social security number of person with **self-employment** income ▶

Before you begin: To determine if you must file Schedule SE, see the instructions.

May I Use Short Schedule SE or Must I Use Long Schedule SE?

Note: Use this flowchart **only if** you must file Schedule SE. If unsure, see *Who Must File Schedule SE* in the instructions.

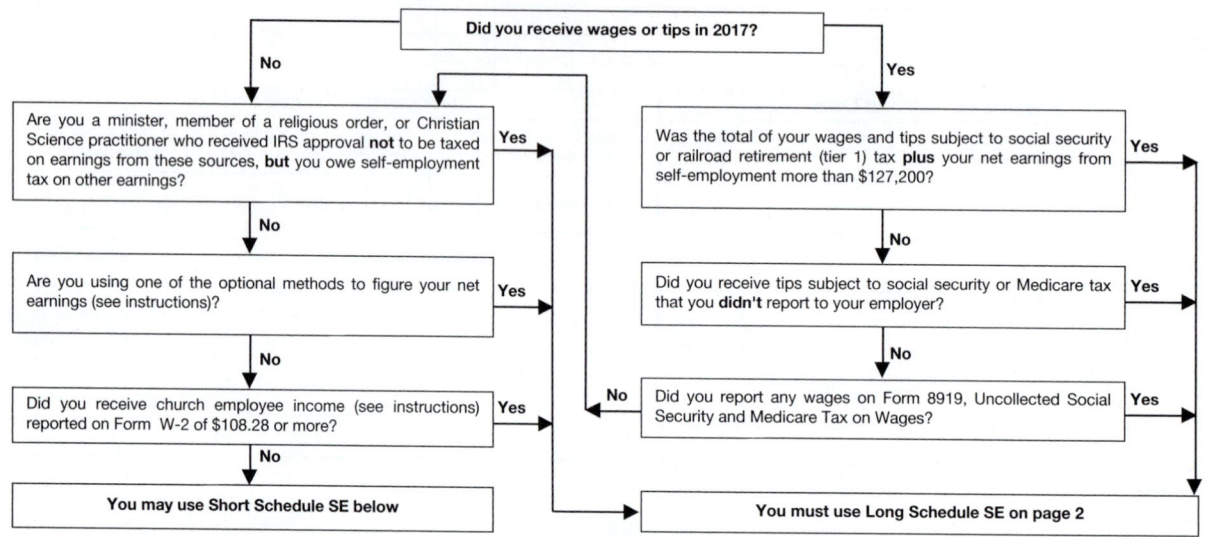

Section A—Short Schedule SE.   Caution: Read above to see if you can use Short Schedule SE.

1a	Net farm profit or (loss) from Schedule F, line 34, and farm partnerships, Schedule K-1 (Form 1065), box 14, code A	**1a**	
b	If you received social security retirement or disability benefits, enter the amount of Conservation Reserve Program payments included on Schedule F, line 4b, or listed on Schedule K-1 (Form 1065), box 20, code Z	**1b** (	)
2	Net profit or (loss) from Schedule C, line 31; Schedule C-EZ, line 3; Schedule K-1 (Form 1065), box 14, code A (other than farming); and Schedule K-1 (Form 1065-B), box 9, code J1. Ministers and members of religious orders, see instructions for types of income to report on this line. See instructions for other income to report	**2**	
3	Combine lines 1a, 1b, and 2	**3**	
4	Multiply line 3 by 92.35% (0.9235). If less than $400, you don't owe self-employment tax; **don't** file this schedule unless you have an amount on line 1b . . . . ▶	**4**	
	Note: If line 4 is less than $400 due to Conservation Reserve Program payments on line 1b, see instructions.		
5	**Self-employment tax.** If the amount on line 4 is: • $127,200 or less, multiply line 4 by 15.3% (0.153). Enter the result here and on **Form 1040, line 57,** or **Form 1040NR, line 55** • More than $127,200, multiply line 4 by 2.9% (0.029). Then, add $15,772.80 to the result. Enter the total here and on **Form 1040, line 57,** or **Form 1040NR, line 55**	**5**	
6	**Deduction for one-half of self-employment tax.** Multiply line 5 by 50% (0.50). Enter the result here and on **Form 1040, line 27,** or **Form 1040NR, line 27** . . . . | **6**		

For Paperwork Reduction Act Notice, see your tax return instructions.   Cat. No. 11358Z   Schedule SE (Form 1040) 2017

Schedule SE (Form 1040) 2017 | Attachment Sequence No. **17** | Page **2**

| Name of person with **self-employment** income (as shown on Form 1040 or Form 1040NR) | Social security number of person with **self-employment** income ▶ | |

Section B—Long Schedule SE
Part I Self-Employment Tax

Note: If your only income subject to self-employment tax is **church employee income,** see instructions. Also see instructions for the definition of church employee income.

A If you are a minister, member of a religious order, or Christian Science practitioner **and** you filed Form 4361, but you had $400 or more of **other** net earnings from self-employment, check here and continue with Part I . . . . ▶ ☐

1a Net farm profit or (loss) from Schedule F, line 34, and farm partnerships, Schedule K-1 (Form 1065), box 14, code A. **Note:** Skip lines 1a and 1b if you use the farm optional method (see instructions) | **1a** | |

b If you received social security retirement or disability benefits, enter the amount of Conservation Reserve Program payments included on Schedule F, line 4b, or listed on Schedule K-1 (Form 1065), box 20, code Z | **1b** | (|) |

2 Net profit or (loss) from Schedule C, line 31; Schedule C-EZ, line 3; Schedule K-1 (Form 1065), box 14, code A (other than farming); and Schedule K-1 (Form 1065-B), box 9, code J1. Ministers and members of religious orders, see instructions for types of income to report on this line. See instructions for other income to report. **Note:** Skip this line if you use the nonfarm optional method (see instructions) . . . . | **2** | |

3 Combine lines 1a, 1b, and 2 . . . . | **3** | |

4a If line 3 is more than zero, multiply line 3 by 92.35% (0.9235). Otherwise, enter amount from line 3 | **4a** | |
Note: If line 4a is less than $400 due to Conservation Reserve Program payments on line 1b, see instructions.

b If you elect one or both of the optional methods, enter the total of lines 15 and 17 here . . | **4b** | |

c Combine lines 4a and 4b. If less than $400, **stop;** you don't owe self-employment tax. **Exception:** If less than $400 and you had **church employee income,** enter -0- and continue ▶ | **4c** | |

5a Enter your **church employee income** from Form W-2. See instructions for definition of church employee income . . . | **5a** | |

b Multiply line 5a by 92.35% (0.9235). If less than $100, enter -0- . . . . | **5b** | |

6 Add lines 4c and 5b . . . . | **6** | |

7 Maximum amount of combined wages and self-employment earnings subject to social security tax or the 6.2% portion of the 7.65% railroad retirement (tier 1) tax for 2017 . . . . . . | **7** | 127,200 | 00 |

8a Total social security wages and tips (total of boxes 3 and 7 on Form(s) W-2) and railroad retirement (tier 1) compensation. If $127,200 or more, skip lines 8b through 10, and go to line 11 | **8a** | |

b Unreported tips subject to social security tax (from Form 4137, line 10) | **8b** | |

c Wages subject to social security tax (from Form 8919, line 10) | **8c** | |

d Add lines 8a, 8b, and 8c . . . . | **8d** | |

9 Subtract line 8d from line 7. If zero or less, enter -0- here and on line 10 and go to line 11 . ▶ | **9** | |

10 Multiply the **smaller** of line 6 or line 9 by 12.4% (0.124) . . . . | **10** | |

11 Multiply line 6 by 2.9% (0.029) . . . . | **11** | |

12 **Self-employment tax.** Add lines 10 and 11. Enter here and on **Form 1040, line 57,** or **Form 1040NR, line 55** | **12** | |

13 **Deduction for one-half of self-employment tax.** Multiply line 12 by 50% (0.50). Enter the result here and on **Form 1040, line 27,** or **Form 1040NR, line 27** . . . . . . | **13** | |

Part II Optional Methods To Figure Net Earnings (see instructions)

Farm Optional Method. You may use this method **only** if **(a)** your gross farm income[1] wasn't more than $7,800, **or (b)** your net farm profits[2] were less than $5,631.

14 Maximum income for optional methods . . . . | **14** | 5,200 | 00 |

15 Enter the **smaller** of: two-thirds ($2/3$) of gross farm income[1] (not less than zero) or $5,200. Also include this amount on line 4b above . . . . | **15** | |

Nonfarm Optional Method. You may use this method **only** if **(a)** your net nonfarm profits[3] were less than $5,631 and also less than 72.189% of your gross nonfarm income,[4] **and (b)** you had net earnings from self-employment of at least $400 in 2 of the prior 3 years. **Caution:** You may use this method no more than five times.

16 Subtract line 15 from line 14 . . . . | **16** | |

17 Enter the **smaller** of: two-thirds ($2/3$) of gross nonfarm income[4] (not less than zero) **or** the amount on line 16. Also include this amount on line 4b above . . . . | **17** | |

[1] From Sch. F, line 9, and Sch. K-1 (Form 1065), box 14, code B.
[2] From Sch. F, line 34, and Sch. K-1 (Form 1065), box 14, code A—minus the amount you would have entered on line 1b had you not used the optional method.

[3] From Sch. C, line 31; Sch. C-EZ, line 3; Sch. K-1 (Form 1065), box 14, code A; and Sch. K-1 (Form 1065-B), box 9, code J1.
[4] From Sch. C, line 7; Sch. C-EZ, line 1; Sch. K-1 (Form 1065), box 14, code C; and Sch. K-1 (Form 1065-B), box 9, code J2.

Schedule SE (Form 1040) 2017

Source: Schedule SE, Form 1040, Department of the Treasury—Internal Revenue Service, 2017

Form **1065**

Department of the Treasury
Internal Revenue Service

U.S. Return of Partnership Income

For calendar year 2017, or tax year beginning _____, 2017, ending _____, 20____

▶ Go to *www.irs.gov/Form1065* for instructions and the latest information.

OMB No. 1545-0123

2017

A Principal business activity		Name of partnership	D Employer identification number
B Principal product or service	**Type or Print**	Number, street, and room or suite no. If a P.O. box, see the instructions.	E Date business started
C Business code number		City or town, state or province, country, and ZIP or foreign postal code	F Total assets (see the instructions) $

G Check applicable boxes: **(1)** ☐ Initial return **(2)** ☐ Final return **(3)** ☐ Name change **(4)** ☐ Address change **(5)** ☐ Amended return
(6) ☐ Technical termination - also check (1) or (2)

H Check accounting method: **(1)** ☐ Cash **(2)** ☐ Accrual **(3)** ☐ Other (specify) ▶ _____

I Number of Schedules K-1. Attach one for each person who was a partner at any time during the tax year ▶ _____

J Check if Schedules C and M-3 are attached . . . . ☐

Caution. *Include **only** trade or business income and expenses on lines 1a through 22 below. See the instructions for more information.*

Income

1a	Gross receipts or sales	1a	
b	Returns and allowances	1b	
c	Balance. Subtract line 1b from line 1a	1c	
2	Cost of goods sold (attach Form 1125-A)	2	
3	Gross profit. Subtract line 2 from line 1c	3	
4	Ordinary income (loss) from other partnerships, estates, and trusts (attach statement) . .	4	
5	Net farm profit (loss) (attach Schedule F (Form 1040))	5	
6	Net gain (loss) from Form 4797, Part II, line 17 (attach Form 4797)	6	
7	Other income (loss) (attach statement)	7	
8	**Total income (loss).** Combine lines 3 through 7	8	

Deductions (see the instructions for limitations)

9	Salaries and wages (other than to partners) (less employment credits)	9	
10	Guaranteed payments to partners	10	
11	Repairs and maintenance	11	
12	Bad debts	12	
13	Rent	13	
14	Taxes and licenses	14	
15	Interest	15	
16a	Depreciation (if required, attach Form 4562)	16a	
b	Less depreciation reported on Form 1125-A and elsewhere on return	16b	16c
17	Depletion (**Do not deduct oil and gas depletion.**)	17	
18	Retirement plans, etc.	18	
19	Employee benefit programs	19	
20	Other deductions (attach statement)	20	
21	**Total deductions.** Add the amounts shown in the far right column for lines 9 through 20 .	21	
22	**Ordinary business income (loss).** Subtract line 21 from line 8	22	

Sign Here

Under penalties of perjury, I declare that I have examined this return, including accompanying schedules and statements, and to the best of my knowledge and belief, it is true, correct, and complete. Declaration of preparer (other than partner or limited liability company member) is based on all information of which preparer has any knowledge.

▶ _____
Signature of partner or limited liability company member

▶ _____ Date

May the IRS discuss this return with the preparer shown below (see instructions)? ☐ Yes ☐ No

Paid Preparer Use Only

Print/Type preparer's name	Preparer's signature	Date	Check ☐ if self-employed	PTIN
Firm's name ▶			Firm's EIN ▶	
Firm's address ▶			Phone no.	

For Paperwork Reduction Act Notice, see separate instructions.   Cat. No. 11390Z   Form **1065** (2017)

Form 1065 (2017)

Schedule B	**Other Information**		Yes	No

1   What type of entity is filing this return? Check the applicable box:

   a ☐ Domestic general partnership   **b** ☐ Domestic limited partnership

   c ☐ Domestic limited liability company   **d** ☐ Domestic limited liability partnership

   e ☐ Foreign partnership   **f** ☐ Other ▶

2   At any time during the tax year, was any partner in the partnership a disregarded entity, a partnership (including an entity treated as a partnership), a trust, an S corporation, an estate (other than an estate of a deceased partner), or a nominee or similar person? . . . .

3   At the end of the tax year:

   a   Did any foreign or domestic corporation, partnership (including any entity treated as a partnership), trust, or tax-exempt organization, or any foreign government own, directly or indirectly, an interest of 50% or more in the profit, loss, or capital of the partnership? For rules of constructive ownership, see instructions. If "Yes," attach Schedule B-1, Information on Partners Owning 50% or More of the Partnership . . . .

   b   Did any individual or estate own, directly or indirectly, an interest of 50% or more in the profit, loss, or capital of the partnership? For rules of constructive ownership, see instructions. If "Yes," attach Schedule B-1, Information on Partners Owning 50% or More of the Partnership . . . .

4   At the end of the tax year, did the partnership:

   a   Own directly 20% or more, or own, directly or indirectly, 50% or more of the total voting power of all classes of stock entitled to vote of any foreign or domestic corporation? For rules of constructive ownership, see instructions. If "Yes," complete (i) through (iv) below . . . .

(i) Name of Corporation	**(ii)** Employer Identification Number (if any)	**(iii)** Country of Incorporation	**(iv)** Percentage Owned in Voting Stock

   b   Own directly an interest of 20% or more, or own, directly or indirectly, an interest of 50% or more in the profit, loss, or capital in any foreign or domestic partnership (including an entity treated as a partnership) or in the beneficial interest of a trust? For rules of constructive ownership, see instructions. If "Yes," complete (i) through (v) below . .

(i) Name of Entity	**(ii)** Employer Identification Number (if any)	**(iii)** Type of Entity	**(iv)** Country of Organization	**(v)** Maximum Percentage Owned in Profit, Loss, or Capital

			Yes	No

5   Did the partnership file Form 8893, Election of Partnership Level Tax Treatment, or an election statement under section 6231(a)(1)(B)(ii) for partnership-level tax treatment, that is in effect for this tax year? See Form 8893 for more details . . . .

6   Does the partnership satisfy **all four** of the following conditions?

   a   The partnership's total receipts for the tax year were less than $250,000.

   b   The partnership's total assets at the end of the tax year were less than $1 million.

   c   Schedules K-1 are filed with the return and furnished to the partners on or before the due date (including extensions) for the partnership return.

   d   The partnership is not filing and is not required to file Schedule M-3 . . . .

     If "Yes," the partnership is not required to complete Schedules L, M-1, and M-2; Item F on page 1 of Form 1065; or Item L on Schedule K-1.

7   Is this partnership a publicly traded partnership as defined in section 469(k)(2)? . . . .

8   During the tax year, did the partnership have any debt that was cancelled, was forgiven, or had the terms modified so as to reduce the principal amount of the debt? . . . .

9   Has this partnership filed, or is it required to file, Form 8918, Material Advisor Disclosure Statement, to provide information on any reportable transaction? . . . .

10   At any time during calendar year 2017, did the partnership have an interest in or a signature or other authority over a financial account in a foreign country (such as a bank account, securities account, or other financial account)? See the instructions for exceptions and filing requirements for FinCEN Form 114, Report of Foreign Bank and Financial Accounts (FBAR). If "Yes," enter the name of the foreign country. ▶

Form **1065** (2017)

651117

☐ Final K-1	☐ Amended K-1	OMB No. 1545-0123

Schedule K-1
(Form 1065)
Department of the Treasury
Internal Revenue Service

2017

For calendar year 2017, or tax year

beginning / / 2017   ending / /

Partner's Share of Income, Deductions, Credits, etc.
▶ See back of form and separate instructions.

Part I	Information About the Partnership

A   Partnership's employer identification number

B   Partnership's name, address, city, state, and ZIP code

C   IRS Center where partnership filed return

D   ☐ Check if this is a publicly traded partnership (PTP)

Part II	Information About the Partner

E   Partner's identifying number

F   Partner's name, address, city, state, and ZIP code

G   ☐ General partner or LLC member-manager   ☐ Limited partner or other LLC member

H   ☐ Domestic partner   ☐ Foreign partner

I1   What type of entity is this partner? _____

I2   If this partner is a retirement plan (IRA/SEP/Keogh/etc.), check here ☐

J   Partner's share of profit, loss, and capital (see instructions):

	Beginning	Ending
Profit	%	%
Loss	%	%
Capital	%	%

K   Partner's share of liabilities at year end:

Nonrecourse . . . . $ _____
Qualified nonrecourse financing . $ _____
Recourse . . . . $ _____

L   Partner's capital account analysis:

Beginning capital account . . . $ _____
Capital contributed during the year $ _____
Current year increase (decrease) . $ _____
Withdrawals & distributions . . $ (_____)
Ending capital account . . . . $ _____

☐ Tax basis   ☐ GAAP   ☐ Section 704(b) book
☐ Other (explain)

M   Did the partner contribute property with a built-in gain or loss?
☐ Yes   ☐ No
If "Yes," attach statement (see instructions)

Part III	Partner's Share of Current Year Income, Deductions, Credits, and Other Items

1 Ordinary business income (loss)	15 Credits
2 Net rental real estate income (loss)	
3 Other net rental income (loss)	16 Foreign transactions
4 Guaranteed payments	
5 Interest income	
6a Ordinary dividends	
6b Qualified dividends	
7 Royalties	
8 Net short-term capital gain (loss)	
9a Net long-term capital gain (loss)	17 Alternative minimum tax (AMT) items
9b Collectibles (28%) gain (loss)	
9c Unrecaptured section 1250 gain	
10 Net section 1231 gain (loss)	18 Tax-exempt income and nondeductible expenses
11 Other income (loss)	
	19 Distributions
12 Section 179 deduction	
13 Other deductions	
	20 Other information
14 Self-employment earnings (loss)	

*See attached statement for additional information.

For IRS Use Only

For Paperwork Reduction Act Notice, see Instructions for Form 1065.   www.irs.gov/Form1065   Cat. No. 11394R   **Schedule K-1 (Form 1065) 2017**

Source: Schedule K-1, Form 1041, Department of the Treasury—Internal Revenue Service, 2017

Form **1120**	**U.S. Corporation Income Tax Return**	OMB No. 1545-0123

Department of the Treasury
Internal Revenue Service

For calendar year 2017 or tax year beginning _____, 2017, ending _____, 20 _____

▶ Go to *www.irs.gov/Form1120* for instructions and the latest information.

2017

A Check if:

1a Consolidated return (attach Form 851) ☐
  b Life/nonlife consoli-dated return ☐
2 Personal holding co. (attach Sch. PH) ☐
3 Personal service corp. (see instructions) ☐
4 Schedule M-3 attached ☐

TYPE OR PRINT

Name

Number, street, and room or suite no. If a P.O. box, see instructions.

City or town, state, or province, country, and ZIP or foreign postal code

B Employer identification number

C Date incorporated

D Total assets (see instructions)
$

E Check if: **(1)** ☐ Initial return **(2)** ☐ Final return **(3)** ☐ Name change **(4)** ☐ Address change

Income

1a	Gross receipts or sales	1a	
b	Returns and allowances	1b	
c	Balance. Subtract line 1b from line 1a	1c	
2	Cost of goods sold (attach Form 1125-A)	2	
3	Gross profit. Subtract line 2 from line 1c	3	
4	Dividends (Schedule C, line 19)	4	
5	Interest	5	
6	Gross rents	6	
7	Gross royalties	7	
8	Capital gain net income (attach Schedule D (Form 1120))	8	
9	Net gain or (loss) from Form 4797, Part II, line 17 (attach Form 4797)	9	
10	Other income (see instructions—attach statement)	10	
11	**Total income.** Add lines 3 through 10 ▶	11	

Deductions (See instructions for limitations on deductions.)

12	Compensation of officers (see instructions—attach Form 1125-E) ▶	12	
13	Salaries and wages (less employment credits)	13	
14	Repairs and maintenance	14	
15	Bad debts	15	
16	Rents	16	
17	Taxes and licenses	17	
18	Interest	18	
19	Charitable contributions	19	
20	Depreciation from Form 4562 not claimed on Form 1125-A or elsewhere on return (attach Form 4562)	20	
21	Depletion	21	
22	Advertising	22	
23	Pension, profit-sharing, etc., plans	23	
24	Employee benefit programs	24	
25	Domestic production activities deduction (attach Form 8903)	25	
26	Other deductions (attach statement)	26	
27	**Total deductions.** Add lines 12 through 26 ▶	27	
28	Taxable income before net operating loss deduction and special deductions. Subtract line 27 from line 11.	28	
29a	Net operating loss deduction (see instructions)	29a	
b	Special deductions (Schedule C, line 20)	29b	
c	Add lines 29a and 29b	29c	

Tax, Refundable Credits, and Payments

30	**Taxable income.** Subtract line 29c from line 28. See instructions	30	
31	Total tax (Schedule J, Part I, line 11)	31	
32	Total payments and refundable credits (Schedule J, Part II, line 21)	32	
33	Estimated tax penalty. See instructions. Check if Form 2220 is attached ▶ ☐	33	
34	**Amount owed.** If line 32 is smaller than the total of lines 31 and 33, enter amount owed	34	
35	**Overpayment.** If line 32 is larger than the total of lines 31 and 33, enter amount overpaid	35	
36	Enter amount from line 35 you want: **Credited to 2018 estimated tax** ▶ Refunded ▶	36	

Sign Here

Under penalties of perjury, I declare that I have examined this return, including accompanying schedules and statements, and to the best of my knowledge and belief, it is true, correct, and complete. Declaration of preparer (other than taxpayer) is based on all information of which preparer has any knowledge.

▶ _____   _____   _____
Signature of officer   Date   Title

May the IRS discuss this return with the preparer shown below? See instructions. ☐ Yes ☐ No

Paid Preparer Use Only

Print/Type preparer's name	Preparer's signature	Date	Check ☐ if self-employed	PTIN
Firm's name ▶			Firm's EIN ▶	
Firm's address ▶			Phone no.	

For Paperwork Reduction Act Notice, see separate instructions.   Cat. No. 11450Q   Form **1120** (2017)

Source: Form 1120, Department of the Treasury—Internal Revenue Service, 2017

U.S. Income Tax Return for an S Corporation

Form **1120S**

Department of the Treasury
Internal Revenue Service

▶ Do not file this form unless the corporation has filed or is attaching Form 2553 to elect to be an S corporation.
▶ Go to *www.irs.gov/Form1120S* for instructions and the latest information.

OMB No. 1545-0123

20**17**

For calendar year 2017 or tax year beginning _____, 2017, ending _____, 20____

A S election effective date	**TYPE OR PRINT**	Name	**D** Employer identification number
B Business activity code number (see instructions)		Number, street, and room or suite no. If a P.O. box, see instructions.	**E** Date incorporated
C Check if Sch. M-3 attached ☐		City or town, state or province, country, and ZIP or foreign postal code	**F** Total assets (see instructions) $

G Is the corporation electing to be an S corporation beginning with this tax year? ☐ Yes ☐ No   If "Yes," attach Form 2553 if not already filed

H Check if: **(1)** ☐ Final return **(2)** ☐ Name change **(3)** ☐ Address change **(4)** ☐ Amended return **(5)** ☐ S election termination or revocation

I Enter the number of shareholders who were shareholders during any part of the tax year . . . . ▶

Caution: Include **only** trade or business income and expenses on lines 1a through 21. See the instructions for more information.

Income

1a	Gross receipts or sales	**1a**	
b	Returns and allowances	**1b**	
c	Balance. Subtract line 1b from line 1a	**1c**	
2	Cost of goods sold (attach Form 1125-A)	**2**	
3	Gross profit. Subtract line 2 from line 1c	**3**	
4	Net gain (loss) from Form 4797, line 17 (attach Form 4797)	**4**	
5	Other income (loss) (see instructions—attach statement) . .	**5**	
6	**Total income (loss).** Add lines 3 through 5 . . . . . ▶	**6**	

Deductions (see instructions for limitations)

7	Compensation of officers (see instructions—attach Form 1125-E) . .	**7**	
8	Salaries and wages (less employment credits)	**8**	
9	Repairs and maintenance	**9**	
10	Bad debts	**10**	
11	Rents	**11**	
12	Taxes and licenses	**12**	
13	Interest	**13**	
14	Depreciation not claimed on Form 1125-A or elsewhere on return (attach Form 4562)	**14**	
15	Depletion **(Do not deduct oil and gas depletion.)** . . .	**15**	
16	Advertising	**16**	
17	Pension, profit-sharing, etc., plans	**17**	
18	Employee benefit programs	**18**	
19	Other deductions (attach statement)	**19**	
20	**Total deductions.** Add lines 7 through 19 . . . . . ▶	**20**	
21	**Ordinary business income (loss).** Subtract line 20 from line 6 . .	**21**	

Tax and Payments

22a	Excess net passive income or LIFO recapture tax (see instructions) . .	**22a**		
b	Tax from Schedule D (Form 1120S)	**22b**		
c	Add lines 22a and 22b (see instructions for additional taxes) . . .		**22c**	
23a	2017 estimated tax payments and 2016 overpayment credited to 2017	**23a**		
b	Tax deposited with Form 7004	**23b**		
c	Credit for federal tax paid on fuels (attach Form 4136) . . .	**23c**		
d	Add lines 23a through 23c		**23d**	
24	Estimated tax penalty (see instructions). Check if Form 2220 is attached . . . . . ▶ ☐		**24**	
25	**Amount owed.** If line 23d is smaller than the total of lines 22c and 24, enter amount owed		**25**	
26	**Overpayment.** If line 23d is larger than the total of lines 22c and 24, enter amount overpaid . .		**26**	
27	Enter amount from line 26 **Credited to 2018 estimated tax** ▶ _____ **Refunded** ▶		**27**	

Sign Here

Under penalties of perjury, I declare that I have examined this return, including accompanying schedules and statements, and to the best of my knowledge and belief, it is true, correct, and complete. Declaration of preparer (other than taxpayer) is based on all information of which preparer has any knowledge.

▶ _____ _____ ▶ _____
Signature of officer   Date   Title

May the IRS discuss this return with the preparer shown below (see instructions)? ☐ Yes ☐ No

Paid Preparer Use Only

Print/Type preparer's name	Preparer's signature	Date	Check ☐ if self-employed	PTIN
Firm's name ▶			Firm's EIN ▶	
Firm's address ▶			Phone no.	

For Paperwork Reduction Act Notice, see separate instructions.   Cat. No. 11510H   Form **1120S** (2017)

Source: Form 1120S, Department of the Treasury—Internal Revenue Service, 2017

671117

☐ Final K-1   ☐ Amended K-1   OMB No. 1545-0123

Schedule K-1
(Form 1120S)

2017

Department of the Treasury
Internal Revenue Service

For calendar year 2017, or tax year

beginning [/ / 2017] ending [/ /]

Shareholder's Share of Income, Deductions,
Credits, etc.   ▶ See back of form and separate instructions.

Part I	**Information About the Corporation**

A Corporation's employer identification number

B Corporation's name, address, city, state, and ZIP code

C IRS Center where corporation filed return

Part II	**Information About the Shareholder**

D Shareholder's identifying number

E Shareholder's name, address, city, state, and ZIP code

F Shareholder's percentage of stock
ownership for tax year . . . . _____ %

For IRS Use Only

Part III	**Shareholder's Share of Current Year Income, Deductions, Credits, and Other Items**	
1	Ordinary business income (loss)	13	Credits
2	Net rental real estate income (loss)	
3	Other net rental income (loss)	
4	Interest income	
5a	Ordinary dividends	
5b	Qualified dividends	14	Foreign transactions
6	Royalties	
7	Net short-term capital gain (loss)	
8a	Net long-term capital gain (loss)	
8b	Collectibles (28%) gain (loss)	
8c	Unrecaptured section 1250 gain	
9	Net section 1231 gain (loss)	
10	Other income (loss)	15	Alternative minimum tax (AMT) items
11	Section 179 deduction	16	Items affecting shareholder basis
12	Other deductions	
		17	Other information

* See attached statement for additional information.

For Paperwork Reduction Act Notice, see the Instructions for Form 1120S.   www.irs.gov/Form1120S   Cat. No. 11520D   **Schedule K-1 (Form 1120S) 2017**

Source: Schedule K-1, Form 1120S, Department of the Treasury—Internal Revenue Service, 2017

SCHEDULE M-3 (Form 1120S)	**Net Income (Loss) Reconciliation for S Corporations With Total Assets of $10 Million or More**	OMB No. 1545-0123
Department of the Treasury Internal Revenue Service	▶ Attach to Form 1120S. ▶ Go to www.irs.gov/Form1120S for instructions and the latest information.	2017

Name of corporation	Employer identification number

Part I   **Financial Information and Net Income (Loss) Reconciliation** (see instructions)

1a Did the corporation prepare a certified audited non-tax-basis income statement for the period ending with or within this tax year? See instructions if multiple non-tax-basis income statements are prepared.

  ☐ **Yes.** Skip line 1b and complete lines 2 through 11 with respect to that income statement.

  ☐ **No.** Go to line 1b.

  b Did the corporation prepare a non-tax-basis income statement for that period?

  ☐ **Yes.** Complete lines 2 through 11 with respect to that income statement.

  ☐ **No.** Skip lines 2 through 3b and enter the corporation's net income (loss) per its books and records on line 4a.

2 Enter the income statement period: Beginning   ___/___/___   Ending   ___/___/___

3a Has the corporation's income statement been restated for the income statement period on line 2?

  ☐ **Yes.** If "Yes," attach an explanation and the amount of each item restated.

  ☐ **No.**

  b Has the corporation's income statement been restated for any of the five income statement periods immediately preceding the period on line 2?

  ☐ **Yes.** If "Yes," attach an explanation and the amount of each item restated.

  ☐ **No.**

4a Worldwide consolidated net income (loss) from income statement source identified in Part I, line 1	**4a**	
b Indicate accounting standard used for line 4a (see instructions):		

  (1) ☐ GAAP   (2) ☐ IFRS

  (3) ☐ Tax-basis   (4) ☐ Other (specify) _____

5a Net income from nonincludible foreign entities (attach statement)	**5a**	( )
b Net loss from nonincludible foreign entities (attach statement and enter as a positive amount)	**5b**	
6a Net income from nonincludible U.S. entities (attach statement)	**6a**	( )
b Net loss from nonincludible U.S. entities (attach statement and enter as a positive amount)	**6b**	
7a Net income (loss) of other foreign disregarded entities (attach statement)	**7a**	
b Net income (loss) of other U.S. disregarded entities (except qualified subchapter S subsidiaries) (attach statement)	**7b**	
c Net income (loss) of other qualified subchapter S subsidiaries (QSubs) (attach statement)	**7c**	
8 Adjustment to eliminations of transactions between includible entities and nonincludible entities (attach statement)	**8**	
9 Adjustment to reconcile income statement period to tax year (attach statement)	**9**	
10 Other adjustments to reconcile to amount on line 11 (attach statement)	**10**	
11 **Net income (loss) per income statement of the corporation.** Combine lines 4 through 10	**11**	

Note: Part I, line 11, must equal Part II, line 26, column (a) or Schedule M-1, line 1. See instructions.

12 Enter the total amount (not just the corporation's share) of the assets and liabilities of all entities included or removed on the following lines:

	Total Assets	Total Liabilities
a Included on Part I, line 4		
b Removed on Part I, line 5		
c Removed on Part I, line 6		
d Included on Part I, line 7		

For Paperwork Reduction Act Notice, see the Instructions for Form 1120S.   Cat. No. 39666W   **Schedule M-3 (Form 1120S) 2017**

Name of corporation	Employer identification number

Part II — Reconciliation of Net Income (Loss) per Income Statement of the Corporation With Total Income (Loss) per Return (see instructions)

Income (Loss) Items (Attach statements for lines 1 through 10)	(a) Income (Loss) per Income Statement	(b) Temporary Difference	(c) Permanent Difference	(d) Income (Loss) per Tax Return
1 Income (loss) from equity method foreign corporations . .				
2 Gross foreign dividends not previously taxed . . .				
3 Subpart F, QEF, and similar income inclusions . .				
4 Gross foreign distributions previously taxed . . .				
5 Income (loss) from equity method U.S. corporations . .				
6 U.S. dividends not eliminated in tax consolidation .				
7 Income (loss) from U.S. partnerships				
8 Income (loss) from foreign partnerships				
9 Income (loss) from other pass-through entities . .				
10 Items relating to reportable transactions				
11 Interest income (see instructions)				
12 Total accrual to cash adjustment				
13 Hedging transactions				
14 Mark-to-market income (loss)				
15 Cost of goods sold (see instructions)	( )			( )
16 Sale versus lease (for sellers and/or lessors) . . .				
17 Section 481(a) adjustments				
18 Unearned/deferred revenue				
19 Income recognition from long-term contracts . . .				
20 Original issue discount and other imputed interest .				
21a Income statement gain/loss on sale, exchange, abandonment, worthlessness, or other disposition of assets other than inventory and pass-through entities				
b Gross capital gains from Schedule D, excluding amounts from pass-through entities				
c Gross capital losses from Schedule D, excluding amounts from pass-through entities, abandonment losses, and worthless stock losses				
d Net gain/loss reported on Form 4797, line 17, excluding amounts from pass-through entities, abandonment losses, and worthless stock losses .				
e Abandonment losses				
f Worthless stock losses (attach statement)				
g Other gain/loss on disposition of assets other than inventory				
22 Other income (loss) items with differences (attach statement)				
23 **Total income (loss) items.** Combine lines 1 through 22				
24 **Total expense/deduction items** (from Part III, line 32)				
25 Other items with no differences				
26 **Reconciliation totals.** Combine lines 23 through 25				

Note: Line 26, column (a), must equal Part I, line 11, and column (d) must equal Form 1120S, Schedule K, line 18.

Name of corporation	Employer identification number

Part III — Reconciliation of Net Income (Loss) per Income Statement of the Corporation With Total Income (Loss) per Return—Expense/Deduction Items (see instructions)

Expense/Deduction Items	(a) Expense per Income Statement	(b) Temporary Difference	(c) Permanent Difference	(d) Deduction per Tax Return
1 U.S. current income tax expense				
2 U.S. deferred income tax expense				
3 State and local current income tax expense				
4 State and local deferred income tax expense				
5 Foreign current income tax expense (other than foreign withholding taxes)				
6 Foreign deferred income tax expense				
7 Equity-based compensation				
8 Meals and entertainment				
9 Fines and penalties				
10 Judgments, damages, awards, and similar costs				
11 Pension and profit-sharing				
12 Other post-retirement benefits				
13 Deferred compensation				
14 Charitable contribution of cash and tangible property				
15 Charitable contribution of intangible property				
16 Current year acquisition or reorganization investment banking fees				
17 Current year acquisition or reorganization legal and accounting fees				
18 Current year acquisition/reorganization other costs				
19 Amortization/impairment of goodwill				
20 Amortization of acquisition, reorganization, and start-up costs				
21 Other amortization or impairment write-offs				
22 Reserved				
23a Depletion—Oil & Gas				
b Depletion—Other than Oil & Gas				
24 Depreciation				
25 Bad debt expense				
26 Interest expense (see instructions)				
27 Corporate owned life insurance premiums				
28 Purchase versus lease (for purchasers and/or lessees)				
29 Research and development costs				
30 Section 118 exclusion (attach statement)				
31 Other expense/deduction items with differences (attach statement)				
32 **Total expense/deduction items.** Combine lines 1 through 31. Enter here and on Part II, line 24, reporting positive amounts as negative and negative amounts as positive				

Schedule M-3 (Form 1120S) 2017

Source: Schedule M-3, Form 1120, Department of the Treasury—Internal Revenue Service, 2017

Appendix B

Tax Terms Glossary

83(b) election a special tax election that employees who receive restricted stock or other property with ownership restrictions can make to accelerate income recognition from the normal date when restrictions lapse to the date when the restricted stock or other property is granted. The election also accelerates the employer's compensation deduction related to the restricted stock or other property.

§162(m) limitation the $1 million deduction limit on nonperformance-based salary paid to certain key executives.

§179 expense an incentive for small businesses that allows them to immediately expense a certain amount of tangible personal property placed in service during the year.

§197 intangibles intangible assets that are purchased that must be amortized over 180 months regardless of their actual useful lives.

§291 depreciation recapture the portion of a corporate taxpayer's gain on real property that is converted from §1231 gain to ordinary income.

§338 election an election by a corporate buyer of 80-percent-or-more of a corporation's stock to treat the acquisition as an asset acquisition and not a stock acquisition.

§338(h)(10) election a joint election by the corporate buyer and corporate seller of the stock of a subsidiary of the seller to treat the acquisition as a sale of the subsidiary's assets by the seller to the buyer.

§481 adjustment a change to taxable income associated with a change in accounting methods.

§1231 assets depreciable or real property used in a taxpayer's trade or business owned for more than one year.

§1231 look-back rule a tax rule requiring taxpayers to treat current year net §1231 gains as ordinary income when the taxpayer has deducted a §1231 loss as an ordinary loss in the five years preceding the current tax year.

§1245 property tangible personal property and intangible property subject to cost recovery deductions.

§1250 property real property subject to cost recovery deductions.

12-month rule regulation that allows prepaid business expenses to be currently deducted when the contract does not extend beyond 12 months and the contract period does not extend beyond the end of the tax year following the year of the payment.

30-day letter the IRS letter received after an audit that instructs the taxpayer that he or she has 30 days to either (1) request a conference with an appeals officer or (2) agree to the proposed adjustment.

90-day letter the IRS letter received after an audit and receipt of the 30-day letter that explains that the taxpayer has 90 days to either (1) pay the proposed deficiency or (2) file a petition in the U.S. Tax Court to hear the case. The 90-day letter is also known as the *statutory notice of deficiency.*

§704(b) capital accounts partners' capital accounts maintained using the accounting rules prescribed in the Section 704(b) regulations. Under these rules, capital accounts reflect the fair market value of property contributed to and distributed property from partnerships.

A

Abandoned spouse a married taxpayer who lives apart from his or her spouse for the last six months of the year (excluding temporary absences), who files a tax return separate from his or her spouse, and who maintains a household for a qualifying child.

Accelerated death benefits early receipt of life insurance proceeds that are not taxable under certain circumstances, such as the taxpayer is medically certified with an illness that is expected to cause death within 24 months.

Accountable plan an employer's reimbursement plan under which employees must submit documentation supporting expenses to receive reimbursement and reimbursements are limited to legitimate business expenses.

Accounting method the procedure for determining the taxable year in which a business recognizes a particular item of income or deduction, thereby dictating the timing of when a taxpayer reports income and deductions.

Accounting period a fixed period in which a business reports income and deductions.

Accrual method a method of accounting that generally recognizes income in the period earned and recognizes deductions in the period that liabilities are incurred.

Accrued market discount a ratable amount of the market discount at the time of purchase (based on the number of days the bond is held over the number of days until maturity when the bond is purchased) that is treated as interest income when a bond with market discount is sold before it matures.

Accumulated adjustments account (AAA) an account that reflects the cumulative income or loss for the time the corporation has been an S corporation.

Accumulated earnings and profits undistributed earnings and profits from years prior to the current year.

Accumulated earnings tax a tax assessed on corporations that retain earnings without a business reason to do so.

Acquiescence issued after the IRS loses a trial-level or circuit court case when the IRS has decided to follow the court's adverse ruling in the future. It does not mean that the IRS agrees with the court's ruling. Instead, it simply means that the IRS will no longer litigate this issue.

Acquisition indebtedness   debt secured by a qualified residence that is incurred in acquiring, constructing, or substantially improving the residence.

Action on decision   an IRS pronouncement that explains the background reasoning behind an IRS acquiescence or nonacquiescence.

Active participant in a rental activity   an individual who owns at least 10 percent of a rental property and participates in the process of making management decisions, such as approving new tenants, deciding on rental terms, and approving repairs and capital expenditures.

Ad valorem taxes   taxes based on the value of property.

Additional Medicare tax   a tax imposed at a rate of .9% for salary or wages or net self-employment earnings in excess of $200,000 ($125,000 for married filing separate; $250,000 of combined salary or wages or net self-employment earnings for married filing joint).

Adequate consideration   a price paid that is equal in value to the service or property received.

Adjusted basis   An asset's carrying value for tax purposes at a given point in time, measured as the initial basis (for example, cost) plus capital improvements less depreciation or amortization. Also called adjusted tax basis.

Adjusted gross estate   gross estate reduced by administrative expenses, debts of the decedent, losses incurred during the administration of the estate, and state death taxes.

Adjusted gross income (AGI)   gross income less deductions for AGI. AGI is an important reference point that is often used in other calculations.

Adjusted tax basis   An asset's carrying value for tax purposes at a given point in time, measured as the initial basis (for example, cost) plus capital improvements less depreciation or amortization.

Adjusted taxable gifts   cumulative taxable gifts from previous years other than gifts already included in the gross estate valued at date of gift values.

Affiliated group   two or more "includible" corporations that are related through common stock ownership and eligible to file a U.S. consolidated tax return. An affiliated group consists of a parent corporation that owns directly 80 percent or more of the voting stock and value of another corporation and one or more subsidiary corporations that meet the 80 percent ownership requirement collectively. Includible corporations are taxable U.S. corporations, excluding real estate investment trusts, regulated investment companies, and life insurance companies.

After-tax rate of return   a taxpayer's before-tax rate of return on an investment minus the taxes paid on the income from the investment. The formula for an after-tax rate of return that is taxed annually is the before-tax rate of return $\times (1 - $ marginal tax rate) [i.e., $r = $ R $\times (1 - t)$]. A taxpayer's after-tax rate of return on an investment held for more than one tax period is $r = (FV/I)^{1/n} - 1$, where r is the after-tax rate of return, FV is the after-tax future value of the investment, I is the original investment amount, and n is the number of periods the investment is held.

Aggregate approach   a theory of taxing partnerships that ignores partnerships as entities and taxes partners as if they directly owned partnership net assets.

Alimony   a support payment of cash made to a former spouse. The payment must be made under a written separation agreement or divorce decree that does not designate the payment as something other than alimony, the payment must be made when the spouses do not live together, and the payments must cease no later than when the recipient dies.

All-events test   requires that income or expenses are recognized when (1) all events have occurred that determine or fix the right to receive the income or liability to make the payments and (2) the amount of the income or expense can be determined with reasonable accuracy.

All-inclusive income concept   a definition of income that says that gross income means all income from whatever source derived.

Allocate   as used in the sourcing rules, the process of associating a deduction with a specific item or items of gross income for purposes of computing foreign source taxable income.

Allocation   the method of dividing or sourcing nonbusiness income to specific states.

Allowance method   method used for financial reporting purposes; under this method, bad debt expense is based on an estimate of the amount of the bad debts in accounts receivable at year-end.

Alternative minimum tax (AMT)   a tax on a broader tax base than the base for the "regular" tax; the additional tax paid when the tentative minimum tax (based on the alternative minimum tax base) exceeds the regular tax (based on the regular tax base). The alternative minimum tax is designed to require taxpayers to pay some minimum level of tax even when they have low or no regular taxable income as a result of certain tax breaks in the tax code.

Alternative minimum tax (AMT) base   alternative minimum taxable income minus the alternative minimum tax exemption.

Alternative minimum tax (AMT) exemption   a deduction to determine the alternative minimum tax base that is phased out based on alternative minimum taxable income.

Alternative minimum tax adjustments   adjustments (positive or negative) to regular taxable income to arrive at the alternative minimum tax base.

Alternative minimum tax system   a secondary or parallel tax system calculated on an *alternative* tax base that more closely reflects economic income than the regular income tax base. The system was designed to ensure that taxpayers generating economic income pay some *minimum* amount of income tax each year.

Alternative valuation date   the date six months after the decedent's date of death.

Amortization   the method of recovering the cost of intangible assets over a specific time period.

Amount realized   the value of everything received by the seller in a transaction (cash, FMV of other property, and relief of liabilities) less selling costs.

Annotated tax service   a tax service arranged by code section. For each code section, an annotated service includes the code section; a listing of the code section history; copies of congressional committee reports that explain changes to the code section; a copy of all the regulations issued for the specific code section; the service's unofficial explanation of the code section; and brief summaries (called annotations) of relevant court cases, revenue rulings, revenue procedures, and letter rulings that address issues specific to the code section.

Annual exclusion   amount of gifts allowed to be made each year per donee (regardless of the number of donees) to prevent the taxation of relatively small gifts ($15,000 per donee per year currently).

Annualized income method   a method for determining a corporation's required estimated tax payments when the taxpayer earns more income later in the year than earlier in the year. Requires corporations to base their first and second required estimated tax installments on their income from the first three months of the year, their third installment based on their taxable income from the first six months of the year, and the final installment based on their taxable income from the first nine months of the year.

Annuity   a stream of equal payments over time.

Applicable credit   also known as the *unified credit*, the amount of current tax on the exemption equivalent; designed to prevent transfer taxation of smaller cumulative transfers.

Apportion   as used in the sourcing rules, the process of calculating the amount of a deduction that is associated with a specific item or items of gross income for purposes of computing foreign source taxable income.

Apportionment   the method of dividing business income of an interstate business among the states where nexus exists.

Arm's length amount price in transactions among unrelated taxpayers, where each transacting party negotiates for his or her own benefit.

Arm's length transactions transactions among unrelated taxpayers, where each transacting party negotiates for his or her own benefit.

Articles of incorporation a document, filed by a corporation's founders with the state, describing the purpose, place of business, and other details of the corporation.

Articles of organization a document, filed by a limited liability company's founders with certain states, describing the purpose, place of business, and other details of the company.

Assignment of income doctrine the judicial doctrine holding that earned income is taxed to the taxpayer providing the service, and that income from property is taxed to the individual who owns the property when the income accrues.

At-risk amount an investor's risk of loss in a worst-case scenario. In a partnership, an amount generally equal to a partner's tax basis exclusive of the partner's share of nonrecourse debt.

At-risk rules tax rules limiting the losses flowing through to partners or S corporation shareholders to their amount "at risk" in the partnership.

Average tax rate a taxpayer's average level of taxation on each dollar of taxable income. Specifically,

$$\text{Average tax rate} = \frac{\text{Total tax}}{\text{Taxable income}}$$

B

Bargain element (of stock options) the difference between the fair market value of the employer's stock and the amount employees pay to acquire the employer's stock.

Barter clubs organizations that facilitate the exchange of rights to goods and services between members.

Base erosion and anti-abuse tax (BEAT) a 10 percent minimum tax imposed on a U.S. corporation's payments of interest and royalties to a related foreign party.

Basis a taxpayer's unrecovered investment in an asset that provides a reference point for measuring gain or loss when an asset is sold.

Before-tax rate of return a taxpayer's rate of return on an investment before paying taxes on the income from the investment.

Beneficiary person for whom trust property is held and administered.

Bond a debt instrument issued for a period of more than one year with the purpose of raising capital by borrowing.

Bond discount the result of issuing bonds for less than their maturity value.

Bond premium the result of issuing bonds for more than their maturity value.

Bonus depreciation additional depreciation allowed in the acquisition year for tangible personal property with a recovery period of 20 years or less.

Book (financial reporting) income the income or loss corporations report on their financial statements using applicable financial accounting standards.

Book equivalent of taxable income a company's pretax income from continuing operations adjusted for permanent differences.

Book–tax difference a difference in the amount of an income item or deduction item taken into account for book purposes compared to the amount taken into account for the same item for tax purposes.

Boot property given or received in an otherwise nontaxable transaction such as a like-kind exchange that may trigger gain to a party to the transaction. The term *boot* derives from a trading expression describing additional property a party to an exchange might throw in "to boot" to equalize the exchange.

Bracket a subset (or portion) of the tax base subject to a specific tax rate. Brackets are common to graduated taxes.

Branch an unincorporated division of a corporation.

Bright line tests technical rules found in the tax law that provide the taxpayer with objective tests to determine the tax consequences of a transaction.

Built-in gain the difference between the fair market value and tax basis of property owned by an entity when the fair market value exceeds the tax basis.

Built-in gains tax a tax levied on S corporations that were formerly C corporations. The tax applies to net unrealized built-in gains at the time the corporation converted from a C corporation to the extent the gains are recognized during the built-in gains tax recognition period. The applicable tax rate is 21 percent.

Built-in gains tax recognition period the first five years a corporation operates as an S corporation after converting from a C corporation.

Built-in loss the difference between the fair market value and tax basis of property owned by an entity when the tax basis exceeds the fair market value.

Bunching itemized deductions a common planning strategy in which a taxpayer pays two year's worth of itemized expenses in one year to exceed the standard deduction in that year.

Business activity a profit-motivated activity that requires a relatively high level of involvement or effort from the taxpayer to generate income.

Business income income derived from business activities.

Business purpose doctrine the judicial doctrine that allows the IRS to challenge and disallow business expenses for transactions with no underlying business motivation.

Business tax credits nonrefundable credits designed to provide incentives for taxpayers to hire certain types of individuals or to participate in certain business activities.

C

C corporation a corporate taxpaying entity with income subject to taxation. Such a corporation is termed a "C" corporation because the corporation and its shareholders are subject to the provisions of Subchapter C of the Internal Revenue Code.

Cafeteria plan an employer plan that allows employees to choose benefits from a menu of nontaxable fringe benefits or receive cash compensation in lieu of the benefits.

Capital account an account reflecting a partner's share of the equity in a partnership. Capital accounts are maintained using tax accounting methods or other methods of accounting, including GAAP, at the discretion of the partnership.

Capital asset in general, an asset other than an asset used in a trade or business or an asset such as an account or note receivable acquired in a business from the sale of services or property.

Capital gain property any asset that would have generated a long-term capital gain if the taxpayer had sold the property for its fair market value.

Capital interest an economic right attached to a partnership interest giving a partner the right to receive cash or property in the event the partnership liquidates. A capital interest is synonymous with the liquidation value of a partnership interest.

Carryover basis the basis of an asset the transferee takes in property received in a nontaxable exchange. The basis of the asset carries over from the transferor to the transferee.

Cash method   the method of accounting that recognizes income in the period in which cash, property, or services are received and recognizes deductions in the period paid.

Cash tax rate   the tax rate computed by dividing a company's taxes paid during the year by its pretax income from continuing operations.

Cashless exercise   a technique where options are exercised and at least a portion of the shares are sold in order to facilitate the purchase.

Ceiling   limitation that is the maximum amount for adjustments to taxable income (or credits). The amounts in excess of the ceiling are either lost or carried to another tax year.

Certainty   one of the criteria used to evaluate tax systems. Certainty means taxpayers should be able to determine when, where, and how much tax to pay.

Certificate of deposit (CD)   an interest-bearing debt instrument offered by banks and savings and loans. Money removed from the CD before maturity is subject to a penalty.

Certificate of limited partnership   a document limited partnerships must file with the state to be formally recognized by the state. The document is similar to articles of incorporation or articles or organization.

Certificate of organization   a document, filed by a limited liability company's founders with certain states, describing the purpose, place of business, and other details of the company.

Character of income   a type of income that is treated differently for tax purposes from other types of income. Common income characters (or types of income) include ordinary, capital, and qualified dividend.

Charitable contribution limit modified taxable income   taxable income for purposes of determining the 10 percent of taxable income deduction limitation for corporate charitable contributions. Computed as taxable income before deducting (1) any charitable contributions, (2) the dividends received deduction, and (3) capital loss carrybacks.

Child tax credit   a $2,000 tax credit, subject to an AGI phase-out, for each qualifying child who is under age 17 at the end of the year and claimed as a dependent of the taxpayer, and a $500 credit, also subject to the AGI phase-out, for other qualified dependents claimed as dependents of the taxpayer.

Circular 230   regulations issued by the IRS that govern tax practice and apply to all persons practicing before the IRS. There are five parts of Circular 230: Subpart A describes who may practice before the IRS (e.g., CPAs, attorneys, enrolled agents) and what practicing before the IRS means (tax return preparation, representing clients before the IRS, etc.). Subpart B describes the duties and restrictions that apply to individuals governed by Circular 230. Subparts C and D explain sanctions and disciplinary proceedings for practitioners violating the Circular 230 provisions. Subpart E concludes with a few miscellaneous provisions (such as the Circular 230 effective date).

Citator   a research tool that allows one to check the status of several types of tax authorities. A citator can be used to review the history of the case to find out, for example, whether it was subsequently appealed and overturned, and to identify subsequent cases that cite the case. Citators can also be used to check the status of revenue rulings, revenue procedures, and other IRS pronouncements.

Civil penalties   monetary penalties imposed when tax practitioners or taxpayers violate tax statutes without reasonable cause—for example, as the result of negligence, intentional disregard of pertinent rules, willful disobedience, or outright fraud.

Claim of right doctrine   judicial doctrine that states that income has been realized if a taxpayer receives income and there are no restrictions on the taxpayer's use of the income (for example, the taxpayer does not have an obligation to repay the amount).

Cliff vesting   a qualified plan provision allowing for benefits to vest all at once after a specified period of time has passed.

Collectibles   a type of capital asset that includes a work of art, a rug or antique, a metal or gem, a stamp or coin, an alcoholic beverage, or other similar items held for investment for more than one year.

Commercial domicile   the state where a business is headquartered and directs operations; this location may be different from the place of incorporation.

Commercial traveler exception   a statutory exception that exempts nonresidents from U.S. taxation of compensation from services if the individual is in the United States 90 days or less and earns compensation of $3,000 or less.

Common-law states   the 41 states that have not adopted community-property laws.

Community property systems   systems in which state laws dictate how the income and property is legally shared between a husband and a wife.

Community-property states   nine states (Arizona, California, Idaho, Louisiana, Nevada, New Mexico, Texas, Washington, and Wisconsin) that automatically equally divide the ownership of property acquired by either spouse during a marriage.

Commuting   traveling from a personal residence to the place of business.

Complex trust   a trust that is not required by the trust instrument to distribute income currently.

Consolidated tax return   a combined U.S. income tax return filed by an affiliated group of corporations.

Consolidation   the combining of the assets and liabilities of two or more corporations into a new entity.

Constructive ownership   rules that cause stock not owned by a taxpayer to be treated as owned by the taxpayer for purposes of meeting certain stock ownership tests.

Constructive receipt doctrine   the judicial doctrine that provides that a taxpayer must recognize income when it is actually or constructively received. Constructive receipt is deemed to have occurred if the income has been credited to the taxpayer's account or if the income is unconditionally available to the taxpayer, the taxpayer is aware of the income's availability, and there are no restrictions on the taxpayer's control over the income.

Continuity of business enterprise (COBE)   a judicial (now regulatory) requirement that the acquiring corporation continue the target corporation's historic business or continue to use a "significant" portion of the target corporation's historic business assets to be tax-deferred.

Continuity of interest (COI)   a judicial (now regulatory) requirement that the transferors of stock in a reorganization collectively retain a continuing ownership (equity) interest in the target corporation's assets or historic business to be tax-deferred.

Contribution to capital   a shareholder's or other person's contribution of cash or other property to a corporation without receipt of an additional equity interest in the corporation.

Controlled foreign corporation (CFC)   a foreign corporation that is more than 50 percent owned by U.S. shareholders.

Convenience   one of the criteria used to evaluate tax systems. Convenience means a tax system should be designed to facilitate the collection of tax revenues without undue hardship on the taxpayer or the government.

Corporation   business entity recognized as a separate entity from its owners under state law.

Corpus   the principal or property transferred to fund a trust or accumulated in the trust.

Correspondence examination   an IRS audit conducted by mail and generally limited to one or two items on the taxpayer's return. Among the three types of audits, correspondence audits are generally the most common, the most narrow in scope, and least complex. The IRS typically requests supporting documentation for one or more items on the taxpayer's return (e.g., documentation of charitable contributions deducted).

Cost depletion   the method of recovering the cost of a natural resource that allows a taxpayer to estimate or determine the number of units that remain in the resource at the beginning of the year and allocate a pro rata share of the remaining basis to each unit of the resource that is extracted or sold during the year.

Cost recovery   the method by which a company expenses the cost of acquiring capital assets. Cost recovery can take the form of depreciation, amortization, or depletion.

Covenant not to compete   a contractual promise to refrain from conducting business or professional activities similar to those of another party.

Criminal penalties   penalties commonly charged in tax evasion cases (i.e., willful intent to defraud the government). They are imposed only after normal due process, including a trial. Compared to civil cases, the standard of conviction is higher in a criminal trial (beyond a reasonable doubt). However, the penalties are also much higher, such as fines up to $100,000 for individuals plus a prison sentence.

Current earnings and profits   a year-to-year calculation maintained by a corporation to determine if a distribution is a dividend. Earnings and profits are computed for the current year by adjusting taxable income to make it more closely resemble economic income.

Current gifts   gifts completed during the calendar year that are not already exempted from the gift tax.

Current income tax expense (benefit)   the amount of taxes paid or payable (refundable) in the current year.

Current tax liability (asset)   the amount of taxes payable (refundable) in the current year.

D

De minimis **fringe benefit**   a nontaxable fringe benefit that allows employees to receive occasional or incidental benefits tax-free.

Debt basis   the outstanding principal of direct loans from an S corporation shareholder to the S corporation. Once taxpayers deduct losses to the extent of their stock basis, they may deduct losses to the extent of their debt basis. When the debt basis has been reduced by losses, it is restored by income/gain allocations.

Deceased spousal unused exclusion (DSUE)   amount of unused applicable credit from predeceased spouse.

Deductible temporary differences   book–tax differences that will result in tax deductible amounts in future years when the related deferred tax asset is recovered.

Deductions   amounts that are subtracted from gross income in calculating taxable income.

Deductions above the line   *for* AGI deductions or deductions subtracted from gross income to determine AGI.

Deductions below the line   *from* AGI deductions or deductions subtracted from AGI to calculate taxable income.

Deduction for qualified business income   subject to limitations, equal to 20 percent of the taxpayer's qualified business income.

Deferral items, deferred income, or deferrals   realized income that will be taxed as income in a subsequent year.

Deferral method   recognizes income from advance payments for goods by the earlier of (1) when the business would recognize the income for tax purposes if it had not received the *advance* payment or (2) when it recognizes the income for financial reporting purposes.

Deferred like-kind exchange   a like-kind exchange where the taxpayer transfers like-kind property before receiving the like-kind property in exchange. The property to be received must be identified within 45 days and received within 180 days of the transfer of the property given up.

Deferred tax asset   the expected future tax benefit attributable to deductible temporary differences and carryforwards.

Deferred tax liability   the expected future tax cost attributable to taxable temporary differences.

Defined benefit plans   employer-provided qualified plans that spell out the specific benefit employees will receive on retirement.

Defined contribution plans   employer-provided qualified plans that specify the maximum annual contributions employers and/or employees may contribute to the plan.

Definitely related deductions   deductions that are associated with the creation of a specific item or items of gross income.

Dependent   a qualifying child or qualifying relative of the taxpayer.

Depletion   the cost recovery method to allocate the cost of natural resources as they are removed.

Depreciation   the cost recovery method to allocate the cost of tangible personal and real property over a specific time period.

Depreciation recapture   the conversion of §1231 gain into ordinary income on a sale (or exchange) based on the amount of accumulated depreciation on the property at the time of sale or exchange.

Determination letters   rulings requested by the taxpayer, issued by local IRS directors, and generally not controversial. An example of a determination letter is the request by an employer for the IRS to rule that the taxpayer's retirement plan is a "qualified plan."

DIF (Discriminant Function) system   the DIF system assigns a score to each tax return that represents the probability that the tax liability on the return has been underreported (a higher score = a higher likelihood of underreporting). The IRS derives the weights assigned to specific tax return attributes from historical IRS audit adjustment data from the National Research Program. The DIF system then uses these (undisclosed) weights to score each tax return based on the tax return's characteristics. Returns with higher DIF scores are then reviewed to determine if an audit is the best course of action.

Direct conversion   when a taxpayer receives noncash property rather than a cash payment as a replacement for property damaged or destroyed in an involuntary conversion.

Direct write-off method   required method for deducting bad debts for tax purposes. Under this method, businesses deduct bad debt only when the debt becomes wholly or partially worthless.

Disability insurance   sometimes called sick pay or wage replacement insurance. It pays the insured for wages lost due to injury or disability.

Discharge of indebtedness   debt forgiveness.

Discount factor   the factor based on the taxpayer's rate of return that is used to determine the present value of future cash inflows (e.g., tax savings) and outflows (taxes paid).

Disproportionate distributions   partnership distributions that change the partners' relative ownership of hot assets.

Disqualifying disposition   the sale of stock acquired using incentive stock options prior to satisfying certain holding period requirements. Failing to satisfy the holding period requirements converts the options into nonqualified stock options.

Disregarded entities   unincorporated entity with one owner that is considered to be the same entity as the owner.

Disregarded entities (international tax)   entities with one owner that are treated as flow-through entities for U.S. income tax purposes.

Distributable net income (DNI)   the maximum amount of the distribution deduction by fiduciaries and the maximum aggregate amount of gross income reportable by beneficiaries.

Distribution deduction   deduction by fiduciaries for distributions of income to beneficiaries that operates to eliminate the potential for double taxation of fiduciary income.

Dividend   a distribution to shareholders of money or property from the corporation's earnings and profits.

Dividends received deduction (DRD)   a corporate deduction for part or all of a dividend received from other domestic corporations.

Document perfection program   a program under which all tax returns are checked for mathematical and tax calculation errors.

Donee   person receiving a gift.

Donor   person making a gift.

Double taxation   the tax burden when an entity's income is subject to two levels of tax. Income of C corporations is subject to double taxation. The first level of tax is at the corporate level and the second level of tax on corporate income occurs at the shareholder level.

DRD modified taxable income   taxable income for purposes of applying the taxable income limitation for the dividends received deduction. Computed as the dividend-receiving corporation's taxable income before deducting the dividends received deduction, any net operating loss deduction, and capital loss carrybacks.

Dwelling unit   property that provides a place suitable for people to occupy (live and sleep).

Dynamic forecasting   the process of forecasting tax revenues that incorporates into the forecast how taxpayers may alter their activities in response to a tax law change.

E

Earmarked tax   a tax assessed for a specific purpose (e.g., for education).

Earned income   compensation and other forms of income received for providing goods or services in the ordinary course of business.

Earned income credit   a refundable credit designed to help offset the effect of employment taxes on compensation paid to low-income taxpayers and to encourage lower income taxpayers to seek employment.

Earnings and profits   a measure of a corporation's earnings that is similar to its economic earnings. Corporate dividends are taxable to shareholders to the extent they come from earnings and profits.

Economic income tax nexus   the concept that businesses without a physical presence in the state may establish income tax nexus in the state through an economic presence there.

Economic performance test   the third requirement that must be met for an accrual method taxpayer to deduct an expense currently. The specific event that satisfies the economic performance test varies based on the type of expense.

Economic substance doctrine   judicially based doctrine that requires transactions to meaningfully change a taxpayer's economic position *and* have a substantial purpose (apart from a federal income tax purpose) in order for a taxpayer to obtain tax benefits.

Economy   one of the criteria used to evaluate tax systems. Economy means a tax system should minimize its compliance and administration costs.

Educational assistance benefit   a nontaxable fringe benefit that allows an employer to provide a certain amount of education benefits on an annual basis.

Effective tax rate   the taxpayer's average rate of taxation on each dollar of total income (taxable and nontaxable income). Specifically,

$$\text{Effective tax rate} = \frac{Total\ tax}{Total\ income}$$

Also, (for income tax footnote purposes) the tax rate computed by dividing a company's income tax provision (expense or benefit) for the year by its pretax income from continuing operations.

Effectively connected income (ECI)   net income that results from the conduct of a U.S. trade or business by a nonresident.

Employee   a person who is hired to provide services to a company on a regular basis in exchange for compensation and who does not provide these services as part of an independent business.

Employment taxes   taxes consisting of the Old Age, Survivors, and Disability Insurance (OASDI) tax, commonly called the Social Security tax, and the Medical Health Insurance (MHI) tax known as the Medicare tax.

Enacted tax rate   the statutory tax rate that will apply in the current or a future period.

Entity approach   a theory of taxing partnerships that treats partnerships as entities separate from partners.

Equity   one of the criteria used to evaluate a tax system. A tax system is considered fair or equitable if the tax is based on the taxpayer's ability to pay; taxpayers with a greater ability to pay tax, pay more tax.

Escrow account (mortgage-related)   a holding account with a taxpayer's mortgage lender. The taxpayer makes mortgage payments to the lender that include payment for the interest and principal and payments for property taxes. The lender maintains the payments for property taxes in the escrow account and uses the funds in the account to pay the property taxes when the taxes are due.

Estate   fiduciary legal entity that comes into existence upon a person's death and is empowered by the probate court to gather and transfer the decedent's real and personal property.

Estate tax   the tax paid for an estate.

Estimated tax payments   quarterly tax payments that a taxpayer makes to the government if the tax withholding is insufficient to meet the taxpayer's tax liability.

Ex-dividend date   the relevant date for determining who receives a dividend from a stock. Anyone purchasing stock before this date will receive current dividends. Otherwise, the purchaser must wait until subsequent dividends are declared before receiving them.

Excess business loss   excess of aggregate business deductions for the year over aggregate business gross income or gain of an individual taxpayer plus a threshold amount depending on filing status.

Excess net passive income   net passive investment income × passive investment income in excess of 25 percent of the S corporation's gross receipts divided by its passive investment income.

Excess net passive income tax   a tax levied on an S corporation that has accumulated earnings and profits from years in which it operated as a C corporation if the corporation reports excess net passive income.

Exchanged basis   the basis of an asset received in a nontaxable exchange. An exchanged basis is generally the basis of the asset given up in a nontaxable exchange. Exchanged basis may also be referred to as a *substituted basis*.

Excise taxes   taxes levied on the retail sale of particular products. They differ from other taxes in that the tax base for an excise tax typically depends on the *quantity* purchased rather than a monetary amount.

Excluded income or exclusions   realized income that is exempted from income taxation.

Executor   the person who takes responsibility for collecting the assets of the decedent, paying the decedent's debts, and distributing the remaining assets to the rightful heirs.

Exemption equivalent   the amount of cumulative taxable transfers a taxpayer can make without exceeding the applicable credit.

Exercise date   the date employees use their stock options to acquire employer stock at a discounted price.

Exercise price   the price at which holders of stock options may purchase stock in the corporation issuing the option.

Explicit taxes   taxes directly imposed by a government.

F

Face value   a specified final amount paid to the owner of a coupon bond on the date of maturity. The face value is also known as the *maturity value*.

Facts and circumstances test   a test used to make a subjective determination such as whether the amount of salary paid to an employee is reasonable. The test requires the taxpayer and the IRS to consider all the relevant facts and circumstances surrounding the situation in order to make a decision. The relevant facts and circumstances are situation-specific.

Family limited partnership   a partnership designed to save estate taxes by dividing a family business into various ownership interests representing control of operations and future income and appreciation of the assets.

Favorable book–tax difference   a book–tax difference that requires a subtraction from book income in determining taxable income.

Federal short-term interest rate   the quarterly interest rate used to determine the interest charged for tax underpayments (federal short-term rate plus 3 percent).

Federal/state adjustments   amounts added to or subtracted from federal taxable income when firms compute taxable income for a particular state.

FICA taxes   FICA (Federal Insurance Contributions Act) taxes is a term used to denote both the Social Security and Medicare taxes upon earned income. For self-employed taxpayers, the terms "FICA tax" and "self-employment tax" are synonymous.

Fiduciary   a person or legal entity that takes possession of property for the benefit of beneficiaries.

Fiduciary duty   a requirement that a fiduciary act in an objective and impartial manner and not favor one beneficiary over another.

Field examination   the least common audit. The IRS conducts these audits at the taxpayer's place of business or the location where the taxpayer's books, records, and source documents are maintained. Field examinations are generally the broadest in scope and most complex of the three audit types. They can last many months to multiple years and generally are limited to business returns and the most complex individual returns.

Filing status   filing status places taxpayers into one of five categories (married filing jointly, married filing separately, qualifying widow or widower, head of household, and single) by marital status and family situation as of the end of the year. Filing status determines whether a taxpayer must file a tax return, appropriate tax rate schedules, standard deduction amounts, and certain deduction and credit limitation thresholds.

Final regulations   regulations that have been issued in final form, and thus, until revoked, they represent the Treasury's interpretation of the Code.

First-in, first-out (FIFO) method   an accounting method that values the cost of assets sold under the assumption that the assets are sold in the same order in which they are purchased (i.e., first purchased, first sold).

Fiscal year   a year that ends on the last day of a month other than December.

Fixed and determinable, annual or periodic income (FDAP)   U.S. source passive income earned by a nonresident.

Flat tax   a tax in which a single tax rate is applied throughout the tax base.

Flexible spending account (FSA)   a plan that allows employees to contribute before-tax dollars that may be used for unreimbursed medical expenses or dependent care.

Flipping   a term used to describe the real estate investment practice of acquiring a home, repairing or remodeling the home, and then immediately, or soon thereafter, selling it (presumably at a profit).

Floor limitation   a minimum amount that an expenditure (or credit or other adjustment to taxable income) must meet before any amount is allowed.

Flow-through entities   legal entities, like partnerships, limited liability companies, and S corporations, that do not pay income tax. Income and losses from flow-through entities are allocated to their owners.

For AGI deductions   deductions that are subtracted from gross income to determine AGI.

For the convenience of the employer benefits   nontaxable benefits employers provide to employees and employee spouses or dependents in the form of meals or lodging if provided on the employer's premises and provided for a purpose that is helpful or convenient for the employer.

Foreign base company sales income   gross profit from the sale of personal property by (to) a U.S. corporation to (from) a CFC, where the product was manufactured outside the country of incorporation of the CFC and resold outside the country of incorporation of the CFC.

Foreign branch company income   a foreign tax credit limitation category added by the Tax Cuts and Jobs Act for years beginning after December 31, 2017.

Foreign derived intangible income (FDII)   net income from certain export sales, services, and licensing of intangibles that is eligible for a 37.5 percent deduction by U.S. corporations.

Foreign joint venture   a 50 percent or less owned foreign entity.

Foreign personal holding company income   a category of foreign source passive income that includes interest, dividends, rents, royalties, and gains from the sale of certain foreign property.

Foreign subsidiary   a more than 50 percent owned foreign corporation.

Foreign tax credit (FTC)   a credit for income taxes paid to a foreign jurisdiction.

Foreign tax credit limitation   the limit put on the use of creditable foreign taxes for the current year.

Form 1065   the form partnerships file annually with the IRS to report partnership ordinary income (loss) and separately stated items for the year.

Form 1120S   the form S corporations file annually with the IRS to report S corporation ordinary income (loss) and separately stated items for the year.

Form 2553   the form filed to elect S corporation status.

Form 7004   the form C corporations, partnerships, and S corporations file to receive an automatic extension to file their annual tax return.

Form W-2   a form filed by the employer for each employee detailing the income, Social Security, and Medicare wages and taxes withheld. Additionally, state income, state taxes withheld, dependent care benefits, and many other tax-related items are reported.

Form W-4   a form used by a taxpayer to supply her employer with the information necessary to determine the amount of tax to withhold from each paycheck.

Fringe benefits   noncash benefits provided to an employee as a form of compensation. As a general rule, fringe benefits are taxable. However, certain fringe benefits are excluded from gross income.

From AGI deductions   deductions subtracted from AGI to calculate taxable income.

FTC basket   a category of income that requires a separate FTC limitation computation.

Full-inclusion method   the method for accounting for advance payments for goods that requires that businesses immediately recognize advance payments as taxable income.

Full-month convention   a convention that allows owners of intangibles to deduct an entire month's amortization in the month of purchase and month of disposition.

Functional currency   the currency of the primary economic environment in which an entity operates (i.e., the currency of the jurisdiction in which an entity primarily generates and expends cash).

Future interest   the right to receive property in the future.

G

GAAP capital accounts   partners' capital accounts maintained using generally accepted accounting principles (GAAP).

General category income   foreign source income that is not considered passive category income for foreign tax credit purposes (generally income from an active trade or business).

General partnership (GP)   a partnership with partners who all have unlimited liability with respect to the liabilities of the entity.

Generation-skipping tax (GST)   supplemental transfer tax designed to prevent the avoidance of estate and gift taxes through transfers that skip a generation of recipients.

Gift   a transfer of property where no, or inadequate, consideration is paid for the property.

Gift tax   the tax paid on a gift.

Global low-taxed intangible income (GILTI)   a new category of subpart F income added by the Tax Cuts and Jobs Act that relates to "high return" income earned by a U.S. corporation's CFC and subject to a low foreign tax rate.

Golsen rule   the rule that states that the U.S. Tax Court will abide by the rulings of the circuit court that has appellate jurisdiction for a case.

Graded vesting   a qualified plan rule that requires an increasing percentage of plan benefits to vest with each additional year of employment.

Graduated taxes   taxes in which the tax base is divided into a series of monetary amounts, or brackets, where each successive bracket is taxed at a different (gradually higher or gradually lower) percentage rate.

Grant date   the date on which employees receive stock options to acquire employer stock at a specified price.

Grant date (stock options)   the date on which employees receive stock options to acquire employer stock at a specified price.

Grantor   person creating a trust.

Gross estate   property owned by the decedent at death and certain property transfers taking effect at death.

Gross income   realized income minus excluded and deferred income.

Gross receipts   the total amount of revenues (including passive investment income) received or accrued under the corporation's accounting method, not reduced by returns, allowances, cost of goods sold, or deductions. Gross receipts include net capital gains from the sales or exchanges of capital assets and gains from the sale or exchange of stock or securities (losses do not offset gains).

Group-term life insurance   term life insurance provided by an employer to a group of employees.

Guaranteed payments   payments made to partners or LLC members that are guaranteed because they are not contingent on partnership profits or losses. They are economically similar to shareholder salary payments.

H

Half-year convention   a depreciation convention that allows owners of tangible personal property to take one-half of a year's worth of depreciation in the year of purchase and in the year of disposition regardless of when the asset was actually placed in service or sold.

Head of household   one of five primary filing statuses. A taxpayer may file as head of household if s/he is unmarried as of the end of the year *and* pays more than half of the cost to maintain a household for a qualifying person who lives with the taxpayer for more than half of the year; or, s/he pays more than half the costs to maintain a household for a parent who qualifies as the taxpayer's dependent.

Health and accident insurance   fringe benefits often offered through employers, including health insurance, group-term life insurance, and accidental death and dismemberment policies.

Heirs   persons who inherit property from the deceased.

Home office deductions   deductions relating to the use of an office in the home. A taxpayer must meet strict requirements to qualify for the deduction.

Horizontal equity   one of the dimensions of equity. Horizontal equity is achieved if taxpayers in similar situations pay the same tax.

Hot assets   unrealized receivables or inventory items defined in §751(a) that give rise to ordinary gains and losses. The exact definition of hot assets depends on whether it is in reference to dispositions of a partnership interest or distributions.

Hybrid entity   an entity for which an election is available to choose the entity's tax status for U.S. tax purposes.

I

Impermissible accounting method   an accounting method prohibited by tax laws.

Implicit taxes   indirect taxes that result from a tax advantage the government grants to certain transactions to satisfy social, economic, or other objectives. They are defined as the reduced before-tax return that a tax-favored asset produces because of its tax-advantaged status.

Imputed income   income from an economic benefit the taxpayer receives indirectly rather than directly. The amount of the income is based on comparable alternatives.

Inbound transaction   a transaction conducted by a foreign person that is subject to U.S. taxation.

Incentive stock option (ISO)   a type of stock option that allows employees to defer the bargain element for regular tax purposes until the stock acquired from option exercises is sold. The bargain element is taxed at capital gains rates provided the stock is retained long enough to satisfy certain holding period requirements. Employers cannot deduct the bargain element as compensation expense.

Income effect   one of the two basic responses that a taxpayer may have when taxes increase. The income effect predicts that when taxpayers are taxed more (e.g., tax rate increases from 25 to 28 percent), they will work harder to generate the same after-tax dollars.

Income tax   a tax in which the tax base is income. Income taxes are imposed by the federal government and by most states.

Income tax nexus   the connection between a business and a tax jurisdiction sufficient to subject the business to the tax jurisdiction's income tax.

Independent contractor   a person who provides services to another entity, usually under terms specified in a contract. The independent contractor has more control over how and when to do the work than does an employee.

Indirect conversion   the receipt of money or other property as a replacement for property that was destroyed or damaged in an involuntary conversion.

Individual retirement account (IRA)   a tax-advantaged account in which individuals who have earned income can save for retirement.

Information matching program   a program that compares the taxpayer's tax return to information submitted to the IRS from other taxpayers (e.g., banks, employers, mutual funds, brokerage companies, mortgage companies). Information matched includes items such as wages (e.g., Form W-2 submitted by employers), interest income (e.g., Form 1099-INT submitted by banks), dividend income (e.g., Form 1099-DIV submitted by brokerage companies), and so forth.

Inheritance   a transfer of property when the owner is deceased (the transfer is made by the decedent's estate).

Initial public offering (IPO)   the first sale of stock by a company to the public.

Inside basis   the tax basis of an entity's assets and liabilities.

Installment sale   a sale for which the taxpayer receives payment in more than one period.

Institutional shareholders   entities, such as investment companies, mutual funds, brokerages, insurance companies, pension funds, investment banks, and endowment funds, with large amounts to invest in corporate stock.

Intangible assets   assets that do not have physical characteristics. Examples include goodwill, covenants not to compete, organizational expenditures, and research and experimentation expenses.

Inter vivos transfers   gifts made by a donor during his or her lifetime.

Internal Revenue Code of 1986   the codified tax laws of the United States. Although the Code is frequently revised, there have been only three different codes since the Code was created in 1939 (i.e., the IRC of 1939, IRC of 1954, and IRC of 1986).

Interpretative regulations   the most common regulations; they represent the Treasury's interpretation of the Code and are issued under the Treasury's general authority to interpret the Code.

Interstate commerce   business conducted between parties in two or more states.

Inventory items   (for sale of partnership interest purposes) classic inventory defined as property held for sale to customers in the ordinary course of business, but also assets that are not capital assets or §1231 assets, which would produce ordinary income if sold by the entity. There are actually two definitions of inventory items in §751. §751(a) inventory items are defined in §751(d) to include all inventory items. The §751(b) definition includes only substantially appreciated inventory.

Investment activity   a profit-seeking activity that is intermittent or occasional in frequency, including the production or collection of income or the management, conservation, or maintenance of property held for the production of income.

Investment expenses   expenses such as safe deposit rental fees, attorney fees, and accounting fees that are necessary to produce portfolio income. Investment expenses are generally not deductible by individuals (except investment interest expense or rental or royalty expenses not associated with a trade or business).

Investment income   income received from portfolio type investments. Portfolio income includes capital gains and losses, interest, dividend, annuity, and royalty income not derived in the ordinary course of a trade or business. When computing the deductibility of investment interest expense, however, capital gains and dividends subject to the preferential tax rate are not treated as investment income unless the taxpayer elects to have this income taxed at ordinary tax rates.

Investment interest expense   interest paid on borrowings or loans that are used to fund portfolio investments. Individuals are allowed an itemized deduction for qualified investment interest paid during the year.

Involuntary conversion   a direct or indirect conversion of property through natural disaster, government condemnation, or accident that allows a taxpayer to defer realized gain if certain requirements are met.

IRS allocation method   allocates expenses associated with rental use of the home between rental use and personal use. The percentage of total expenses allocated to rental use is the ratio of the number of rental use days for the property to the total days the property was used during the year.

Itemized deductions   certain types of expenditures that Congress allows taxpayers to deduct as *from* AGI deductions.

J

Joint tenancy   joint ownership of property by two or more people.

Joint tenancy with the right of survivorship   title to property that provides the co-owners with equal rights to it and that automatically transfers to the survivor(s) at the death of a co-owner.

K

Kiddie tax   a tax imposed at trusts and estates tax rates on a child's unearned income.

L

Last will and testament   the document that directs the transfer of ownership of the decedent's assets to the heirs.

Last-in, first-out (LIFO) method   an accounting method that values the cost of assets sold under the assumption that assets are sold in the reverse order in which they are purchased (i.e., last purchased, first sold).

Late filing penalty   a penalty assessed if a taxpayer does not file a tax return by the required date (the original due date plus extension).

Late payment penalty   a tax penalty equal to .5 percent of the amount of tax owed for each month (or fraction thereof) that the tax is not paid.

Least aggregate deferral   an approach to determine a partnership's required year-end if a majority of the partners don't have the same year-end and if the principal partners don't have the same year-end. As the name implies, this approach minimizes the combined tax deferral of the partners.

Legislative grace   the concept that taxpayers receive certain tax benefits only because Congress writes laws that allow taxpayers to receive the tax benefits.

Legislative regulations   the rarest type of regulation, issued when Congress specifically directs the Treasury Department to create regulations to address an issue in an area of law. In these instances, the Treasury is actually writing the law instead of interpreting the Code. Because legislative regulations actually represent tax law instead of an interpretation of tax law, legislative regulations have more authoritative weight than interpretative and procedural regulations.

Life estate   the right to possess property and/or collect income from property for the duration of someone's life.

Life insurance trust   a trust that is funded with an irrevocable transfer of a life insurance policy and that gives the trustee the power to redesignate beneficiaries.

LIFO recapture amount   the excess of a C corporation's inventory basis under the FIFO method in excess of the inventory basis under the LIFO method in its final tax year as a C corporation before it becomes an S corporation.

LIFO recapture tax   a tax levied on a C corporation that elects to be taxed as an S corporation when it is using the LIFO method for accounting for inventories.

Like-kind exchange   a nontaxable (or partially taxable) trade or exchange of assets that are similar or related in use.

Limited liability company (LLC)   a type of flow-through entity for federal income tax purposes. By state law, the owners of the LLC have limited liability with respect to the entity's debts or liabilities. Limited liability companies are generally taxed as partnerships for federal income tax purposes.

Limited partnership (LP)   a partnership with at least one general partner with unlimited liability for the entity's debts and at least one limited partner with liability limited to the limited partner's investment in the partnership.

Liquidating distribution   a distribution that terminates an owner's interest in the entity.

Liquidation value   the amount a partner would receive if the partnership were to sell all its assets, pay its debts, and distribute its remaining assets to the partners in exchange for their partnership interests.

Listed property   business assets that are often used for personal purposes. Depreciation on listed property is limited to the business-use portion of the asset.

Local taxes   taxes imposed by local governments (cities, counties, school districts, etc.).

Long-term capital gains or losses   gains or losses from the sale of capital assets held for more than 12 months.

Luxury automobile   an automobile on which the amount of annual depreciation expense is limited because the cost of the automobile exceeds a certain threshold. The definition excludes vehicles with gross vehicle weight exceeding 6,000 pounds.

M

M adjustments   *see* Schedule M adjustments.

Majority interest taxable year   the common tax year of a group of partners who jointly hold greater than 50 percent of the profits and capital interests in the partnership.

Marginal tax rate   the tax rate that applies to the *next additional increment* of a taxpayer's taxable income (or to deductions). Specifically,

$$\text{Marginal tax rate} = \frac{\Delta Tax}{\Delta Taxable\ income}$$
$$= \frac{(New\ total\ tax - Old\ total\ tax)}{(New\ taxable\ income - Old\ taxable\ income)}$$

where "old" refers to the current tax and "new" refers to the revised tax after incorporating the additional income (or deductions) in question.

Marital deduction   the deduction for transfers of qualified property to a spouse.

Market discount   the difference between the amount paid for a bond in a market purchase rather than at original issuance when the amount paid is less than the maturity value of the bond.

Market premium   the difference between the amount paid for a bond in a market purchase rather than at original issuance when the amount paid is greater than the maturity value of the bond.

Marriage benefit   the tax savings married couples receive by filing a joint return relative to the tax they would have paid had they each filed as single taxpayers. This typically occurs when one spouse is either not working or earns significantly less than the other spouse.

Marriage penalty   the extra tax cost a married couple pays by filing a joint return relative to what they would have paid had they each filed as single taxpayers. This typically occurs when both spouses earn approximately the same amount of income.

Married filing jointly   one of five primary filing statuses. A taxpayer may file jointly if s/he is legally married as of the end of the year (or one spouse died during the year and the surviving spouse did not remarry) and both spouses agree to jointly file. Married couples filing joint returns combine their income and deductions and share joint and several liability for the resulting tax.

Married filing separately   one of five primary filing statuses. When married couples file separately, each spouse reports the income he or she received during the year and the deductions he or she paid on a tax return separate from the other spouse.

Maturity   the amount of time to the expiration date, or maturity date, of a debt instrument. The maturity of a debt instrument is generally the life of the instrument, at which point a payment of the face value is due or the instrument terminates.

Maturity value   the amount paid to a bondholder when the bond matures and the bondholder redeems the bond for cash.

Maximum 15 percent rate amount   threshold for the 15 percent rate to apply to long-term capital gains. Any 0/15/20 percent capital gains included that results in taxable income above the maximum zero rate amount and up to the maximum 15 percent rate amount are taxed at 15 percent. The threshold is based on a taxpayer's filing status and income.

Maximum zero percent rate amount   threshold for the zero percent rate to apply to long-term capital gains. Any 0/15/20 percent capital gains included in taxable income up to the maximum zero percent amount are taxed at 0 percent. It is based on a taxpayer's filing status and income level.

Medicare tax   the Medical Health Insurance (MHI) tax. This tax helps pay medical costs for qualifying individuals. The Medicare tax rate for employees and employers is 1.45 percent on salary or wages. An additional Medicare tax of .9 percent is assessed on employees (not employers) on salary or wages in excess of $200,000 ($125,000 for married filing separate; $250,000 of combined salary or wages for married filing joint). Self-employed taxpayers pay both the employee and employer Medicare tax and additional Medicare tax.

Merger   the acquisition by one (acquiring) corporation of the assets and liabilities of another (target) corporation. No new entity is created in the transaction.

Mid-month convention   a convention that allows owners of real property to take one-half of a month's depreciation during the month when the property was placed in service and in the month it was disposed of.

Mid-quarter convention   a depreciation convention for tangible personal property that allows for one-half of a quarter's worth of depreciation in the quarter of purchase and in the quarter of disposition. This convention must be used when more than 40 percent of tangible personal property is placed into service in the fourth quarter of the tax year.

Minimum tax credit credit available in certain situations for the alternative minimum tax paid. The credit can be used only when the regular tax exceeds the tentative minimum tax.

Miscellaneous itemized deductions itemized deductions such as gambling losses, casualty and theft losses on investment property, and the unrecovered cost of a life annuity (if the taxpayer died before recovering the full cost of the annuity).

Mixed-motive expenditures activities that involve a mixture of business and personal objectives.

Modified Accelerated Cost Recovery System (MACRS) the current tax depreciation system for tangible personal and real property. Depreciation under MACRS is calculated by finding the depreciation method, the recovery period, and the applicable convention.

Municipal bond the common name for state and local government debt.

Mutual fund a diversified portfolio of securities owned and managed by a regulated investment company.

N

Negative basis adjustment (for special basis adjustment purposes) the sum of the recognized loss and the amount of the basis increase made by an owner receiving the distribution.

Net capital gain the excess of net long-term capital gain for the taxable year over net short-term capital loss for such year.

Net capital loss carryback the amount of a corporation's net capital loss from one year that it uses to offset net capital gains in any of the three preceding tax years.

Net capital loss carryover the amount of a corporation's or an individual's net capital loss from one year that it may use to offset net capital gains in future years.

Net earnings from self-employment the amount of earnings subject to self-employment income taxes. The amount is 92.35 percent of a taxpayer's self-employment income.

Net investment income (for determining deductibility of investment interest expense) gross investment income reduced by deductible investment expenses.

Net investment income tax a 3.8 percent tax on the lesser of (a) net investment income or (b) the excess of modified adjusted gross income over $250,000 for married-joint filers and surviving spouses, $125,000 for married-separate filers, and $200,000 for other taxpayers.

Net long-term capital gain the excess of long-term capital gains for the taxable year over the long-term capital losses for such year.

Net long-term capital loss the excess of long-term capital losses for the taxable year over the long-term capital gains for such year.

Net operating loss (NOL) the excess of allowable deductions over gross income.

Net operating loss carryback the amount of a pre-2018 net operating loss that a corporation elects to carry back to the two previous years to offset taxable income in those years.

Net operating loss carryover the amount of a current-year net operating loss that is carried forward for up to 20 years to offset taxable income in those years. (20 years for pre-2018 losses; unlimited for post-2017 losses)

Net passive investment income passive investment income less any expenses connected with producing it.

Net short-term capital gain the excess of short-term capital gains for the taxable year over the short-term capital losses for such year.

Net short-term capital loss the excess of short-term capital losses for the taxable year over the short-term capital gains for such year.

Net unearned income unearned income in excess of a specified threshold amount of a child under the age of 19 or under the age of 24 if a full-time student.

Net unrealized built-in gain the net gain (if any) an S corporation that was formerly a C corporation would recognize if it sold each asset at its fair market value. It is measured on the first day of the corporation's first year as an S corporation.

Nexus the connection between a business and a tax jurisdiction sufficient to subject the business to the tax jurisdiction's tax system. Also, the connection that is required to exist between a jurisdiction and a potential taxpayer such that the jurisdiction asserts the right to impose a tax.

No-additional-cost services a nontaxable fringe benefit that provides employer services to employees with little cost to the employer (e.g., airline tickets or phone service).

Nonacquiescence issued after the IRS loses a trial-level or circuit court case when the IRS has decided to continue to litigate this issue.

Nonbusiness income all income except for business income—generally, investment income and rental income.

Nondeductible terminable interests transfers of property interests to a spouse that do not qualify for a marital deduction, because the interest of the spouse terminates when some event occurs or after a specified amount of time and the property is then transferred to another person.

Nondomiciliary business a business operating in a state other than its commercial domicile.

Nonqualified deferred compensation compensation provided for under a nonqualified plan allowing employees to defer compensation to a future period.

Nonqualified stock option (NQO) a type of stock option requiring employees to treat the bargain element from options exercised as ordinary income in the tax year options are exercised. Correspondingly, employers may deduct the bargain element as compensation expense in the tax year options are exercised.

Nonrecaptured net §1231 loss a net §1231 loss that is deducted as an ordinary loss in one year and has not caused subsequent §1231 gain to be taxed as ordinary income.

Nonrecognition provisions tax laws that allow taxpayers to permanently exclude income from taxation or to defer recognizing realized income until a subsequent period.

Nonrecognition transaction a transaction where at least a portion of the realized gain or loss is not currently recognized.

Nonrecourse debt debt for which no partner bears any economic risk of loss. Mortgages on real property are a common form of nonrecourse debt.

Nonrefundable credits tax credits that reduce a taxpayer's gross tax liability but are limited to the amount of gross tax liability. Any credit not used in the current year is lost.

Nonresident alien a non-U.S. citizen who does not meet the criteria to be treated as a resident for U.S. tax purposes.

Nonservice partner a partner who receives a partnership interest in exchange for property rather than services.

Nontaxable fringe benefit an employer provided benefit that may be excluded from an employee's income.

Not definitely related deductions deductions that are not associated with a specific item or items of gross income in computing the foreign tax credit limitation.

Office examination   the second most common audit. As the name suggests, the IRS conducts these audits at the local IRS office. These audits are typically broader in scope and more complex than correspondence examinations. Small businesses, taxpayers operating sole proprietorships, and middle- to high-income individual taxpayers are more likely, if audited, to have office examinations.

Operating distributions   payments from an entity to its owners that represent a distribution of entity profits. Distributions generally fall into the category of operating distributions when the owners continue their interests in the entity after the distribution.

Operating income   the annual income from a trade or business or rental activity.

Operating loss   the annual loss from a trade or business or rental activity.

Option exercise   the use of a stock option to acquire employer stock at a specified price.

Ordinary and necessary   an expense that is normal or appropriate and that is helpful or conducive to the business activity.

Ordinary asset   an asset created or used in a taxpayer's trade or business (e.g., accounts receivable or inventory) that generates ordinary income (or loss) on disposition.

Ordinary business income (loss)   a partnership's or S corporation's remaining income or loss after separately stated items are removed. It is also referred to as nonseparately stated income (loss).

Ordinary income property   property that if sold would generate income taxed at ordinary rates.

Organizational expenses   expenses associated with legally forming a partnership (such as attorneys' and accountants' fees).

Organizational expenditures   expenses that are (1) connected directly to the creation of a corporation or partnership, (2) chargeable to a capital account, and (3) generally amortized over 180 months (limited immediate expensing may be available).

Original issue discount (OID)   a type of bond issued for less than the maturity or face value of the bond.

Outbound transaction   a transaction conducted outside the United States by a U.S. person that is subject to U.S. taxation.

Outside basis   an investor's tax basis in the stock of a corporation or the interest in a partnership or LLC.

Partial liquidation   a distribution made by a corporation to shareholders that results from a contraction of the corporation's activities.

Partnership agreement   an agreement among the partners in a partnership stipulating the partners' rights and responsibilities in the partnership.

Partnership interest   an intangible asset reflecting the economic rights a partner has with respect to a partnership, including the right to receive assets in liquidation of the partnership (called a *capital interest*) and the right to be allocated profits and losses (called a *profits interest*).

Passive activity loss (PAL) rules   tax rules designed to limit taxpayers' ability to deduct losses from activities in which they don't materially participate against income from other sources.

Passive category income   foreign source personal holding company income, such as interest, dividends, rents, royalties, annuities, and gains from sale of certain assets, that is combined in computing the FTC limitation.

Passive investment income (PII)   royalties, rents, dividends, interest (including tax-exempt interest), annuities, and gains from the sale or exchange of stock or securities.

Passive investments   direct or indirect investments (other than through a C corporation) in a trade or business or rental activity in which the taxpayer does not materially participate.

Payment liabilities   liabilities of accrual method businesses for which economic performance occurs when the business actually *pays* the liability for, among others: worker's compensation; tort; breach of contract or violation of law; rebates and refunds; awards, prizes, and jackpots; insurance, warranties, and service contracts provided *to* the business; and taxes.

Percentage depletion   a method of recovering the cost of a natural resource that allows a taxpayer to recover or expense an amount based on a statutorily determined percentage.

Permanent book–tax differences   items of income or deductions for either book purposes or for tax purposes during the year but not both. Permanent differences do not reverse over time, so over the long run, the total amount of income or deduction for the item is different for book and tax purposes.

Permanent establishment   generally, a fixed place of business through which an enterprise carries out its business. Examples include a place of management, a branch, an office, and a factory.

Permissible accounting method   accounting method allowed under the tax law. Permissible accounting methods are adopted the first time a taxpayer uses the method on a tax return.

Person   an individual, trust, estate, partnership, association, company, or corporation.

Personal expenses   expenses incurred for personal motives. Personal expenses are not deductible for tax purposes.

Personal holding companies   closely held corporations generating primarily investment income.

Personal holding company tax   penalty tax on the undistributed income of a personal holding company.

Personal property   all tangible property other than real property.

Personal property tax   a tax on the fair market value of all types of tangible and intangible property, except real property.

Point   one percent of the principal amount of a loan. A home buyer might pay points to compensate the lender for services or for a lower interest rate.

Portfolio investments   investments producing dividends, interest, royalties, annuities, or capital gains.

Positive basis adjustment   (for special basis adjustment purposes) the sum of the gain recognized by the owners receiving distributed property and the amount of any required basis reduction.

Post-termination transition period (PTTP)   the period that begins on the day after the last day of a corporation's last taxable year as an S corporation and generally ends on the later of (a) one year after the last S corporation day, or (b) the due date for filing the return for the last year as an S corporation (including extensions).

Preferential tax rate   a tax rate that is lower than the tax rate applied to ordinary income.

Preferentially taxed income   income taxed at a preferential rate such as long-term capital gains and qualified dividends.

Present interest   right to presently enjoy property or receive income from the property.

Present value   the concept that $1 today is worth more than $1 in the future. For example, assuming an investor can earn a 5 percent after-tax return, $1 invested today should be worth $1.05 in one year. Hence, $1 today is equivalent to $1.05 in one year.

Primary authorities official sources of the tax law generated by the legislative branch (i.e., statutory authority issued by Congress), judicial branch (i.e., rulings by the U.S. District Court, U.S. Tax Court, U.S. Court of Federal Claims, U.S. Circuit Courts of Appeals, or U.S. Supreme Court), or executive/administrative branch (i.e., Treasury or IRS pronouncements).

Principal partner a partner having a 5 percent or more interest in partnership capital or profits.

Principal residence the main place of residence for a taxpayer during the taxable year.

Private activity bond a bond issued by a municipality but proceeds of which are used to fund privately owned activity.

Private letter rulings IRS pronouncements issued in response to a taxpayer request for a ruling on specific issues for the taxpayer. They are common for proposed transactions with potentially large tax implications. For the requesting taxpayer, a private letter ruling has very high authority. For all other taxpayers, private letter rulings have little authoritative weight.

Private nonoperating foundations privately sponsored foundations that disburse funds to other charities.

Private operating foundations privately sponsored foundations that actually fund and conduct charitable activities.

Probate the process in the probate court of gathering property possessed by or titled in the name of a decedent at the time of death, paying the debts of the decedent, and transferring the ownership of any remaining property to the decedent's heirs.

Probate estate property possessed by or titled in the name of a decedent at the time of death.

Procedural regulations regulations that explain Treasury Department procedures as they relate to administering the Code.

Production of income a for-profit activity that doesn't rise to the level of a trade or business.

Profits interest an interest in a partnership giving a partner the right to share in future profits but not the right to share in the current value of a partnership's assets. Profits interests are generally not taxable in the year they are received.

Progressive tax rate structure a tax rate structure that imposes an increasing marginal tax rate as the tax base increases. As the tax base increases, both the marginal tax rate and the taxes paid increase.

Proportional tax rate structure also known as a *flat tax*, this tax rate structure imposes a constant tax rate throughout the tax base. As the tax base increases, the taxes paid increase proportionally.

Proposed regulations regulations issued in proposed form; they do not carry the same authoritative weight as temporary or final regulations. All regulations are issued in proposed form first to allow public comment on them.

Public Law 86-272 federal law passed by Congress that provides additional protection for sellers of tangible personal property against income tax nexus.

 Q

Qualified business asset investment (QBAI) the tax basis of tangible personal property used in a trade or business that forms the basis for determining the deductions allowed for foreign derived intangible income and global low taxed intangible income.

Qualified business income net business income from a qualified trade or business conducted in the United States. This is the tax base for the deduction for qualified business income.

Qualified dividends paid by domestic or certain qualified foreign corporations that are eligible for lower capital gains rates.

Qualified educational loans loans whose proceeds are used to pay qualified education expenses.

Qualified employee discount a nontaxable fringe benefit that provides a discount on employer goods (not to be discounted below the employer's cost) and services (up to a 20 percent discount) to employees.

Qualified equity grant a broad-based equity grant of either stock options or restricted stock units by a private corporation. Eligible employees may make an inclusion deferral election that may defer the income attributable to the qualified equity for up to five years.

Qualified moving expense reimbursement a nontaxable fringe benefit that allows employers to pay moving-related expenses on behalf of employees.

Qualified nonrecourse financing nonrecourse debt secured by real property from a commercial lender unrelated to the borrower.

Qualified replacement property property acquired to replace property damaged or destroyed in an involuntary conversion. It must be of a similar or related use to the original property even if the replacement property is real property (e.g., rental real estate for rental real estate).

Qualified residence the taxpayer's principal residence and one other residence.

Qualified retirement accounts plans meeting certain requirements that allow compensation placed in the account to be tax-deferred until the taxpayer withdraws money from the account.

Qualified retirement plans employer-sponsored retirement plans that meet government-imposed funding and antidiscrimination requirements.

Qualified small business stock stock received at original issue from a corporation with a gross tax basis in its assets both before and after the issuance of no more than $50,000,000 and with 80 percent of the value of its assets used in the active conduct of certain qualified trades or businesses.

Qualified trade or business for purposes of the deduction for qualified business income, any trade or business other than a specified trade or business.

Qualified transportation fringe benefit a nontaxable fringe benefit provided by employers in the form of mass transit passes, parking, or company-owned carpool benefits.

Qualifying child an individual who qualifies as a dependent of a taxpayer by meeting a relationship, age, residence, and support test with respect to the taxpayer.

Qualifying relative an individual who is not a qualifying child of another taxpayer and who meets a relationship, support, and gross income test and thus qualifies to be a dependent of another taxpayer.

Qualifying widow or widower one of five primary filing statuses. Applies for up to two years after the year in which the taxpayer's spouse dies (the taxpayer files married filing jointly in the year of the spouse's death) as long as the taxpayer remains unmarried and maintains a household for a dependent child.

Question of fact a research question that hinges upon the facts and circumstances of the taxpayer's transaction.

Question of law a research question that hinges upon the interpretation of the law, such as interpreting a particular phrase in a code section.

 R

Real property land and structures permanently attached to land.

Real property tax a tax on the fair market value of land and structures permanently attached to land.

Realization gain or loss that results from an exchange of property rights in a transaction.

Realization principle   the proposition that income only exists when there is a transaction with another party resulting in a measurable change in property rights.

Realized gain or loss   the difference between the amount realized and the adjusted basis of an asset sold or otherwise disposed of.

Realized income   income generated in a transaction with a second party in which there is a measurable change in property rights between parties.

Reasonable in amount   an expenditure is reasonable when the amount paid is neither extravagant nor exorbitant.

Recapture   the recharacterization of income from capital gain to ordinary income.

Recognized gain or loss   the gain or loss included in gross income on a taxpayer's tax return. This is usually the realized gain or loss unless a nonrecognition provision applies.

Recourse debt   debt held by a partnership for which at least one partner has economic risk of loss.

Recovery period   a length of time prescribed by statute in which business property is depreciated or amortized.

Recurring item   an election under economic performance to currently deduct an accrued liability if the liability is expected to persist in the future and is either not material or a current deduction better matches revenue.

Refinance   when a taxpayer pays off a current loan with the proceeds of a second loan.

Regressive tax rate structure   a tax rate structure that imposes a decreasing marginal tax rate as the tax base increases. As the tax base increases, the taxes paid increase, but the marginal tax rate decreases.

Regulations   the Treasury Department's official interpretation of the Internal Revenue Code. Regulations are the highest authority issued by the IRS.

Related-party transaction   financial activities among family members, among owners and their businesses, or among businesses owned by the same owners.

Remainder   the right to ownership of a property that transfers to a new owner, the remainderman, following a temporary interest.

Remainderman   the person entitled to a remainder interest.

Reorganization   a tax-deferred transaction (acquisition, disposition, recapitalization, or change of name or place of incorporation) that meets one of the seven statutory definitions found in §368(a)(1).

Requisite service period   The period or periods during which an employee is required to provide service in exchange for an award under a share-based payment arrangement (ASC 718, Glossary).

Research and experimentation (R&E) costs   expenses for research including costs of research laboratories (salaries, materials, and other related expenses). Taxpayers can elect to amortize research and development costs over not less than 60 months from the time benefits are first derived from the research.

Residence-based jurisdiction   taxation of income based on the taxpayer's residence.

Resident alien   an individual who is not a U.S. citizen but is treated as a resident for U.S. tax purposes.

Restricted stock   stock employees receive as compensation that may be sold only after the passage of time or after certain performance targets are achieved. Because employees are not entitled to immediately sell the restricted stock they receive, the value of the stock is generally not taxable to employees or deductible by employers until the selling restrictions lapse.

Restricted stock units   a form of stock equity compensation. Restricted stock units are valued in terms of company stock, but because the restricted stock is not issued at the grant date there are no immediate

tax consequences. Many plans allow the employee to choose whether to settle the grant in either stock or cash.

Return of capital   the portion of proceeds from a sale (or distribution) representing a return of the original cost of the underlying property.

Revenue procedures   second in administrative authoritative weight after regulations. Revenue procedures are much more detailed than regulations and explain in greater detail IRS practice and procedures in administering the tax law. Revenue procedures have the same authoritative weight as revenue rulings.

Revenue rulings   second in administrative authoritative weight after regulations. Revenue rulings address the specific application of the Code and regulations to a specific factual situation. Revenue rulings have the same authoritative weight as revenue procedures.

Reverse hybrid entity   a "check-the-box" entity owned by multiple persons for which corporation status is elected.

Reversion   terms by which ownership of property returns to the original owner following a temporary interest.

Rollover   a transfer of funds from a qualified retirement plan to another qualified retirement plan, from a qualified retirement plan to a Roth or traditional IRA, or from a traditional IRA to a Roth IRA.

Roth 401(k)   a type of defined contribution plan that allows employees to contribute on an after-tax basis and receive distributions tax-free.

Roth IRA   an individually managed retirement plan permitting individuals to contribute on an after-tax basis and receive distributions tax-free.

 S

S corporation   a corporation under state law that has elected to be taxed under the rules provided in Subchapter S of the Internal Revenue Code. Under Subchapter S, an S corporation is taxed as a flow-through entity.

Safe-harbor provision   provision of the tax law that reduces or eliminates a taxpayer's liability under the law if the taxpayer meets certain requirements.

Salary   a fixed regular payment by an employer to an employee in exchange for the employee's services; usually paid on a monthly basis, but typically expressed as an annual amount.

Sales tax   a tax imposed on the retail price of goods (plus certain services). Retailers are responsible for collecting and remitting the tax; typically sales tax is collected at the point of sale.

Sales tax nexus   the connection between a business and a tax jurisdiction sufficient to subject the business to the tax jurisdiction's sales tax.

Same-day sale   a phrase used to describe a situation where a taxpayer exercises stock options and then immediately sells the stock received through the option exercise.

Schedule C   a schedule on which a taxpayer reports the income and deductions for a sole proprietorship.

Schedule K   a schedule filed with a partnership's annual tax return listing its ordinary income (loss) and its separately stated items.

Schedule M adjustments   book–tax differences that corporations report on the Schedule M-1 or M-3 of Form 1120 as adjustments to book income to reconcile to taxable income.

Secondary authorities   unofficial tax authorities that interpret and explain the primary authorities, such as tax research services, tax articles, newsletters, and textbooks. Secondary authorities may be very helpful in understanding a tax issue, but they hold little weight in a tax dispute (hence, the term *unofficial* tax authorities).

Self-employment taxes   Social Security and Medicare taxes paid by the self-employed on a taxpayer's net earnings from self-employment. For self-employed taxpayers, the terms "self-employment tax" and "FICA tax" are synonymous.

SEP IRA   a simplified employee pension (SEP) that is administered through an individual retirement account (IRA). Available to self-employed taxpayers.

Separate tax return   a state tax return methodology requiring that each related entity with nexus must file a separate tax return.

Separately stated items   income, expenses, gains, losses, credits, and other items that are excluded from a partnership's or S corporation's operating income (loss) and disclosed to partners in a partnership or shareholders of an S corporation separately because their tax effects may be different for each partner or shareholder.

Serial gift   transfer tax strategy that uses the annual exclusion to convert a potentially large taxable transfer into a tax-exempt transfer by dividing it into multiple inter vivos gifts spread over several periods or donees.

Service partner   a partner who receives a partnership interest by contributing services rather than cash or property.

Settlement statement   a statement that details the monies paid out and received by the buyer and seller in a real estate transaction.

Short-term capital gains or losses   gains or losses from the sale of capital assets held for one year or less.

Simple trust   a trust that must distribute all accounting income currently and cannot make charitable contributions.

Sin taxes   taxes imposed on the purchase of goods (e.g., alcohol, tobacco products, etc.) that are considered socially less desirable.

Single   one of five primary filing statuses. A taxpayer files as single if s/he is unmarried as of the end of the year and does not qualify for any of the other filing statuses. A taxpayer is considered single if s/he is unmarried or legally separated from his or her spouse under a divorce or separate maintenance decree.

Single-member LLC   a limited liability company with only one member. Single-member LLCs with individual owners are taxed as sole proprietorships and as disregarded entities otherwise.

Social Security tax   the Old Age, Survivors, and Disability Insurance (OASDI) tax. The tax is intended to provide basic pension coverage for the retired and disabled. Employees pay Social Security tax at a rate of 6.2 percent on the wage base (employers also pay 6.2 percent). Self-employed taxpayers are subject to a Social Security tax at a rate of 12.4 percent on their net earnings from self-employment. The base on which Social Security taxes are paid is limited to an annually determined amount of wages and/or net earnings from self-employment.

Sole proprietorship   a business entity that is not legally separate from the individual owner of the business. The income of a sole proprietorship is taxed and paid directly by the owner.

Solicitation   selling activities or activities ancillary to selling that are protected under Public Law 86-272.

Source-based jurisdiction   taxation of income based on where the income is earned.

Special allocations   allocations of income, gain, expense, loss, etc., that are allocated to the owners of an entity in a manner out of proportion with the owners' interests in the entity. Special allocations can be made by entities treated as partnerships for federal income tax purposes.

Special basis adjustment   an optional (sometimes mandatory) election to adjust the entity asset bases as a result of an owner's disposition of an interest in the entity or distributions from the entity to its owners.

Specific identification method   an elective method for determining the cost of an asset sold. Under this method, the taxpayer specifically chooses the assets that are to be sold.

Specified service trade or business   any trade or business involving the performance of services in the fields of health, law, consulting, athletics, financial services, brokerage services, or any trade or business where the principal asset of such trade or business is the reputation or skill of one or more of its employees or owners, or which involves the performance of services that consist of investing and investment management trading, or dealing in securities, partnership interests, or commodities. Architecture and engineering services (their services build things) are specifically excluded from the definition of specified service trade or business.

Spot rate   the foreign currency exchange rate on a specific day.

Spousal IRA   an IRA account for the spouse with the lesser amount of earned income. Contributions in this account belong to this spouse no matter where the funds for the contribution came from.

Standard deduction   a fixed deduction offered in lieu of itemized deductions. The amount of the standard deduction depends on the taxpayer's filing status.

Stare decisis   a doctrine meaning that a court will rule consistently with (a) its previous rulings (i.e., unless, due to evolving interpretations of the tax law over time, it decides to overturn an earlier decision) and (b) the rulings of higher courts with appellate jurisdiction (i.e., the courts to which its cases are appealed).

Start-up costs   expenses that would be classified as business expenses except that the expenses are incurred before the business begins. These costs are generally capitalized and amortized over 180 months, but limited immediate expensing may be available.

State tax   a tax imposed by one of the 50 U.S. states.

State tax base   the federal taxable income plus or minus required state adjustments.

Statements on Standards for Tax Services (SSTS)   standards of practice for tax professionals issued by the AICPA. Currently, there are seven SSTS that describe the tax professional standards when recommending a tax return position, answering questions on a tax return, preparing a tax return using data supplied by a client, using estimates on a tax return, taking a tax return position inconsistent with a previous year's tax return, discovering a tax return error, and giving tax advice to taxpayers.

Static forecasting   the process of forecasting tax revenues based on the existing state of transactions while ignoring how taxpayers may alter their activities in response to a tax law change.

Statute of limitations   defines the period in which the taxpayer can file an amended tax return or the IRS can assess a tax deficiency for a specific tax year. For both amended tax returns filed by a taxpayer and proposed tax assessments by the IRS, the statute of limitations generally ends three years from the *later* of (1) the date the tax return was actually filed or (2) the tax return's original due date.

Step-transaction doctrine   judicial doctrine that allows the IRS to collapse a series of related transactions into one transaction to determine the tax consequences of the transaction.

Stock dividend   a distribution of additional shares of stock to the shareholders of a corporation in the form of a stock dividend or stock split.

Stock redemption   a property distribution made to shareholders in return for some or all of their stock in the distributing corporation that is not in partial or complete liquidation of the corporation.

Stock split   a stock redemption in which a corporation exchanges a ratio of shares of stock (e.g., 2 for 1) for each share held by the shareholder.

Stock-for-stock acquisition   an exchange of solely voting stock by the acquiring corporation in exchange for stock of the target corporation, after which the acquiring corporation controls (owns 80 percent or more of) the target corporation. Often referred to as a "Type B reorganization."

Strike price   *see* exercise price.

Structural tax rate   the tax rate computed by dividing a company's income tax provision adjusted for nonrecurring permanent differences by its pretax income from continuing operations.

Subchapter K   the portion of the Internal Revenue Code dealing with partnerships tax law.

Subchapter S   the portion of the Internal Revenue Code containing tax rules for S corporations and their shareholders.

Subpart F income   income earned by a controlled foreign corporation that is not eligible for deferral from U.S. taxation.

Substance-over-form doctrine   judicial doctrine that allows the IRS to consider the transaction's substance regardless of its form and, where appropriate, reclassify the transaction according to its substance.

Substantial authority   the standard used to determine whether a tax practitioner may recommend and a taxpayer may take a tax return position without being subject to IRS penalty under IRC §6694 and IRC §6662, respectively. A good CPA evaluates whether supporting authority is substantial or not based upon the supporting and opposing authorities' weight and relevance. Substantial authority suggests that the probability that the taxpayer's position will be sustained upon audit or litigation is in the 35 to 40 percent range or above.

Substantial basis reduction   negative basis adjustment of more than $250,000 resulting from a distribution from an entity taxed as a partnership to its owners.

Substantial built-in loss   exists when a partnership's adjusted basis in its property exceeds the property's fair market value by more than $250,000 when a transfer of an interest occurs or if the purchasing partner would be allocated a loss of more than $250,000 if the partnership assets were sold for fair market value immediately after the transfer.

Substantially appreciated inventory   (for partnership disproportionate distributions purposes) inventory with a fair market value that exceeds its basis by more than 120 percent.

Substituted basis   the transfer of the tax basis of stock or other property given up in an exchange to stock or other property received in return.

Substitution effect   one of the two basic responses that a taxpayer may have when taxes increase. The substitution effect predicts that, when taxpayers are taxed more, rather than work more, they will substitute nontaxable activities (e.g., leisure pursuits) for taxable ones because the marginal value of taxable activities has decreased.

Sufficiency   a standard for evaluating a good tax system. Sufficiency is defined as assessing the aggregate size of the tax revenues that must be generated and ensuring that the tax system provides these revenues.

Syndication costs   costs partnerships incur to promote the sale of partnership interests to the public. Syndication expenses must be capitalized and are not amortizable.

T

Tax   a payment required by a government that is unrelated to any specific benefit or service received from the government.

Tax accounting balance sheet   a balance sheet that records a company's assets and liabilities at their tax bases instead of their financial accounting bases.

Tax avoidance   the legal act of arranging one's transactions or affairs to reduce taxes paid.

Tax base   the item that is being taxed (e.g., purchase price of a good, taxable income, etc.).

Tax basis   the amount of a taxpayer's unrecovered cost of or investment in an asset; *see also* adjusted tax basis.

Tax benefit rule   holds that a refund of an amount deducted in a previous period is only included in income to the extent that the deduction reduced taxable income.

Tax bracket   a range of taxable income taxed at a specified rate.

Tax capital accounts   partners' capital accounts initially determined using the tax basis of contributed property and maintained using tax accounting income and expense recognition principles.

Tax carryforwards   tax deductions or credits that cannot be used on the current-year tax return and that can be carried forward to reduce taxable income or taxes payable in a future year.

Tax Court allocation method   allocates expenses associated with rental use of the home between rental use and personal use. Property taxes and mortgage interest are allocated to rental use of the home based on the ratio of the number of rental use days to the total days in the year. All other expenses are allocated to rental use based on the ratio of the number of rental use days to total days the property was used during the year.

Tax credits   items that directly reduce a taxpayer's tax liability.

Tax evasion   the willful attempt to defraud the government (i.e., by not paying taxes legally owed). Tax evasion falls outside the confines of legal tax avoidance.

Tax haven   generally, a country offering very favorable tax laws for foreign businesses and individuals.

Tax rate   the level of taxes imposed on the tax base, usually expressed as a percentage.

Tax rate schedule   a schedule of progressive tax rates and the income ranges to which the rates apply that taxpayers may use to compute their gross tax liability.

Tax shelter   an investment or other arrangement designed to produce tax benefits without any expectation of economic profits.

Tax tables   IRS-provided tables that specify the federal income tax liability for individuals with taxable income within a specific range. The tables differ by filing status and reflect tax rates that increase with taxable income.

Tax treaties   agreements negotiated between countries that describe the tax treatment of entities subject to tax in both countries (e.g., U.S. citizens earning investment income in Spain). The U.S. president has the authority to enter into a tax treaty with another country after receiving the Senate's advice.

Tax year   a fixed period in which a business reports income and deductions, generally 12 months.

Taxable estate   adjusted gross estate reduced by the marital deduction and the charitable deduction.

Taxable fringe benefit   a noncash fringe benefit provided by employers to an employee that is included in taxable income (e.g., auto allowance or group-term life over $50,000).

Taxable gifts   the amount left after adjusting current gifts for gift splitting, annual exclusions, the marital deduction, and the charitable deduction.

Taxable income   the tax base for the income tax.

Taxable temporary differences   book–tax differences that will result in taxable amounts in future years when the related deferred tax liability is settled.

Technical advice memorandum   ruling issued by the IRS national office, requested by an IRS agent, and generated for a completed transaction.

Temporary book–tax differences   book–tax differences that reverse over time such that, over the long term, corporations recognize the same amount of income or deductions for the items on their financial statements as they recognize on their tax returns.

Temporary regulations   regulations issued with a limited life (three years for regulations issued after November 20, 1988). During their life, temporary regulations carry the same authoritative weight as final regulations.

Tenancy in common   ownership in which owners hold divided rights to property and have the ability to transfer these rights during their life or upon their death.

Tentative minimum tax (TMT)   the tax on the AMT tax base under the alternative minimum tax system.

Terminable interest   a right to property that terminates at a specified time or upon the occurrence of a specified event, such as a life estate.

Testamentary transfers   transfers that take place upon the death of the donor.

Third-party intermediaries   people or organizations that facilitate the transfer of property between taxpayers in a like-kind exchange. Typically, the intermediary receives the cash from selling the property received from the taxpayer and uses it to acquire like-kind property identified by the taxpayer.

Throwback rule   the rule that sales into a state without nexus are included with sales from the state the property was shipped from.

Topical tax service   a tax service arranged by subject (i.e., topic). For each topic, topical services identify tax issues that relate to each topic and then explain and cite authorities relevant to the issue (code sections, regulations, court cases, revenue rulings, etc.).

Trade or business   a profit-motivated activity characterized by a sustained, continuous, high level of individual involvement or effort.

Trade show rule   a rule that permits businesses to have physical presence at conventions and trade shows, generally up to two weeks a year, without creating nexus.

Traditional 401(k)   a popular type of defined contribution plan with before-tax employee and employer contributions and taxable distributions.

Traditional IRA   an individually managed retirement account with deductible contributions and taxable distributions.

Transfer taxes   taxes on the transfer of wealth from one taxpayer to another. The estate and gift taxes are two examples of transfer taxes.

Travel expenses   expenditures incurred while "away from home overnight," including the cost of transportation, meals, lodging, and incidental expenses.

Treasury bond   a debt instrument issued by the U.S. Treasury at face value, at a discount, or at a premium, with a set interest rate and maturity date that pays interest semiannually. Treasury bonds have terms of 30 years.

Treasury note   a debt instrument issued by the U.S. Treasury at face value, at a discount, or at a premium, with a set interest rate and maturity date that pays interest semiannually. Treasury notes have terms of 2, 5, or 10 years.

Triple i agreement   a 10-year agreement filed with the IRS in which the taxpayer agrees to notify the IRS that he or she has acquired a prohibited interest after waiving the family attribution rules in a complete redemption.

Trust   fiduciary entity created to hold and administer the property for other persons according to the terms of a trust instrument.

Trustee   the person responsible for administering a trust.

U

U.S. Circuit Courts of Appeals   the first level of appeals courts after the trial-level courts. There are 13 U.S. Circuit Courts of Appeal; 1 for the Federal Circuit and 12 assigned to hear cases that originate from a specific circuit (e.g., the 11th Circuit Court of Appeals only hears cases originating within the 11th Circuit).

U.S. Constitution   the founding law of the United States, ratified in 1789.

U.S. Court of Federal Claims   one of the three trial-level courts. It is a national court that only hears monetary claims against the federal government.

U.S. District Court   one of three trial-level courts. It is the only court that allows a jury trial. There is at least one district court in each state.

U.S. savings bonds   debt instruments issued by the U.S. Treasury at face value or at a discount, with a set maturity date. Interest earned from U.S. bonds is paid either at maturity or when the bonds are converted to cash before maturity.

U.S. Supreme Court   the highest court in the United States. The Supreme Court hears only a few tax cases a year with great significance to a broad cross-section of taxpayers or cases litigating issues in which there has been disagreement among the circuit courts. For most tax cases, the Supreme Court refuses to hear the case (i.e., the *writ of certiorari* is denied) and, thus, litigation ends with the circuit court decision.

U.S. Tax Court   a national court that only hears tax cases and where the judges are tax experts. The U.S. Tax Court is the only court that allows tax cases to be heard *before* the taxpayer pays the disputed liability and the only court with a small claims division (hearing claims involving disputed liabilities of $50,000 or less).

Uncertain tax position   a tax return position for which a corporation does not have a high degree of certainty as to its tax consequences.

Underpayment penalty   the penalty that applies when taxpayers fail to adequately prepay their tax liability. The underpayment penalty is determined by multiplying the federal short-term interest rate plus 3 percentage points by the amount of tax underpayment per quarter.

Unearned income   income from property that accrues as time passes without effort on the part of the owner of the property.

Unemployment tax   the tax that pays for temporary unemployment benefits for individuals terminated from their jobs without cause.

Unfavorable book–tax difference   any book–tax difference that requires an add back to book income in computing taxable income. This type of adjustment is unfavorable because it increases taxable income relative to book income.

Uniform cost capitalization (UNICAP) rules   specify that inventories must be accounted for using full absorption rules to allocate the indirect costs of productive activities to inventory.

Unitary tax return   a state tax return methodology requiring the activities of a group of related entities to be reported on a single tax return. The criteria for determining whether a group of entities must file a unitary tax return are functional integration, centralization of management, and economies of scale.

Unrealized receivables   any rights to receive payment for (1) goods delivered, or to be delivered, or (2) services rendered, or to be rendered. Unrealized receivables also include other assets to the extent that they would produce ordinary income if sold for their fair market value.

Unrecaptured §1250 gain   a type of §1231 gain derived from the sale of real estate held by a noncorporate taxpayer for more than one year in a trade or business or as rental property attributable to tax depreciation deducted at ordinary tax rates. This gain is taxable at a maximum 25 percent capital gains rate.

Use tax   a tax imposed on the retail price of goods owned, possessed, or consumed within a state that were *not* purchased within the state.

V

Valuation allowance the portion of a deferred tax asset for which management determines it is more likely than not that a tax benefit will not be realized on a future tax return.

Value-added tax a tax imposed on the producer of goods (and services) based on the value added to the goods (services) at each stage of production. Value-added taxes are common in Europe.

Vertical equity one of the dimensions of equity. Vertical equity is achieved when taxpayers with greater ability to pay tax, pay more tax relative to taxpayers with a lesser ability to pay tax.

Vesting the process of becoming legally entitled to receive a particular benefit without risk of forfeiture; gaining ownership.

Vesting date the date on which the taxpayer becomes legally entitled to receive a particular benefit without risk of forfeiture.

Vesting period period of employment over which employees earn the right to own and exercise stock options.

W

Wages a payment by an employer to an employee in exchange for the employee's services; typically expressed in an hourly, daily, or piecework rate.

Wash sale the sale of an investment if that same investment (or substantially identical investment) is purchased within 30 days before or after the sale date. Losses on wash sales are deferred.

Wherewithal to pay the ability or resources to pay taxes due from a particular transaction.

Withholdings taxes collected and remitted to the government by an employer from an employee's wages.

Working condition fringe benefit a nontaxable fringe benefit provided by employers that would be deductible as an ordinary and necessary business expense if paid by an employee (e.g., reimbursement for professional dues).

Writ of certiorari a document filed to request the U.S. Supreme Court to hear a case.

Z

Zero-coupon bond a type of bond issued at a discount that pays interest only at maturity.

Appendix C

Comprehensive Tax Return Problems

In order to provide you with the most up-to-date IRS tax information, Appendix C for the Spilker 2019 *Taxation* series has been moved online.

Instructors may access Appendix C through the Instructor Resource Center in your Connect course's Library tab, or, if you are a non-Connect user, through a password-protected url. Please contact your McGraw-Hill representative for more information—http://shop.mheducation.com/store/paris/user/findltr.html.

Students may access Appendix C through **Additional Student Resources** found in the ebook, or may request the web link to Appendix C from their instructors.

Appendix D

Tax Rates

2018 Tax Rate Schedules

Individuals

Schedule X-Single

If taxable income is over:	But not over:	The tax is:
$ 0	$ 9,525	10% of taxable income
$ 9,525	$ 38,700	$952.50 plus 12% of the excess over $9,525
$ 38,700	$ 82,500	$4,453.50 plus 22% of the excess over $38,700
$ 82,500	$157,500	$14,089.50 plus 24% of the excess over $82,500
$157,500	$200,000	$32,089.50 plus 32% of the excess over $157,500
$200,000	$500,000	$45,689.50 plus 35% of the excess over $200,000
$500,000	—	$150,689.50 plus 37% of the excess over $500,000

Schedule Z-Head of Household

If taxable income is over:	But not over:	The tax is:
$ 0	$ 13,600	10% of taxable income
$ 13,600	$ 51,800	$1,360 plus 12% of the excess over $13,600
$ 51,800	$ 82,500	$5,944 plus 22% of the excess over $51,800
$ 82,500	$157,500	$12,698 plus 24% of the excess over $82,500
$157,500	$200,000	$30,698 plus 32% of the excess over $157,500
$200,000	$500,000	$44,298 plus 35% of the excess over $200,000
$500,000	—	$149,298 plus 37% of the excess over $500,000

Schedule Y-1-Married Filing Jointly or Qualifying Widow(er)

If taxable income is over:	But not over:	The tax is:
$ 0	$ 19,050	10% of taxable income
$ 19,050	$ 77,400	$1,905 plus 12% of the excess over $19,050
$ 77,400	$165,000	$8,907 plus 22% of the excess over $77,400
$165,000	$315,000	$28,179 plus 24% of the excess over $165,000
$315,000	$400,000	$64,179 plus 32% of the excess over $315,000
$400,000	$600,000	$91,379 plus 35% of the excess over $400,000
$600,000	—	$161,379 plus 37% of the excess over $600,000

Schedule Y-2-Married Filing Separately

If taxable income is over:	But not over:	The tax is:
$ 0	$ 9,525	10% of taxable income
$ 9,525	$ 38,700	$952.50 plus 12% of the excess over $9,525
$ 38,700	$ 82,500	$4,453.50 plus 22% of the excess over $38,700
$ 82,500	$157,500	$14,089.50 plus 24% of the excess over $82,500
$157,500	$200,000	$32,089.50 plus 32% of the excess over $157,500
$200,000	$300,000	$45,689.50 plus 35% of the excess over $200,000
$300,000	—	$80,689.50 plus 37% of the excess over $300,000

Estates and Trusts

If taxable income is over:	But not over:	The tax is:
$ 0	$ 2,550	10% of taxable income
$ 2,550	$ 9,150	$255 plus 24% of the excess over $2,550
$ 9,150	$12,500	$1,839 plus 35% of the excess over $9,150
$12,500		$3,011.50 plus 37% of the excess over $12,500

Tax Rates for Net Capital Gains and Qualified Dividends

Rate*	Taxable Income				
	Married Filing Jointly	Married Filing Separately	Single	Head of Household	Trusts and Estates
0%	$0 – $77,200	$0 – $38,600	$0 – $38,600	$0 – $51,700	$0 – $2,600
15%	$77,201 – $479,000	$38,601 – $239,500	$38,601 – $425,800	$51,701 – $452,400	$2,601 – $12,700
20%	$479,000+	$239,500+	$425,801+	$452,401+	$12,701+

*This rate applies to the net capital gains and qualified dividends that fall within the range of taxable income specified in the table (net capital gains and qualified dividends are included in taxable income last for this purpose).

Basic Standard Deduction Amounts*

Filing Status	2017 Amount	2018 Amount
Married Filing Jointly	$12,700	$24,000
Qualifying Widow or Widower	$12,700	$24,000
Married Filing Separately	$ 6,350	$12,000
Head of Household	$ 9,350	$18,000
Single	$ 6,350	$12,000

*For individuals claimed as a dependent on another return, the 2018 standard deduction is the greater of (1) $1,050 or (2) $350 plus earned income not to exceed the standard deduction amount of those who are not dependents.

Amount of Each Additional Standard Deduction for Taxpayers Who Are Age 65 or Blind

	2017 Amount	2018 Amount
Married taxpayers	$1,250	$1,300
Single taxpayer or head of household	$1,550	$1,600

Exemption Amount

2017	2018
$4,050	$4,150*

*Used for qualifying relative gross income test.

Corporations

Rate	Taxable Income
21%	All

Code Index

Page numbers followed by n refer to footnotes.

Subject Index

Page numbers followed by n refer to footnotes.